Oh My Goddess!

OMNIBUS 1

ああっ女神さまっ

 D1282455

STORY AND ART BY
Kosuke Fujishima

TRANSLATION BY
**Dana Lewis, Alan Gleason,
and Toren Smith**

LETTERING AND TOUCHUP BY
**Susie Lee AND Betty Dong
WITH Tom2K**

DARK HORSE MANGA

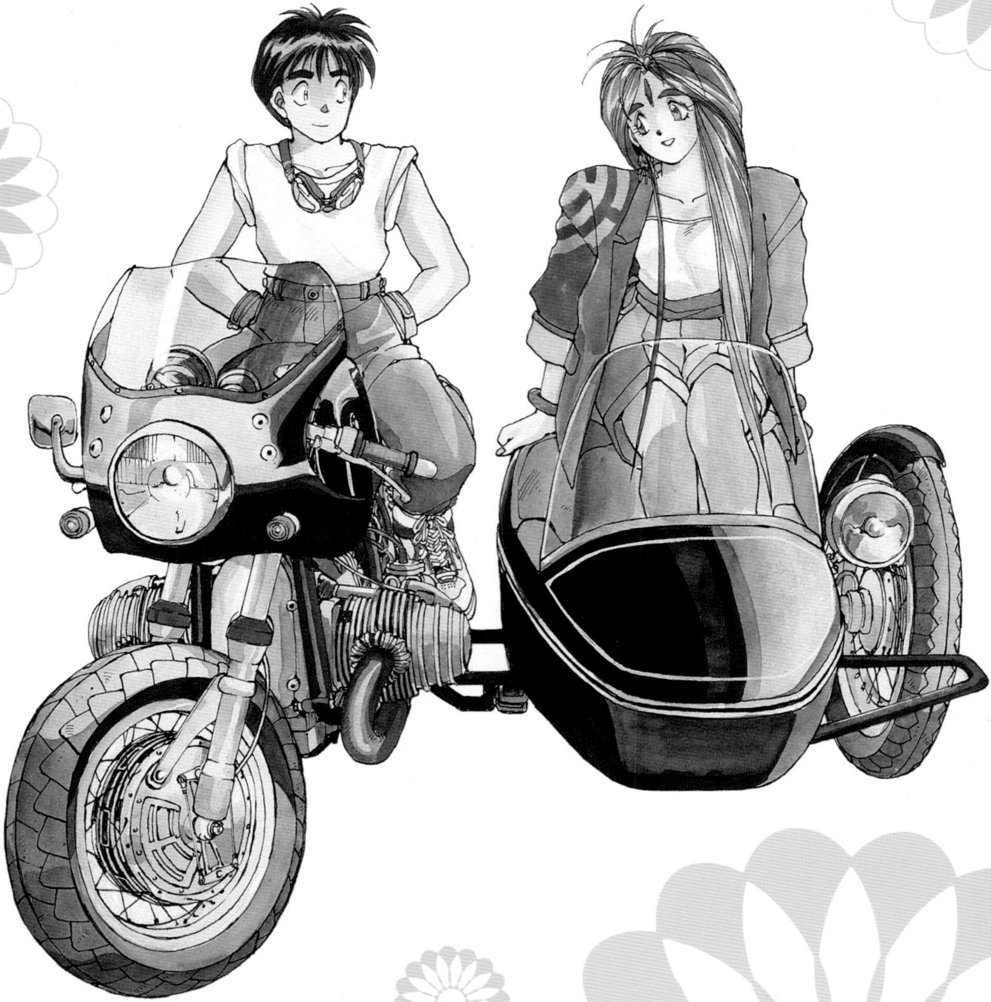

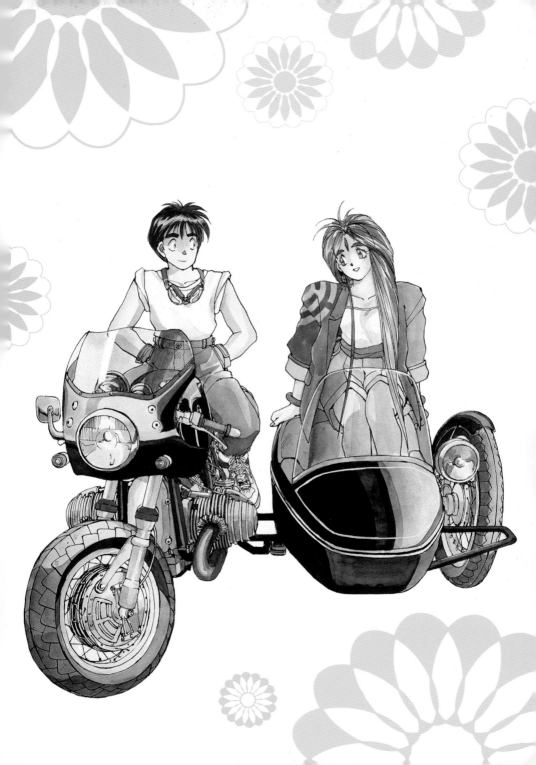

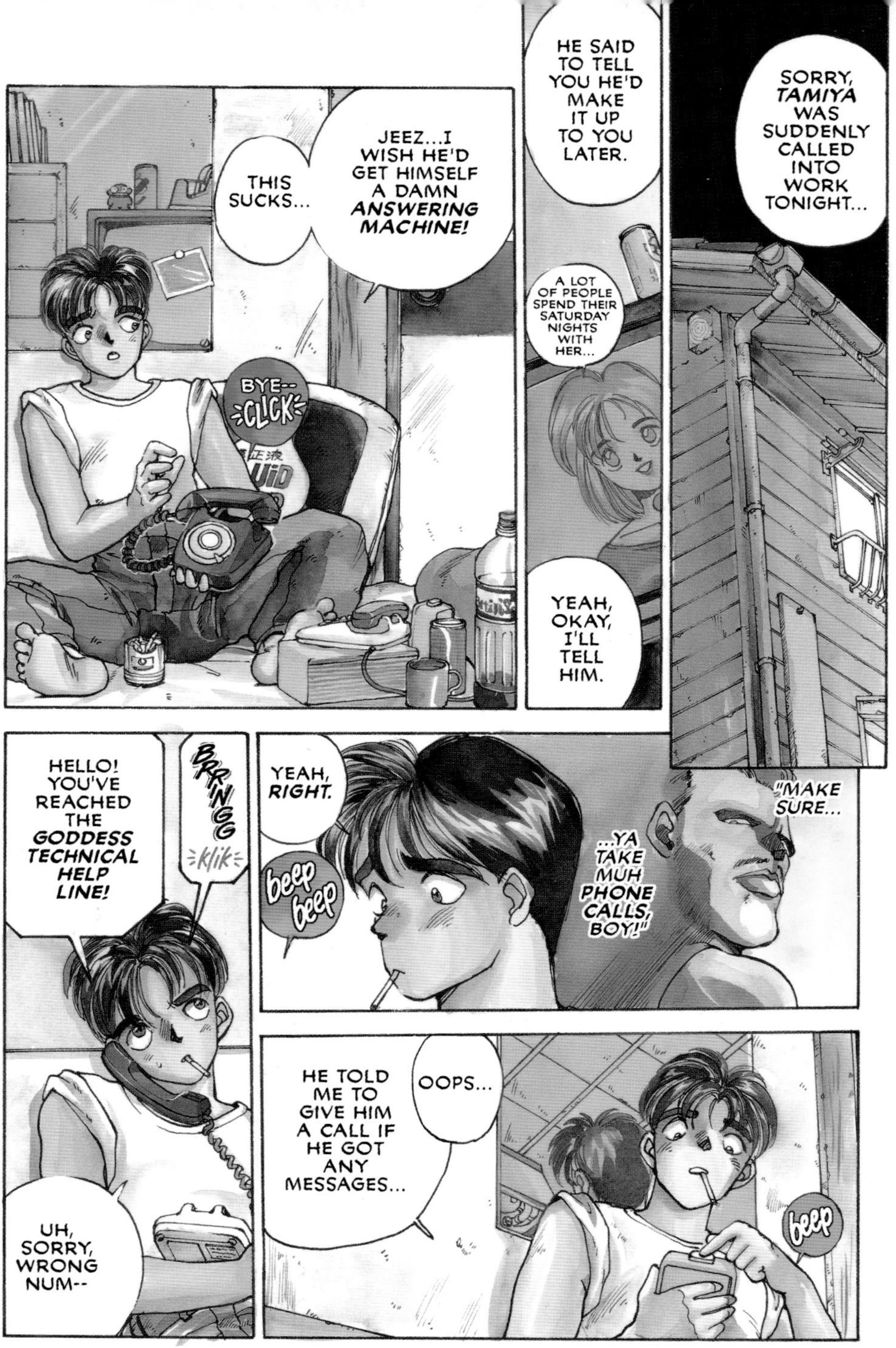
SORRY, TAMIYA WAS SUDDENLY CALLED INTO WORK TONIGHT...
HE SAID TO TELL YOU HE'D MAKE IT UP TO YOU LATER.
A LOT OF PEOPLE SPEND THEIR SATURDAY NIGHTS WITH HER...
YEAH, OKAY, I'LL TELL HIM.
JEEZ...I WISH HE'D GET HIMSELF A DAMN ANSWERING MACHINE!
THIS SUCKS...
BYE-- CLICK
"MAKE SURE...
...YA TAKE MUH PHONE CALLS, BOY!"
YEAH, RIGHT.
beep beep
beep
OOPS...
HE TOLD ME TO GIVE HIM A CALL IF HE GOT ANY MESSAGES...
BRRINGG
klik
HELLO! YOU'VE REACHED THE GODDESS TECHNICAL HELP LINE!
UH, SORRY, WRONG NUM--

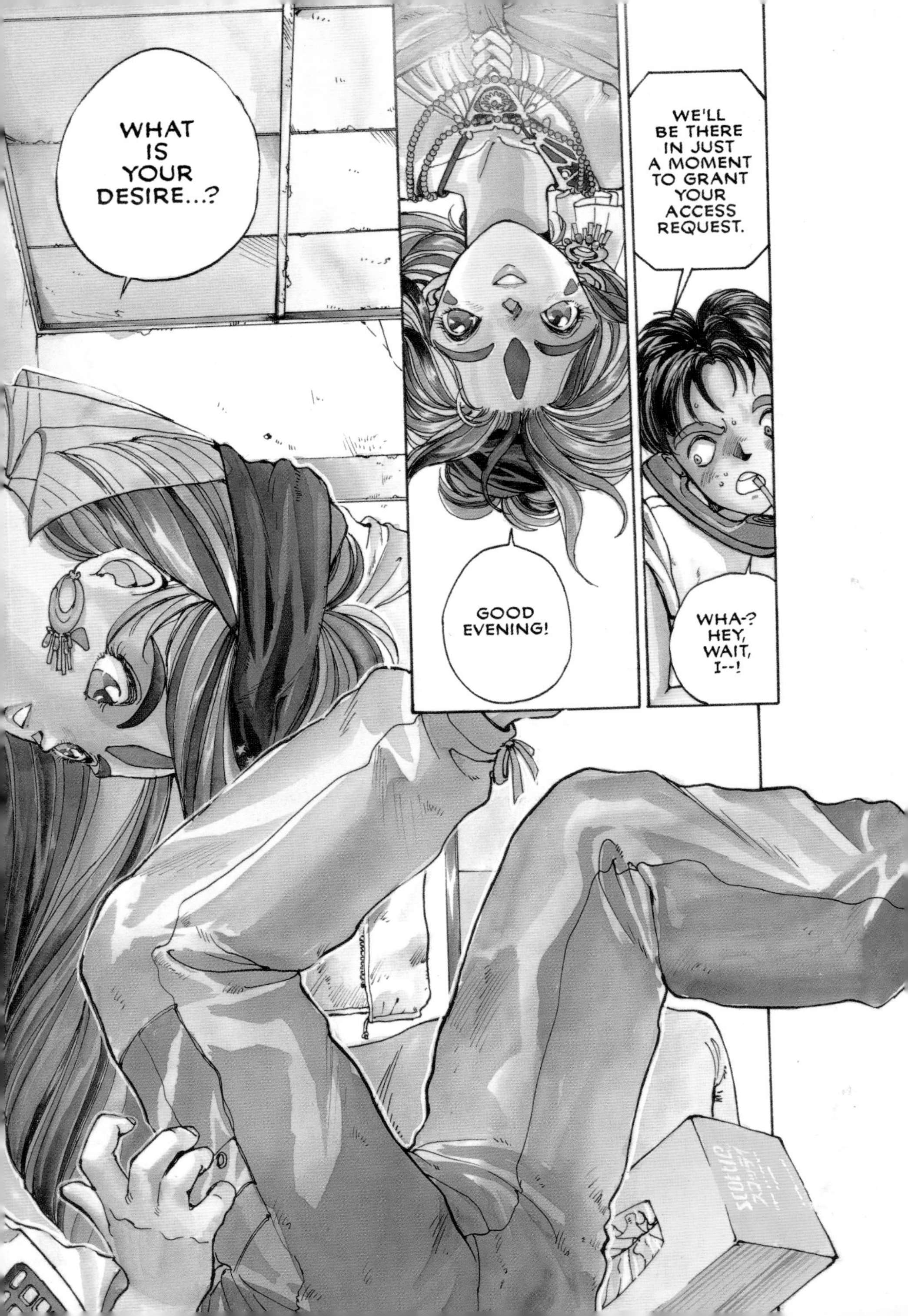
WE'LL BE THERE IN JUST A MOMENT TO GRANT YOUR ACCESS REQUEST.
WHA-? HEY, WAIT, I--!
GOOD EVENING!
WHAT IS YOUR DESIRE...?

CHAPTER 1

The Number You Have Dialed Is Incorrect

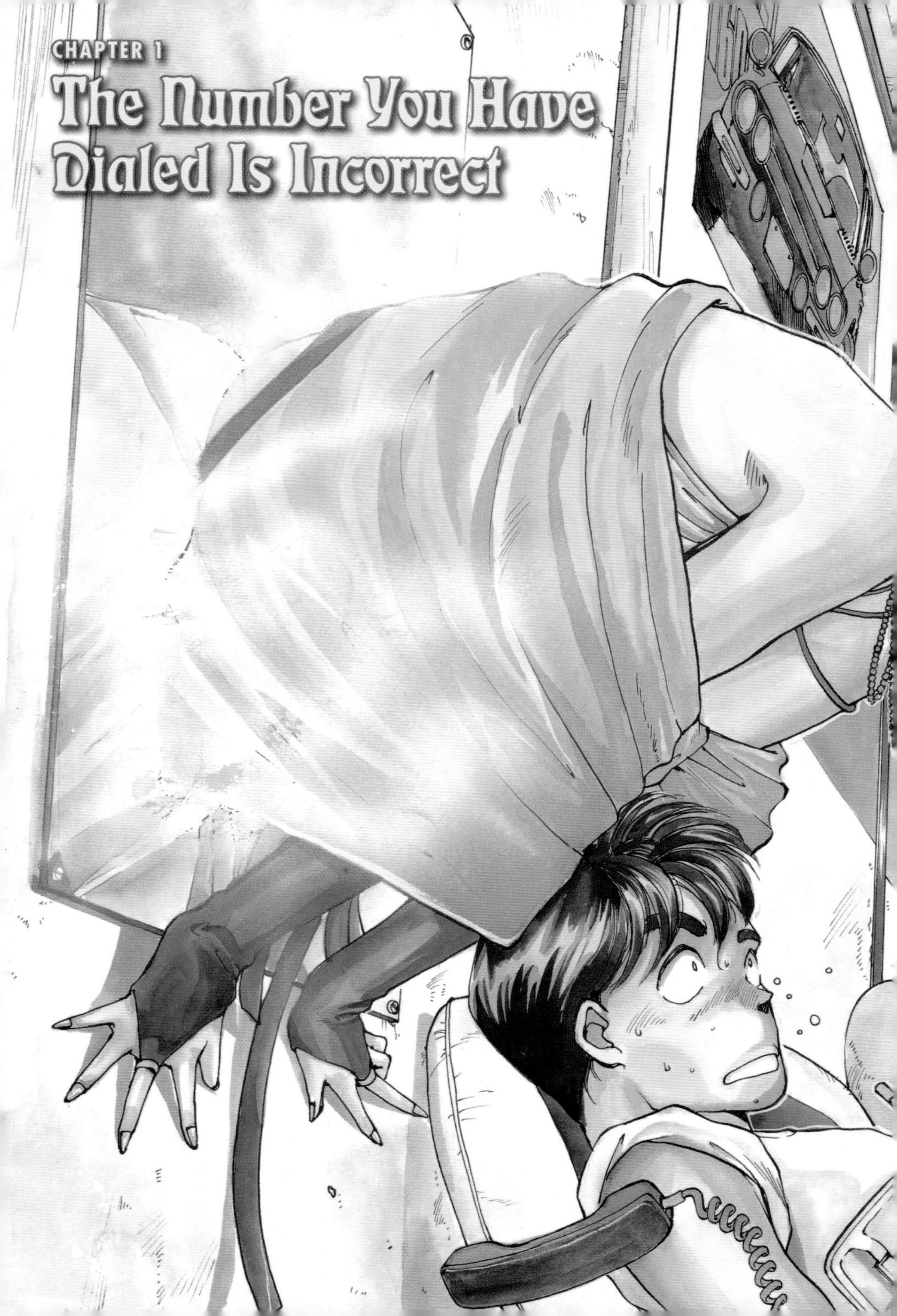

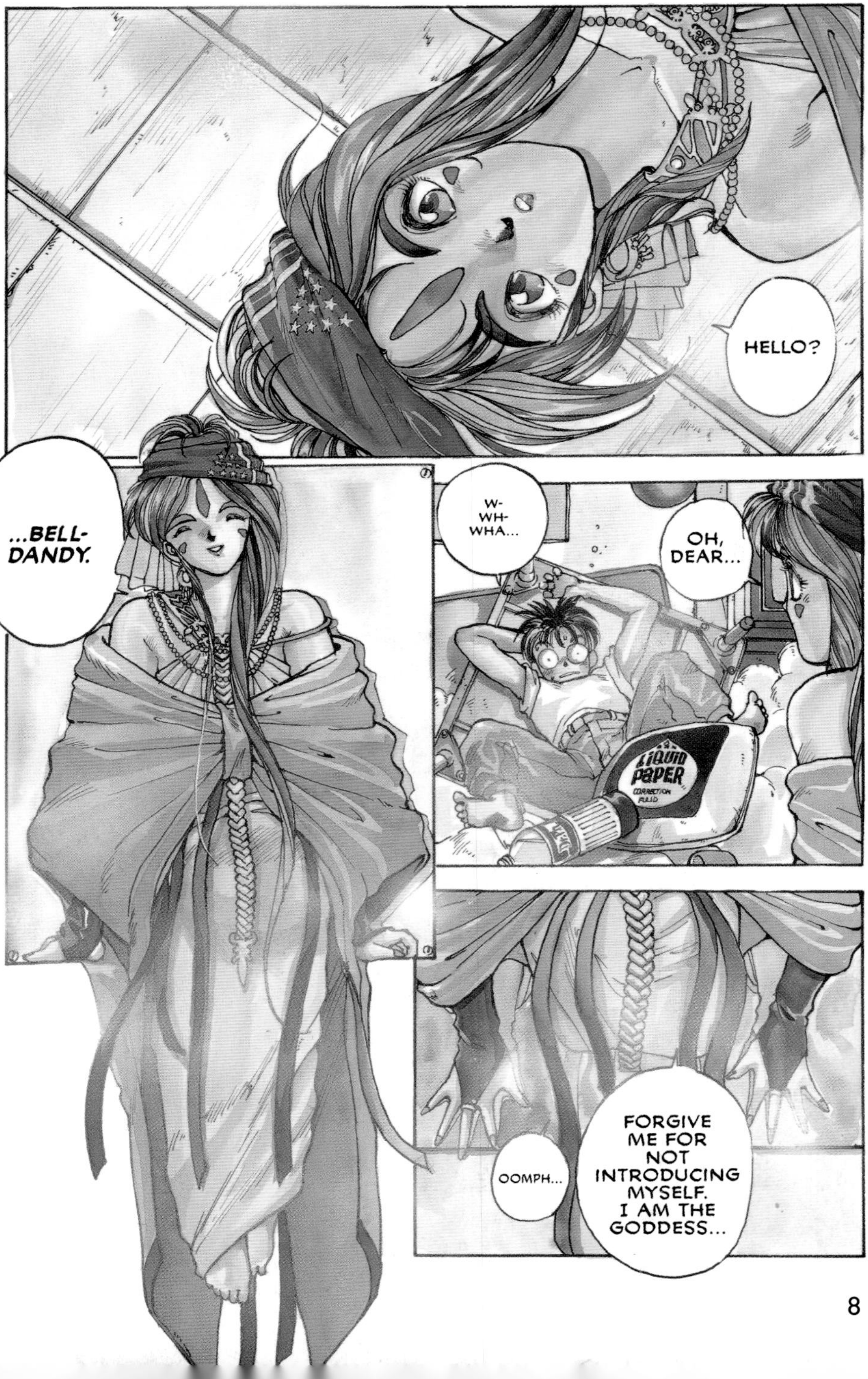
HELLO?
OH, DEAR...
W- WH- WHA...
FORGIVE ME FOR NOT INTRODUCING MYSELF. I AM THE GODDESS...
OOMPH...
...BELL-DANDY.

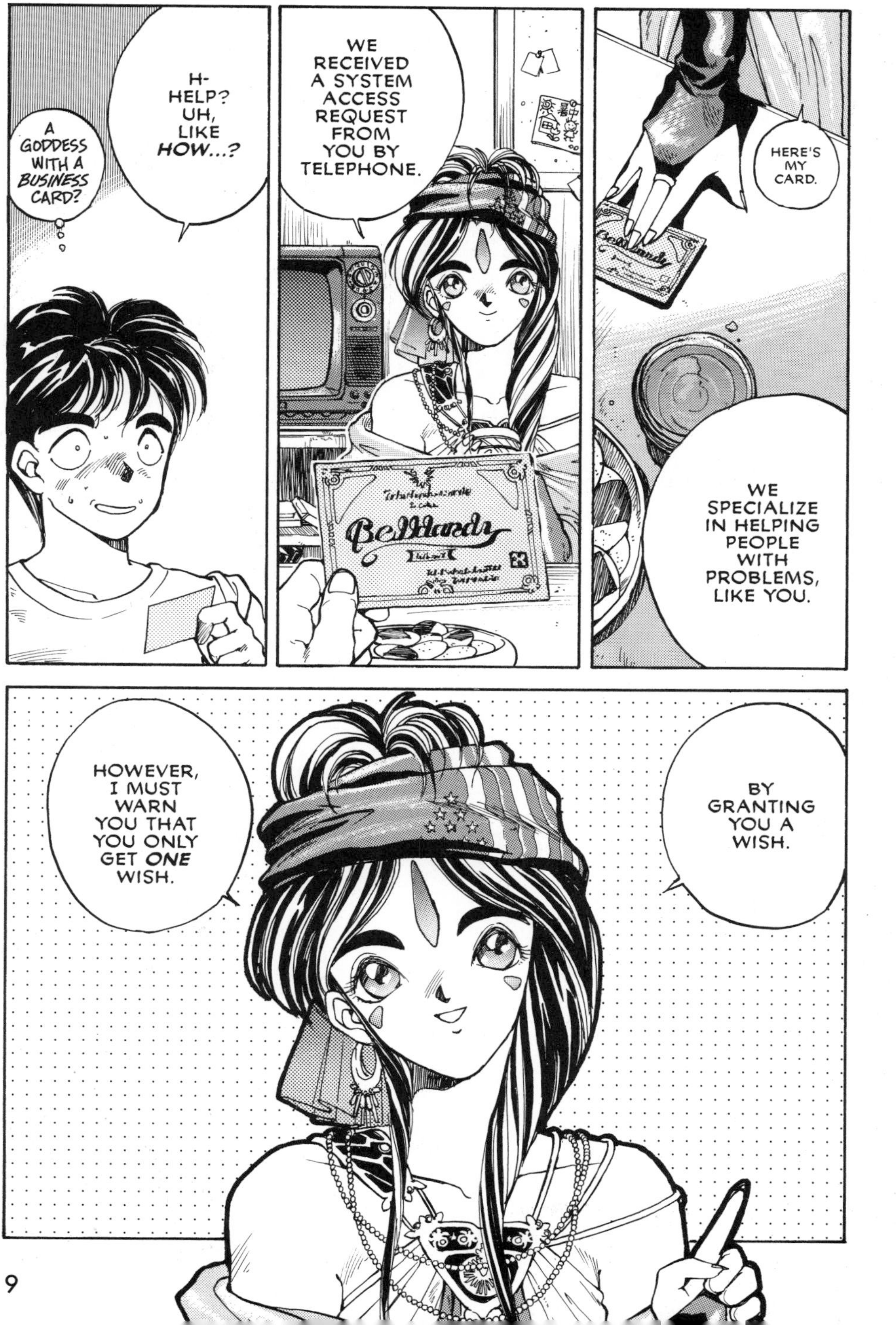
HERE'S MY CARD.
WE SPECIALIZE IN HELPING PEOPLE WITH PROBLEMS, LIKE YOU.
WE RECEIVED A SYSTEM ACCESS REQUEST FROM YOU BY TELEPHONE.
H-HELP? UH, LIKE *HOW*...?
A GODDESS WITH A *BUSINESS* CARD?
BY GRANTING YOU A WISH.
HOWEVER, I MUST WARN YOU THAT YOU ONLY GET *ONE* WISH.

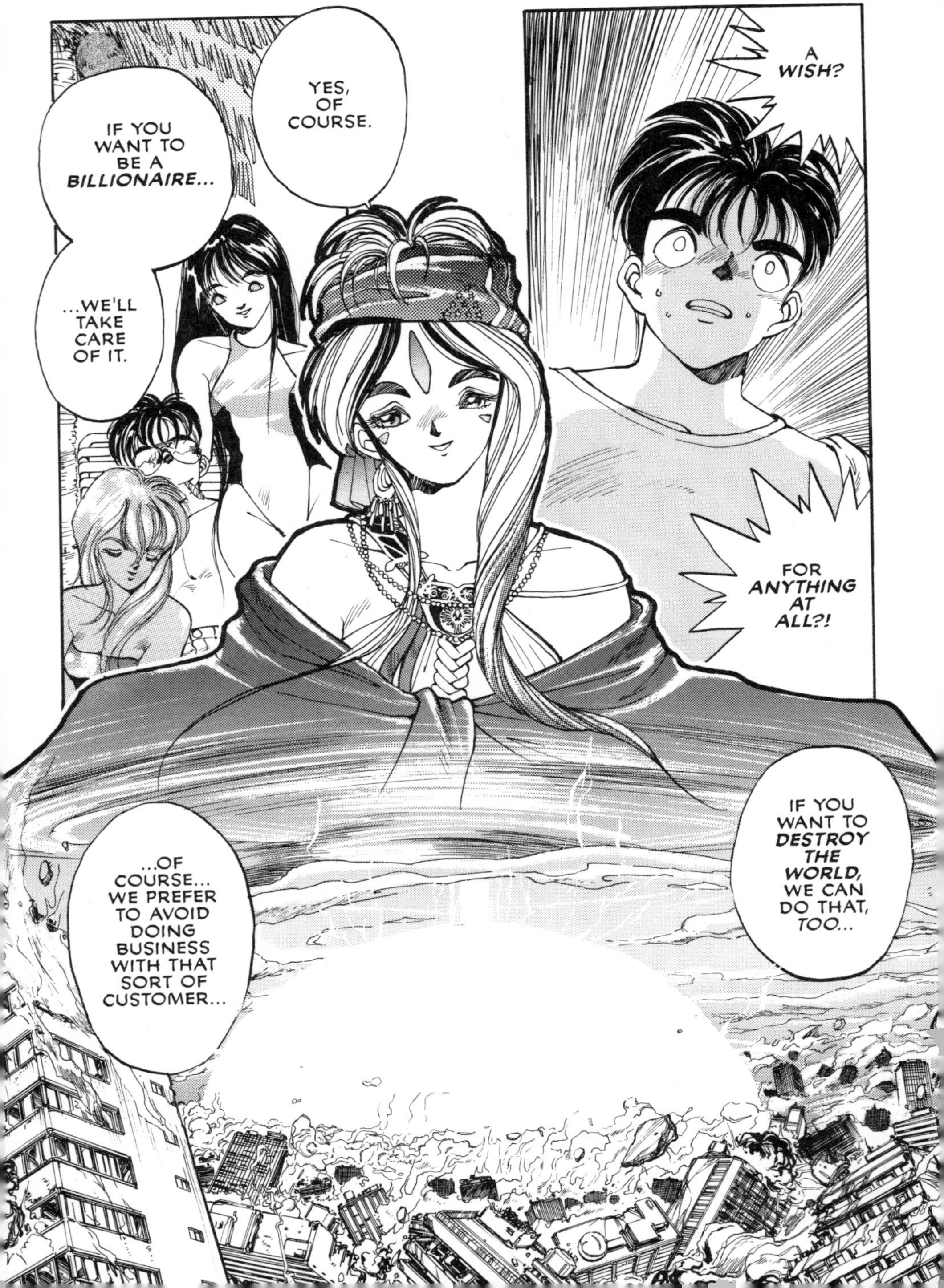
A *WISH?*
FOR *ANYTHING AT ALL?!*
YES, OF COURSE.
IF YOU WANT TO BE A *BILLIONAIRE...*
...WE'LL TAKE CARE OF IT.
IF YOU WANT TO *DESTROY THE WORLD,* WE CAN DO THAT, *TOO...*
...OF COURSE... WE PREFER TO AVOID DOING BUSINESS WITH THAT SORT OF CUSTOMER...

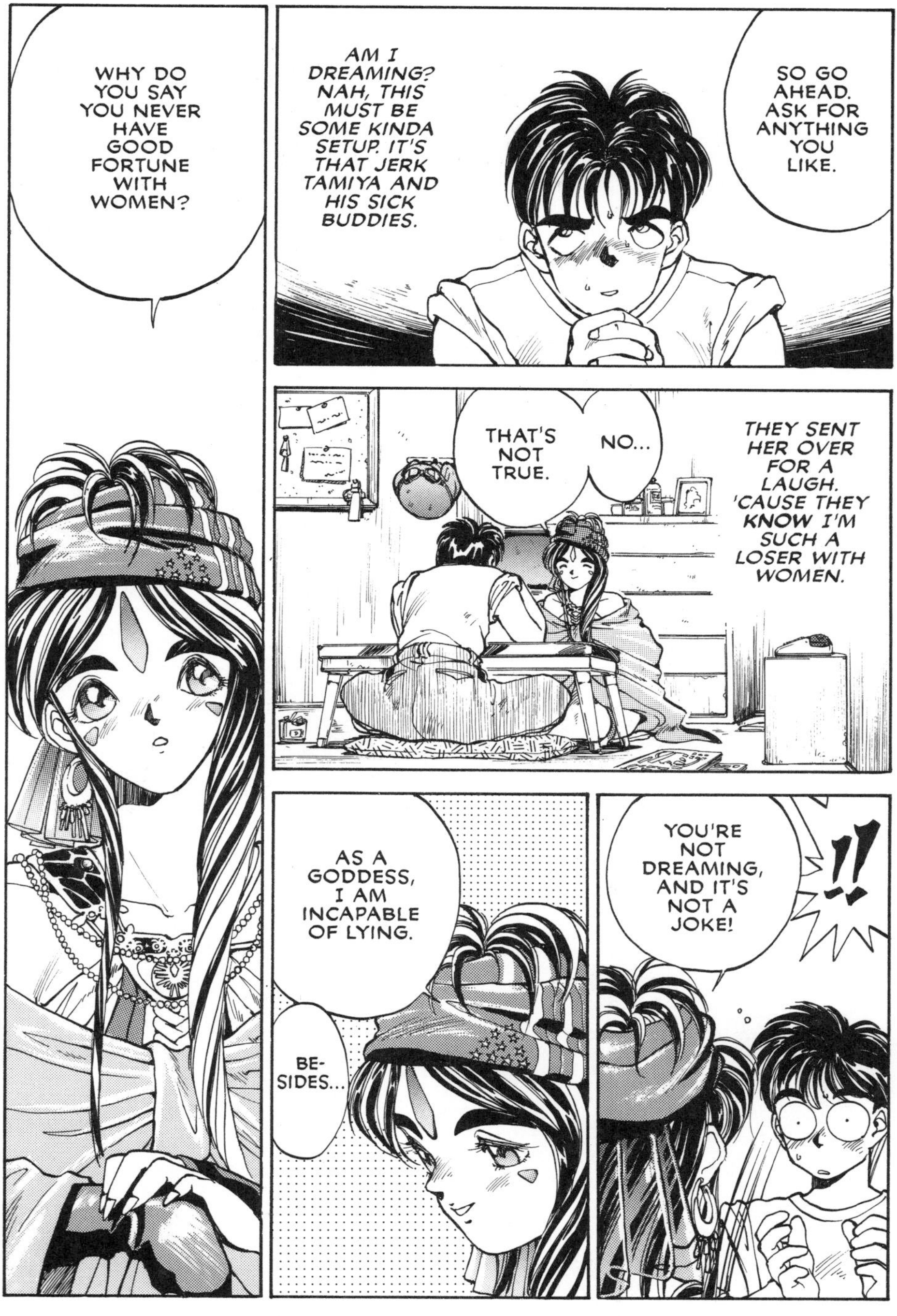
SO GO AHEAD. ASK FOR ANYTHING YOU LIKE.
AM I DREAMING? NAH, THIS MUST BE SOME KINDA SETUP. IT'S THAT JERK TAMIYA AND HIS SICK BUDDIES.
THEY SENT HER OVER FOR A LAUGH. 'CAUSE THEY KNOW I'M SUCH A LOSER WITH WOMEN.
NO...
THAT'S NOT TRUE.
!!
YOU'RE NOT DREAMING, AND IT'S NOT A JOKE!
AS A GODDESS, I AM INCAPABLE OF LYING.
BE-SIDES...
WHY DO YOU SAY YOU NEVER HAVE GOOD FORTUNE WITH WOMEN?

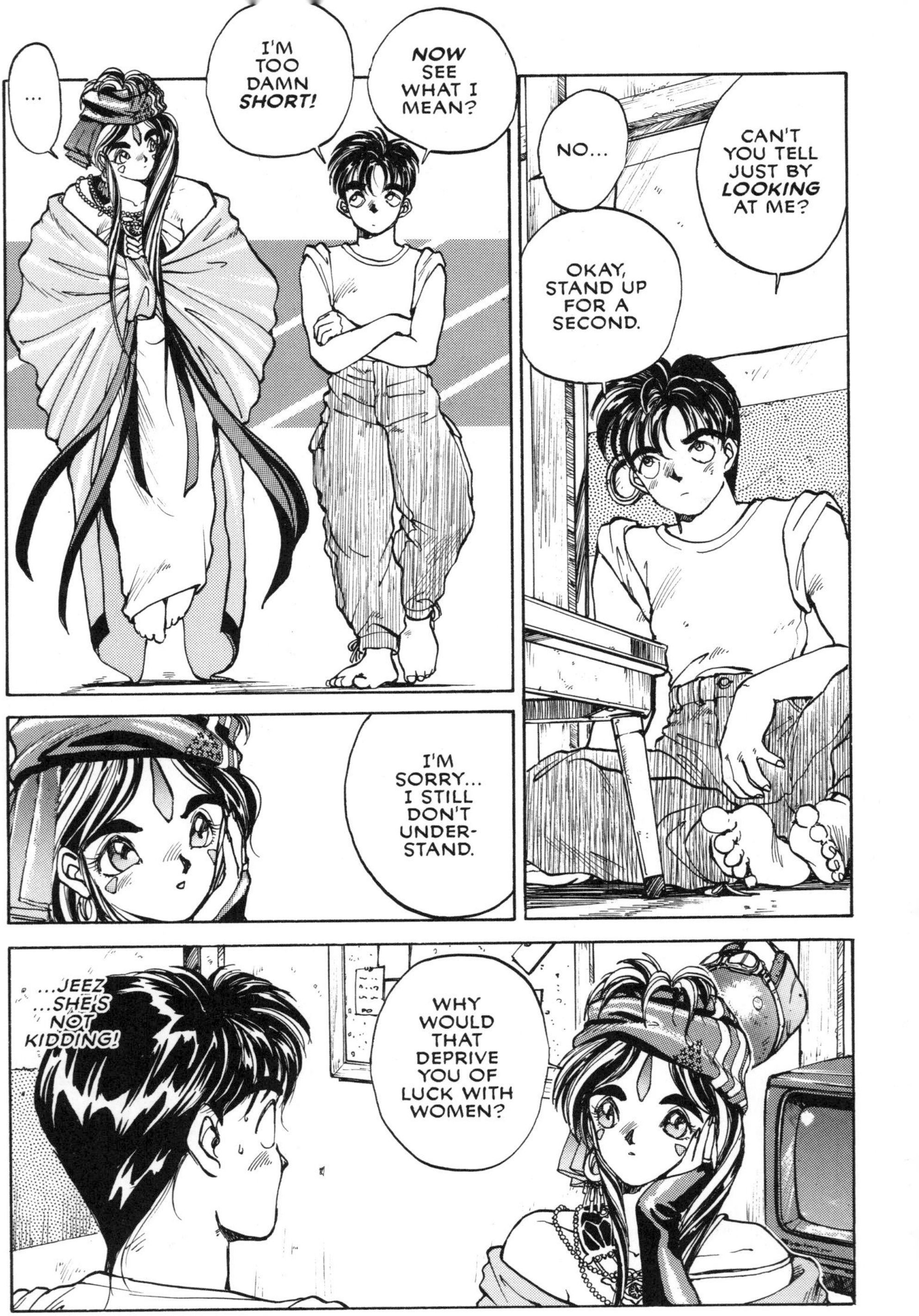
CAN'T YOU TELL JUST BY *LOOKING* AT ME?
NO...
OKAY, STAND UP FOR A SECOND.
NOW SEE WHAT I MEAN?
I'M TOO DAMN *SHORT!*
...
I'M SORRY... I STILL DON'T UNDER-STAND.
WHY WOULD THAT DEPRIVE YOU OF LUCK WITH WOMEN?
...JEEZ ...SHE'S NOT KIDDING!

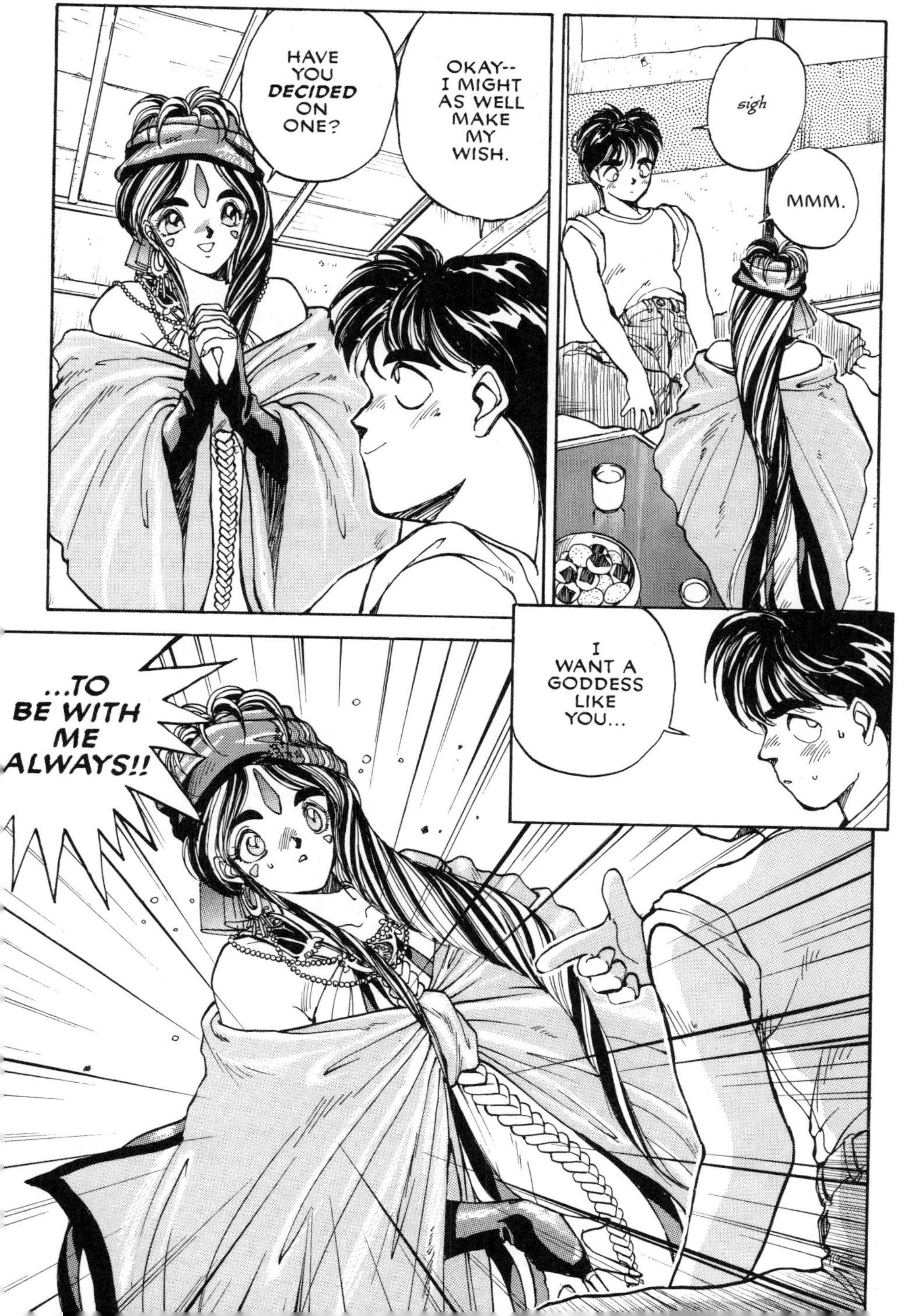
sigh
MMM.
HAVE YOU *DECIDED* ON ONE?
OKAY-- I MIGHT AS WELL MAKE MY WISH.
I WANT A GODDESS LIKE YOU...
...TO BE WITH ME ALWAYS!!

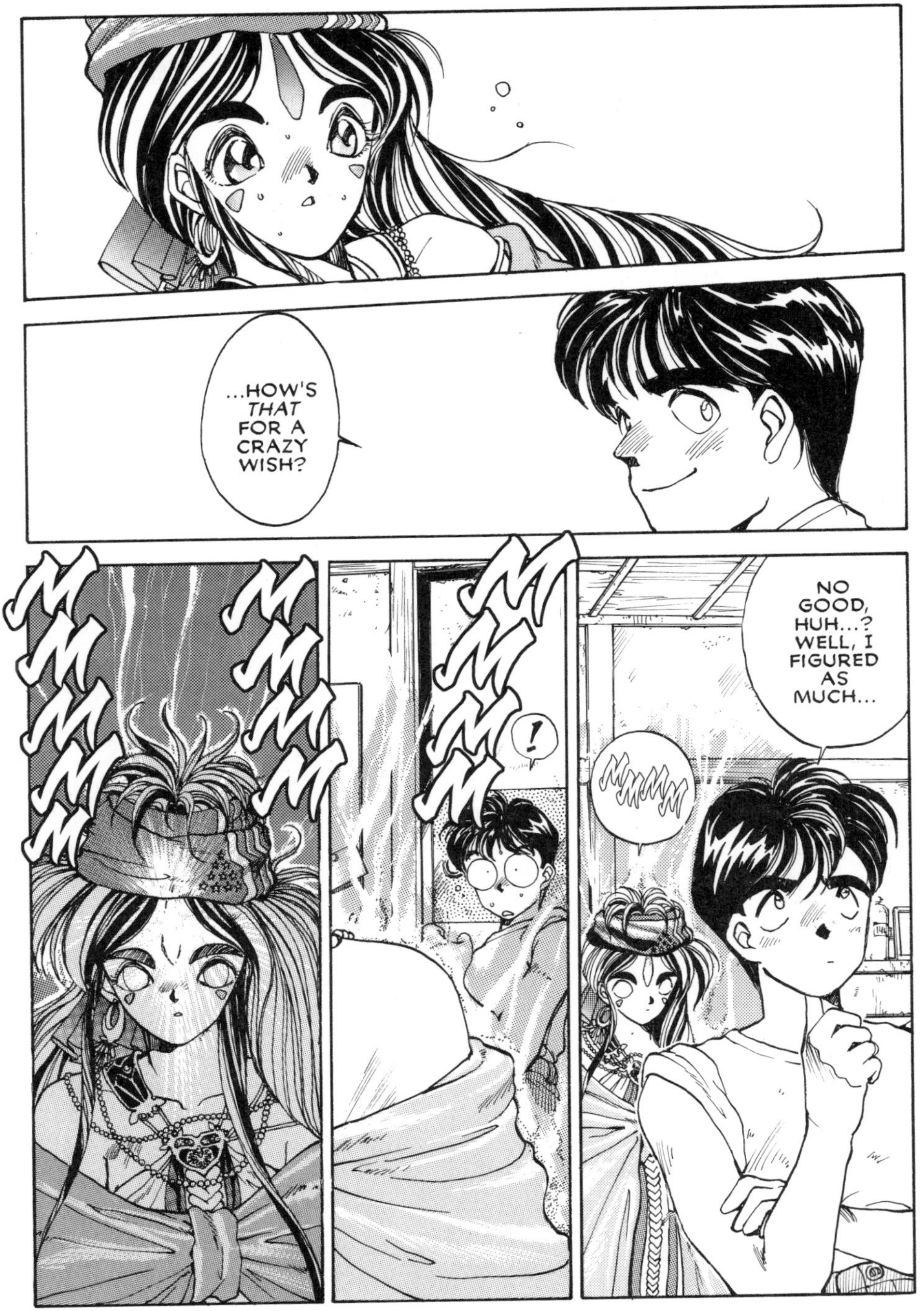
...HOW'S *THAT* FOR A CRAZY WISH?
NO GOOD, HUH...? WELL, I FIGURED AS MUCH...
MMMM
MMMMM
!
MMMMM
MMMM

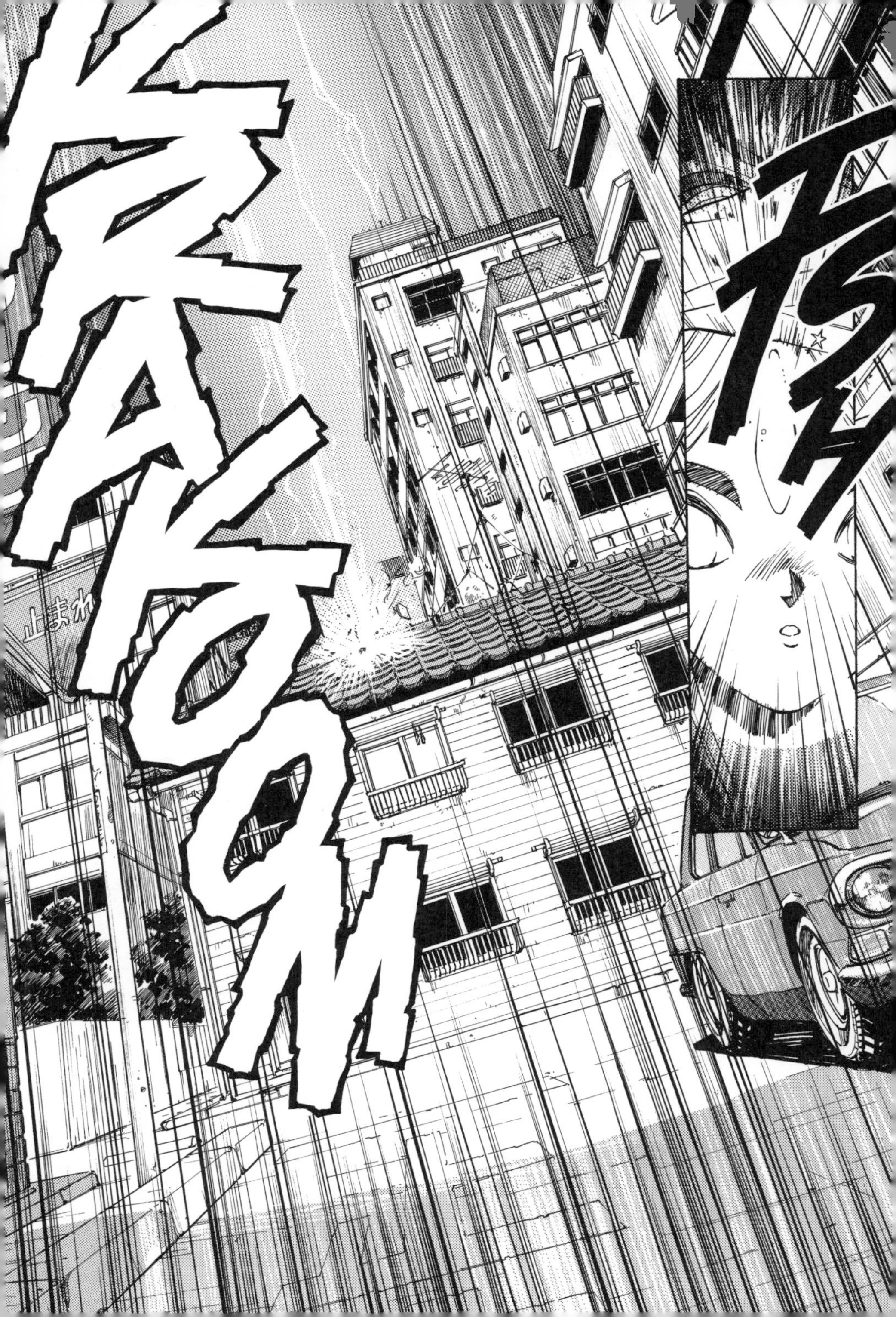
TSH
KAKOOM

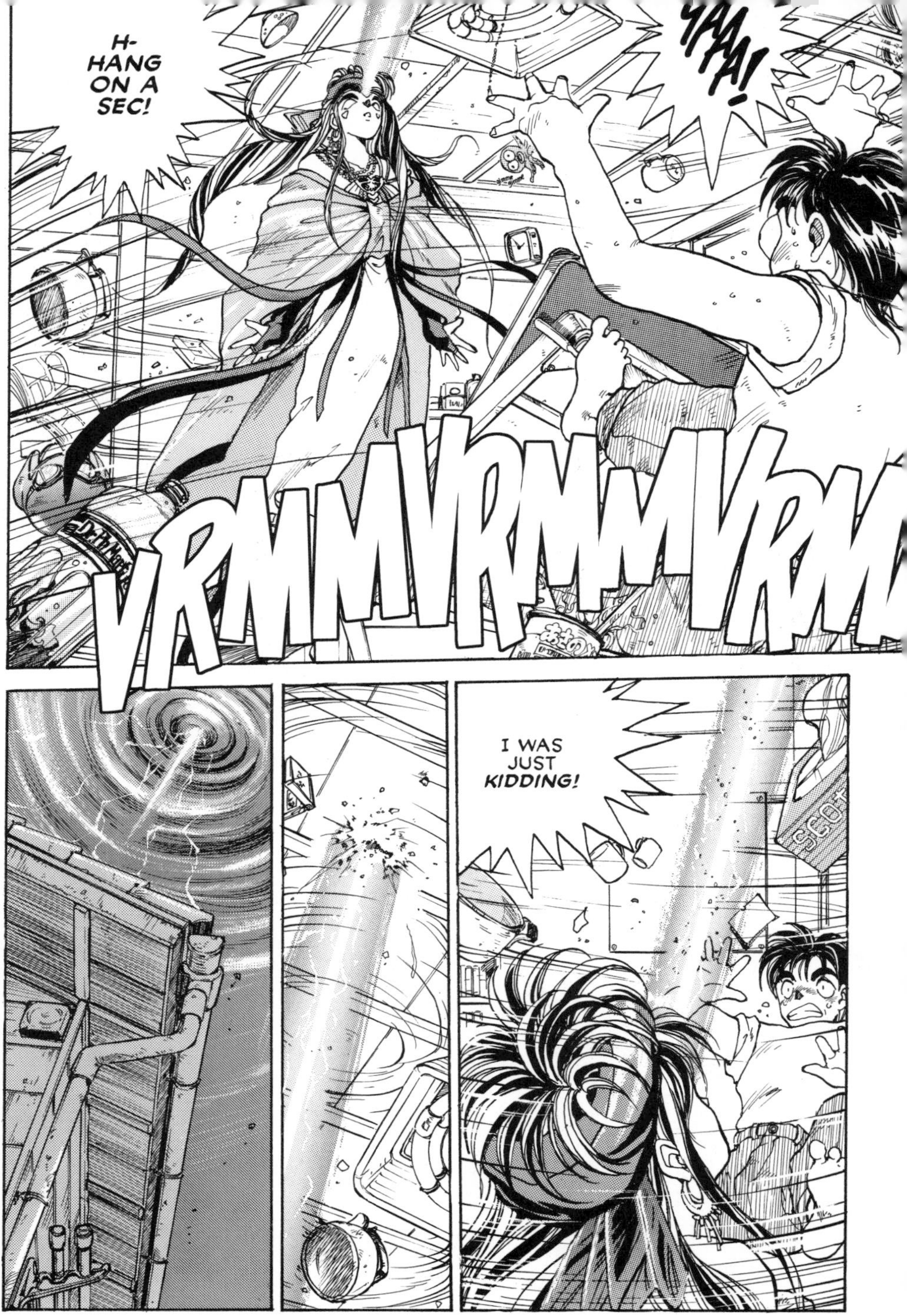
YAAAA!
H-HANG ON A SEC!
VRMMVRMMVRM
I WAS JUST KIDDING!

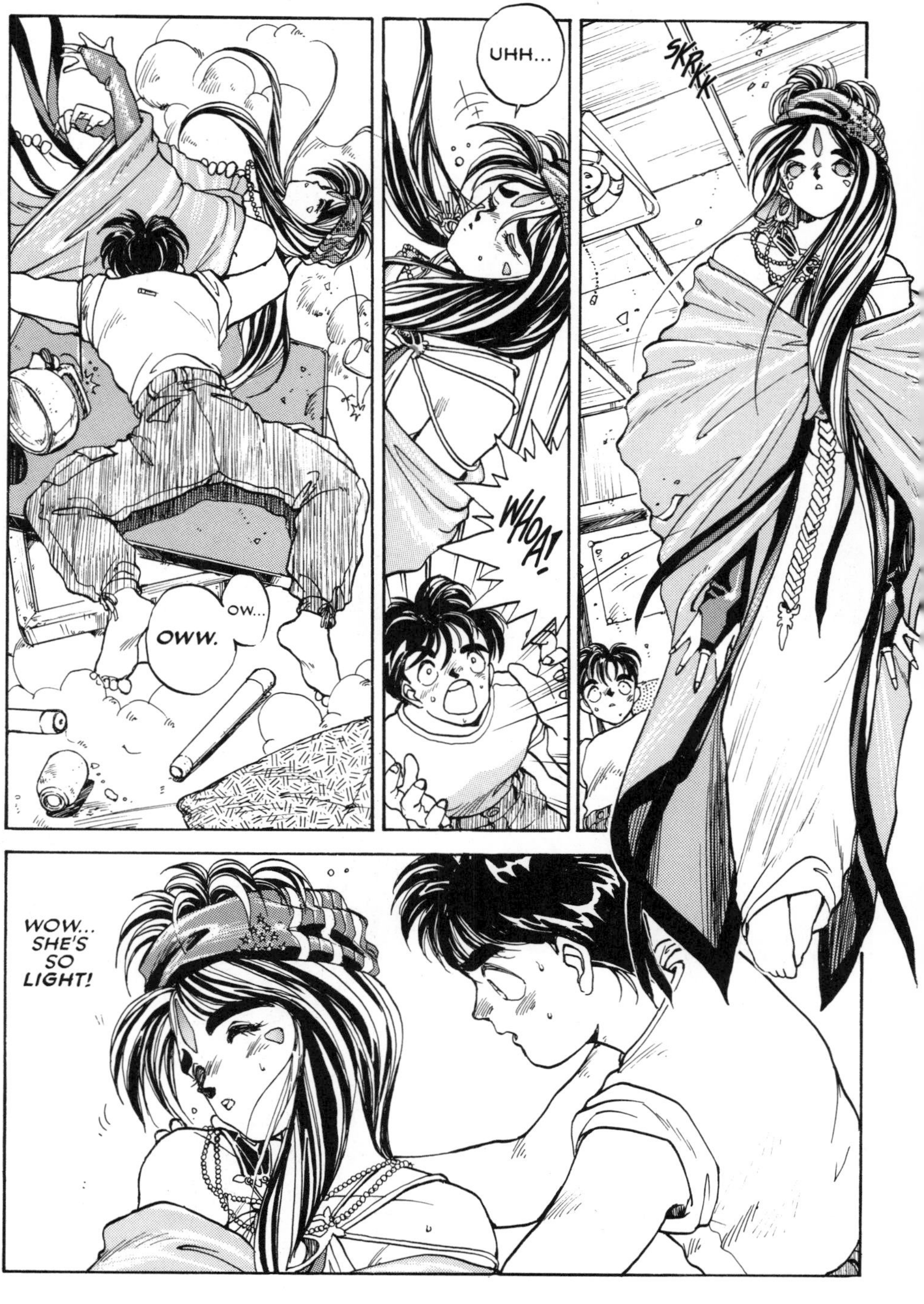
SKRKK
UHH...
WHOA!
OW...
OWW.
WOW... SHE'S SO LIGHT!

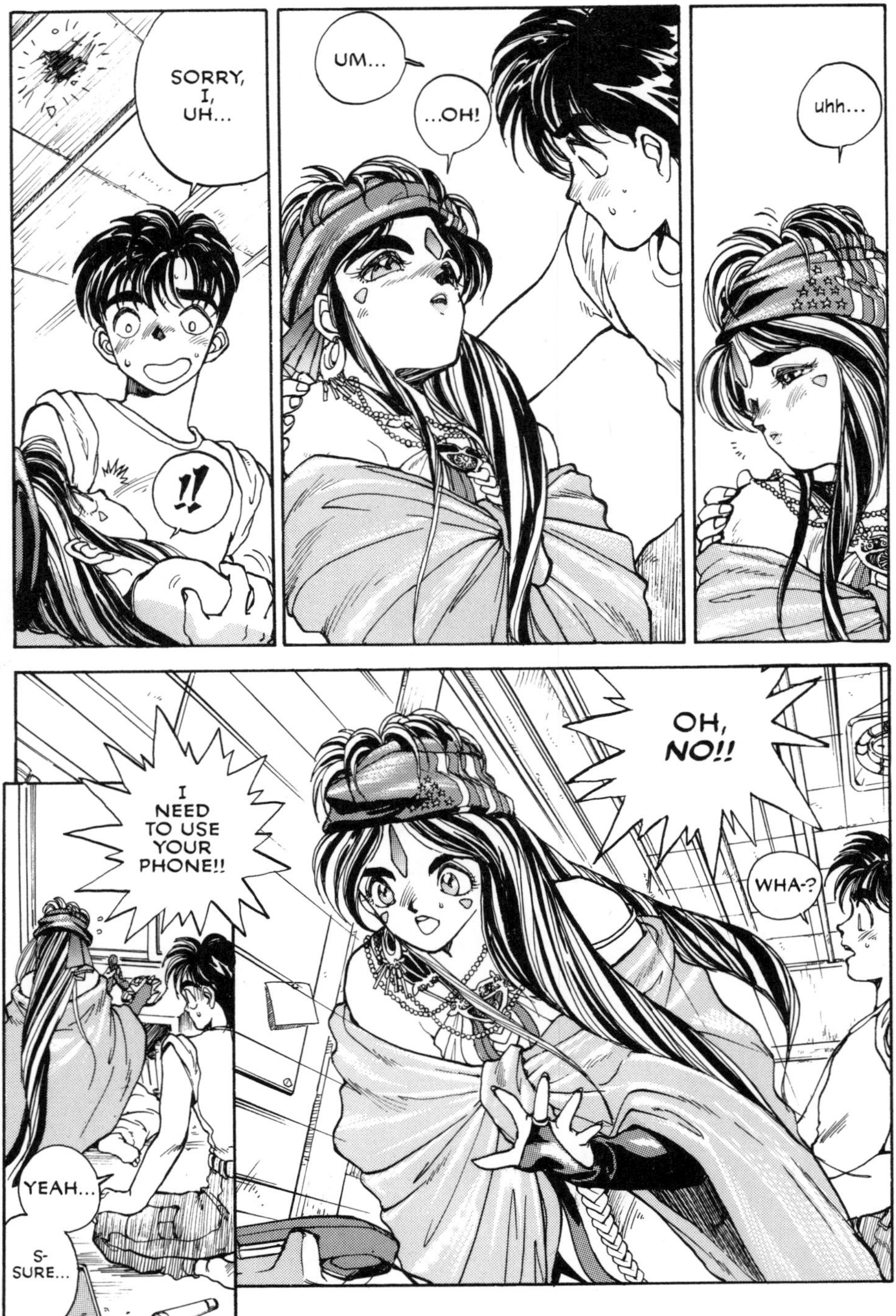
uhh...
UM...
...OH!
SORRY, I, UH...
!!
OH, NO!!
I NEED TO USE YOUR PHONE!!
WHA-?
YEAH...
S-SURE...

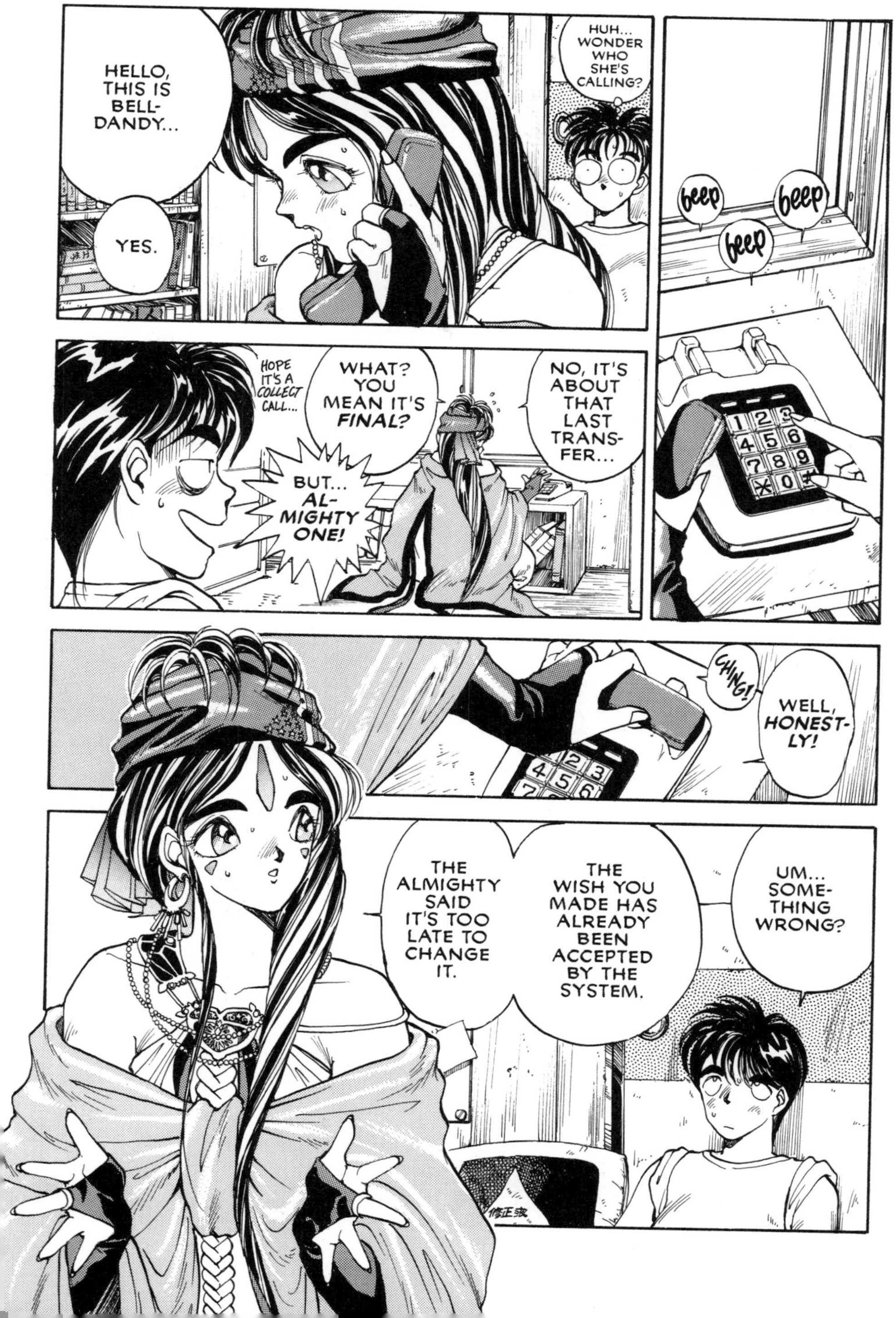
beep
beep
beep
HUH... WONDER WHO SHE'S CALLING?
HELLO, THIS IS BELL-DANDY...
YES.
NO, IT'S ABOUT THAT LAST TRANS-FER...
WHAT? YOU MEAN IT'S *FINAL?*
HOPE IT'S A COLLECT CALL...
BUT... ***AL-MIGHTY ONE!***
CHING!
WELL, ***HONEST-LY!***
UM... SOME-THING WRONG?
THE WISH YOU MADE HAS ALREADY BEEN ACCEPTED BY THE SYSTEM.
THE ALMIGHTY SAID IT'S TOO LATE TO CHANGE IT.
修正液

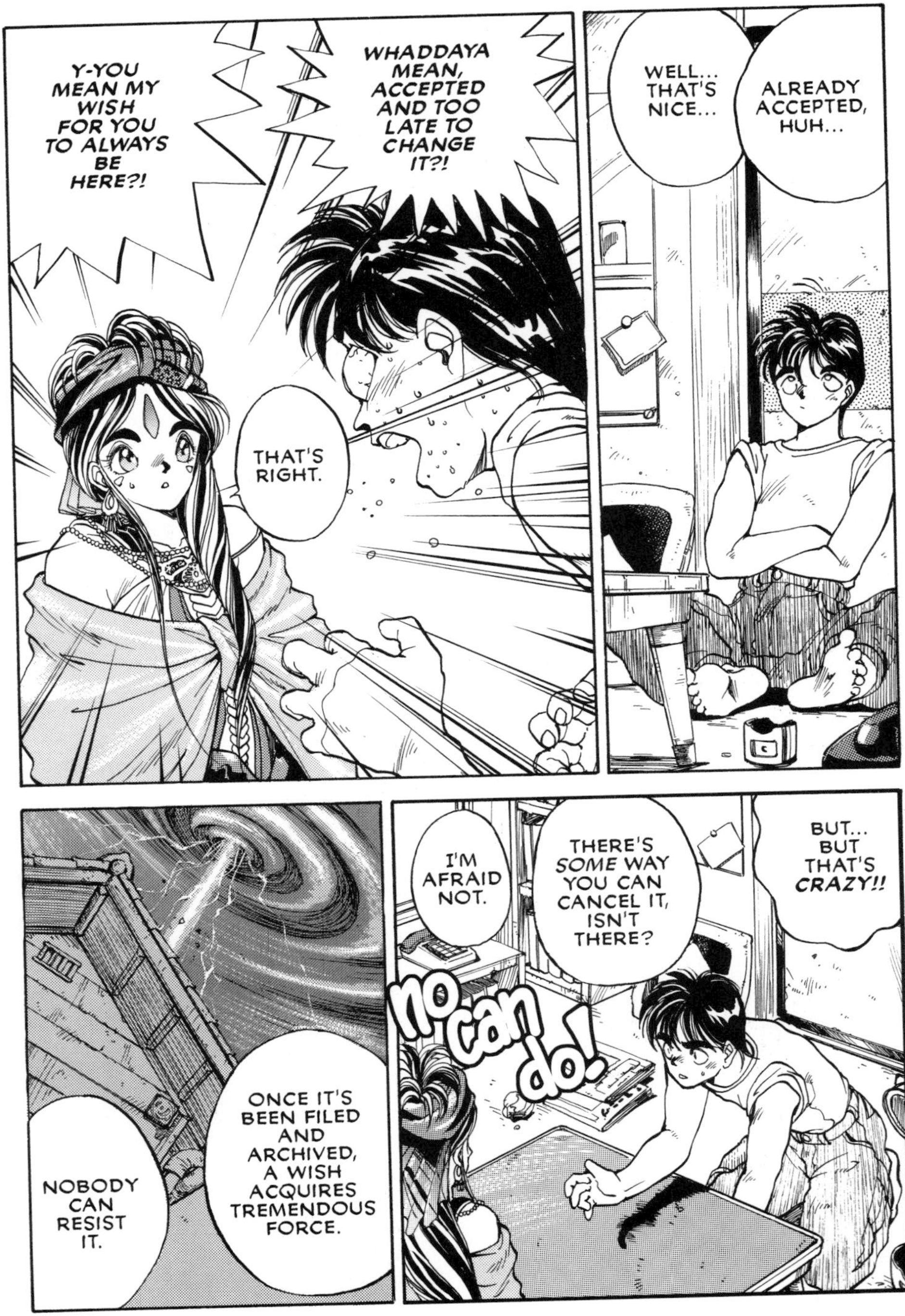
ALREADY ACCEPTED, HUH...
WELL... THAT'S NICE...
WHADDAYA MEAN, ACCEPTED AND TOO LATE TO CHANGE IT?!
Y-YOU MEAN MY WISH FOR YOU TO ALWAYS BE HERE?!
THAT'S RIGHT.
BUT... BUT THAT'S CRAZY!!
THERE'S SOME WAY YOU CAN CANCEL IT, ISN'T THERE?
I'M AFRAID NOT.
no can do!
ONCE IT'S BEEN FILED AND ARCHIVED, A WISH ACQUIRES TREMENDOUS FORCE.
NOBODY CAN RESIST IT.

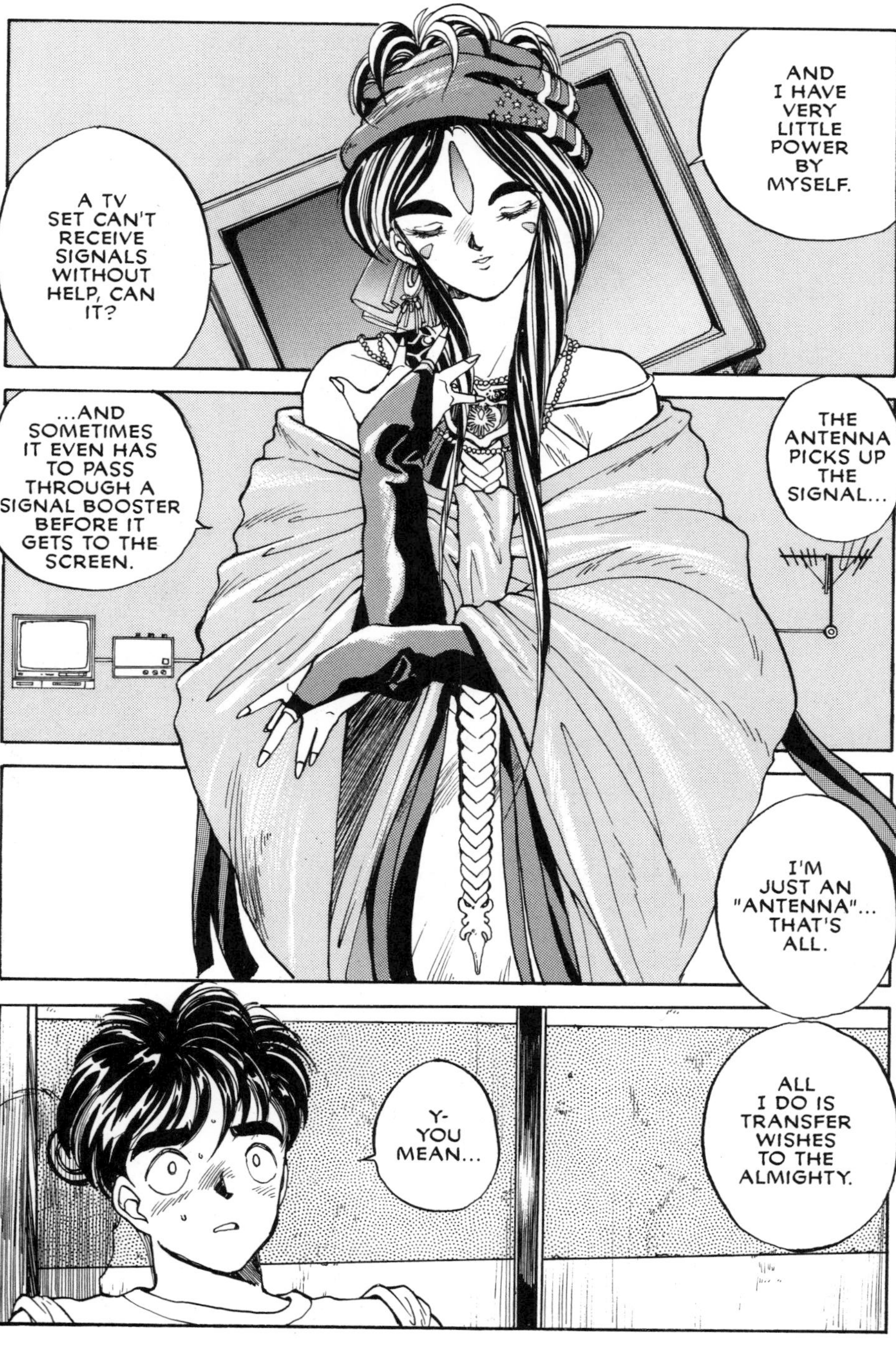
AND I HAVE VERY LITTLE POWER BY MYSELF.
A TV SET CAN'T RECEIVE SIGNALS WITHOUT HELP, CAN IT?
THE ANTENNA PICKS UP THE SIGNAL...
...AND SOMETIMES IT EVEN HAS TO PASS THROUGH A SIGNAL BOOSTER BEFORE IT GETS TO THE SCREEN.
I'M JUST AN "ANTENNA"... THAT'S ALL.
ALL I DO IS TRANSFER WISHES TO THE ALMIGHTY.
Y- YOU MEAN...

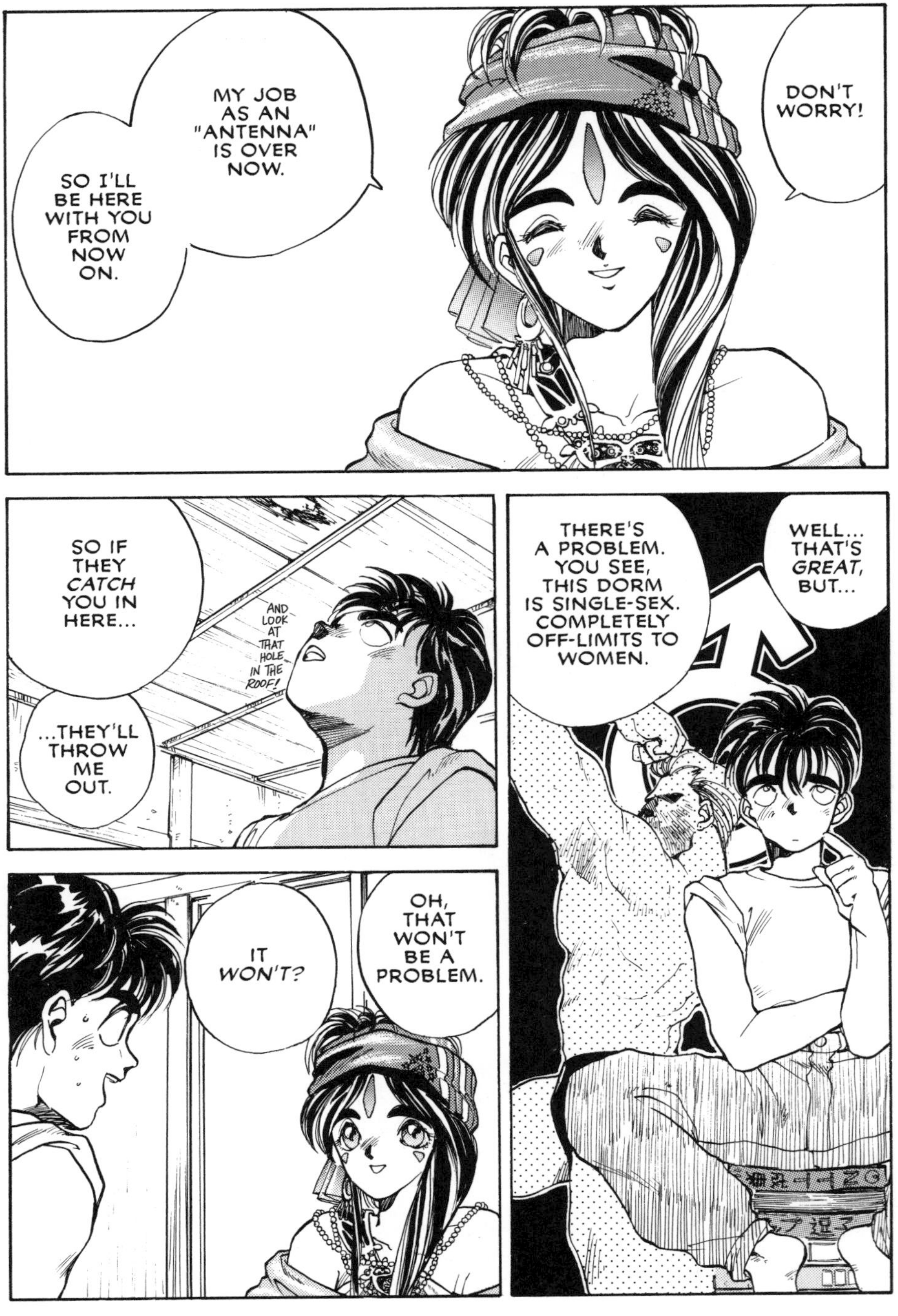
DON'T WORRY!
MY JOB AS AN "ANTENNA" IS OVER NOW.
SO I'LL BE HERE WITH YOU FROM NOW ON.
WELL... THAT'S *GREAT*, BUT...
THERE'S A PROBLEM. YOU SEE, THIS DORM IS SINGLE-SEX. COMPLETELY OFF-LIMITS TO WOMEN.
SO IF THEY *CATCH* YOU IN HERE...
...THEY'LL THROW ME OUT.
AND LOOK AT THAT HOLE IN THE ROOF!
OH, THAT WON'T BE A PROBLEM.
IT *WON'T?*

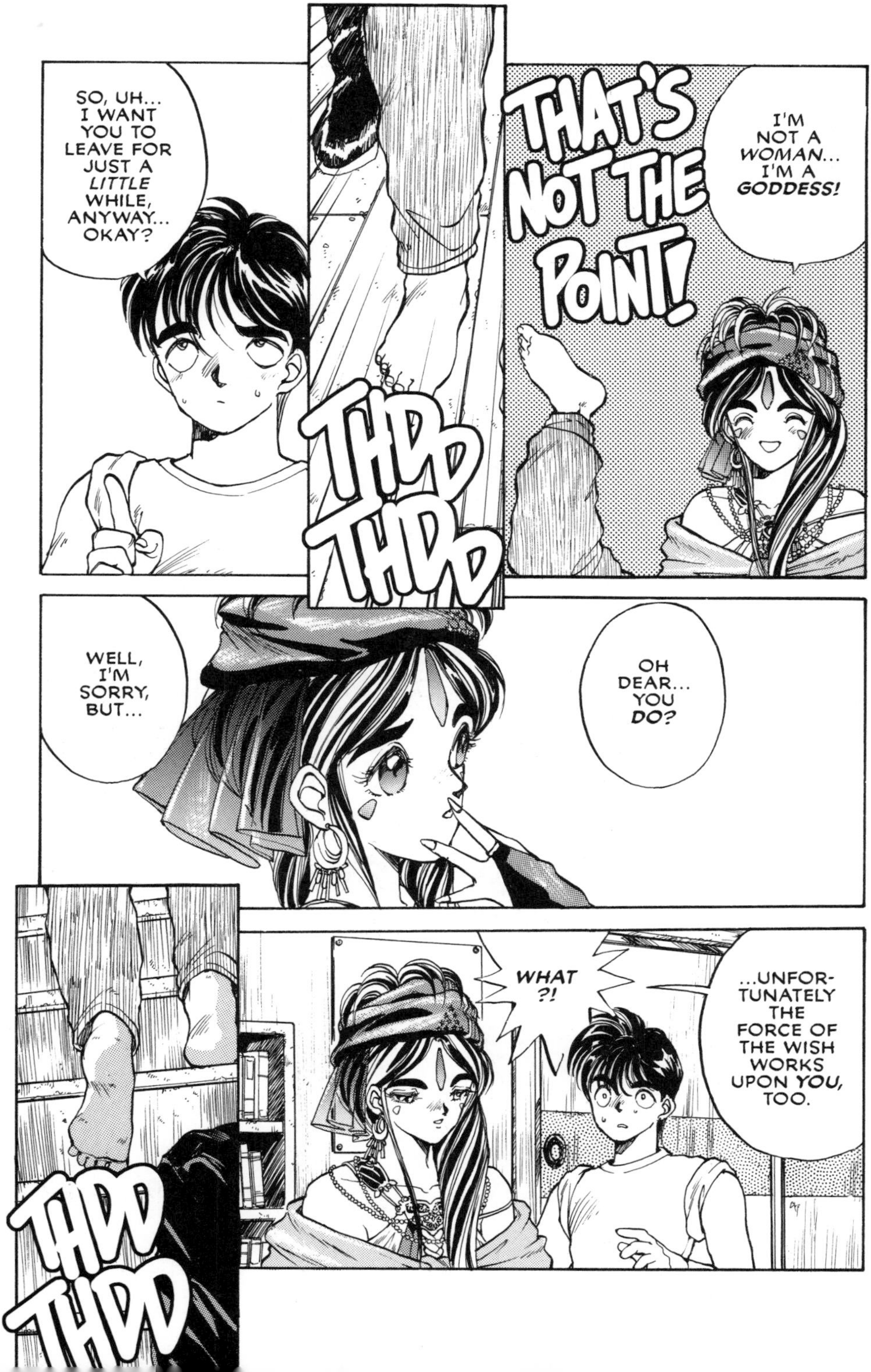
I'M NOT A WOMAN... I'M A GODDESS!
THAT'S NOT THE POINT!
THDD THDD
SO, UH... I WANT YOU TO LEAVE FOR JUST A LITTLE WHILE, ANYWAY... OKAY?
OH DEAR... YOU DO?
WELL, I'M SORRY, BUT...
...UNFORTUNATELY THE FORCE OF THE WISH WORKS UPON YOU, TOO.
WHAT ?!
THDD THDD

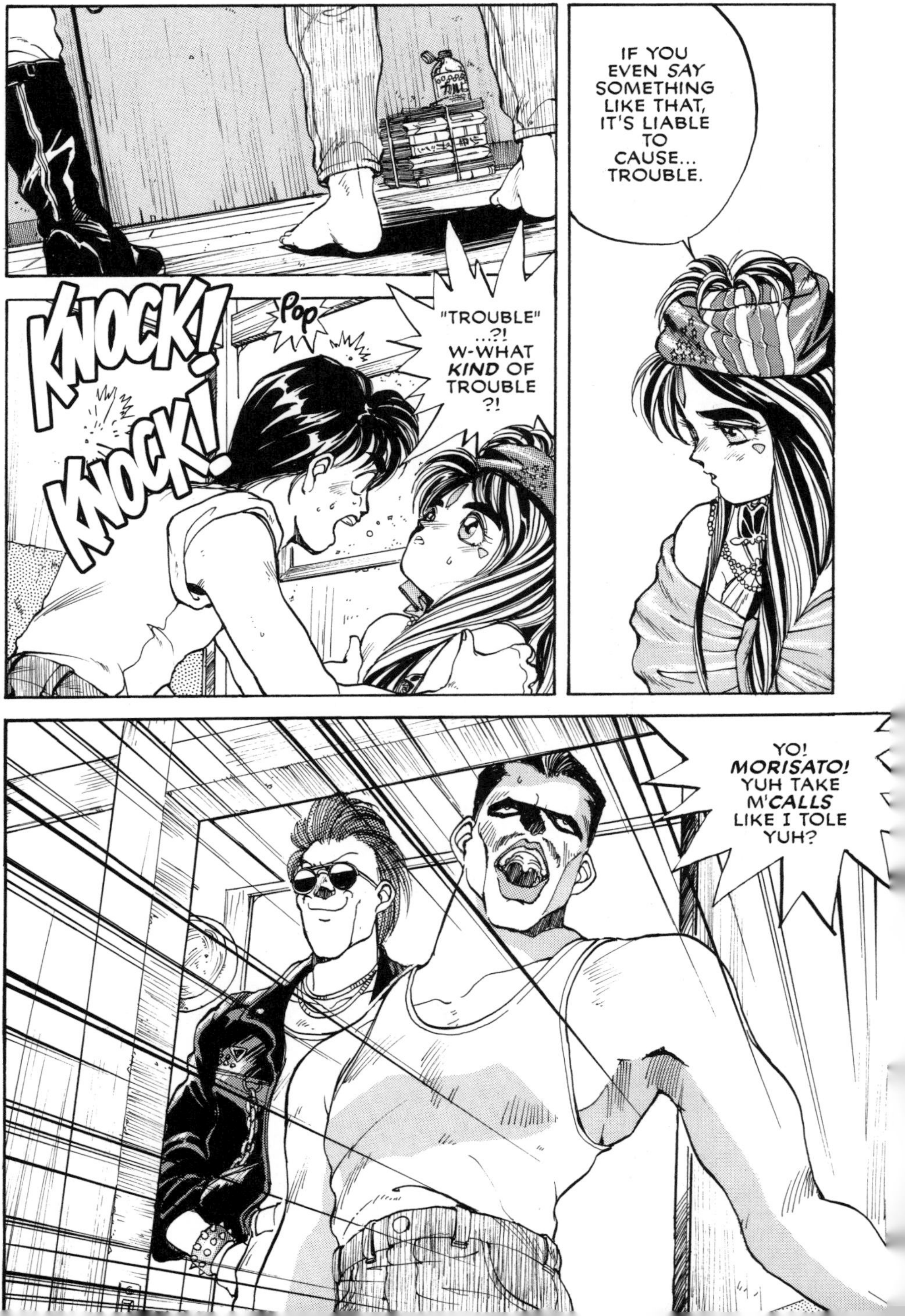
IF YOU EVEN SAY SOMETHING LIKE THAT, IT'S LIABLE TO CAUSE... TROUBLE.
Pop
"TROUBLE" ...?! W-WHAT KIND OF TROUBLE ?!
KNOCK! KNOCK!
YO! MORISATO! YUH TAKE M'CALLS LIKE I TOLE YUH?

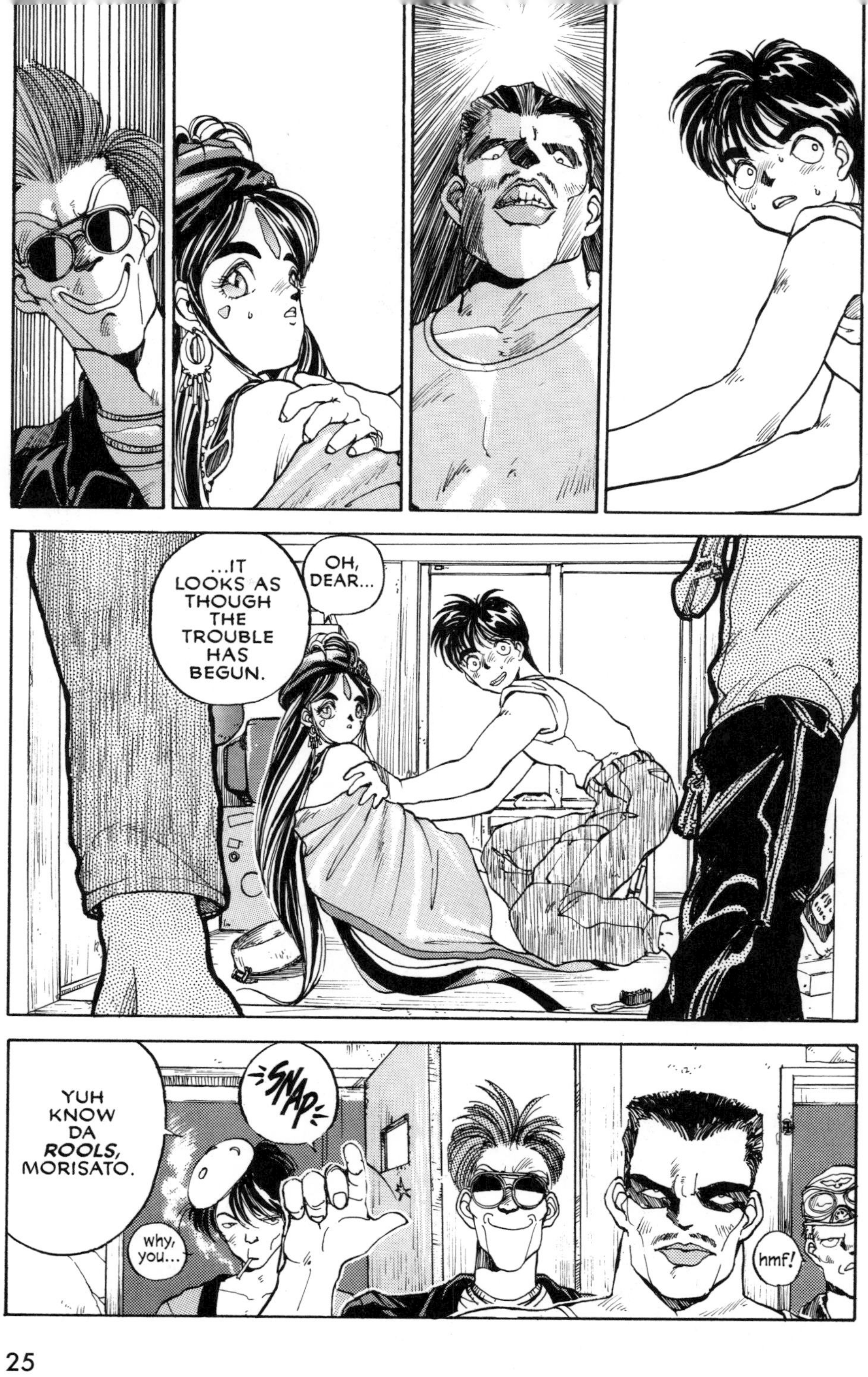
OH, DEAR...
...IT LOOKS AS THOUGH THE TROUBLE HAS BEGUN.
hmf!
SNAP
YUH KNOW DA *ROOLS,* MORISATO.
why, you...

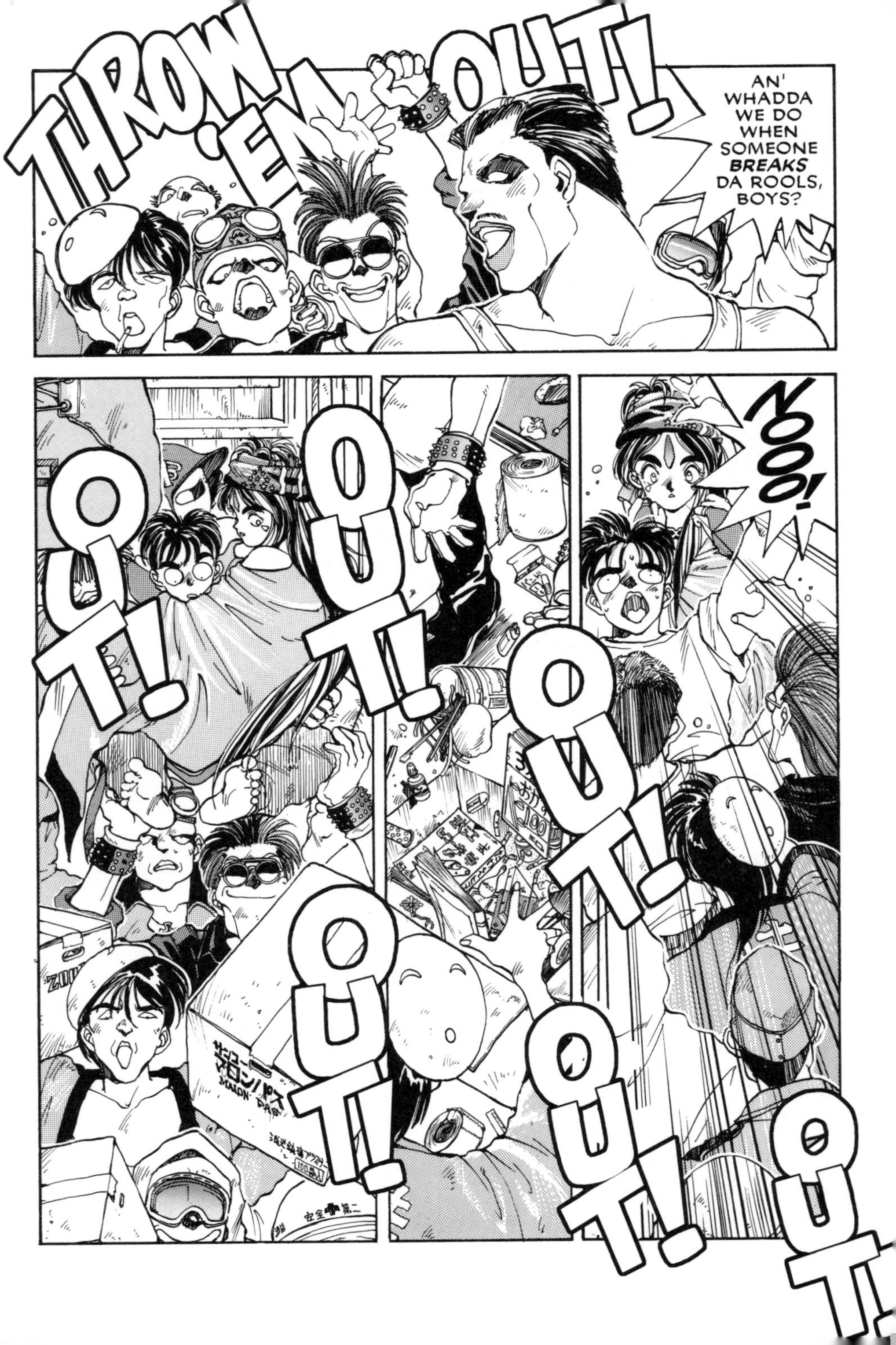
AN' WHADDA WE DO WHEN SOMEONE BREAKS DA ROOLS, BOYS?
THROW 'EM OUT!
NOOOO!
OUT!
OUT!
OUT!
OUT!
OUT!
OUT!

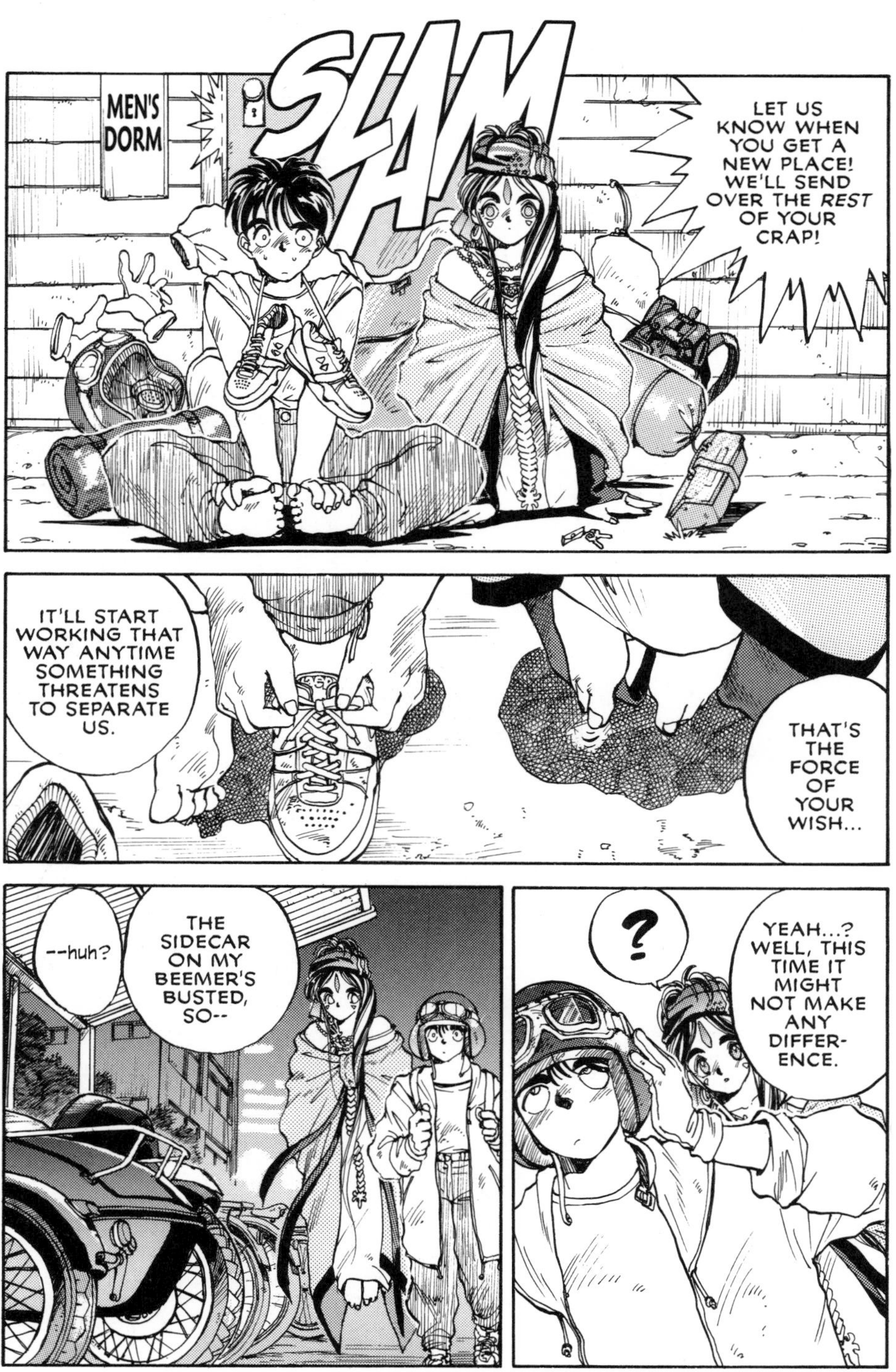
SLAM
LET US KNOW WHEN YOU GET A NEW PLACE! WE'LL SEND OVER THE *REST* OF YOUR CRAP!
MEN'S DORM
THAT'S THE FORCE OF YOUR WISH...
IT'LL START WORKING THAT WAY ANYTIME SOMETHING THREATENS TO SEPARATE US.
YEAH...? WELL, THIS TIME IT MIGHT NOT MAKE ANY DIFFER-ENCE.
?
THE SIDECAR ON MY BEEMER'S BUSTED, SO--
--huh?

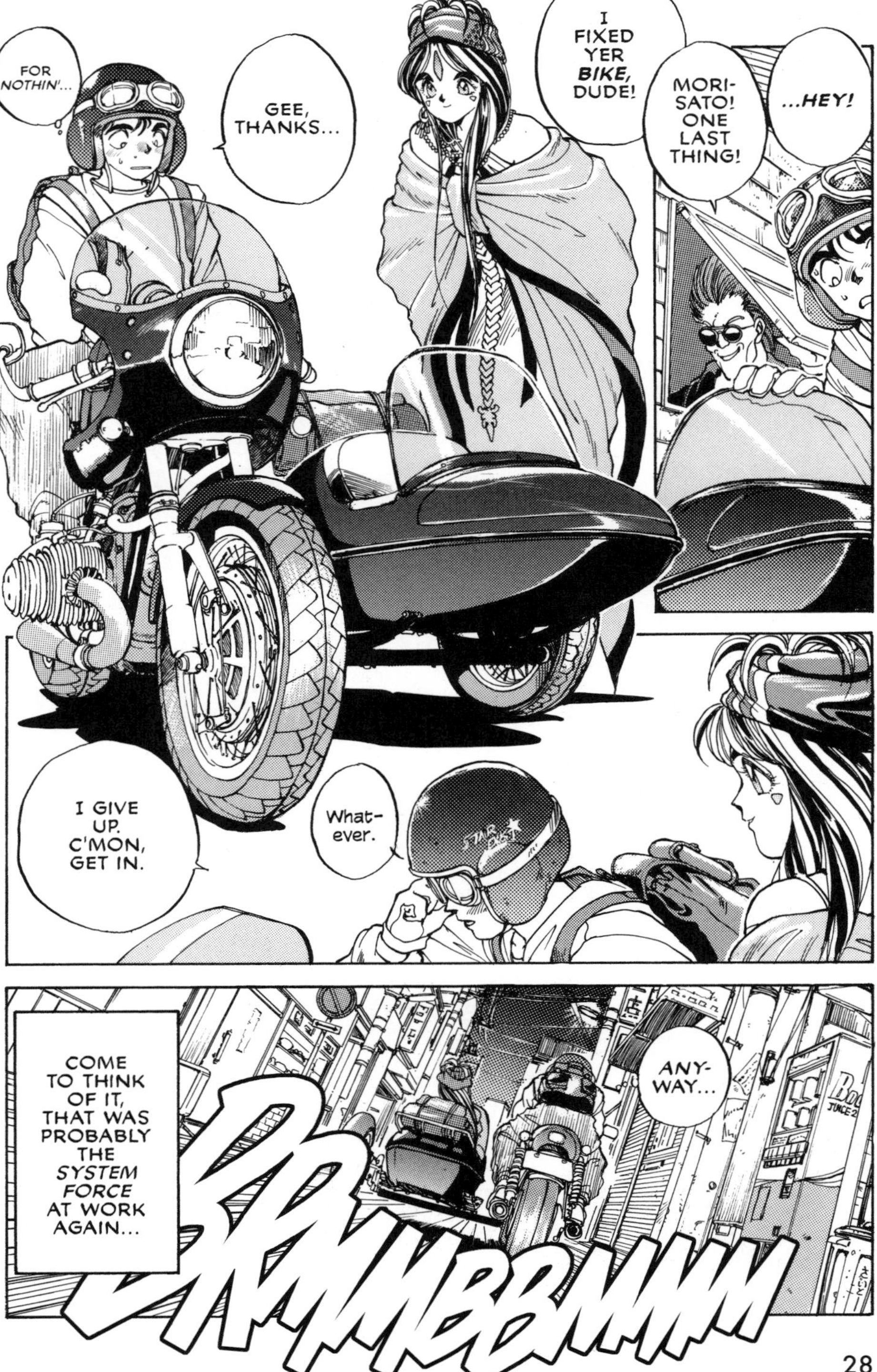
...HEY!
MORI-SATO! ONE LAST THING!
I FIXED YER BIKE, DUDE!
GEE, THANKS...
FOR NOTHIN'...
What-ever.
I GIVE UP. C'MON, GET IN.
ANY-WAY...
COME TO THINK OF IT, THAT WAS PROBABLY THE *SYSTEM FORCE* AT WORK AGAIN...

CHAPTER 2

Lair of the Anime Mania

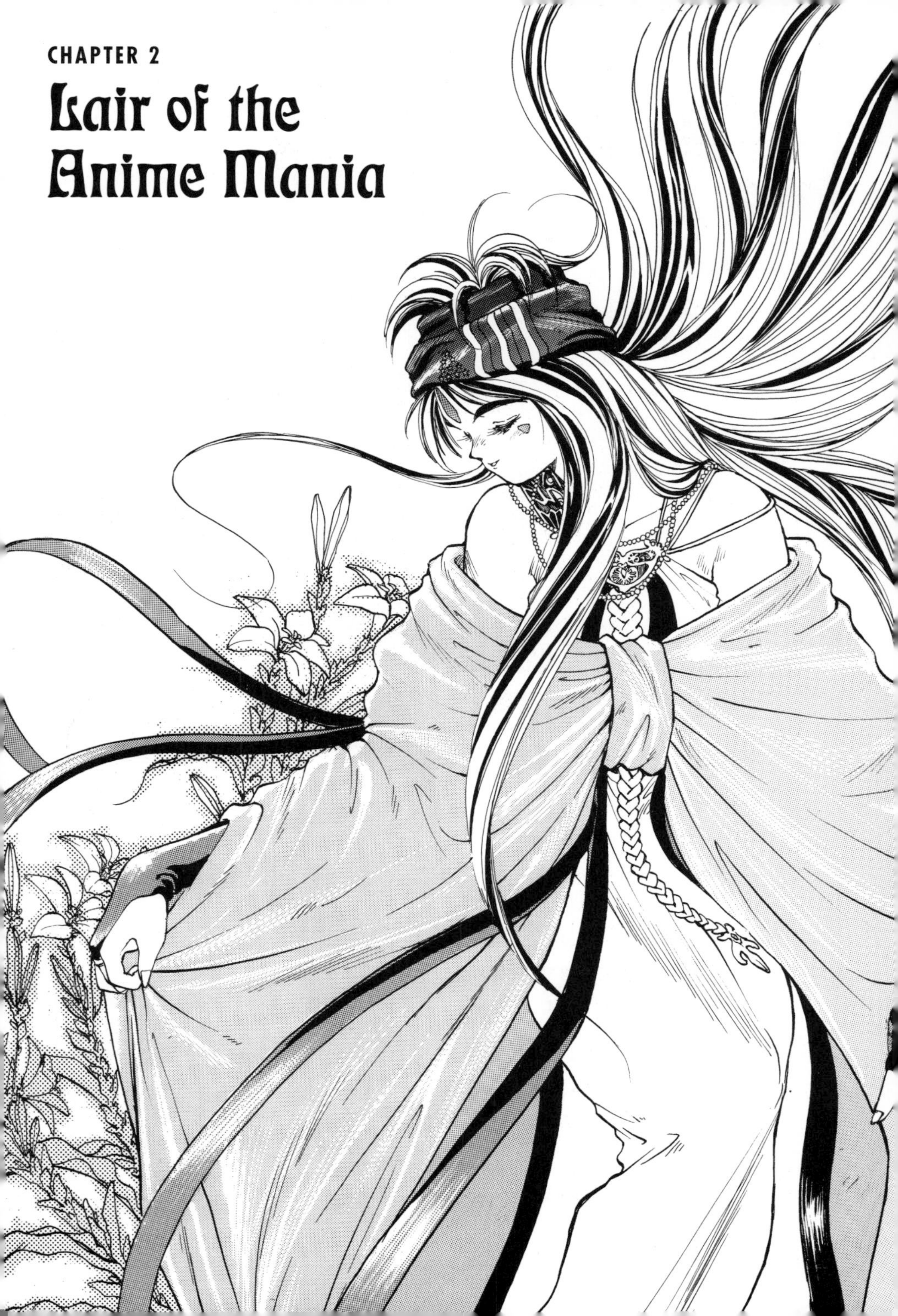

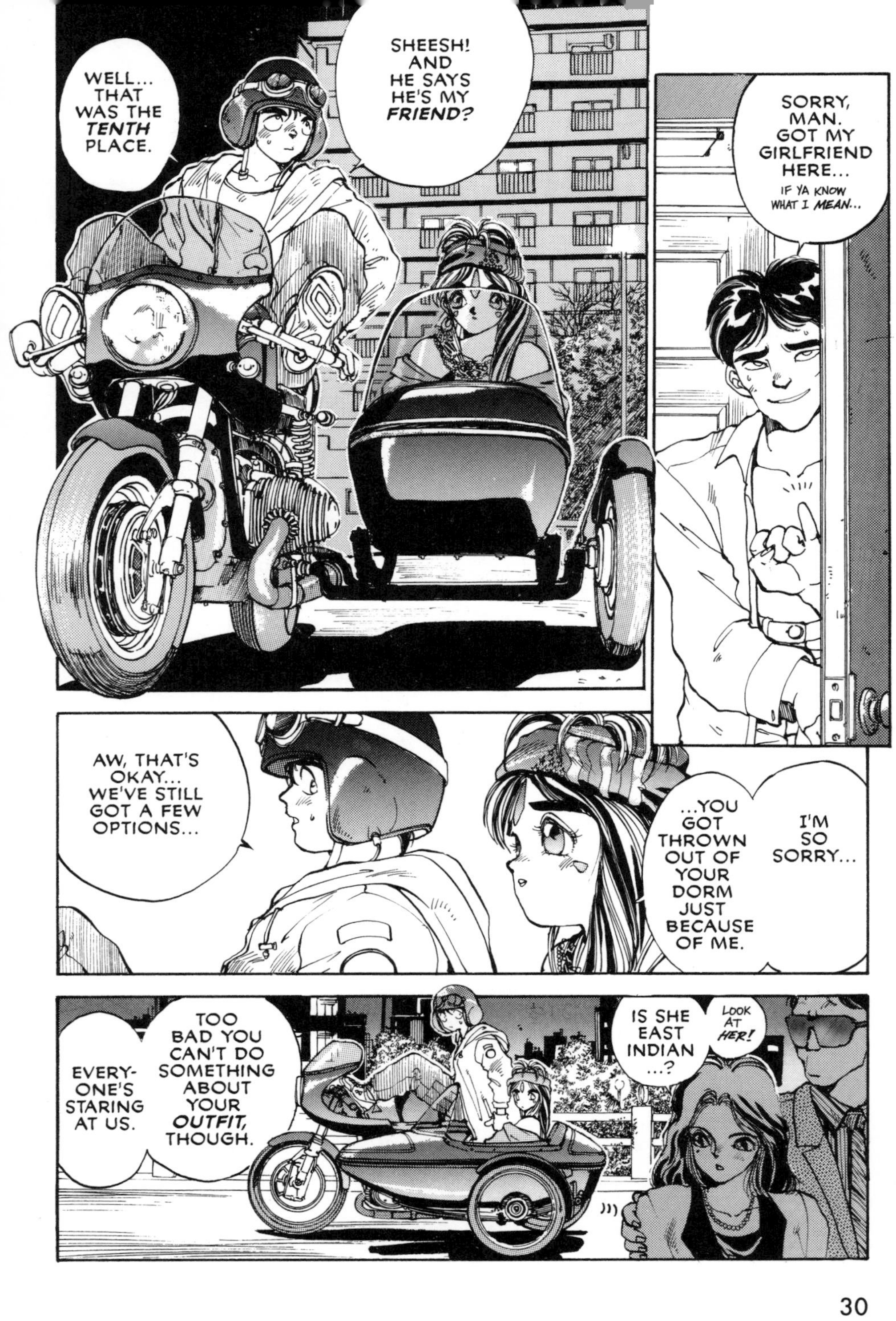
SORRY, MAN. GOT MY GIRLFRIEND HERE... IF YA KNOW WHAT I *MEAN*...
SHEESH! AND HE SAYS HE'S MY *FRIEND*?
WELL... THAT WAS THE *TENTH* PLACE.
I'M SO SORRY...
...YOU GOT THROWN OUT OF YOUR DORM JUST BECAUSE OF ME.
AW, THAT'S OKAY... WE'VE STILL GOT A FEW OPTIONS...
LOOK AT *HER!*
IS SHE EAST INDIAN ...?
TOO BAD YOU CAN'T DO SOMETHING ABOUT YOUR *OUTFIT,* THOUGH.
EVERY-ONE'S STARING AT US.

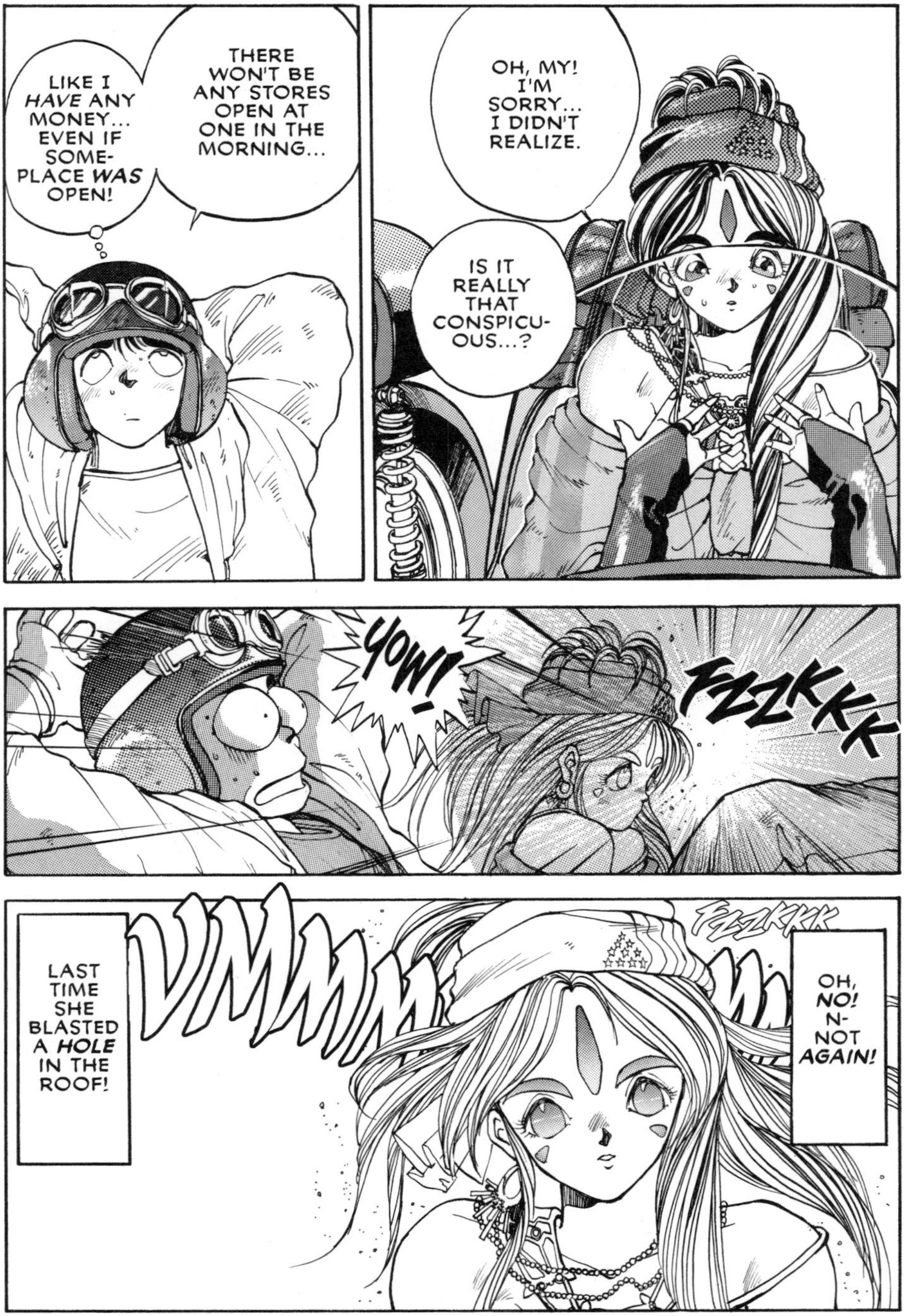
OH, MY! I'M SORRY... I DIDN'T REALIZE.
IS IT REALLY THAT CONSPICU-OUS...?
THERE WON'T BE ANY STORES OPEN AT ONE IN THE MORNING...
LIKE I *HAVE* ANY MONEY... EVEN IF SOME-PLACE ***WAS*** OPEN!
FZZKKKK
YOW!
FZZKKK
OH, ***NO!*** N-NOT ***AGAIN!***
VMMMM
LAST TIME SHE BLASTED A ***HOLE*** IN THE ROOF!

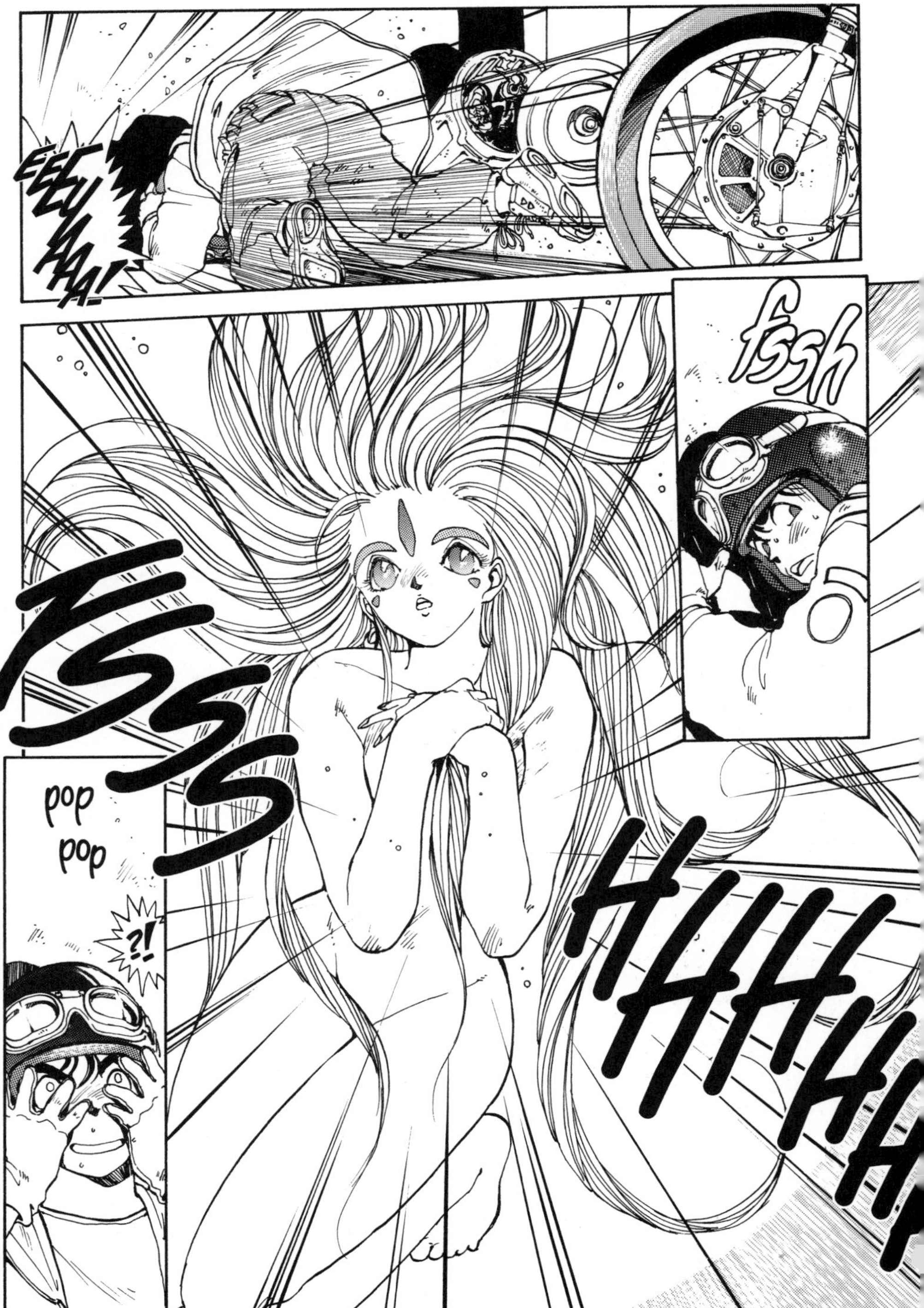
EEEYAAAA!
fssh
FSSSHHHHH
pop pop
?!

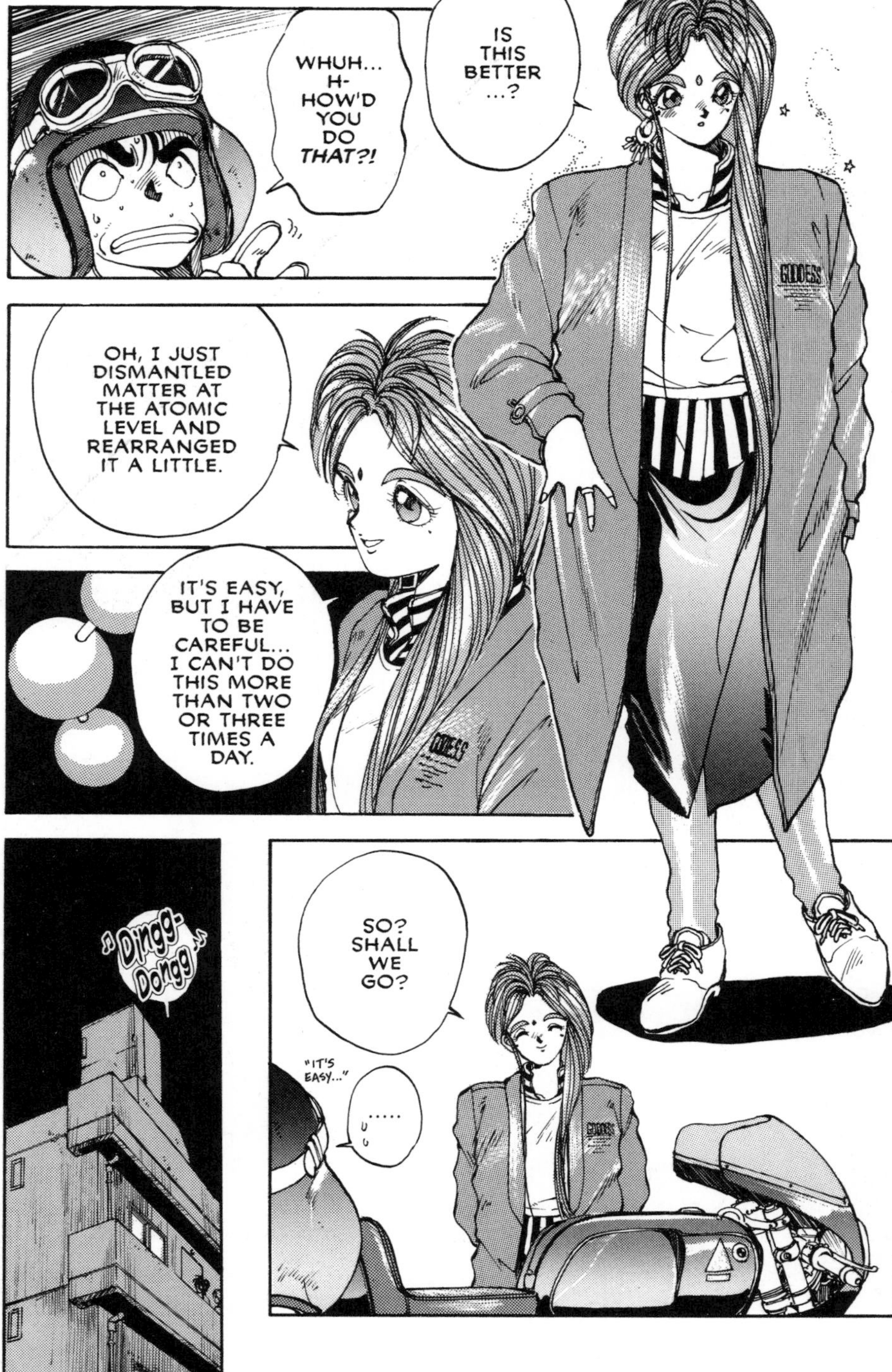
IS THIS BETTER ...?
WHUH... H-HOW'D YOU DO THAT?!
OH, I JUST DISMANTLED MATTER AT THE ATOMIC LEVEL AND REARRANGED IT A LITTLE.
IT'S EASY, BUT I HAVE TO BE CAREFUL... I CAN'T DO THIS MORE THAN TWO OR THREE TIMES A DAY.
SO? SHALL WE GO?
"IT'S EASY..."
.....
Dingg-Dongg

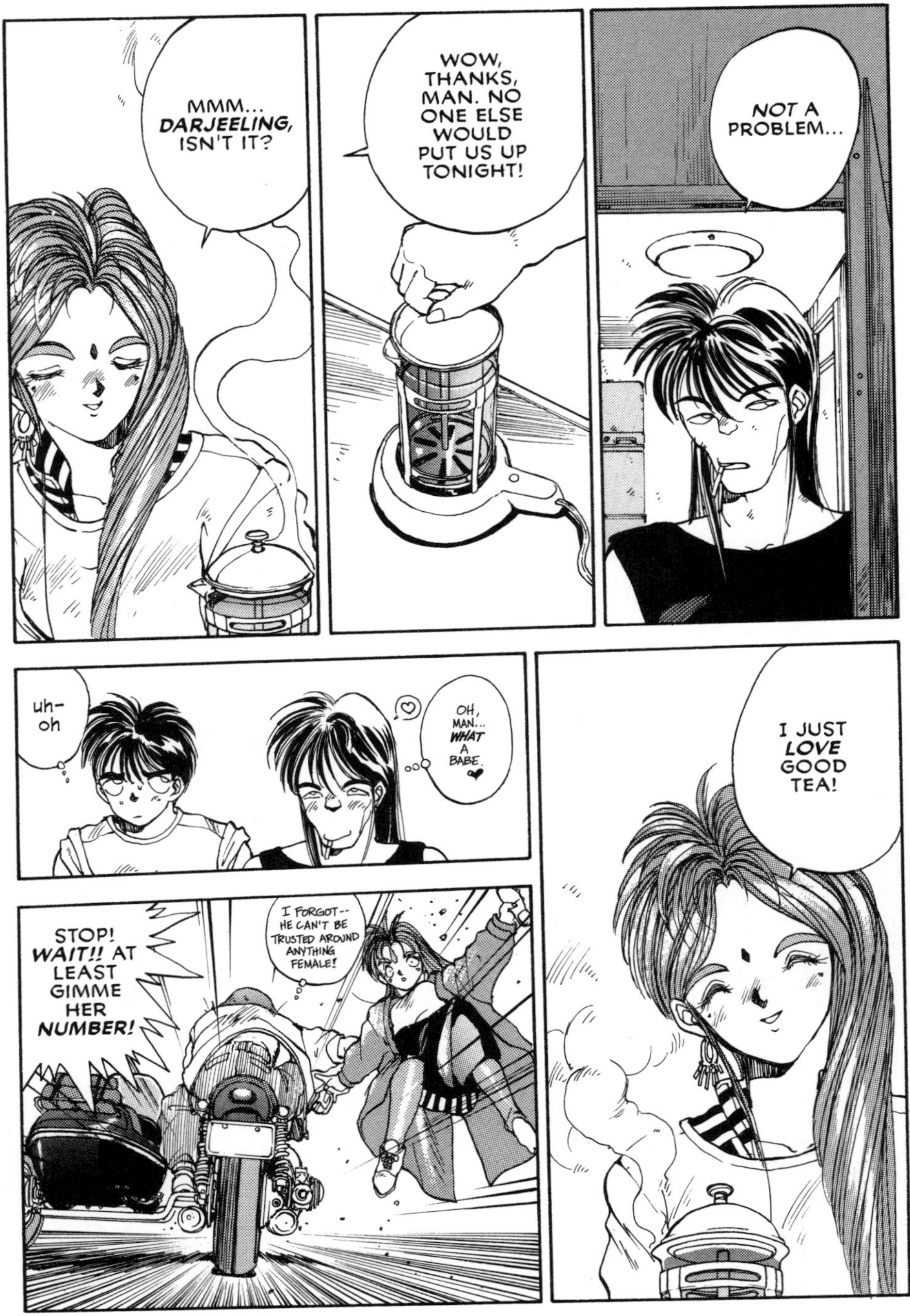
NOT A PROBLEM...
WOW, THANKS, MAN. NO ONE ELSE WOULD PUT US UP TONIGHT!
MMM... DARJEELING, ISN'T IT?
I JUST LOVE GOOD TEA!
OH, MAN... WHAT A BABE
uh-oh
I FORGOT-- HE CAN'T BE TRUSTED AROUND ANYTHING FEMALE!
STOP! WAIT!! AT LEAST GIMME HER NUMBER!

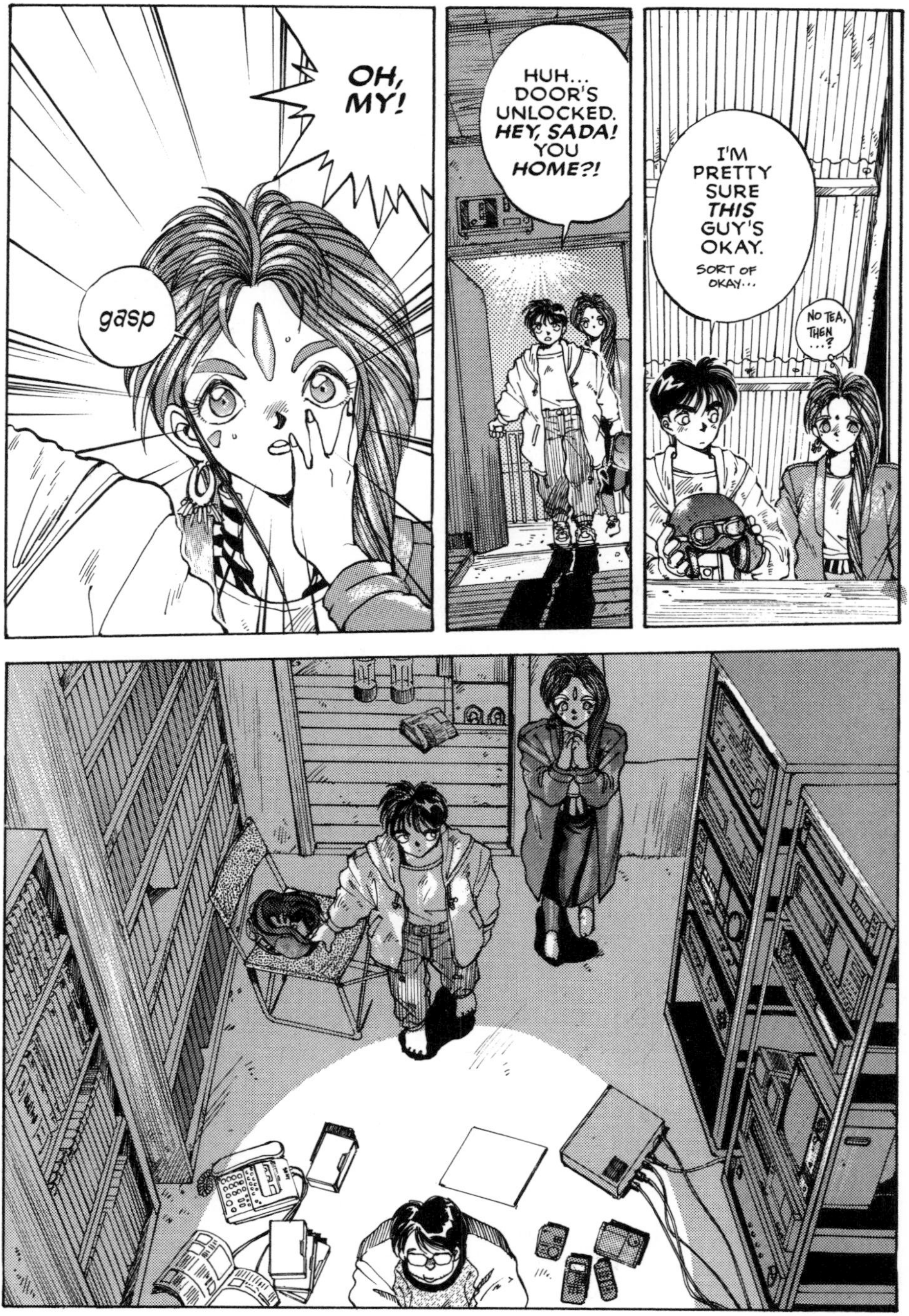
I'M PRETTY SURE THIS GUY'S OKAY.
SORT OF OKAY...
NO TEA, THEN...?
HUH... DOOR'S UNLOCKED. HEY, SADA! YOU HOME?!
OH, MY!
gasp

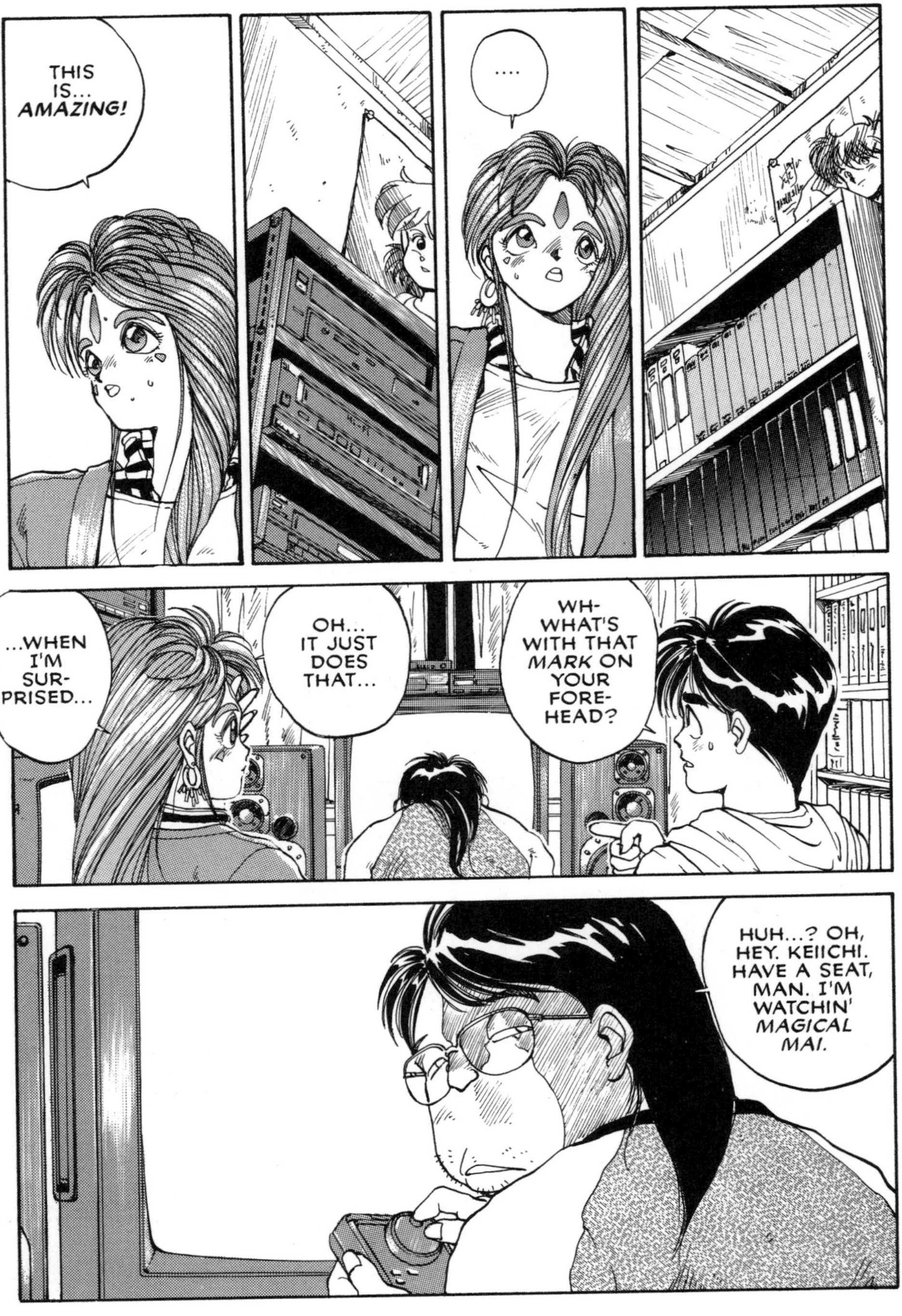
....
THIS IS... AMAZING!
WH-WHAT'S WITH THAT MARK ON YOUR FOREHEAD?
OH... IT JUST DOES THAT...
...WHEN I'M SURPRISED...
HUH...? OH, HEY. KEIICHI. HAVE A SEAT, MAN. I'M WATCHIN' MAGICAL MAI.

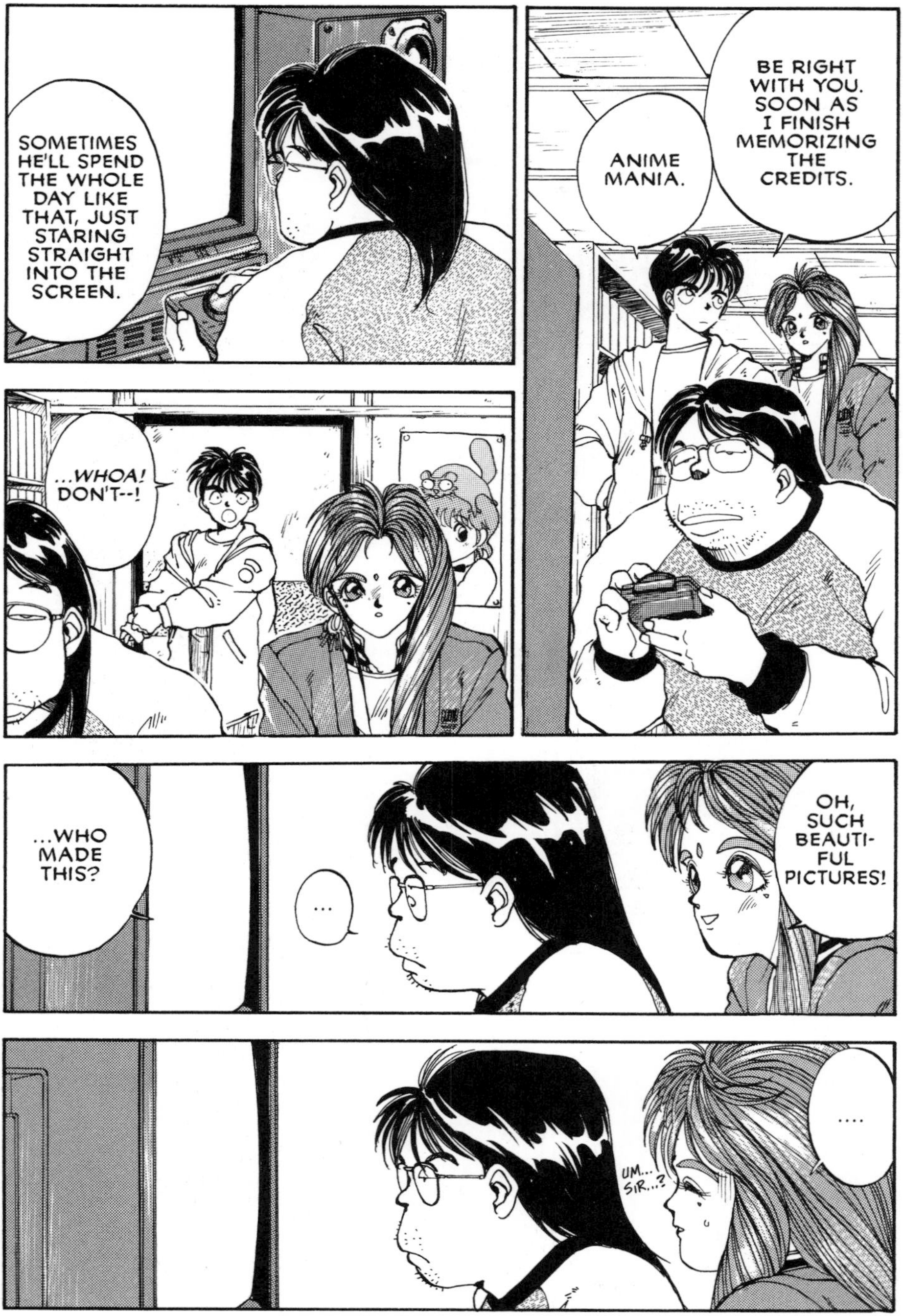

BE RIGHT WITH YOU. SOON AS I FINISH MEMORIZING THE CREDITS.
ANIME MANIA.
SOMETIMES HE'LL SPEND THE WHOLE DAY LIKE THAT, JUST STARING STRAIGHT INTO THE SCREEN.
...WHOA! DON'T--!
OH, SUCH BEAUTIFUL PICTURES!
...
...WHO MADE THIS?
....
UM... SIR...?

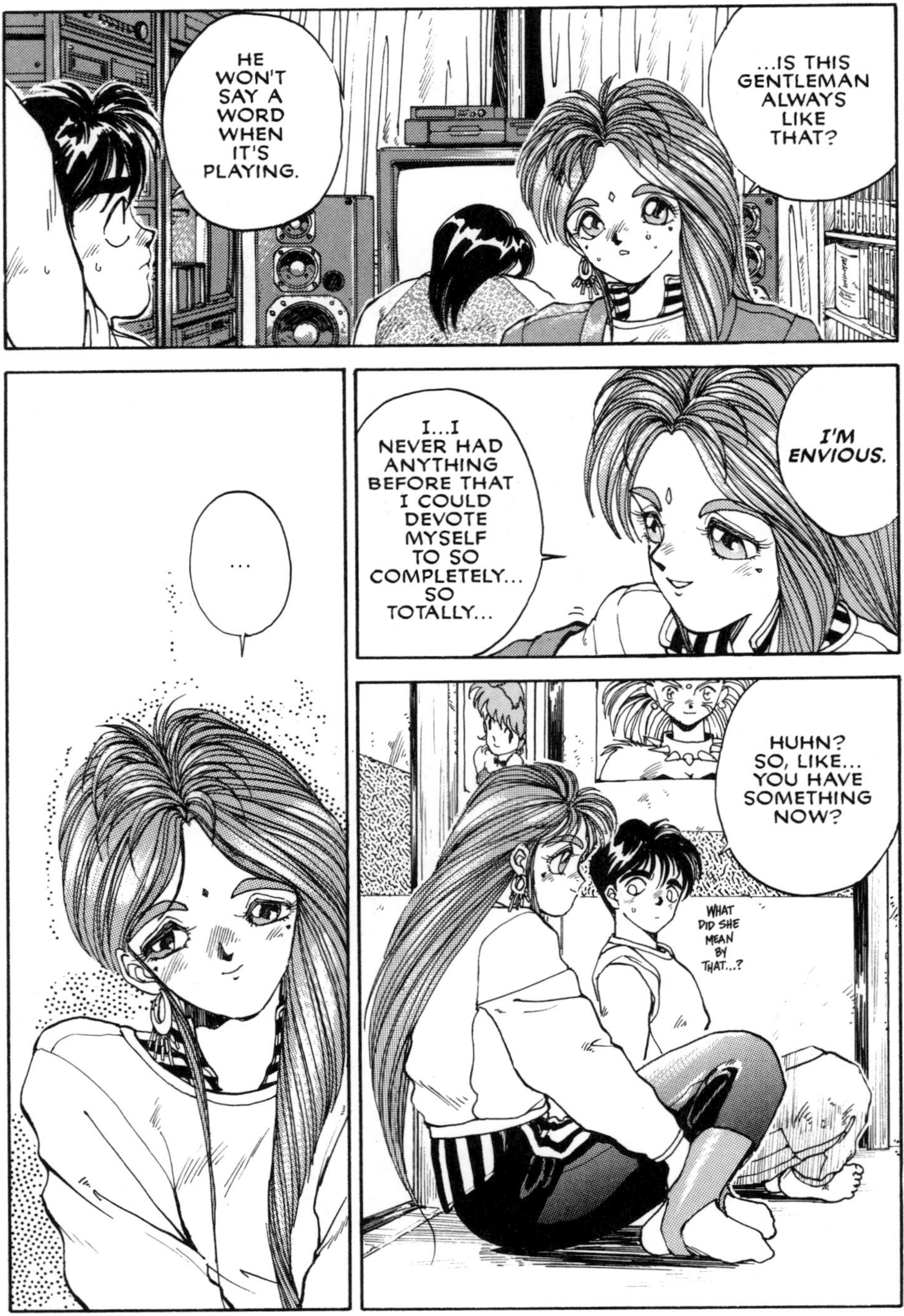
...IS THIS GENTLEMAN ALWAYS LIKE THAT?
HE WON'T SAY A WORD WHEN IT'S PLAYING.
I'M ENVIOUS.
I...I NEVER HAD ANYTHING BEFORE THAT I COULD DEVOTE MYSELF TO SO COMPLETELY... SO TOTALLY...
HUHN? SO, LIKE... YOU HAVE SOMETHING NOW?
WHAT DID SHE MEAN BY THAT...?
...

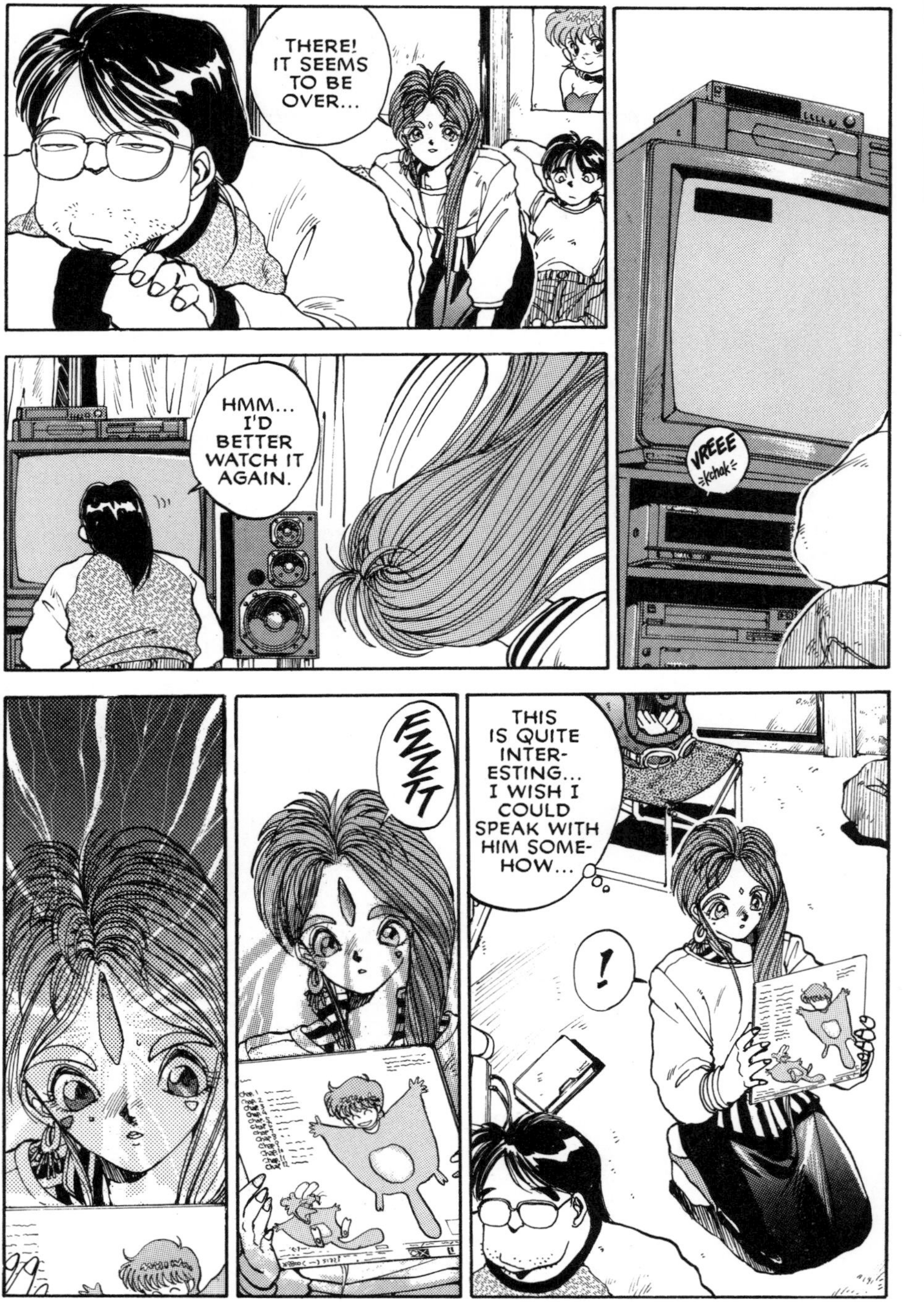
VREEE
kchak
THERE! IT SEEMS TO BE OVER...
HMM... I'D BETTER WATCH IT AGAIN.
THIS IS QUITE INTER-ESTING... I WISH I COULD SPEAK WITH HIM SOME-HOW...
!
EZZZT

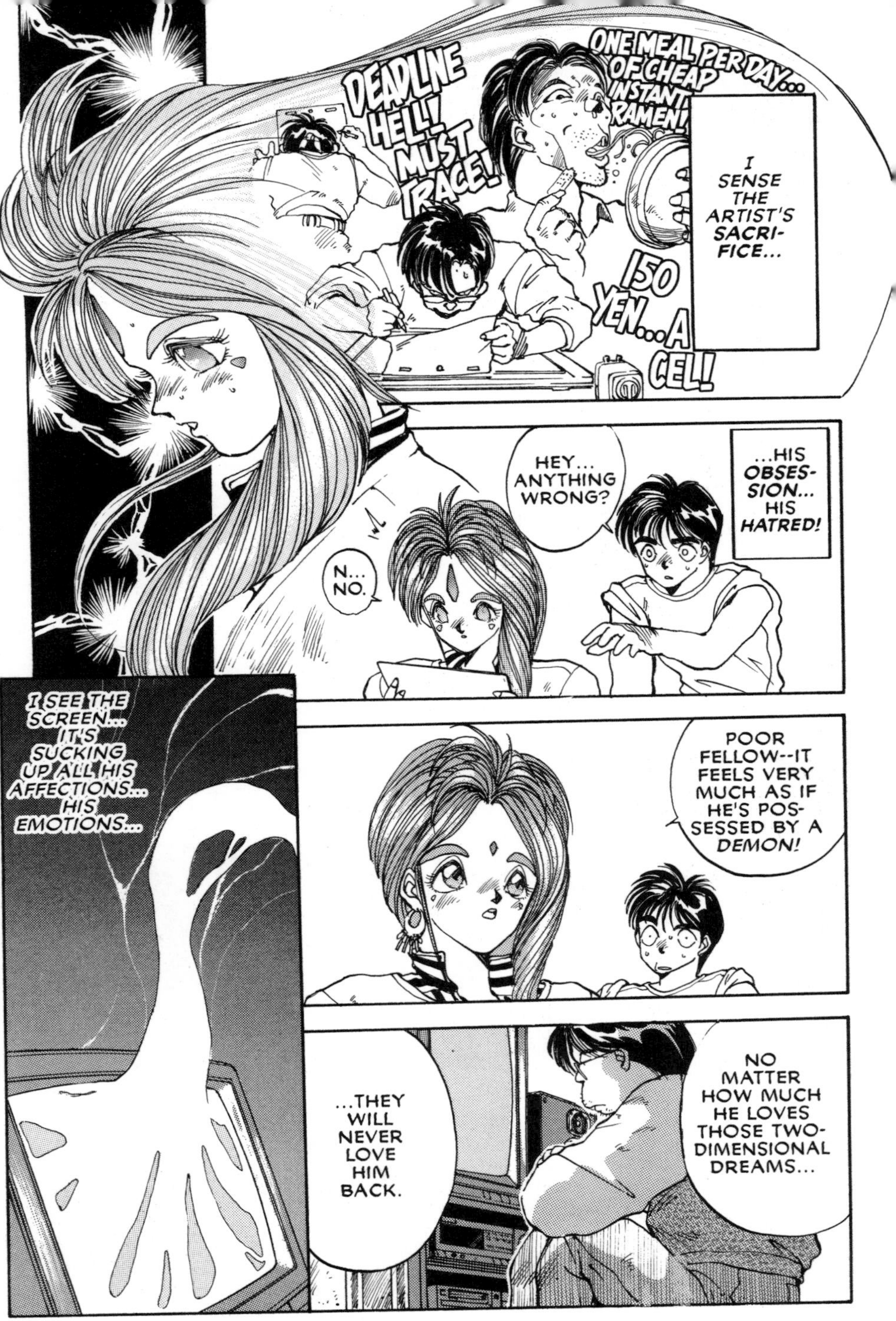
ONE MEAL PER DAY... OF CHEAP INSTANT RAMEN!
I SENSE THE ARTIST'S SACRIFICE...
150 YEN...A CEL!
DEADLINE HELL! MUST TRACE!
...HIS OBSESSION... HIS HATRED!
HEY... ANYTHING WRONG?
N... NO.
POOR FELLOW--IT FEELS VERY MUCH AS IF HE'S POSSESSED BY A DEMON!
NO MATTER HOW MUCH HE LOVES THOSE TWO-DIMENSIONAL DREAMS...
...THEY WILL NEVER LOVE HIM BACK.
I SEE THE SCREEN... IT'S SUCKING UP ALL HIS AFFECTIONS... HIS EMOTIONS...

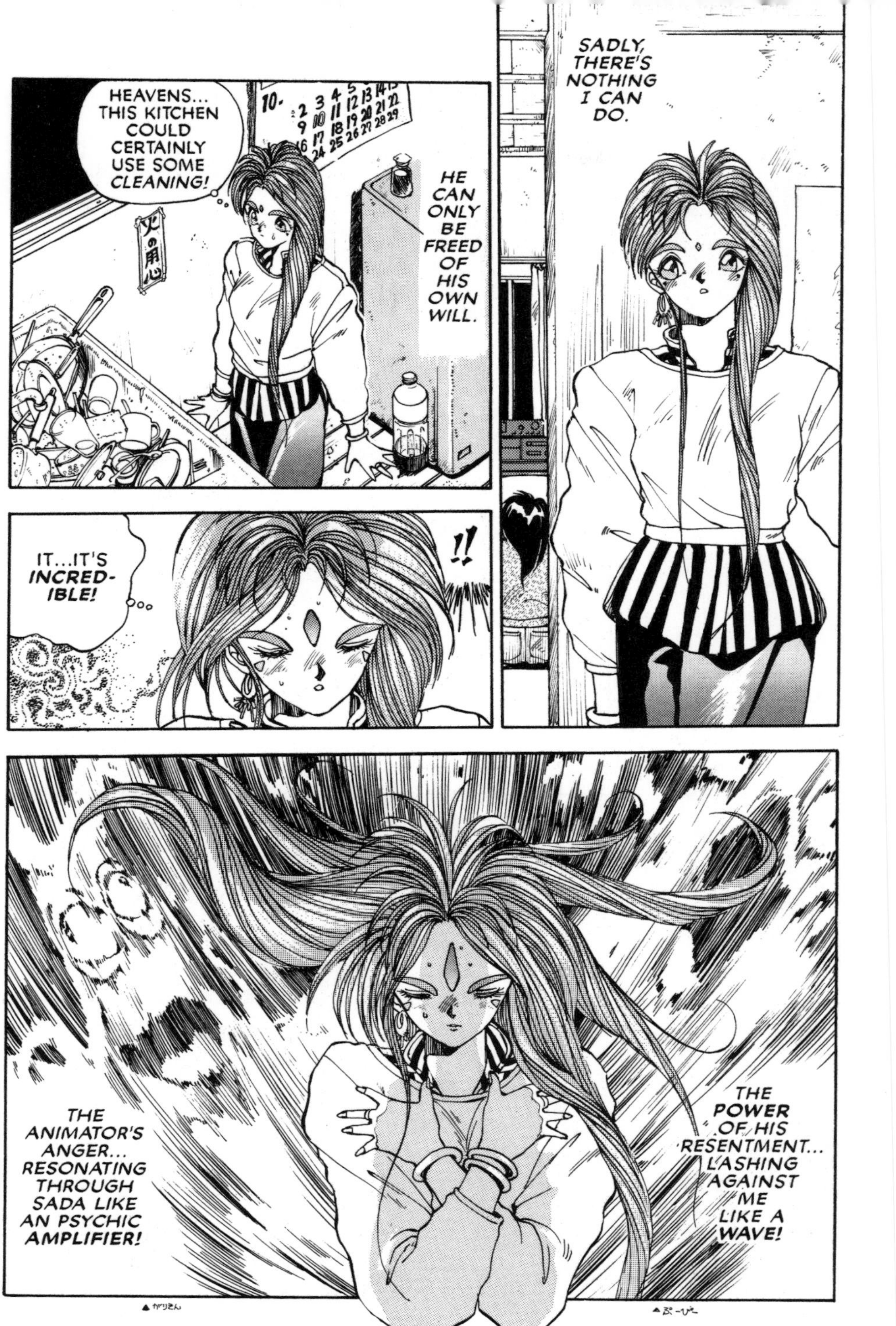

SADLY, THERE'S NOTHING I CAN DO.
HE CAN ONLY BE FREED OF HIS OWN WILL.
HEAVENS... THIS KITCHEN COULD CERTAINLY USE SOME *CLEANING!*
火の用心
!!
IT...IT'S *INCRED-IBLE!*
THE *POWER* OF HIS *RESENTMENT...* LASHING AGAINST ME LIKE A *WAVE!*
THE ANIMATOR'S ANGER... RESONATING THROUGH SADA LIKE AN PSYCHIC AMPLIFIER!

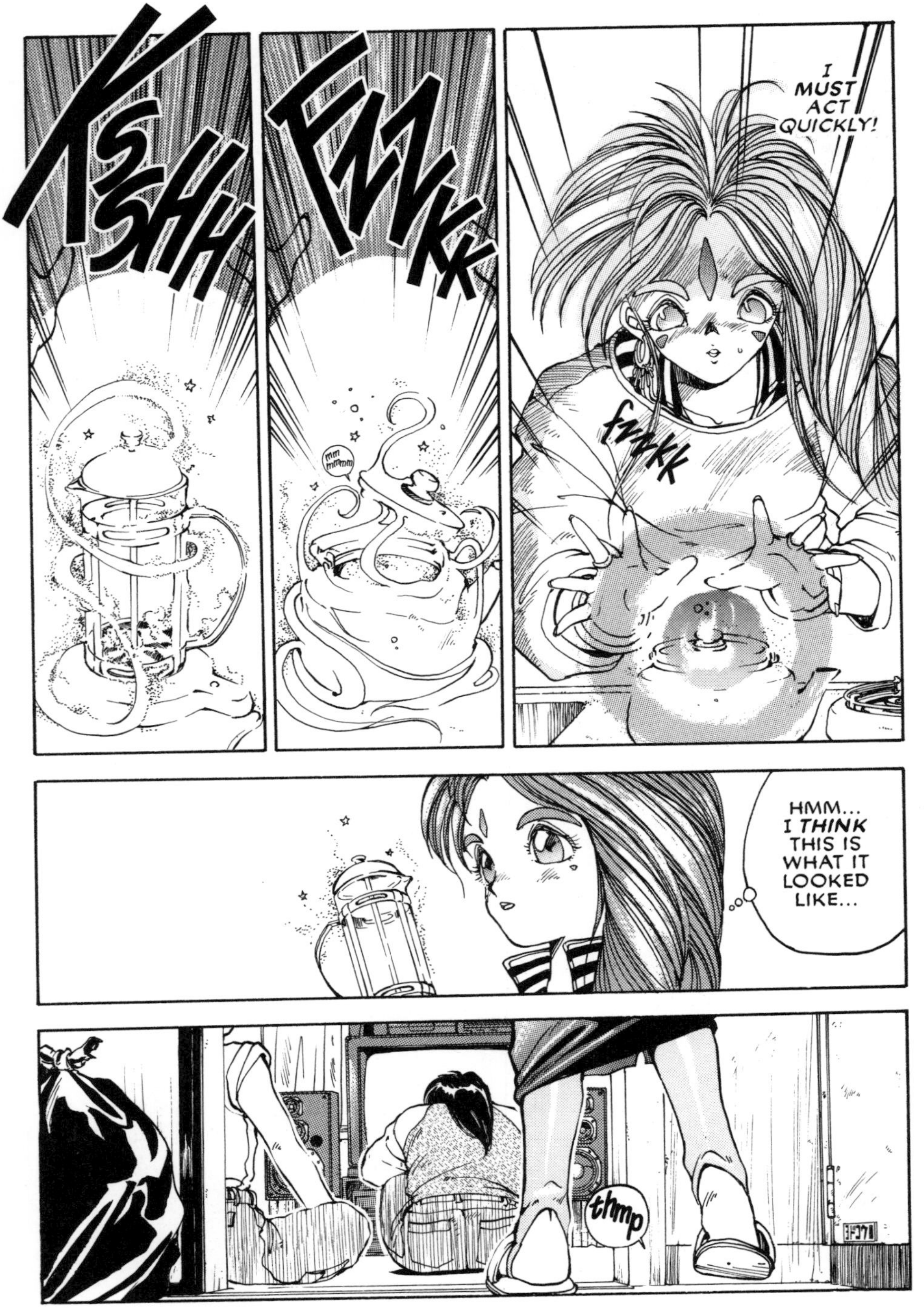
I MUST ACT QUICKLY!
fwnkk
FZNKK
mm mmmm
KSHH
HMM... I *THINK* THIS IS WHAT IT LOOKED LIKE...
thmp

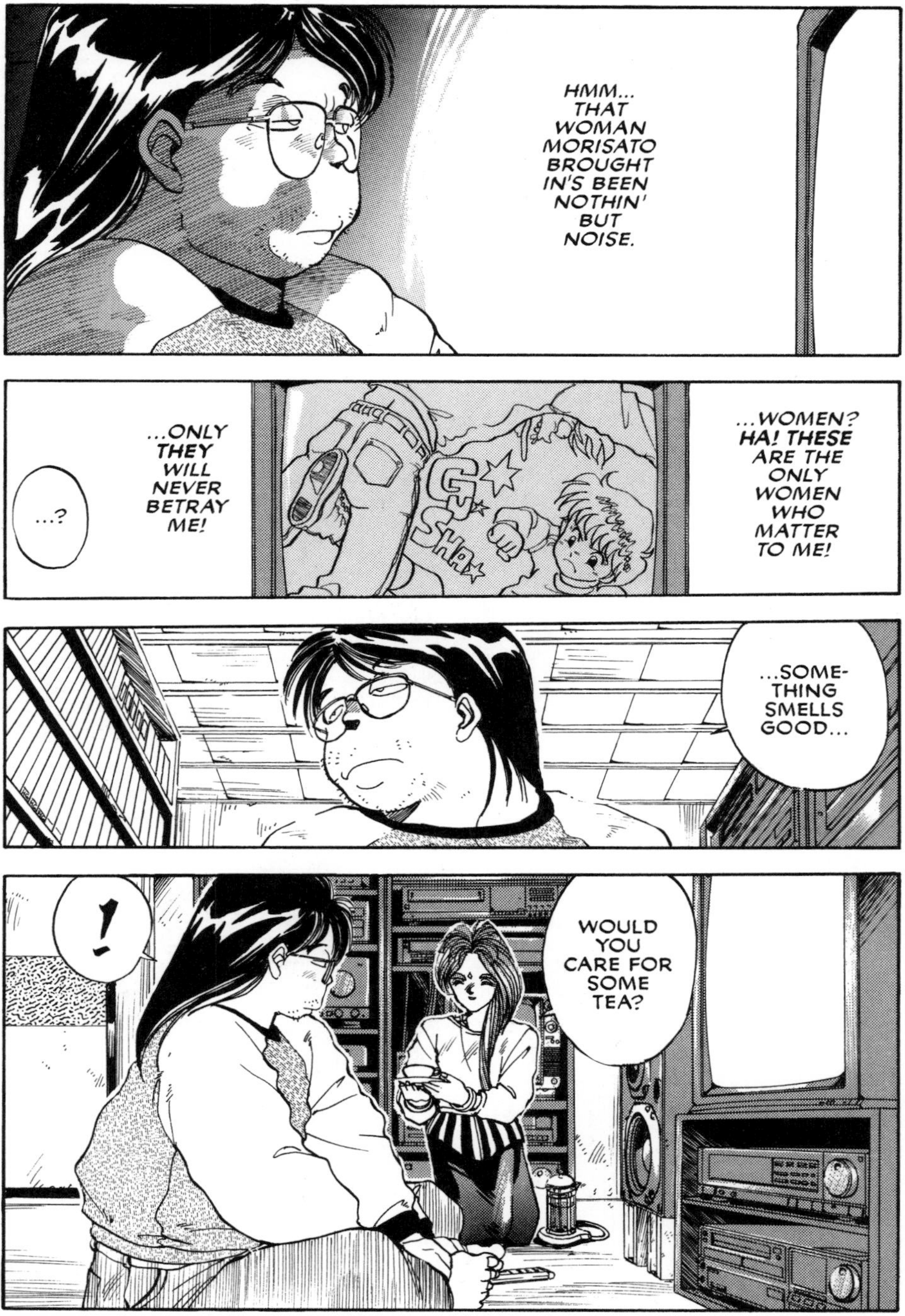
HMM... THAT WOMAN MORISATO BROUGHT IN'S BEEN NOTHIN' BUT NOISE.
...WOMEN? HA! THESE ARE THE ONLY WOMEN WHO MATTER TO ME!
GUSHA
...ONLY THEY WILL NEVER BETRAY ME!
...?
...SOME-THING SMELLS GOOD...
WOULD YOU CARE FOR SOME TEA?
!

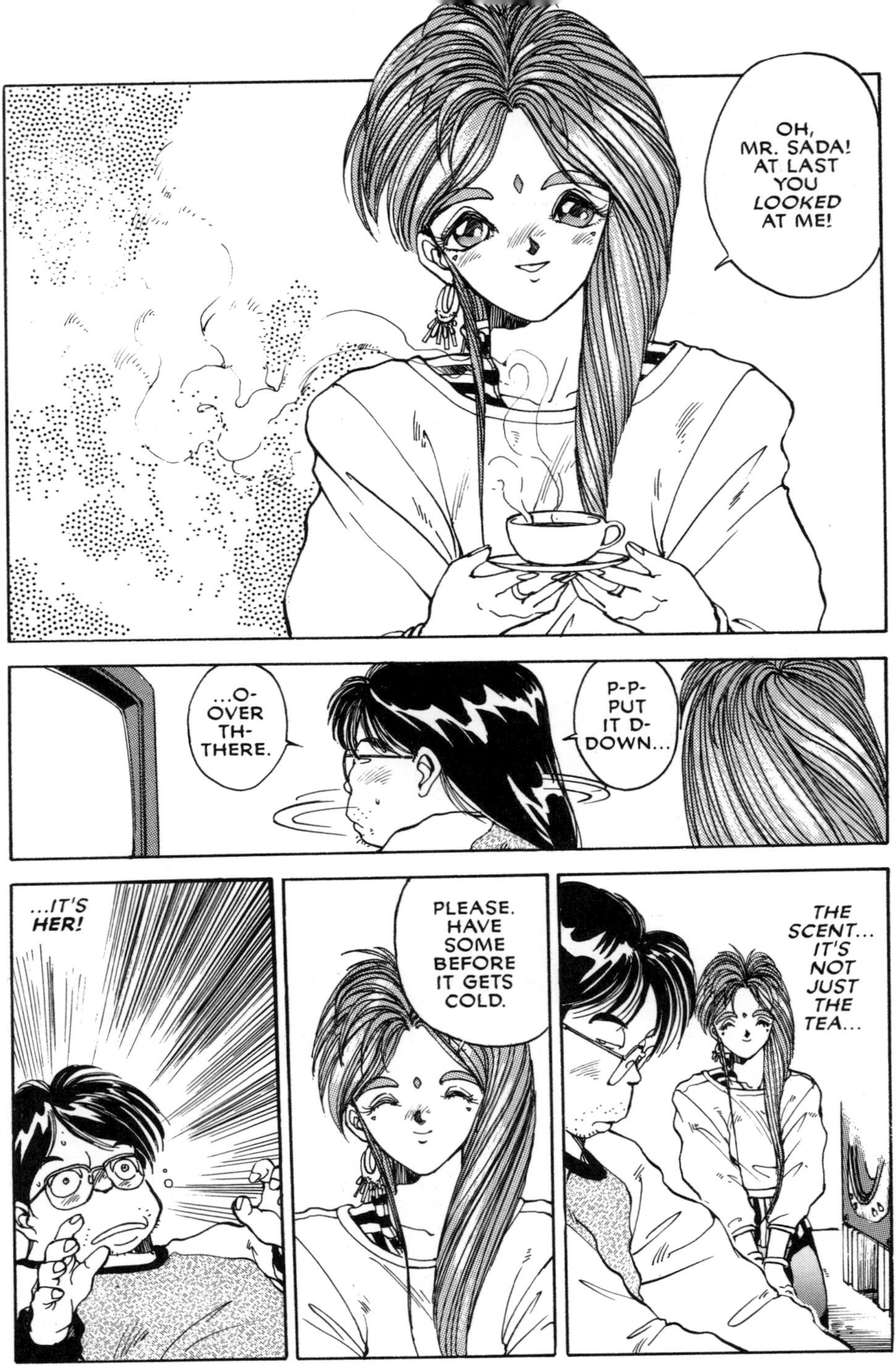
OH, MR. SADA! AT LAST YOU *LOOKED* AT ME!
P-P-PUT IT D-DOWN...
...O-OVER TH-THERE.
THE SCENT... IT'S NOT JUST THE TEA...
PLEASE. HAVE SOME BEFORE IT GETS COLD.
*...IT'S **HER!***

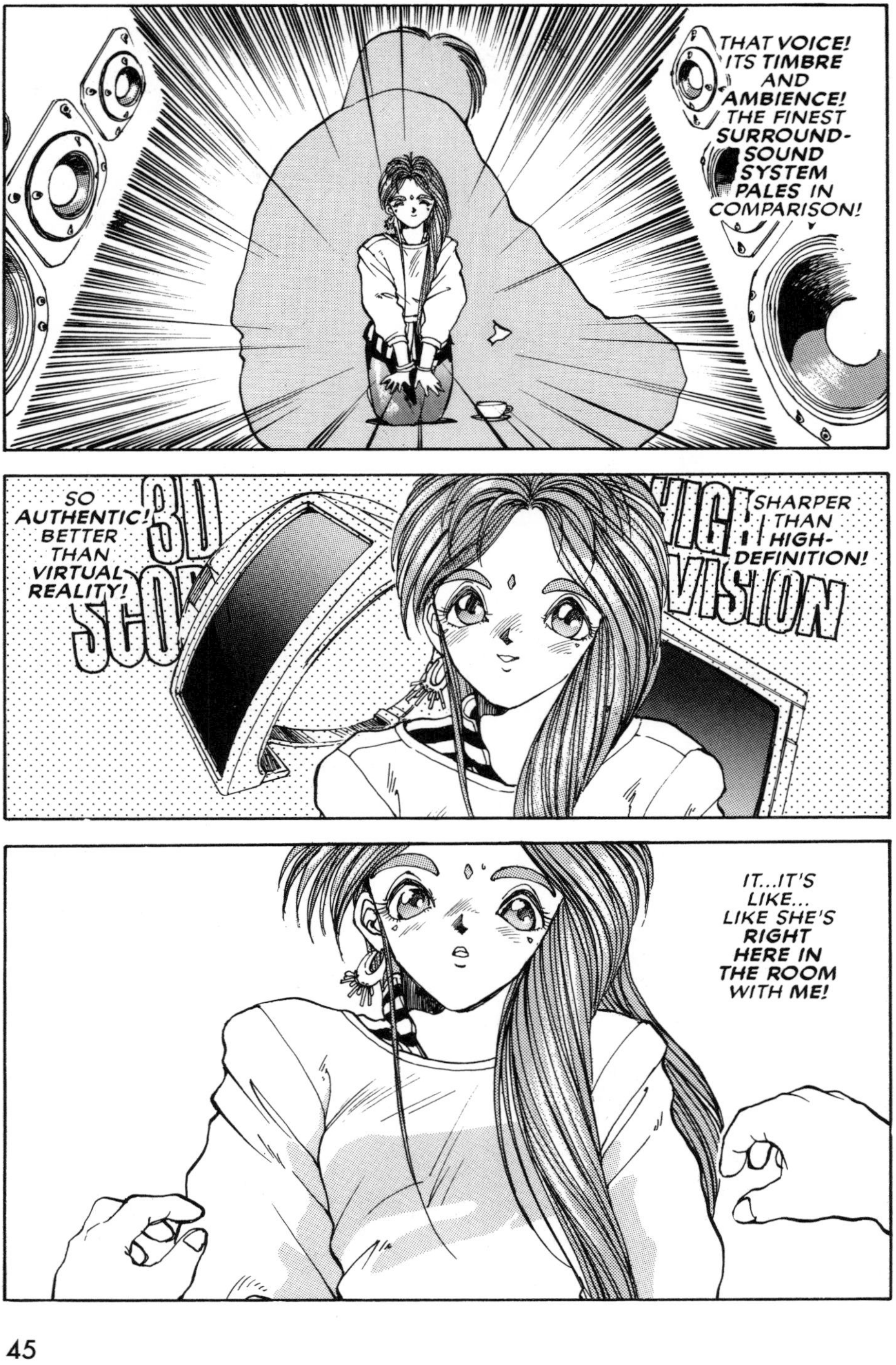
THAT VOICE! ITS TIMBRE AND AMBIENCE! THE FINEST SURROUND-SOUND SYSTEM PALES IN COMPARISON!
SHARPER THAN HIGH-DEFINITION!
VISION
3D
SO AUTHENTIC! BETTER THAN VIRTUAL REALITY!
IT...IT'S LIKE... LIKE SHE'S RIGHT HERE IN THE ROOM WITH ME!

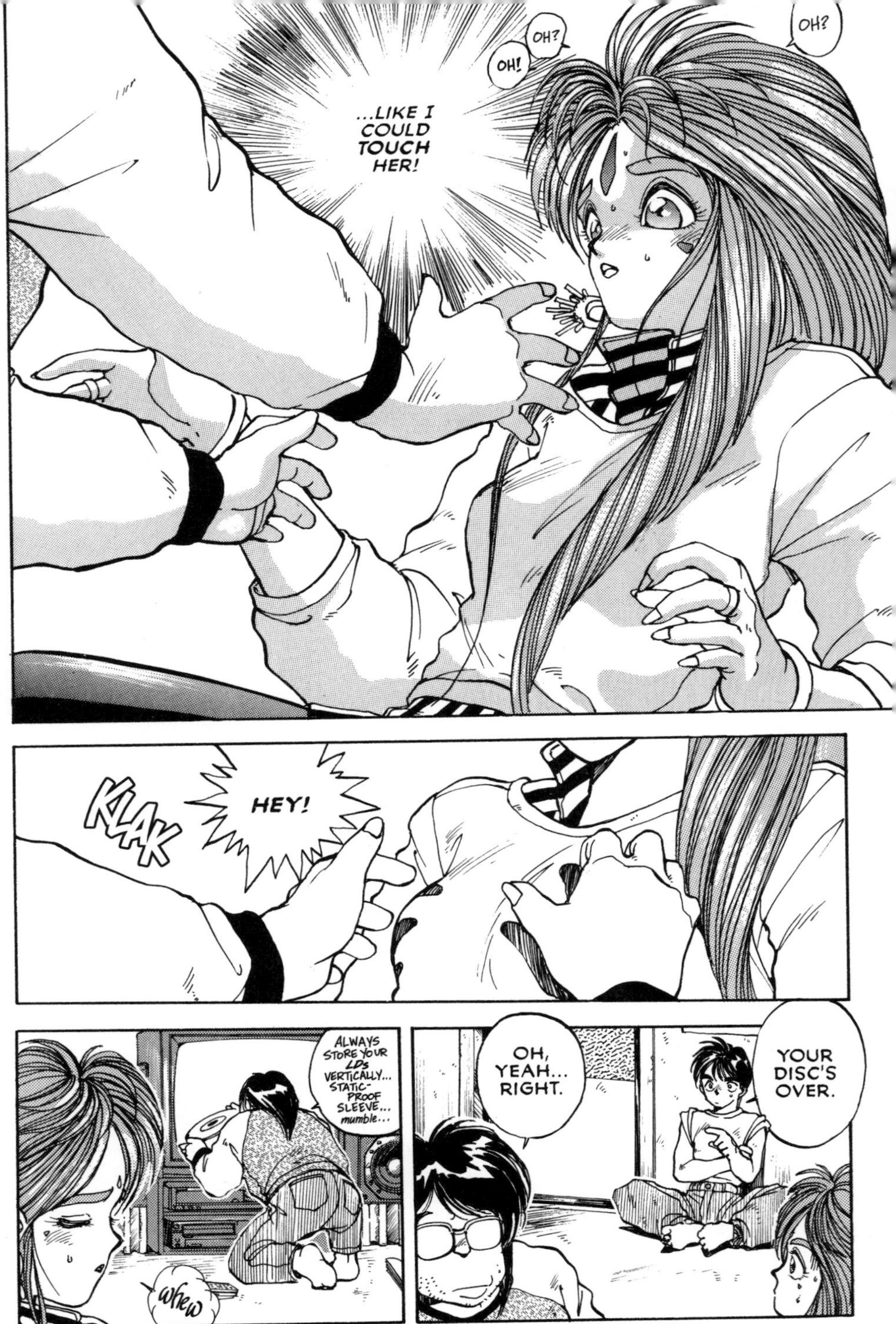
OH?
OH?
OH!
...LIKE I COULD TOUCH HER!
HEY!
KLAK
YOUR DISC'S OVER.
OH, YEAH... RIGHT.
ALWAYS STORE YOUR LDs VERTICALLY... STATIC-PROOF SLEEVE... mumble...
whew

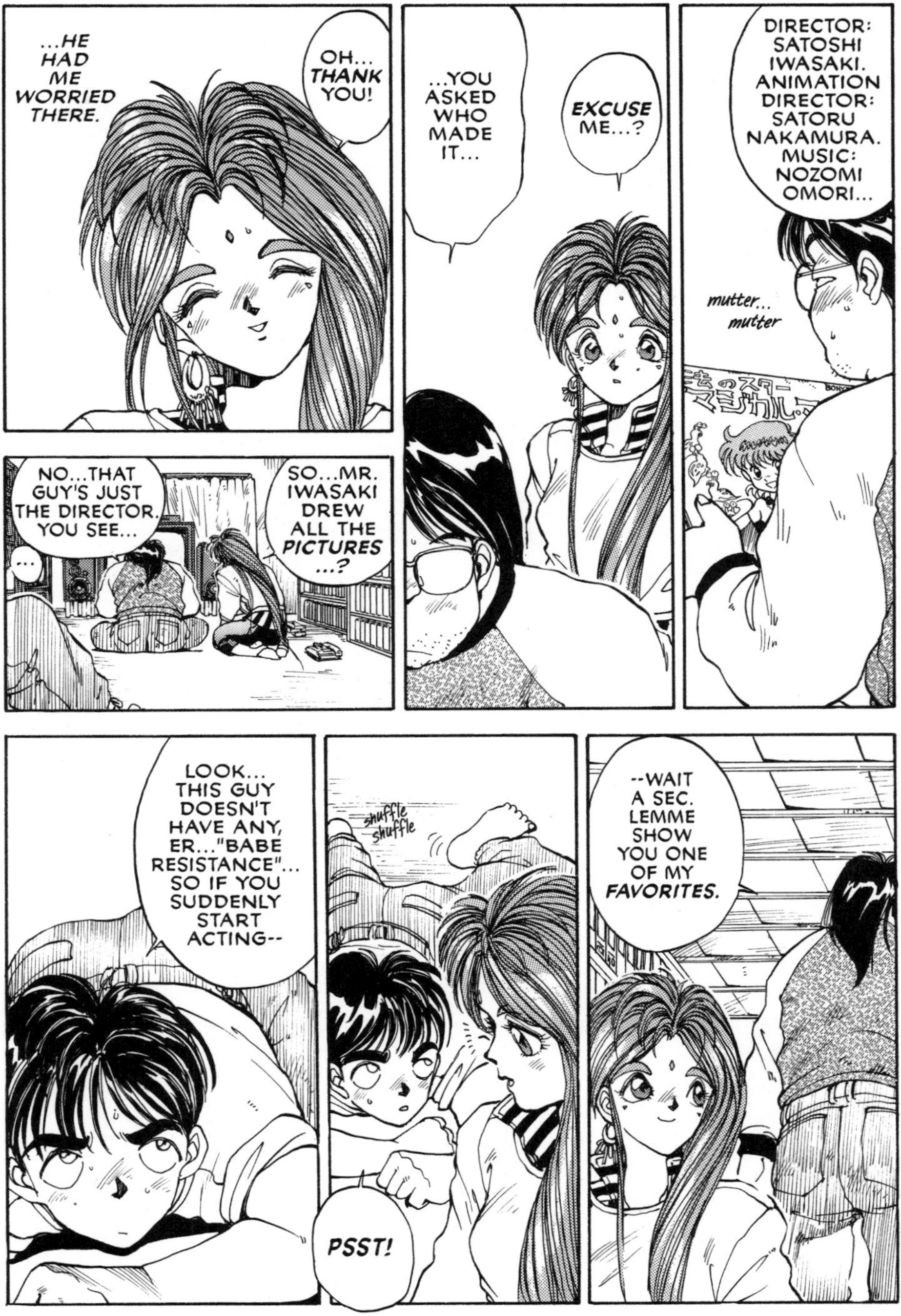
DIRECTOR: SATOSHI IWASAKI. ANIMATION DIRECTOR: SATORU NAKAMURA. MUSIC: NOZOMI OMORI...
mutter... mutter
EXCUSE ME...?
...YOU ASKED WHO MADE IT...
OH... THANK YOU!
...HE HAD ME WORRIED THERE.
SO...MR. IWASAKI DREW ALL THE PICTURES ...?
NO...THAT GUY'S JUST THE DIRECTOR. YOU SEE...
...
--WAIT A SEC. LEMME SHOW YOU ONE OF MY FAVORITES.
shuffle shuffle
PSST!
LOOK... THIS GUY DOESN'T HAVE ANY, ER..."BABE RESISTANCE"... SO IF YOU SUDDENLY START ACTING--

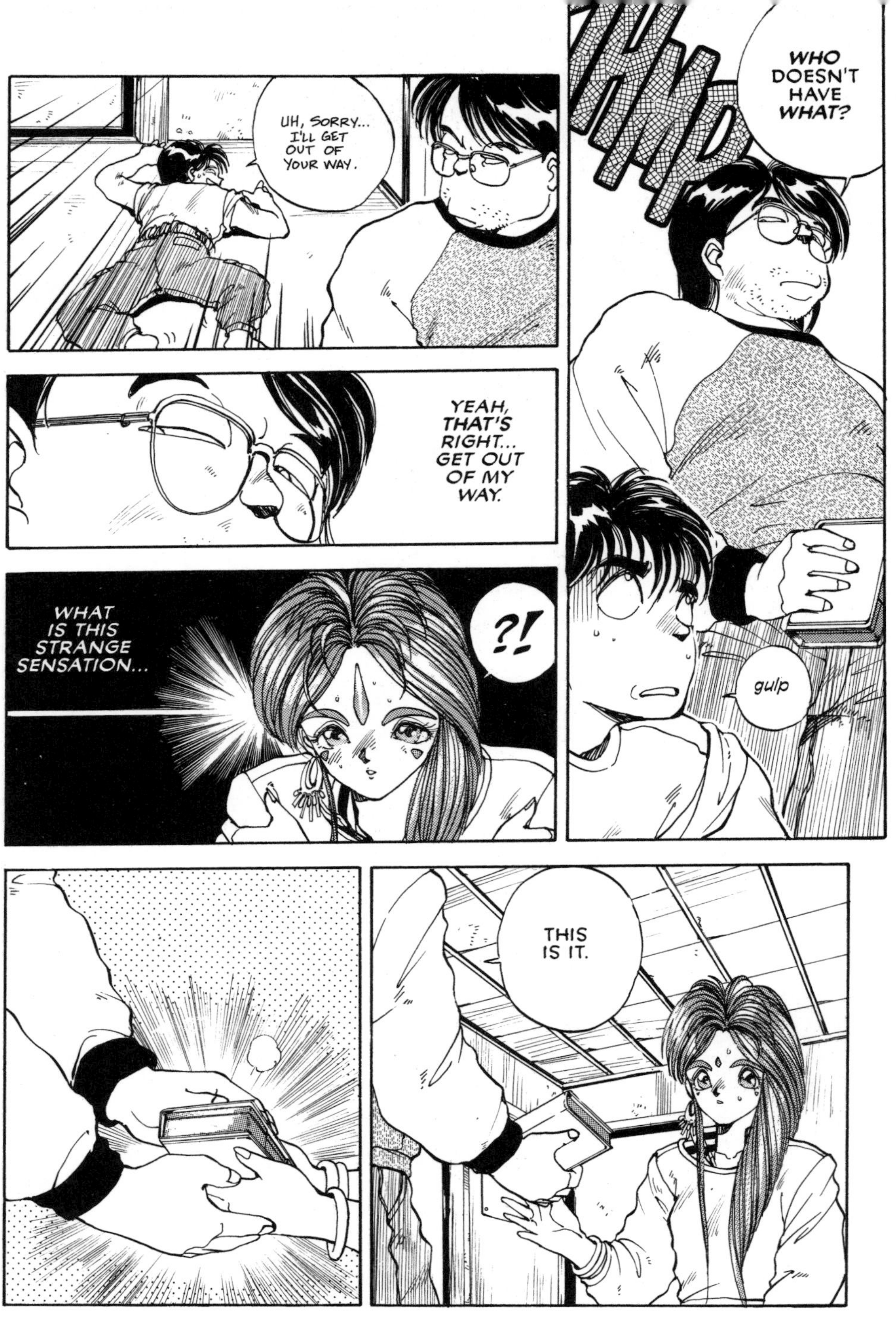
THMP
WHO DOESN'T HAVE WHAT?
gulp
UH, SORRY... I'LL GET OUT OF YOUR WAY.
YEAH, THAT'S RIGHT... GET OUT OF MY WAY.
?!
WHAT IS THIS STRANGE SENSATION...
THIS IS IT.

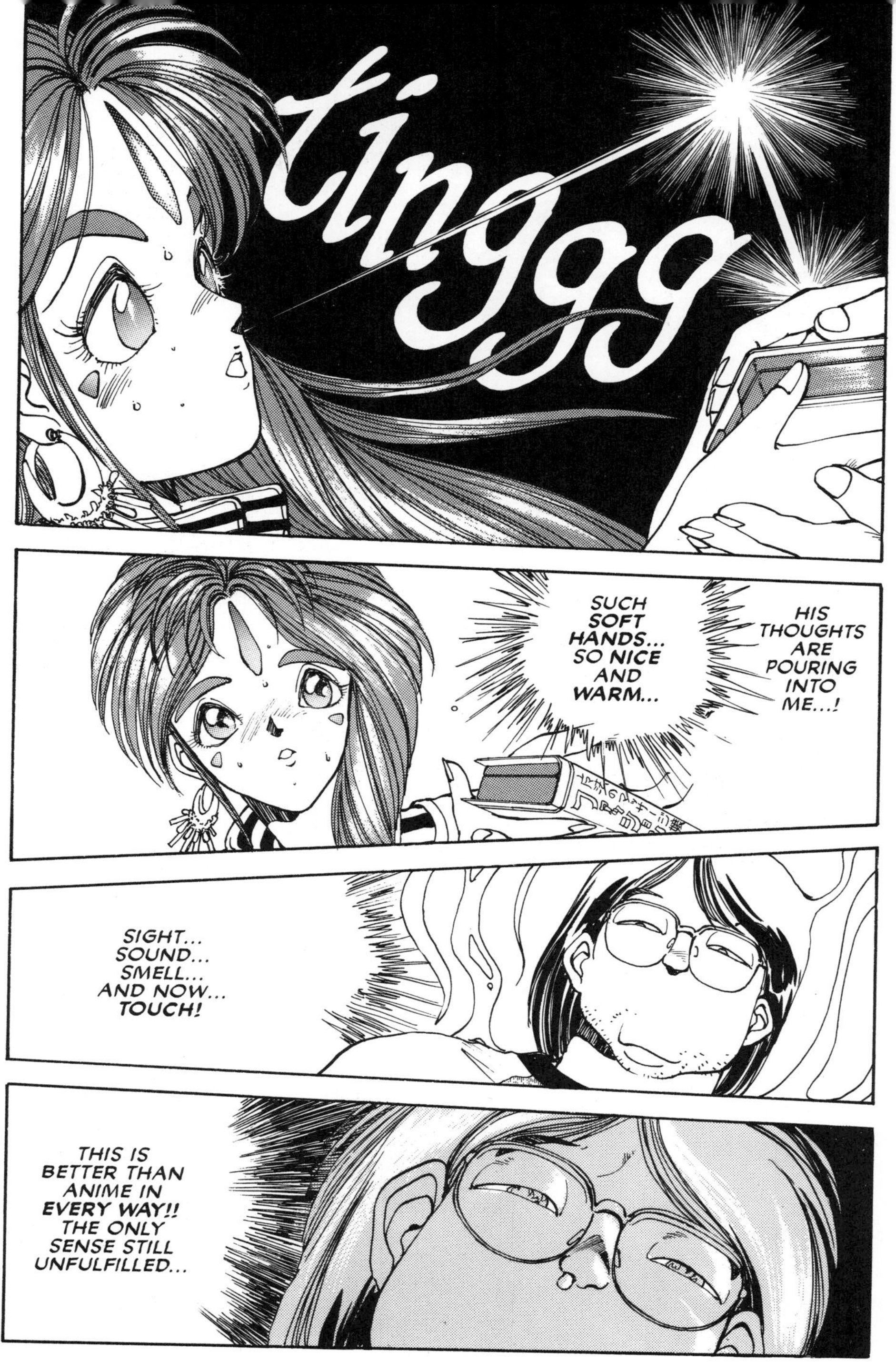
tinggg
HIS THOUGHTS ARE POURING INTO ME...!
SUCH SOFT HANDS... SO NICE AND WARM...
SIGHT... SOUND... SMELL... AND NOW... TOUCH!
THIS IS BETTER THAN ANIME IN EVERY WAY!! THE ONLY SENSE STILL UNFULFILLED...

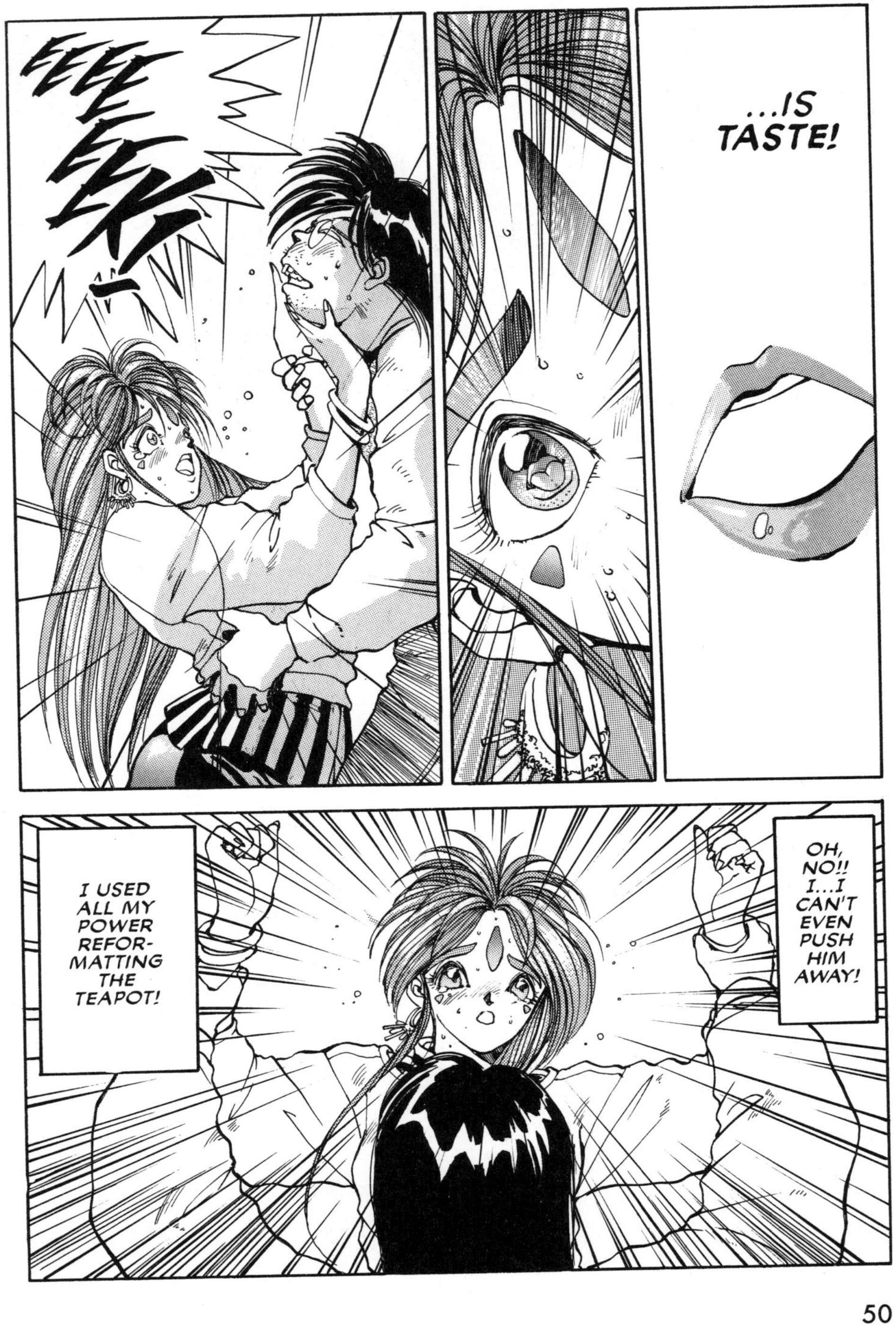
...IS TASTE!
EEEEEEK!
OH, NO!! I...I CAN'T EVEN PUSH HIM AWAY!
I USED ALL MY POWER REFOR-MATTING THE TEAPOT!

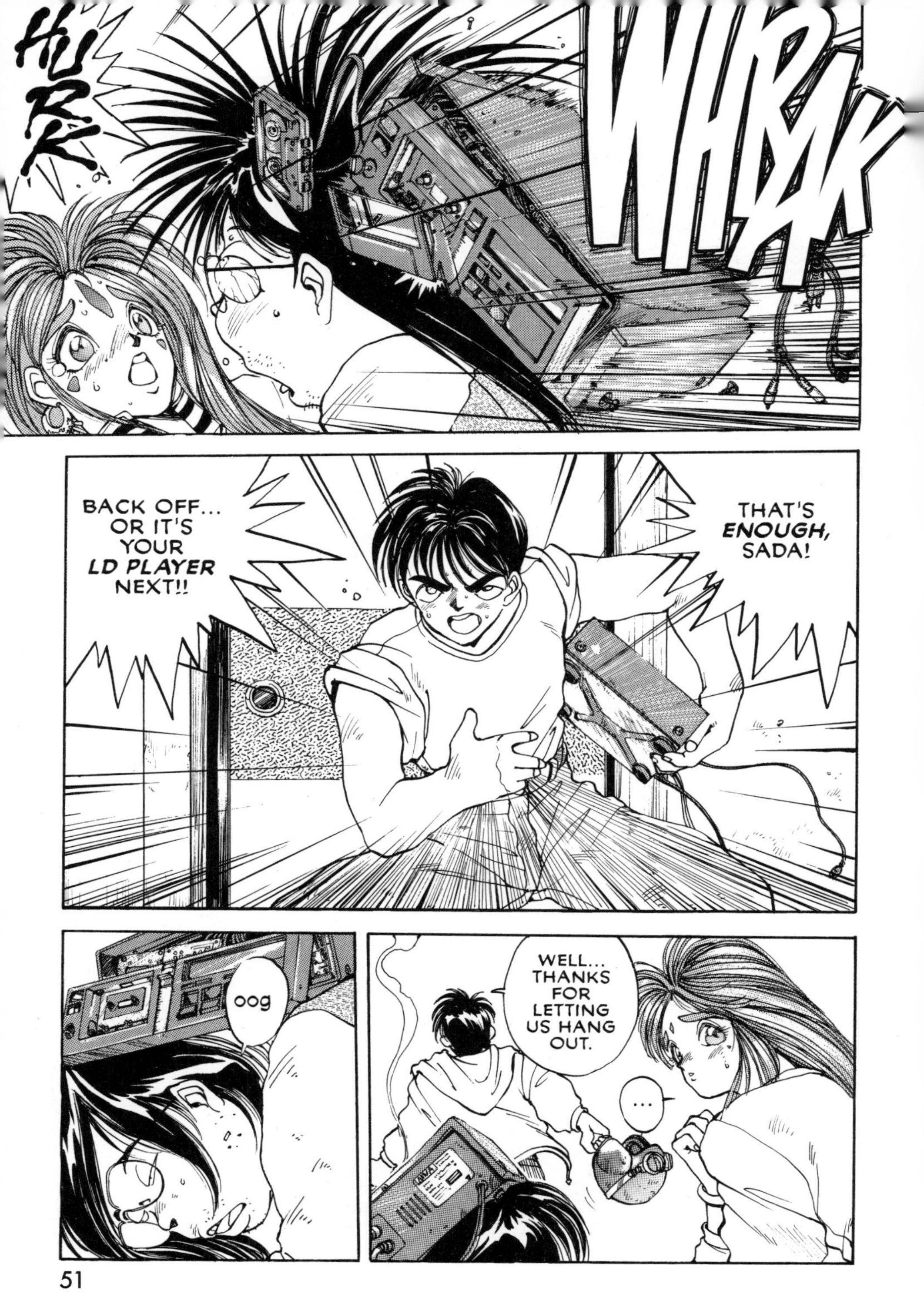
WHRAK
HURK!
THAT'S ENOUGH, SADA!
BACK OFF... OR IT'S YOUR LD PLAYER NEXT!!
WELL... THANKS FOR LETTING US HANG OUT.
...
oog

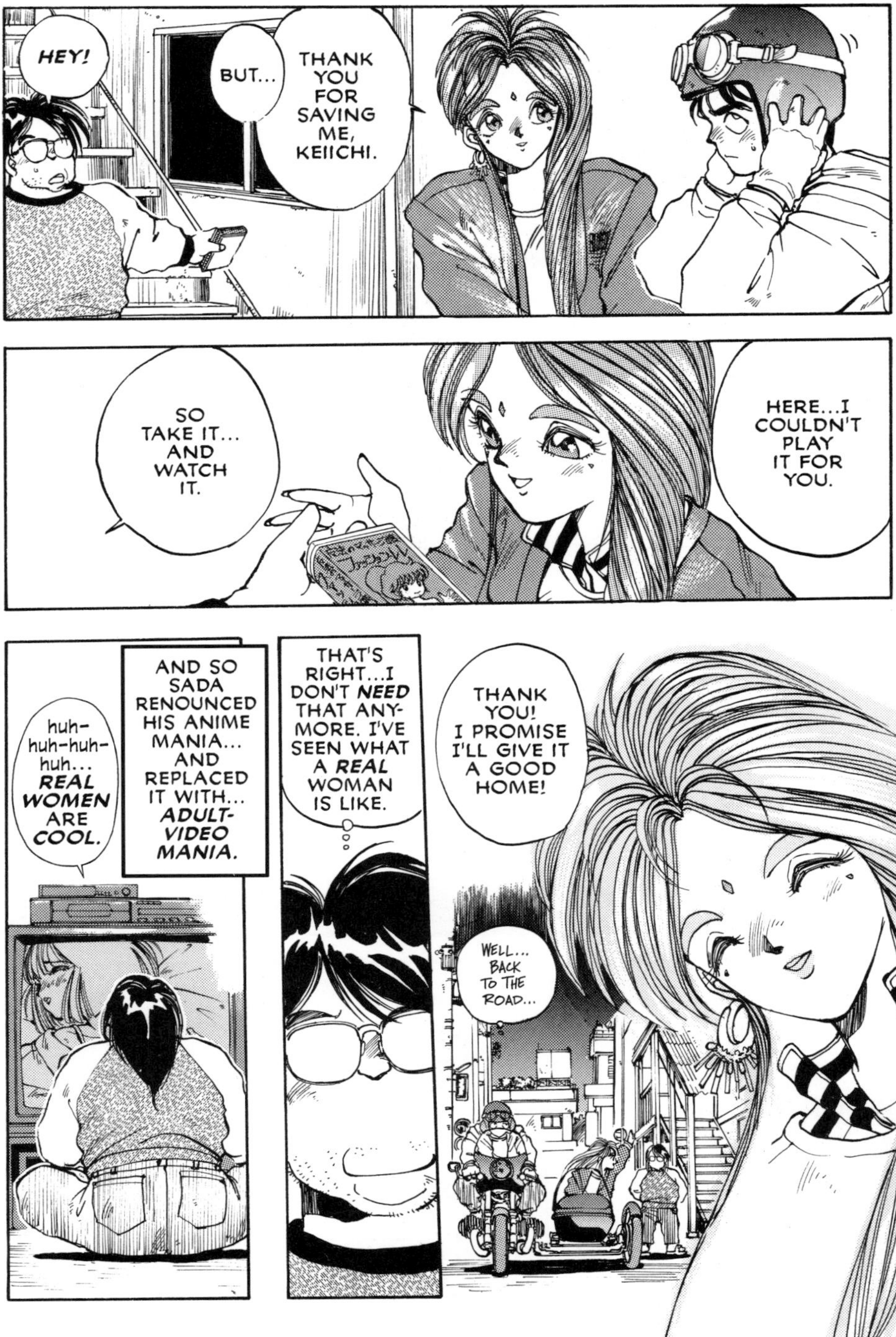
THANK YOU FOR SAVING ME, KEIICHI.
BUT...
HEY!
HERE...I COULDN'T PLAY IT FOR YOU.
SO TAKE IT... AND WATCH IT.
THANK YOU! I PROMISE I'LL GIVE IT A GOOD HOME!
WELL... BACK TO THE ROAD...
THAT'S RIGHT...I DON'T NEED THAT ANY-MORE. I'VE SEEN WHAT A REAL WOMAN IS LIKE.
AND SO SADA RENOUNCED HIS ANIME MANIA... AND REPLACED IT WITH... ADULT-VIDEO MANIA.
huh-huh-huh-huh... REAL WOMEN ARE COOL.

OH MY GODDESS!

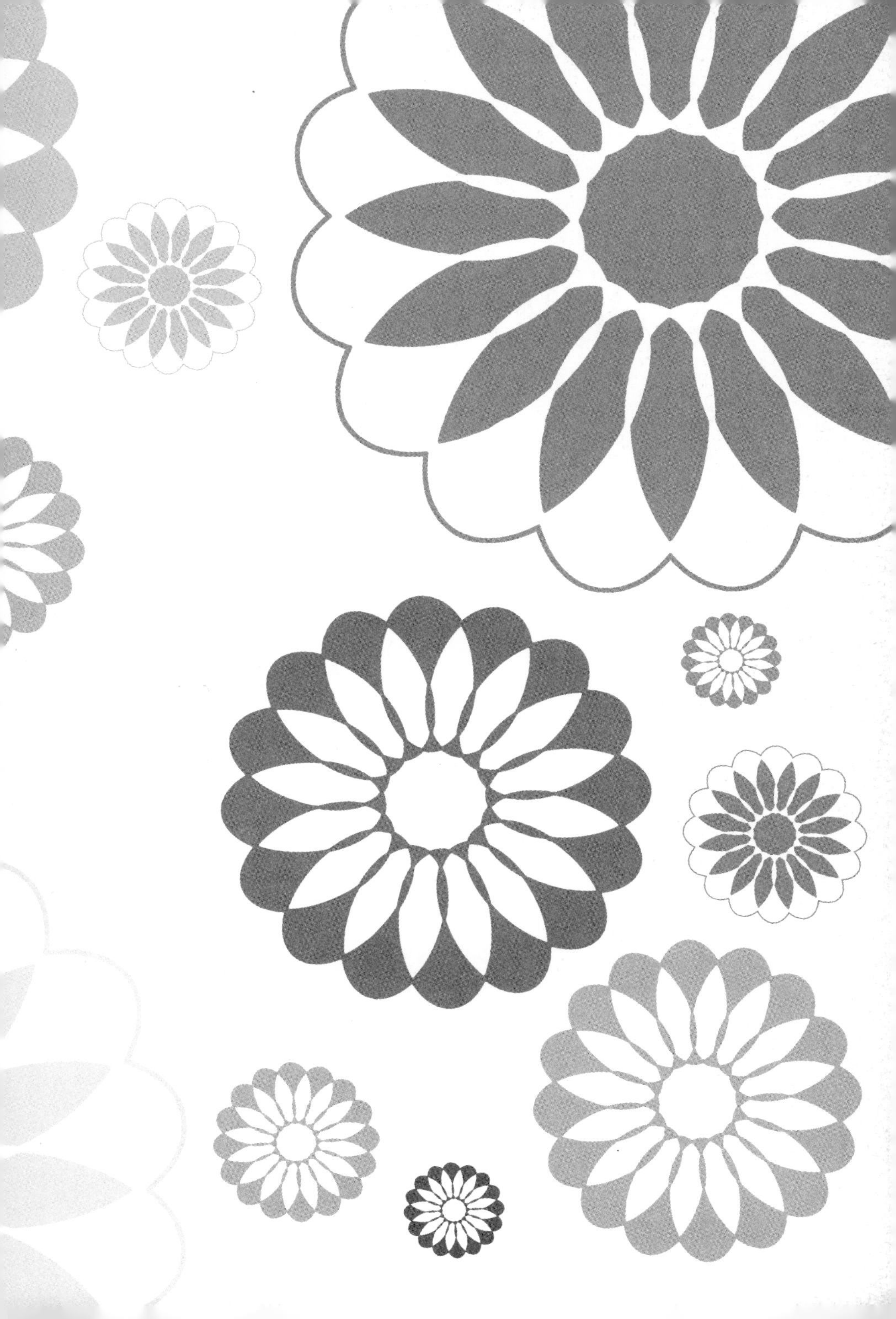

CHAPTER 3

A Man's Home Is His... Temple?

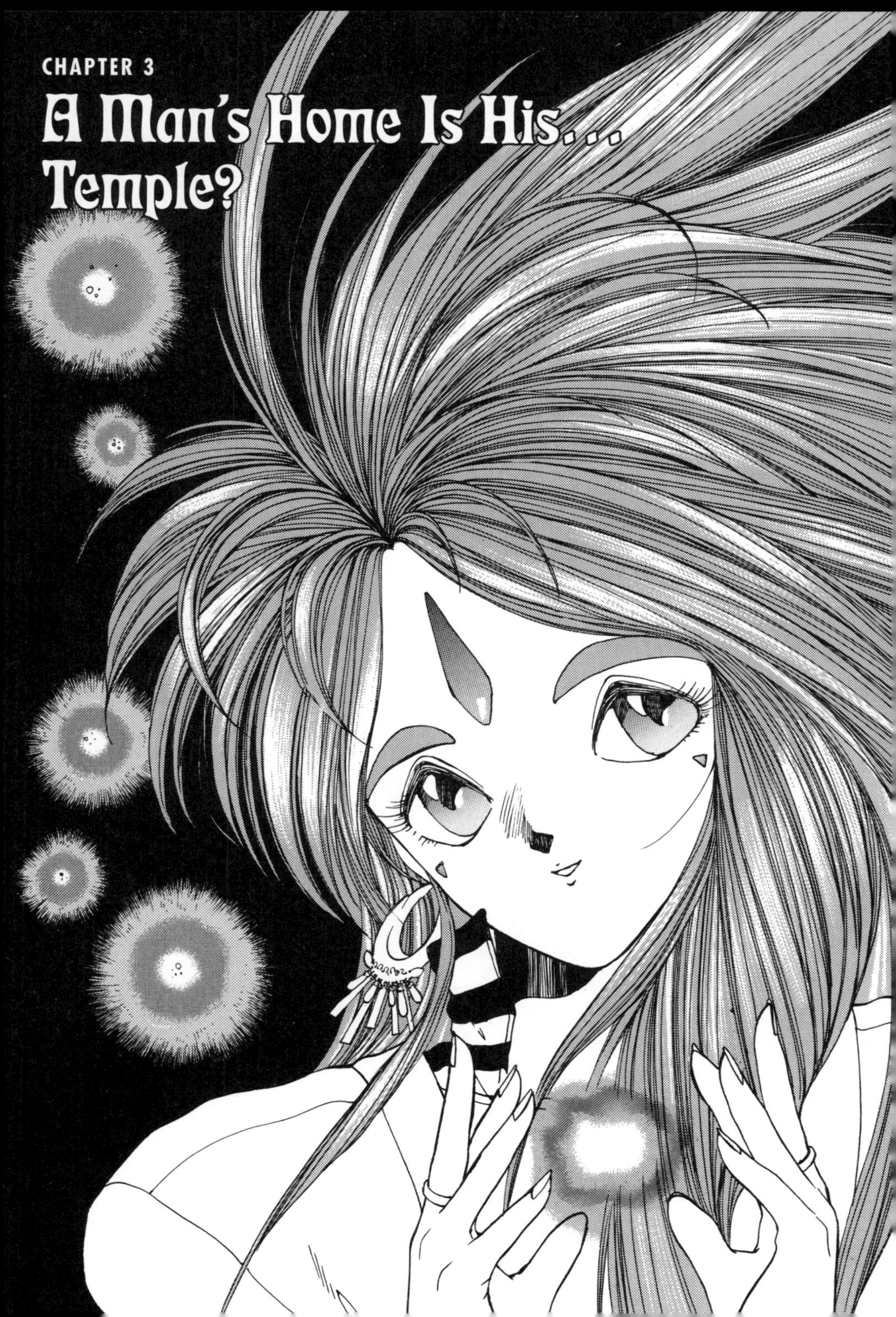

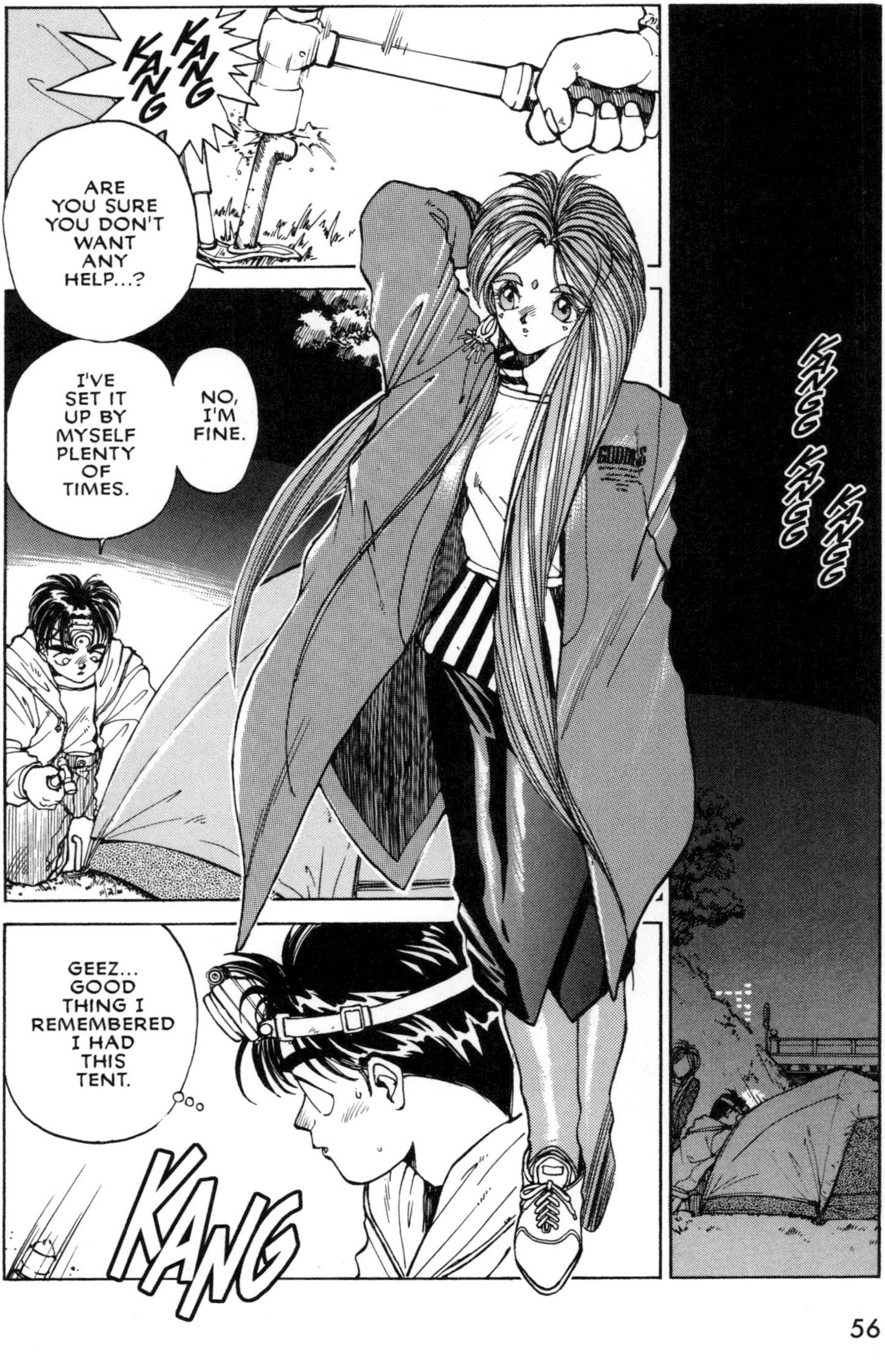
KANGG KANGG KANGG
KANG KANG
ARE YOU SURE YOU DON'T WANT ANY HELP...?
NO, I'M FINE.
I'VE SET IT UP BY MYSELF PLENTY OF TIMES.
GEEZ... GOOD THING I REMEMBERED I HAD THIS TENT.
KANG

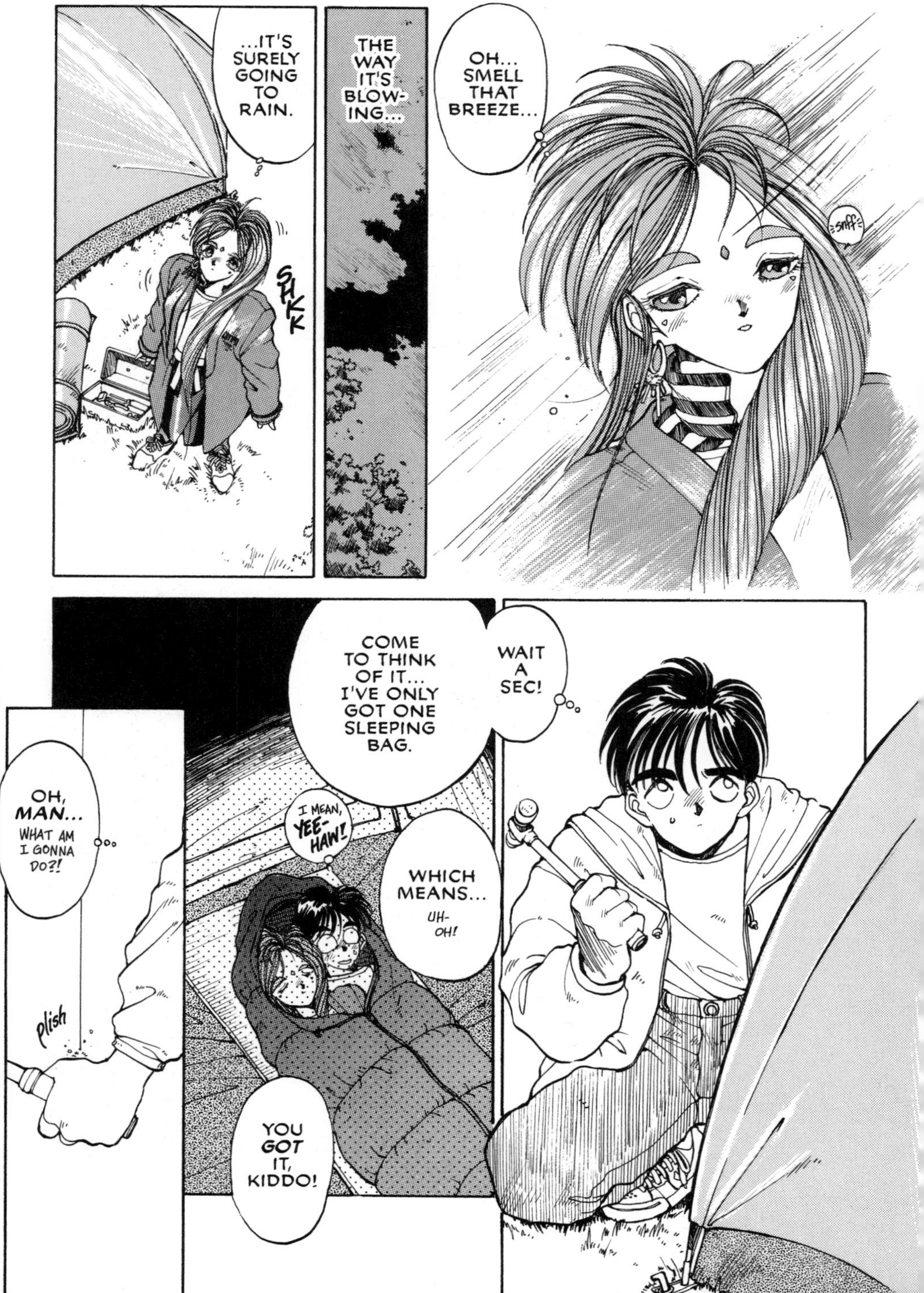
OH... SMELL THAT BREEZE...
snff
THE WAY IT'S BLOWING...
...IT'S SURELY GOING TO RAIN.
SHKK
WAIT A SEC!
COME TO THINK OF IT... I'VE ONLY GOT ONE SLEEPING BAG.
WHICH MEANS...
UH-OH!
I MEAN, YEE-HAW!
YOU GOT IT, KIDDO!
OH, MAN... WHAT AM I GONNA DO?!
plish

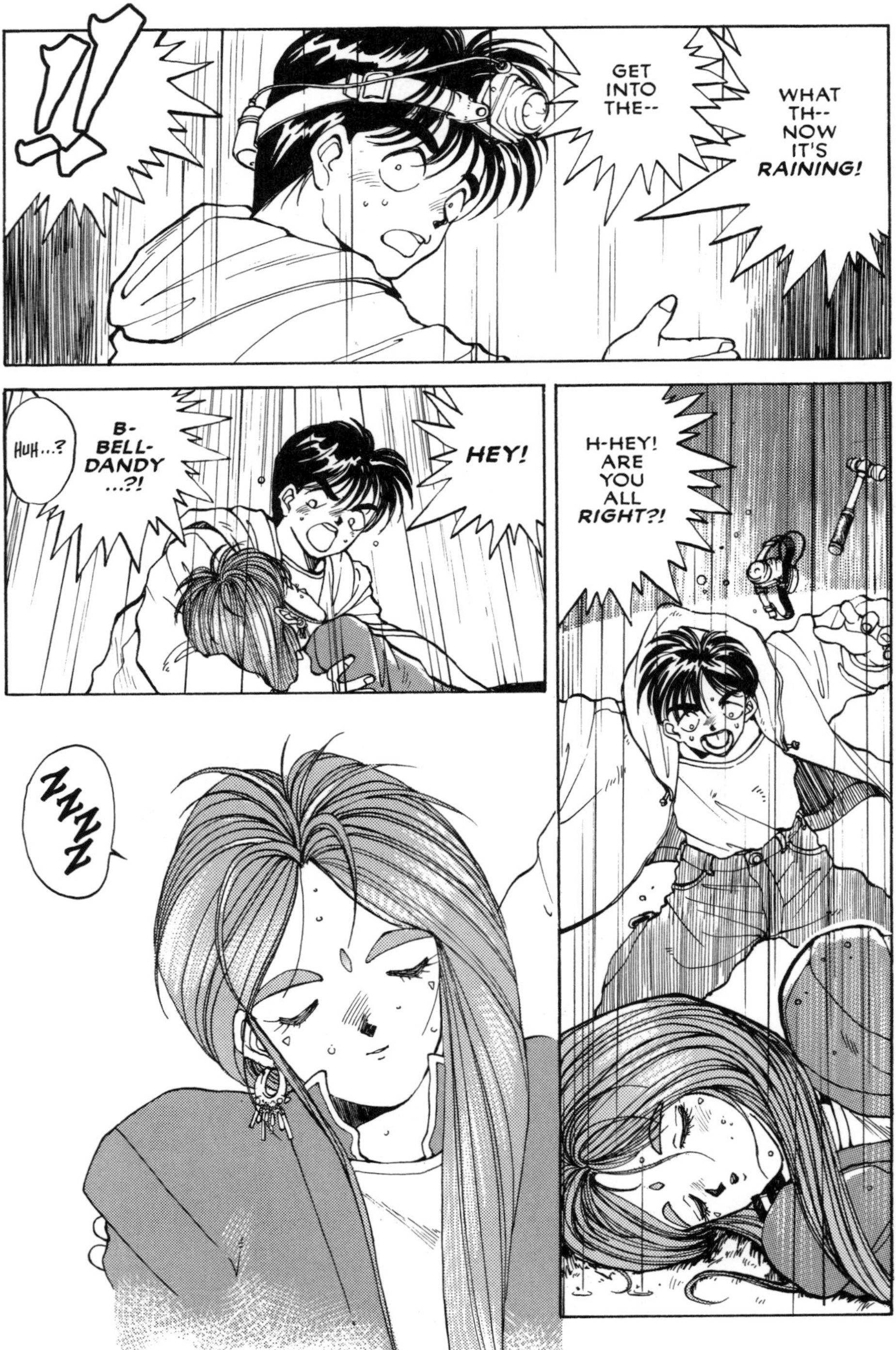
WHAT TH-- NOW IT'S RAINING!
GET INTO THE--
!!
H-HEY! ARE YOU ALL RIGHT?!
HEY!
B-BELL-DANDY ...?!
HUH...?
ZZZZ

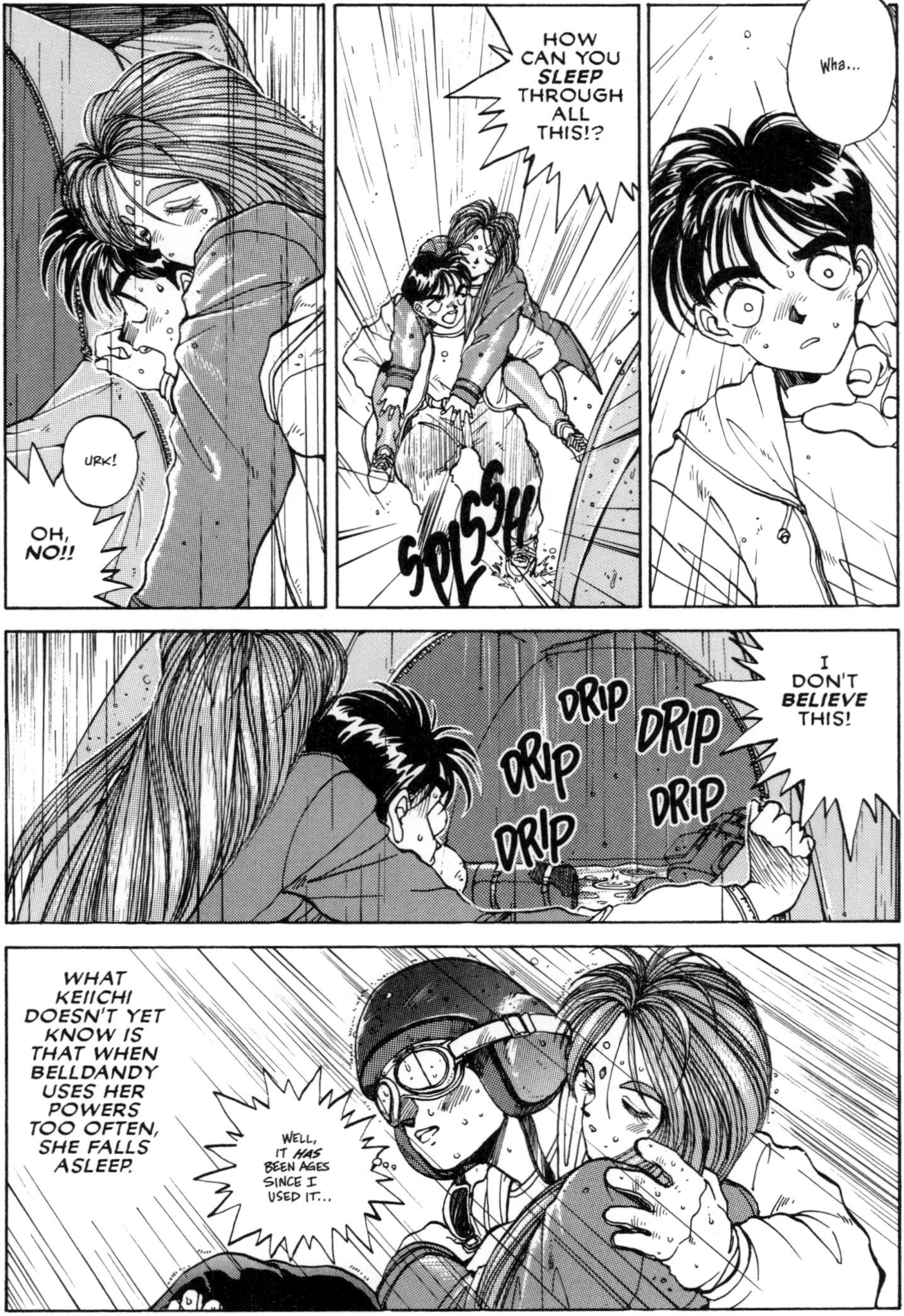
Wha...
HOW CAN YOU SLEEP THROUGH ALL THIS!?
SPLSSH
URK!
OH, NO!!
I DON'T BELIEVE THIS!
DRIP DRIP DRIP DRIP DRIP
WELL, IT HAS BEEN AGES SINCE I USED IT...
WHAT KEIICHI DOESN'T YET KNOW IS THAT WHEN BELLDANDY USES HER POWERS TOO OFTEN, SHE FALLS ASLEEP.

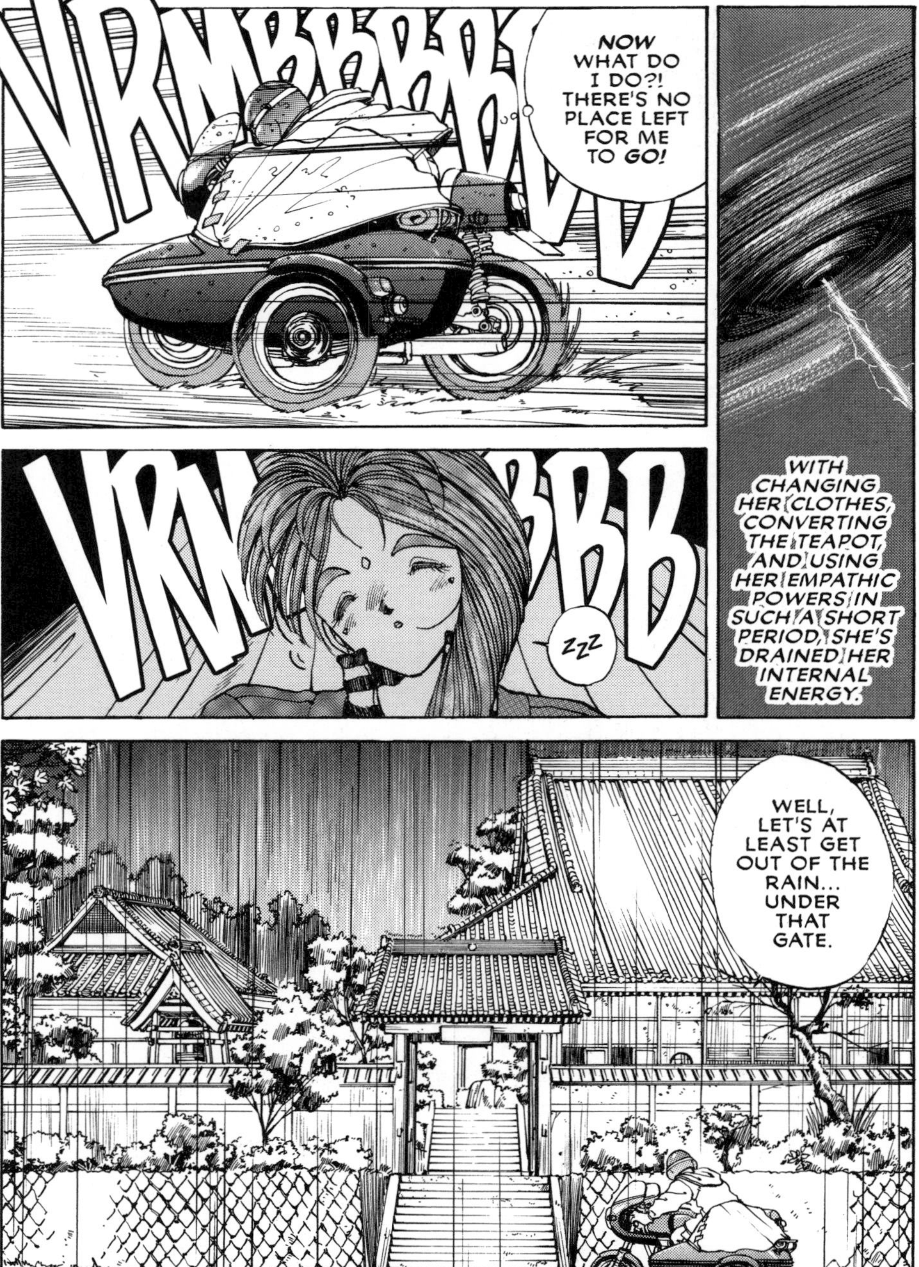
WITH CHANGING HER CLOTHES, CONVERTING THE TEAPOT, AND USING HER EMPATHIC POWERS IN SUCH A SHORT PERIOD, SHE'S DRAINED HER INTERNAL ENERGY.
NOW WHAT DO I DO?! THERE'S NO PLACE LEFT FOR ME TO GO!
ZZZ
WELL, LET'S AT LEAST GET OUT OF THE RAIN... UNDER THAT GATE.

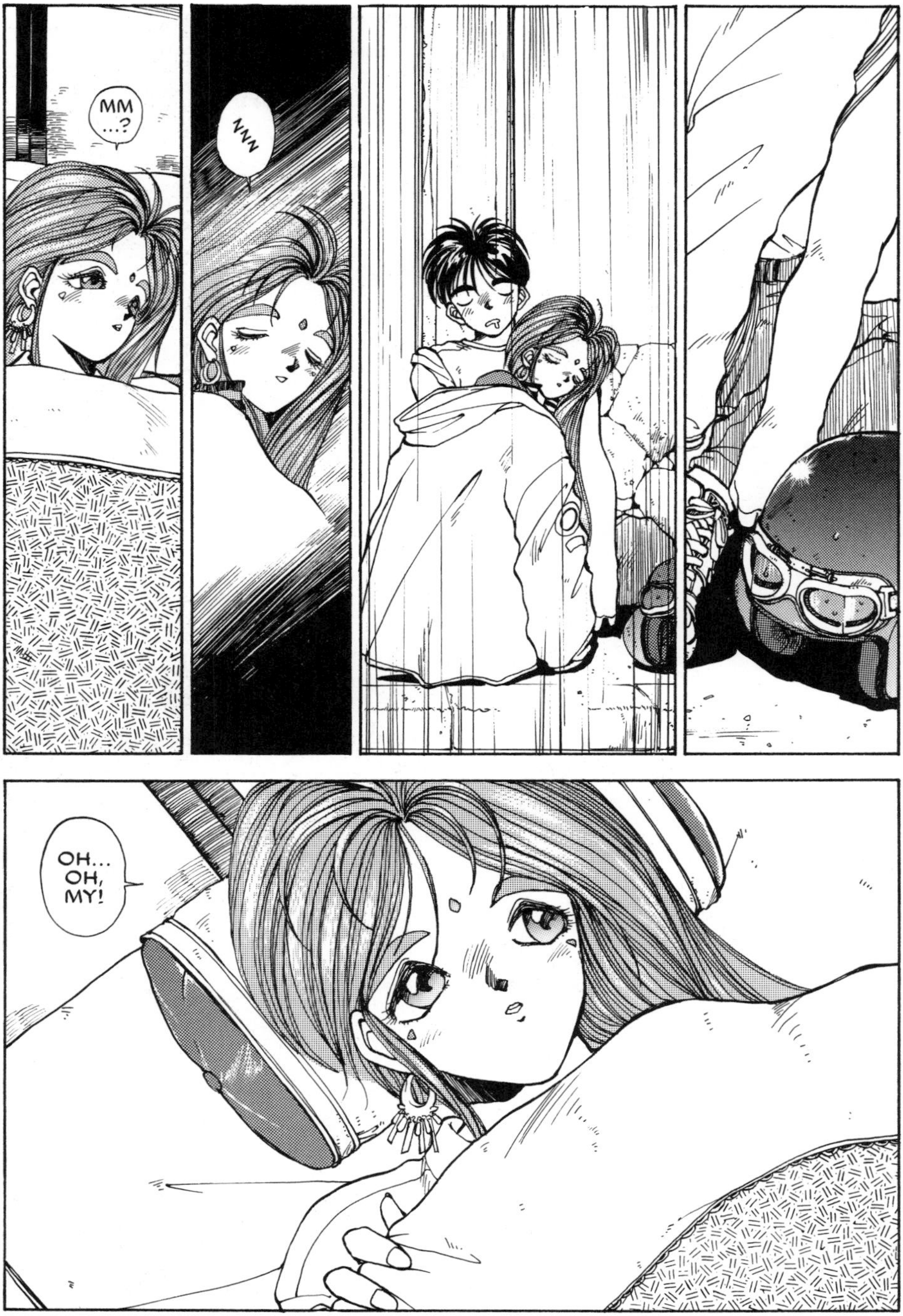
ZZZ
MM ...?
OH... OH, MY!

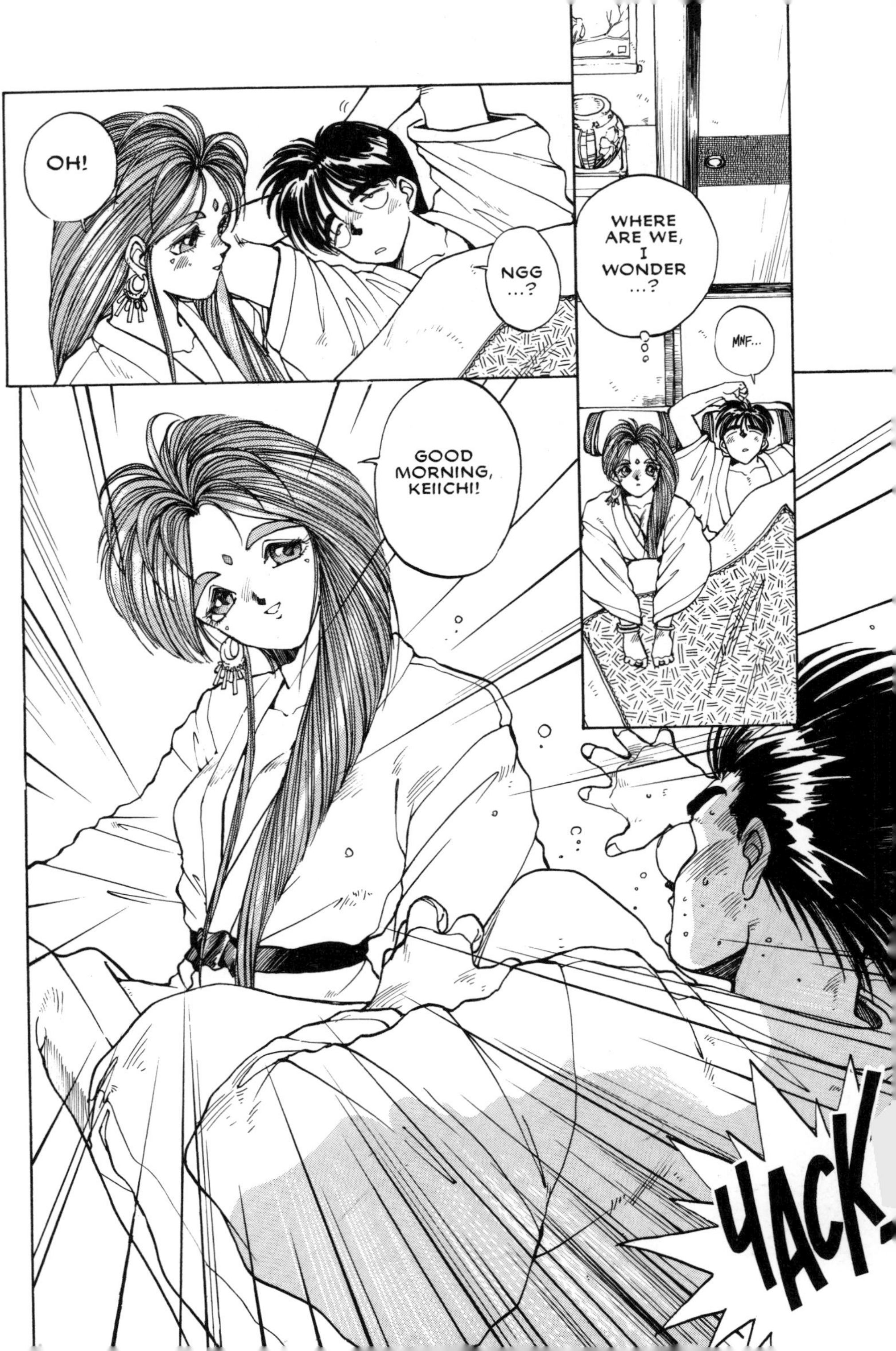
WHERE ARE WE, I WONDER ...?
MNF...
NGG ...?
OH!
GOOD MORNING, KEIICHI!
YACK!

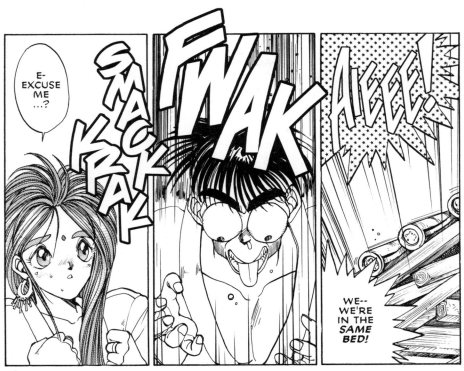

AIEEE!
WE-- WE'RE IN THE *SAME BED!*
FWAK
SMACK
KRAK
E- EXCUSE ME ...?
HRM.
MY APOLOGIES, YOUNG LADY. I'M AFRAID I MAY HAVE INADVERTENTLY PUT YOU IN A DIFFICULT POSITION.
WHEN YOU ARRIVED TOGETHER LAST NIGHT, I JUST ASSUMED THE TWO OF YOU WERE... LOVERS.
SORRY ABOUT THAT.

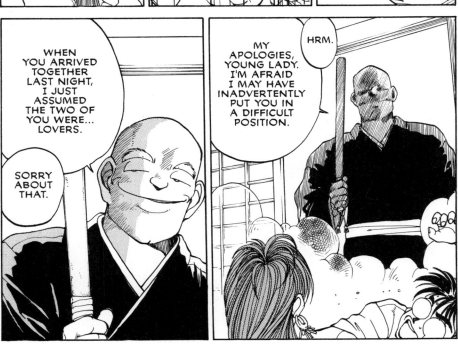

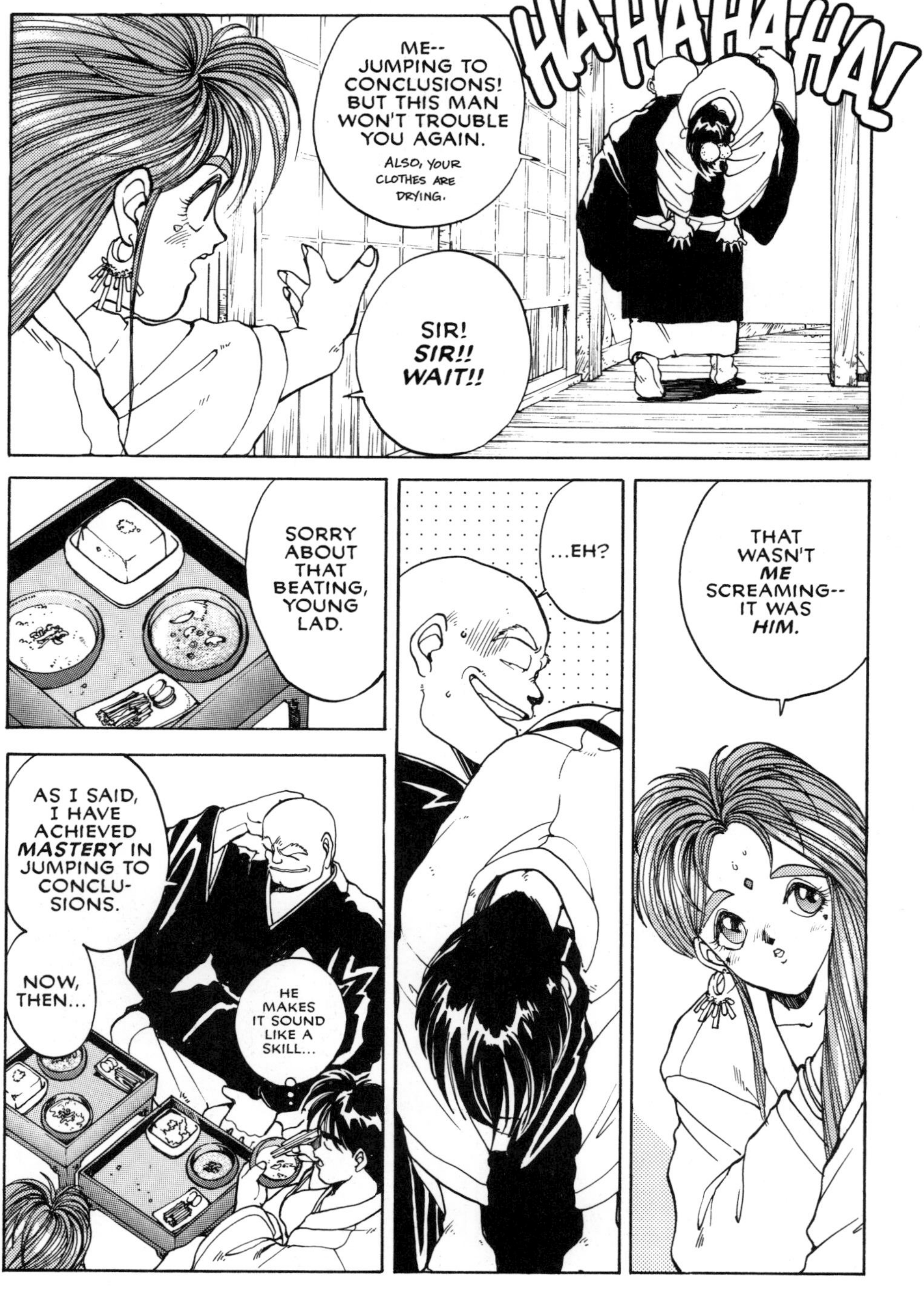
HAHAHAHA!
ME-- JUMPING TO CONCLUSIONS! BUT THIS MAN WON'T TROUBLE YOU AGAIN.
ALSO, YOUR CLOTHES ARE DRYING.
SIR! *SIR!!* *WAIT!!*
THAT WASN'T *ME* SCREAMING-- IT WAS *HIM.*
...EH?
SORRY ABOUT THAT BEATING, YOUNG LAD.
AS I SAID, I HAVE ACHIEVED **MASTERY** IN JUMPING TO CONCLU- SIONS.
NOW, THEN...
HE MAKES IT SOUND LIKE A SKILL...

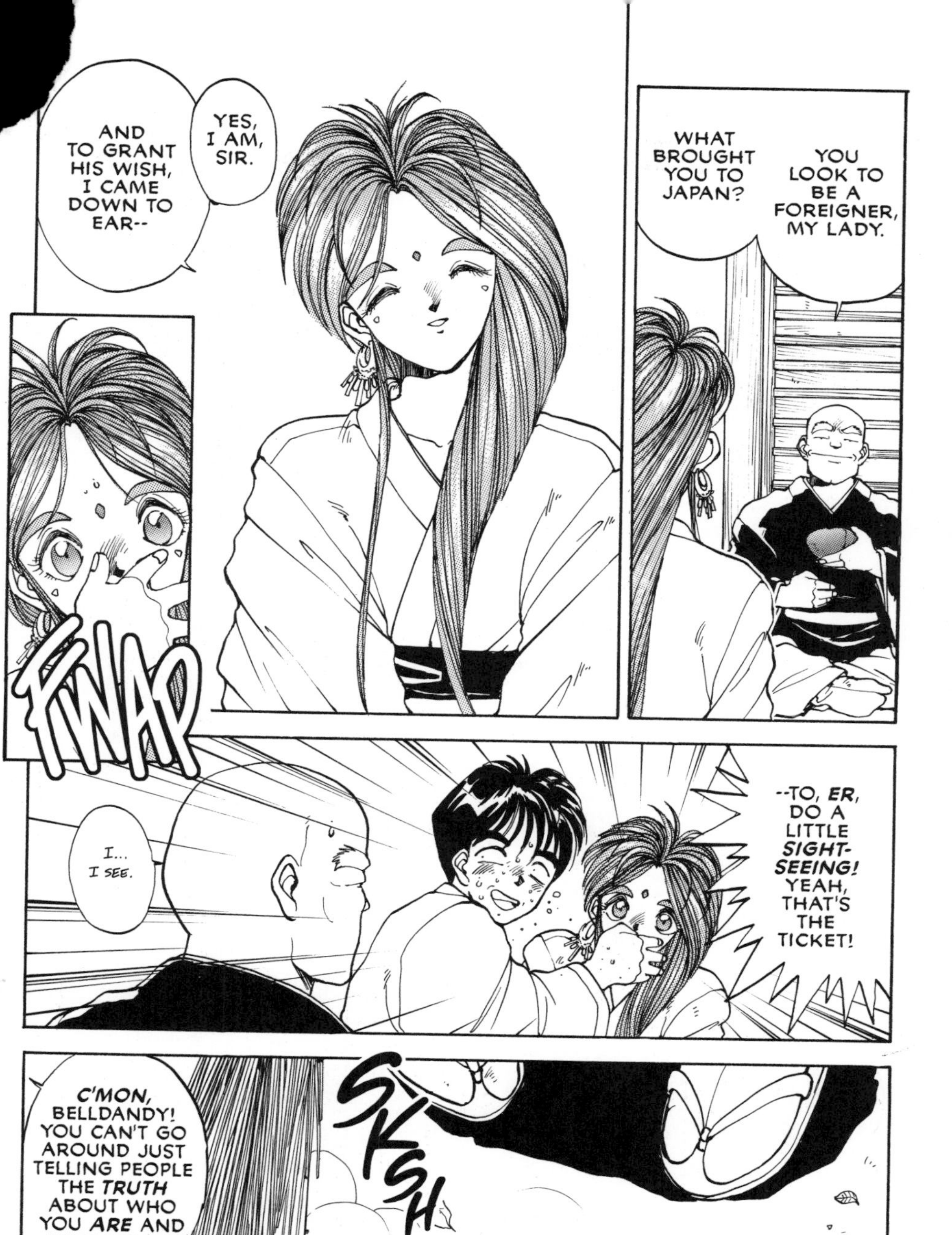
YOU LOOK TO BE A FOREIGNER, MY LADY.
WHAT BROUGHT YOU TO JAPAN?
YES, I AM, SIR.
AND TO GRANT HIS WISH, I CAME DOWN TO EAR--
FWAP
--TO, *ER*, DO A LITTLE *SIGHT-SEEING!* YEAH, THAT'S THE TICKET!
I... I SEE.
SKSH
C'MON, BELLDANDY! YOU CAN'T GO AROUND JUST TELLING PEOPLE THE *TRUTH* ABOUT WHO YOU *ARE* AND WHY YOU'RE *HERE!*

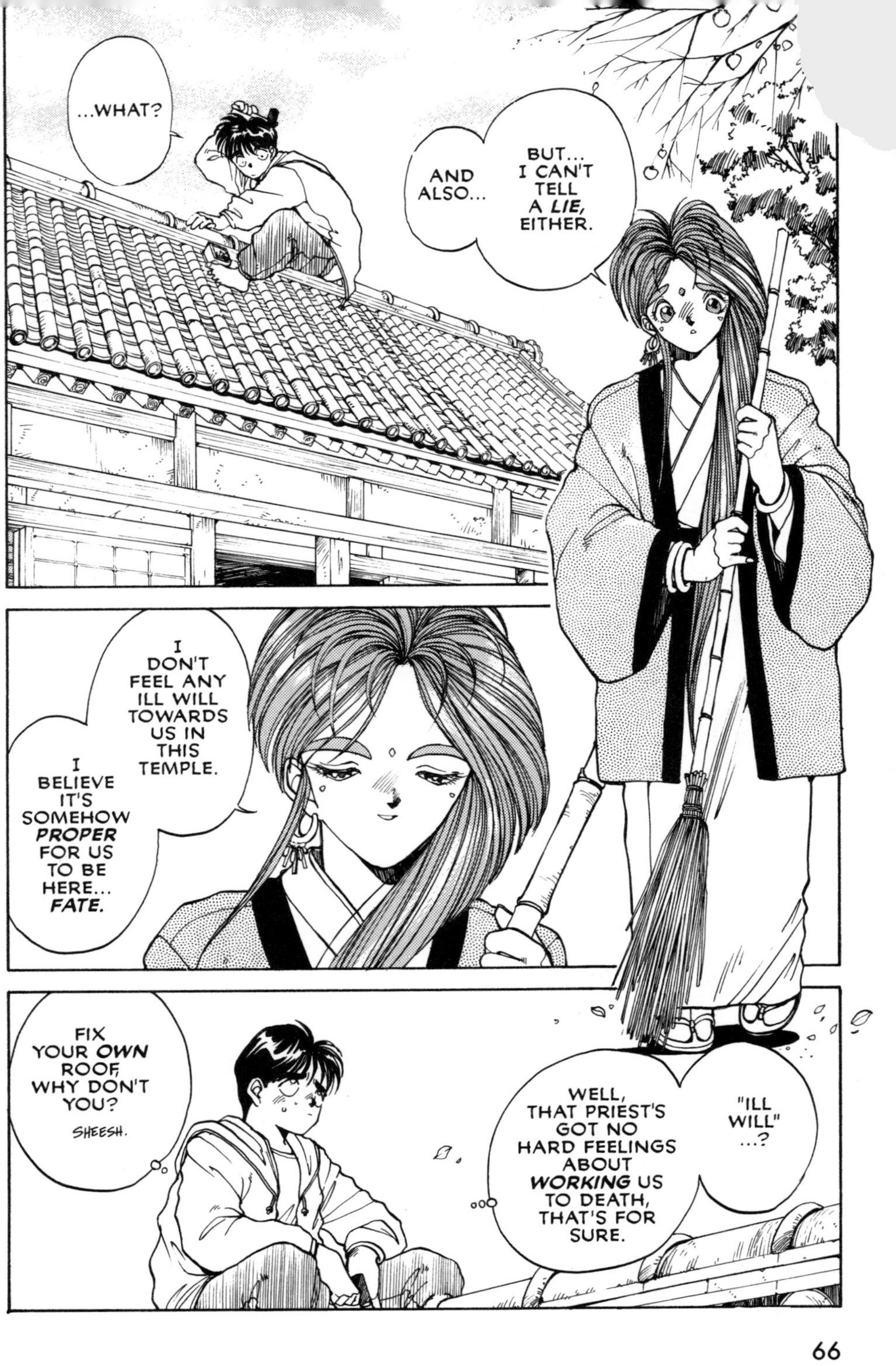
BUT... I CAN'T TELL A *LIE,* EITHER.
AND ALSO...
...WHAT?
I DON'T FEEL ANY ILL WILL TOWARDS US IN THIS TEMPLE.
I BELIEVE IT'S SOMEHOW *PROPER* FOR US TO BE HERE... *FATE.*
"ILL WILL" ...?
WELL, THAT PRIEST'S GOT NO HARD FEELINGS ABOUT *WORKING* US TO DEATH, THAT'S FOR SURE.
FIX YOUR *OWN* ROOF, WHY DON'T YOU?
SHEESH.

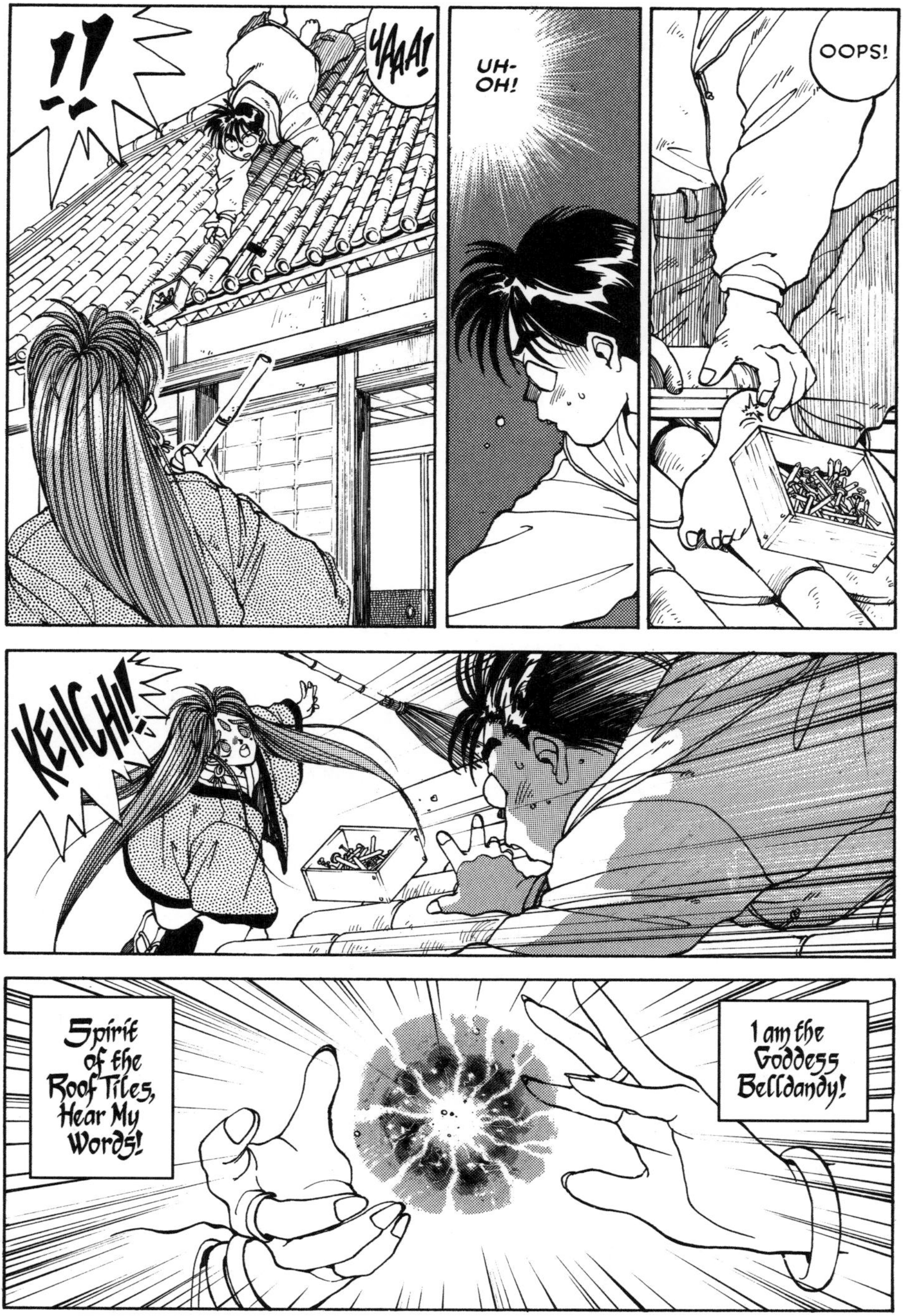
OOPS!
UH-OH!
YAAAA!
!!
KEIICHI!
I am the Goddess Belldandy!
Spirit of the Roof Tiles, Hear My Words!

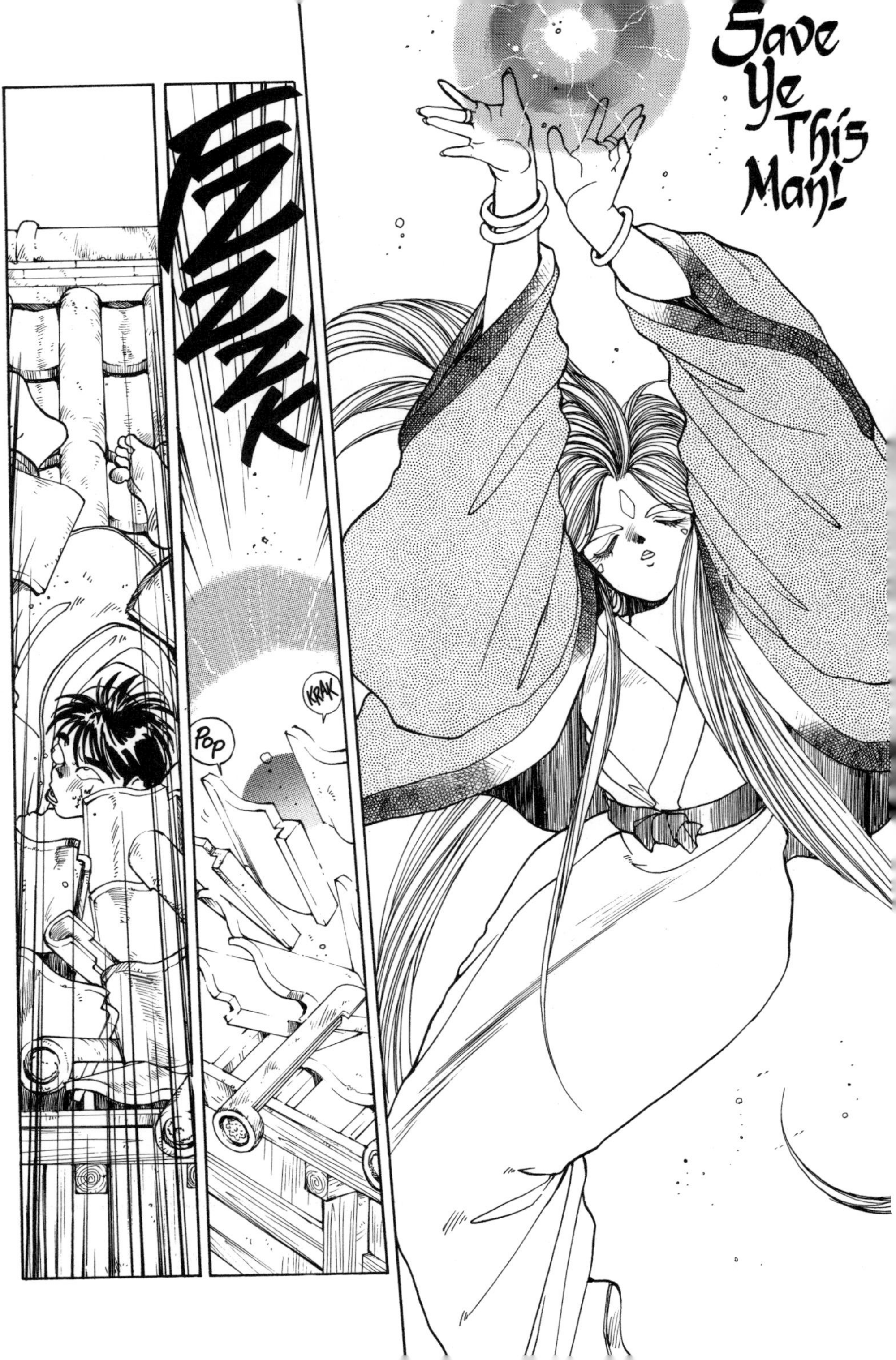
Save Ye This Man!
FZZZZK
KRAK
POP

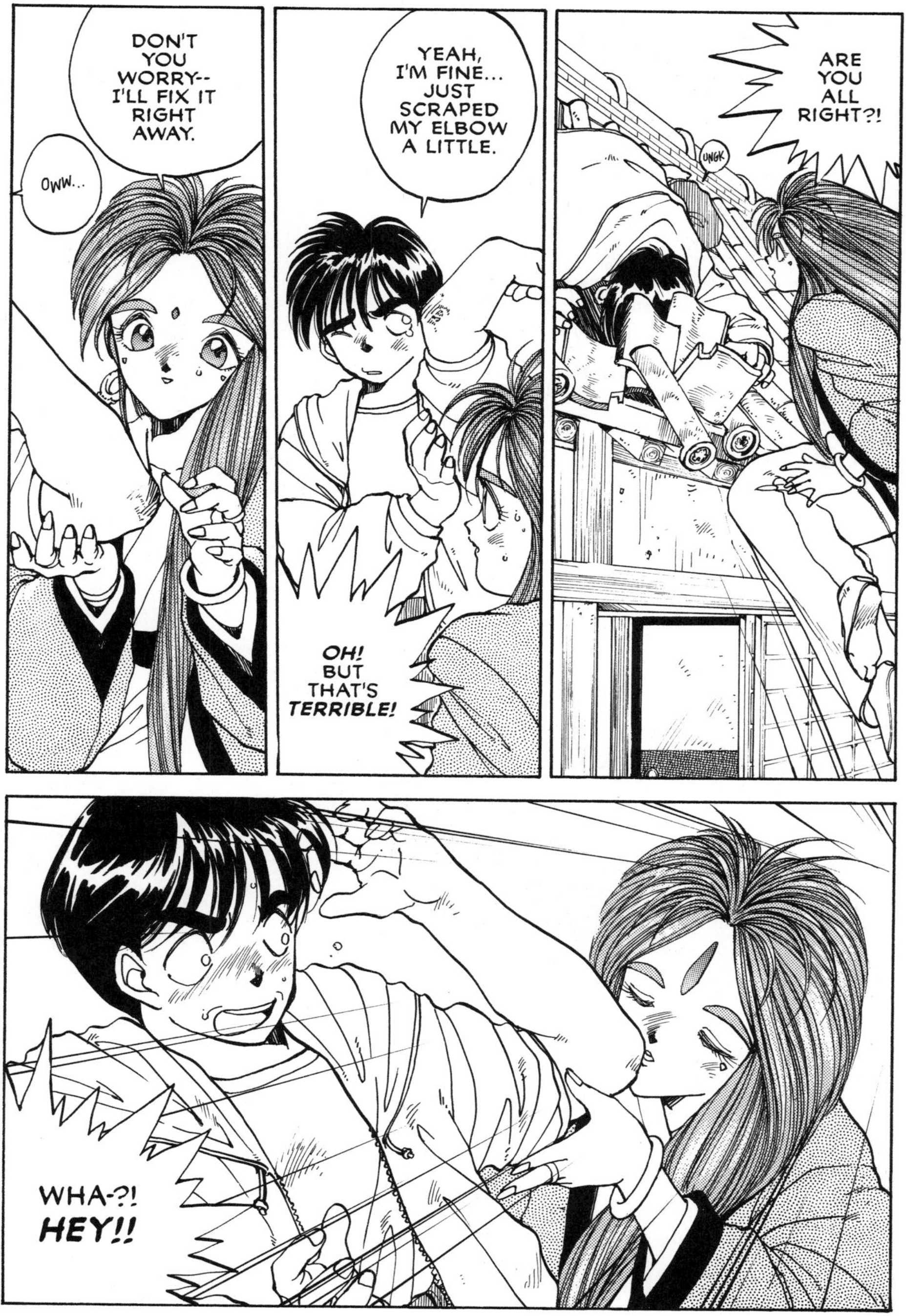
ARE YOU ALL RIGHT?!
UNGK
YEAH, I'M FINE... JUST SCRAPED MY ELBOW A LITTLE.
OH! BUT THAT'S TERRIBLE!
DON'T YOU WORRY-- I'LL FIX IT RIGHT AWAY.
OWW...
WHA-?! HEY!!

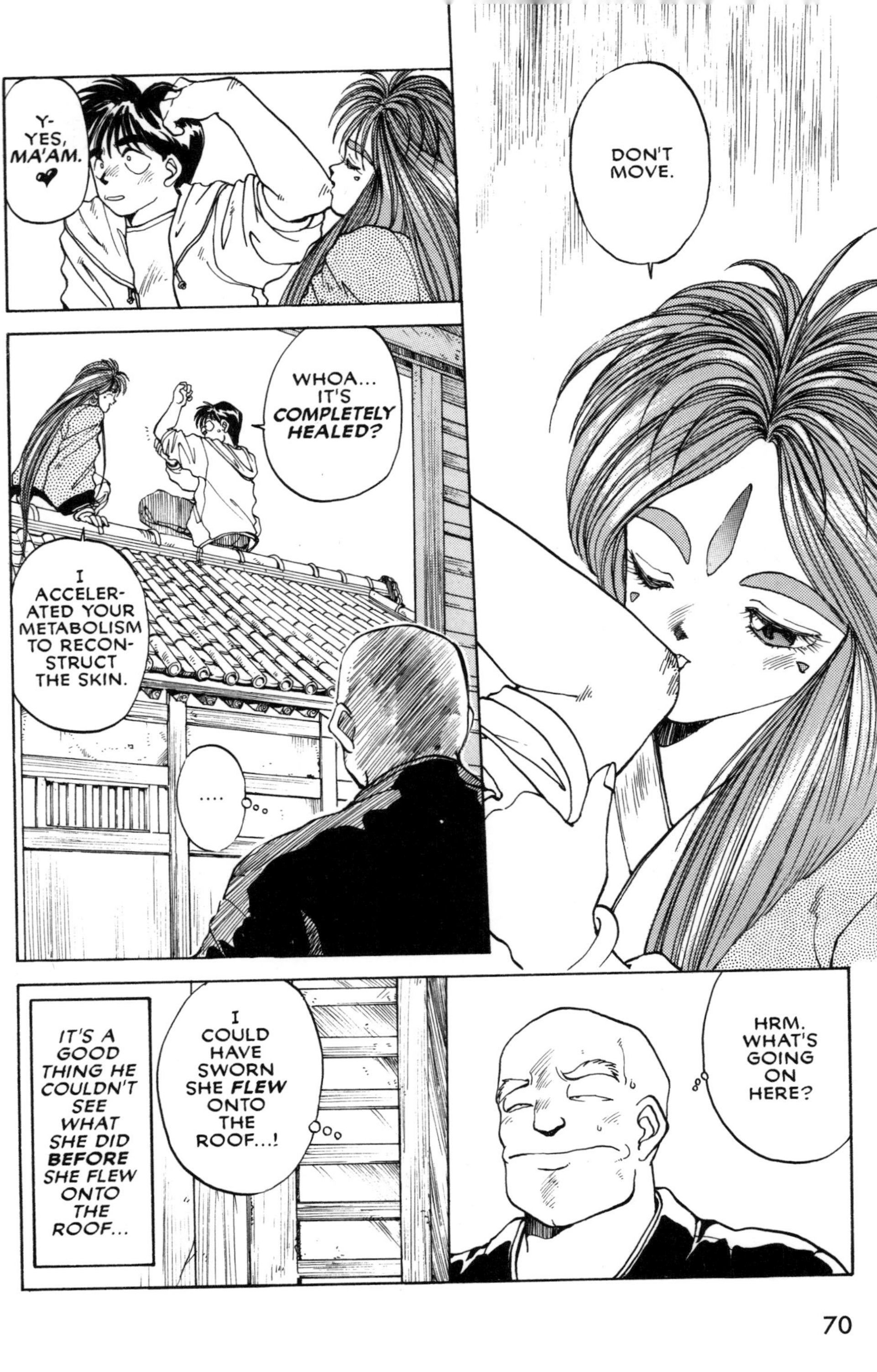
DON'T MOVE.
Y-YES, MA'AM. ♥
WHOA... IT'S COMPLETELY HEALED?
I ACCELERATED YOUR METABOLISM TO RECONSTRUCT THE SKIN.
....
HRM. WHAT'S GOING ON HERE?
I COULD HAVE SWORN SHE FLEW ONTO THE ROOF...!
IT'S A GOOD THING HE COULDN'T SEE WHAT SHE DID BEFORE SHE FLEW ONTO THE ROOF...

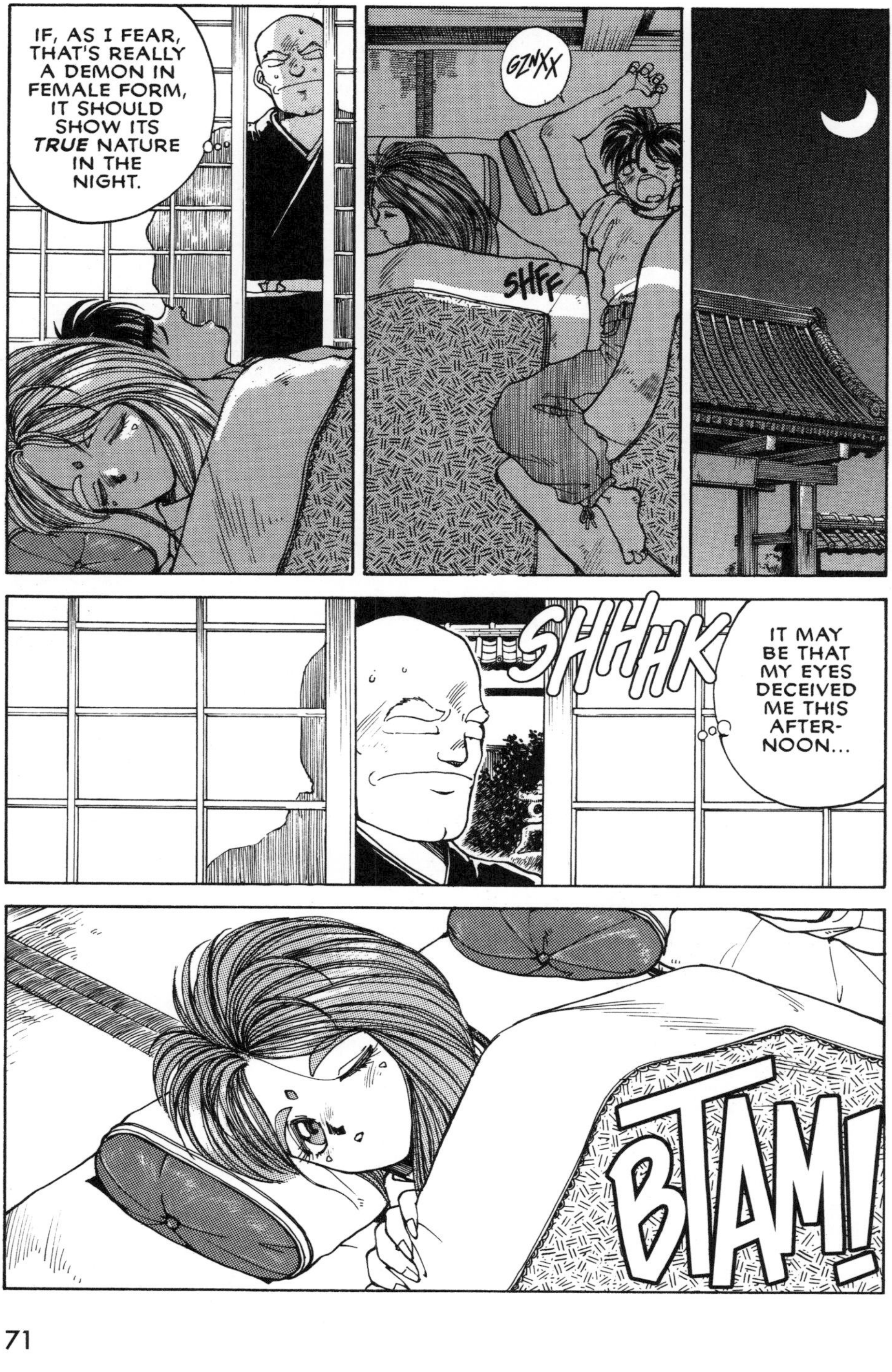
GZNXX
SHFF
IF, AS I FEAR, THAT'S REALLY A DEMON IN FEMALE FORM, IT SHOULD SHOW ITS *TRUE* NATURE IN THE NIGHT.
IT MAY BE THAT MY EYES DECEIVED ME THIS AFTER-NOON...
SHHHK
BTAM!

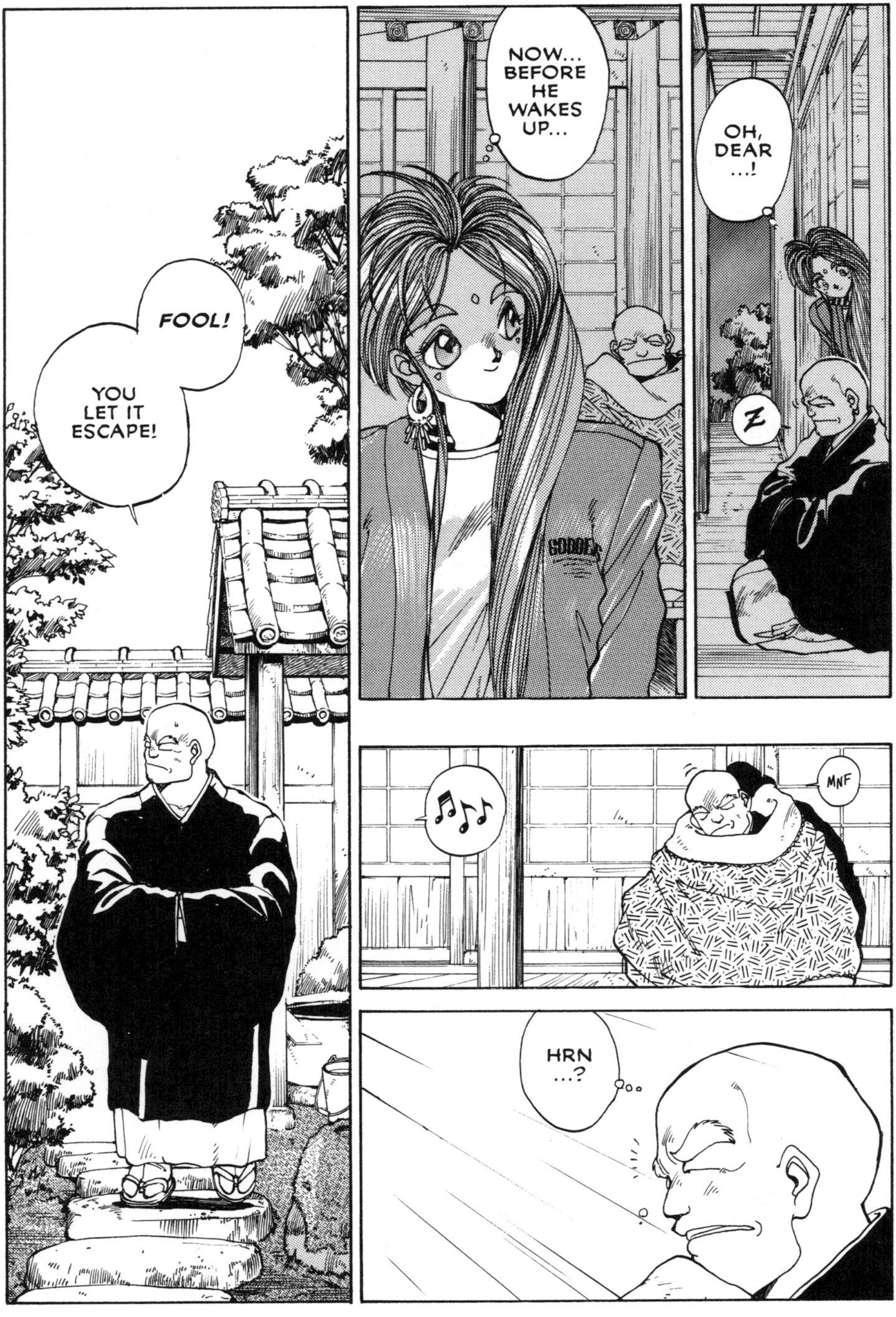
OH, DEAR ...!
Z
NOW... BEFORE HE WAKES UP...
MNF
HRN ...?
FOOL!
YOU LET IT ESCAPE!

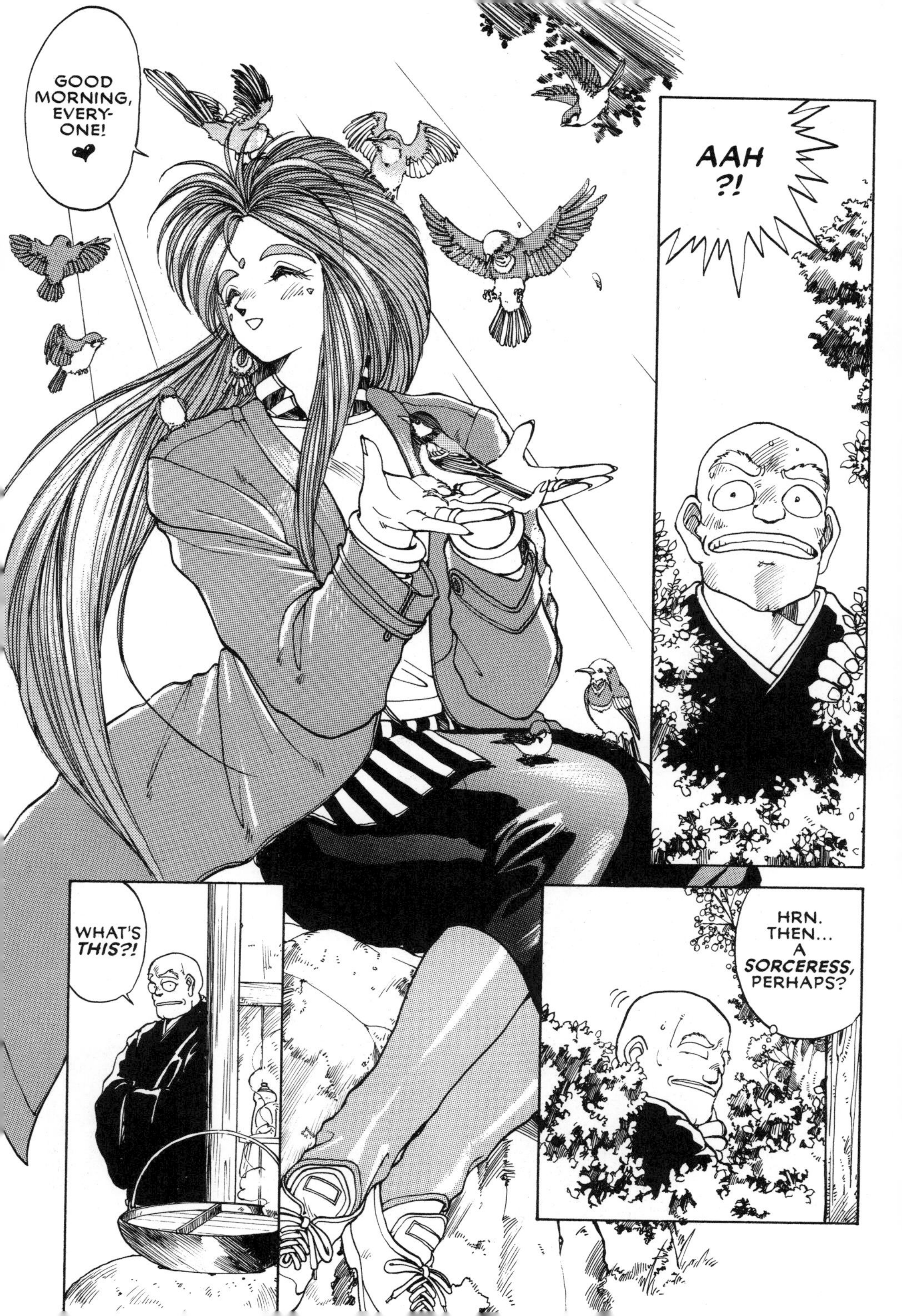
GOOD MORNING, EVERY-ONE! ❤
AAH ?!
HRN. THEN... A *SORCERESS,* PERHAPS?
WHAT'S *THIS?!*

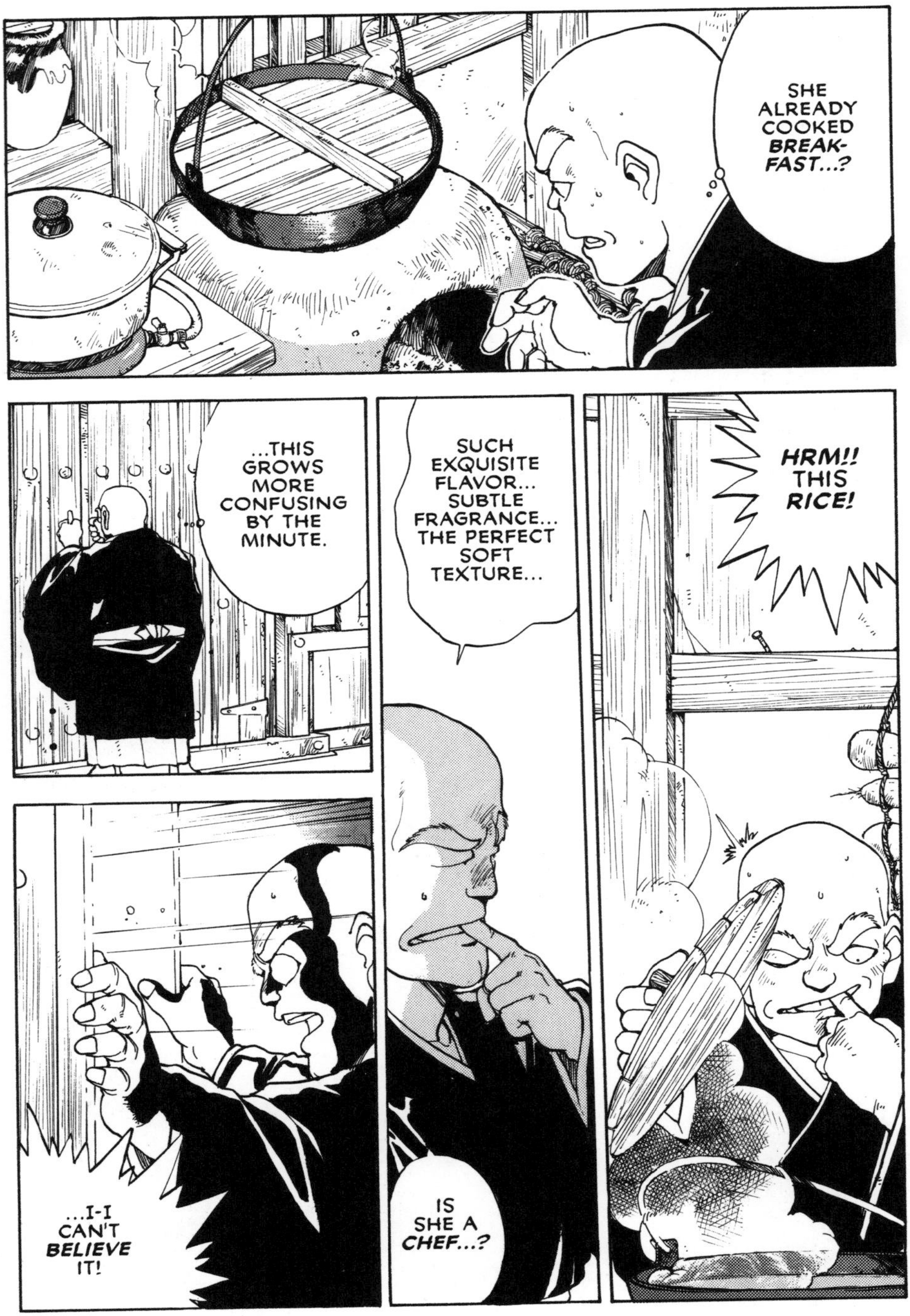
SHE ALREADY COOKED BREAKFAST...?
HRM!! THIS RICE!
SUCH EXQUISITE FLAVOR... SUBTLE FRAGRANCE... THE PERFECT SOFT TEXTURE...
IS SHE A CHEF...?
...THIS GROWS MORE CONFUSING BY THE MINUTE.
...I-I CAN'T BELIEVE IT!

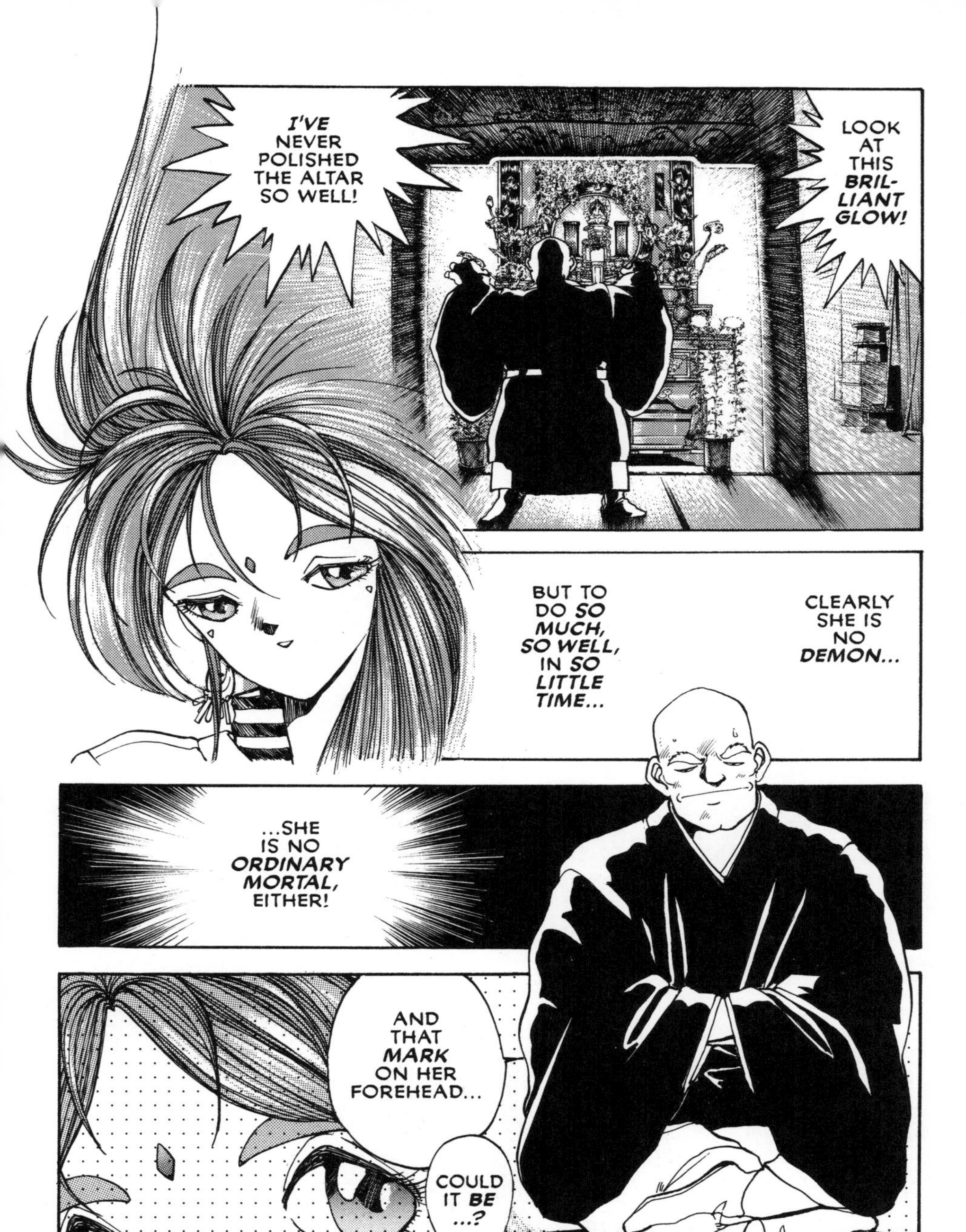
LOOK AT THIS BRIL-LIANT GLOW!
I'VE NEVER POLISHED THE ALTAR SO WELL!
CLEARLY SHE IS NO DEMON...
BUT TO DO SO MUCH, SO WELL, IN SO LITTLE TIME...
...SHE IS NO ORDINARY MORTAL, EITHER!
AND THAT MARK ON HER FOREHEAD...
COULD IT BE ...?

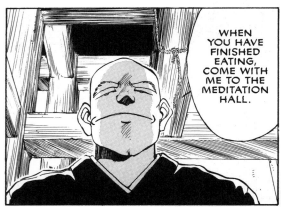

I WONDER WHERE THE PRIEST WENT?
IT'S LONG PAST BREAK-FAST TIME...
MNPH?
WHEN YOU HAVE FINISHED EATING, COME WITH ME TO THE MEDITATION HALL.
BUT FIRST-- CHOW TIME!
HEY! DON'T HOG IT ALL!
NOW, NOW.
SPLOT
YOU SHOULD BE FASTING TO PURIFY YOURSELF, LAD!
...DID I SIGN UP FOR THIS...?

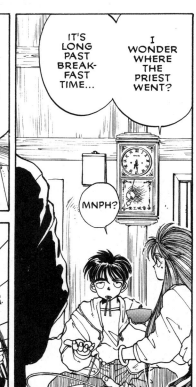

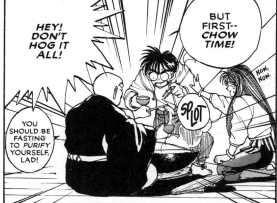

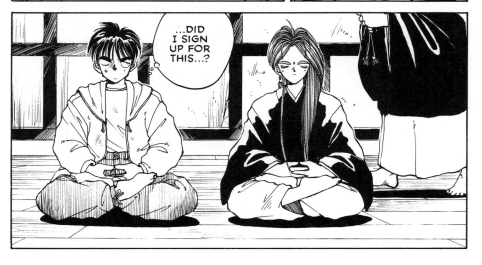

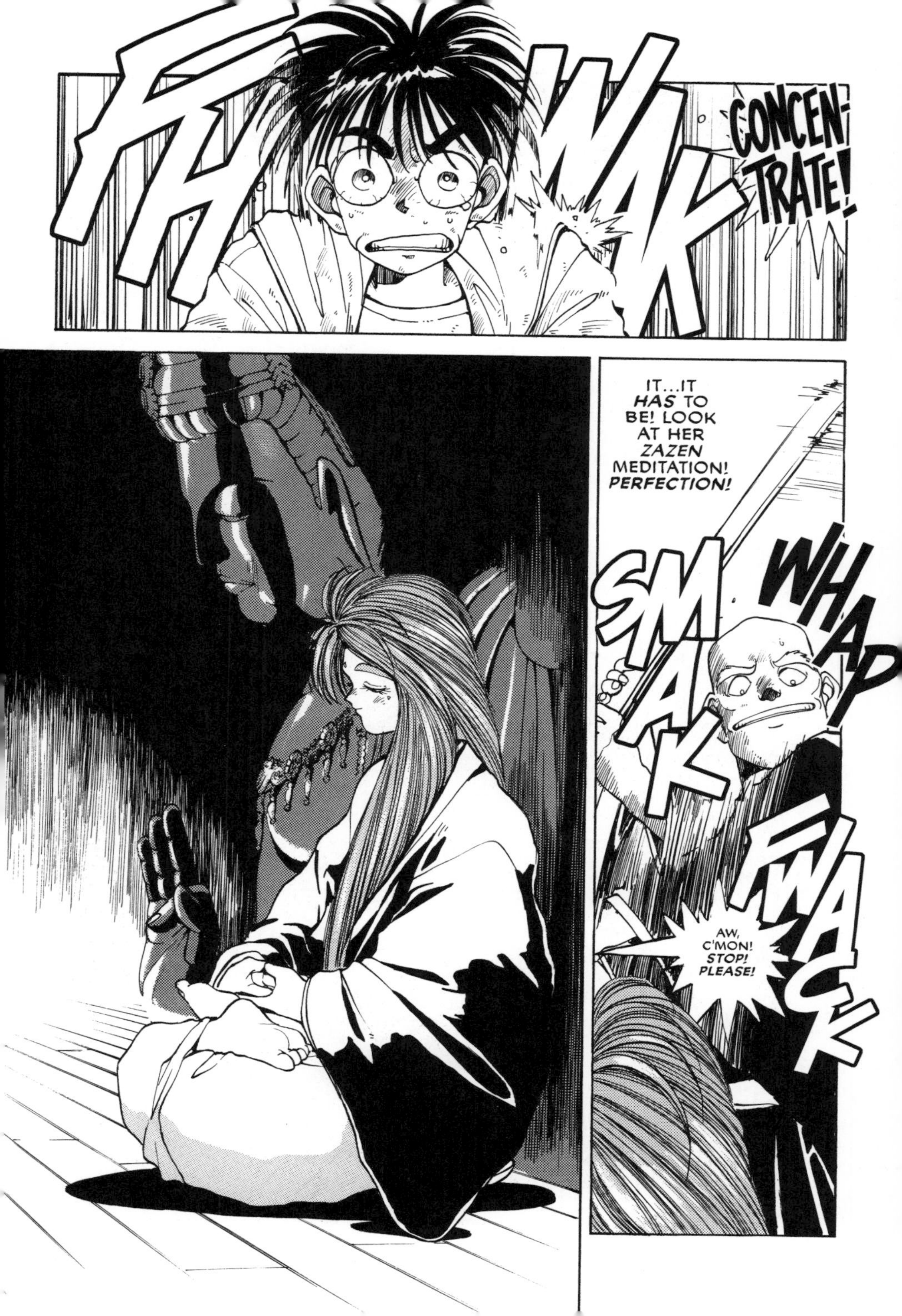
FHWAK
CONCEN-TRATE!
IT...IT *HAS* TO BE! LOOK AT HER *ZAZEN* MEDITATION! ***PERFECTION!***
WHAP
SMAK
FWACK
AW, C'MON! ***STOP!*** PLEASE!

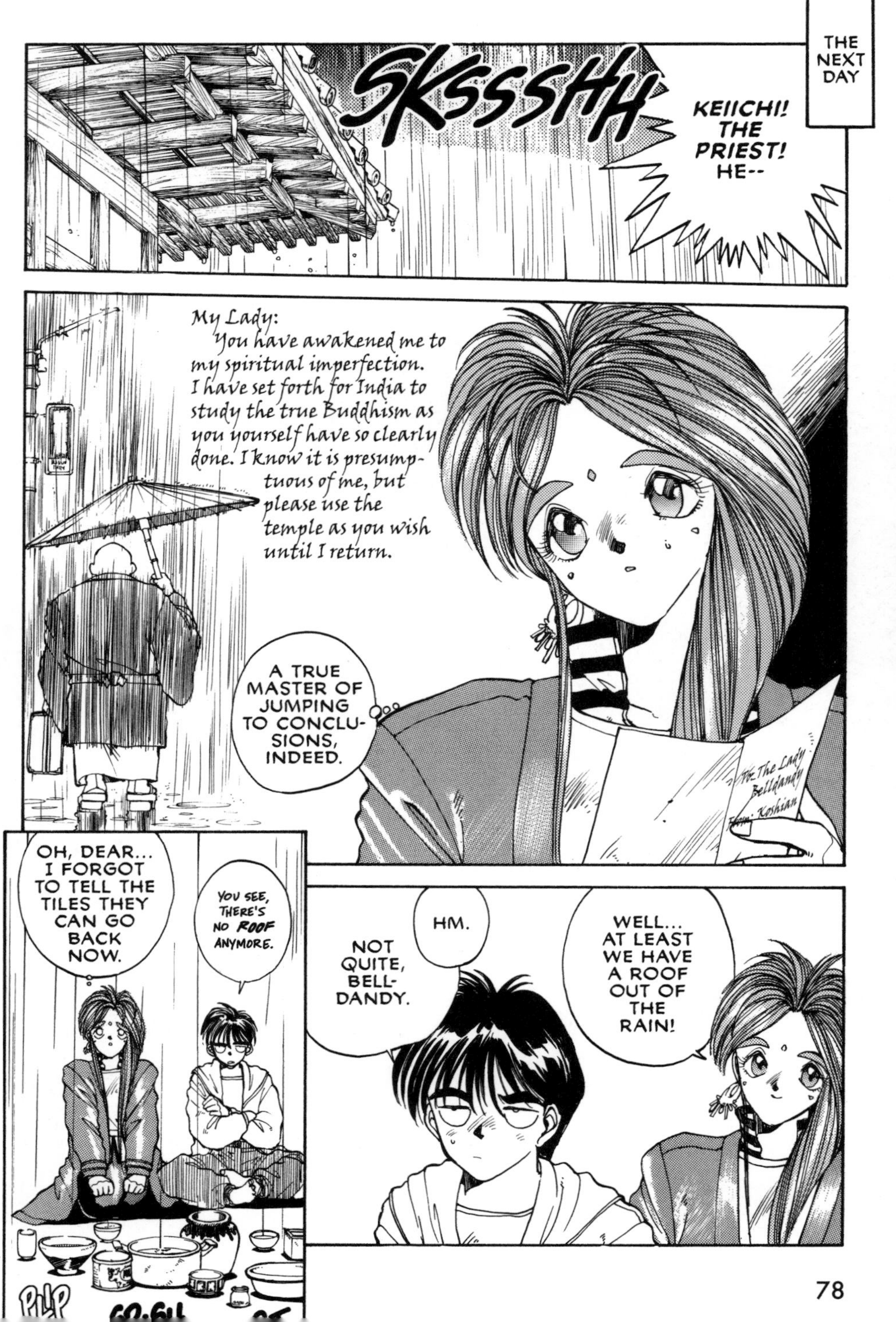
THE NEXT DAY
SKSSSHH
KEIICHI! THE PRIEST! HE--
My Lady:
You have awakened me to my spiritual imperfection. I have set forth for India to study the true Buddhism as you yourself have so clearly done. I know it is presumptuous of me, but please use the temple as you wish until I return.
A TRUE MASTER OF JUMPING TO CONCLUSIONS, INDEED.
To: The Lady Belldandy
From: Koshian
WELL... AT LEAST WE HAVE A ROOF OUT OF THE RAIN!
HM.
NOT QUITE, BELL-DANDY.
YOU SEE, THERE'S NO ROOF ANYMORE.
OH, DEAR... I FORGOT TO TELL THE TILES THEY CAN GO BACK NOW.
PILP

CHAPTER 4

College-Exchange Goddess

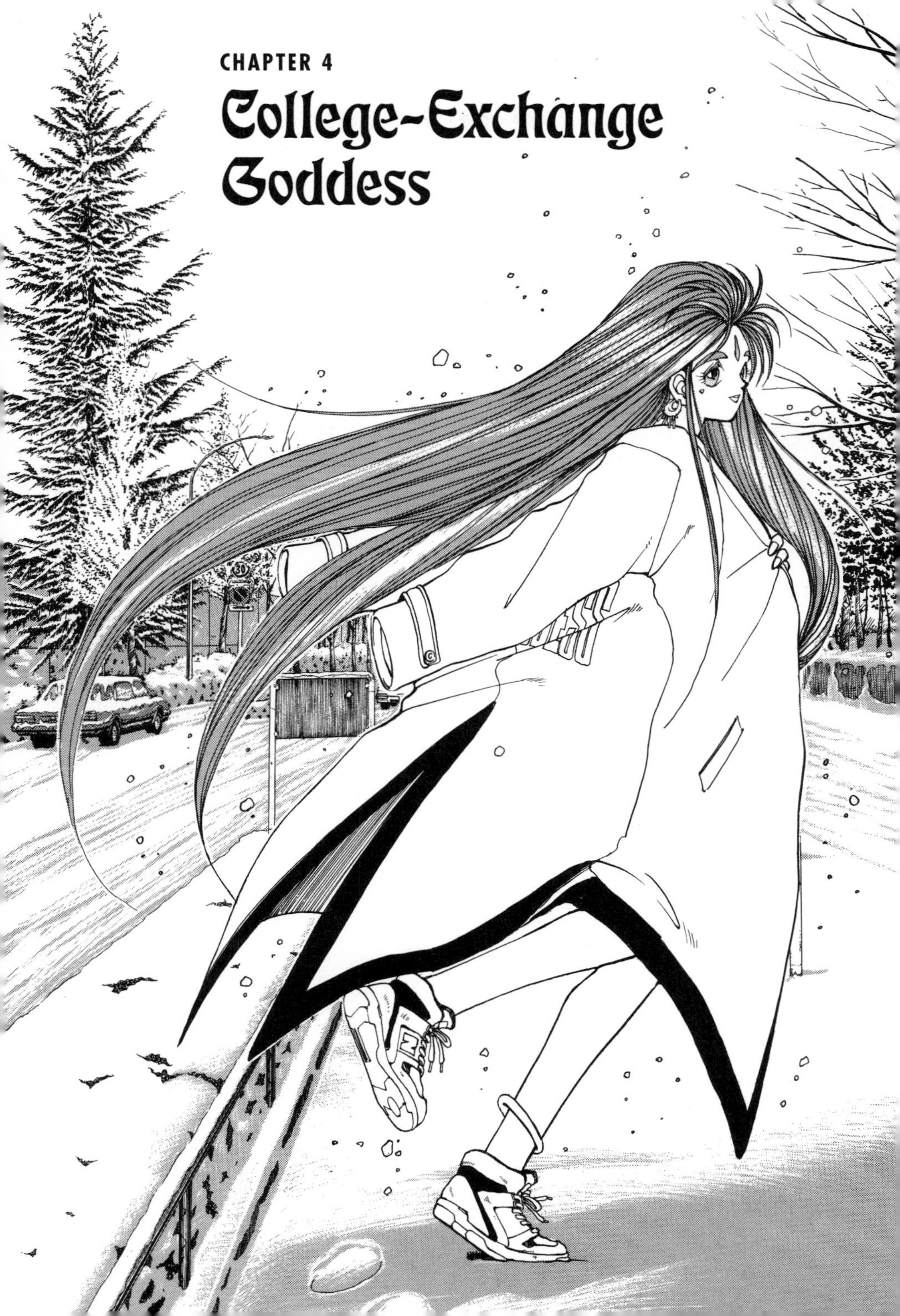

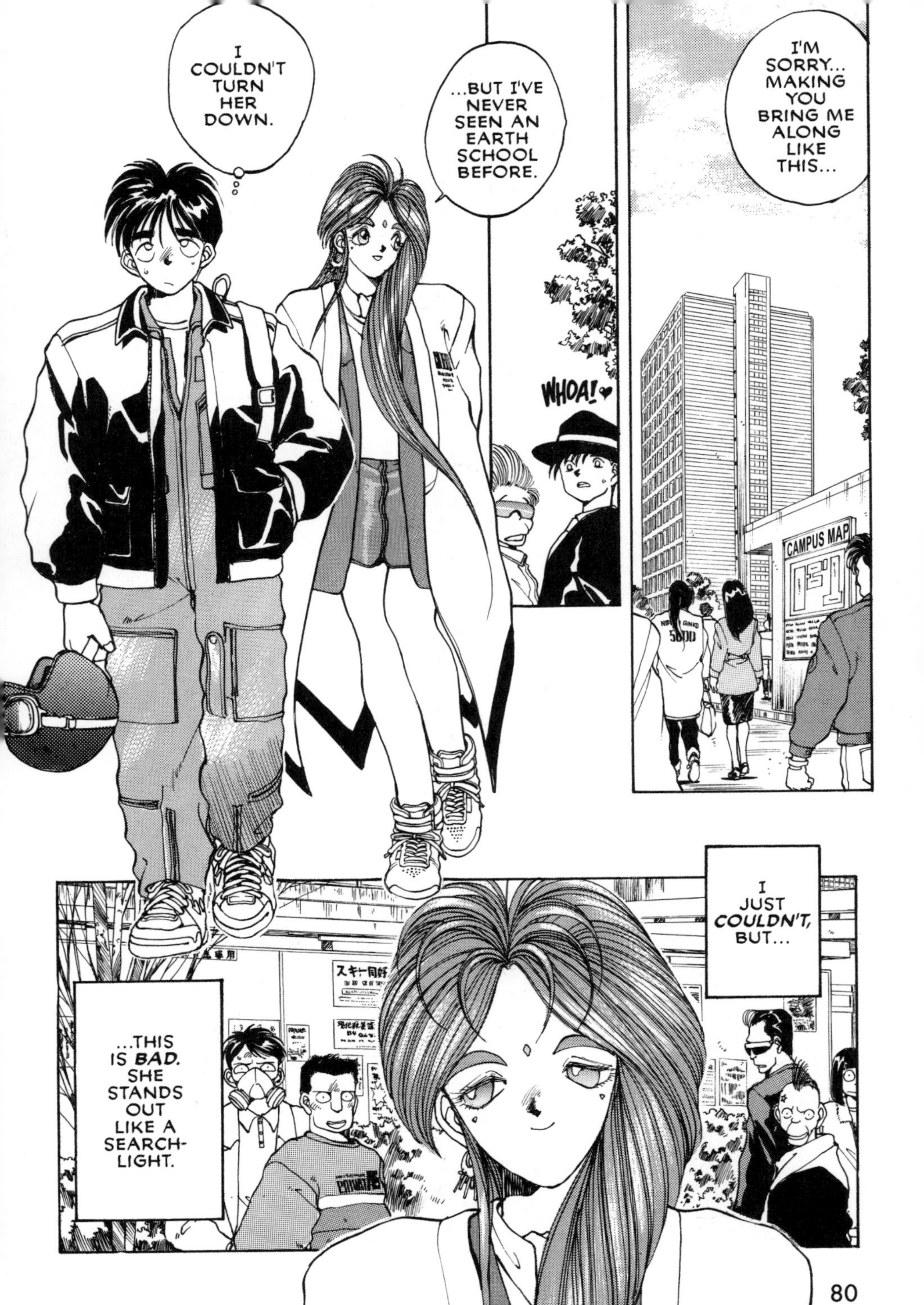
I'M SORRY... MAKING YOU BRING ME ALONG LIKE THIS...
CAMPUS MAP
WHOA!
...BUT I'VE NEVER SEEN AN EARTH SCHOOL BEFORE.
I COULDN'T TURN HER DOWN.
I JUST *COULDN'T,* BUT...
...THIS IS *BAD.* SHE STANDS OUT LIKE A SEARCH-LIGHT.

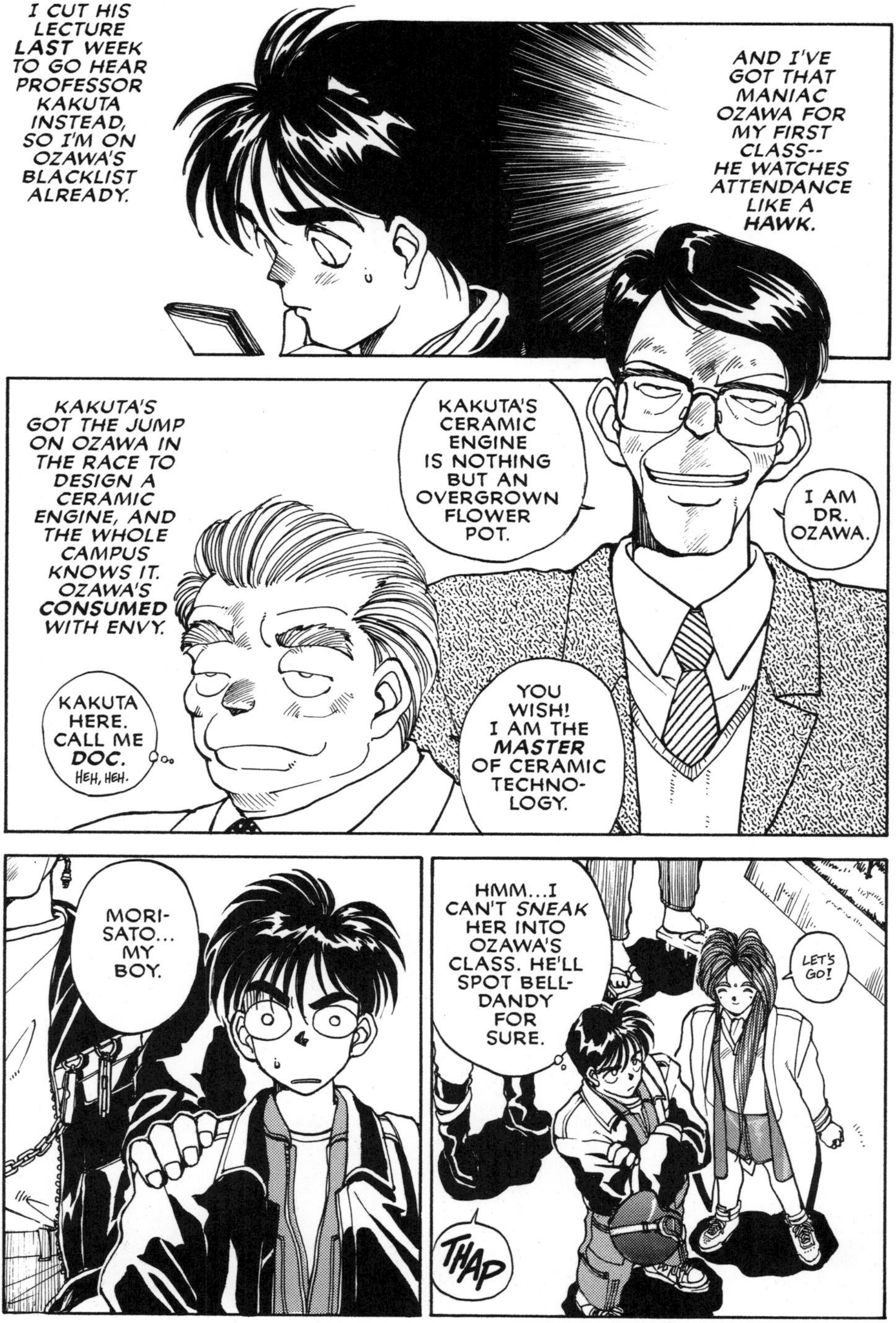
AND I'VE GOT THAT MANIAC OZAWA FOR MY FIRST CLASS-- HE WATCHES ATTENDANCE LIKE A HAWK.
I CUT HIS LECTURE LAST WEEK TO GO HEAR PROFESSOR KAKUTA INSTEAD, SO I'M ON OZAWA'S BLACKLIST ALREADY.
I AM DR. OZAWA.
KAKUTA'S CERAMIC ENGINE IS NOTHING BUT AN OVERGROWN FLOWER POT.
KAKUTA'S GOT THE JUMP ON OZAWA IN THE RACE TO DESIGN A CERAMIC ENGINE, AND THE WHOLE CAMPUS KNOWS IT. OZAWA'S CONSUMED WITH ENVY.
YOU WISH! I AM THE MASTER OF CERAMIC TECHNOLOGY.
KAKUTA HERE. CALL ME DOC. HEH, HEH.
LET'S GO!
HMM...I CAN'T SNEAK HER INTO OZAWA'S CLASS. HE'LL SPOT BELLDANDY FOR SURE.
THAP
MORISATO... MY BOY.

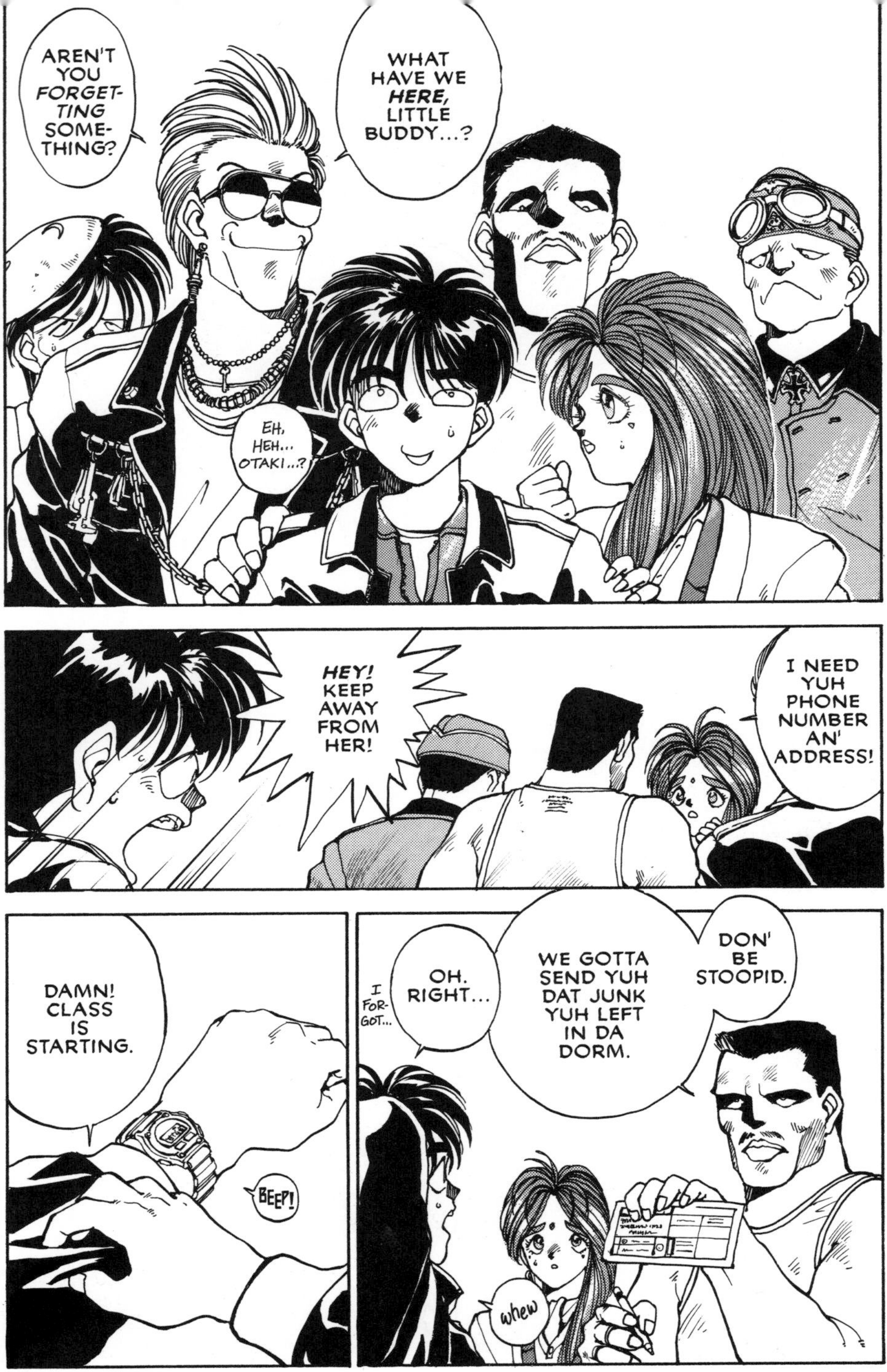
WHAT HAVE WE *HERE,* LITTLE BUDDY...?
AREN'T YOU *FORGET-TING* SOME-THING?
EH, HEH... OTAKI...?
I NEED YUH PHONE NUMBER AN' ADDRESS!
HEY! KEEP AWAY FROM HER!
DON' BE STOOPID.
WE GOTTA SEND YUH DAT JUNK YUH LEFT IN DA DORM.
OH. RIGHT...
I FOR-GOT...
whew
DAMN! CLASS IS STARTING.
BEEP!

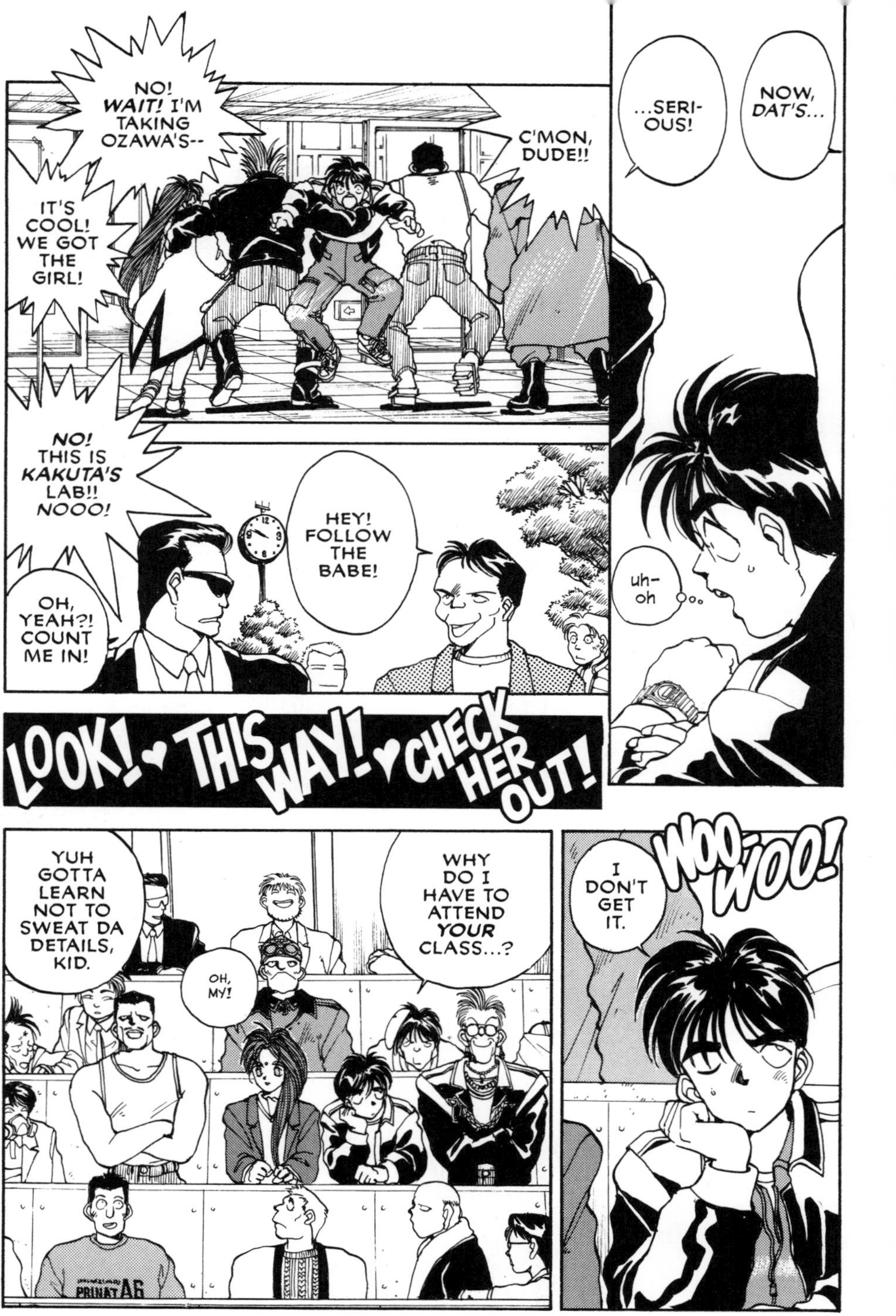
NOW, DAT'S...
...SERI-OUS!
uh-oh
NO! WAIT! I'M TAKING OZAWA'S--
C'MON, DUDE!!
IT'S COOL! WE GOT THE GIRL!
HEY! FOLLOW THE BABE!
OH, YEAH?! COUNT ME IN!
NO! THIS IS KAKUTA'S LAB!! NOOO!
LOOK! ♥ THIS WAY! ♥ CHECK HER OUT!
WOO-WOO!
I DON'T GET IT.
WHY DO I HAVE TO ATTEND YOUR CLASS...?
YUH GOTTA LEARN NOT TO SWEAT DA DETAILS, KID.
OH, MY!
PRINAT A6

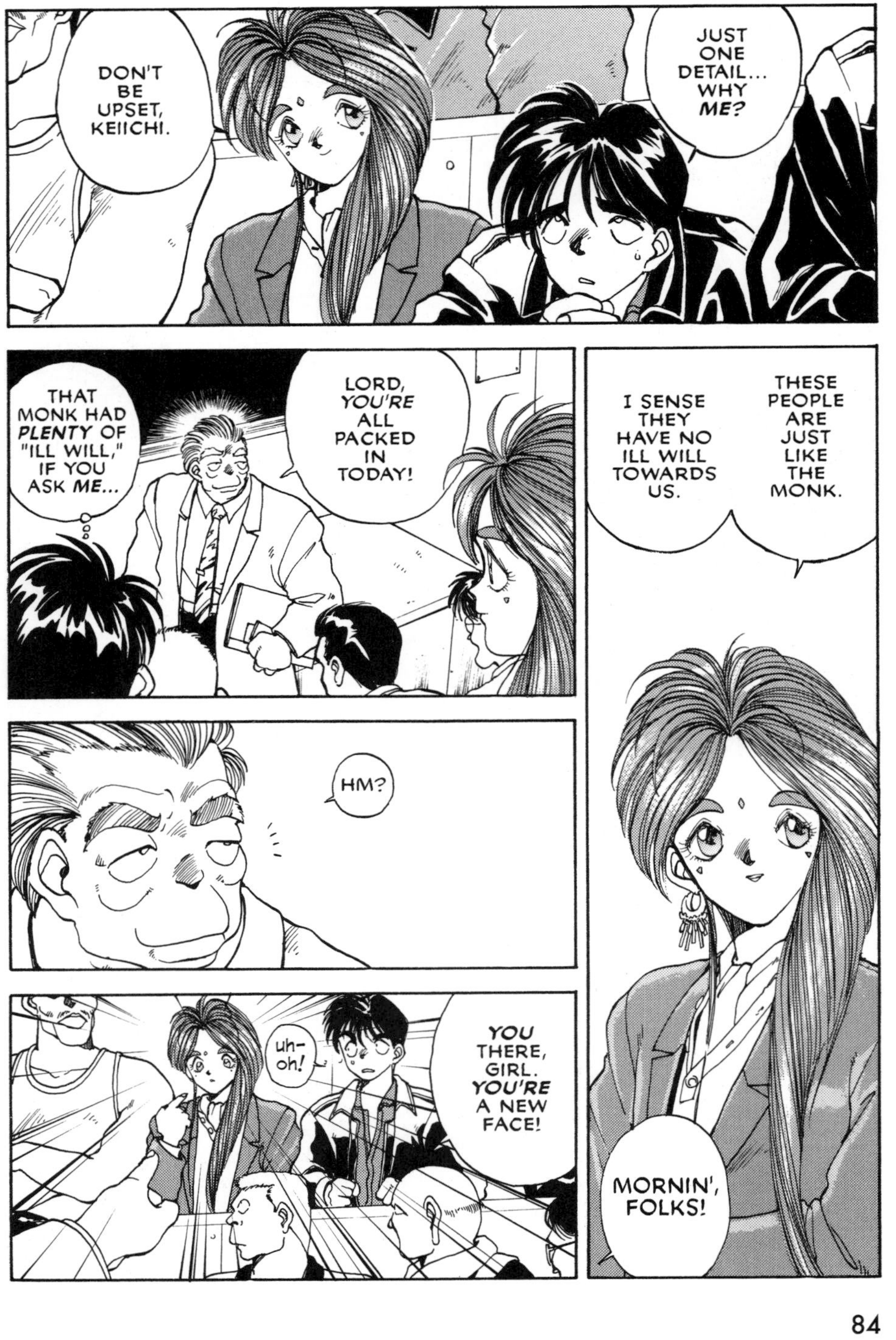
JUST ONE DETAIL... WHY *ME?*
DON'T BE UPSET, KEIICHI.
THESE PEOPLE ARE JUST LIKE THE MONK.
I SENSE THEY HAVE NO ILL WILL TOWARDS US.
MORNIN', FOLKS!
LORD, *YOU'RE* ALL PACKED IN TODAY!
THAT MONK HAD *PLENTY* OF "ILL WILL," IF YOU ASK *ME*...
HM?
YOU THERE, GIRL. *YOU'RE* A NEW FACE!
uh-oh!

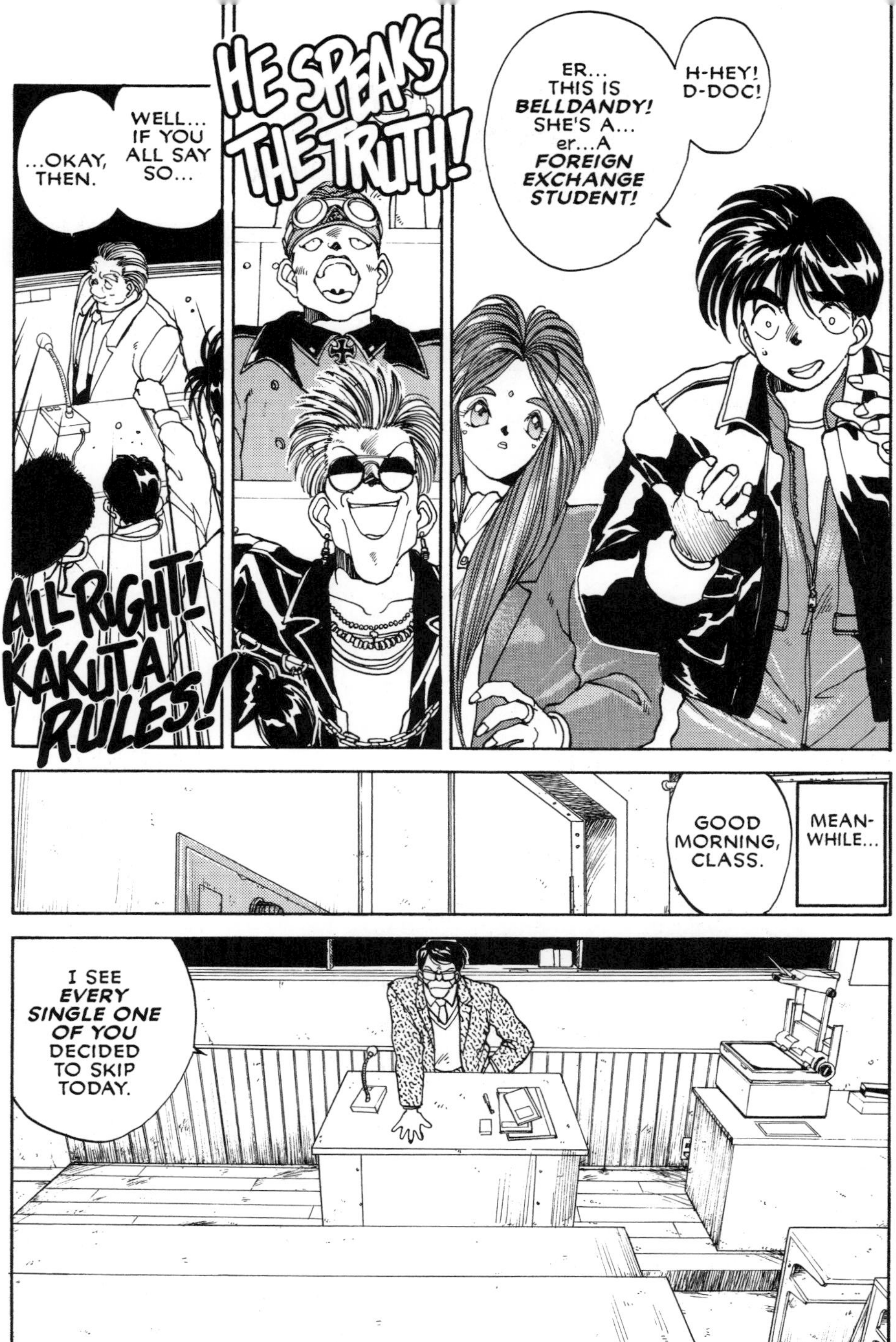
H-HEY! D-DOC!
ER... THIS IS BELLDANDY! SHE'S A... er...A FOREIGN EXCHANGE STUDENT!
HE SPEAKS THE TRUTH!
ALL RIGHT! KAKUTA RULES!
WELL... IF YOU ALL SAY SO...
...OKAY, THEN.
MEAN-WHILE...
GOOD MORNING, CLASS.
I SEE EVERY SINGLE ONE OF YOU DECIDED TO SKIP TODAY.

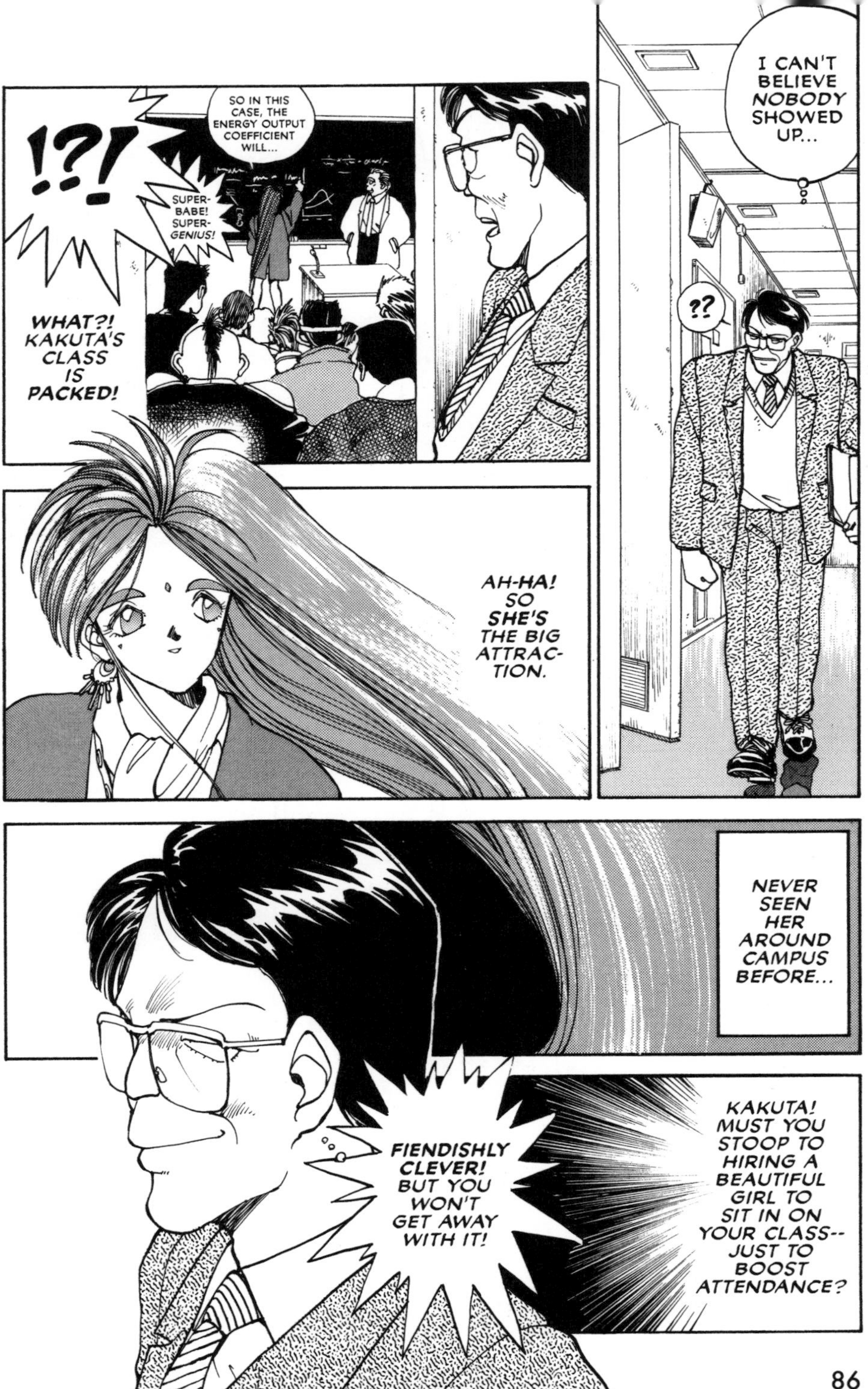
I CAN'T BELIEVE NOBODY SHOWED UP...
??
SO IN THIS CASE, THE ENERGY OUTPUT COEFFICIENT WILL...
!?!
SUPER-BABE! SUPER-GENIUS!
WHAT?! KAKUTA'S CLASS IS PACKED!
AH-HA! SO SHE'S THE BIG ATTRACTION.
NEVER SEEN HER AROUND CAMPUS BEFORE...
KAKUTA! MUST YOU STOOP TO HIRING A BEAUTIFUL GIRL TO SIT IN ON YOUR CLASS-- JUST TO BOOST ATTENDANCE?
FIENDISHLY CLEVER! BUT YOU WON'T GET AWAY WITH IT!

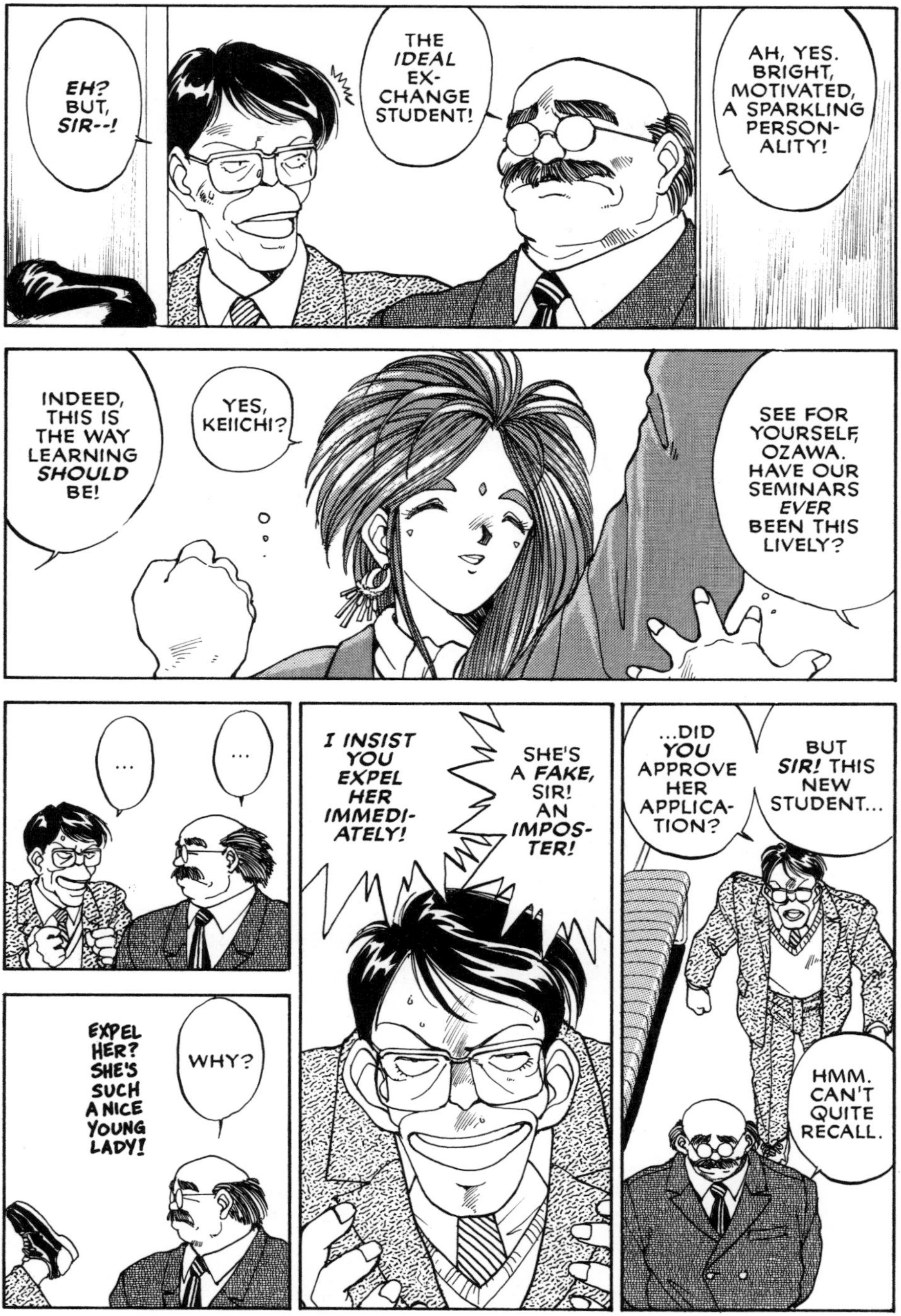
AH, YES. BRIGHT, MOTIVATED, A SPARKLING PERSONALITY!
THE IDEAL EXCHANGE STUDENT!
EH? BUT, SIR--!
SEE FOR YOURSELF, OZAWA. HAVE OUR SEMINARS EVER BEEN THIS LIVELY?
YES, KEIICHI?
INDEED, THIS IS THE WAY LEARNING SHOULD BE!
BUT SIR! THIS NEW STUDENT...
...DID YOU APPROVE HER APPLICATION?
HMM. CAN'T QUITE RECALL.
SHE'S A FAKE, SIR! AN IMPOSTER!
I INSIST YOU EXPEL HER IMMEDIATELY!
...
...
WHY?
EXPEL HER? SHE'S SUCH A NICE YOUNG LADY!

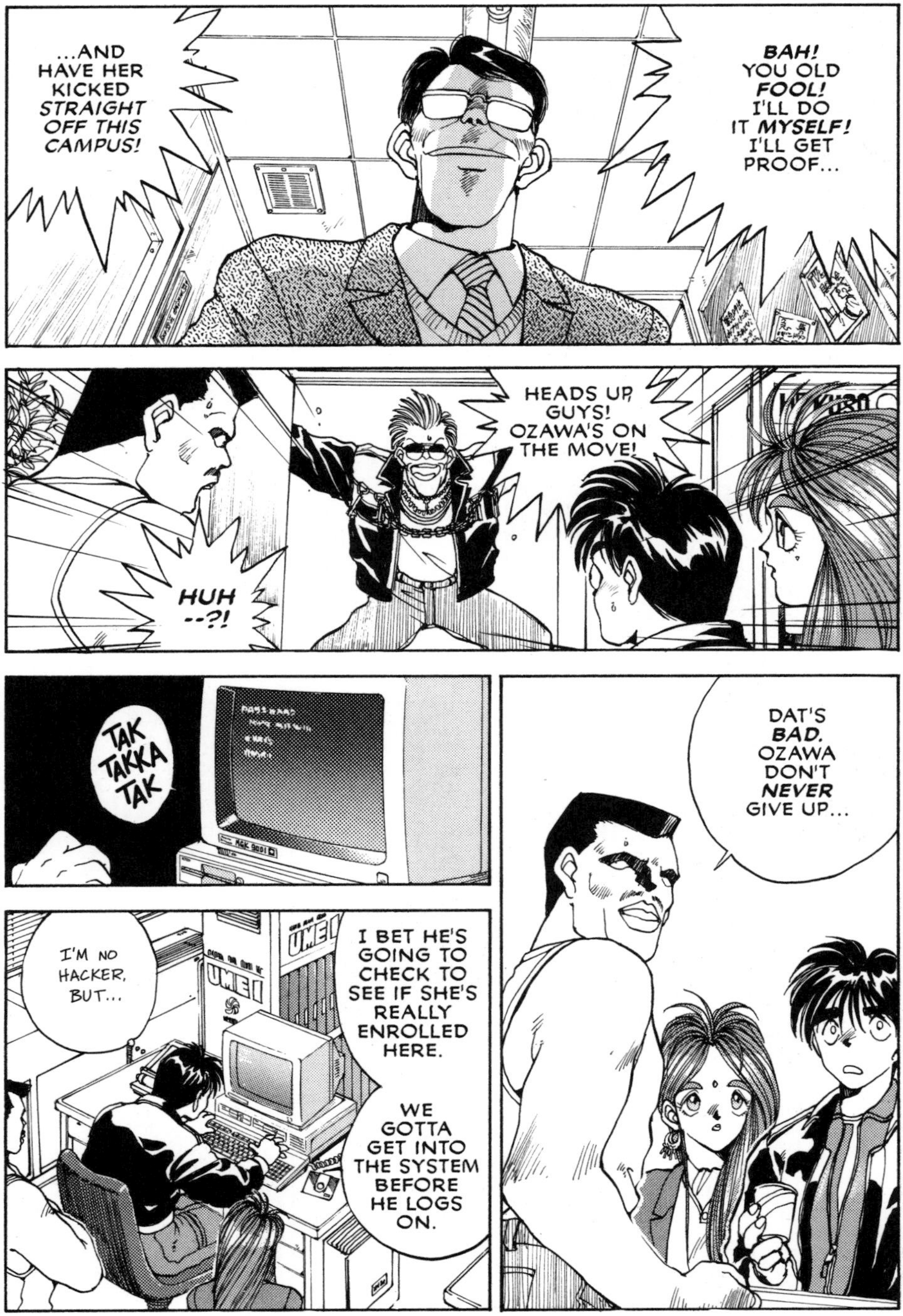
BAH! YOU OLD FOOL! I'LL DO IT MYSELF! I'LL GET PROOF...
...AND HAVE HER KICKED STRAIGHT OFF THIS CAMPUS!
HEADS UP, GUYS! OZAWA'S ON THE MOVE!
HUH --?!
DAT'S BAD. OZAWA DON'T NEVER GIVE UP...
TAK TAKKA TAK
I'M NO HACKER, BUT...
I BET HE'S GOING TO CHECK TO SEE IF SHE'S REALLY ENROLLED HERE.
WE GOTTA GET INTO THE SYSTEM BEFORE HE LOGS ON.

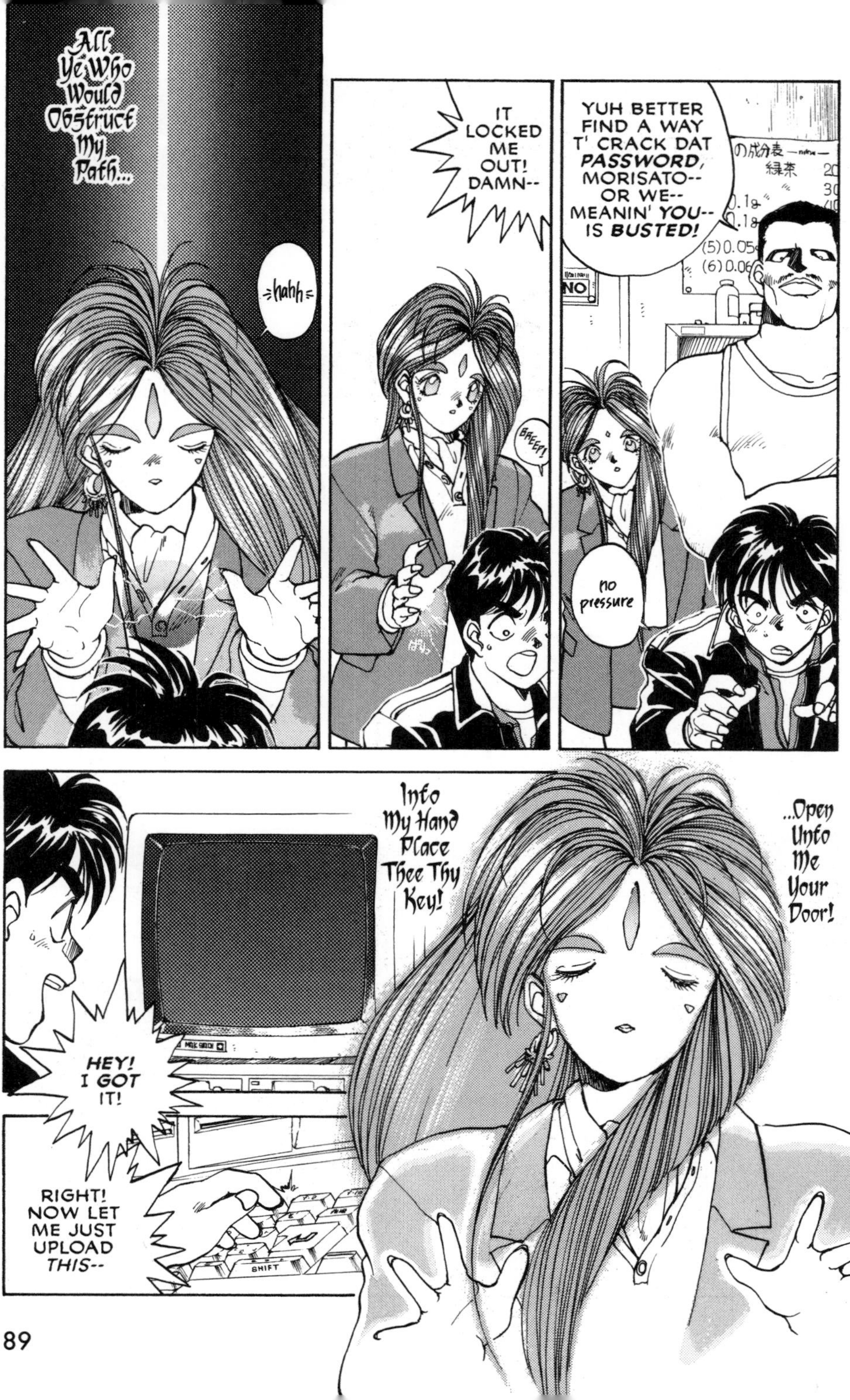
YUH BETTER FIND A WAY T' CRACK DAT PASSWORD, MORISATO-- OR WE-- MEANIN' YOU-- IS BUSTED!
NO
no pressure
IT LOCKED ME OUT! DAMN--
BREEP!
All Ye Who Would Obstruct My Path...
hahh
...Open Unto Me Your Door!
Into My Hand Place Thee Thy Key!
HEY! I GOT IT!
RIGHT! NOW LET ME JUST UPLOAD THIS--
SHIFT

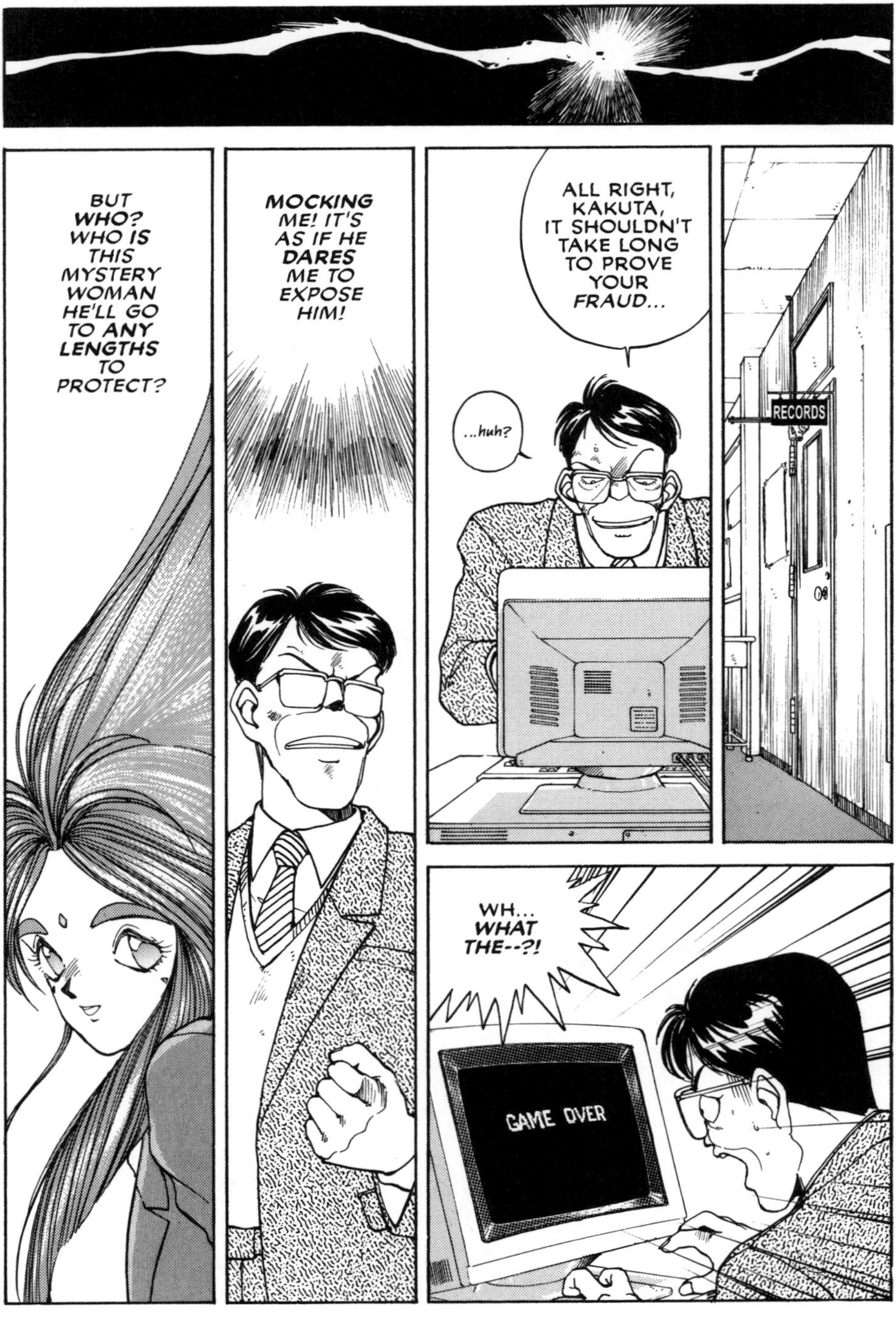
RECORDS
ALL RIGHT, KAKUTA, IT SHOULDN'T TAKE LONG TO PROVE YOUR *FRAUD*...
...huh?
WH... *WHAT THE--?!*
GAME OVER
MOCKING ME! IT'S AS IF HE *DARES* ME TO EXPOSE HIM!
BUT *WHO?* WHO *IS* THIS MYSTERY WOMAN HE'LL GO TO *ANY LENGTHS* TO PROTECT?

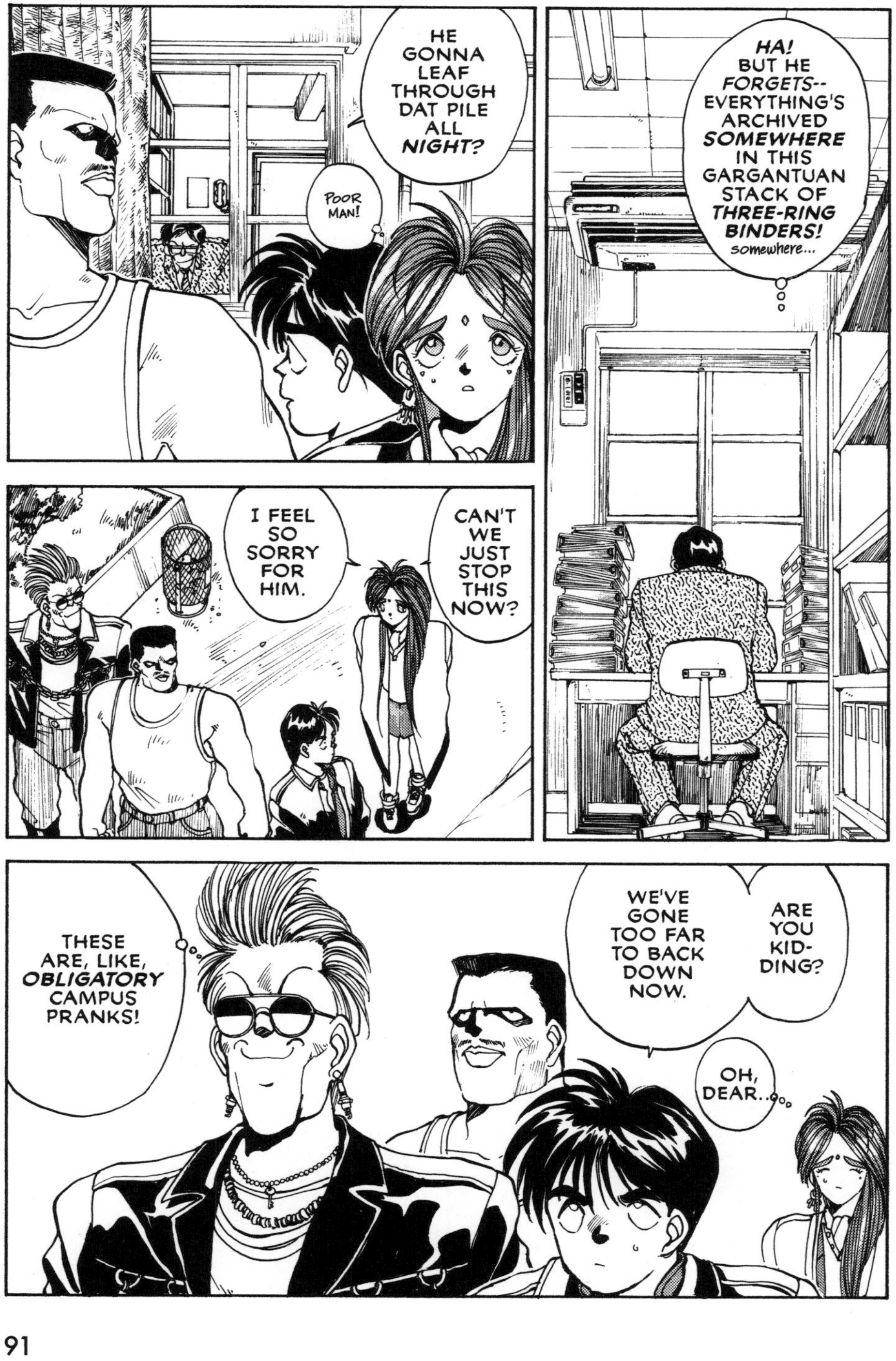
HA! BUT HE FORGETS-- EVERYTHING'S ARCHIVED SOMEWHERE IN THIS GARGANTUAN STACK OF THREE-RING BINDERS! somewhere...
HE GONNA LEAF THROUGH DAT PILE ALL NIGHT?
POOR MAN!
CAN'T WE JUST STOP THIS NOW?
I FEEL SO SORRY FOR HIM.
ARE YOU KID-DING?
WE'VE GONE TOO FAR TO BACK DOWN NOW.
THESE ARE, LIKE, OBLIGATORY CAMPUS PRANKS!
OH, DEAR...

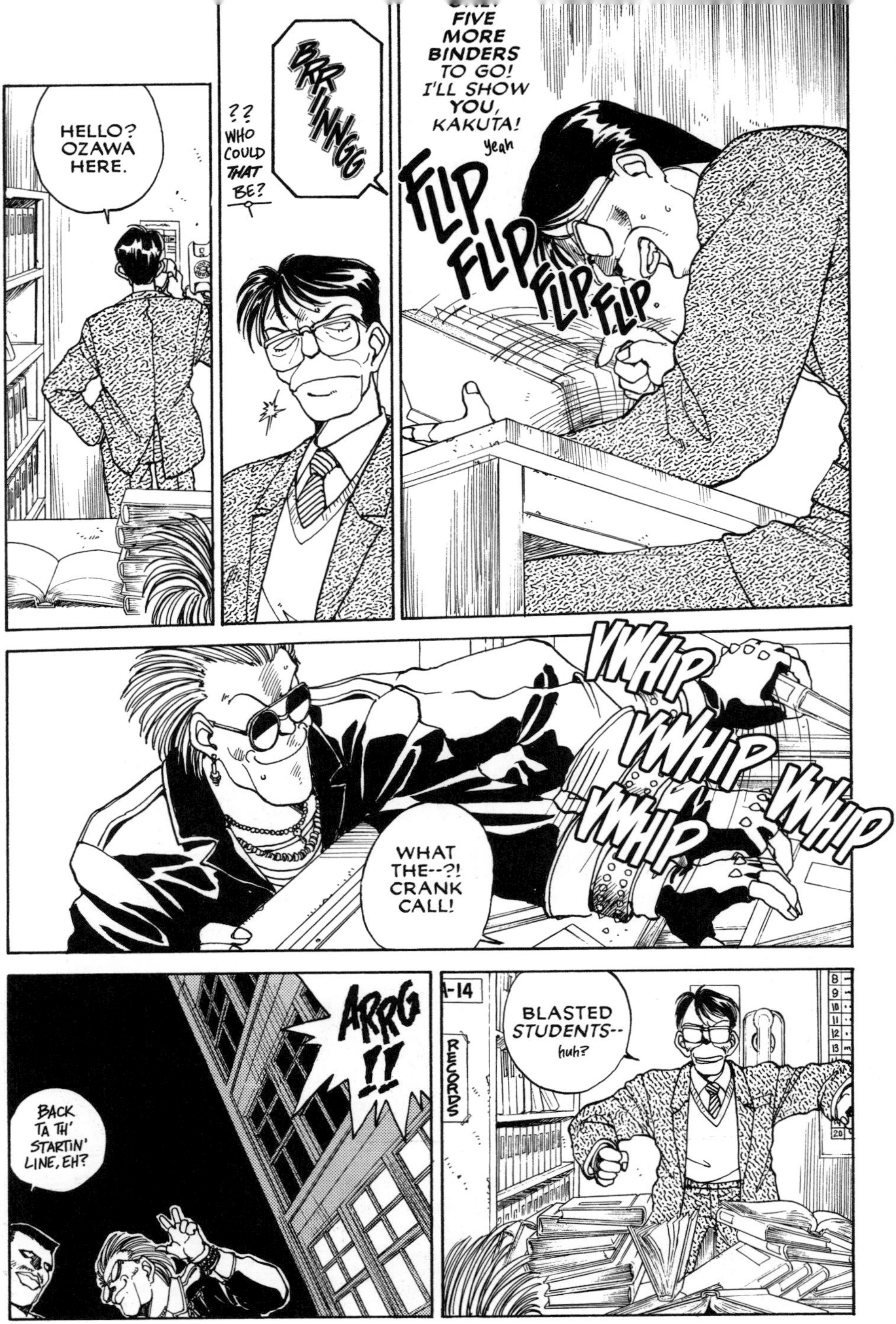
FIVE MORE BINDERS TO GO! I'LL SHOW YOU, KAKUTA!
yeah
FLIP FLIP FLIP FLIP
BRRRINNGG
?? WHO COULD THAT BE?
HELLO? OZAWA HERE.
VWHIP VWHIP VWHIP VWHIP
WHAT THE--?! CRANK CALL!
A-14
RECORDS
BLASTED STUDENTS-- huh?
ARRG !!
BACK TA TH' STARTIN' LINE, EH?

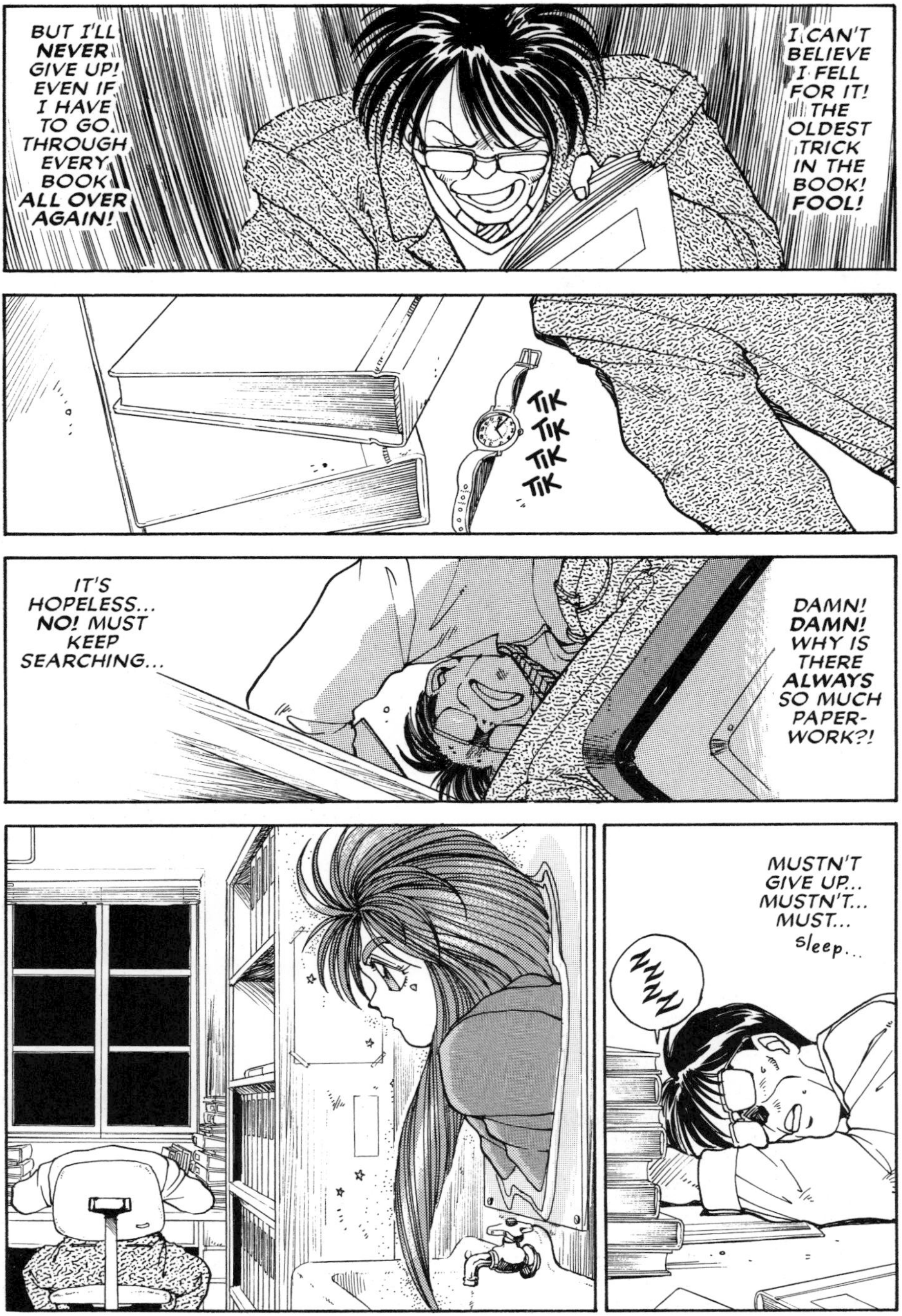
I CAN'T BELIEVE I FELL FOR IT! THE OLDEST TRICK IN THE BOOK! FOOL!
BUT I'LL NEVER GIVE UP! EVEN IF I HAVE TO GO THROUGH EVERY BOOK ALL OVER AGAIN!
TIK TIK TIK TIK
DAMN! DAMN! WHY IS THERE ALWAYS SO MUCH PAPER-WORK?!
IT'S HOPELESS... NO! MUST KEEP SEARCHING...
MUSTN'T GIVE UP... MUSTN'T... MUST... sleep...
NNNN

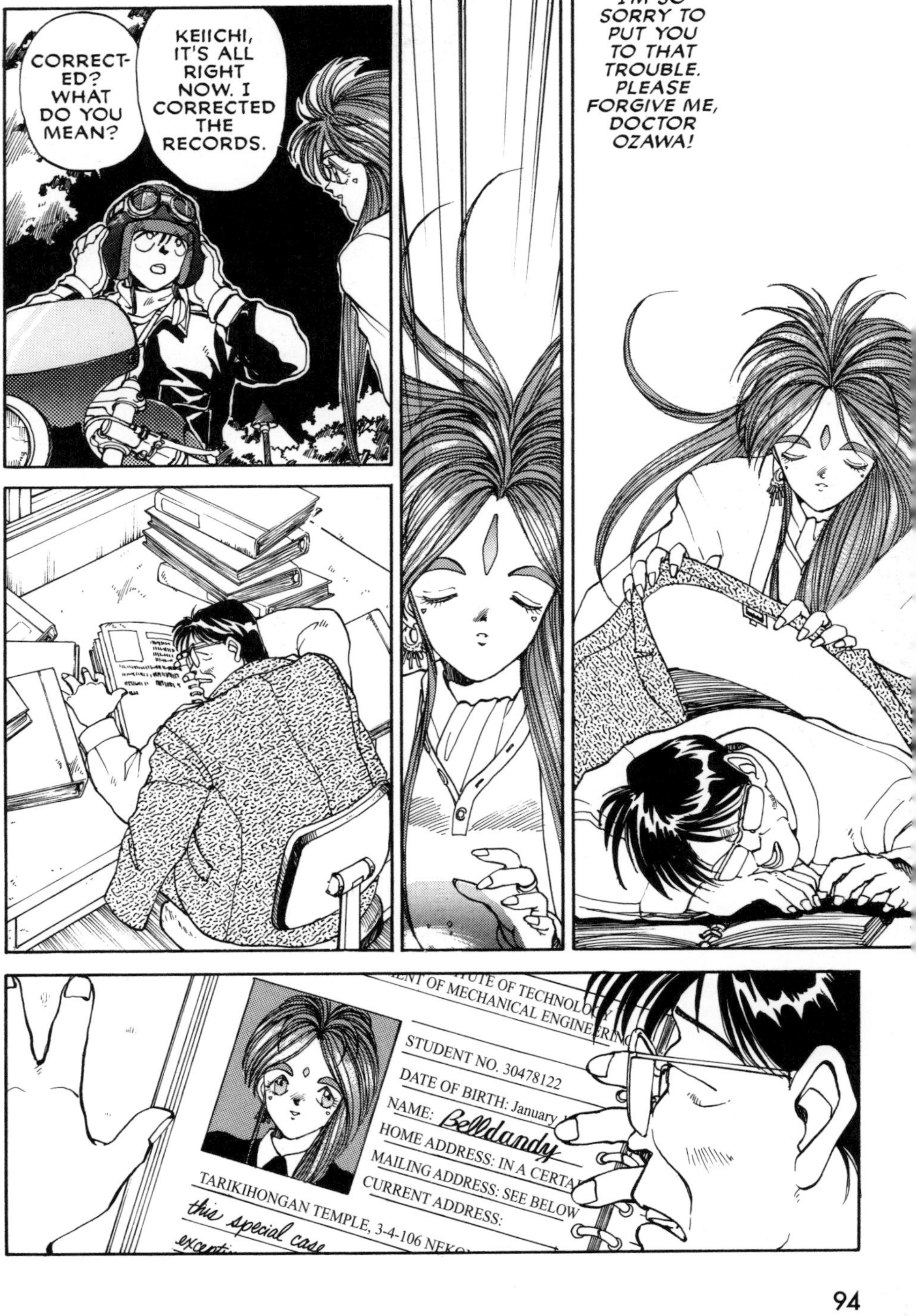
I'M SO SORRY TO PUT YOU TO THAT TROUBLE. PLEASE FORGIVE ME, DOCTOR OZAWA!
KEIICHI, IT'S ALL RIGHT NOW. I CORRECTED THE RECORDS.
CORRECTED? WHAT DO YOU MEAN?
TUTE OF TECHNOLOGY
ENT OF MECHANICAL ENGINEERIN
STUDENT NO. 30478122
DATE OF BIRTH: January
NAME: Belldandy
HOME ADDRESS: IN A CERTA
MAILING ADDRESS: SEE BELOW
CURRENT ADDRESS:
TARIKIHONGAN TEMPLE, 3-4-106 NEKO
this special case

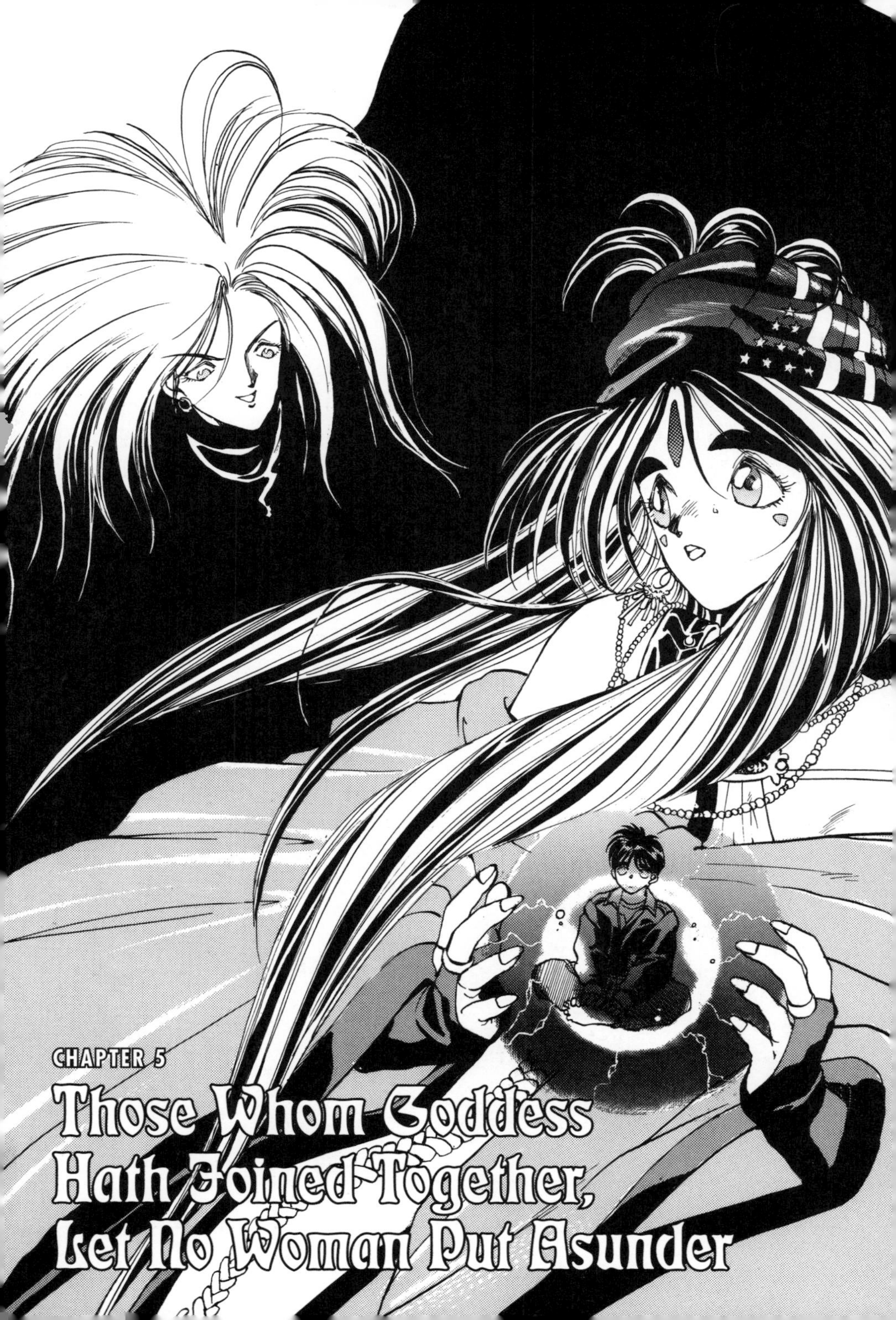

CHAPTER 5

Those Whom Goddess Hath Joined Together, Let No Woman Put Asunder

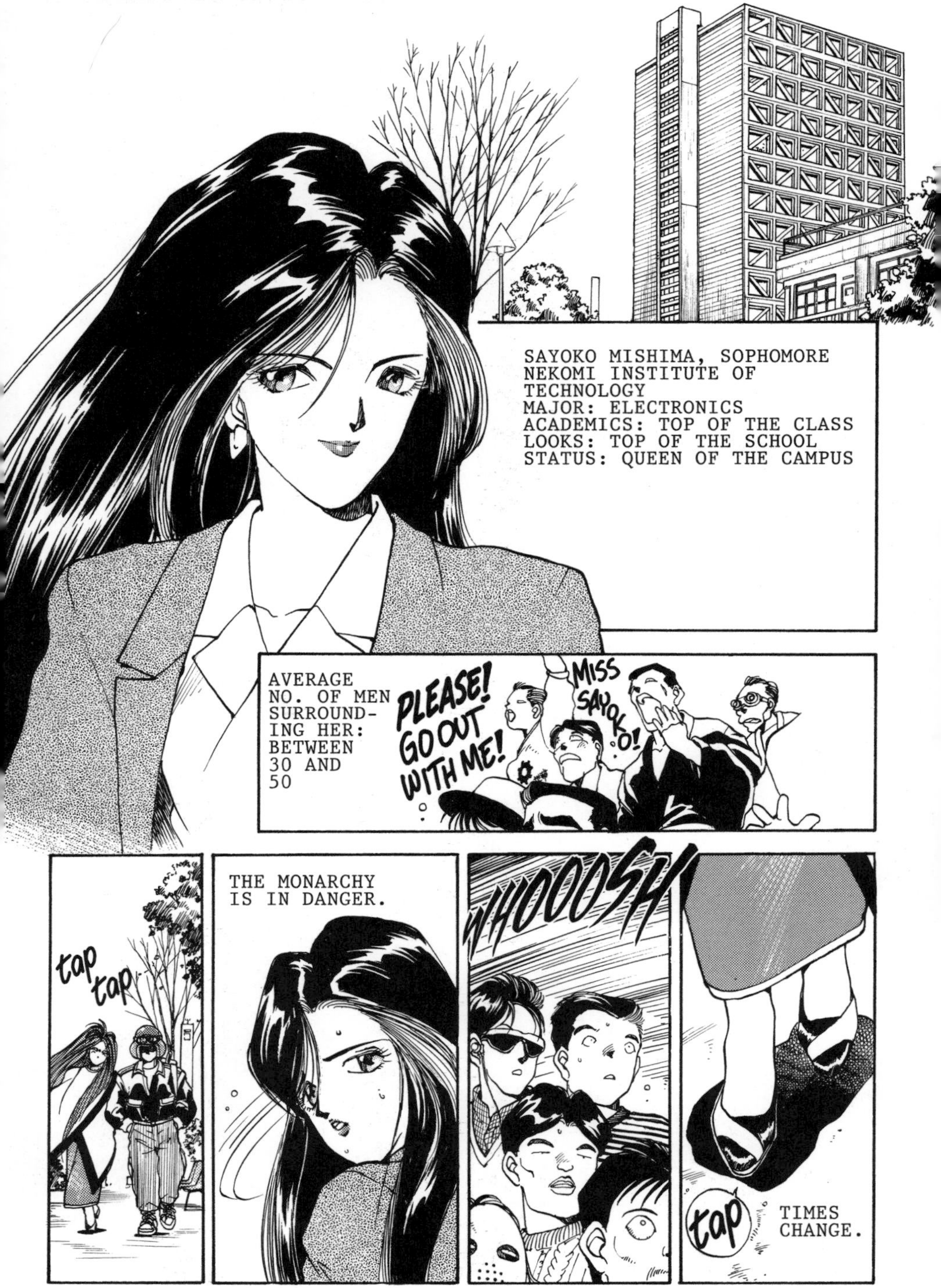
SAYOKO MISHIMA, SOPHOMORE
NEKOMI INSTITUTE OF TECHNOLOGY
MAJOR: ELECTRONICS
ACADEMICS: TOP OF THE CLASS
LOOKS: TOP OF THE SCHOOL
STATUS: QUEEN OF THE CAMPUS
MISS SAYOKO!
PLEASE! GO OUT WITH ME!
AVERAGE NO. OF MEN SURROUNDING HER: BETWEEN 30 AND 50
tap
TIMES CHANGE.
WHOOOSH
THE MONARCHY IS IN DANGER.
tap tap

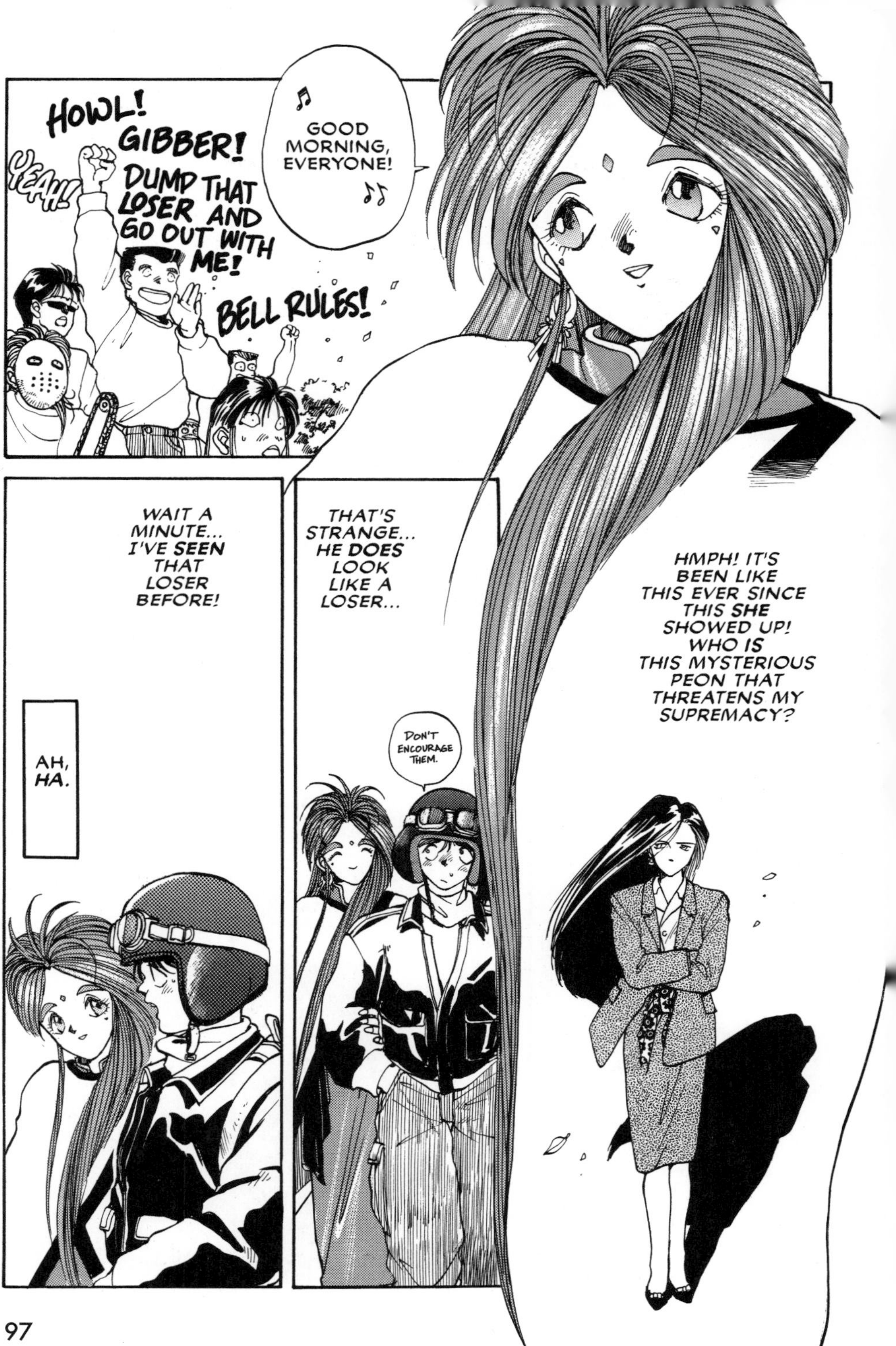
GOOD MORNING, EVERYONE!
HOWL!
GIBBER!
YEAH!
DUMP THAT LOSER AND GO OUT WITH ME!
BELL RULES!
HMPH! IT'S BEEN LIKE THIS EVER SINCE THIS SHE SHOWED UP! WHO IS THIS MYSTERIOUS PEON THAT THREATENS MY SUPREMACY?
THAT'S STRANGE... HE DOES LOOK LIKE A LOSER...
DON'T ENCOURAGE THEM.
WAIT A MINUTE... I'VE SEEN THAT LOSER BEFORE!
AH, HA.

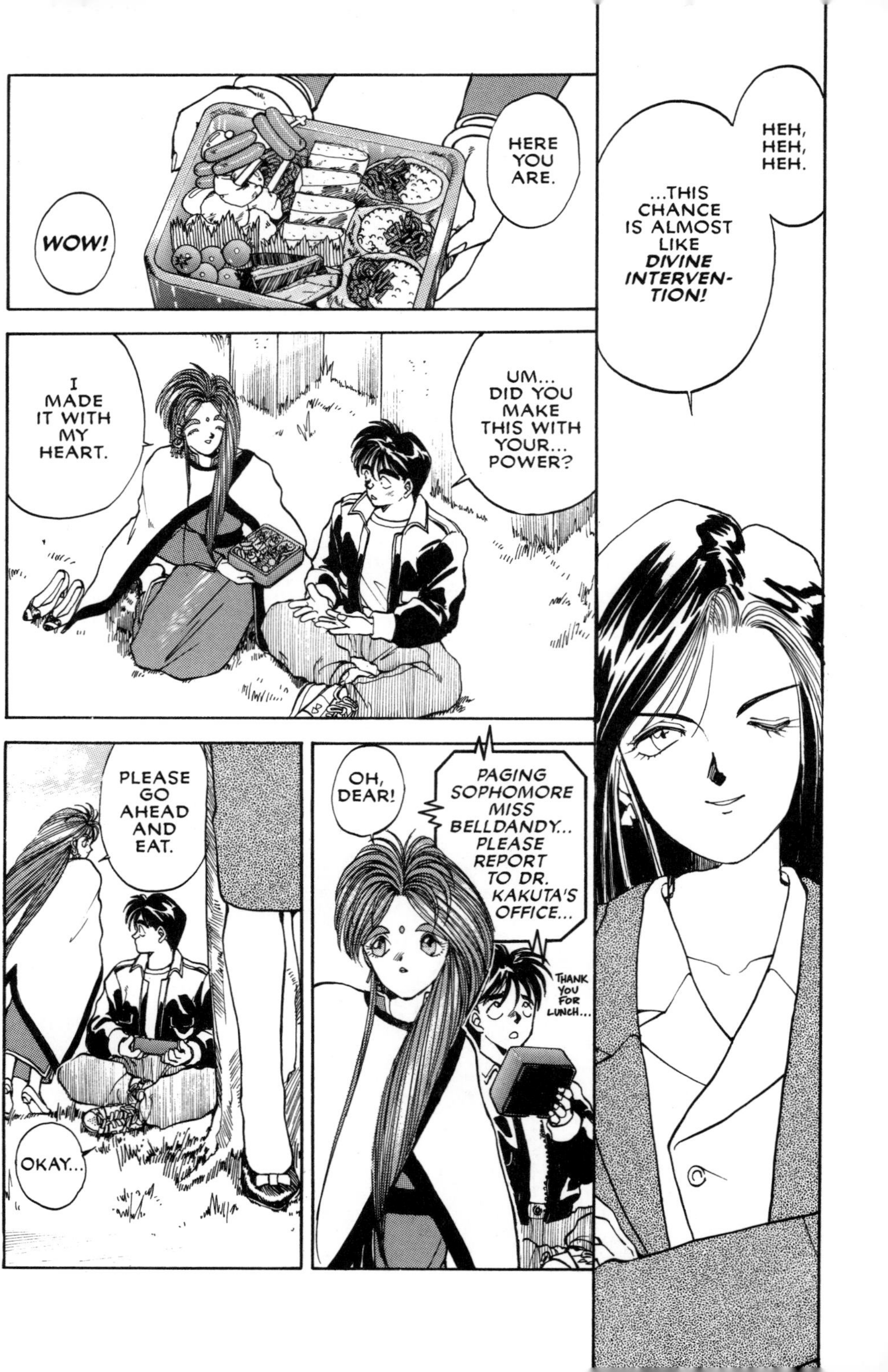
HEH, HEH, HEH.
...THIS CHANCE IS ALMOST LIKE DIVINE INTERVENTION!
HERE YOU ARE.
WOW!
UM... DID YOU MAKE THIS WITH YOUR... POWER?
I MADE IT WITH MY HEART.
PAGING SOPHOMORE MISS BELLDANDY... PLEASE REPORT TO DR. KAKUTA'S OFFICE...
OH, DEAR!
THANK YOU FOR LUNCH...
PLEASE GO AHEAD AND EAT.
OKAY...

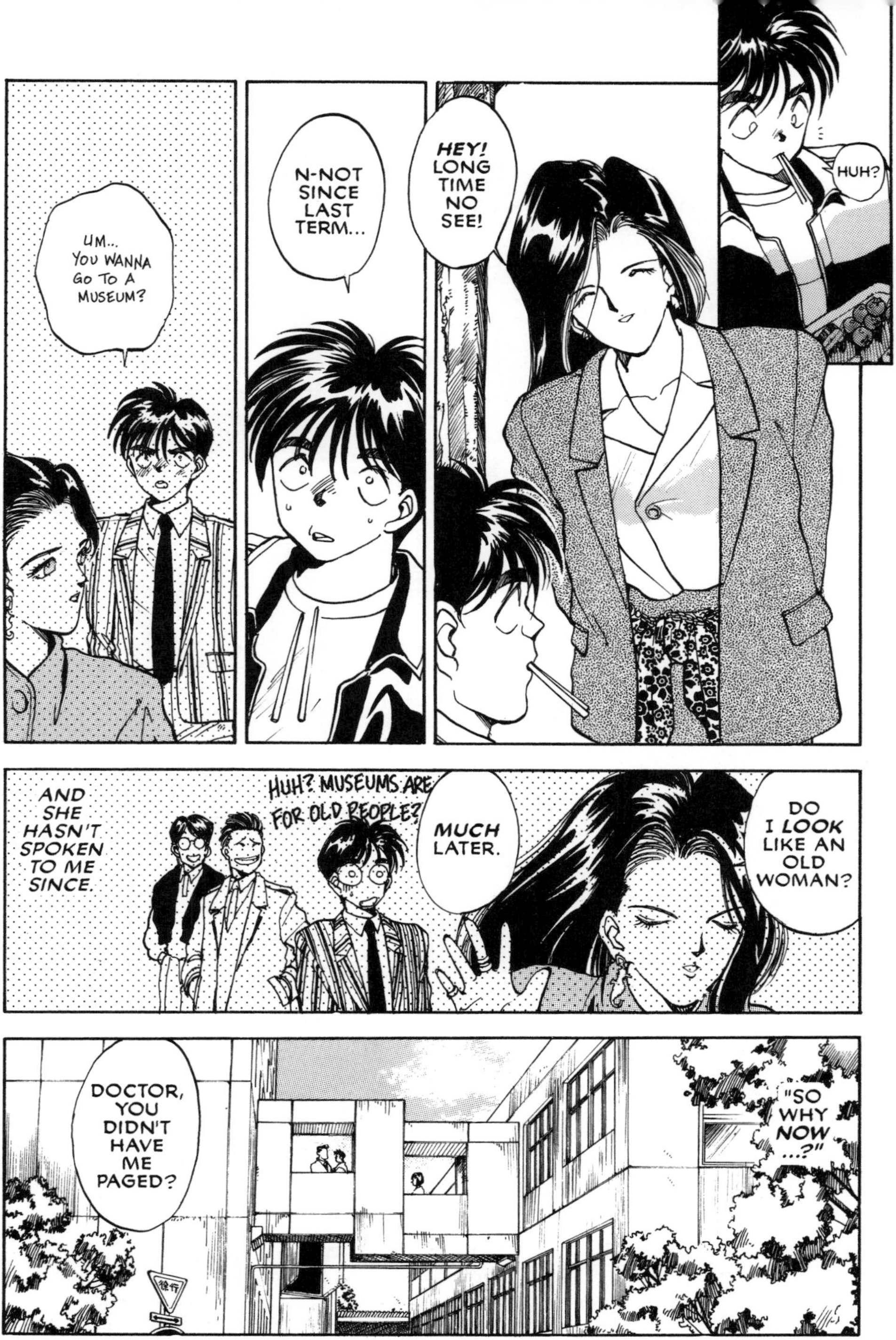
HUH?
HEY! LONG TIME NO SEE!
N-NOT SINCE LAST TERM...
UM... YOU WANNA GO TO A MUSEUM?
DO I LOOK LIKE AN OLD WOMAN?
MUCH LATER.
HUH? MUSEUMS ARE FOR OLD PEOPLE?
AND SHE HASN'T SPOKEN TO ME SINCE.
"SO WHY NOW ...?"
DOCTOR, YOU DIDN'T HAVE ME PAGED?
徐行

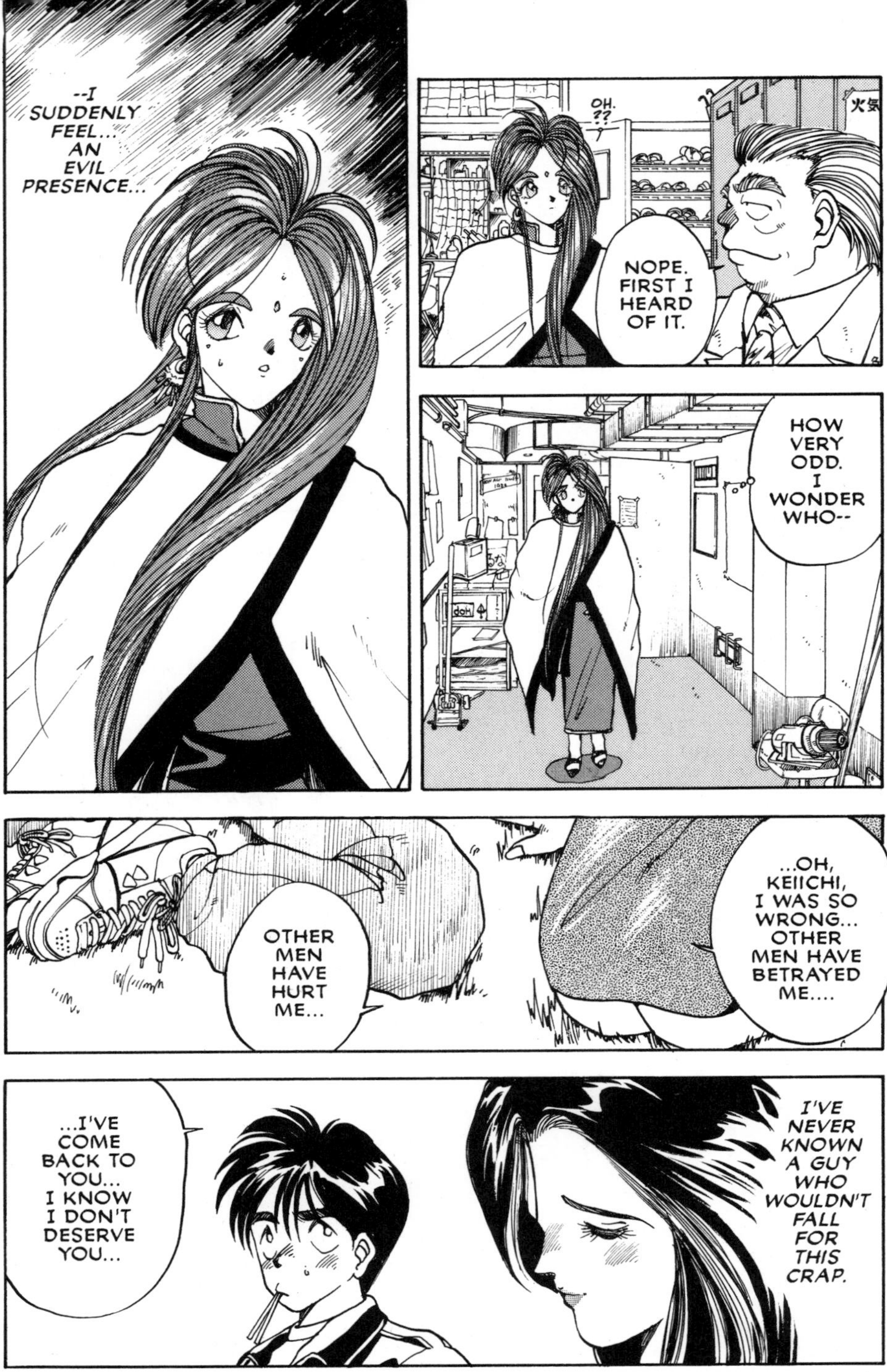
OH. ??
NOPE. FIRST I HEARD OF IT.
HOW VERY ODD. I WONDER WHO--
--I SUDDENLY FEEL... AN EVIL PRESENCE...
...OH, KEIICHI, I WAS SO WRONG... OTHER MEN HAVE BETRAYED ME....
OTHER MEN HAVE HURT ME...
I'VE NEVER KNOWN A GUY WHO WOULDN'T FALL FOR THIS CRAP.
...I'VE COME BACK TO YOU... I KNOW I DON'T DESERVE YOU...

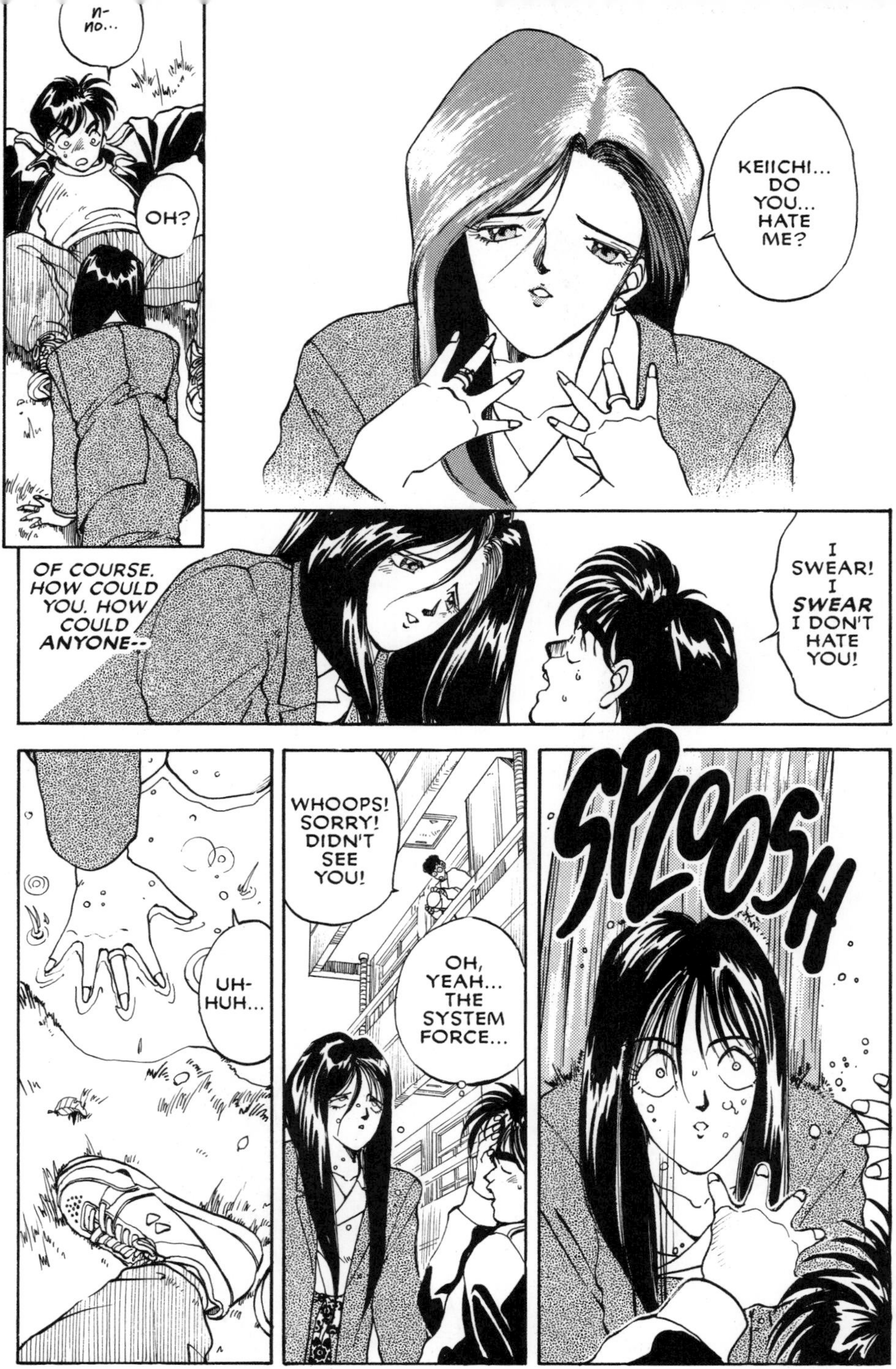
KEIICHI... DO YOU... HATE ME?
n-no...
OH?
I SWEAR! I SWEAR I DON'T HATE YOU!
OF COURSE. HOW COULD YOU. HOW COULD ANYONE--
SPLOOSH
WHOOPS! SORRY! DIDN'T SEE YOU!
OH, YEAH... THE SYSTEM FORCE...
UH-HUH...

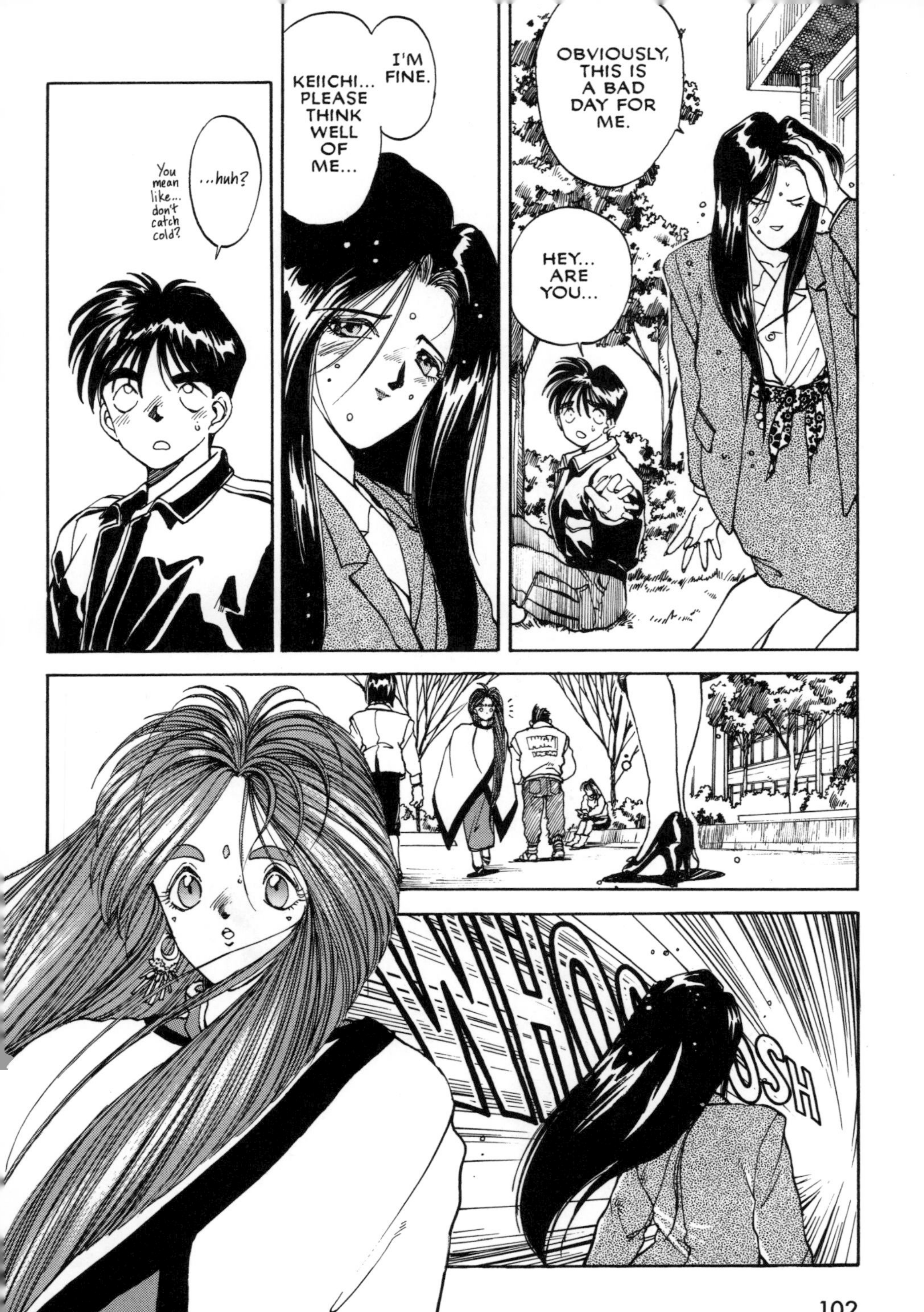
OBVIOUSLY, THIS IS A BAD DAY FOR ME.
HEY... ARE YOU...
I'M FINE.
KEIICHI... PLEASE THINK WELL OF ME...
...huh?
You mean like... don't catch cold?
WHOOSH

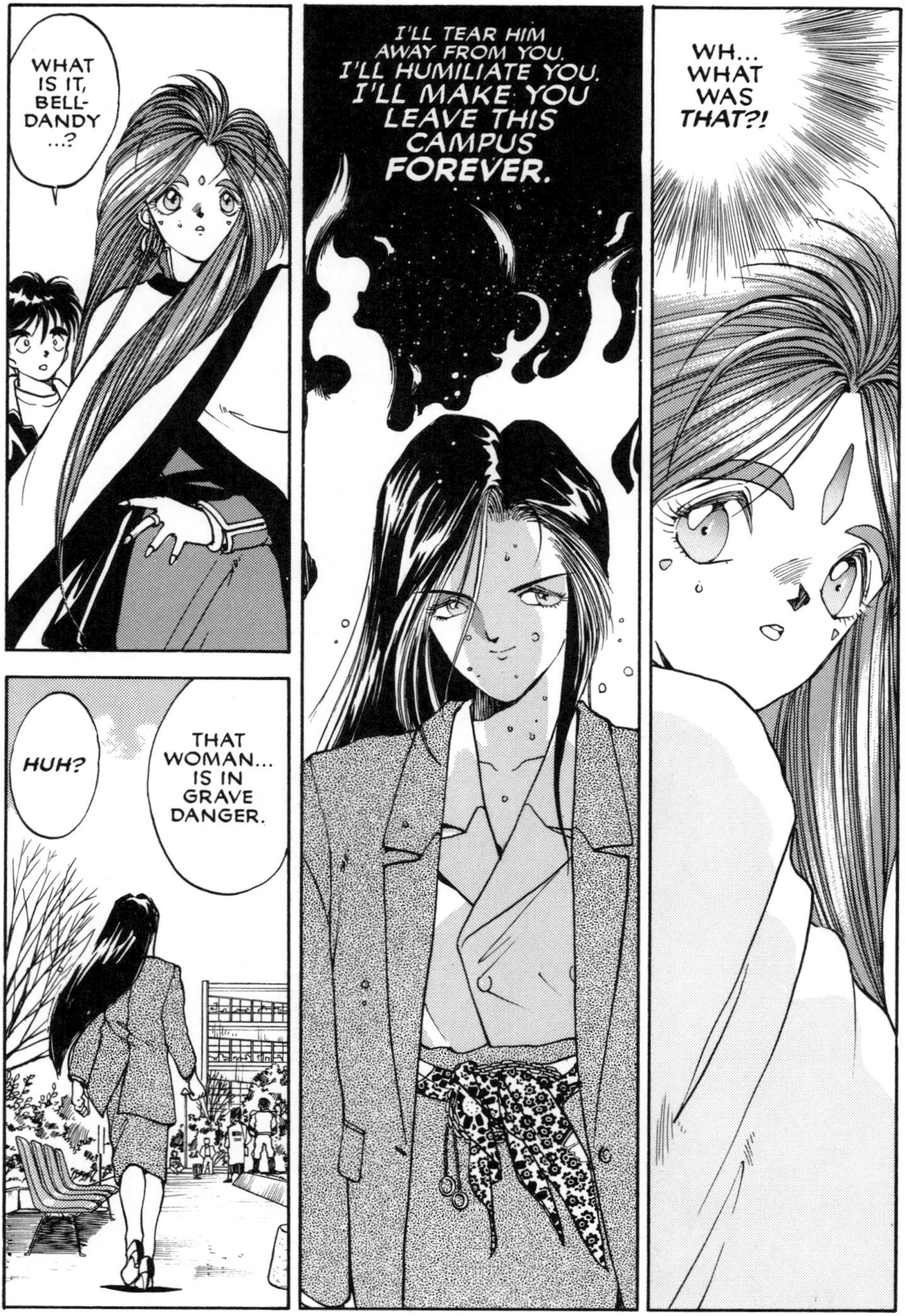
WH... WHAT WAS *THAT?!*
I'LL TEAR HIM AWAY FROM YOU. I'LL HUMILIATE YOU. I'LL MAKE YOU LEAVE THIS CAMPUS **FOREVER.**
WHAT IS IT, BELL-DANDY ...?
THAT WOMAN... IS IN GRAVE DANGER.
HUH?

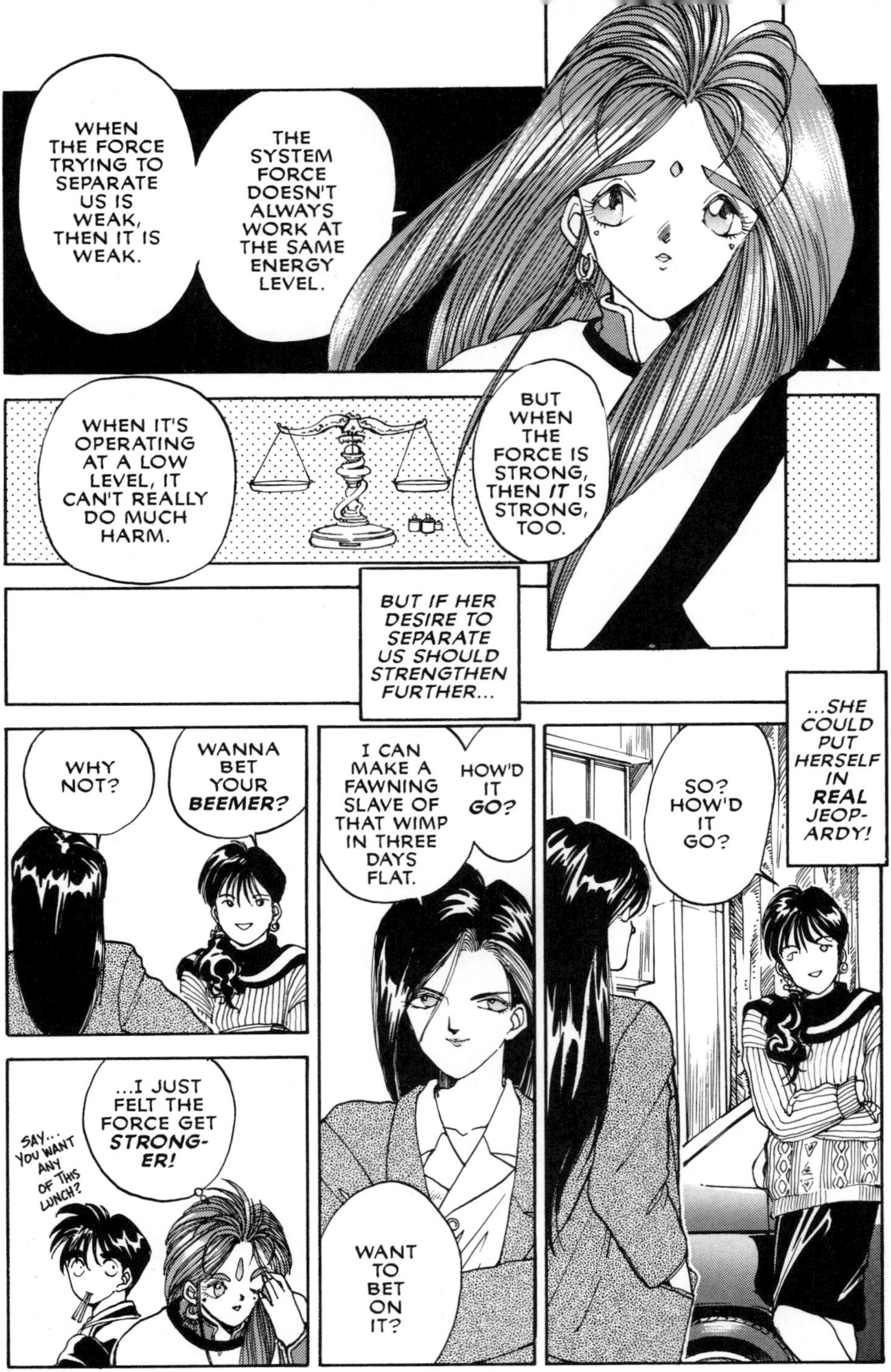
THE SYSTEM FORCE DOESN'T ALWAYS WORK AT THE SAME ENERGY LEVEL.
WHEN THE FORCE TRYING TO SEPARATE US IS WEAK, THEN IT IS WEAK.
BUT WHEN THE FORCE IS STRONG, THEN *IT* IS STRONG, TOO.
WHEN IT'S OPERATING AT A LOW LEVEL, IT CAN'T REALLY DO MUCH HARM.
BUT IF HER DESIRE TO SEPARATE US SHOULD STRENGTHEN FURTHER...
*...SHE COULD PUT HERSELF IN **REAL** JEOPARDY!*
SO? HOW'D IT GO?
HOW'D IT ***GO?***
I CAN MAKE A FAWNING SLAVE OF THAT WIMP IN THREE DAYS FLAT.
WANT TO BET ON IT?
WANNA BET YOUR ***BEEMER?***
WHY NOT?
...I JUST FELT THE FORCE GET ***STRONGER!***
SAY... YOU WANT ANY OF THIS LUNCH?

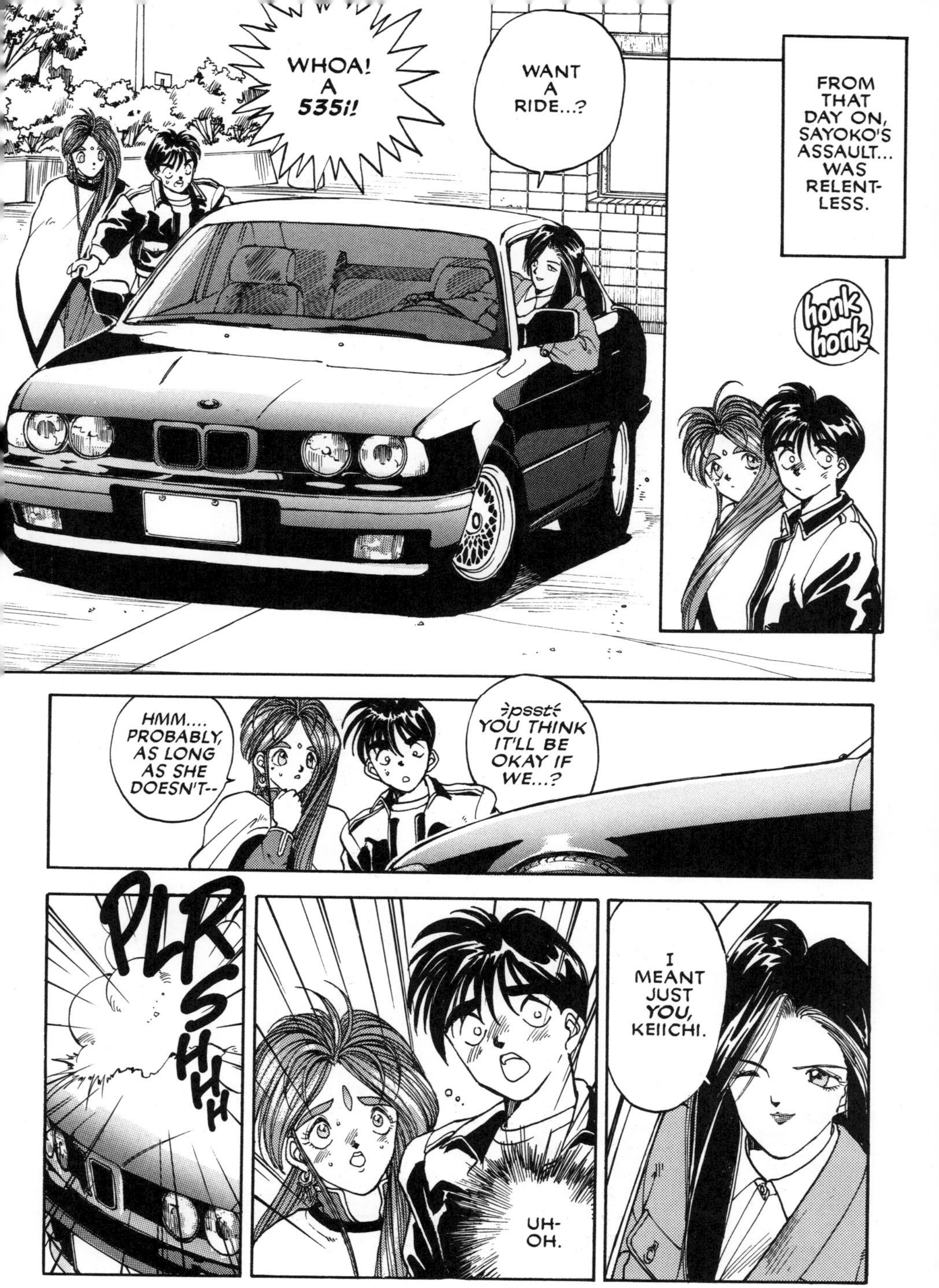
FROM THAT DAY ON, SAYOKO'S ASSAULT... WAS RELENTLESS.
honk honk
WANT A RIDE...?
WHOA! A 535i!
psst YOU THINK IT'LL BE OKAY IF WE...?
HMM.... PROBABLY, AS LONG AS SHE DOESN'T--
I MEANT JUST YOU, KEIICHI.
UH-OH.
PLRSHHH

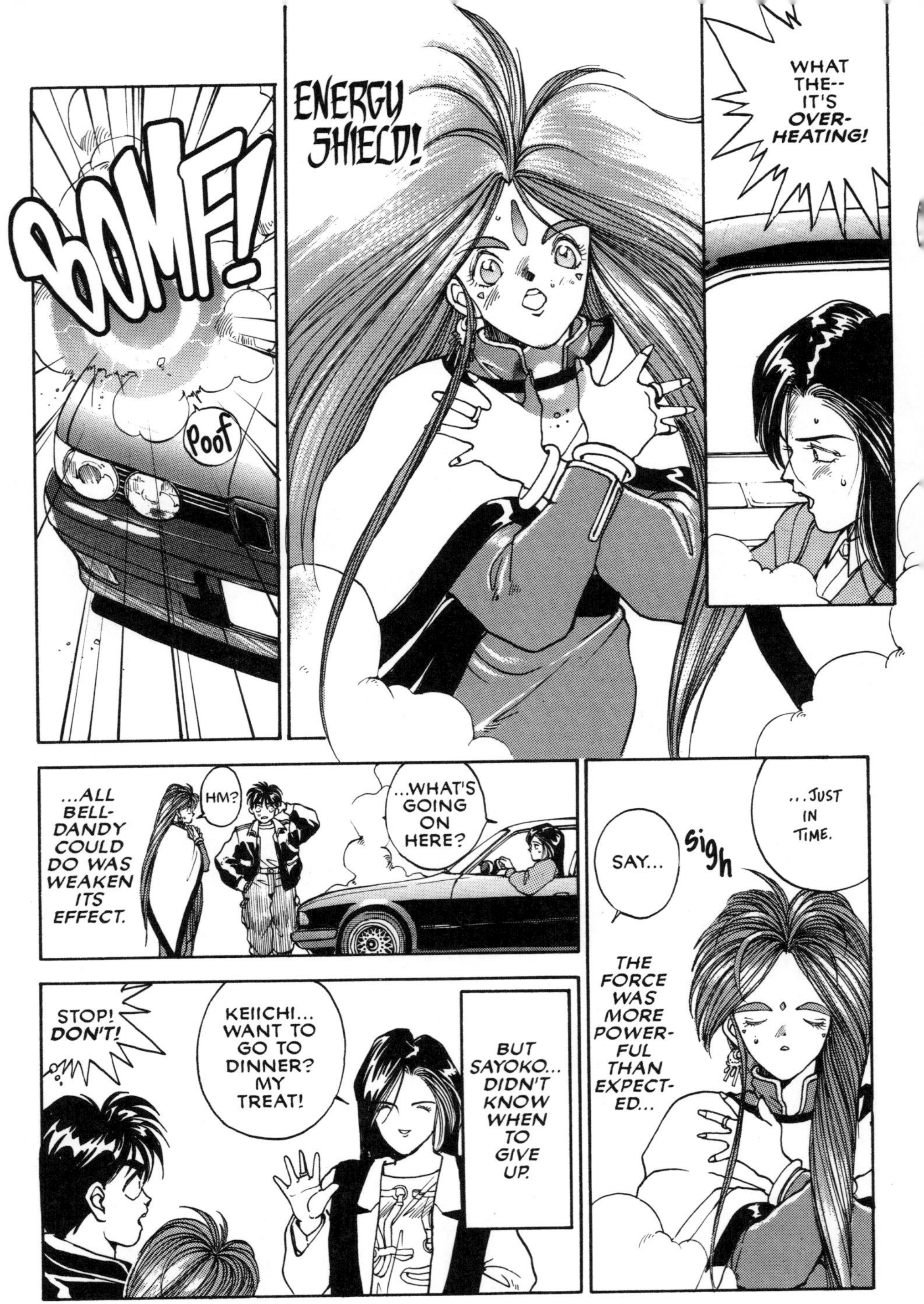
WHAT THE-- IT'S OVER-HEATING!
ENERGY SHIELD!
BOMF!
Poof
...JUST IN TIME.
sigh
SAY...
THE FORCE WAS MORE POWER-FUL THAN EXPECT-ED...
...WHAT'S GOING ON HERE?
HM?
...ALL BELL-DANDY COULD DO WAS WEAKEN ITS EFFECT.
BUT SAYOKO... DIDN'T KNOW WHEN TO GIVE UP.
KEIICHI... WANT TO GO TO DINNER? MY TREAT!
STOP! DON'T!

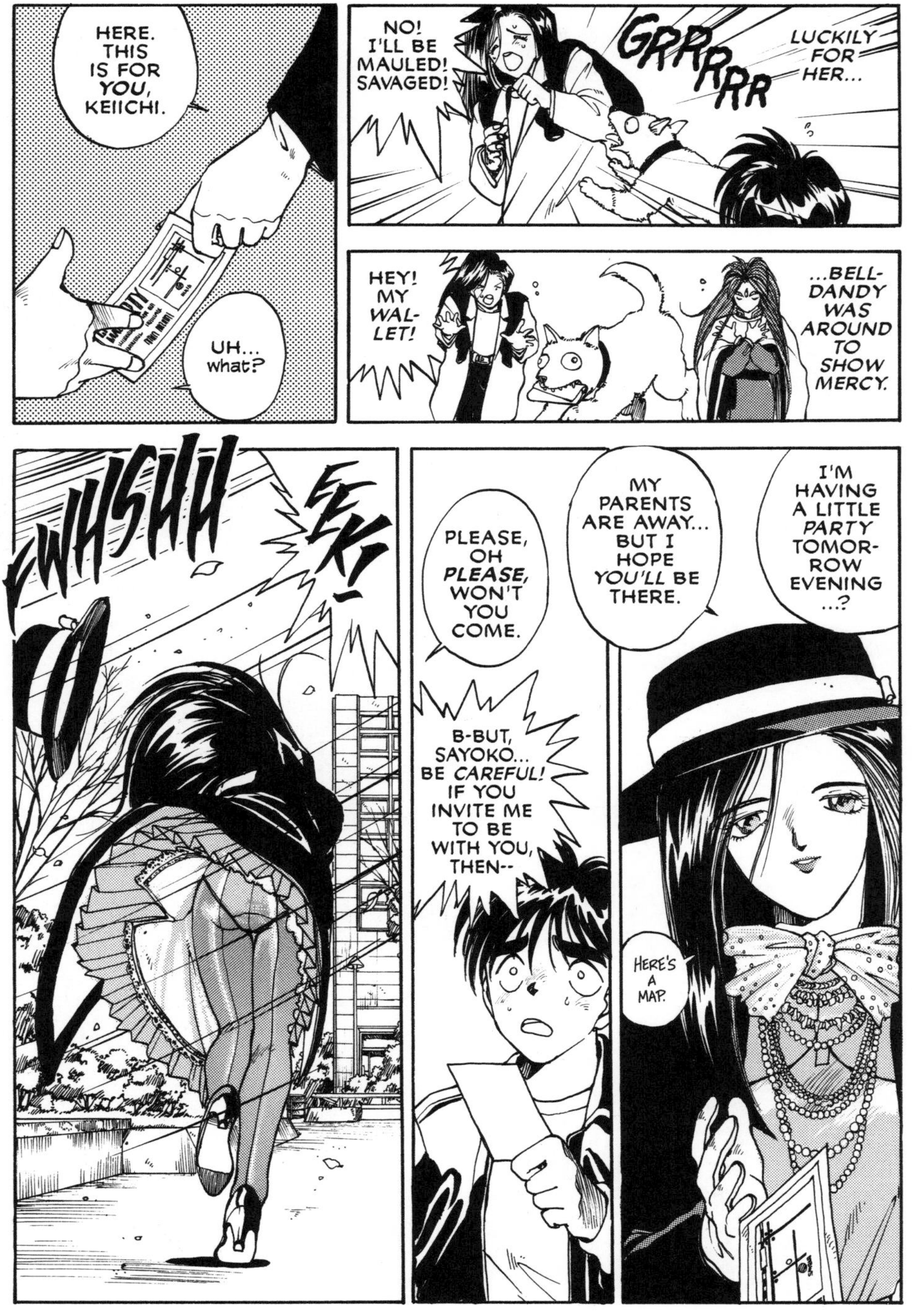
LUCKILY FOR HER...
GRRRRRR
NO! I'LL BE MAULED! SAVAGED!
...BELL-DANDY WAS AROUND TO SHOW MERCY.
HEY! MY WAL-LET!
HERE. THIS IS FOR *YOU*, KEIICHI.
UH... what?
I'M HAVING A LITTLE *PARTY* TOMOR-ROW EVENING ...?
HERE'S A MAP.
MY PARENTS ARE AWAY... BUT I HOPE *YOU'LL* BE THERE.
PLEASE, OH ***PLEASE,*** WON'T YOU COME.
B-BUT, SAYOKO... BE *CAREFUL!* IF YOU INVITE ME TO BE WITH YOU, THEN--
EEK!
FWHSHH

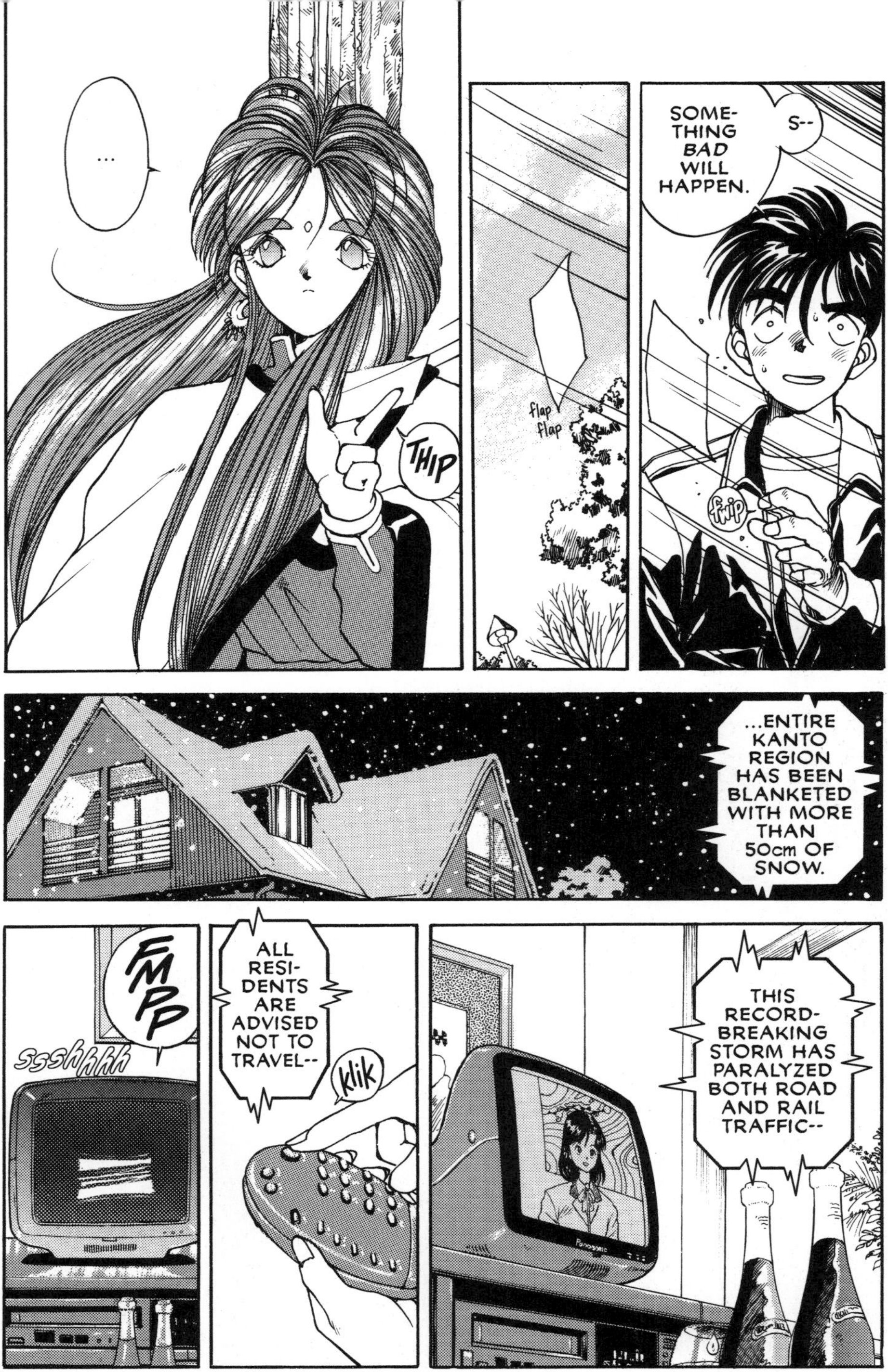
S--
SOMETHING *BAD* WILL HAPPEN.
fwip
flap flap
...
THIP
...ENTIRE KANTO REGION HAS BEEN BLANKETED WITH MORE THAN 50cm OF SNOW.
THIS RECORD-BREAKING STORM HAS PARALYZED BOTH ROAD AND RAIL TRAFFIC--
ALL RESIDENTS ARE ADVISED NOT TO TRAVEL--
klik
FMPP
ssshhhh

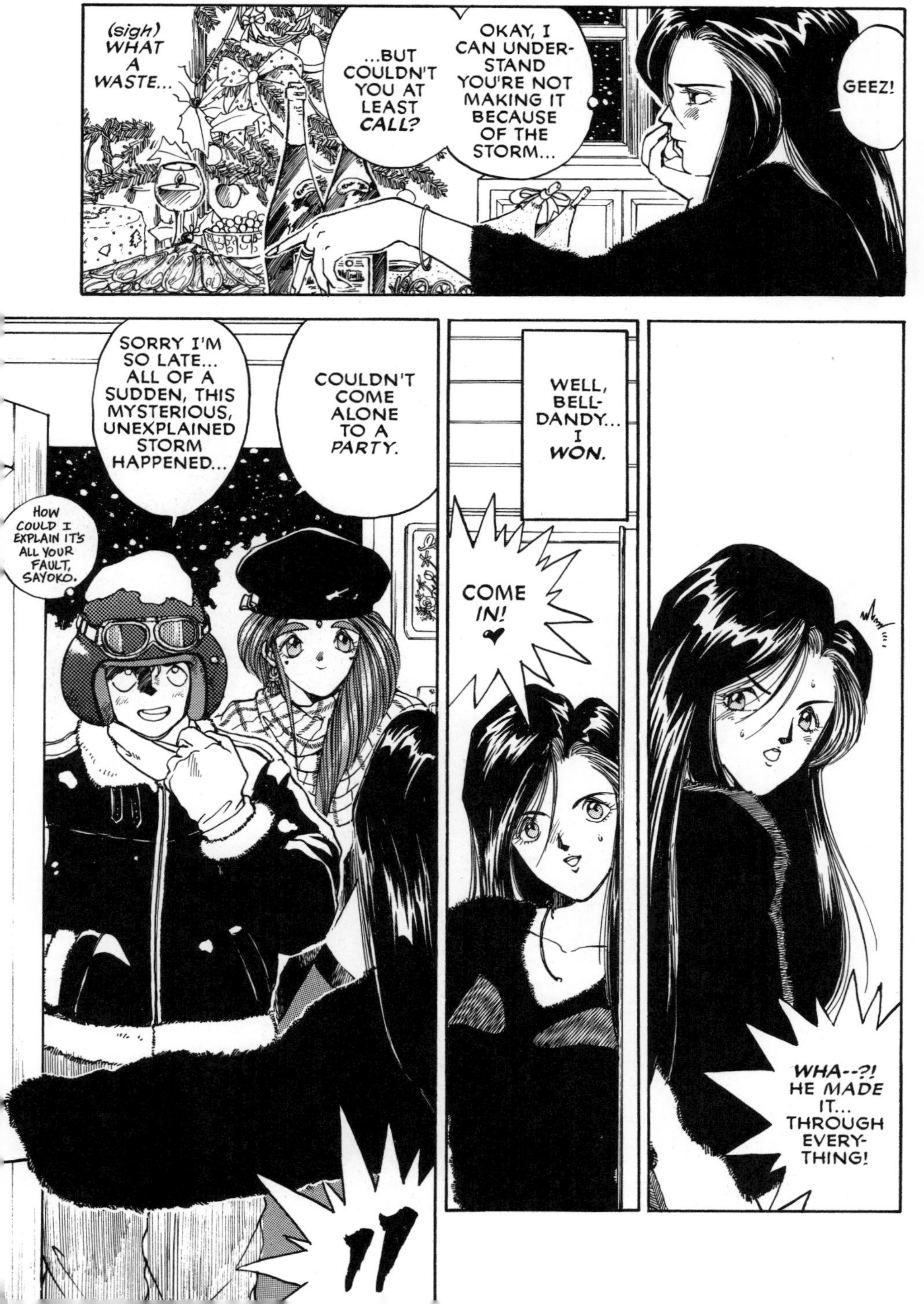
GEEZ!
OKAY, I CAN UNDER-STAND YOU'RE NOT MAKING IT BECAUSE OF THE STORM...
...BUT COULDN'T YOU AT LEAST *CALL?*
(sigh) WHAT A WASTE...
WHA--?! HE *MADE* IT... THROUGH EVERY-THING!
WELL, BELL-DANDY... I **WON.**
COME *IN!*
COULDN'T COME ALONE TO A *PARTY.*
SORRY I'M SO LATE... ALL OF A SUDDEN, THIS MYSTERIOUS, UNEXPLAINED STORM HAPPENED...
HOW COULD I EXPLAIN IT'S ALL YOUR FAULT, SAYOKO.

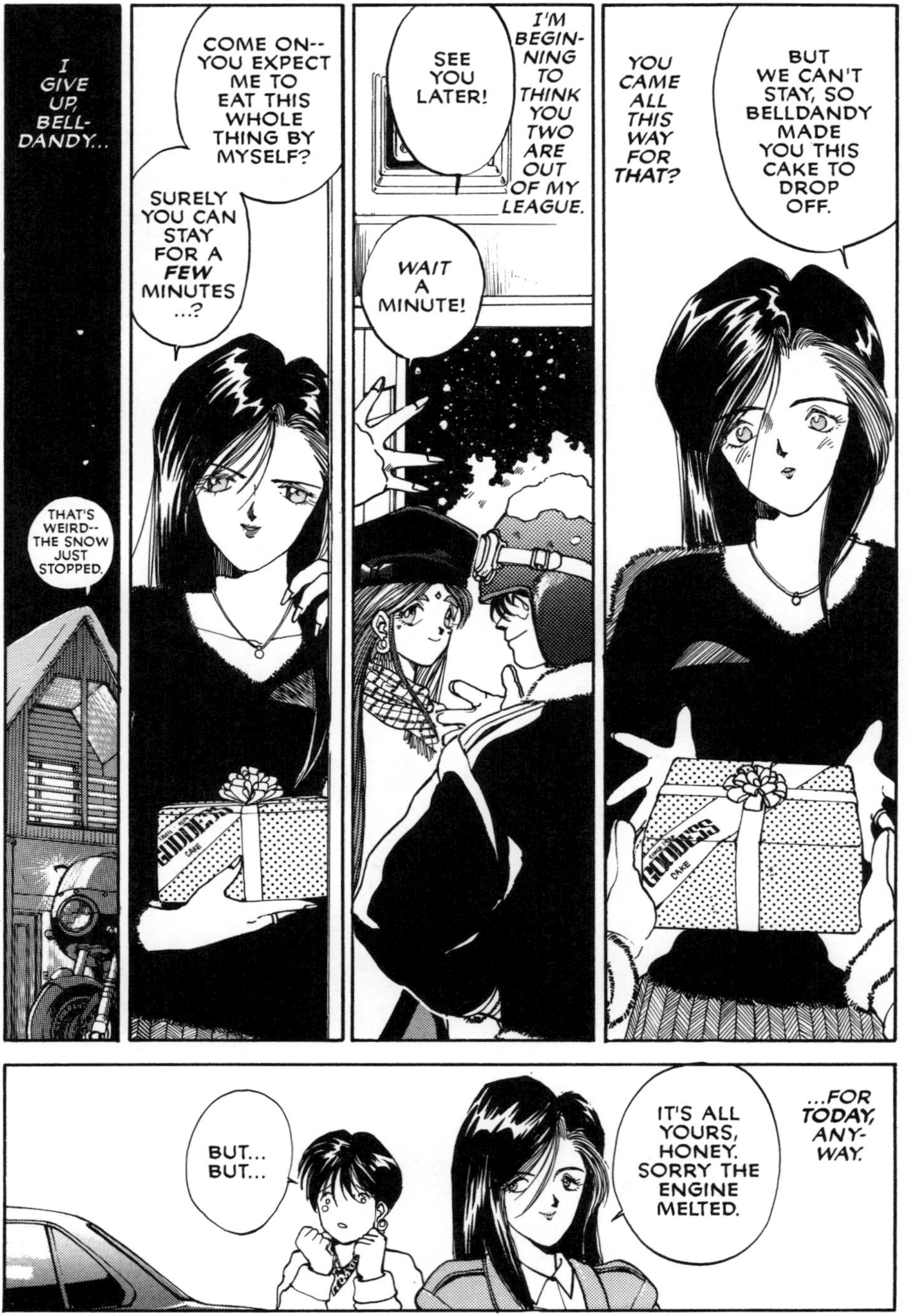
BUT WE CAN'T STAY, SO BELLDANDY MADE YOU THIS CAKE TO DROP OFF.
YOU CAME ALL THIS WAY FOR THAT?
I'M BEGINNING TO THINK YOU TWO ARE OUT OF MY LEAGUE.
SEE YOU LATER!
WAIT A MINUTE!
COME ON-- YOU EXPECT ME TO EAT THIS WHOLE THING BY MYSELF?
SURELY YOU CAN STAY FOR A *FEW* MINUTES ...?
I GIVE UP, BELL-DANDY...
THAT'S WEIRD-- THE SNOW JUST STOPPED.
...FOR *TODAY,* ANY-WAY.
IT'S ALL YOURS, HONEY. SORRY THE ENGINE MELTED.
BUT... BUT...

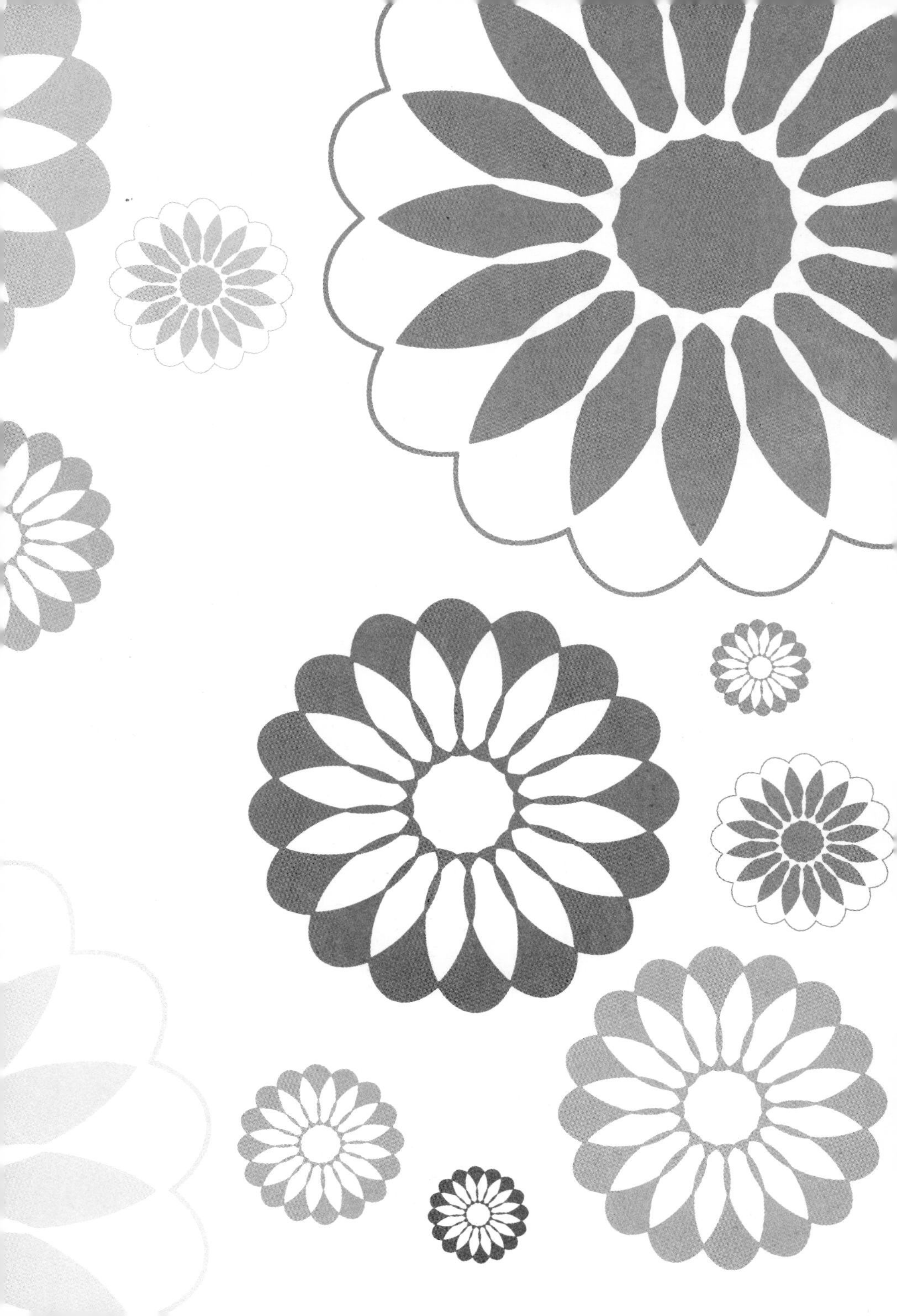

OH MY GODDESS!

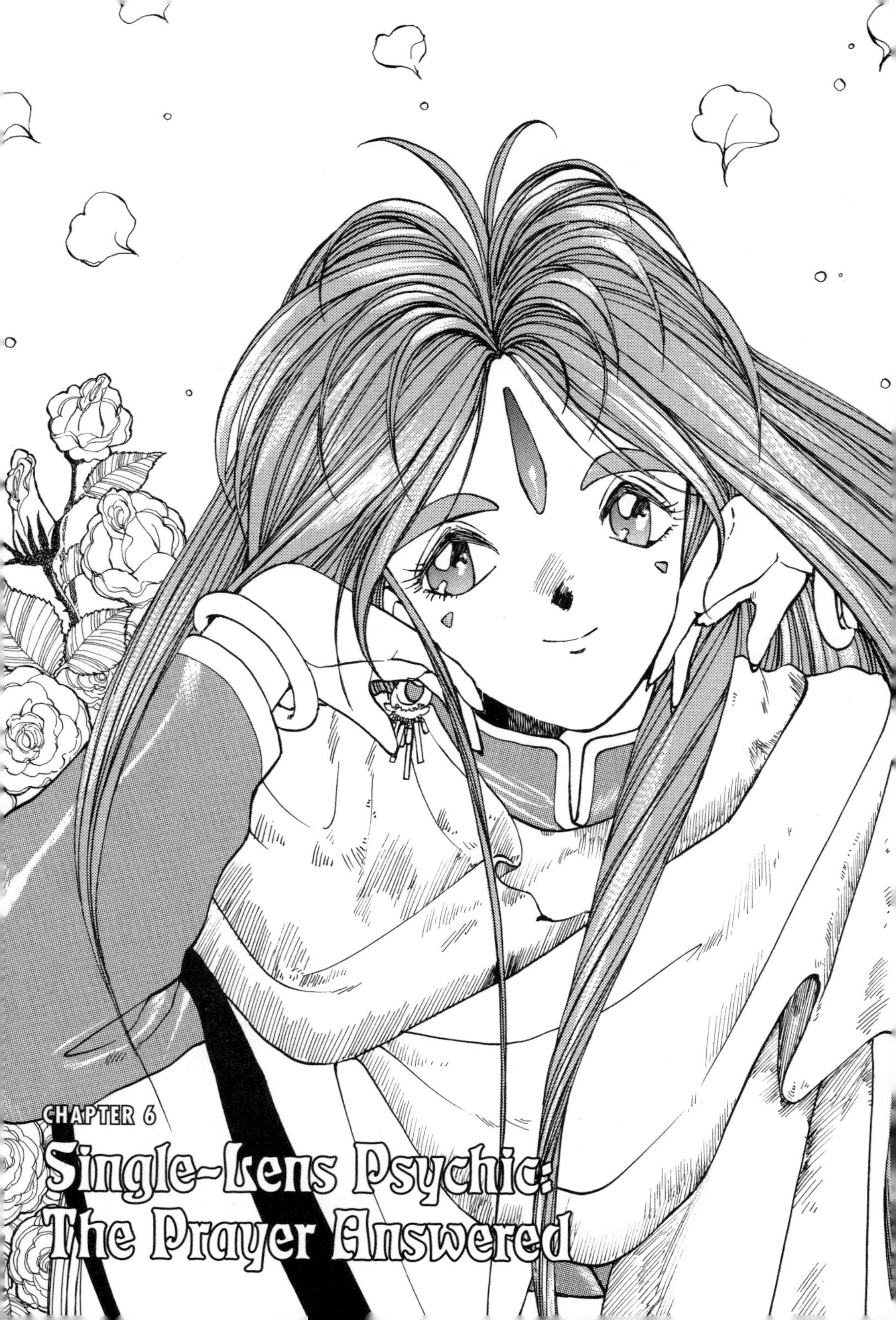
CHAPTER 6
Single-Lens Psychic:
The Prayer Answered

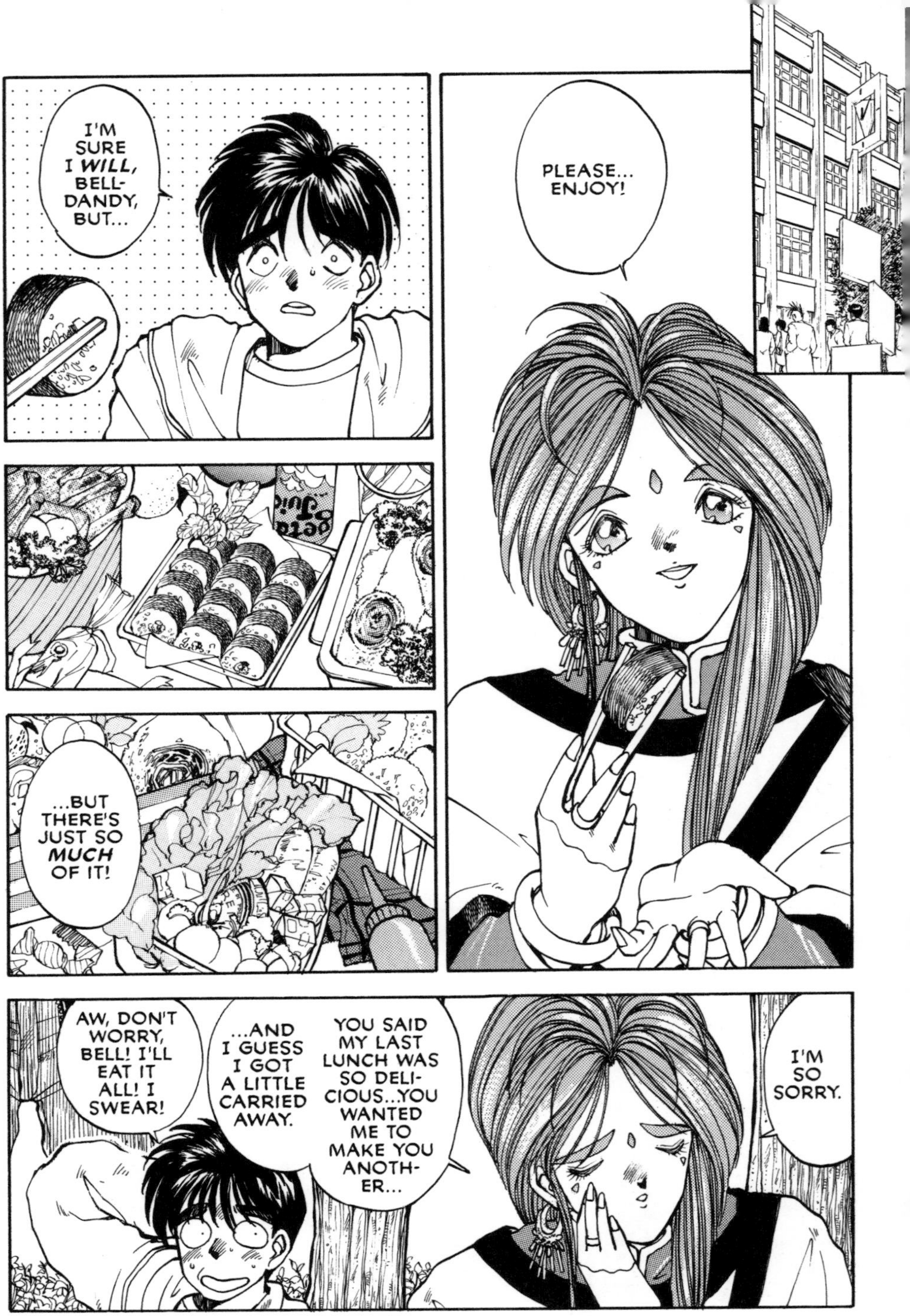
PLEASE... ENJOY!
I'M SURE I *WILL*, BELL-DANDY, BUT...
...BUT THERE'S JUST SO *MUCH* OF IT!
I'M SO SORRY.
YOU SAID MY LAST LUNCH WAS SO DELI-CIOUS...YOU WANTED ME TO MAKE YOU ANOTH-ER...
...AND I GUESS I GOT A LITTLE CARRIED AWAY.
AW, DON'T WORRY, BELL! I'LL EAT IT ALL! I SWEAR!

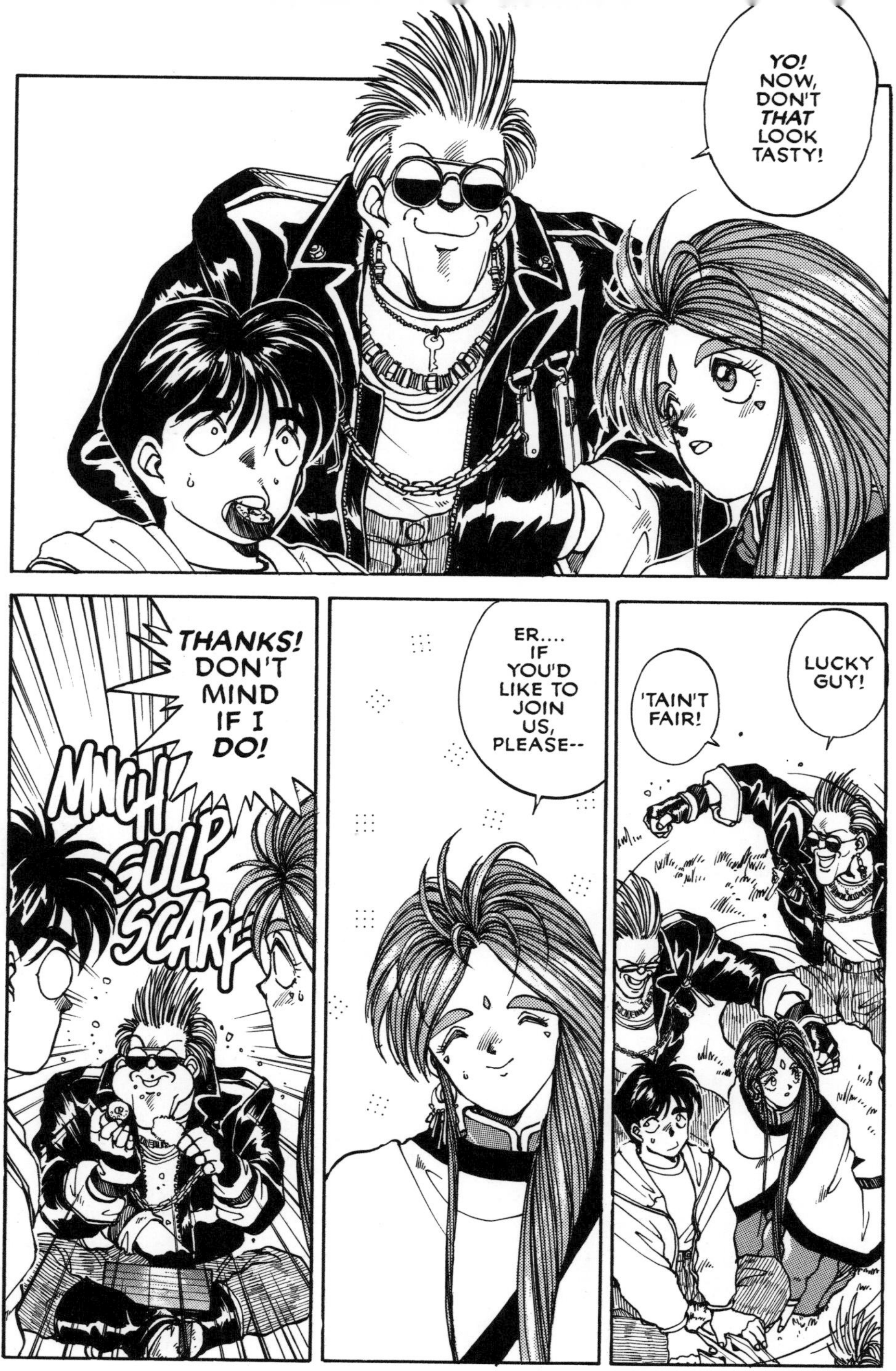
YO! NOW, DON'T THAT LOOK TASTY!
LUCKY GUY!
'TAIN'T FAIR!
ER.... IF YOU'D LIKE TO JOIN US, PLEASE--
THANKS! DON'T MIND IF I DO!
MNCH
GULP
SCARF

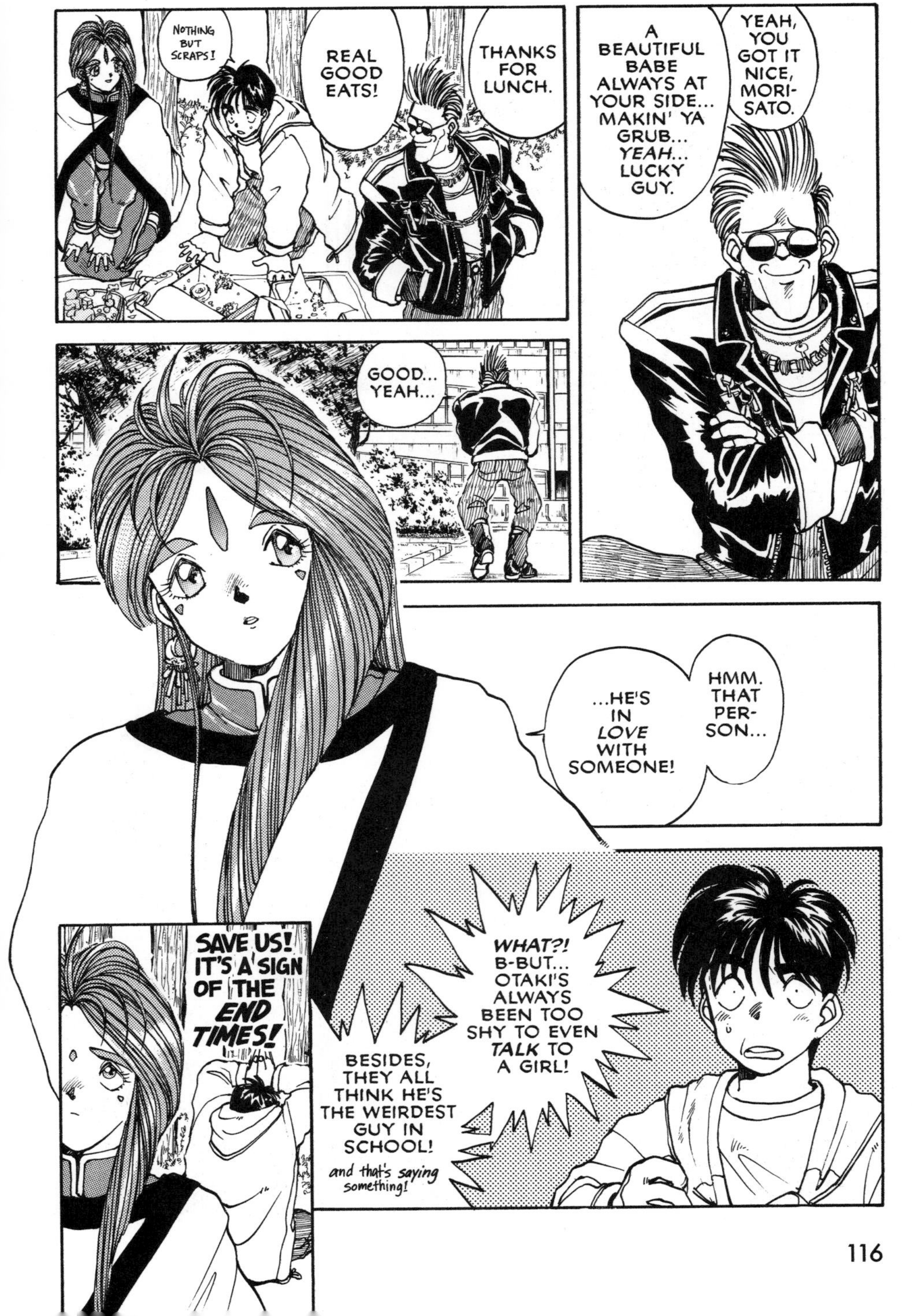
YEAH, YOU GOT IT NICE, MORI-SATO.
A BEAUTIFUL BABE ALWAYS AT YOUR SIDE... MAKIN' YA GRUB... *YEAH*... LUCKY GUY.
THANKS FOR LUNCH.
REAL GOOD EATS!
NOTHING BUT SCRAPS!
GOOD... YEAH...
HMM. THAT PER-SON...
...HE'S IN *LOVE* WITH SOMEONE!
WHAT?! B-BUT... OTAKI'S ALWAYS BEEN TOO SHY TO EVEN *TALK* TO A GIRL!
BESIDES, THEY ALL THINK HE'S THE WEIRDEST GUY IN SCHOOL!
and that's saying something!
SAVE US! IT'S A SIGN OF THE *END TIMES!*

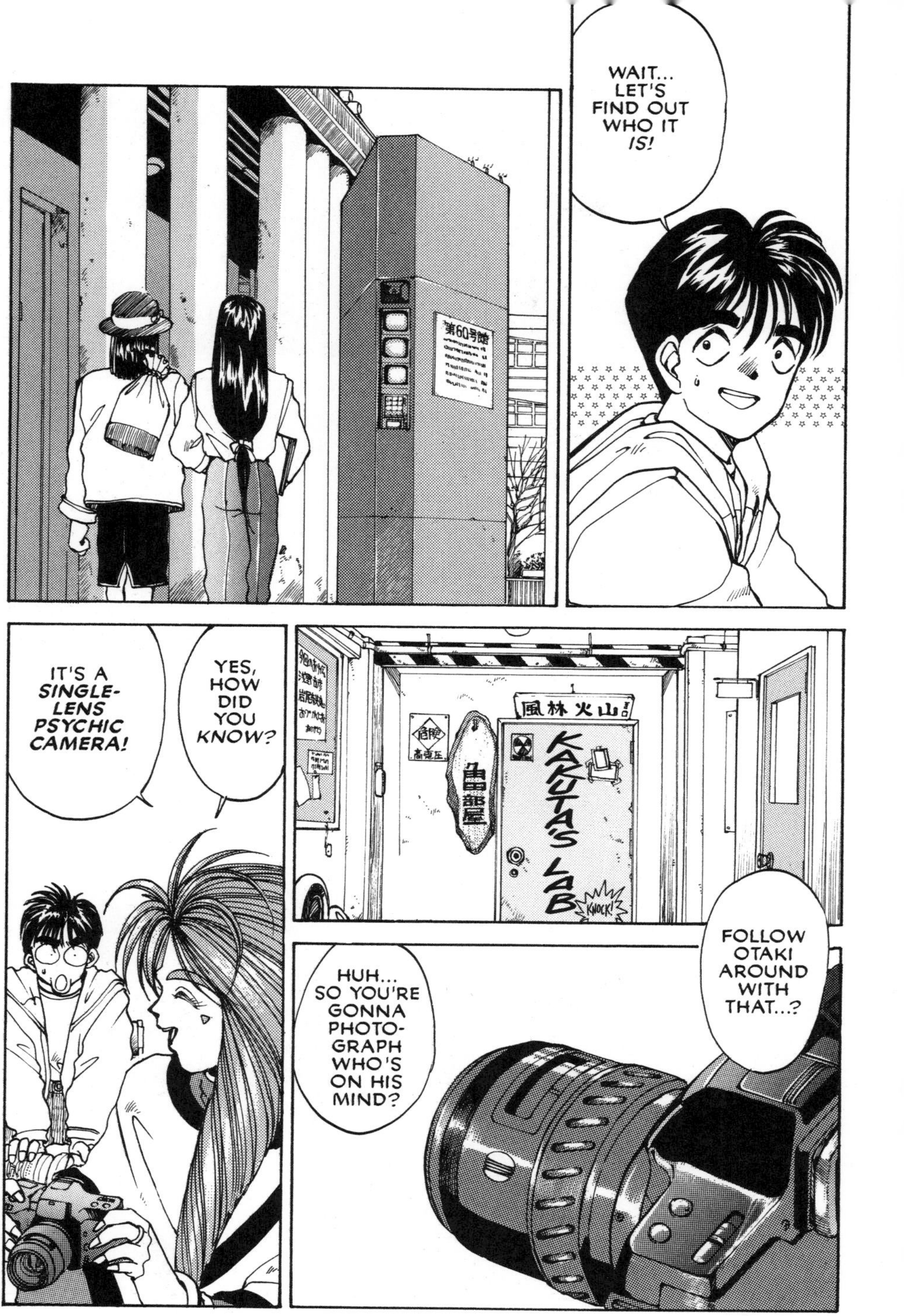
WAIT... LET'S FIND OUT WHO IT *IS!*
第60号館
風林火山
危険
高電圧
KAKUTA'S LAB
KNOCK!
FOLLOW OTAKI AROUND WITH THAT...?
HUH... SO YOU'RE GONNA PHOTOGRAPH WHO'S ON HIS MIND?
YES, HOW DID YOU KNOW?
IT'S A *SINGLE-LENS PSYCHIC CAMERA!*

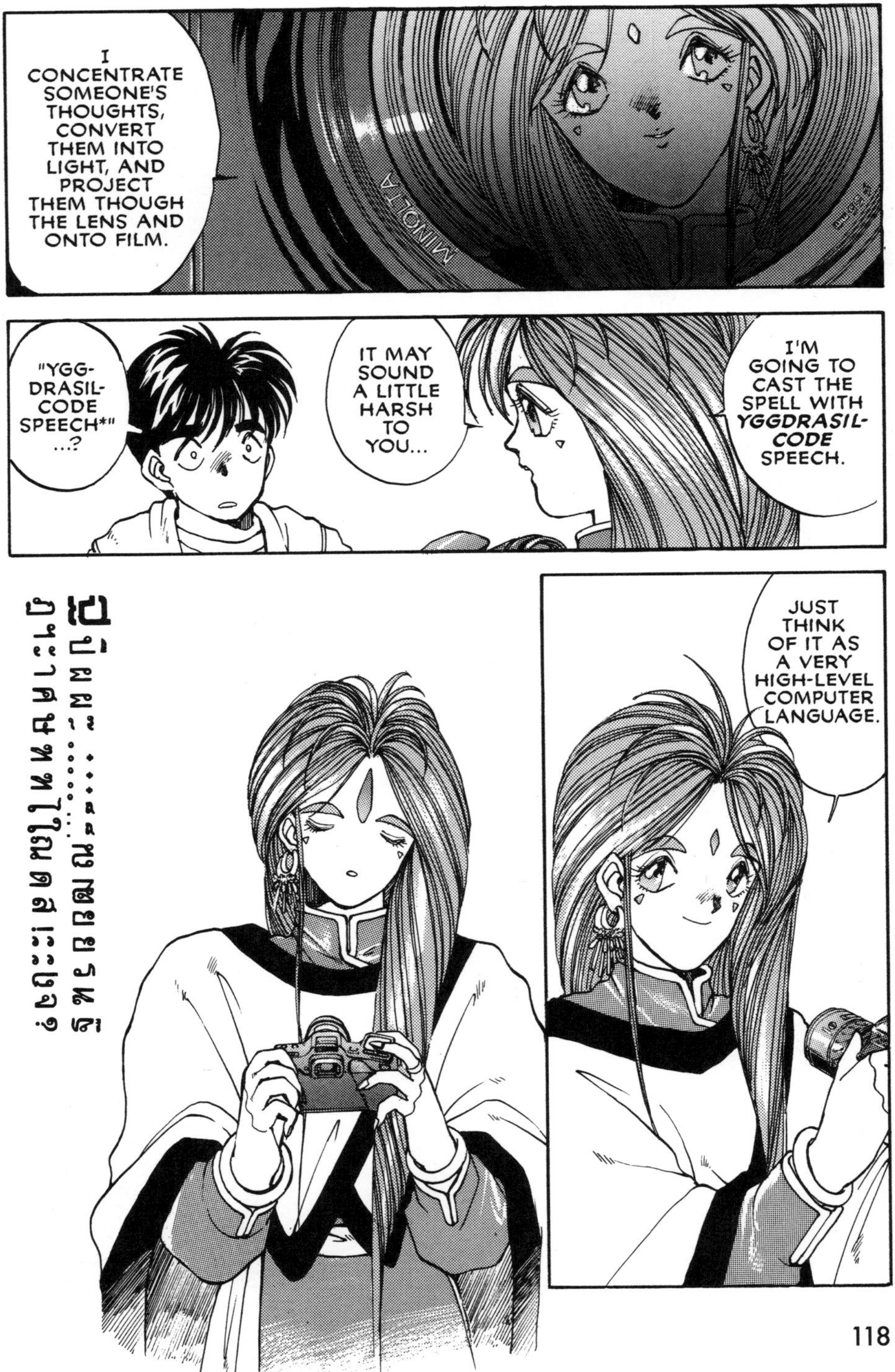
I CONCENTRATE SOMEONE'S THOUGHTS, CONVERT THEM INTO LIGHT, AND PROJECT THEM THOUGH THE LENS AND ONTO FILM.
MINOLTA
I'M GOING TO CAST THE SPELL WITH ***YGGDRASIL-CODE*** SPEECH.
IT MAY SOUND A LITTLE HARSH TO YOU...
"YGG-DRASIL-CODE SPEECH*" ...?
JUST THINK OF IT AS A VERY HIGH-LEVEL COMPUTER LANGUAGE.

*EACH PULSE-CODE MODULATION EQUALS 5,000 WORDS!

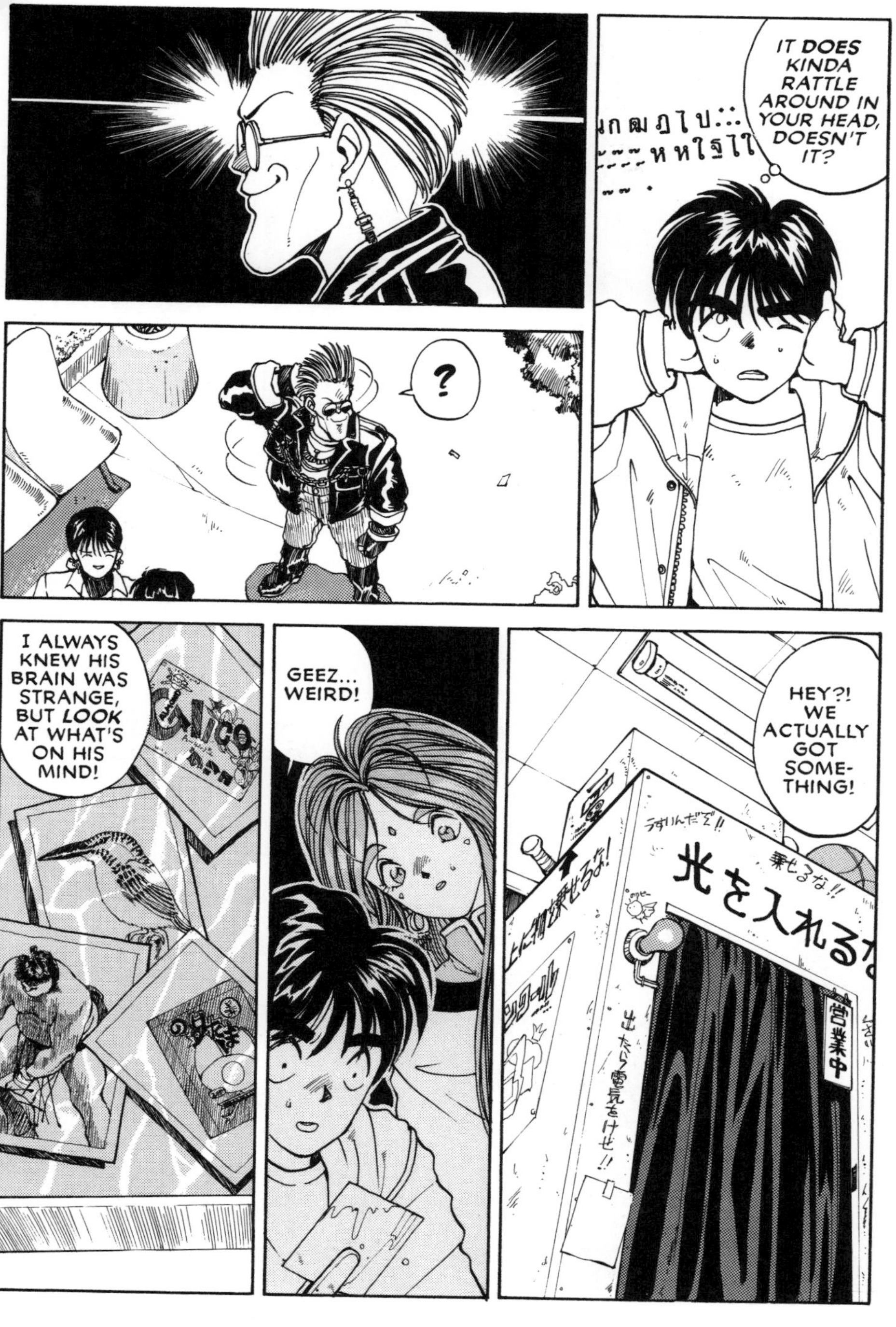
IT DOES KINDA RATTLE AROUND IN YOUR HEAD, DOESN'T IT?
?
HEY?! WE ACTUALLY GOT SOME-THING!
光を入れるな
営業中
GEEZ... WEIRD!
I ALWAYS KNEW HIS BRAIN WAS STRANGE, BUT LOOK AT WHAT'S ON HIS MIND!

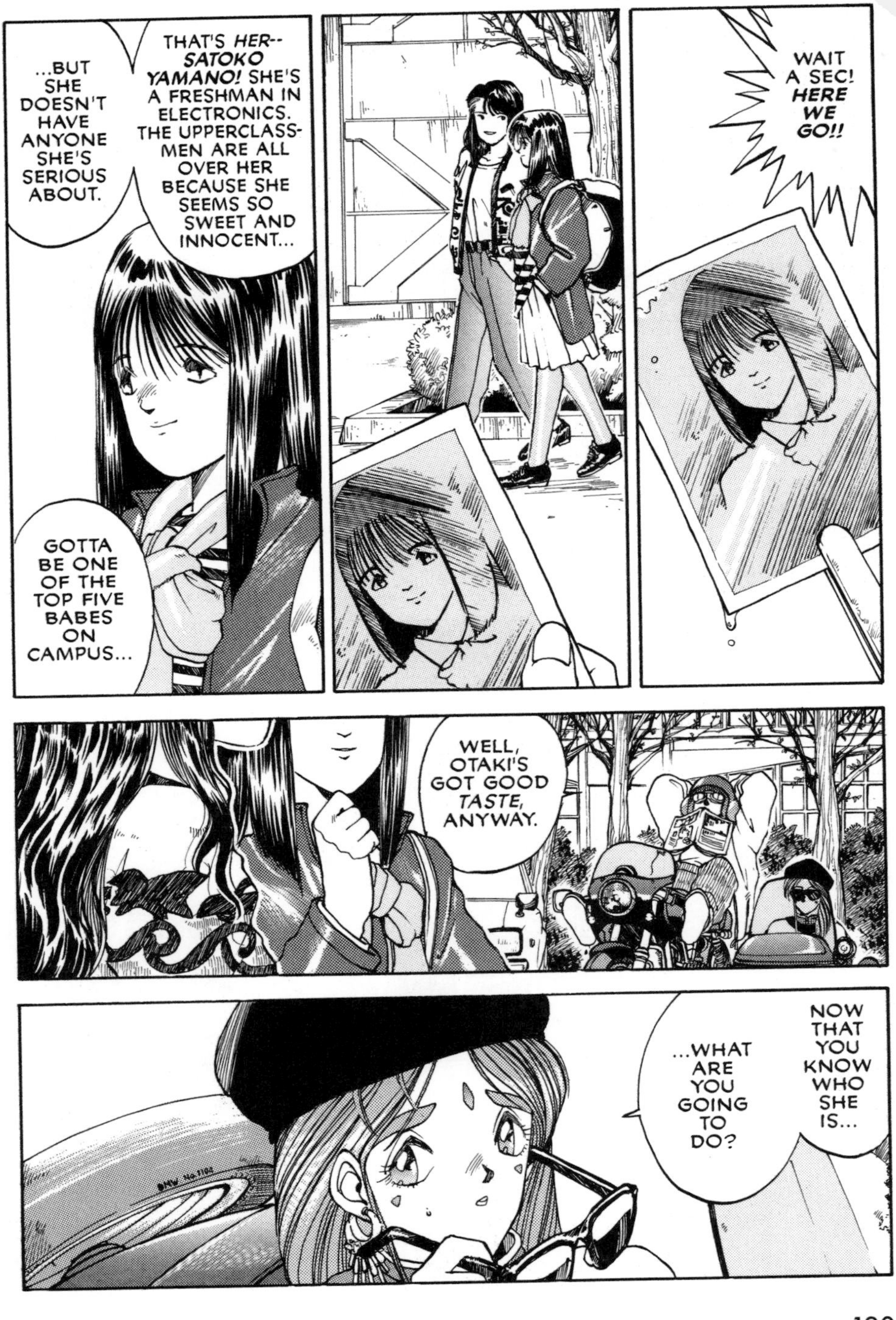
WAIT A SEC! HERE WE GO!!
THAT'S HER-- SATOKO YAMANO! SHE'S A FRESHMAN IN ELECTRONICS. THE UPPERCLASSMEN ARE ALL OVER HER BECAUSE SHE SEEMS SO SWEET AND INNOCENT...
...BUT SHE DOESN'T HAVE ANYONE SHE'S SERIOUS ABOUT.
GOTTA BE ONE OF THE TOP FIVE BABES ON CAMPUS...
WELL, OTAKI'S GOT GOOD TASTE, ANYWAY.
NOW THAT YOU KNOW WHO SHE IS...
...WHAT ARE YOU GOING TO DO?

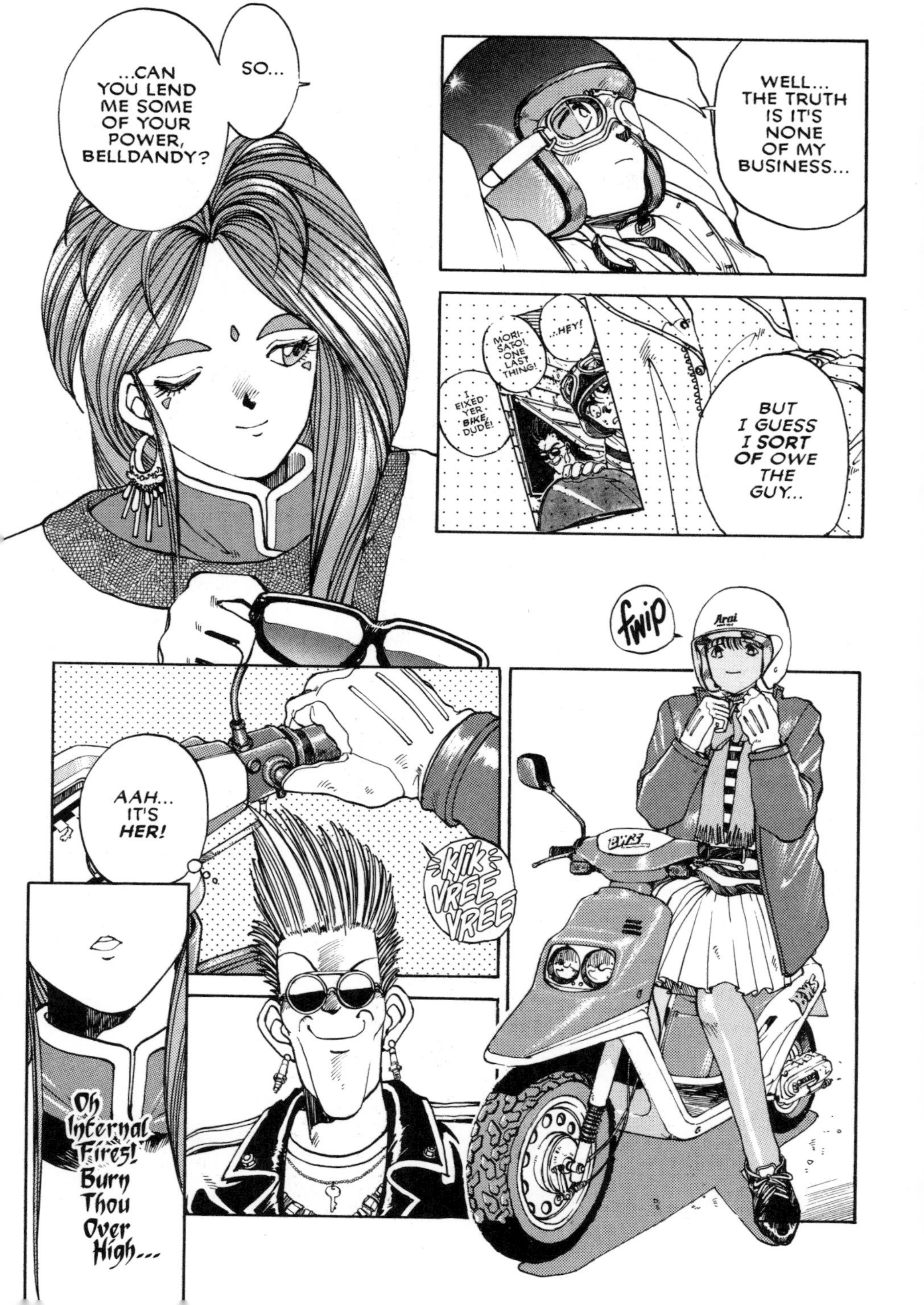
WELL... THE TRUTH IS IT'S NONE OF MY BUSINESS...
...HEY!
MORI-SATO! ONE LAST THING!
I... FIXED YER BIKE, DUDE!
BUT I GUESS I SORT OF OWE THE GUY...
SO...
...CAN YOU LEND ME SOME OF YOUR POWER, BELLDANDY?
fwip
Arai
AAH... IT'S HER!
klik VREE VREE
Oh Internal Fires! Burn Thou Over High...

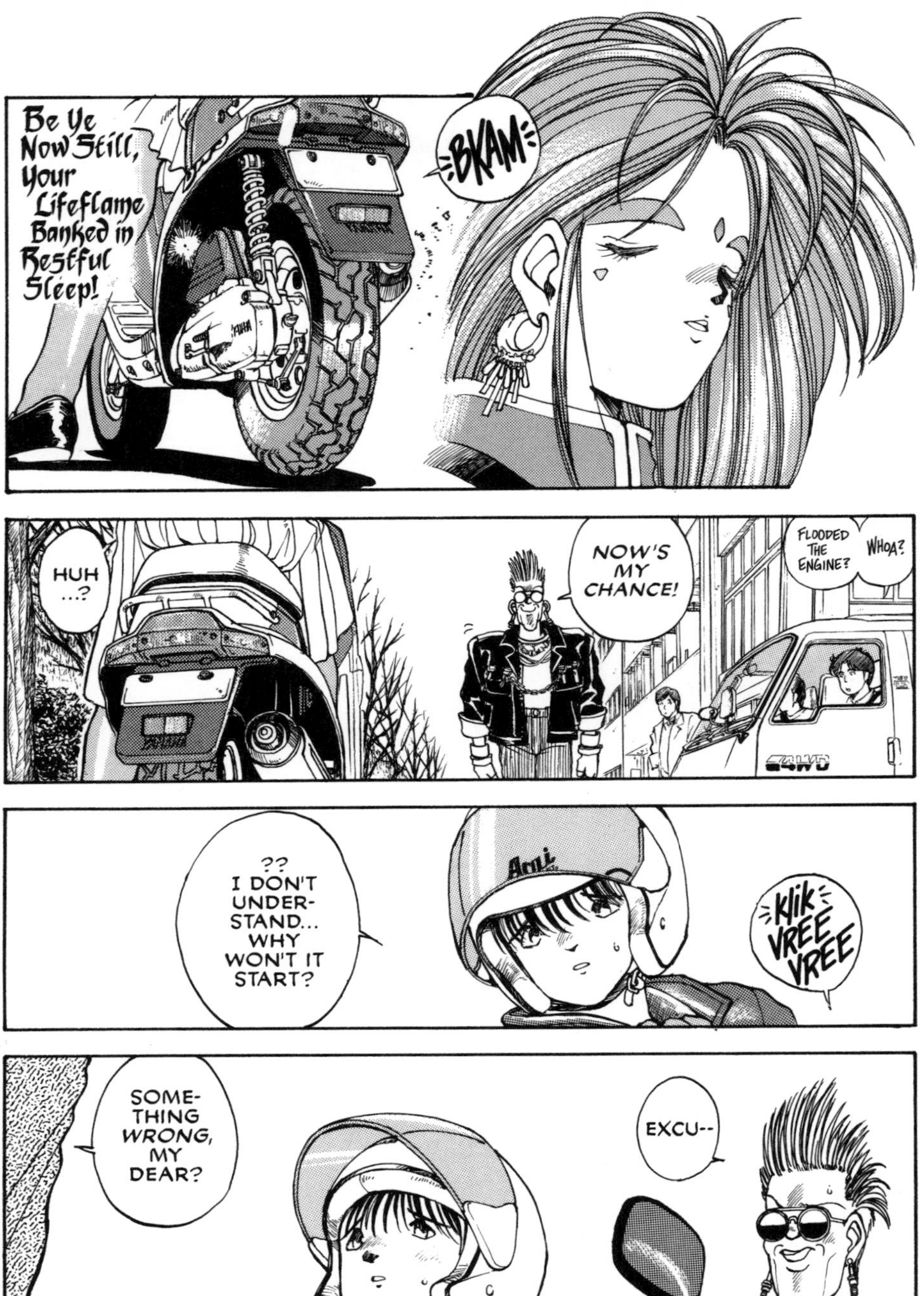
BKAM
Be Ye Now Still, Your Lifeflame Banked in Restful Sleep!
WHOA?
FLOODED THE ENGINE?
NOW'S MY CHANCE!
HUH ...?
klik VREE VREE
?? I DON'T UNDER-STAND... WHY WON'T IT START?
EXCU--
SOME-THING WRONG, MY DEAR?

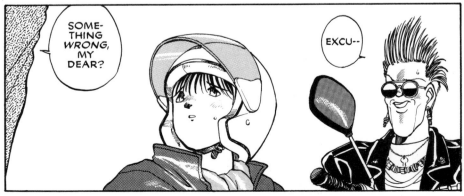

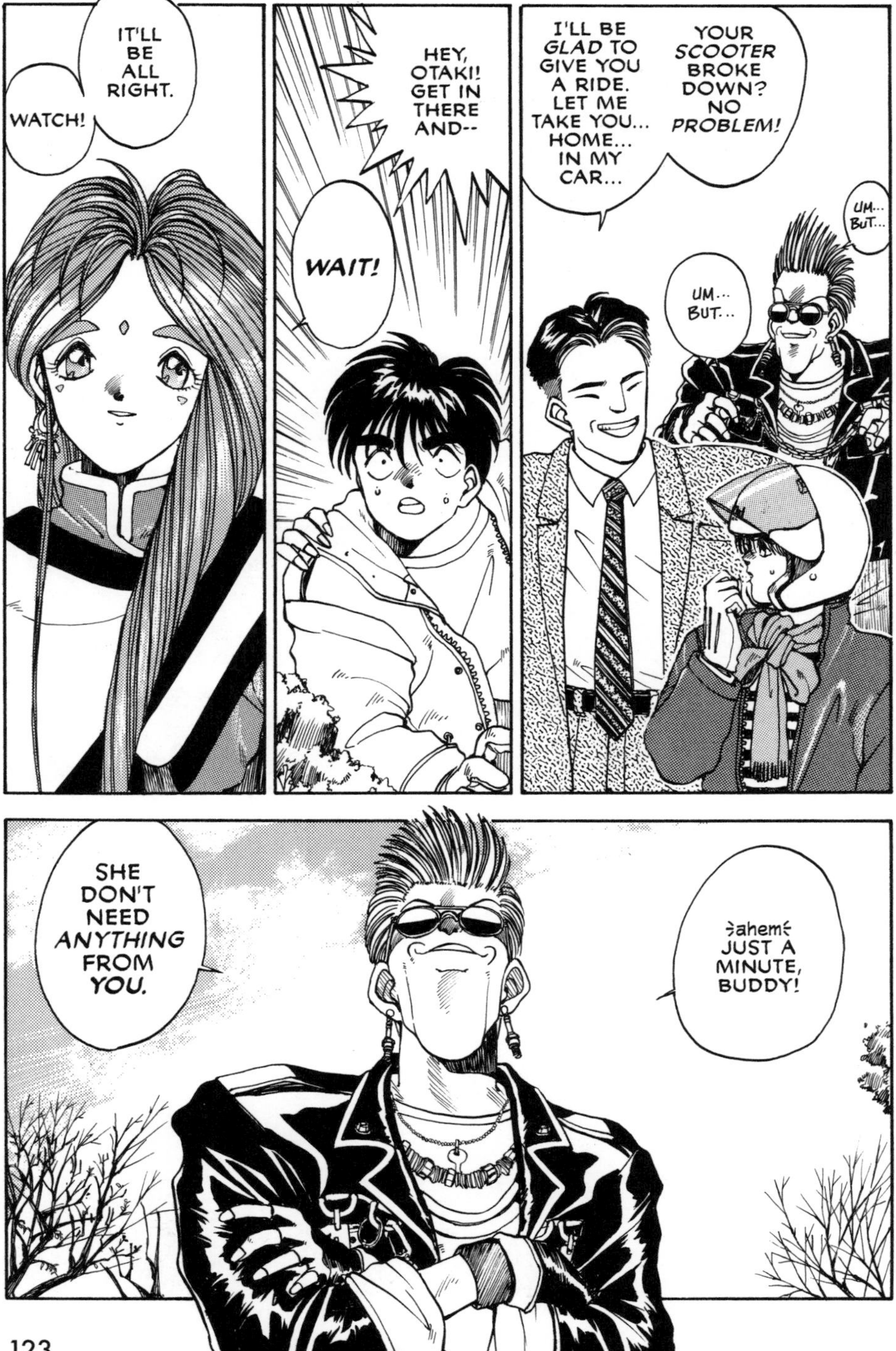
YOUR SCOOTER BROKE DOWN? NO PROBLEM!
I'LL BE GLAD TO GIVE YOU A RIDE. LET ME TAKE YOU... HOME... IN MY CAR...
UM... BUT...
UM... BUT...
HEY, OTAKI! GET IN THERE AND--
WAIT!
IT'LL BE ALL RIGHT.
WATCH!
ahem JUST A MINUTE, BUDDY!
SHE DON'T NEED ANYTHING FROM YOU.

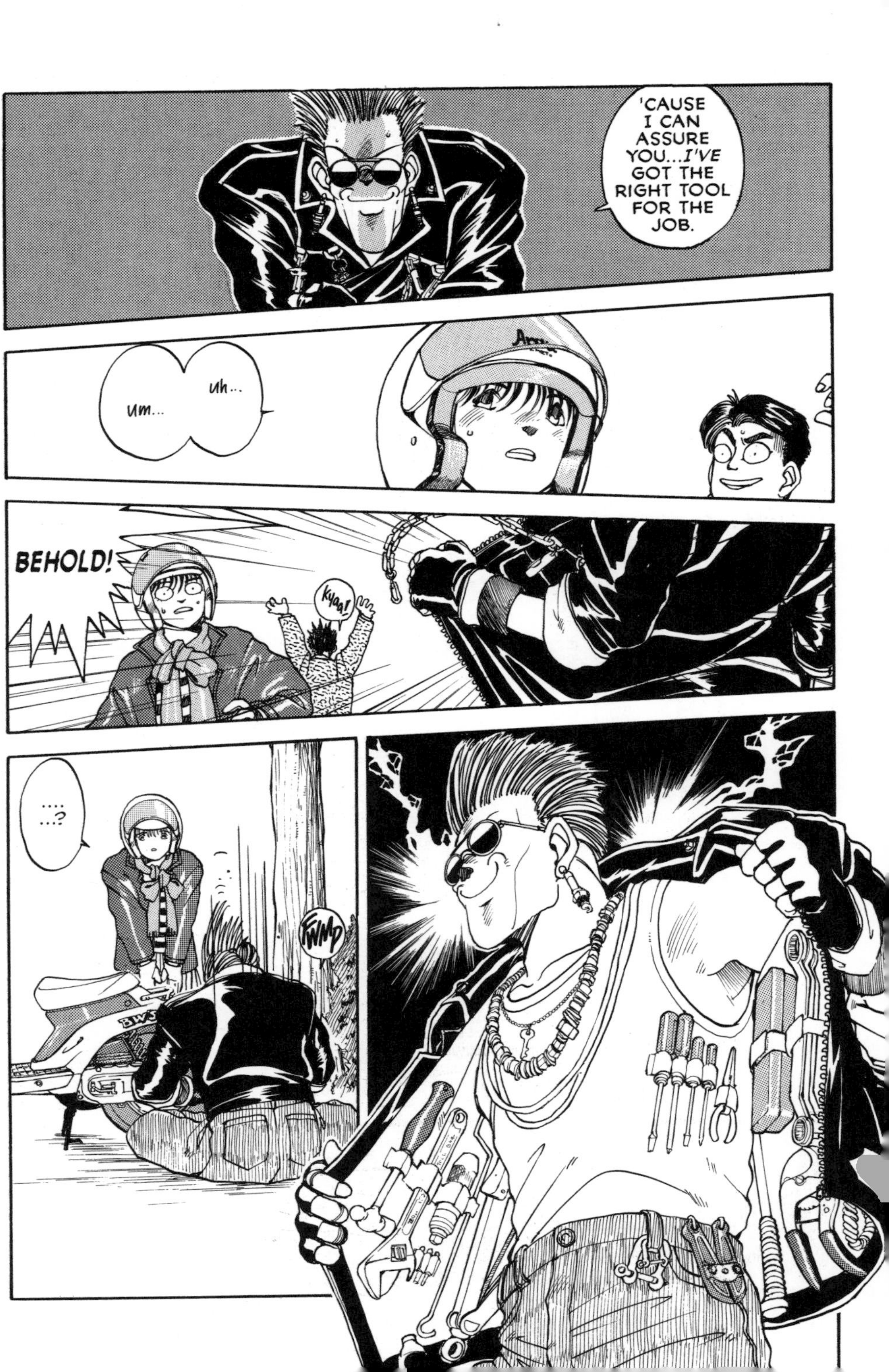
'CAUSE I CAN ASSURE YOU...*I'VE* GOT THE RIGHT TOOL FOR THE JOB.
uh...
um...
Kyaa!
BEHOLD!
FWMP
....
...?

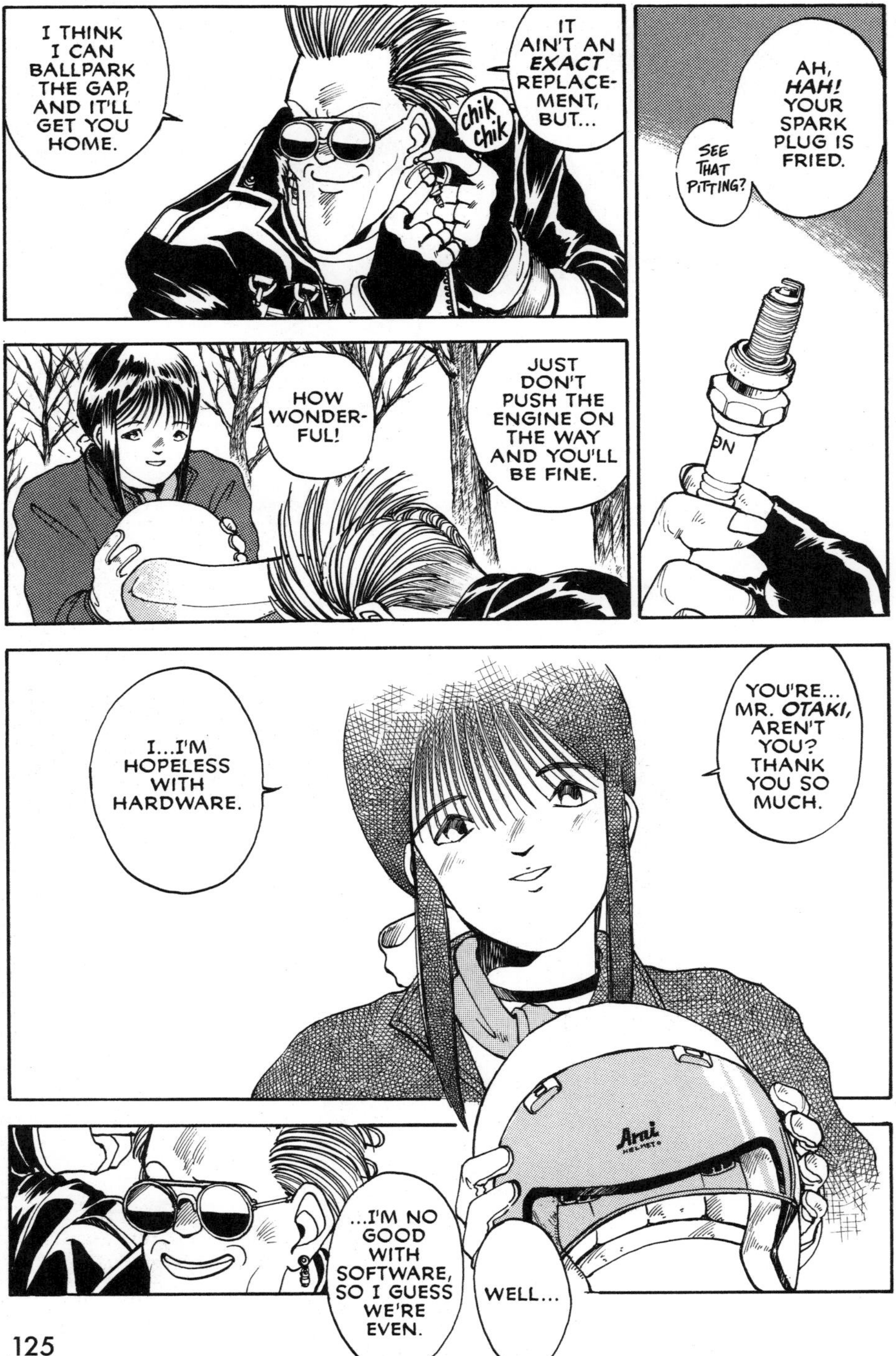
AH, HAH! YOUR SPARK PLUG IS FRIED.
SEE THAT PITTING?
IT AIN'T AN EXACT REPLACEMENT, BUT...
chik chik
I THINK I CAN BALLPARK THE GAP, AND IT'LL GET YOU HOME.
JUST DON'T PUSH THE ENGINE ON THE WAY AND YOU'LL BE FINE.
HOW WONDERFUL!
YOU'RE... MR. OTAKI, AREN'T YOU? THANK YOU SO MUCH.
I...I'M HOPELESS WITH HARDWARE.
WELL...
...I'M NO GOOD WITH SOFTWARE, SO I GUESS WE'RE EVEN.

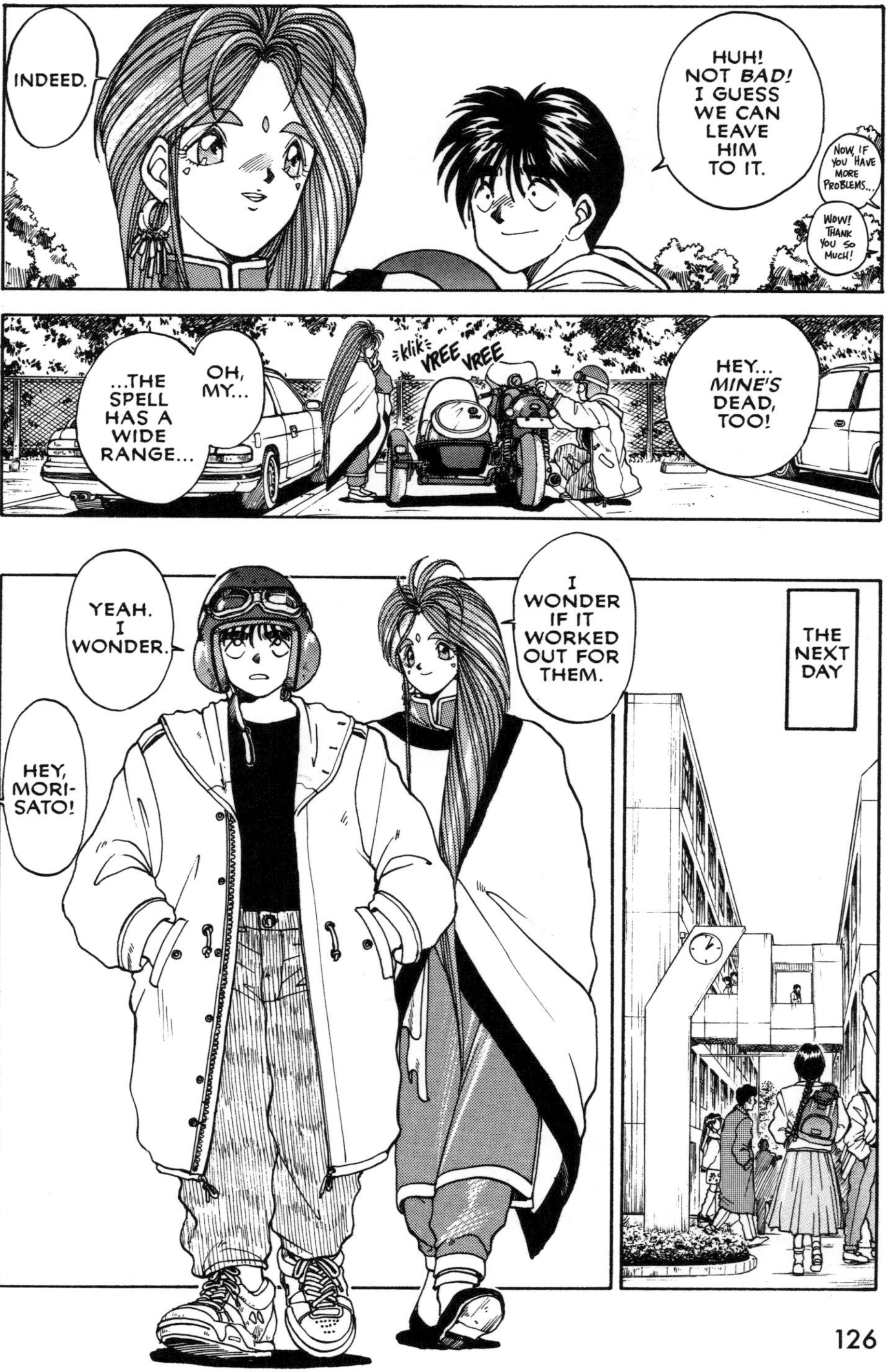
HUH! NOT BAD! I GUESS WE CAN LEAVE HIM TO IT.
NOW, IF YOU HAVE MORE PROBLEMS...
WOW! THANK YOU SO MUCH!
INDEED.
HEY... MINE'S DEAD, TOO!
klik
VREE VREE
OH, MY...
...THE SPELL HAS A WIDE RANGE...
THE NEXT DAY
I WONDER IF IT WORKED OUT FOR THEM.
YEAH. I WONDER.
HEY, MORI-SATO!

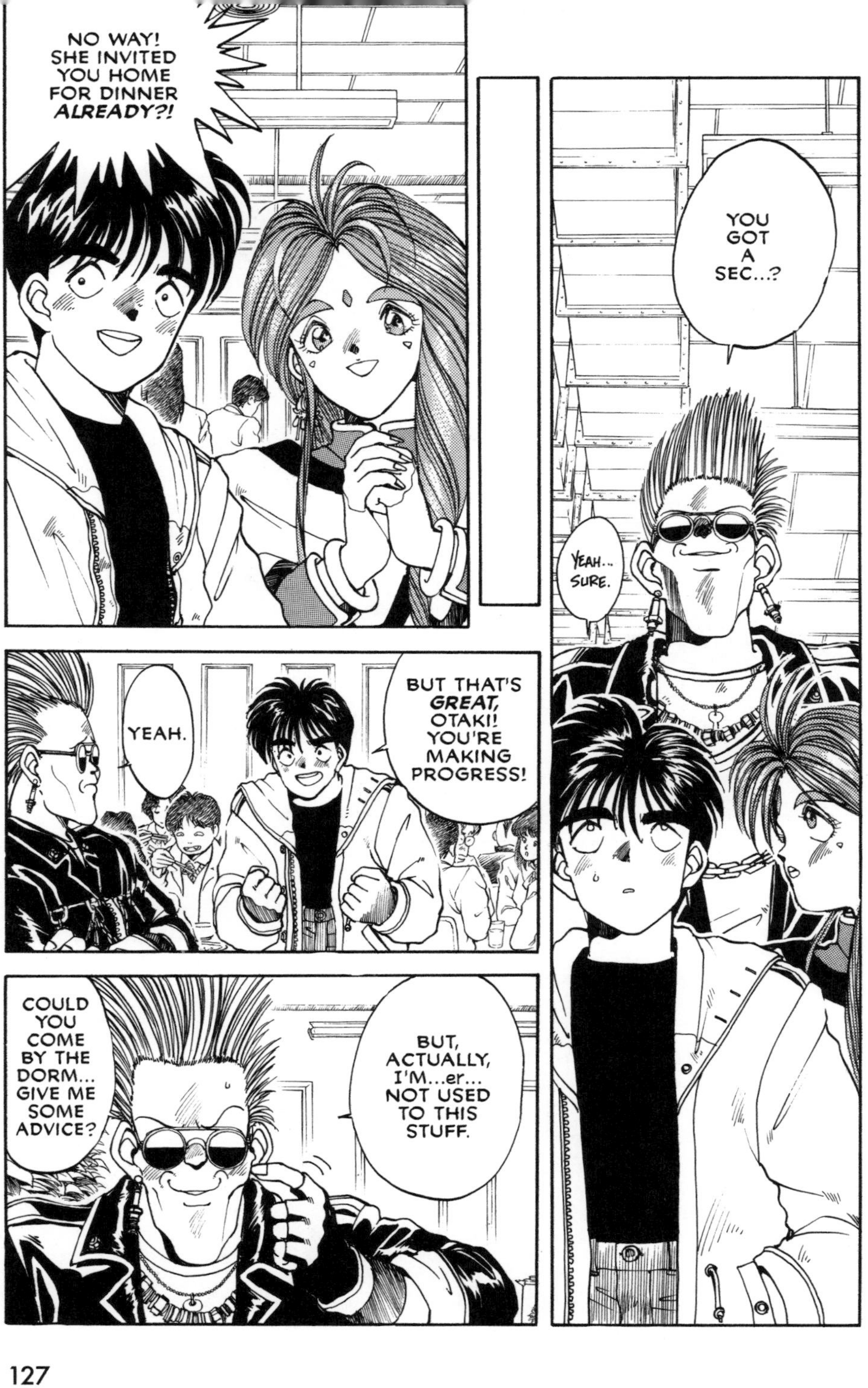
YOU GOT A SEC...?
YEAH... SURE.
NO WAY! SHE INVITED YOU HOME FOR DINNER ALREADY?!
BUT THAT'S GREAT, OTAKI! YOU'RE MAKING PROGRESS!
YEAH.
BUT, ACTUALLY, I'M...er... NOT USED TO THIS STUFF.
COULD YOU COME BY THE DORM... GIVE ME SOME ADVICE?

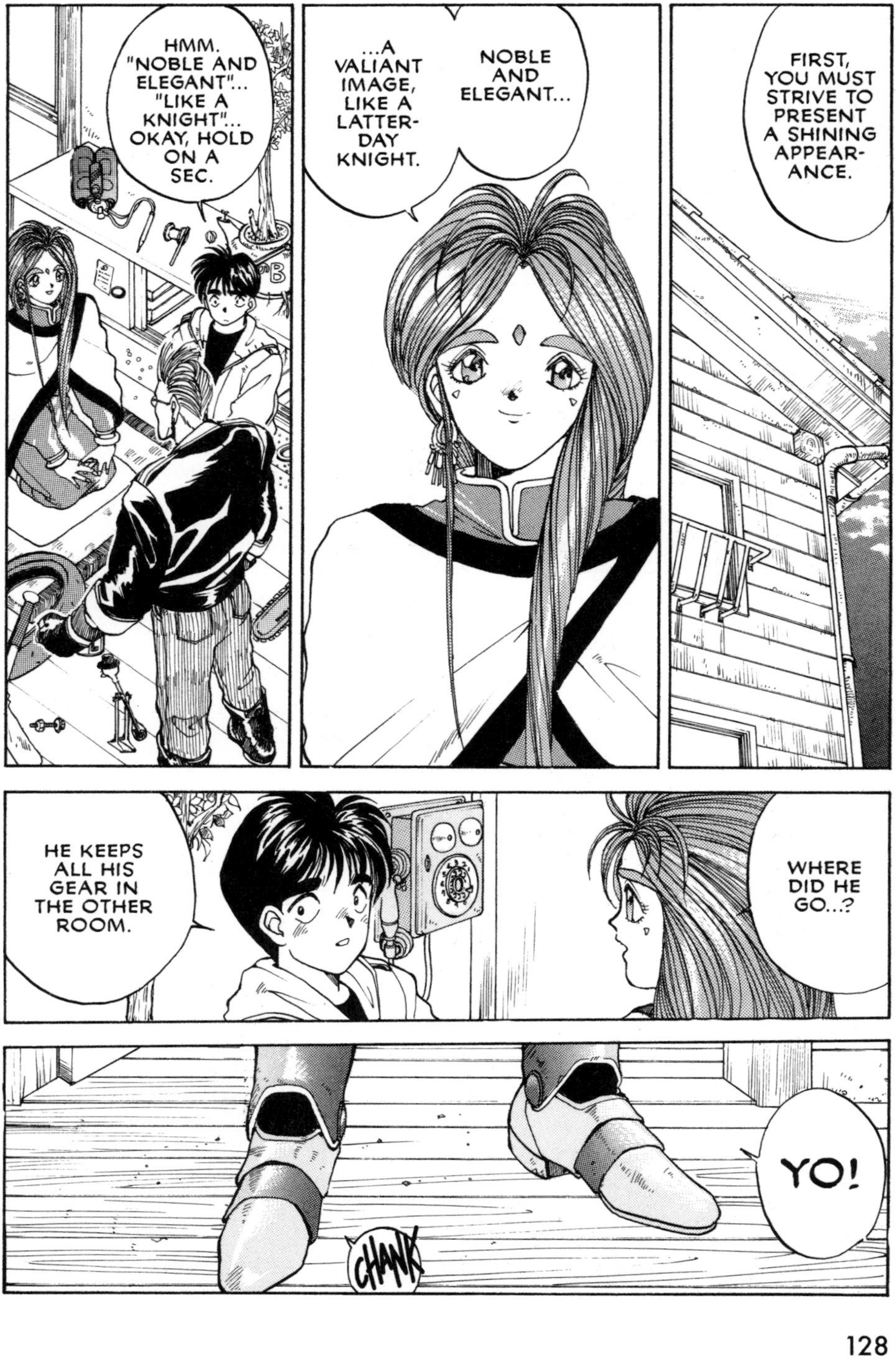
FIRST, YOU MUST STRIVE TO PRESENT A SHINING APPEAR-ANCE.
NOBLE AND ELEGANT...
...A VALIANT IMAGE, LIKE A LATTER-DAY KNIGHT.
HMM. "NOBLE AND ELEGANT"... "LIKE A KNIGHT"... OKAY, HOLD ON A SEC.
WHERE DID HE GO...?
HE KEEPS ALL HIS GEAR IN THE OTHER ROOM.
YO!
CHANK

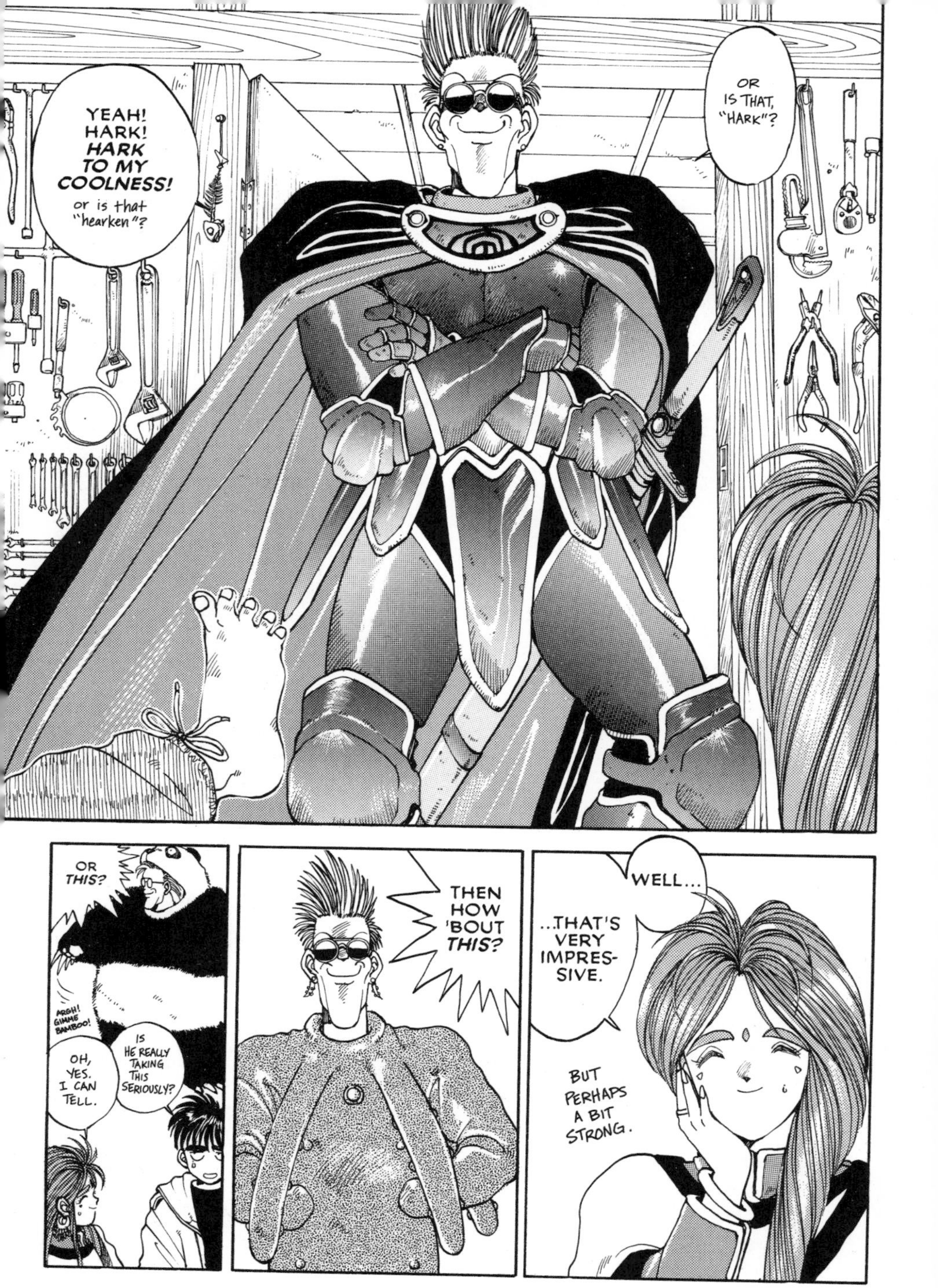
OR IS THAT, "HARK"?
YEAH! HARK! ***HARK TO MY COOLNESS!*** or is that "hearken"?
WELL...
...THAT'S VERY IMPRESSIVE.
BUT PERHAPS A BIT STRONG.
THEN HOW 'BOUT ***THIS?***
OR ***THIS?***
ARGH! GIMME BAMBOO!
IS HE REALLY TAKING THIS SERIOUSLY?
OH, YES. I CAN TELL.

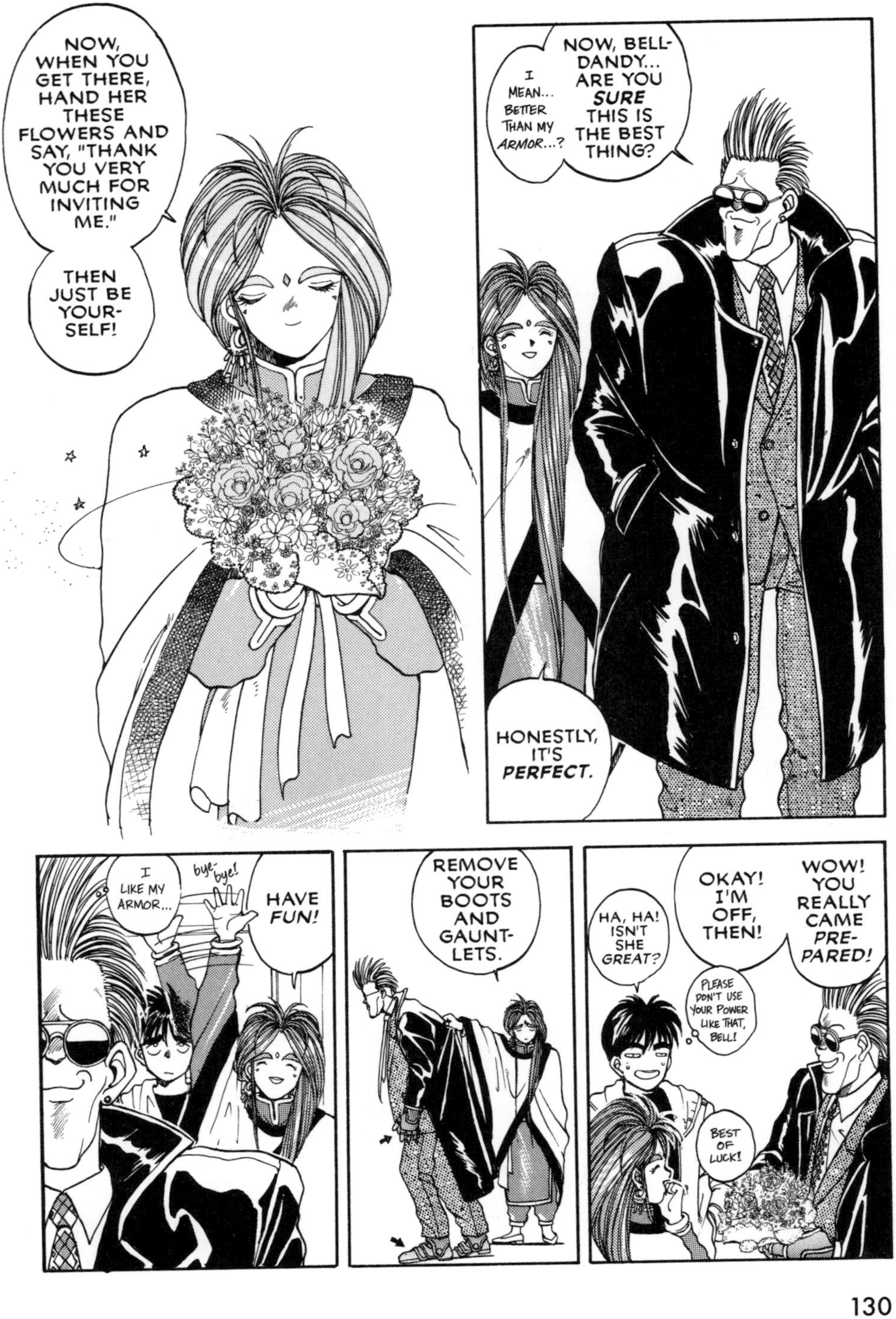
NOW, BELL-DANDY... ARE YOU *SURE* THIS IS THE BEST THING?
I MEAN... BETTER THAN MY *ARMOR*...?
HONESTLY, IT'S *PERFECT*.
NOW, WHEN YOU GET THERE, HAND HER THESE FLOWERS AND SAY, "THANK YOU VERY MUCH FOR INVITING ME."
THEN JUST BE YOURSELF!
WOW! YOU REALLY CAME *PREPARED!*
OKAY! I'M OFF, THEN!
HA, HA! ISN'T SHE *GREAT?*
PLEASE DON'T USE YOUR POWER LIKE THAT, BELL!
BEST OF LUCK!
REMOVE YOUR BOOTS AND GAUNTLETS.
HAVE *FUN!*
bye-bye!
I LIKE MY ARMOR...

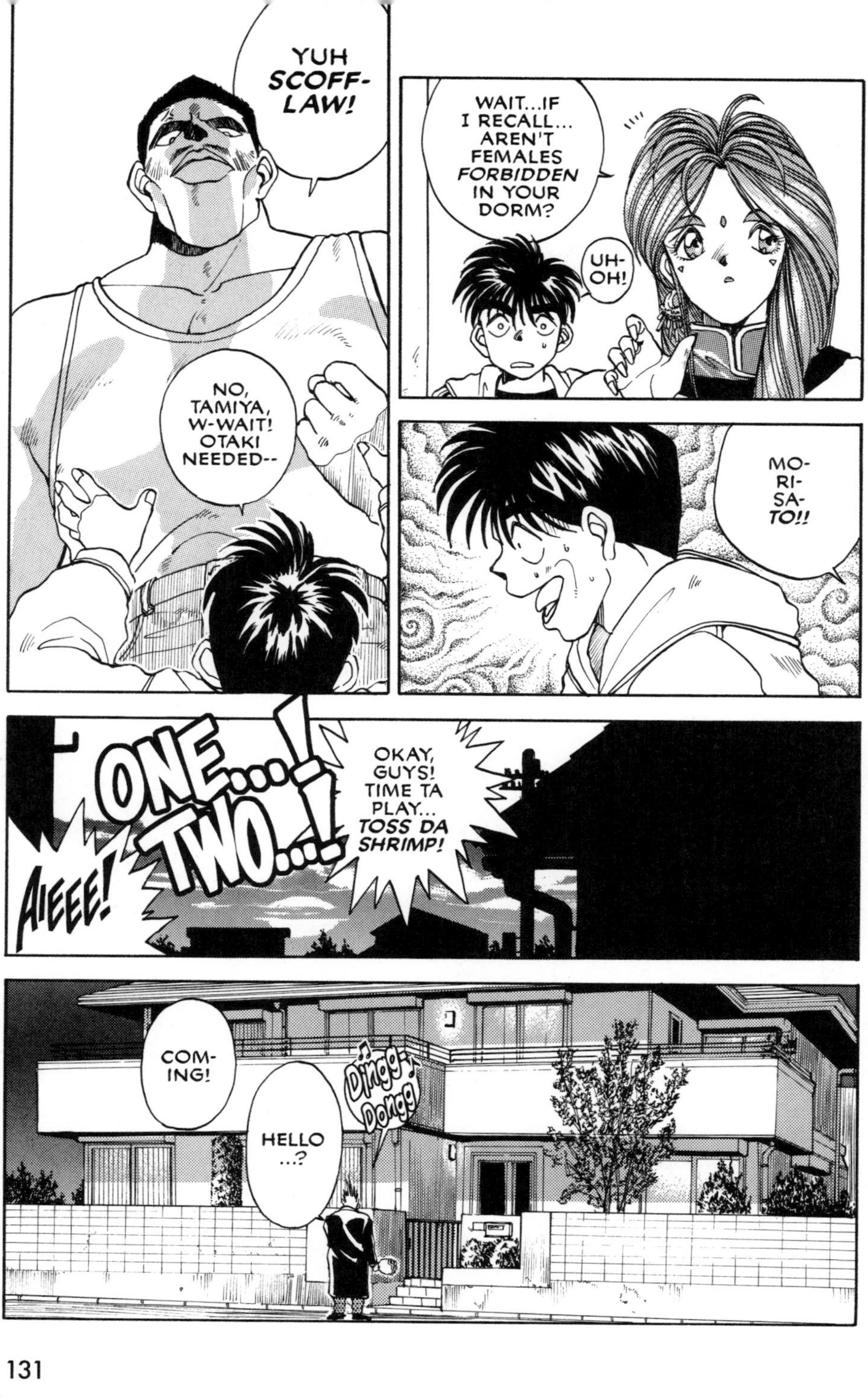
WAIT...IF I RECALL... AREN'T FEMALES FORBIDDEN IN YOUR DORM?
UH-OH!
MO-RI-SA-TO!!
YUH SCOFF-LAW!
NO, TAMIYA, W-WAIT! OTAKI NEEDED--
OKAY, GUYS! TIME TA PLAY... TOSS DA SHRIMP!
ONE...!
TWO...!
AIEEE!
Dingg-Dongg
COMING!
HELLO ...?

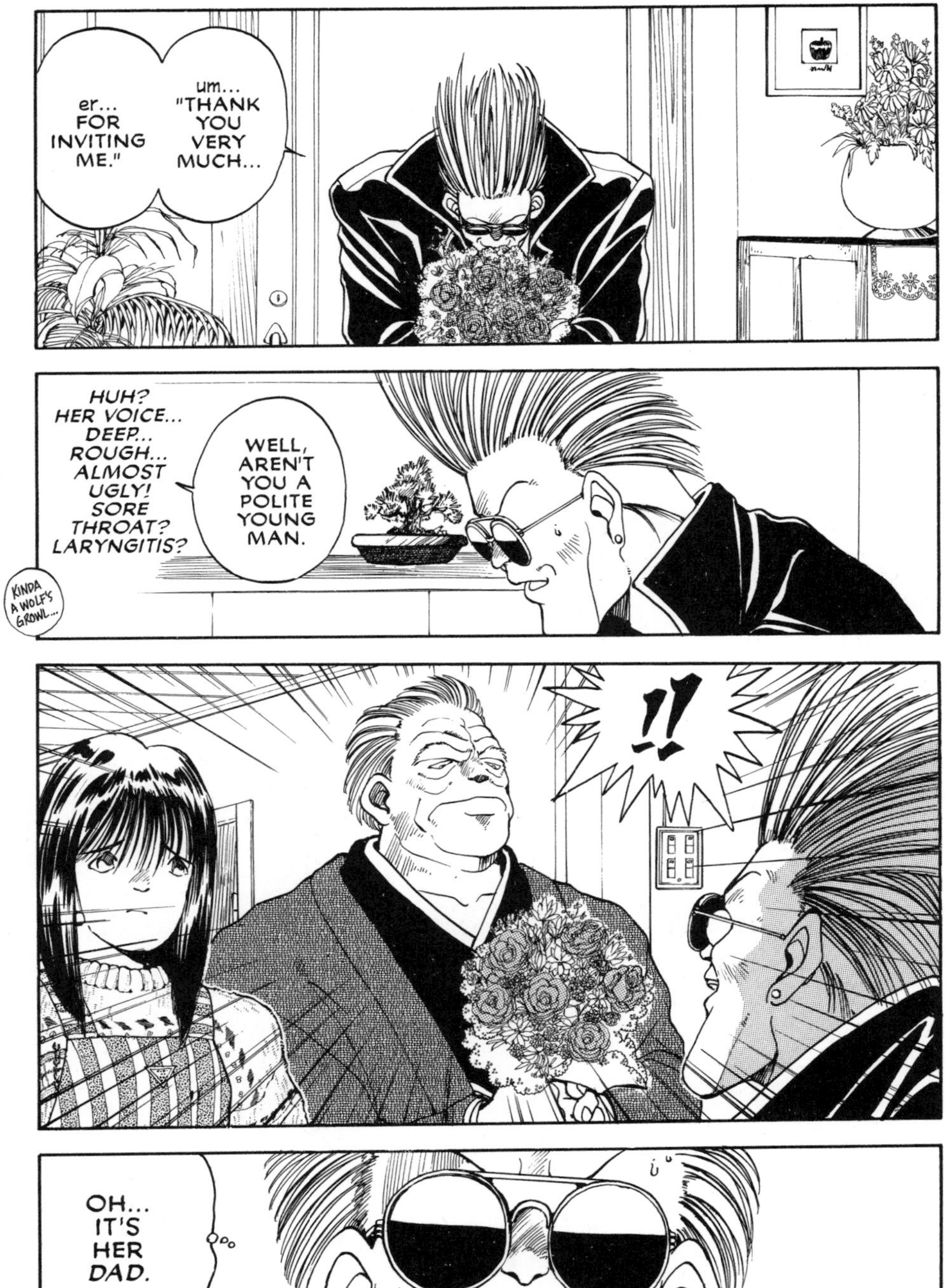
um... "THANK YOU VERY MUCH...
er... FOR INVITING ME."
WELL, AREN'T YOU A POLITE YOUNG MAN.
HUH? HER VOICE... DEEP... ROUGH... ALMOST UGLY! SORE THROAT? LARYNGITIS?
KINDA A WOLF'S GROWL...
!!
OH... IT'S HER DAD.

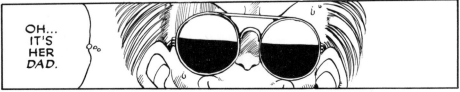

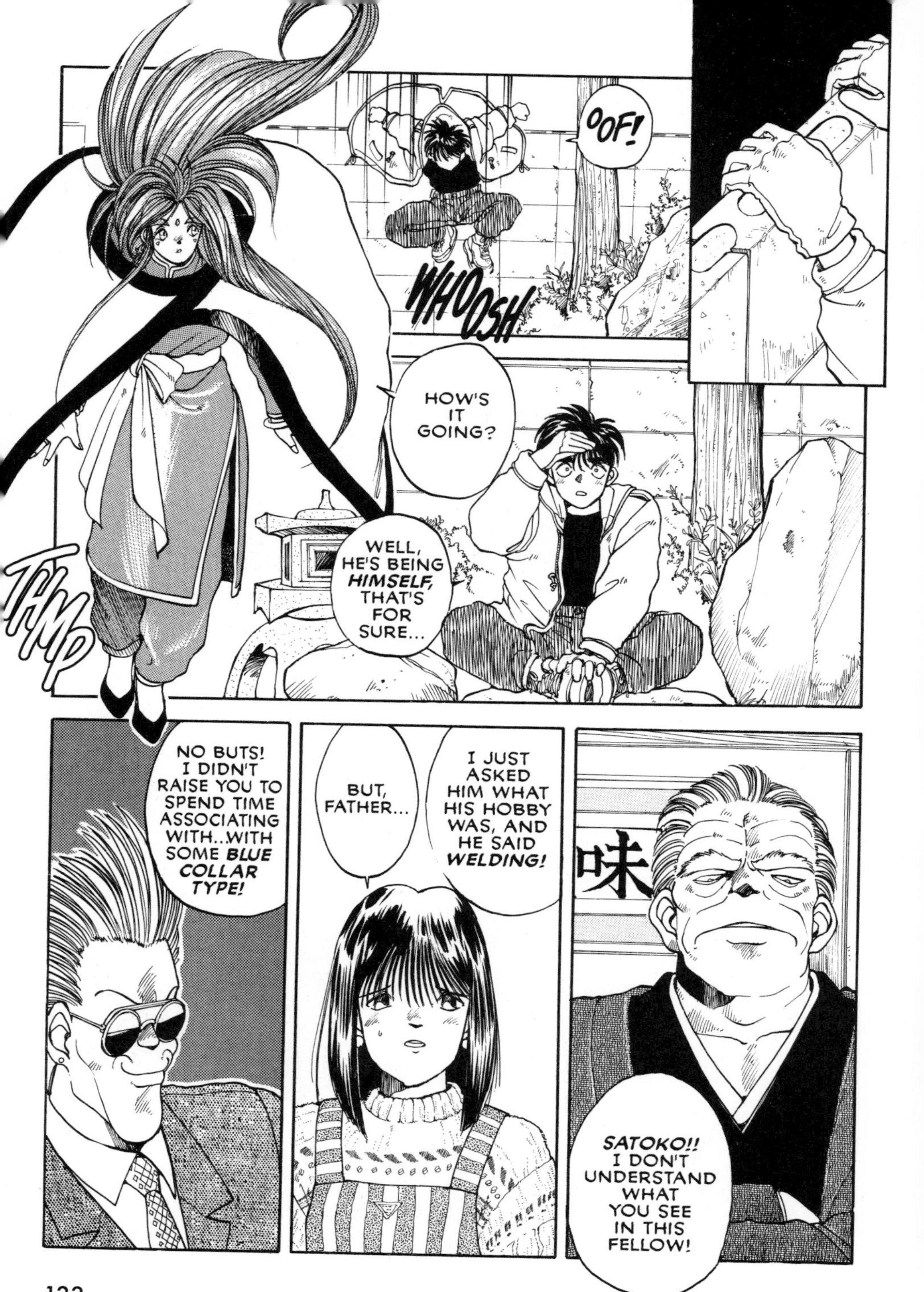
OOF!
WHOOSH
HOW'S IT GOING?
WELL, HE'S BEING *HIMSELF,* THAT'S FOR SURE...
THMP
SATOKO!! I DON'T UNDERSTAND WHAT YOU SEE IN THIS FELLOW!
味
I JUST ASKED HIM WHAT HIS HOBBY WAS, AND HE SAID *WELDING!*
BUT, FATHER...
NO BUTS! I DIDN'T RAISE YOU TO SPEND TIME ASSOCIATING WITH...WITH SOME *BLUE COLLAR TYPE!*

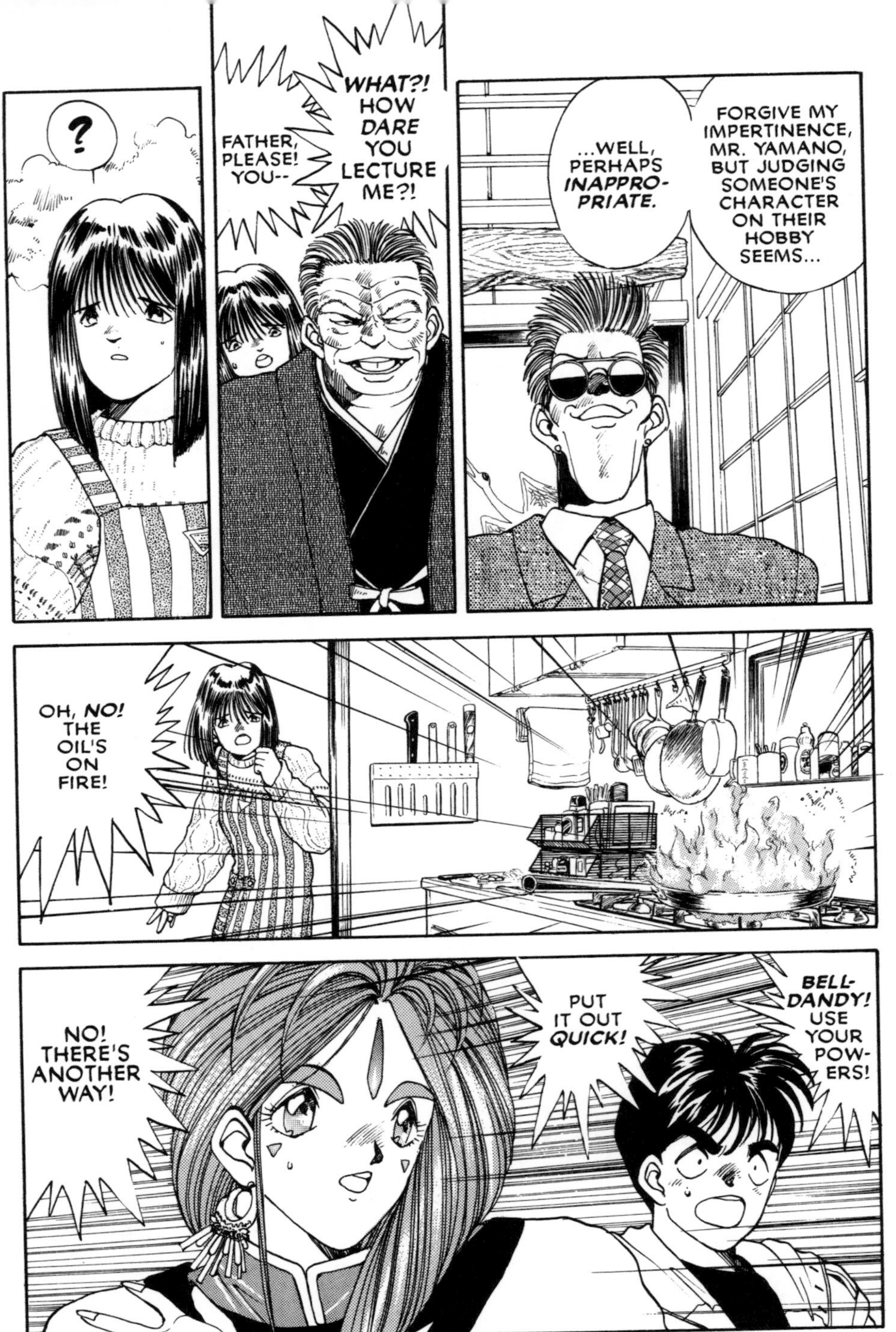
FORGIVE MY IMPERTINENCE, MR. YAMANO, BUT JUDGING SOMEONE'S CHARACTER ON THEIR HOBBY SEEMS...
...WELL, PERHAPS INAPPROPRIATE.
WHAT?! HOW DARE YOU LECTURE ME?!
FATHER, PLEASE! YOU--
?
OH, NO! THE OIL'S ON FIRE!
BELLDANDY! USE YOUR POWERS!
PUT IT OUT QUICK!
NO! THERE'S ANOTHER WAY!

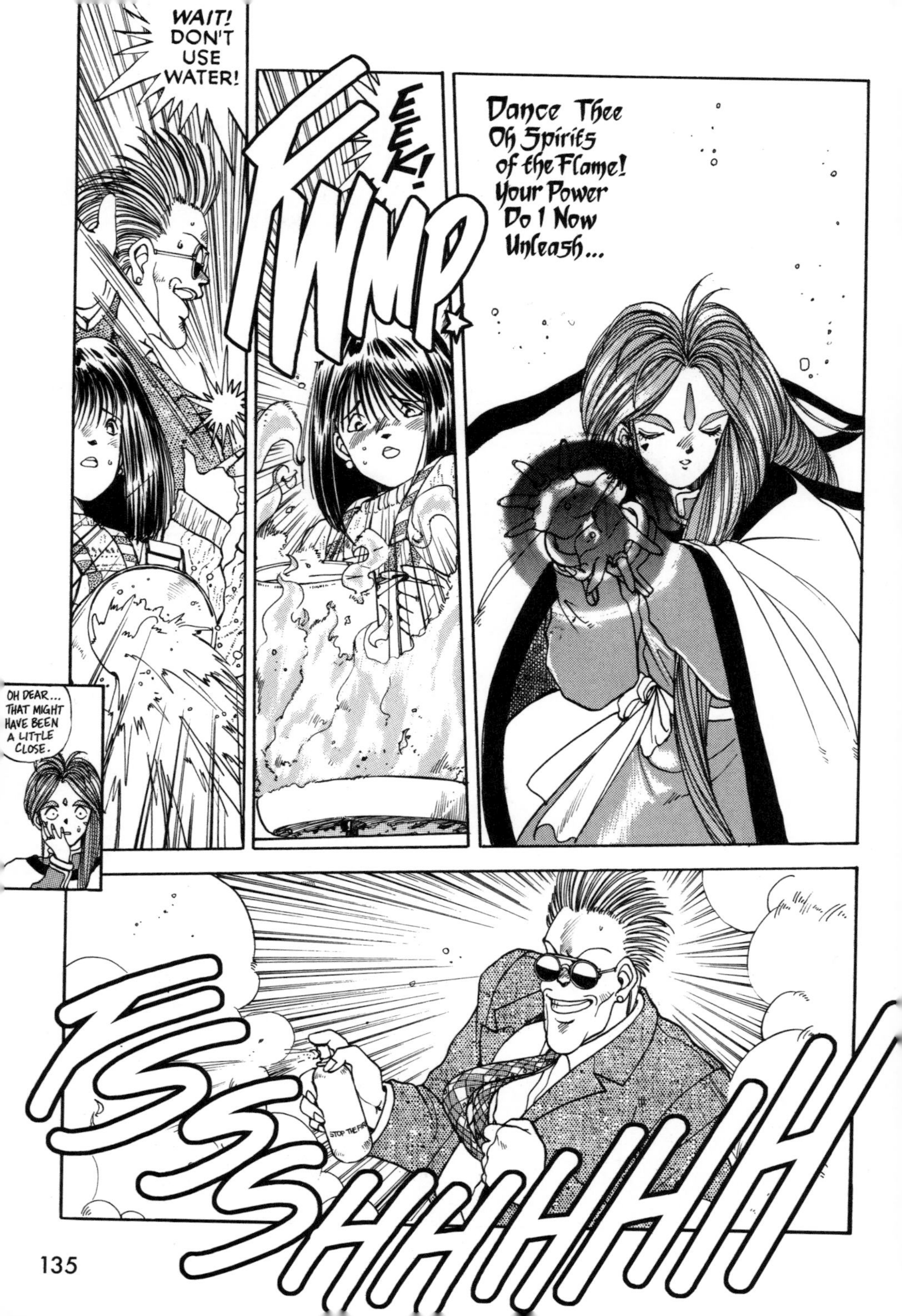
Dance Thee Oh Spirits of the Flame! Your Power Do I Now Unleash...
EEEK!
FWMP!
WAIT! DON'T USE WATER!
OH DEAR... THAT MIGHT HAVE BEEN A LITTLE CLOSE.
FSSSHHHHHH

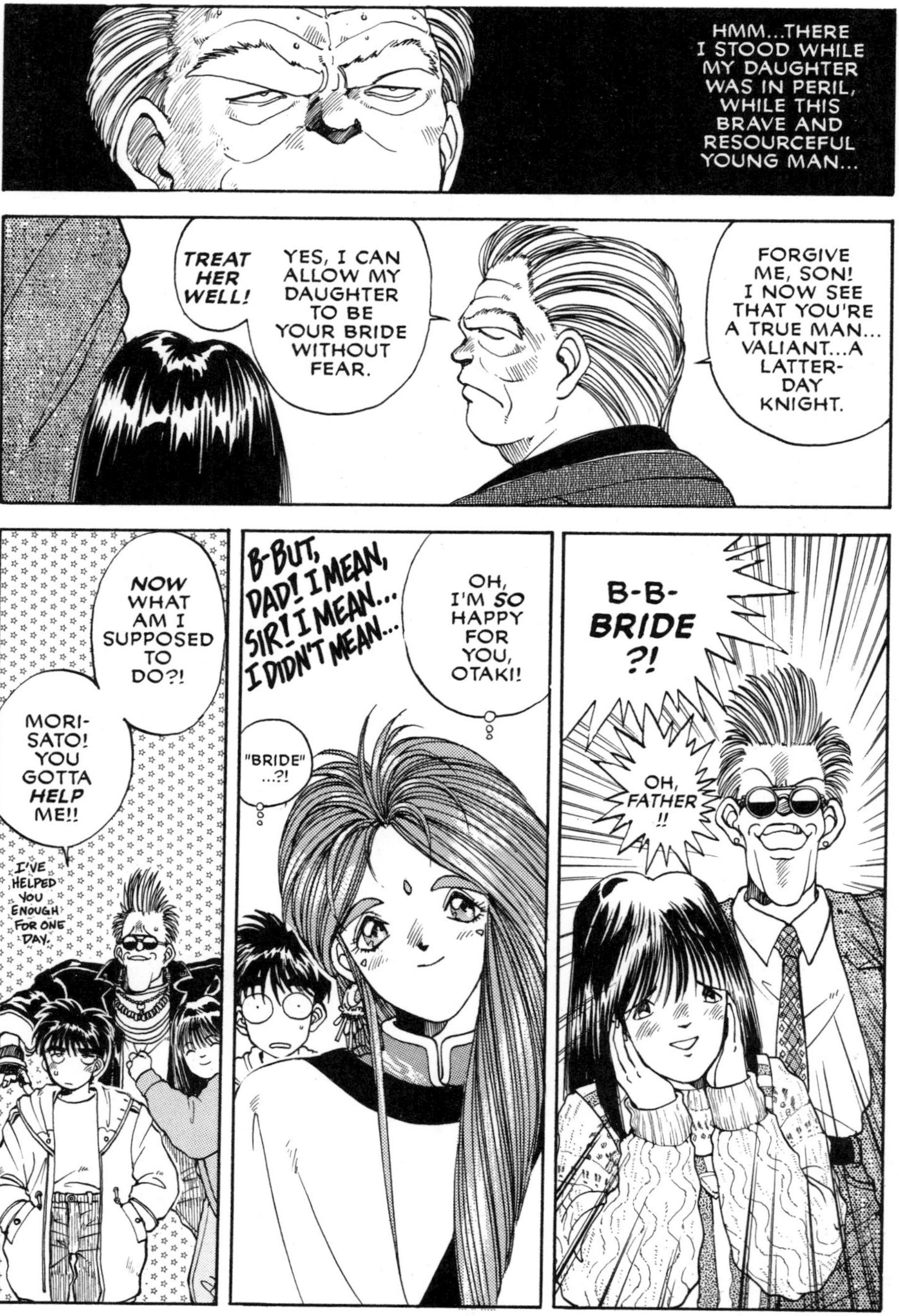
HMM...THERE I STOOD WHILE MY DAUGHTER WAS IN PERIL, WHILE THIS BRAVE AND RESOURCEFUL YOUNG MAN...
FORGIVE ME, SON! I NOW SEE THAT YOU'RE A TRUE MAN... VALIANT...A LATTER-DAY KNIGHT.
YES, I CAN ALLOW MY DAUGHTER TO BE YOUR BRIDE WITHOUT FEAR.
TREAT HER WELL!
B-B-BRIDE?!
OH, FATHER!!
OH, I'M SO HAPPY FOR YOU, OTAKI!
B-BUT, DAD! I MEAN, SIR! I MEAN... I DIDN'T MEAN...
"BRIDE"...?!
NOW WHAT AM I SUPPOSED TO DO?!
MORI-SATO! YOU GOTTA HELP ME!!
I'VE HELPED YOU ENOUGH FOR ONE DAY.

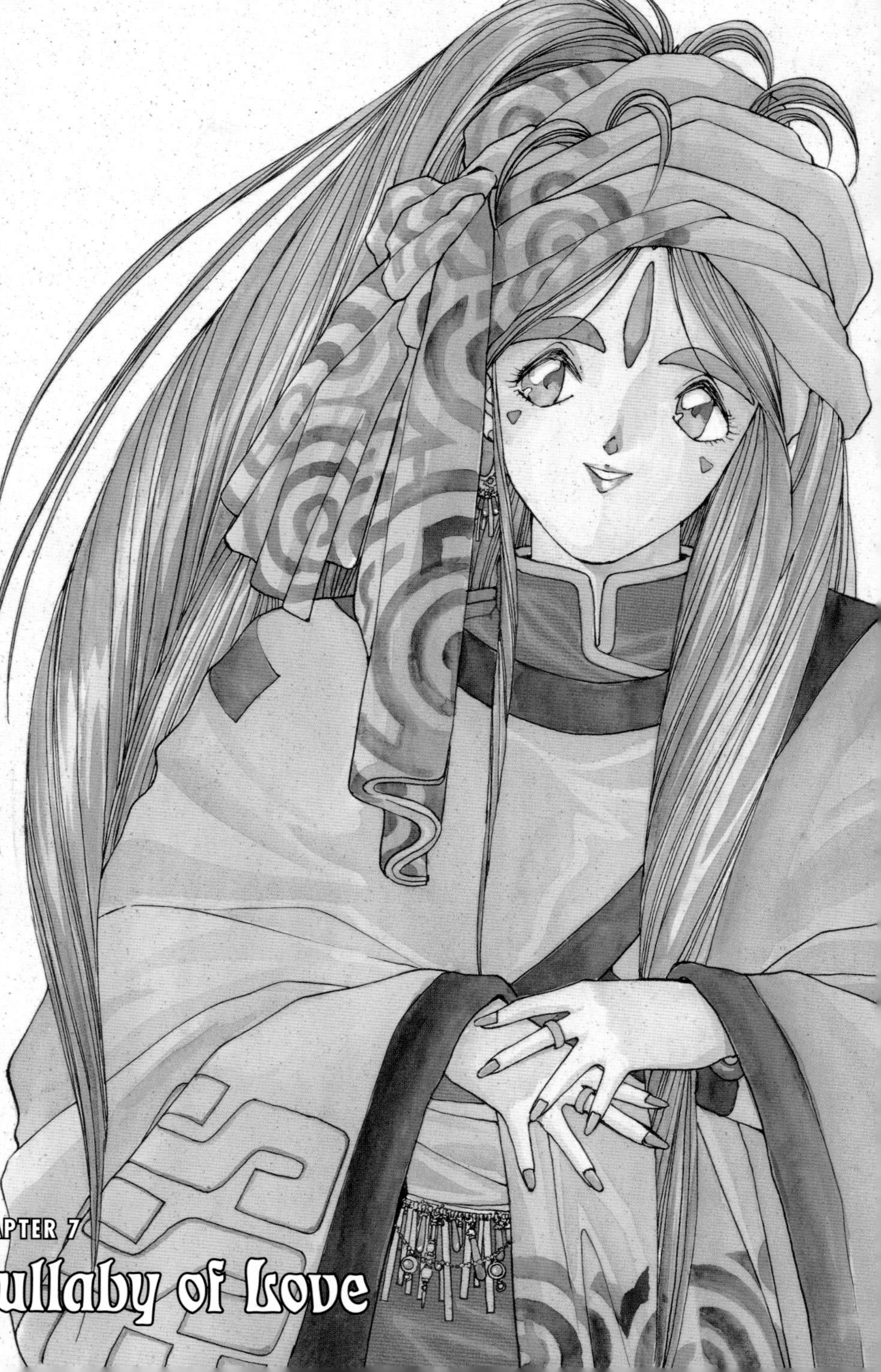

CHAPTER 7
Lullaby of Love

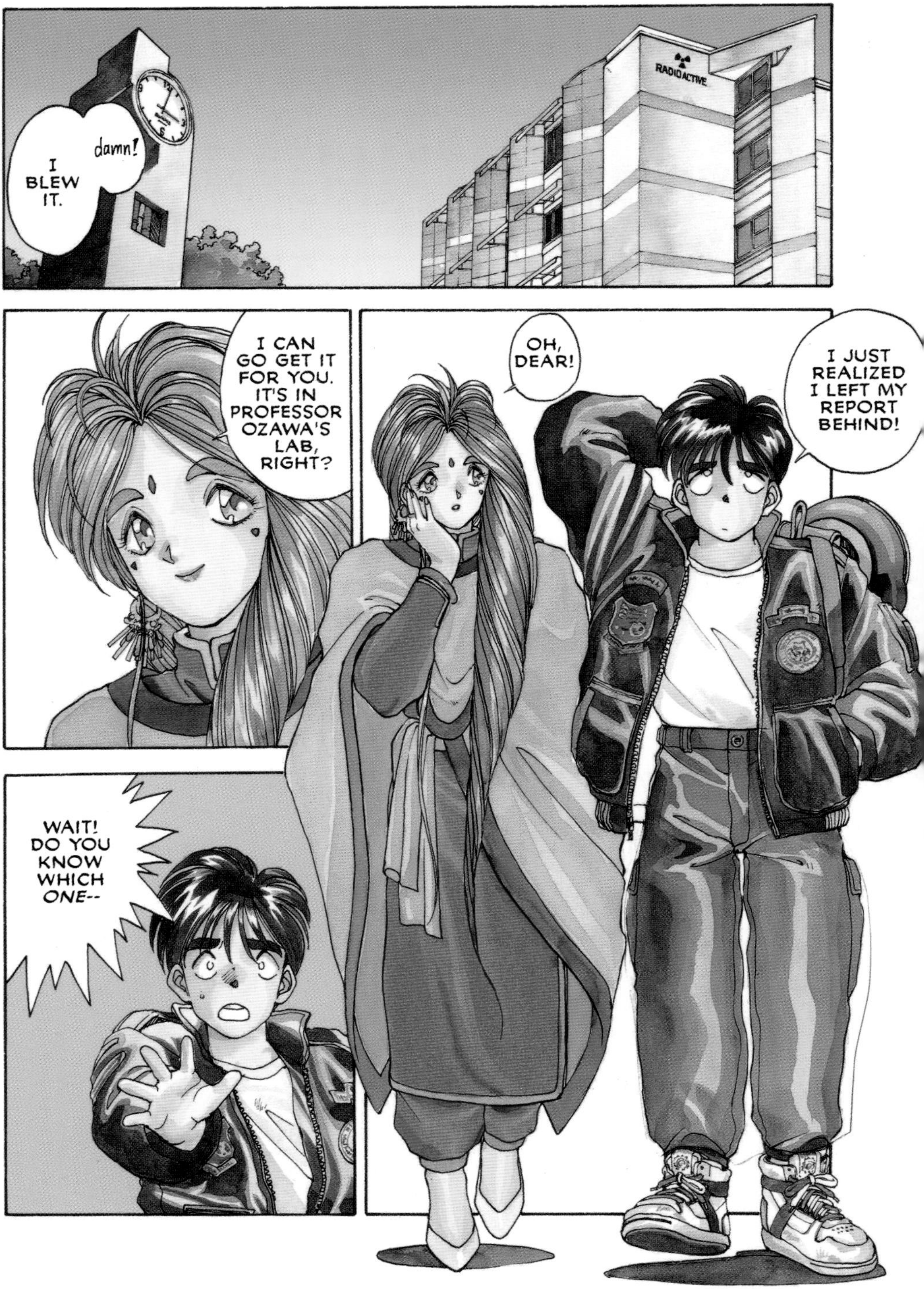
RADIO ACTIVE
damn!
I BLEW IT.
I JUST REALIZED I LEFT MY REPORT BEHIND!
OH, DEAR!
I CAN GO GET IT FOR YOU. IT'S IN PROFESSOR OZAWA'S LAB, RIGHT?
WAIT! DO YOU KNOW WHICH *ONE*--

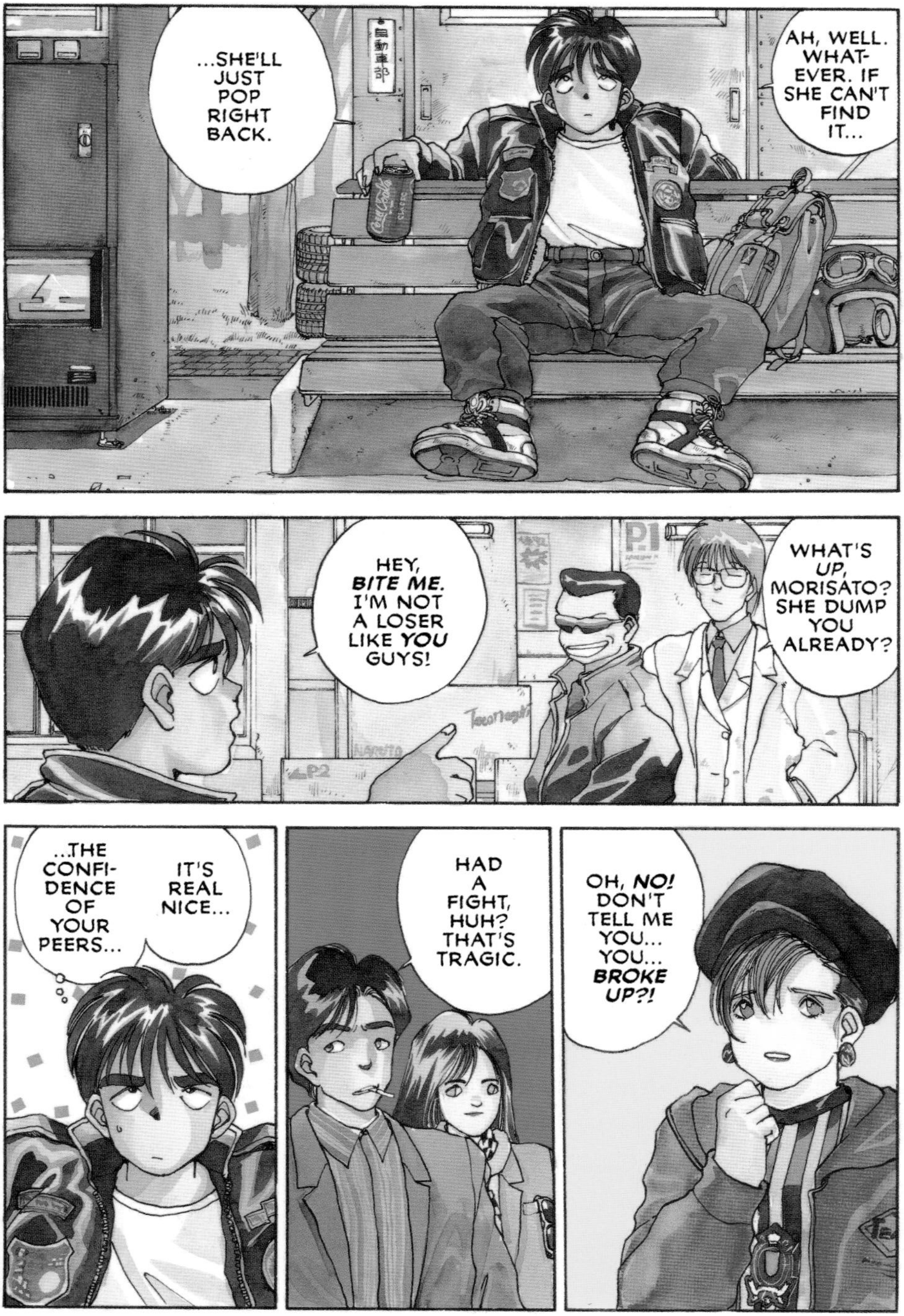
AH, WELL. WHATEVER. IF SHE CAN'T FIND IT...
...SHE'LL JUST POP RIGHT BACK.
WHAT'S *UP*, MORISATO? SHE DUMP YOU ALREADY?
HEY, ***BITE ME.*** I'M NOT A LOSER LIKE ***YOU*** GUYS!
OH, ***NO!*** DON'T TELL ME YOU... YOU... ***BROKE UP?!***
HAD A FIGHT, HUH? THAT'S TRAGIC.
IT'S REAL NICE...
...THE CONFIDENCE OF YOUR PEERS...

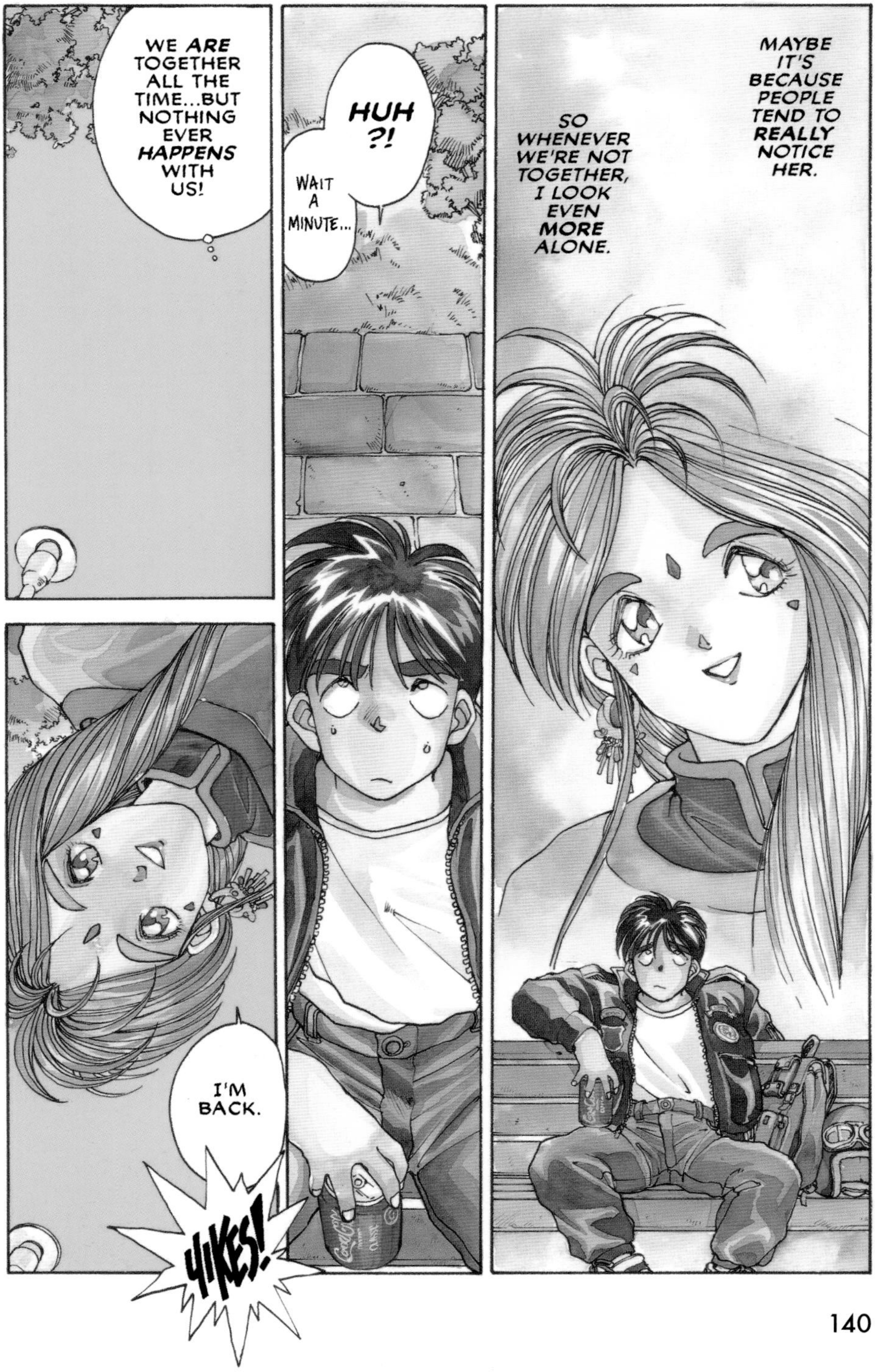
MAYBE IT'S BECAUSE PEOPLE TEND TO REALLY NOTICE HER.
SO WHENEVER WE'RE NOT TOGETHER, I LOOK EVEN MORE ALONE.
HUH ?!
WAIT A MINUTE...
WE ARE TOGETHER ALL THE TIME...BUT NOTHING EVER HAPPENS WITH US!
I'M BACK.
YIKES!

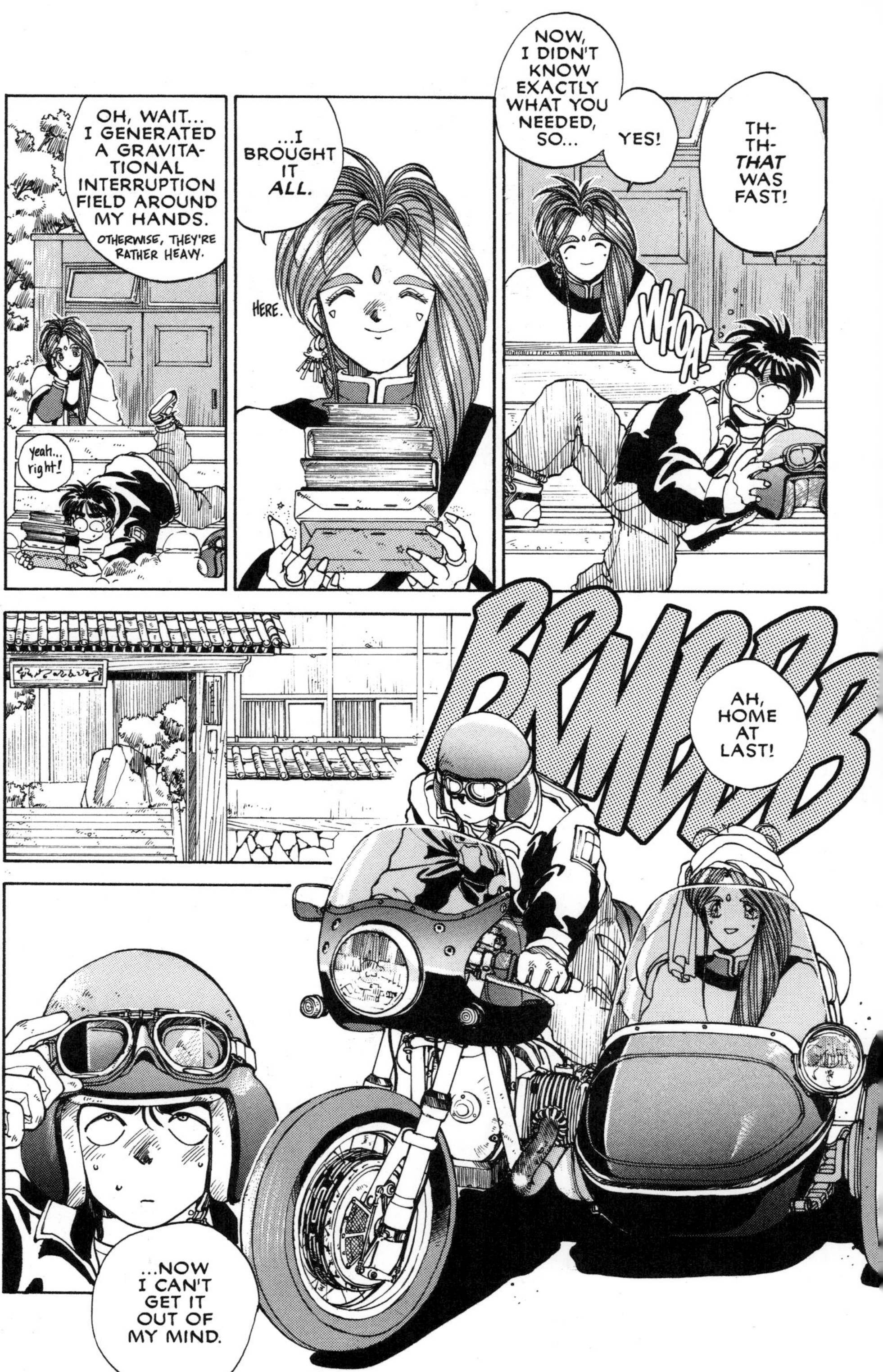
TH-TH-*THAT* WAS FAST!
YES!
NOW, I DIDN'T KNOW EXACTLY WHAT YOU NEEDED, SO...
WHOA!
...I BROUGHT IT *ALL.*
HERE.
OH, WAIT... I GENERATED A GRAVITATIONAL INTERRUPTION FIELD AROUND MY HANDS.
OTHERWISE, THEY'RE RATHER HEAVY.
yeah... right!
AH, HOME AT LAST!
...NOW I CAN'T GET IT OUT OF MY MIND.

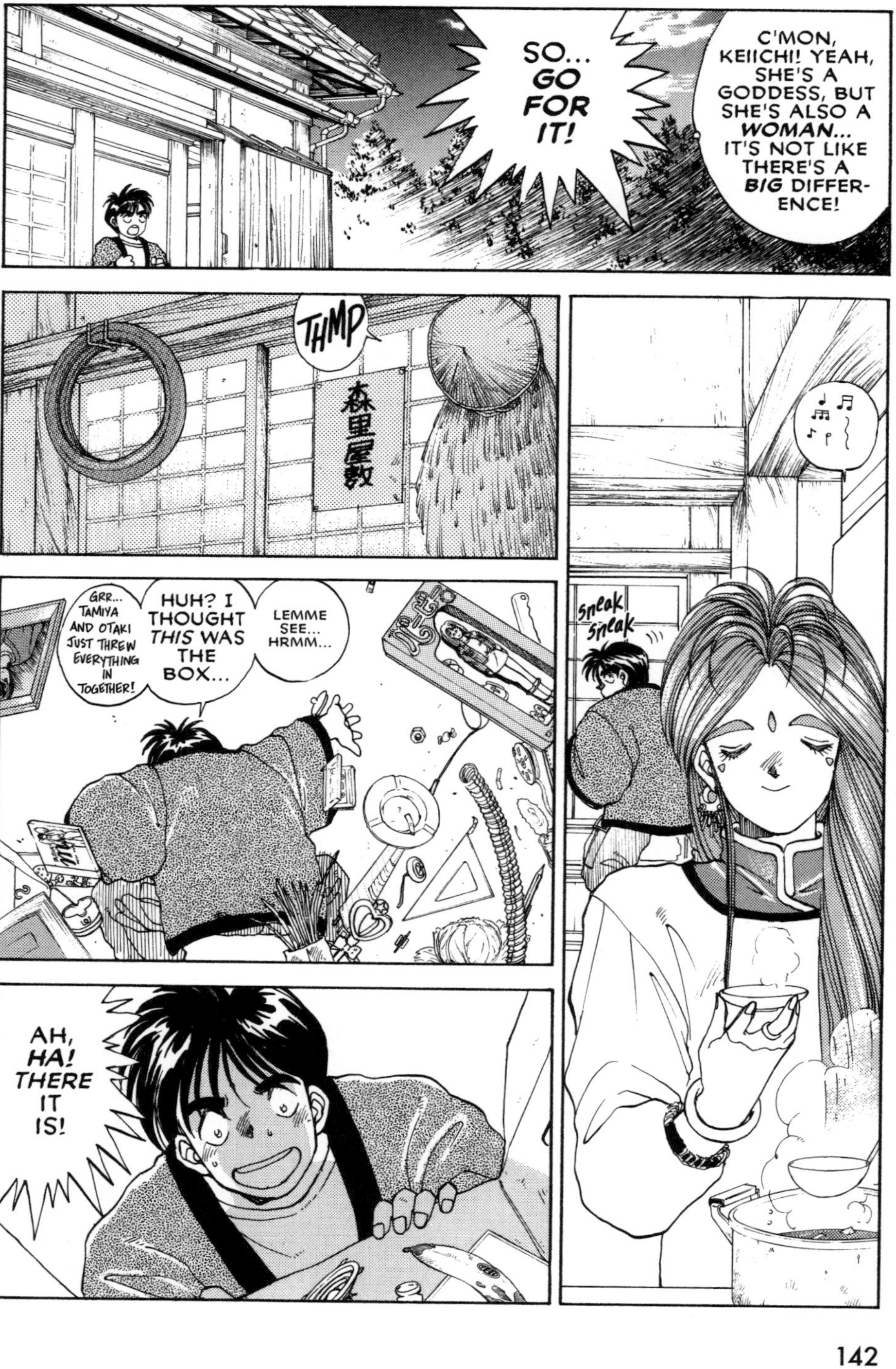
C'MON, KEIICHI! YEAH, SHE'S A GODDESS, BUT SHE'S ALSO A WOMAN... IT'S NOT LIKE THERE'S A BIG DIFFERENCE!
SO... GO FOR IT!
SNEAK SNEAK
THMP
森里屋敷
LEMME SEE... HRMM...
HUH? I THOUGHT THIS WAS THE BOX...
GRR... TAMIYA AND OTAKI JUST THREW EVERYTHING IN TOGETHER!
AH, HA! THERE IT IS!

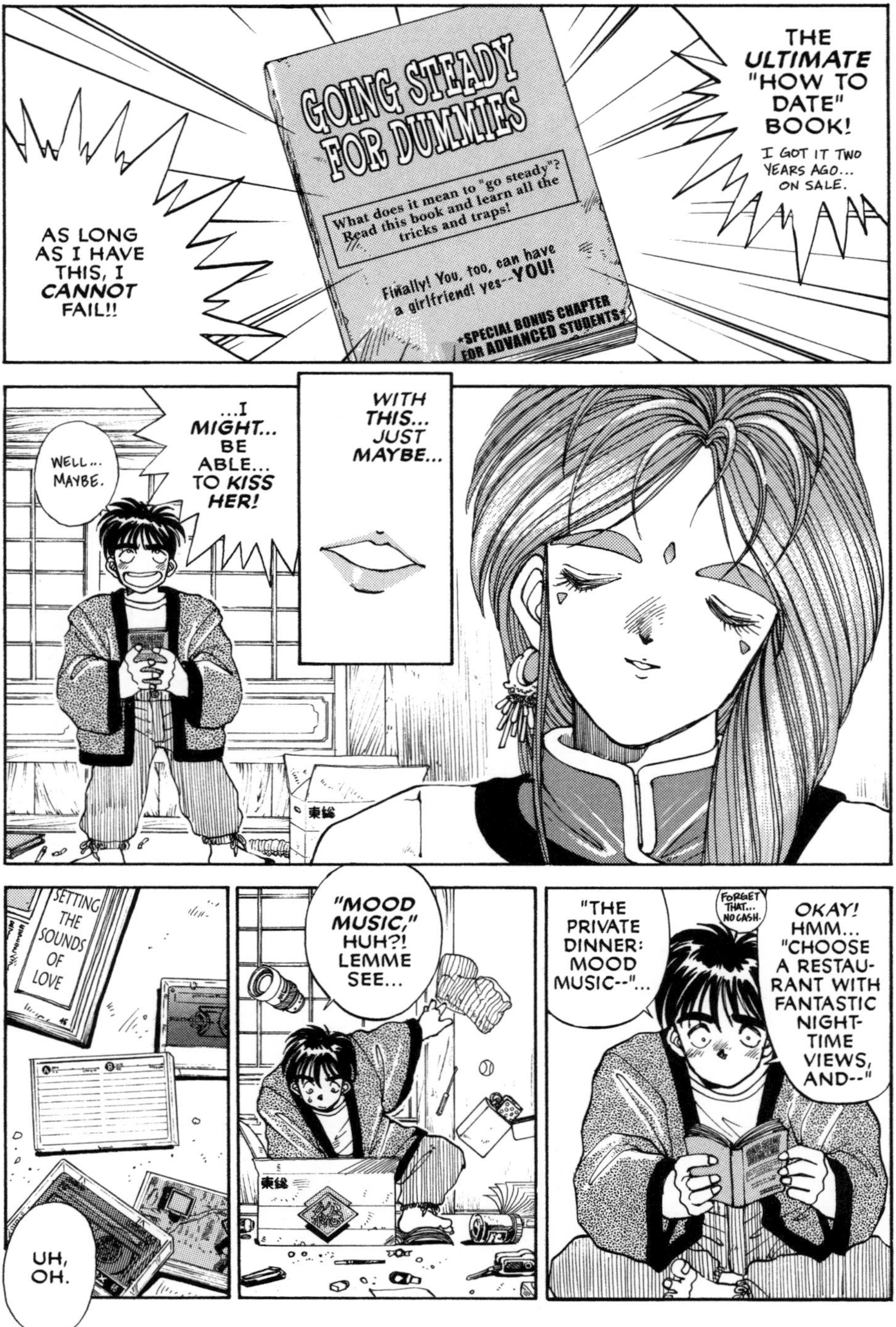
THE ULTIMATE "HOW TO DATE" BOOK!
I GOT IT TWO YEARS AGO... ON SALE.
GOING STEADY FOR DUMMIES
What does it mean to "go steady"? Read this book and learn all the tricks and traps!
Finally! You, too, can have a girlfriend! yes--YOU!
SPECIAL BONUS CHAPTER FOR ADVANCED STUDENTS
AS LONG AS I HAVE THIS, I CANNOT FAIL!!
WITH THIS... JUST MAYBE...
...I MIGHT... BE ABLE... TO KISS HER!
WELL... MAYBE.
OKAY! HMM... "CHOOSE A RESTAURANT WITH FANTASTIC NIGHT-TIME VIEWS, AND--"
FORGET THAT... NO CASH.
"THE PRIVATE DINNER: MOOD MUSIC--"...
"MOOD MUSIC," HUH?! LEMME SEE...
SETTING THE SOUNDS OF LOVE
UH, OH.

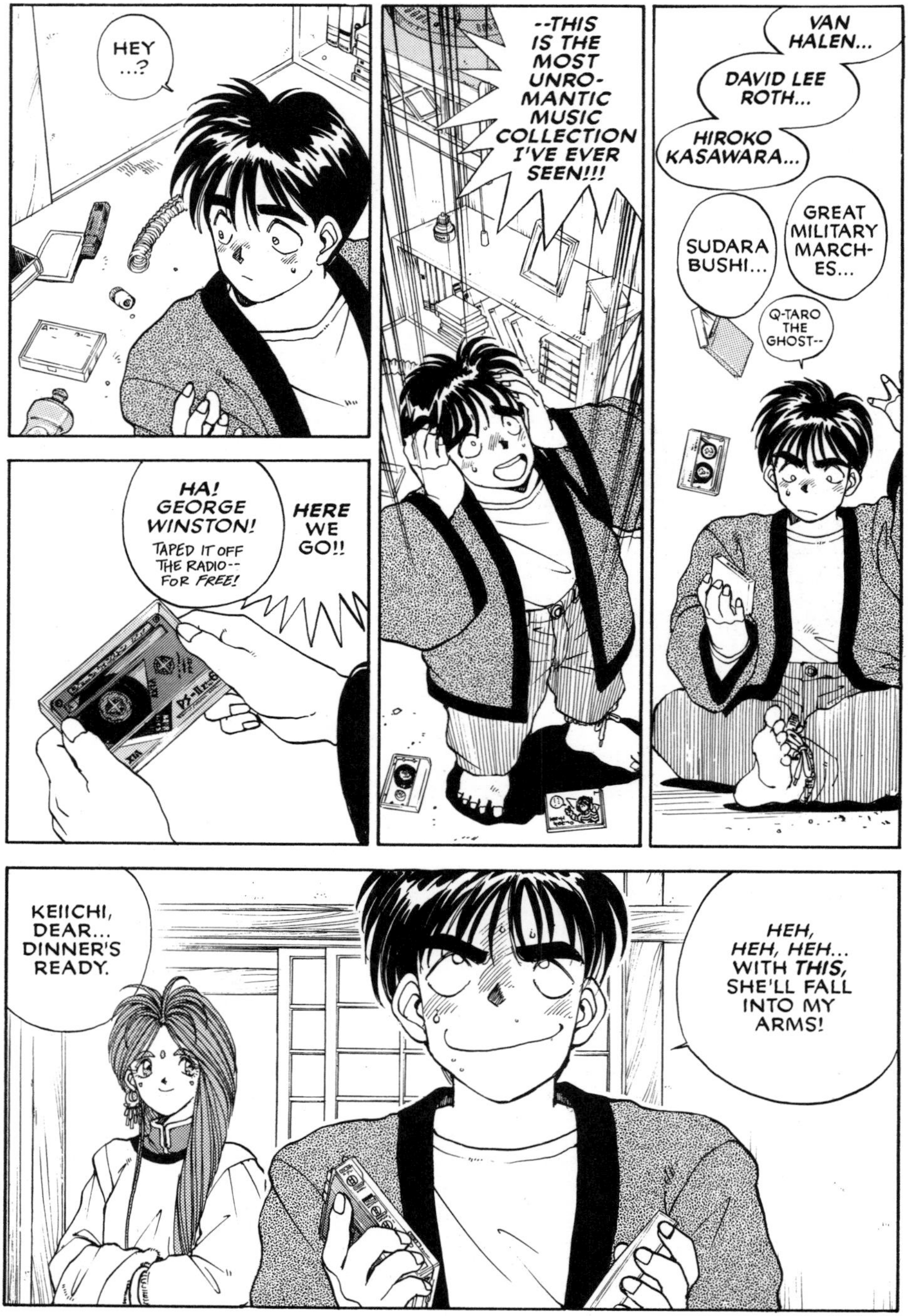
VAN HALEN...
DAVID LEE ROTH...
HIROKO KASAWARA...
GREAT MILITARY MARCH-ES...
SUDARA BUSHI...
Q-TARO THE GHOST--
--THIS IS THE MOST UNRO-MANTIC MUSIC COLLECTION I'VE EVER SEEN!!!
HEY ...?
HERE WE GO!!
HA! GEORGE WINSTON!
TAPED IT OFF THE RADIO-- FOR *FREE!*
HEH, HEH, HEH... WITH *THIS,* SHE'LL FALL INTO MY ARMS!
KEIICHI, DEAR... DINNER'S READY.

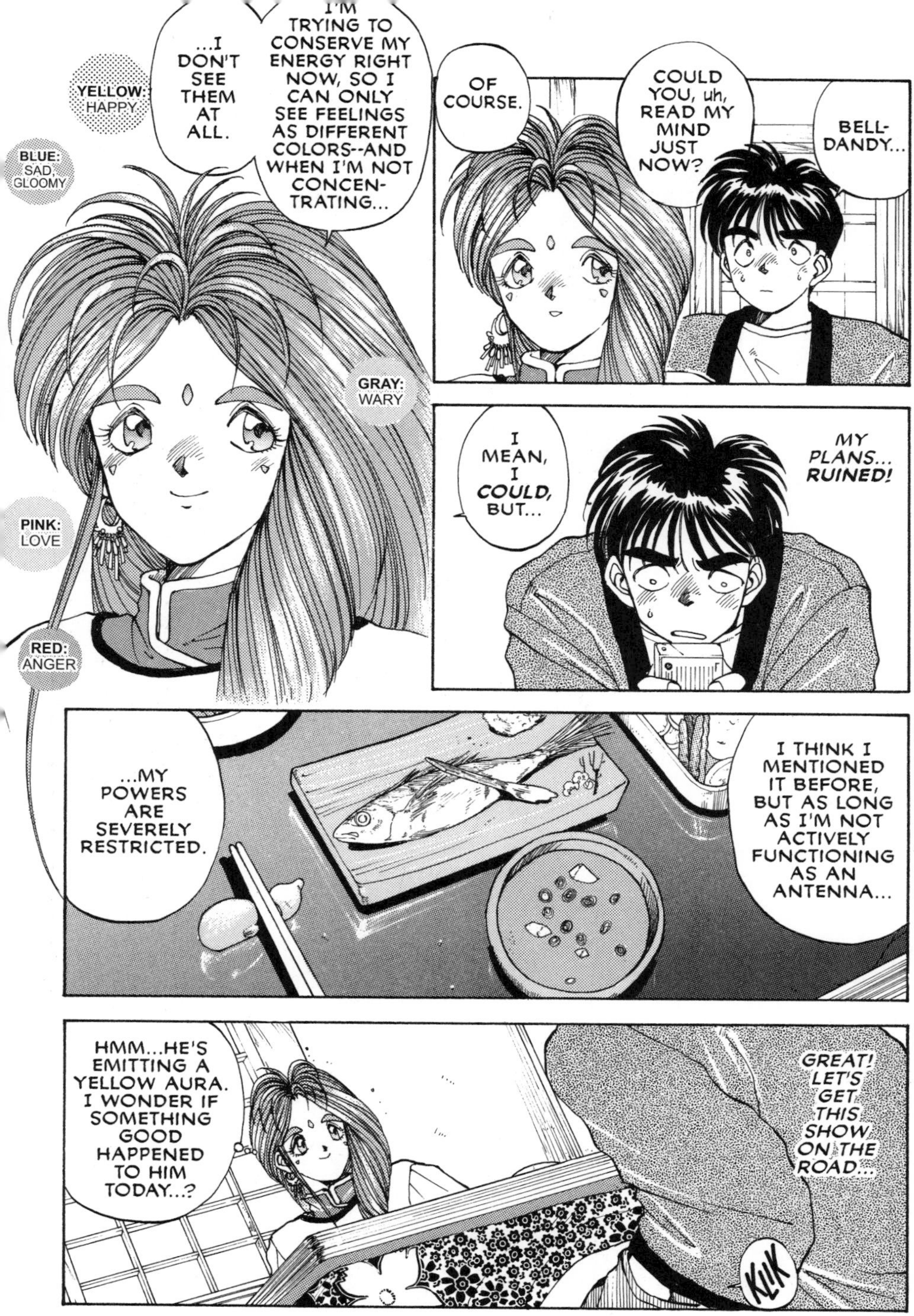
BELL-DANDY...
COULD YOU, uh, READ MY MIND JUST NOW?
OF COURSE.
MY PLANS... RUINED!
I MEAN, I COULD, BUT...
I'M TRYING TO CONSERVE MY ENERGY RIGHT NOW, SO I CAN ONLY SEE FEELINGS AS DIFFERENT COLORS--AND WHEN I'M NOT CONCENTRATING...
...I DON'T SEE THEM AT ALL.
YELLOW: HAPPY
BLUE: SAD, GLOOMY
GRAY: WARY
PINK: LOVE
RED: ANGER
I THINK I MENTIONED IT BEFORE, BUT AS LONG AS I'M NOT ACTIVELY FUNCTIONING AS AN ANTENNA...
...MY POWERS ARE SEVERELY RESTRICTED.
GREAT! LET'S GET THIS SHOW ON THE ROAD...
KLIK
HMM...HE'S EMITTING A YELLOW AURA. I WONDER IF SOMETHING GOOD HAPPENED TO HIM TODAY...?

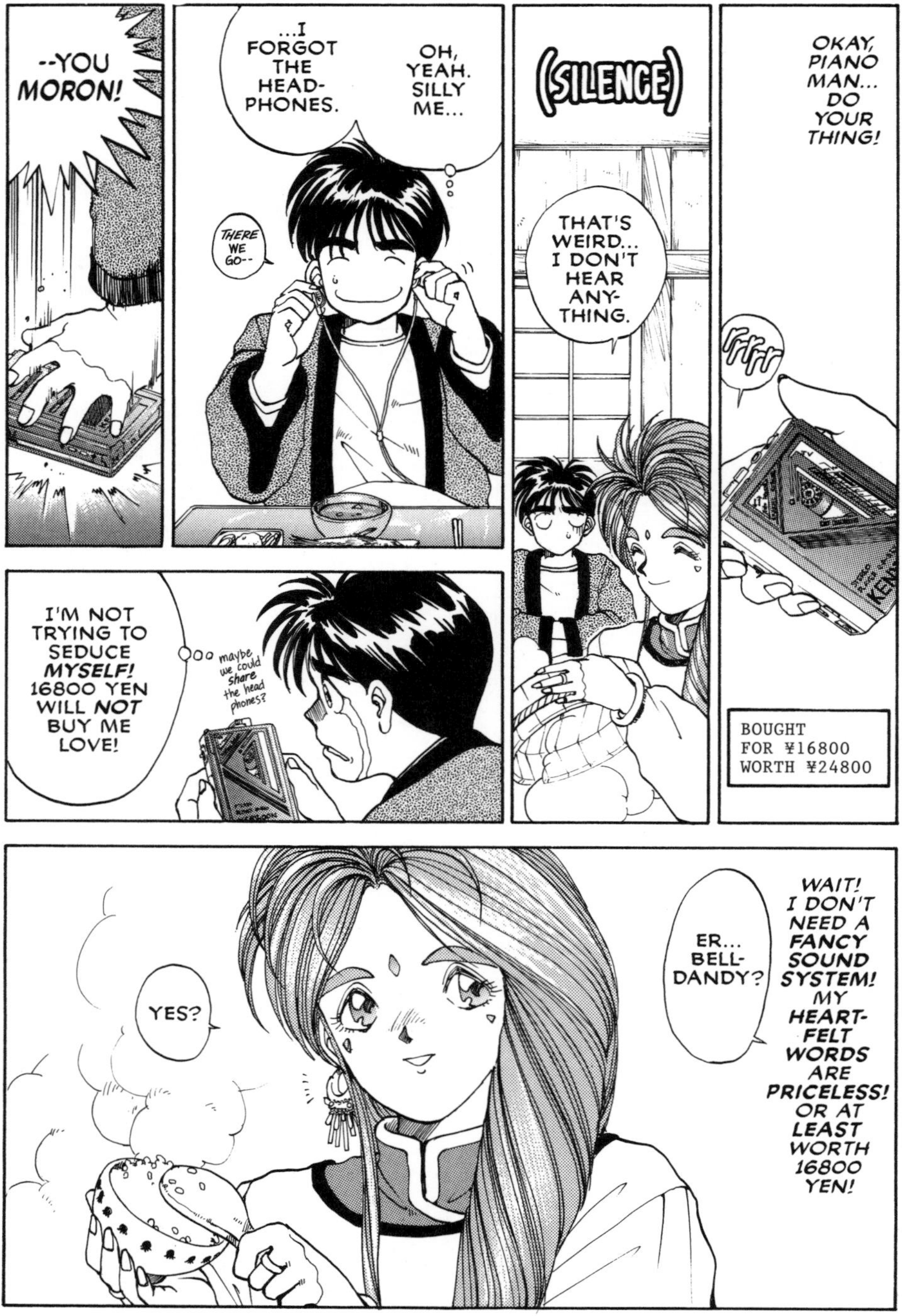
OKAY, PIANO MAN... DO YOUR THING!
rrrr
BOUGHT FOR ¥16800 WORTH ¥24800
(SILENCE)
THAT'S WEIRD... I DON'T HEAR ANYTHING.
OH, YEAH. SILLY ME...
...I FORGOT THE HEAD-PHONES.
THERE WE GO--
--YOU MORON!
maybe we could share the head phones?
I'M NOT TRYING TO SEDUCE MYSELF! 16800 YEN WILL NOT BUY ME LOVE!
WAIT! I DON'T NEED A FANCY SOUND SYSTEM! MY HEART-FELT WORDS ARE PRICELESS! OR AT LEAST WORTH 16800 YEN!
ER... BELL-DANDY?
YES?

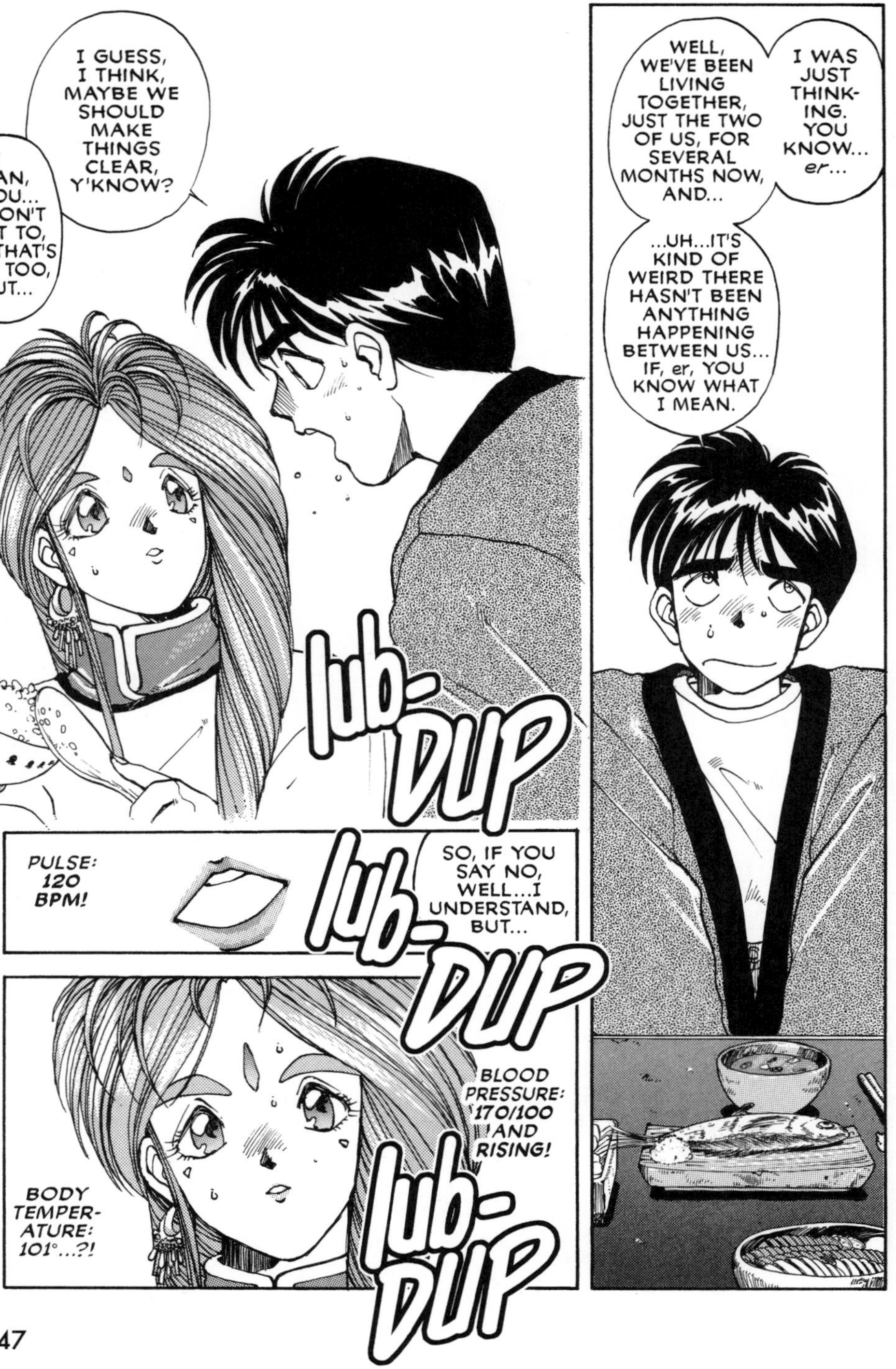
I WAS JUST THINKING. YOU KNOW... er...
WELL, WE'VE BEEN LIVING TOGETHER, JUST THE TWO OF US, FOR SEVERAL MONTHS NOW, AND...
...UH...IT'S KIND OF WEIRD THERE HASN'T BEEN ANYTHING HAPPENING BETWEEN US... IF, er, YOU KNOW WHAT I MEAN.
I GUESS, I THINK, MAYBE WE SHOULD MAKE THINGS CLEAR, Y'KNOW?
I MEAN, IF YOU... uh...DON'T WANT TO, THEN THAT'S OKAY TOO, B-BUT...
lub-DUP
SO, IF YOU SAY NO, WELL...I UNDERSTAND, BUT...
PULSE: 120 BPM!
lub-DUP
BLOOD PRESSURE: 170/100 AND RISING!
BODY TEMPERATURE: 101°...?!
lub-DUP

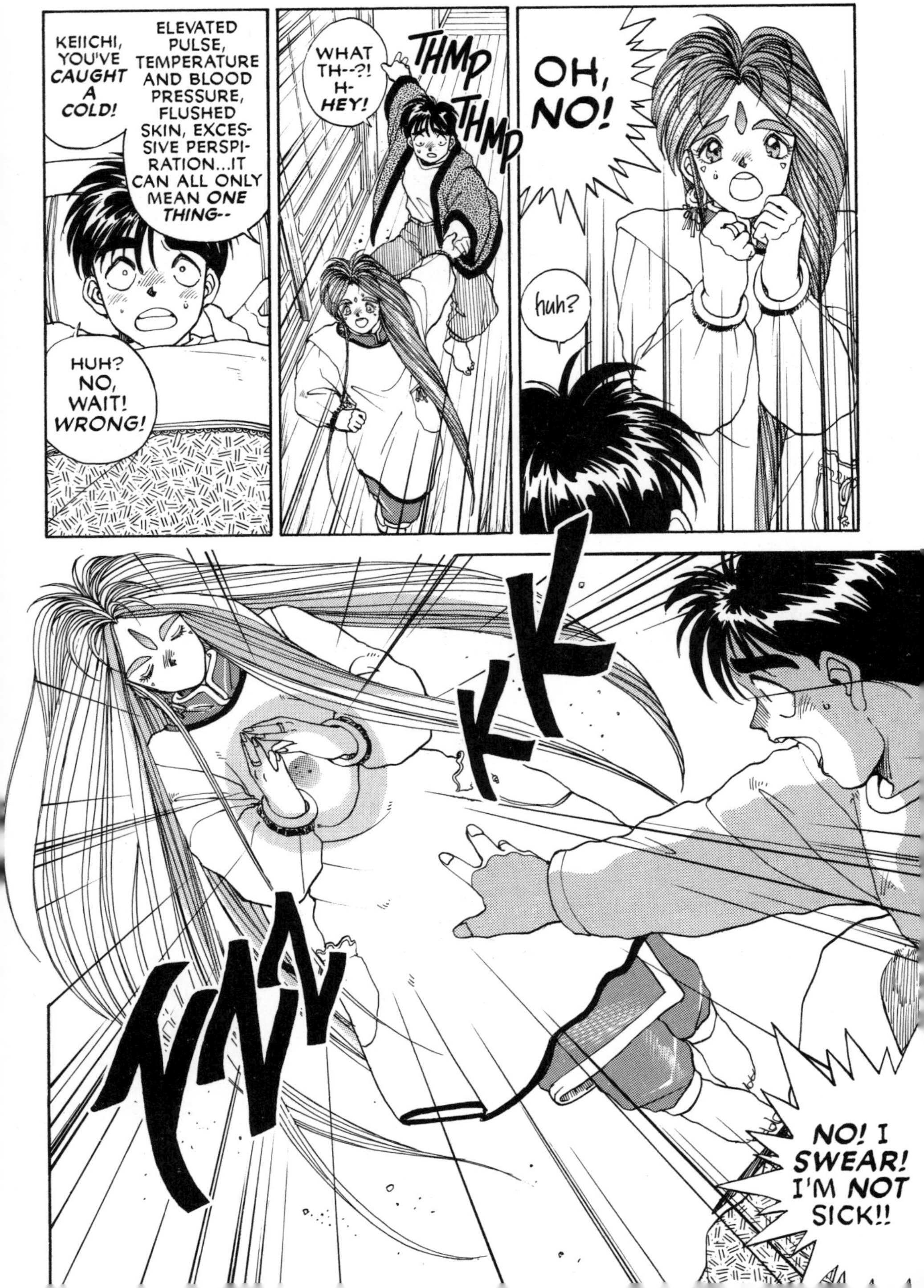
OH, NO!
huh?
THMP THMP
WHAT TH--?! H-HEY!
ELEVATED PULSE, TEMPERATURE AND BLOOD PRESSURE, FLUSHED SKIN, EXCESSIVE PERSPIRATION...IT CAN ALL ONLY MEAN ONE THING--
KEIICHI, YOU'VE CAUGHT A COLD!
HUH? NO, WAIT! WRONG!
KK
NO! I SWEAR! I'M NOT SICK!!

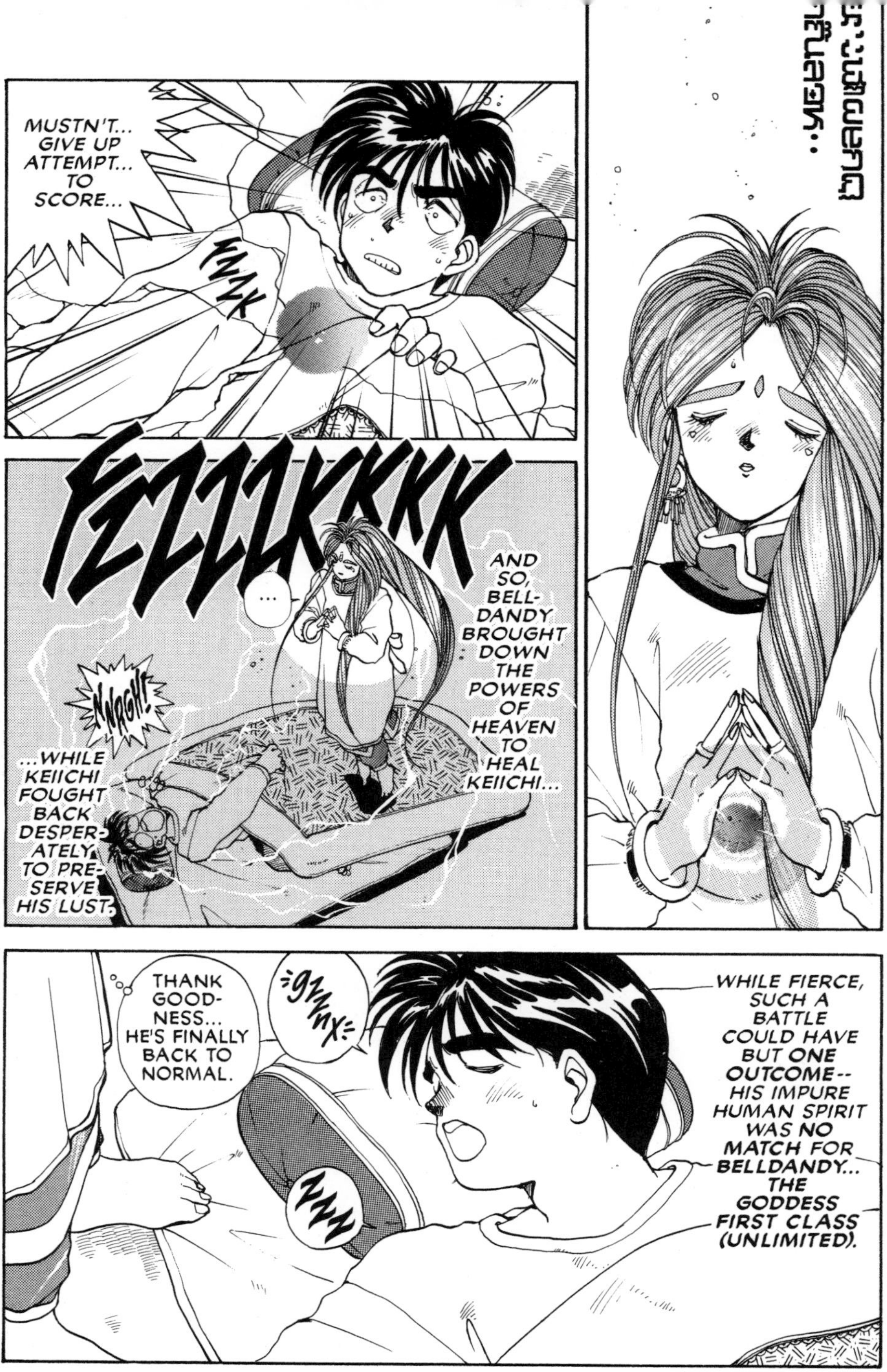
MUSTN'T... GIVE UP ATTEMPT... TO SCORE...
FZZZKKKK
AND SO, BELLDANDY BROUGHT DOWN THE POWERS OF HEAVEN TO HEAL KEIICHI...
...
N'NRGH!
...WHILE KEIICHI FOUGHT BACK DESPERATELY TO PRESERVE HIS LUST.
WHILE FIERCE, SUCH A BATTLE COULD HAVE BUT ONE OUTCOME-- HIS IMPURE HUMAN SPIRIT WAS NO MATCH FOR BELLDANDY... THE GODDESS FIRST CLASS (UNLIMITED).
gnnx
THANK GOODNESS... HE'S FINALLY BACK TO NORMAL.

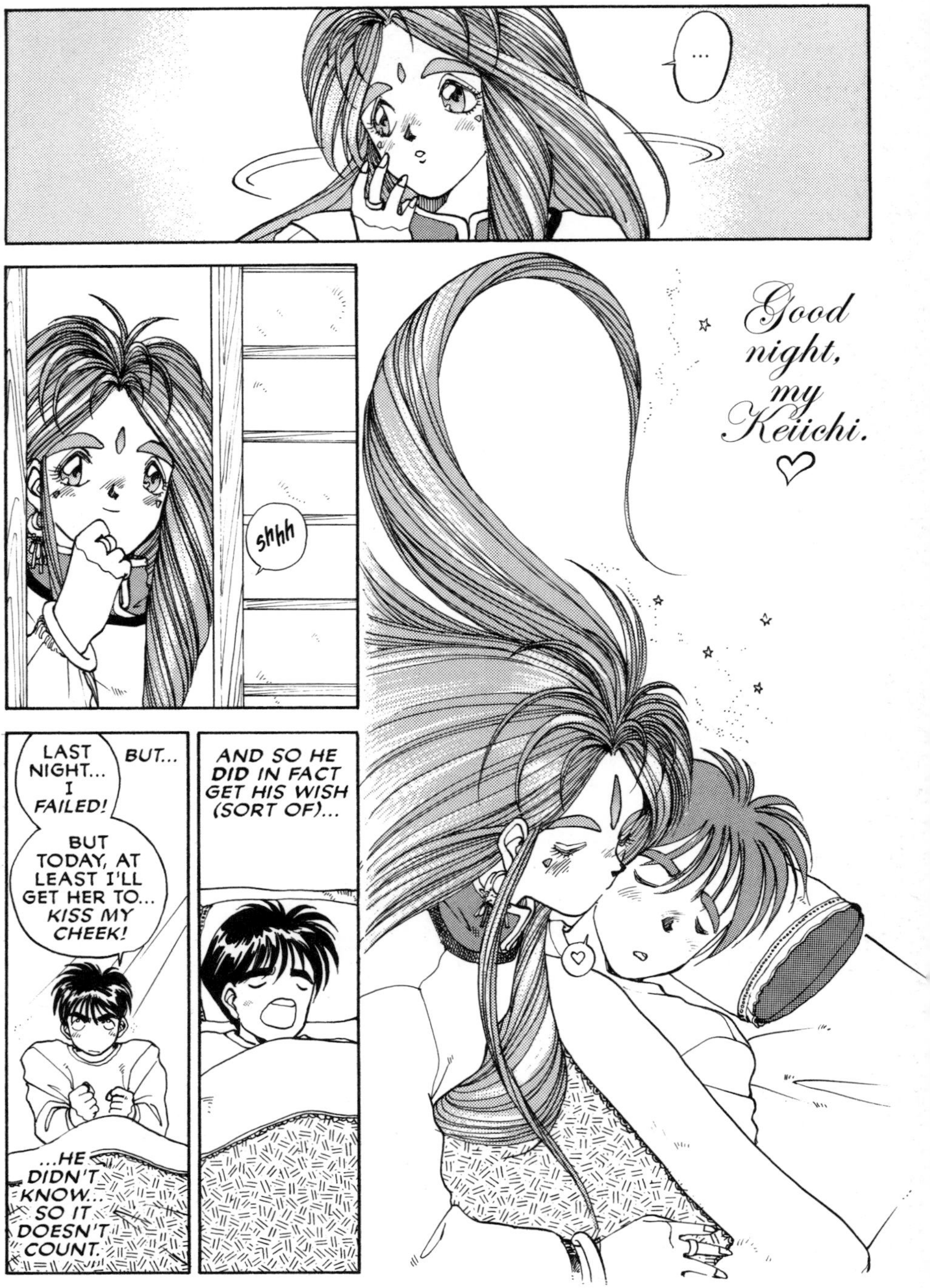
...
Good night, my Keiichi. ♡
shhh
AND SO HE DID IN FACT GET HIS WISH (SORT OF)...
BUT...
LAST NIGHT... I FAILED!
BUT TODAY, AT LEAST I'LL GET HER TO... KISS MY CHEEK!
...HE DIDN'T KNOW... SO IT DOESN'T COUNT.

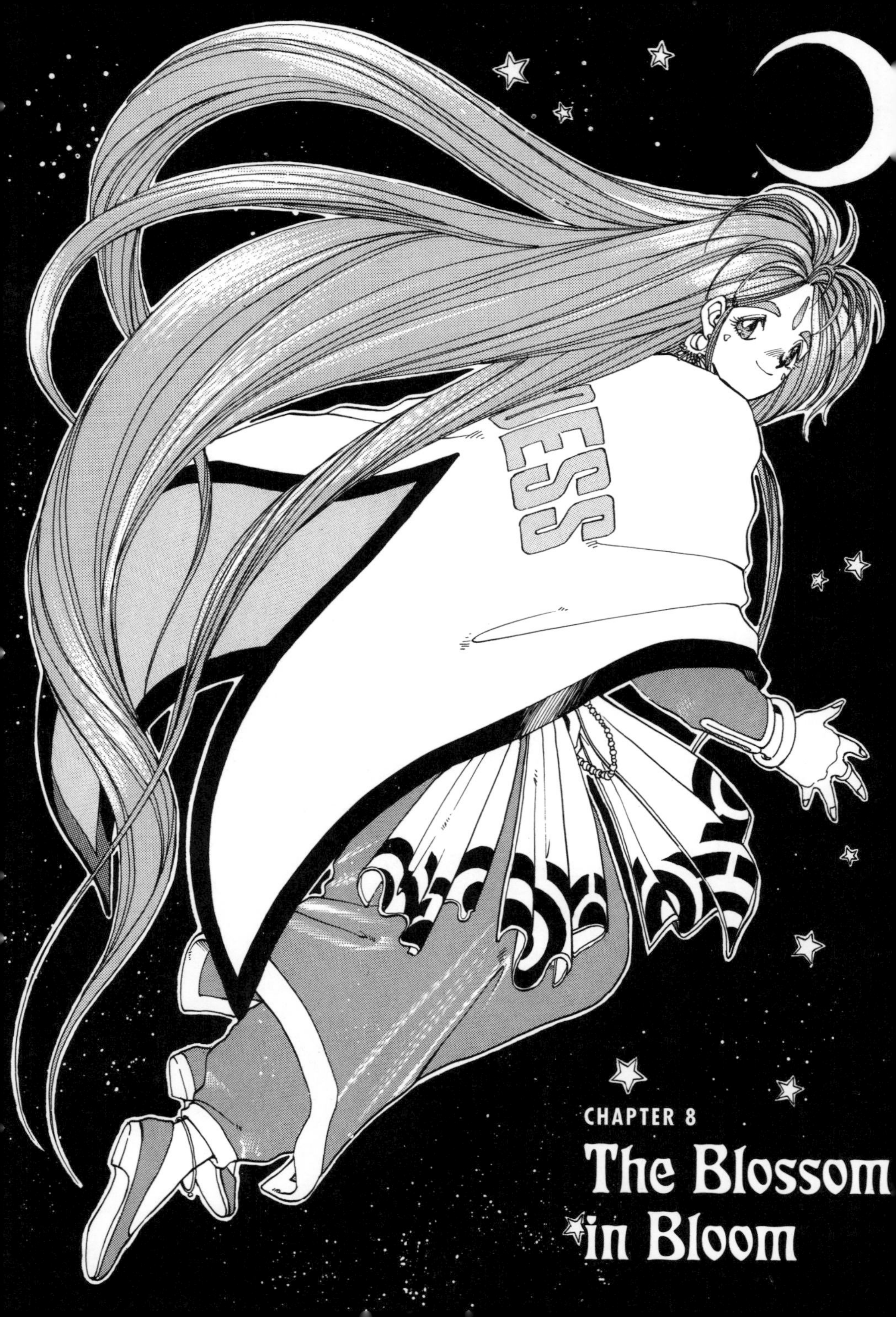
DESS

CHAPTER 8

The Blossom in Bloom

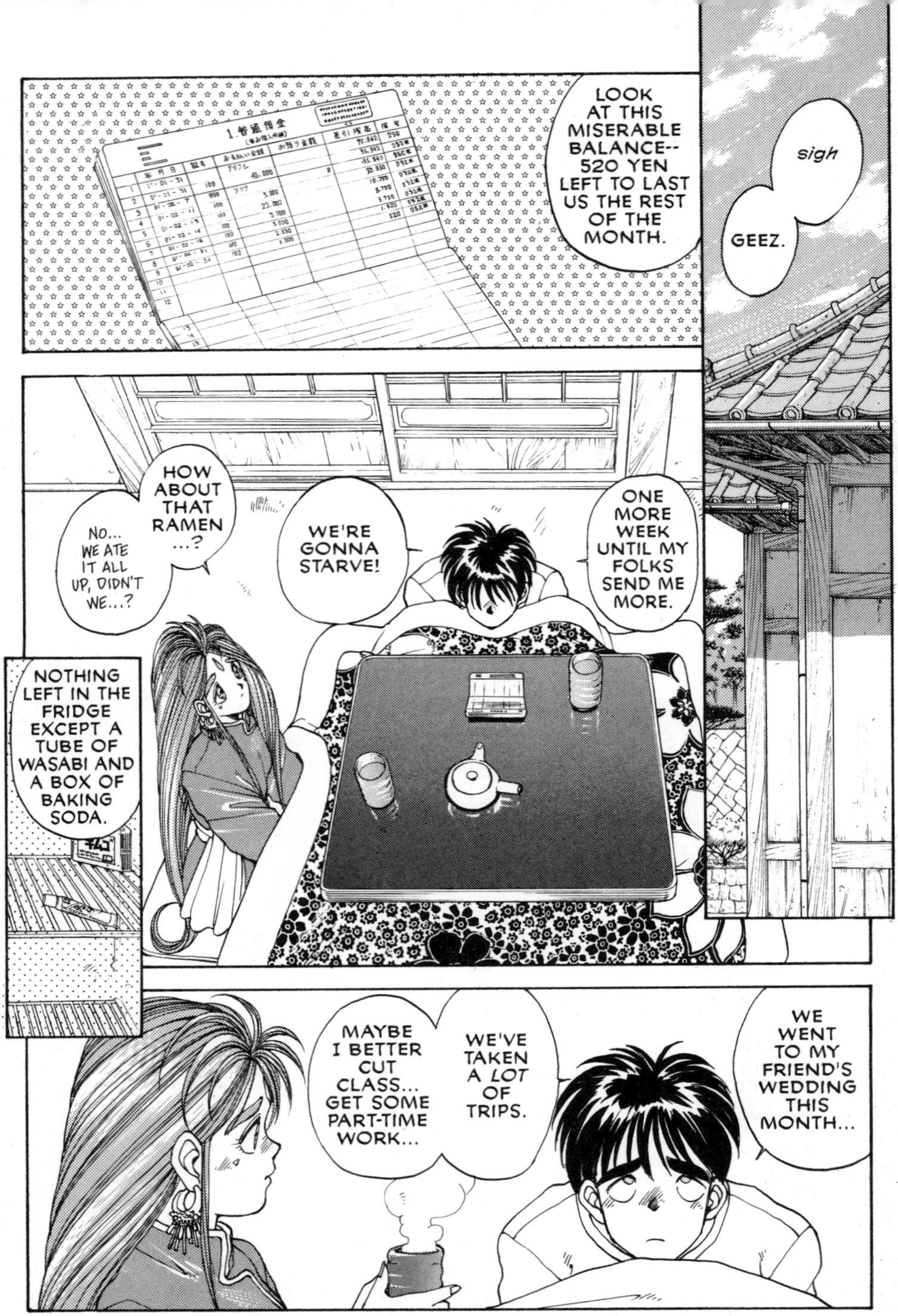
sigh
GEEZ.
LOOK AT THIS MISERABLE BALANCE-- 520 YEN LEFT TO LAST US THE REST OF THE MONTH.
ONE MORE WEEK UNTIL MY FOLKS SEND ME MORE.
WE'RE GONNA STARVE!
HOW ABOUT THAT RAMEN ...?
NO... WE ATE IT ALL UP, DIDN'T WE...?
NOTHING LEFT IN THE FRIDGE EXCEPT A TUBE OF WASABI AND A BOX OF BAKING SODA.
WE WENT TO MY FRIEND'S WEDDING THIS MONTH...
WE'VE TAKEN A *LOT* OF TRIPS.
MAYBE I BETTER CUT CLASS... GET SOME PART-TIME WORK...

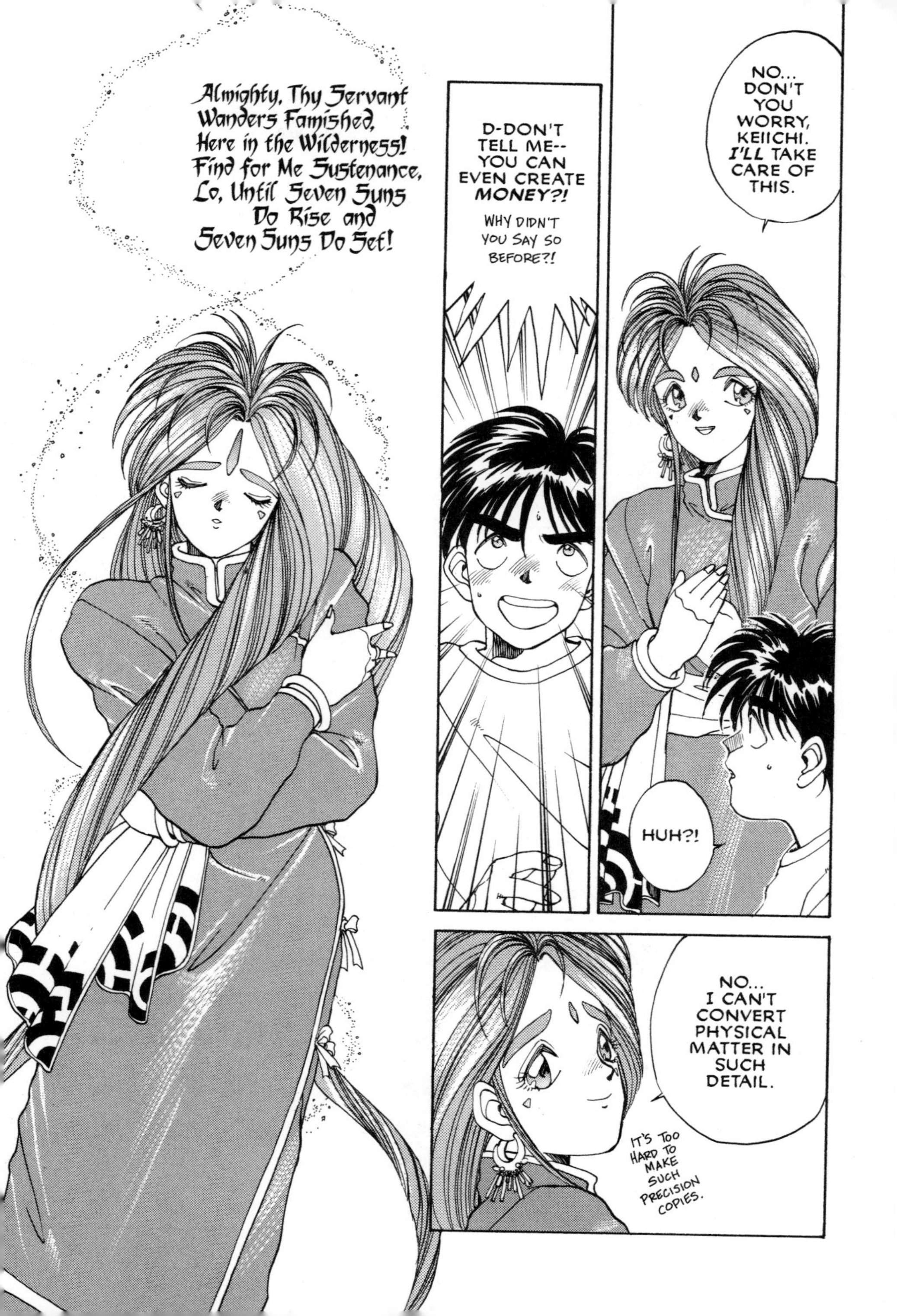
NO... DON'T YOU WORRY, KEIICHI. I'LL TAKE CARE OF THIS.
HUH?!
D-DON'T TELL ME-- YOU CAN EVEN CREATE MONEY?!
WHY DIDN'T YOU SAY SO BEFORE?!
NO... I CAN'T CONVERT PHYSICAL MATTER IN SUCH DETAIL.
IT'S TOO HARD TO MAKE SUCH PRECISION COPIES.
Almighty, Thy Servant Wanders Famished, Here in the Wilderness! Find for Me Sustenance, Lo, Until Seven Suns Do Rise and Seven Suns Do Set!

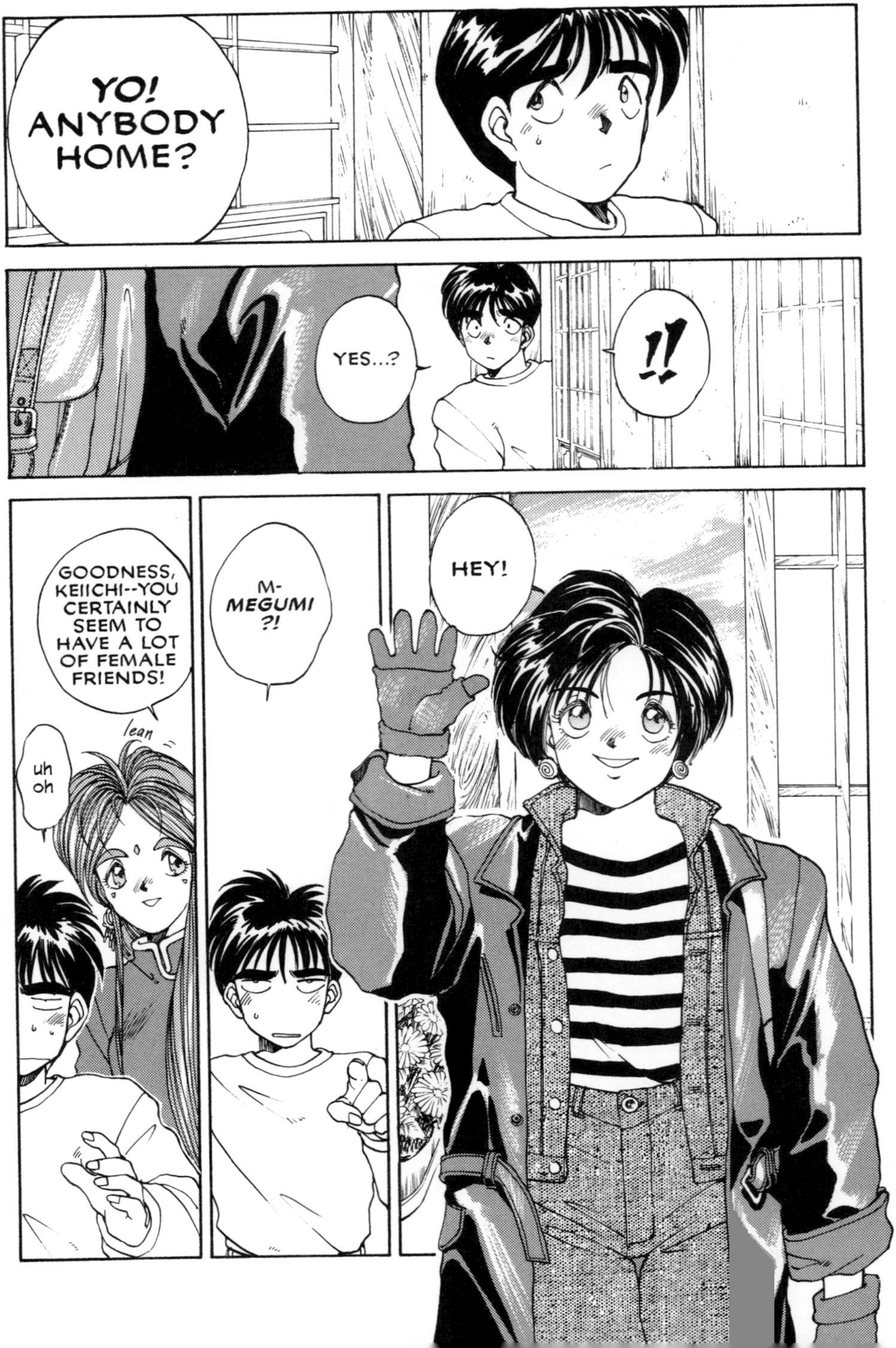
YO! ANYBODY HOME?
!!
YES...?
HEY!
M-MEGUMI?!
GOODNESS, KEIICHI--YOU CERTAINLY SEEM TO HAVE A LOT OF FEMALE FRIENDS!
lean
uh oh

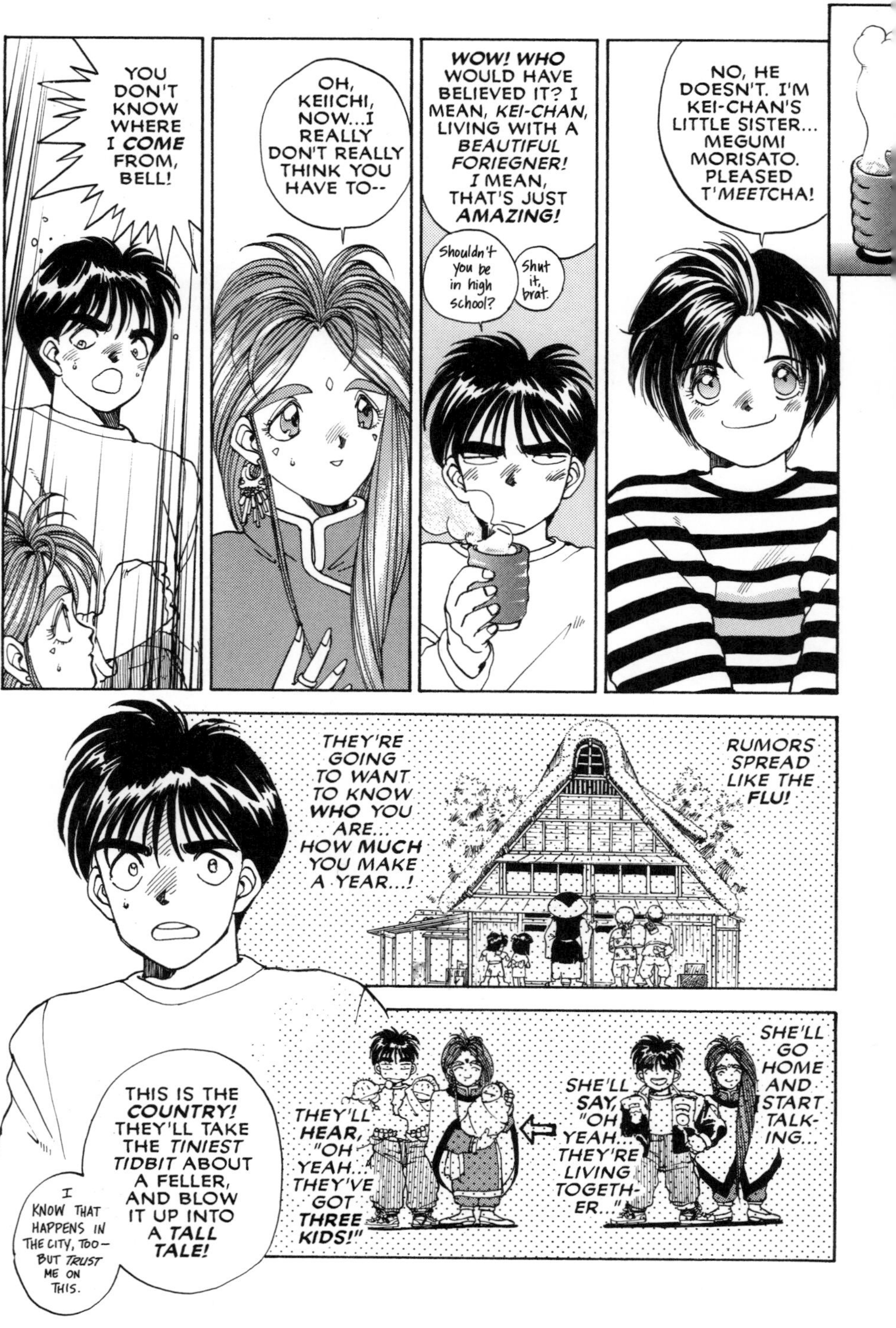
NO, HE DOESN'T. I'M KEI-CHAN'S LITTLE SISTER... MEGUMI MORISATO. PLEASED T'MEETCHA!
WOW! WHO WOULD HAVE BELIEVED IT? I MEAN, KEI-CHAN, LIVING WITH A BEAUTIFUL FORIEGNER! I MEAN, THAT'S JUST AMAZING!
Shut it, brat.
Shouldn't you be in high school?
OH, KEIICHI, NOW...I REALLY DON'T REALLY THINK YOU HAVE TO--
YOU DON'T KNOW WHERE I COME FROM, BELL!
RUMORS SPREAD LIKE THE FLU!
THEY'RE GOING TO WANT TO KNOW WHO YOU ARE... HOW MUCH YOU MAKE A YEAR...!
SHE'LL GO HOME AND START TALK-ING...
SHE'LL SAY, "OH YEAH... THEY'RE LIVING TOGETH-ER..."
THEY'LL HEAR, "OH YEAH... THEY'VE GOT THREE KIDS!"
THIS IS THE COUNTRY! THEY'LL TAKE THE TINIEST TIDBIT ABOUT A FELLER, AND BLOW IT UP INTO A TALL TALE!
I KNOW THAT HAPPENS IN THE CITY, TOO—BUT TRUST ME ON THIS.

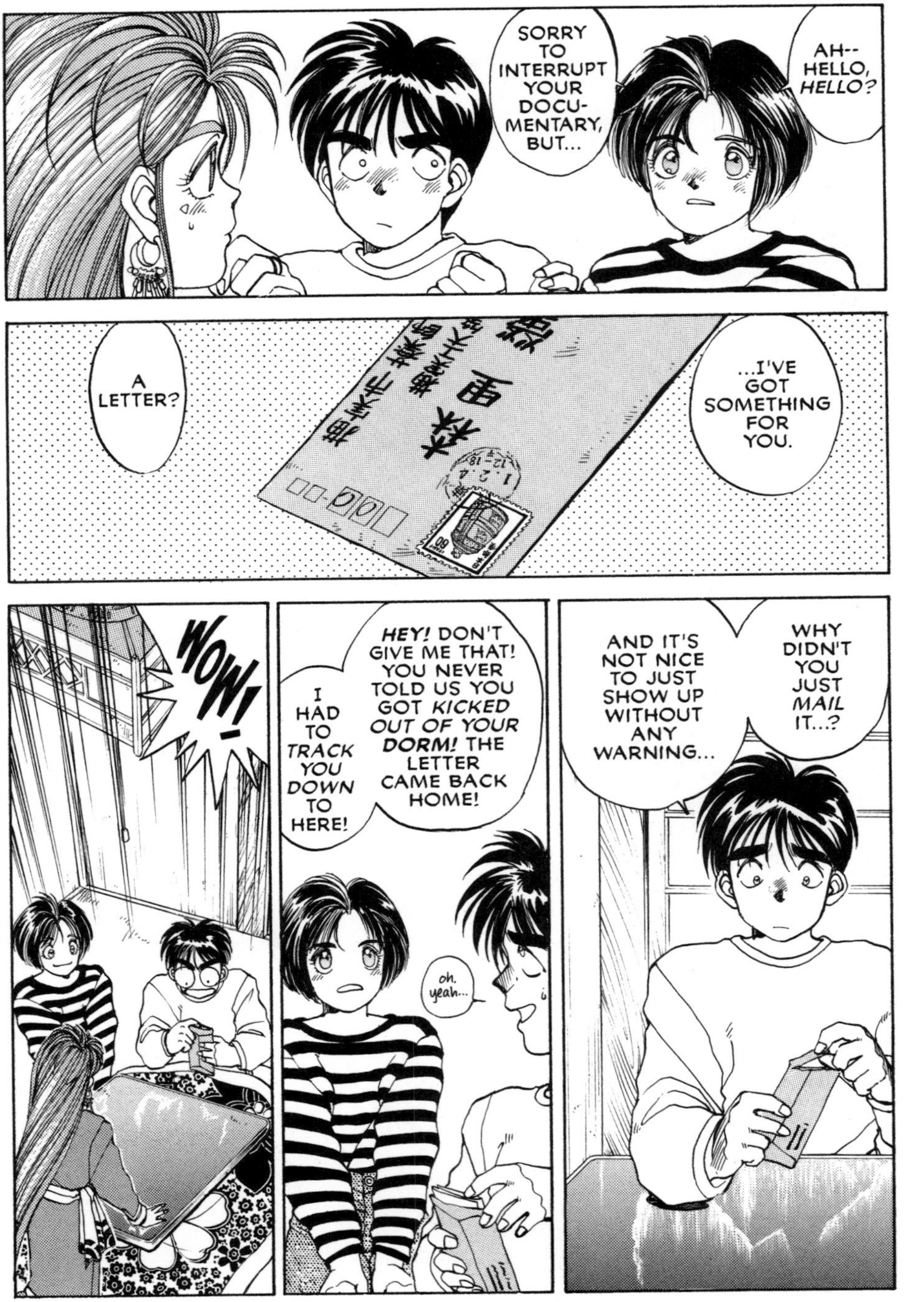
AH-- HELLO, *HELLO?*
SORRY TO INTERRUPT YOUR DOCUMENTARY, BUT...
...I'VE GOT SOMETHING FOR YOU.
A LETTER?
WHY DIDN'T YOU JUST *MAIL* IT...?
AND IT'S NOT NICE TO JUST SHOW UP WITHOUT ANY WARNING...
HEY! DON'T GIVE ME THAT! YOU NEVER TOLD US YOU GOT *KICKED OUT OF YOUR **DORM!*** THE LETTER CAME BACK HOME!
I HAD TO *TRACK* YOU DOWN TO HERE!
oh, yeah...
WOW!

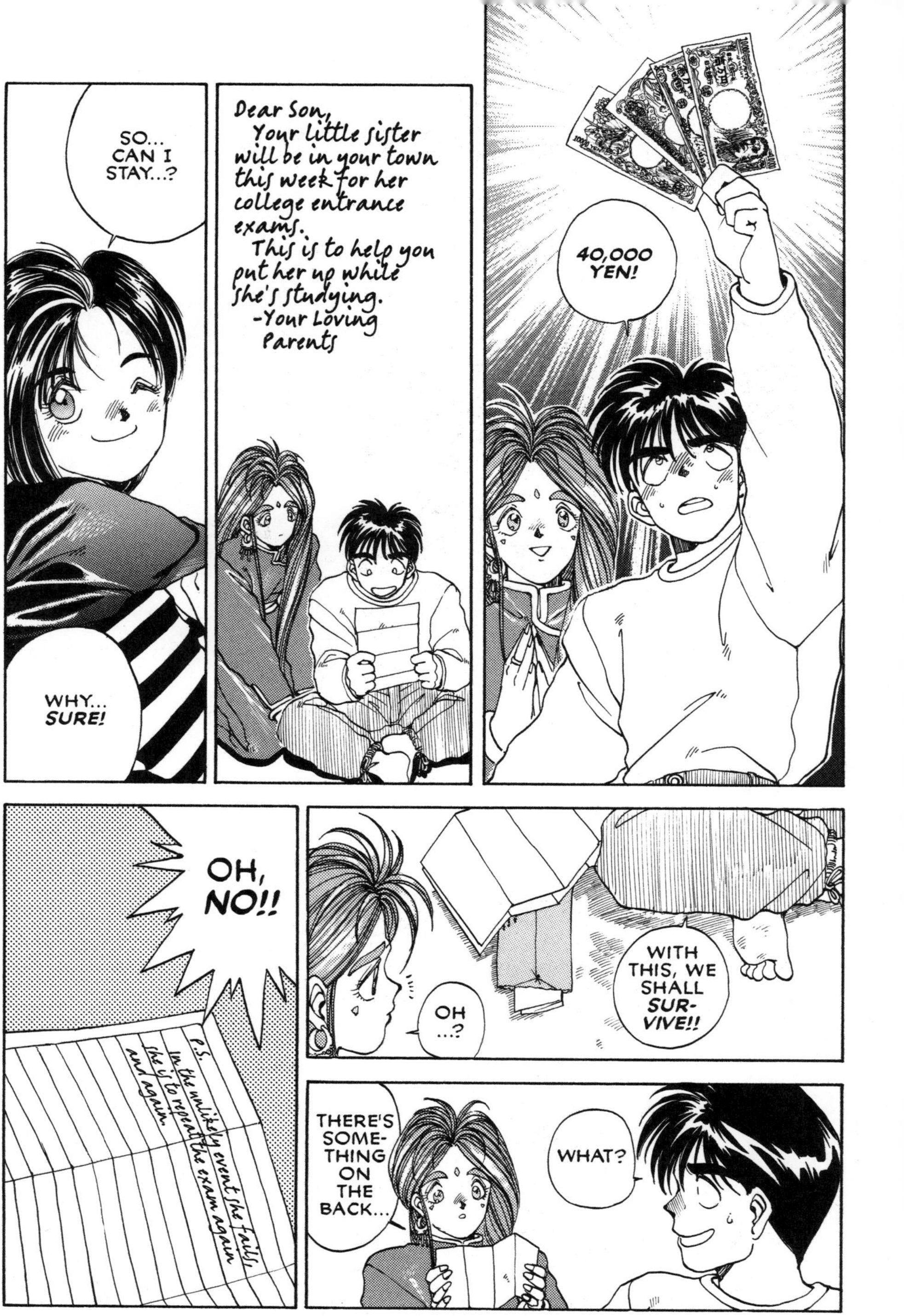
40,000 YEN!
Dear Son,
Your little sister will be in your town this week for her college entrance exams.
This is to help you put her up while she's studying.
-Your Loving Parents
SO... CAN I STAY...?
WHY... SURE!
WITH THIS, WE SHALL SUR-VIVE!!
OH ...?
WHAT?
THERE'S SOME-THING ON THE BACK...
OH, NO!!
P.S.
In the unlikely event she fails, she is to repeat the exam again and again.

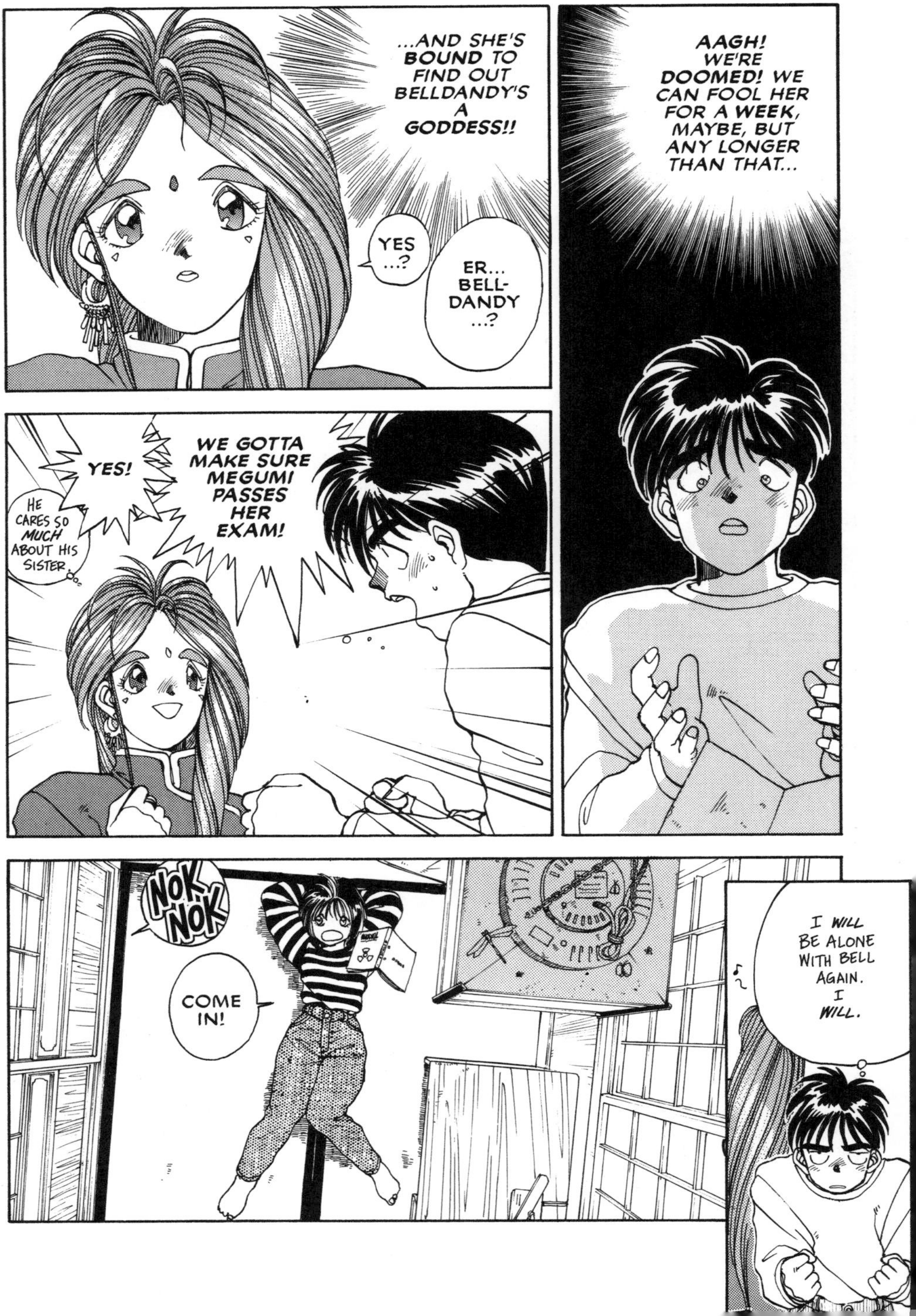
AAGH! WE'RE DOOMED! WE CAN FOOL HER FOR A WEEK, MAYBE, BUT ANY LONGER THAN THAT...
...AND SHE'S BOUND TO FIND OUT BELLDANDY'S A GODDESS!!
ER... BELL-DANDY ...?
YES ...?
WE GOTTA MAKE SURE MEGUMI PASSES HER EXAM!
YES!
HE CARES SO MUCH ABOUT HIS SISTER.
I WILL BE ALONE WITH BELL AGAIN. I WILL.
NOK NOK
COME IN!

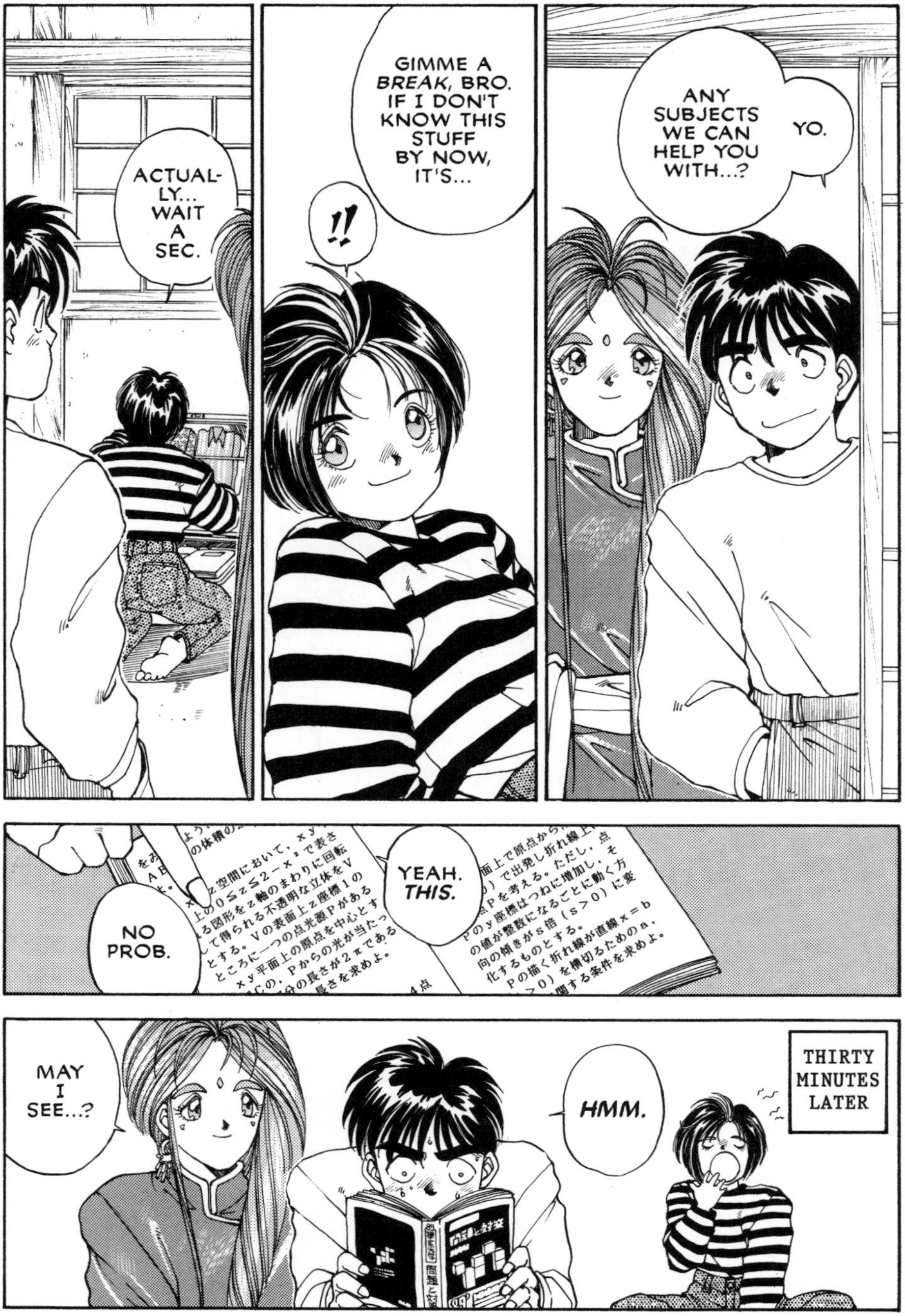

YO.
ANY SUBJECTS WE CAN HELP YOU WITH...?
GIMME A *BREAK*, BRO. IF I DON'T KNOW THIS STUFF BY NOW, IT'S...
!!
ACTUAL-LY... WAIT A SEC.
YEAH. *THIS.*
NO PROB.
THIRTY MINUTES LATER
HMM.
MAY I SEE...?

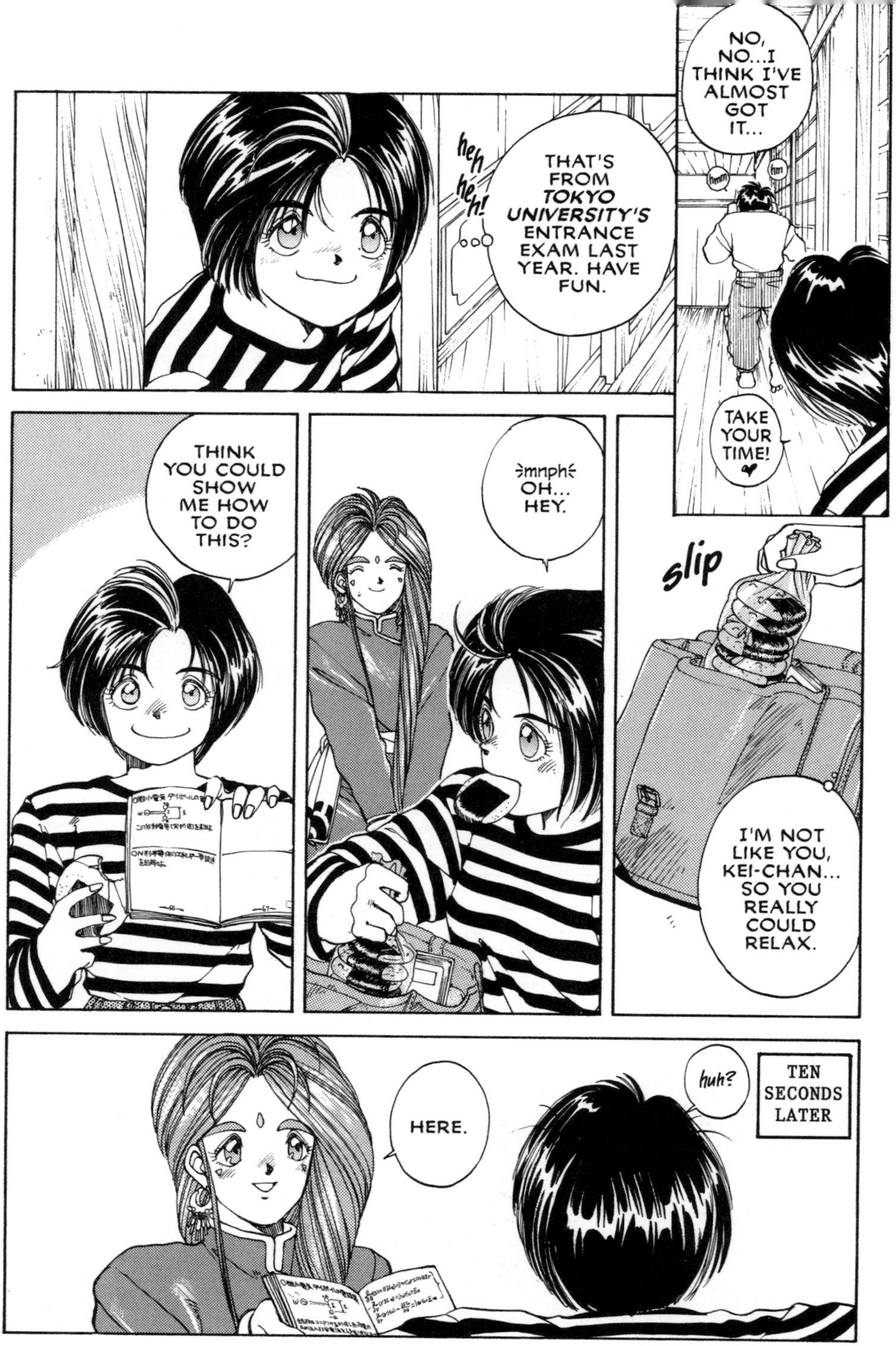
NO, NO...I THINK I'VE ALMOST GOT IT...
hm
hmm
TAKE YOUR TIME!
THAT'S FROM *TOKYO UNIVERSITY'S* ENTRANCE EXAM LAST YEAR. HAVE FUN.
heh heh!
slip
I'M NOT LIKE YOU, KEI-CHAN... SO YOU REALLY COULD RELAX.
mnph
OH... HEY.
THINK YOU COULD SHOW ME HOW TO DO THIS?
TEN SECONDS LATER
huh?
HERE.

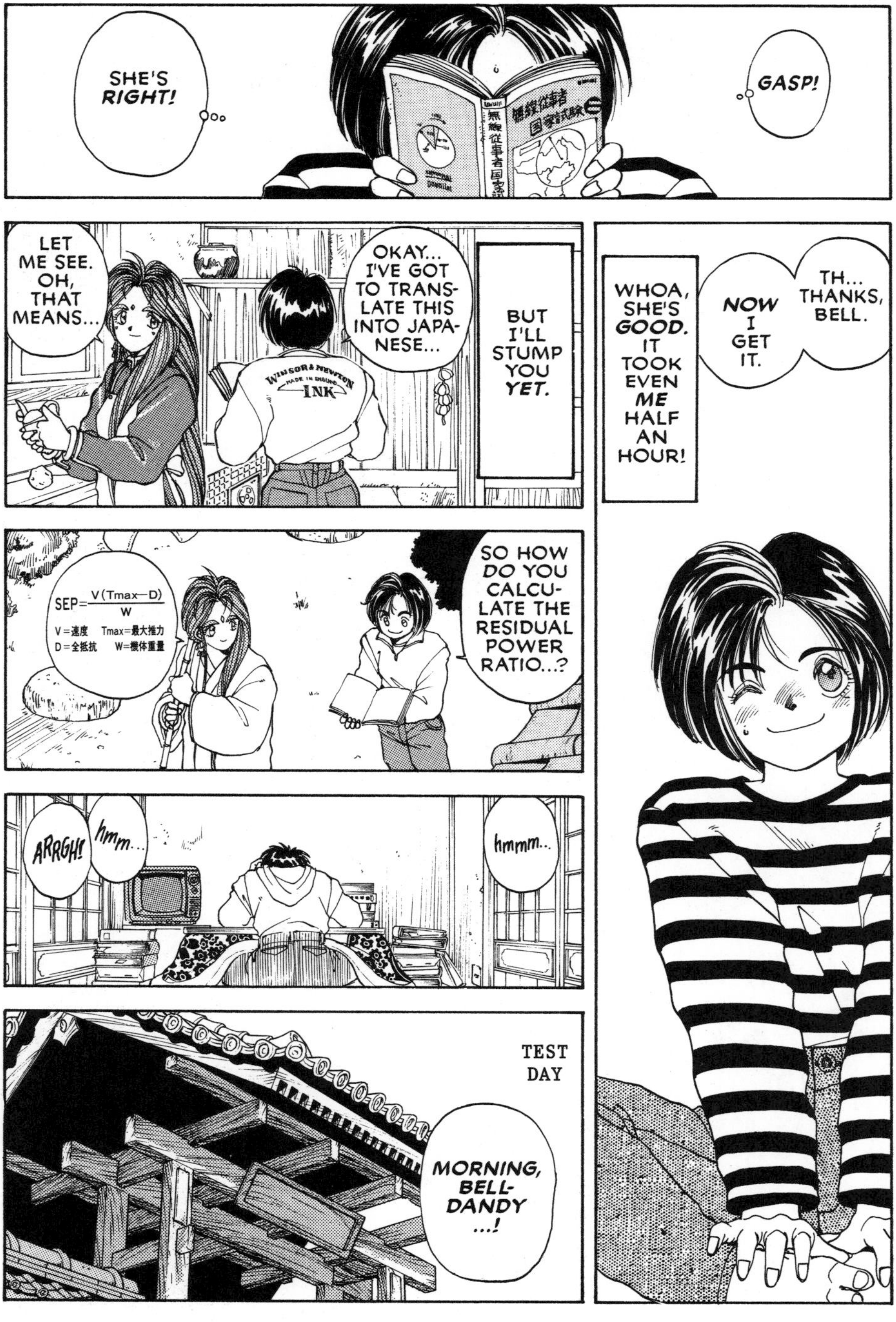
GASP!
SHE'S RIGHT!
TH... THANKS, BELL.
NOW I GET IT.
WHOA, SHE'S GOOD. IT TOOK EVEN ME HALF AN HOUR!
BUT I'LL STUMP YOU YET.
OKAY... I'VE GOT TO TRANS-LATE THIS INTO JAPA-NESE...
WINSOR & NEWTON MADE IN ENGLAND INK
LET ME SEE. OH, THAT MEANS...
SO HOW DO YOU CALCULATE THE RESIDUAL POWER RATIO...?
SEP=V(Tmax—D)/W
V=速度 Tmax=最大推力
D=全抵抗 W=機体重量
hmmm...
hmm...
ARRGH!
TEST DAY
MORNING, BELL-DANDY...!

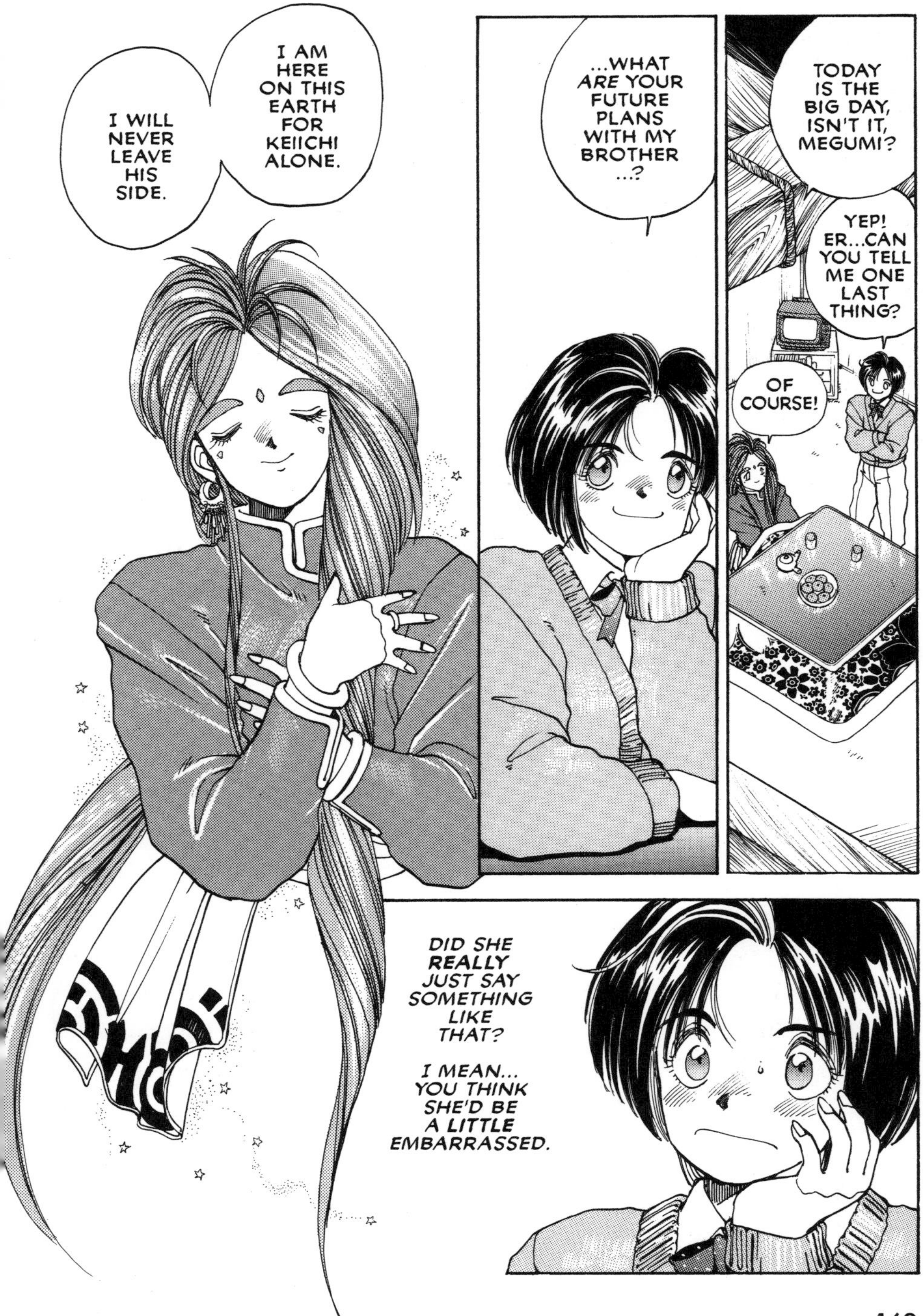
TODAY IS THE BIG DAY, ISN'T IT, MEGUMI?
YEP! ER...CAN YOU TELL ME ONE LAST THING?
OF COURSE!
...WHAT *ARE* YOUR FUTURE PLANS WITH MY BROTHER ...?
I AM HERE ON THIS EARTH FOR KEIICHI ALONE.
I WILL NEVER LEAVE HIS SIDE.
DID SHE **REALLY** JUST SAY SOMETHING LIKE THAT?
I MEAN... YOU THINK SHE'D BE A **LITTLE** EMBARRASSED.

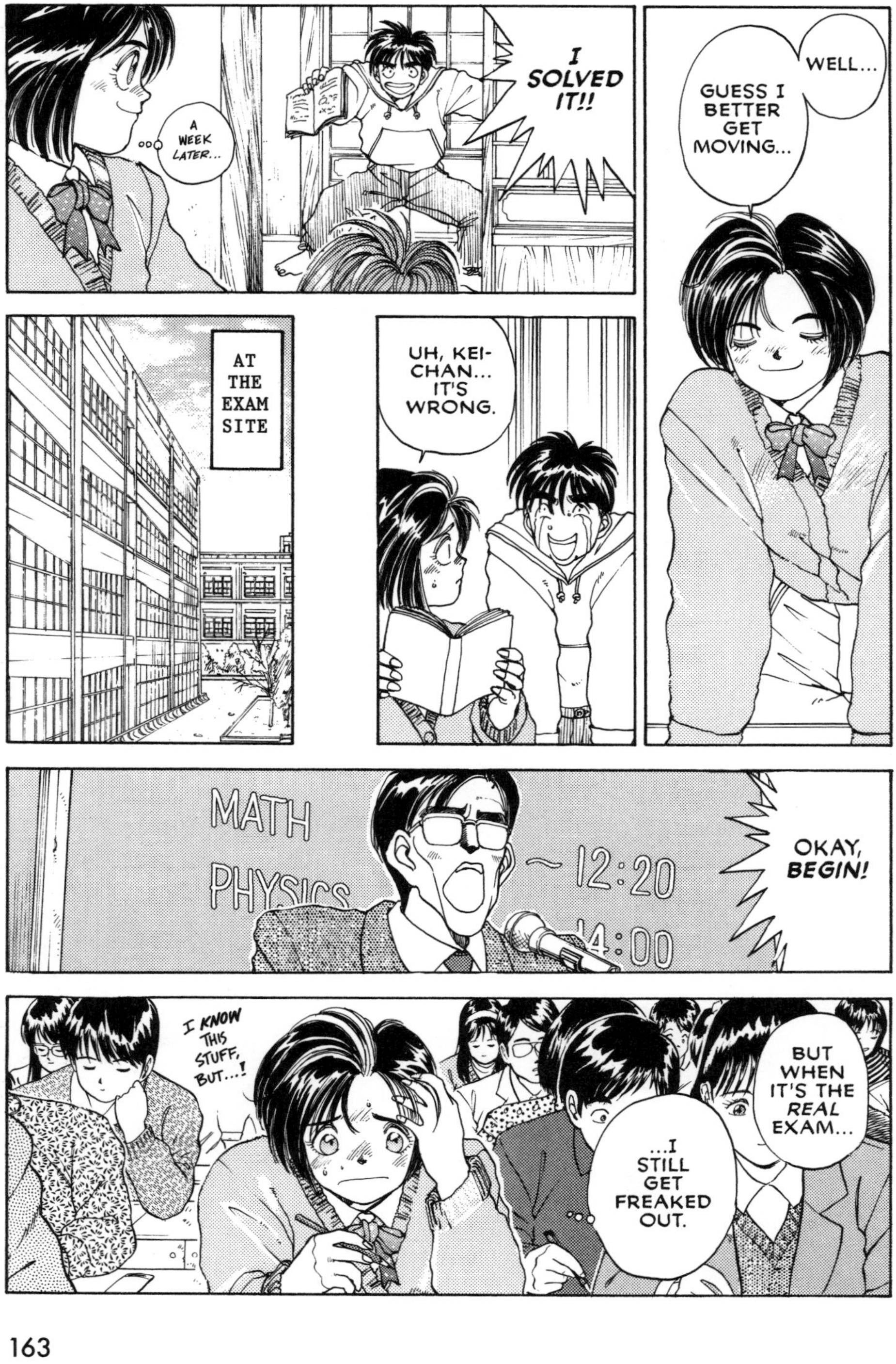
WELL...
GUESS I BETTER GET MOVING...
I SOLVED IT!!
A WEEK LATER...
UH, KEI-CHAN... IT'S WRONG.
AT THE EXAM SITE
OKAY, BEGIN!
MATH
PHYSICS
~ 12:20
14:00
BUT WHEN IT'S THE REAL EXAM...
...I STILL GET FREAKED OUT.
I KNOW THIS STUFF, BUT...!

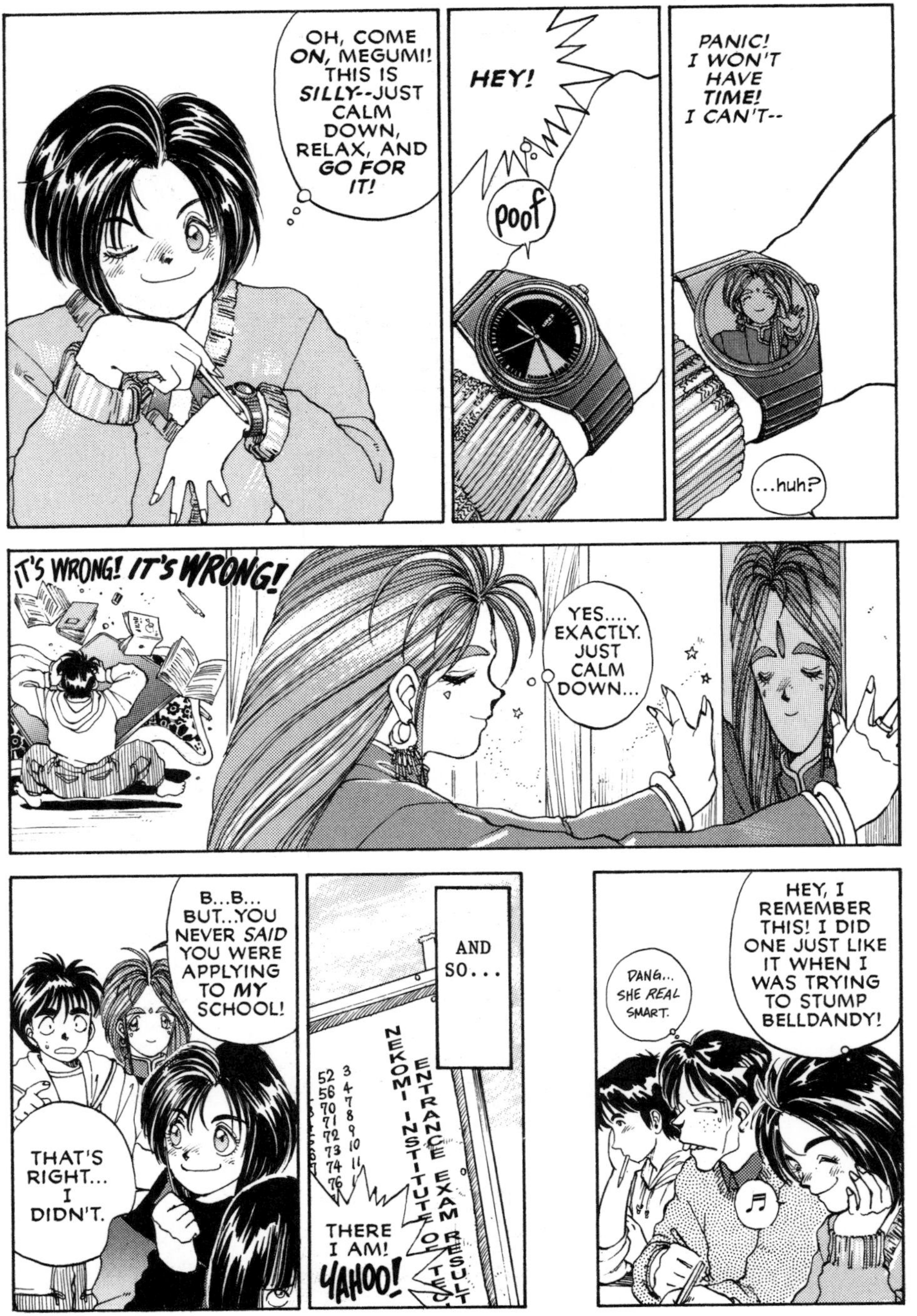
PANIC! I WON'T HAVE TIME! I CAN'T--
...huh?
HEY!
poof
OH, COME ON, MEGUMI! THIS IS SILLY--JUST CALM DOWN, RELAX, AND GO FOR IT!
YES.... EXACTLY. JUST CALM DOWN...
IT'S WRONG! IT'S WRONG!
HEY, I REMEMBER THIS! I DID ONE JUST LIKE IT WHEN I WAS TRYING TO STUMP BELLDANDY!
DANG... SHE REAL SMART.
AND SO...
ENTRANCE EXAM RESULT
NEKOMI INSTITUTE OF
THERE I AM!
YAHOO!
B...B... BUT...YOU NEVER SAID YOU WERE APPLYING TO MY SCHOOL!
THAT'S RIGHT... I DIDN'T.

OH MY GODDESS!

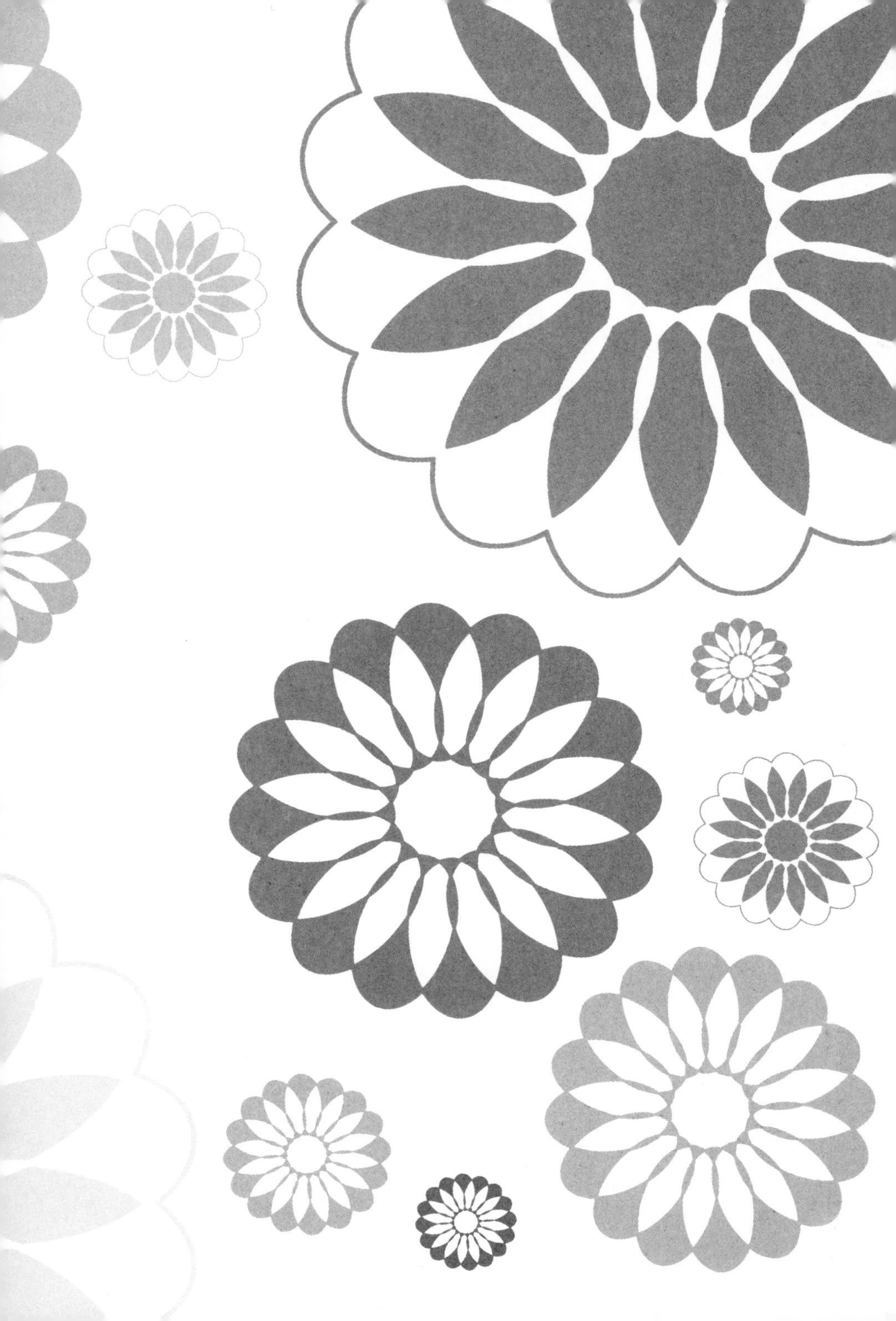

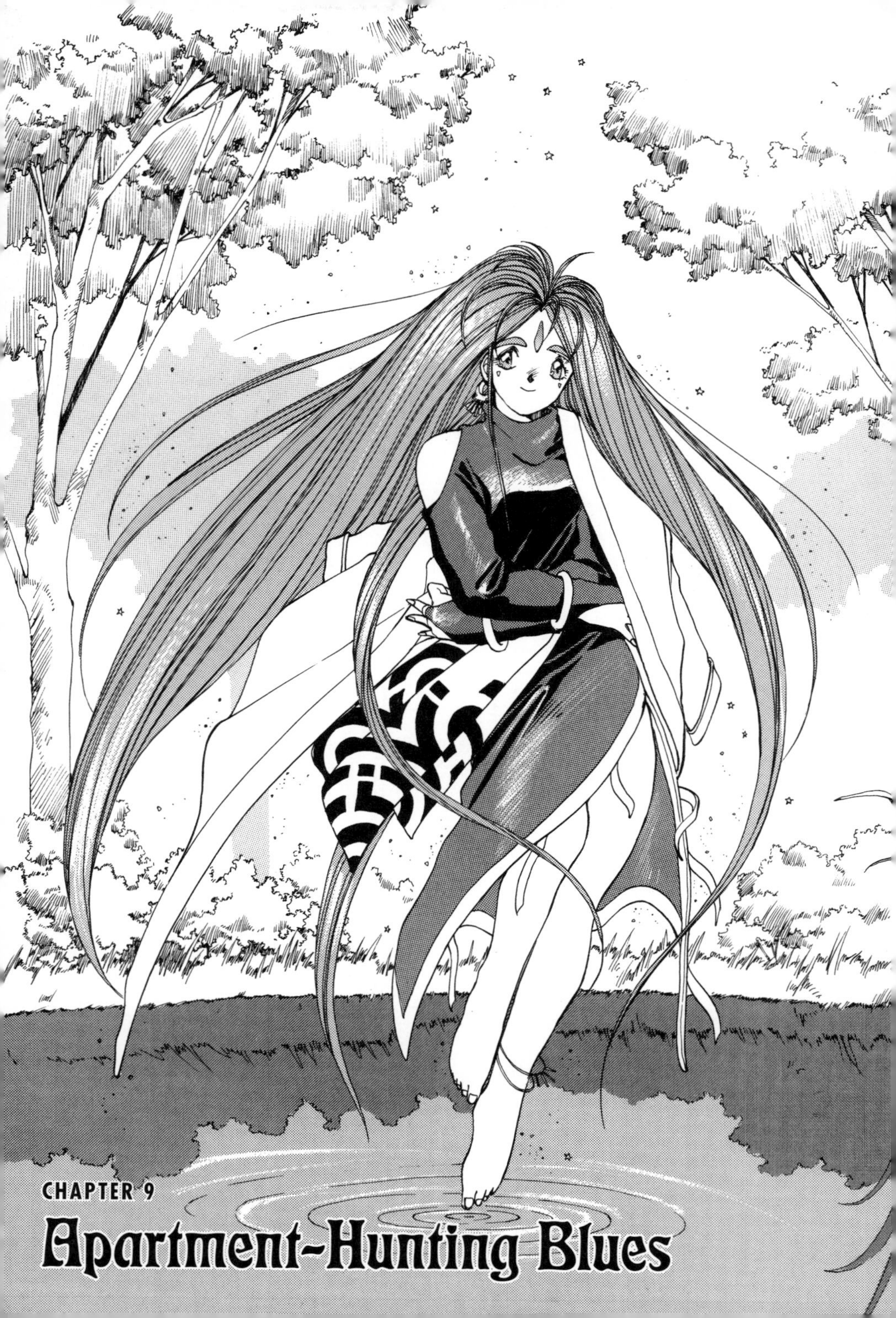

CHAPTER 9

Apartment-Hunting Blues

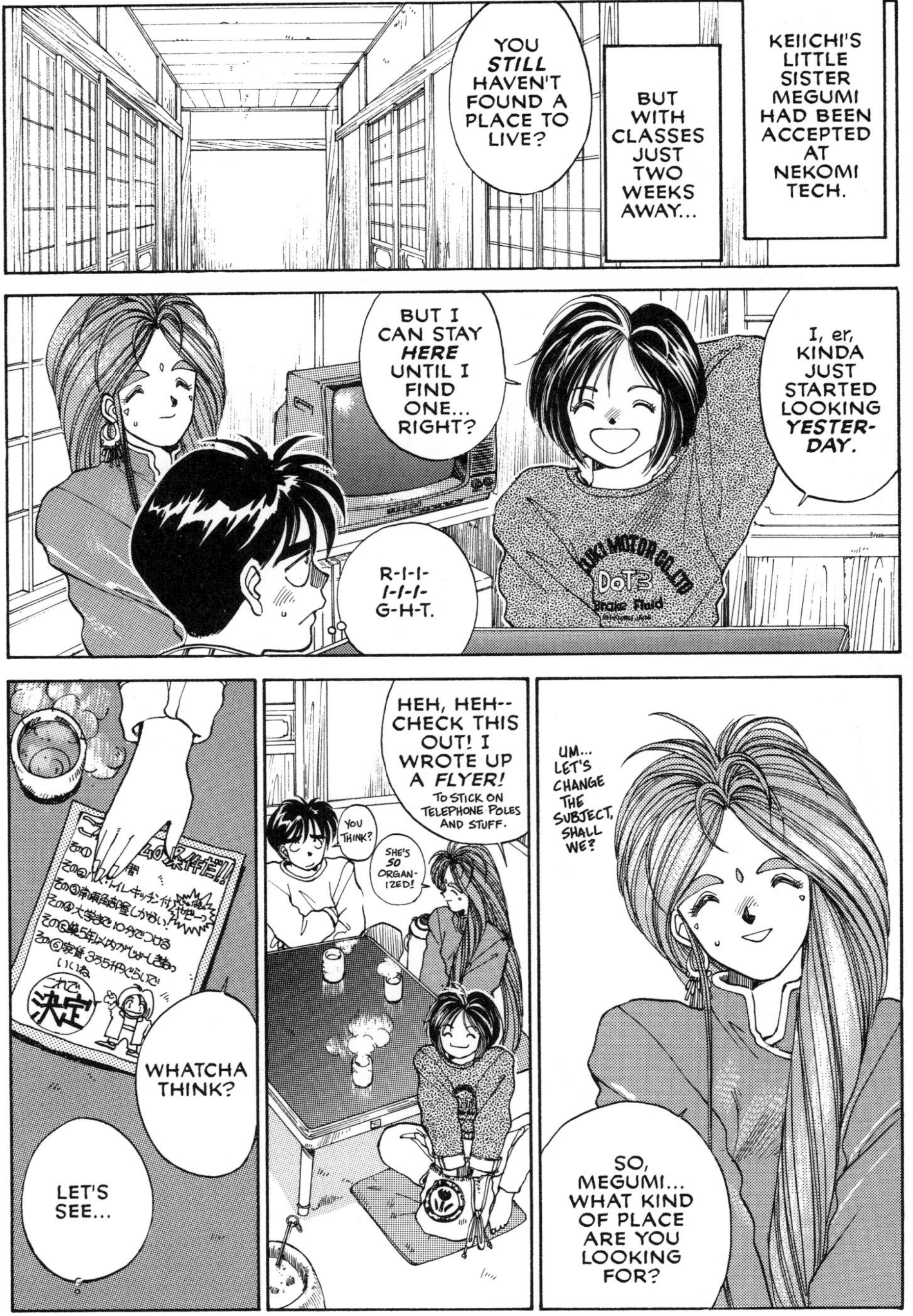
KEIICHI'S LITTLE SISTER MEGUMI HAD BEEN ACCEPTED AT NEKOMI TECH.
BUT WITH CLASSES JUST TWO WEEKS AWAY...
YOU *STILL* HAVEN'T FOUND A PLACE TO LIVE?
I, er, KINDA JUST STARTED LOOKING *YESTER-DAY.*
BUT I CAN STAY *HERE* UNTIL I FIND ONE... RIGHT?
R-I-I-*I-I-I*-G-H-T.
UM... LET'S CHANGE THE SUBJECT, SHALL WE?
SO, MEGUMI... WHAT KIND OF PLACE ARE YOU LOOKING FOR?
HEH, HEH-- CHECK THIS OUT! I WROTE UP A *FLYER!* TO STICK ON TELEPHONE POLES AND STUFF.
SHE'S *SO* ORGANIZED!
YOU THINK?
WHATCHA THINK?
LET'S SEE...

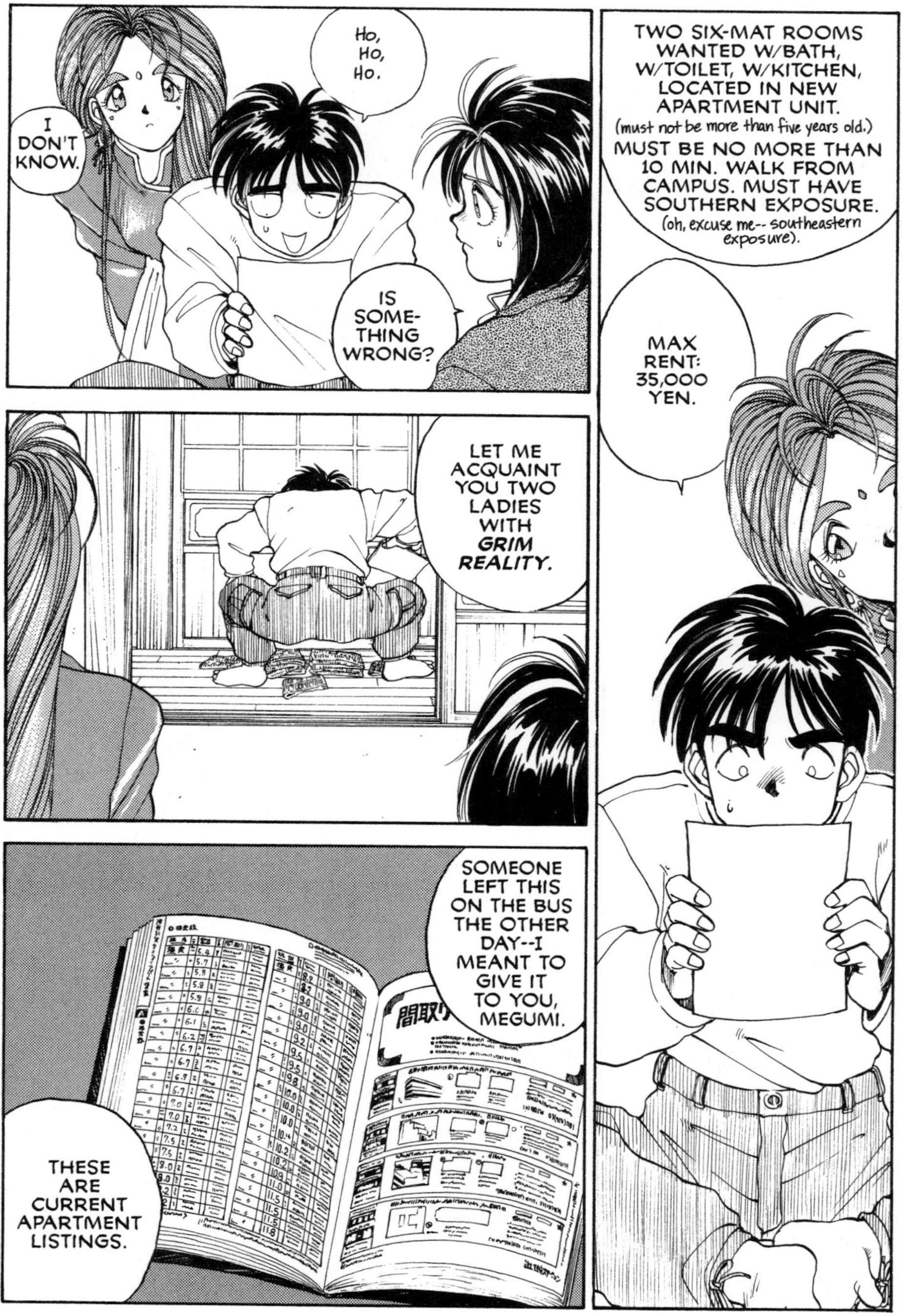
TWO SIX-MAT ROOMS WANTED W/BATH, W/TOILET, W/KITCHEN, LOCATED IN NEW APARTMENT UNIT. (must not be more than five years old.) MUST BE NO MORE THAN 10 MIN. WALK FROM CAMPUS. MUST HAVE SOUTHERN EXPOSURE. (oh, excuse me-- southeastern exposure).
MAX RENT: 35,000 YEN.
Ho, Ho, Ho.
IS SOMETHING WRONG?
I DON'T KNOW.
LET ME ACQUAINT YOU TWO LADIES WITH ***GRIM REALITY.***
SOMEONE LEFT THIS ON THE BUS THE OTHER DAY--I MEANT TO GIVE IT TO YOU, MEGUMI.
THESE ARE CURRENT APARTMENT LISTINGS.

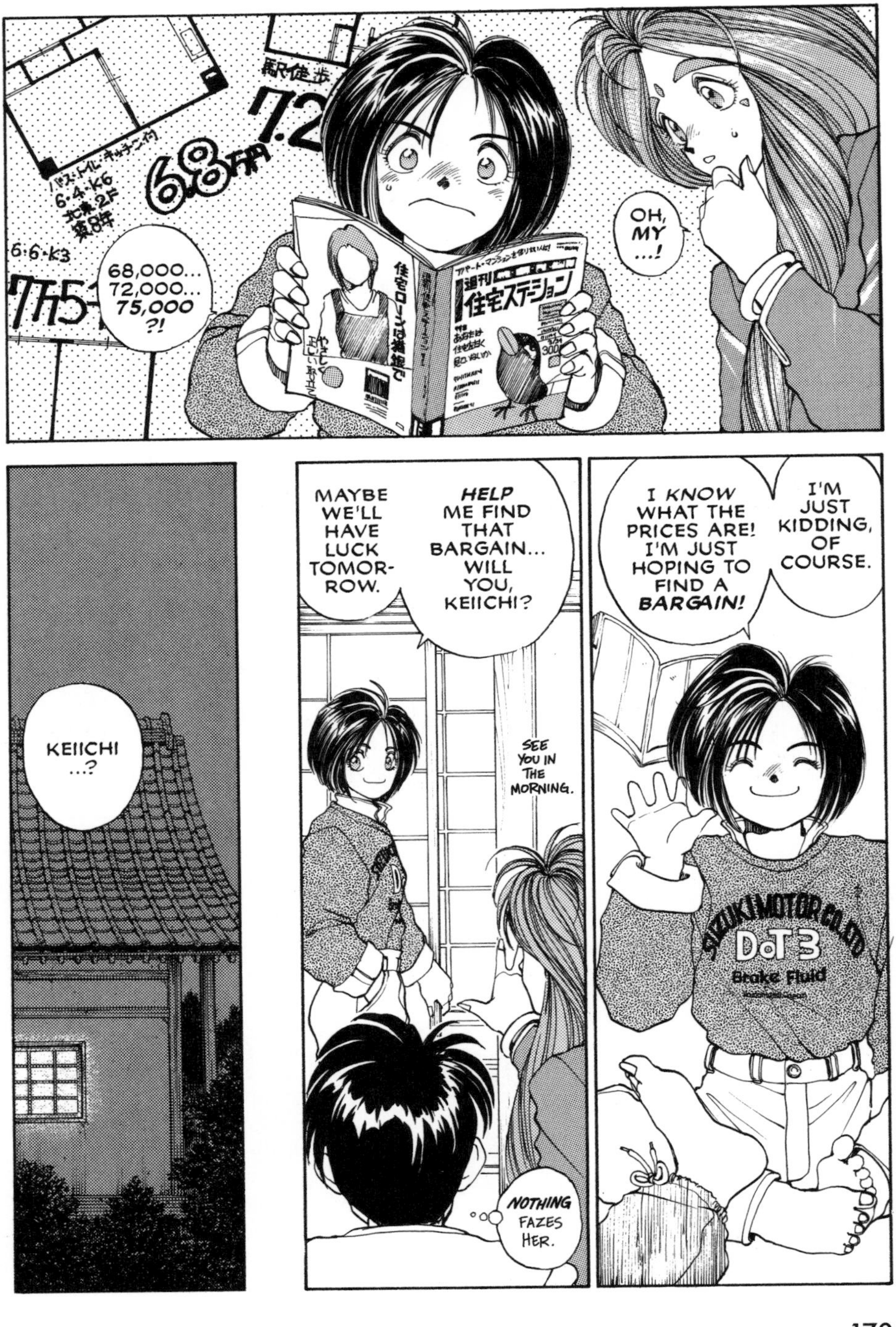
OH, MY ...!
68,000... 72,000... 75,000 ?!
I'M JUST KIDDING, OF COURSE.
I KNOW WHAT THE PRICES ARE! I'M JUST HOPING TO FIND A BARGAIN!
HELP ME FIND THAT BARGAIN... WILL YOU, KEIICHI?
MAYBE WE'LL HAVE LUCK TOMOR-ROW.
SEE YOU IN THE MORNING.
NOTHING FAZES HER.
KEIICHI ...?

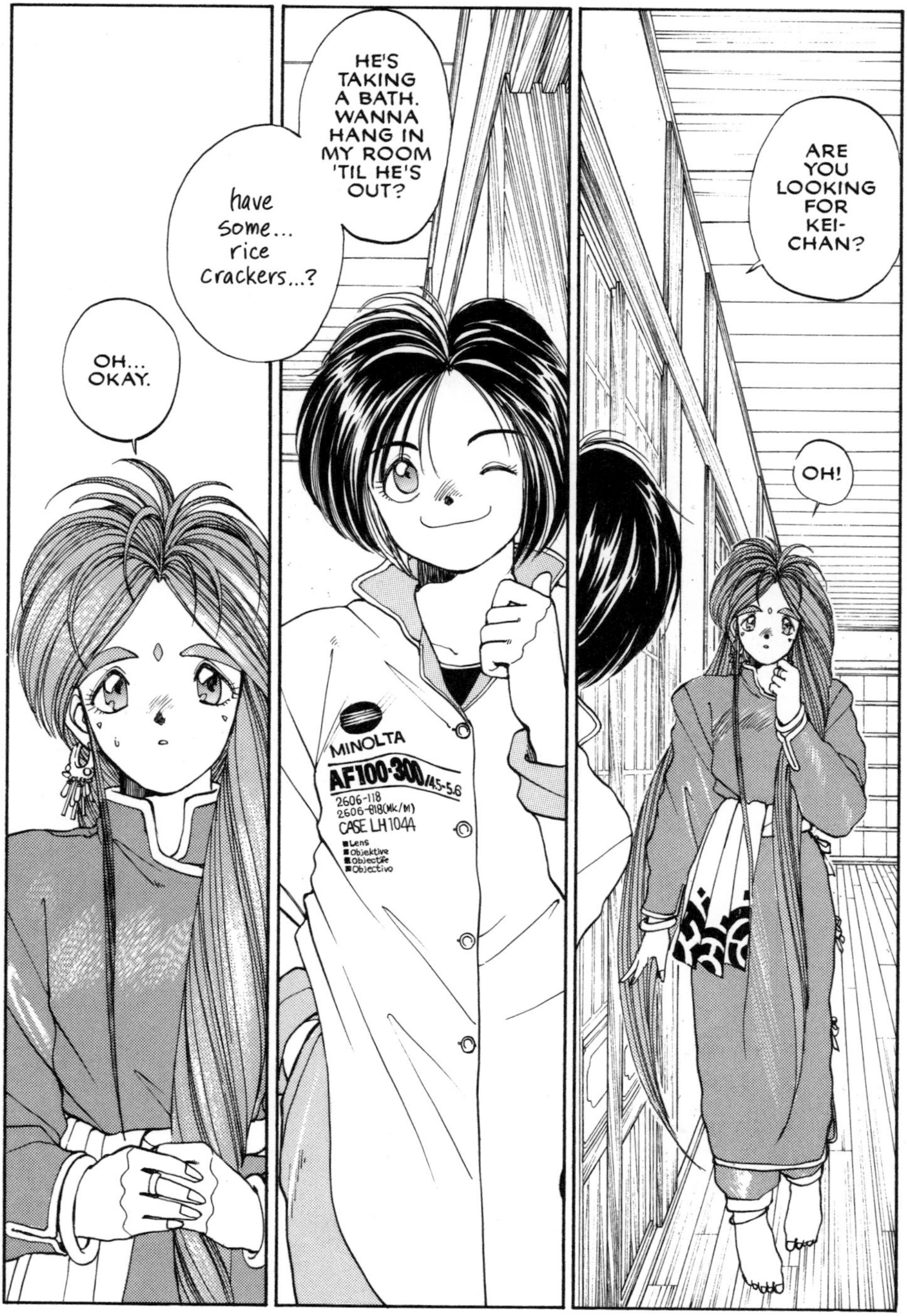
ARE YOU LOOKING FOR KEI-CHAN?
OH!
HE'S TAKING A BATH. WANNA HANG IN MY ROOM 'TIL HE'S OUT?
have some... rice crackers...?
MINOLTA
AF100-300/4.5-5.6
2606-118
2606-818(Mk/M)
CASE LH1044
Lens
Objektive
Objectife
Objectivo
OH... OKAY.

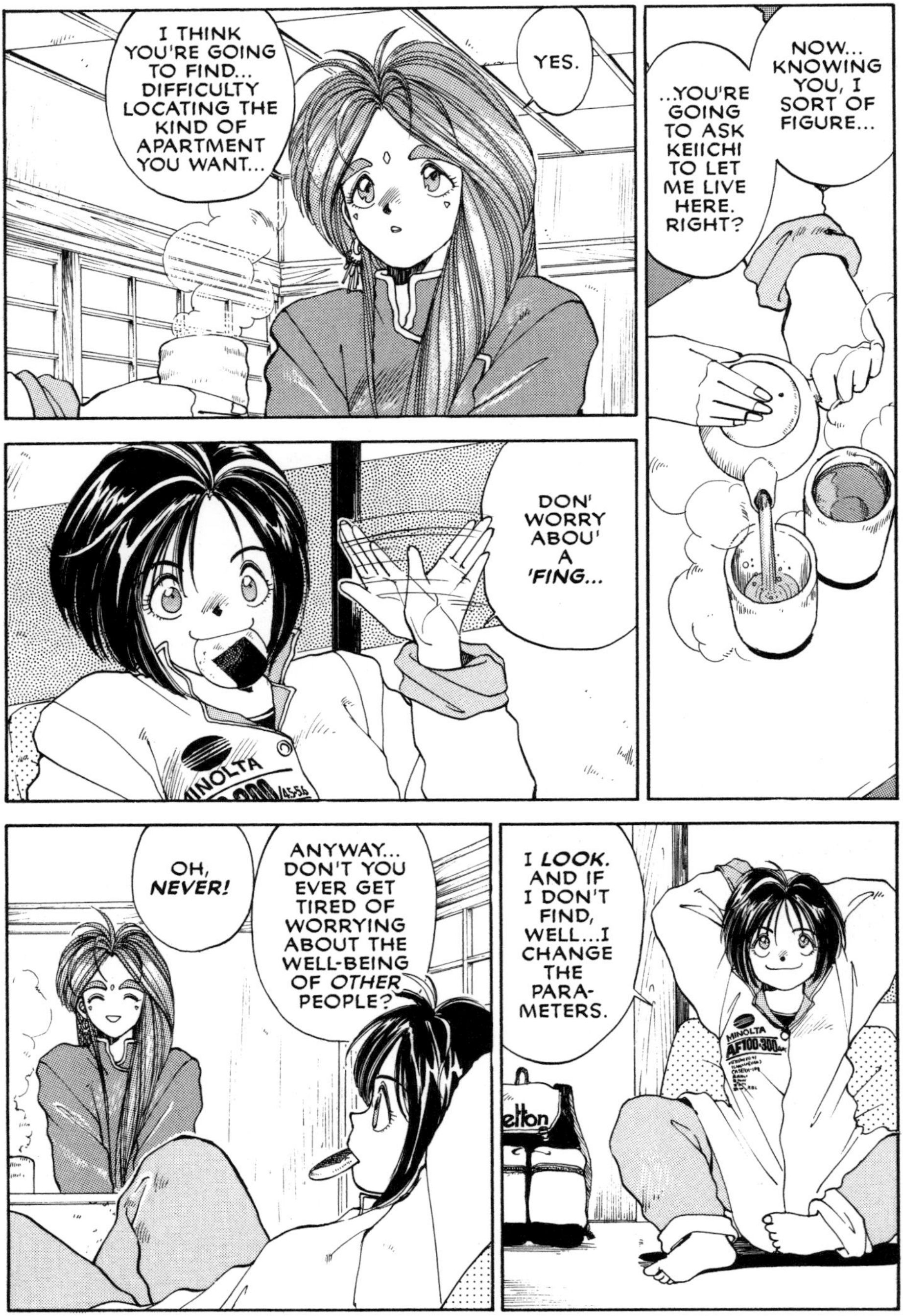
NOW... KNOWING YOU, I SORT OF FIGURE...
...YOU'RE GOING TO ASK KEIICHI TO LET ME LIVE HERE. RIGHT?
YES.
I THINK YOU'RE GOING TO FIND... DIFFICULTY LOCATING THE KIND OF APARTMENT YOU WANT...
DON' WORRY ABOU' A *'FING...*
MINOLTA
I *LOOK.* AND IF I DON'T FIND, WELL...I CHANGE THE PARA-METERS.
MINOLTA
AF100·300
ANYWAY... DON'T YOU EVER GET TIRED OF WORRYING ABOUT THE WELL-BEING OF *OTHER* PEOPLE?
OH, *NEVER!*

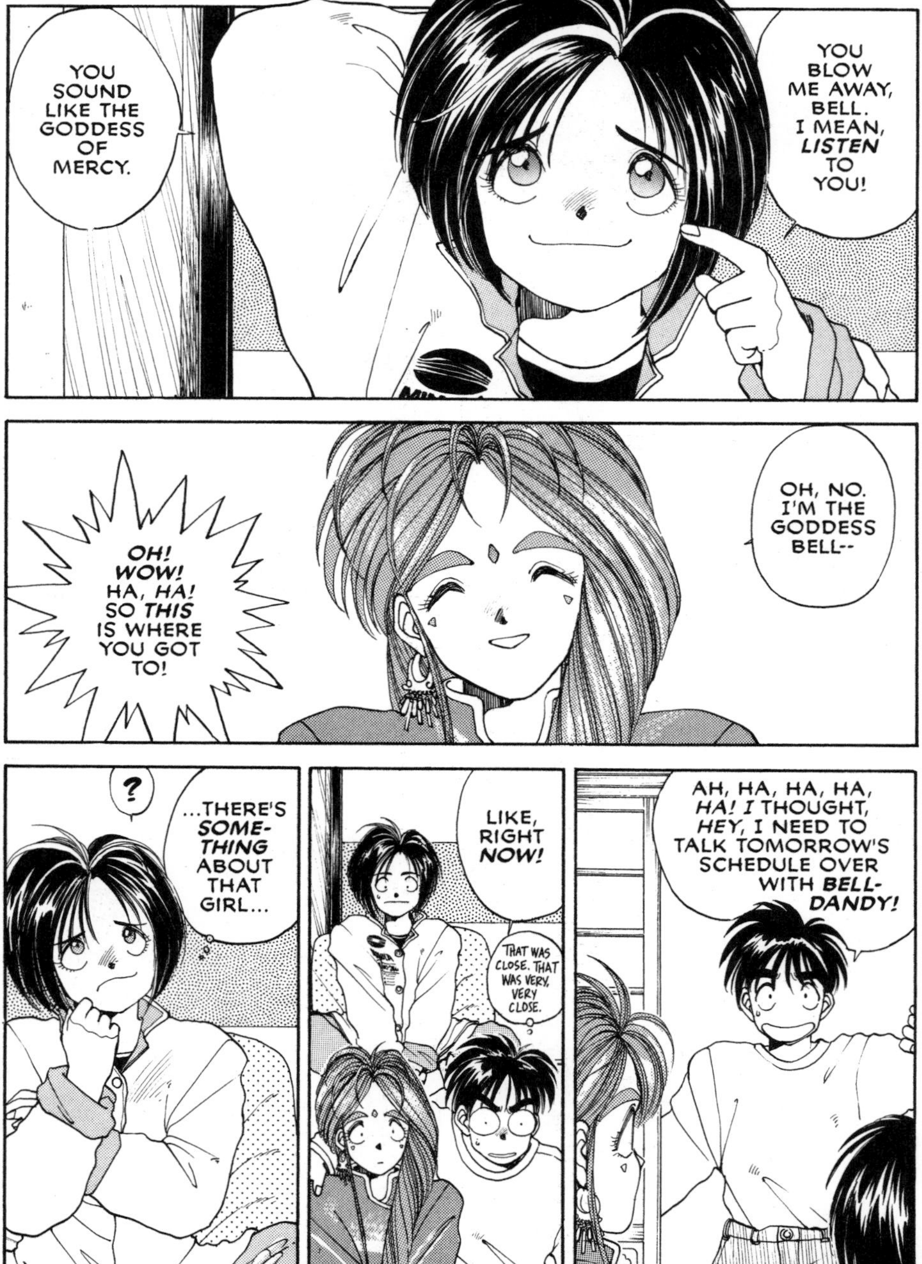
YOU BLOW ME AWAY, BELL. I MEAN, LISTEN TO YOU!
YOU SOUND LIKE THE GODDESS OF MERCY.
OH, NO. I'M THE GODDESS BELL--
OH! WOW! HA, HA! SO THIS IS WHERE YOU GOT TO!
AH, HA, HA, HA, HA! I THOUGHT, HEY, I NEED TO TALK TOMORROW'S SCHEDULE OVER WITH BELL-DANDY!
LIKE, RIGHT NOW!
THAT WAS CLOSE. THAT WAS VERY, VERY CLOSE.
?
...THERE'S SOMETHING ABOUT THAT GIRL...

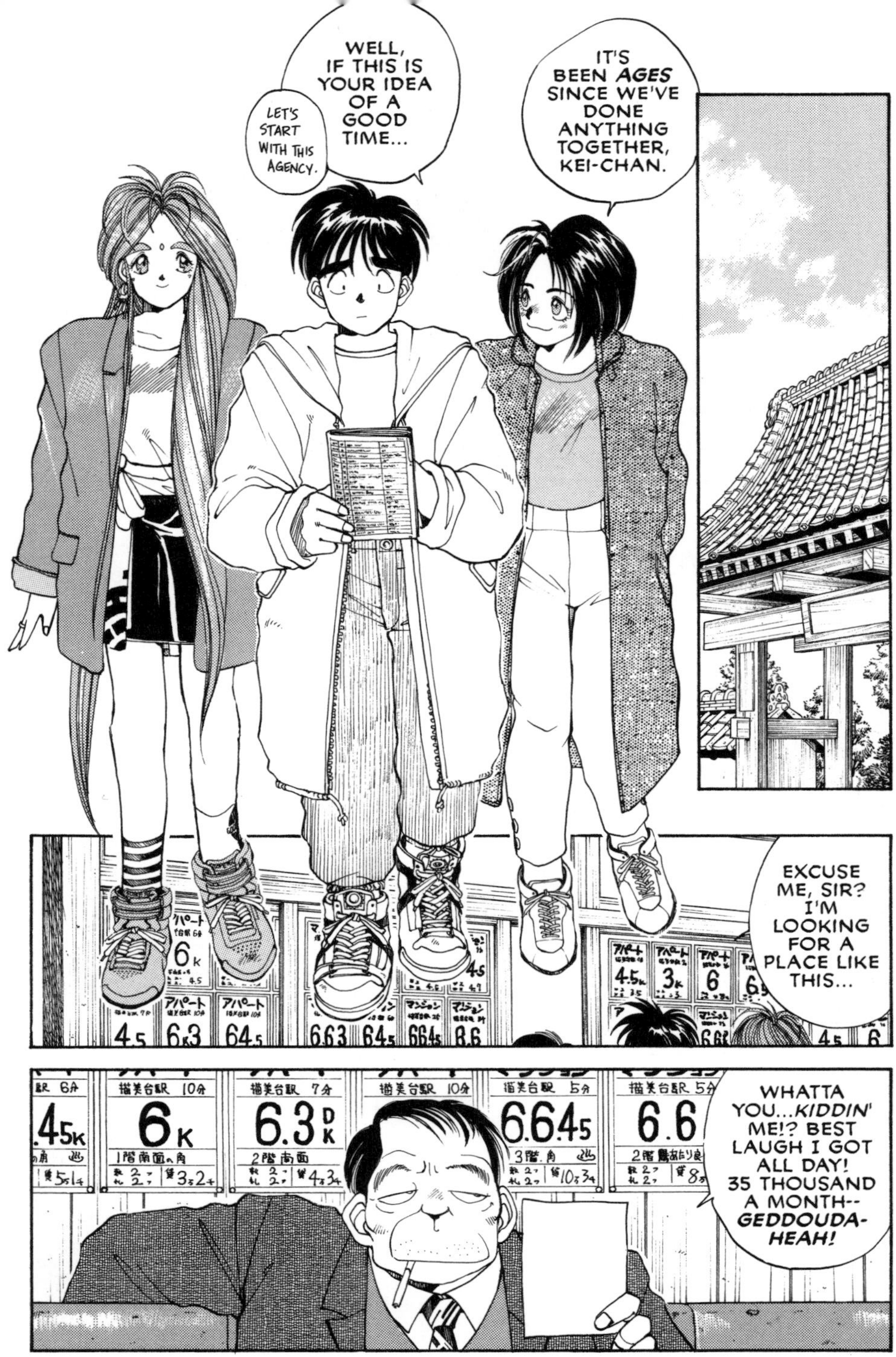
IT'S BEEN AGES SINCE WE'VE DONE ANYTHING TOGETHER, KEI-CHAN.
WELL, IF THIS IS YOUR IDEA OF A GOOD TIME...
LET'S START WITH THIS AGENCY.
EXCUSE ME, SIR? I'M LOOKING FOR A PLACE LIKE THIS...
WHATTA YOU...KIDDIN' ME!? BEST LAUGH I GOT ALL DAY! 35 THOUSAND A MONTH-- GEDDOUDA-HEAH!

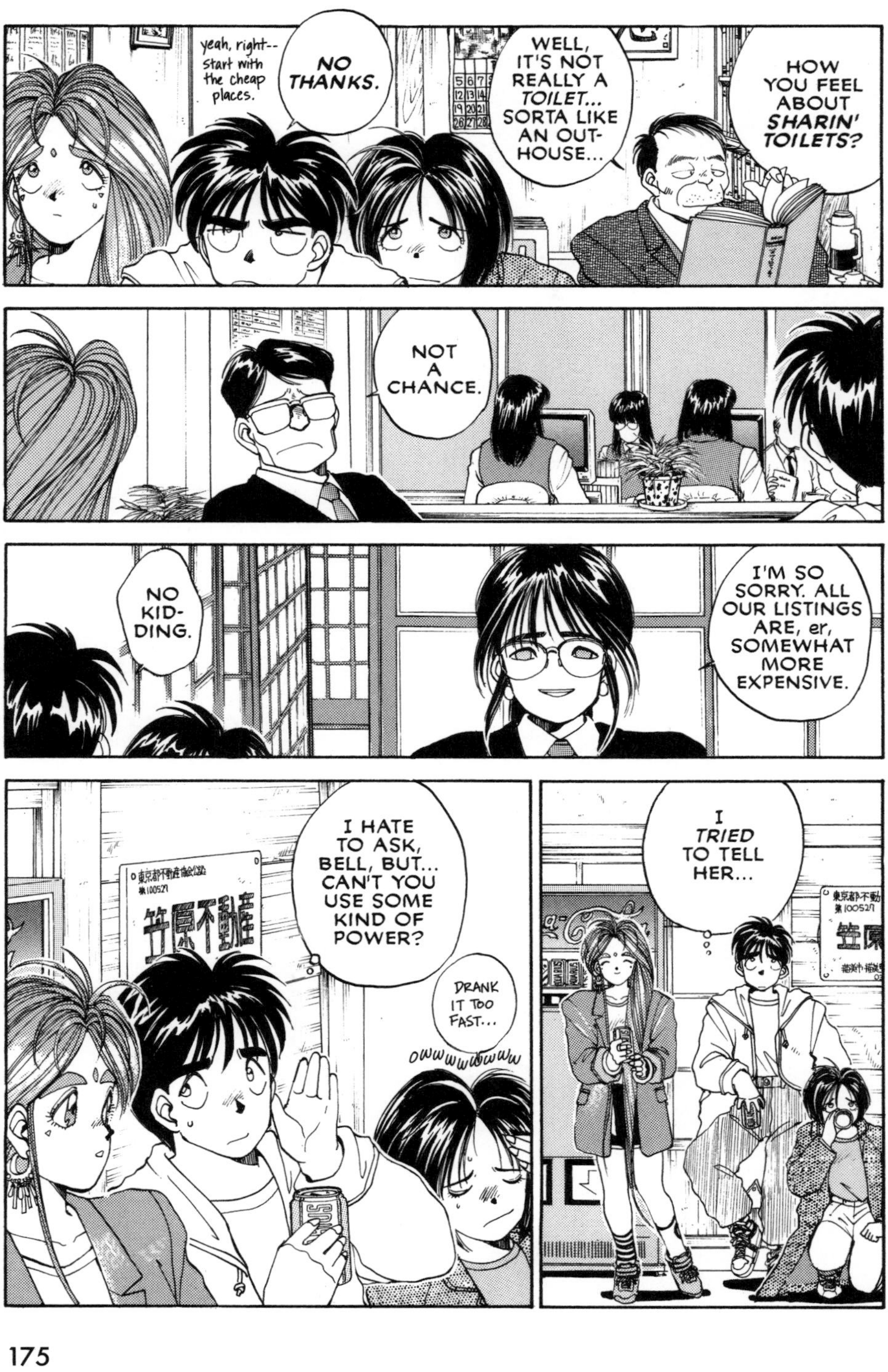
HOW YOU FEEL ABOUT *SHARIN'* *TOILETS?*
WELL, IT'S NOT REALLY A *TOILET*... SORTA LIKE AN OUT-HOUSE...
NO THANKS.
yeah, right-- start with the cheap places.
NOT A CHANCE.
I'M SO SORRY. ALL OUR LISTINGS ARE, er, SOMEWHAT MORE EXPENSIVE.
NO KID-DING.
I *TRIED* TO TELL HER...
東京都不動
第100527
笠原
I HATE TO ASK, BELL, BUT... CAN'T YOU USE SOME KIND OF POWER?
第100527
笠原不動産
DRANK IT TOO FAST...
OWWWWWWWW

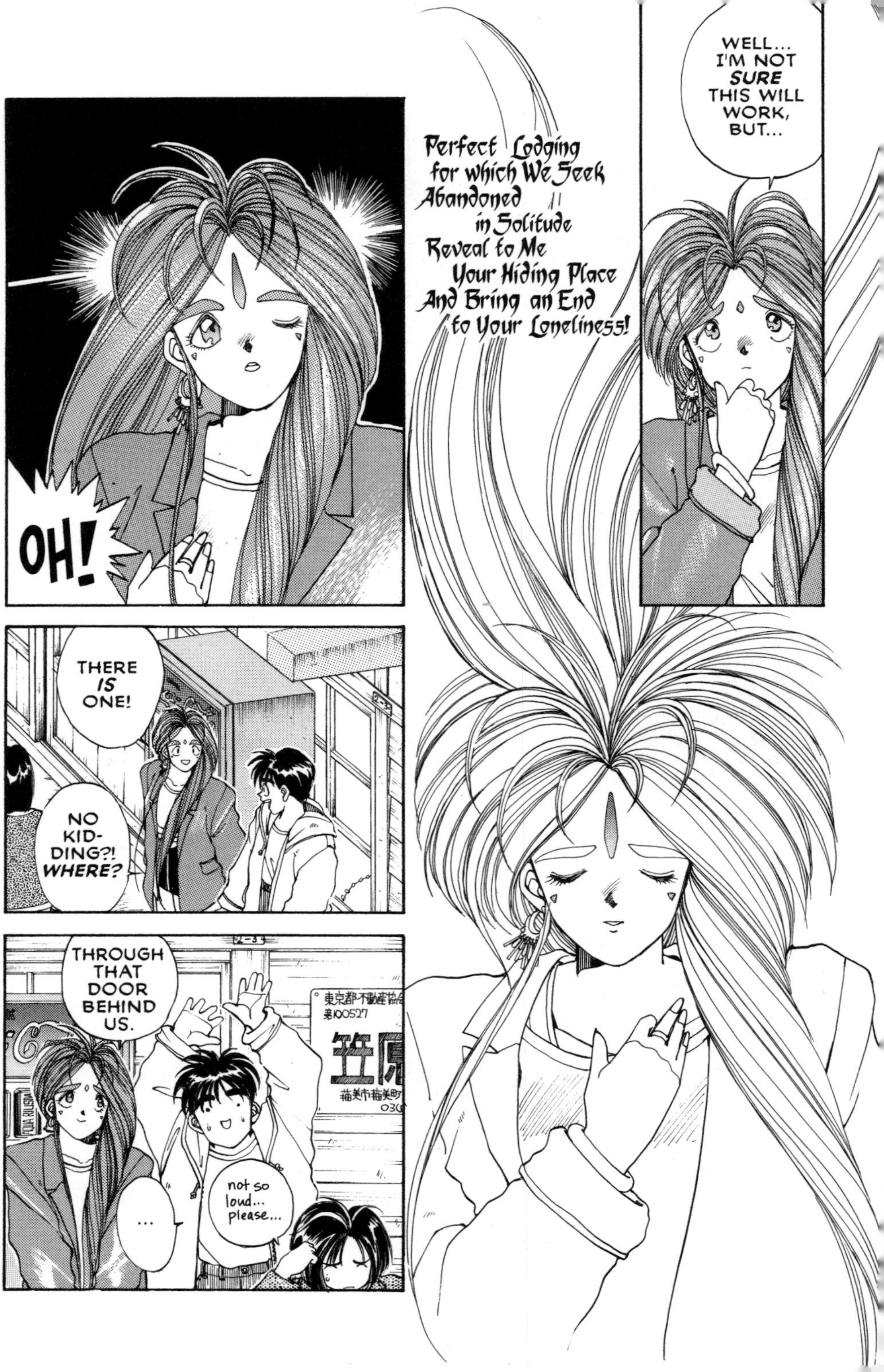
WELL... I'M NOT *SURE* THIS WILL WORK, BUT...
Perfect Lodging for which We Seek Abandoned in Solitude Reveal to Me Your Hiding Place And Bring an End to Your Loneliness!
OH!
THERE *IS* ONE!
NO KID-DING?! *WHERE?*
THROUGH THAT DOOR BEHIND US.
...
not so loud... please...

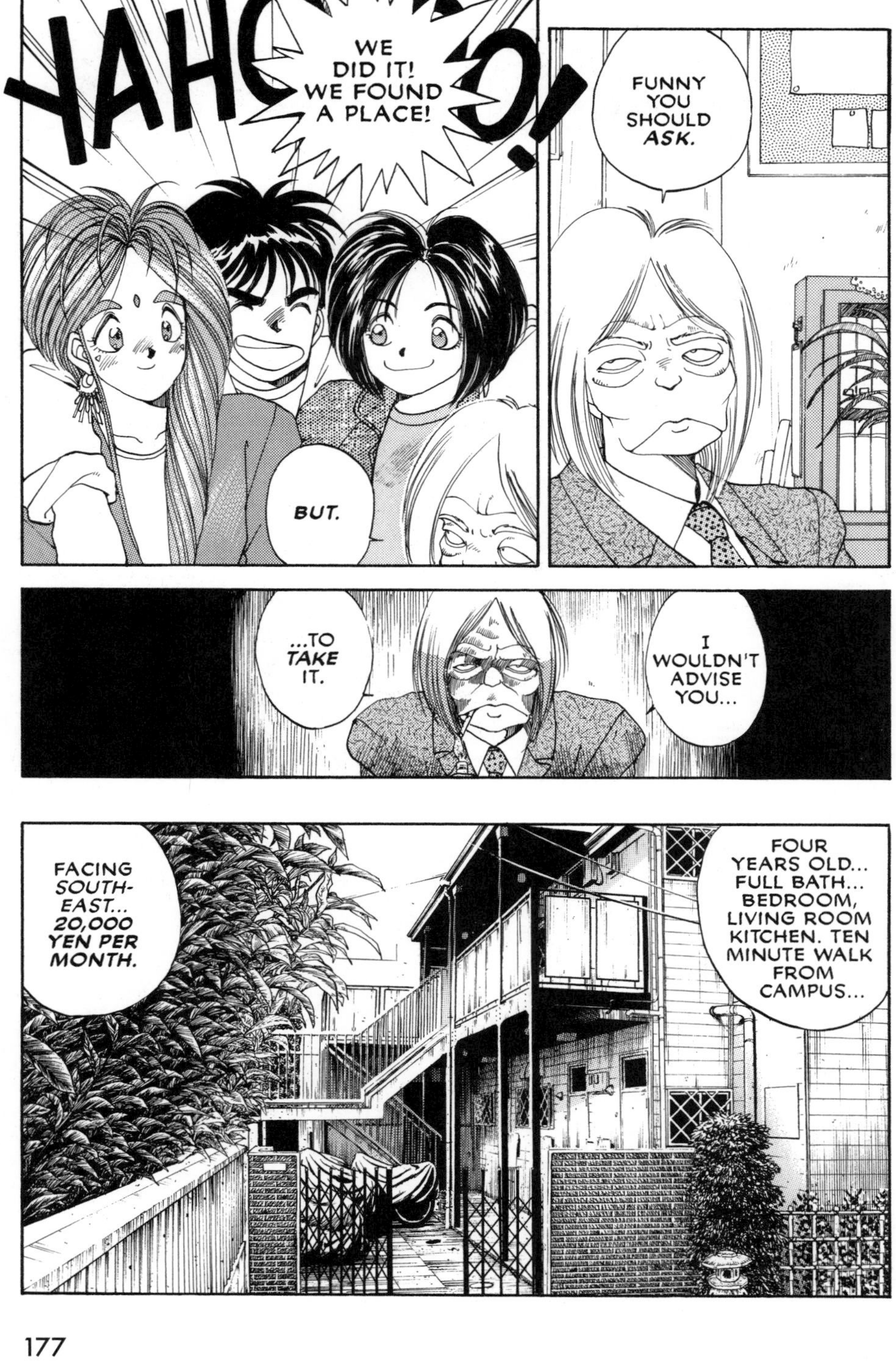
FUNNY YOU SHOULD ASK.
YAHOOO!
WE DID IT! WE FOUND A PLACE!
BUT.
I WOULDN'T ADVISE YOU...
...TO TAKE IT.
FOUR YEARS OLD... FULL BATH... BEDROOM, LIVING ROOM KITCHEN. TEN MINUTE WALK FROM CAMPUS...
FACING SOUTH-EAST... 20,000 YEN PER MONTH.

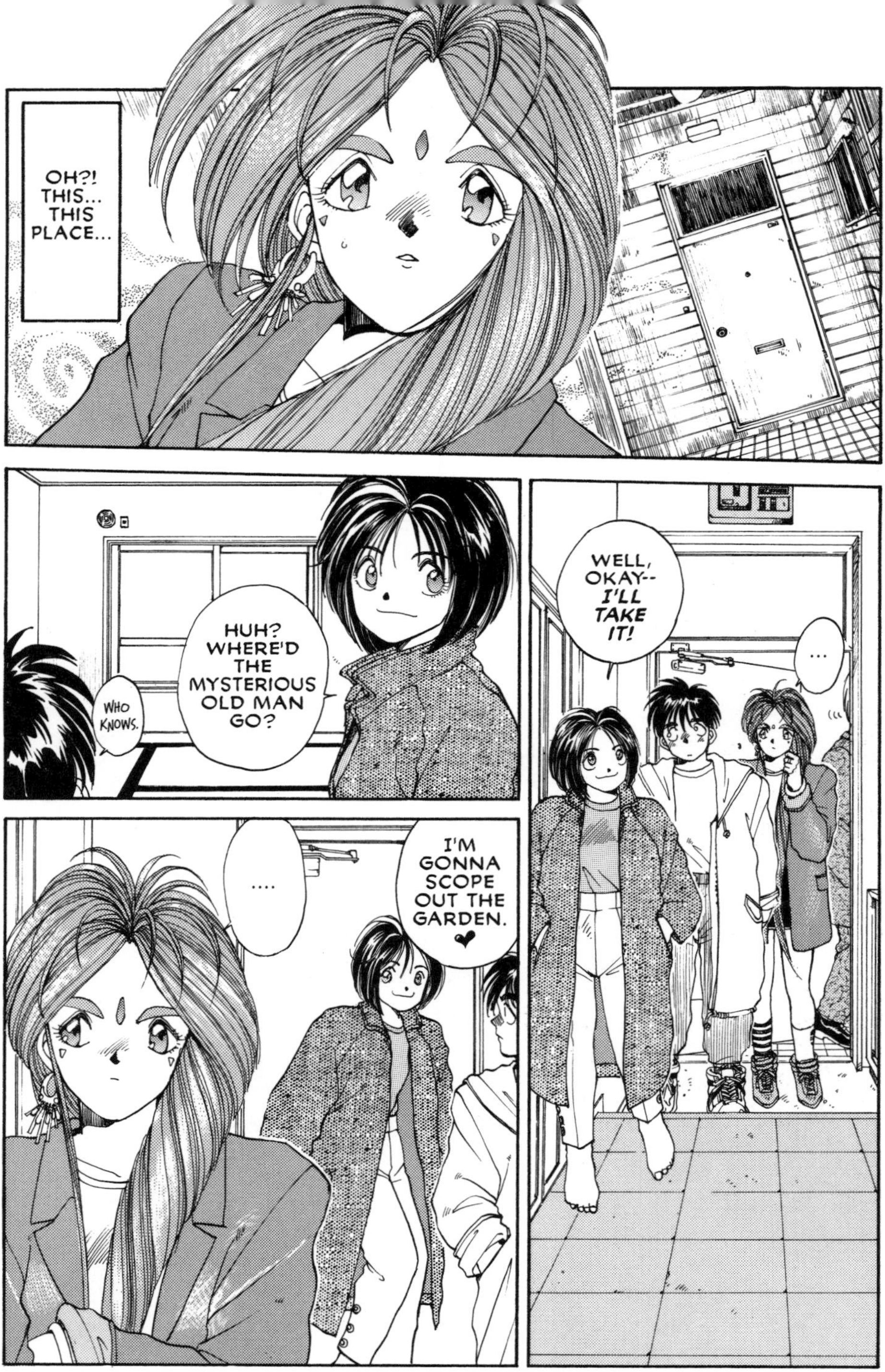
OH?! THIS... THIS PLACE...
WELL, OKAY-- *I'LL TAKE IT!*
...
HUH? WHERE'D THE MYSTERIOUS OLD MAN GO?
WHO KNOWS.
I'M GONNA SCOPE OUT THE GARDEN. ❤
....

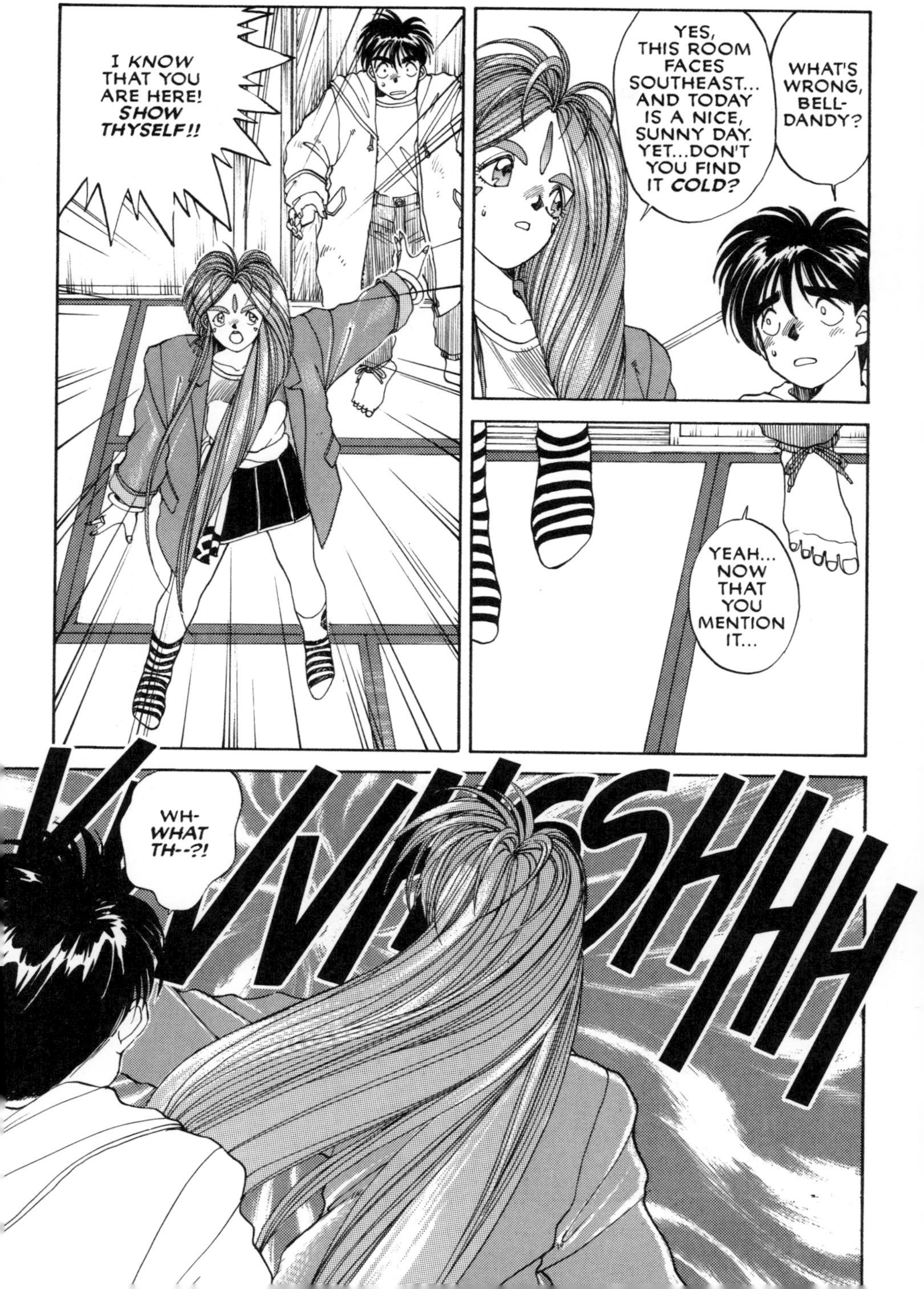
WHAT'S WRONG, BELL-DANDY?
YES, THIS ROOM FACES SOUTHEAST... AND TODAY IS A NICE, SUNNY DAY. YET...DON'T YOU FIND IT *COLD?*
YEAH... NOW THAT YOU MENTION IT...
I *KNOW* THAT YOU ARE HERE! ***SHOW THYSELF!!***
WH-WHAT TH--?!

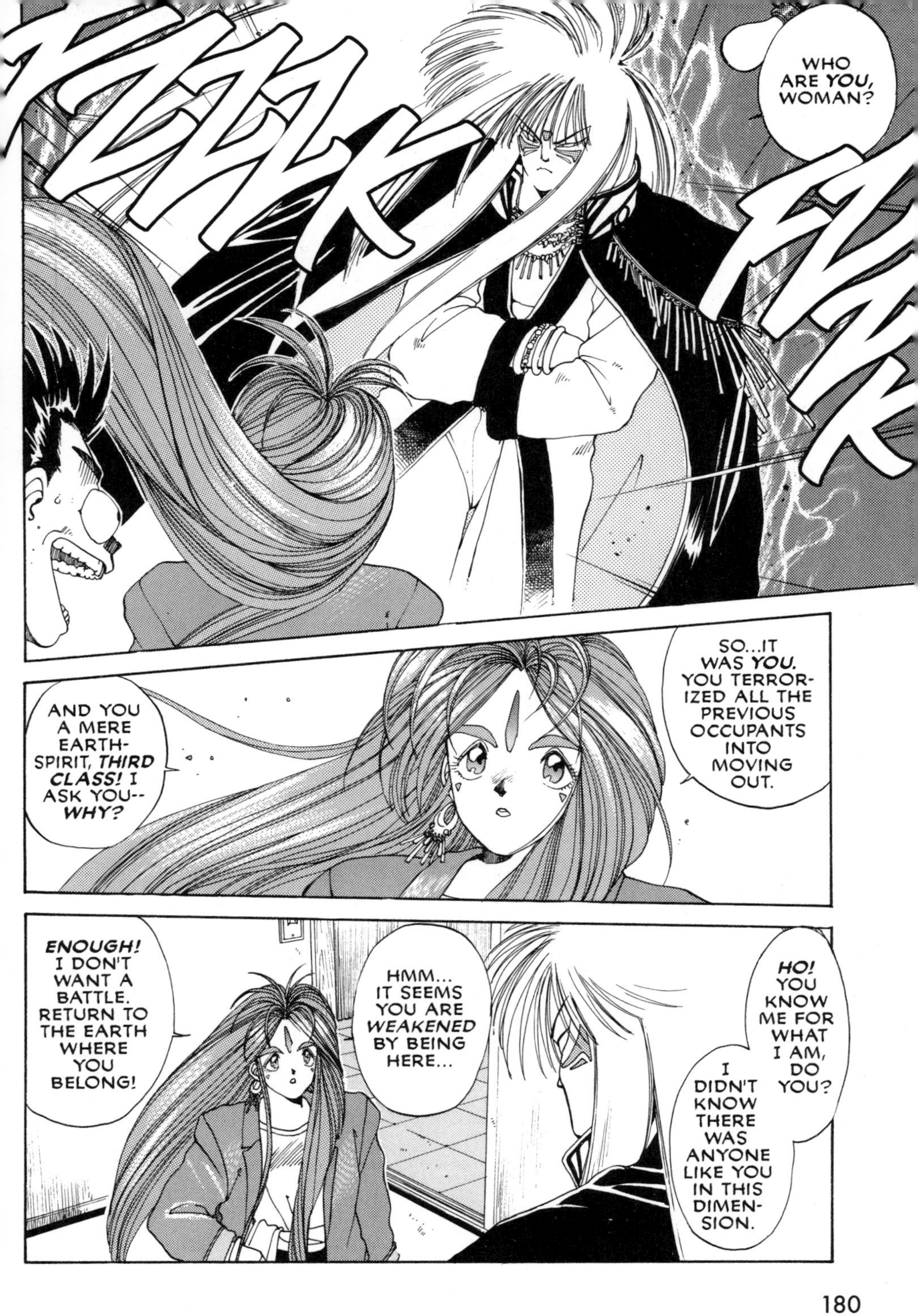
WHO ARE *YOU*, WOMAN?
SO...IT WAS *YOU*. YOU TERRORIZED ALL THE PREVIOUS OCCUPANTS INTO MOVING OUT.
AND YOU A MERE EARTH-SPIRIT, *THIRD CLASS!* I ASK YOU-- *WHY?*
HO! YOU KNOW ME FOR WHAT I AM, DO YOU?
I DIDN'T KNOW THERE WAS ANYONE LIKE YOU IN THIS DIMENSION.
HMM... IT SEEMS YOU ARE *WEAKENED* BY BEING HERE...
ENOUGH! I DON'T WANT A BATTLE. RETURN TO THE EARTH WHERE YOU BELONG!

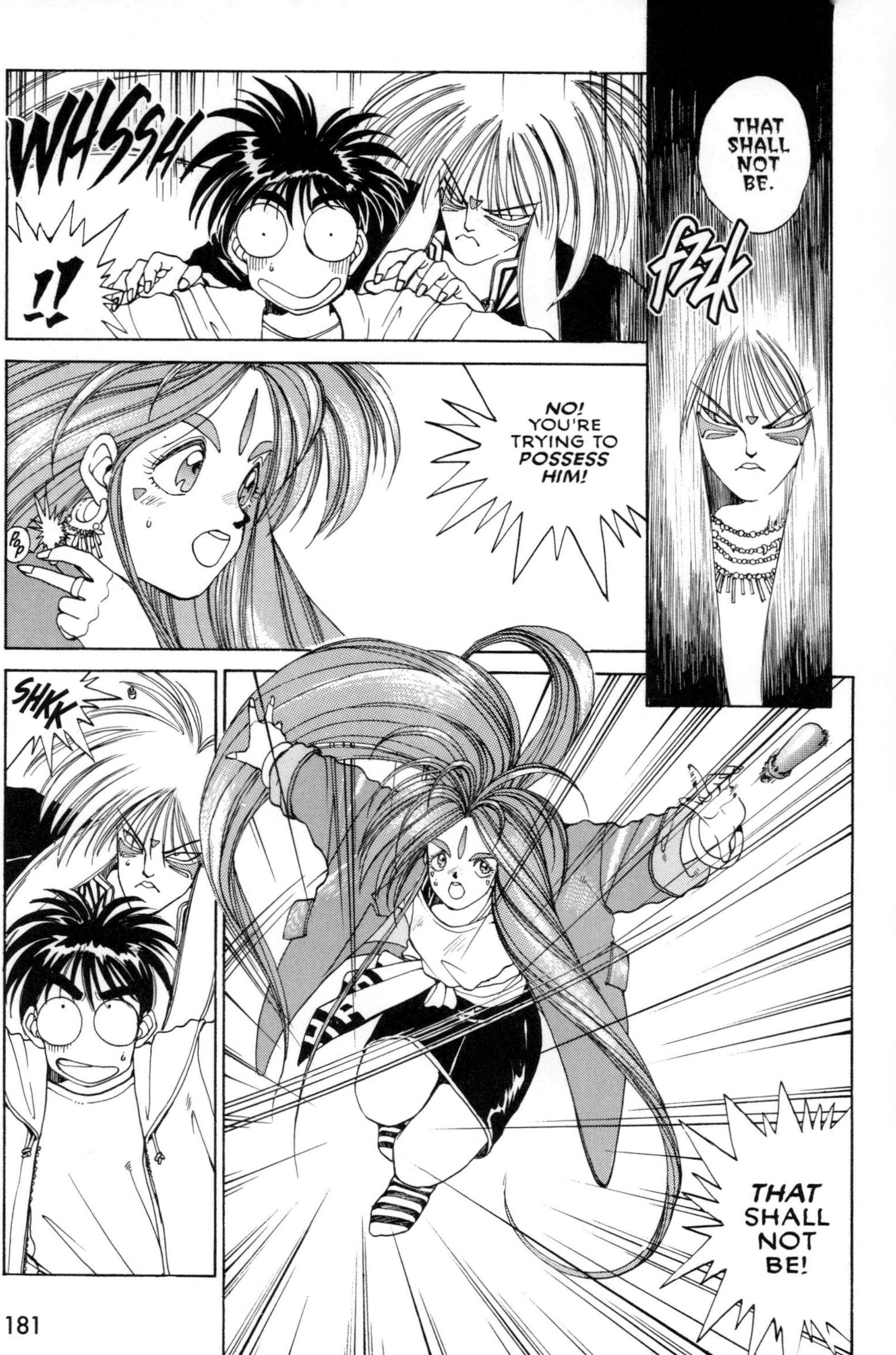
THAT SHALL NOT BE.
FZK
WHSSH
!!
NO! YOU'RE TRYING TO POSSESS HIM!
THAT SHALL NOT BE!
SHKK

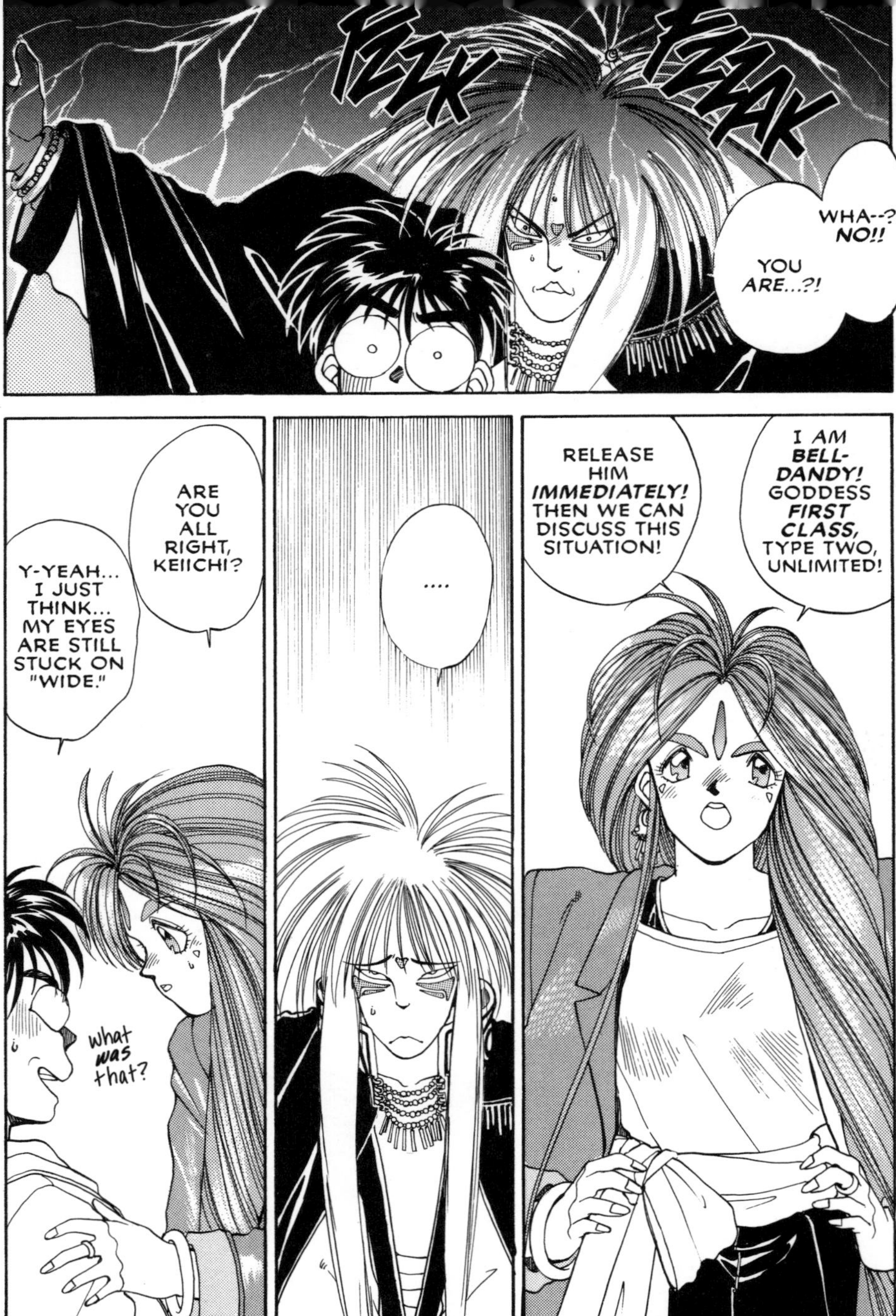
FZZAK
FZZK
WHA--?! NO!!
YOU ARE...?!
I AM BELL-DANDY! GODDESS FIRST CLASS, TYPE TWO, UNLIMITED!
RELEASE HIM IMMEDIATELY! THEN WE CAN DISCUSS THIS SITUATION!
....
ARE YOU ALL RIGHT, KEIICHI?
Y-YEAH... I JUST THINK... MY EYES ARE STILL STUCK ON "WIDE."
what was that?

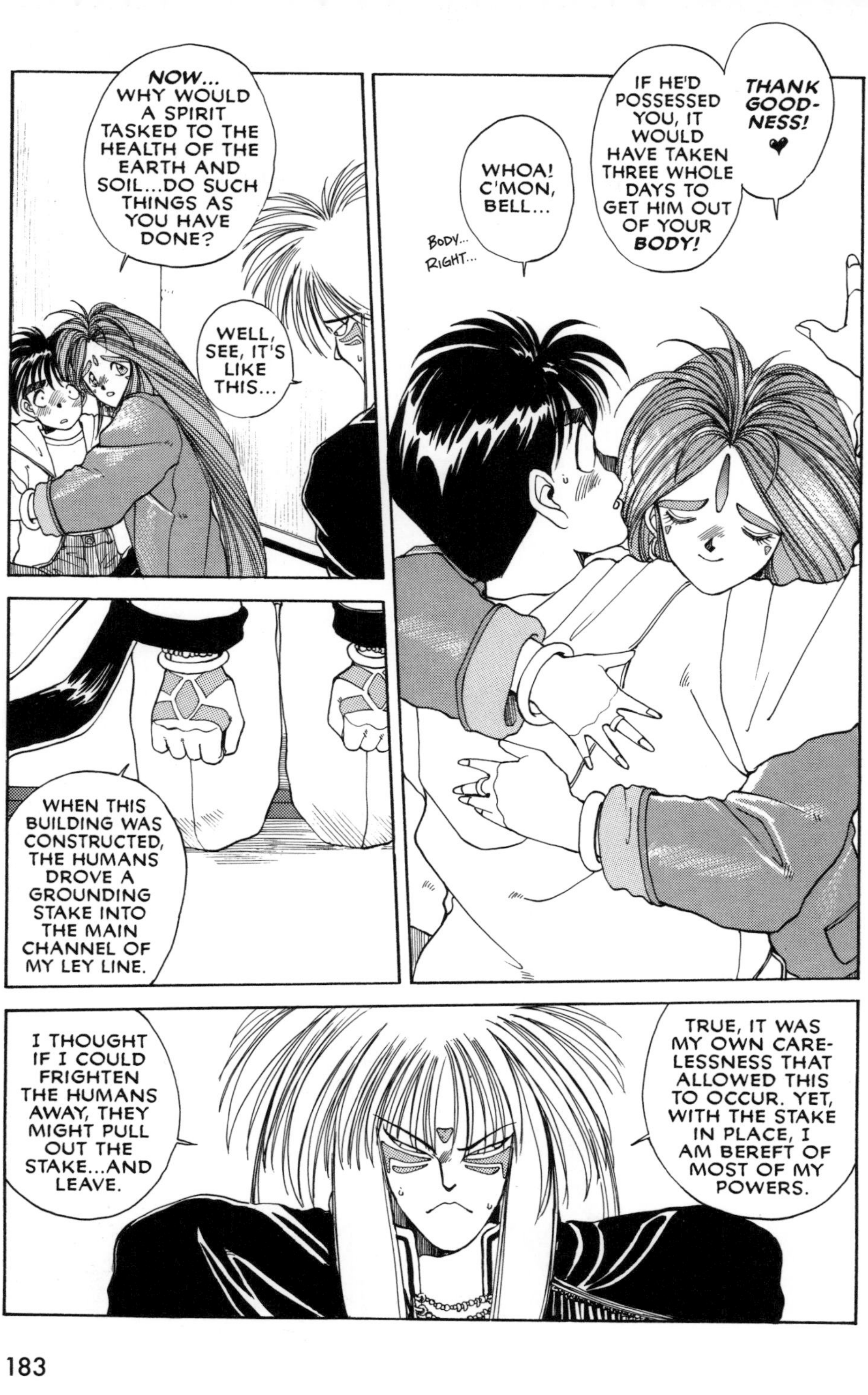
THANK GOODNESS! ♥
IF HE'D POSSESSED YOU, IT WOULD HAVE TAKEN THREE WHOLE DAYS TO GET HIM OUT OF YOUR BODY!
WHOA! C'MON, BELL...
BODY... RIGHT...
NOW... WHY WOULD A SPIRIT TASKED TO THE HEALTH OF THE EARTH AND SOIL...DO SUCH THINGS AS YOU HAVE DONE?
WELL, SEE, IT'S LIKE THIS...
WHEN THIS BUILDING WAS CONSTRUCTED, THE HUMANS DROVE A GROUNDING STAKE INTO THE MAIN CHANNEL OF MY LEY LINE.
TRUE, IT WAS MY OWN CARELESSNESS THAT ALLOWED THIS TO OCCUR. YET, WITH THE STAKE IN PLACE, I AM BEREFT OF MOST OF MY POWERS.
I THOUGHT IF I COULD FRIGHTEN THE HUMANS AWAY, THEY MIGHT PULL OUT THE STAKE...AND LEAVE.

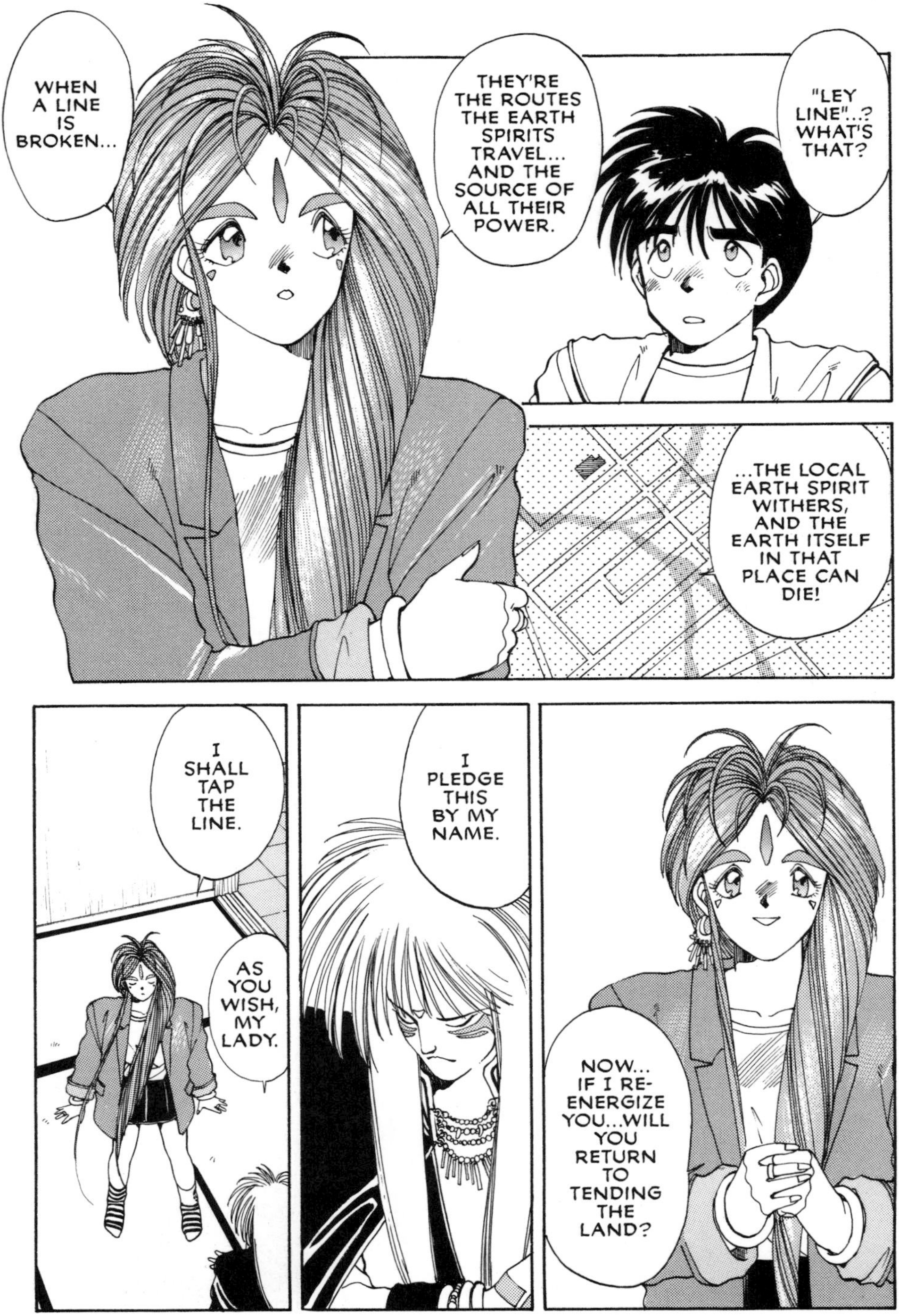
"LEY LINE"..? WHAT'S THAT?
THEY'RE THE ROUTES THE EARTH SPIRITS TRAVEL... AND THE SOURCE OF ALL THEIR POWER.
WHEN A LINE IS BROKEN...
...THE LOCAL EARTH SPIRIT WITHERS, AND THE EARTH ITSELF IN THAT PLACE CAN DIE!
NOW... IF I RE-ENERGIZE YOU...WILL YOU RETURN TO TENDING THE LAND?
I PLEDGE THIS BY MY NAME.
I SHALL TAP THE LINE.
AS YOU WISH, MY LADY.

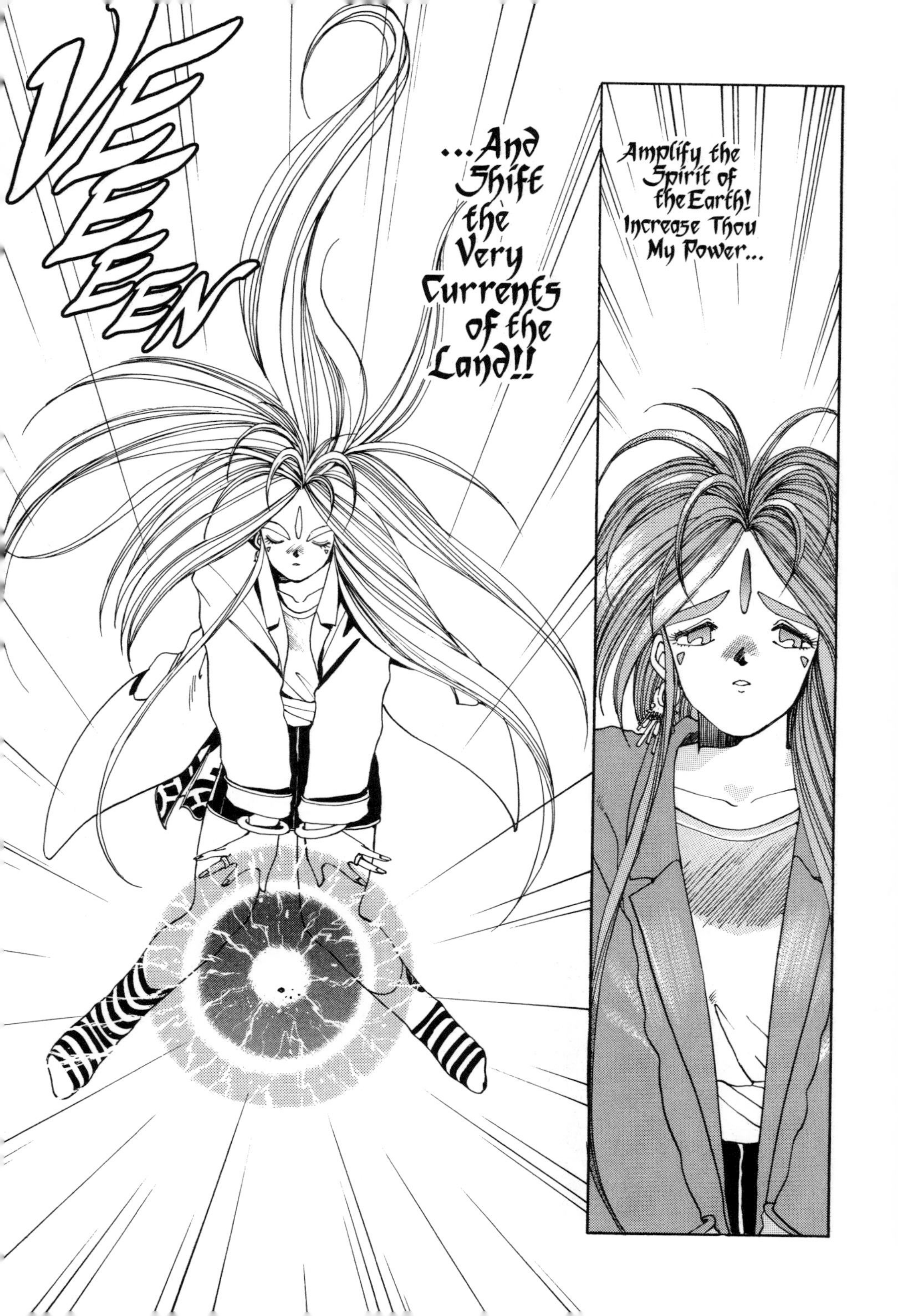
Amplify the Spirit of the Earth! Increase Thou My Power...
...And Shift the Very Currents of the Land!!
VEEEEN

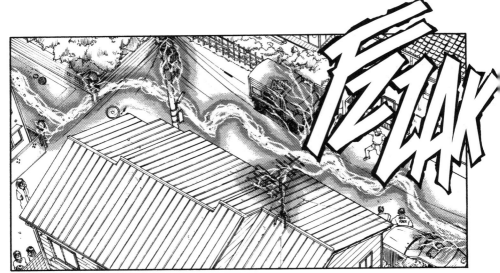

MY LADY... I AM IN YOUR DEBT.

OW!

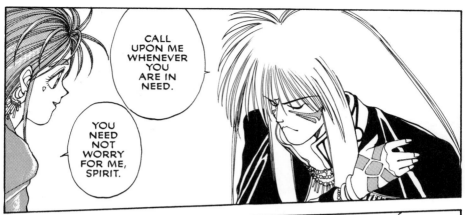

CALL UPON ME WHENEVER YOU ARE IN NEED.
YOU NEED NOT WORRY FOR ME, SPIRIT.
BUT ACTUALLY... A FRIEND OF MINE WILL BE MOVING IN HERE.
CAN YOU PROTECT *HER*...?
UPON MY HONOR!
IN THAT CASE, NAME YOUR CHOSEN FORM...
HEY!
TMP
SHE'S COMING *BACK!* SHE...
KEI-CHAN... DID YOU *SEE* THAT?
see **what?**

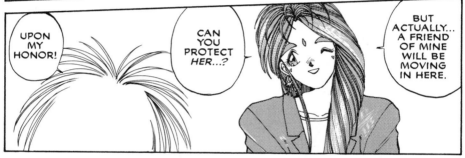

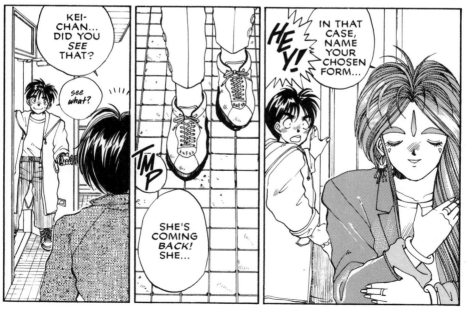

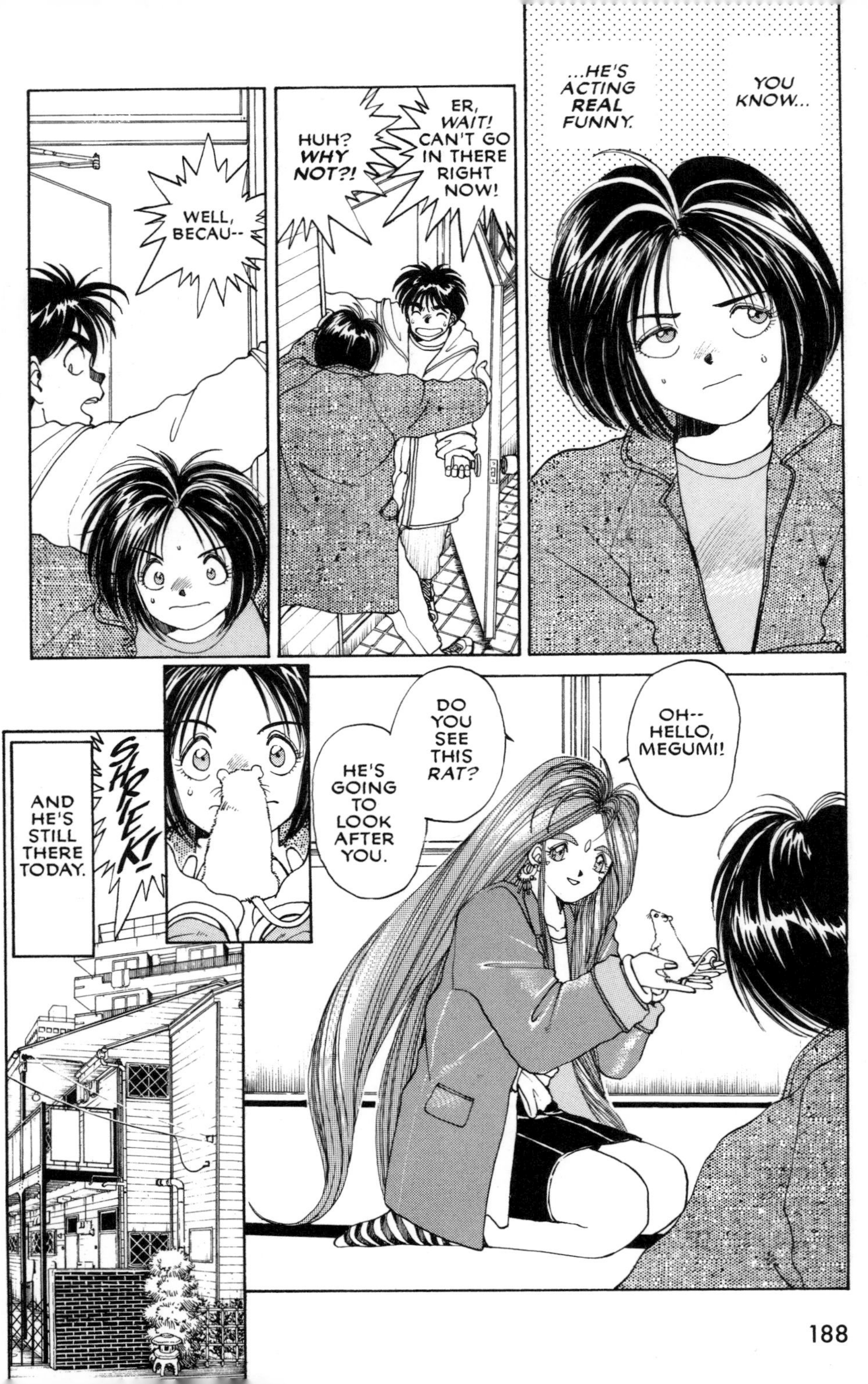
YOU KNOW...
...HE'S ACTING *REAL* FUNNY.
ER, *WAIT!* CAN'T GO IN THERE RIGHT NOW!
HUH? *WHY NOT?!*
WELL, BECAU--
OH-- HELLO, MEGUMI!
DO YOU SEE THIS *RAT?*
HE'S GOING TO LOOK AFTER YOU.
SHRIEK!
AND HE'S STILL THERE TODAY.

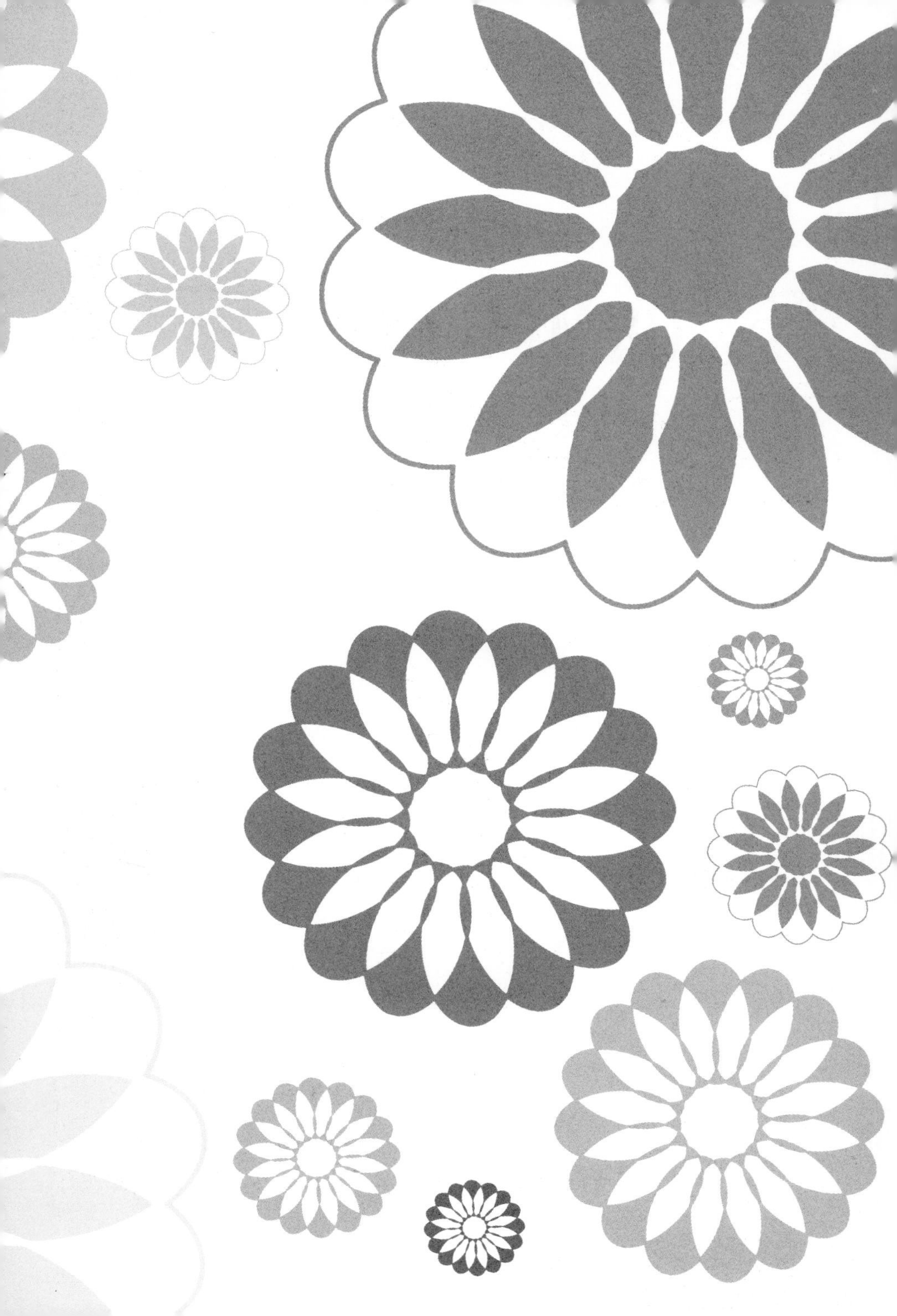

OH MY GODDESS!

CHAPTER 10

An Honest Match

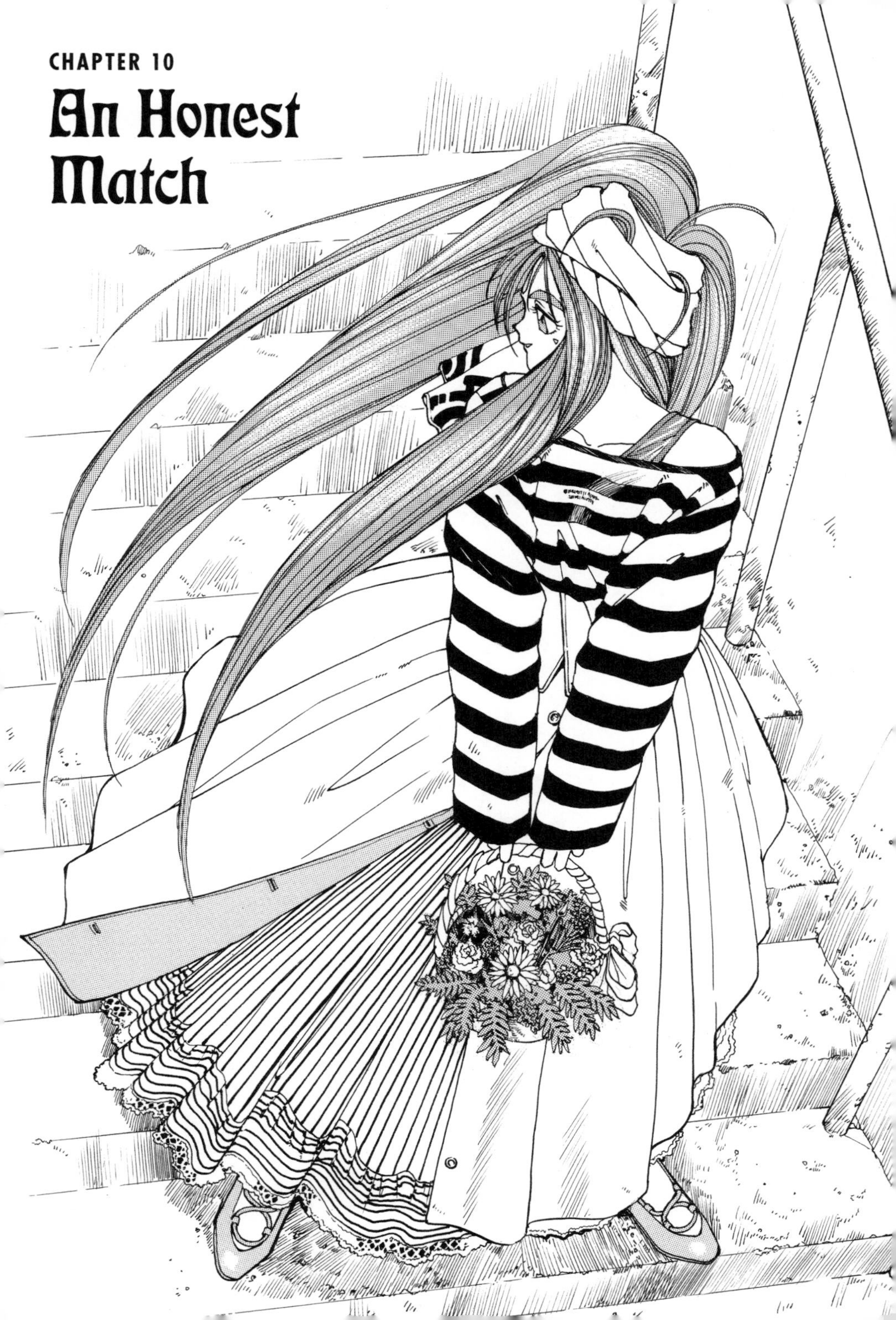

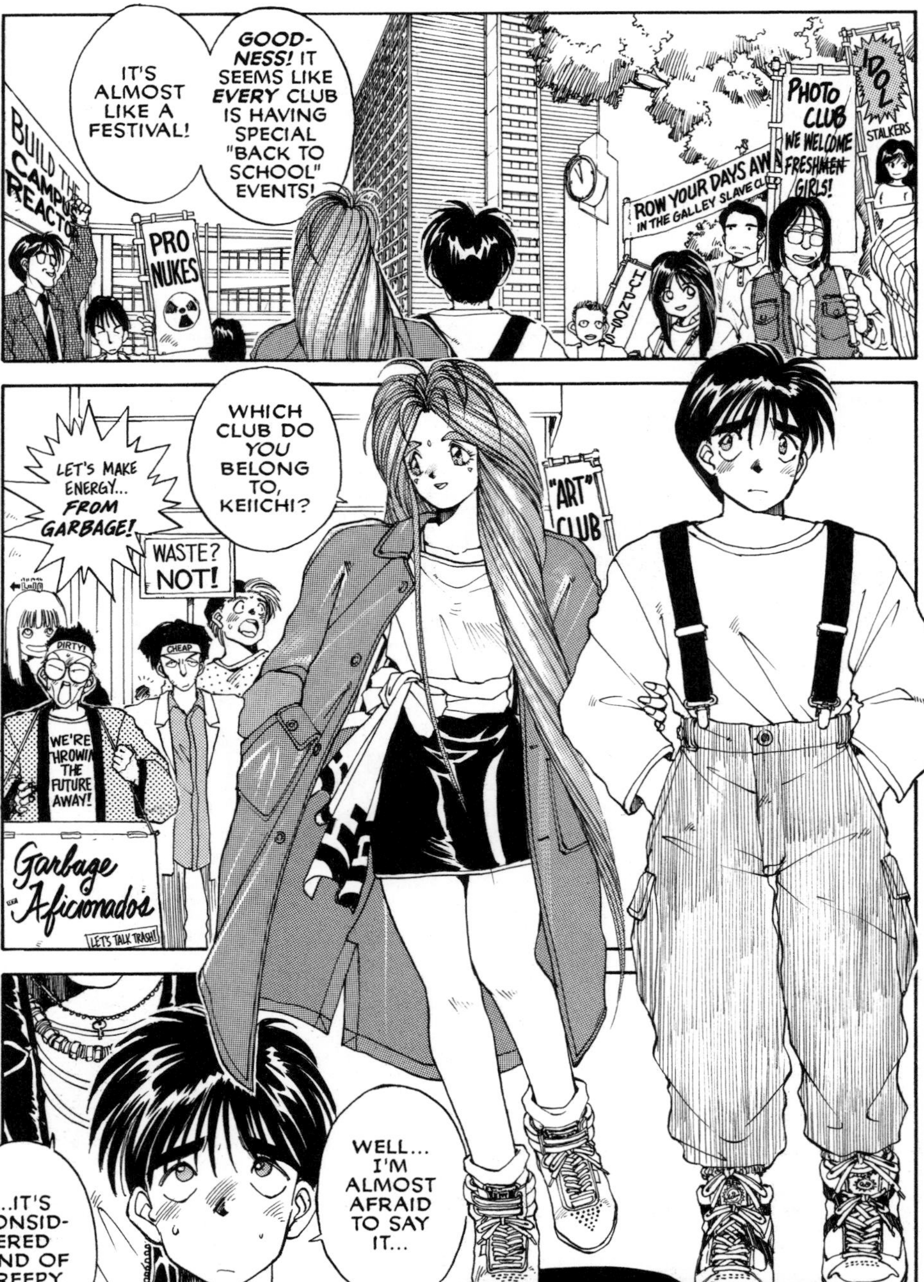

IDOL STALKERS
PHOTO CLUB WE WELCOME FRESHMEN GIRLS!
ROW YOUR DAYS AWA IN THE GALLEY SLAVE CL
HYPNOSIS
GOODNESS! IT SEEMS LIKE EVERY CLUB IS HAVING SPECIAL "BACK TO SCHOOL" EVENTS!
IT'S ALMOST LIKE A FESTIVAL!
PRO NUKES
BUILD THE CAMPU REACTO
WHICH CLUB DO YOU BELONG TO, KEIICHI?
"ART" CLUB
LET'S MAKE ENERGY... FROM GARBAGE!
WASTE? NOT!
CHEAP
DIRTY!
WE'RE THROWIN THE FUTURE AWAY!
Garbage Aficionados
LET'S TALK TRASH!
WELL... I'M ALMOST AFRAID TO SAY IT...
...IT'S CONSID-ERED KIND OF CREEPY.

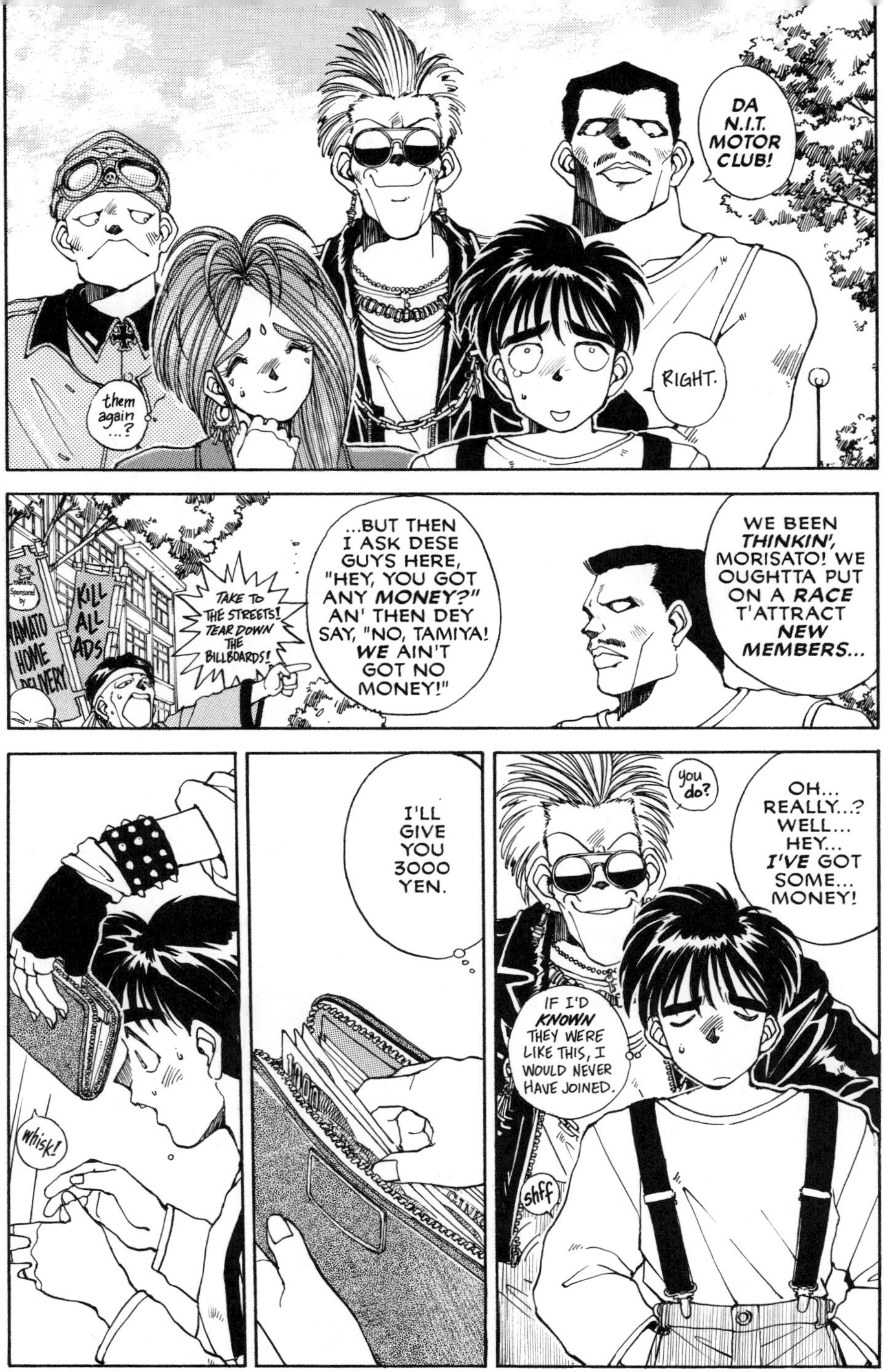
DA N.I.T. MOTOR CLUB!
RIGHT.
them again ...?
WE BEEN THINKIN', MORISATO! WE OUGHTTA PUT ON A RACE T'ATTRACT NEW MEMBERS...
...BUT THEN I ASK DESE GUYS HERE, "HEY, YOU GOT ANY MONEY?" AN' THEN DEY SAY, "NO, TAMIYA! WE AIN'T GOT NO MONEY!"
TAKE TO THE STREETS! TEAR DOWN THE BILLBOARDS!
KILL ALL ADS!
Sponsored by
OH... REALLY...? WELL... HEY... I'VE GOT SOME... MONEY!
you do?
IF I'D KNOWN THEY WERE LIKE THIS, I WOULD NEVER HAVE JOINED.
shff
I'LL GIVE YOU 3000 YEN.
whisk!

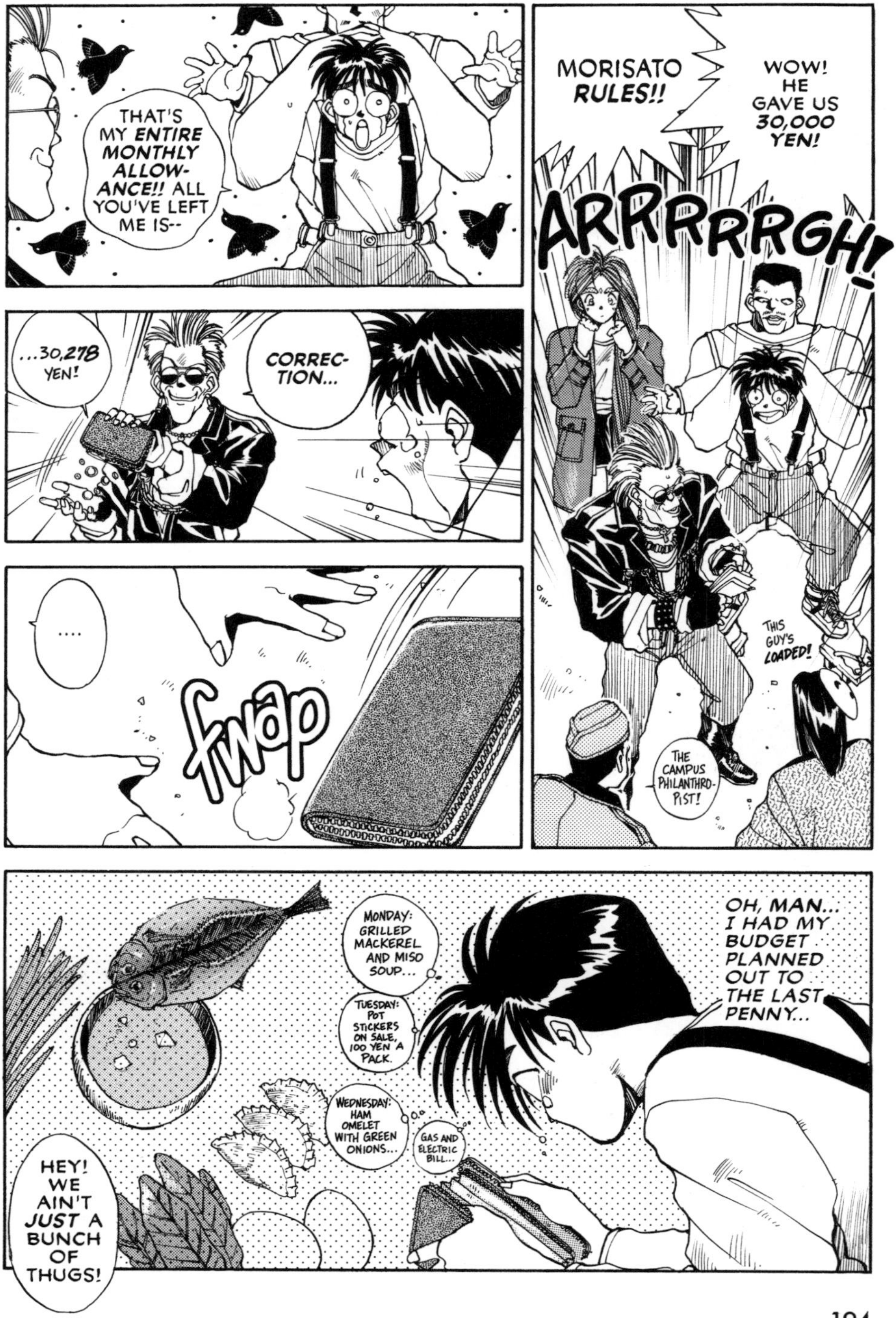
WOW! HE GAVE US 30,000 YEN!
MORISATO RULES!!
ARRRRRGH!
THIS GUY'S LOADED!
THE CAMPUS PHILANTHRO-PIST!
THAT'S MY ENTIRE MONTHLY ALLOW-ANCE!! ALL YOU'VE LEFT ME IS--
CORRECTION...
...30,278 YEN!
....
fwap
OH, MAN... I HAD MY BUDGET PLANNED OUT TO THE LAST PENNY...
MONDAY: GRILLED MACKEREL AND MISO SOUP...
TUESDAY: POT STICKERS ON SALE, 100 YEN A PACK.
WEDNESDAY: HAM OMELET WITH GREEN ONIONS...
GAS AND ELECTRIC BILL...
HEY! WE AIN'T JUST A BUNCH OF THUGS!

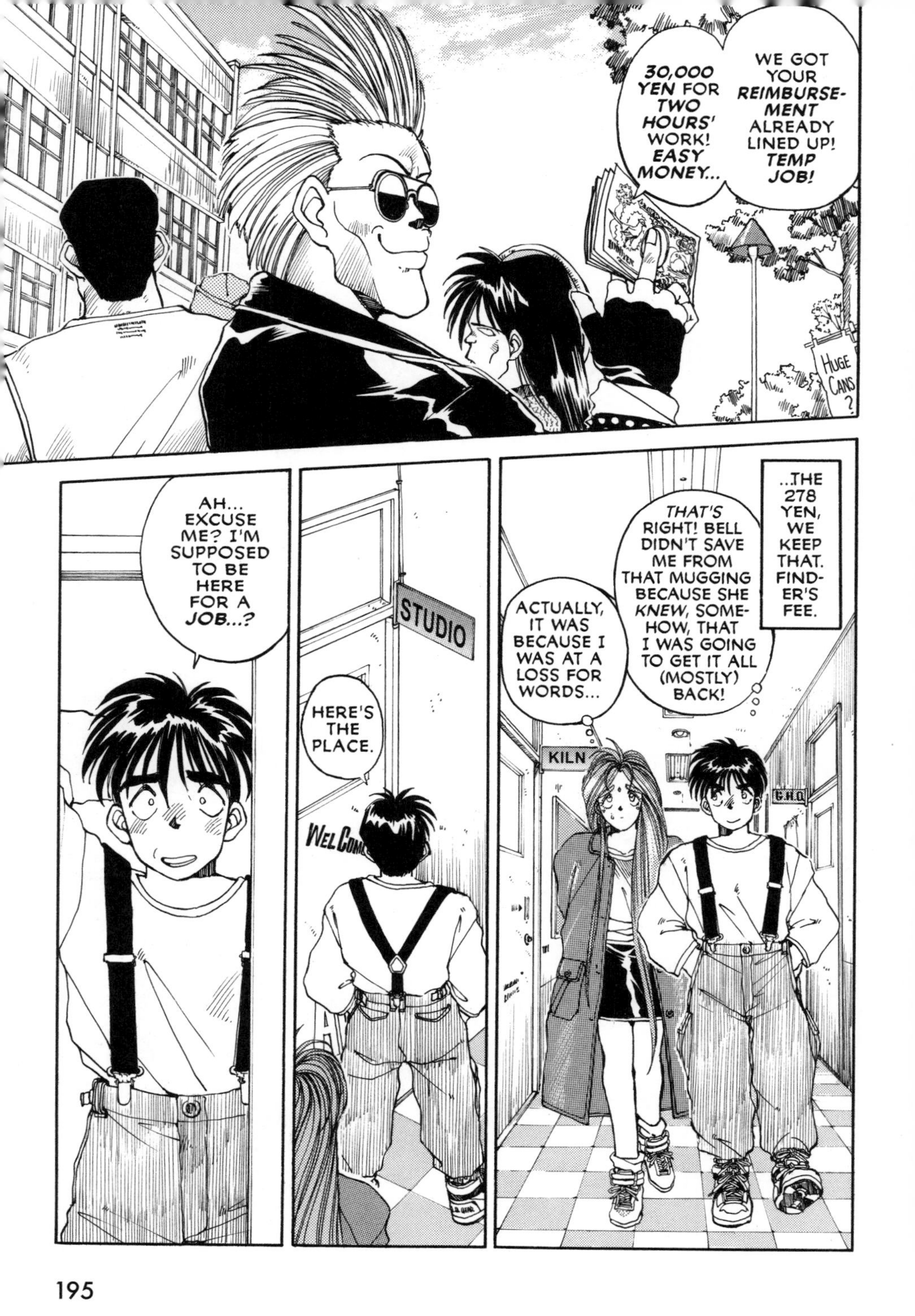
WE GOT YOUR REIMBURSEMENT ALREADY LINED UP! TEMP JOB!
30,000 YEN FOR TWO HOURS' WORK! EASY MONEY...
HUGE CANS ?
...THE 278 YEN, WE KEEP THAT. FINDER'S FEE.
THAT'S RIGHT! BELL DIDN'T SAVE ME FROM THAT MUGGING BECAUSE SHE KNEW, SOMEHOW, THAT I WAS GOING TO GET IT ALL (MOSTLY) BACK!
ACTUALLY, IT WAS BECAUSE I WAS AT A LOSS FOR WORDS...
KILN
G.H.Q.
STUDIO
HERE'S THE PLACE.
AH... EXCUSE ME? I'M SUPPOSED TO BE HERE FOR A JOB...?

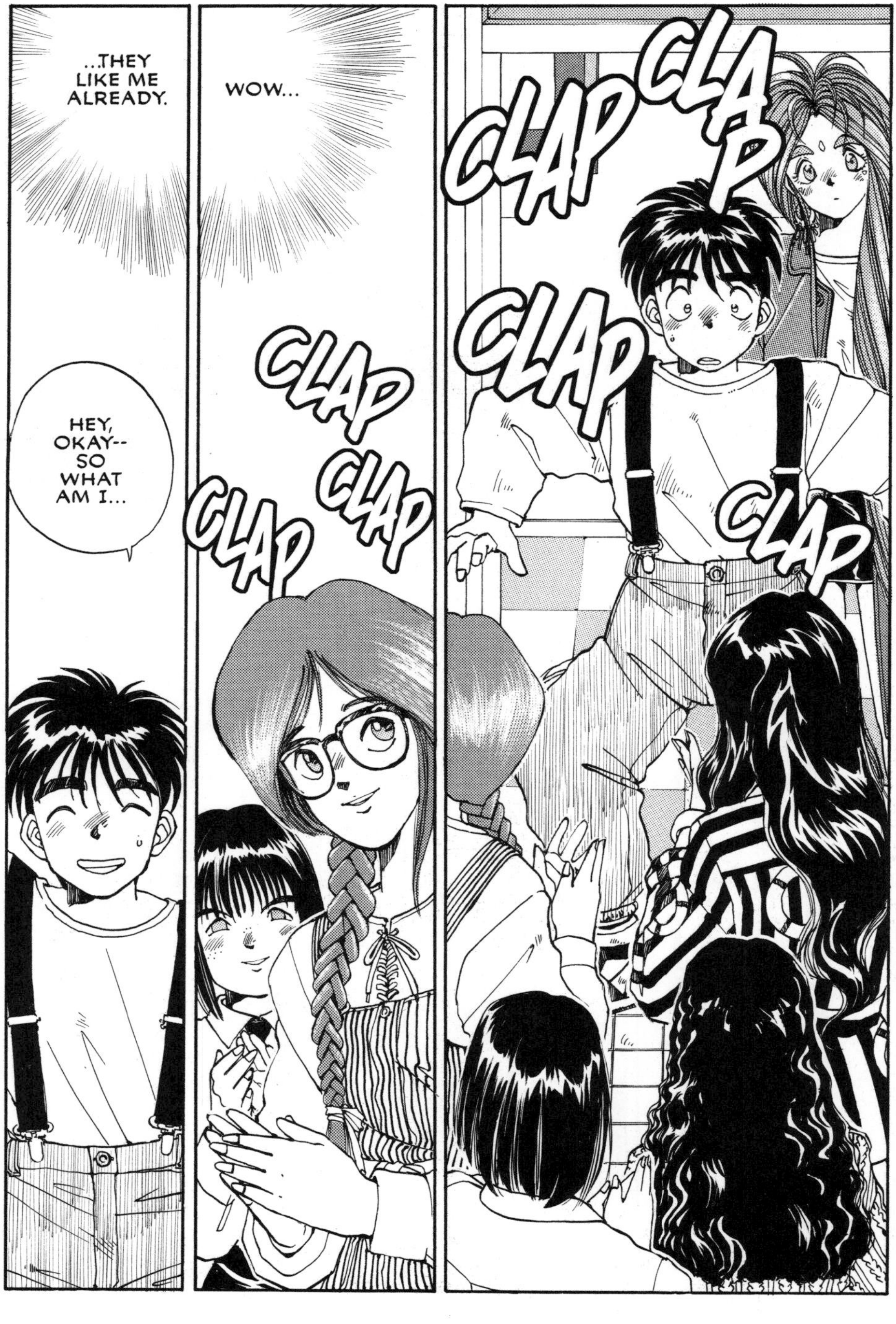
CLAP
CLAP
CLAP
CLAP
WOW...
CLAP
CLAP
CLAP
...THEY LIKE ME ALREADY.
HEY, OKAY-- SO WHAT AM I...

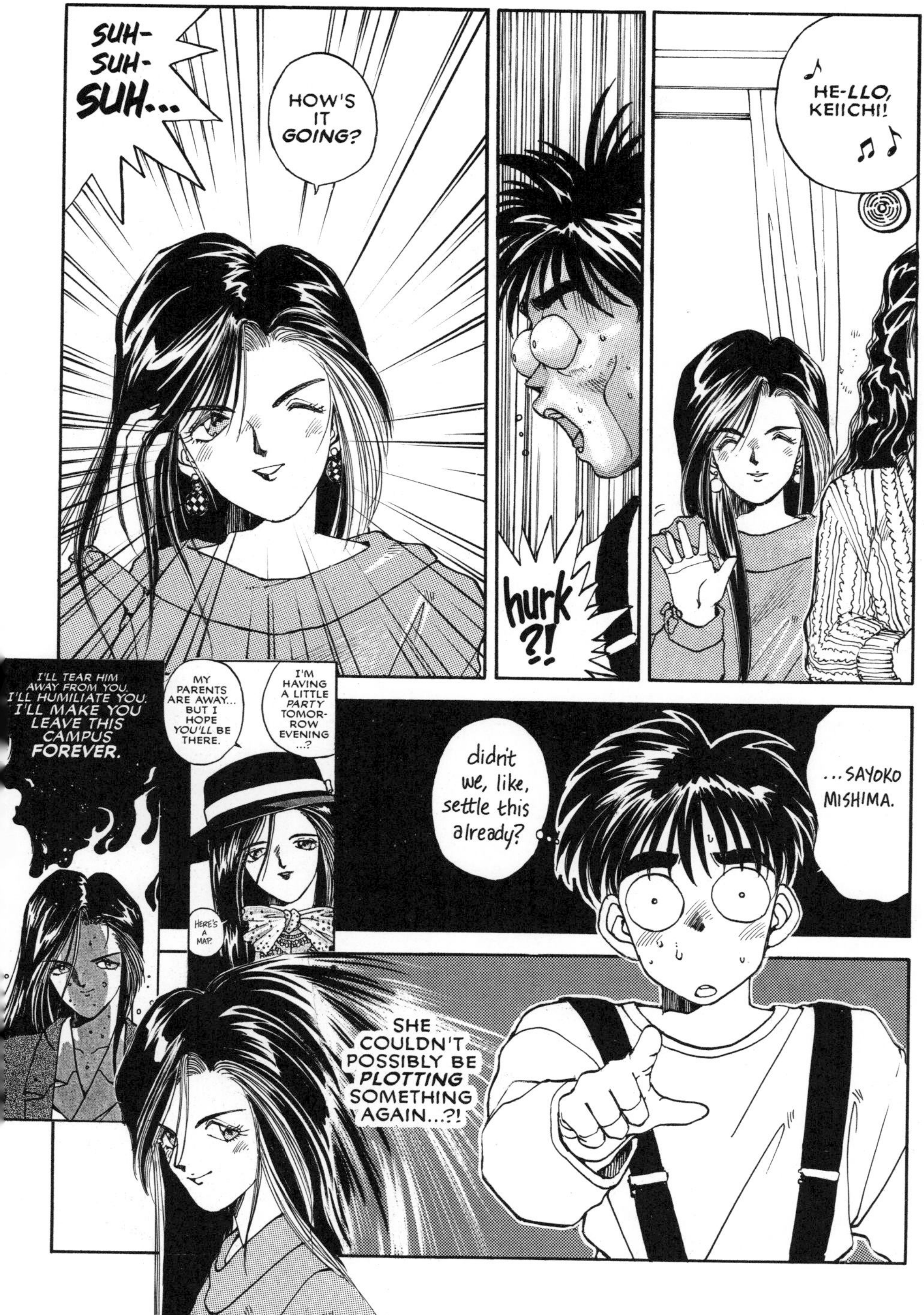
♪ HE-*LLO*, KEIICHI! ♫ ♪
hurk ?!
HOW'S IT *GOING?*
SUH-SUH-SUH...
...SAYOKO MISHIMA.
didn't we, like, settle this already?
I'M HAVING A LITTLE *PARTY* TOMORROW EVENING ...?
MY PARENTS ARE AWAY... BUT I HOPE *YOU'LL* BE THERE.
HERE'S A MAP.
I'LL TEAR HIM AWAY FROM YOU. I'LL HUMILIATE YOU. I'LL MAKE YOU LEAVE THIS CAMPUS **FOREVER.**
SHE COULDN'T POSSIBLY BE *PLOTTING* SOMETHING AGAIN...?!

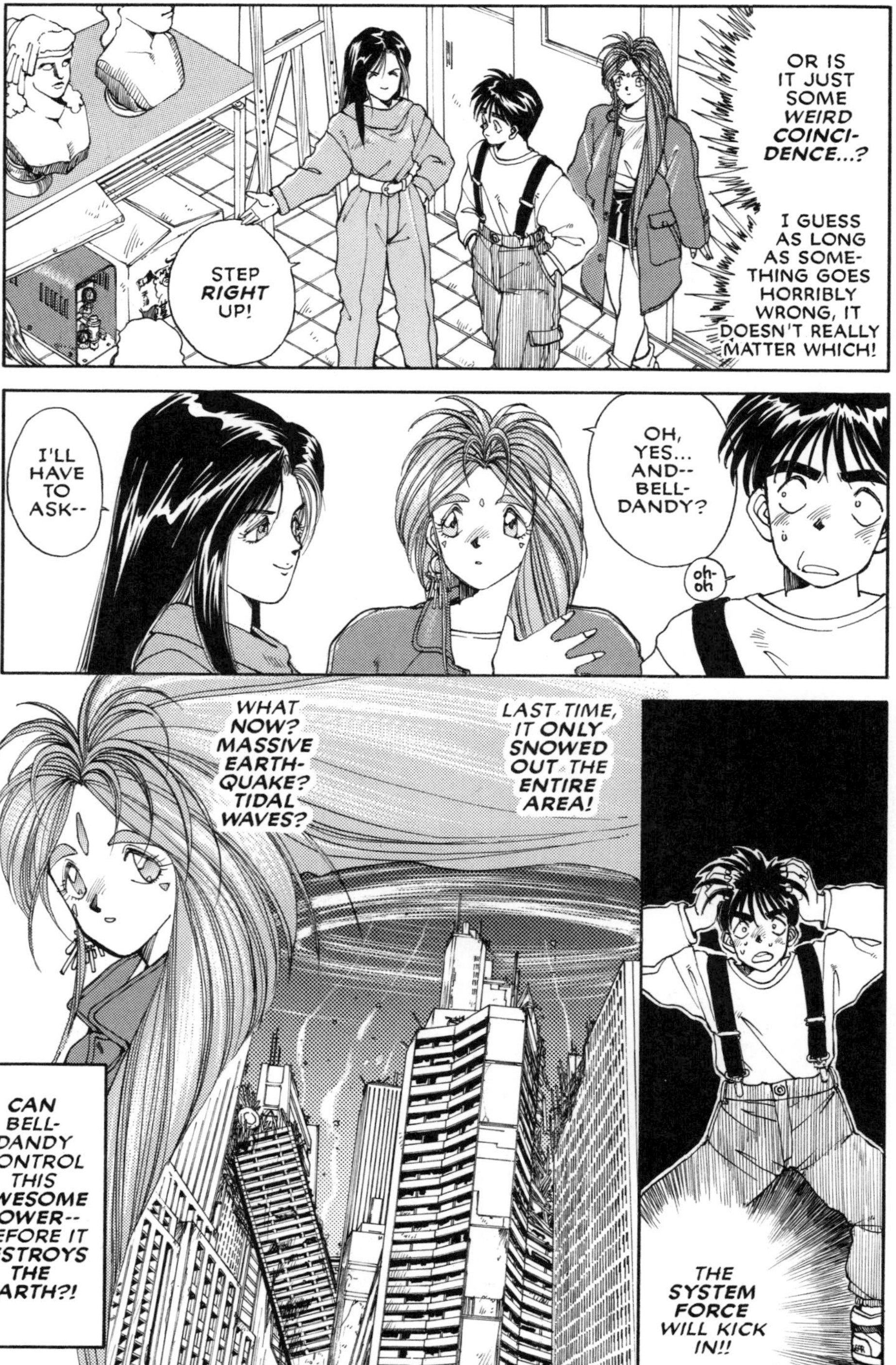
OR IS IT JUST SOME WEIRD COINCIDENCE...?
I GUESS AS LONG AS SOME-THING GOES HORRIBLY WRONG, IT DOESN'T REALLY MATTER WHICH!
STEP RIGHT UP!
OH, YES... AND-- BELL-DANDY?
oh-oh
I'LL HAVE TO ASK--
THE SYSTEM FORCE WILL KICK IN!!
LAST TIME, IT ONLY SNOWED OUT THE ENTIRE AREA!
WHAT NOW? MASSIVE EARTH-QUAKE? TIDAL WAVES?
CAN BELL-DANDY CONTROL THIS AWESOME POWER-- BEFORE IT DESTROYS THE EARTH?!

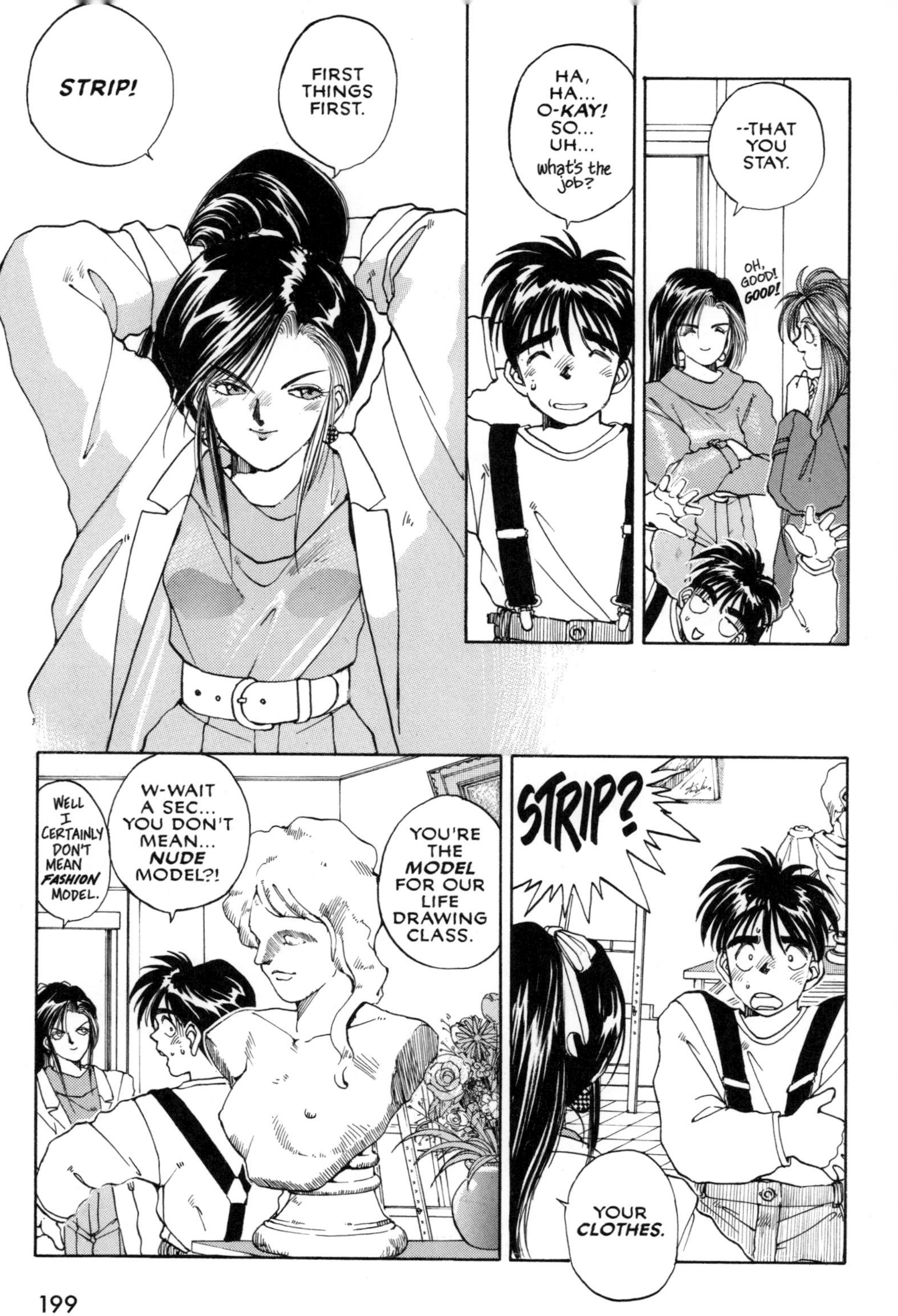
--THAT YOU STAY.
OH, GOOD! GOOD!
HA, HA... O-KAY! SO... UH... what's the job?
FIRST THINGS FIRST.
STRIP!
STRIP?
YOUR CLOTHES.
YOU'RE THE MODEL FOR OUR LIFE DRAWING CLASS.
W-WAIT A SEC... YOU DON'T MEAN... NUDE MODEL?!
WELL I CERTAINLY DON'T MEAN FASHION MODEL.

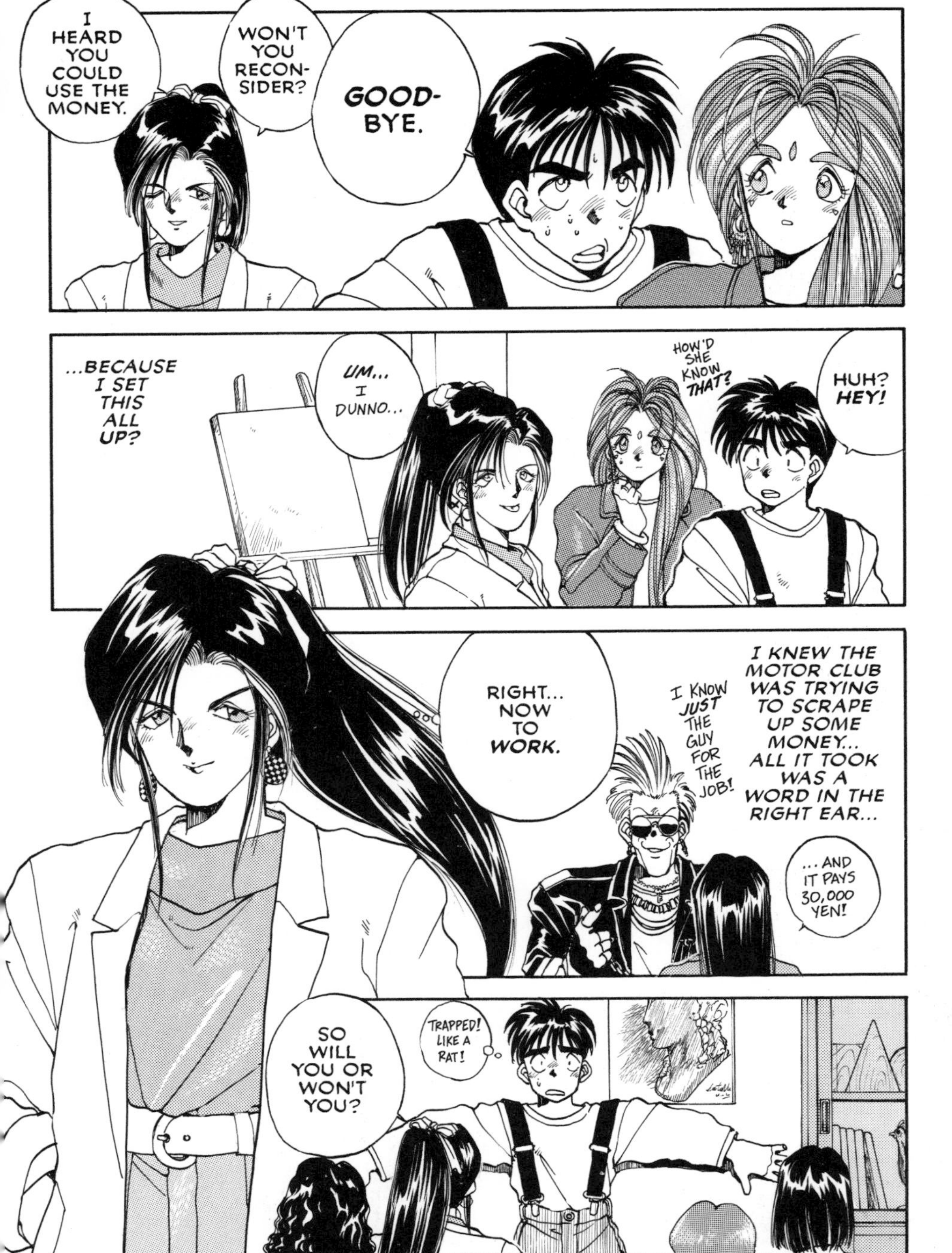
GOOD-BYE.
WON'T YOU RECONSIDER?
I HEARD YOU COULD USE THE MONEY.
HUH? HEY!
HOW'D SHE KNOW THAT?
UM... I DUNNO...
...BECAUSE I SET THIS ALL UP?
I KNEW THE MOTOR CLUB WAS TRYING TO SCRAPE UP SOME MONEY... ALL IT TOOK WAS A WORD IN THE RIGHT EAR...
I KNOW JUST THE GUY FOR THE JOB!
...AND IT PAYS 30,000 YEN!
RIGHT... NOW TO WORK.
TRAPPED! LIKE A RAT!
SO WILL YOU OR WON'T YOU?

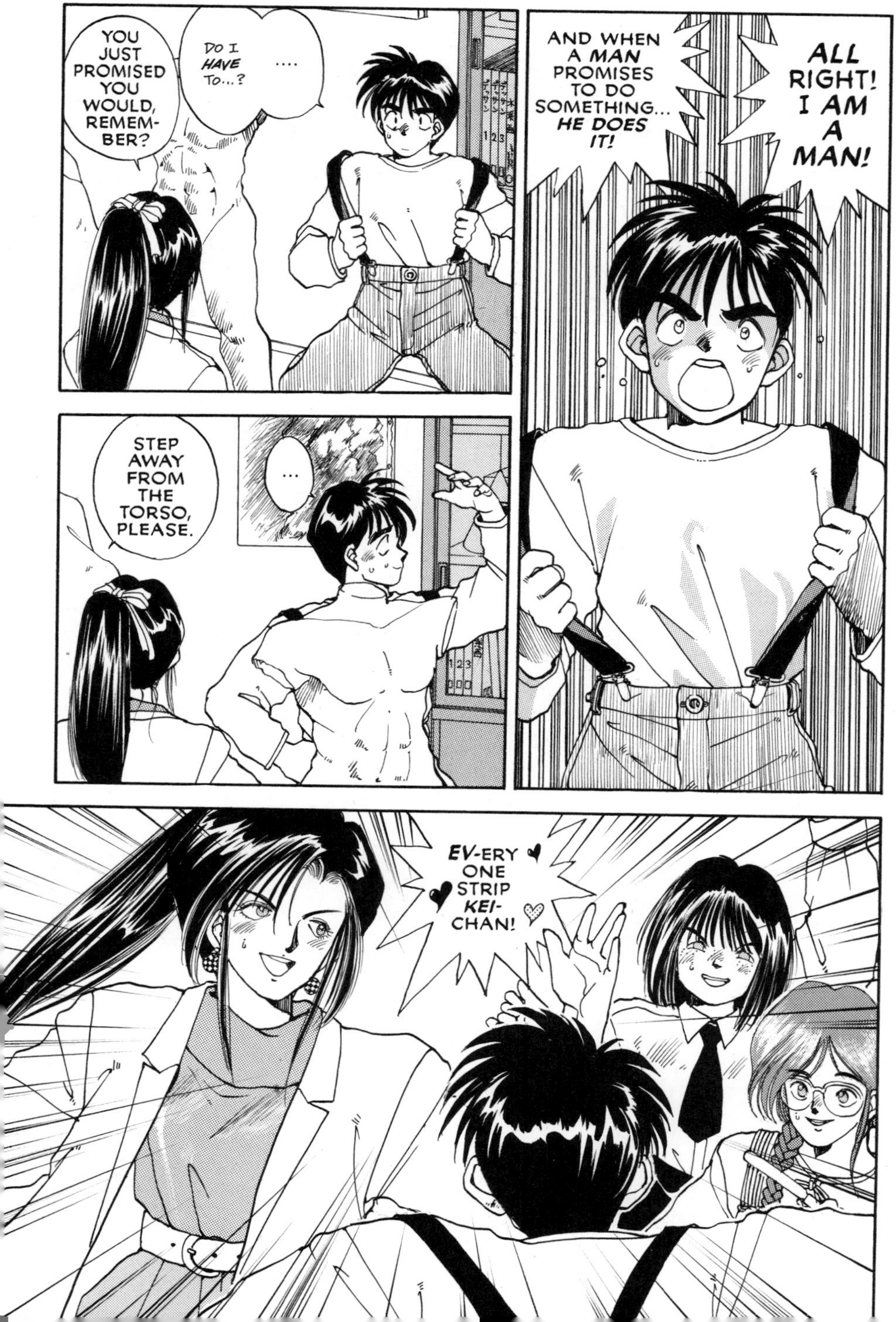
AND WHEN A *MAN* PROMISES TO DO SOMETHING... *HE DOES IT!*
ALL RIGHT! I AM A MAN!
....
DO I *HAVE* TO...?
YOU JUST PROMISED YOU WOULD, REMEMBER?
...
STEP AWAY FROM THE TORSO, PLEASE.
EV-ERY ONE STRIP *KEI*-CHAN!

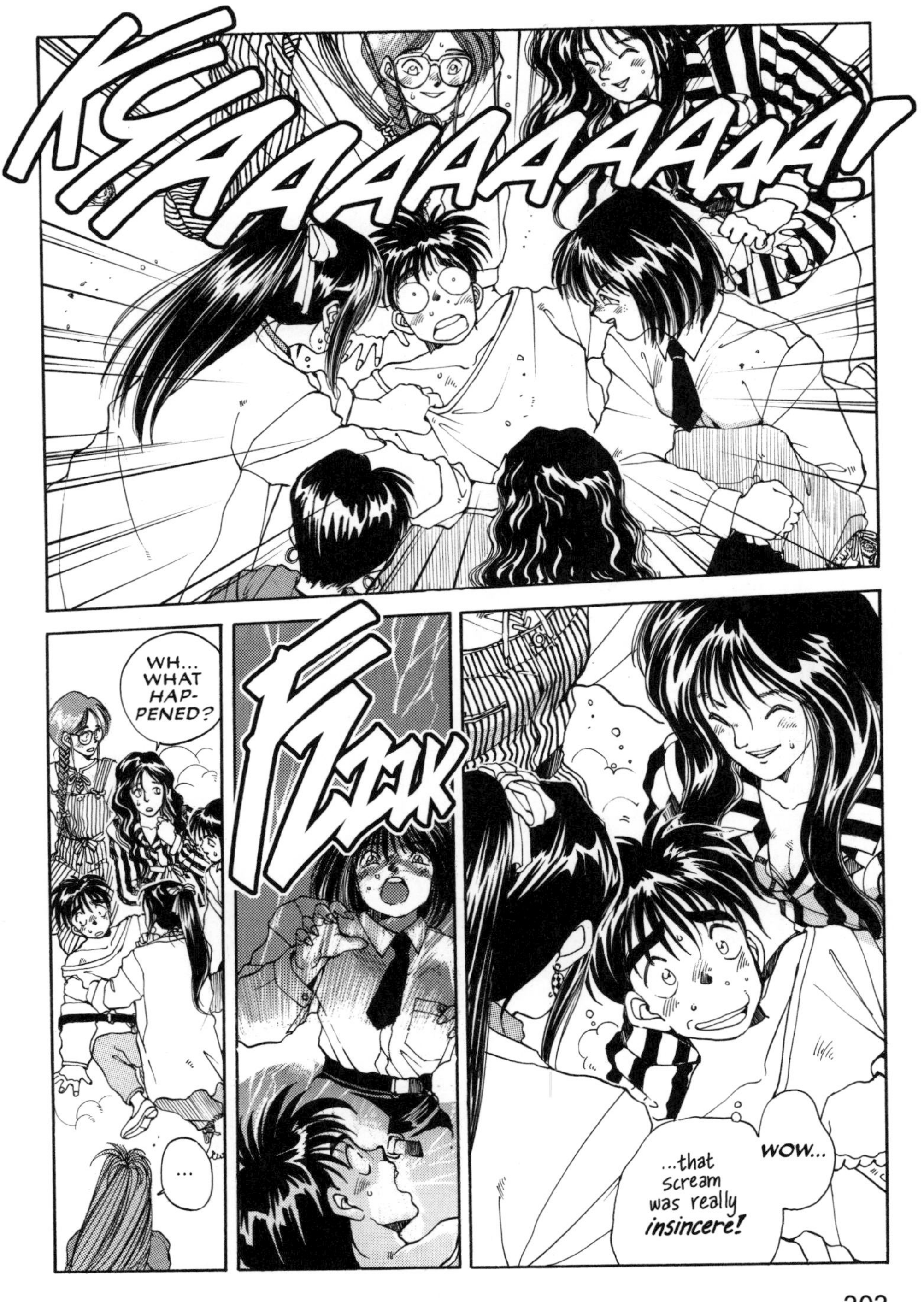
KYAAAAAAAAAAA!
WOW...
...that scream was really *insincere!*
FZZAK
WH... WHAT HAP-PENED?
...

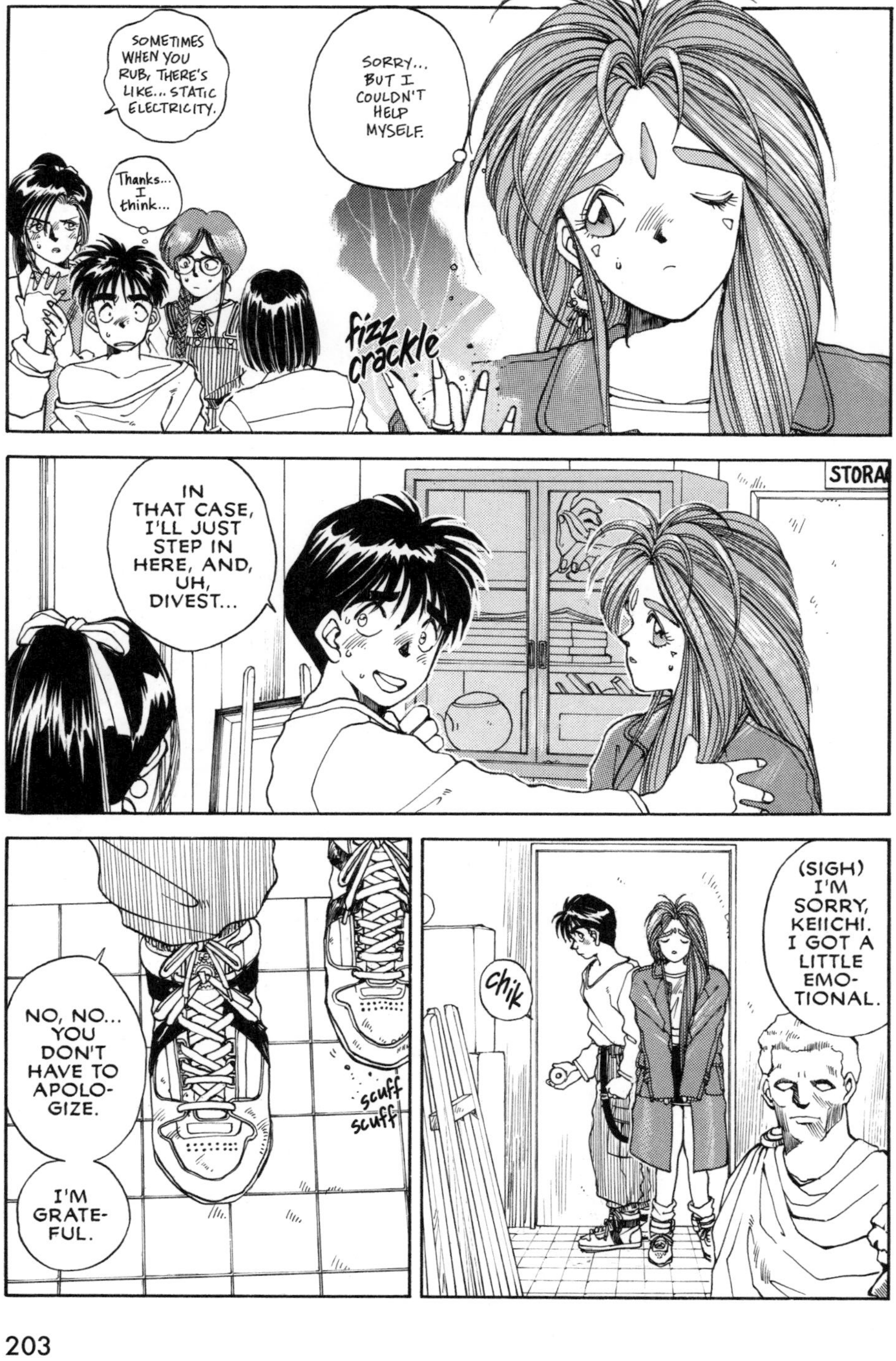
SORRY... BUT I COULDN'T HELP MYSELF.
SOMETIMES WHEN YOU RUB, THERE'S LIKE... STATIC ELECTRICITY.
Thanks... I think...
fizz crackle
IN THAT CASE, I'LL JUST STEP IN HERE, AND, UH, DIVEST...
(SIGH) I'M SORRY, KEIICHI. I GOT A LITTLE EMO-TIONAL.
chik
NO, NO... YOU DON'T HAVE TO APOLO-GIZE.
I'M GRATE-FUL.
scuff scuff

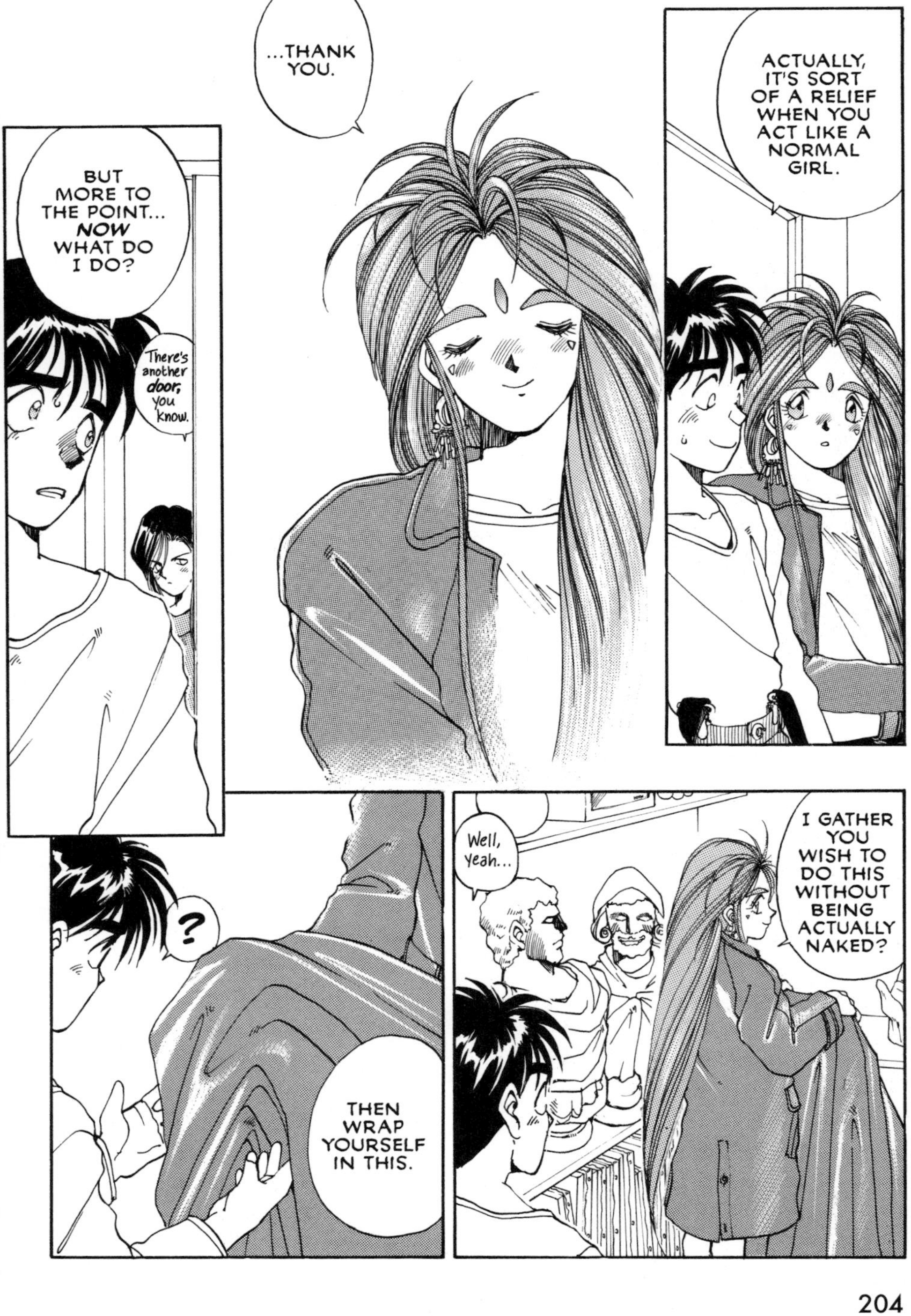
ACTUALLY, IT'S SORT OF A RELIEF WHEN YOU ACT LIKE A NORMAL GIRL.
...THANK YOU.
BUT MORE TO THE POINT... **NOW** WHAT DO I DO?
There's another *door,* you know.
I GATHER YOU WISH TO DO THIS WITHOUT BEING ACTUALLY NAKED?
Well, yeah...
?
THEN WRAP YOURSELF IN THIS.

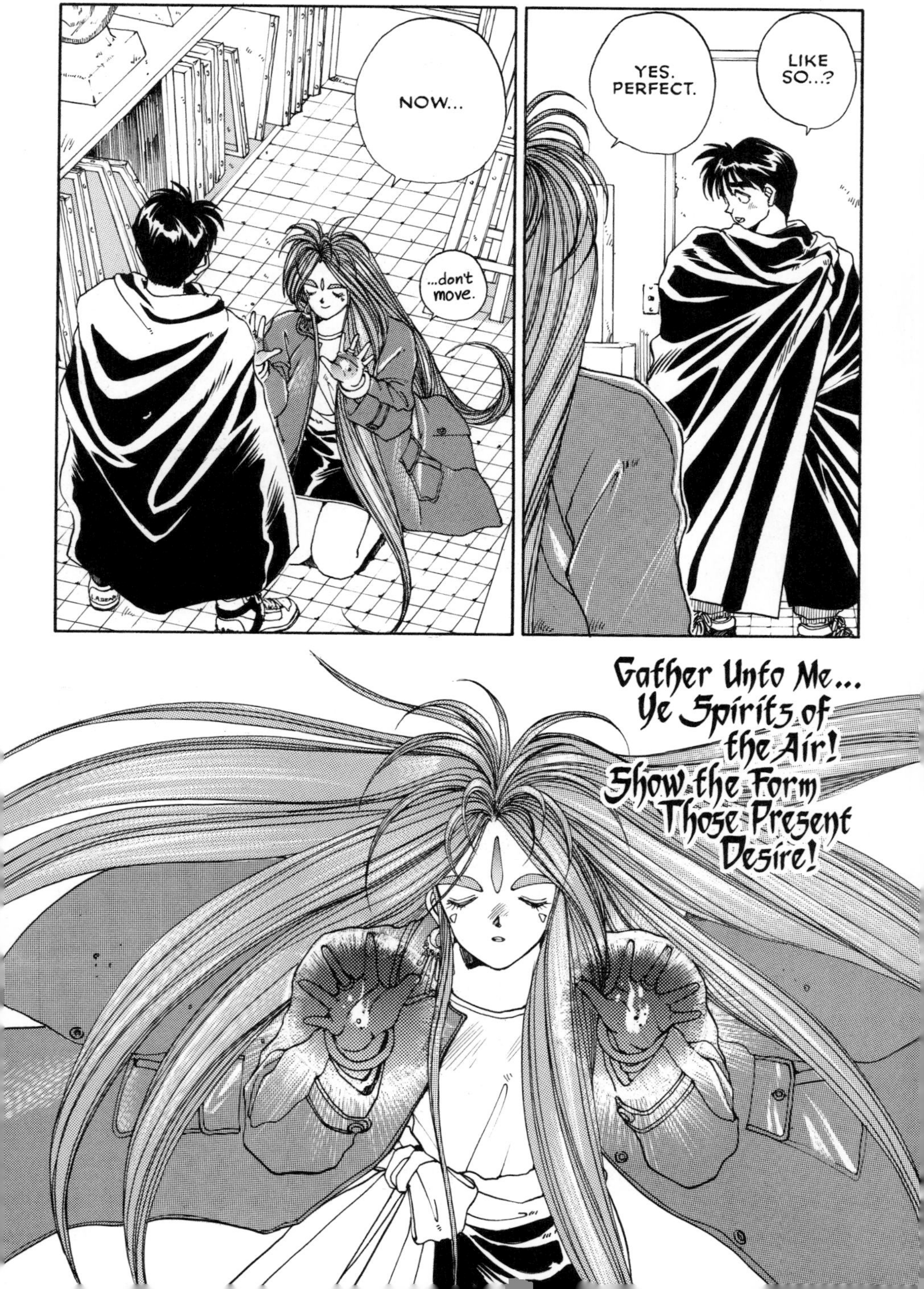
LIKE SO...?
YES. PERFECT.
NOW...
...don't move.
Gather Unto Me... Ye Spirits of the Air! Show the Form Those Present Desire!

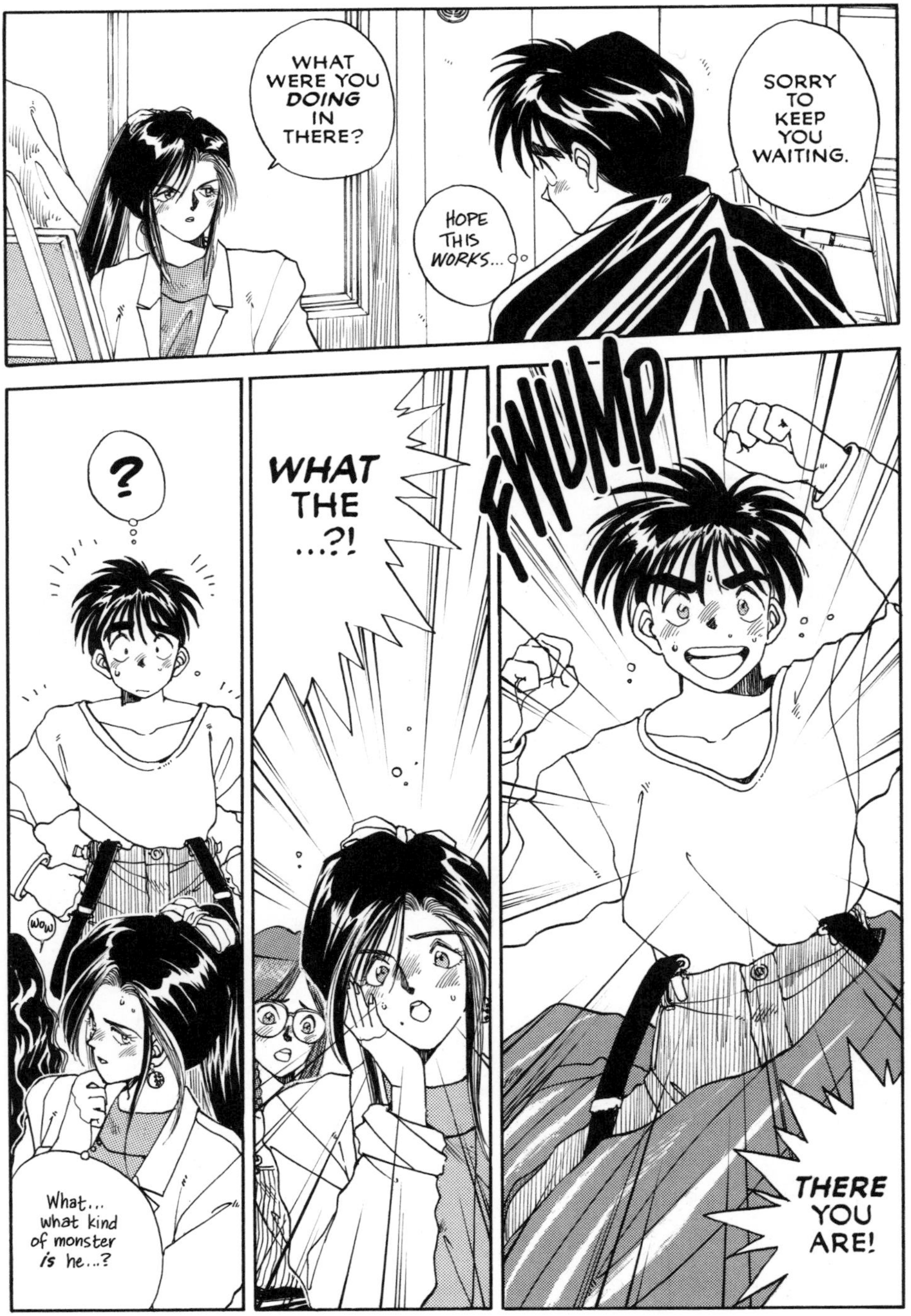
SORRY TO KEEP YOU WAITING.
WHAT WERE YOU *DOING* IN THERE?
HOPE THIS *WORKS*...
FWUMP
THERE YOU ARE!
WHAT THE ...?!
?
wow
What... what kind of monster *is* he...?

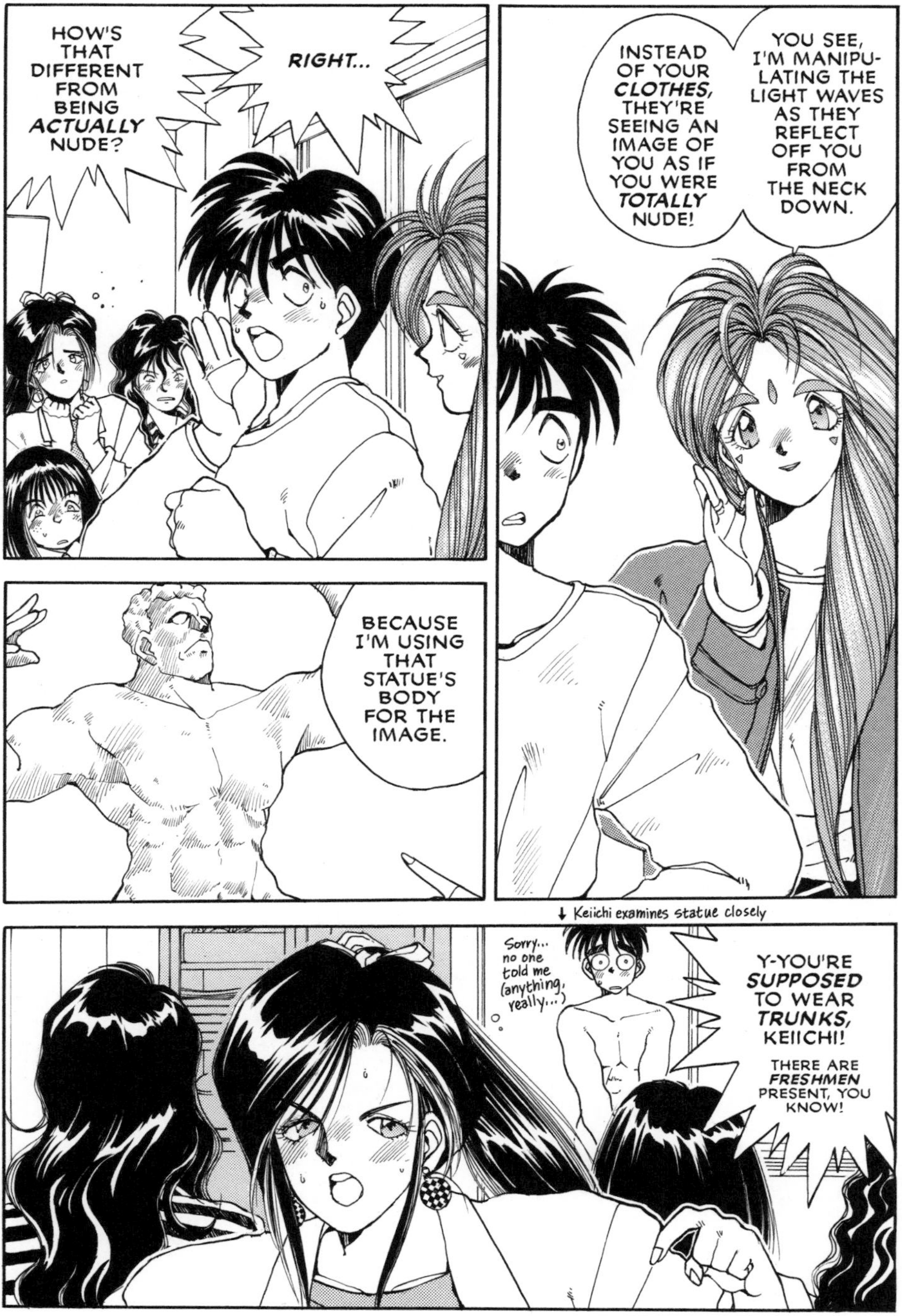
YOU SEE, I'M MANIPULATING THE LIGHT WAVES AS THEY REFLECT OFF YOU FROM THE NECK DOWN.
INSTEAD OF YOUR CLOTHES, THEY'RE SEEING AN IMAGE OF YOU AS IF YOU WERE TOTALLY NUDE!
RIGHT...
HOW'S THAT DIFFERENT FROM BEING ACTUALLY NUDE?
BECAUSE I'M USING THAT STATUE'S BODY FOR THE IMAGE.
↓ Keiichi examines statue closely
Y-YOU'RE SUPPOSED TO WEAR TRUNKS, KEIICHI!
THERE ARE FRESHMEN PRESENT, YOU KNOW!
Sorry... no one told me (anything, really...)

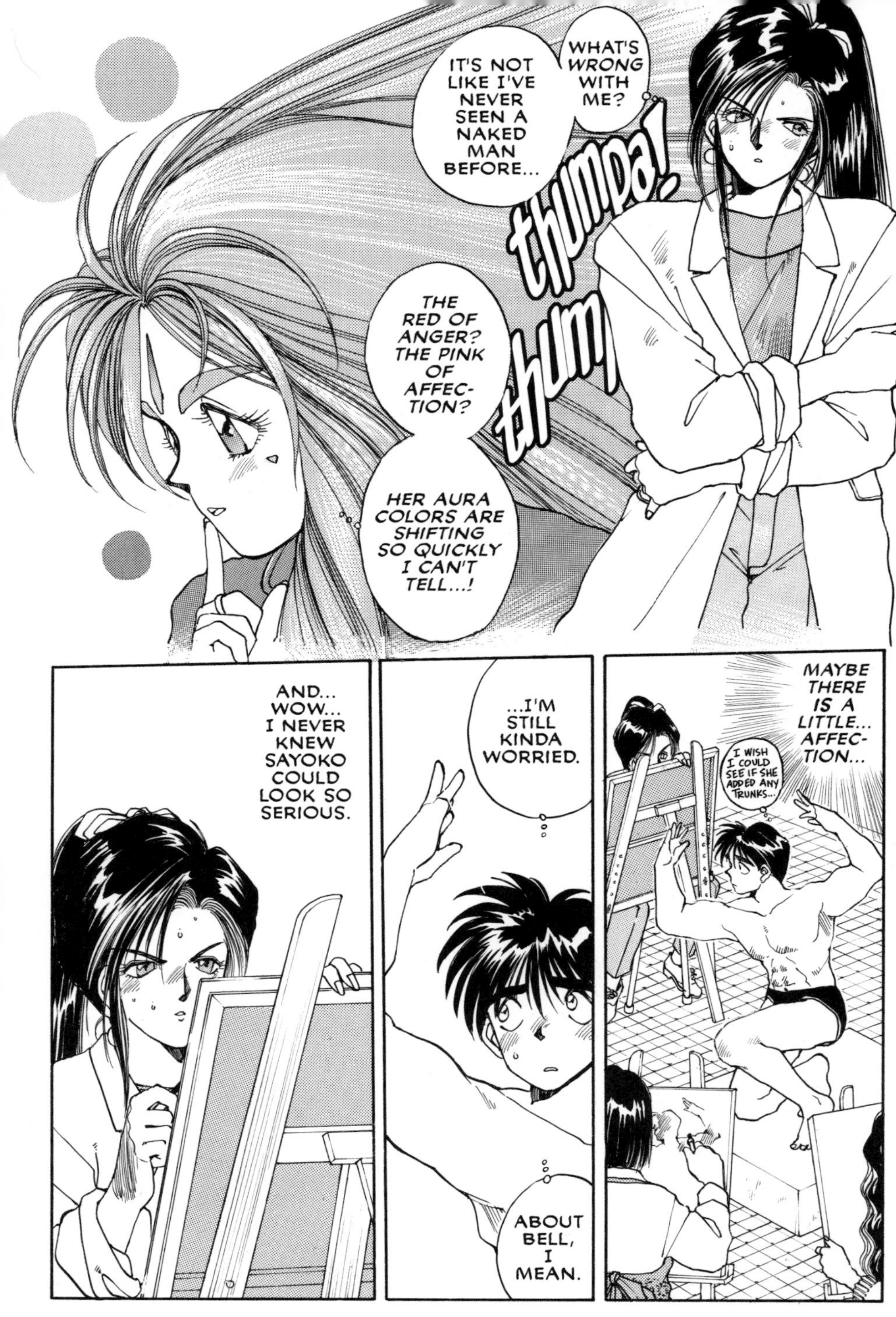
WHAT'S WRONG WITH ME?
IT'S NOT LIKE I'VE NEVER SEEN A NAKED MAN BEFORE...
thumpa! thump
THE RED OF ANGER? THE PINK OF AFFEC-TION?
HER AURA COLORS ARE SHIFTING SO QUICKLY I CAN'T TELL...!
MAYBE THERE IS A LITTLE... AFFEC-TION...
I WISH I COULD SEE IF SHE ADDED ANY TRUNKS...
...I'M STILL KINDA WORRIED.
ABOUT BELL, I MEAN.
AND... WOW... I NEVER KNEW SAYOKO COULD LOOK SO SERIOUS.

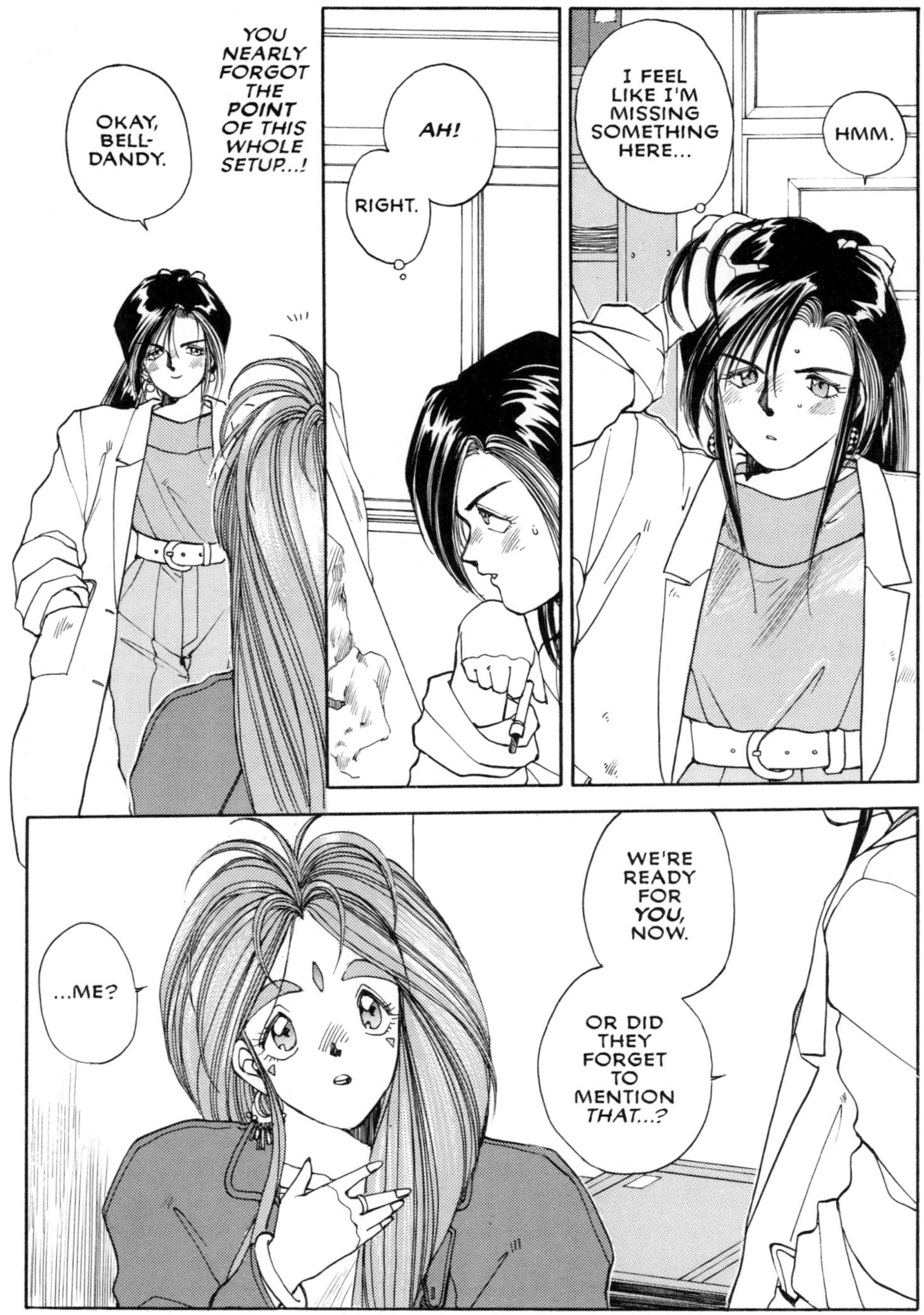
HMM.
I FEEL LIKE I'M MISSING SOMETHING HERE...
AH!
RIGHT.
YOU NEARLY FORGOT THE *POINT* OF THIS WHOLE SETUP...!
OKAY, BELL-DANDY.
WE'RE READY FOR *YOU,* NOW.
OR DID THEY FORGET TO MENTION *THAT*...?
...ME?

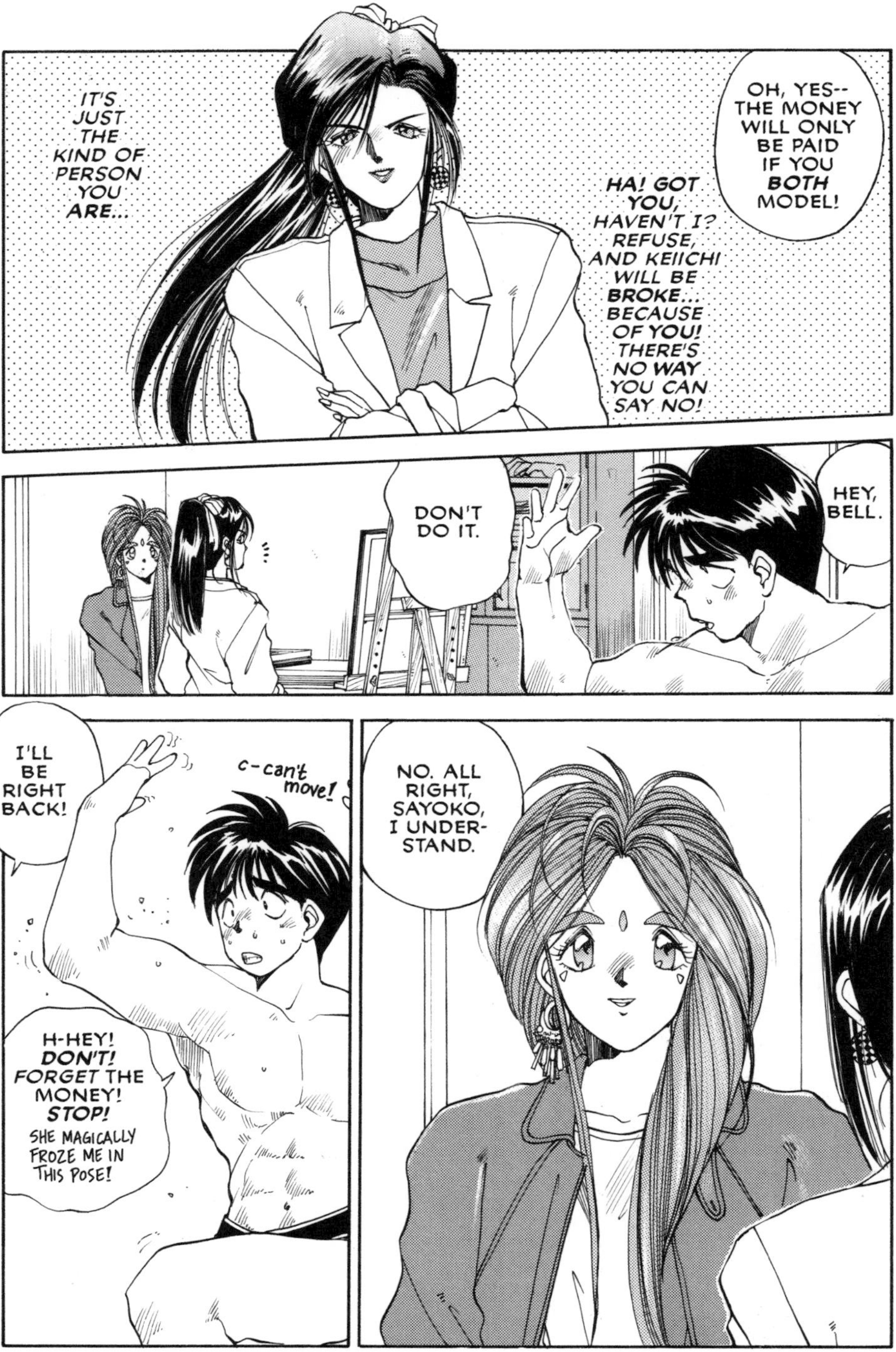
OH, YES-- THE MONEY WILL ONLY BE PAID IF YOU BOTH MODEL!
HA! GOT YOU, HAVEN'T I? REFUSE, AND KEIICHI WILL BE BROKE... BECAUSE OF YOU! THERE'S NO WAY YOU CAN SAY NO!
IT'S JUST THE KIND OF PERSON YOU ARE...
HEY, BELL.
DON'T DO IT.
NO. ALL RIGHT, SAYOKO, I UNDER-STAND.
I'LL BE RIGHT BACK!
c-can't move!
H-HEY! DON'T! FORGET THE MONEY! STOP!
SHE MAGICALLY FROZE ME IN THIS POSE!

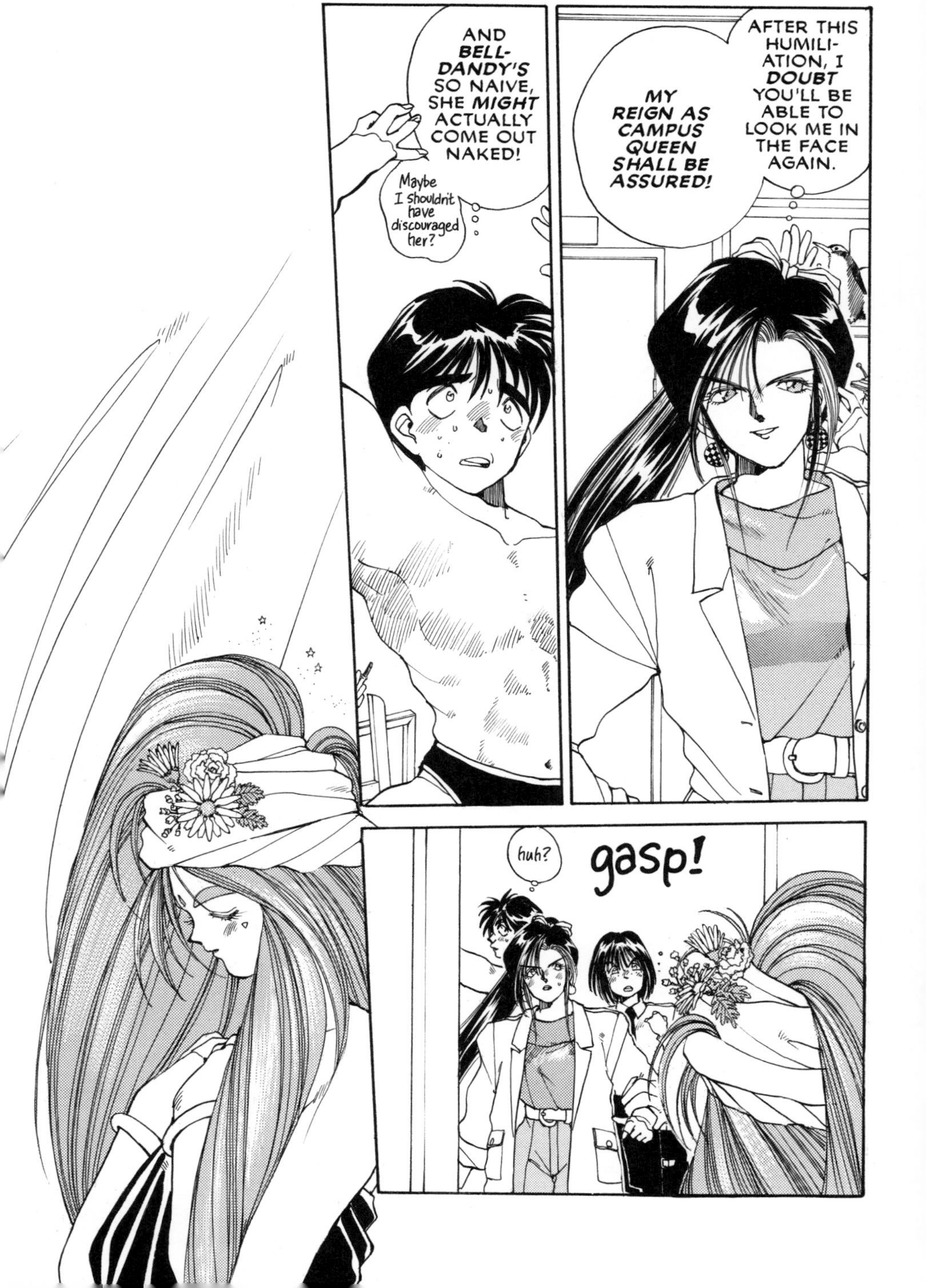
AFTER THIS HUMILI-ATION, I DOUBT YOU'LL BE ABLE TO LOOK ME IN THE FACE AGAIN.
MY REIGN AS CAMPUS QUEEN SHALL BE ASSURED!
AND BELL-DANDY'S SO NAIVE, SHE MIGHT ACTUALLY COME OUT NAKED!
Maybe I shouldn't have discouraged her?
gasp!
huh?

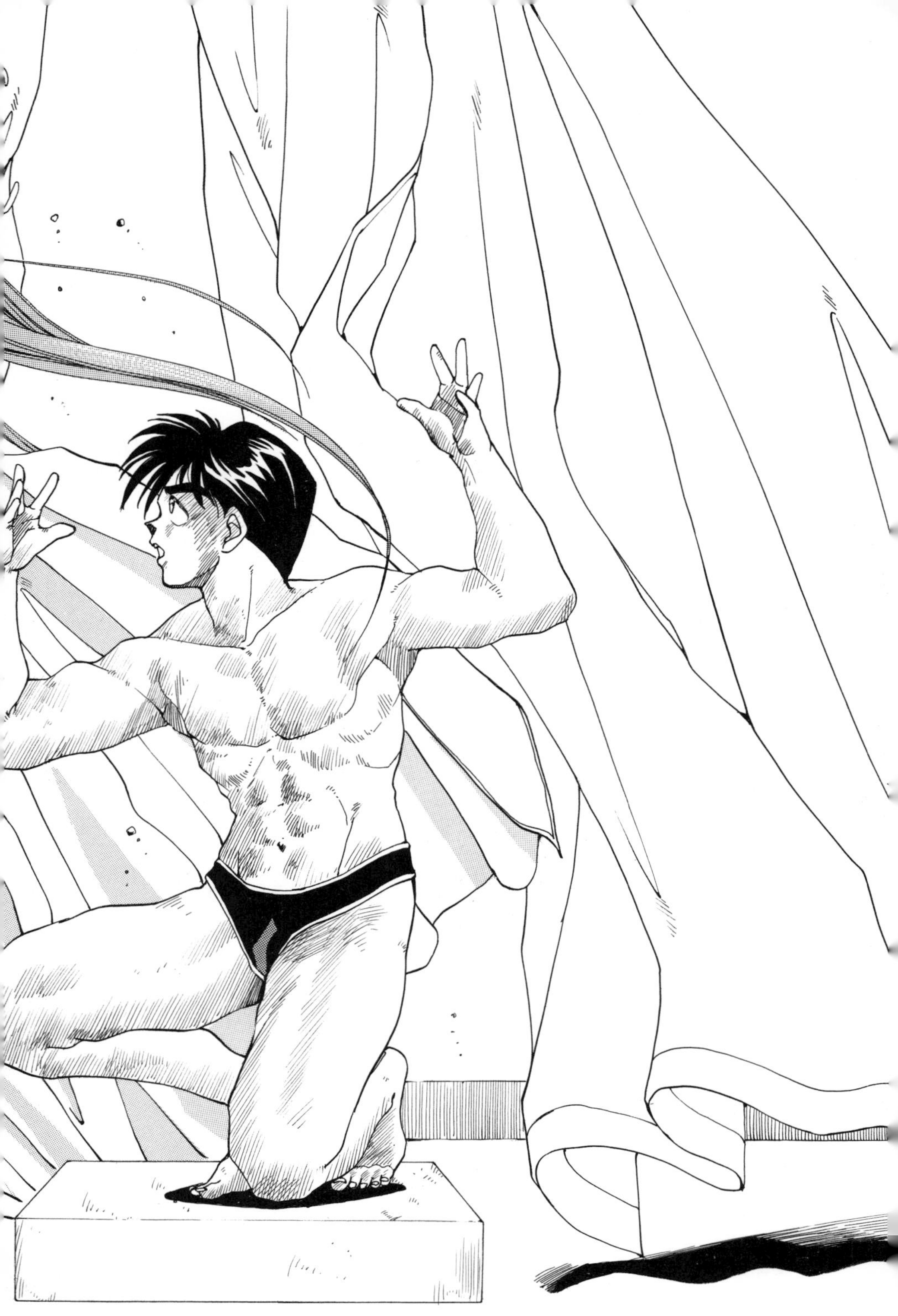

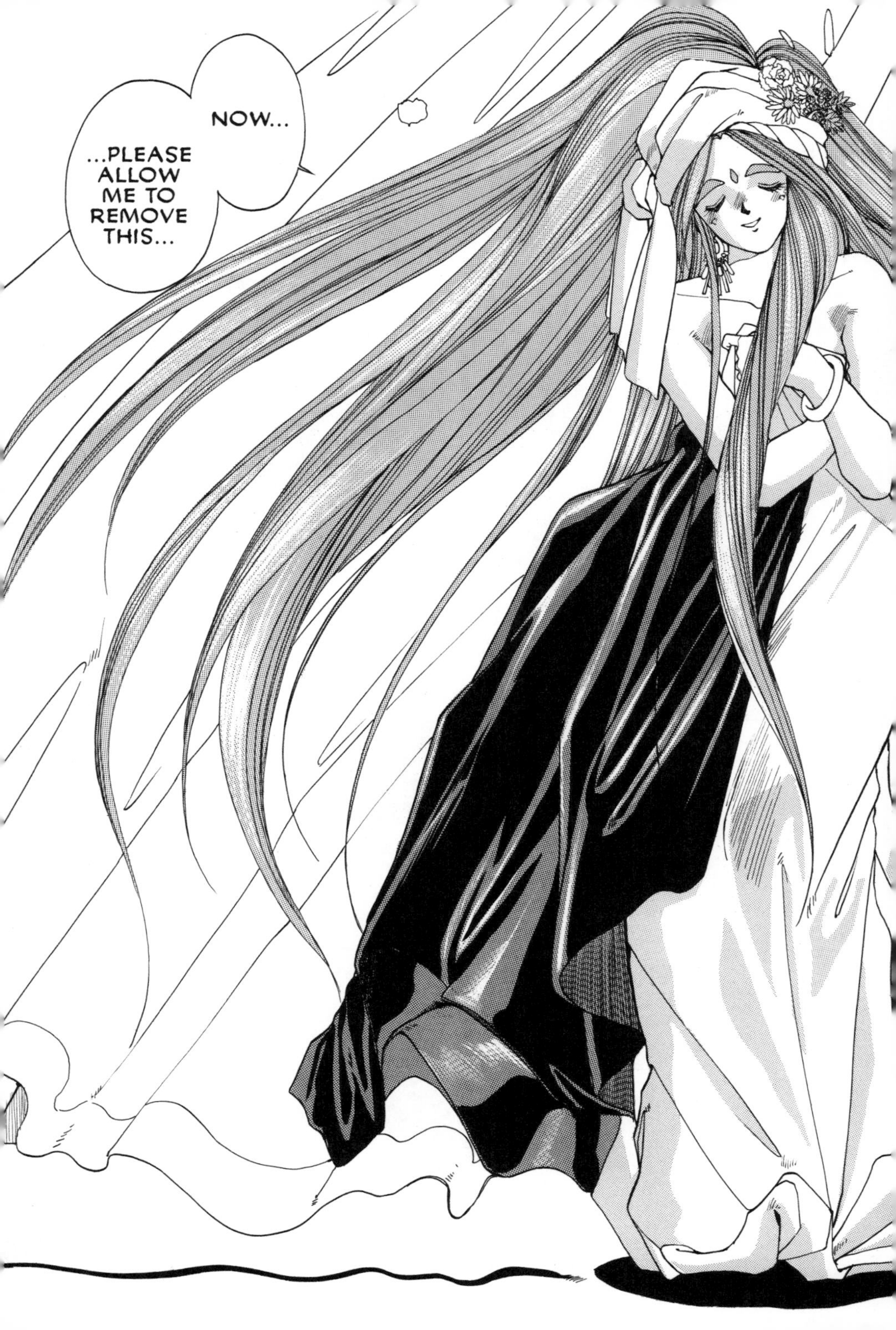
NOW...
...PLEASE ALLOW ME TO REMOVE THIS...

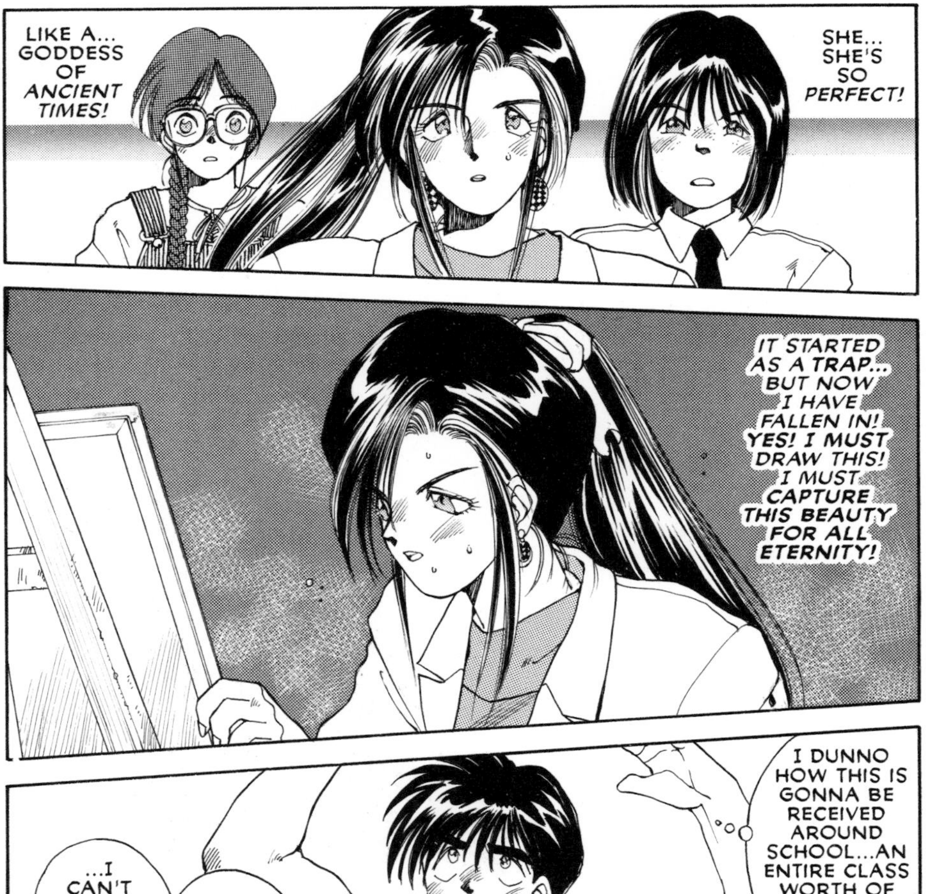
SHE... SHE'S SO *PERFECT!*
LIKE A... GODDESS OF *ANCIENT TIMES!*
IT STARTED AS A *TRAP...* BUT NOW I HAVE FALLEN IN! *YES! I MUST* DRAW THIS! I MUST *CAPTURE THIS BEAUTY FOR ALL ETERNITY!*
I DUNNO HOW THIS IS GONNA BE RECEIVED AROUND SCHOOL...AN ENTIRE CLASS WORTH OF *NUDE PICTURES* OF US...
THE ABSOLUTE WORST PART IS...
...I CAN'T SEE WHAT THEY'RE SEEING.

NEXT DAY, THE SPELL HAD WORN OFF...

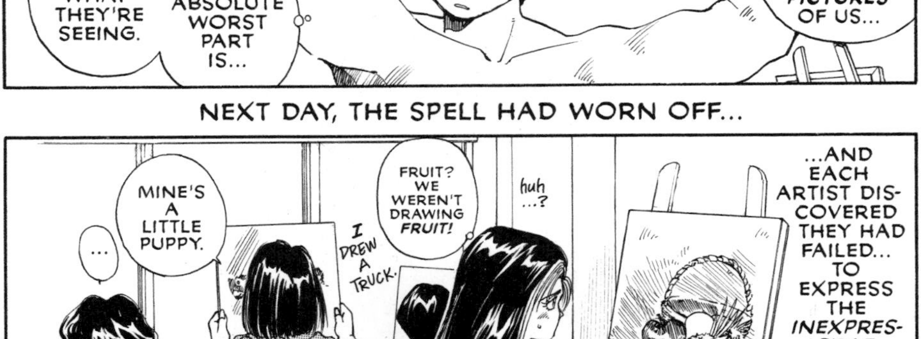
...AND EACH ARTIST DIS-COVERED THEY HAD FAILED... TO EXPRESS THE *INEXPRES-SIBLE.*
huh ...?
FRUIT? WE WEREN'T DRAWING *FRUIT!*
I DREW A TRUCK.
MINE'S A LITTLE PUPPY.
...

OH MY GODDESS!

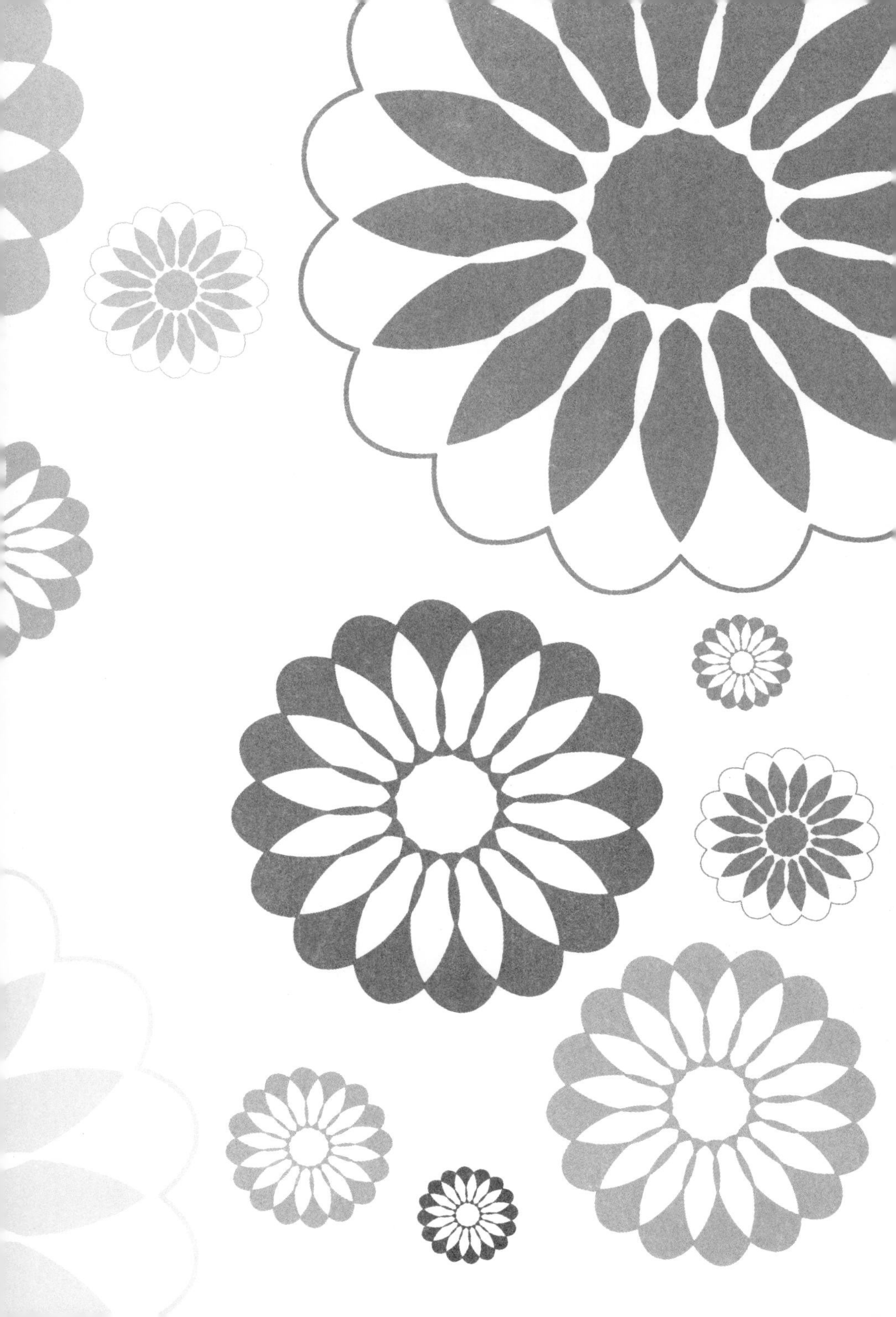

CHAPTER 11

This Life Is Wonderful

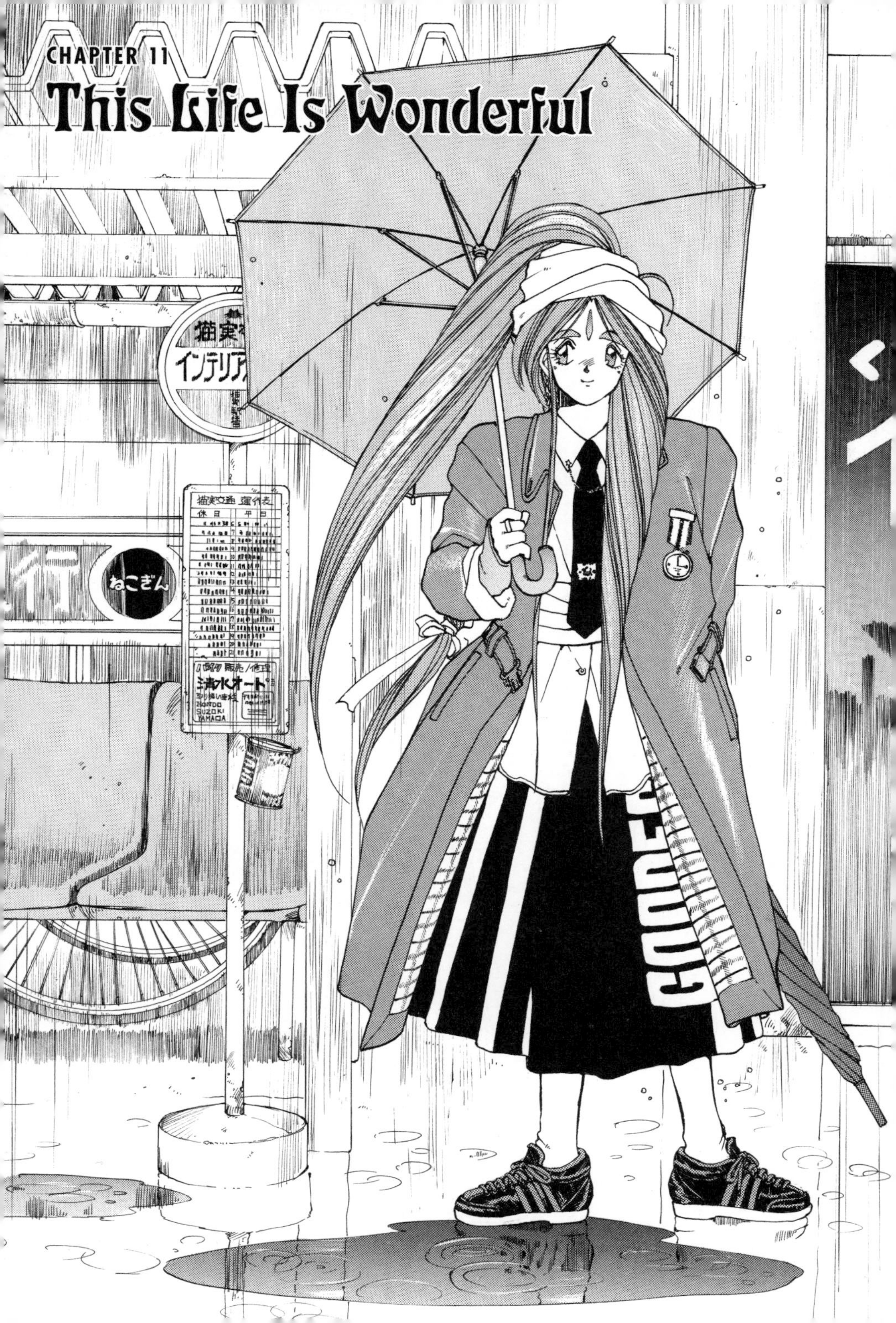
インテリア
ねこぎん

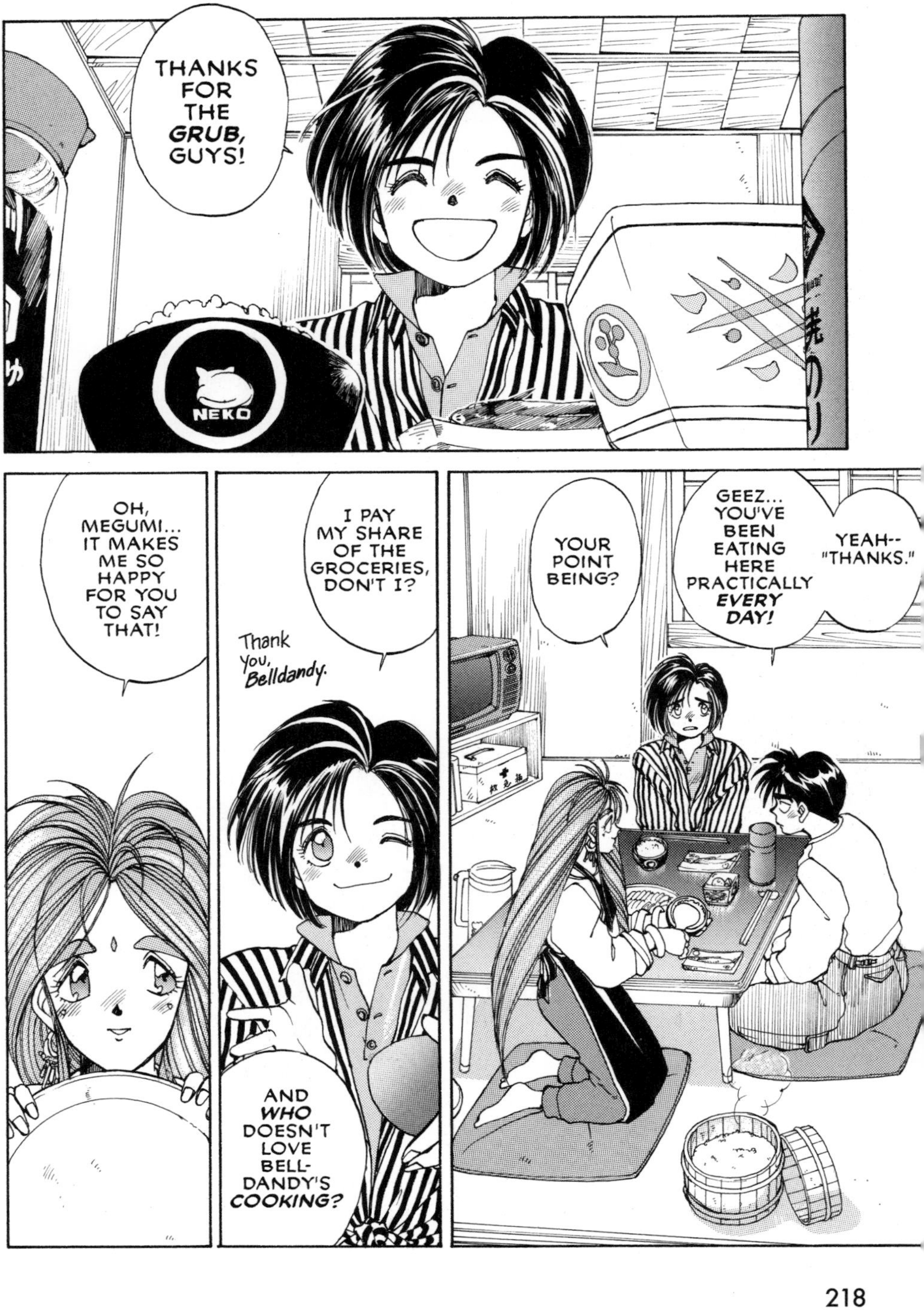
THANKS FOR THE GRUB, GUYS!
NEKO
YEAH-- "THANKS."
GEEZ... YOU'VE BEEN EATING HERE PRACTICALLY EVERY DAY!
YOUR POINT BEING?
I PAY MY SHARE OF THE GROCERIES, DON'T I?
Thank you, Belldandy.
AND WHO DOESN'T LOVE BELL-DANDY'S COOKING?
OH, MEGUMI... IT MAKES ME SO HAPPY FOR YOU TO SAY THAT!

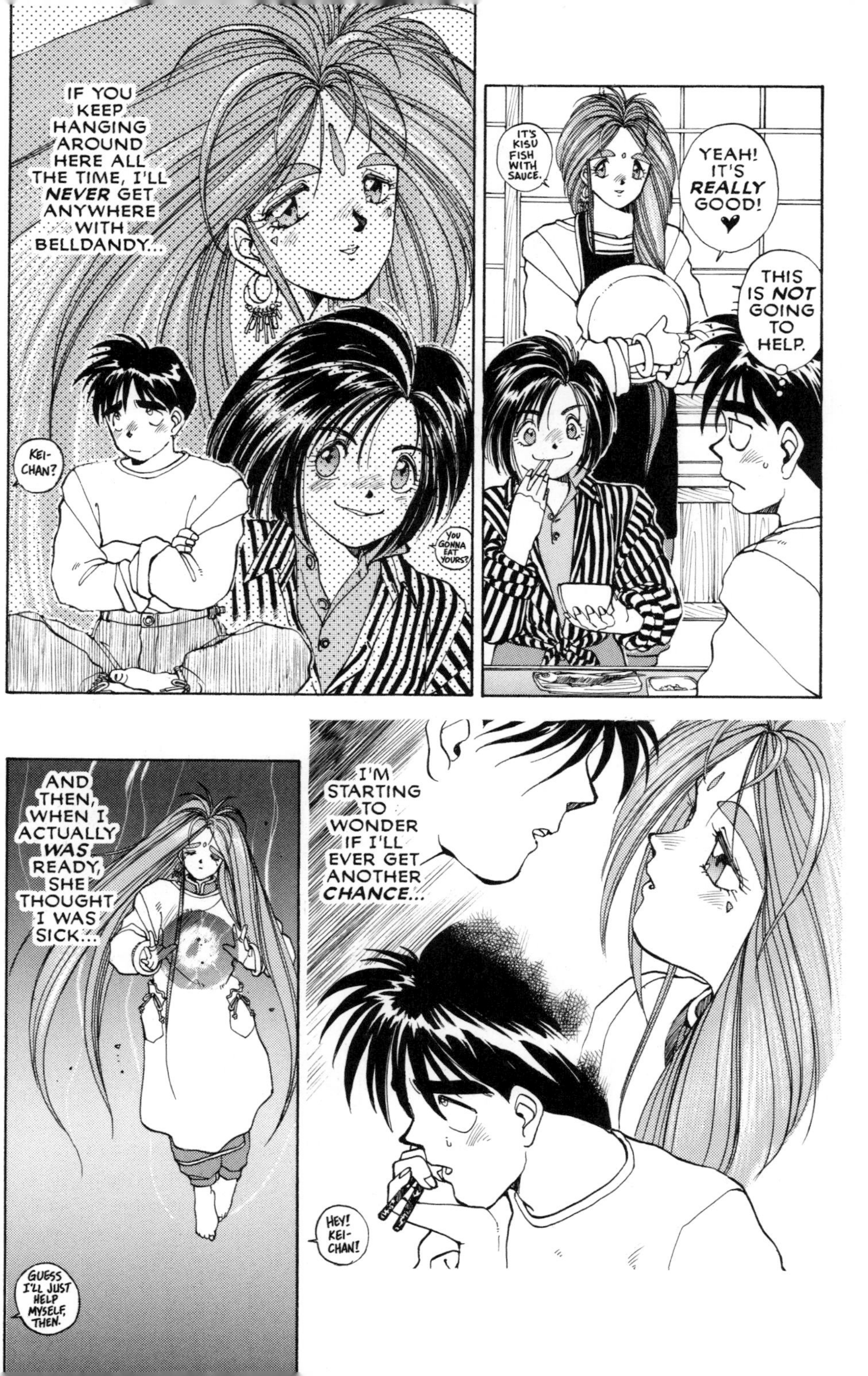
YEAH! IT'S REALLY GOOD! ♥
IT'S KISU FISH WITH SAUCE.
THIS IS NOT GOING TO HELP.
IF YOU KEEP HANGING AROUND HERE ALL THE TIME, I'LL NEVER GET ANYWHERE WITH BELLDANDY...
YOU GONNA EAT YOURS?
KEI-CHAN?
I'M STARTING TO WONDER IF I'LL EVER GET ANOTHER CHANCE...
HEY! KEI-CHAN!
AND THEN, WHEN I ACTUALLY WAS READY, SHE THOUGHT I WAS SICK...
GUESS I'LL JUST HELP MYSELF, THEN.

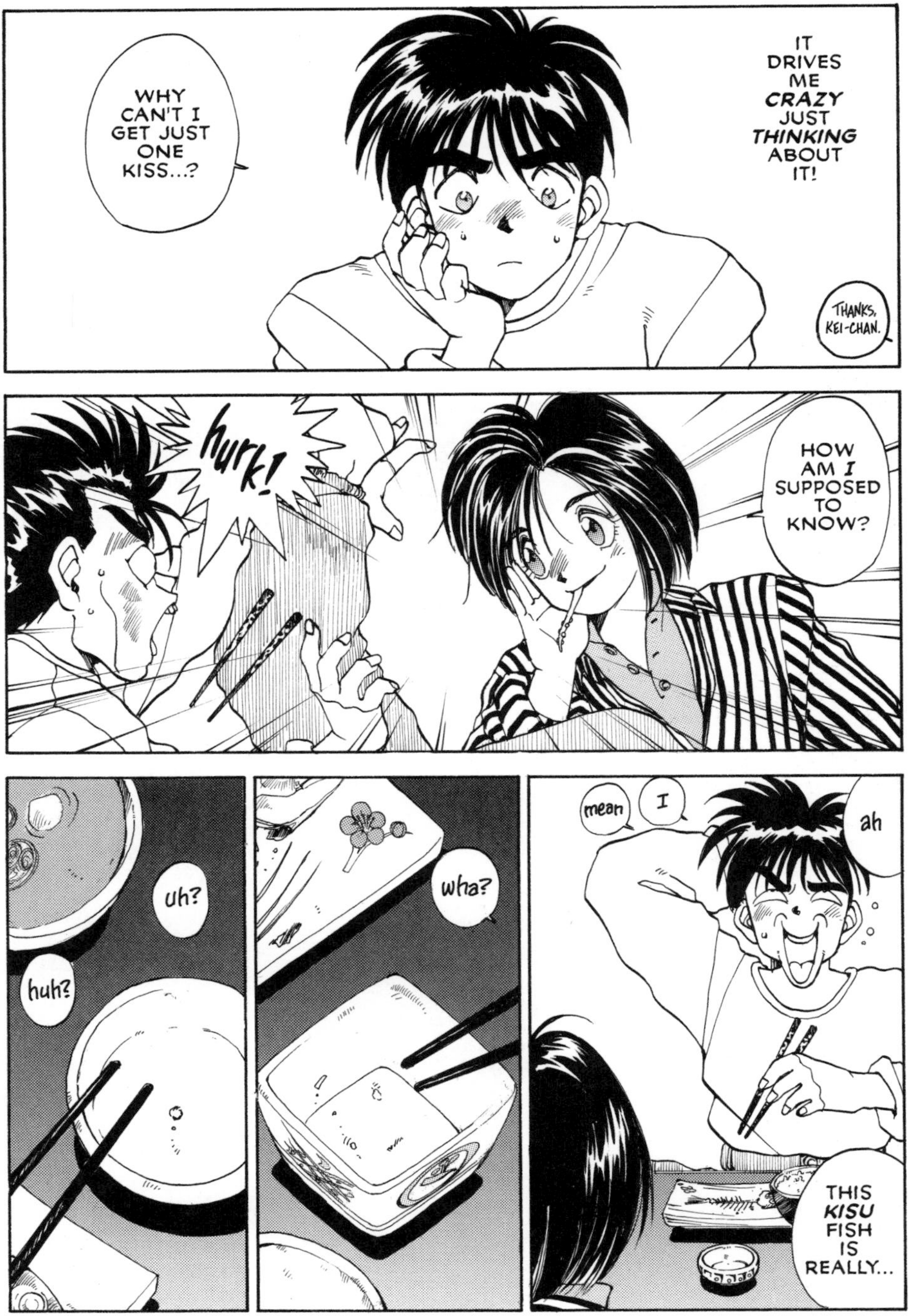
IT DRIVES ME *CRAZY* JUST *THINKING* ABOUT IT!
WHY CAN'T I GET JUST ONE KISS...?
THANKS, KEI-CHAN.
HOW AM *I* SUPPOSED TO KNOW?
hurk!
ah
I
mean
THIS *KISU* FISH IS REALLY...
wha?
uh?
huh?

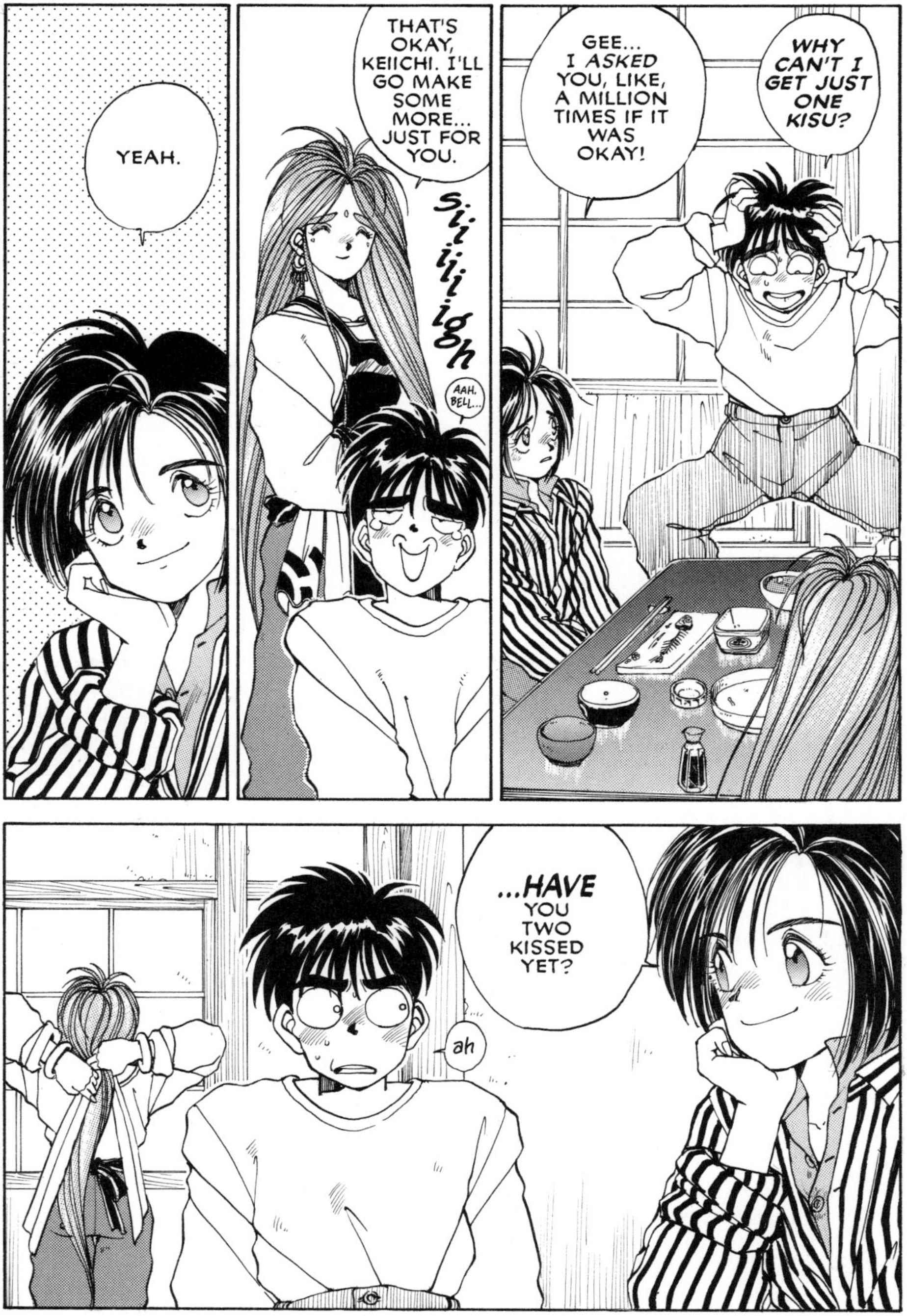
WHY CAN'T I GET JUST ONE KISU?
GEE... I ASKED YOU, LIKE, A MILLION TIMES IF IT WAS OKAY!
THAT'S OKAY, KEIICHI. I'LL GO MAKE SOME MORE... JUST FOR YOU.
Siiiiiigh
AAH, BELL...
YEAH.
...HAVE YOU TWO KISSED YET?
ah

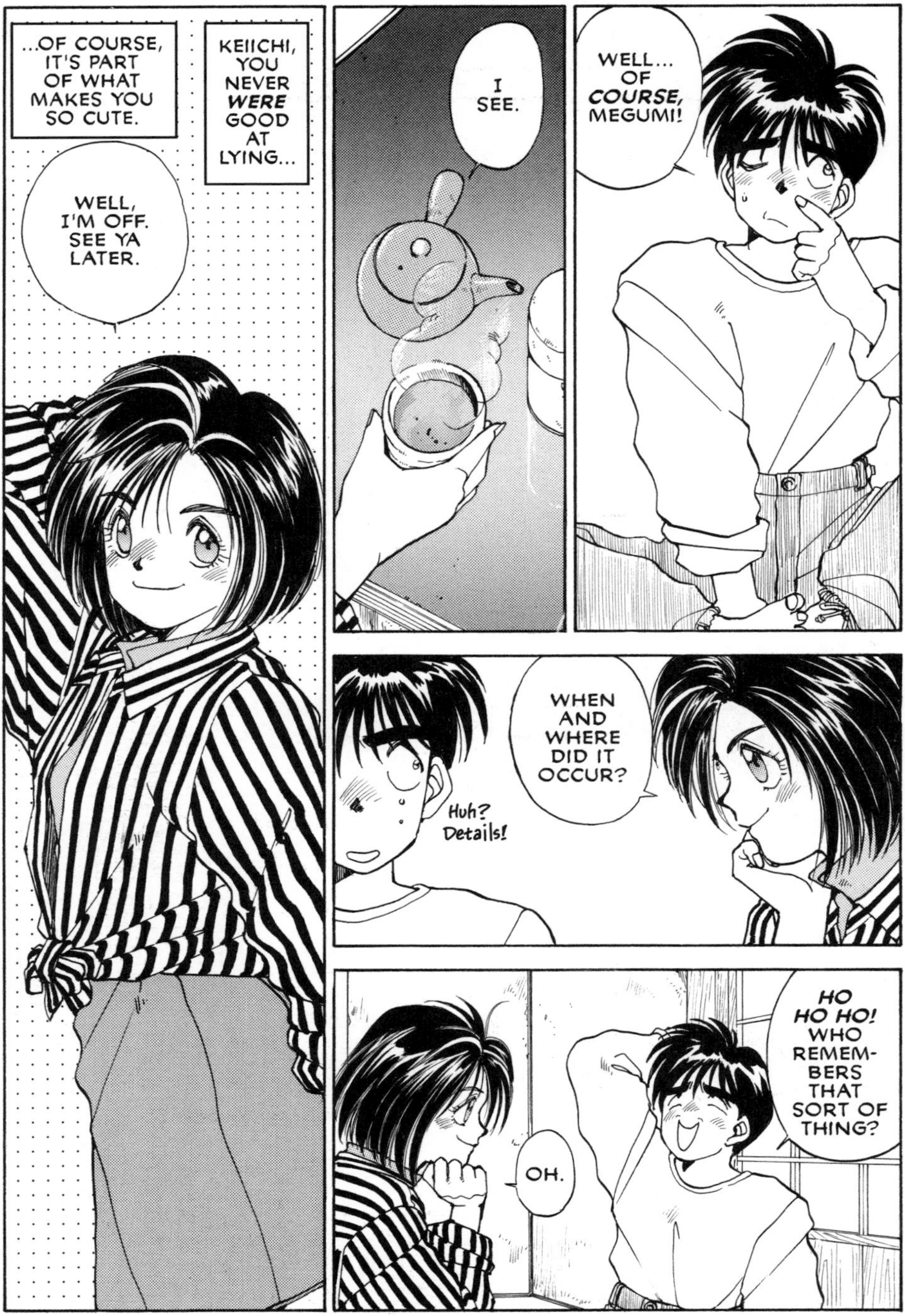
WELL... OF COURSE, MEGUMI!
I SEE.
WHEN AND WHERE DID IT OCCUR?
Huh? Details!
HO HO HO! WHO REMEM-BERS THAT SORT OF THING?
OH.
KEIICHI, YOU NEVER WERE GOOD AT LYING...
...OF COURSE, IT'S PART OF WHAT MAKES YOU SO CUTE.
WELL, I'M OFF. SEE YA LATER.

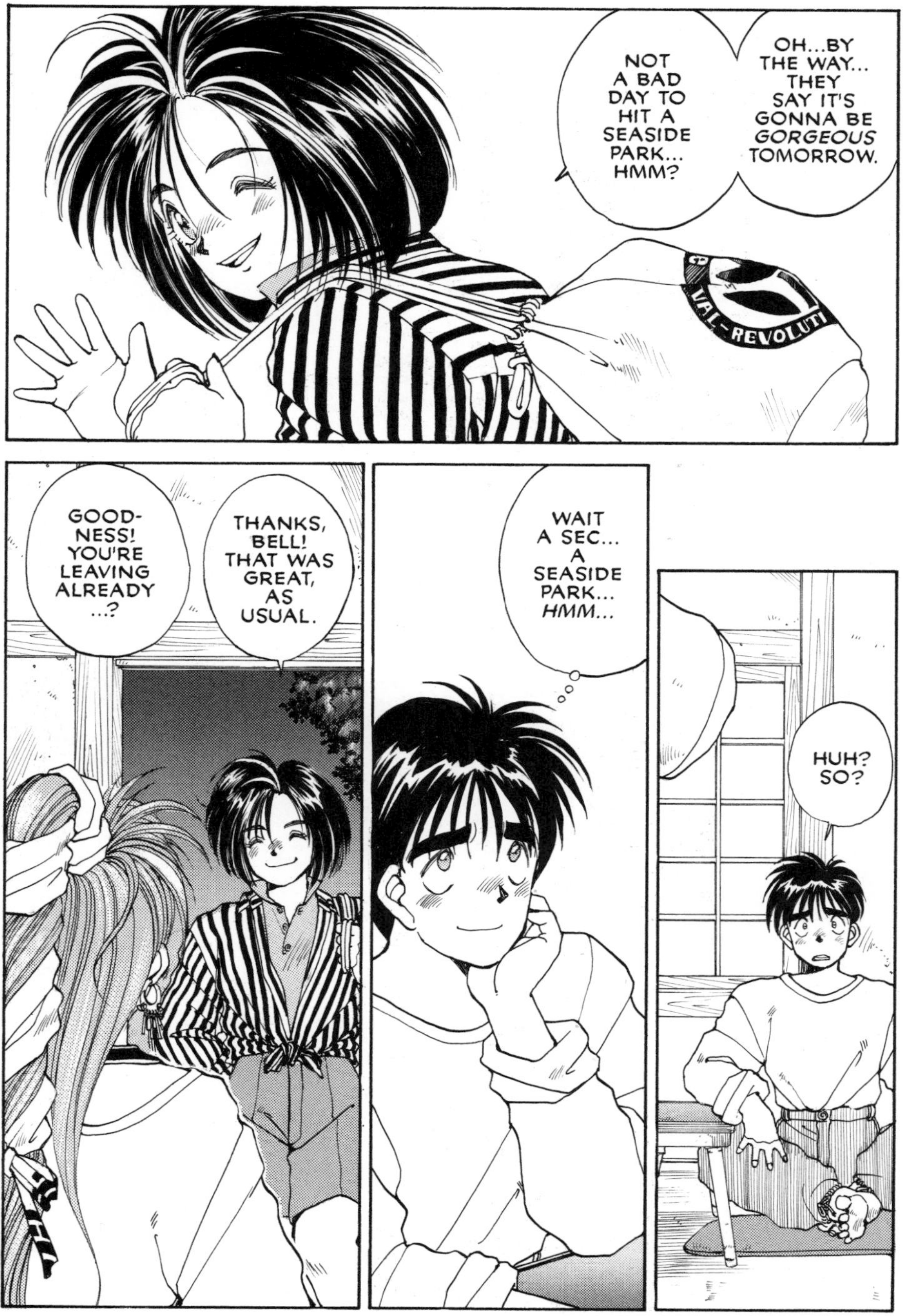
OH...BY THE WAY... THEY SAY IT'S GONNA BE *GORGEOUS* TOMORROW.
NOT A BAD DAY TO HIT A SEASIDE PARK... HMM?
VAL-REVOLUTI
HUH? SO?
WAIT A SEC... A SEASIDE PARK... *HMM*...
THANKS, BELL! THAT WAS GREAT, AS USUAL.
GOODNESS! YOU'RE LEAVING ALREADY ...?

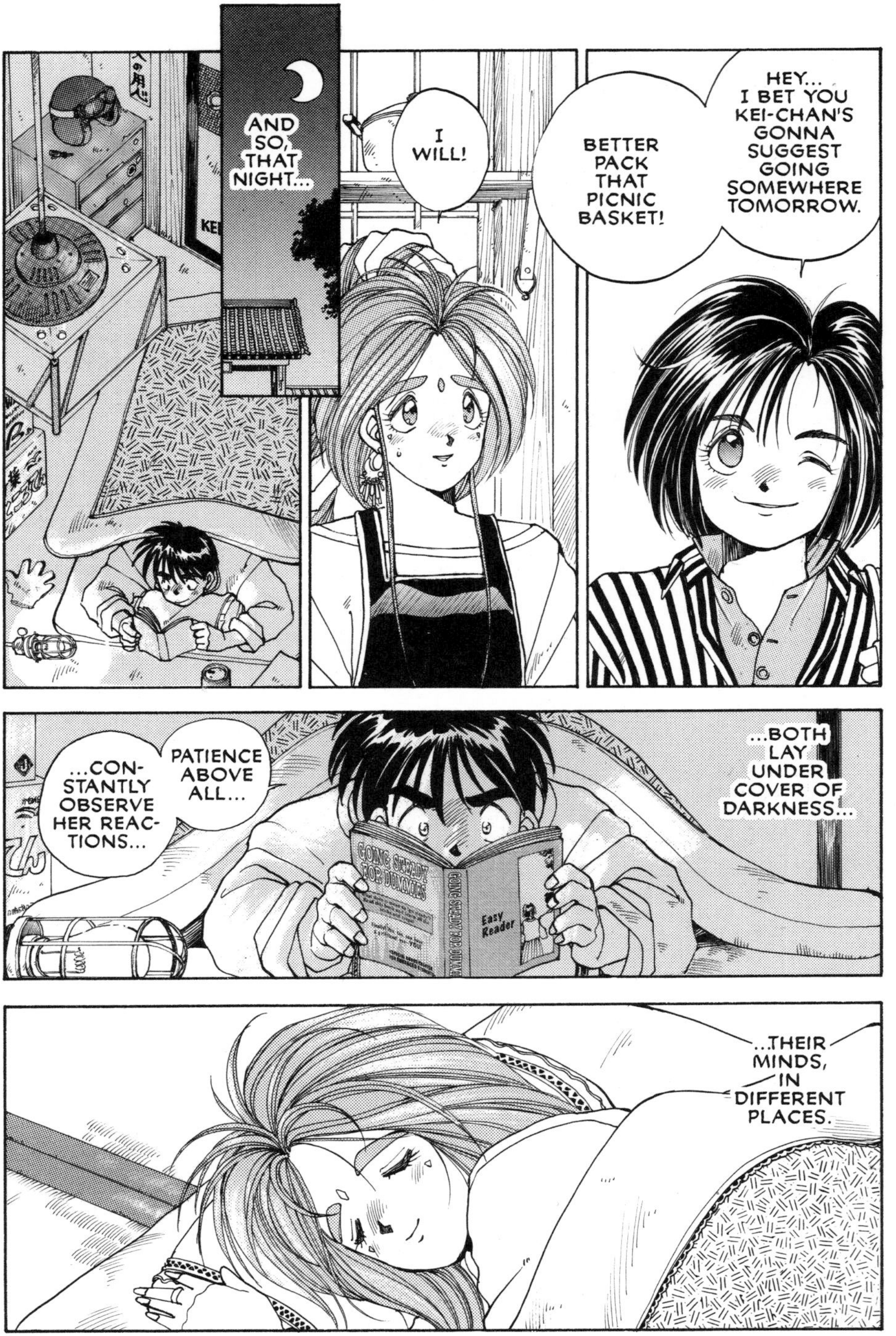
HEY... I BET YOU KEI-CHAN'S GONNA SUGGEST GOING SOMEWHERE TOMORROW.
BETTER PACK THAT PICNIC BASKET!
I WILL!
AND SO, THAT NIGHT...
...BOTH LAY UNDER COVER OF DARKNESS...
PATIENCE ABOVE ALL...
...CON-STANTLY OBSERVE HER REAC-TIONS...
GOING STEADY FOR DUMMIES
Easy Reader
...THEIR MINDS, IN DIFFERENT PLACES.

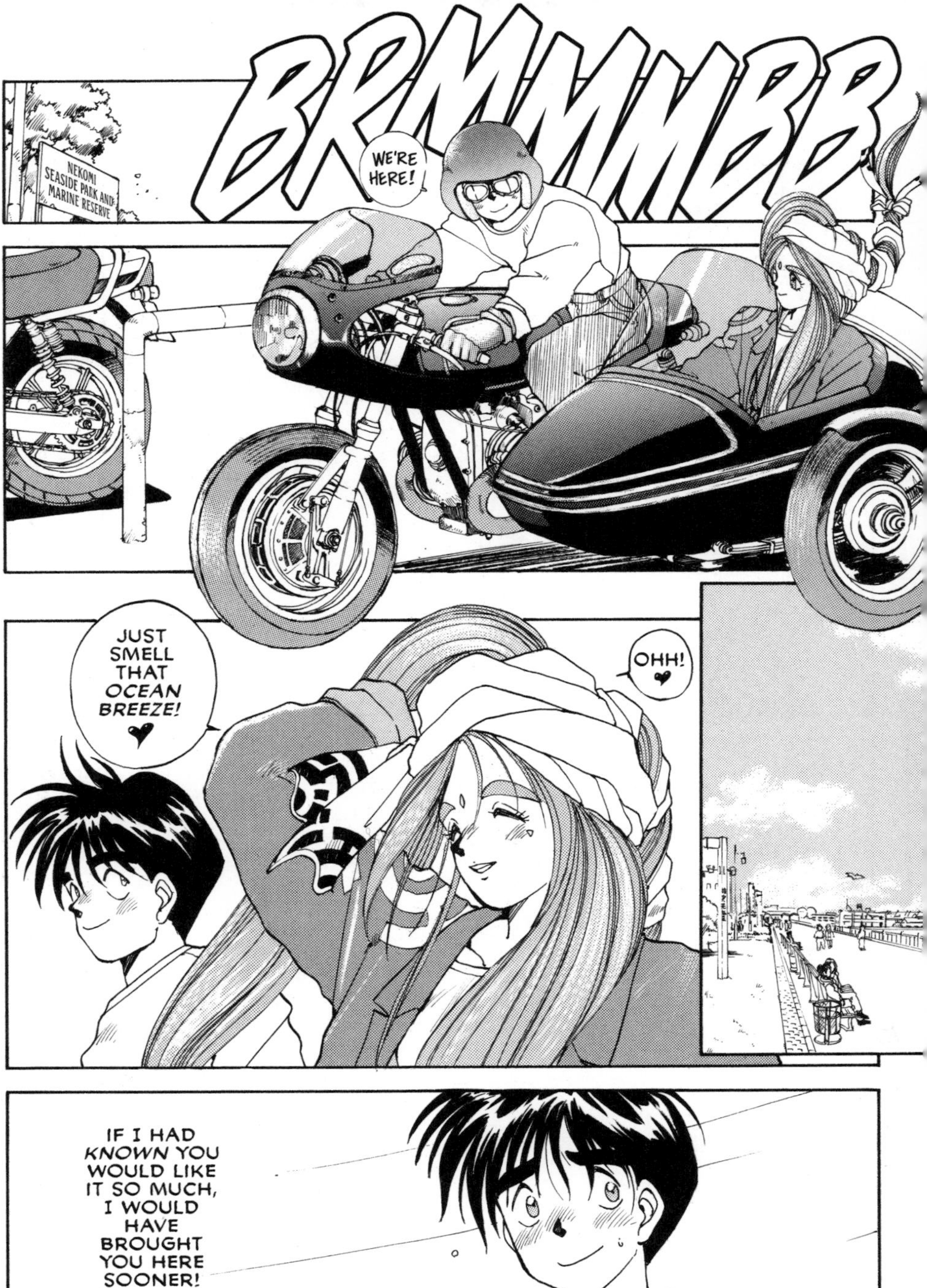
BRMMMBB
WE'RE HERE!
NEKOMI SEASIDE PARK AND MARINE RESERVE
OHH! ♥
JUST SMELL THAT *OCEAN BREEZE!* ♥
IF I HAD *KNOWN* YOU WOULD LIKE IT SO MUCH, I WOULD HAVE BROUGHT YOU HERE SOONER!

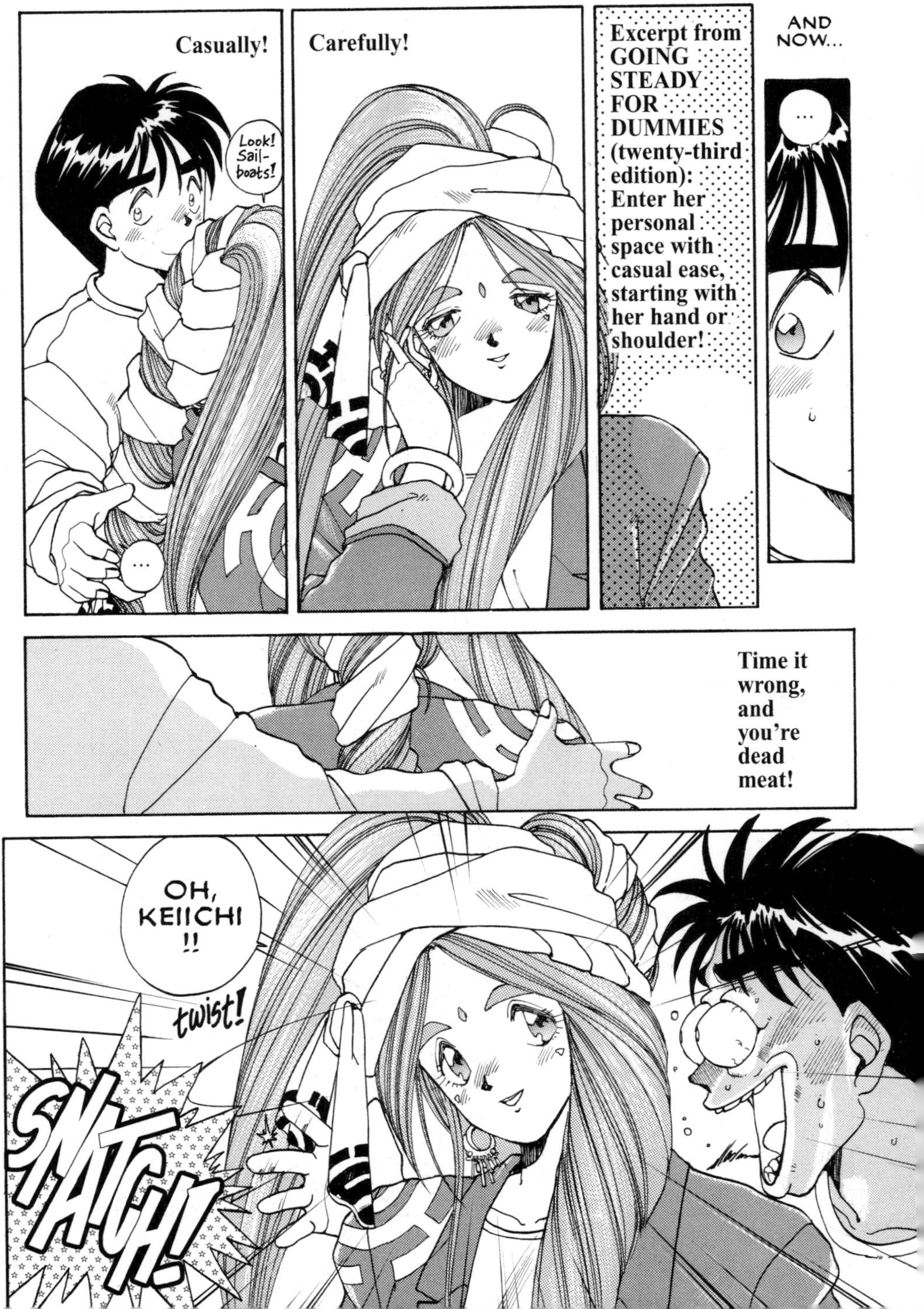
AND NOW...
...
Excerpt from GOING STEADY FOR DUMMIES (twenty-third edition): Enter her personal space with casual ease, starting with her hand or shoulder!
Carefully!
Casually!
Look! Sail-boats!
...
Time it wrong, and you're dead meat!
OH, KEIICHI !!
twist!
SNATCH!!

WOULD YOU LIKE SOME ICE CREAM?
G-G-G-GOOD IDEA!
Why'd you take your **hand** away, **stupid?!**
HERE YA GO.
330 YEN.
?
THIS IS ALL *YOUR* FAULT!
UM...
WOULD YOU MIND IF I PAID...?
huh?
WHEN WE WERE MODELING, THEY SEEMED SO EN- TRANCED...
...THEY PAID ME A *BONUS* FEE!

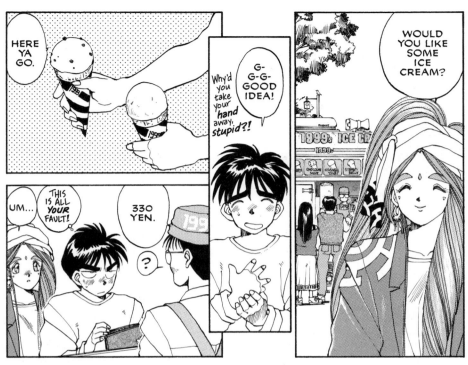

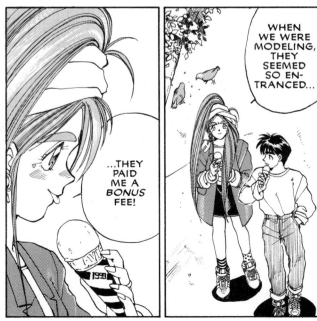

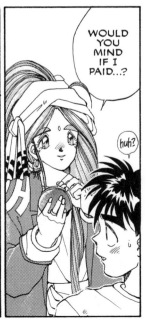

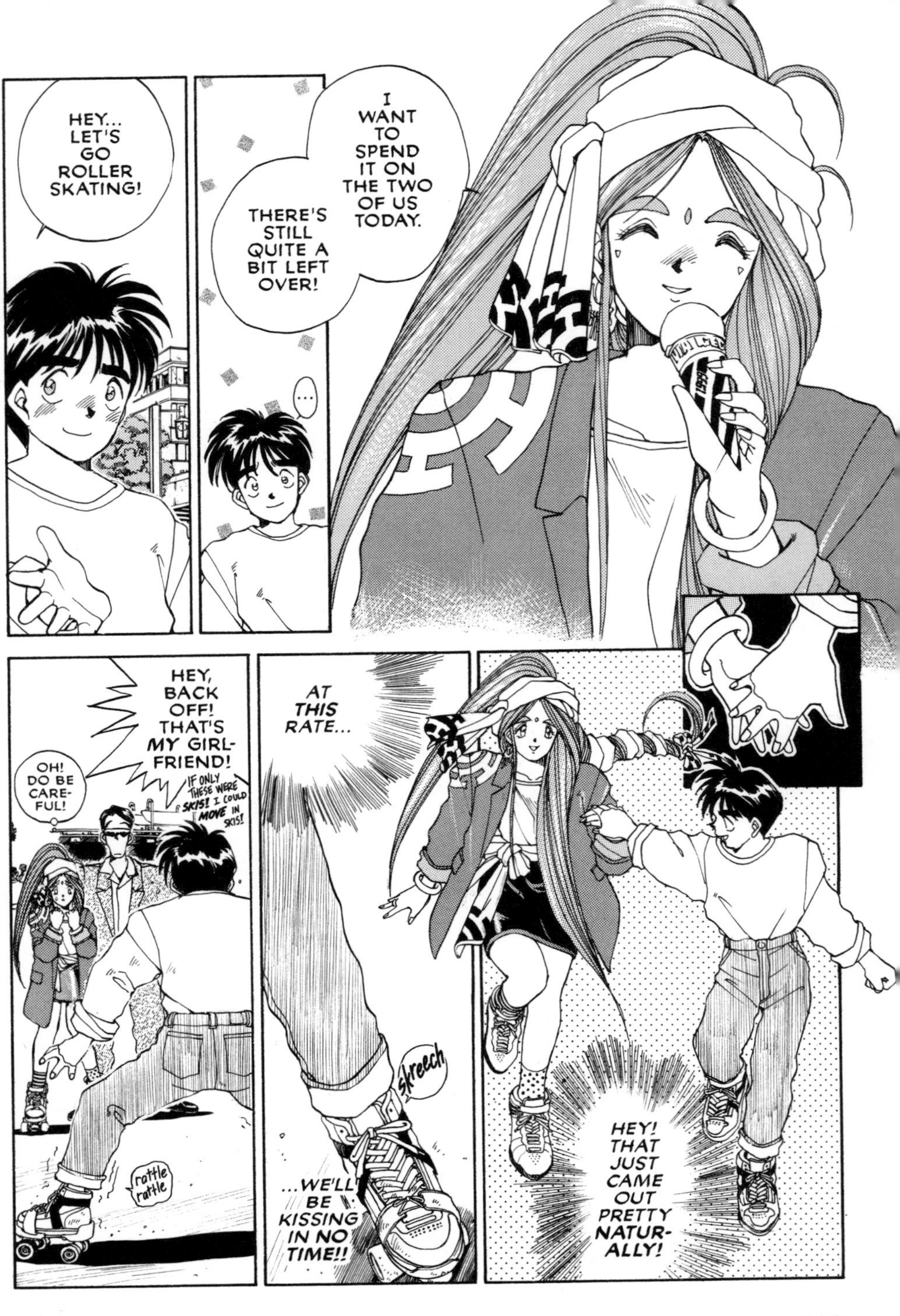
I WANT TO SPEND IT ON THE TWO OF US TODAY.
THERE'S STILL QUITE A BIT LEFT OVER!
...
HEY... LET'S GO ROLLER SKATING!
HEY! THAT JUST CAME OUT PRETTY NATURALLY!
AT THIS RATE...
skreech
...WE'LL BE KISSING IN NO TIME!!
HEY, BACK OFF! THAT'S MY GIRL-FRIEND!
IF ONLY THESE WERE SKIS! I COULD MOVE IN SKIS!
OH! DO BE CARE-FUL!
rattle rattle

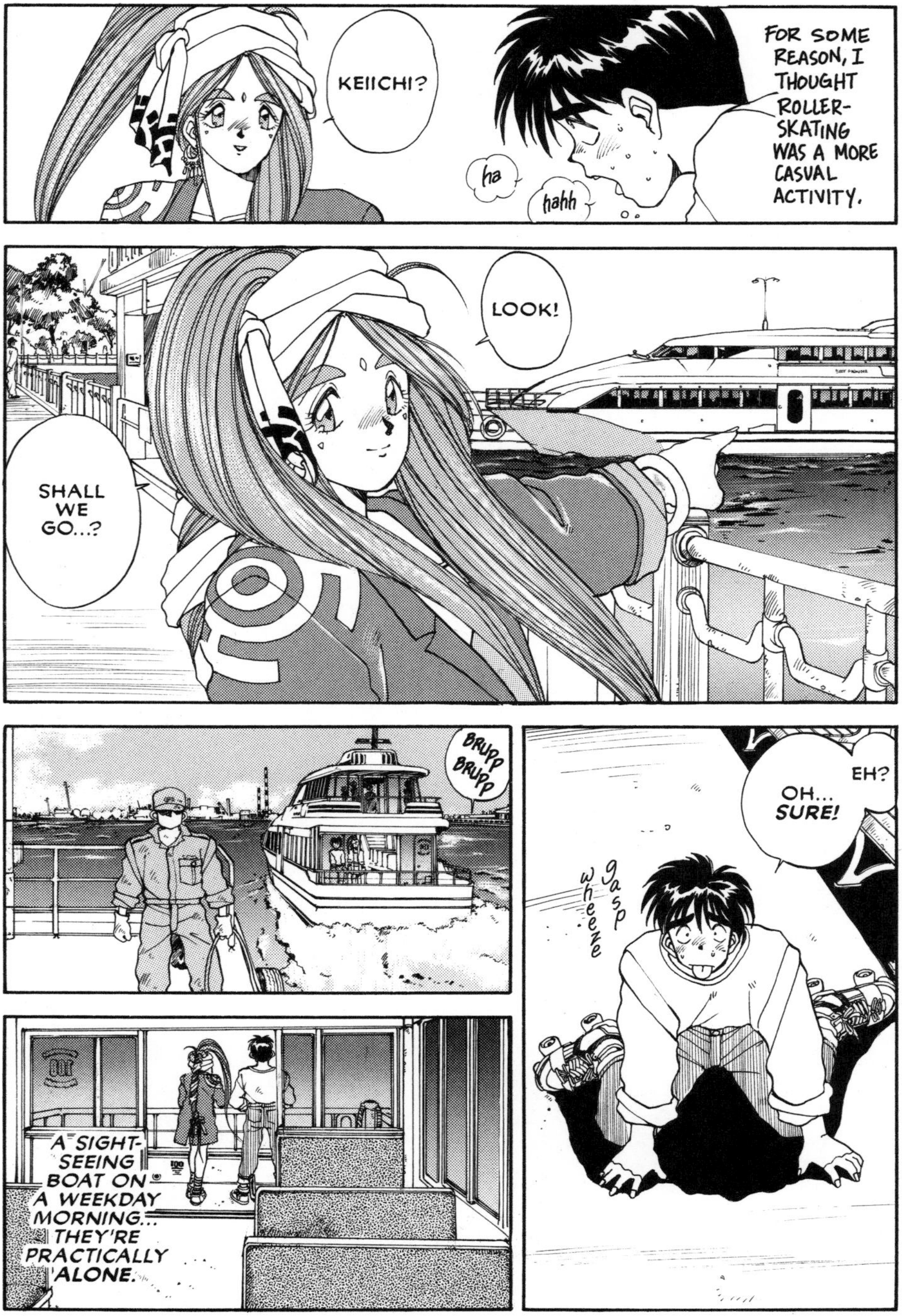
FOR SOME REASON, I THOUGHT ROLLER-SKATING WAS A MORE CASUAL ACTIVITY.
ha
hahh
KEIICHI?
LOOK!
SHALL WE GO...?
EH?
OH... SURE!
gasp
wheeze
BRUPP BRUPP
A SIGHT-SEEING BOAT ON A WEEKDAY MORNING... THEY'RE PRACTICALLY ALONE.

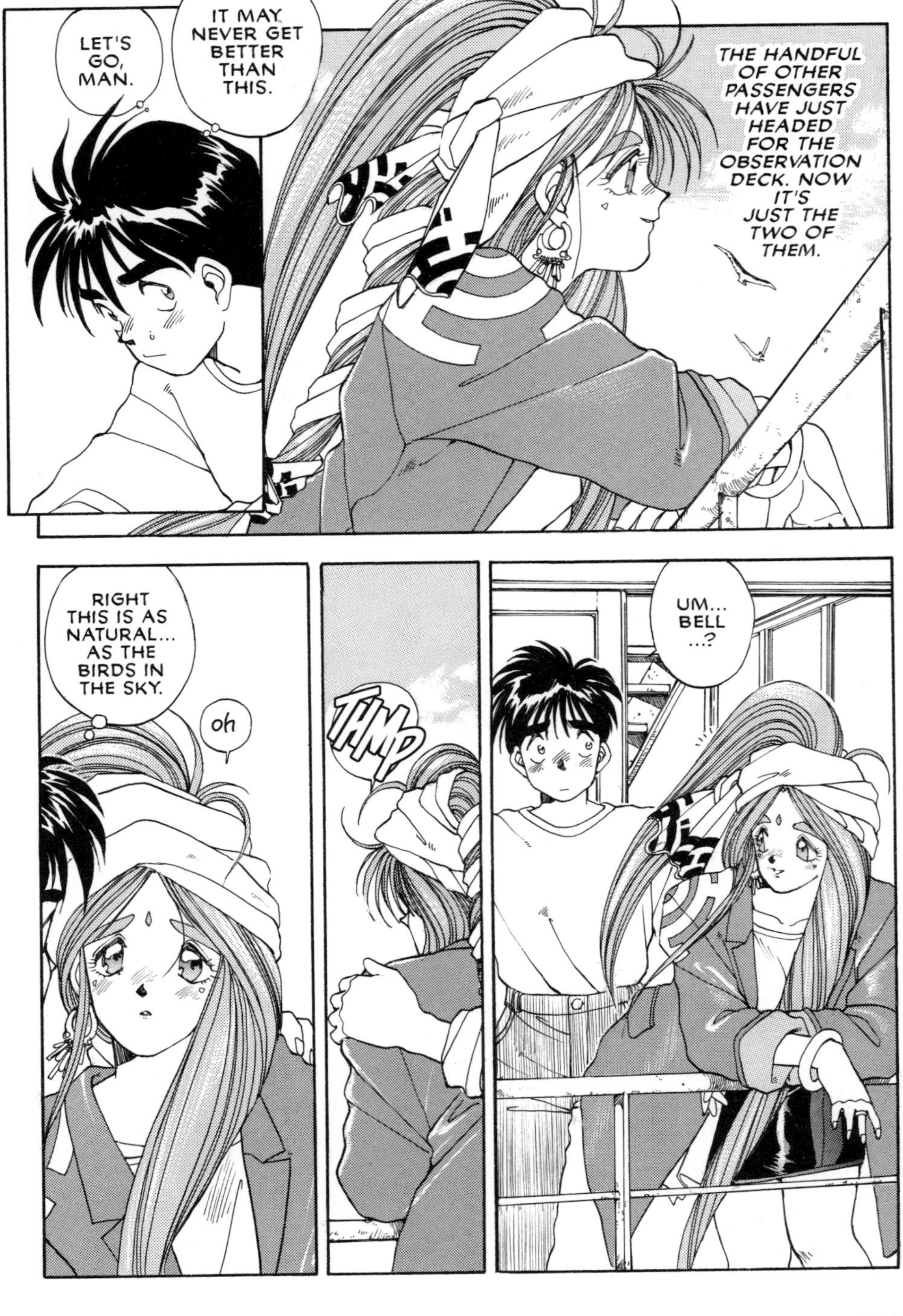
THE HANDFUL OF OTHER PASSENGERS HAVE JUST HEADED FOR THE OBSERVATION DECK. NOW IT'S JUST THE TWO OF THEM.
IT MAY NEVER GET BETTER THAN THIS.
LET'S GO, MAN.
UM... BELL ...?
THMP
RIGHT THIS IS AS NATURAL... AS THE BIRDS IN THE SKY.
oh

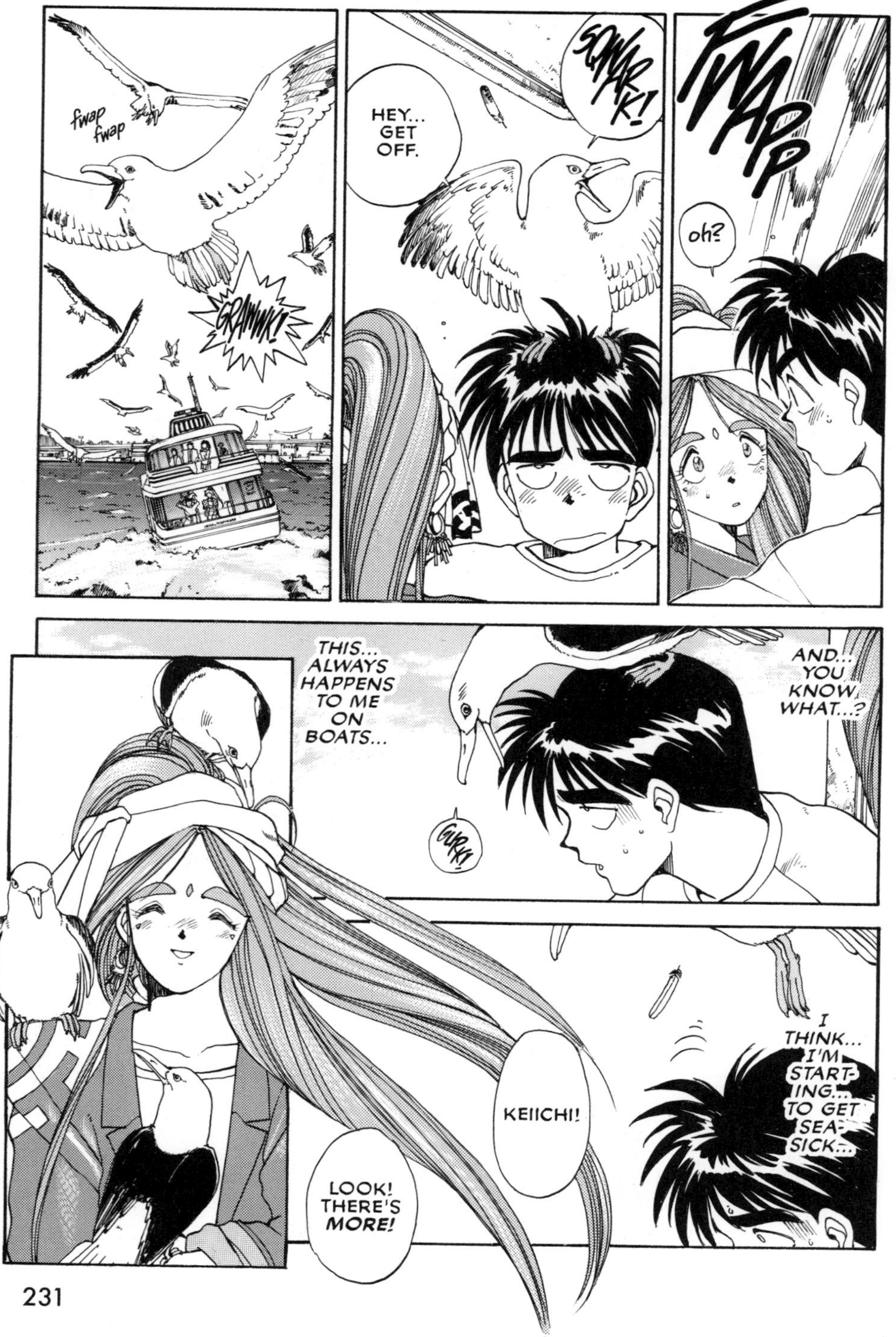
fwap fwap
GRAWWK!
SQWARK!
HEY... GET OFF.
FWAPP
oh?
THIS... ALWAYS HAPPENS TO ME ON BOATS...
GURK!
AND... YOU KNOW WHAT...?
KEIICHI!
LOOK! THERE'S MORE!
I THINK... I'M START-ING... TO GET SEA-SICK...

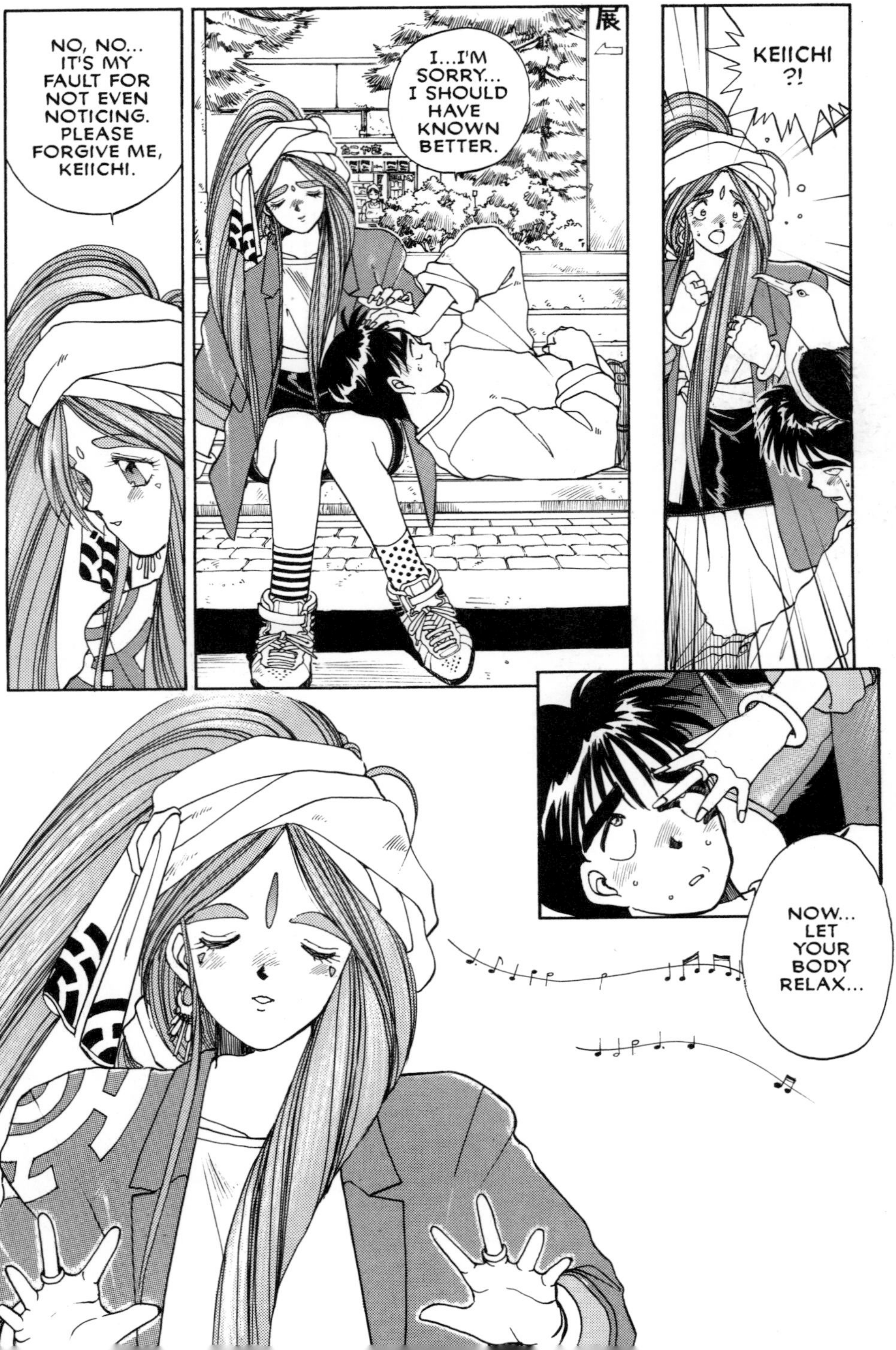
KEIICHI ?!
展
I...I'M SORRY... I SHOULD HAVE KNOWN BETTER.
NO, NO... IT'S MY FAULT FOR NOT EVEN NOTICING. PLEASE FORGIVE ME, KEIICHI.
NOW... LET YOUR BODY RELAX...

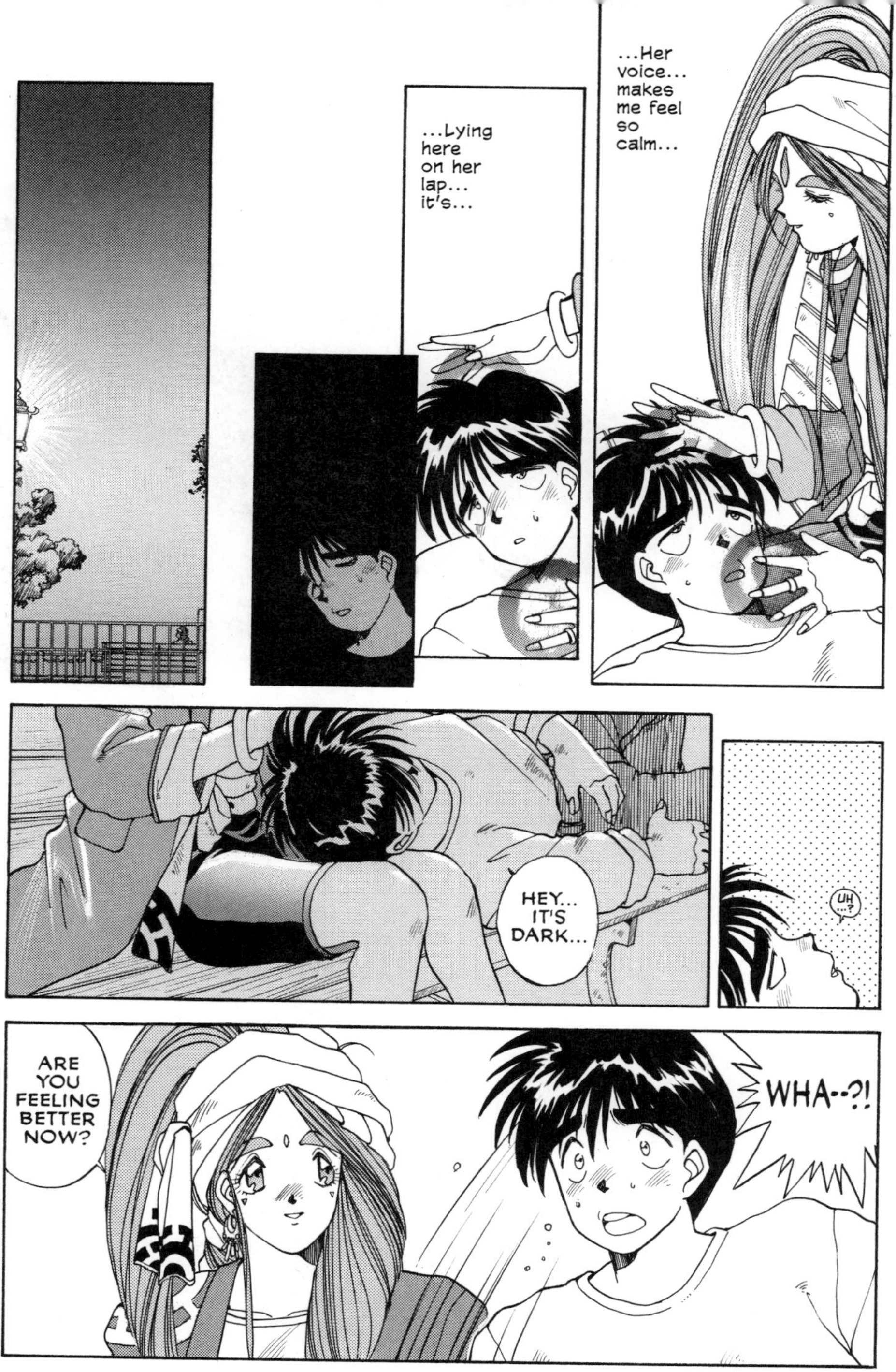

...Her voice... makes me feel so calm...
...Lying here on her lap... it's...
UH...?
HEY... IT'S DARK...
WHA--?!
ARE YOU FEELING BETTER NOW?

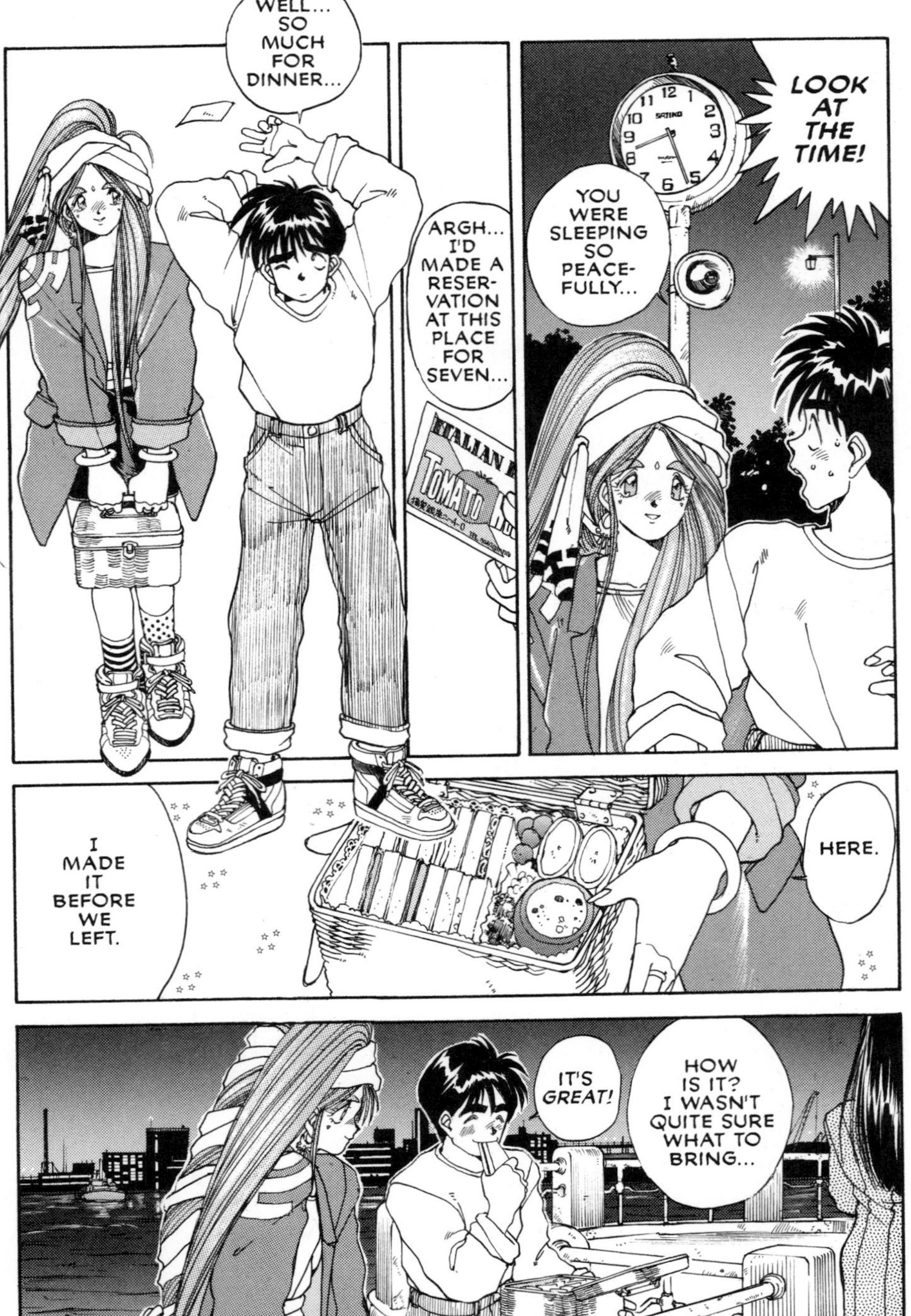
LOOK AT THE TIME!
YOU WERE SLEEPING SO PEACEFULLY...
ARGH... I'D MADE A RESERVATION AT THIS PLACE FOR SEVEN...
WELL... SO MUCH FOR DINNER...
ITALIAN
TOMATO
HERE.
I MADE IT BEFORE WE LEFT.
HOW IS IT? I WASN'T QUITE SURE WHAT TO BRING...
IT'S *GREAT!*

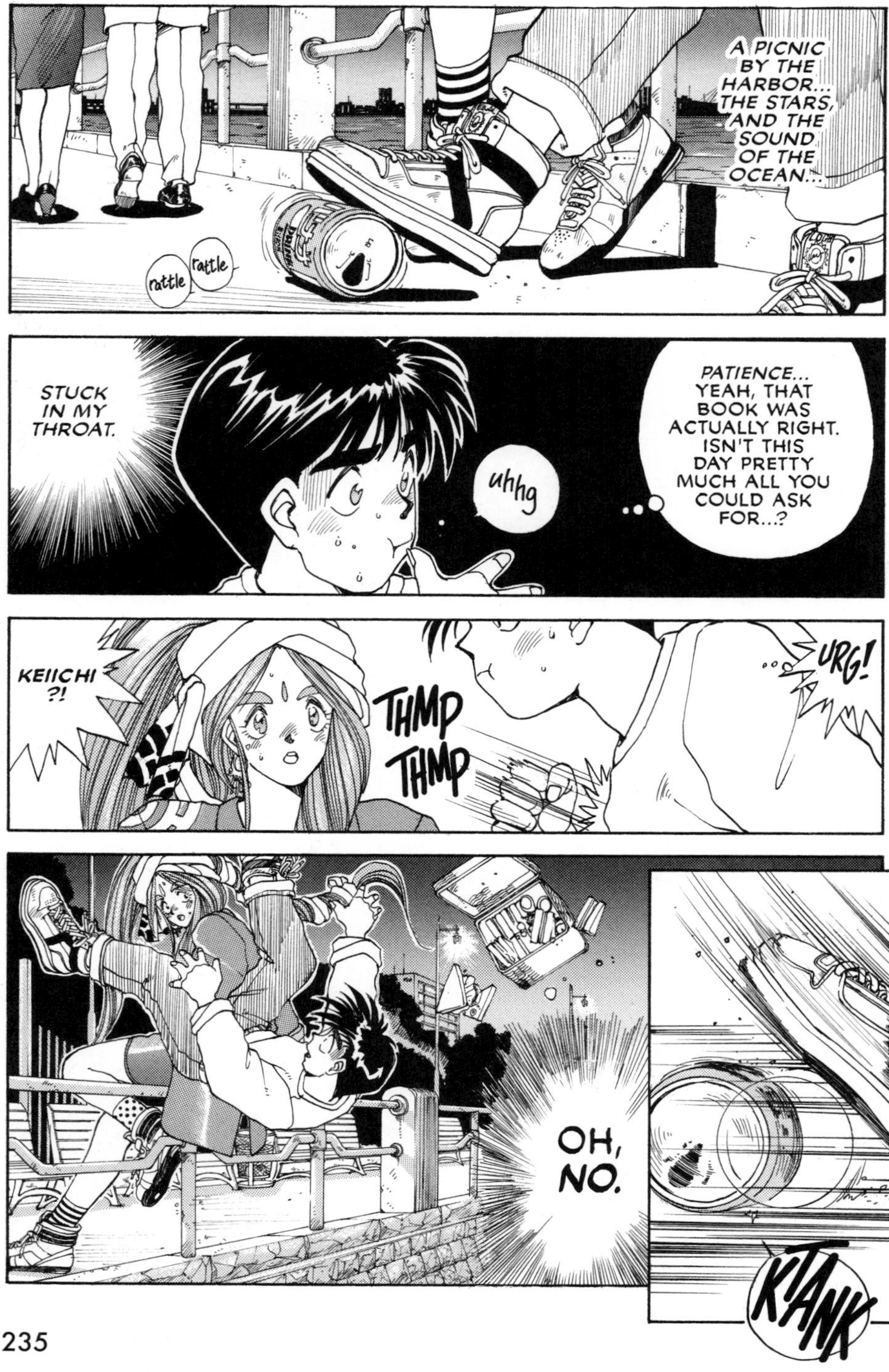
A PICNIC BY THE HARBOR... THE STARS, AND THE SOUND OF THE OCEAN...
rattle
rattle
PATIENCE... YEAH, THAT BOOK WAS ACTUALLY RIGHT. ISN'T THIS DAY PRETTY MUCH ALL YOU COULD ASK FOR...?
uhhg
STUCK IN MY THROAT.
URG!
THMP THMP
KEIICHI ?!
KTANK
OH, NO.

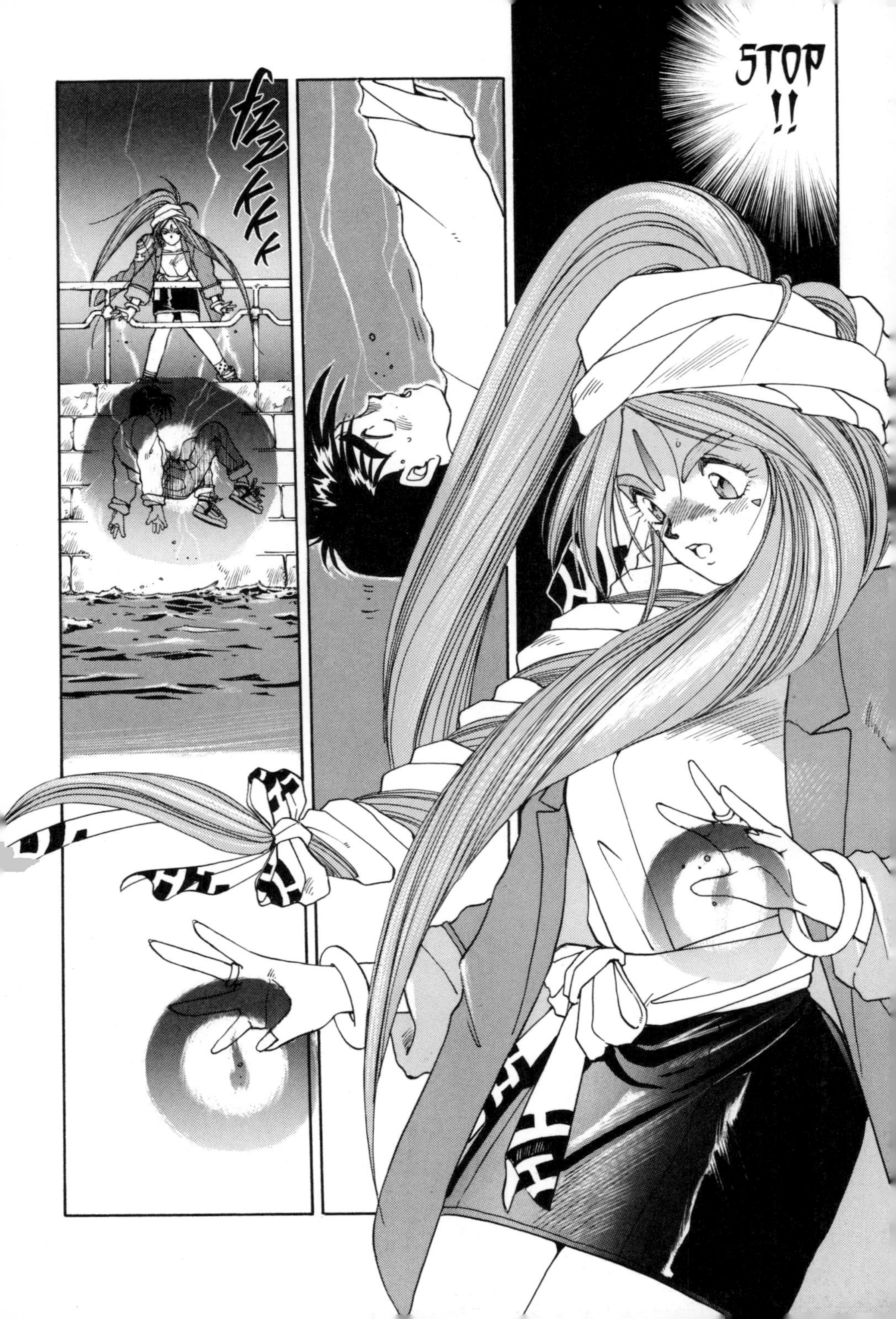

STOP!!
FZZZKKKK

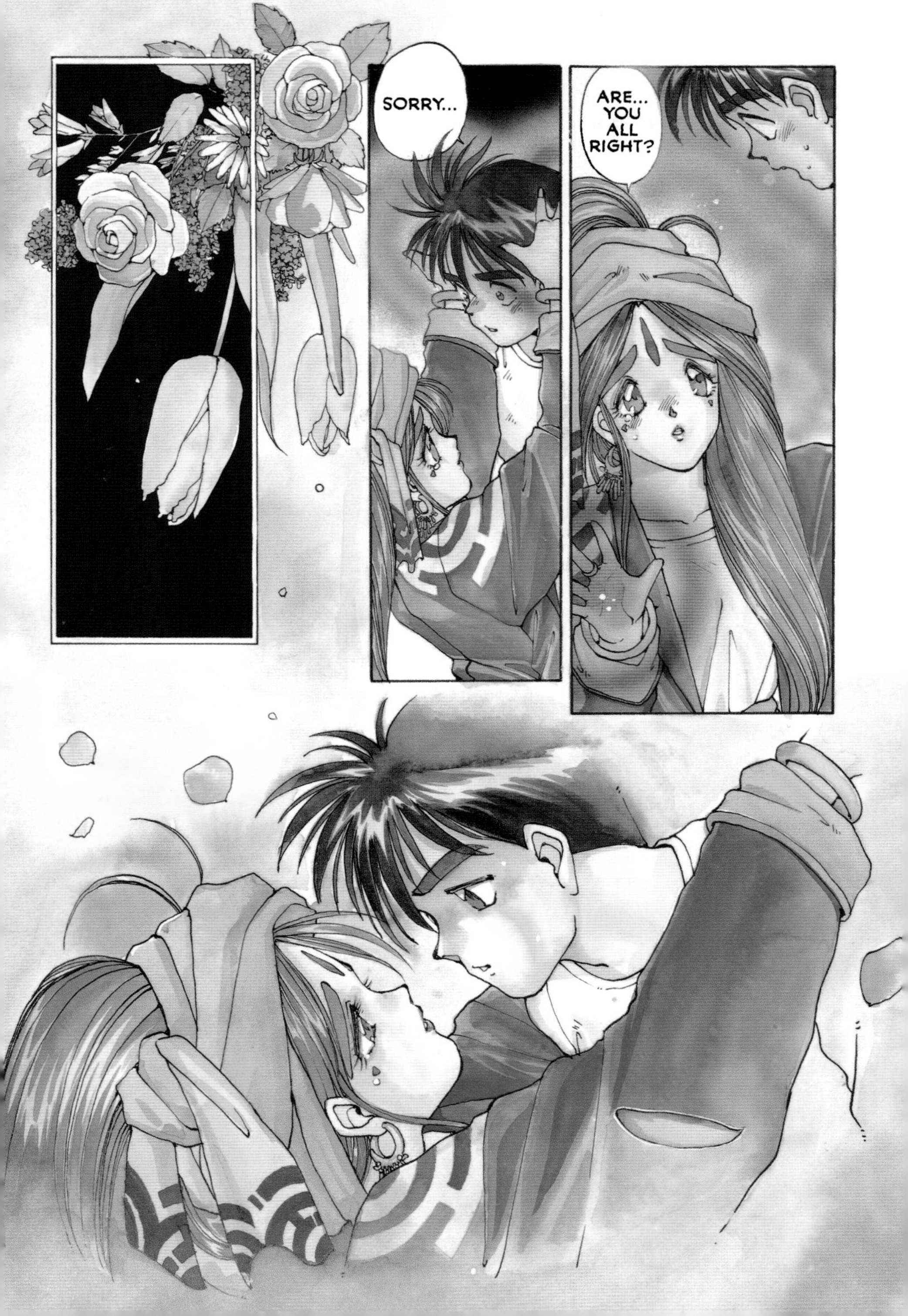
ARE... YOU ALL RIGHT?
SORRY...

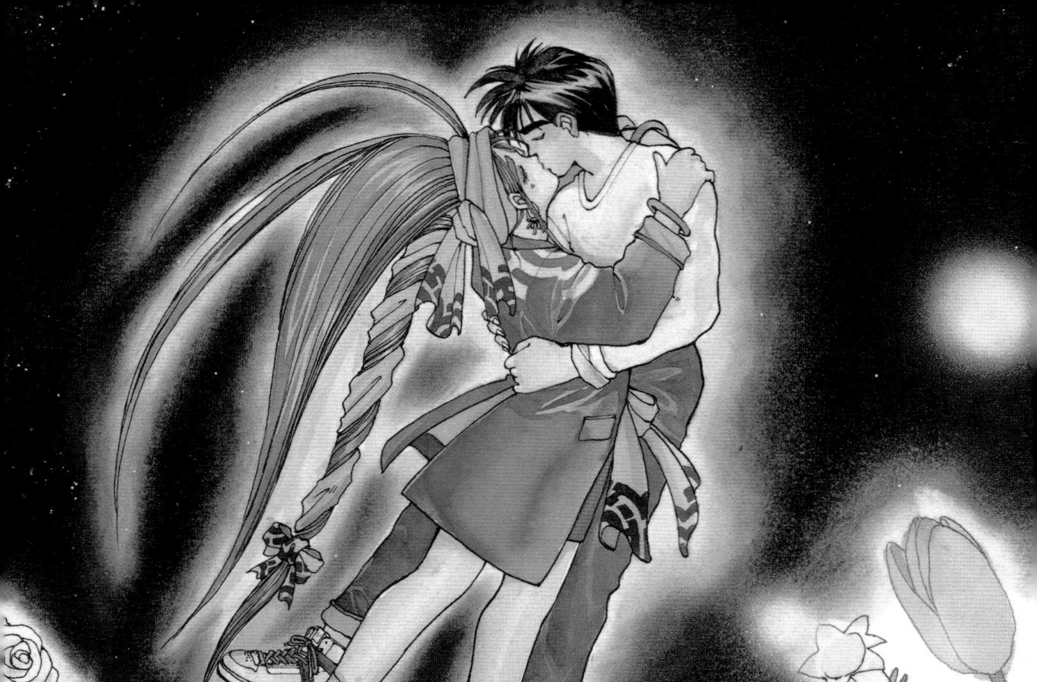

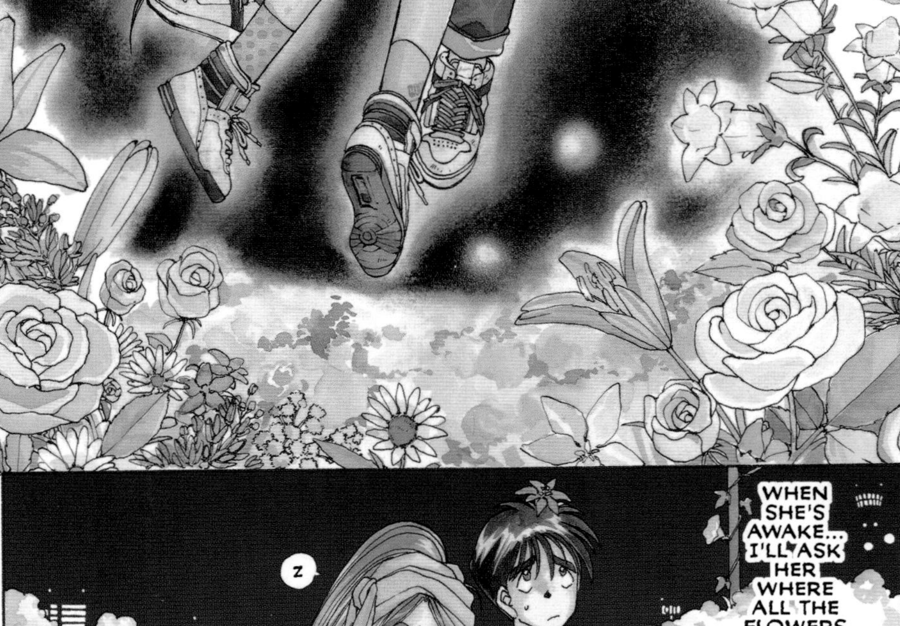

WHEN SHE'S AWAKE... I'LL ASK HER WHERE ALL THE FLOWERS CAME FROM.
Z

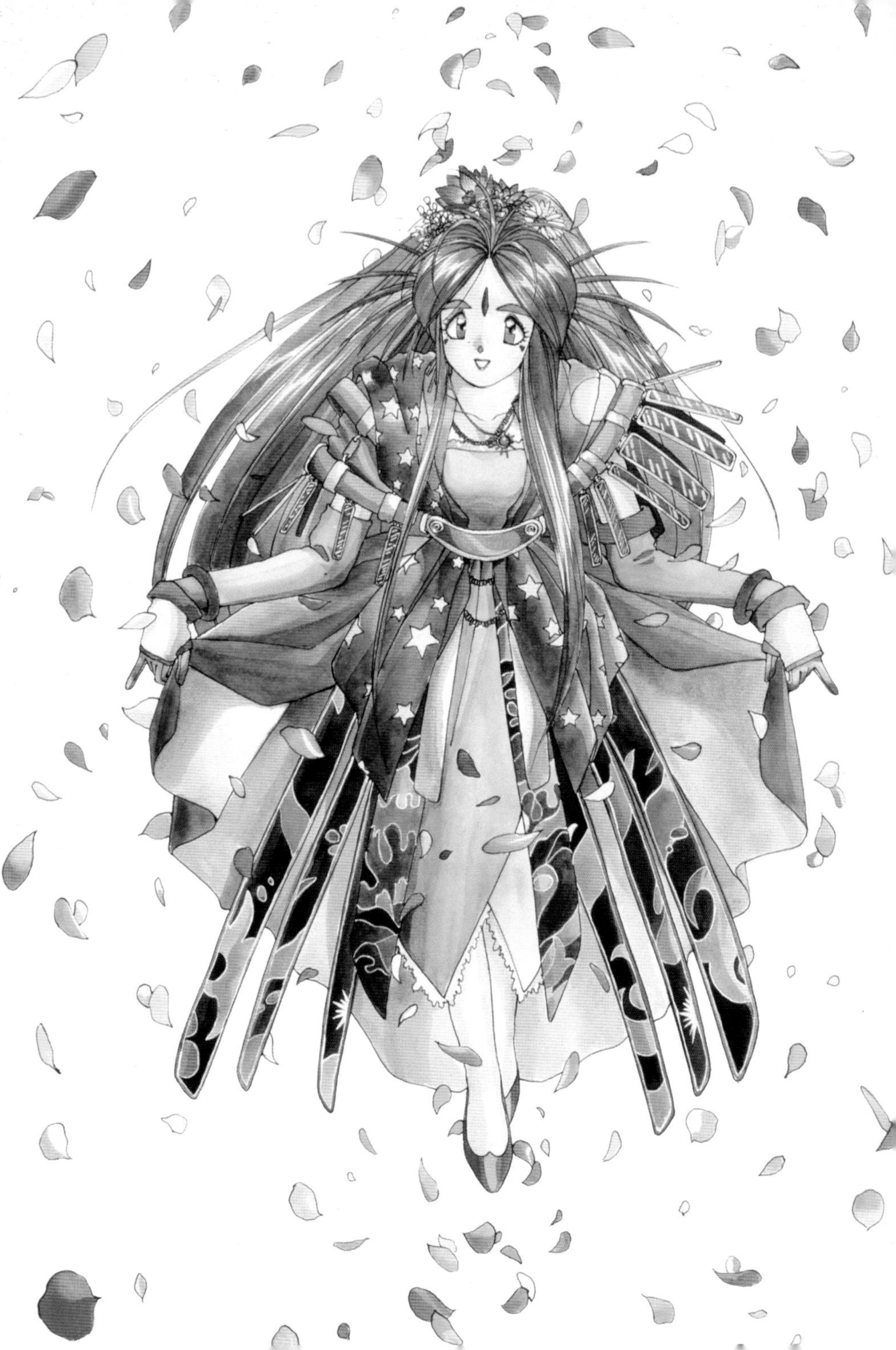

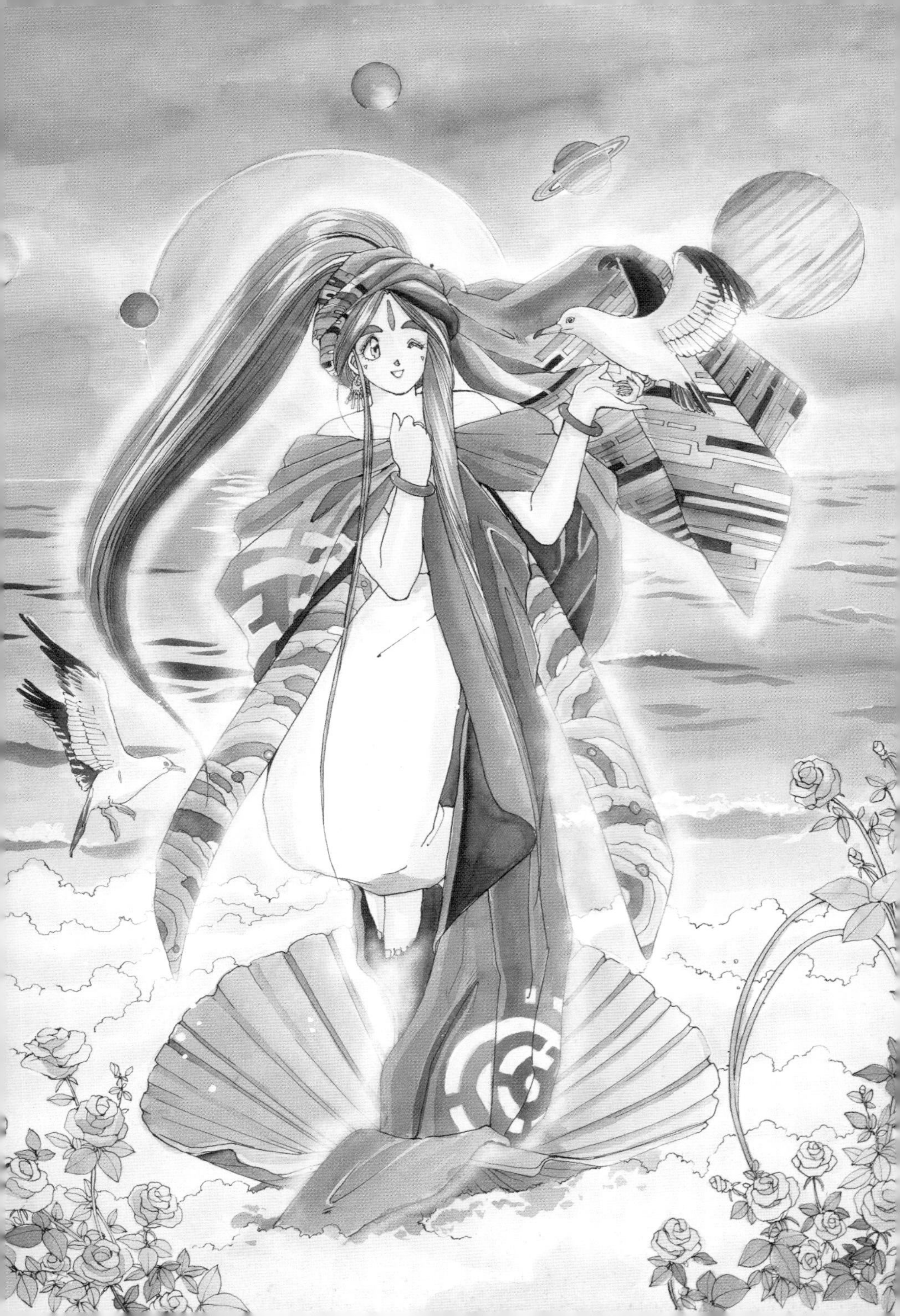

CHAPTER 12

Love Is the Prize

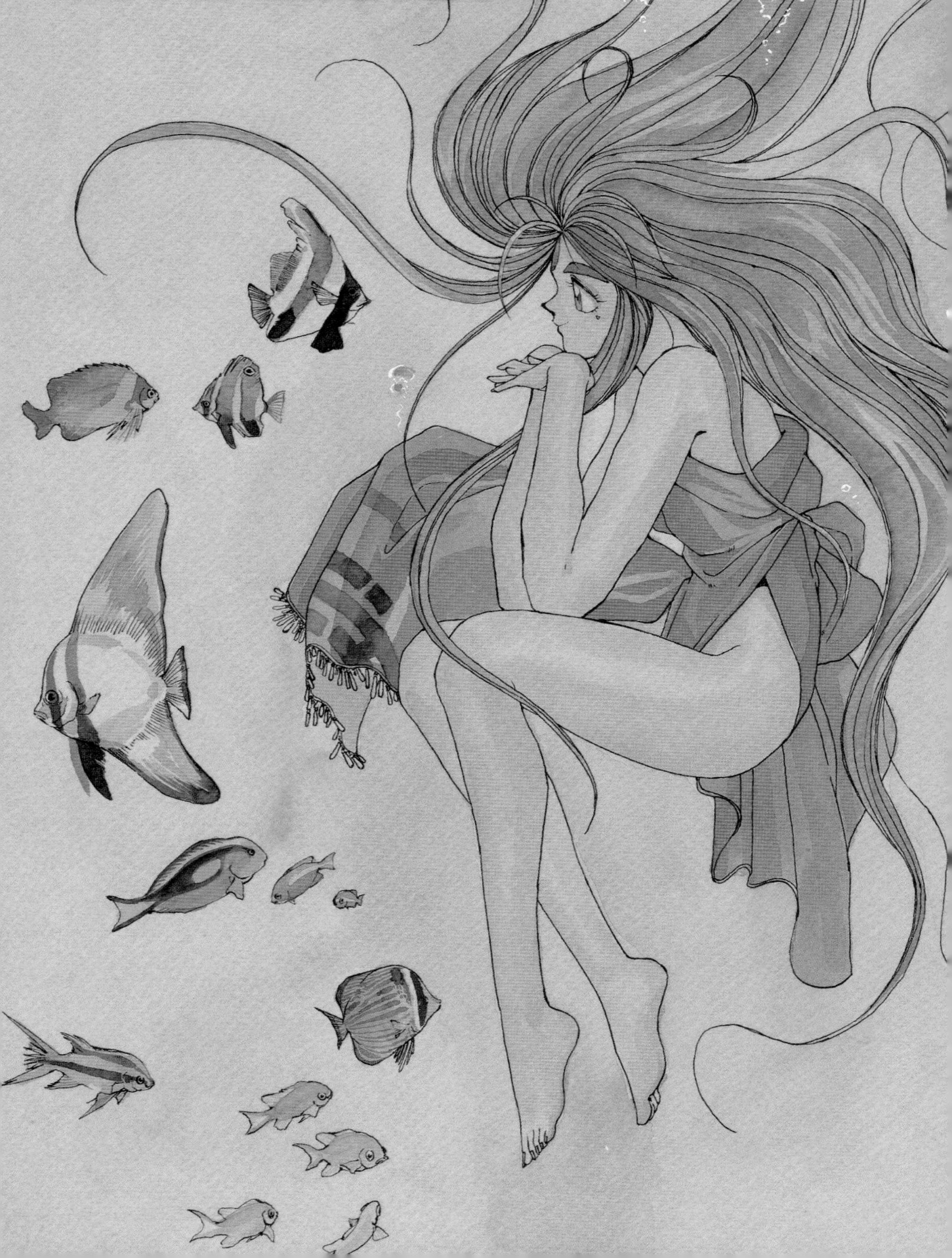

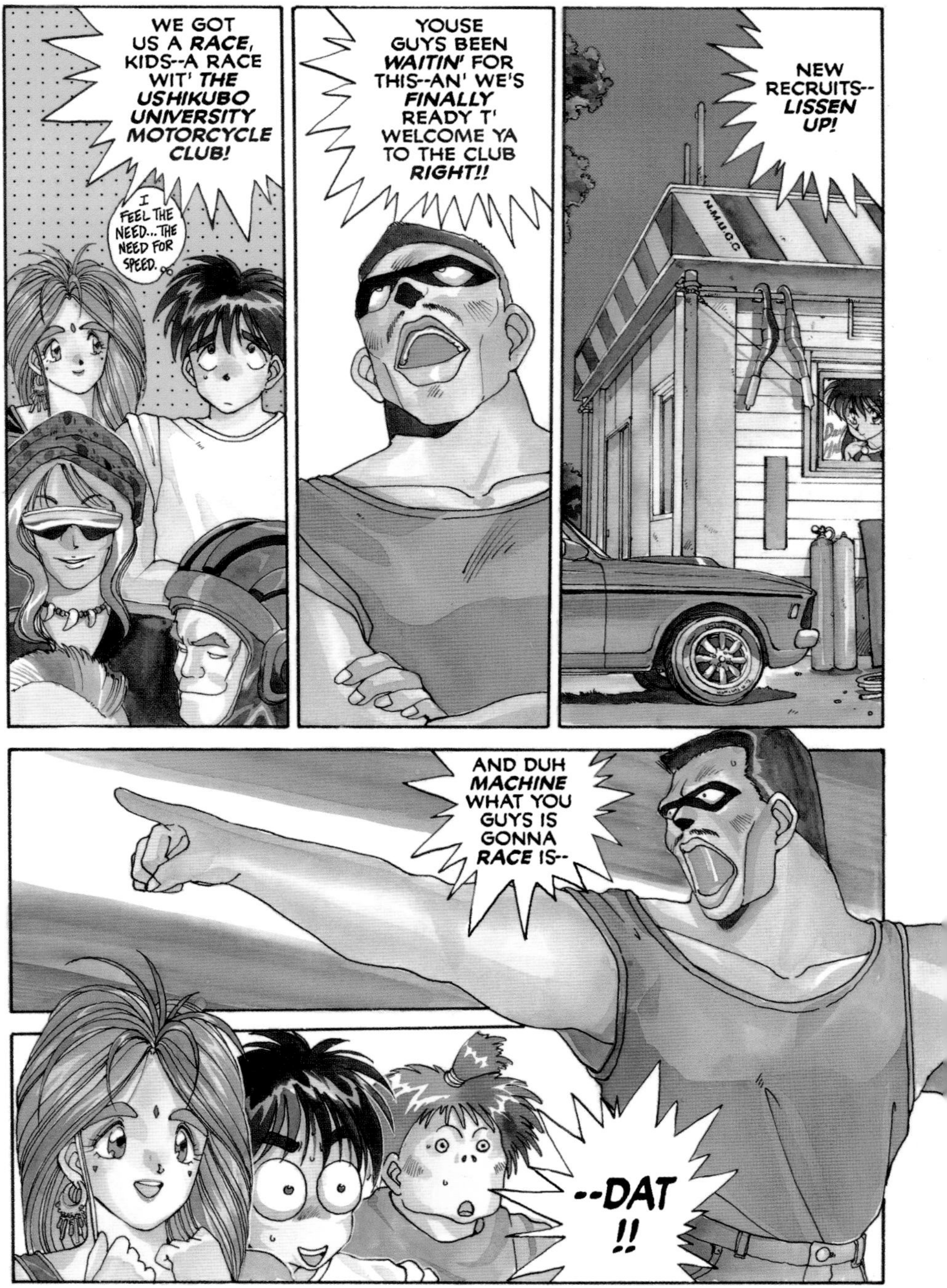
NEW RECRUITS--LISSEN UP!
YOUSE GUYS BEEN WAITIN' FOR THIS--AN' WE'S FINALLY READY T' WELCOME YA TO THE CLUB RIGHT!!
WE GOT US A RACE, KIDS--A RACE WIT' THE USHIKUBO UNIVERSITY MOTORCYCLE CLUB!
I FEEL THE NEED... THE NEED FOR SPEED.
AND DUH MACHINE WHAT YOU GUYS IS GONNA RACE IS--
--DAT!!

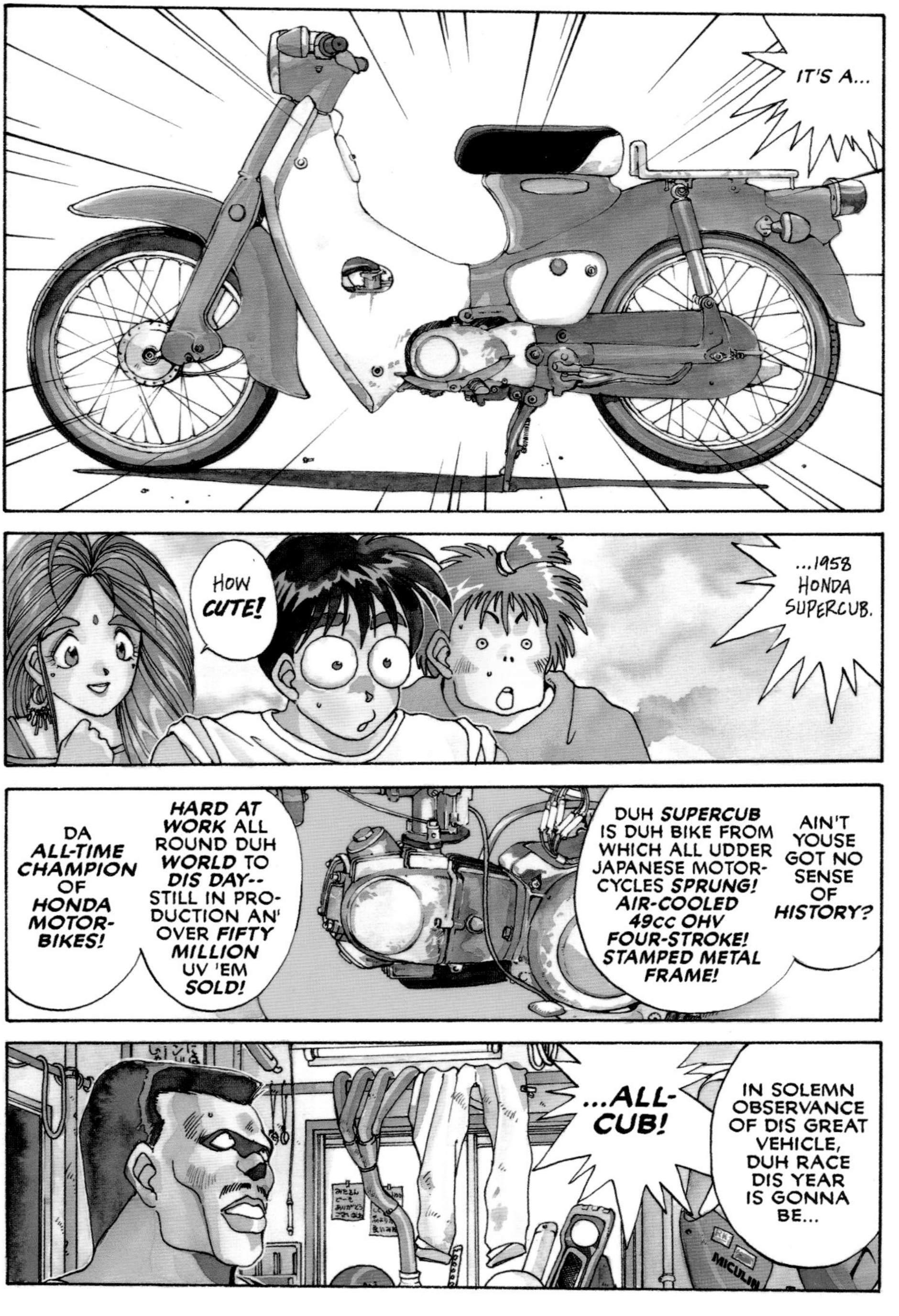
IT'S A...
...1958 HONDA SUPERCUB.
HOW CUTE!
AIN'T YOUSE GOT NO SENSE OF HISTORY?
DUH SUPERCUB IS DUH BIKE FROM WHICH ALL UDDER JAPANESE MOTORCYCLES SPRUNG! AIR-COOLED 49cc OHV FOUR-STROKE! STAMPED METAL FRAME!
HARD AT WORK ALL ROUND DUH WORLD TO DIS DAY-- STILL IN PRODUCTION AN' OVER FIFTY MILLION UV 'EM SOLD!
DA ALL-TIME CHAMPION OF HONDA MOTORBIKES!
IN SOLEMN OBSERVANCE OF DIS GREAT VEHICLE, DUH RACE DIS YEAR IS GONNA BE...
...ALL-CUB!

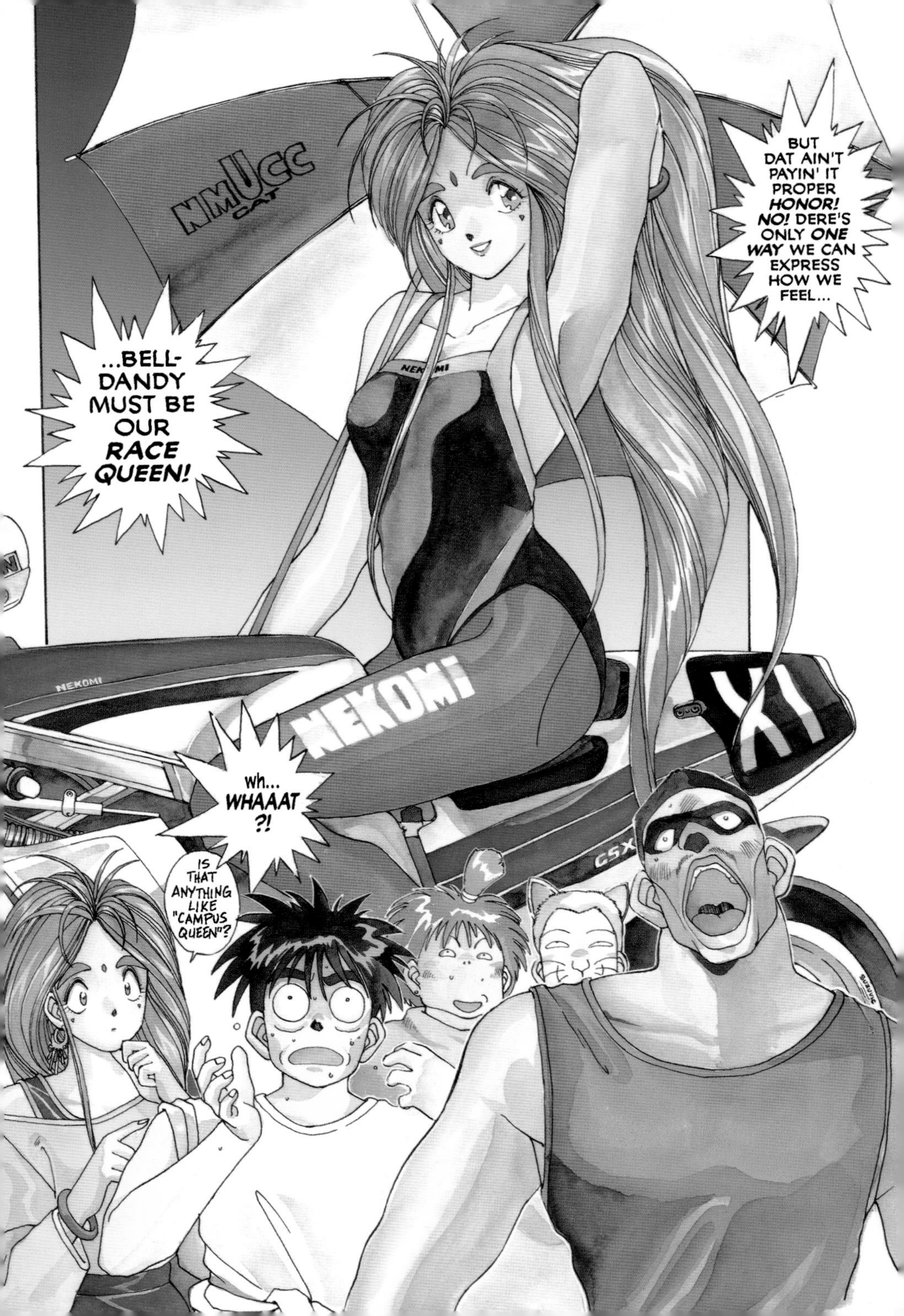
BUT DAT AIN'T PAYIN' IT PROPER HONOR! NO! DERE'S ONLY ONE WAY WE CAN EXPRESS HOW WE FEEL...
...BELL-DANDY MUST BE OUR RACE QUEEN!
NMUCC CAT
NEKOMI
XI
wh... WHAAAT ?!
IS THAT ANYTHING LIKE "CAMPUS QUEEN"?

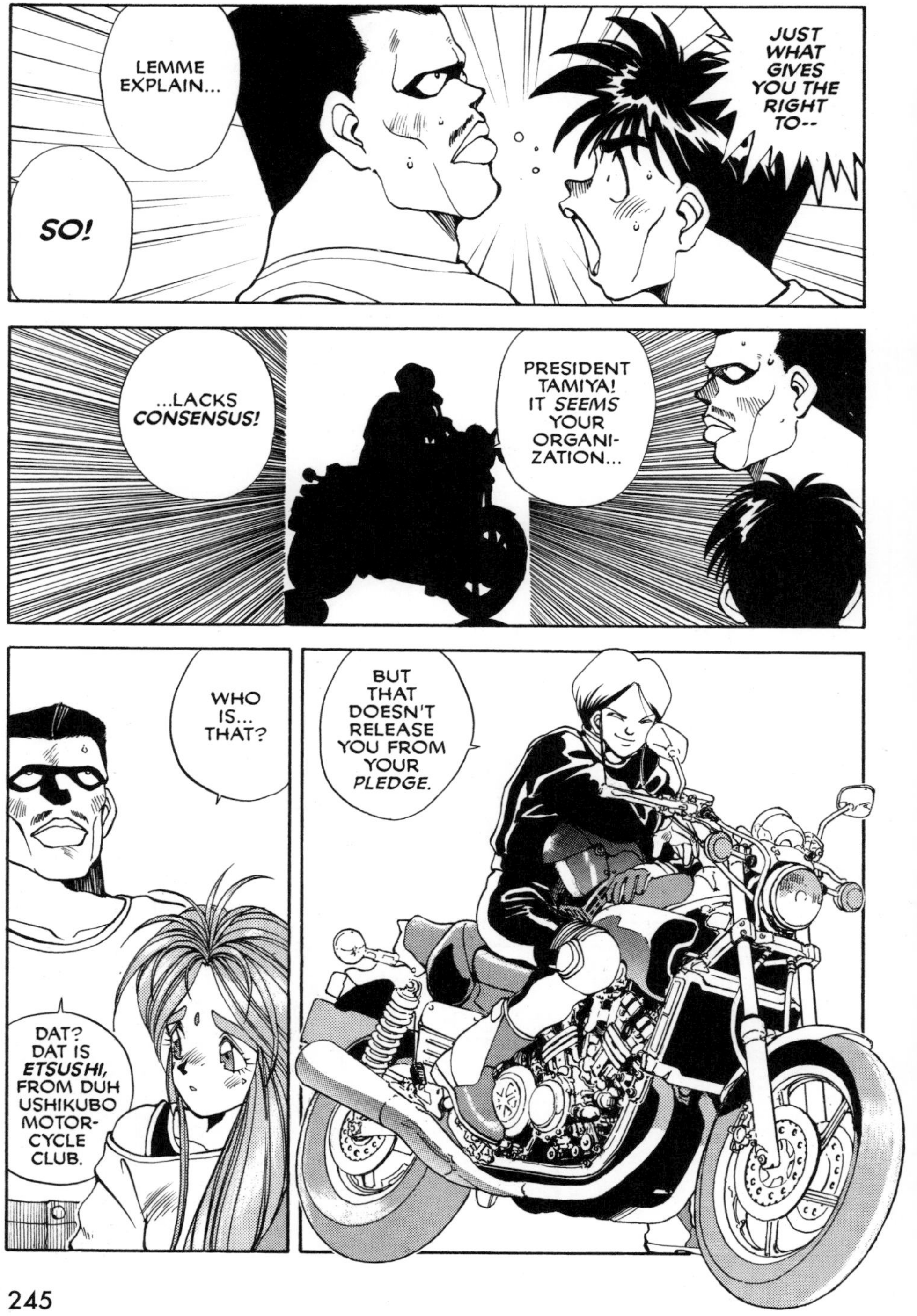
JUST WHAT GIVES YOU THE RIGHT TO--
LEMME EXPLAIN...
SO!
PRESIDENT TAMIYA! IT SEEMS YOUR ORGANIZATION...
...LACKS CONSENSUS!
BUT THAT DOESN'T RELEASE YOU FROM YOUR PLEDGE.
WHO IS... THAT?
DAT? DAT IS ETSUSHI, FROM DUH USHIKUBO MOTORCYCLE CLUB.

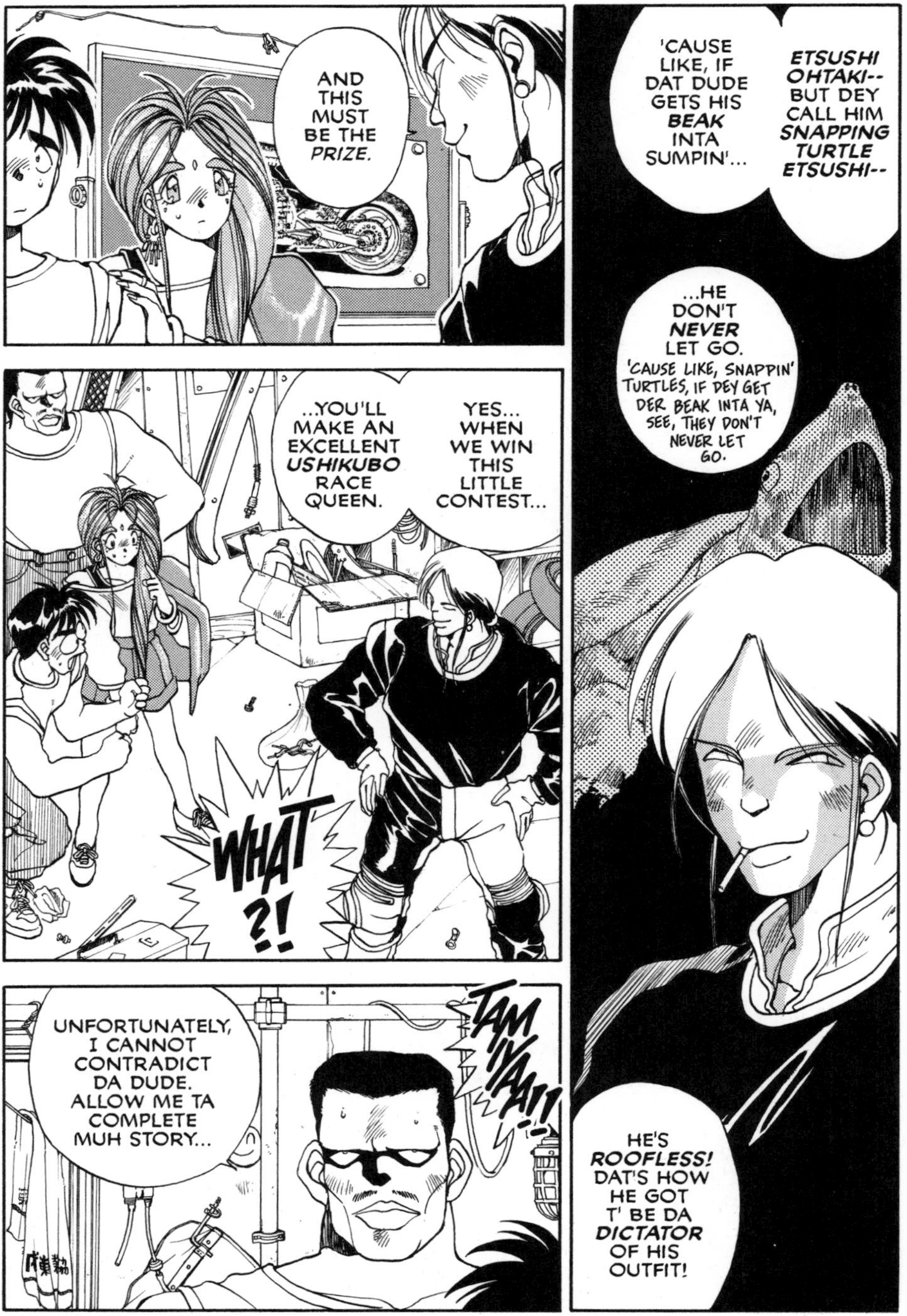
ETSUSHI OHTAKI-- BUT DEY CALL HIM SNAPPING TURTLE ETSUSHI--
'CAUSE LIKE, IF DAT DUDE GETS HIS BEAK INTA SUMPIN'...
...HE DON'T NEVER LET GO.
'CAUSE LIKE, SNAPPIN' TURTLES, IF DEY GET DER BEAK INTA YA, SEE, THEY DON'T NEVER LET GO.
HE'S ROOFLESS! DAT'S HOW HE GOT T' BE DA DICTATOR OF HIS OUTFIT!
AND THIS MUST BE THE PRIZE.
YES... WHEN WE WIN THIS LITTLE CONTEST...
...YOU'LL MAKE AN EXCELLENT USHIKUBO RACE QUEEN.
WHAT?!
TAMIYAA!!
UNFORTUNATELY, I CANNOT CONTRADICT DA DUDE. ALLOW ME TA COMPLETE MUH STORY...

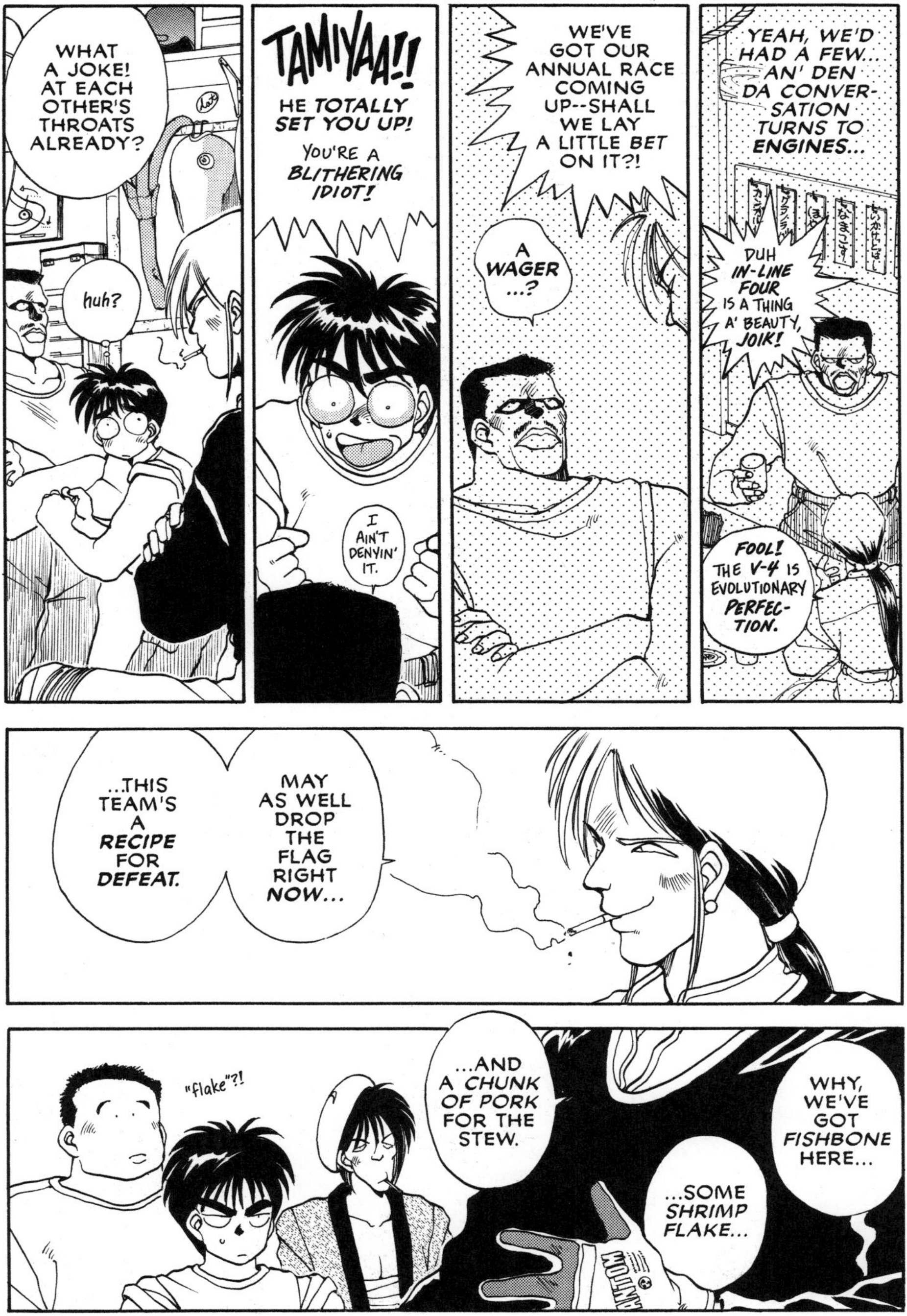
YEAH, WE'D HAD A FEW... AN' DEN DA CONVERSATION TURNS TO ENGINES...
DUH IN-LINE FOUR IS A THING A' BEAUTY, JOIK!
FOOL! THE V-4 IS EVOLUTIONARY PERFECTION.
WE'VE GOT OUR ANNUAL RACE COMING UP--SHALL WE LAY A LITTLE BET ON IT?!
A WAGER ...?
TAMIYAA!!
HE TOTALLY SET YOU UP!
YOU'RE A BLITHERING IDIOT!
I AIN'T DENYIN' IT.
WHAT A JOKE! AT EACH OTHER'S THROATS ALREADY?
huh?
MAY AS WELL DROP THE FLAG RIGHT NOW...
...THIS TEAM'S A RECIPE FOR DEFEAT.
WHY, WE'VE GOT FISHBONE HERE...
...SOME SHRIMP FLAKE...
...AND A CHUNK OF PORK FOR THE STEW.
"flake"?!

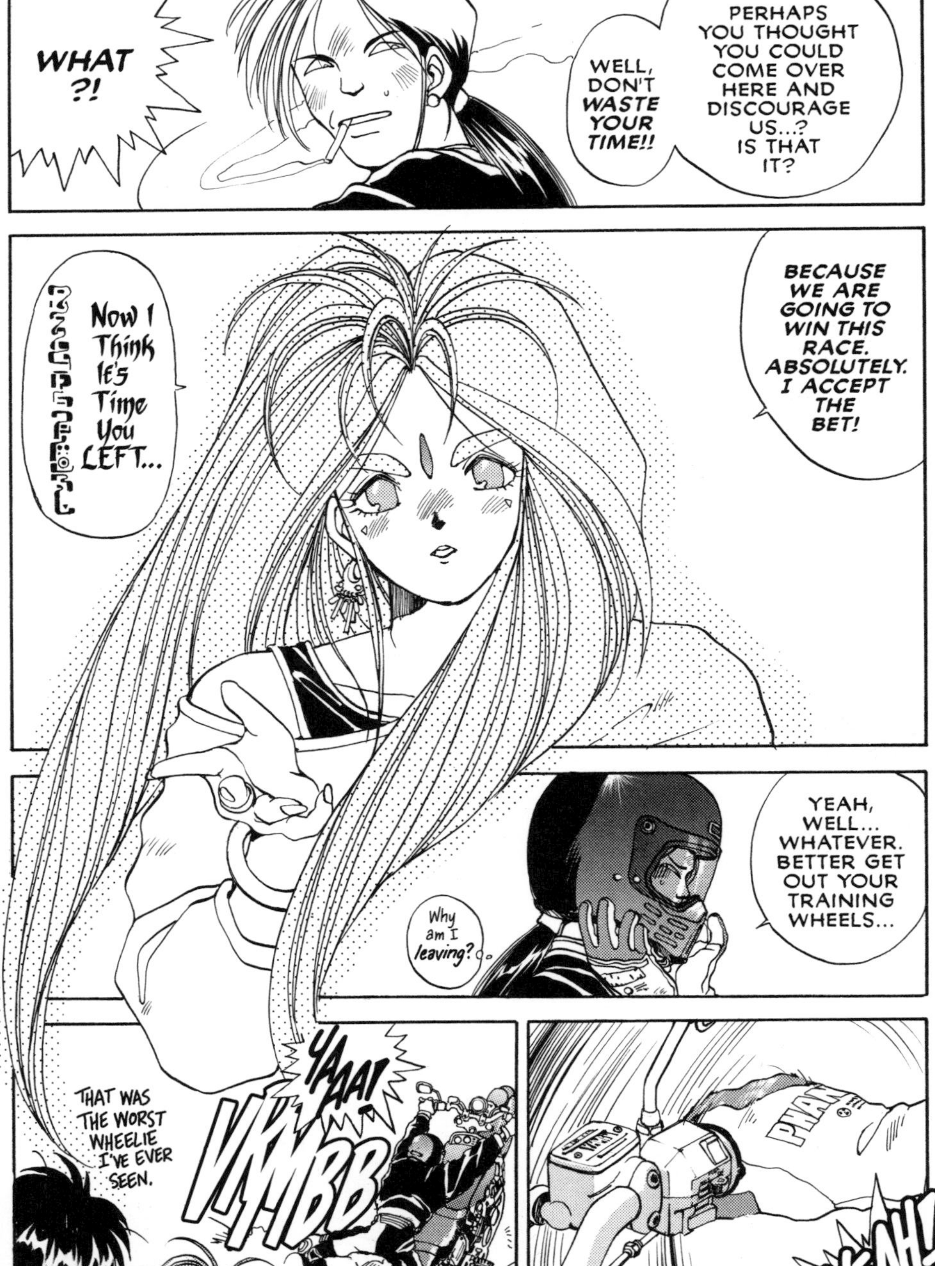
PERHAPS YOU THOUGHT YOU COULD COME OVER HERE AND DISCOURAGE US...? IS THAT IT?
WELL, DON'T WASTE YOUR TIME!!
WHAT ?!
BECAUSE WE ARE GOING TO WIN THIS RACE. ABSOLUTELY. I ACCEPT THE BET!
Now I Think It's Time You LEFT...
YEAH, WELL... WHATEVER. BETTER GET OUT YOUR TRAINING WHEELS...
Why am I leaving?
YEAH!
YAAAI!
VMBB
THAT WAS THE WORST WHEELIE I'VE EVER SEEN.

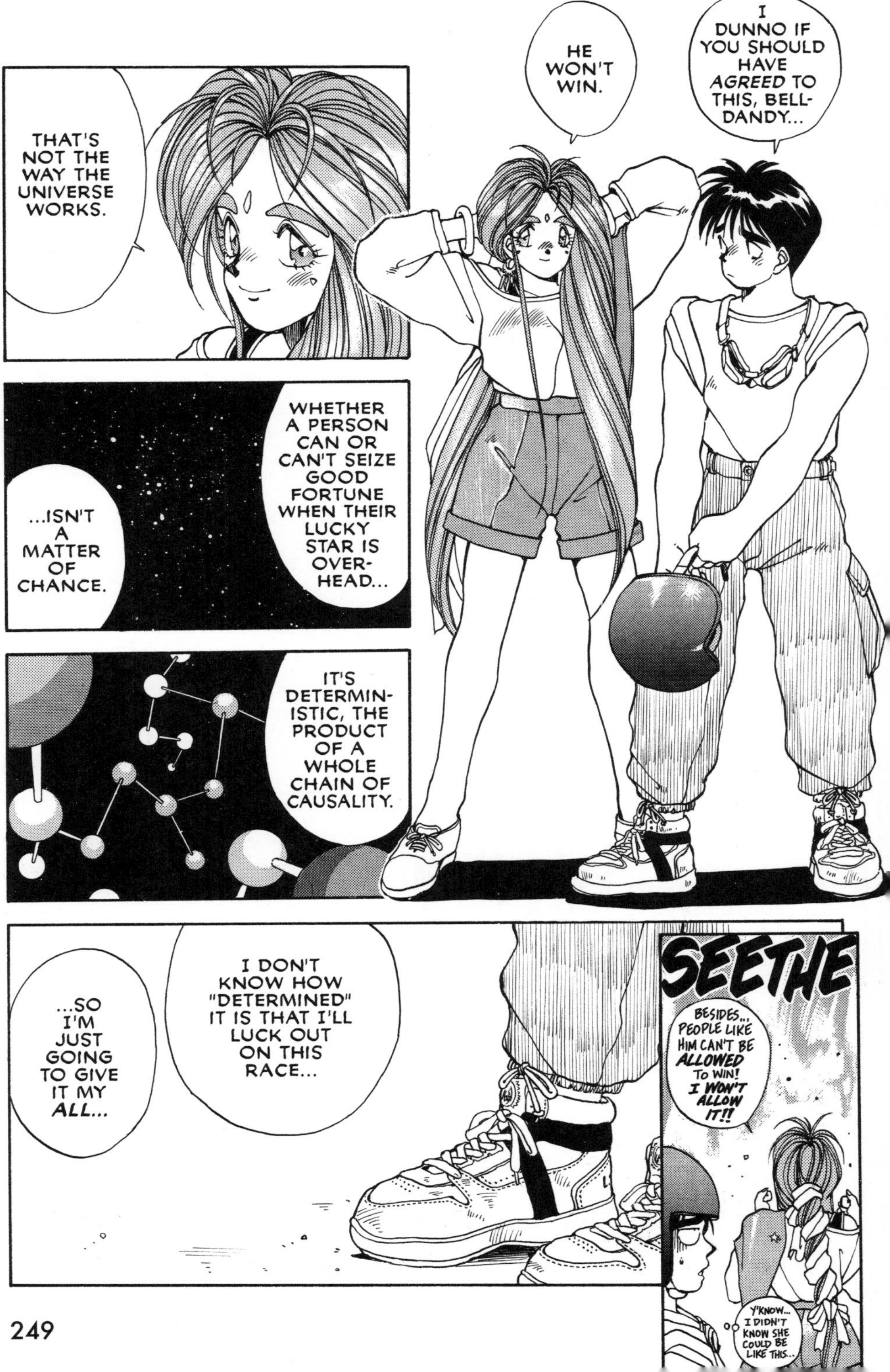
I DUNNO IF YOU SHOULD HAVE AGREED TO THIS, BELL-DANDY...
HE WON'T WIN.
THAT'S NOT THE WAY THE UNIVERSE WORKS.
WHETHER A PERSON CAN OR CAN'T SEIZE GOOD FORTUNE WHEN THEIR LUCKY STAR IS OVER-HEAD...
...ISN'T A MATTER OF CHANCE.
IT'S DETERMIN-ISTIC, THE PRODUCT OF A WHOLE CHAIN OF CAUSALITY.
SEETHE
BESIDES... PEOPLE LIKE HIM CAN'T BE ALLOWED TO WIN! I WON'T ALLOW IT!!
Y'KNOW... I DIDN'T KNOW SHE COULD BE LIKE THIS...
I DON'T KNOW HOW "DETERMINED" IT IS THAT I'LL LUCK OUT ON THIS RACE...
...SO I'M JUST GOING TO GIVE IT MY ALL...

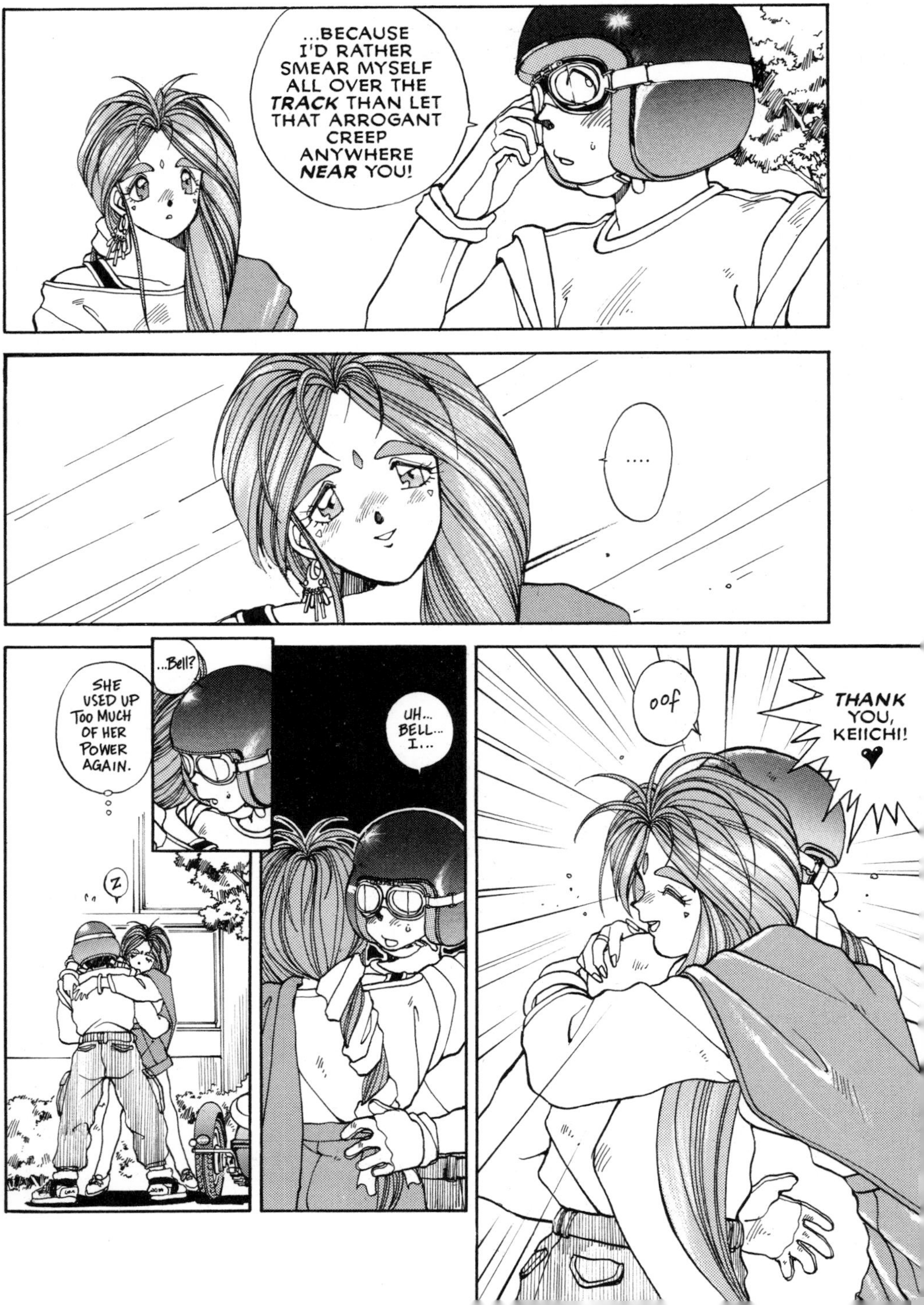
...BECAUSE I'D RATHER SMEAR MYSELF ALL OVER THE TRACK THAN LET THAT ARROGANT CREEP ANYWHERE NEAR YOU!
....
THANK YOU, KEIICHI!
oof
UH... BELL... I...
...Bell?
SHE USED UP TOO MUCH OF HER POWER AGAIN.
Z

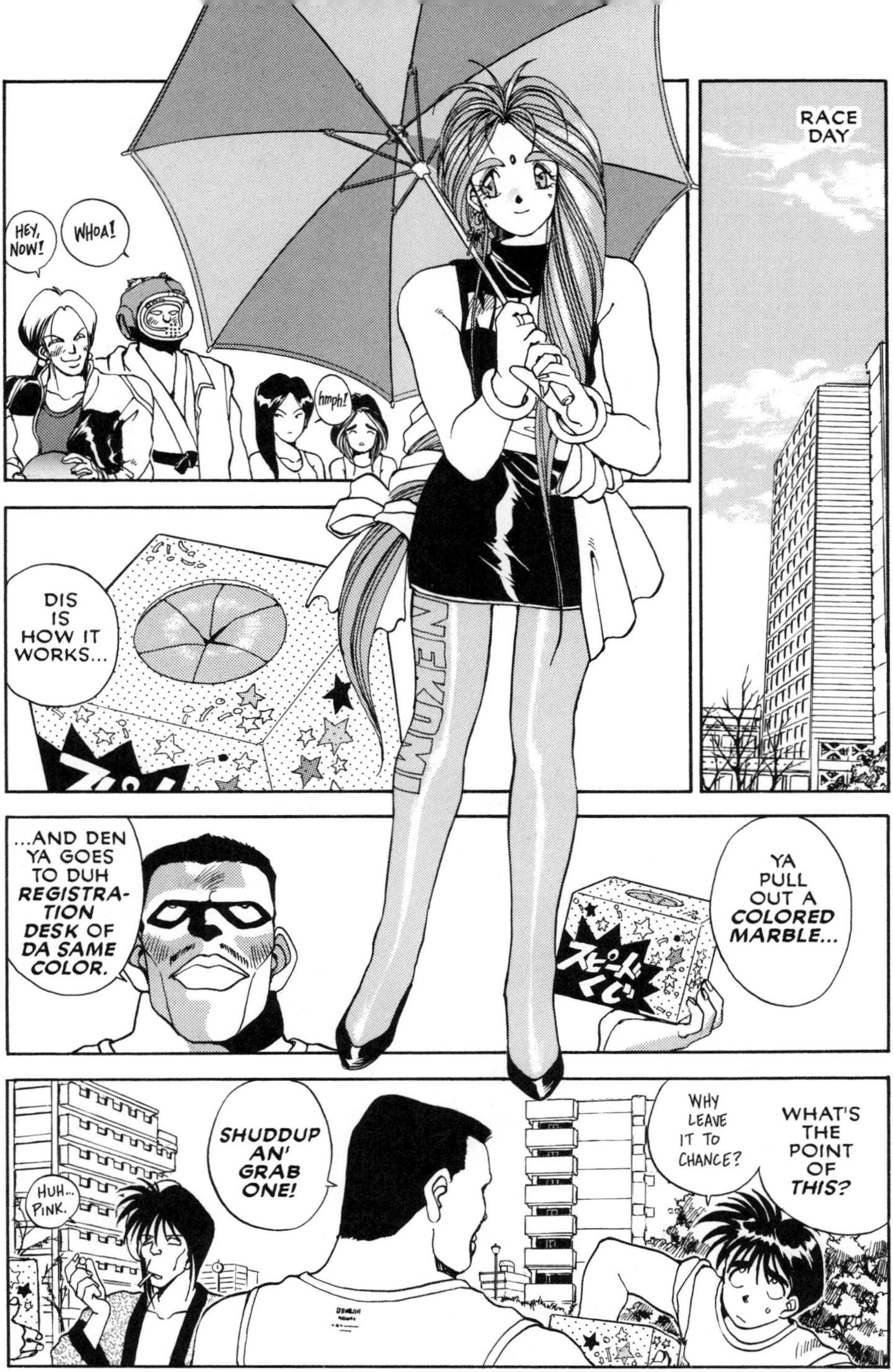
RACE DAY
WHOA!
HEY, NOW!
hmph!
DIS IS HOW IT WORKS...
YA PULL OUT A COLORED MARBLE...
スピードくじ
...AND DEN YA GOES TO DUH REGISTRATION DESK OF DA SAME COLOR.
WHAT'S THE POINT OF THIS?
WHY LEAVE IT TO CHANCE?
SHUDDUP AN' GRAB ONE!
HUH... PINK.

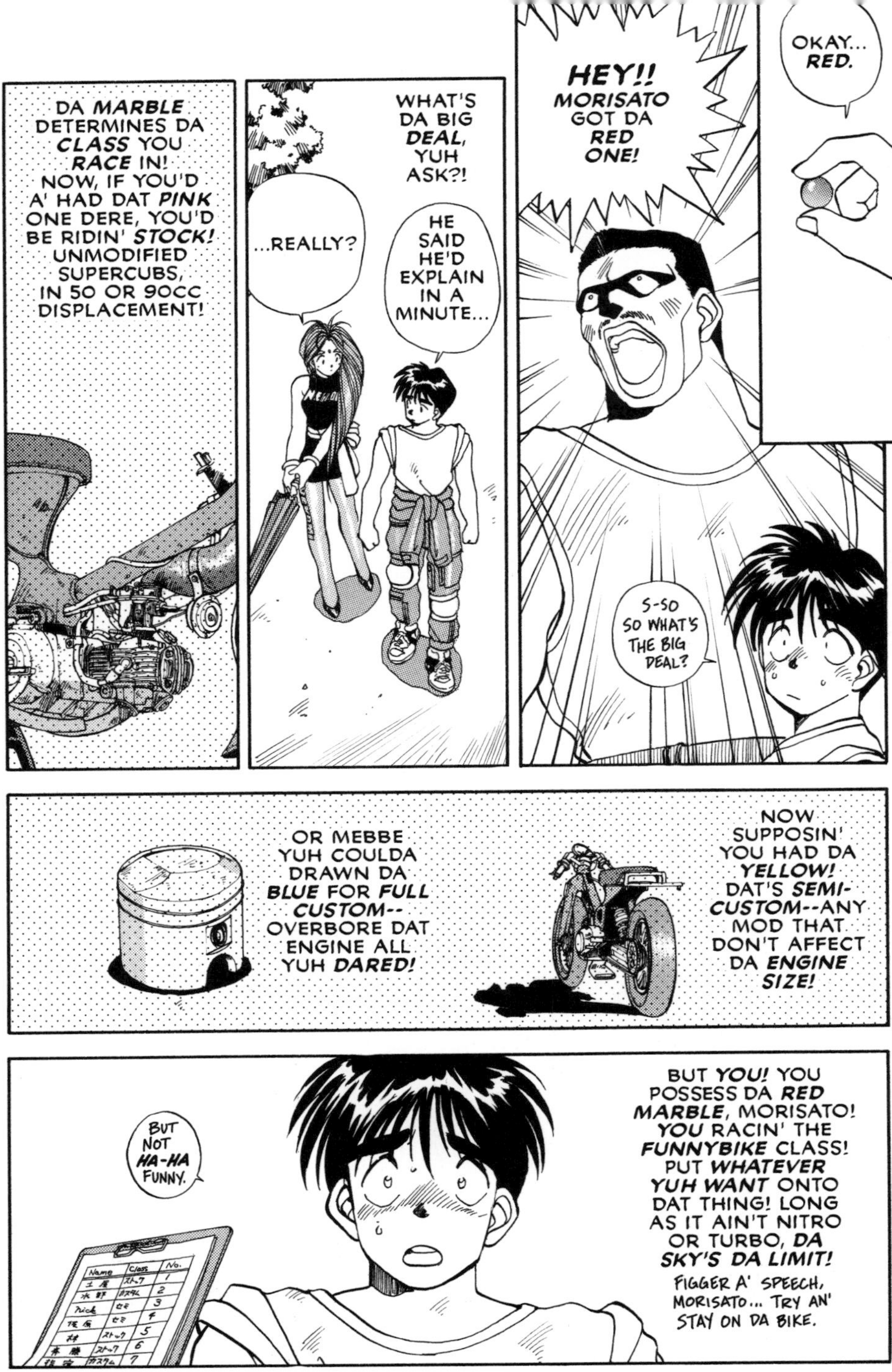
OKAY... RED.
HEY!! MORISATO GOT DA RED ONE!
S-SO SO WHAT'S THE BIG DEAL?
WHAT'S DA BIG DEAL, YUH ASK?!
...REALLY?
HE SAID HE'D EXPLAIN IN A MINUTE...
DA MARBLE DETERMINES DA CLASS YOU RACE IN! NOW, IF YOU'D A' HAD DAT PINK ONE DERE, YOU'D BE RIDIN' STOCK! UNMODIFIED SUPERCUBS, IN 50 OR 90CC DISPLACEMENT!
NOW SUPPOSIN' YOU HAD DA YELLOW! DAT'S SEMI-CUSTOM--ANY MOD THAT DON'T AFFECT DA ENGINE SIZE!
OR MEBBE YUH COULDA DRAWN DA BLUE FOR FULL CUSTOM--OVERBORE DAT ENGINE ALL YUH DARED!
BUT YOU! YOU POSSESS DA RED MARBLE, MORISATO! YOU RACIN' THE FUNNYBIKE CLASS! PUT WHATEVER YUH WANT ONTO DAT THING! LONG AS IT AIN'T NITRO OR TURBO, DA SKY'S DA LIMIT!
FIGGER A' SPEECH, MORISATO... TRY AN' STAY ON DA BIKE.
BUT NOT HA-HA FUNNY.

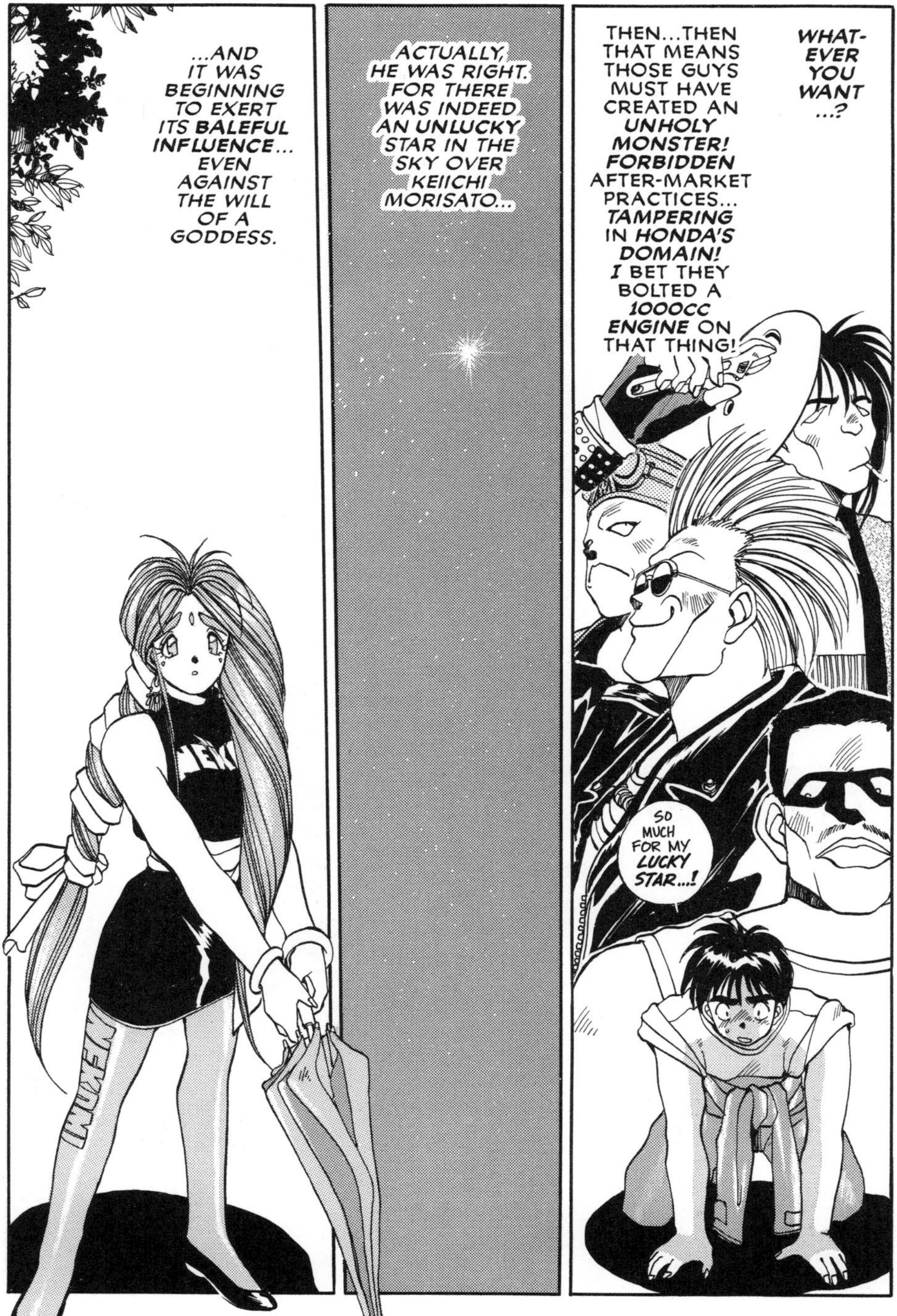
WHAT-EVER YOU WANT ...?
THEN...THEN THAT MEANS THOSE GUYS MUST HAVE CREATED AN UNHOLY MONSTER! FORBIDDEN AFTER-MARKET PRACTICES... TAMPERING IN HONDA'S DOMAIN! I BET THEY BOLTED A 1000CC ENGINE ON THAT THING!
SO MUCH FOR MY LUCKY STAR...!
ACTUALLY, HE WAS RIGHT. FOR THERE WAS INDEED AN UNLUCKY STAR IN THE SKY OVER KEIICHI MORISATO...
...AND IT WAS BEGINNING TO EXERT ITS BALEFUL INFLUENCE... EVEN AGAINST THE WILL OF A GODDESS.

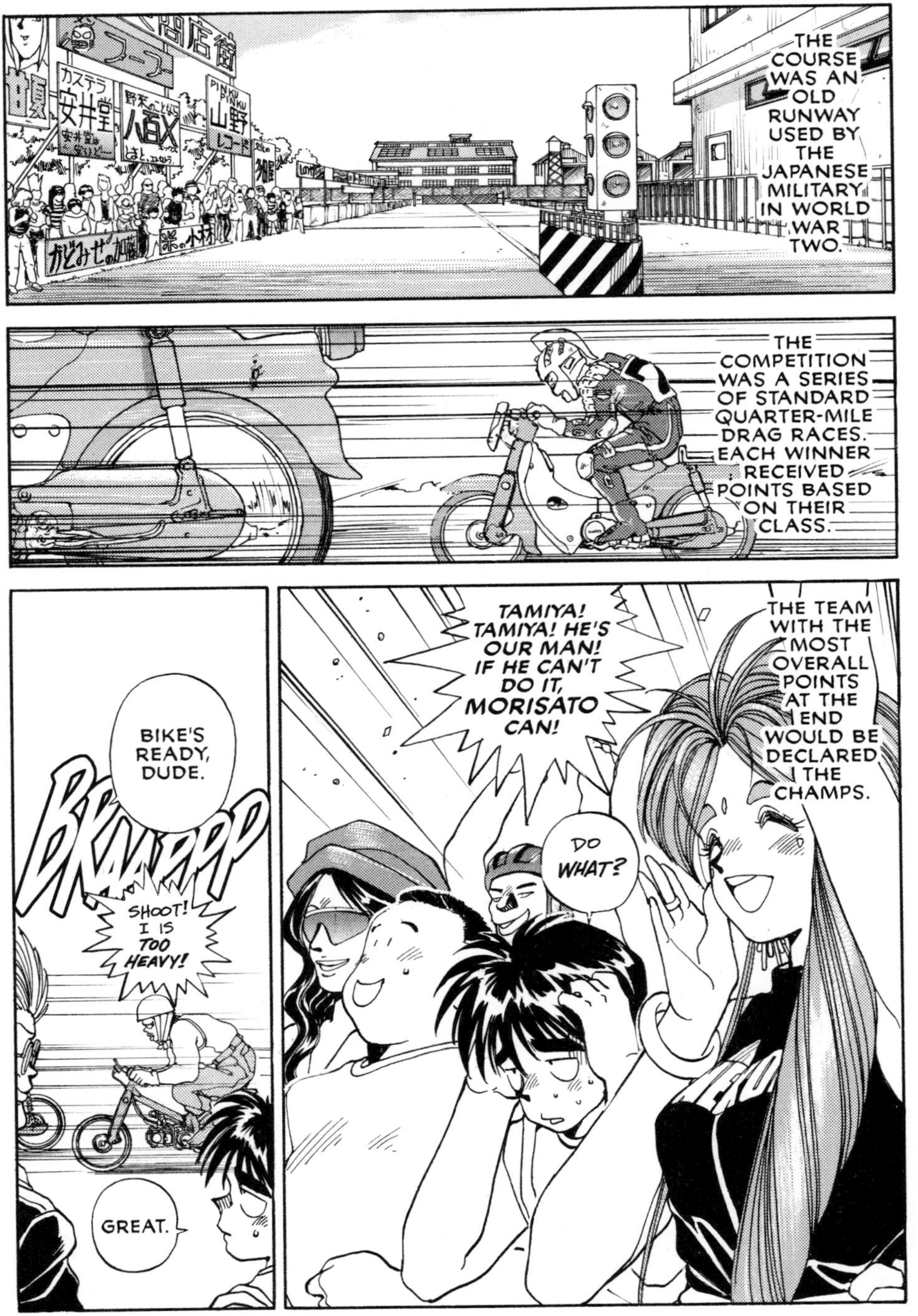
THE COURSE WAS AN OLD RUNWAY USED BY THE JAPANESE MILITARY IN WORLD WAR TWO.
THE COMPETITION WAS A SERIES OF STANDARD QUARTER-MILE DRAG RACES. EACH WINNER RECEIVED POINTS BASED ON THEIR CLASS.
THE TEAM WITH THE MOST OVERALL POINTS AT THE END WOULD BE DECLARED THE CHAMPS.
TAMIYA! TAMIYA! HE'S OUR MAN! IF HE CAN'T DO IT, MORISATO CAN!
DO WHAT?
BIKE'S READY, DUDE.
SHOOT! I IS TOO HEAVY!
GREAT.

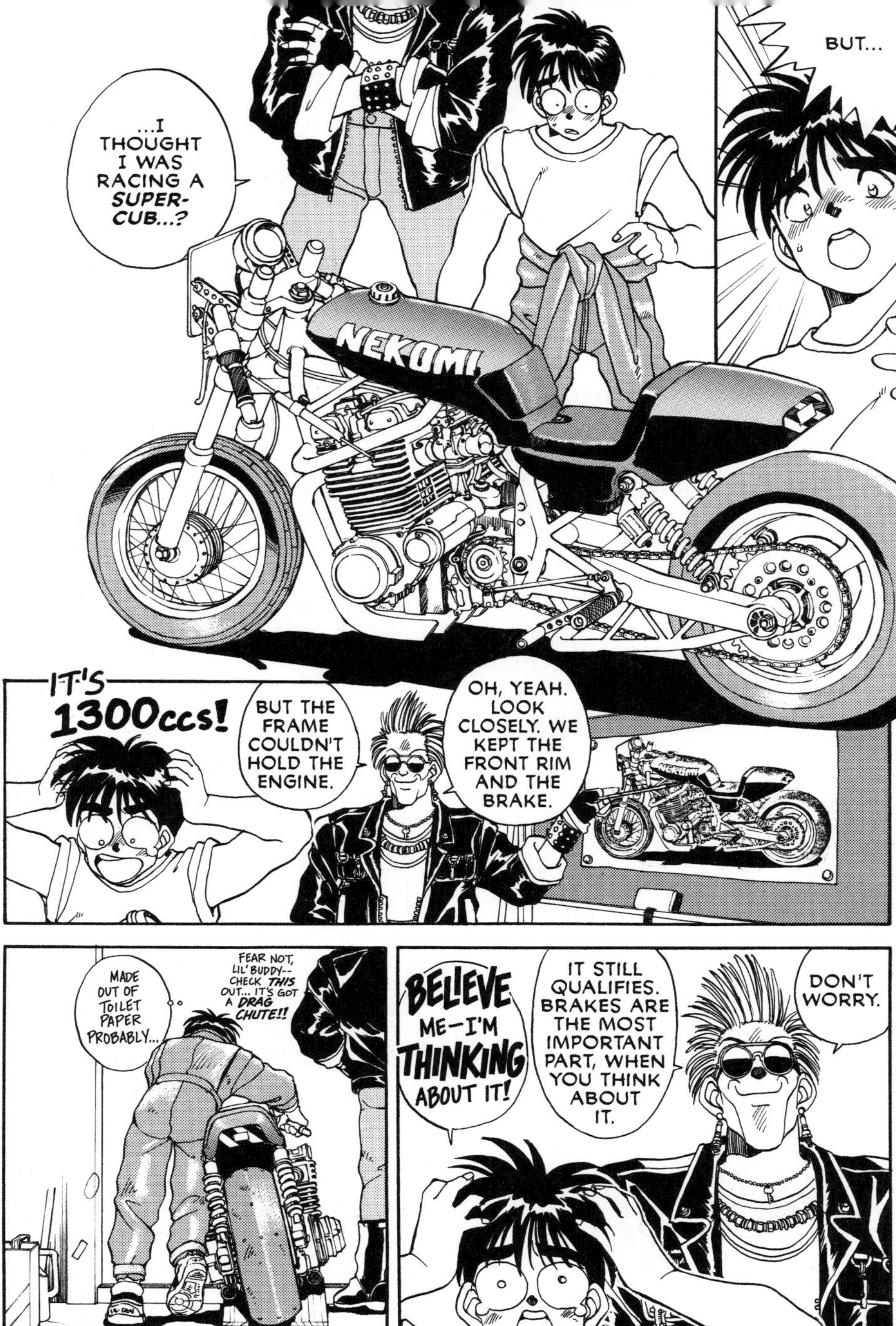

BUT...
...I THOUGHT I WAS RACING A SUPER-CUB...?
NEKOMI
OH, YEAH. LOOK CLOSELY. WE KEPT THE FRONT RIM AND THE BRAKE.
BUT THE FRAME COULDN'T HOLD THE ENGINE.
IT'S 1300ccs!
DON'T WORRY.
IT STILL QUALIFIES. BRAKES ARE THE MOST IMPORTANT PART, WHEN YOU THINK ABOUT IT.
BELIEVE ME—I'M THINKING ABOUT IT!
FEAR NOT, LIL' BUDDY-- CHECK THIS OUT... IT'S GOT A DRAG CHUTE!!
MADE OUT OF TOILET PAPER PROBABLY...

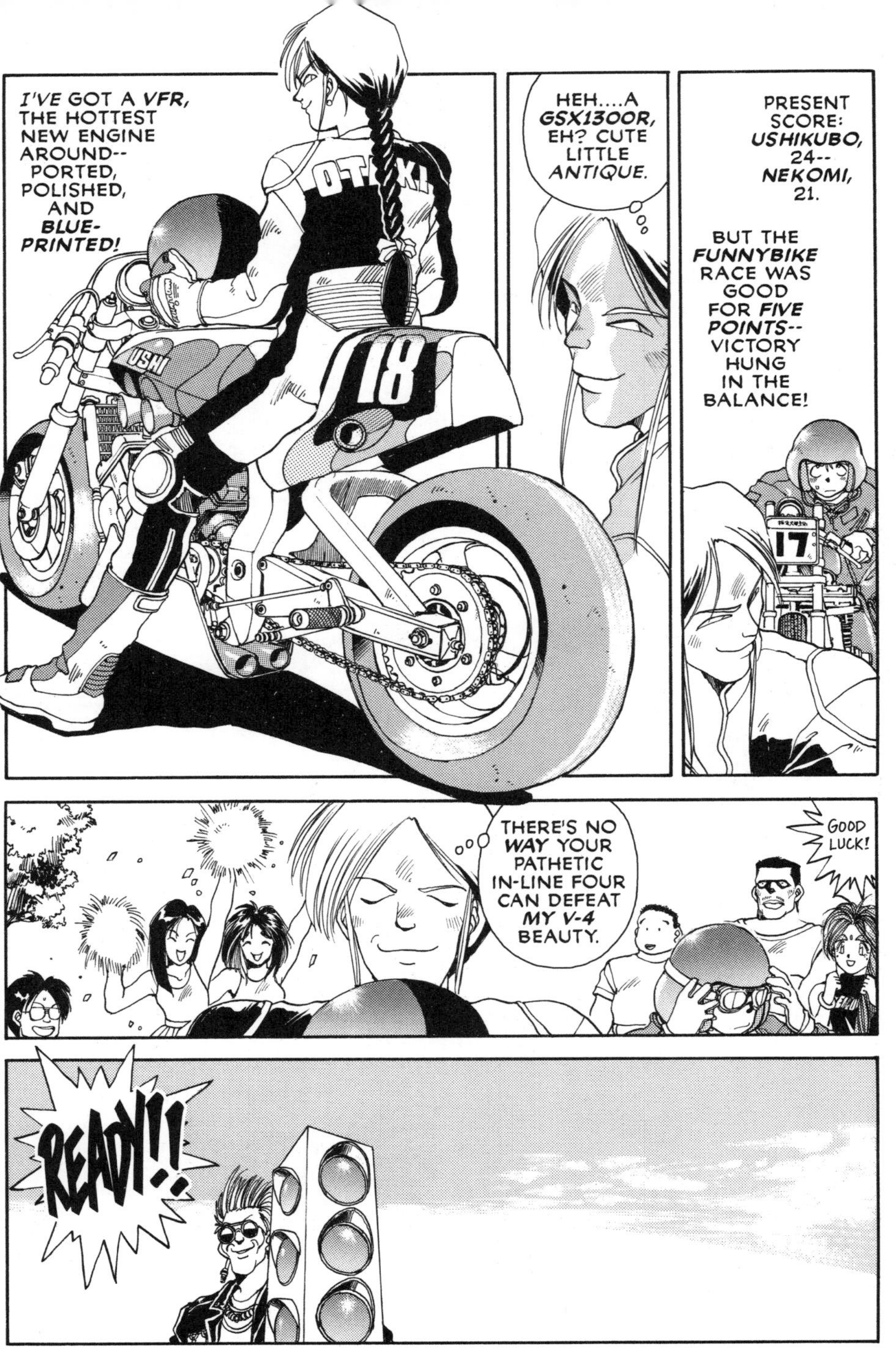
PRESENT SCORE: USHIKUBO, 24-- NEKOMI, 21.
BUT THE FUNNYBIKE RACE WAS GOOD FOR FIVE POINTS-- VICTORY HUNG IN THE BALANCE!
HEH....A GSX1300R, EH? CUTE LITTLE ANTIQUE.
I'VE GOT A VFR, THE HOTTEST NEW ENGINE AROUND-- PORTED, POLISHED, AND BLUE-PRINTED!
GOOD LUCK!
THERE'S NO WAY YOUR PATHETIC IN-LINE FOUR CAN DEFEAT MY V-4 BEAUTY.
READY!!

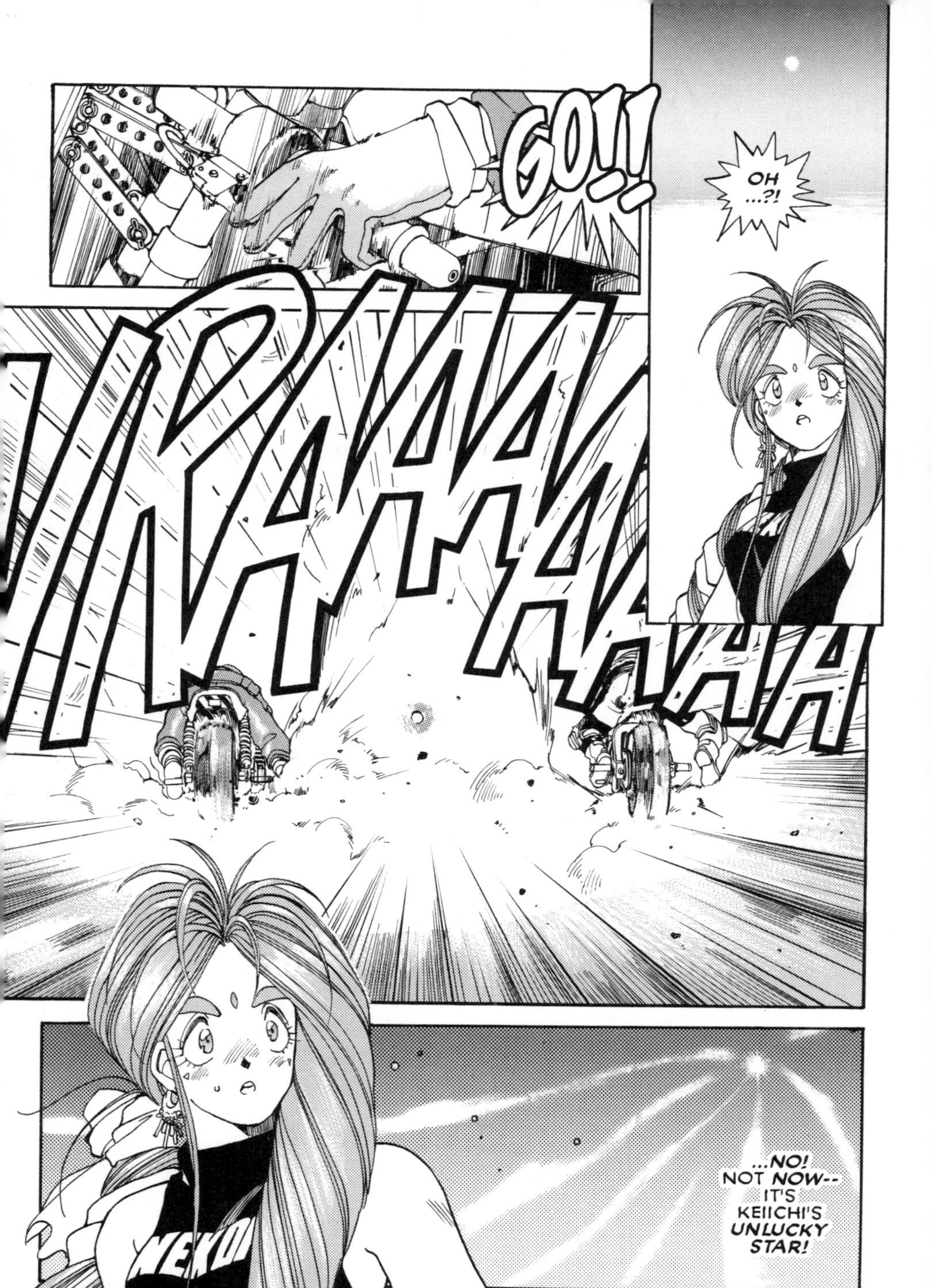
OH ...?!
GO!!
VRAAAAAAH
...NO! NOT NOW-- IT'S KEIICHI'S UNLUCKY STAR!

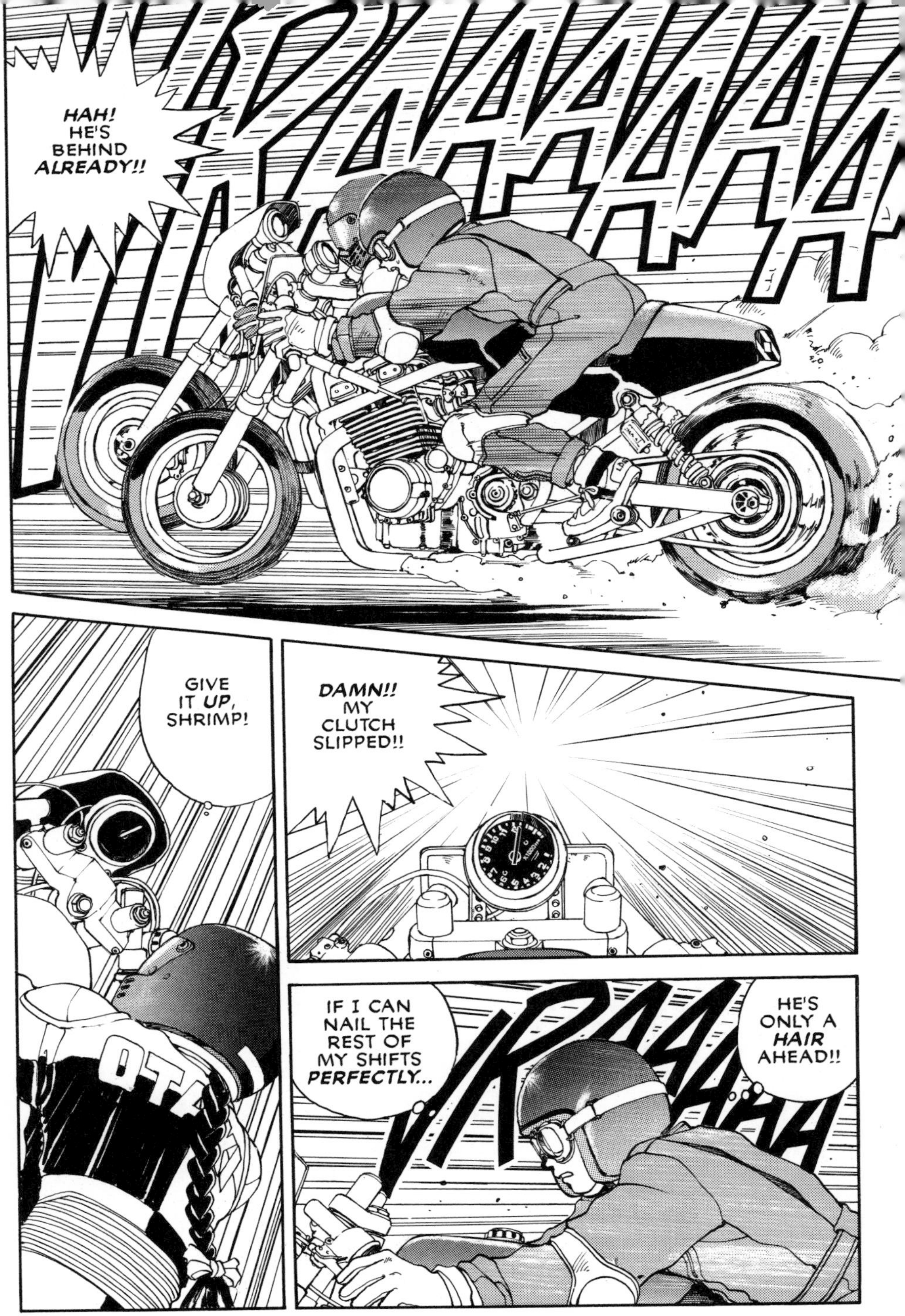
HAH! HE'S BEHIND ALREADY!!
DAMN!! MY CLUTCH SLIPPED!!
HE'S ONLY A HAIR AHEAD!!
IF I CAN NAIL THE REST OF MY SHIFTS PERFECTLY...
GIVE IT UP, SHRIMP!

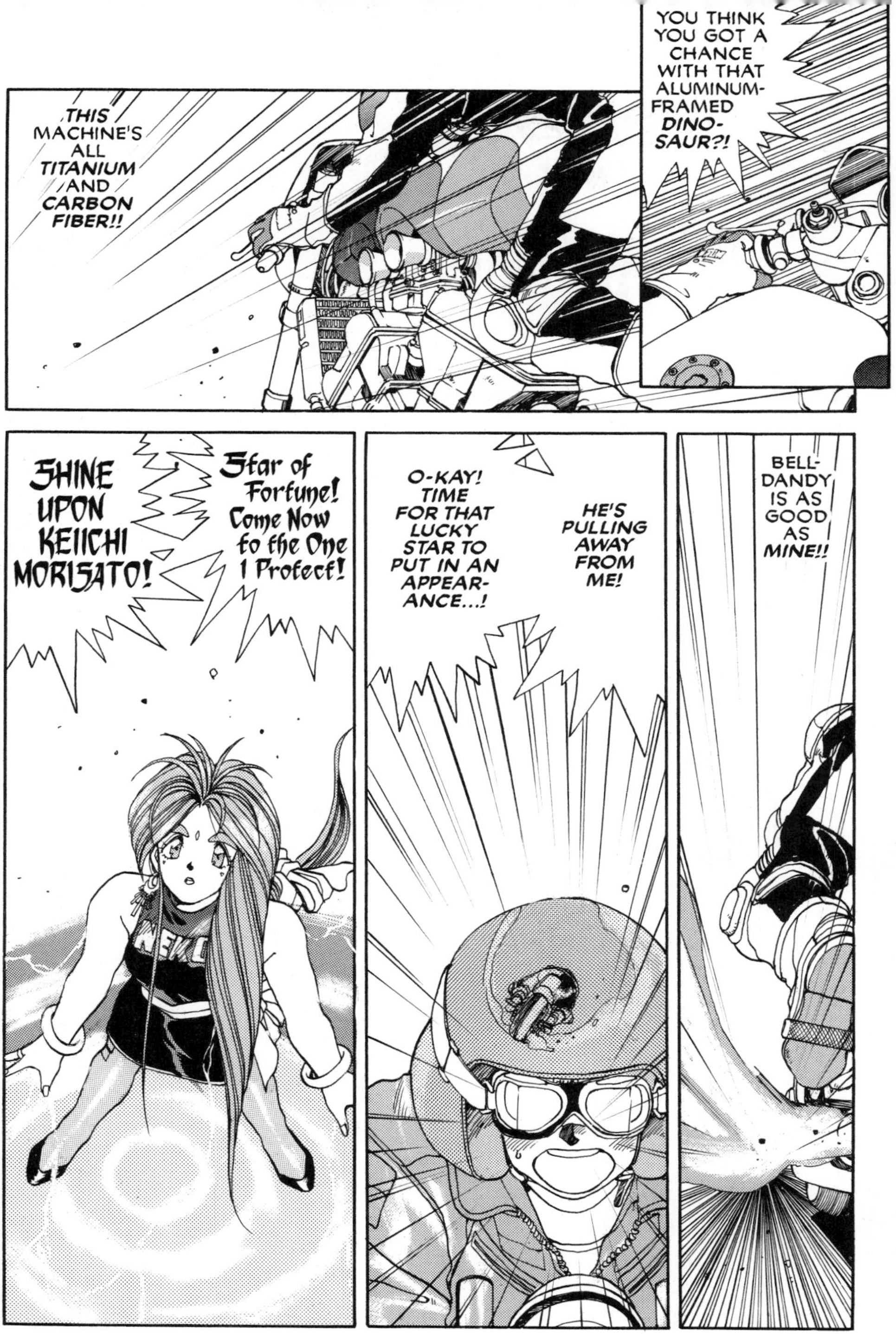
YOU THINK YOU GOT A CHANCE WITH THAT ALUMINUM-FRAMED DINOSAUR?!
THIS MACHINE'S ALL TITANIUM AND CARBON FIBER!!
BELL-DANDY IS AS GOOD AS MINE!!
HE'S PULLING AWAY FROM ME!
O-KAY! TIME FOR THAT LUCKY STAR TO PUT IN AN APPEAR-ANCE...!
Star of Fortune! Come Now to the One I Protect!
SHINE UPON KEIICHI MORISATO!

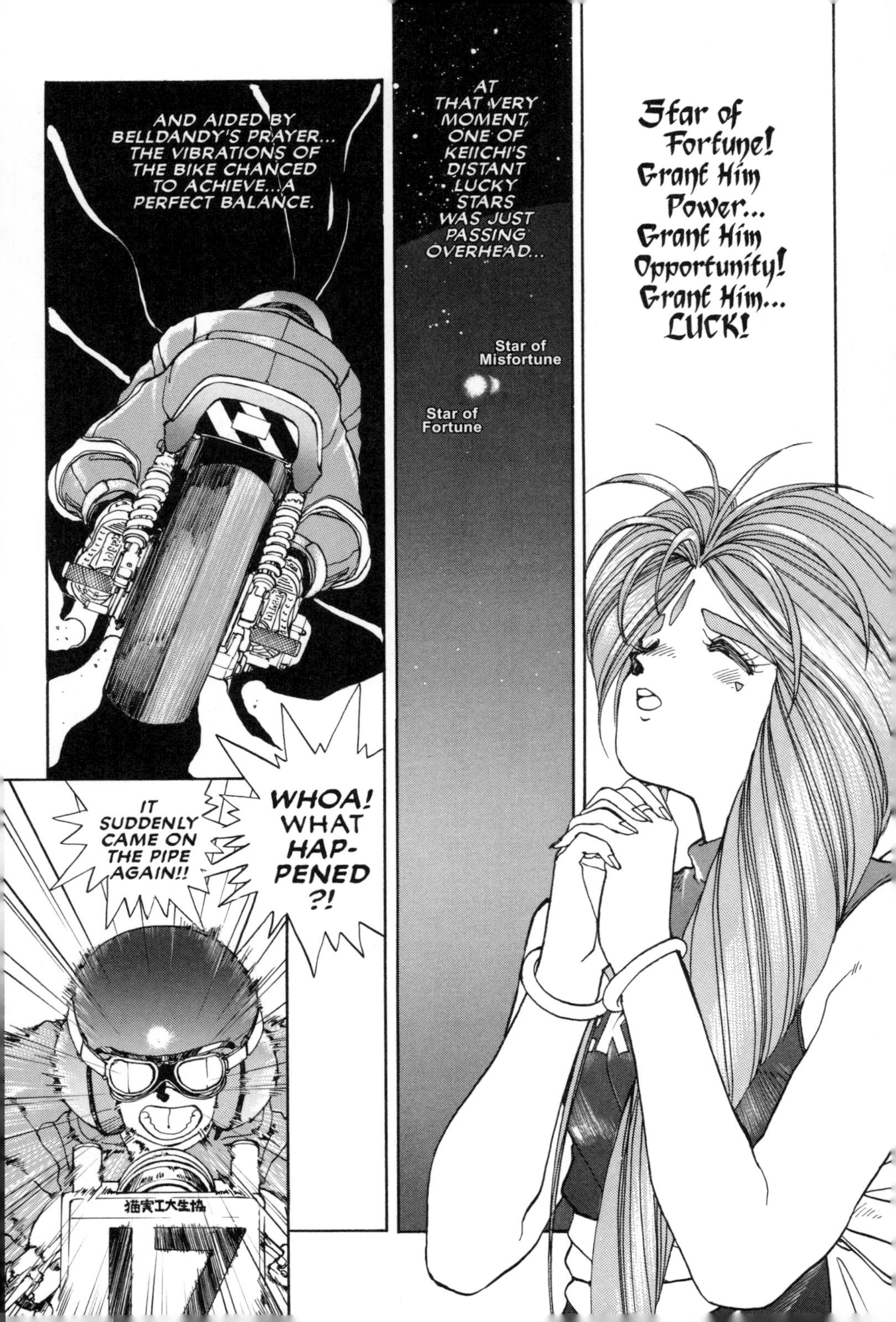
Star of Fortune! Grant Him Power... Grant Him Opportunity! Grant Him... LUCK!
AT THAT VERY MOMENT, ONE OF KEIICHI'S DISTANT LUCKY STARS WAS JUST PASSING OVERHEAD...
Star of Misfortune
Star of Fortune
AND AIDED BY BELLDANDY'S PRAYER... THE VIBRATIONS OF THE BIKE CHANCED TO ACHIEVE...A PERFECT BALANCE.
WHOA! WHAT HAP-PENED?!
IT SUDDENLY CAME ON THE PIPE AGAIN!!
猫実工大生協
17

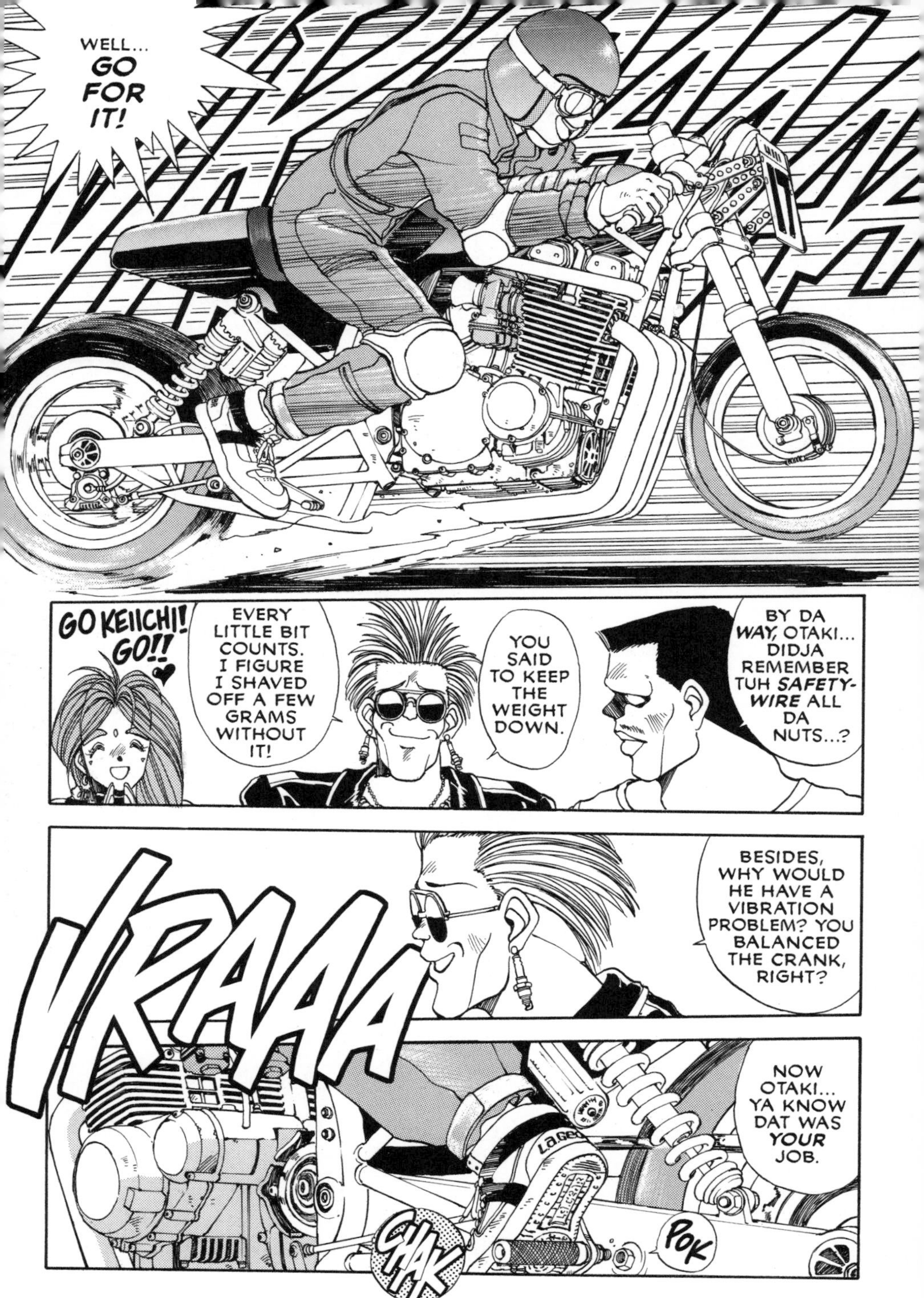
WELL... GO FOR IT!
BY DA WAY, OTAKI... DIDJA REMEMBER TUH SAFETY-WIRE ALL DA NUTS...?
YOU SAID TO KEEP THE WEIGHT DOWN.
EVERY LITTLE BIT COUNTS. I FIGURE I SHAVED OFF A FEW GRAMS WITHOUT IT!
GO KEIICHI! GO!!
BESIDES, WHY WOULD HE HAVE A VIBRATION PROBLEM? YOU BALANCED THE CRANK, RIGHT?
VRAAAA
NOW OTAKI... YA KNOW DAT WAS YOUR JOB.
POK
CHAK

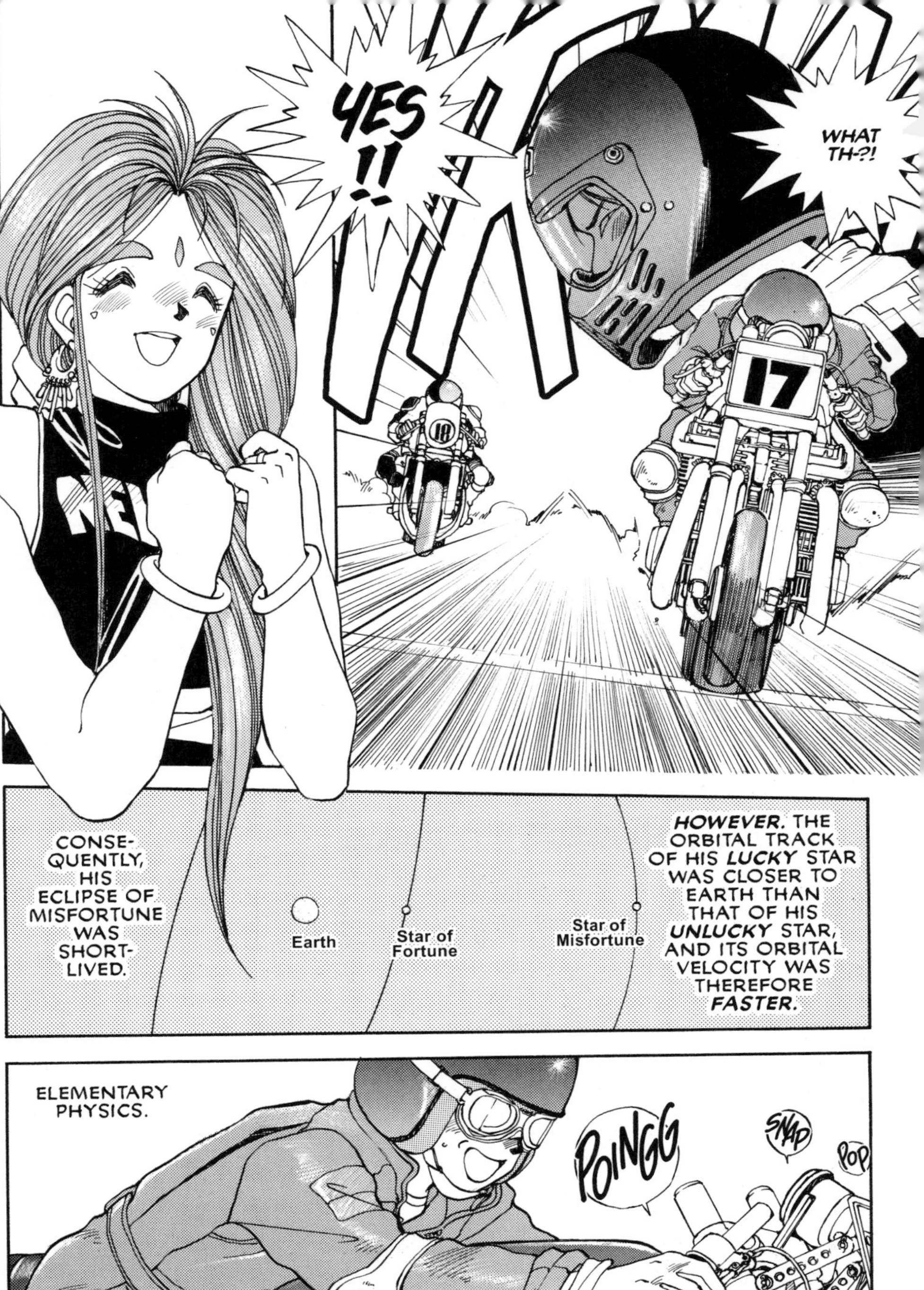

YES !!
WHAT TH-?!
17
18
HOWEVER. THE ORBITAL TRACK OF HIS LUCKY STAR WAS CLOSER TO EARTH THAN THAT OF HIS UNLUCKY STAR, AND ITS ORBITAL VELOCITY WAS THEREFORE FASTER.
Star of Misfortune
Star of Fortune
Earth
CONSE-QUENTLY, HIS ECLIPSE OF MISFORTUNE WAS SHORT-LIVED.
POP
SNAP
POINGG
ELEMENTARY PHYSICS.

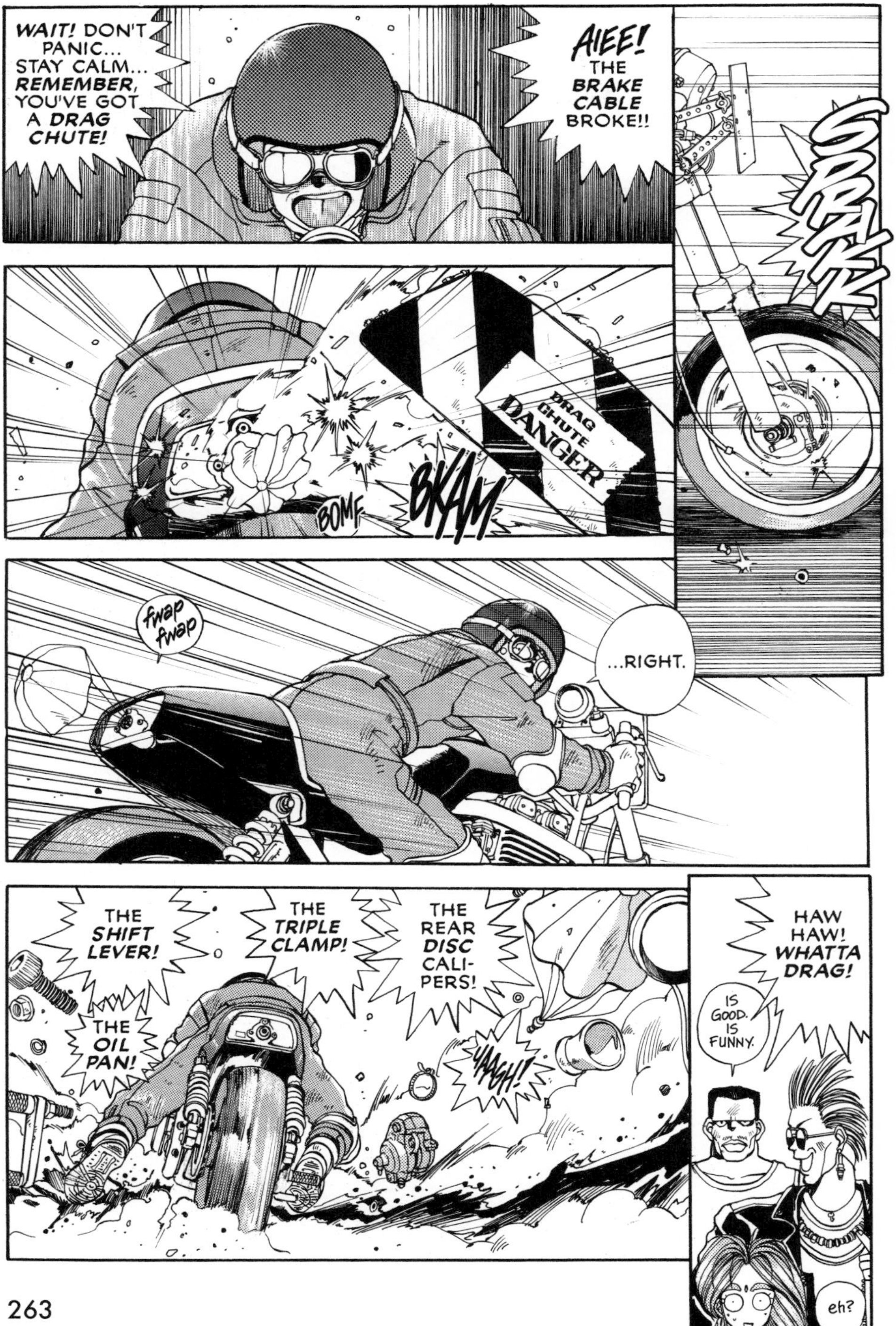
SPRAKK
AIEE! THE BRAKE CABLE BROKE!!
WAIT! DON'T PANIC... STAY CALM... REMEMBER, YOU'VE GOT A DRAG CHUTE!
DRAG CHUTE DANGER
BKAM
BOMF
...RIGHT.
fwap fwap
HAW HAW! WHATTA DRAG!
IS GOOD. IS FUNNY.
eh?
THE REAR DISC CALI-PERS!
THE TRIPLE CLAMP!
THE SHIFT LEVER!
YAAGH!
THE OIL PAN!

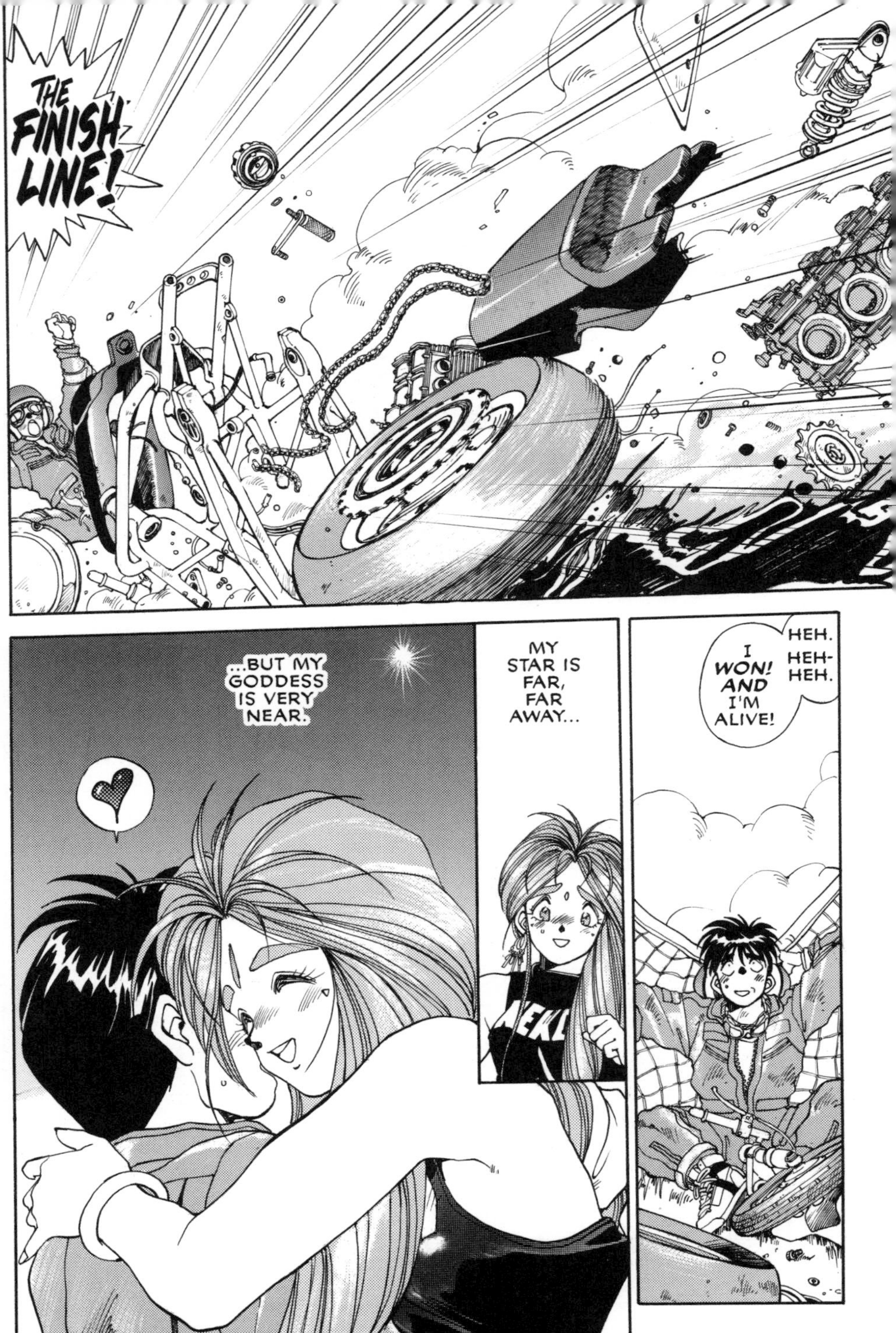
THE FINISH LINE!
HEH. HEH-HEH.
I WON! AND I'M ALIVE!
MY STAR IS FAR, FAR AWAY...
...BUT MY GODDESS IS VERY NEAR.

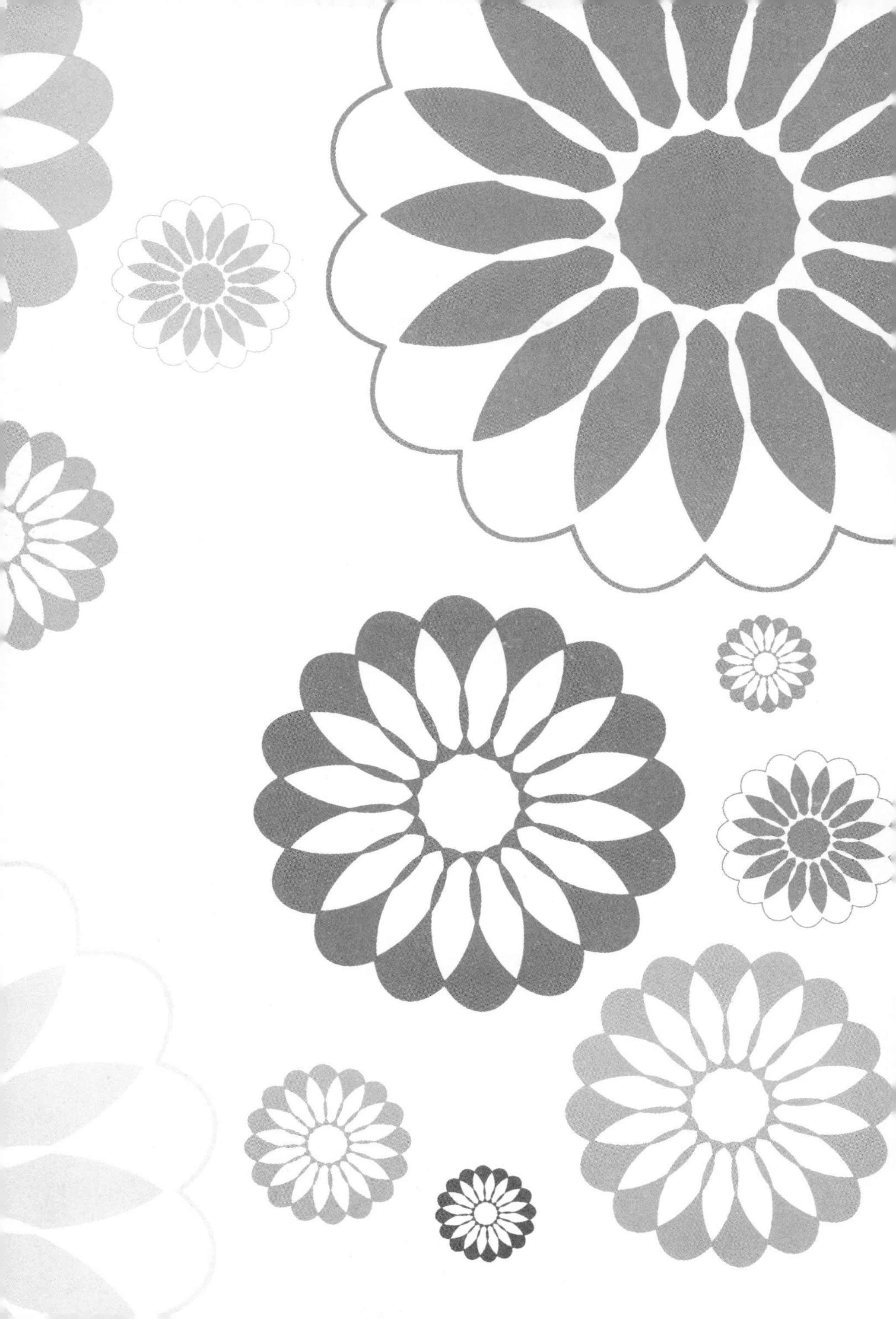

OH MY GODDESS!

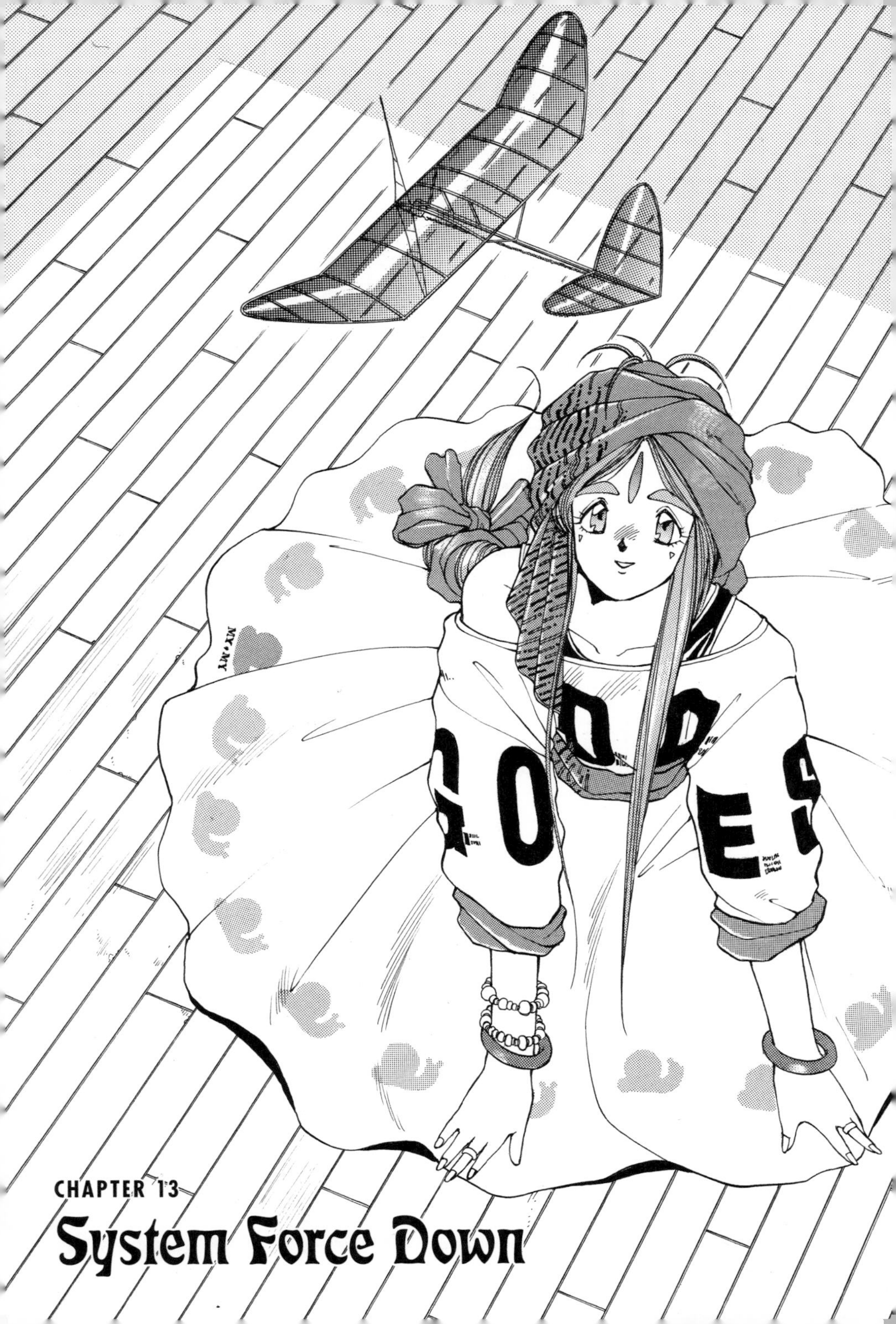

CHAPTER 13

System Force Down

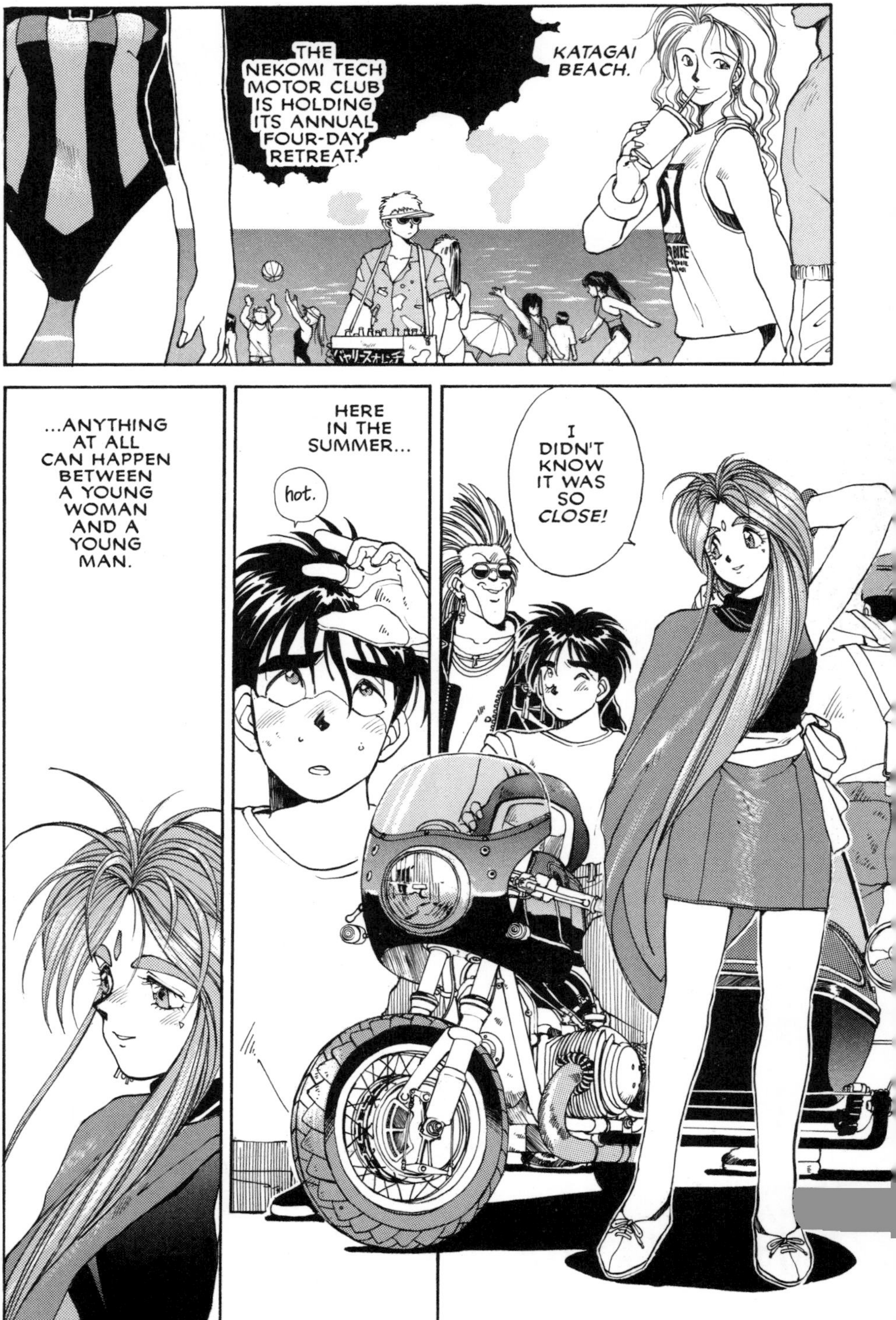
KATAGAI BEACH.
THE NEKOMI TECH MOTOR CLUB IS HOLDING ITS ANNUAL FOUR-DAY RETREAT.
I DIDN'T KNOW IT WAS SO CLOSE!
HERE IN THE SUMMER...
hot.
...ANYTHING AT ALL CAN HAPPEN BETWEEN A YOUNG WOMAN AND A YOUNG MAN.

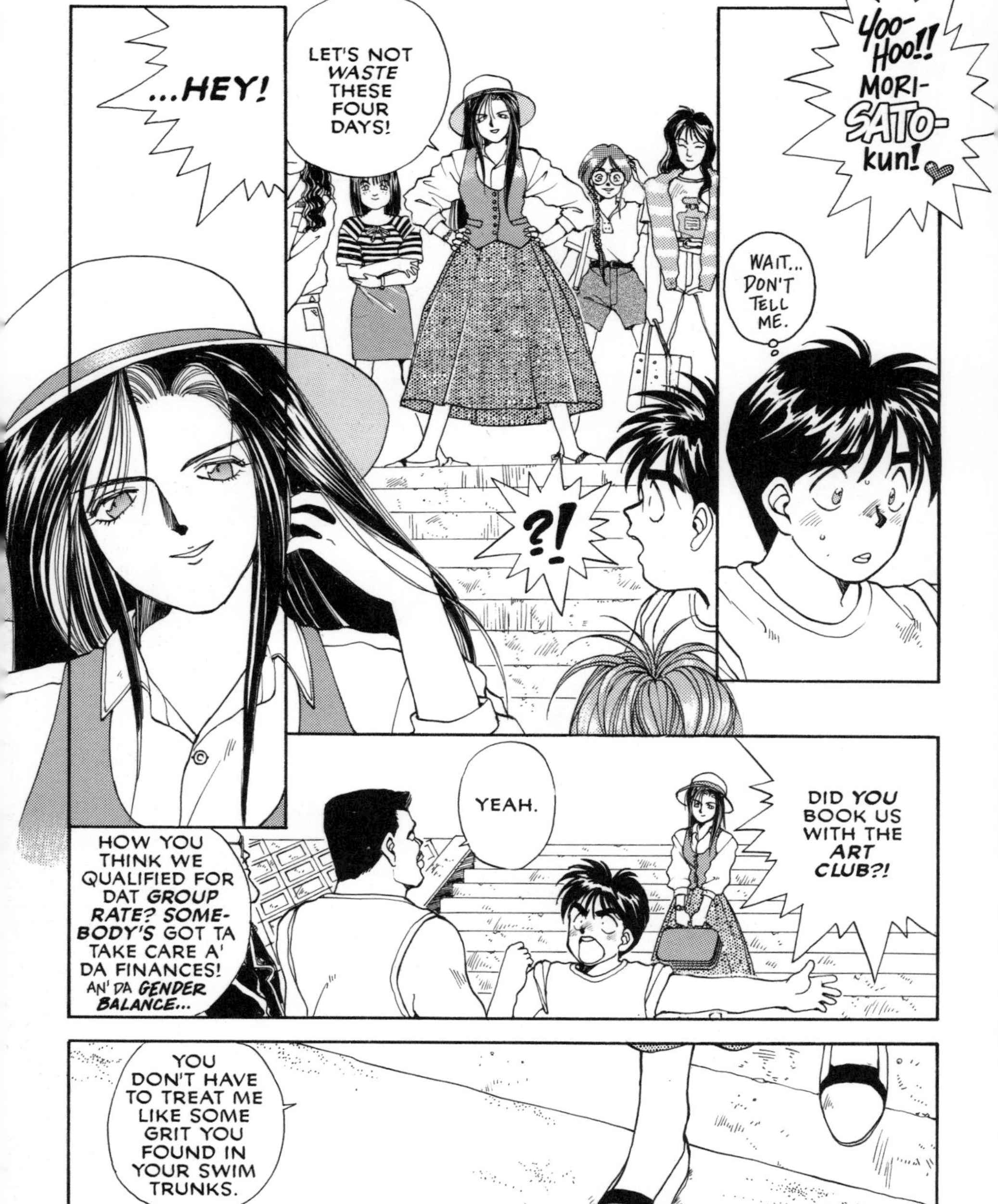

YOO-HOO!! MORI-SATO-kun!
WAIT... DON'T TELL ME.
LET'S NOT WASTE THESE FOUR DAYS!
?!
...HEY!
DID YOU BOOK US WITH THE ART CLUB?!
YEAH.
HOW YOU THINK WE QUALIFIED FOR DAT GROUP RATE? SOMEBODY'S GOT TA TAKE CARE A' DA FINANCES! AN' DA GENDER BALANCE...
YOU DON'T HAVE TO TREAT ME LIKE SOME GRIT YOU FOUND IN YOUR SWIM TRUNKS.
shff

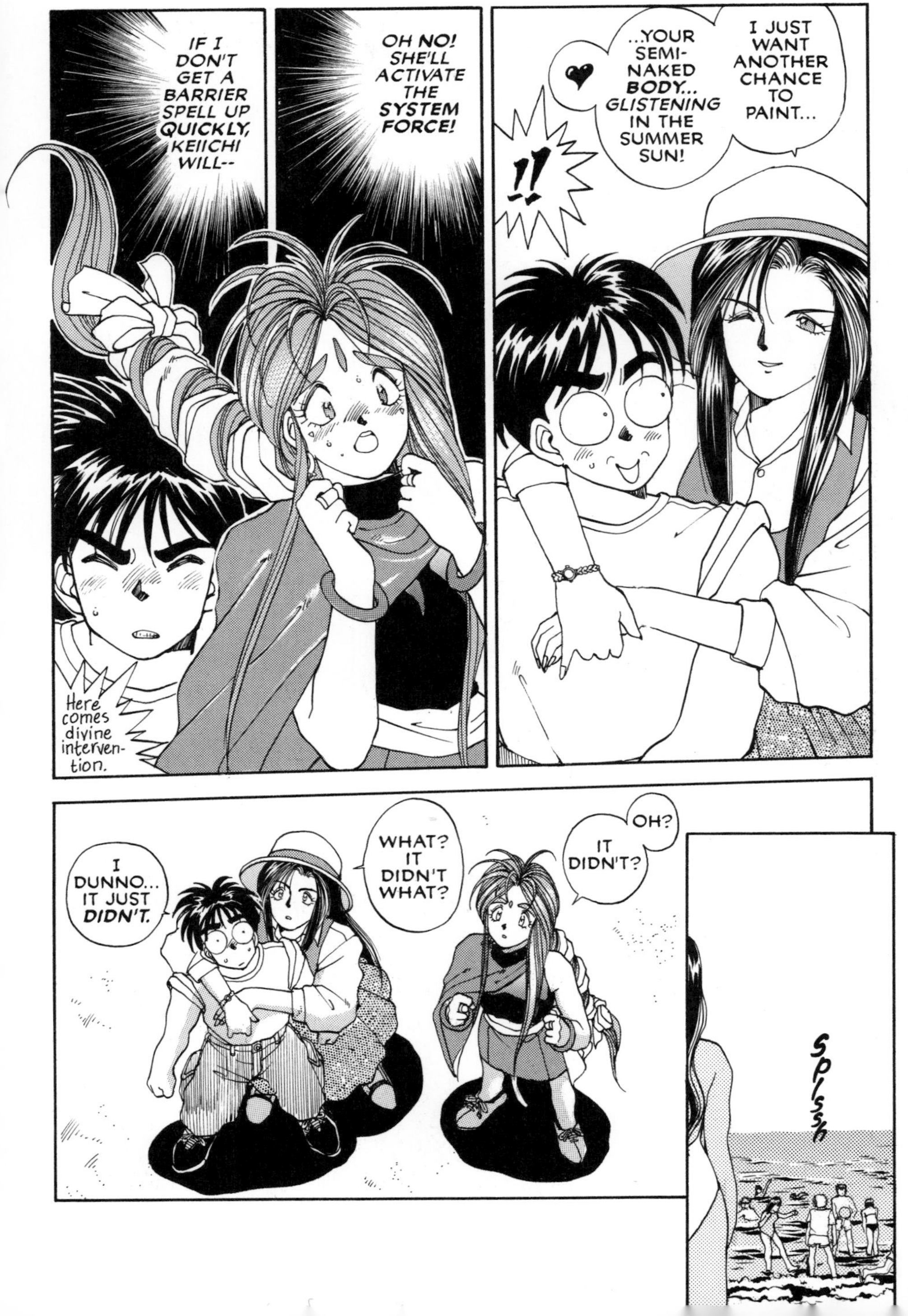
I JUST WANT ANOTHER CHANCE TO PAINT...
...YOUR SEMI-NAKED BODY... GLISTENING IN THE SUMMER SUN!
!!
OH NO! SHE'LL ACTIVATE THE SYSTEM FORCE!
IF I DON'T GET A BARRIER SPELL UP QUICKLY, KEIICHI WILL--
Here comes divine intervention.
SPLSSH
OH?
IT DIDN'T?
WHAT? IT DIDN'T WHAT?
I DUNNO... IT JUST DIDN'T.

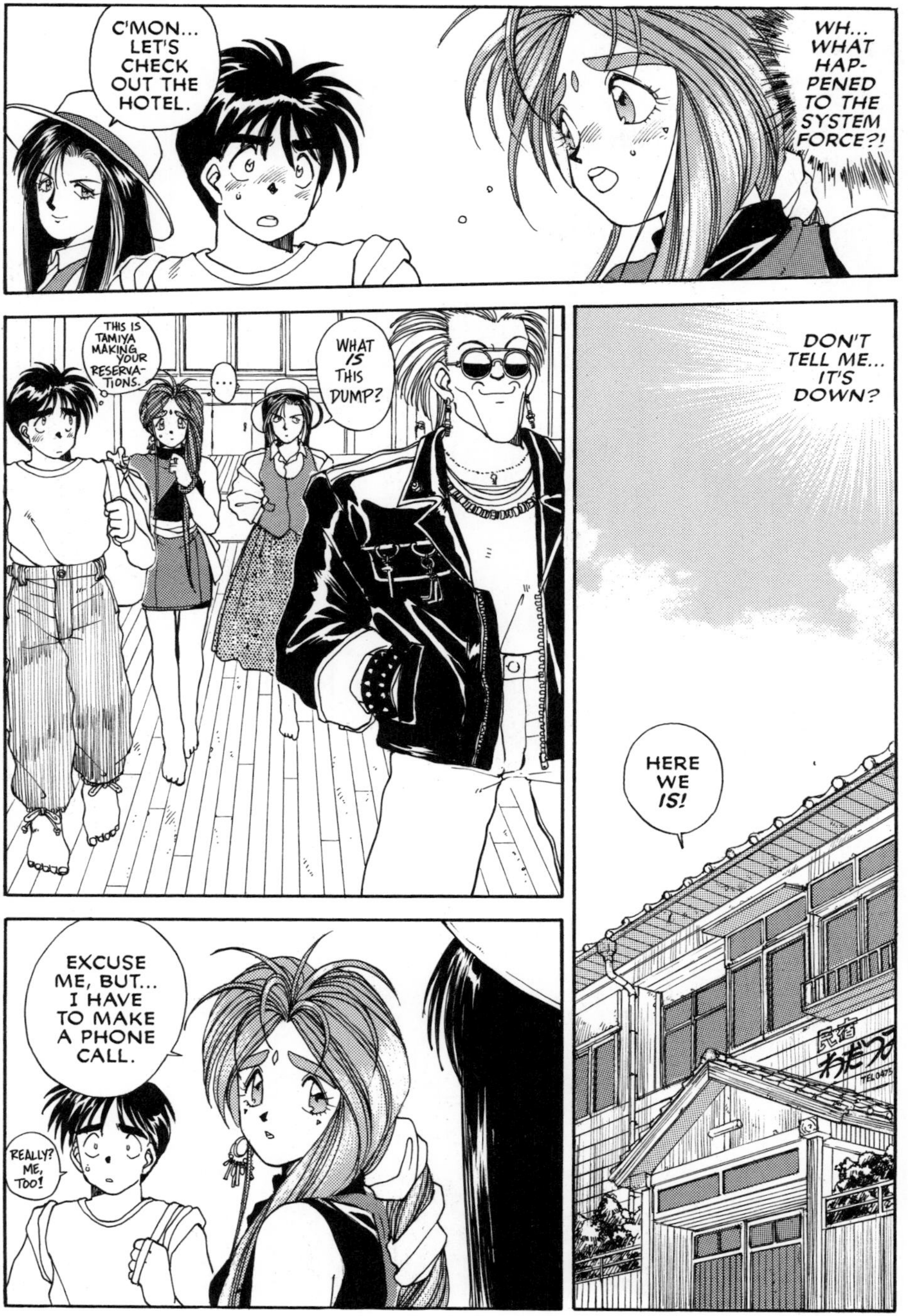
WH... WHAT HAPPENED TO THE SYSTEM FORCE?!
C'MON... LET'S CHECK OUT THE HOTEL.
DON'T TELL ME... IT'S DOWN?
HERE WE *IS!*
WHAT *IS* THIS DUMP?
...
THIS IS TAMIYA MAKING YOUR RESERVATIONS.
EXCUSE ME, BUT... I HAVE TO MAKE A PHONE CALL.
REALLY? ME, TOO!

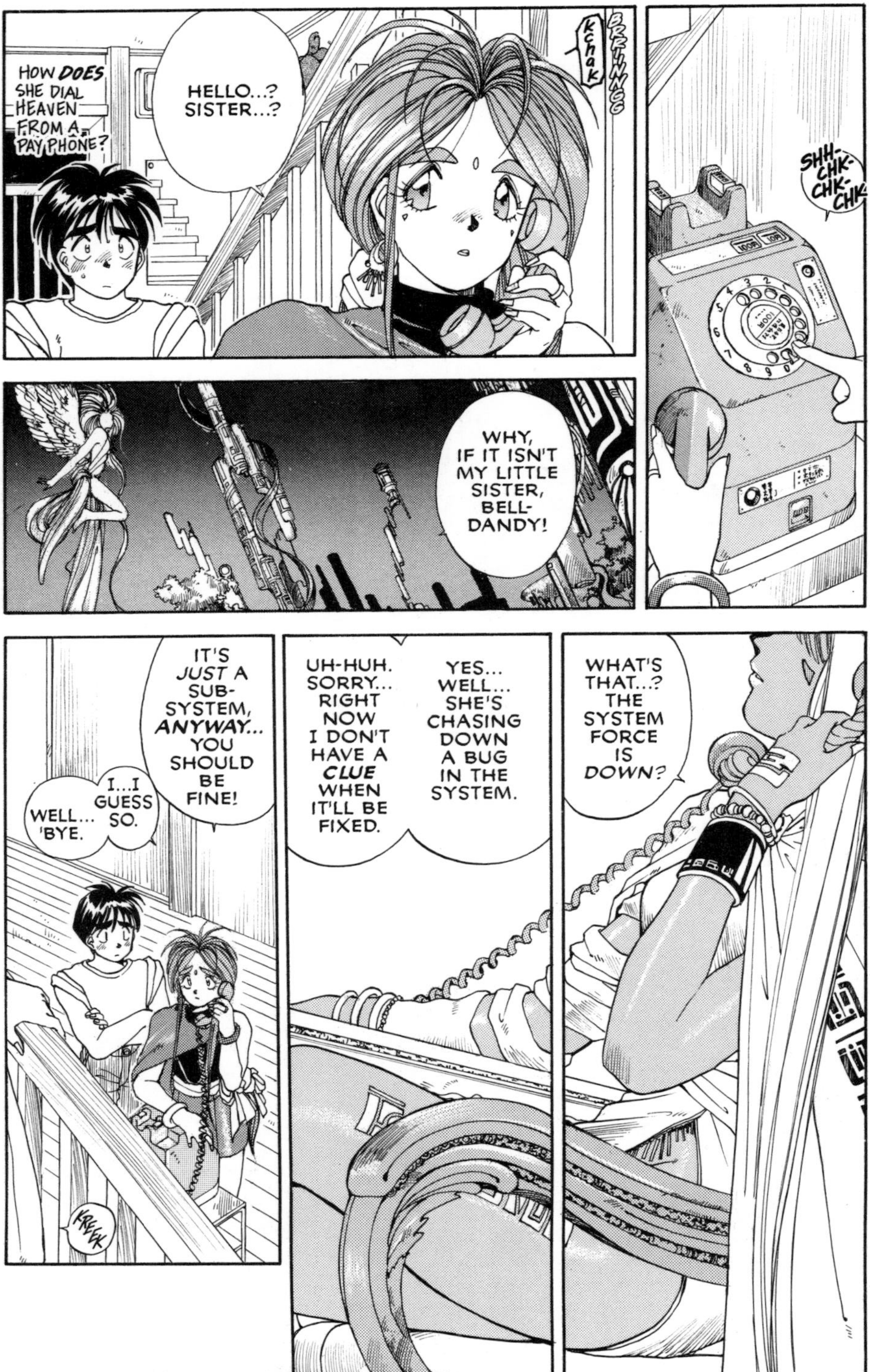
SHH-CHK-CHK-CHK
BRRINNGG
kchak
HELLO...? SISTER...?
HOW DOES SHE DIAL HEAVEN FROM A PAY PHONE?
WHY, IF IT ISN'T MY LITTLE SISTER, BELL-DANDY!
WHAT'S THAT...? THE SYSTEM FORCE IS DOWN?
YES... WELL... SHE'S CHASING DOWN A BUG IN THE SYSTEM.
UH-HUH. SORRY... RIGHT NOW I DON'T HAVE A CLUE WHEN IT'LL BE FIXED.
IT'S JUST A SUB-SYSTEM, ANYWAY... YOU SHOULD BE FINE!
I...I GUESS SO.
WELL... 'BYE.
KREEK

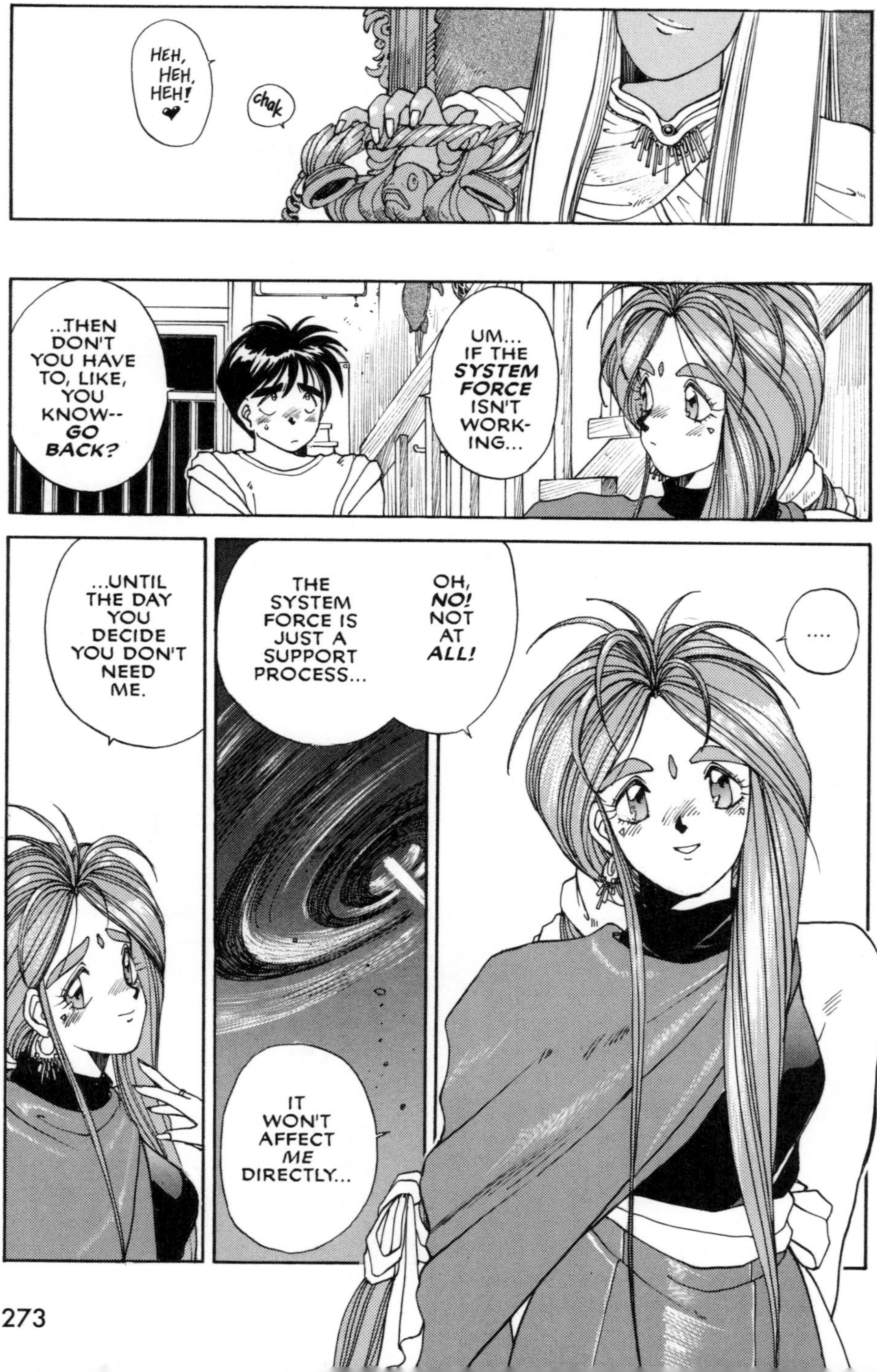
chak
HEH, HEH, HEH! ❤
UM... IF THE *SYSTEM FORCE* ISN'T WORKING...
...THEN DON'T YOU HAVE TO, LIKE, YOU KNOW-- *GO BACK?*
....
OH, *NO!* NOT AT *ALL!*
THE SYSTEM FORCE IS JUST A SUPPORT PROCESS...
IT WON'T AFFECT *ME* DIRECTLY...
...UNTIL THE DAY YOU DECIDE YOU DON'T NEED ME.

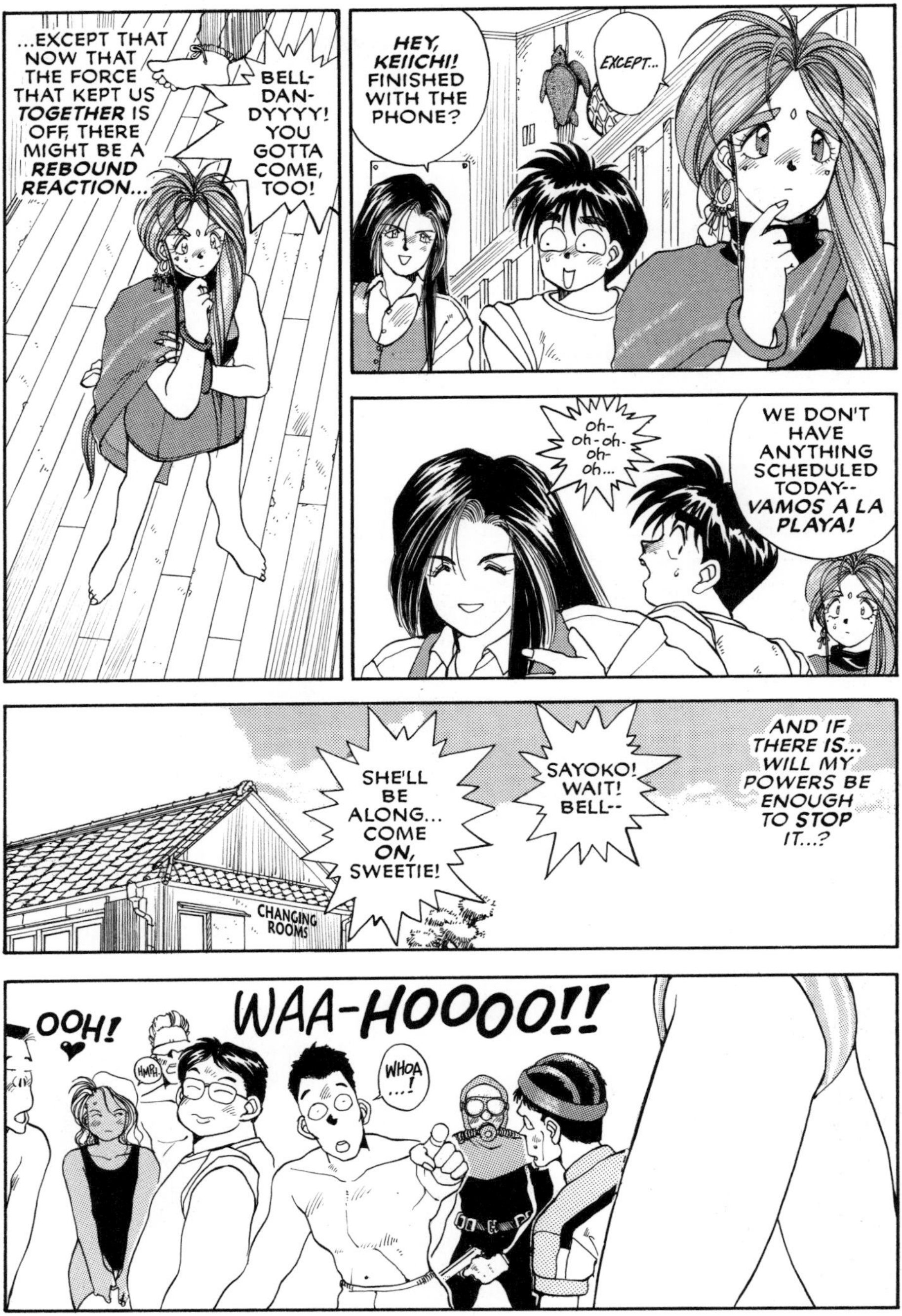
EXCEPT...
HEY, KEIICHI! FINISHED WITH THE PHONE?
WE DON'T HAVE ANYTHING SCHEDULED TODAY-- VAMOS A LA PLAYA!
oh-oh-oh-oh-oh...
BELL-DANDYYYY! YOU GOTTA COME, TOO!
...EXCEPT THAT NOW THAT THE FORCE THAT KEPT US TOGETHER IS OFF, THERE MIGHT BE A REBOUND REACTION...
AND IF THERE IS... WILL MY POWERS BE ENOUGH TO STOP IT...?
SAYOKO! WAIT! BELL--
SHE'LL BE ALONG... COME ON, SWEETIE!
CHANGING ROOMS
WAA-HOOOO!!
WHOA ...!
HMPH
OOH!

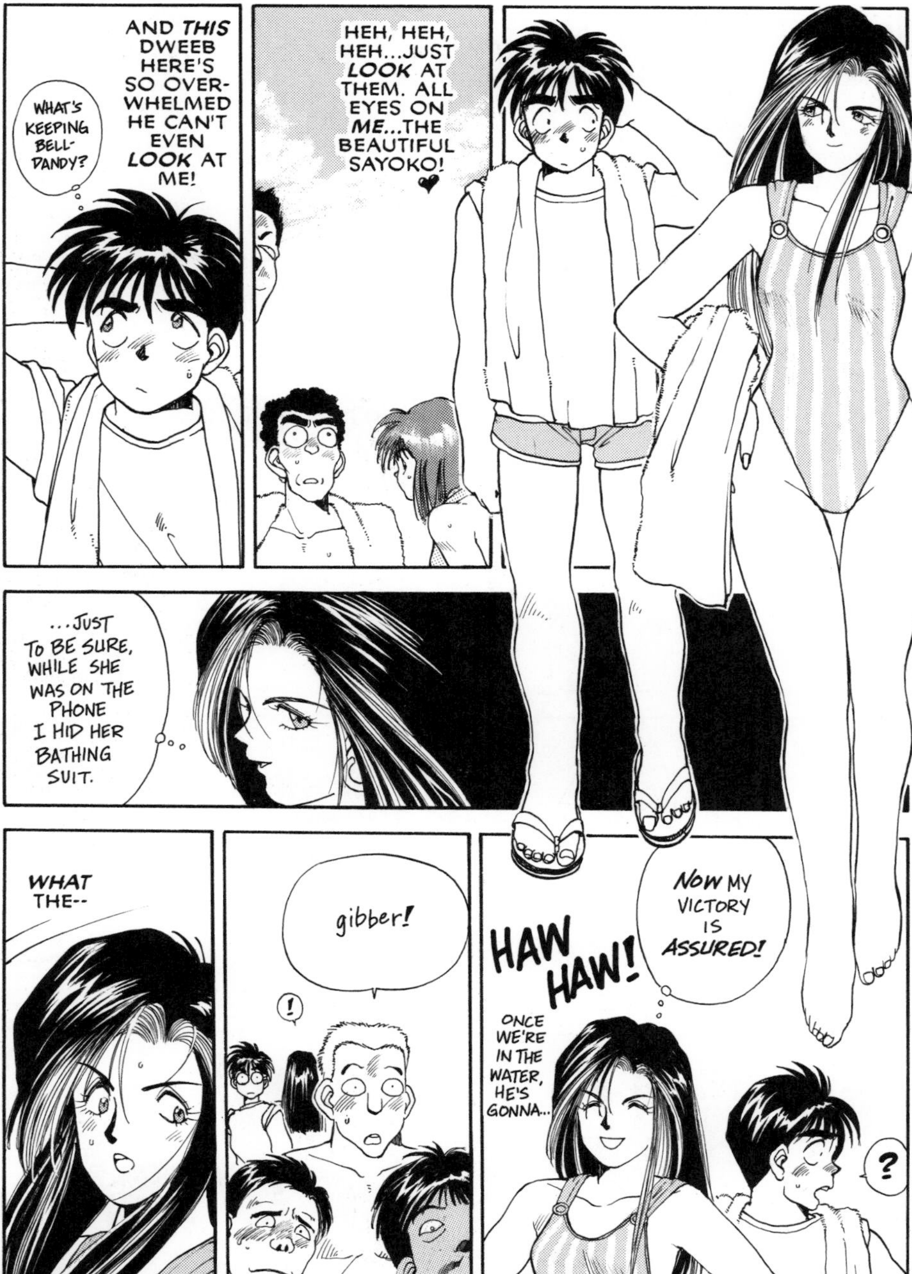
HEH, HEH, HEH...JUST LOOK AT THEM. ALL EYES ON ME...THE BEAUTIFUL SAYOKO! ❤
AND THIS DWEEB HERE'S SO OVER-WHELMED HE CAN'T EVEN LOOK AT ME!
WHAT'S KEEPING BELL-DANDY?
...JUST TO BE SURE, WHILE SHE WAS ON THE PHONE I HID HER BATHING SUIT.
NOW MY VICTORY IS ASSURED!
HAW HAW!
ONCE WE'RE IN THE WATER, HE'S GONNA...
?
gibber!
!
WHAT THE--

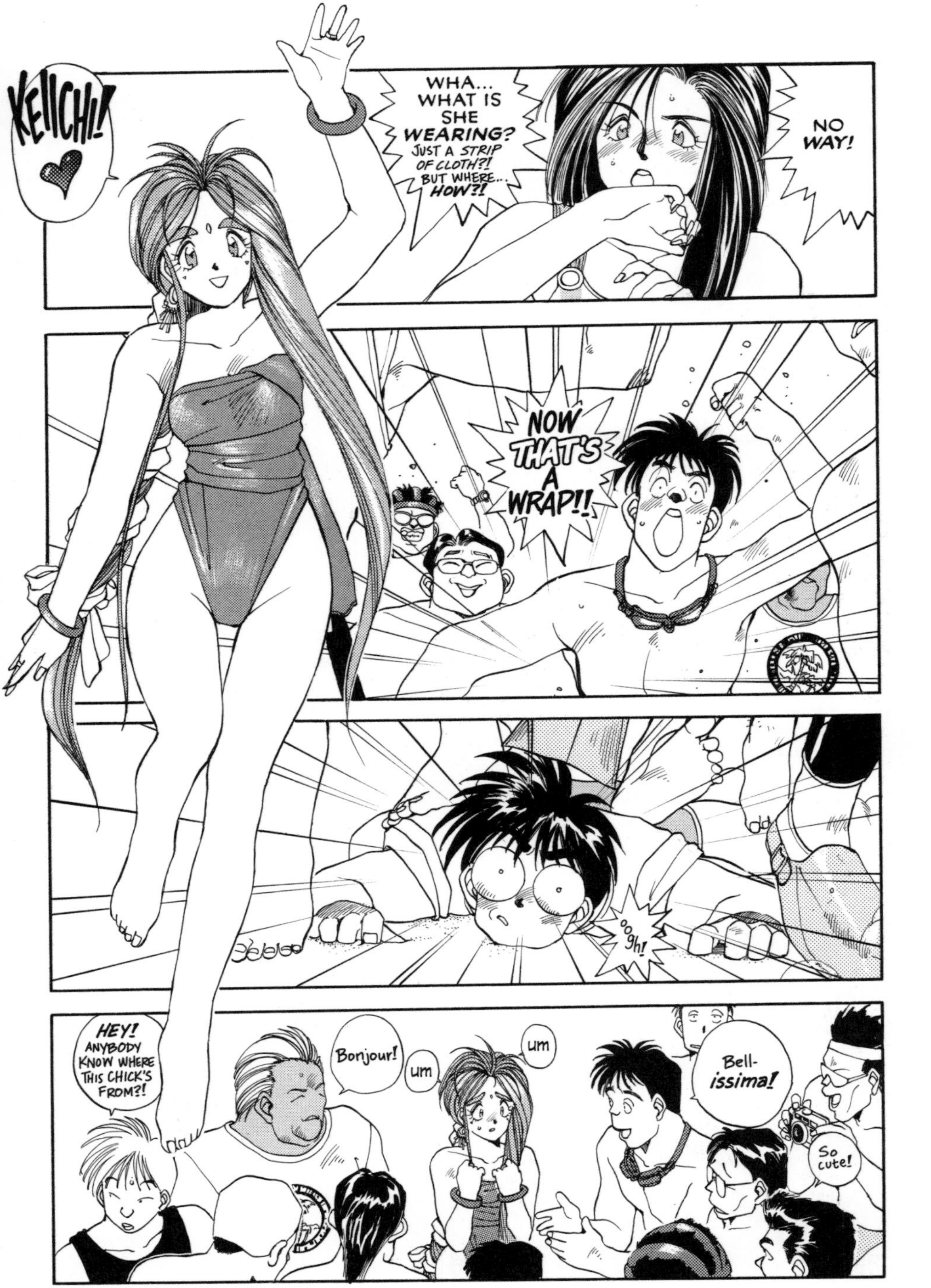
NO WAY!
WHA... WHAT IS SHE WEARING? JUST A STRIP OF CLOTH?! BUT WHERE... HOW?!
KEIICHI! ♥
NOW THAT'S A WRAP!!
oogh!
Bell-issima!
So cute!
um
um
Bonjour!
HEY! ANYBODY KNOW WHERE THIS CHICK'S FROM?!

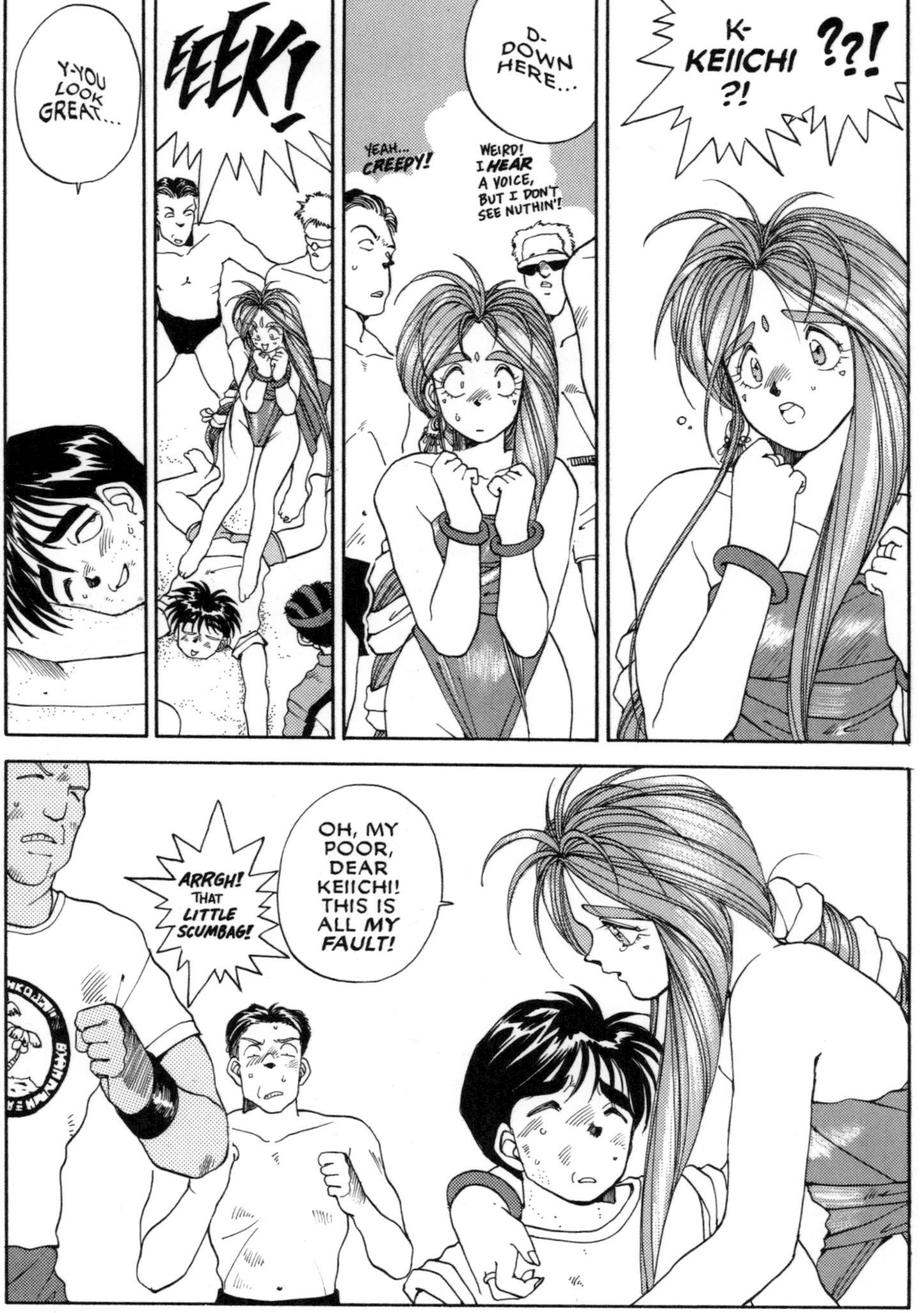
K-KEIICHI ?!
??!
D-DOWN HERE...
WEIRD! I HEAR A VOICE, BUT I DON'T SEE NUTHIN'!
YEAH... CREEPY!
EEEK!
Y-YOU LOOK GREAT...
OH, MY POOR, DEAR KEIICHI! THIS IS ALL MY FAULT!
ARRGH! THAT LITTLE SCUMBAG!

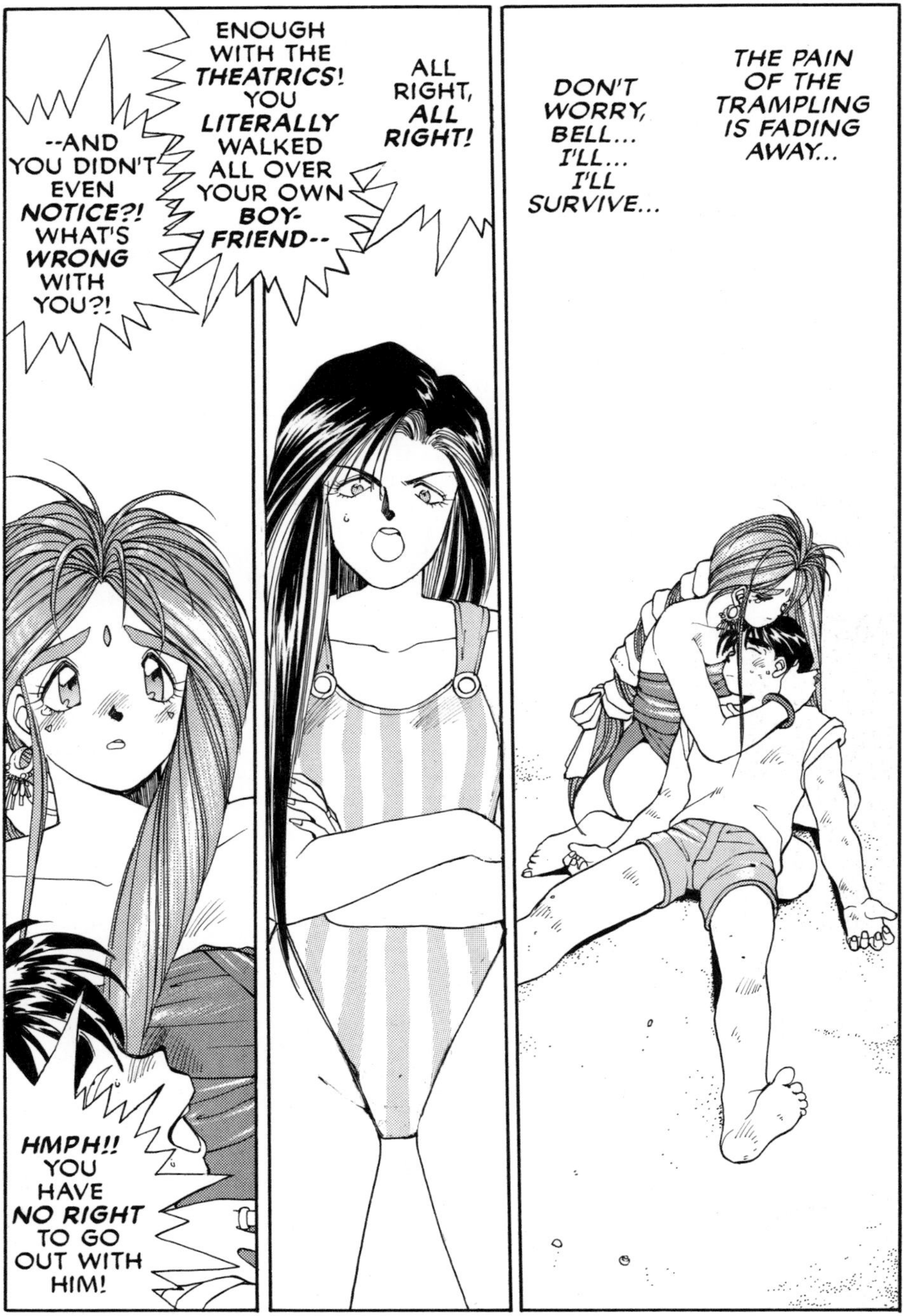
THE PAIN OF THE TRAMPLING IS FADING AWAY...
DON'T WORRY, BELL... I'LL... I'LL SURVIVE...
ALL RIGHT, ALL RIGHT!
ENOUGH WITH THE THEATRICS! YOU LITERALLY WALKED ALL OVER YOUR OWN BOY-FRIEND--
--AND YOU DIDN'T EVEN NOTICE?! WHAT'S WRONG WITH YOU?!
HMPH!! YOU HAVE NO RIGHT TO GO OUT WITH HIM!

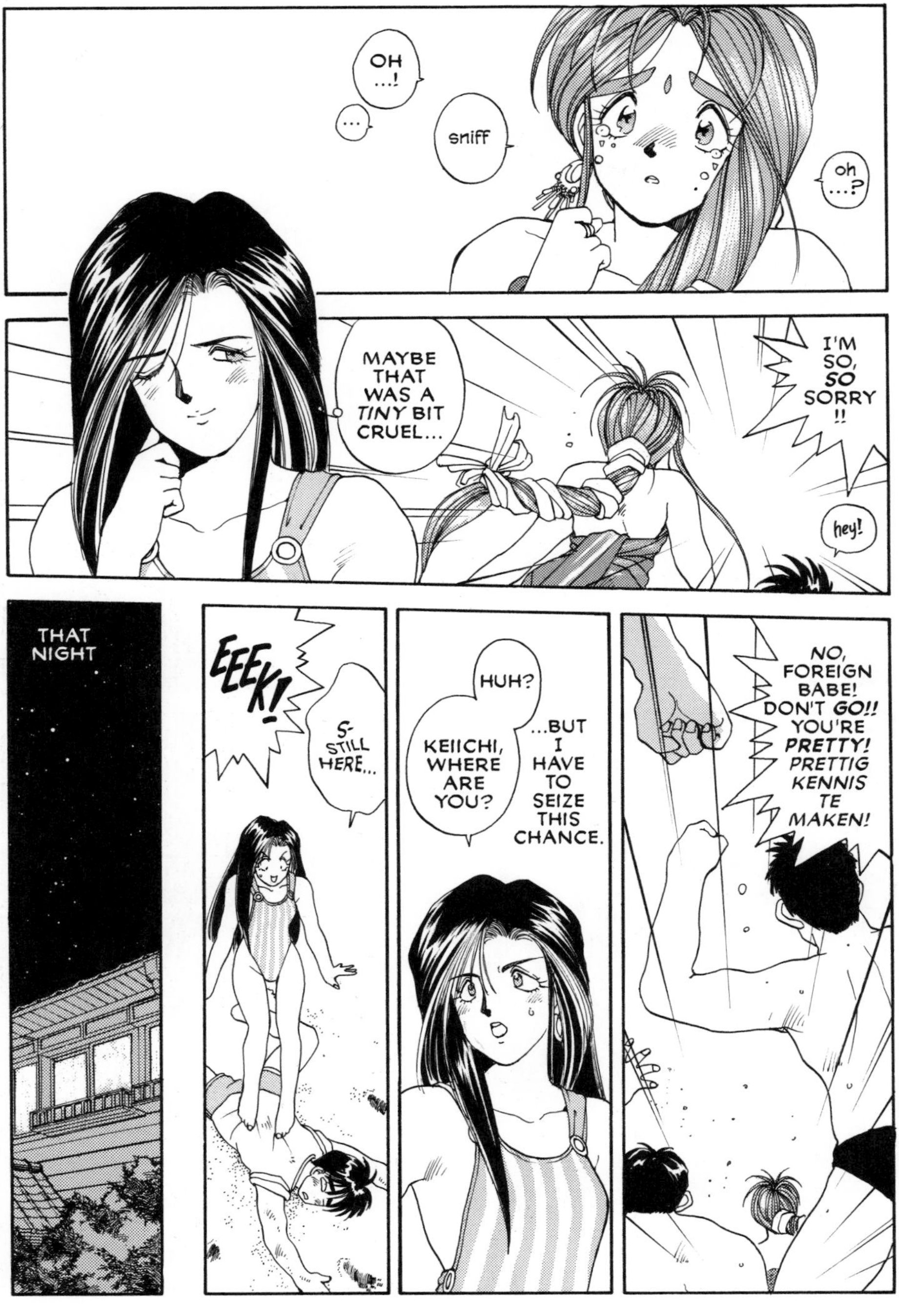
oh ...?
sniff
OH ...!
...
I'M SO, SO SORRY !!
hey!
MAYBE THAT WAS A TINY BIT CRUEL...
NO, FOREIGN BABE! DON'T GO!! YOU'RE PRETTY! PRETTIG KENNIS TE MAKEN!
HUH?
...BUT I HAVE TO SEIZE THIS CHANCE.
KEIICHI, WHERE ARE YOU?
EEEK!
S-STILL HERE...
THAT NIGHT

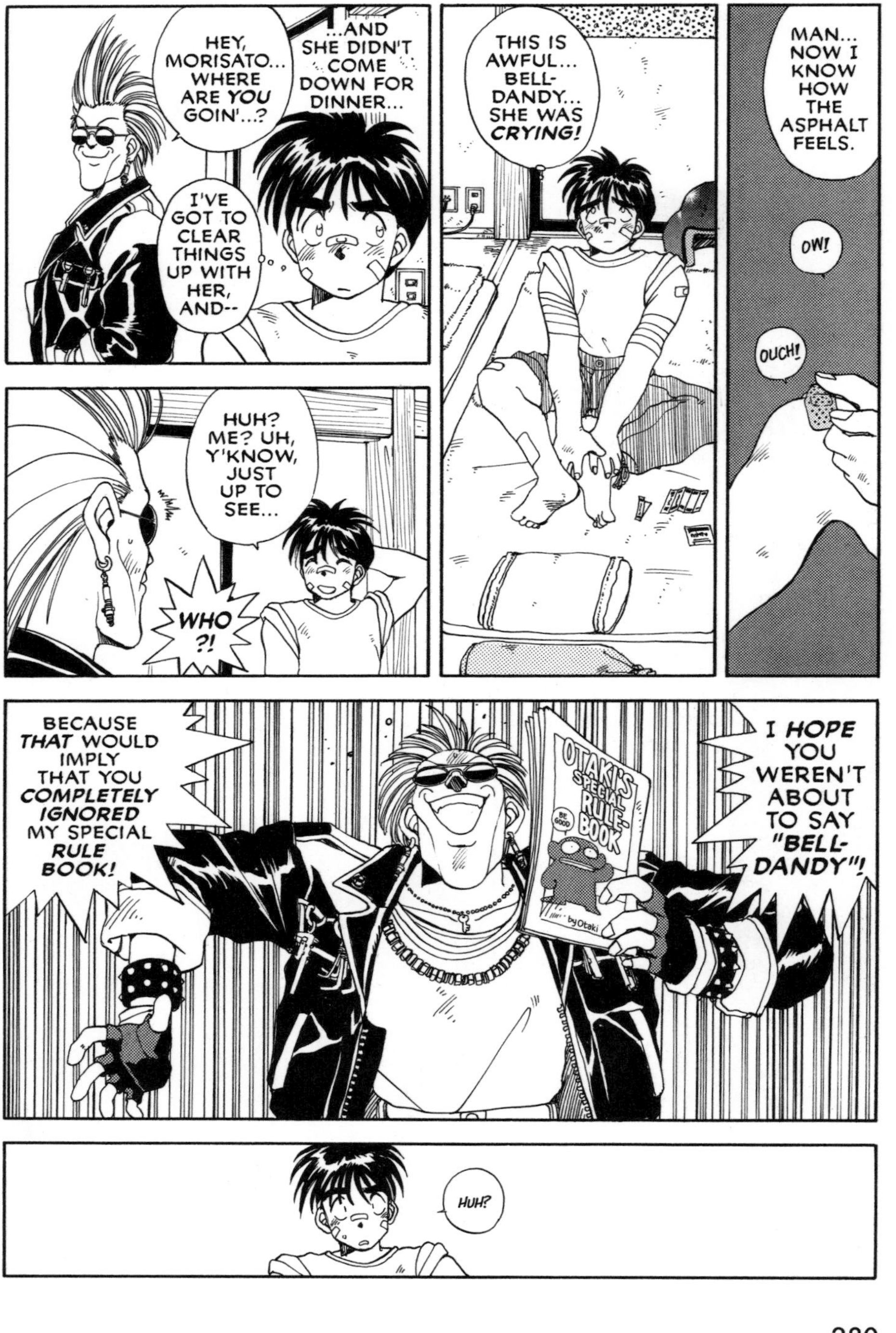
MAN... NOW I KNOW HOW THE ASPHALT FEELS.
OW!
OUCH!
THIS IS AWFUL... BELL-DANDY... SHE WAS CRYING!
...AND SHE DIDN'T COME DOWN FOR DINNER...
HEY, MORISATO... WHERE ARE YOU GOIN'...?
I'VE GOT TO CLEAR THINGS UP WITH HER, AND--
HUH? ME? UH, Y'KNOW, JUST UP TO SEE...
WHO ?!
I HOPE YOU WEREN'T ABOUT TO SAY "BELL-DANDY"!
OTAKI'S SPECIAL RULE-BOOK
BE GOOD
by Otaki
BECAUSE THAT WOULD IMPLY THAT YOU COMPLETELY IGNORED MY SPECIAL RULE BOOK!
HUH?

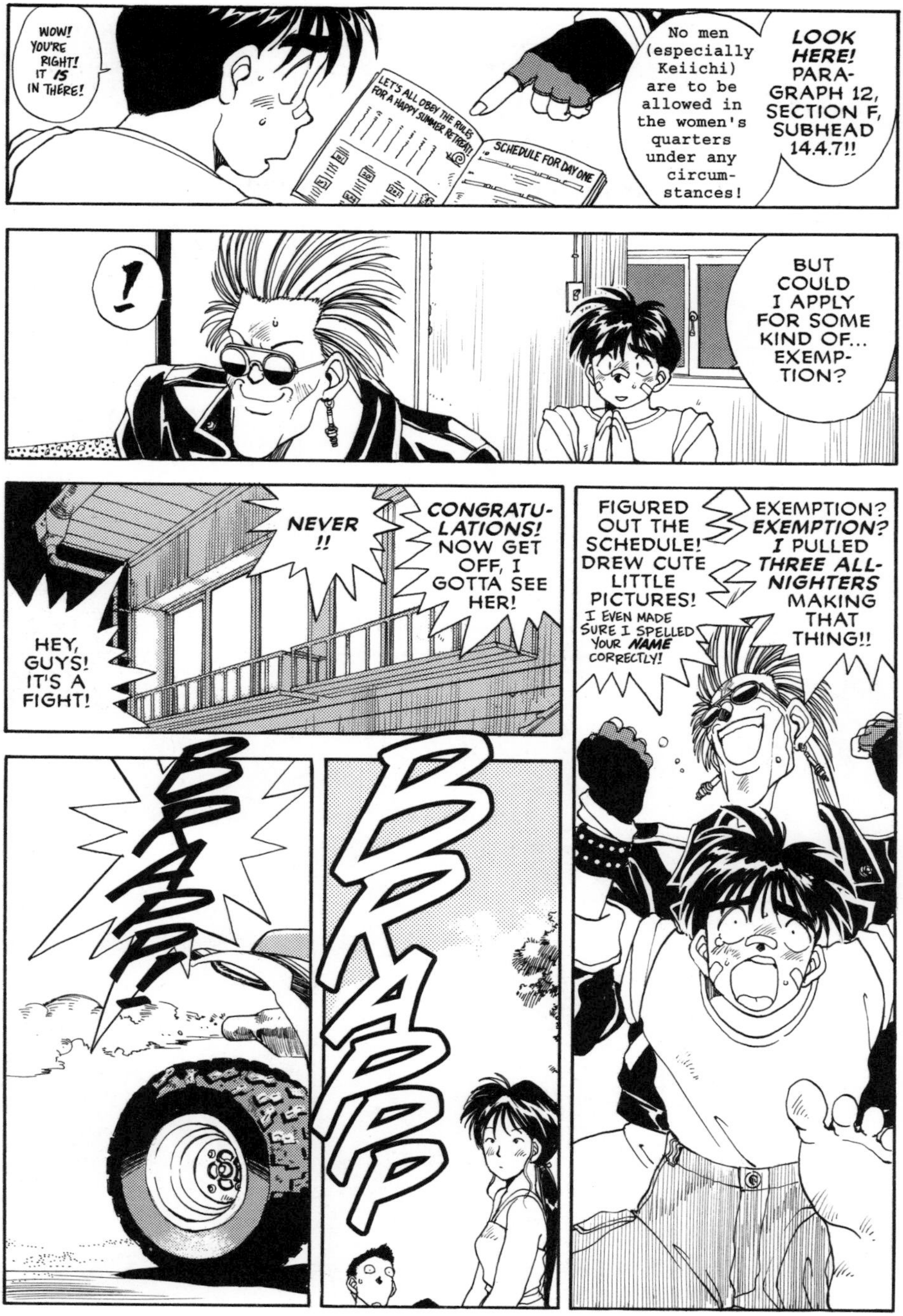
LOOK HERE! PARAGRAPH 12, SECTION F, SUBHEAD 14.4.7!!
No men (especially Keiichi) are to be allowed in the women's quarters under any circumstances!
LET'S ALL OBEY THE RULES FOR A HAPPY SUMMER RETREAT!
SCHEDULE FOR DAY ONE
WOW! YOU'RE RIGHT! IT IS IN THERE!
BUT COULD I APPLY FOR SOME KIND OF... EXEMPTION?
!
EXEMPTION? EXEMPTION? I PULLED THREE ALL-NIGHTERS MAKING THAT THING!!
FIGURED OUT THE SCHEDULE! DREW CUTE LITTLE PICTURES!
I EVEN MADE SURE I SPELLED YOUR NAME CORRECTLY!
CONGRATULATIONS! NOW GET OFF, I GOTTA SEE HER!
NEVER!!
HEY, GUYS! IT'S A FIGHT!
BRAAPPP
BRAPP!

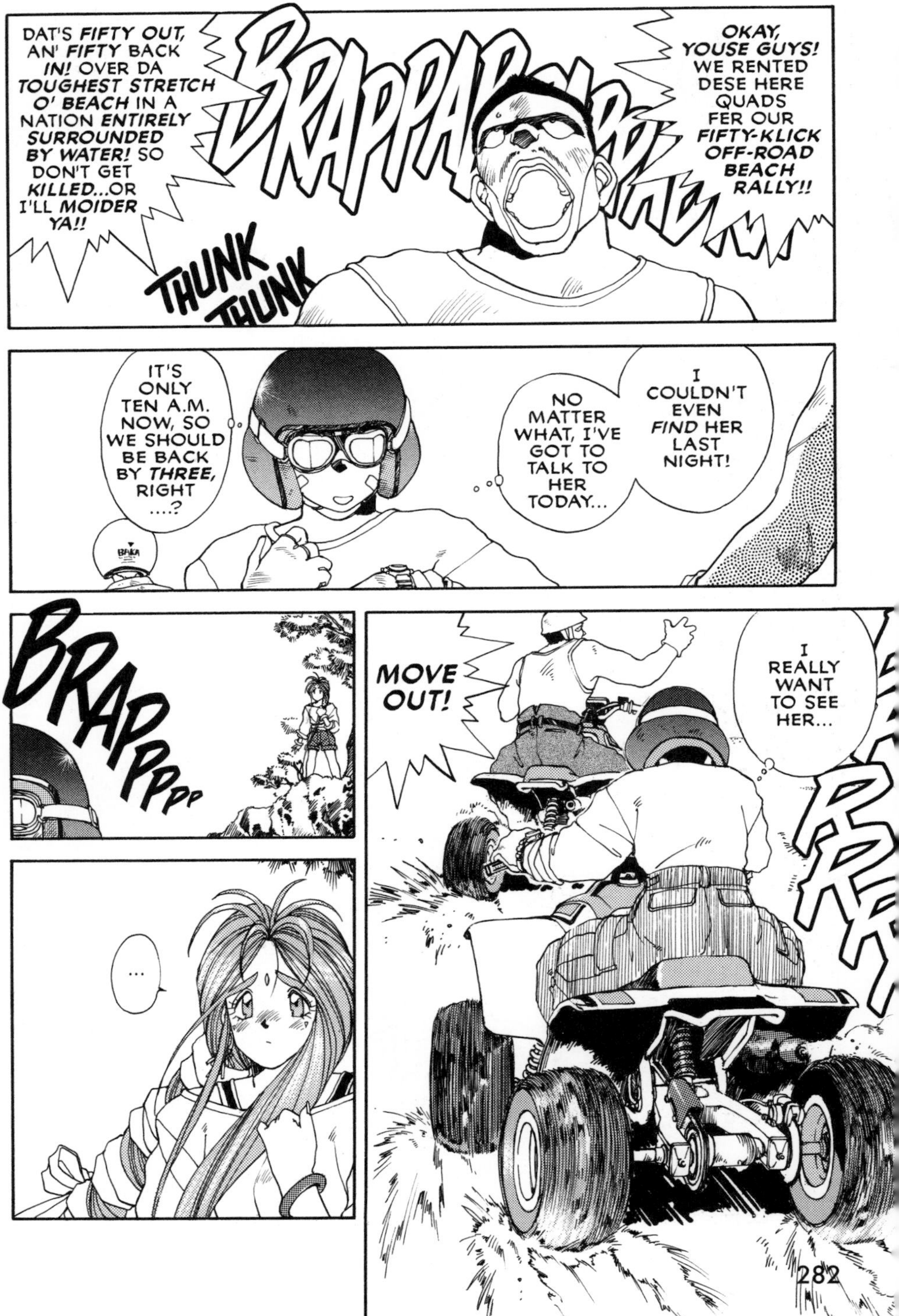
OKAY, YOUSE GUYS! WE RENTED DESE HERE QUADS FER OUR FIFTY-KLICK OFF-ROAD BEACH RALLY!!
DAT'S FIFTY OUT, AN' FIFTY BACK IN! OVER DA TOUGHEST STRETCH O' BEACH IN A NATION ENTIRELY SURROUNDED BY WATER! SO DON'T GET KILLED...OR I'LL MOIDER YA!!
BRAPPAP
THUNK THUNK
I COULDN'T EVEN FIND HER LAST NIGHT!
NO MATTER WHAT, I'VE GOT TO TALK TO HER TODAY...
IT'S ONLY TEN A.M. NOW, SO WE SHOULD BE BACK BY THREE, RIGHT ....?
BAKA
I REALLY WANT TO SEE HER...
MOVE OUT!
BRAPPPPP
...

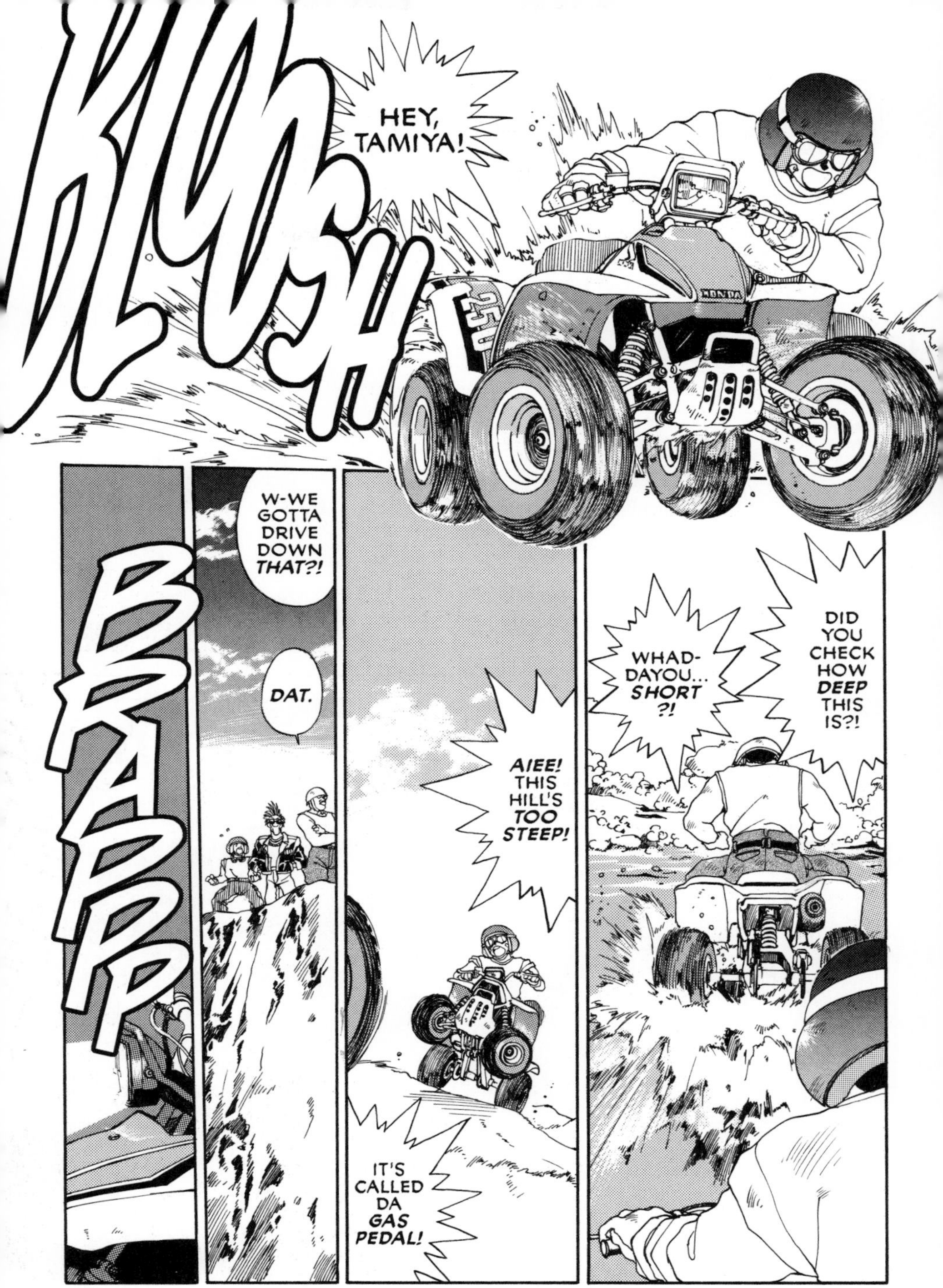
HEY, TAMIYA!
KLOOSH
DID YOU CHECK HOW DEEP THIS IS?!
WHAD-DAYOU... SHORT?!
AIEE! THIS HILL'S TOO STEEP!
IT'S CALLED DA GAS PEDAL!
W-WE GOTTA DRIVE DOWN THAT?!
DAT.
BRAPPP

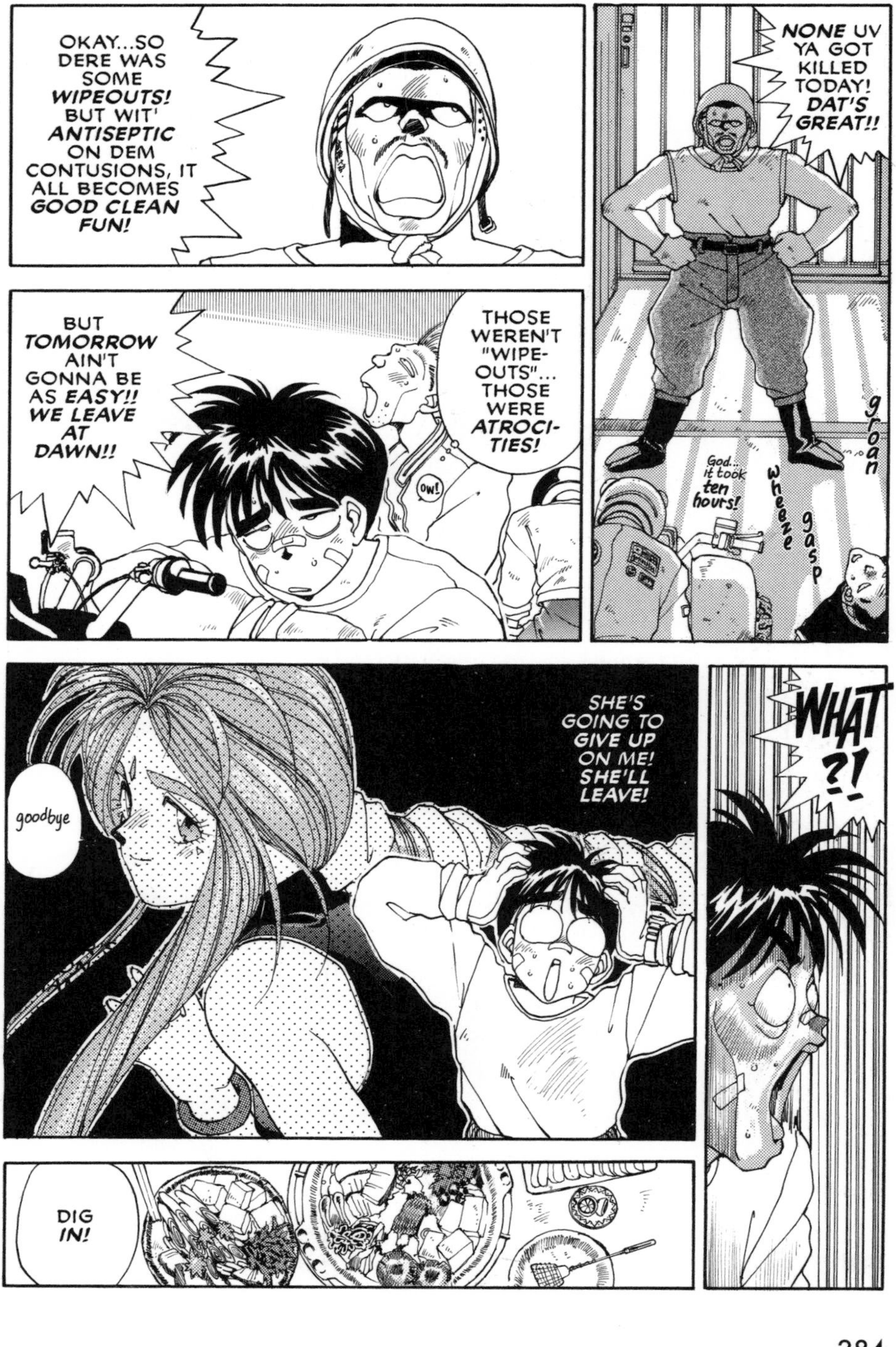
NONE UV YA GOT KILLED TODAY! DAT'S GREAT!!
groan
God... it took ten hours!
wheeze
gasp
OKAY...SO DERE WAS SOME WIPEOUTS! BUT WIT' ANTISEPTIC ON DEM CONTUSIONS, IT ALL BECOMES GOOD CLEAN FUN!
THOSE WEREN'T "WIPE-OUTS"... THOSE WERE ATROCI-TIES!
OW!
BUT TOMORROW AIN'T GONNA BE AS EASY!! WE LEAVE AT DAWN!!
WHAT ?!
SHE'S GOING TO GIVE UP ON ME! SHE'LL LEAVE!
goodbye
DIG IN!

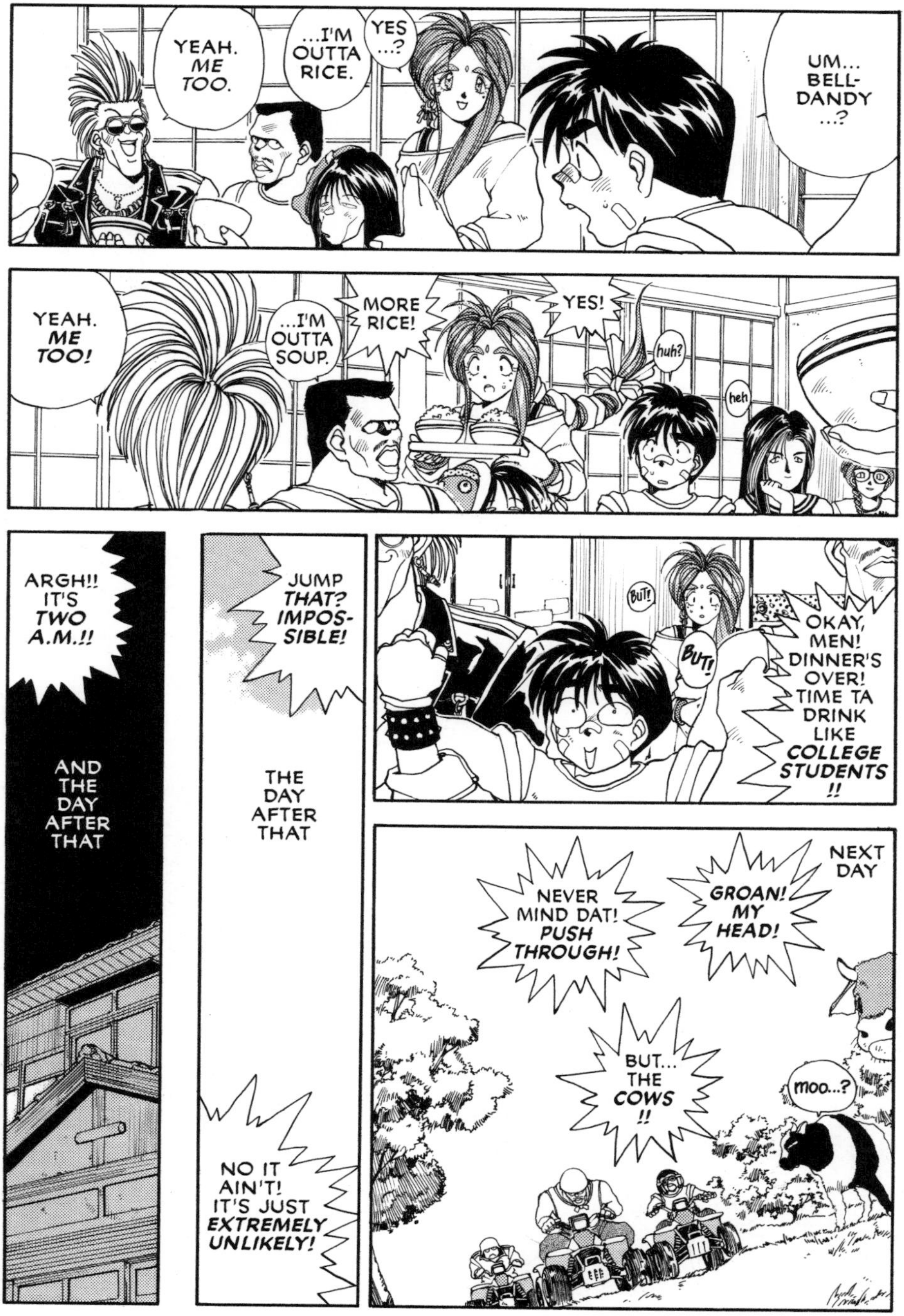
UM... BELL-DANDY ...?
YES ...?
...I'M OUTTA RICE.
YEAH. ME TOO.
heh
huh?
YES!
MORE RICE!
...I'M OUTTA SOUP.
YEAH. ME TOO!
OKAY, MEN! DINNER'S OVER! TIME TA DRINK LIKE COLLEGE STUDENTS !!
BUT!
BUT!
NEXT DAY
GROAN! MY HEAD!
NEVER MIND DAT! PUSH THROUGH!
moo...?
BUT... THE COWS !!
JUMP THAT? IMPOSSIBLE!
THE DAY AFTER THAT
NO IT AIN'T! IT'S JUST EXTREMELY UNLIKELY!
ARGH!! IT'S TWO A.M.!!
AND THE DAY AFTER THAT

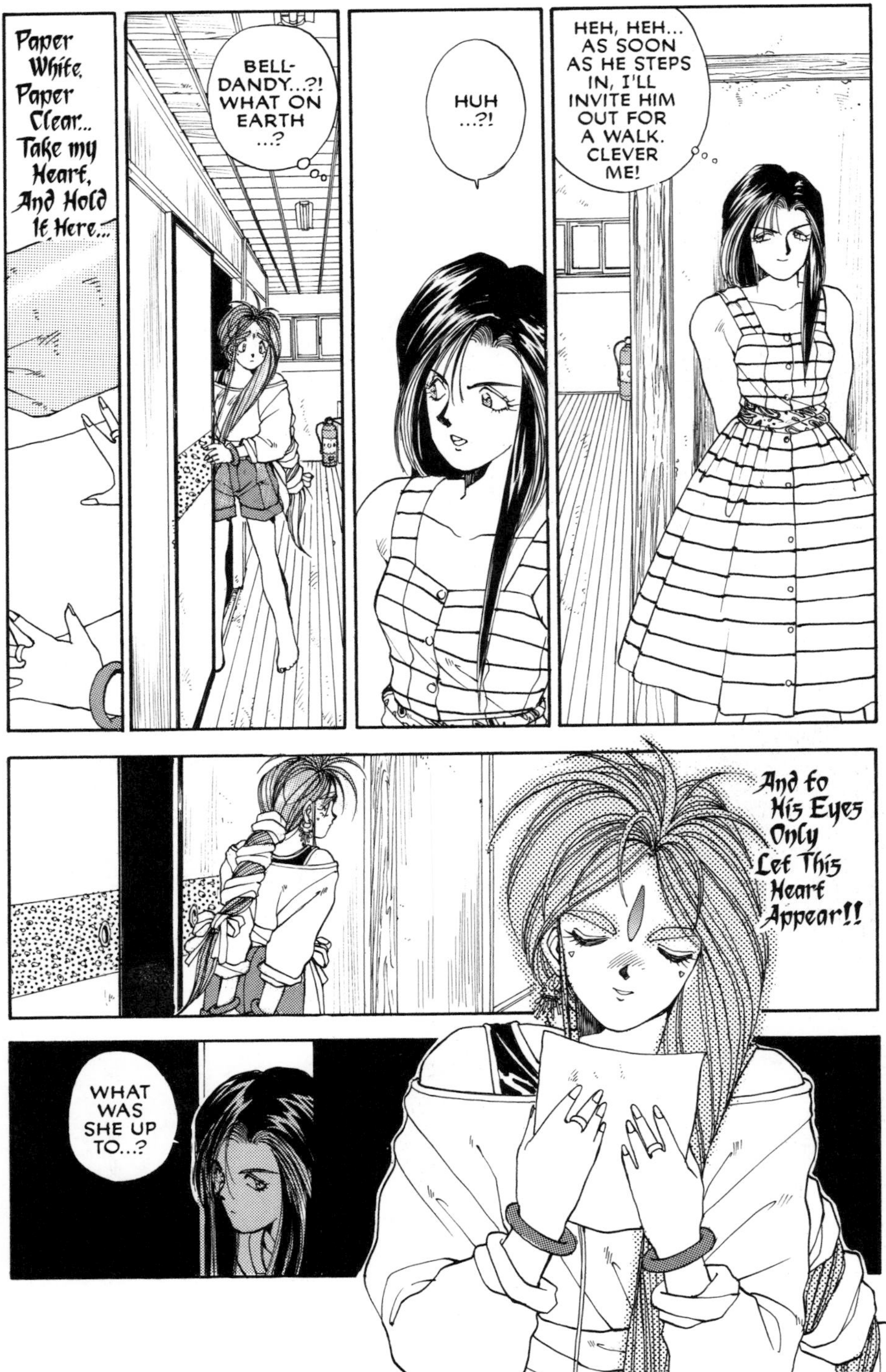
HEH, HEH... AS SOON AS HE STEPS IN, I'LL INVITE HIM OUT FOR A WALK. CLEVER ME!
HUH ...?!
BELL-DANDY...?! WHAT ON EARTH ...?
Paper White, Paper Clear... Take my Heart, And Hold It Here...
And to His Eyes Only Let This Heart Appear!!
WHAT WAS SHE UP TO...?

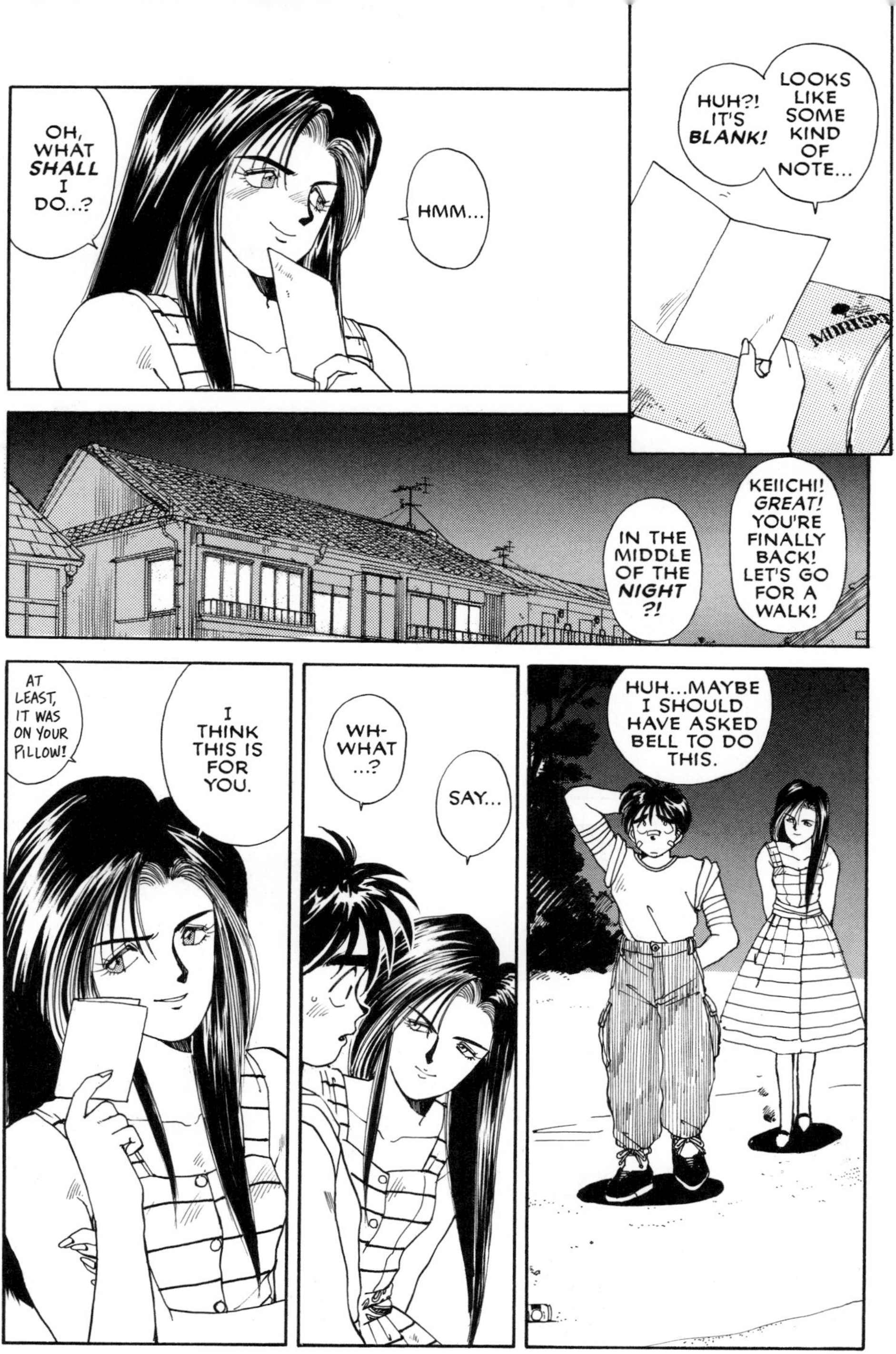
LOOKS LIKE SOME KIND OF NOTE...
HUH?! IT'S *BLANK!*
HMM...
OH, WHAT *SHALL* I DO...?
KEIICHI! *GREAT!* YOU'RE FINALLY BACK! LET'S GO FOR A WALK!
IN THE MIDDLE OF THE *NIGHT* ?!
HUH...MAYBE I SHOULD HAVE ASKED BELL TO DO THIS.
SAY...
WH-WHAT ...?
I THINK THIS IS FOR YOU.
AT LEAST, IT WAS ON YOUR PILLOW!

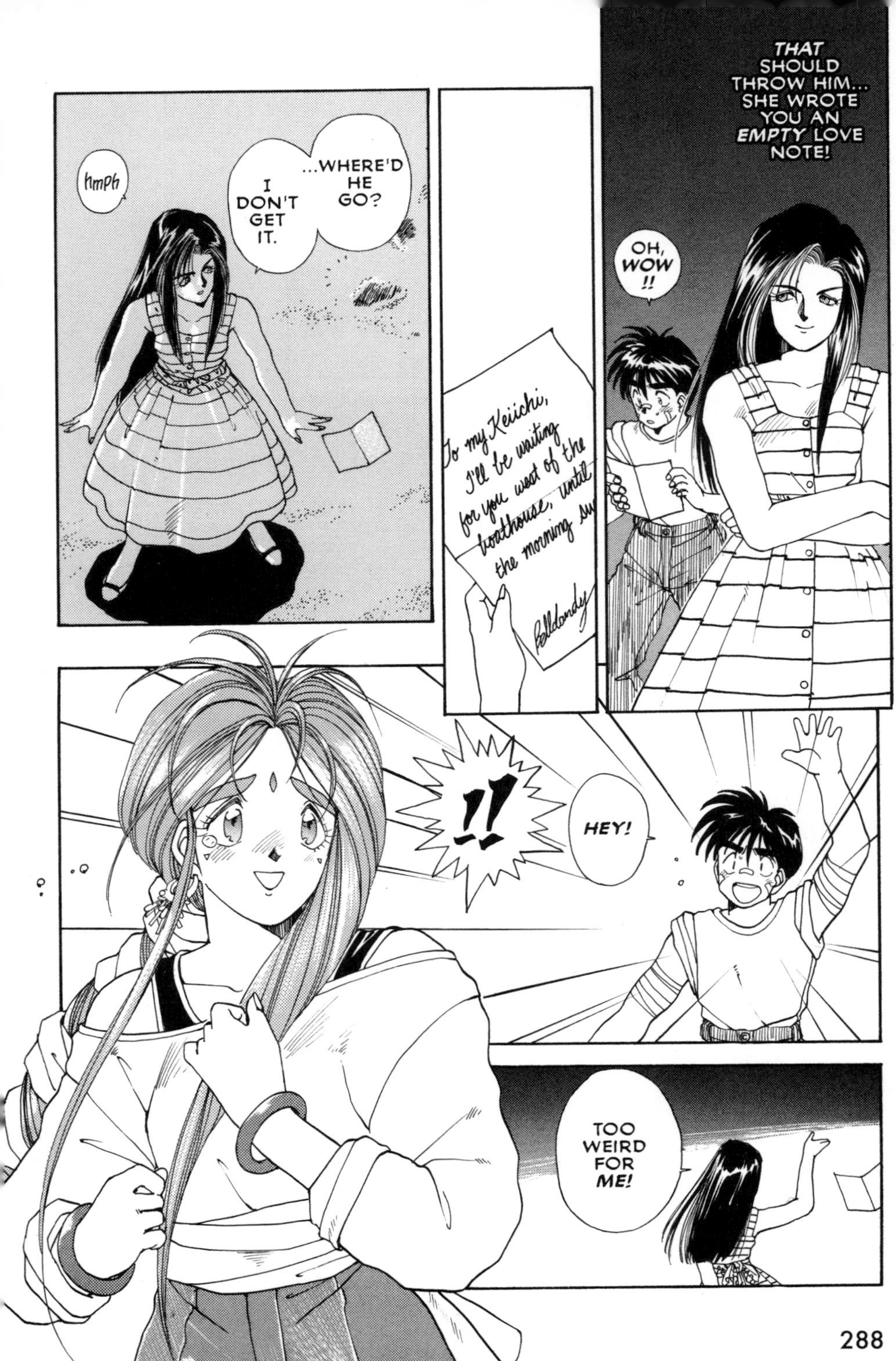
THAT SHOULD THROW HIM... SHE WROTE YOU AN EMPTY LOVE NOTE!
OH, WOW !!
To my Keiichi, I'll be waiting for you west of the boathouse, until the morning su
Belldandy
...WHERE'D HE GO?
I DON'T GET IT.
hmph
HEY!
!!
TOO WEIRD FOR ME!

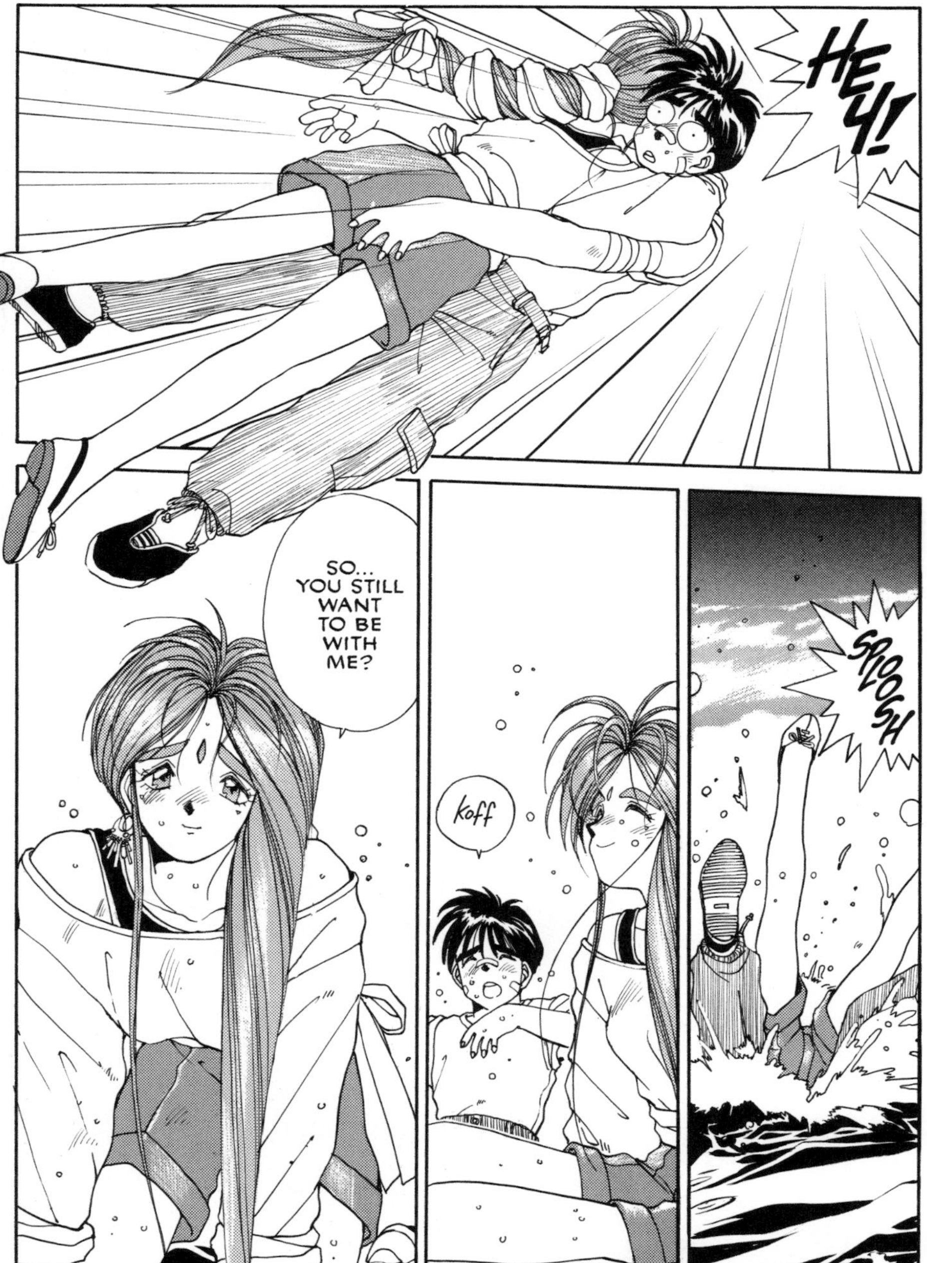
HEY!
SPLOOSH
koff
SO... YOU STILL WANT TO BE WITH ME?

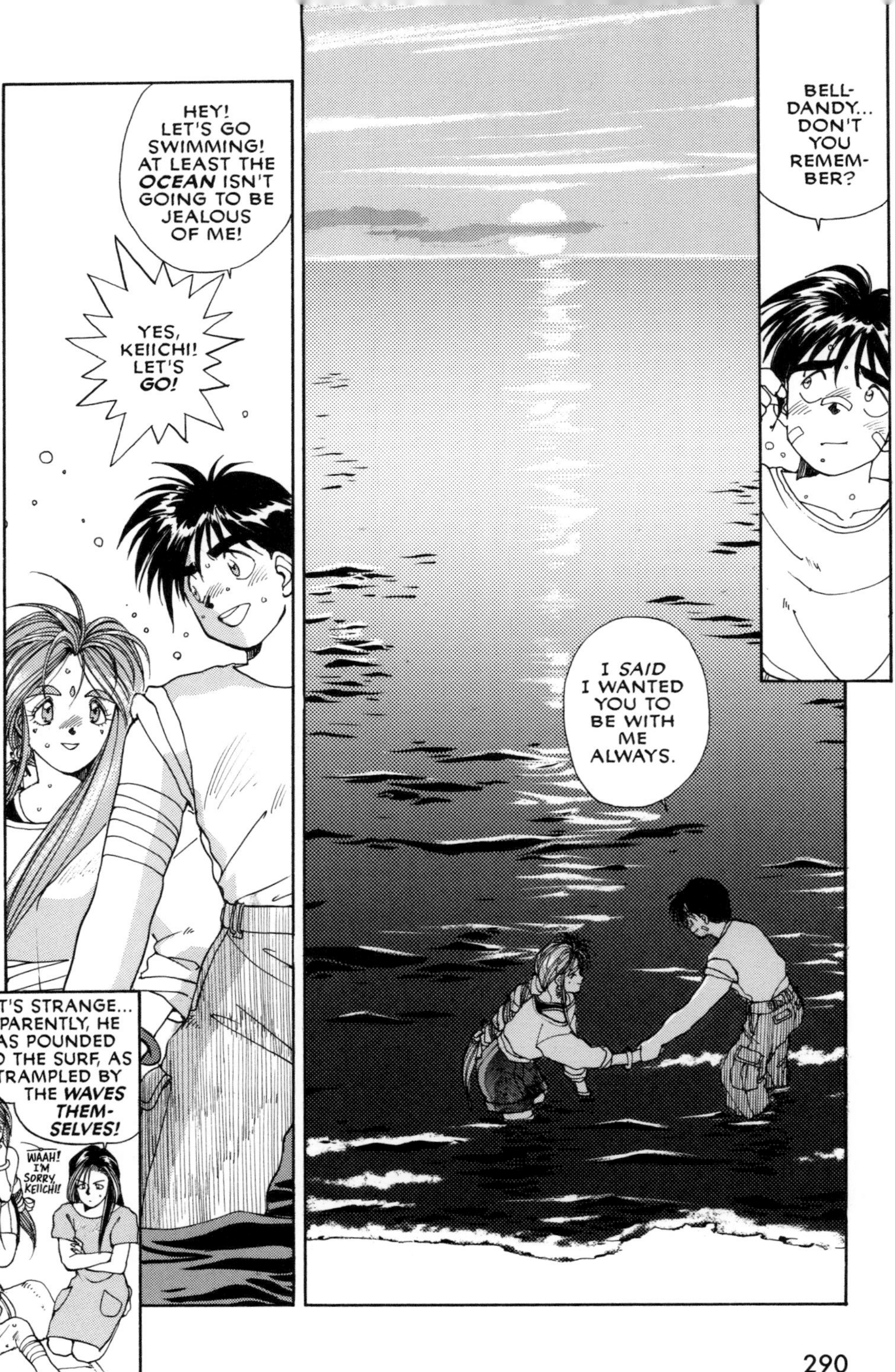
BELL-DANDY... DON'T YOU REMEMBER?
I *SAID* I WANTED YOU TO BE WITH ME ALWAYS.
HEY! LET'S GO SWIMMING! AT LEAST THE ***OCEAN*** ISN'T GOING TO BE JEALOUS OF ME!
YES, KEIICHI! LET'S ***GO!***
THAT'S STRANGE... APPARENTLY, HE WAS POUNDED INTO THE SURF, AS IF TRAMPLED BY THE ***WAVES THEMSELVES!***
WAAH! I'M SORRY, KEIICHI!

OH MY GODDESS!

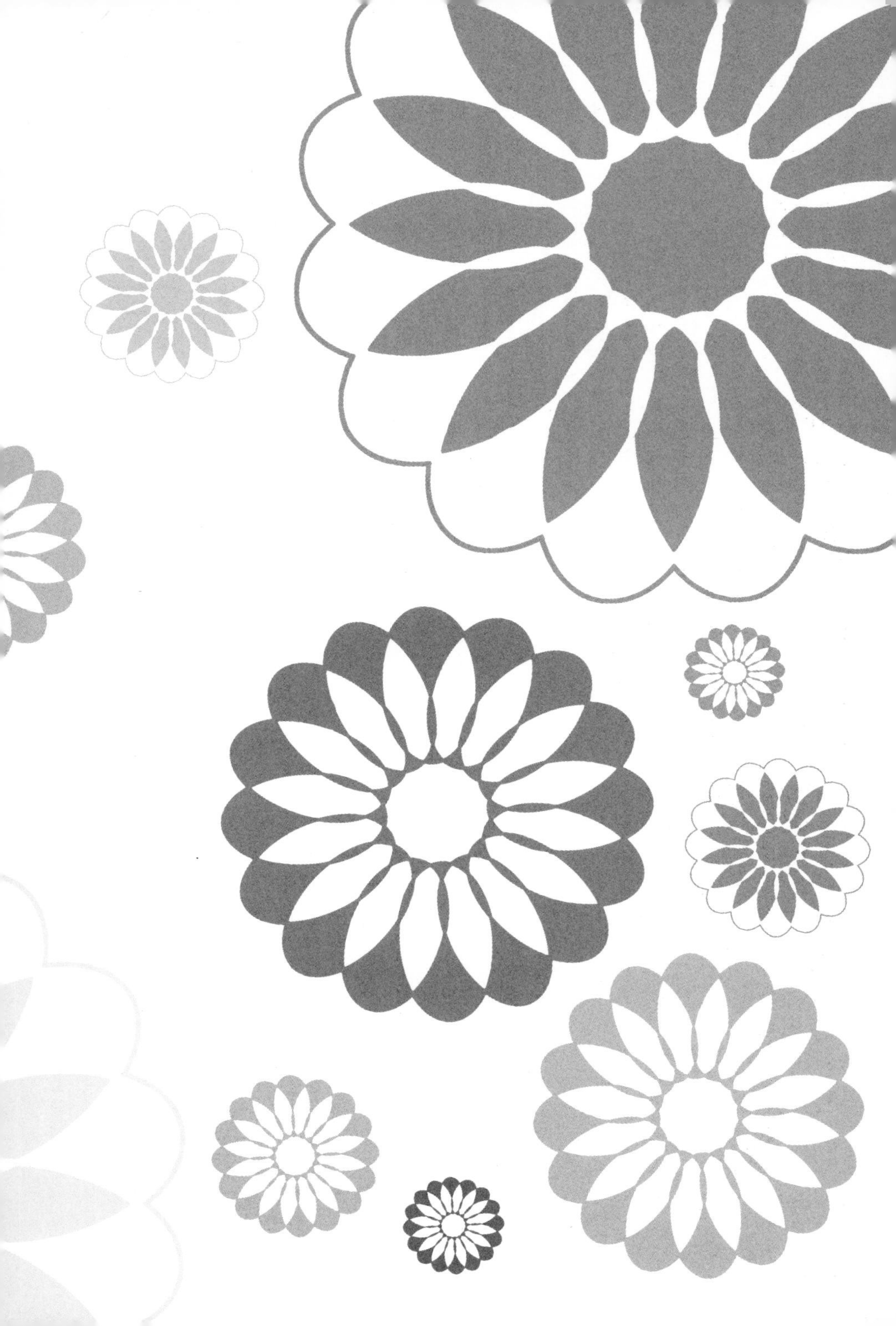

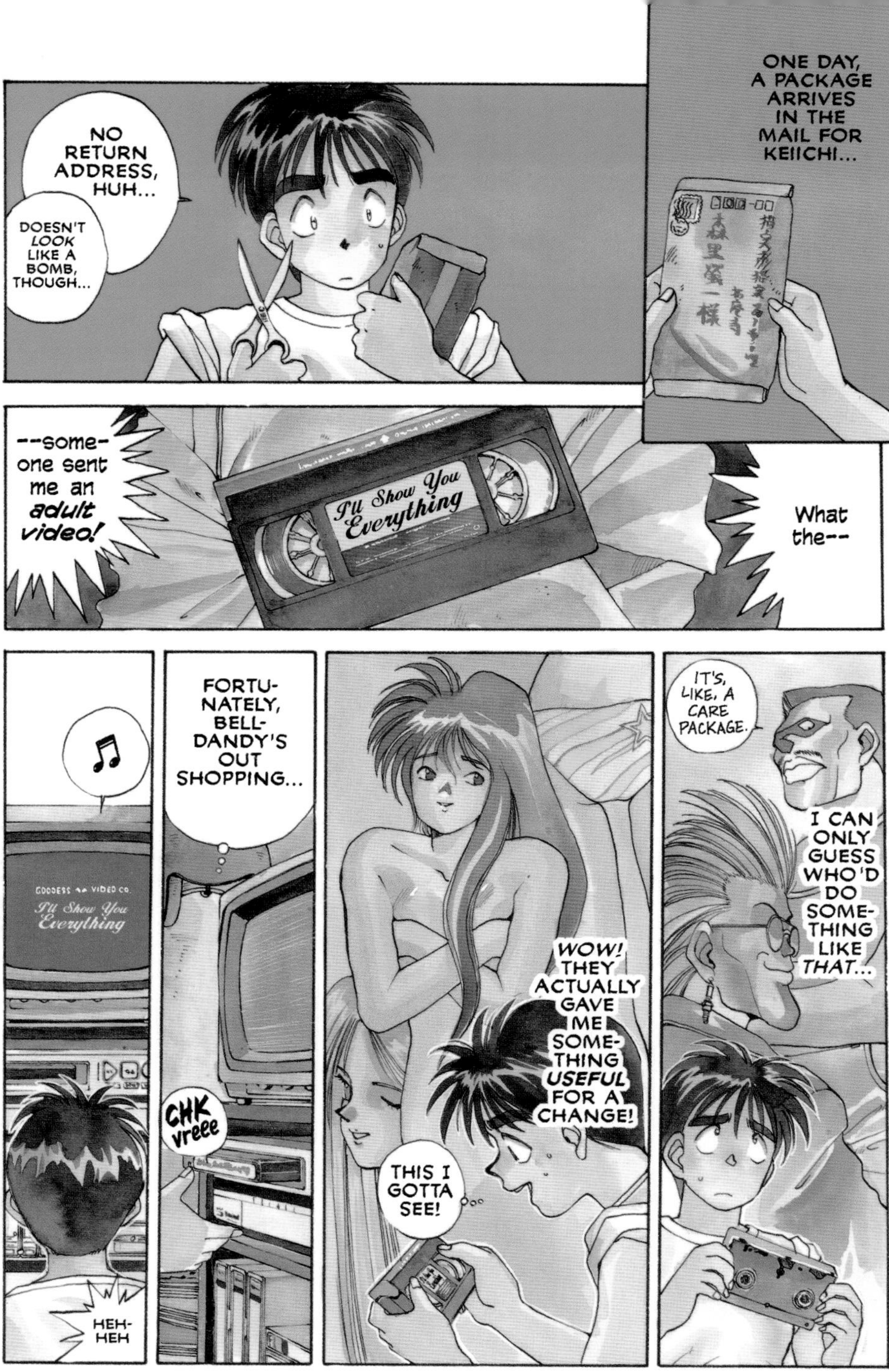
ONE DAY, A PACKAGE ARRIVES IN THE MAIL FOR KEIICHI...
NO RETURN ADDRESS, HUH...
DOESN'T *LOOK* LIKE A BOMB, THOUGH...
What the--
--someone sent me an ***adult video!***
I'll Show You Everything
IT'S, LIKE, A CARE PACKAGE.
I CAN ONLY GUESS WHO'D DO SOMETHING LIKE *THAT*...
WOW! THEY ACTUALLY GAVE ME SOMETHING *USEFUL* FOR A CHANGE!
THIS I GOTTA SEE!
FORTUNATELY, BELL-DANDY'S OUT SHOPPING...
CHK vreee
♫
GODDESS VIDEO CO.
I'll Show You Everything
HEH-HEH

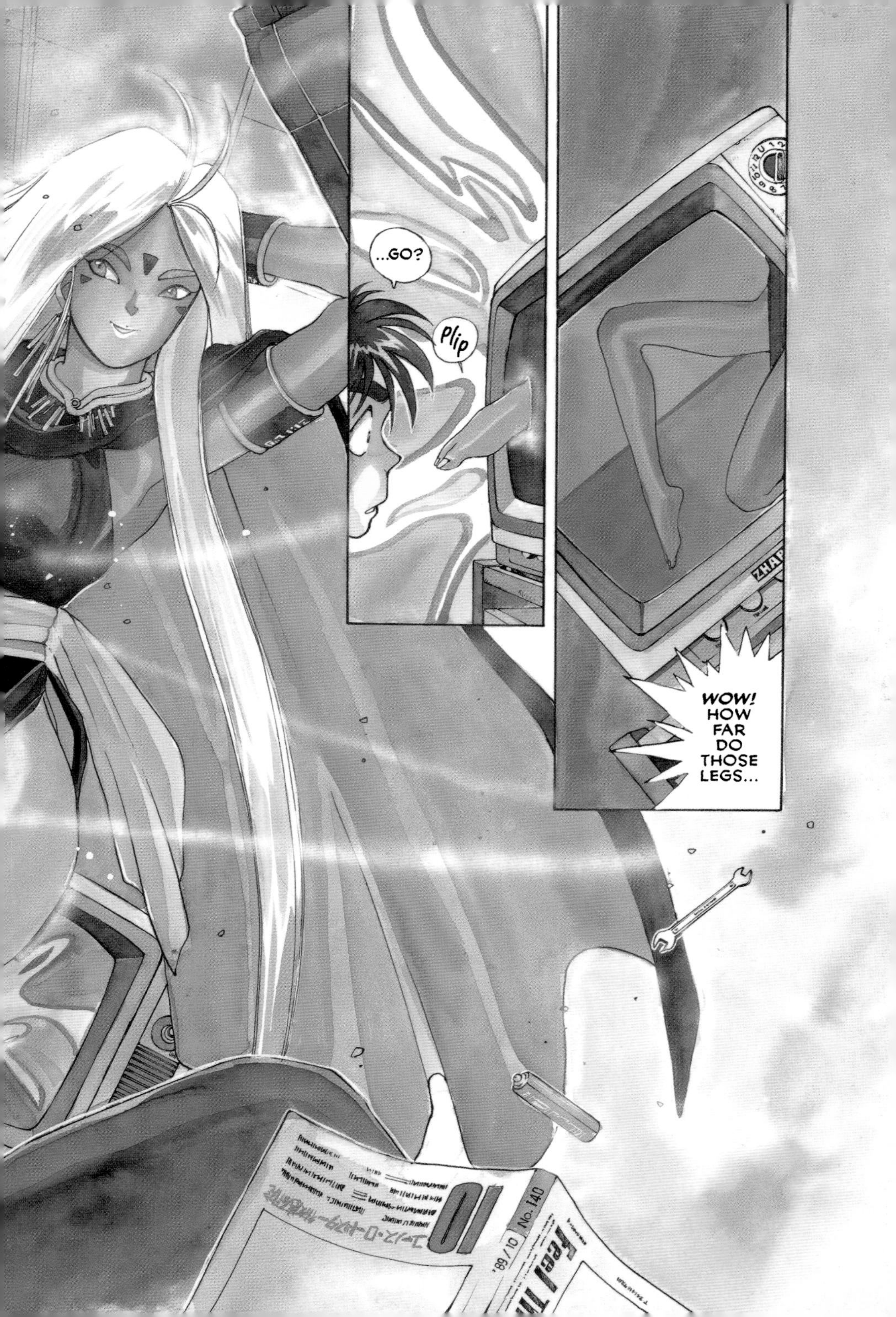
WOW! HOW FAR DO THOSE LEGS...
...GO?
plip

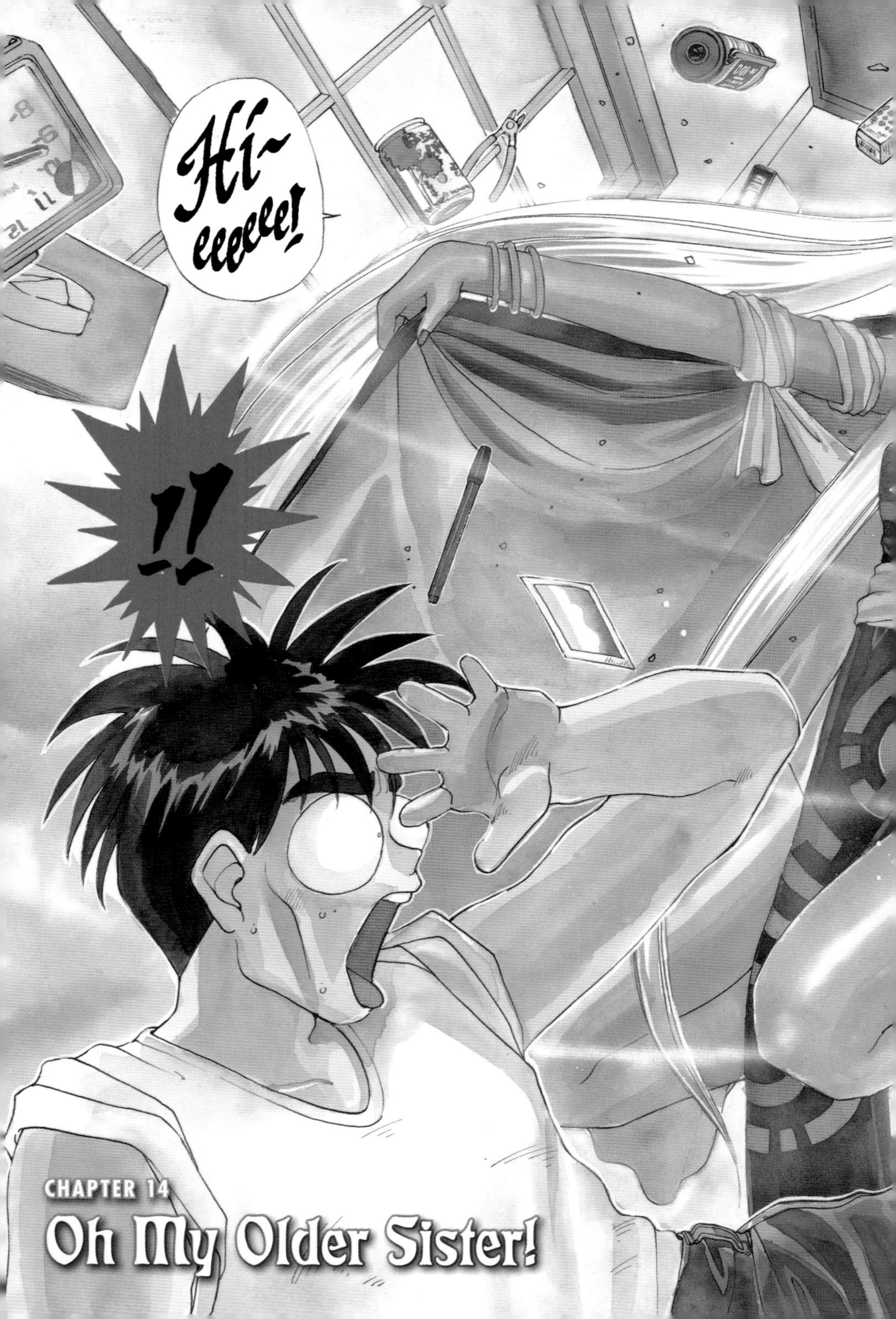

Hi~eeeeee!
!!
CHAPTER 14
Oh My Older Sister!

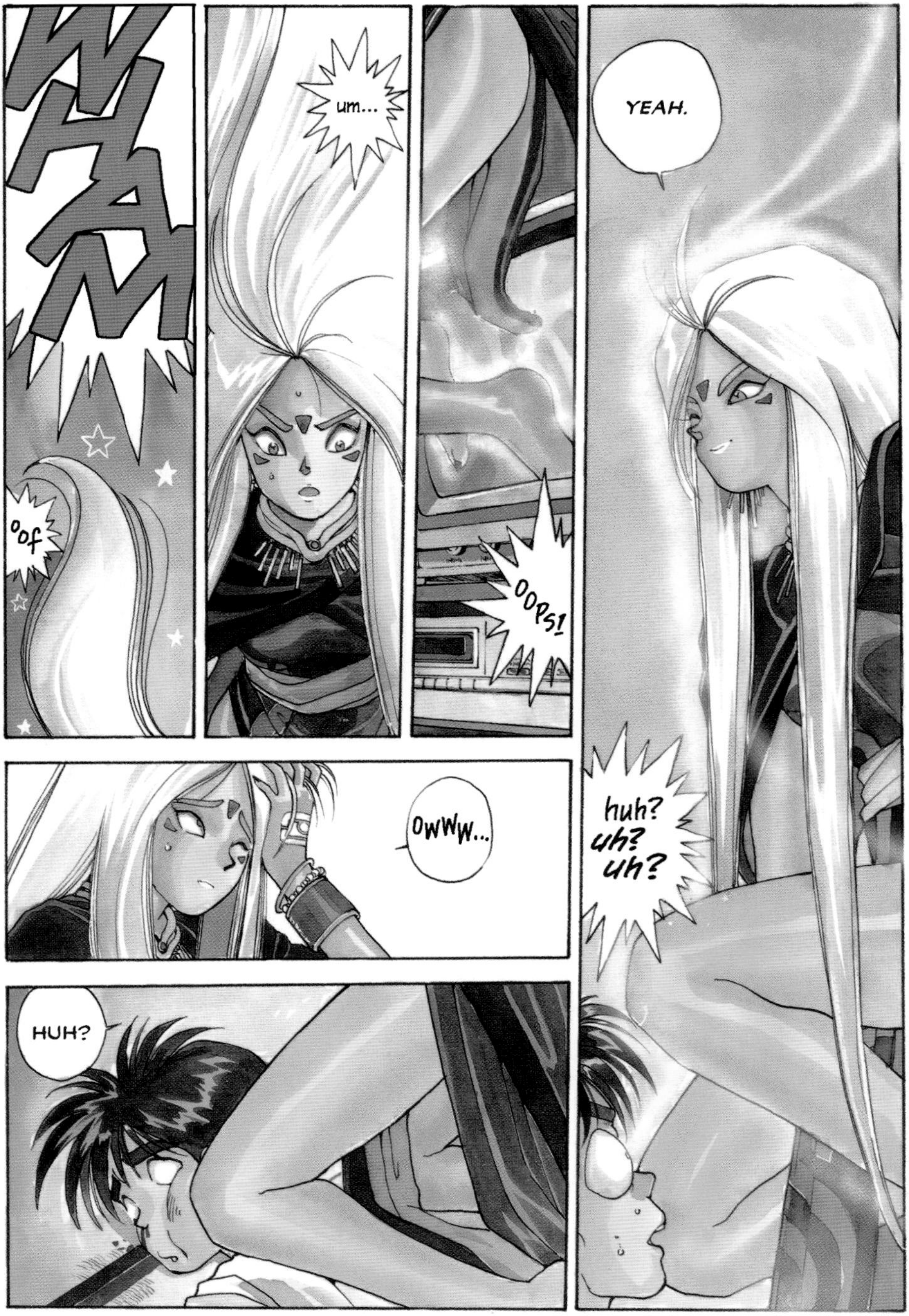
YEAH.
huh? uh? uh?
OOPS!
um...
WHAM
oof
OWWW...
HUH?

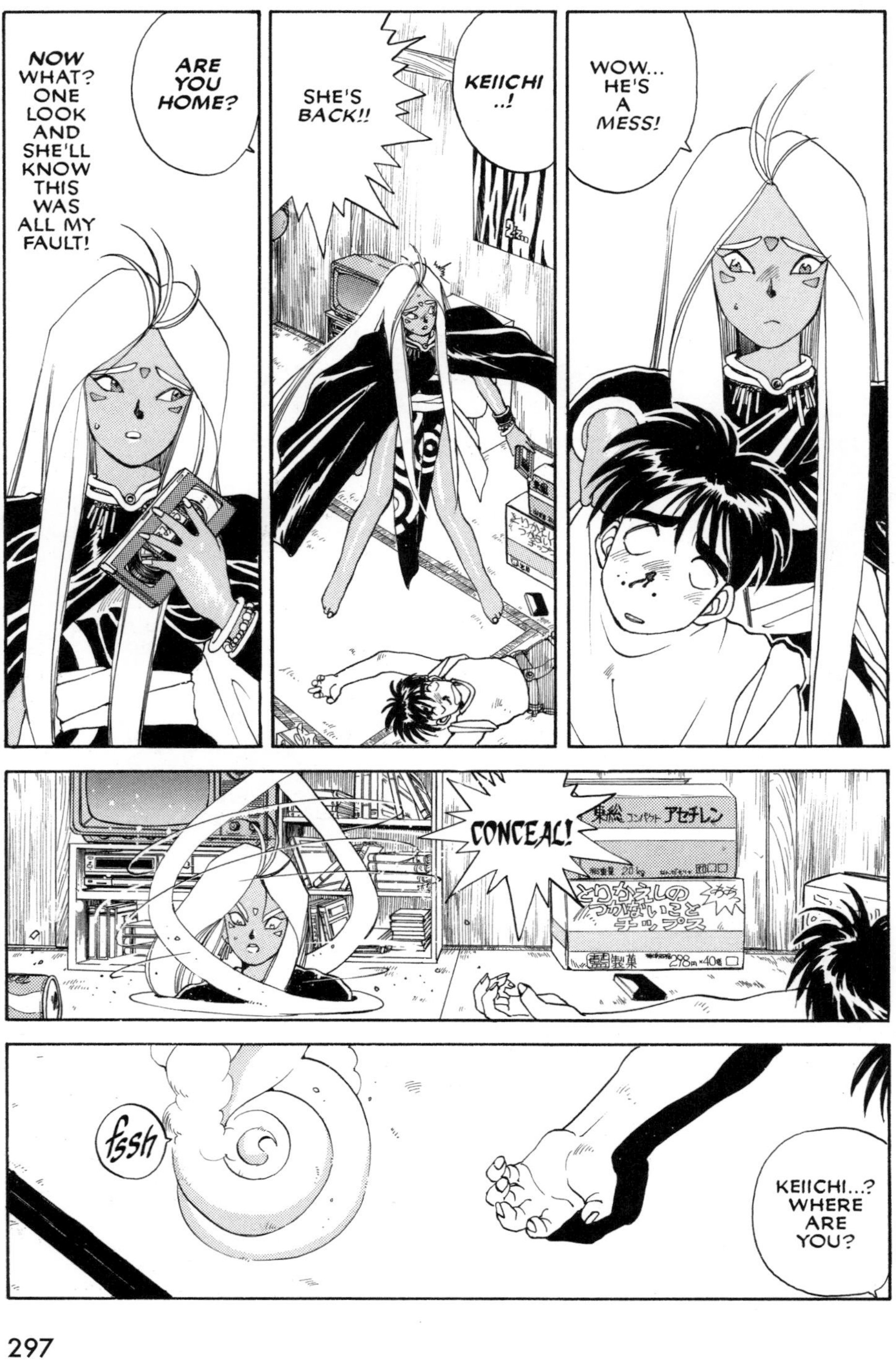
WOW... HE'S A MESS!
KEIICHI ..!
SHE'S BACK!!
ARE YOU HOME?
NOW WHAT? ONE LOOK AND SHE'LL KNOW THIS WAS ALL MY FAULT!
東松 コンパクト アセチレン
CONCEAL!
とりかえしのつかないことチップス
KEIICHI...? WHERE ARE YOU?
fssh

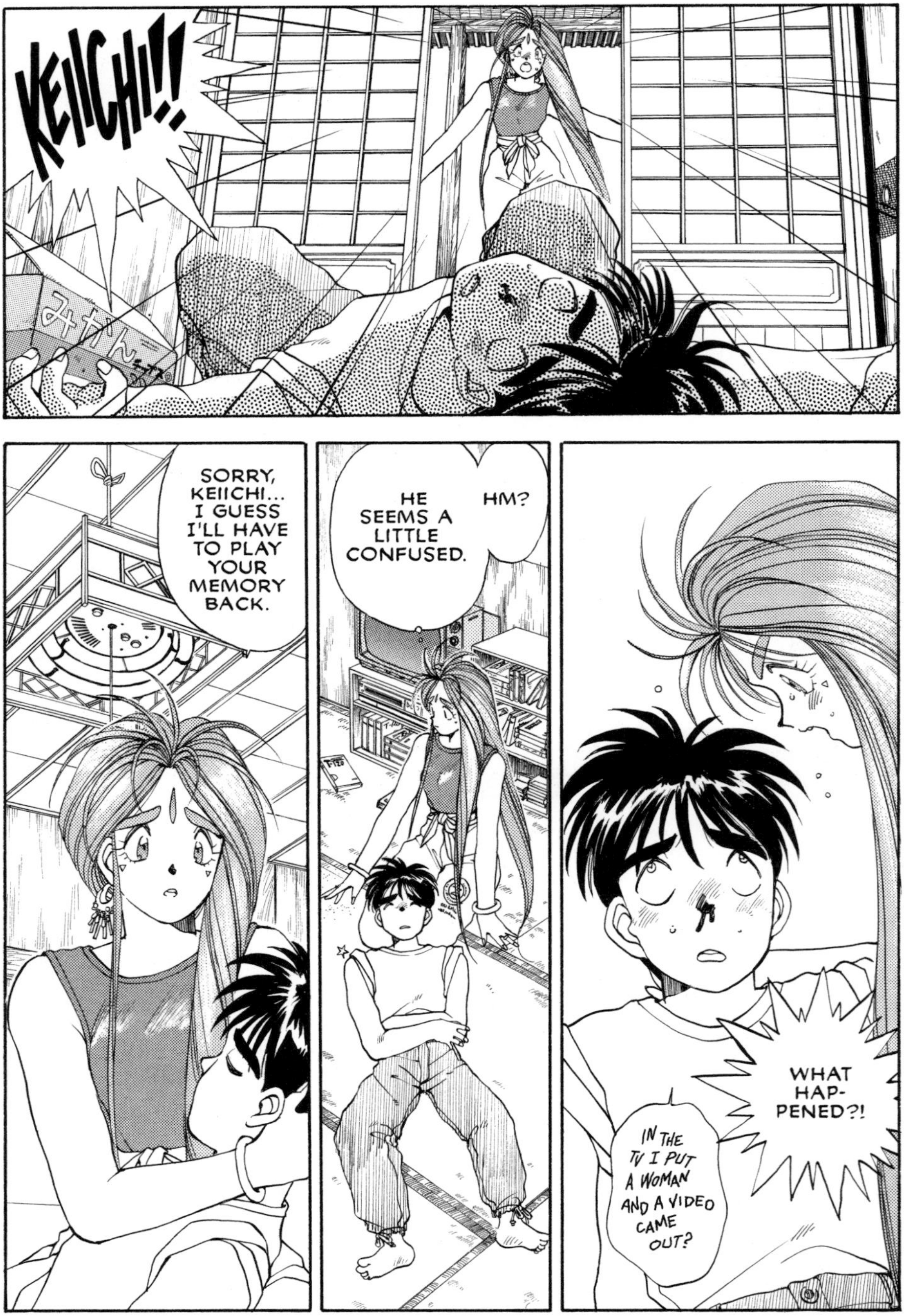
KEIICHI!!
みかん
WHAT HAP-PENED?!
IN THE TV I PUT A WOMAN AND A VIDEO CAME OUT?
HM?
HE SEEMS A LITTLE CONFUSED.
SORRY, KEIICHI... I GUESS I'LL HAVE TO PLAY YOUR MEMORY BACK.

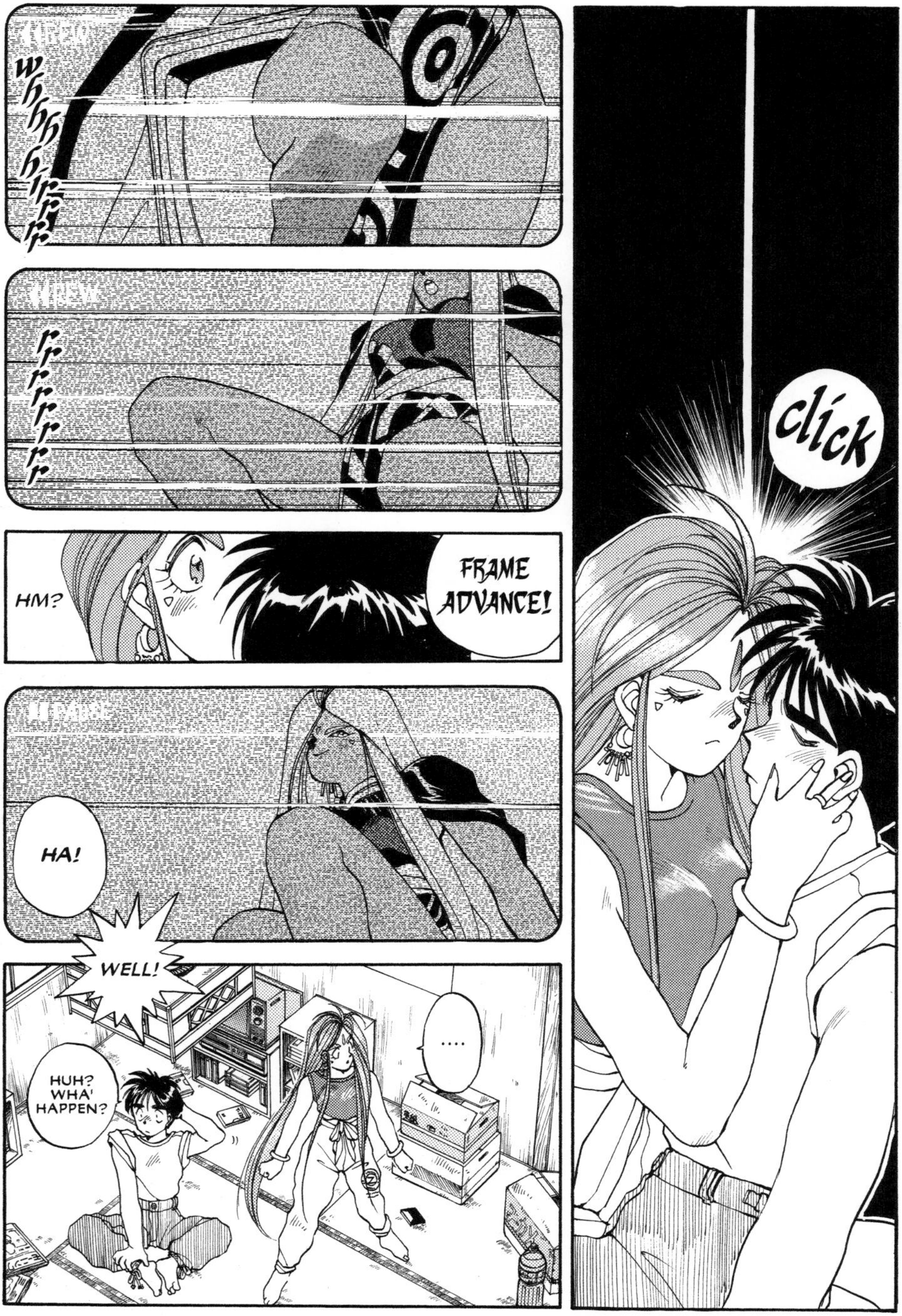
click
whhhhirrrr
rrrrrrrr
FRAME ADVANCE!
HM?
HA!
WELL!
....
HUH? WHA' HAPPEN?

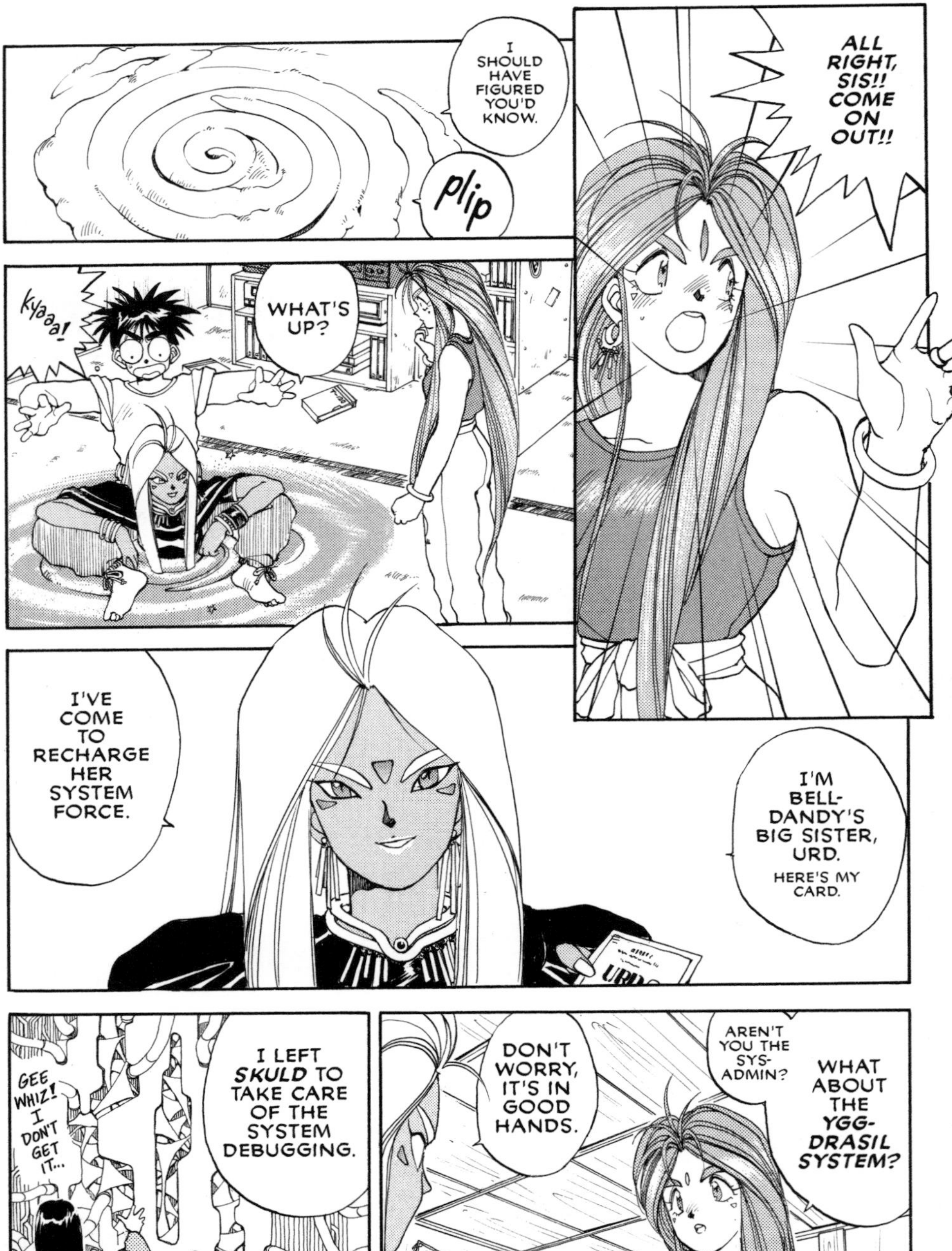
ALL RIGHT, SIS!! COME ON OUT!!
I SHOULD HAVE FIGURED YOU'D KNOW.
plip
WHAT'S UP?
kyaaa!
I'M BELL-DANDY'S BIG SISTER, URD.
HERE'S MY CARD.
I'VE COME TO RECHARGE HER SYSTEM FORCE.
WHAT ABOUT THE YGG-DRASIL SYSTEM?
AREN'T YOU THE SYS-ADMIN?
DON'T WORRY, IT'S IN GOOD HANDS.
I LEFT SKULD TO TAKE CARE OF THE SYSTEM DEBUGGING.
GEE WHIZ! I DON'T GET IT...

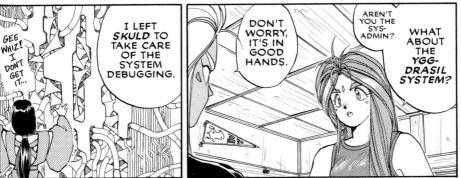

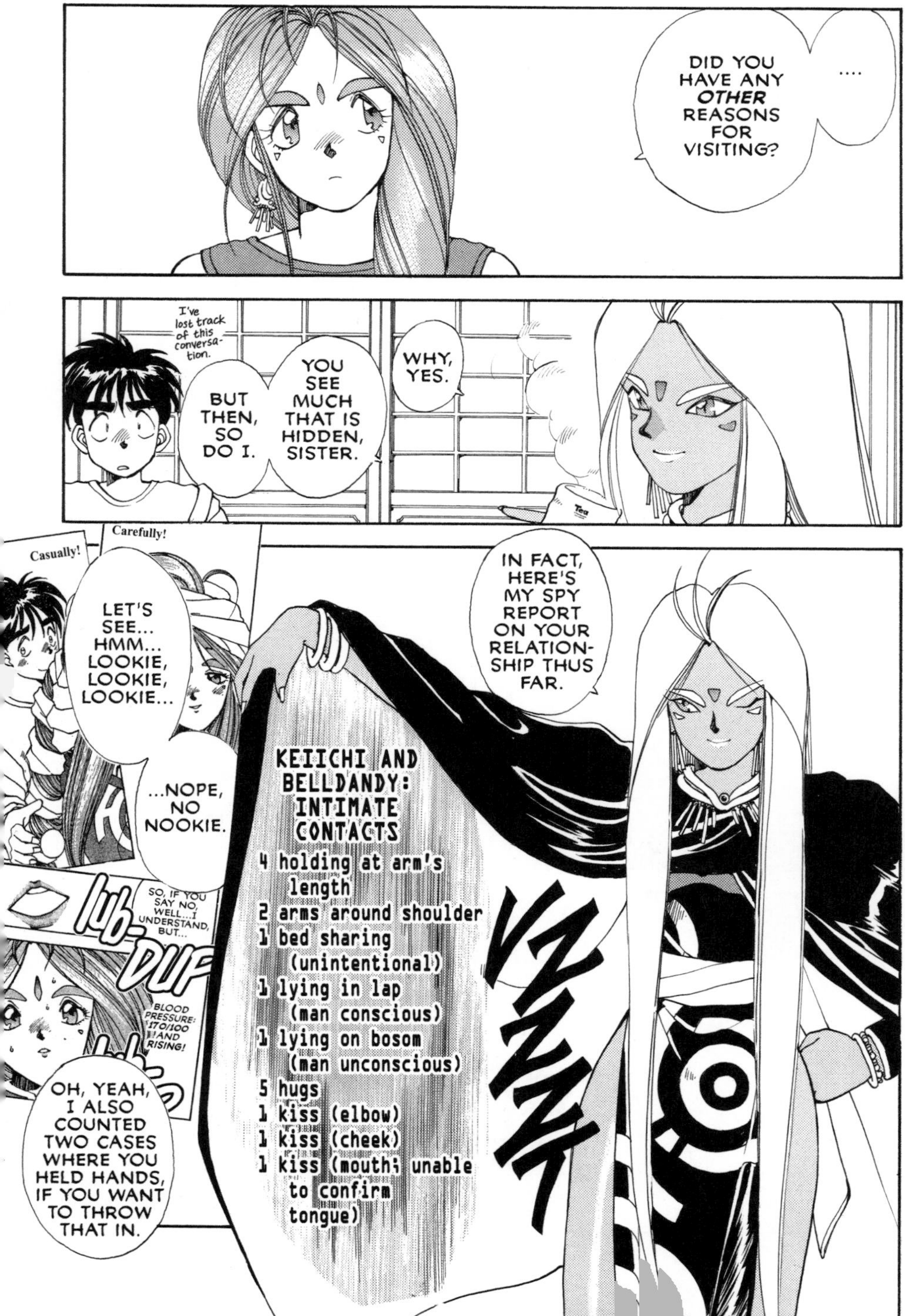
....
DID YOU HAVE ANY *OTHER* REASONS FOR VISITING?
WHY, YES.
YOU SEE MUCH THAT IS HIDDEN, SISTER.
BUT THEN, SO DO I.
I've lost track of this conversation.
IN FACT, HERE'S MY SPY REPORT ON YOUR RELATIONSHIP THUS FAR.
KEIICHI AND BELLDANDY: INTIMATE CONTACTS
4 holding at arm's length
2 arms around shoulder
1 bed sharing (unintentional)
1 lying in lap (man conscious)
1 lying on bosom (man unconscious)
5 hugs
1 kiss (elbow)
1 kiss (cheek)
1 kiss (mouth; unable to confirm tongue)
VZNNK
Carefully!
Casually!
LET'S SEE... HMM... LOOKIE, LOOKIE, LOOKIE...
...NOPE, NO NOOKIE.
lub-DUP
SO, IF YOU SAY NO, WELL...I UNDERSTAND, BUT...
BLOOD PRESSURE: 170/100 AND RISING!
OH, YEAH, I ALSO COUNTED TWO CASES WHERE YOU HELD HANDS, IF YOU WANT TO THROW THAT IN.

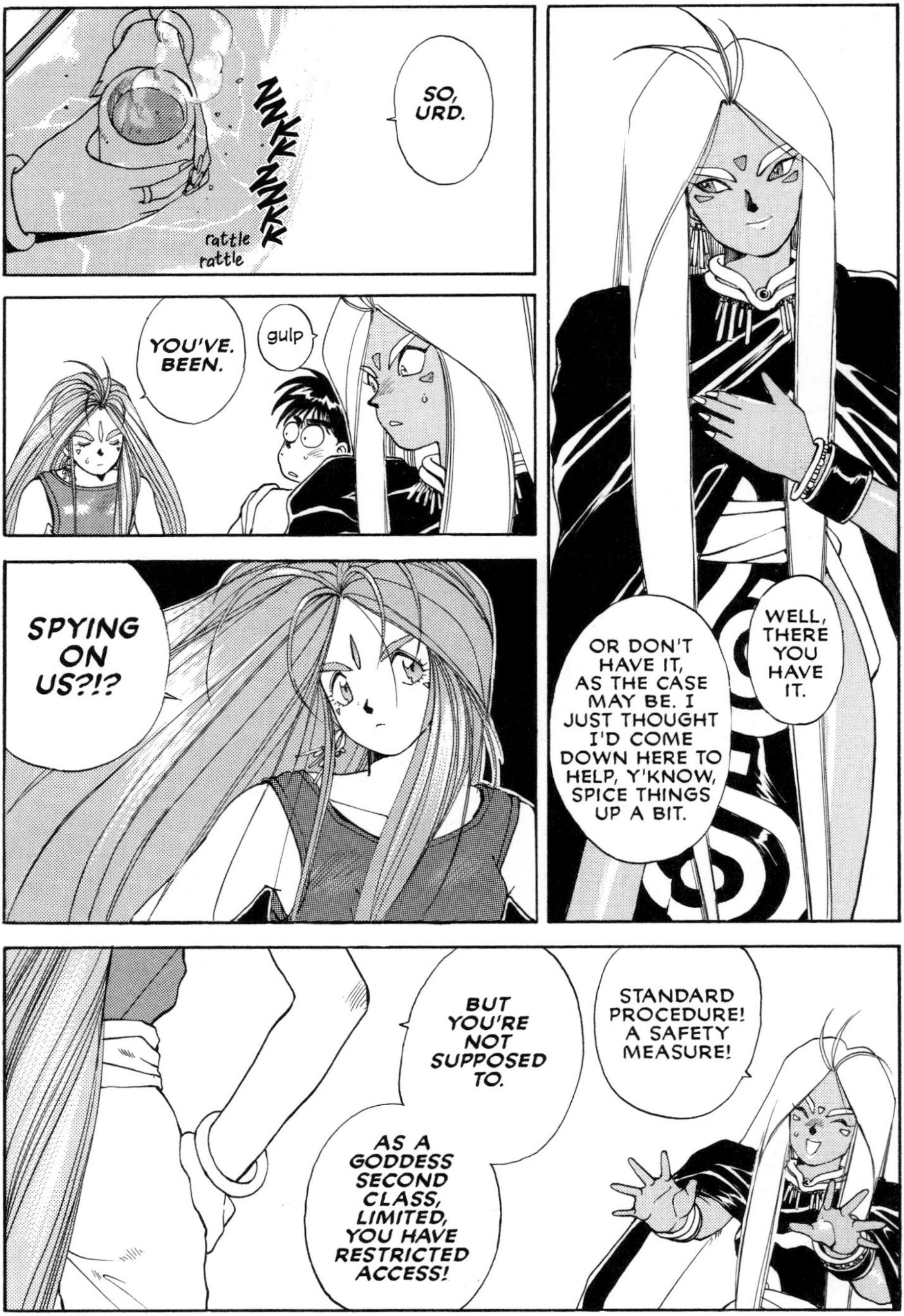
ZZZKKK ZZZKKK
rattle rattle
SO, URD.
YOU'VE. BEEN.
gulp
SPYING ON US?!?
WELL, THERE YOU HAVE IT.
OR DON'T HAVE IT, AS THE CASE MAY BE. I JUST THOUGHT I'D COME DOWN HERE TO HELP, Y'KNOW, SPICE THINGS UP A BIT.
BUT YOU'RE NOT SUPPOSED TO.
AS A GODDESS SECOND CLASS, LIMITED, YOU HAVE RESTRICTED ACCESS!
STANDARD PROCEDURE! A SAFETY MEASURE!

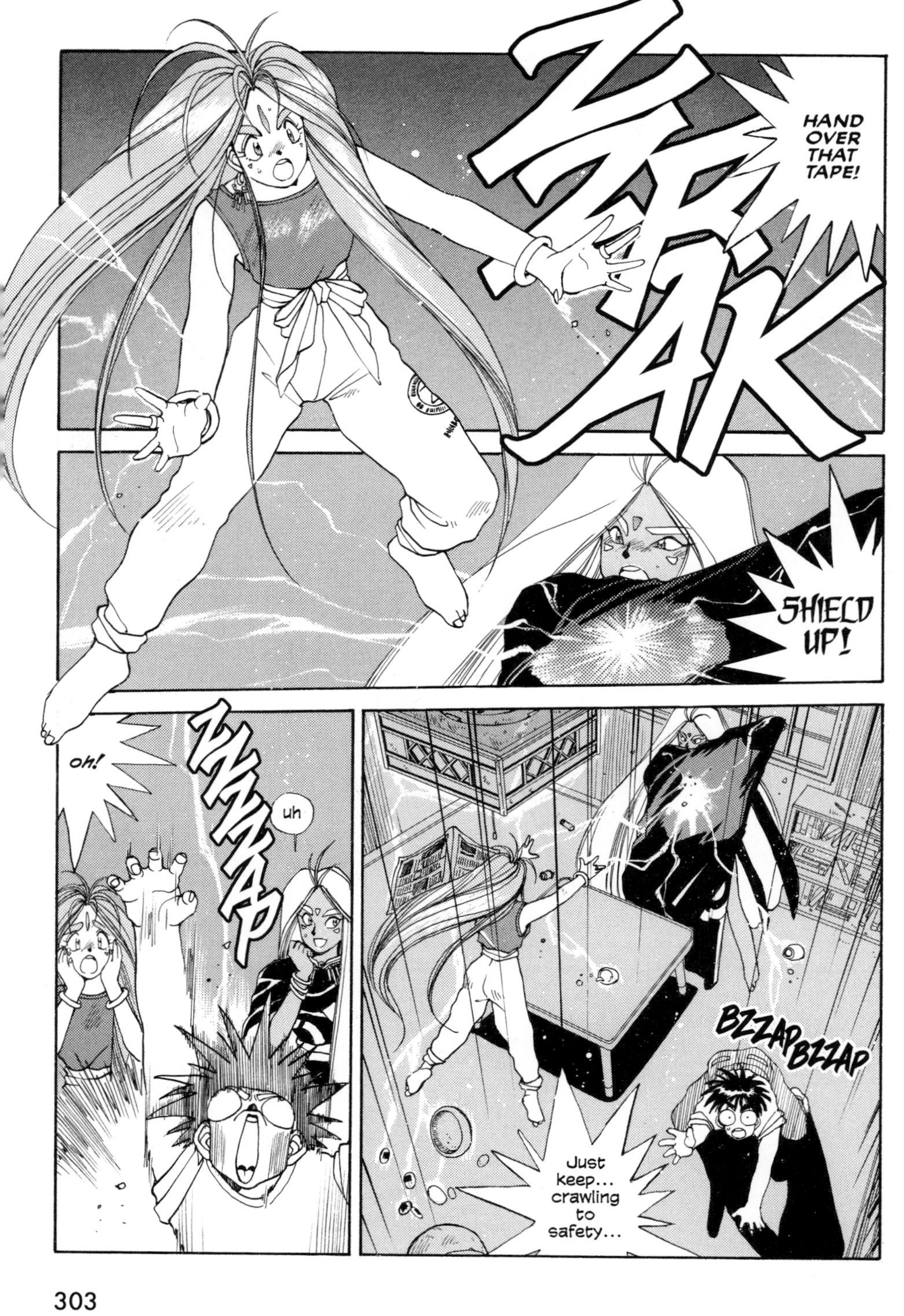
HAND OVER THAT TAPE!
SHIELD UP!
BZZAP BZZAP
Just keep... crawling to safety...
uh
oh!

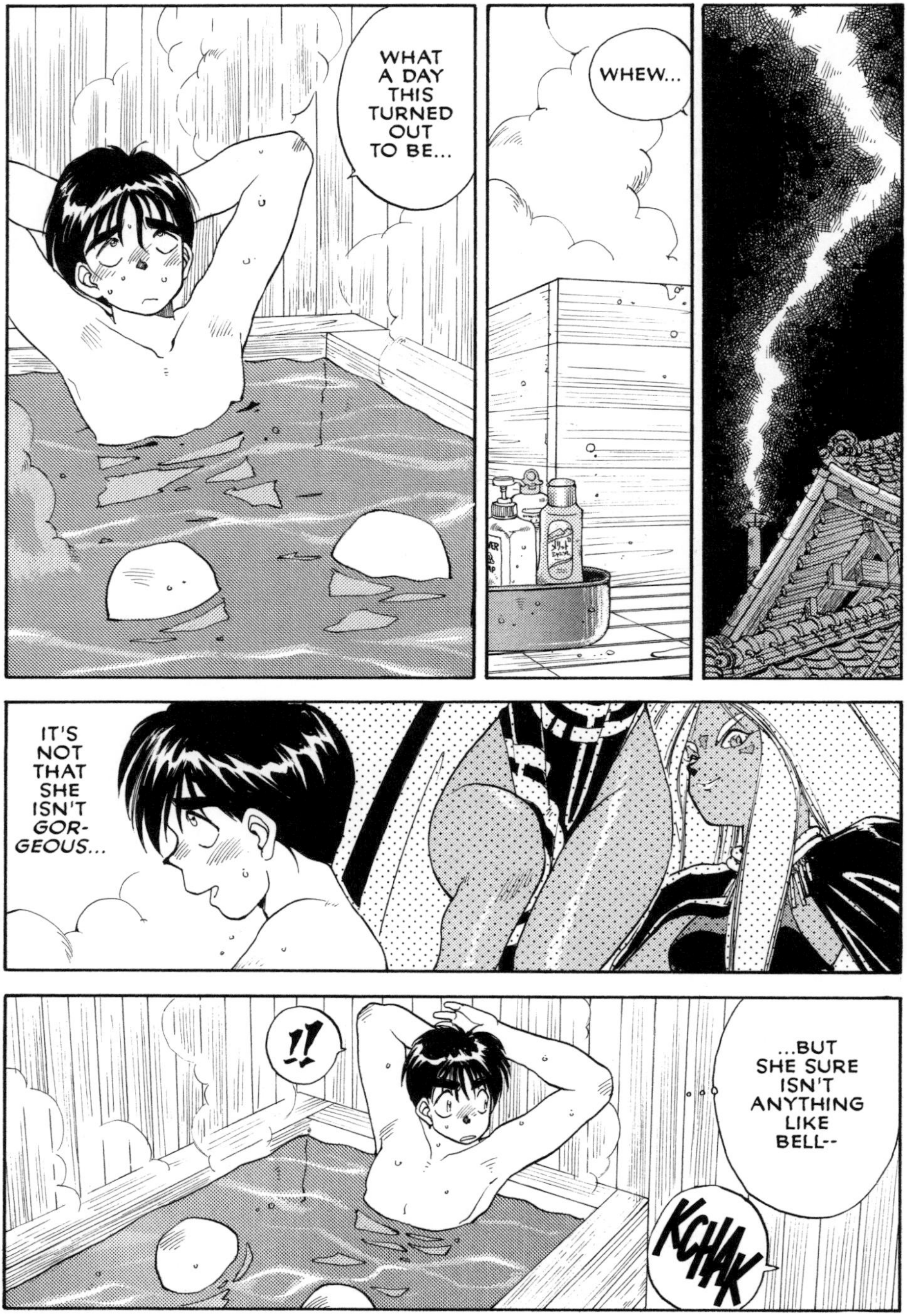
WHEW...
WHAT A DAY THIS TURNED OUT TO BE...
IT'S NOT THAT SHE ISN'T *GORGEOUS*...
...BUT SHE SURE ISN'T ANYTHING LIKE BELL--
KCHAK
!!

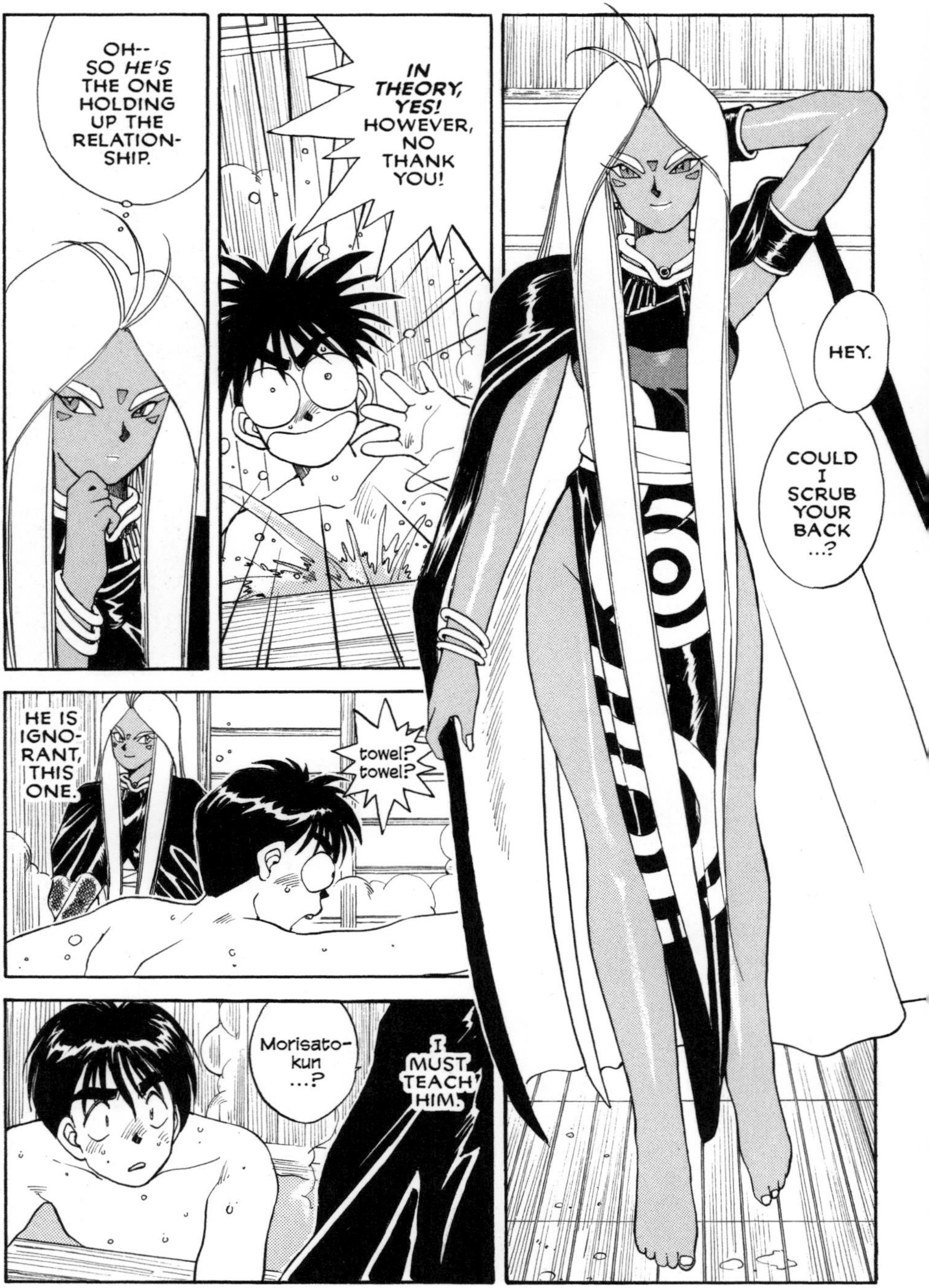
HEY.
COULD I SCRUB YOUR BACK ...?
IN THEORY, YES! HOWEVER, NO THANK YOU!
OH-- SO *HE'S* THE ONE HOLDING UP THE RELATION-SHIP.
towel? towel?
HE IS IGNO-RANT, THIS ONE.
I MUST TEACH HIM.
Morisato-kun ...?

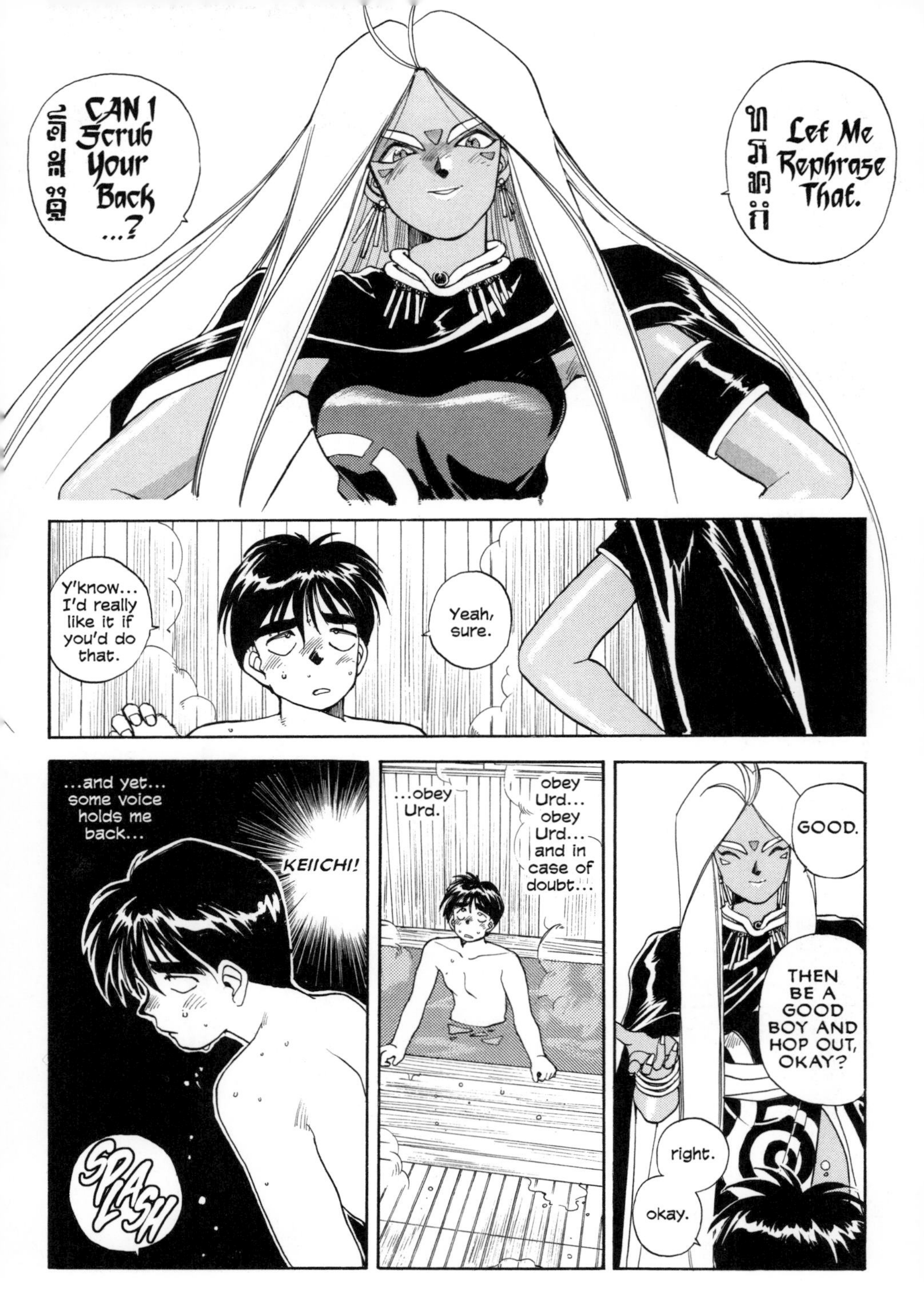
Let Me Rephrase That.
CAN I Scrub Your Back ...?
Yeah, sure.
Y'know... I'd really like it if you'd do that.
GOOD.
THEN BE A GOOD BOY AND HOP OUT, OKAY?
right.
okay.
obey Urd... obey Urd... and in case of doubt...
...obey Urd.
...and yet... some voice holds me back...
KEIICHI!
SPLASH

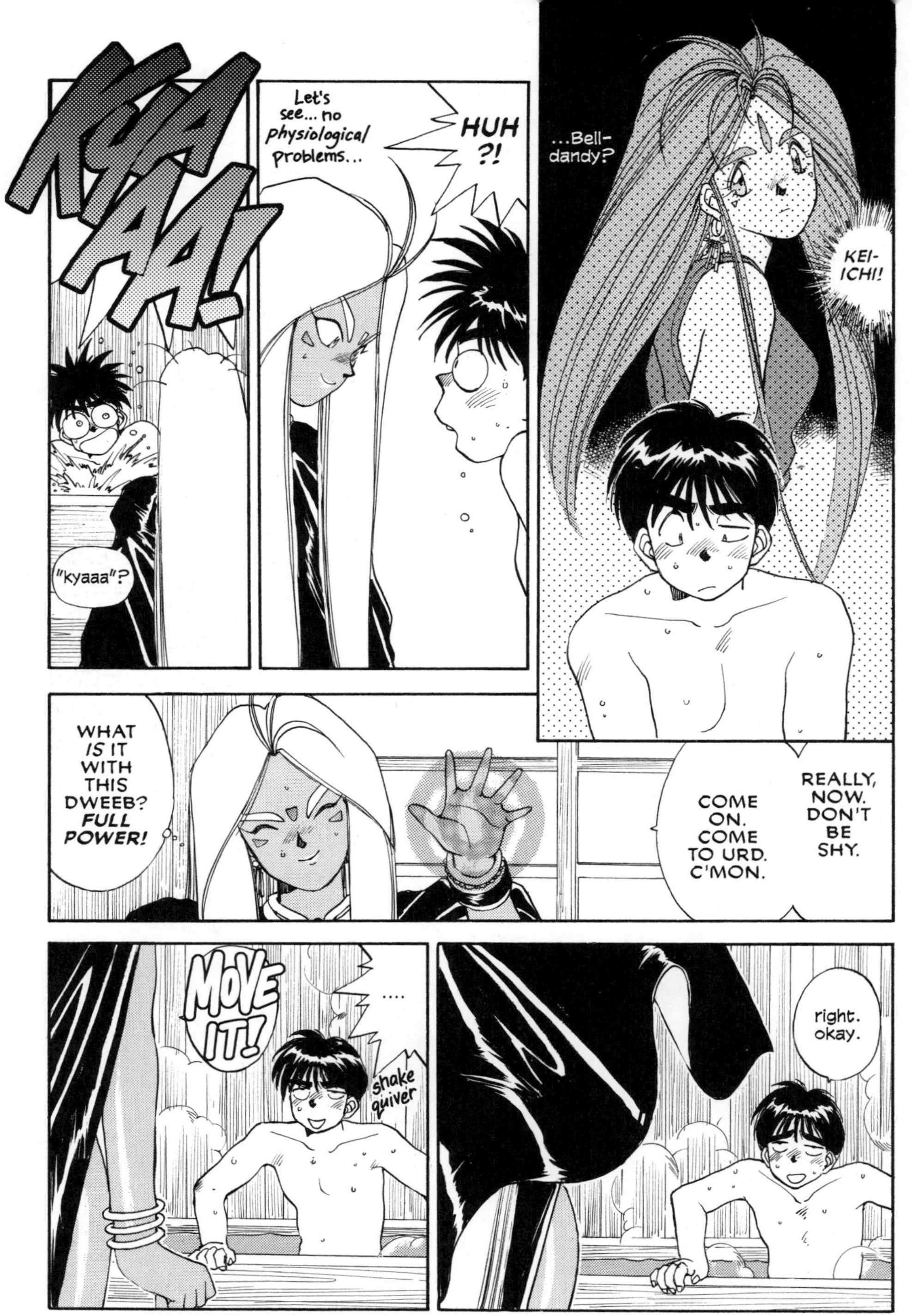
...Bell-dandy?
KEI-ICHI!
HUH ?!
Let's see... no physiological problems...
KYAAA!
"kyaaa"?
REALLY, NOW. DON'T BE SHY.
COME ON. COME TO URD. C'MON.
WHAT IS IT WITH THIS DWEEB? FULL POWER!
right. okay.
....
MOVE IT!
shake quiver

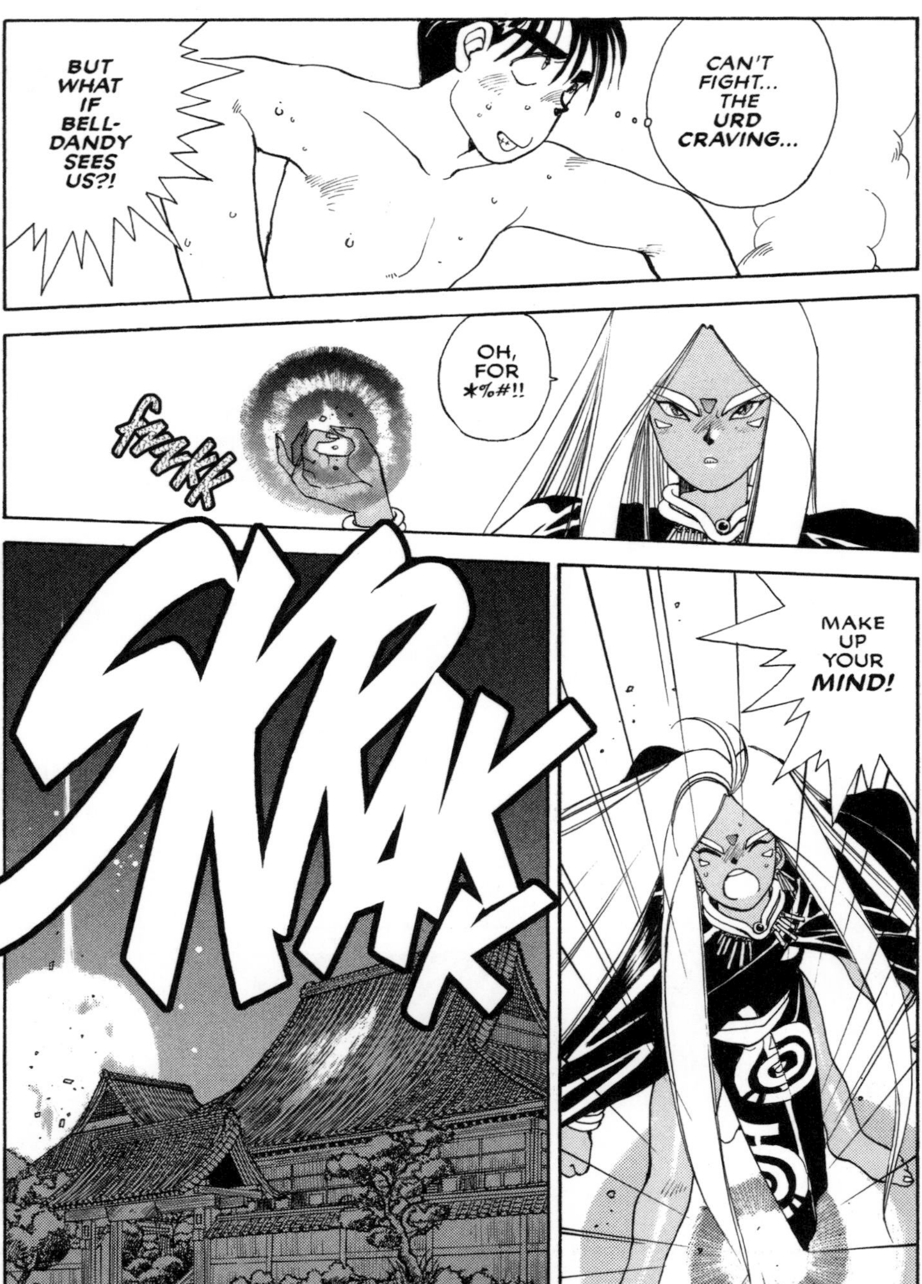
CAN'T FIGHT... THE URD CRAVING...
BUT WHAT IF BELL-DANDY SEES US?!
OH, FOR *%#!!
MAKE UP YOUR MIND!
SKRAKK

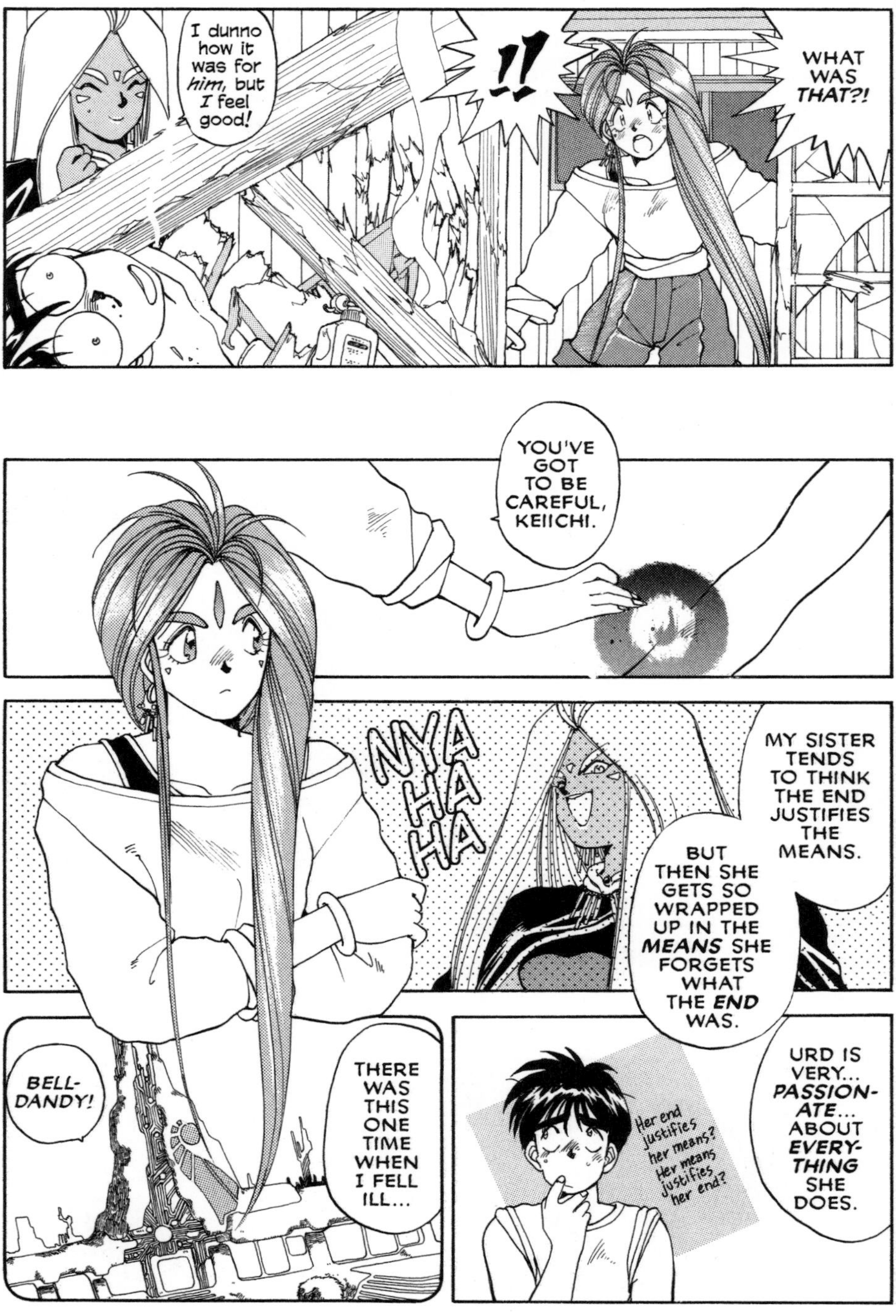
WHAT WAS THAT?!
!!
I dunno how it was for him, but I feel good!
YOU'VE GOT TO BE CAREFUL, KEIICHI.
MY SISTER TENDS TO THINK THE END JUSTIFIES THE MEANS.
BUT THEN SHE GETS SO WRAPPED UP IN THE MEANS SHE FORGETS WHAT THE END WAS.
NYA HA HA
URD IS VERY... PASSIONATE... ABOUT EVERYTHING SHE DOES.
Her end justifies her means? Her means justifies her end?
THERE WAS THIS ONE TIME WHEN I FELL ILL...
BELL-DANDY!

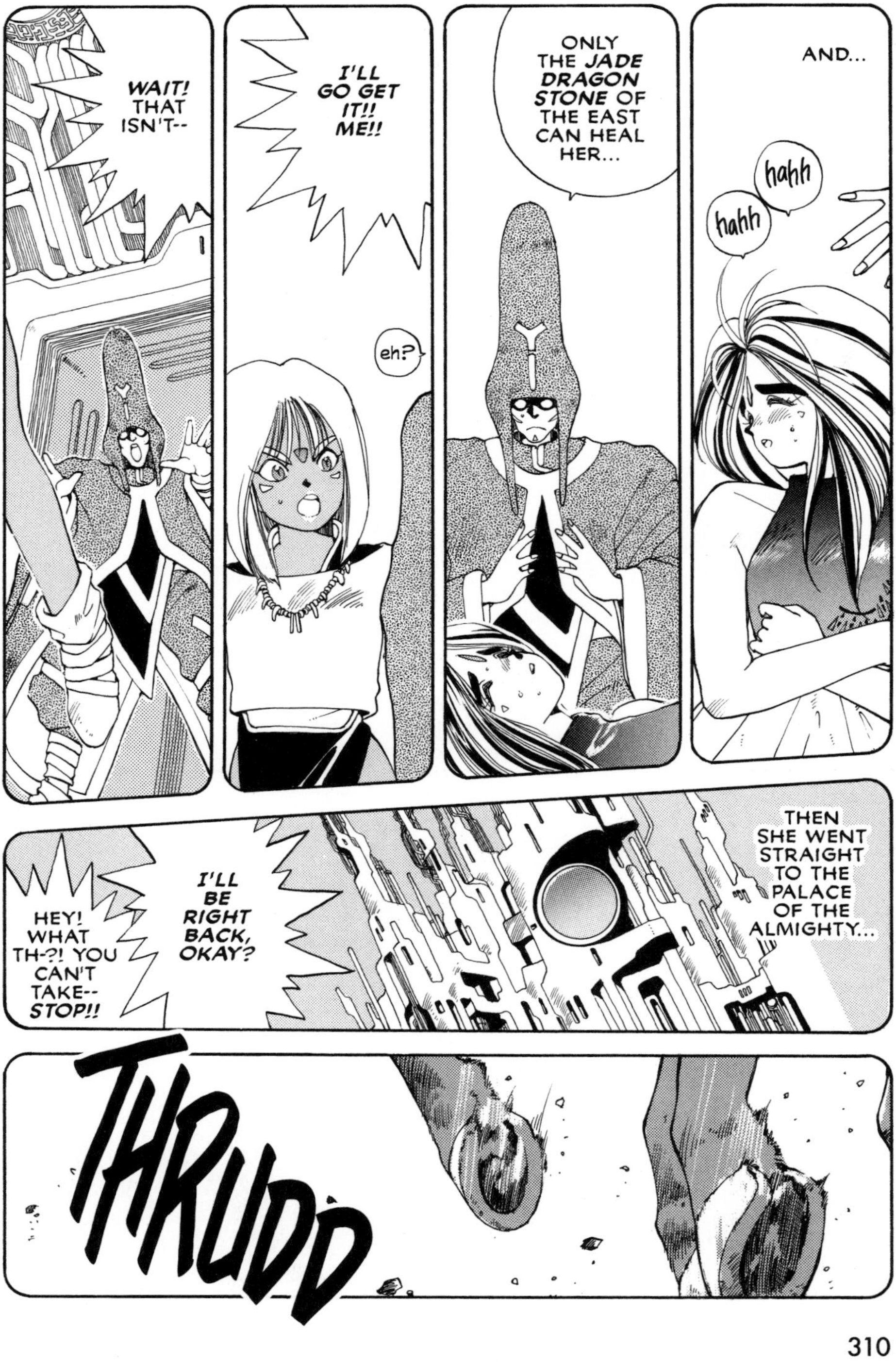

AND...
hahh
hahh
ONLY THE JADE DRAGON STONE OF THE EAST CAN HEAL HER...
I'LL GO GET IT!! ME!!
eh?
WAIT! THAT ISN'T--
THEN SHE WENT STRAIGHT TO THE PALACE OF THE ALMIGHTY...
I'LL BE RIGHT BACK, OKAY?
HEY! WHAT TH-?! YOU CAN'T TAKE-- STOP!!
THRUDD

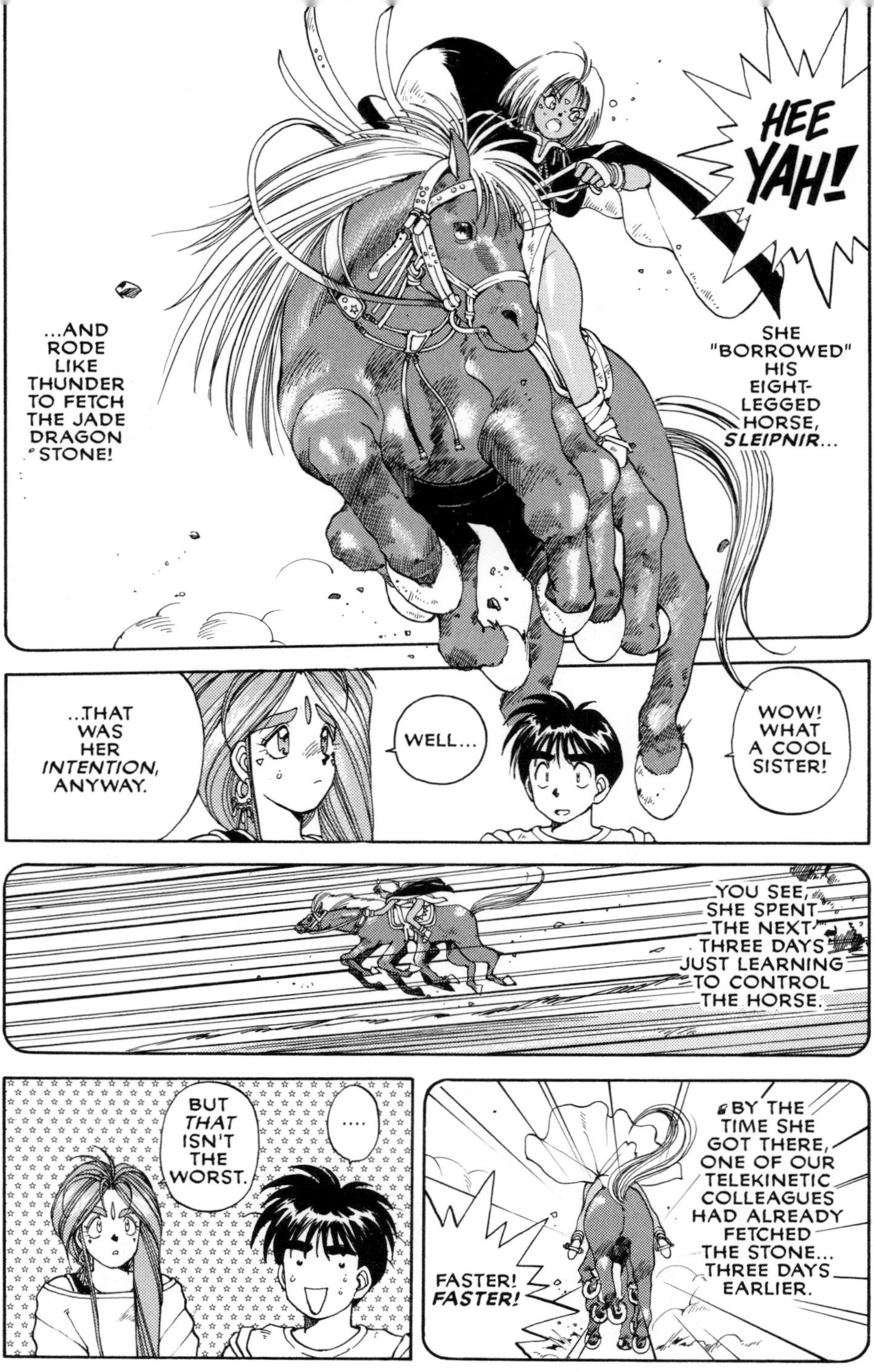
HEE YAH!
SHE "BORROWED" HIS EIGHT-LEGGED HORSE, SLEIPNIR...
...AND RODE LIKE THUNDER TO FETCH THE JADE DRAGON STONE!
WOW! WHAT A COOL SISTER!
WELL...
...THAT WAS HER INTENTION, ANYWAY.
YOU SEE, SHE SPENT THE NEXT THREE DAYS JUST LEARNING TO CONTROL THE HORSE.
BY THE TIME SHE GOT THERE, ONE OF OUR TELEKINETIC COLLEAGUES HAD ALREADY FETCHED THE STONE... THREE DAYS EARLIER.
FASTER! FASTER!
....
BUT THAT ISN'T THE WORST.

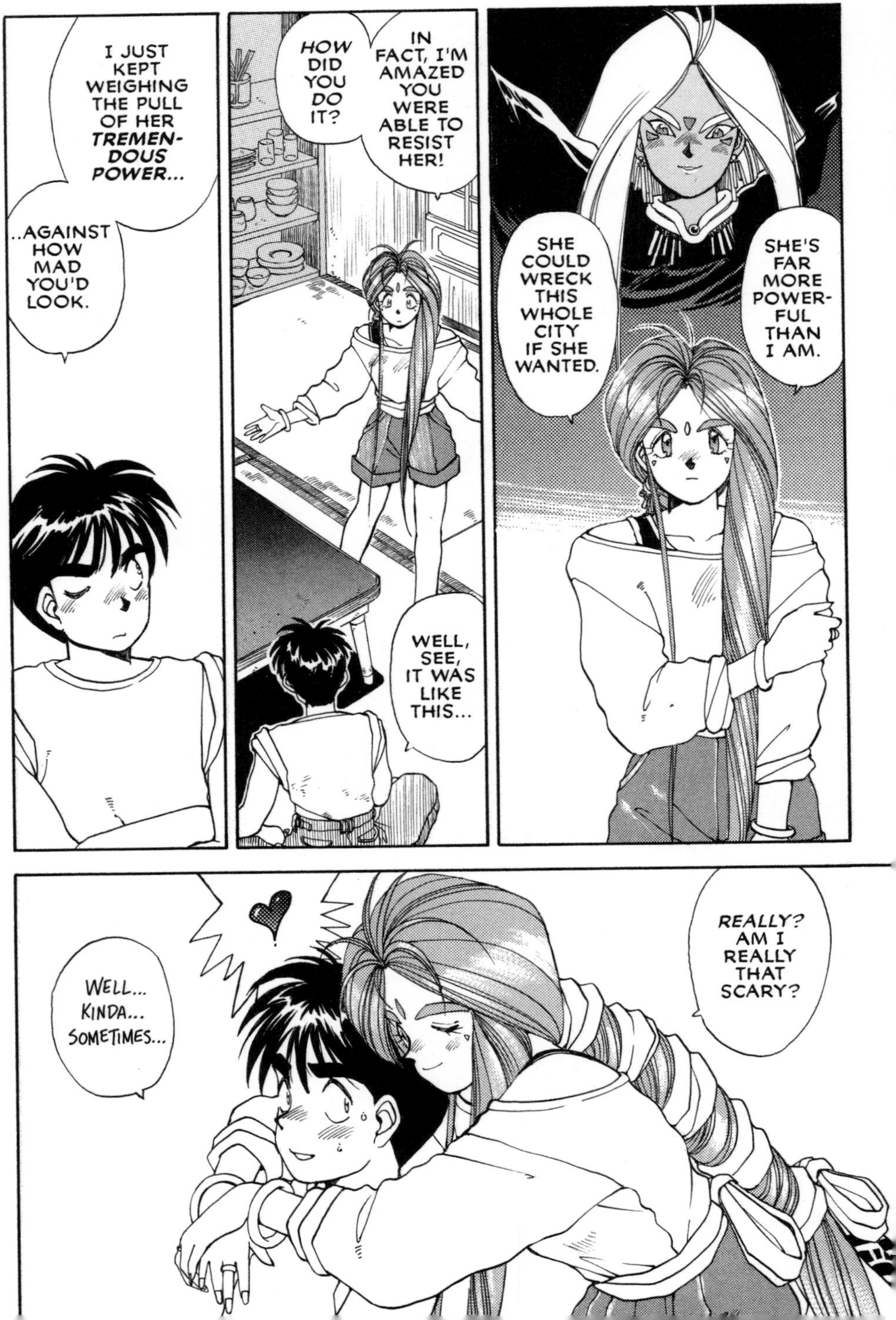
SHE'S FAR MORE POWERFUL THAN I AM.
SHE COULD WRECK THIS WHOLE CITY IF SHE WANTED.
IN FACT, I'M AMAZED YOU WERE ABLE TO RESIST HER!
HOW DID YOU DO IT?
WELL, SEE, IT WAS LIKE THIS...
I JUST KEPT WEIGHING THE PULL OF HER TREMENDOUS POWER...
..AGAINST HOW MAD YOU'D LOOK.
REALLY? AM I REALLY THAT SCARY?
WELL... KINDA... SOMETIMES...

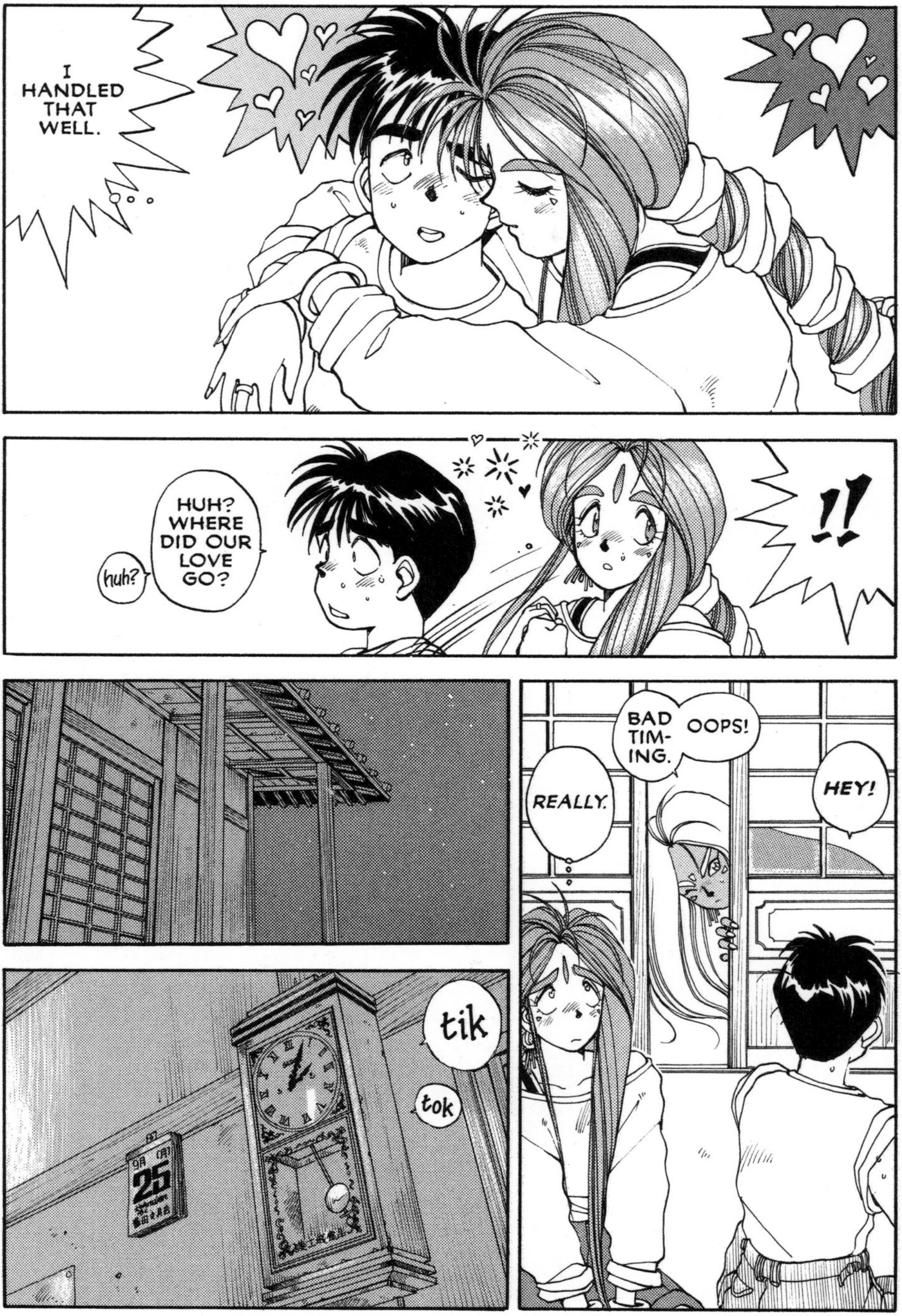
I HANDLED THAT WELL.
!!
HUH? WHERE DID OUR LOVE GO?
huh?
OOPS!
BAD TIM-ING.
HEY!
REALLY.
tik
tok

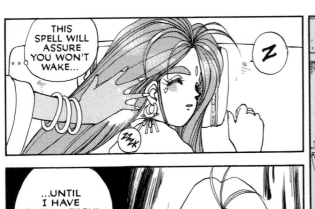

heh!
THIS SPELL WILL ASSURE YOU WON'T WAKE...
Z
...UNTIL I HAVE GIVEN KEIICHI THAT... *FORBIDDEN KNOWLEDGE.*
WHEN YOU THINK ABOUT IT, I LOST OUT *TWICE* TODAY...
mnch
mnch
ANY MORE CHIPS IN THAT BAG...?

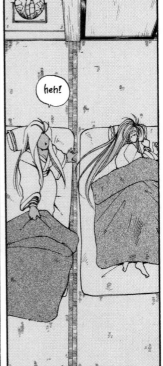

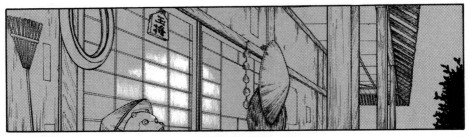

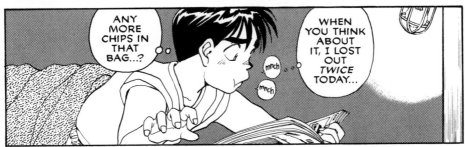

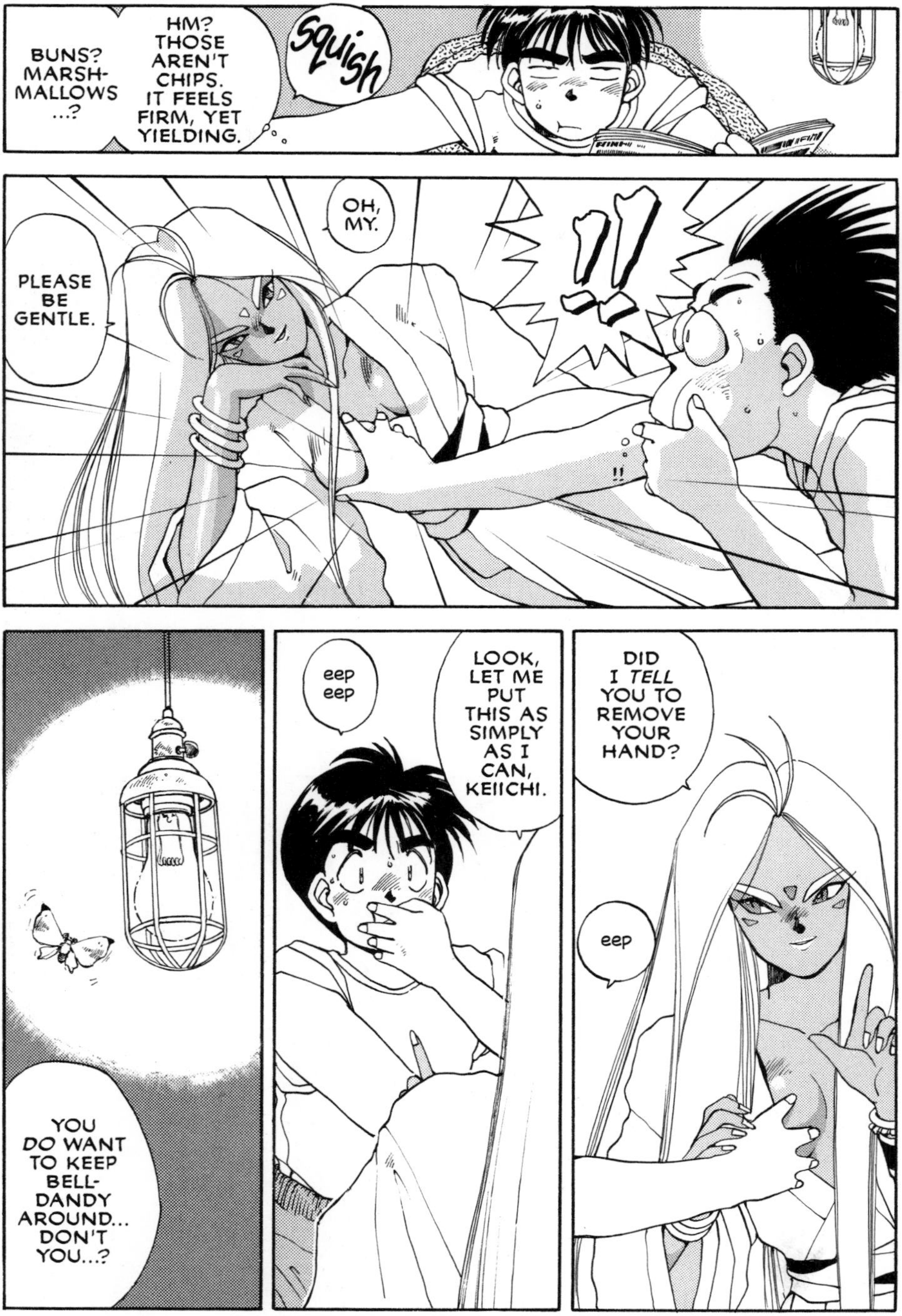
squish
HM? THOSE AREN'T CHIPS. IT FEELS FIRM, YET YIELDING.
BUNS? MARSH-MALLOWS ...?
!!
OH, MY.
PLEASE BE GENTLE.
!!
DID I *TELL* YOU TO REMOVE YOUR HAND?
eep
LOOK, LET ME PUT THIS AS SIMPLY AS I CAN, KEIICHI.
eep eep
YOU *DO* WANT TO KEEP BELL-DANDY AROUND... DON'T YOU...?

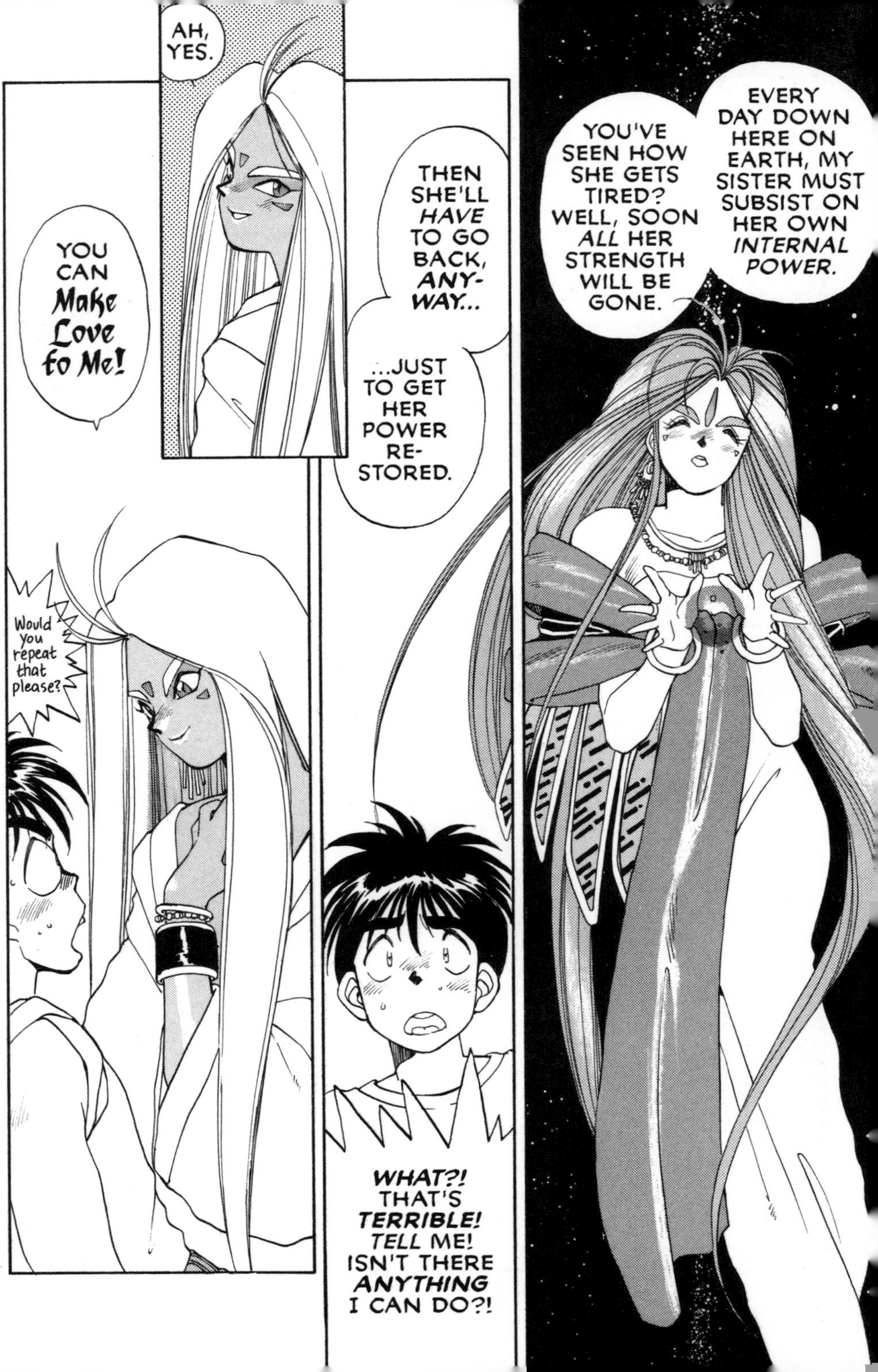
EVERY DAY DOWN HERE ON EARTH, MY SISTER MUST SUBSIST ON HER OWN *INTERNAL POWER.*
YOU'VE SEEN HOW SHE GETS TIRED? WELL, SOON *ALL* HER STRENGTH WILL BE GONE.
THEN SHE'LL *HAVE* TO GO BACK, *ANY-WAY...*
...JUST TO GET HER POWER RE-STORED.
WHAT?! THAT'S ***TERRIBLE!*** ***TELL*** ME! ISN'T THERE ***ANYTHING*** I CAN DO?!
AH, YES.
YOU CAN Make Love to Me!
Would you repeat that please?

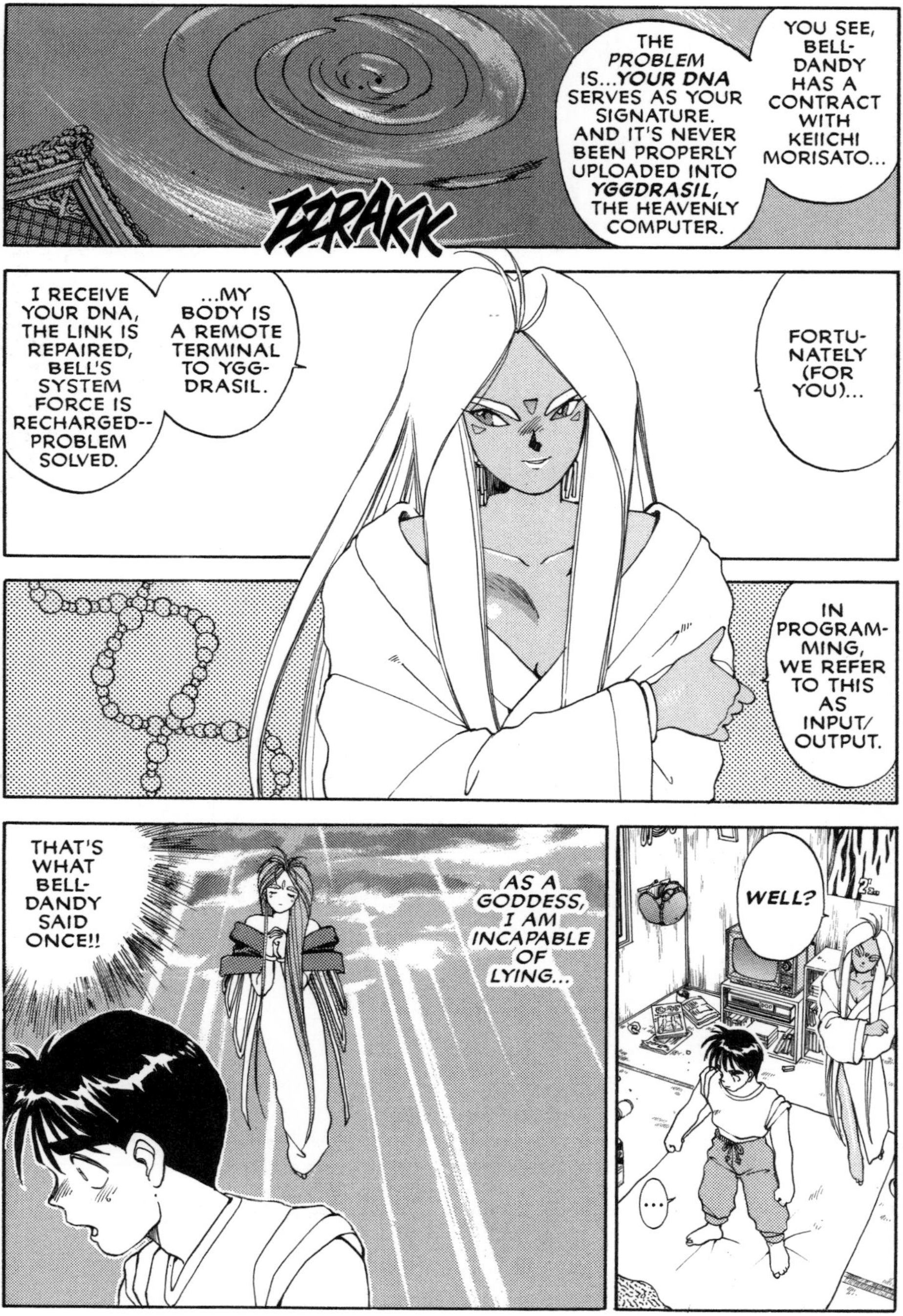
YOU SEE, BELL-DANDY HAS A CONTRACT WITH KEIICHI MORISATO...
THE *PROBLEM* IS...***YOUR DNA*** SERVES AS YOUR SIGNATURE. AND IT'S NEVER BEEN PROPERLY UPLOADED INTO ***YGGDRASIL,*** THE HEAVENLY COMPUTER.
ZZRAKK
FORTU-NATELY (FOR YOU)...
...MY BODY IS A REMOTE TERMINAL TO YGG-DRASIL.
I RECEIVE YOUR DNA, THE LINK IS REPAIRED, BELL'S SYSTEM FORCE IS RECHARGED--PROBLEM SOLVED.
IN PROGRAM-MING, WE REFER TO THIS AS INPUT/OUTPUT.
WELL?
...
AS A GODDESS, I AM INCAPABLE OF LYING...
THAT'S WHAT BELL-DANDY SAID ONCE!!

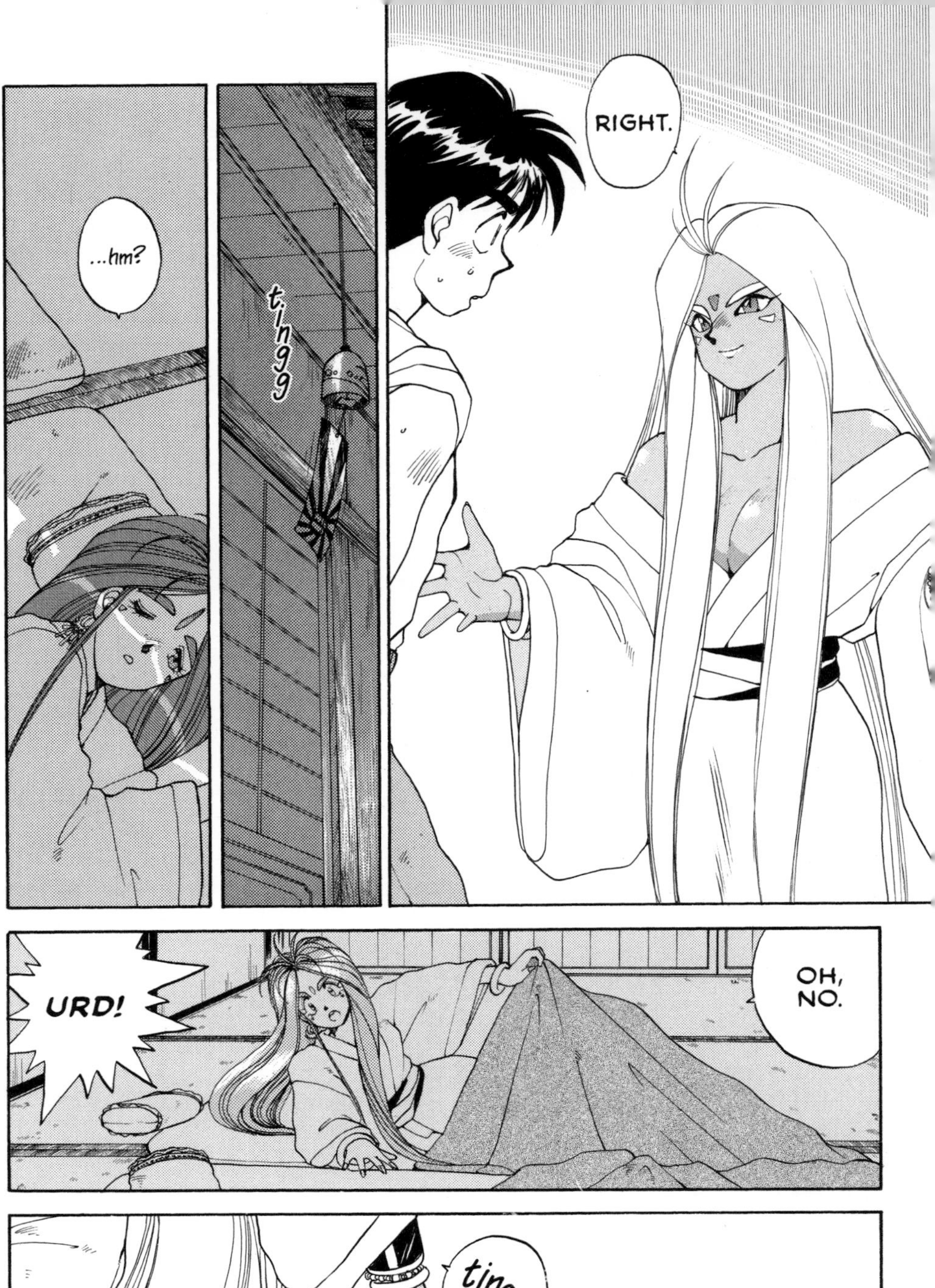
RIGHT.
tingg
...hm?
OH, NO.
URD!
tingg

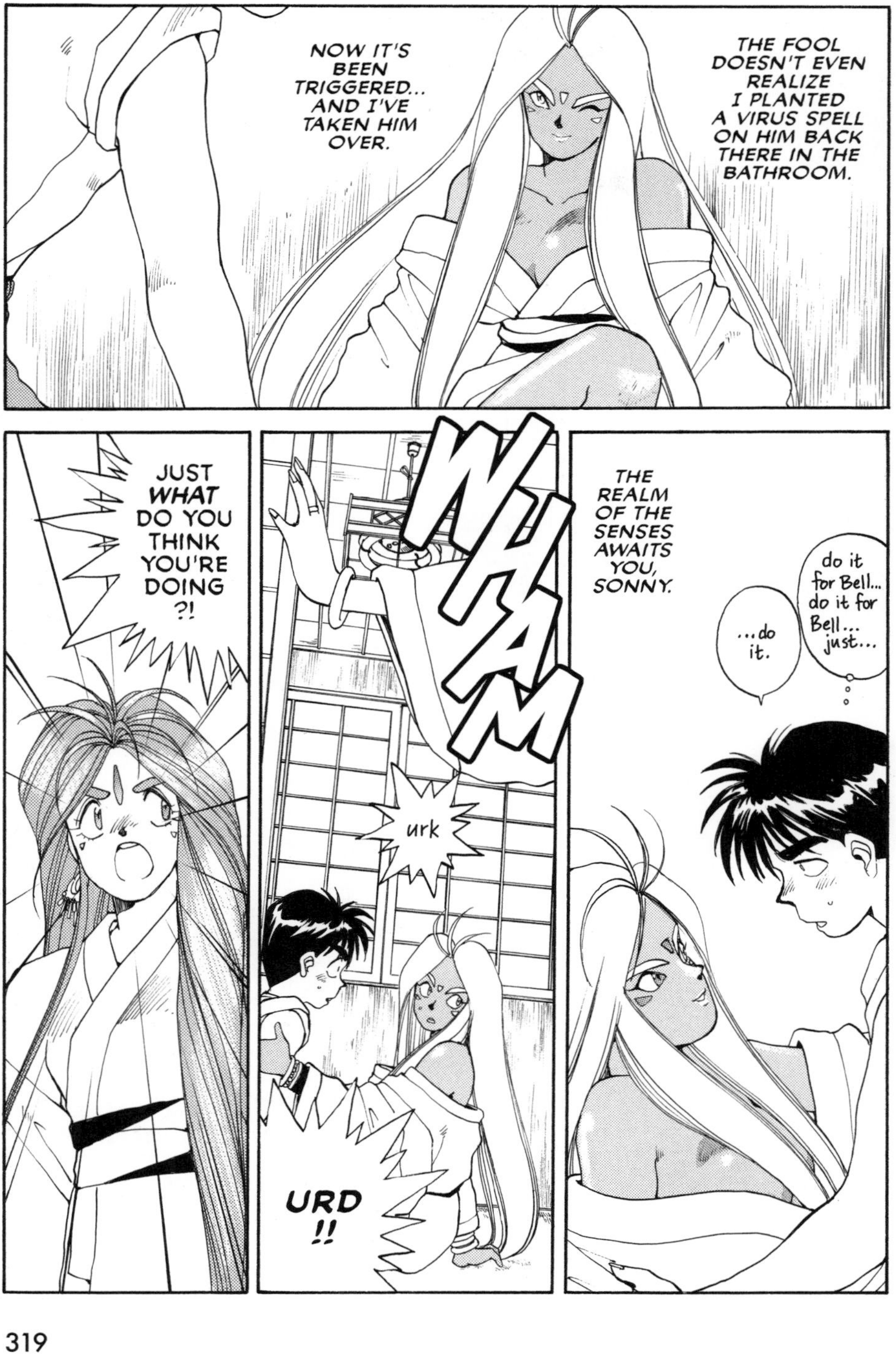
THE FOOL DOESN'T EVEN REALIZE I PLANTED A VIRUS SPELL ON HIM BACK THERE IN THE BATHROOM.
NOW IT'S BEEN TRIGGERED... AND I'VE TAKEN HIM OVER.
THE REALM OF THE SENSES AWAITS YOU, SONNY.
do it for Bell... do it for Bell... just...
...do it.
WHAM
urk
URD !!
JUST WHAT DO YOU THINK YOU'RE DOING ?!

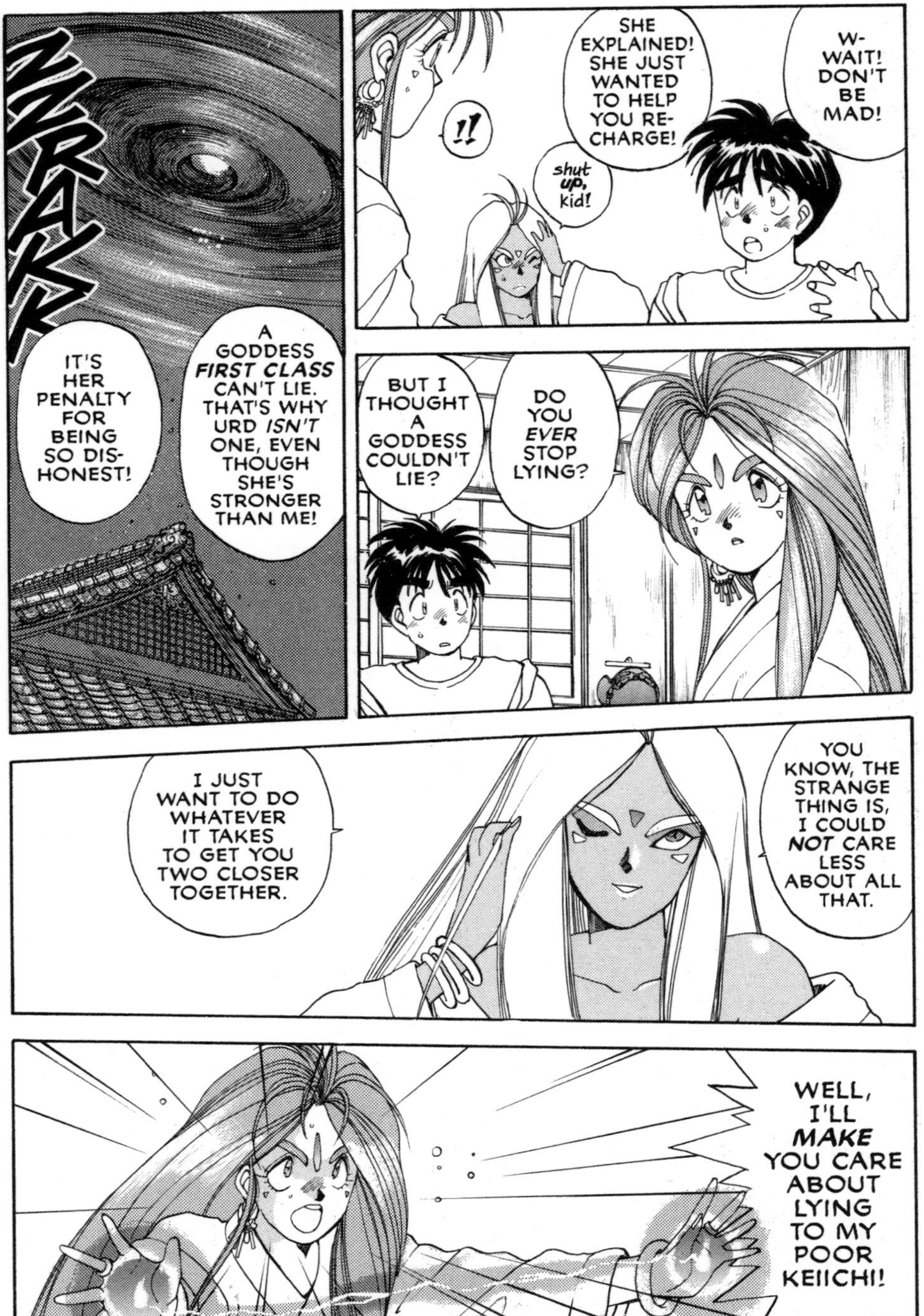
W-WAIT! DON'T BE MAD!
SHE EXPLAINED! SHE JUST WANTED TO HELP YOU RE-CHARGE!
!!
shut up, kid!
DO YOU EVER STOP LYING?
BUT I THOUGHT A GODDESS COULDN'T LIE?
ZZRAKK
A GODDESS FIRST CLASS CAN'T LIE. THAT'S WHY URD ISN'T ONE, EVEN THOUGH SHE'S STRONGER THAN ME!
IT'S HER PENALTY FOR BEING SO DISHONEST!
YOU KNOW, THE STRANGE THING IS, I COULD NOT CARE LESS ABOUT ALL THAT.
I JUST WANT TO DO WHATEVER IT TAKES TO GET YOU TWO CLOSER TOGETHER.
WELL, I'LL MAKE YOU CARE ABOUT LYING TO MY POOR KEIICHI!

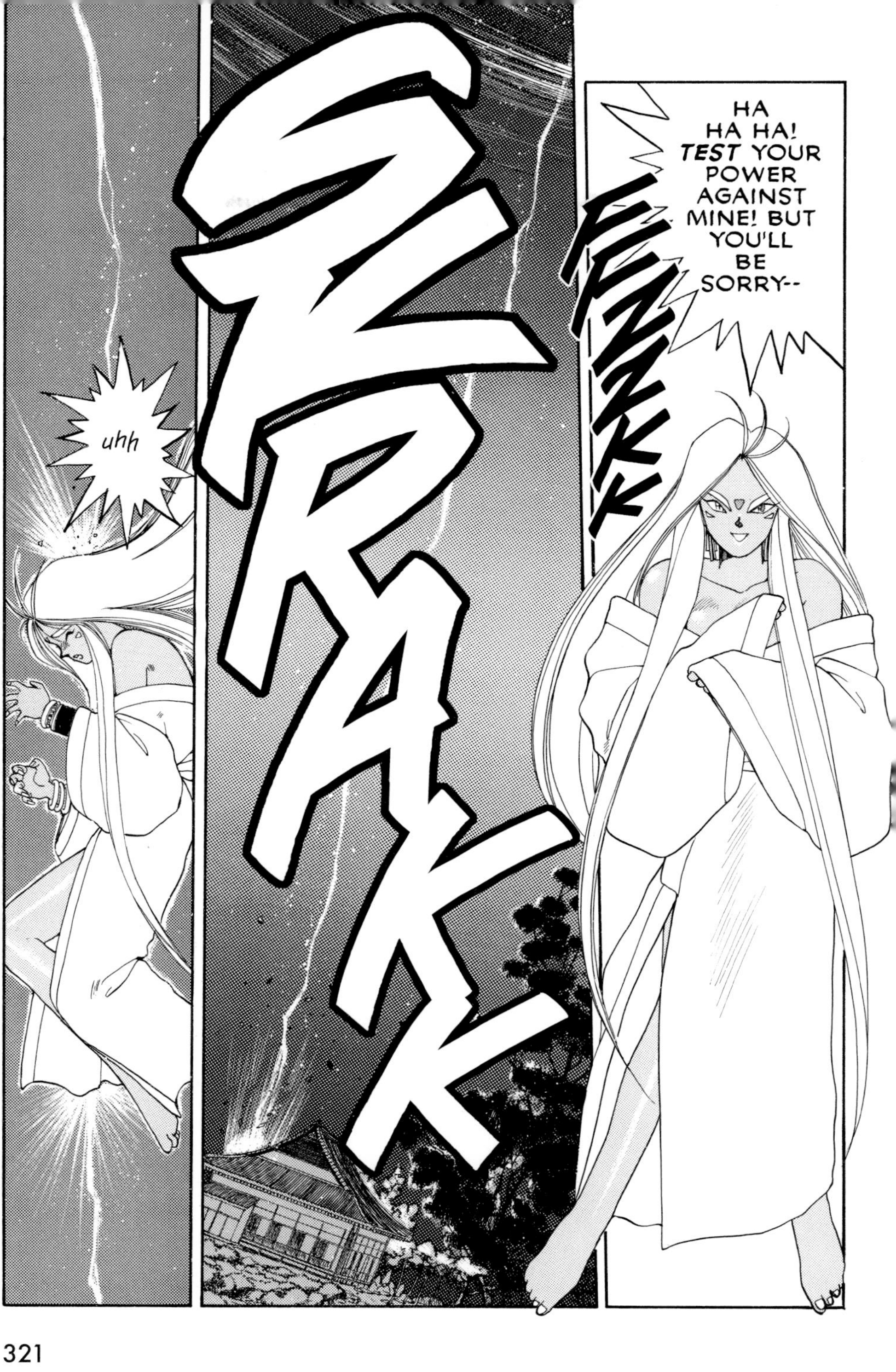
HA HA HA! *TEST* YOUR POWER AGAINST MINE! BUT YOU'LL BE SORRY--
ZRAKKK
uhh

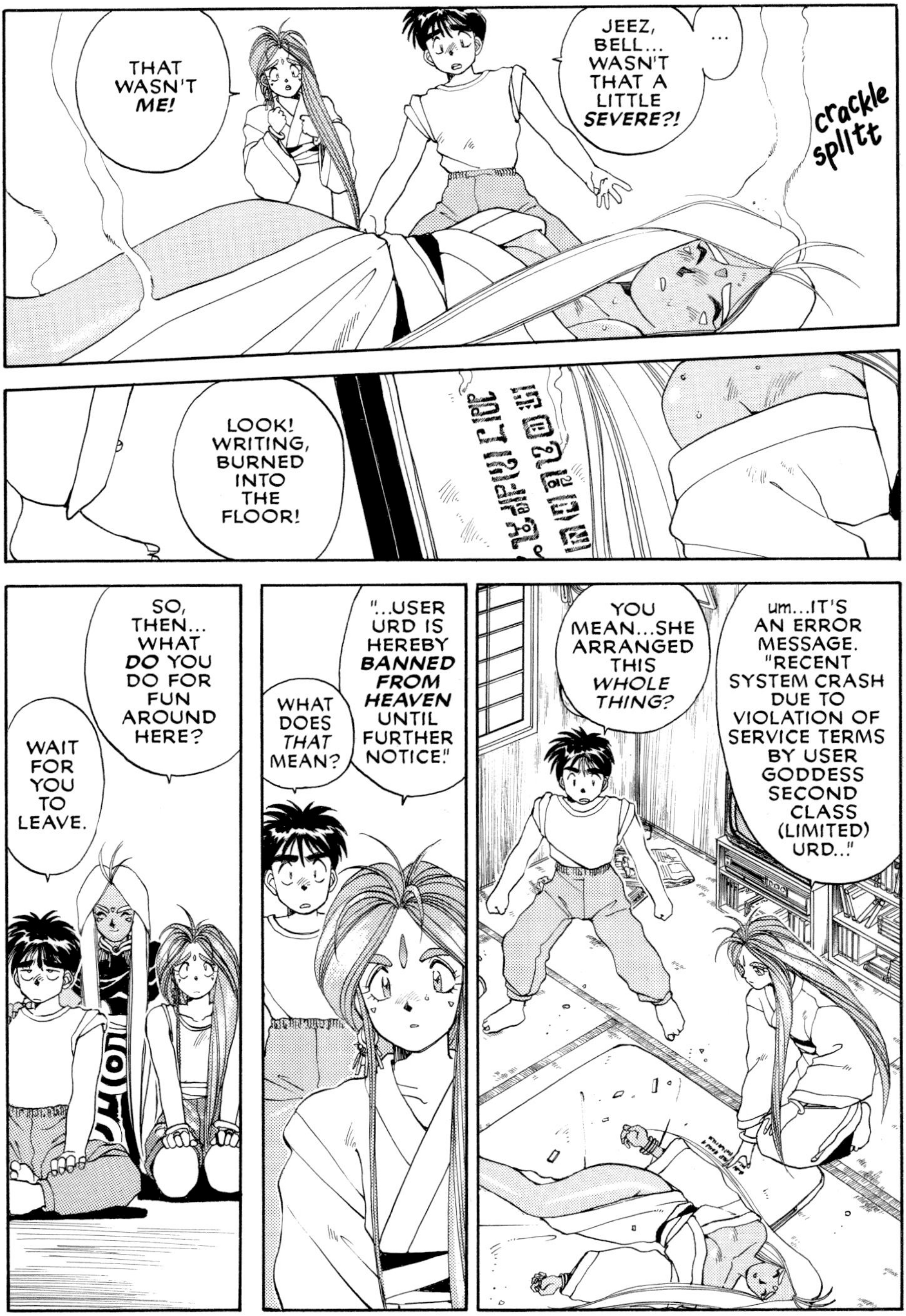
...
JEEZ, BELL... WASN'T THAT A LITTLE SEVERE?!
crackle spl/tt
THAT WASN'T ME!
LOOK! WRITING, BURNED INTO THE FLOOR!
um...IT'S AN ERROR MESSAGE. "RECENT SYSTEM CRASH DUE TO VIOLATION OF SERVICE TERMS BY USER GODDESS SECOND CLASS (LIMITED) URD..."
YOU MEAN...SHE ARRANGED THIS WHOLE THING?
"...USER URD IS HEREBY BANNED FROM HEAVEN UNTIL FURTHER NOTICE."
WHAT DOES THAT MEAN?
SO, THEN... WHAT DO YOU DO FOR FUN AROUND HERE?
WAIT FOR YOU TO LEAVE.

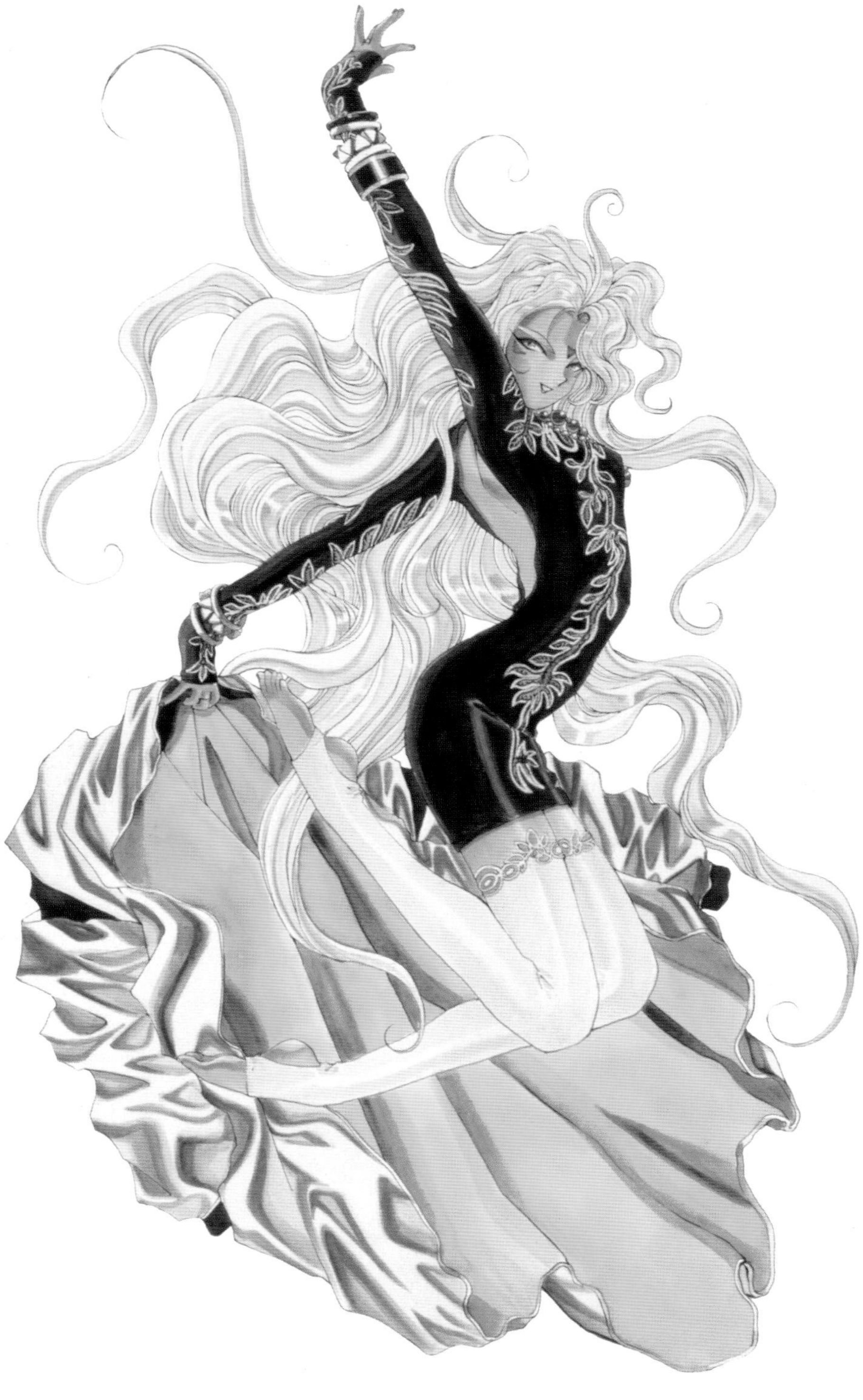

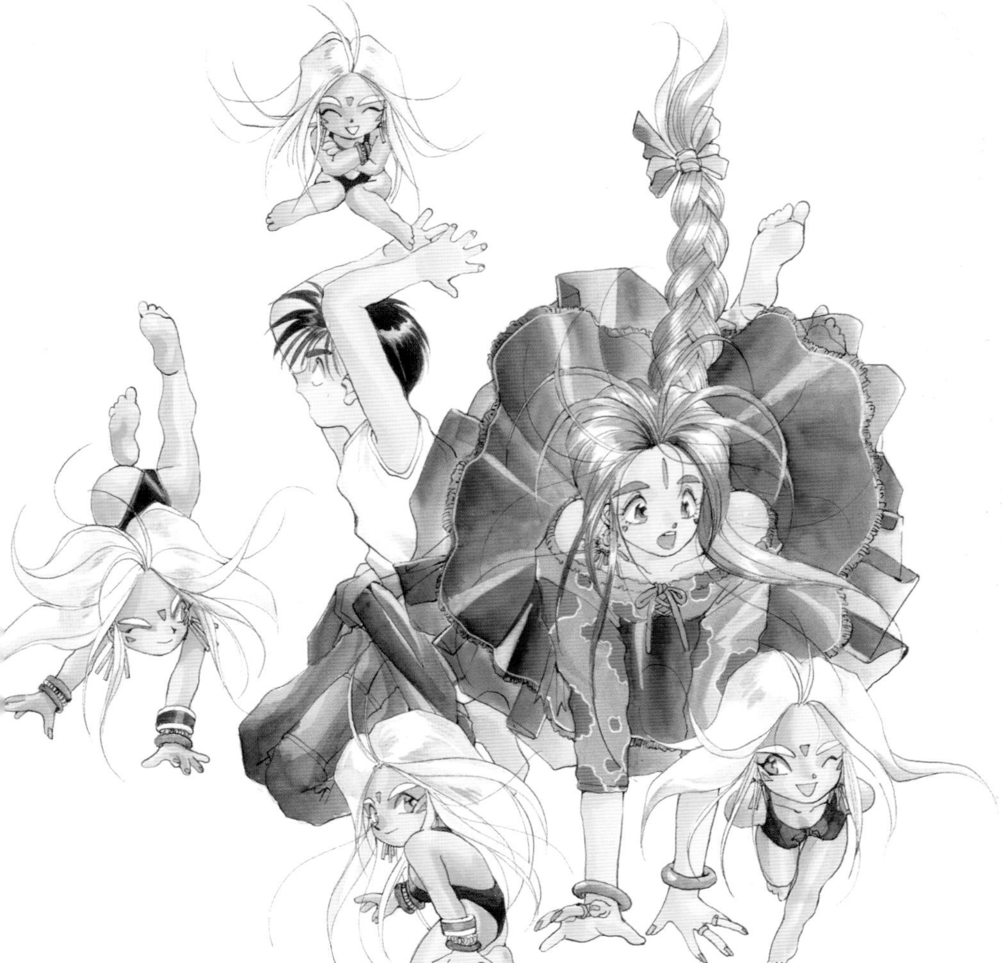

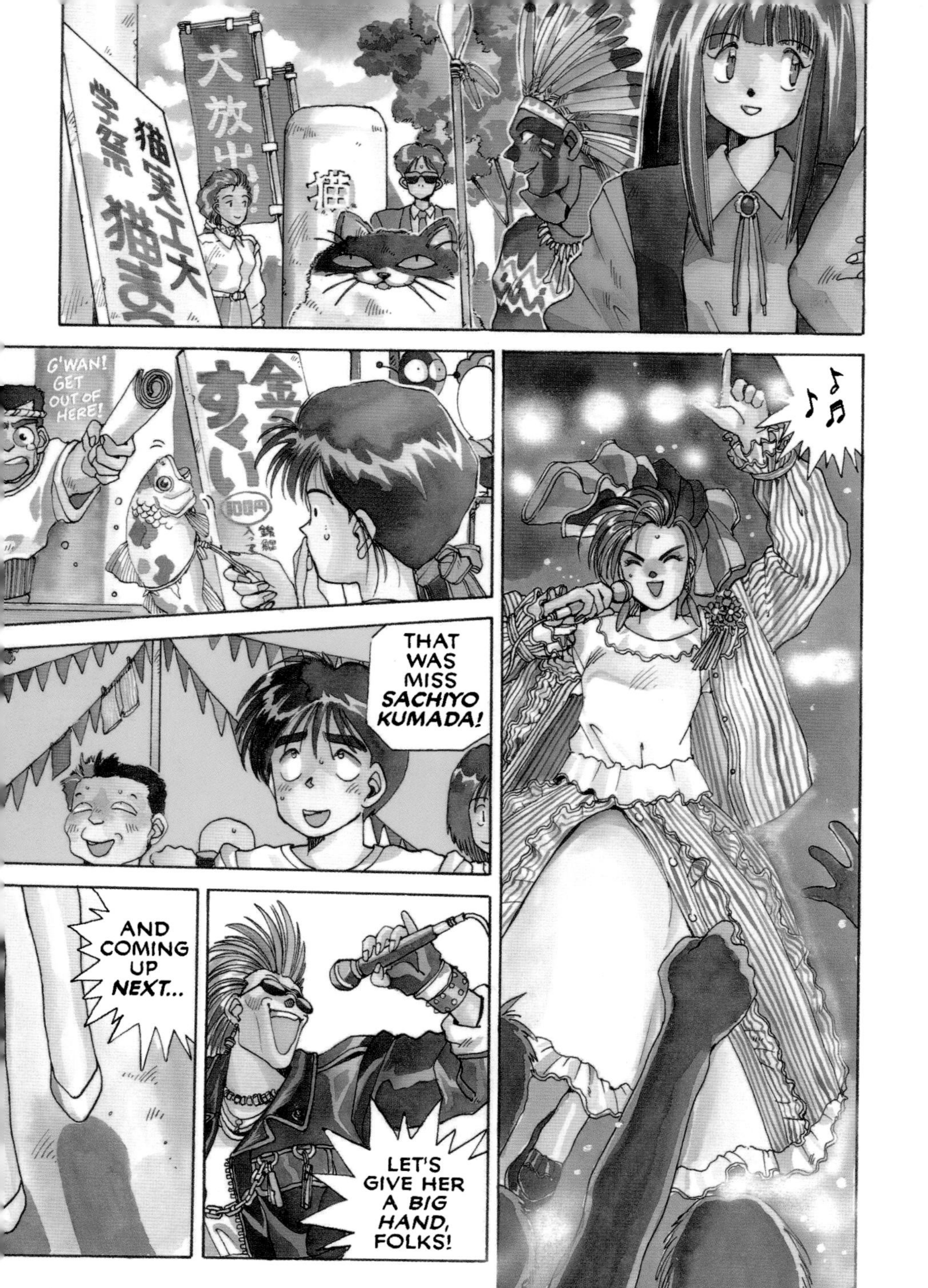
大放出!!
猫実工大
学祭
猫
金魚すくい!
100円
G'WAN! GET OUT OF HERE!
THAT WAS MISS *SACHIYO KUMADA!*
LET'S GIVE HER A *BIG HAND,* FOLKS!
AND COMING UP *NEXT...*

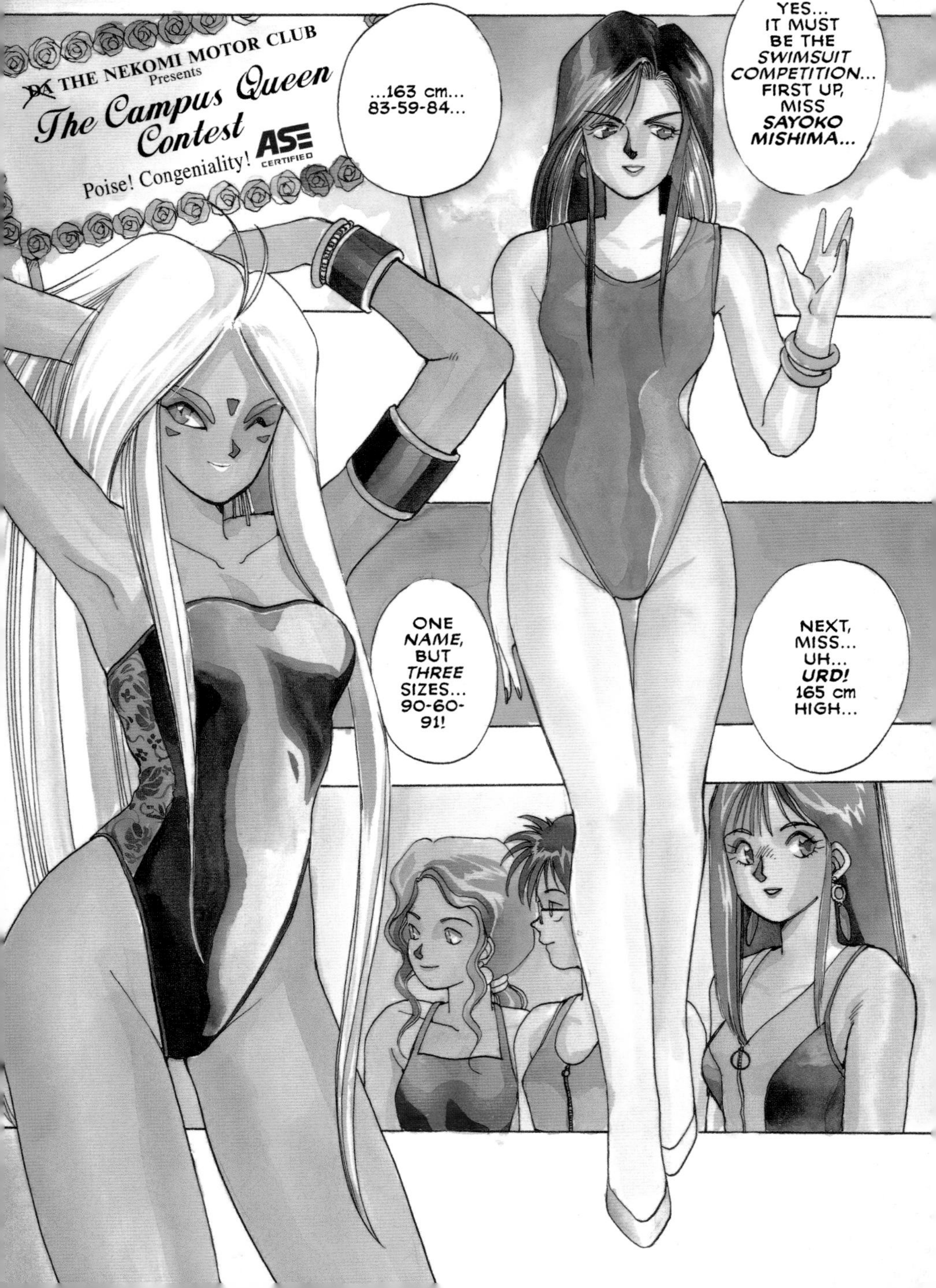

YES... IT MUST BE THE SWIMSUIT COMPETITION... FIRST UP, MISS SAYOKO MISHIMA...
...163 cm... 83-59-84...
DA THE NEKOMI MOTOR CLUB Presents
The Campus Queen Contest
ASE CERTIFIED
Poise! Congeniality!
NEXT, MISS... UH... URD! 165 cm HIGH...
ONE NAME, BUT THREE SIZES... 90-60-91!

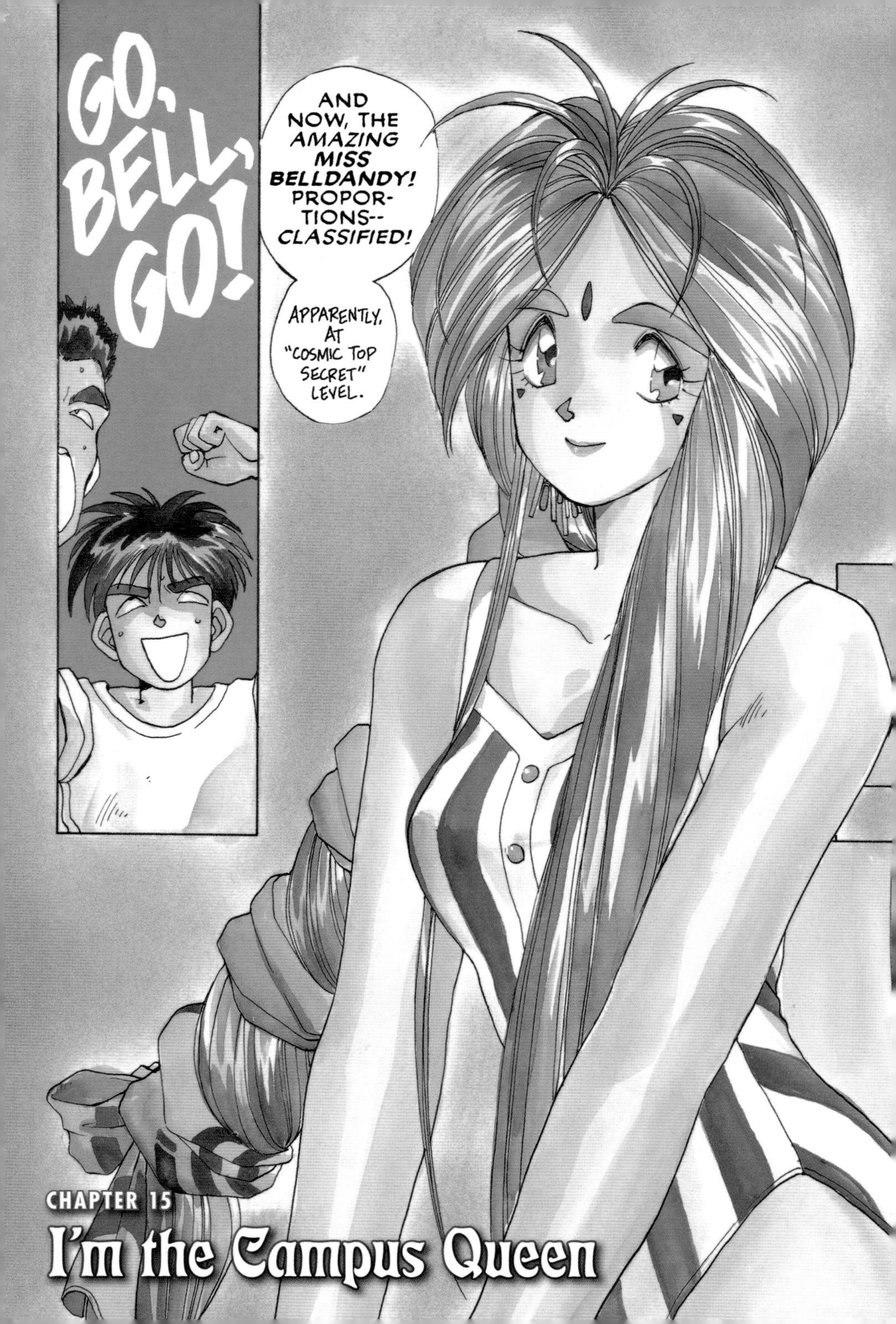
AND NOW, THE AMAZING MISS BELLDANDY! PROPORTIONS-- CLASSIFIED!
APPARENTLY, AT "COSMIC TOP SECRET" LEVEL.
GO, BELL, GO!

CHAPTER 15

I'm the Campus Queen

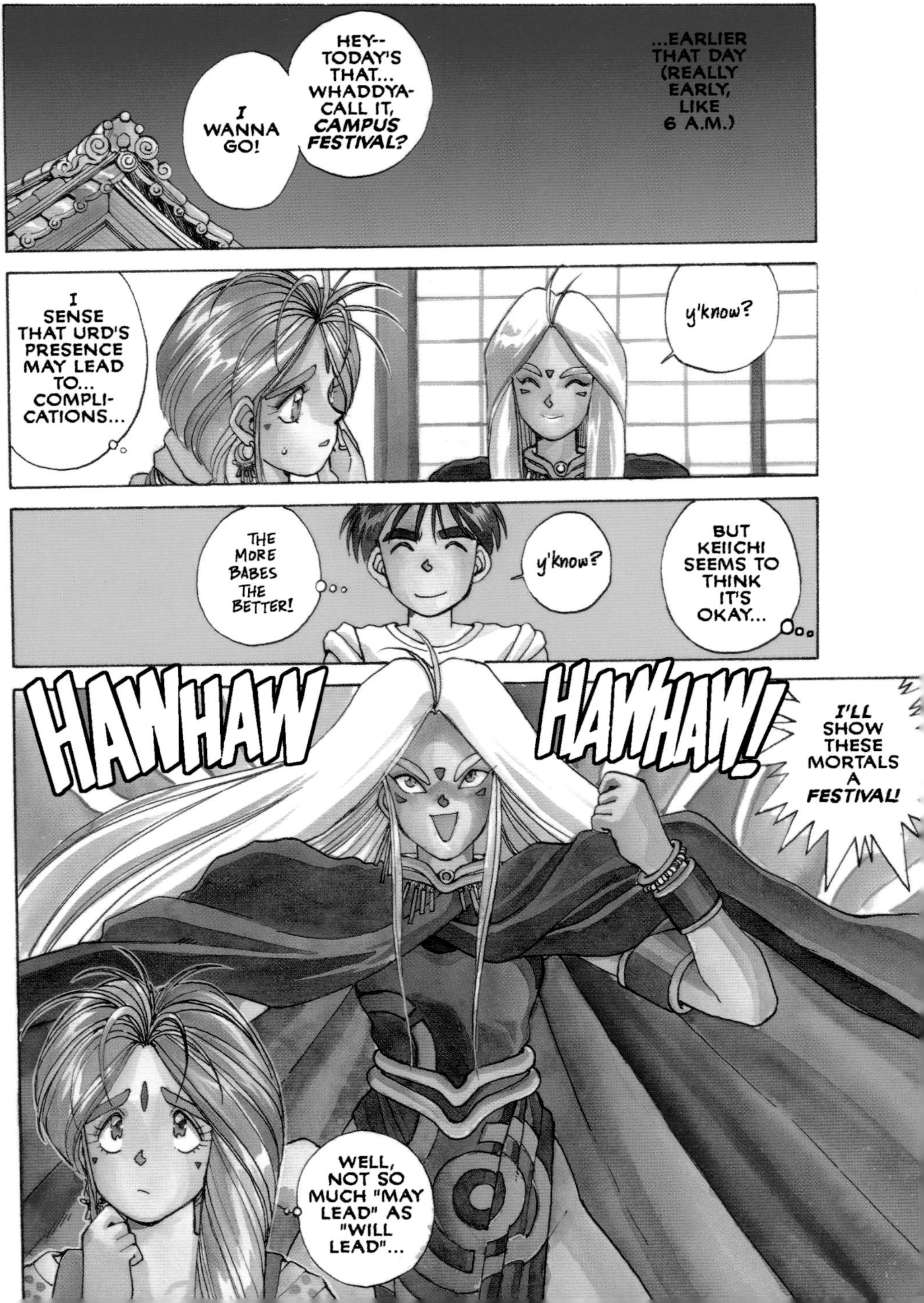

...EARLIER THAT DAY (REALLY EARLY, LIKE 6 A.M.)
HEY-- TODAY'S THAT... WHADDYA-CALL IT, CAMPUS FESTIVAL?
I WANNA GO!
y'know?
I SENSE THAT URD'S PRESENCE MAY LEAD TO... COMPLICATIONS...
BUT KEIICHI SEEMS TO THINK IT'S OKAY...
y'know?
THE MORE BABES THE BETTER!
I'LL SHOW THESE MORTALS A FESTIVAL!
HAWHAW!
HAWHAW
WELL, NOT SO MUCH "MAY LEAD" AS "WILL LEAD"...

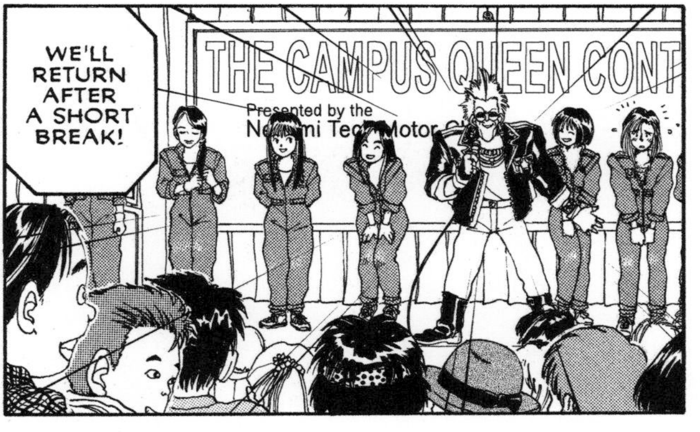
WE'LL RETURN AFTER A SHORT BREAK!
THE CAMPUS QUEEN CONT
Presented by the

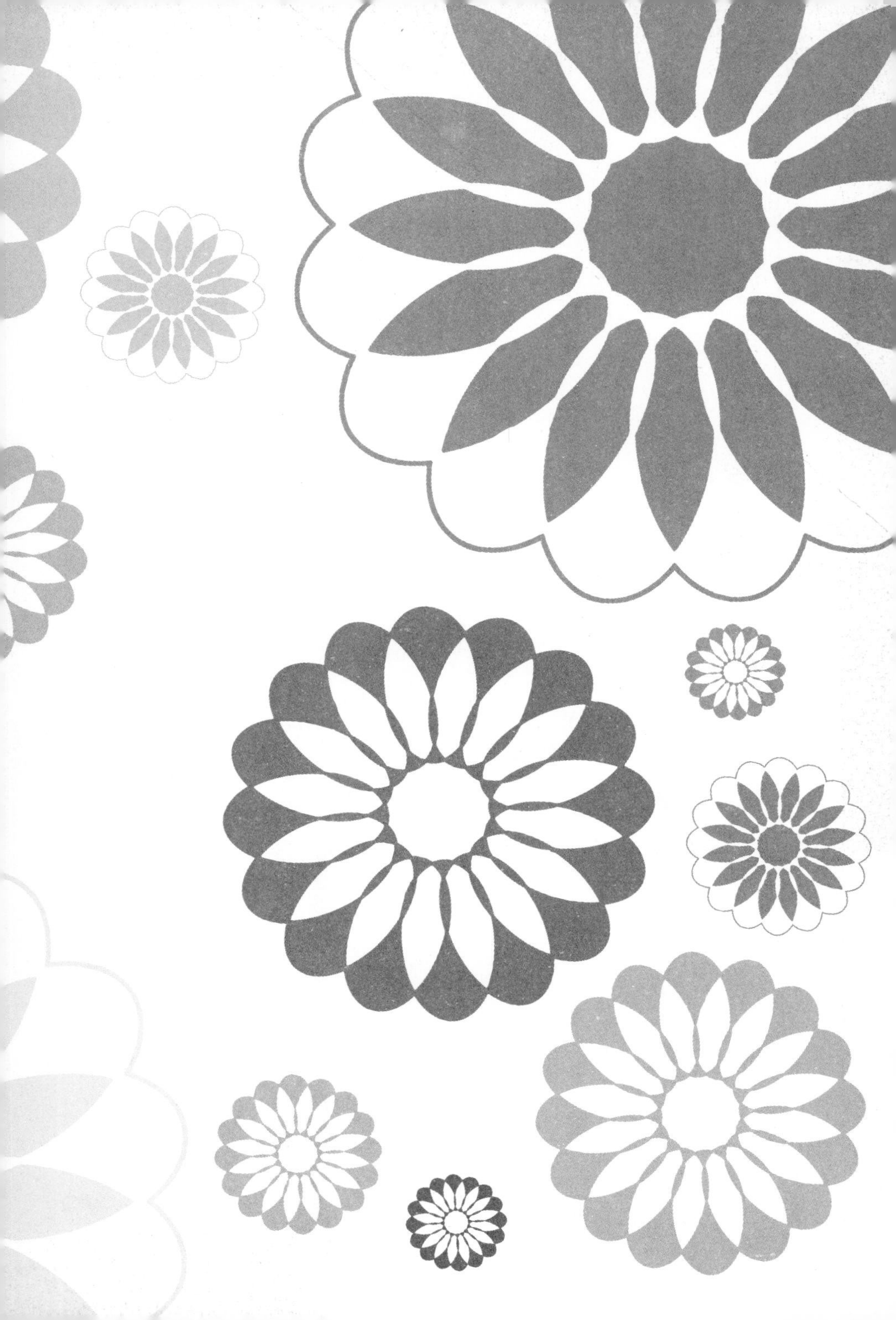

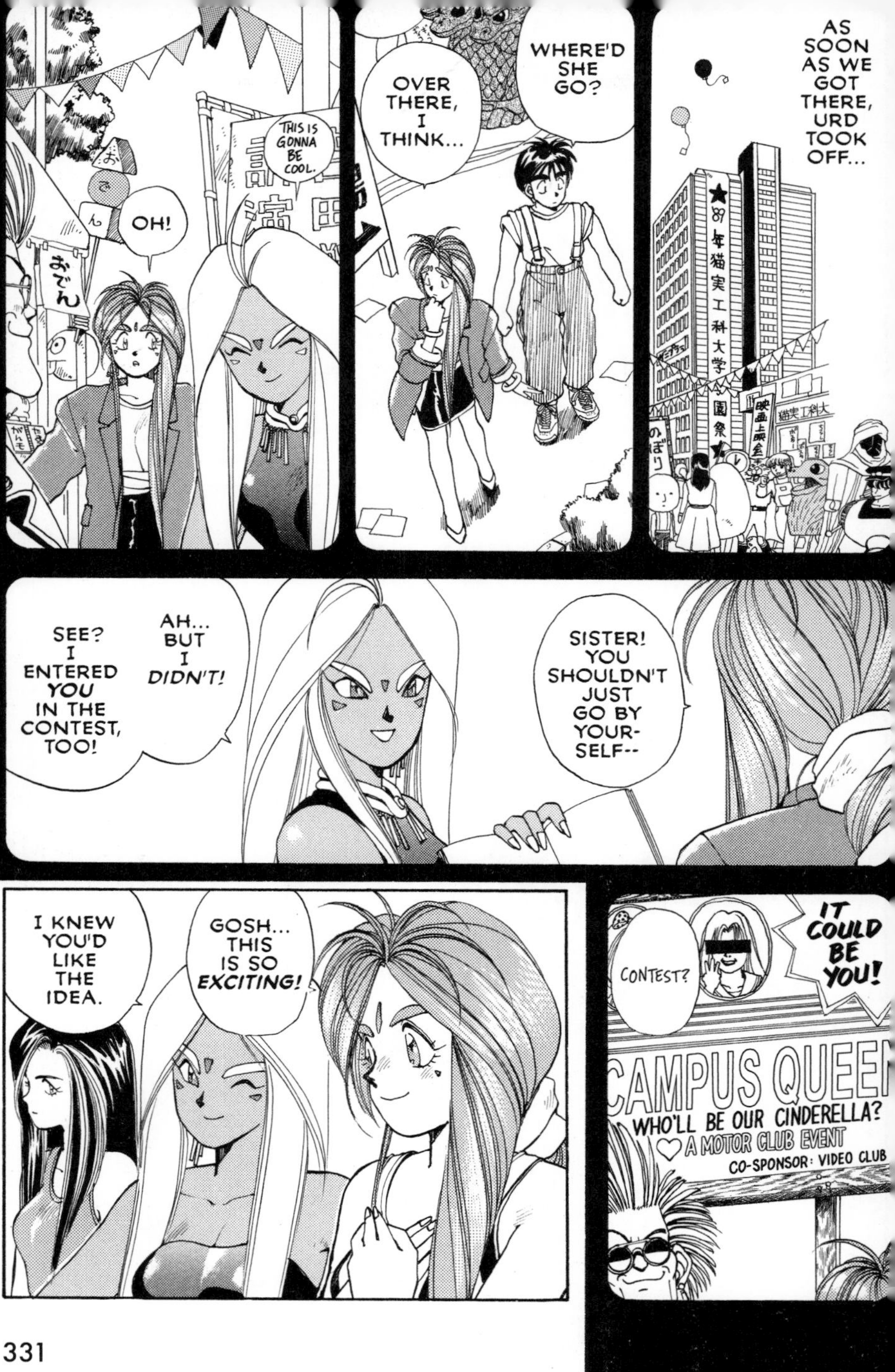
AS SOON AS WE GOT THERE, URD TOOK OFF...
映画上映会
猫実工科大
WHERE'D SHE GO?
OVER THERE, I THINK...
THIS IS GONNA BE COOL.
OH!
おでん
SISTER! YOU SHOULDN'T JUST GO BY YOURSELF--
AH... BUT I *DIDN'T!*
SEE? I ENTERED *YOU* IN THE CONTEST, TOO!
IT COULD BE YOU!
CONTEST?
CAMPUS QUEE
WHO'LL BE OUR CINDERELLA?
A MOTOR CLUB EVENT
CO-SPONSOR: VIDEO CLUB
GOSH... THIS IS SO *EXCITING!*
I KNEW YOU'D LIKE THE IDEA.

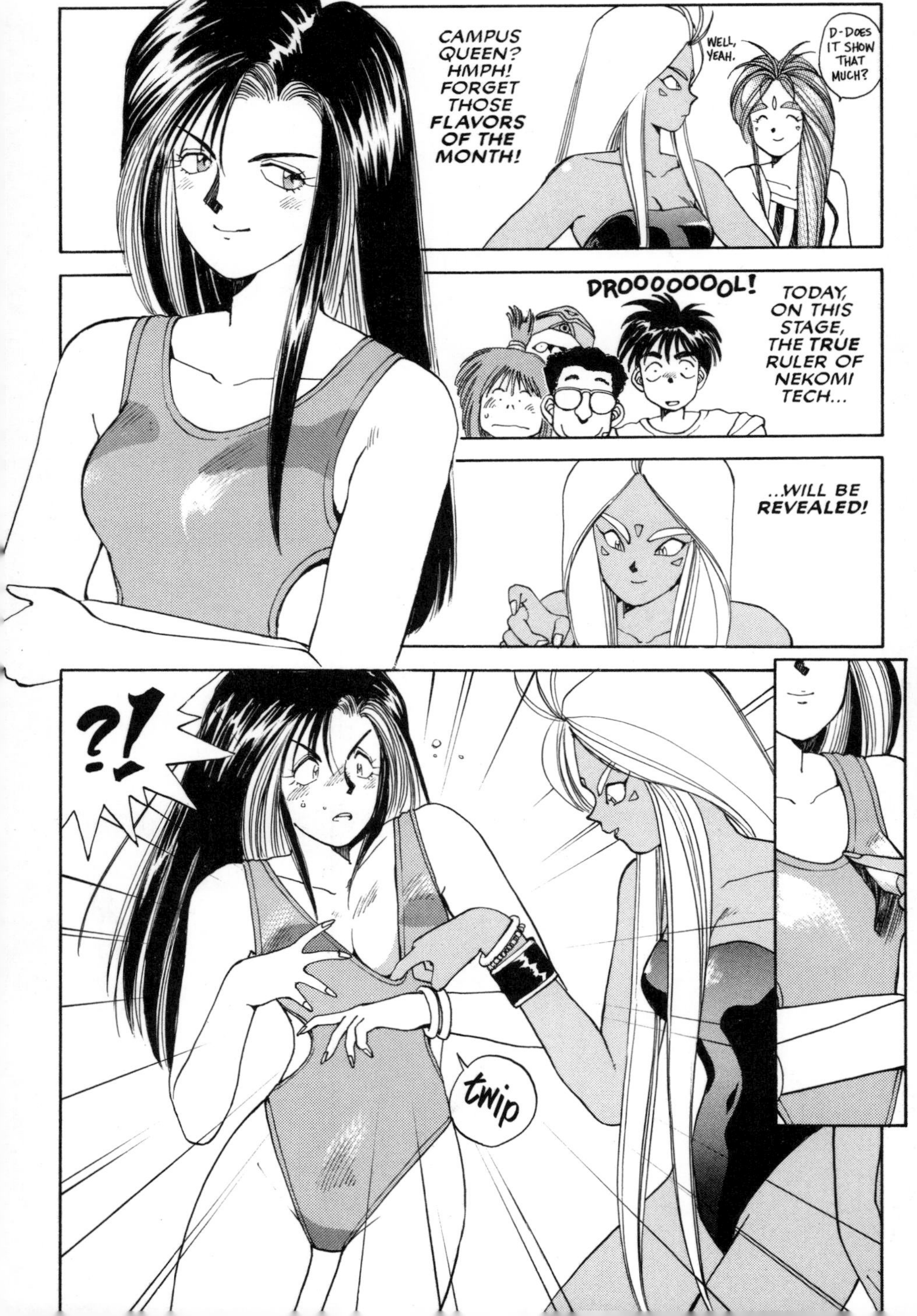
D-DOES IT SHOW THAT MUCH?
WELL, YEAH.
CAMPUS QUEEN? HMPH! FORGET THOSE FLAVORS OF THE MONTH!
TODAY, ON THIS STAGE, THE TRUE RULER OF NEKOMI TECH...
DROOOOOOOL!
...WILL BE REVEALED!
?!
twip

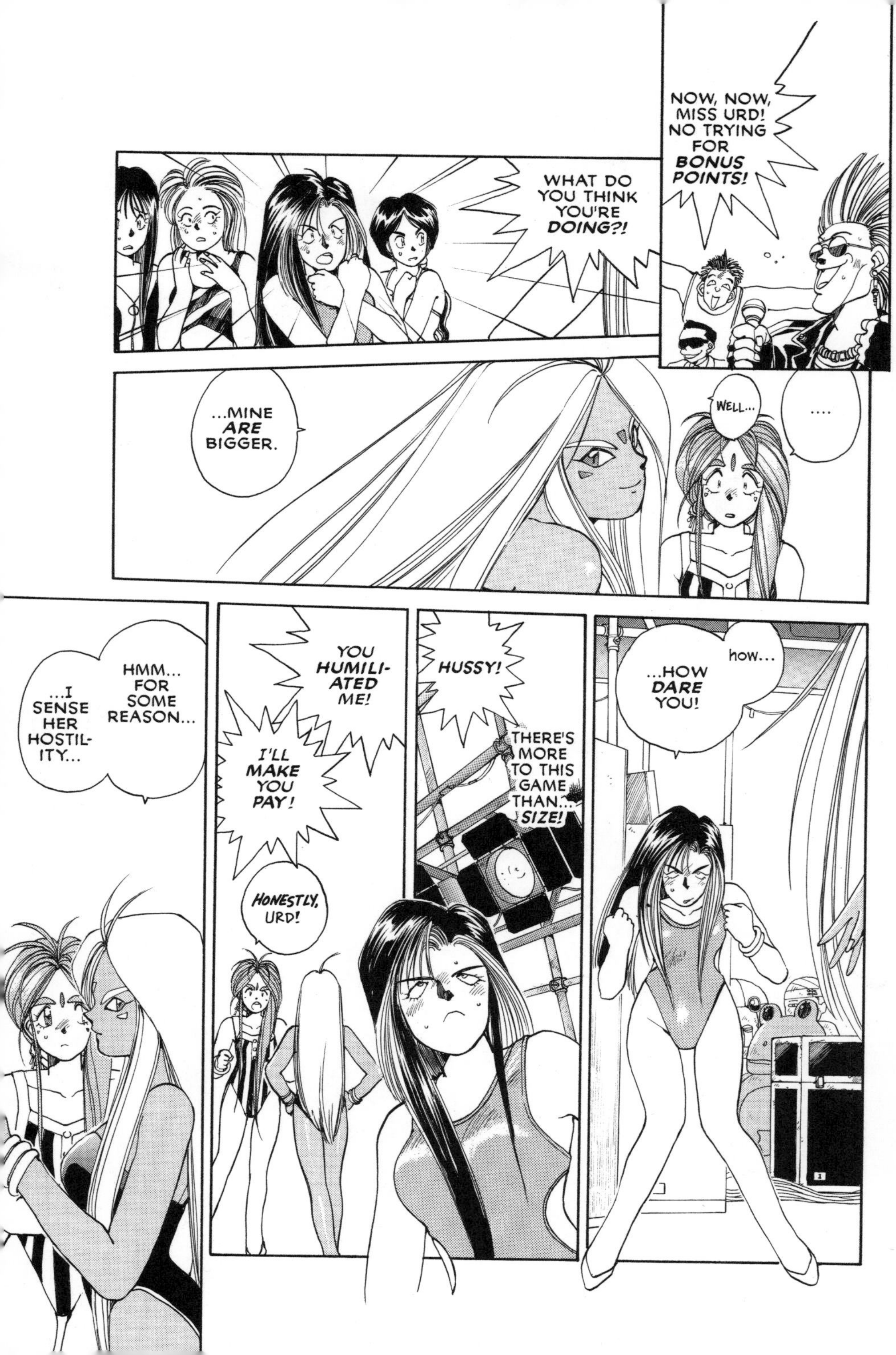
NOW, NOW, MISS URD! NO TRYING FOR BONUS POINTS!
WHAT DO YOU THINK YOU'RE DOING?!
....
WELL...
...MINE ARE BIGGER.
how...
...HOW DARE YOU!
HUSSY!
THERE'S MORE TO THIS GAME THAN... SIZE!
YOU HUMILI- ATED ME!
I'LL MAKE YOU PAY!
HONESTLY, URD!
HMM... FOR SOME REASON...
...I SENSE HER HOSTIL- ITY...

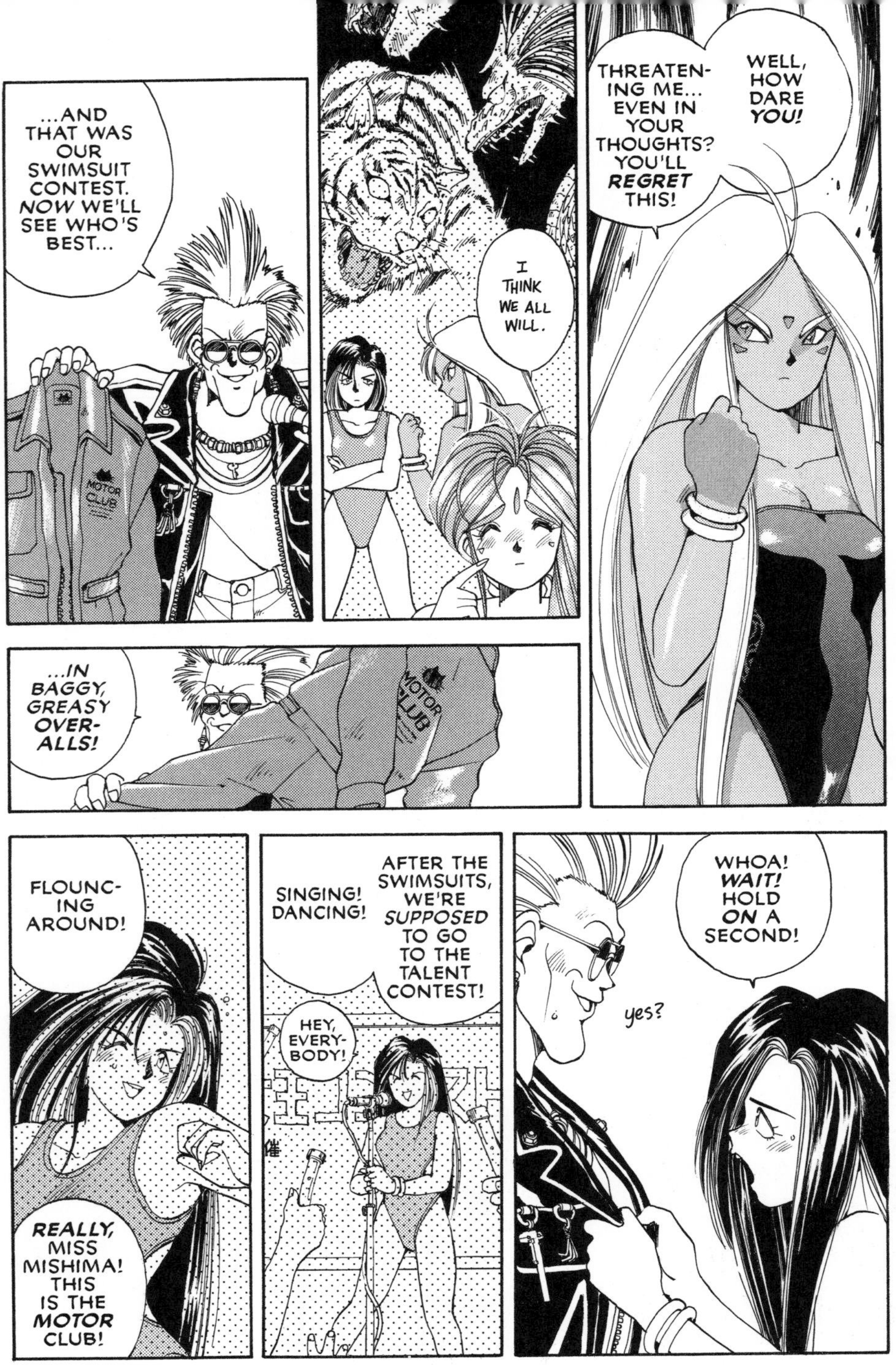
WELL, HOW DARE YOU!
THREATENING ME... EVEN IN YOUR THOUGHTS? YOU'LL REGRET THIS!
I THINK WE ALL WILL.
...AND THAT WAS OUR SWIMSUIT CONTEST. NOW WE'LL SEE WHO'S BEST...
...IN BAGGY, GREASY OVERALLS!
WHOA! WAIT! HOLD ON A SECOND!
yes?
AFTER THE SWIMSUITS, WE'RE SUPPOSED TO GO TO THE TALENT CONTEST!
SINGING! DANCING!
HEY, EVERYBODY!
FLOUNCING AROUND!
REALLY, MISS MISHIMA! THIS IS THE MOTOR CLUB!

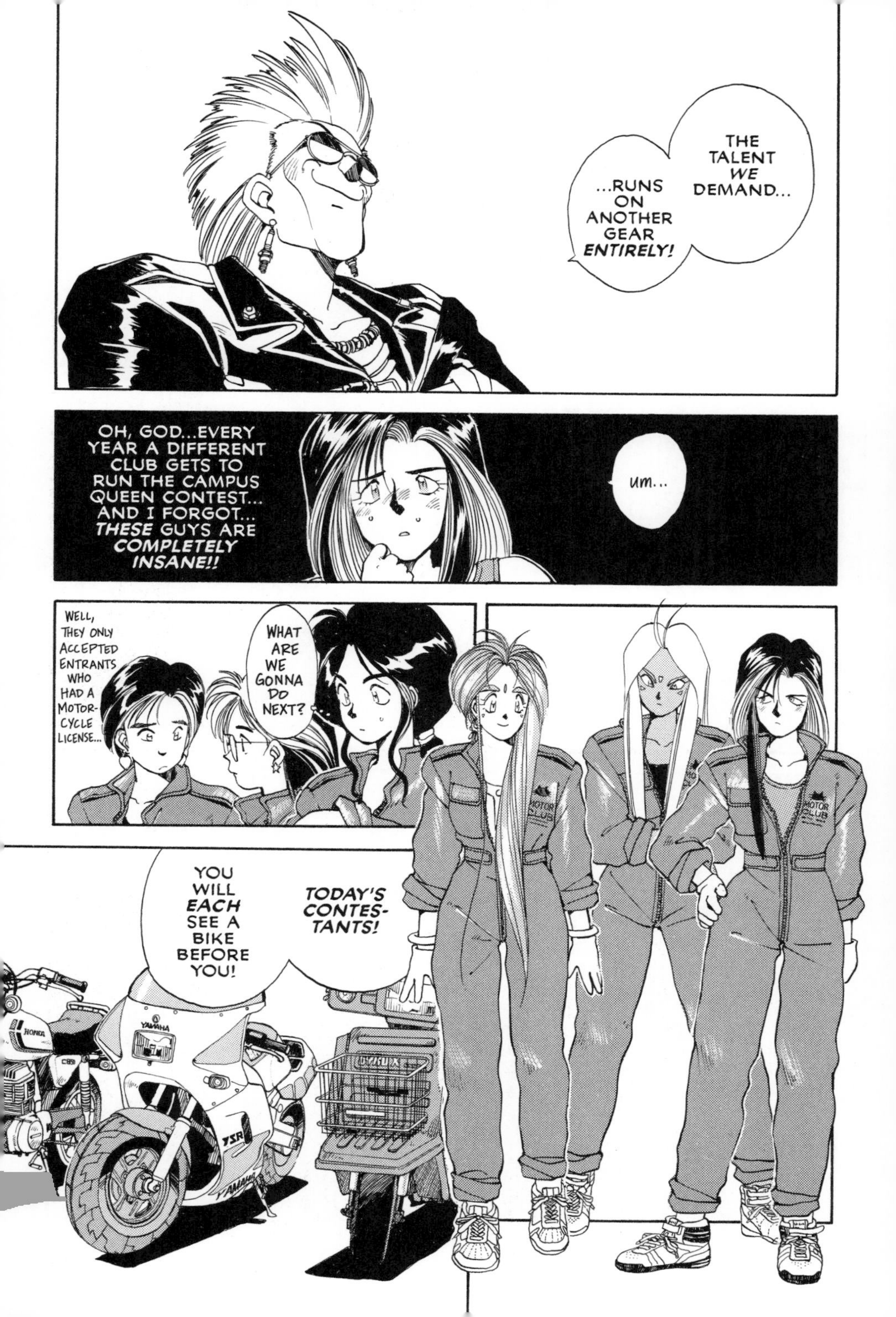
THE TALENT *WE* DEMAND...
...RUNS ON ANOTHER GEAR *ENTIRELY!*
um...
OH, GOD...EVERY YEAR A DIFFERENT CLUB GETS TO RUN THE CAMPUS QUEEN CONTEST... AND I FORGOT... *THESE* GUYS ARE *COMPLETELY INSANE!!*
WHAT ARE WE GONNA DO NEXT?
WELL, THEY ONLY ACCEPTED ENTRANTS WHO HAD A MOTOR-CYCLE LICENSE...
TODAY'S CONTES-TANTS!
YOU WILL *EACH* SEE A BIKE BEFORE YOU!

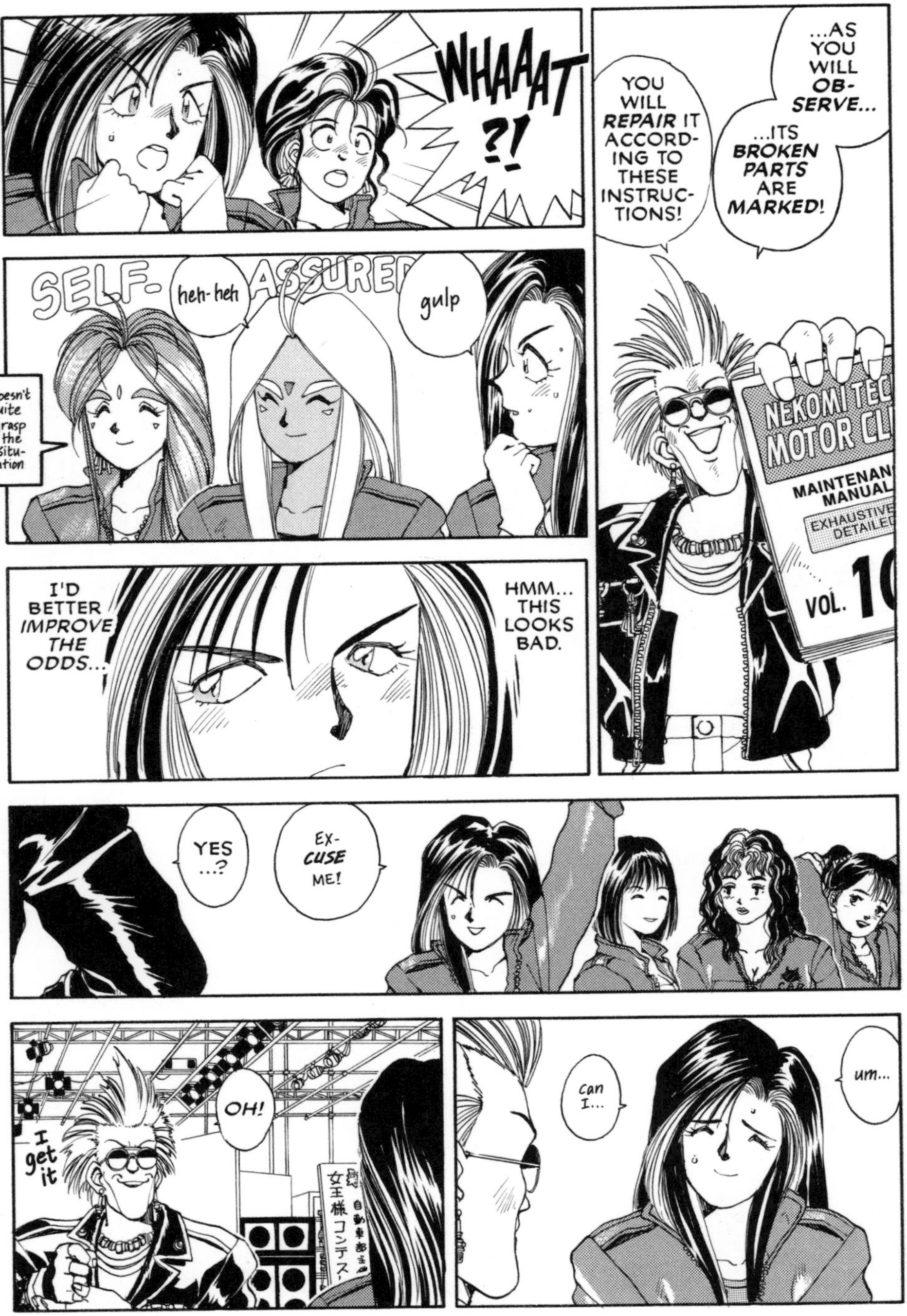
...AS YOU WILL OBSERVE...
...ITS BROKEN PARTS ARE MARKED!
YOU WILL REPAIR IT ACCORDING TO THESE INSTRUCTIONS!
NEKOMI TEC
MOTOR CL
MAINTENAN
MANUAL
EXHAUSTIVE
DETAILED
VOL. 10
WHAAAT ?!
SELF-ASSURED
gulp
heh-heh
Doesn't quite grasp the situation
HMM... THIS LOOKS BAD.
I'D BETTER IMPROVE THE ODDS...
EX-CUSE ME!
YES ...?
um...
Can I...
OH!
I get it

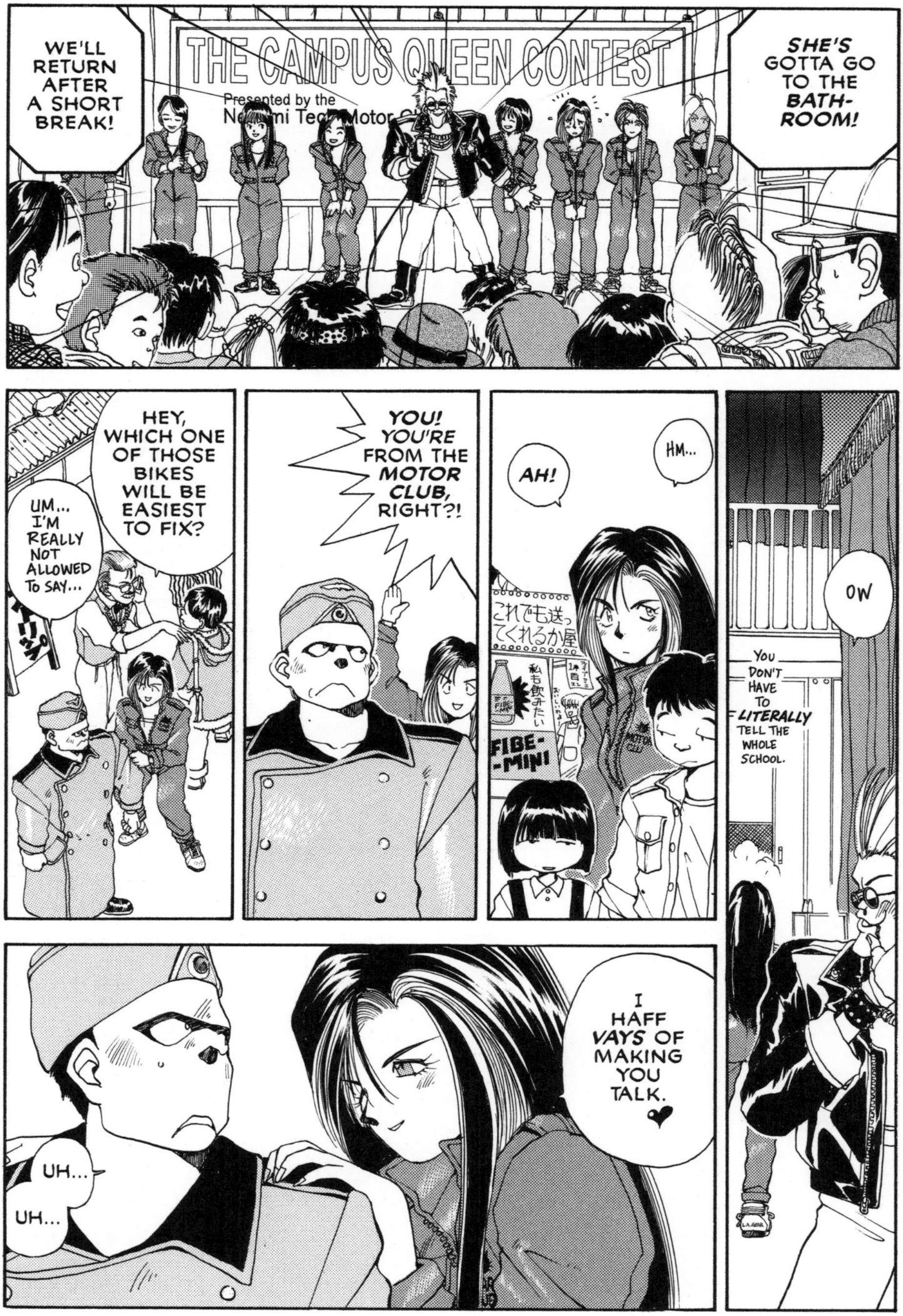
SHE'S GOTTA GO TO THE BATH-ROOM!
THE CAMPUS QUEEN CONTEST
Presented by the
WE'LL RETURN AFTER A SHORT BREAK!
OW
YOU DON'T HAVE TO LITERALLY TELL THE WHOLE SCHOOL.
HM...
AH!
これでも送ってくれるか屋
私も飲みたい
FIBE-MINI
YOU! YOU'RE FROM THE MOTOR CLUB, RIGHT?!
HEY, WHICH ONE OF THOSE BIKES WILL BE EASIEST TO FIX?
UM... I'M REALLY NOT ALLOWED TO SAY...
I HAFF VAYS OF MAKING YOU TALK. ♥
UH...
UH...

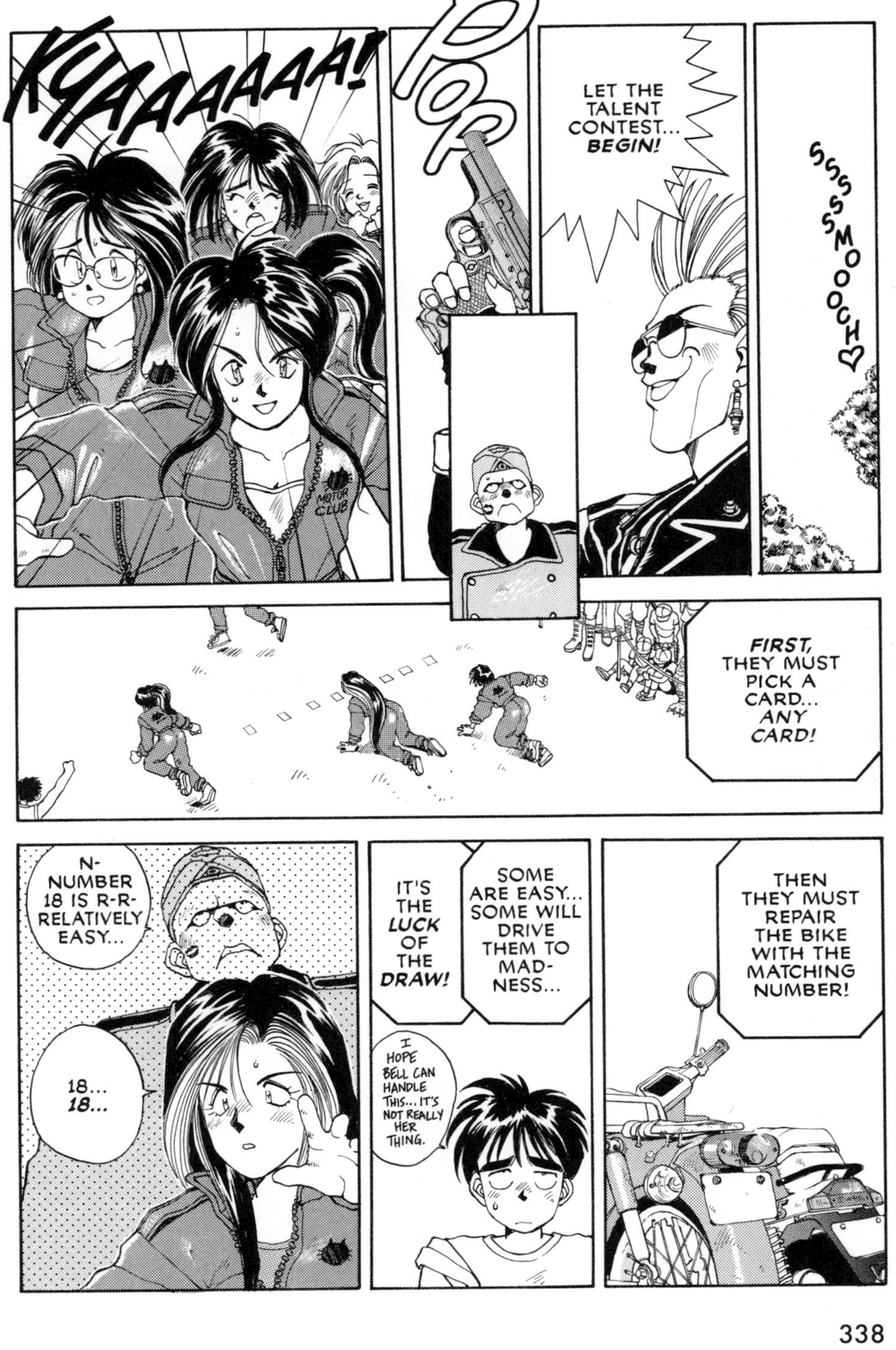
SSSSMOOOCH♡
LET THE TALENT CONTEST... *BEGIN!*
POP
KYAAAAAAA!
FIRST, THEY MUST PICK A CARD... *ANY CARD!*
THEN THEY MUST REPAIR THE BIKE WITH THE MATCHING NUMBER!
SOME ARE EASY... SOME WILL DRIVE THEM TO MAD-NESS...
IT'S THE *LUCK* OF THE *DRAW!*
I HOPE BELL CAN HANDLE THIS... IT'S NOT REALLY HER THING.
N-NUMBER 18 IS R-R-RELATIVELY EASY...
18... *18...*

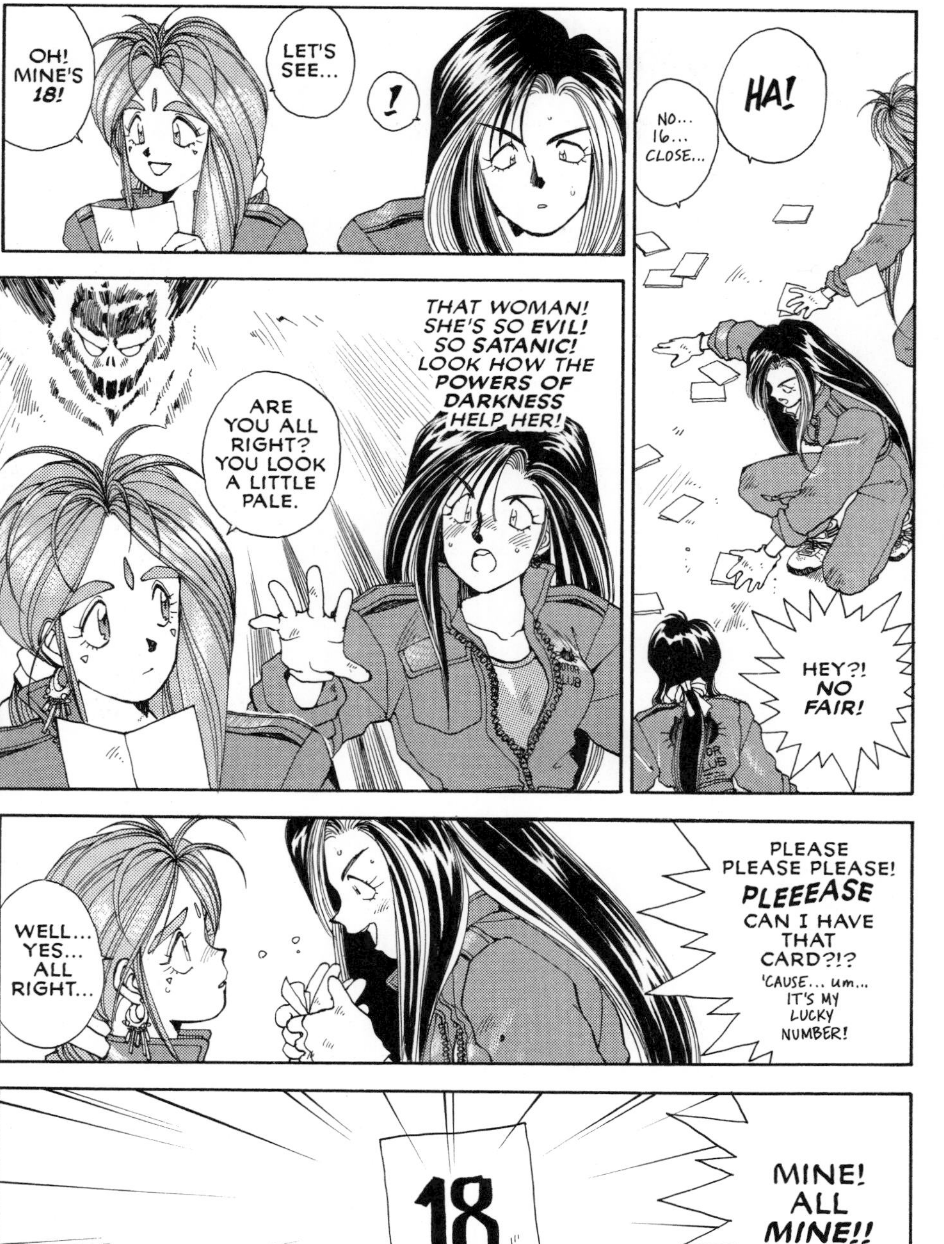
HA!
NO... 16... CLOSE...
HEY?! NO FAIR!
LET'S SEE...
OH! MINE'S 18!
!
THAT WOMAN! SHE'S SO EVIL! SO SATANIC! LOOK HOW THE POWERS OF DARKNESS HELP HER!
ARE YOU ALL RIGHT? YOU LOOK A LITTLE PALE.
PLEASE PLEASE PLEASE! PLEEEASE CAN I HAVE THAT CARD?!? 'CAUSE... um... IT'S MY LUCKY NUMBER!
WELL... YES... ALL RIGHT...
18
MINE! ALL MINE!!

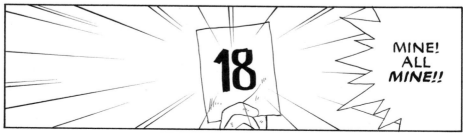

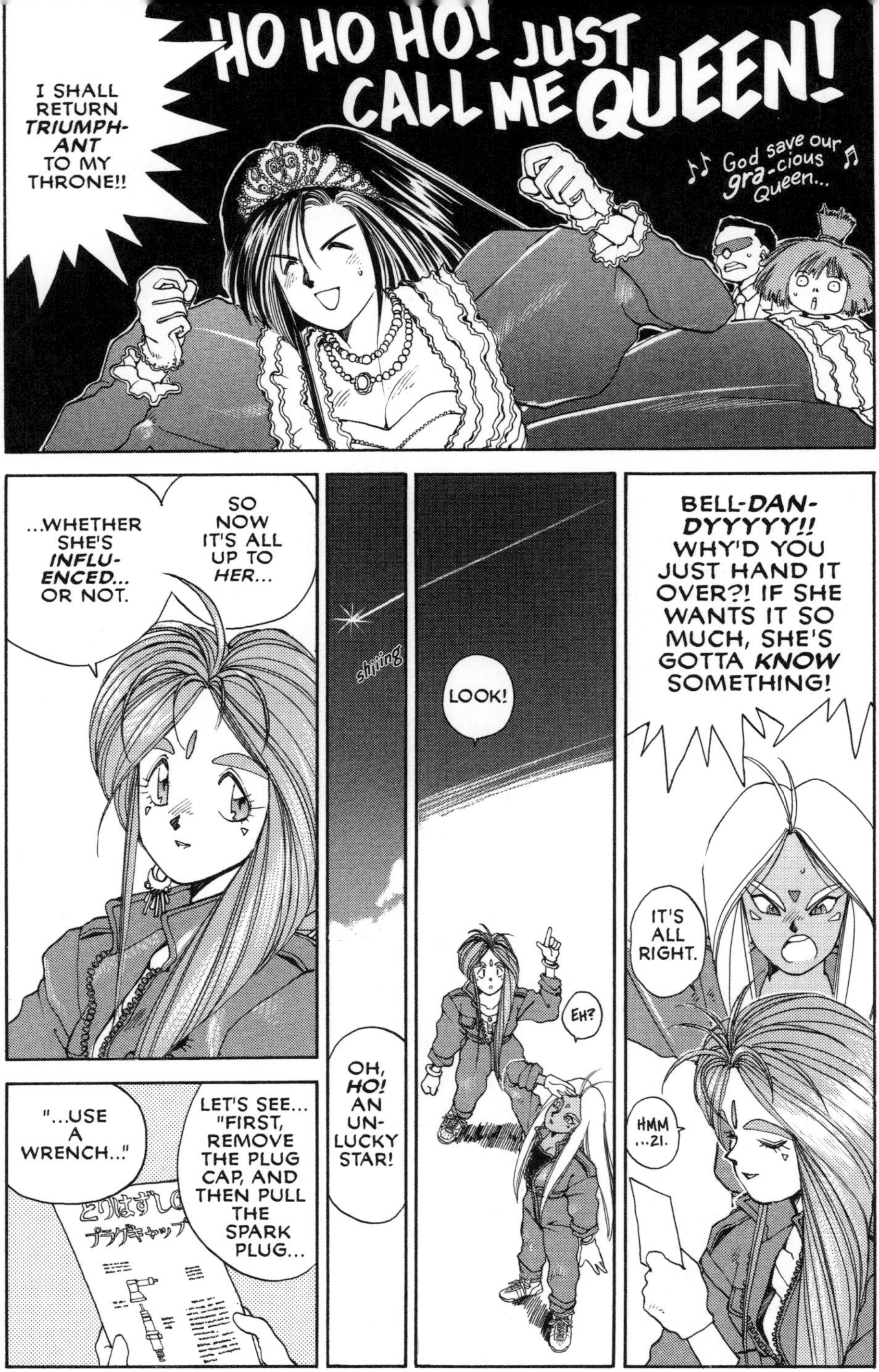

HO HO HO! JUST CALL ME QUEEN!
♪♪ God save our gra-cious Queen... ♫
I SHALL RETURN TRIUMPHANT TO MY THRONE!!
BELL-DANDYYYY!! WHY'D YOU JUST HAND IT OVER?! IF SHE WANTS IT SO MUCH, SHE'S GOTTA KNOW SOMETHING!
IT'S ALL RIGHT.
HMM ...21.
LOOK!
EH?
shiiing
OH, HO! AN UN-LUCKY STAR!
SO NOW IT'S ALL UP TO HER...
...WHETHER SHE'S INFLU-ENCED... OR NOT.
LET'S SEE... "FIRST, REMOVE THE PLUG CAP, AND THEN PULL THE SPARK PLUG...
"...USE A WRENCH..."
とりはずし
プラグキャップ

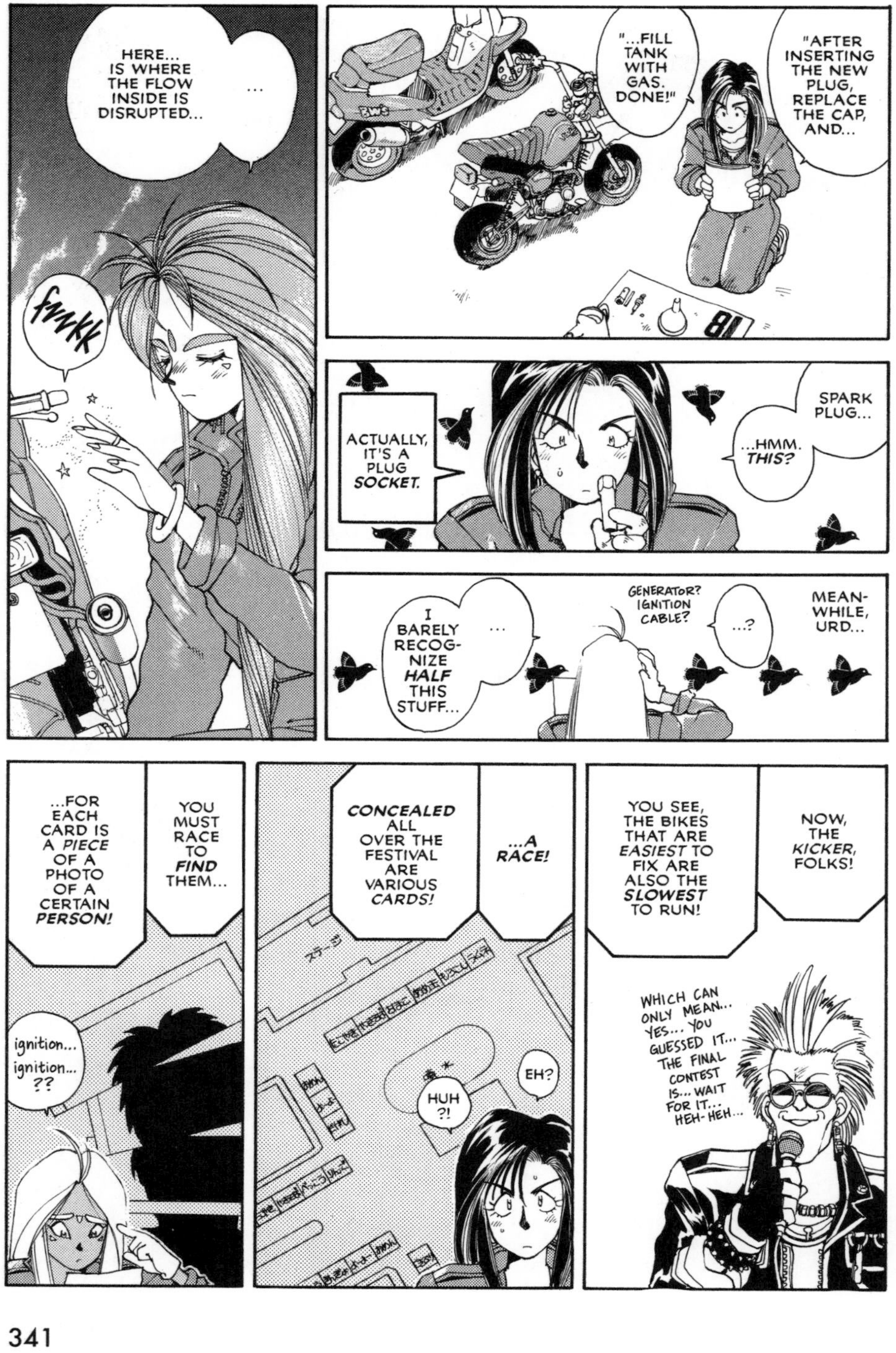
"AFTER INSERTING THE NEW PLUG, REPLACE THE CAP, AND...
"...FILL TANK WITH GAS. DONE!"
SPARK PLUG...
...HMM. *THIS?*
ACTUALLY, IT'S A PLUG **SOCKET.**
MEAN-WHILE, URD...
GENERATOR? IGNITION CABLE?
...?
...
I BARELY RECOGNIZE **HALF** THIS STUFF...
HERE... IS WHERE THE FLOW INSIDE IS DISRUPTED...
...
fwikk
NOW, THE *KICKER*, FOLKS!
YOU SEE, THE BIKES THAT ARE *EASIEST* TO FIX ARE ALSO THE **SLOWEST** TO RUN!
WHICH CAN ONLY MEAN... YES... YOU GUESSED IT... THE FINAL CONTEST IS... WAIT FOR IT... HEH-HEH...
...A RACE!
CONCEALED ALL OVER THE FESTIVAL ARE VARIOUS ***CARDS!***
EH?
HUH ?!
YOU MUST RACE TO ***FIND*** THEM...
...FOR EACH CARD IS A *PIECE* OF A PHOTO OF A CERTAIN ***PERSON!***
ignition... ignition... ??

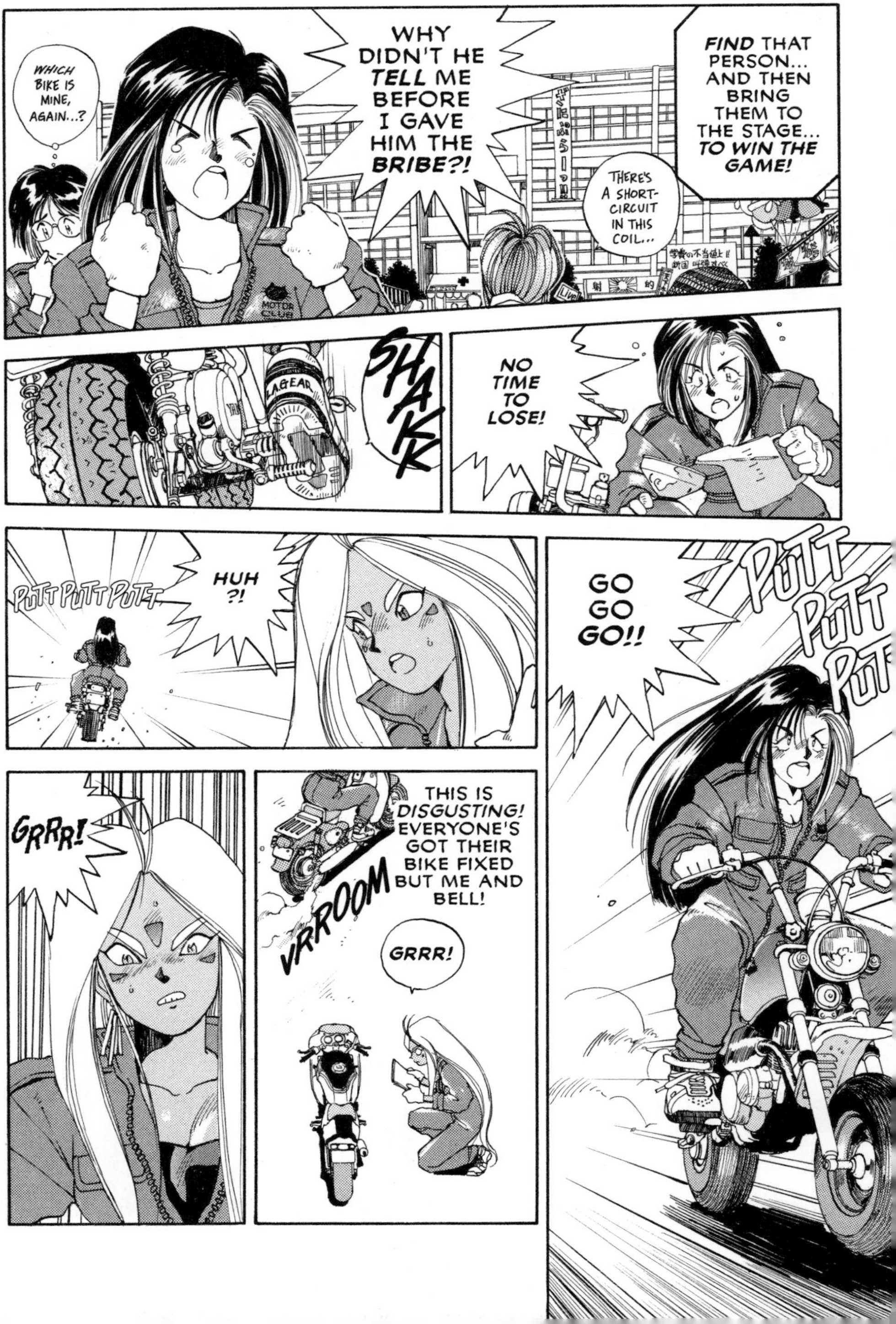
FIND THAT PERSON... AND THEN BRING THEM TO THE STAGE... TO WIN THE GAME!
THERE'S A SHORT-CIRCUIT IN THIS COIL...
WHY DIDN'T HE TELL ME BEFORE I GAVE HIM THE BRIBE?!
WHICH BIKE IS MINE, AGAIN...?
NO TIME TO LOSE!
SHAKK
L.A.GEAR
PUTT PUTT PUTT
GO GO GO!!
HUH ?!
PUTT PUTT PUTT
THIS IS DISGUSTING! EVERYONE'S GOT THEIR BIKE FIXED BUT ME AND BELL!
VRROOM
GRRR!
GRRR!

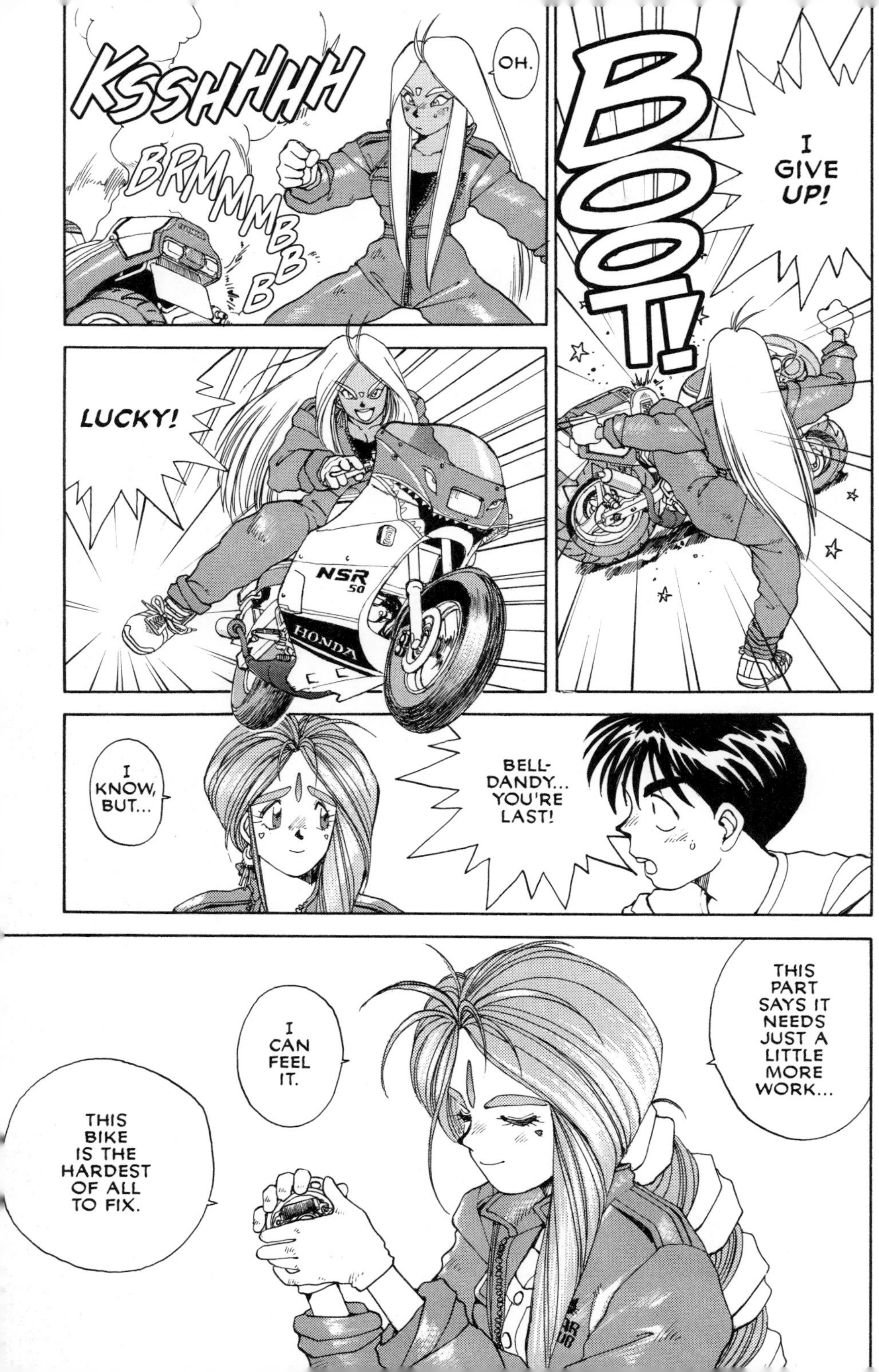
BOOT!
I GIVE UP!
OH.
KSSHHHH
BRMMMMBBBB
LUCKY!
BELL-DANDY... YOU'RE LAST!
I KNOW, BUT...
THIS PART SAYS IT NEEDS JUST A LITTLE MORE WORK...
I CAN FEEL IT.
THIS BIKE IS THE HARDEST OF ALL TO FIX.

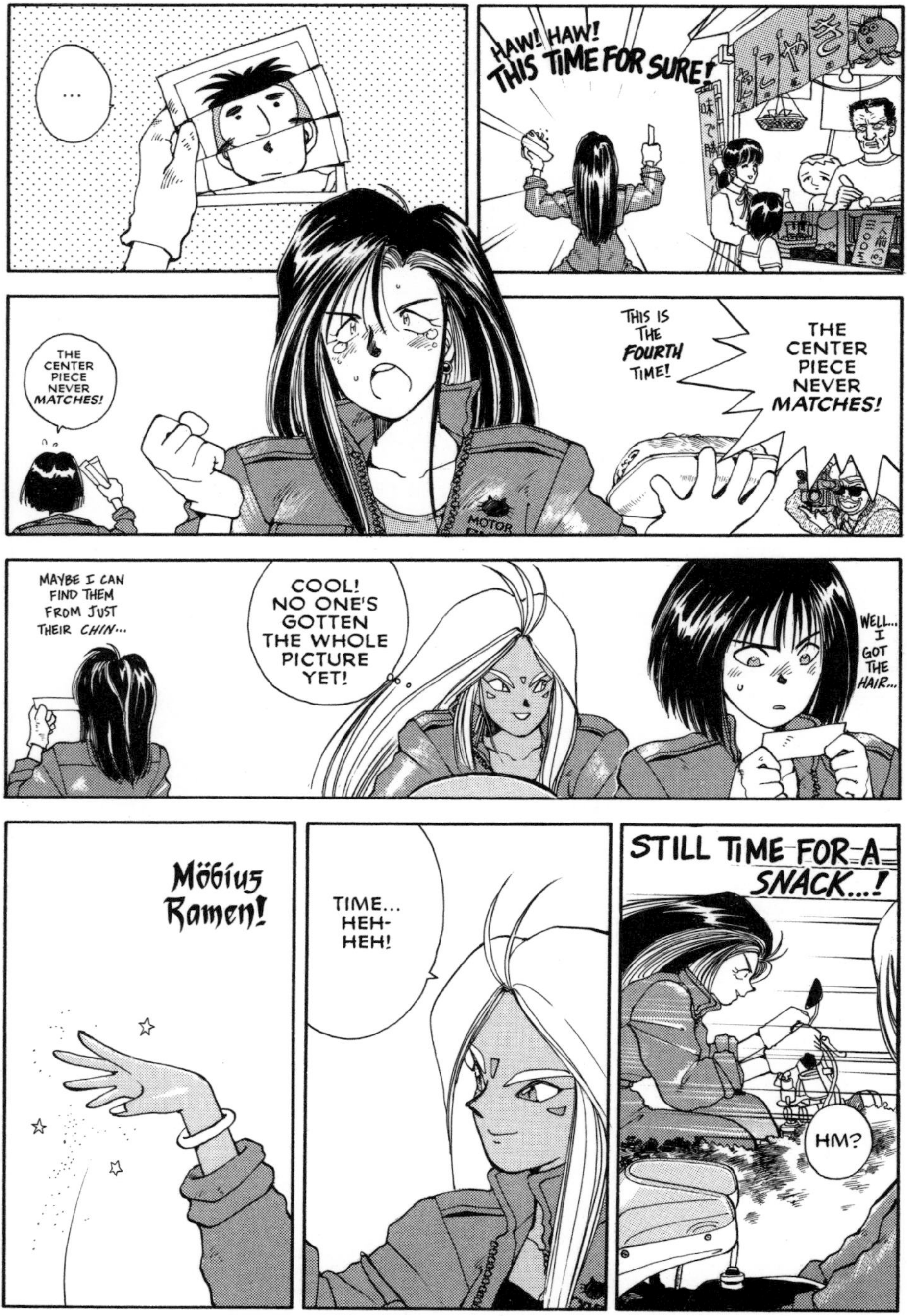
HAW! HAW!
THIS TIME FOR SURE!
...
THE CENTER PIECE NEVER MATCHES!
THIS IS THE FOURTH TIME!
THE CENTER PIECE NEVER MATCHES!
WELL... I GOT THE HAIR...
COOL! NO ONE'S GOTTEN THE WHOLE PICTURE YET!
MAYBE I CAN FIND THEM FROM JUST THEIR CHIN...
STILL TIME FOR A SNACK...!
HM?
TIME... HEH-HEH!
Möbius Ramen!

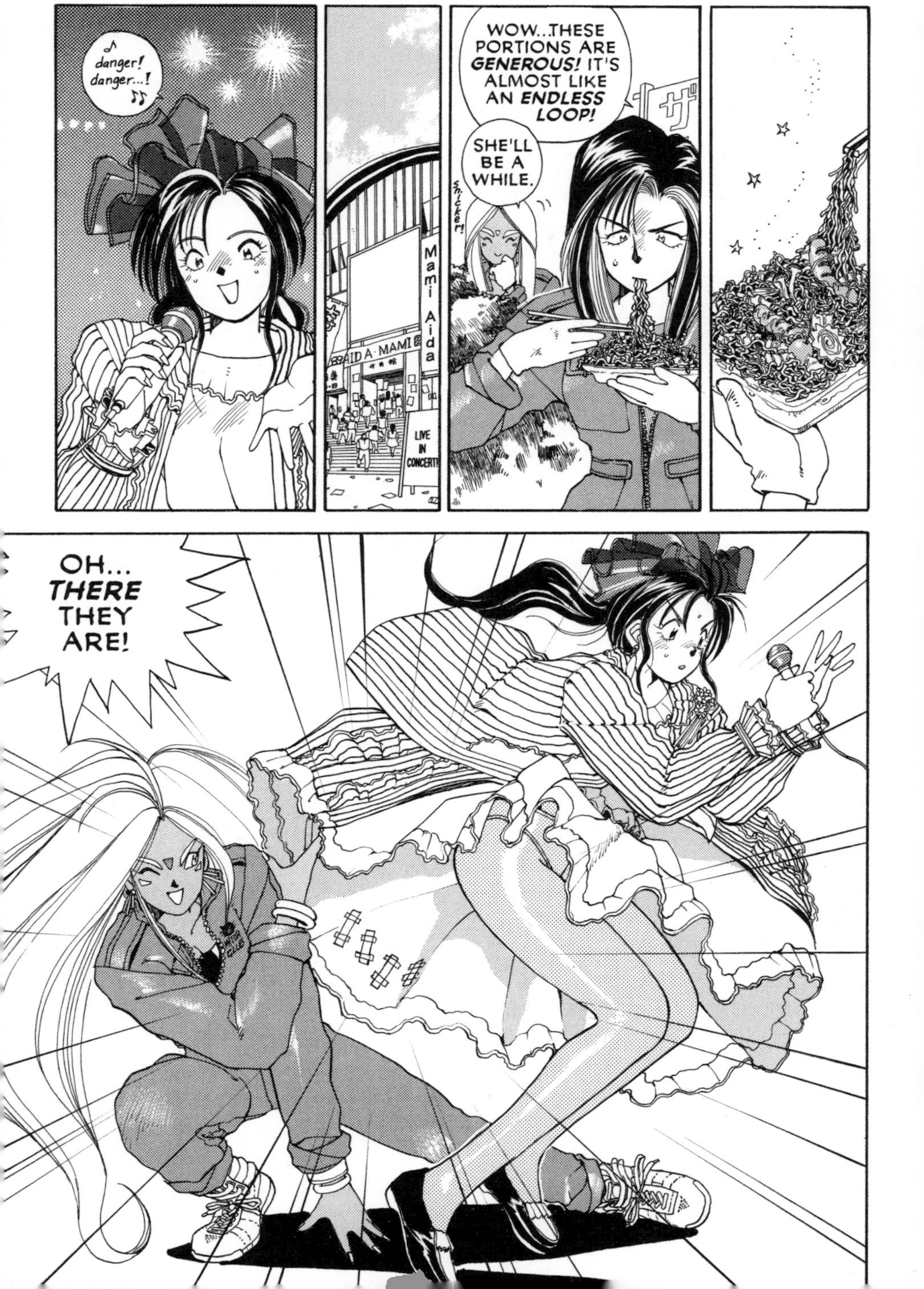
WOW...THESE PORTIONS ARE GENEROUS! IT'S ALMOST LIKE AN ENDLESS LOOP!
ザ
SHE'LL BE A WHILE.
snicker!
Mami Aida
AIDA MAMI
LIVE IN CONCERT!
danger! danger...!
OH... THERE THEY ARE!

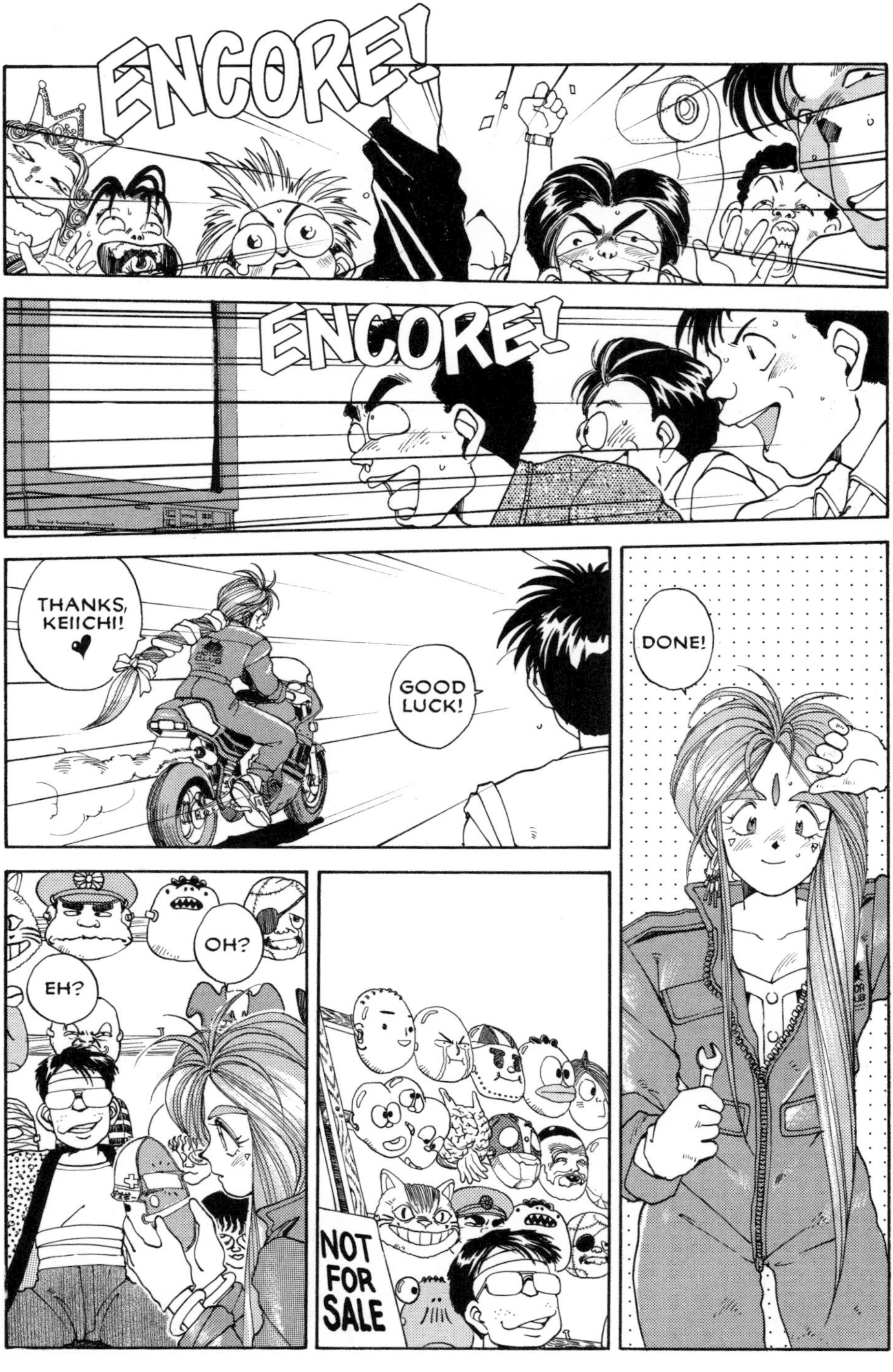
ENCORE!
ENCORE!
DONE!
GOOD LUCK!
THANKS, KEIICHI!
NOT FOR SALE
OH?
EH?

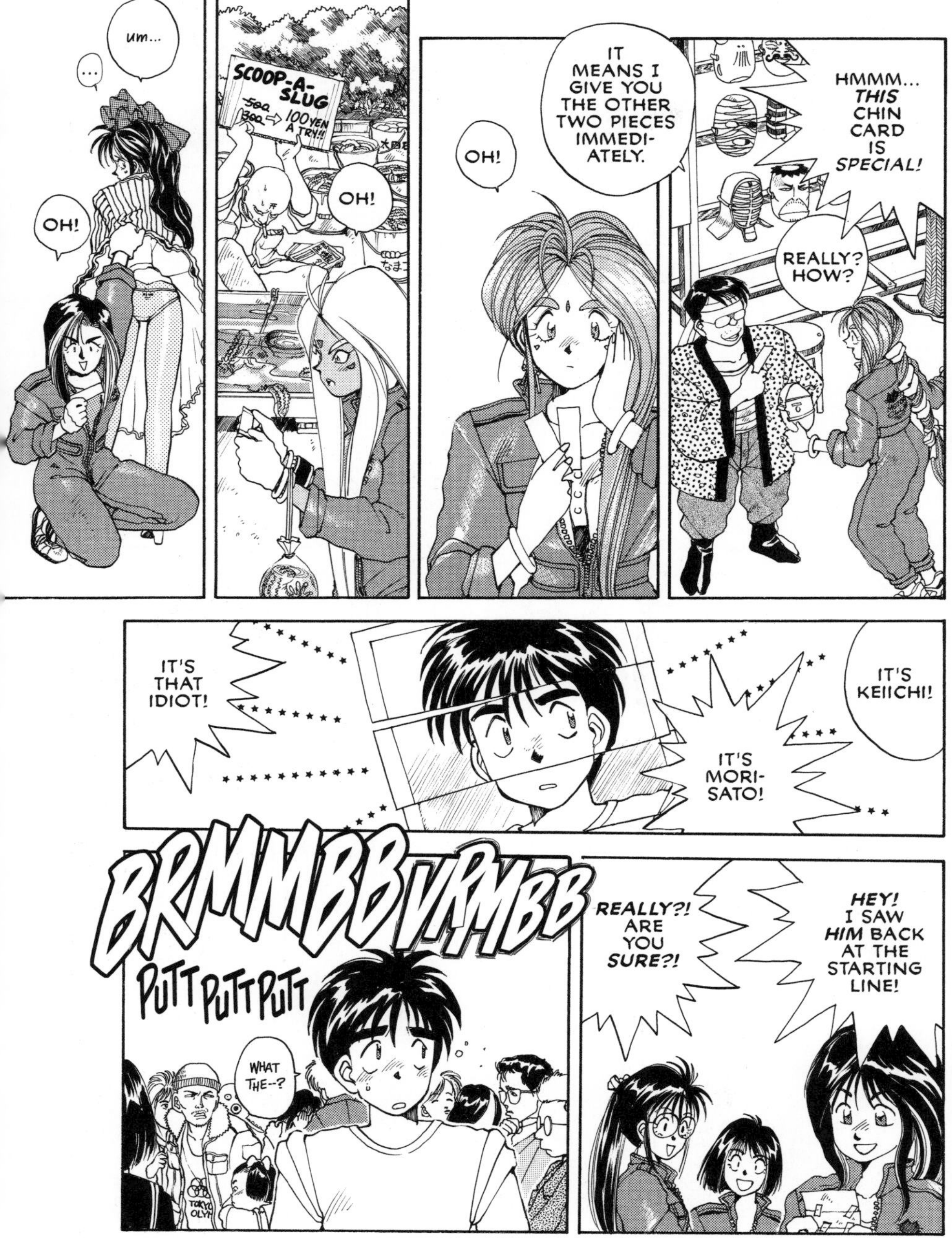
HMMM... THIS CHIN CARD IS SPECIAL!
REALLY? HOW?
IT MEANS I GIVE YOU THE OTHER TWO PIECES IMMEDI-ATELY.
OH!
SCOOP-A-SLUG
500 300 → 100 YEN A TRY!!
OH!
um...
...
OH!
IT'S KEIICHI!
IT'S MORI-SATO!
IT'S THAT IDIOT!
HEY! I SAW HIM BACK AT THE STARTING LINE!
REALLY?! ARE YOU SURE?!
BRMMBBVRMBB
PUTT PUTT PUTT
WHAT THE--?

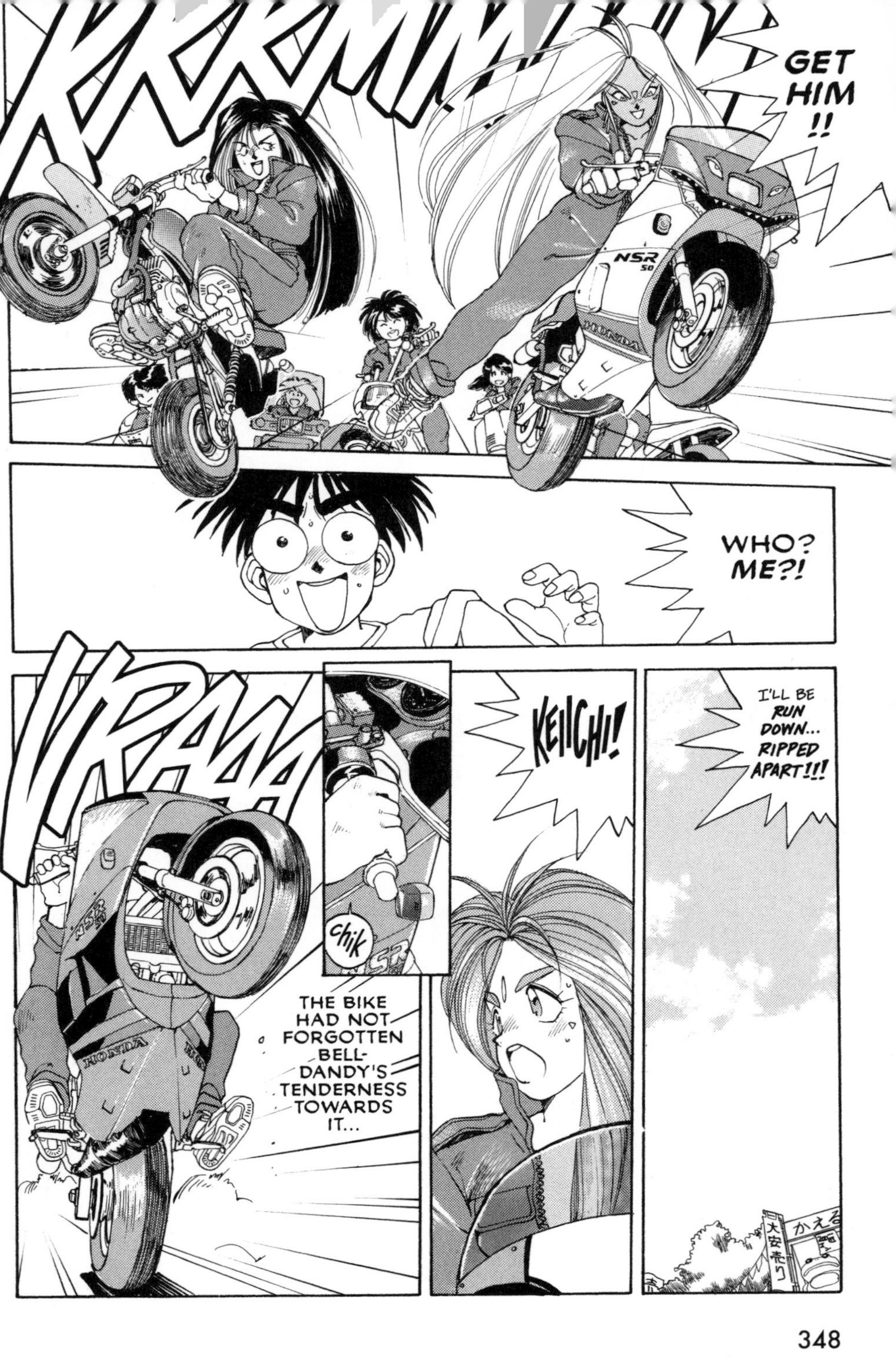
GET HIM !!
WHO? ME?!
I'LL BE RUN DOWN... RIPPED APART!!!
KEIICHI!
chik
THE BIKE HAD NOT FORGOTTEN BELL-DANDY'S TENDERNESS TOWARDS IT...

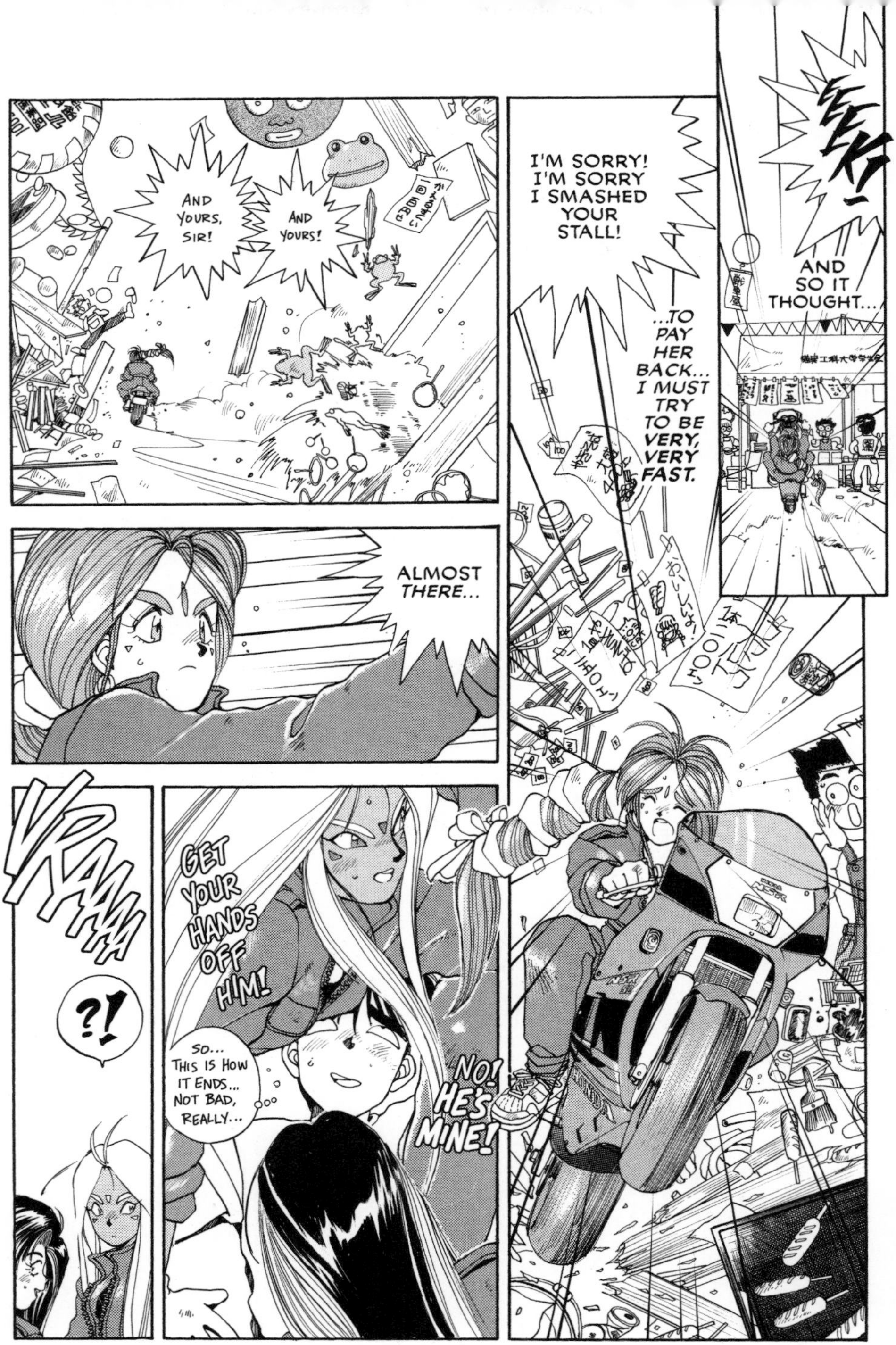
EEK!
AND SO IT THOUGHT...
I'M SORRY! I'M SORRY I SMASHED YOUR STALL!
...TO PAY HER BACK... I MUST TRY TO BE VERY, VERY FAST.
AND YOURS, SIR!
AND YOURS!
ALMOST THERE...
GET YOUR HANDS OFF HIM!
NO! HE'S MINE!
SO... THIS IS HOW IT ENDS... NOT BAD, REALLY...
VRAAAAA
?!

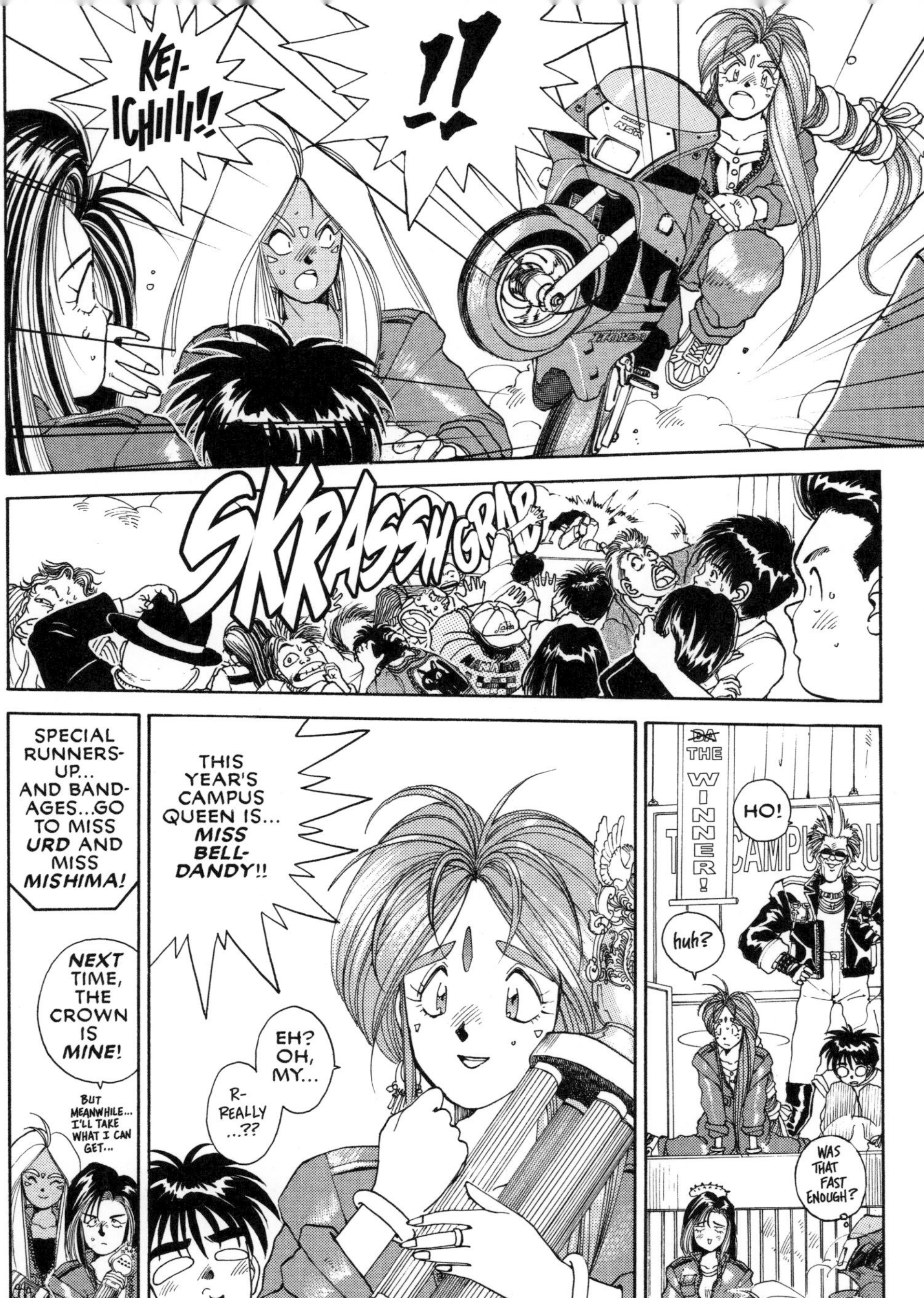
!!
KEI-ICHIIII!!
SKRASSH
GRAB
DA THE WINNER!
HO!
huh?
WAS THAT FAST ENOUGH?
THIS YEAR'S CAMPUS QUEEN IS... MISS BELL-DANDY!!
EH? OH, MY...
R-REALLY ...??
SPECIAL RUNNERS-UP... AND BANDAGES...GO TO MISS URD AND MISS MISHIMA!
NEXT TIME, THE CROWN IS MINE!
BUT MEANWHILE... I'LL TAKE WHAT I CAN GET...

OH MY GODDESS!

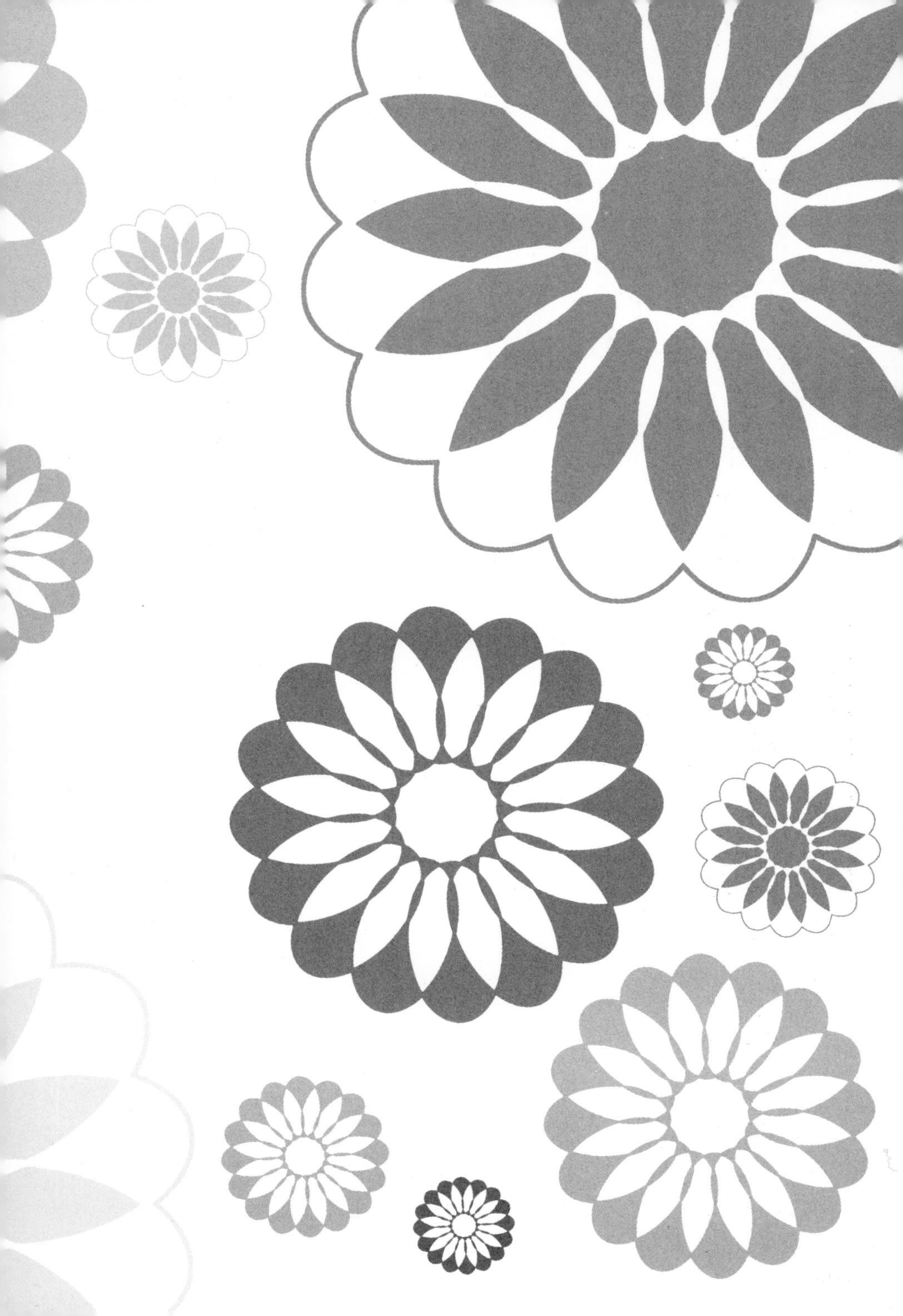

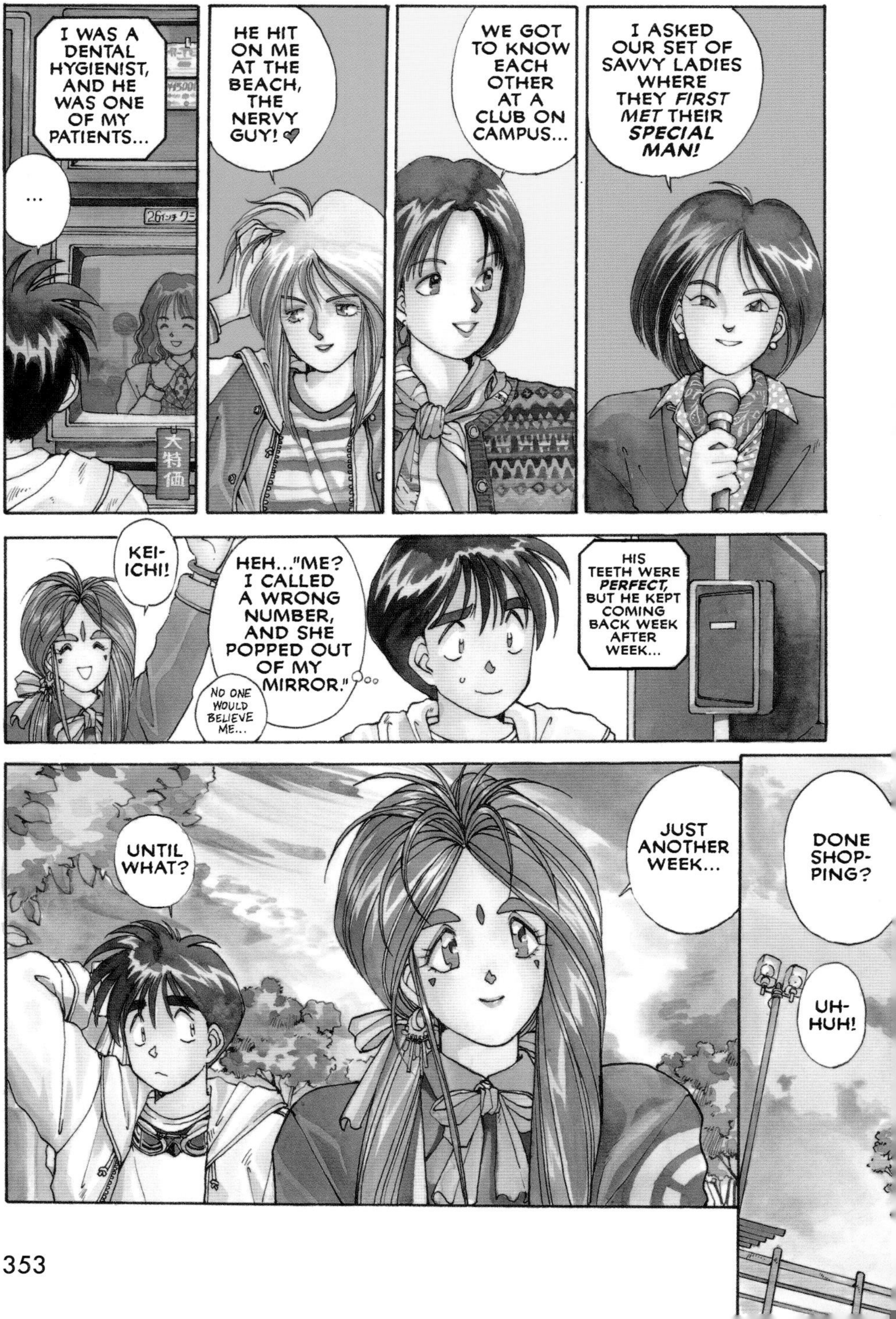
I ASKED OUR SET OF SAVVY LADIES WHERE THEY *FIRST MET* THEIR ***SPECIAL MAN!***
WE GOT TO KNOW EACH OTHER AT A CLUB ON CAMPUS...
HE HIT ON ME AT THE BEACH, THE NERVY GUY! ♥
I WAS A DENTAL HYGIENIST, AND HE WAS ONE OF MY PATIENTS...
...
大特価
HIS TEETH WERE ***PERFECT,*** BUT HE KEPT COMING BACK WEEK AFTER WEEK...
HEH..."ME? I CALLED A WRONG NUMBER, AND SHE POPPED OUT OF MY MIRROR."
NO ONE WOULD BELIEVE ME...
KEI-ICHI!
DONE SHOP-PING?
UH-HUH!
JUST ANOTHER WEEK...
UNTIL WHAT?

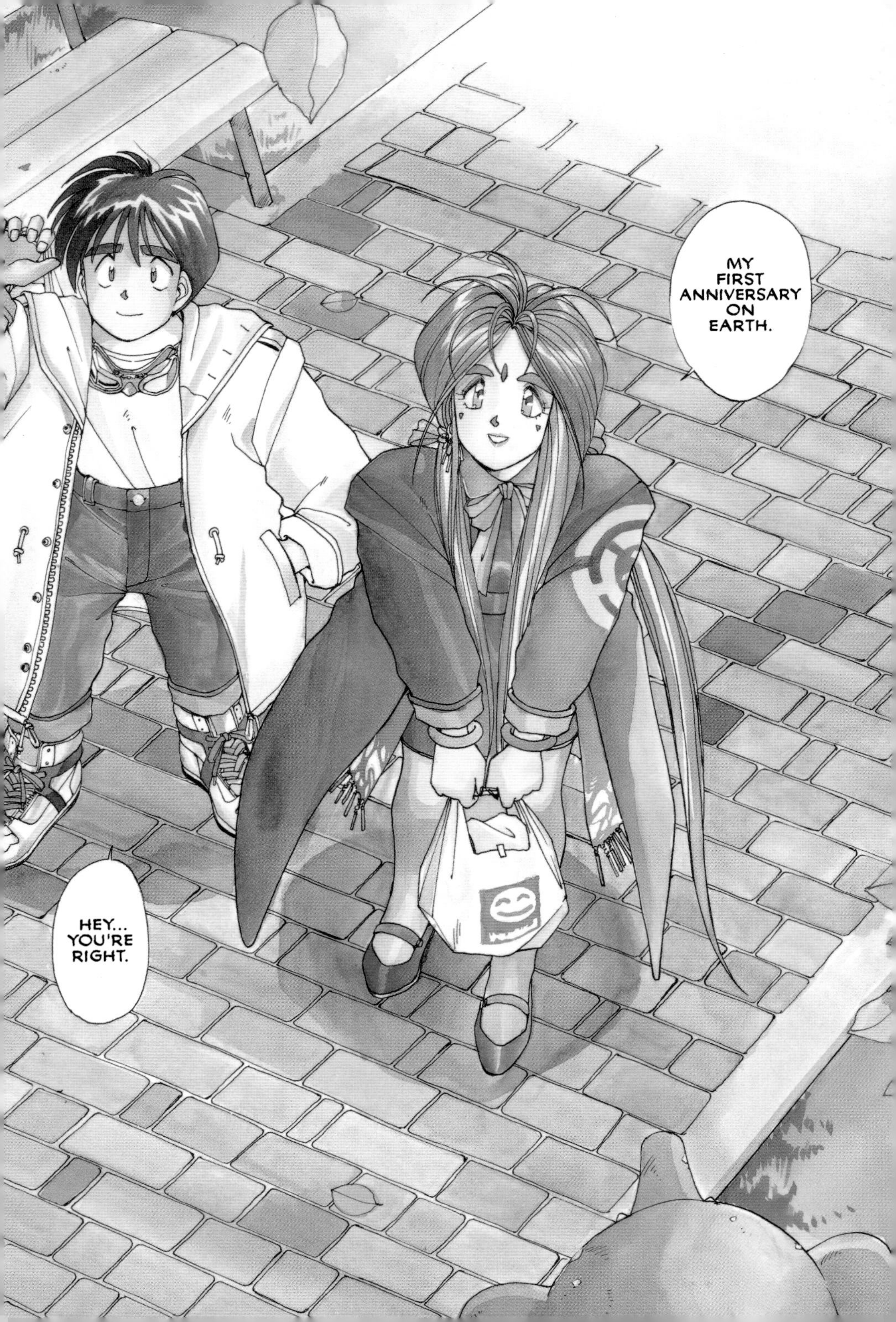
MY FIRST ANNIVERSARY ON EARTH.
HEY... YOU'RE RIGHT.

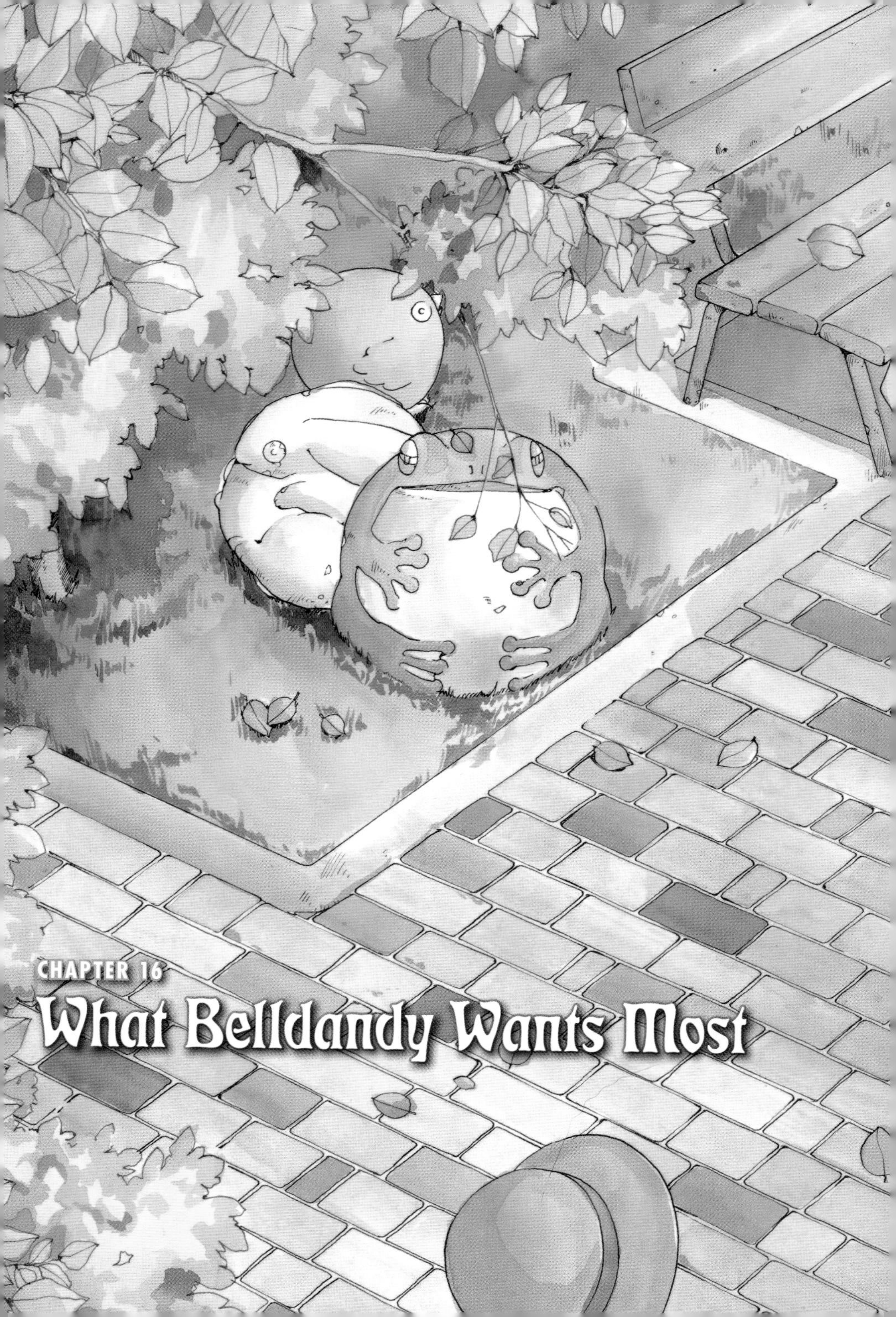

CHAPTER 16

What Belldandy Wants Most

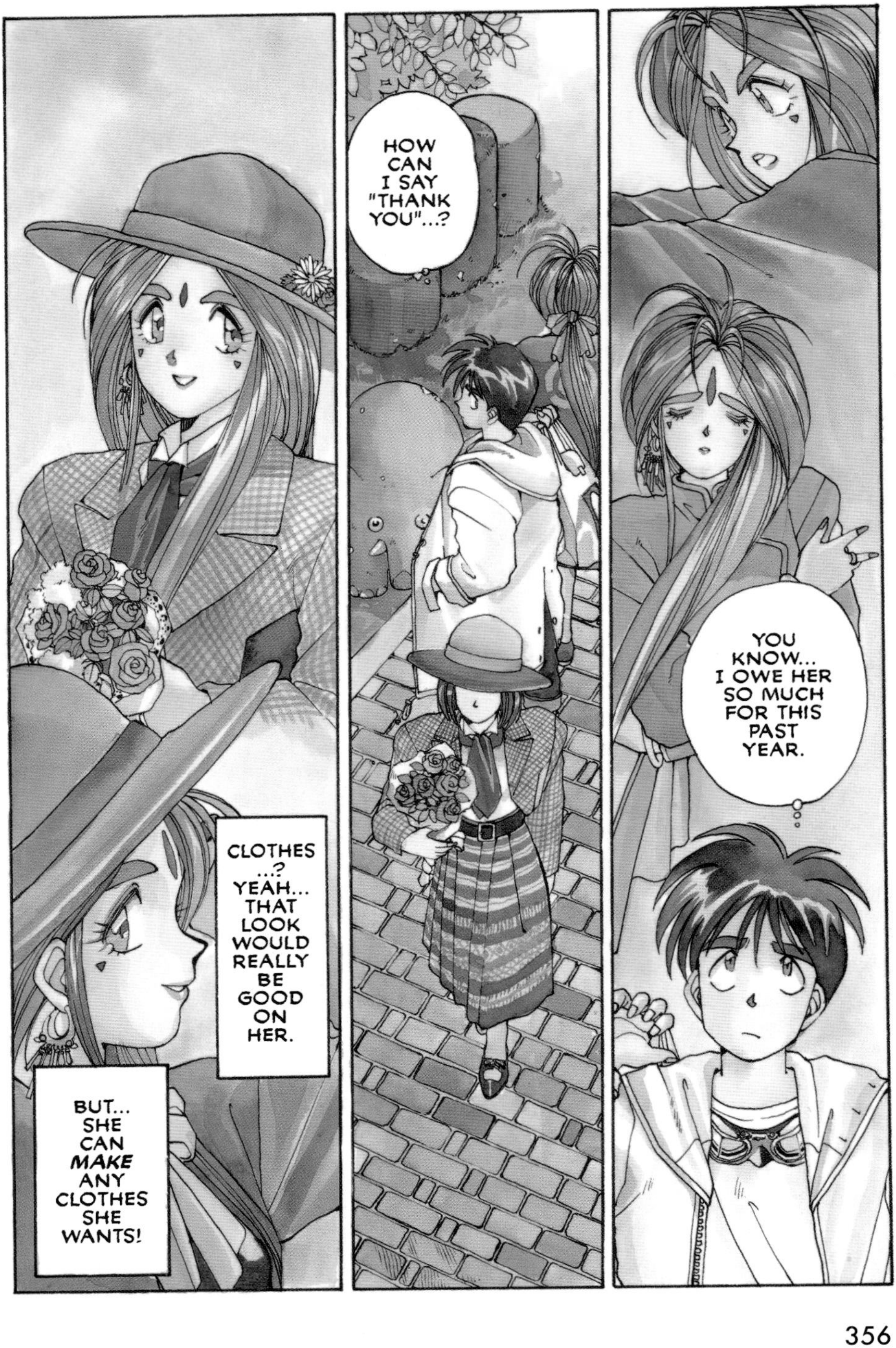
YOU KNOW... I OWE HER SO MUCH FOR THIS PAST YEAR.
HOW CAN I SAY "THANK YOU"...?
CLOTHES ...? YEAH... THAT LOOK WOULD REALLY BE GOOD ON HER.
BUT... SHE CAN *MAKE* ANY CLOTHES SHE WANTS!

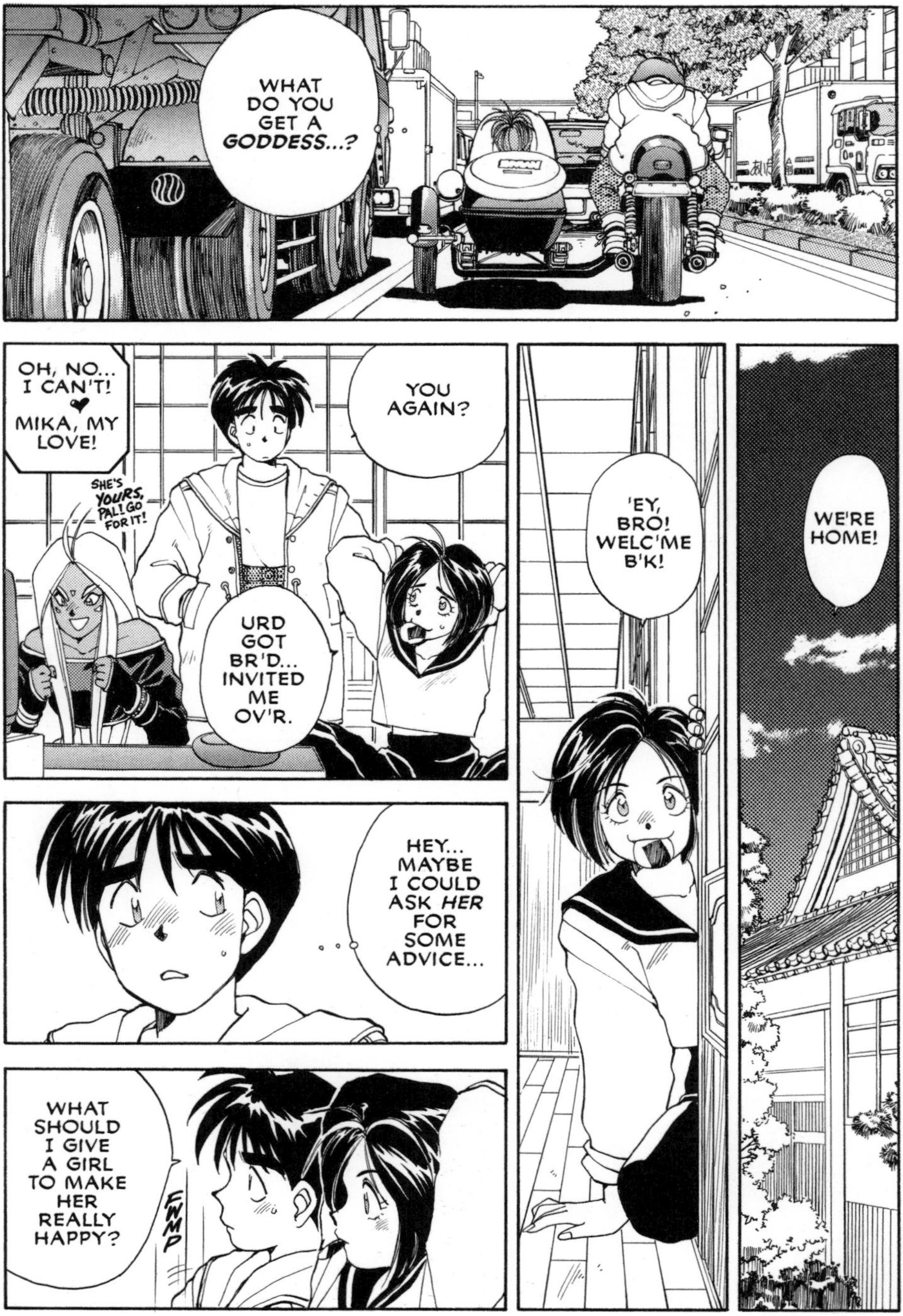
WHAT DO YOU GET A *GODDESS...?*
WE'RE HOME!
'EY, BRO! WELC'ME B'K!
YOU AGAIN?
OH, NO... I CAN'T! ❤ MIKA, MY LOVE!
SHE'S *YOURS,* PAL! GO FOR IT!
URD GOT BR'D... INVITED ME OV'R.
HEY... MAYBE I COULD ASK *HER* FOR SOME ADVICE...
WHAT SHOULD I GIVE A GIRL TO MAKE HER REALLY HAPPY?
FWMP

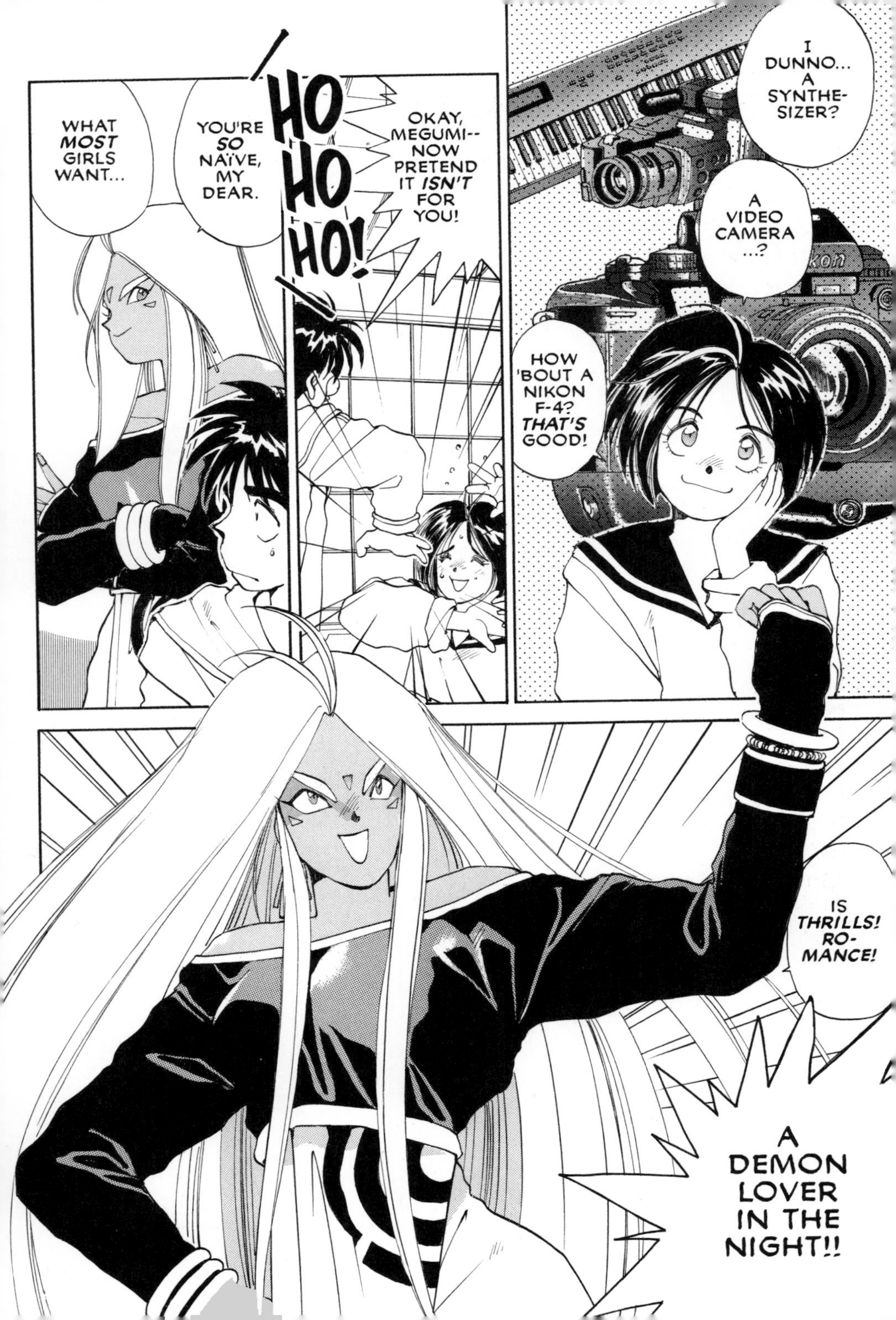
I DUNNO... A SYNTHESIZER?
A VIDEO CAMERA ...?
HOW 'BOUT A NIKON F-4? THAT'S GOOD!
OKAY, MEGUMI-- NOW PRETEND IT ISN'T FOR YOU!
HO HO HO!
YOU'RE SO NAÏVE, MY DEAR.
WHAT MOST GIRLS WANT...
IS THRILLS! ROMANCE!
A DEMON LOVER IN THE NIGHT!!

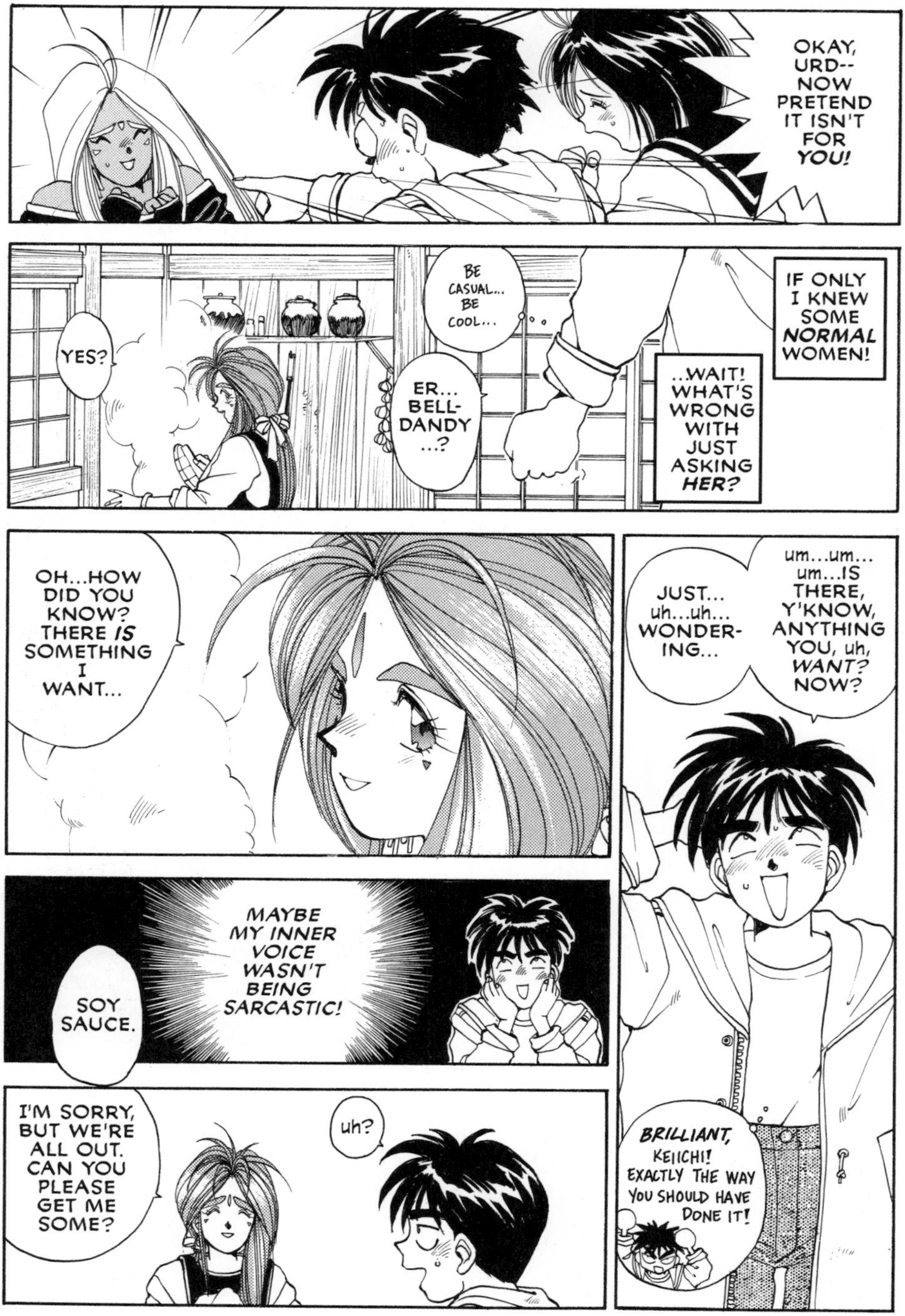
OKAY, URD-- NOW PRETEND IT ISN'T FOR YOU!
IF ONLY I KNEW SOME NORMAL WOMEN!
...WAIT! WHAT'S WRONG WITH JUST ASKING HER?
BE CASUAL... BE COOL...
ER... BELL-DANDY ...?
YES?
um...um... um...IS THERE, Y'KNOW, ANYTHING YOU, uh, WANT? NOW?
JUST... uh...uh... WONDER-ING...
BRILLIANT, KEIICHI! EXACTLY THE WAY YOU SHOULD HAVE DONE IT!
OH...HOW DID YOU KNOW? THERE IS SOMETHING I WANT...
MAYBE MY INNER VOICE WASN'T BEING SARCASTIC!
SOY SAUCE.
uh?
I'M SORRY, BUT WE'RE ALL OUT. CAN YOU PLEASE GET ME SOME?

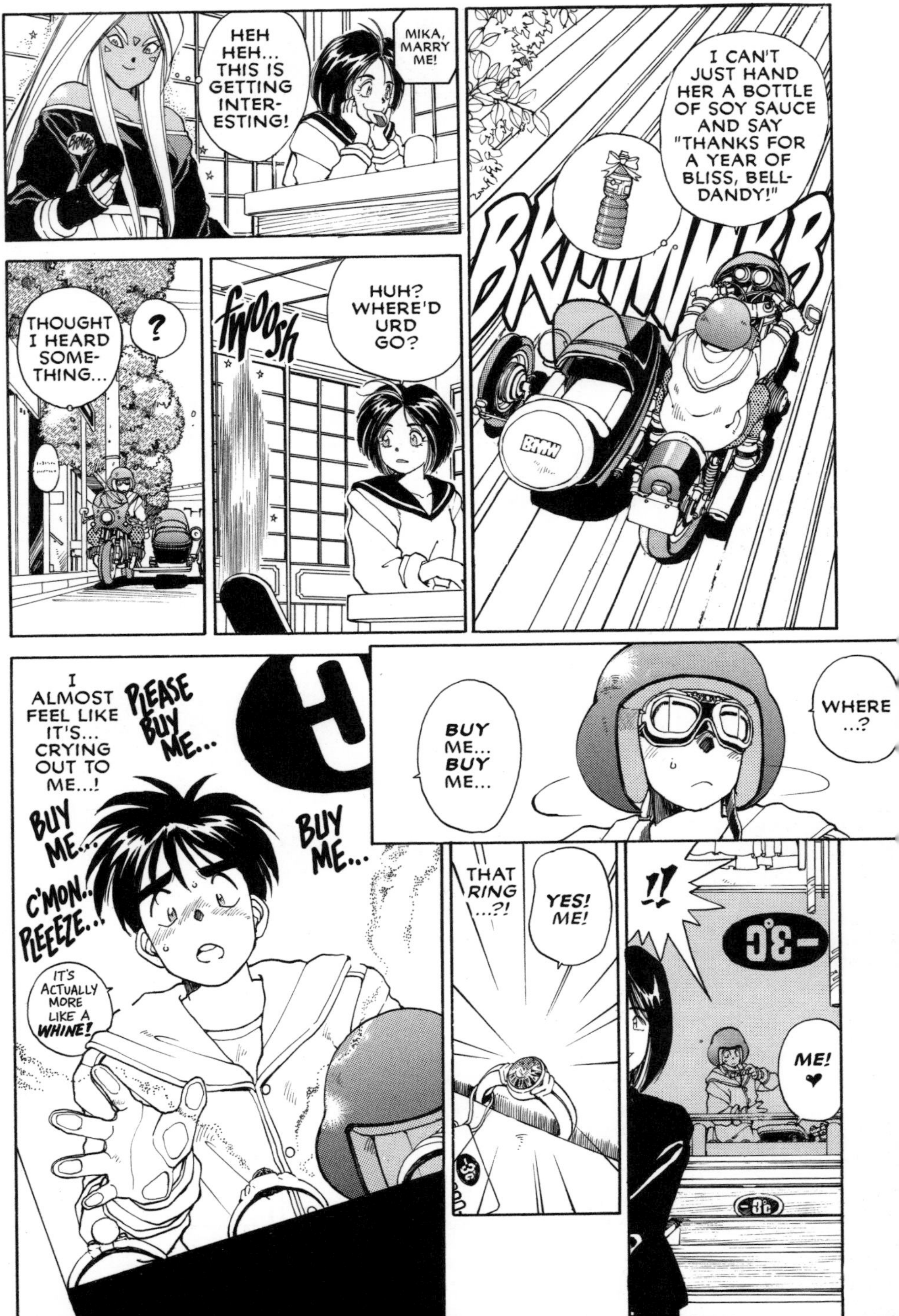
I CAN'T JUST HAND HER A BOTTLE OF SOY SAUCE AND SAY "THANKS FOR A YEAR OF BLISS, BELL-DANDY!"
MIKA, MARRY ME!
HEH HEH... THIS IS GETTING INTER-ESTING!
fwoosh
HUH? WHERE'D URD GO?
?
THOUGHT I HEARD SOME-THING...
WHERE ...?
BUY ME... BUY ME...
!!
ME! ❤
YES! ME!
THAT RING ...?!
PLEASE BUY ME...
I ALMOST FEEL LIKE IT'S... CRYING OUT TO ME...!
BUY ME...
BUY ME...
C'MON.. PLEEEEZE...
IT'S ACTUALLY MORE LIKE A WHINE!

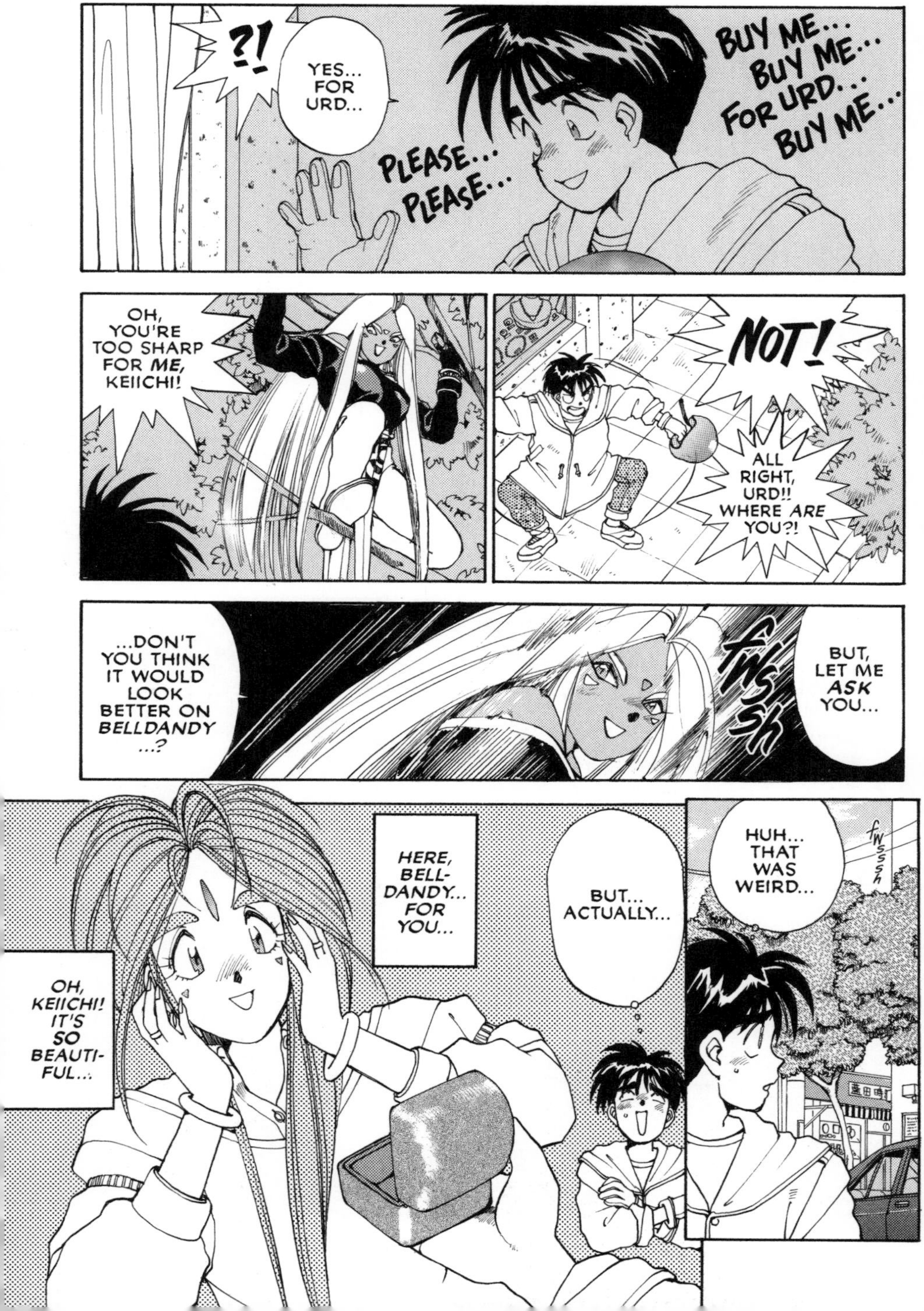
BUY ME... BUY ME... FOR URD... BUY ME...
YES... FOR URD...
?!
PLEASE... PLEASE...
NOT!
ALL RIGHT, URD!! WHERE ARE YOU?!
OH, YOU'RE TOO SHARP FOR ME, KEIICHI!
BUT, LET ME ASK YOU...
fwssh
...DON'T YOU THINK IT WOULD LOOK BETTER ON BELLDANDY ...?
HUH... THAT WAS WEIRD...
fwsssh
BUT... ACTUALLY...
HERE, BELL-DANDY... FOR YOU...
OH, KEIICHI! IT'S SO BEAUTI-FUL...

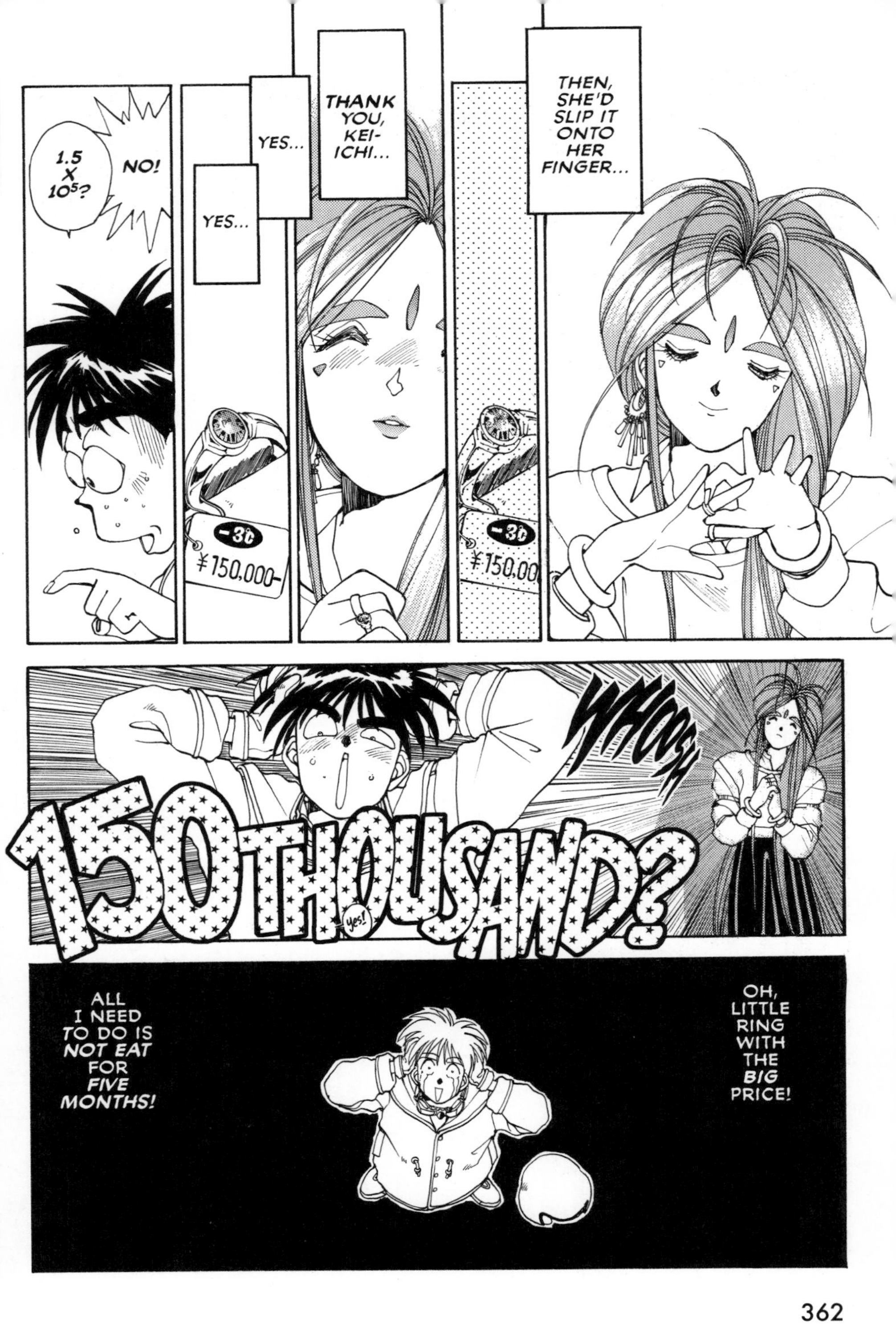
THEN, SHE'D SLIP IT ONTO HER FINGER...
¥150,00
THANK YOU, KEI-ICHI...
YES...
YES...
¥150,000-
NO!
1.5 X 10⁵?
WHOOSH
150 THOUSAND?
Yes!
OH, LITTLE RING WITH THE BIG PRICE!
ALL I NEED TO DO IS NOT EAT FOR FIVE MONTHS!

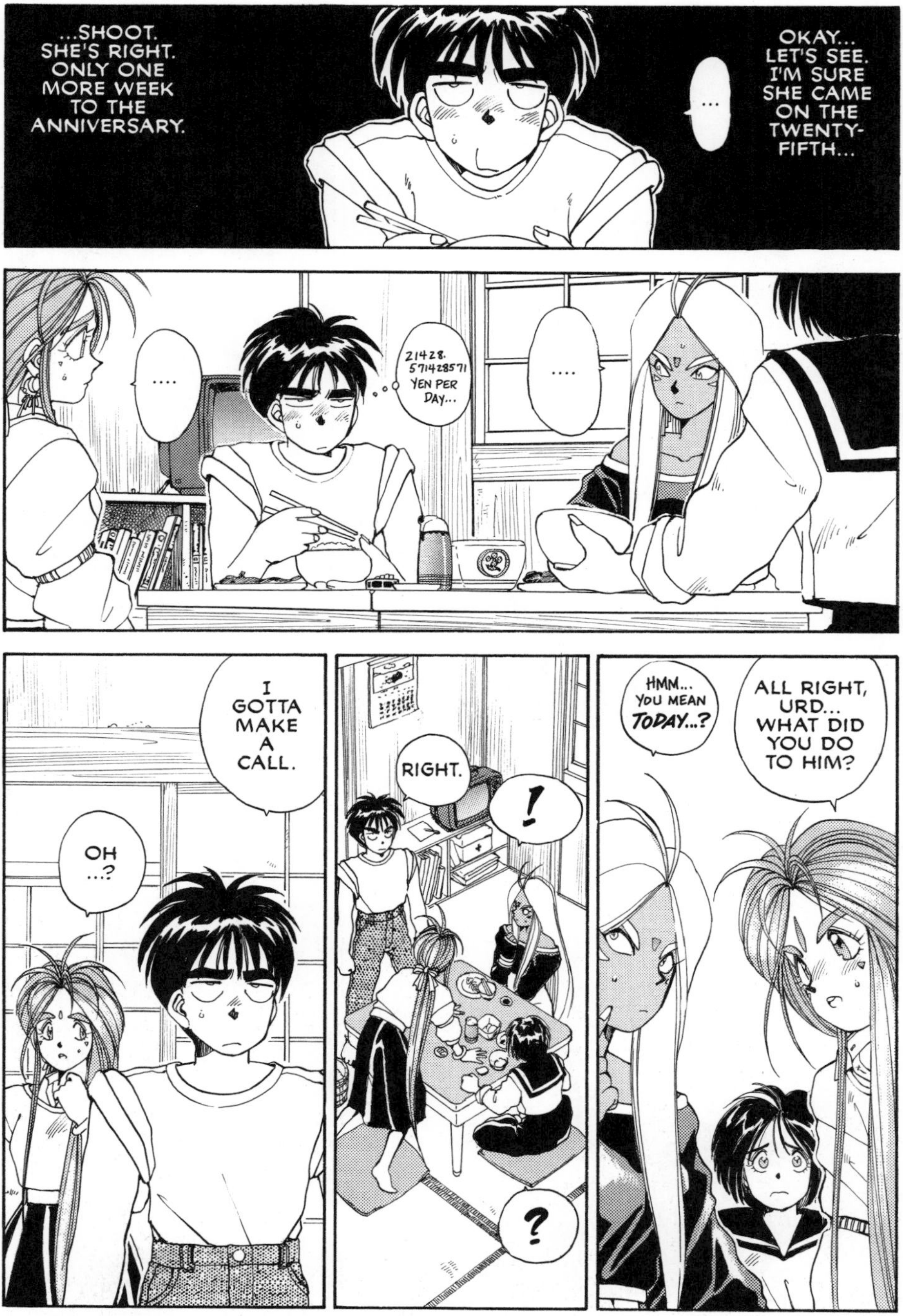
OKAY... LET'S SEE. I'M SURE SHE CAME ON THE TWENTY-FIFTH...
...
...SHOOT. SHE'S RIGHT. ONLY ONE MORE WEEK TO THE ANNIVERSARY.
....
21428.571428571 YEN PER DAY...
....
ALL RIGHT, URD... WHAT DID YOU DO TO HIM?
HMM... YOU MEAN *TODAY*...?
RIGHT.
!
?
I GOTTA MAKE A CALL.
OH ...?

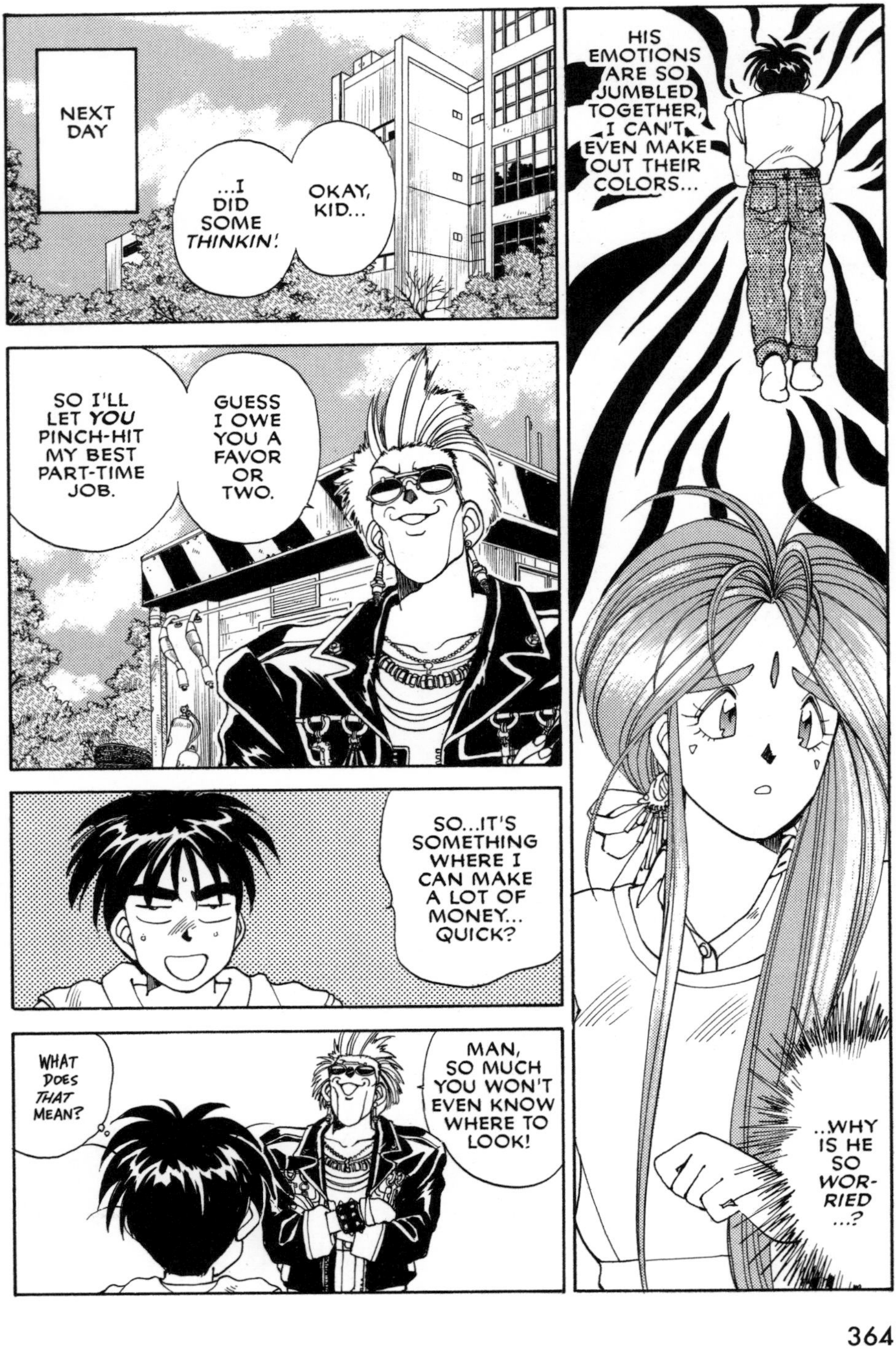

HIS EMOTIONS ARE SO JUMBLED TOGETHER, I CAN'T EVEN MAKE OUT THEIR COLORS...
..WHY IS HE SO *WOR-RIED* ...?
NEXT DAY
OKAY, KID...
...I DID SOME *THINKIN'!*
GUESS I OWE YOU A FAVOR OR TWO.
SO I'LL LET **YOU** PINCH-HIT MY BEST PART-TIME JOB.
SO...IT'S SOMETHING WHERE I CAN MAKE A LOT OF MONEY... QUICK?
MAN, SO MUCH YOU WON'T EVEN KNOW WHERE TO LOOK!
WHAT DOES *THAT* MEAN?

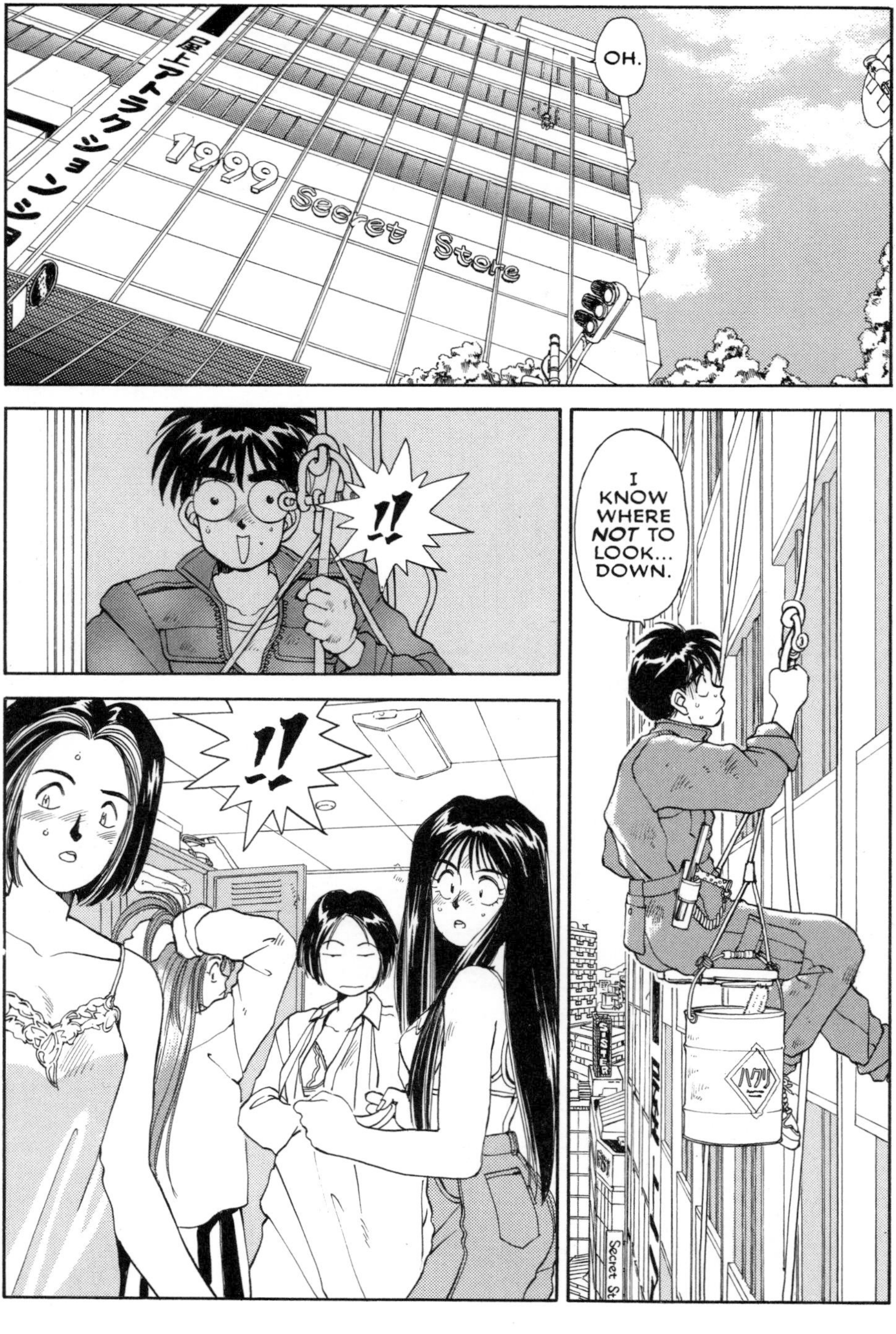
1999 Secret Store
OH.
I KNOW WHERE *NOT* TO LOOK... DOWN.
ハクリ
Secret St
!!
!!

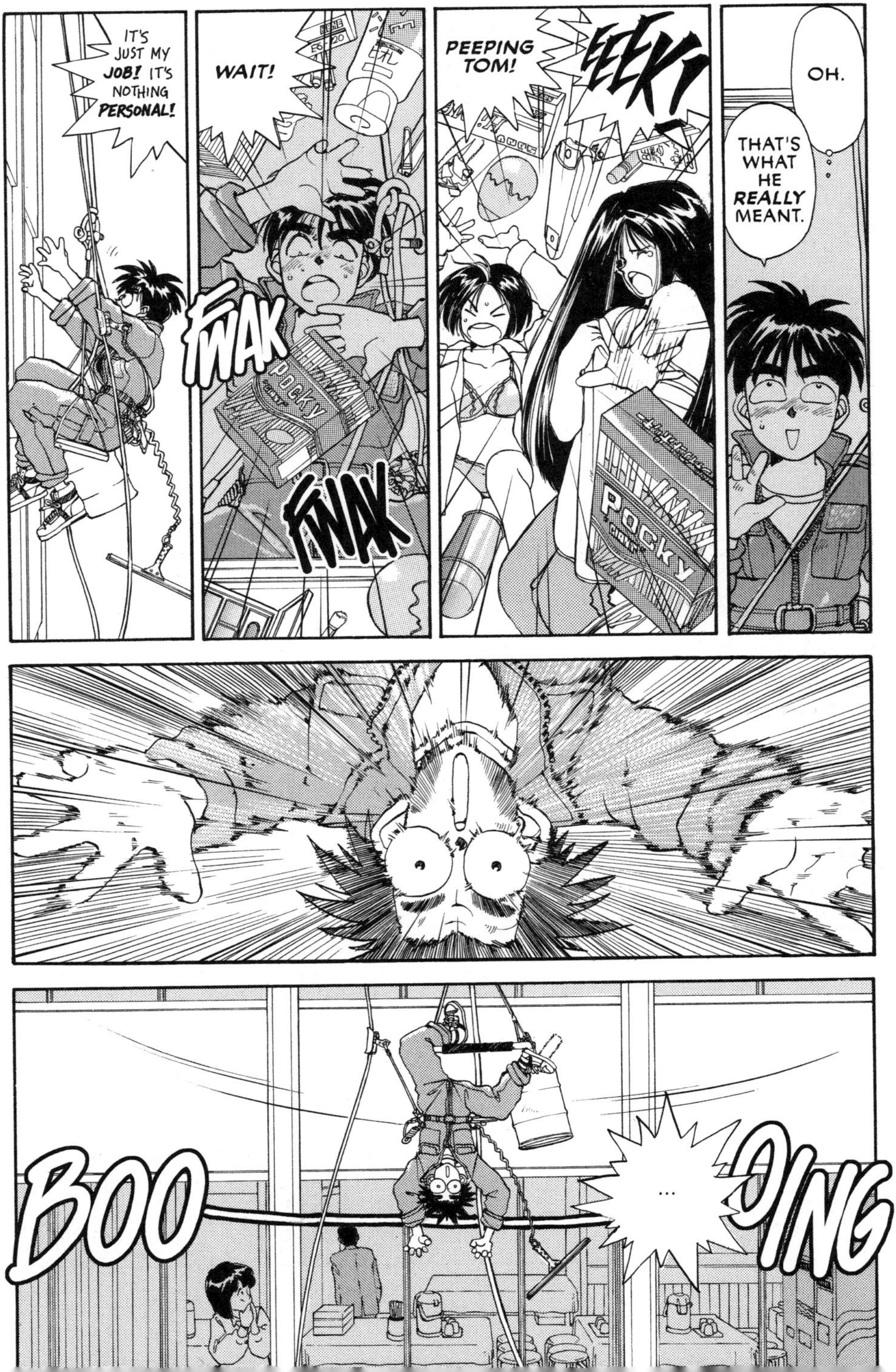
OH.
THAT'S WHAT HE REALLY MEANT.
EEEK!
PEEPING TOM!
WAIT!
FWAK
FWAK
IT'S JUST MY JOB! IT'S NOTHING PERSONAL!
BOO
...
OING

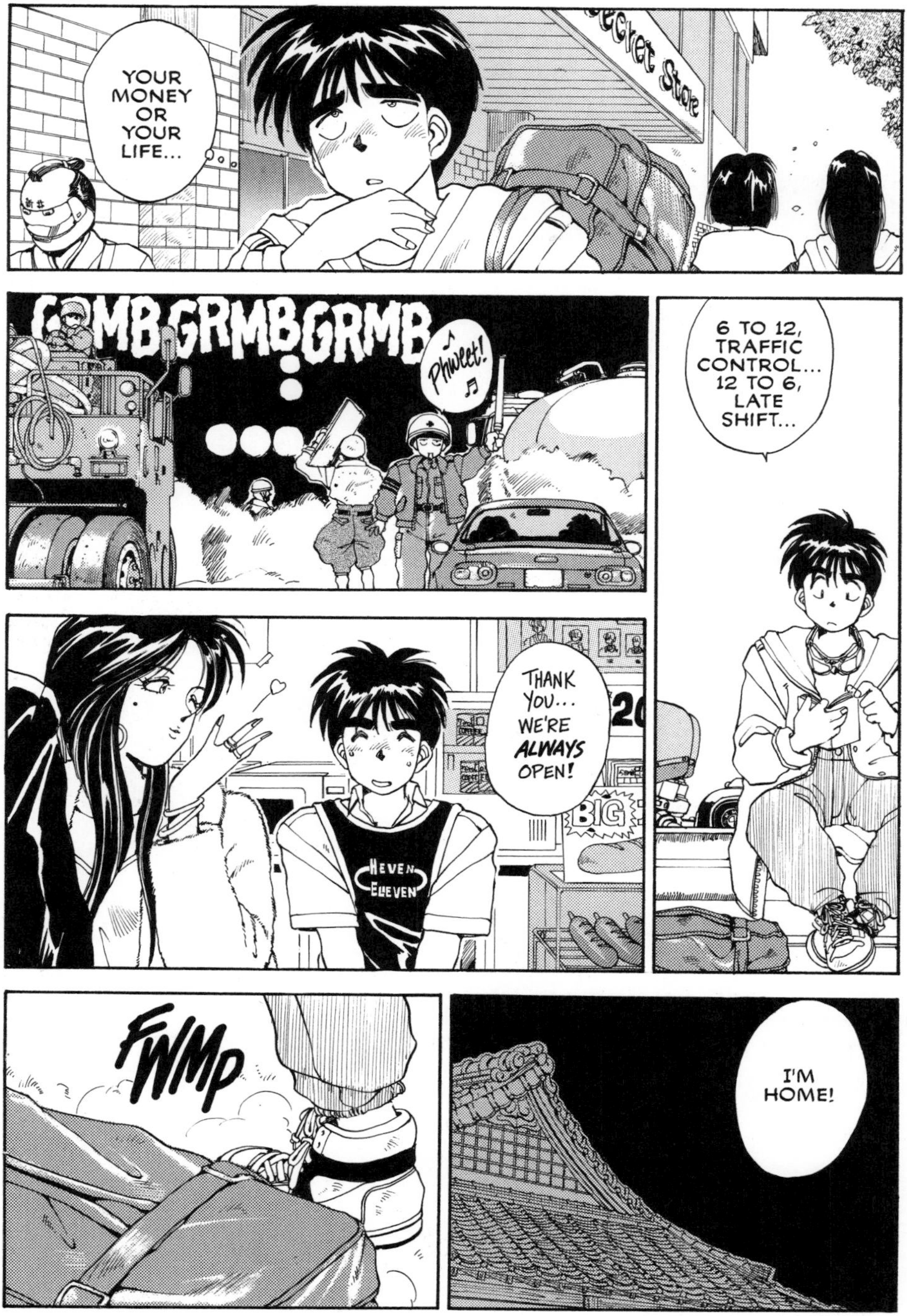
YOUR MONEY OR YOUR LIFE...
6 TO 12, TRAFFIC CONTROL... 12 TO 6, LATE SHIFT...
GRMB GRMB GRMB
Phweet!
THANK YOU... WE'RE ALWAYS OPEN!
HEVEN ELEVEN
BIG
I'M HOME!
FWMP

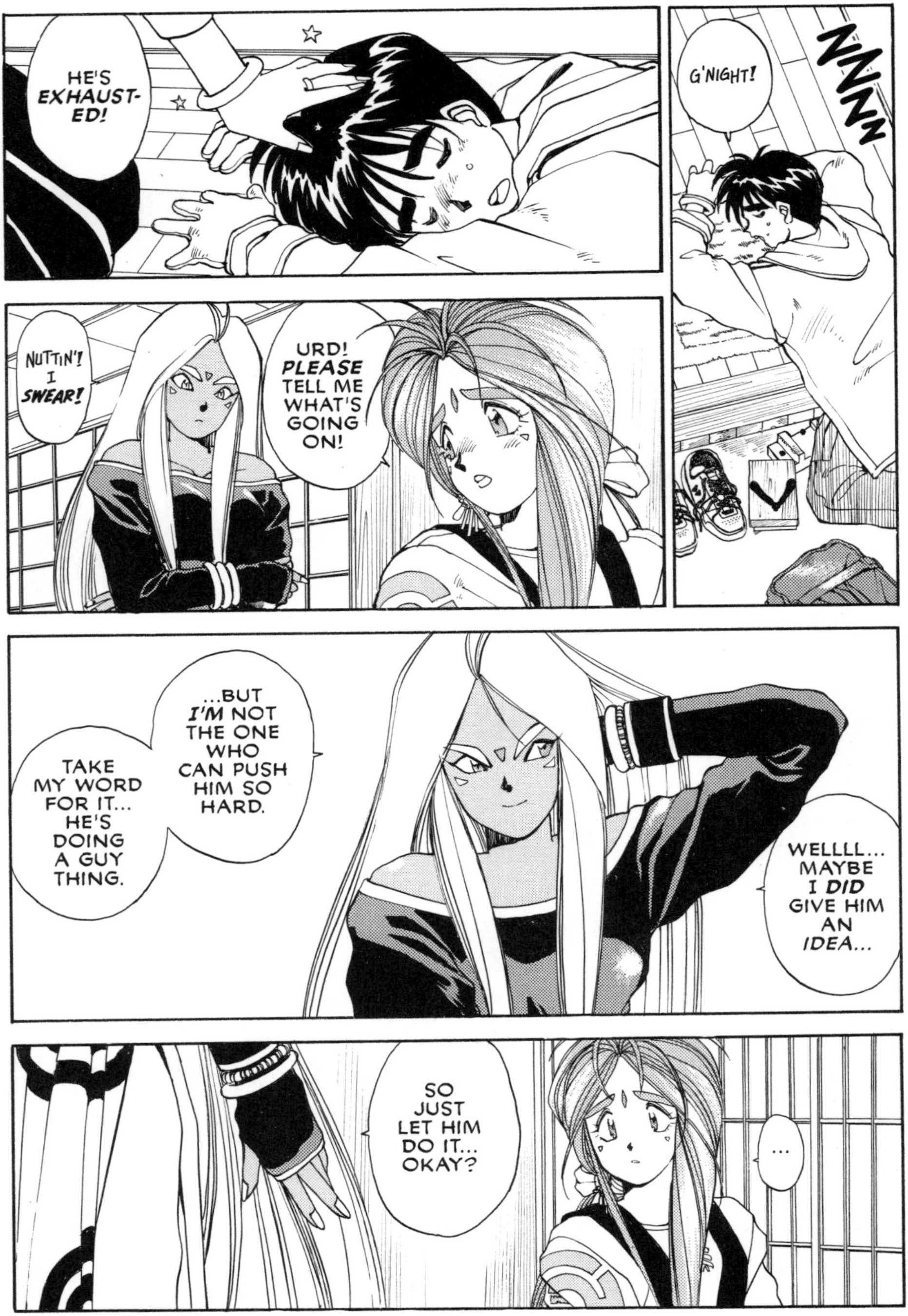
G'NIGHT!
ZZZZ
HE'S EXHAUST-ED!
URD! PLEASE TELL ME WHAT'S GOING ON!
NUTTIN'! I SWEAR!
WELLLL... MAYBE I DID GIVE HIM AN IDEA...
...BUT I'M NOT THE ONE WHO CAN PUSH HIM SO HARD.
TAKE MY WORD FOR IT... HE'S DOING A GUY THING.
...
SO JUST LET HIM DO IT... OKAY?

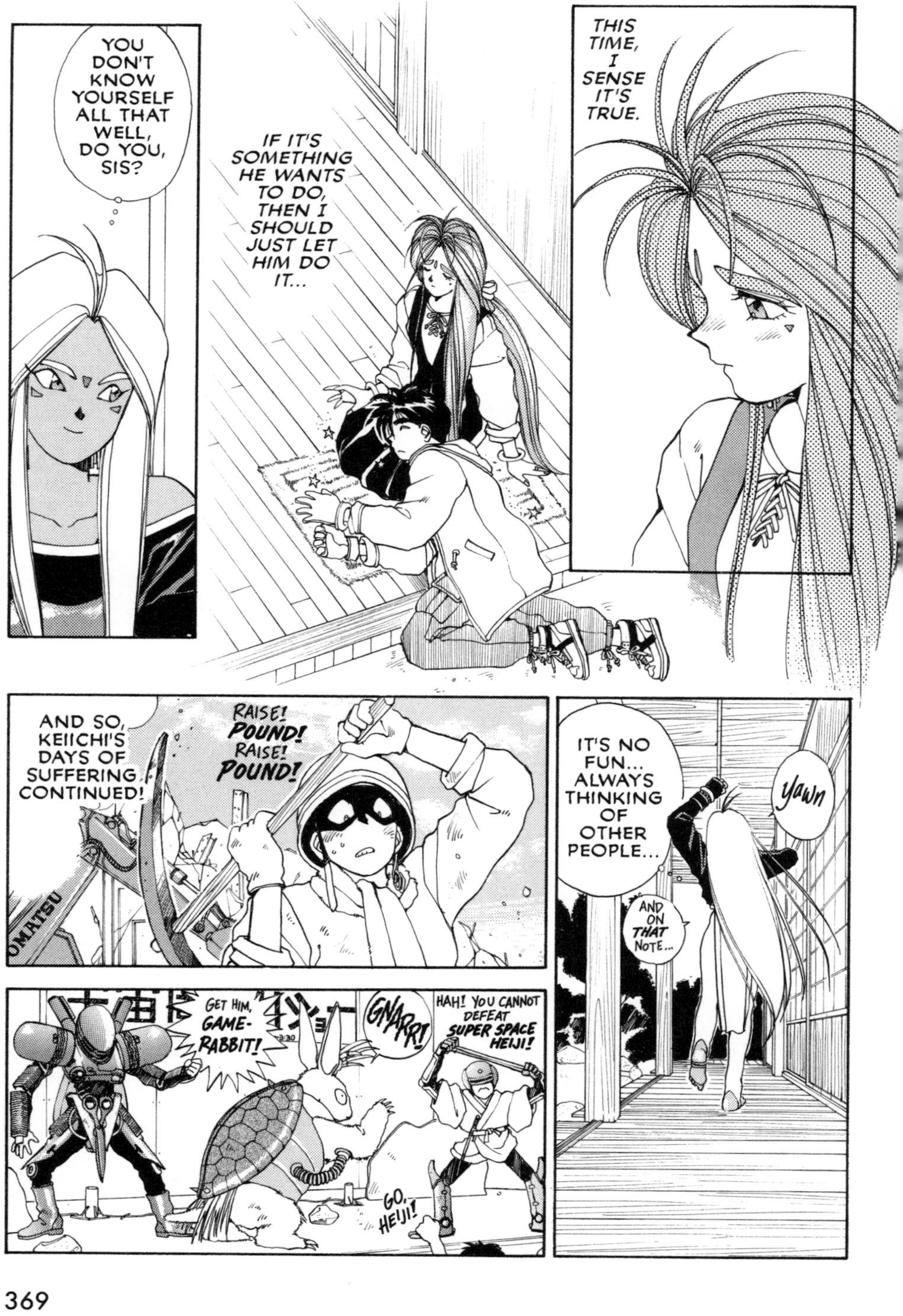
THIS TIME, I SENSE IT'S TRUE.
IF IT'S SOMETHING HE WANTS TO DO, THEN I SHOULD JUST LET HIM DO IT...
YOU DON'T KNOW YOURSELF ALL THAT WELL, DO YOU, SIS?
Yawn
IT'S NO FUN... ALWAYS THINKING OF OTHER PEOPLE...
AND ON THAT NOTE...
RAISE! POUND! RAISE! POUND!
AND SO, KEIICHI'S DAYS OF SUFFERING CONTINUED!
HAH! YOU CANNOT DEFEAT SUPER SPACE HEIJI!
GNARR!
GET HIM, GAME-RABBIT!
GO, HEIJI!

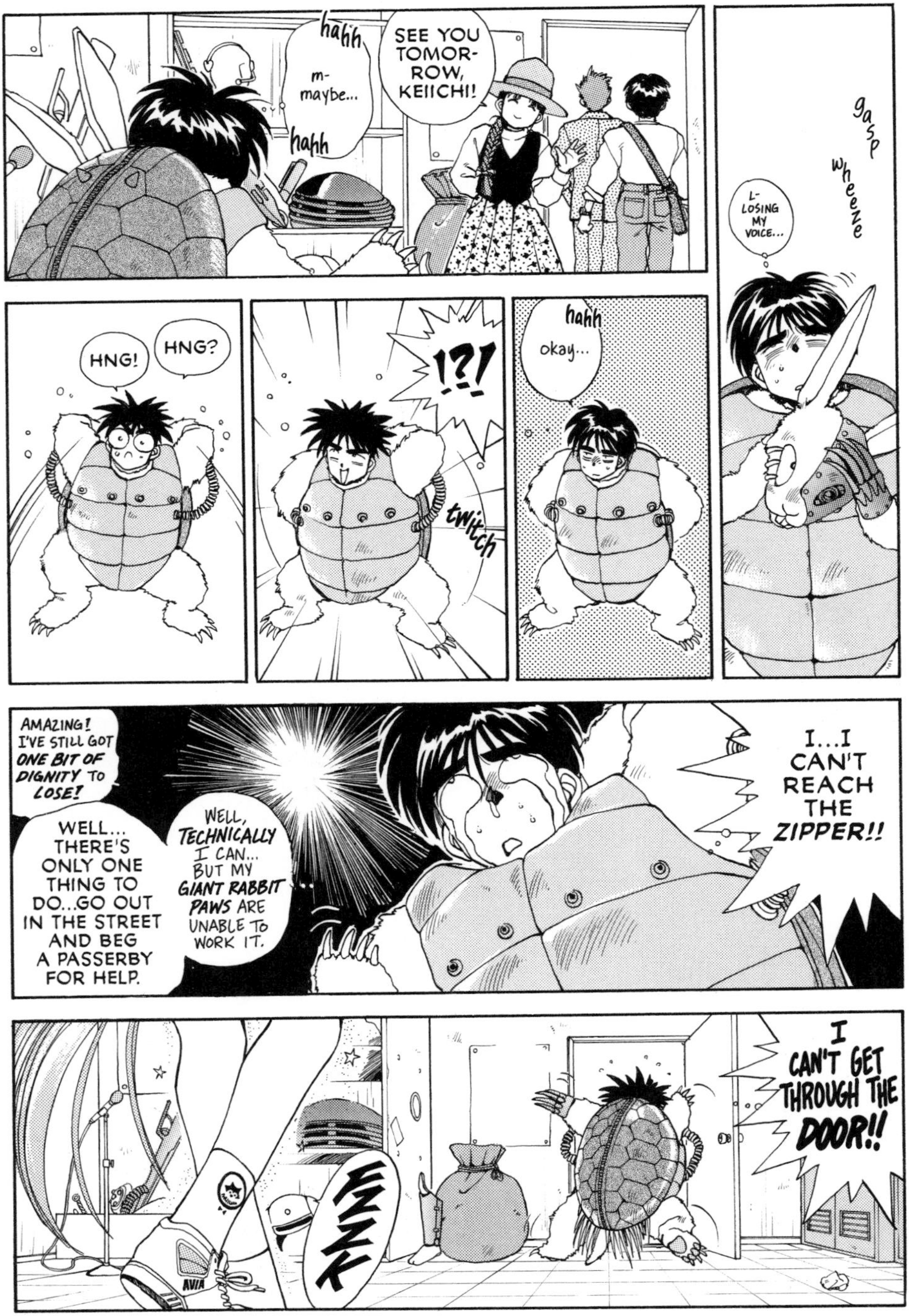
gasp
wheeze
L-LOSING MY VOICE...
SEE YOU TOMORROW, KEIICHI!
hahh
m-maybe...
hahh
hahh
okay...
!?!
twitch
HNG?
HNG!
I...I CAN'T REACH THE ZIPPER!!
WELL, TECHNICALLY I CAN... BUT MY GIANT RABBIT PAWS ARE UNABLE TO WORK IT.
WELL... THERE'S ONLY ONE THING TO DO...GO OUT IN THE STREET AND BEG A PASSERBY FOR HELP.
AMAZING! I'VE STILL GOT ONE BIT OF DIGNITY TO LOSE!
I CAN'T GET THROUGH THE DOOR!!
ZZZK
AVIA

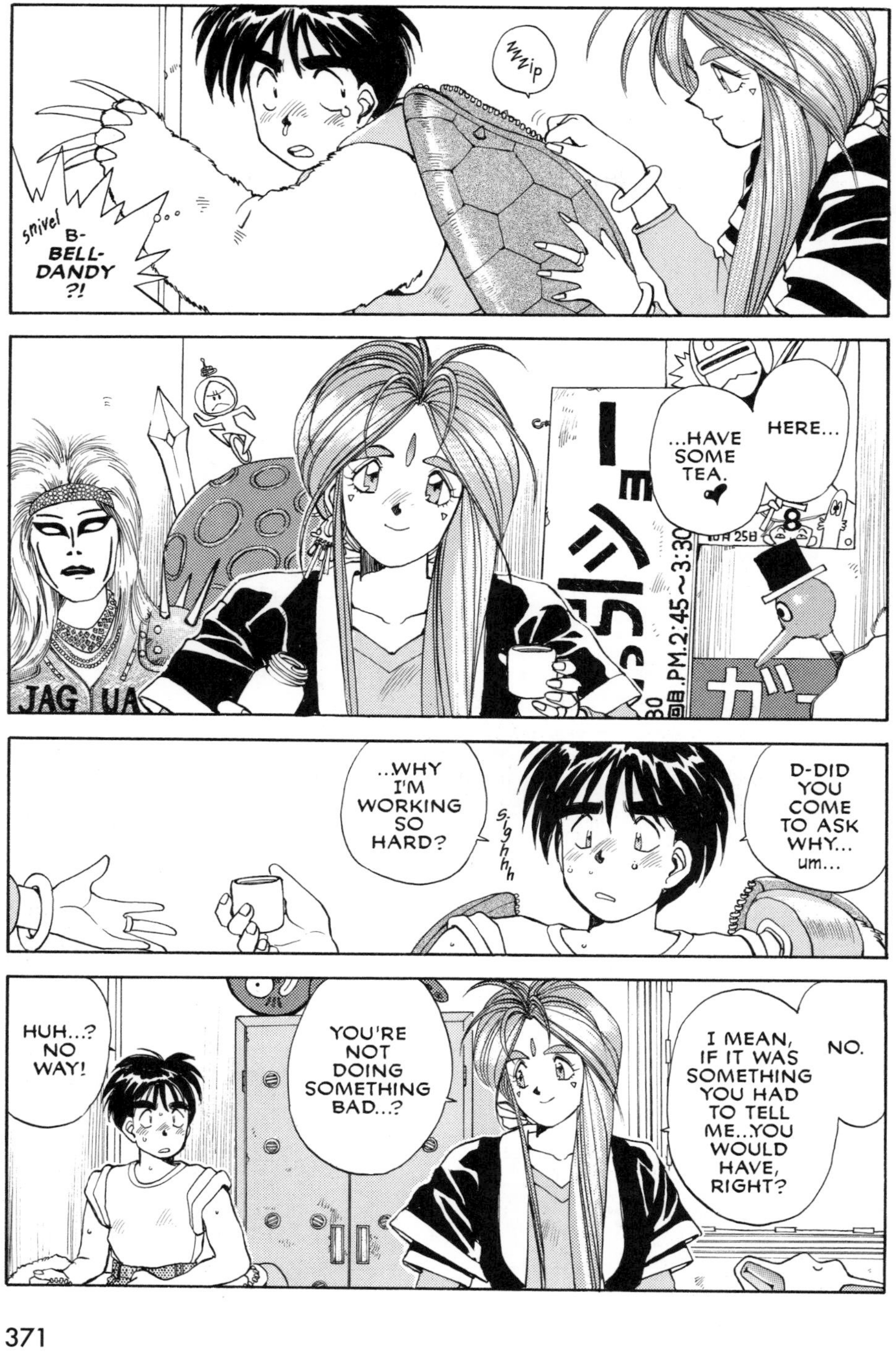
zzzip
snivel
B-BELL-DANDY?!
HERE...
...HAVE SOME TEA.
JAG UA
D-DID YOU COME TO ASK WHY... um...
sighhh
...WHY I'M WORKING SO HARD?
NO.
I MEAN, IF IT WAS SOMETHING YOU HAD TO TELL ME...YOU WOULD HAVE, RIGHT?
YOU'RE NOT DOING SOMETHING BAD...?
HUH...? NO WAY!

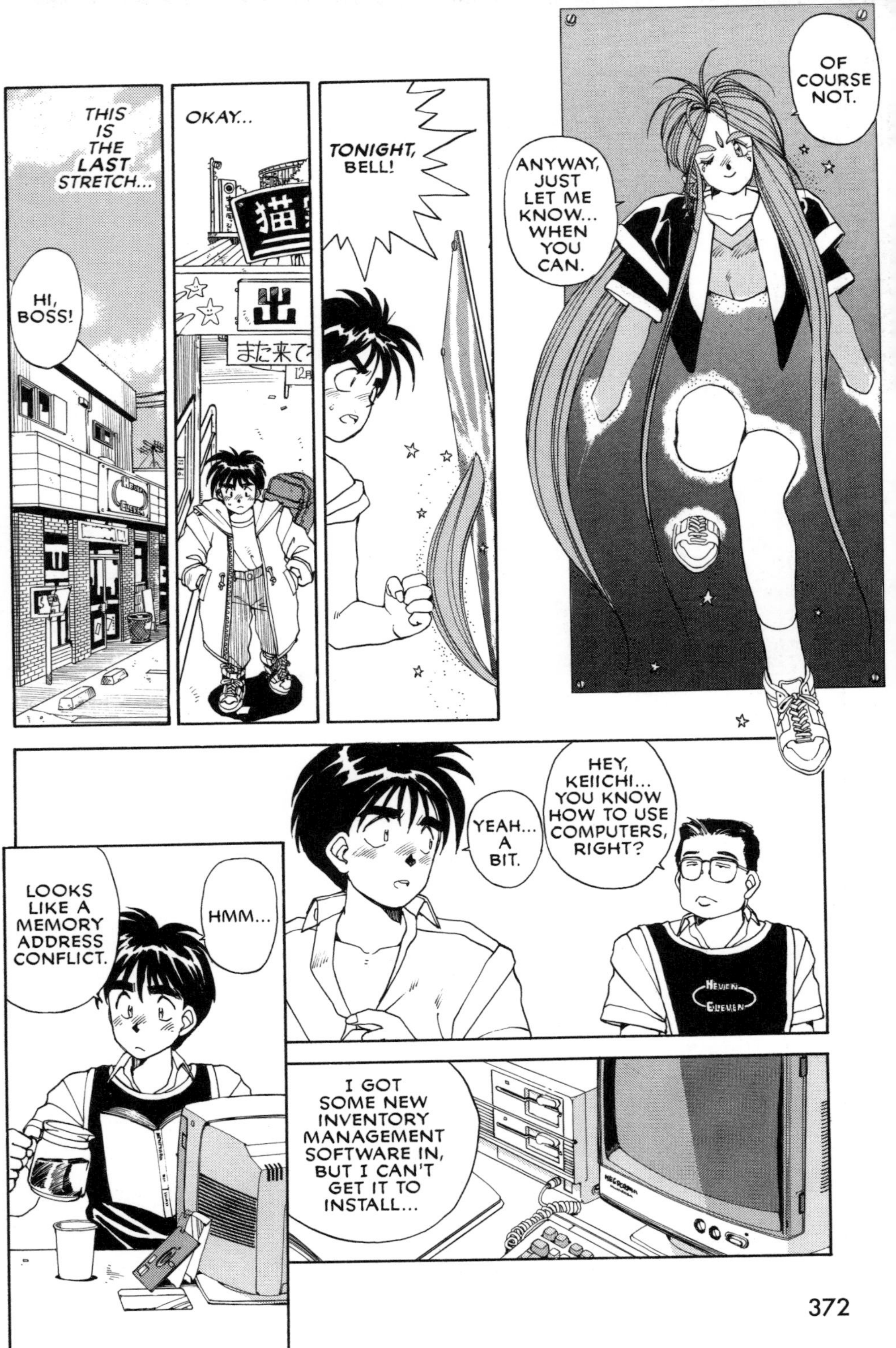
OF COURSE NOT.
ANYWAY, JUST LET ME KNOW... WHEN YOU CAN.
TONIGHT, BELL!
OKAY...
THIS IS THE LAST STRETCH...
HI, BOSS!
HEY, KEIICHI... YOU KNOW HOW TO USE COMPUTERS, RIGHT?
YEAH... A BIT.
I GOT SOME NEW INVENTORY MANAGEMENT SOFTWARE IN, BUT I CAN'T GET IT TO INSTALL...
HMM...
LOOKS LIKE A MEMORY ADDRESS CONFLICT.

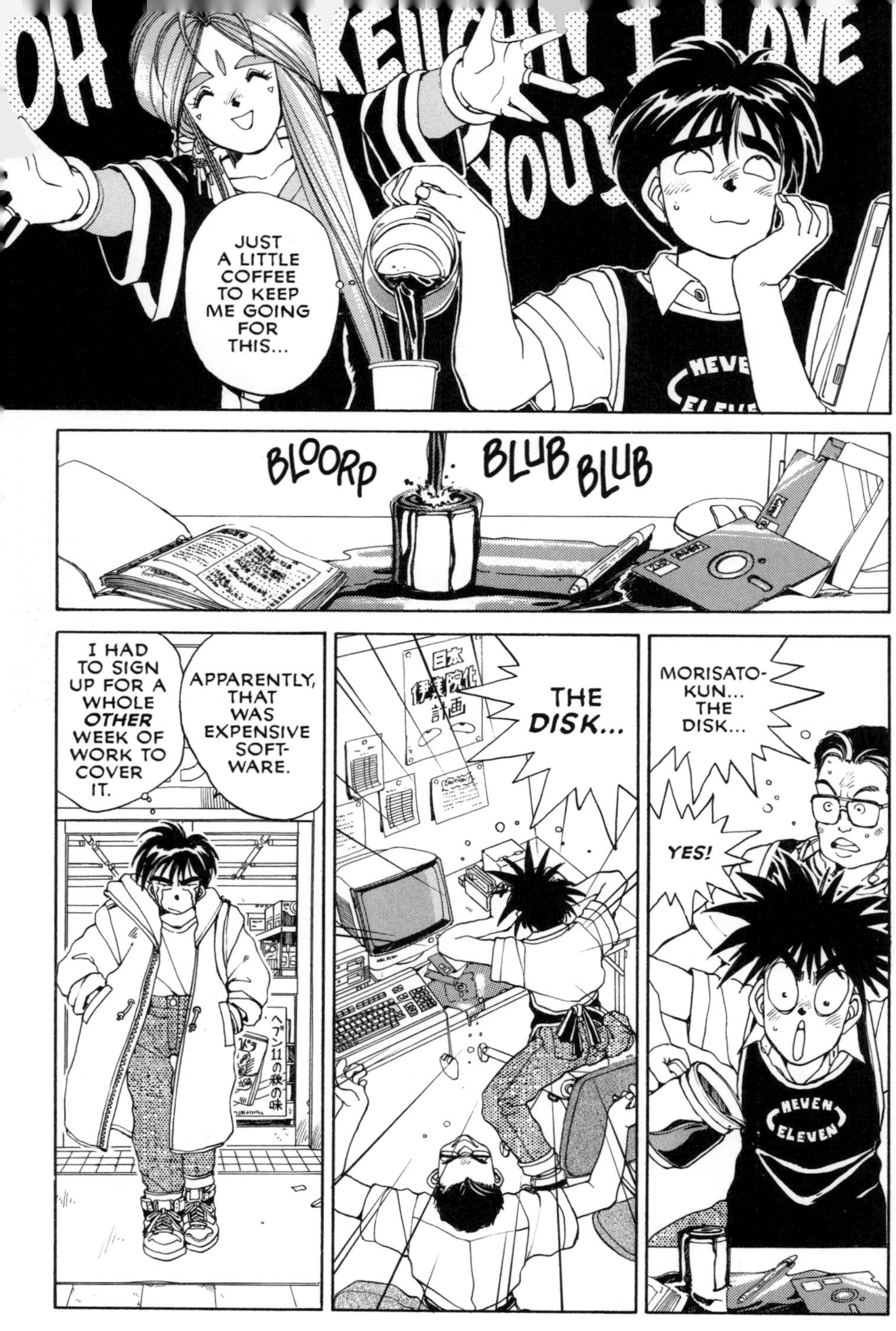
OH KEIICHI! I LOVE YOU!
JUST A LITTLE COFFEE TO KEEP ME GOING FOR THIS...
HEVEN ELEVEN
BLOORP
BLUB BLUB
MORISATO-KUN... THE DISK...
YES!
HEVEN ELEVEN
THE DISK...
APPARENTLY, THAT WAS EXPENSIVE SOFT-WARE.
I HAD TO SIGN UP FOR A WHOLE OTHER WEEK OF WORK TO COVER IT.
ヘブン11の秋の味

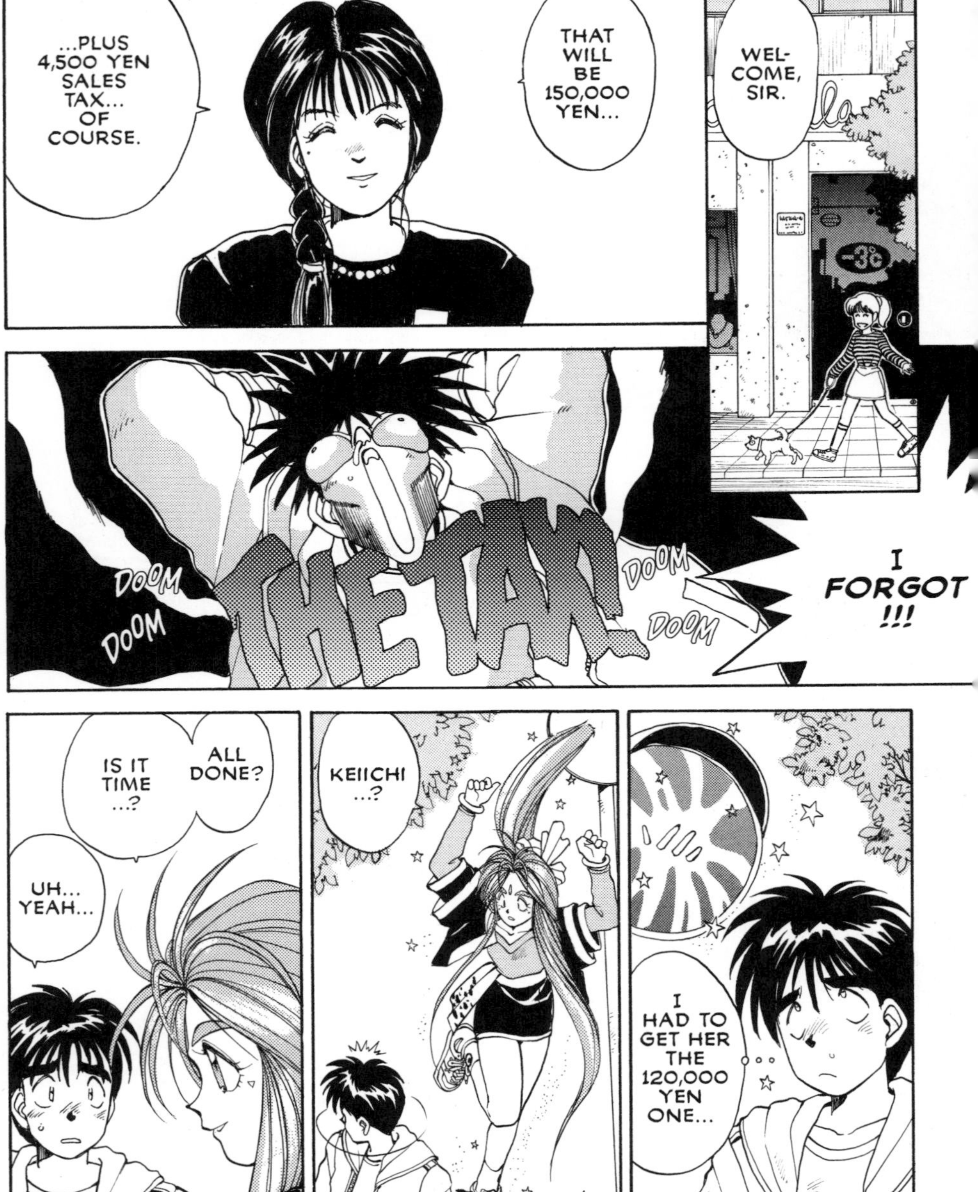
WEL-COME, SIR.
THAT WILL BE 150,000 YEN...
...PLUS 4,500 YEN SALES TAX... OF COURSE.
I FORGOT !!!
DOOM
DOOM
THE TAX
DOOM
DOOM
I HAD TO GET HER THE 120,000 YEN ONE...
KEIICHI ...?
ALL DONE?
IS IT TIME ...?
UH... YEAH...

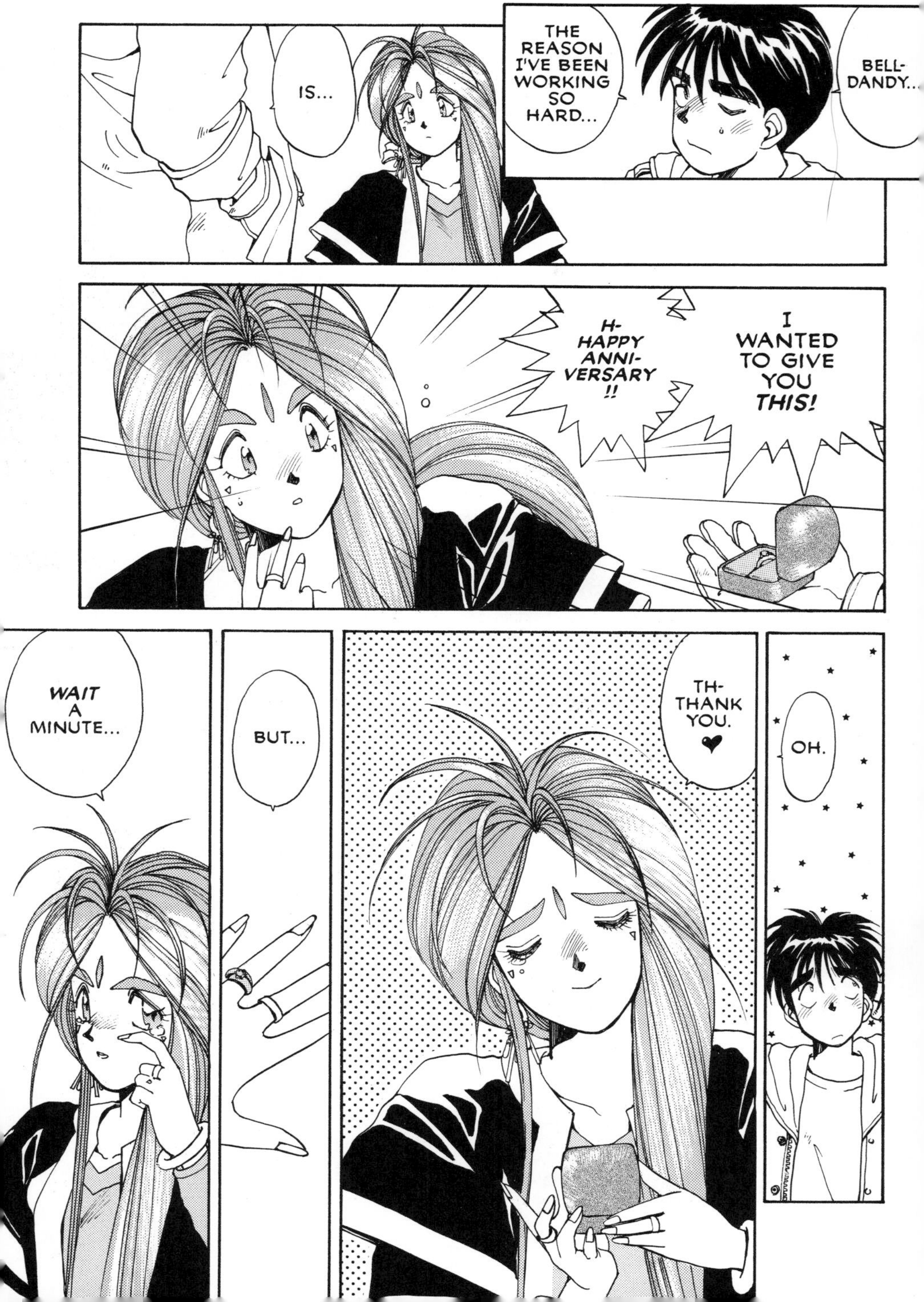
BELL-DANDY...
THE REASON I'VE BEEN WORKING SO HARD...
IS...
I WANTED TO GIVE YOU *THIS!*
H-HAPPY ANNI-VERSARY!!
OH.
TH-THANK YOU. ❤
BUT...
WAIT A MINUTE...

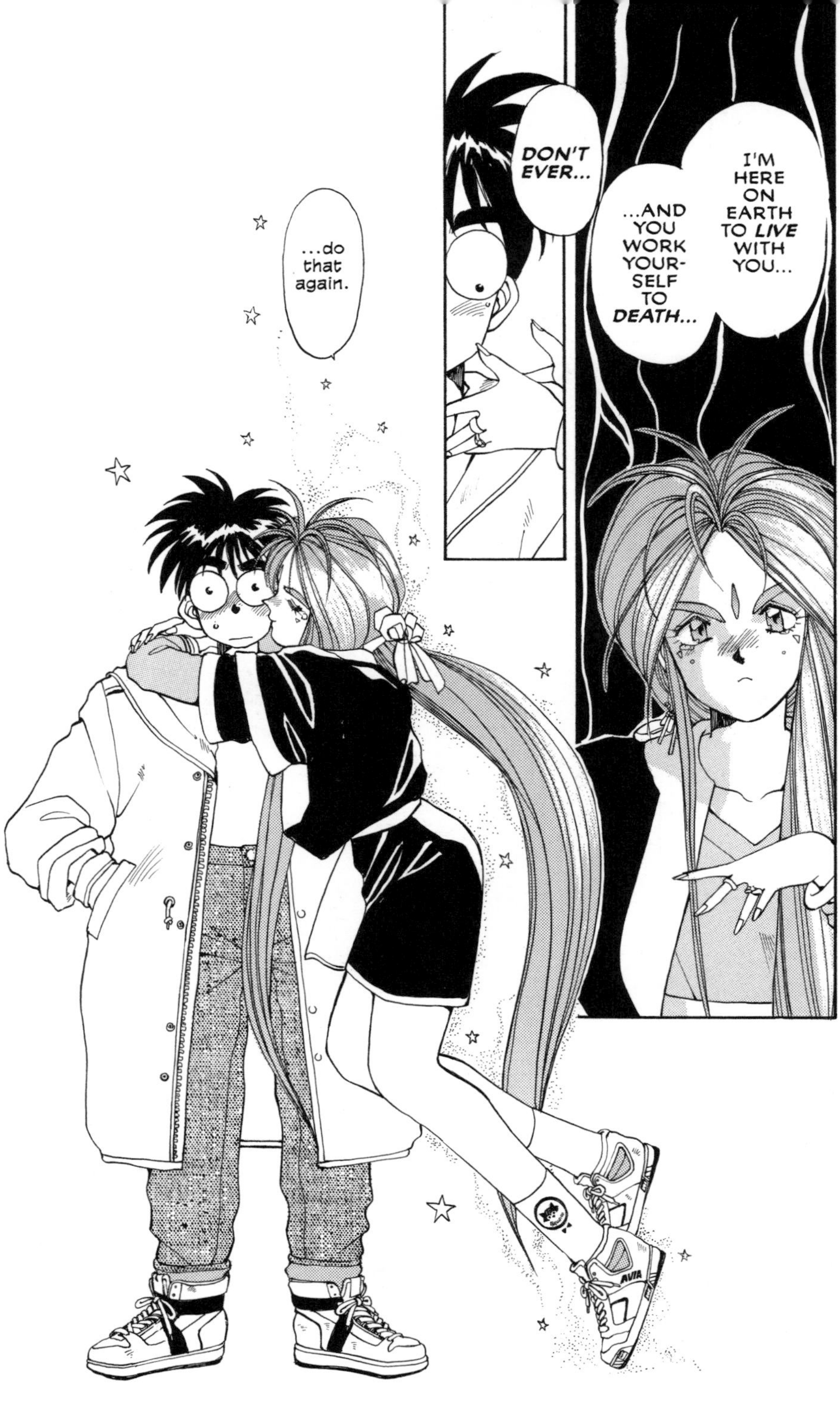
I'M HERE ON EARTH TO *LIVE* WITH YOU...
...AND YOU WORK YOUR-SELF TO *DEATH*...
DON'T EVER...
...do that again.

OH MY MANGA ART-IST!

Goddess Side Story

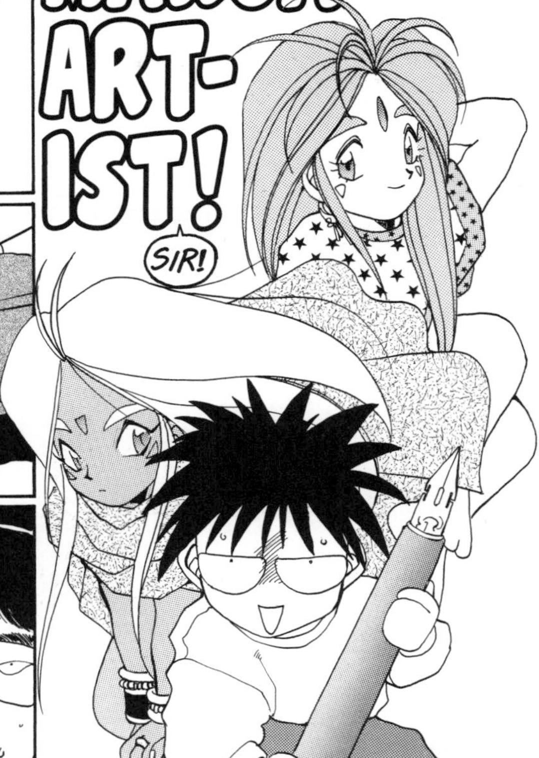
SIR!

STORY AND ART BY

KOSUKE FUJISHIMA

A Satan-Like Gentleman

THE SHIELD

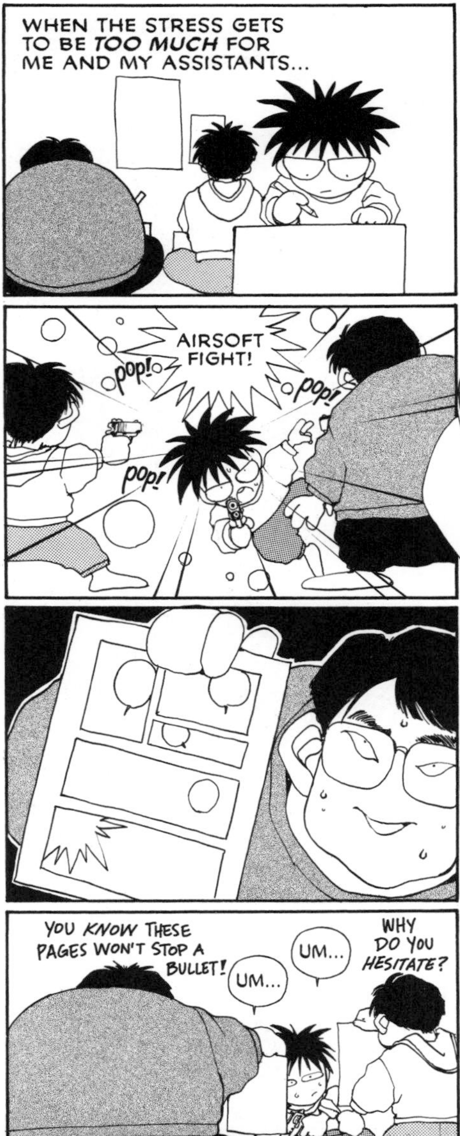
WHEN THE STRESS GETS TO BE *TOO MUCH* FOR ME AND MY ASSISTANTS...
POP!
AIRSOFT FIGHT!
POP!
POP!
WHY DO YOU *HESITATE?*
UM...
UM...
YOU *KNOW* THESE PAGES WON'T STOP A BULLET!

THE TRAP

hey...
hey...
hey... hey...
WHAT?
we've all tried it...
...
THIS DRINK, WHICH SHALL REMAIN ANONYMOUS, IS FAMOUS FOR ITS TASTE.
it's really...
AWFUL
AND YET, SOMEHOW, IT'S VERY POPULAR IN FUJISHIMA'S NEIGHBOR-HOOD.

THE PAPER

WE HAVE A BIRD IN OUR STUDIO NAMED *TIGER CHERRY*.
HE MAKES SMALL CONTRI-BUTIONS TO OUR WORK.
SQUAK!
flap flap
AWK! AWWK!
flap flap
UH...
sob
plop

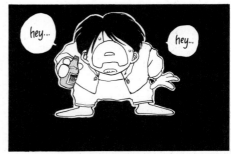

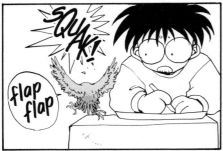

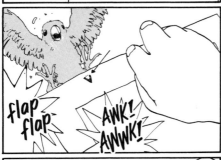

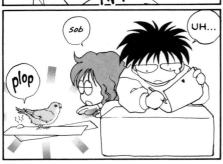

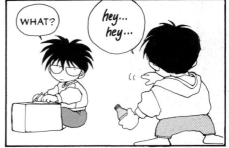

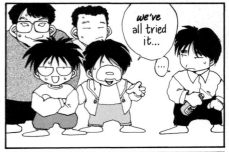

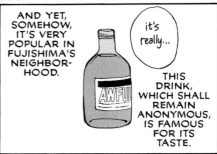

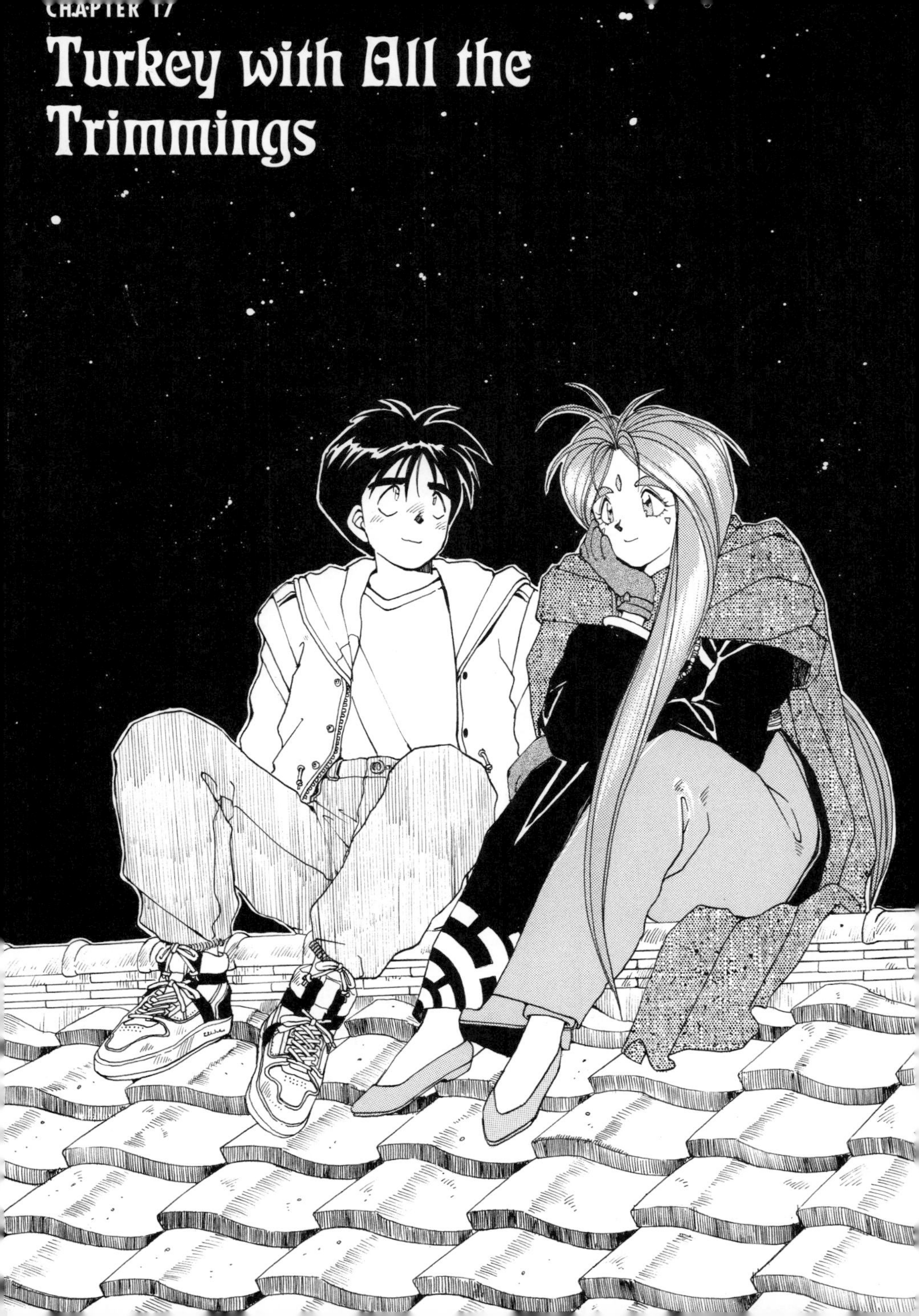
CHAPTER 17
Turkey with All the Trimmings

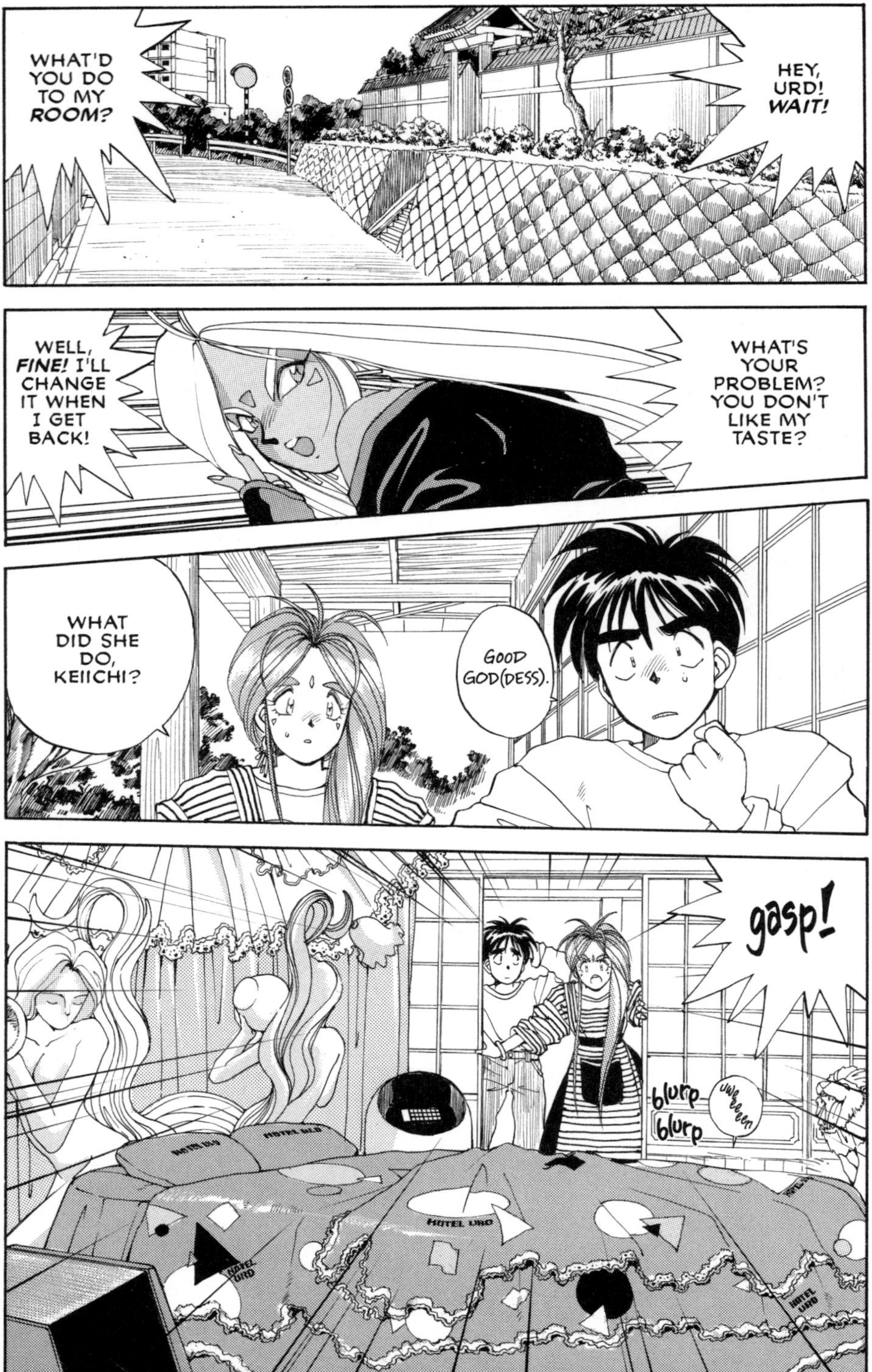
HEY, URD! WAIT!
WHAT'D YOU DO TO MY ROOM?
WHAT'S YOUR PROBLEM? YOU DON'T LIKE MY TASTE?
WELL, FINE! I'LL CHANGE IT WHEN I GET BACK!
GOOD GOD(DESS).
WHAT DID SHE DO, KEIICHI?
gasp!
uweeeen
blurp
blurp

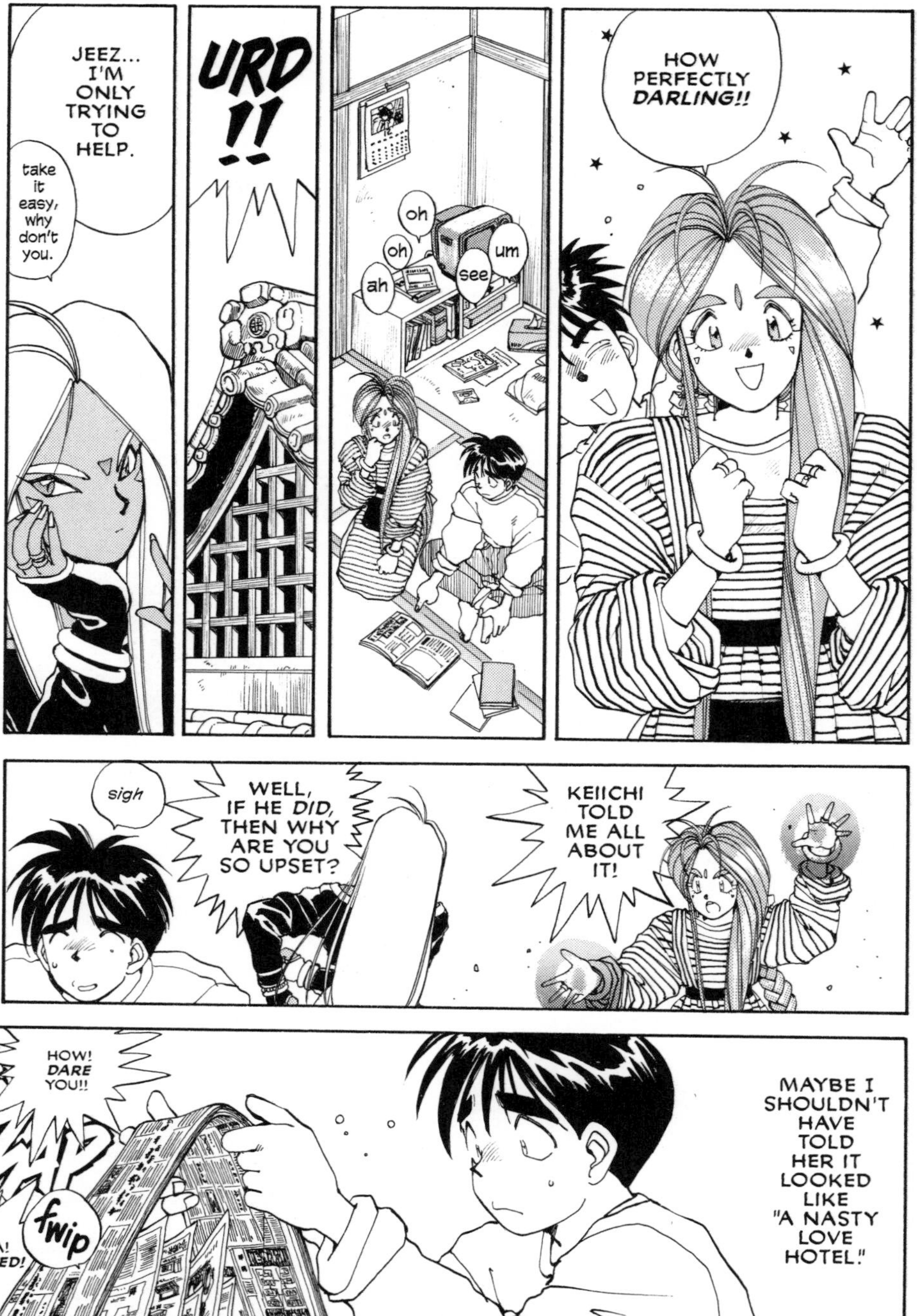

HOW PERFECTLY *DARLING!!*
oh
um
oh
see
ah
URD!!
JEEZ... I'M ONLY TRYING TO HELP.
take it easy, why don't you.
KEIICHI TOLD ME ALL ABOUT IT!
WELL, IF HE *DID,* THEN WHY ARE YOU SO UPSET?
sigh
MAYBE I SHOULDN'T HAVE TOLD HER IT LOOKED LIKE "A NASTY LOVE HOTEL."
HOW! *DARE* YOU!!
fwip
HA! *MISSED!*

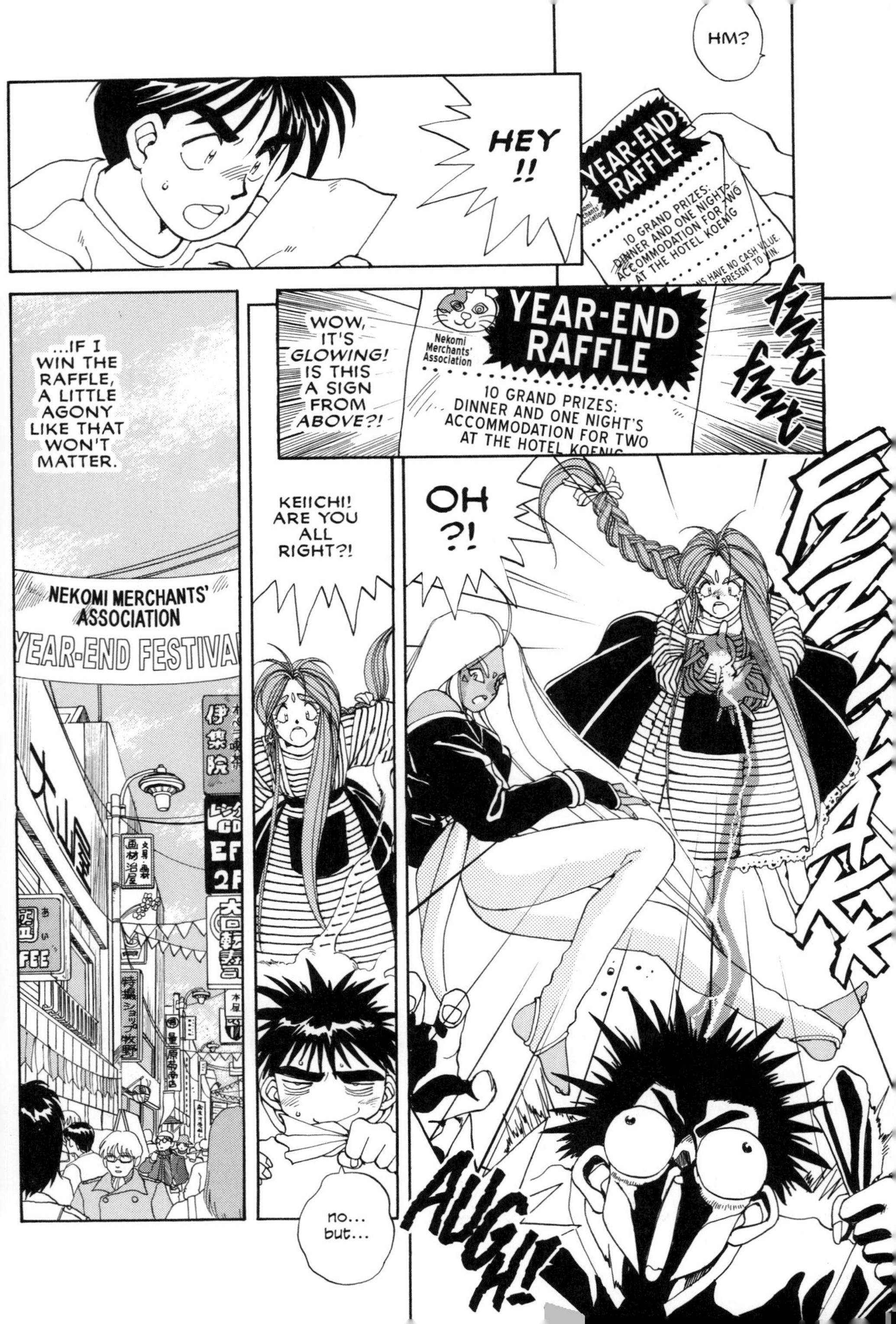
HM?
YEAR-END RAFFLE
Nekomi Merchants' Association
10 GRAND PRIZES: DINNER AND ONE NIGHT'S ACCOMMODATION FOR TWO AT THE HOTEL KOENIG
HEY !!
YEAR-END RAFFLE
Nekomi Merchants' Association
10 GRAND PRIZES: DINNER AND ONE NIGHT'S ACCOMMODATION FOR TWO
WOW, IT'S *GLOWING!* IS THIS A SIGN FROM *ABOVE?!*
OH ?!
AUGH!
KEIICHI! ARE YOU ALL RIGHT?!
no... but...
...IF I WIN THE RAFFLE, A LITTLE AGONY LIKE THAT WON'T MATTER.
NEKOMI MERCHANTS' ASSOCIATION
YEAR-END FESTIVAL

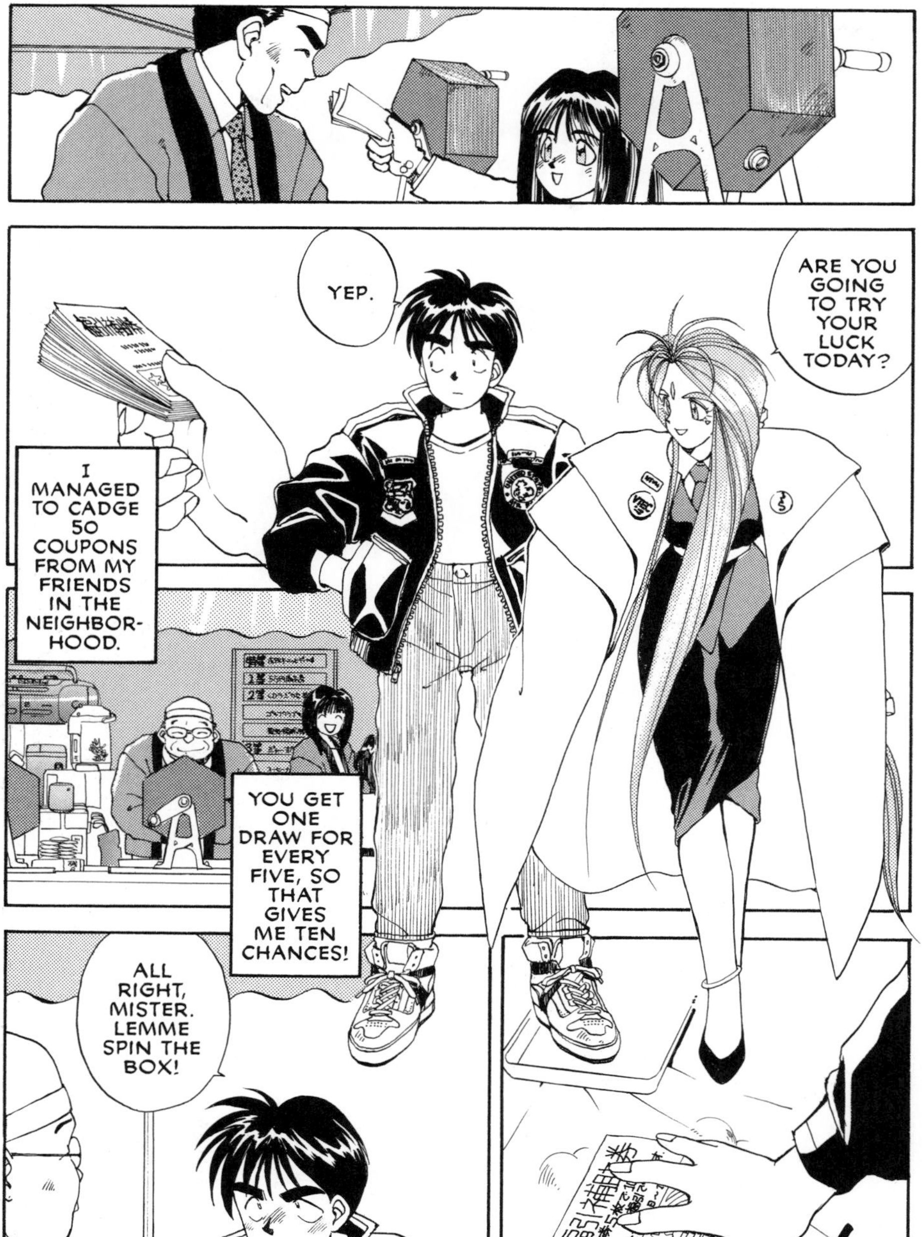
ARE YOU GOING TO TRY YOUR LUCK TODAY?
YEP.
I MANAGED TO CADGE 50 COUPONS FROM MY FRIENDS IN THE NEIGHBOR-HOOD.
YOU GET ONE DRAW FOR EVERY FIVE, SO THAT GIVES ME TEN CHANCES!
whap
ALL RIGHT, MISTER. LEMME SPIN THE BOX!

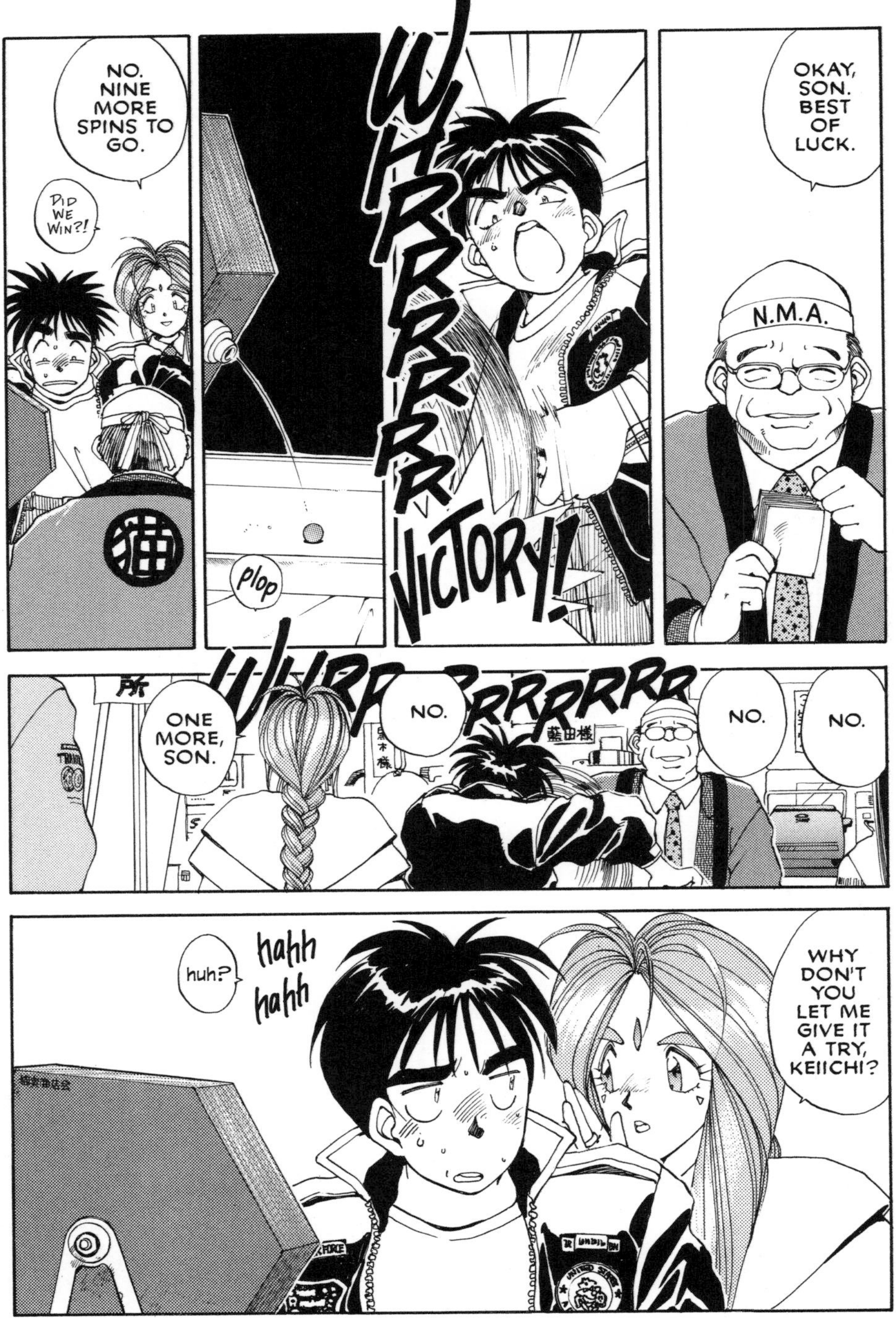
OKAY, SON. BEST OF LUCK.
N.M.A.
WHRRRRRR
VICTORY!
plop
NO. NINE MORE SPINS TO GO.
DID WE WIN?!
NO.
NO.
NO.
ONE MORE, SON.
WHY DON'T YOU LET ME GIVE IT A TRY, KEIICHI?
hahh hahh
huh?

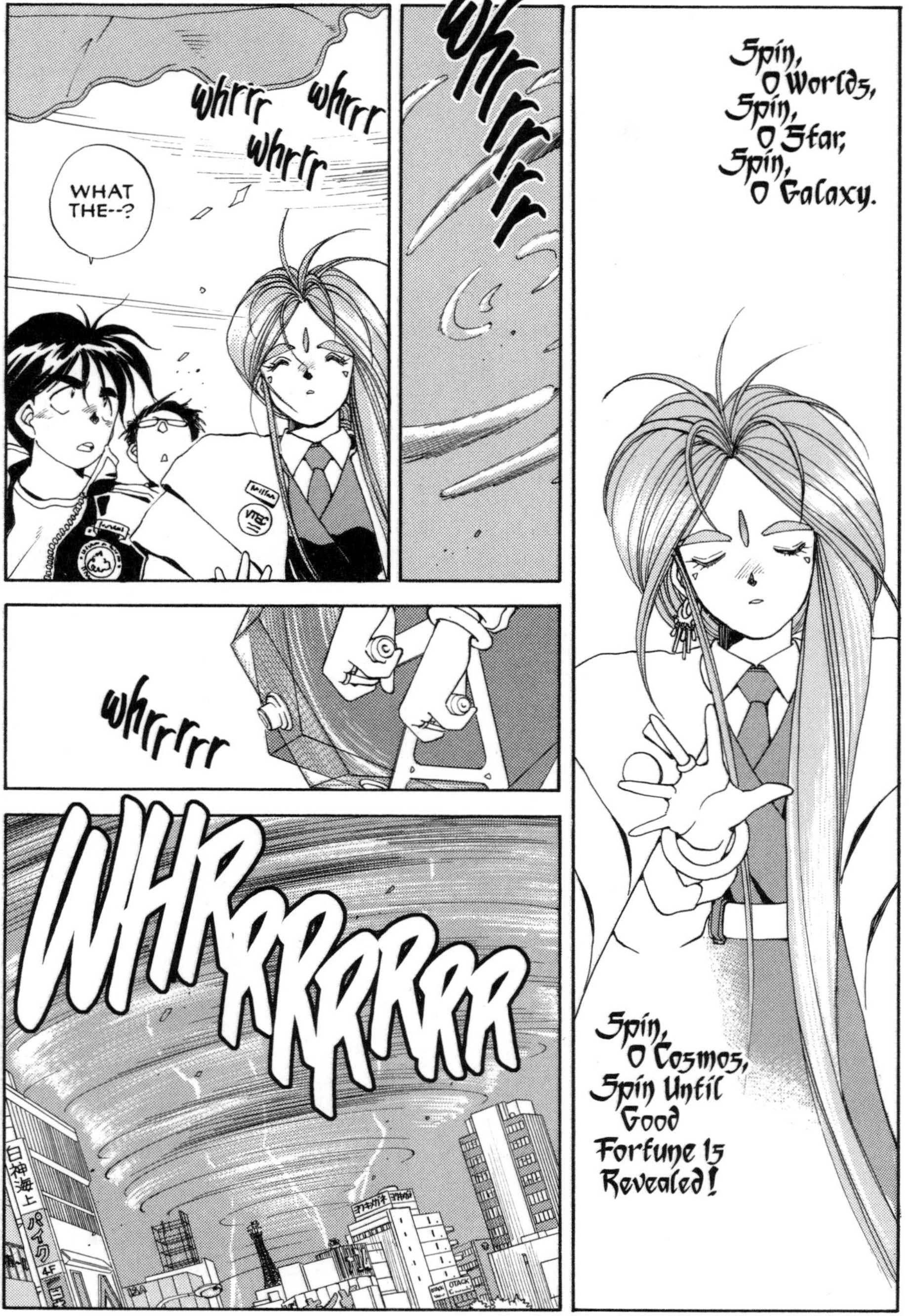
Spin, O Worlds, Spin, O Star; Spin, O Galaxy.
Spin, O Cosmos, Spin Until Good Fortune Is Revealed!
whrrrrrr
whrrr
whrrr
whrrr
WHAT THE--?
whrrrrr
WHRRRRRRR
白神海上
パイク
4F

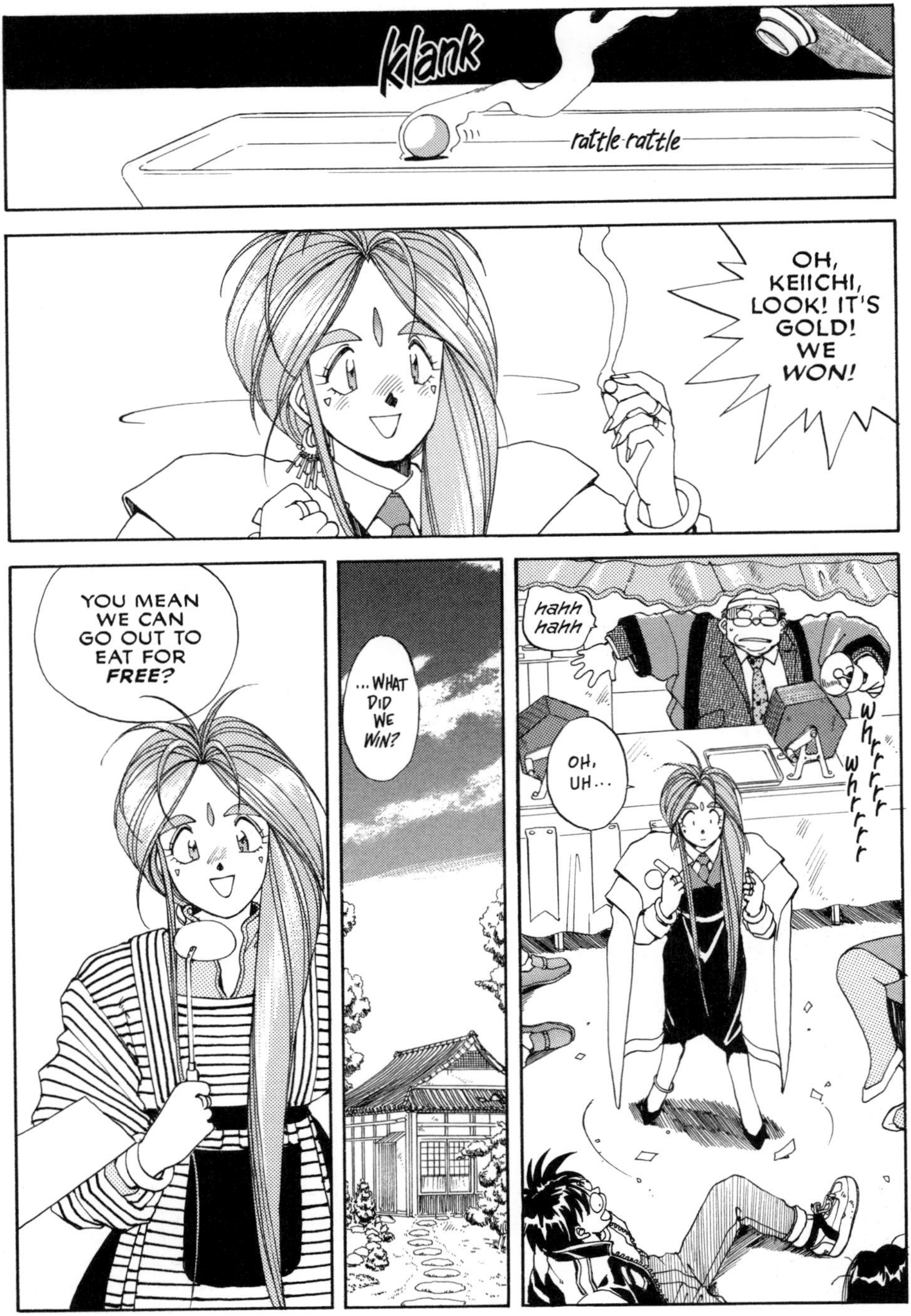
klank
rattle rattle
OH, KEIICHI, LOOK! IT'S GOLD! WE WON!
hahh hahh
whrrrr whrrrr whrrrr
OH, UH...
...WHAT DID WE WIN?
YOU MEAN WE CAN GO OUT TO EAT FOR FREE?

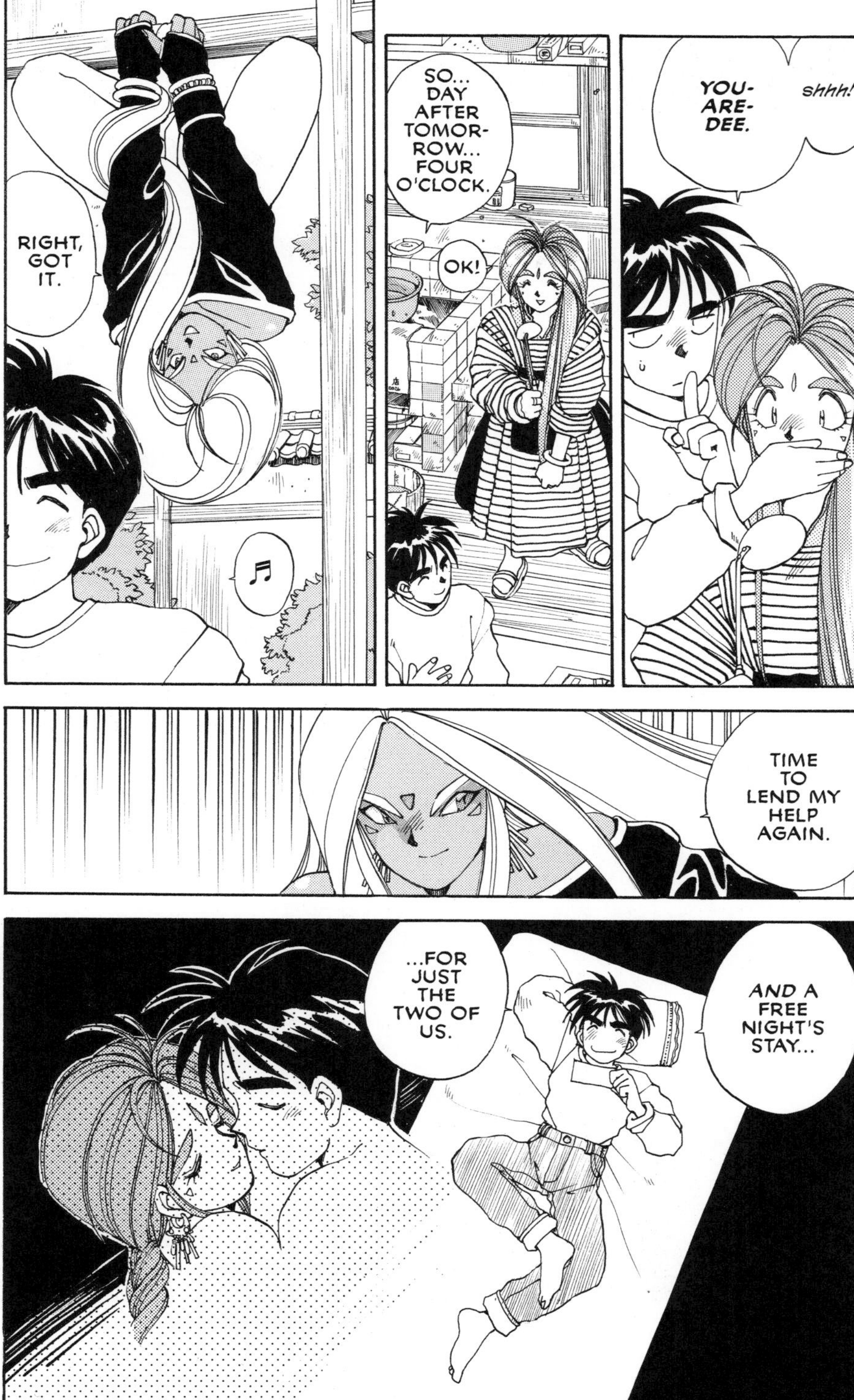
YOU-ARE-DEE.
shhh!
SO... DAY AFTER TOMORROW... FOUR O'CLOCK.
OK!
RIGHT, GOT IT.
♬
TIME TO LEND MY HELP AGAIN.
AND A FREE NIGHT'S STAY...
...FOR JUST THE TWO OF US.

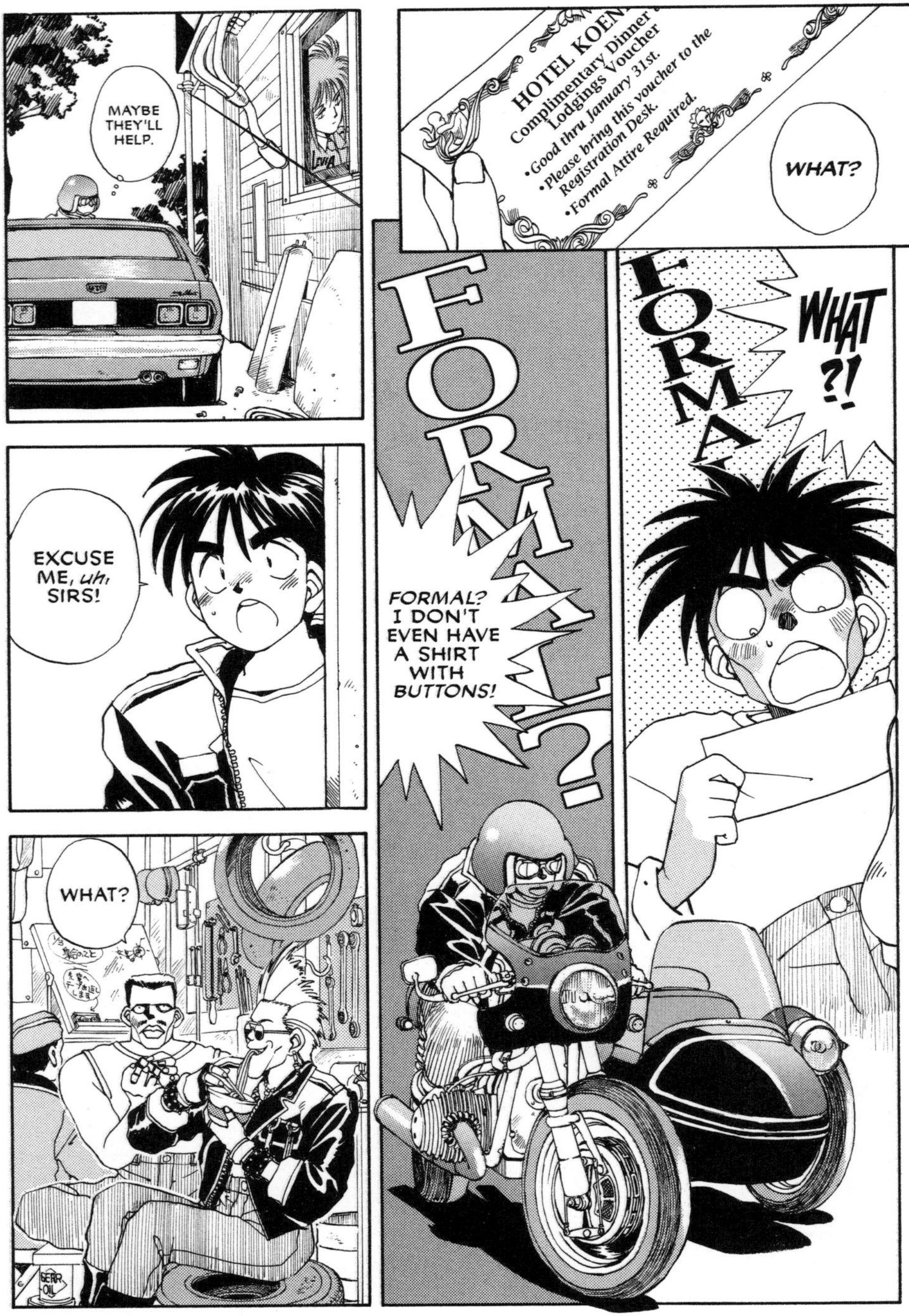
HOTEL KOEN
Complimentary Dinner & Lodgings Voucher
•Good thru January 31st.
•Please bring this voucher to the Registration Desk.
•Formal Attire Required.
WHAT?
FORMA
WHAT ?!
FORMAL?
FORMAL? I DON'T EVEN HAVE A SHIRT WITH BUTTONS!
MAYBE THEY'LL HELP.
EXCUSE ME, uh, SIRS!
WHAT?

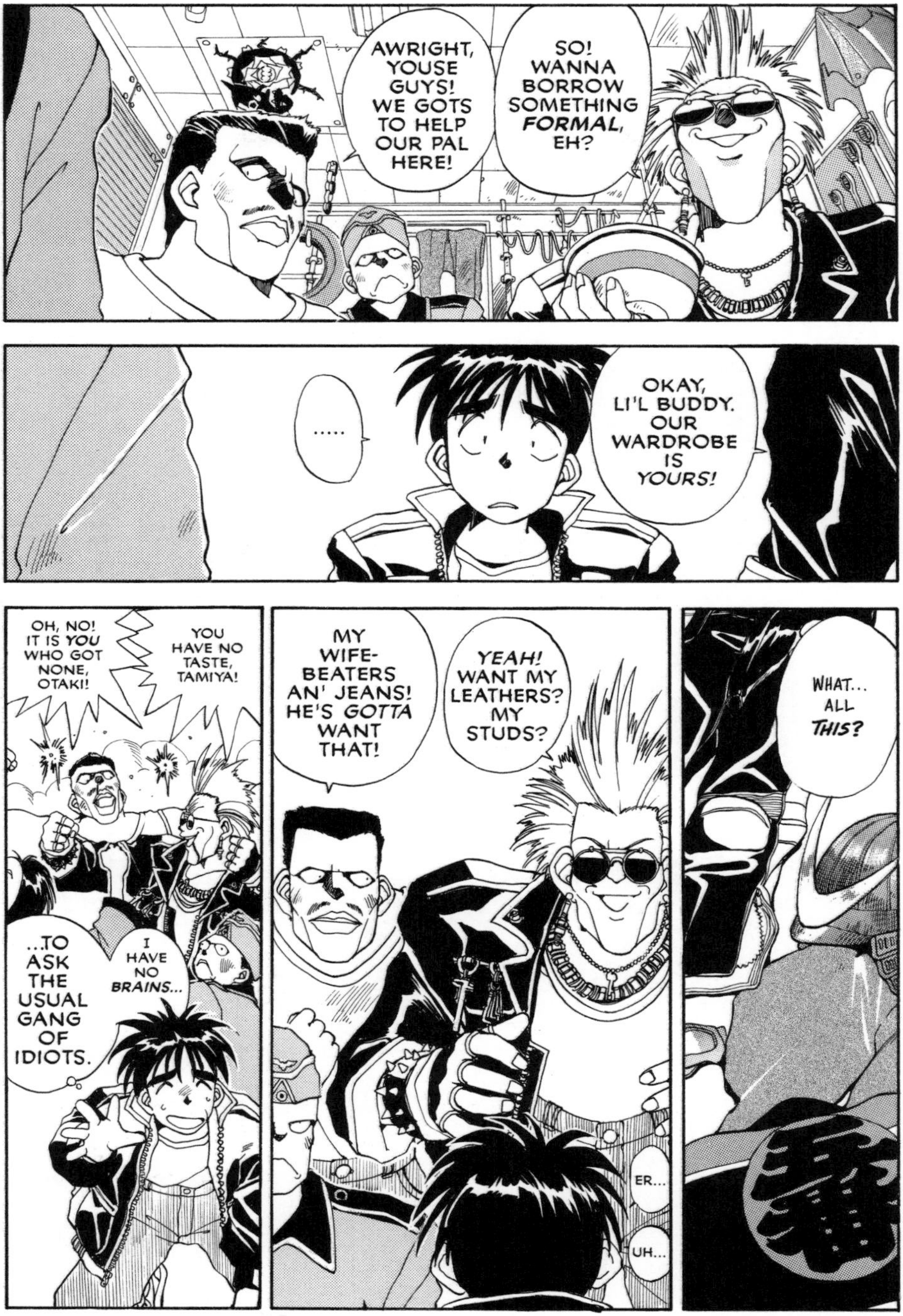
SO! WANNA BORROW SOMETHING FORMAL, EH?
AWRIGHT, YOUSE GUYS! WE GOTS TO HELP OUR PAL HERE!
OKAY, LI'L BUDDY. OUR WARDROBE IS YOURS!
.....
WHAT... ALL THIS?
YEAH! WANT MY LEATHERS? MY STUDS?
MY WIFE-BEATERS AN' JEANS! HE'S GOTTA WANT THAT!
ER...
UH...
YOU HAVE NO TASTE, TAMIYA!
OH, NO! IT IS YOU WHO GOT NONE, OTAKI!
I HAVE NO BRAINS...
...TO ASK THE USUAL GANG OF IDIOTS.

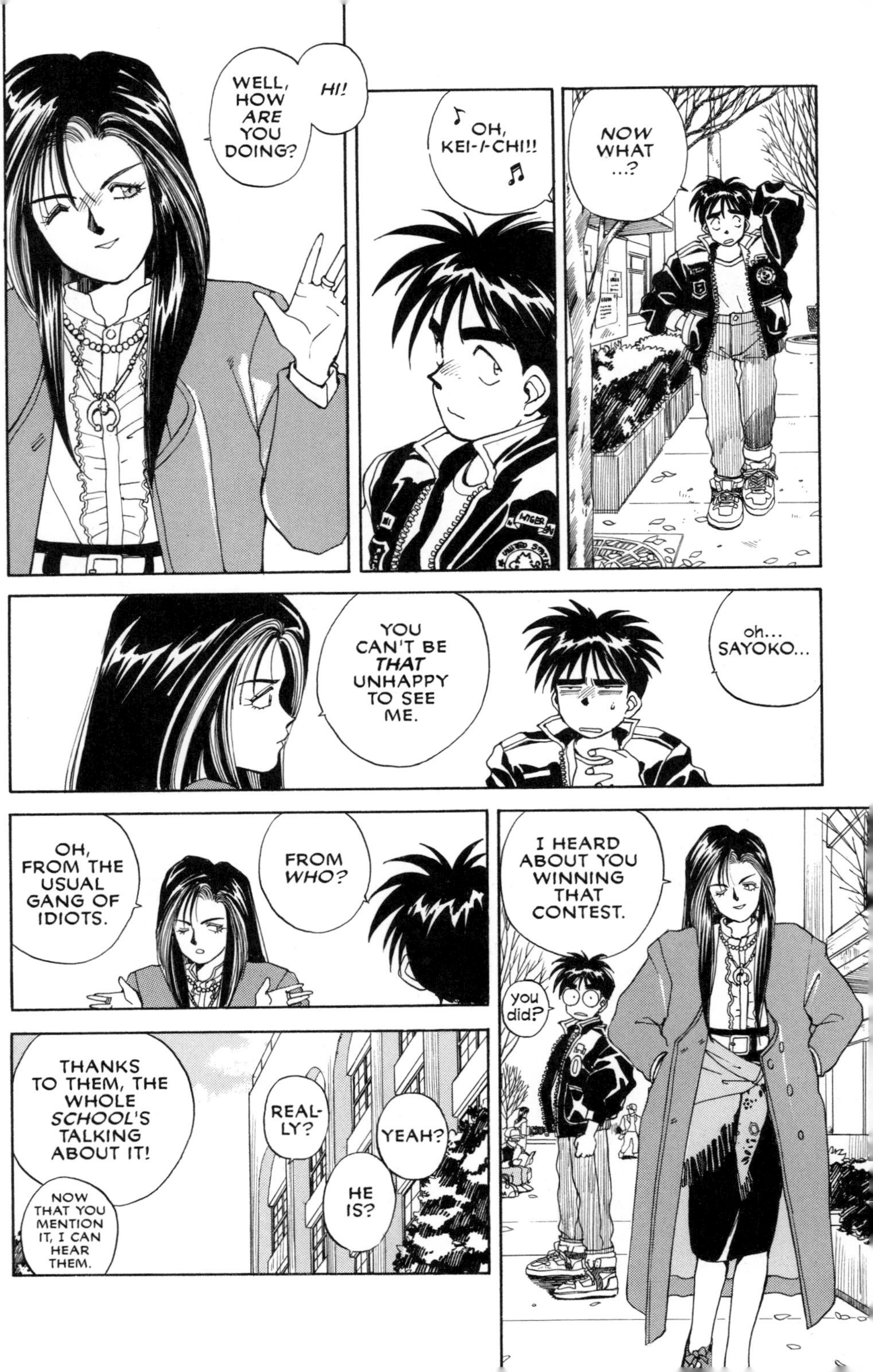

NOW WHAT ...?
OH, KEI-I-CHI!! ♪ ♫
HI!
WELL, HOW ARE YOU DOING?
oh... SAYOKO...
YOU CAN'T BE THAT UNHAPPY TO SEE ME.
I HEARD ABOUT YOU WINNING THAT CONTEST.
you did?
FROM WHO?
OH, FROM THE USUAL GANG OF IDIOTS.
THANKS TO THEM, THE WHOLE SCHOOL'S TALKING ABOUT IT!
REAL-LY?
YEAH?
HE IS?
NOW THAT YOU MENTION IT, I CAN HEAR THEM.

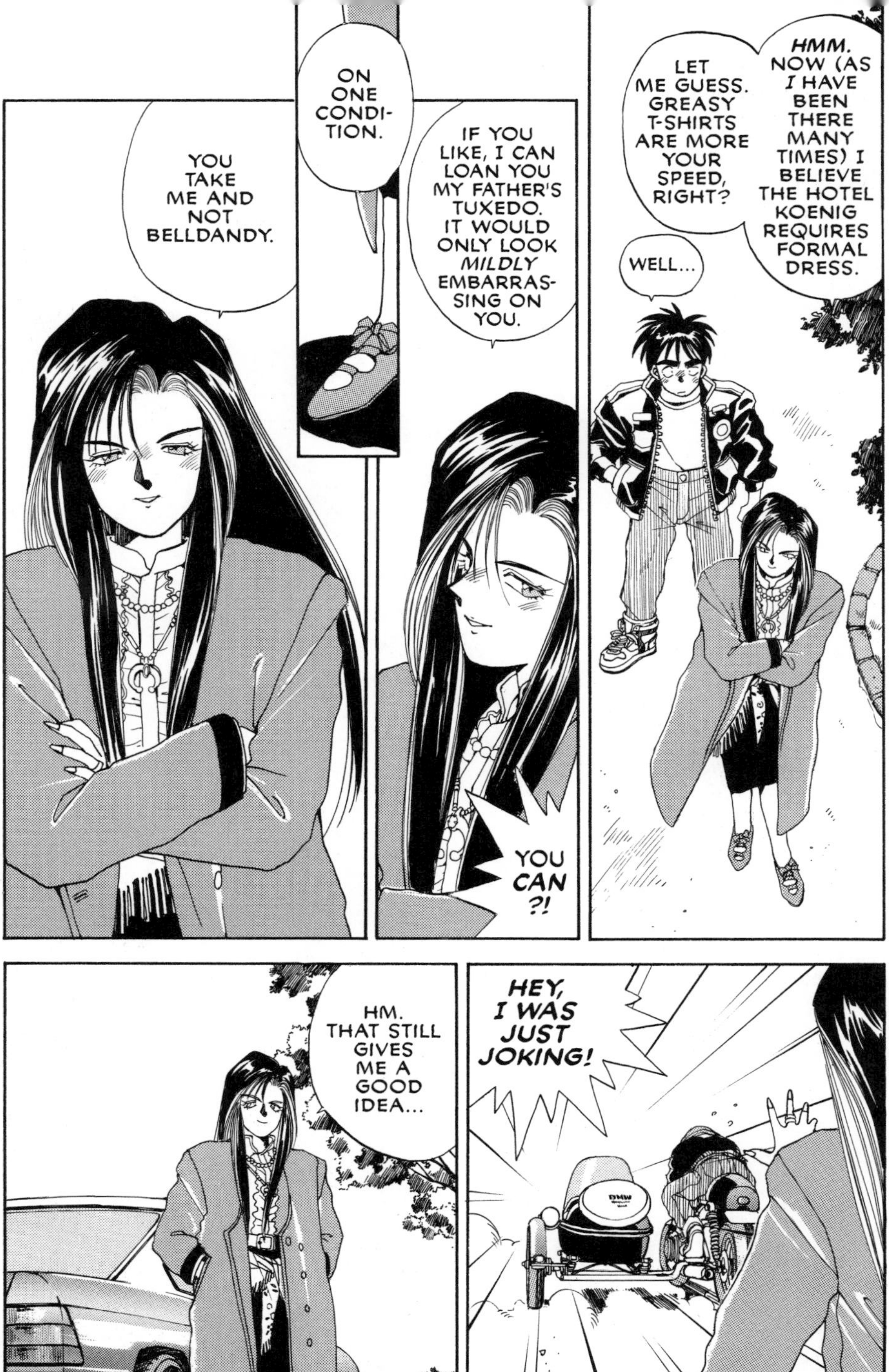
HMM. NOW (AS I HAVE BEEN THERE MANY TIMES) I BELIEVE THE HOTEL KOENIG REQUIRES FORMAL DRESS.
LET ME GUESS. GREASY T-SHIRTS ARE MORE YOUR SPEED, RIGHT?
WELL...
IF YOU LIKE, I CAN LOAN YOU MY FATHER'S TUXEDO. IT WOULD ONLY LOOK *MILDLY* EMBARRASSING ON YOU.
YOU *CAN* ?!
ON ONE CONDITION.
YOU TAKE ME AND NOT BELLDANDY.
HEY, I WAS JUST JOKING!
HM. THAT STILL GIVES ME A GOOD IDEA...

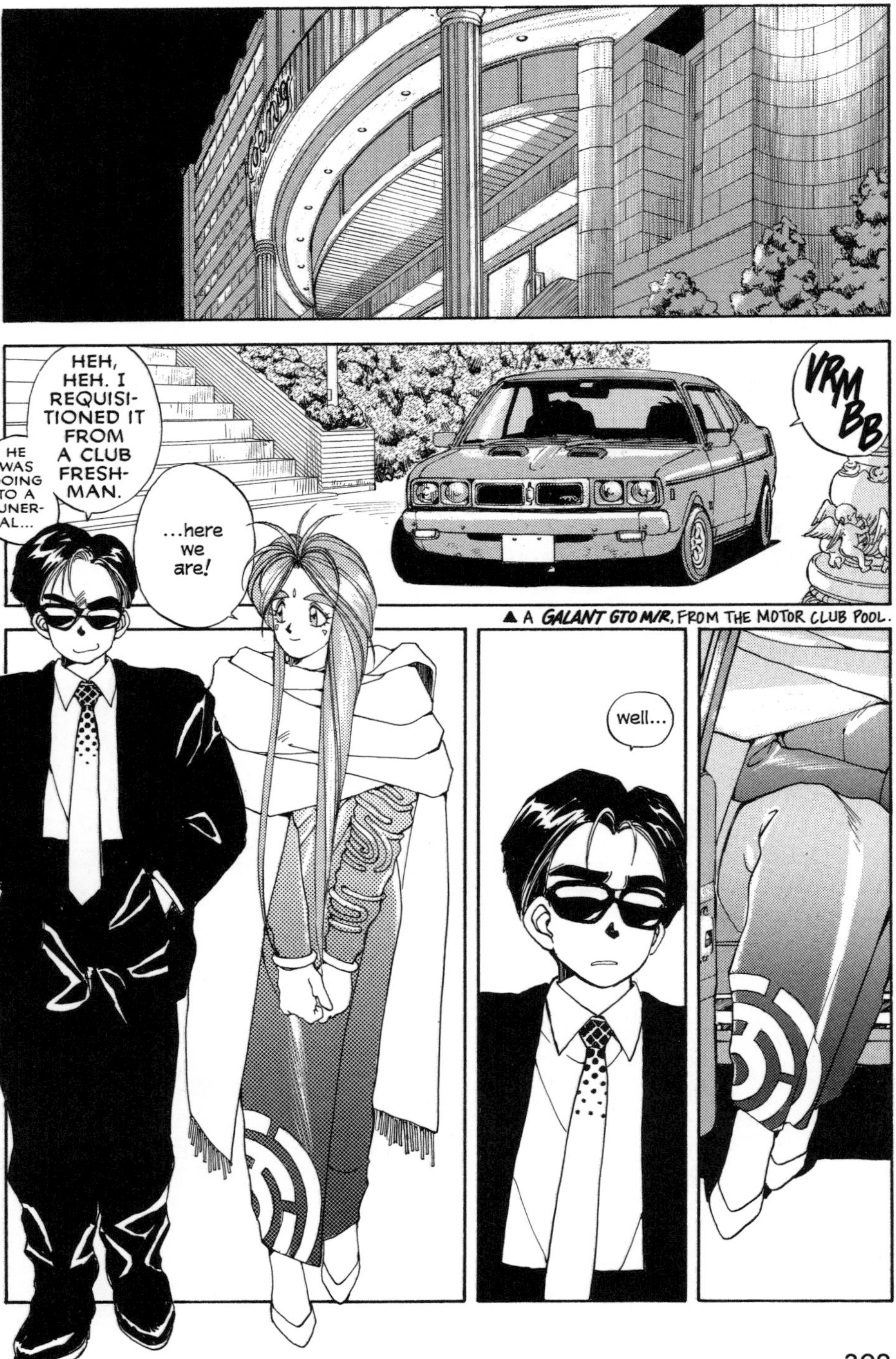
VRMBB
HEH, HEH. I REQUISITIONED IT FROM A CLUB FRESHMAN.
HE WAS GOING TO A FUNERAL...
well...
...here we are!
▲ A *GALANT GTO M/R*, FROM THE MOTOR CLUB POOL.

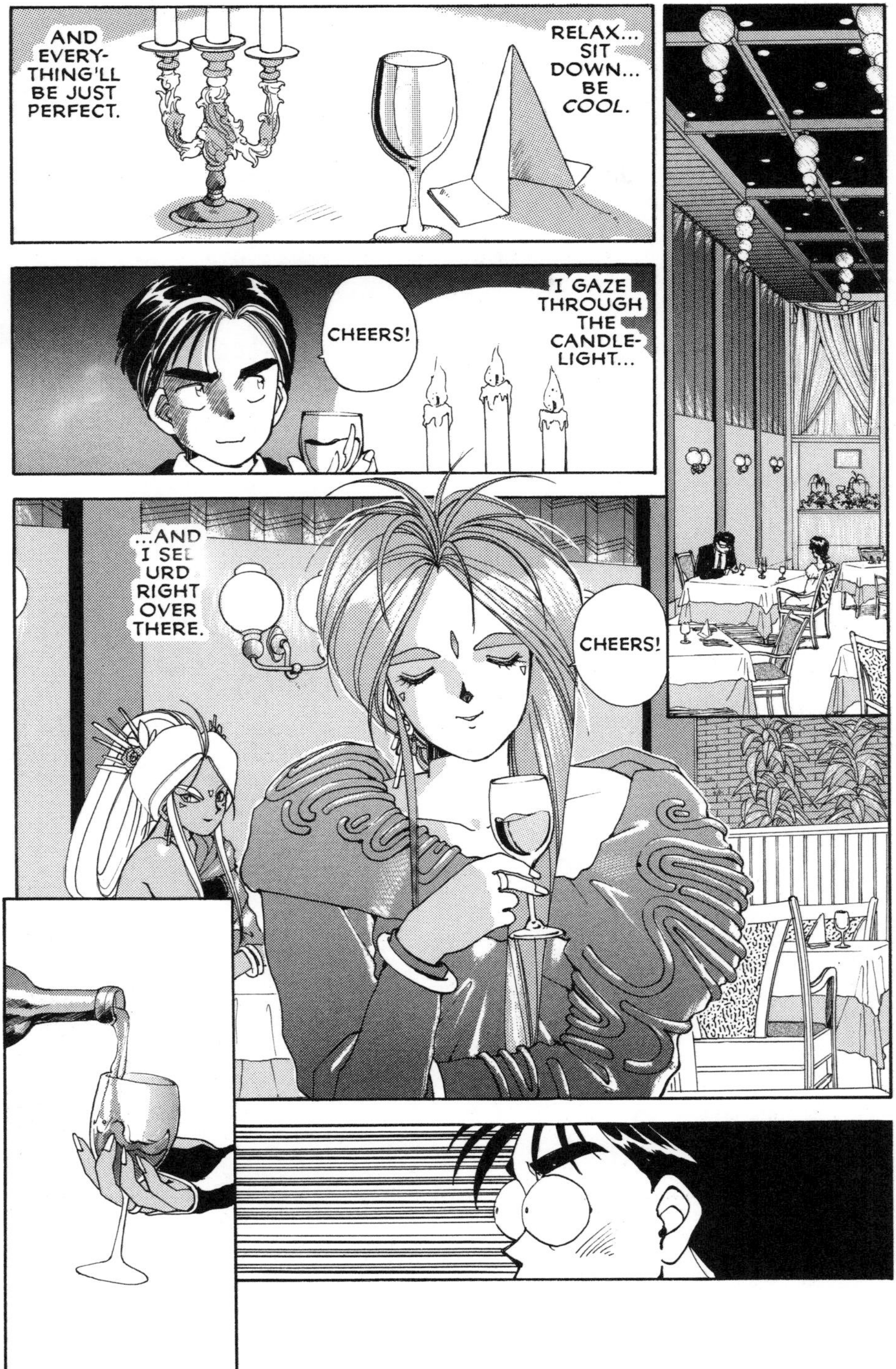
RELAX... SIT DOWN... BE *COOL.*
AND EVERY-THING'LL BE JUST PERFECT.
I GAZE THROUGH THE CANDLE-LIGHT...
CHEERS!
CHEERS!
...AND I SEE URD RIGHT OVER THERE.

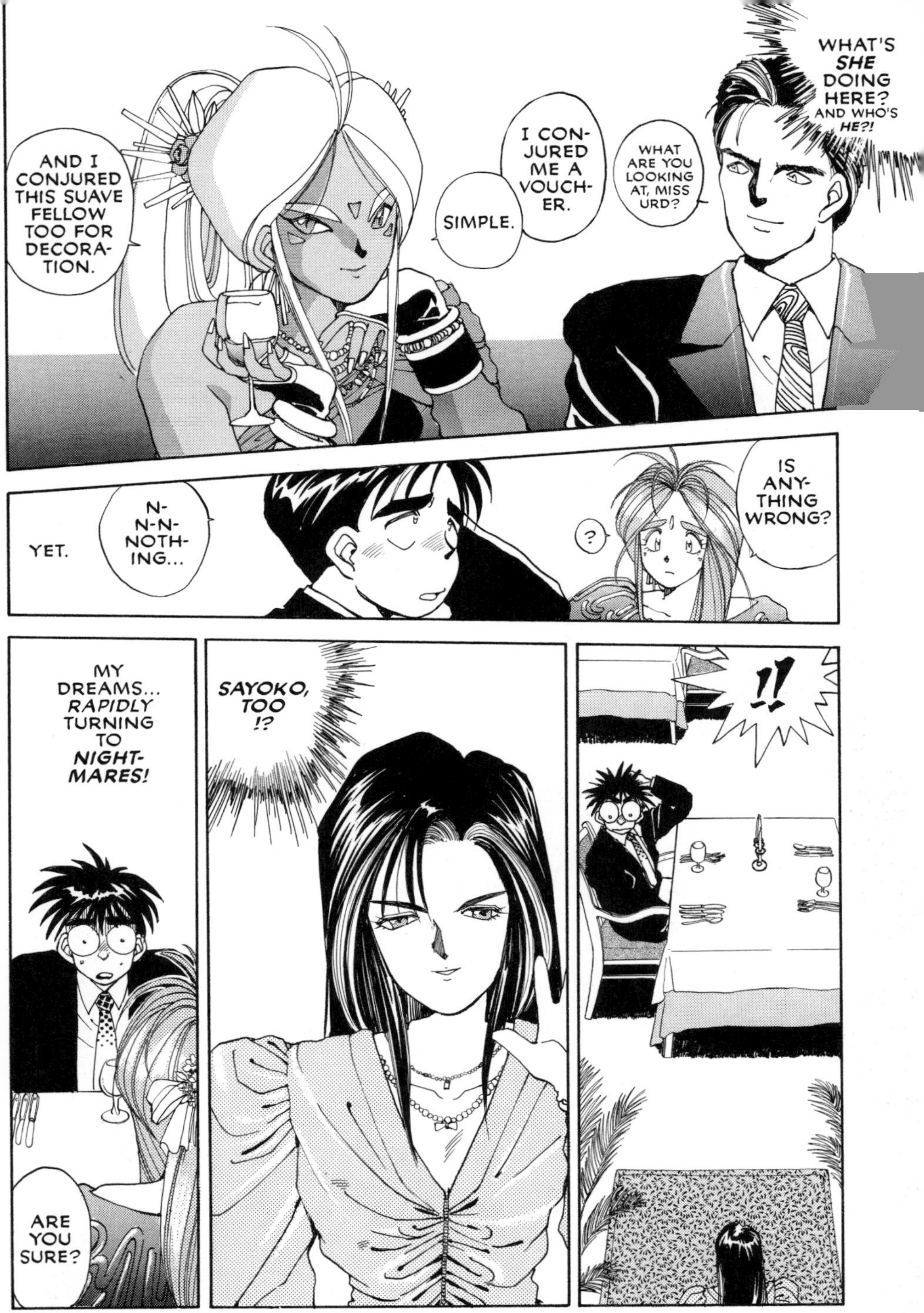
WHAT'S SHE DOING HERE? AND WHO'S HE?!
WHAT ARE YOU LOOKING AT, MISS URD?
I CON-JURED ME A VOUCH-ER.
SIMPLE.
AND I CONJURED THIS SUAVE FELLOW TOO FOR DECORA-TION.
IS ANY-THING WRONG?
?
N-N-N-NOTH-ING...
YET.
!!
SAYOKO, TOO !?
MY DREAMS... RAPIDLY TURNING TO NIGHT-MARES!
ARE YOU SURE?

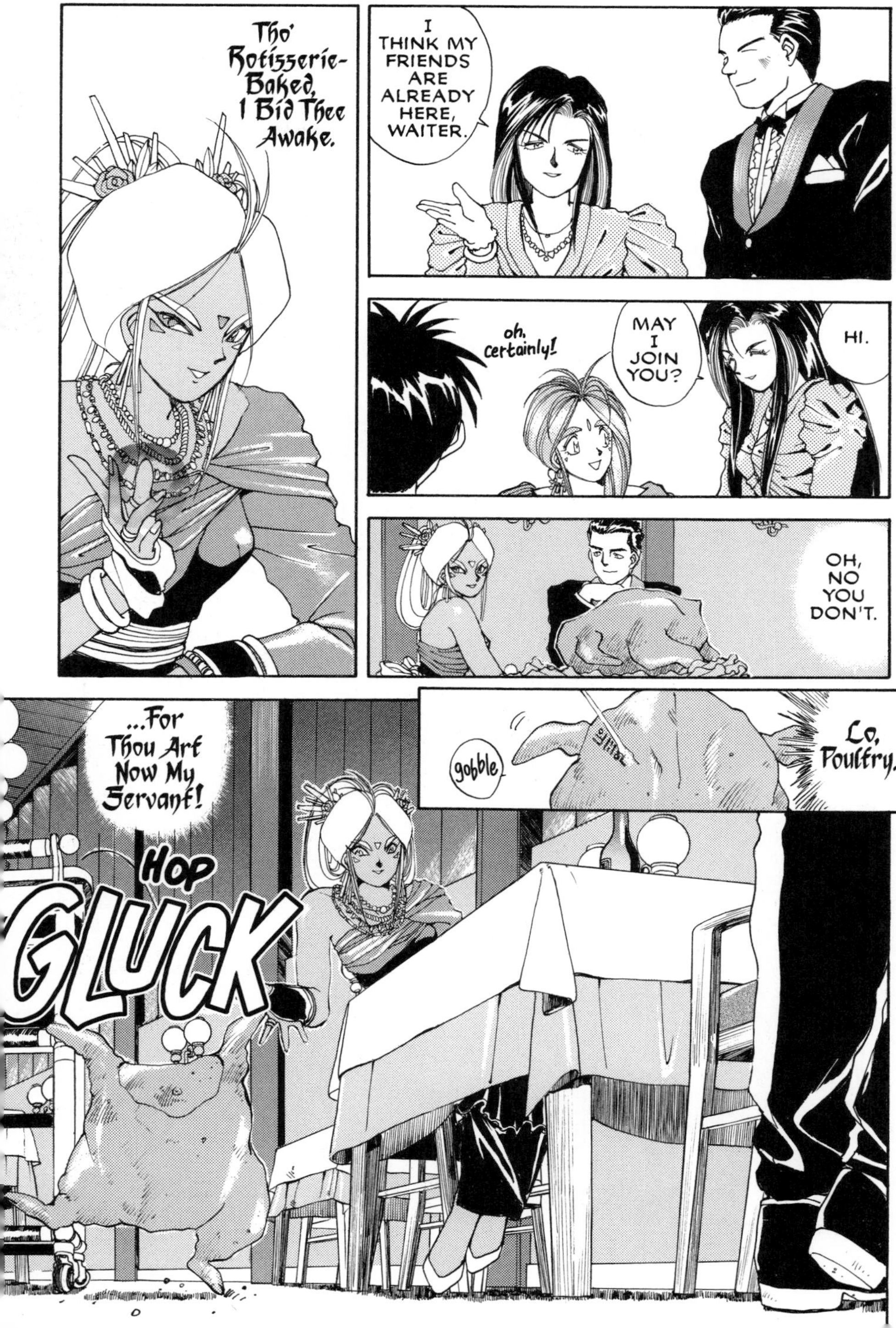
I THINK MY FRIENDS ARE ALREADY HERE, WAITER.
HI.
MAY I JOIN YOU?
oh, certainly!
OH, NO YOU DON'T.
Tho' Rotisserie-Baked, I Bid Thee Awake.
Lo, Poultry...
gobble
...For Thou Art Now My Servant!
HOP
GLUCK

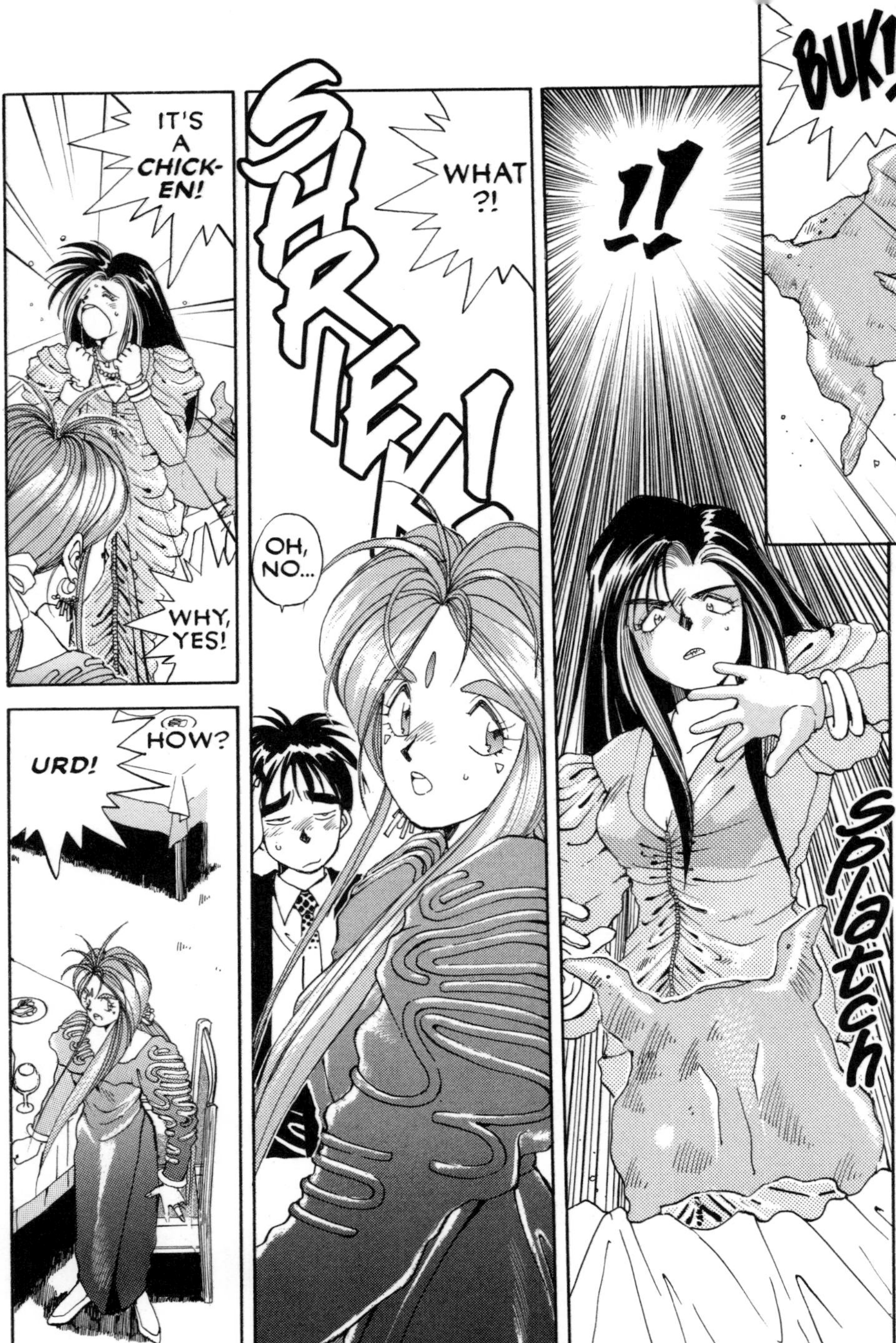

BUK!
!!
Splatch
SHRIEK!
WHAT ?!
OH, NO...
IT'S A CHICKEN!
WHY, YES!
HOW?
URD!

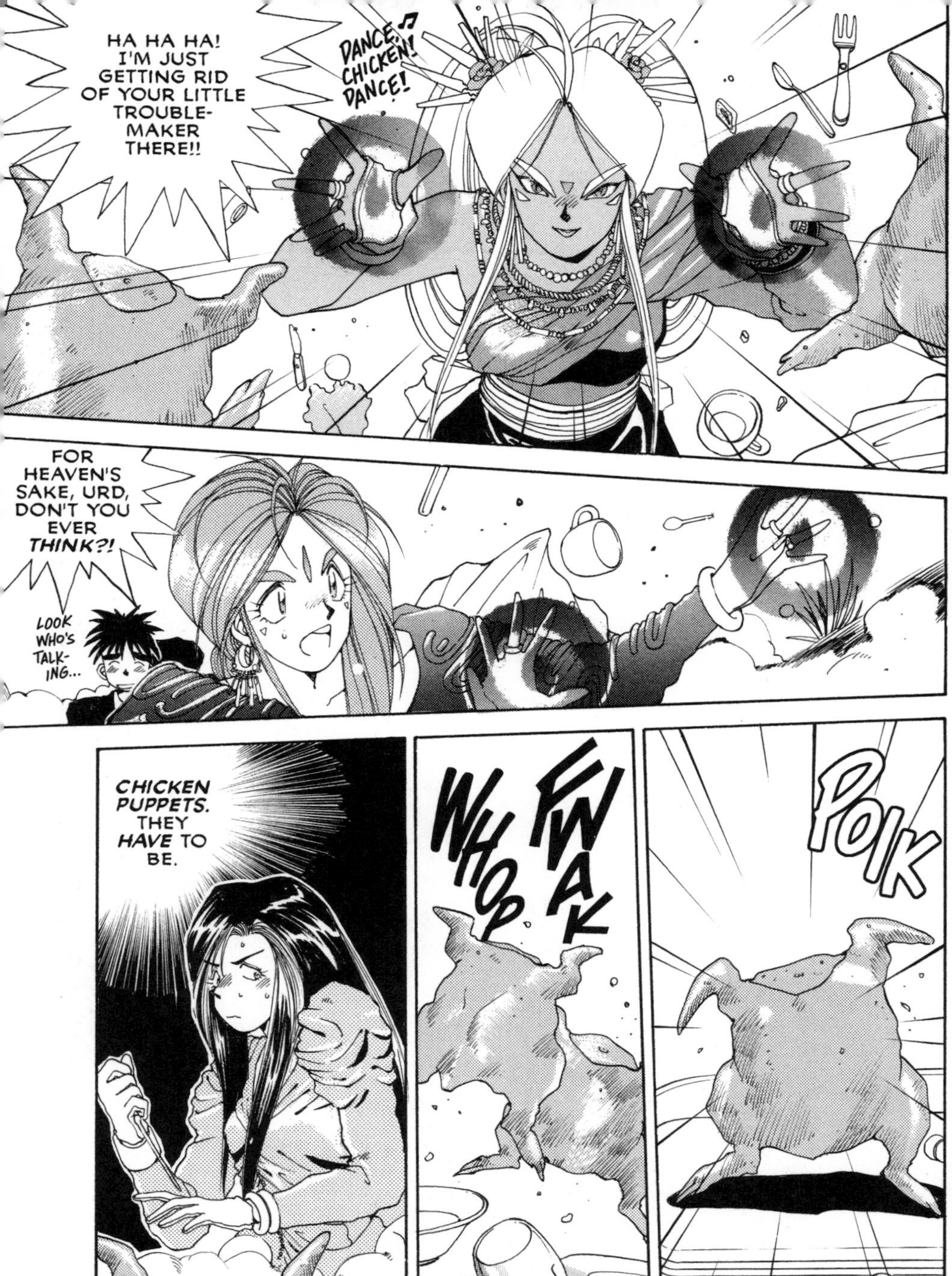
DANCE, CHICKEN! DANCE!
HA HA HA! I'M JUST GETTING RID OF YOUR LITTLE TROUBLE-MAKER THERE!!
FOR HEAVEN'S SAKE, URD, DON'T YOU EVER *THINK?!*
LOOK WHO'S TALK-ING...
POIK
FWAK
WHOP
CHICKEN PUPPETS. THEY *HAVE* TO BE.

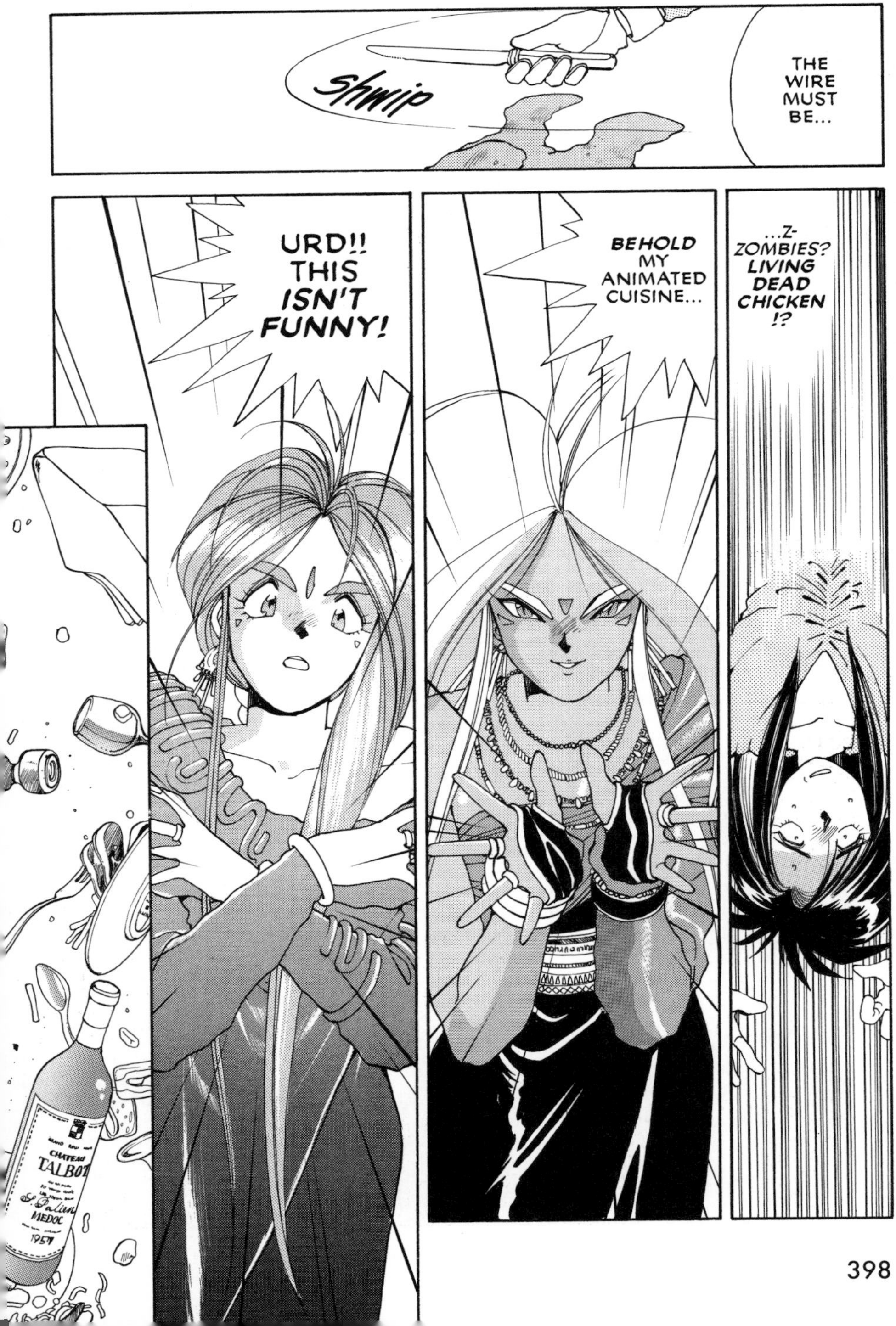
THE WIRE MUST BE...
shwip
...Z-ZOMBIES? LIVING DEAD CHICKEN !?
BEHOLD MY ANIMATED CUISINE...
URD!! THIS ISN'T FUNNY!
CHATEAU
TALBOT
MEDOC
1957

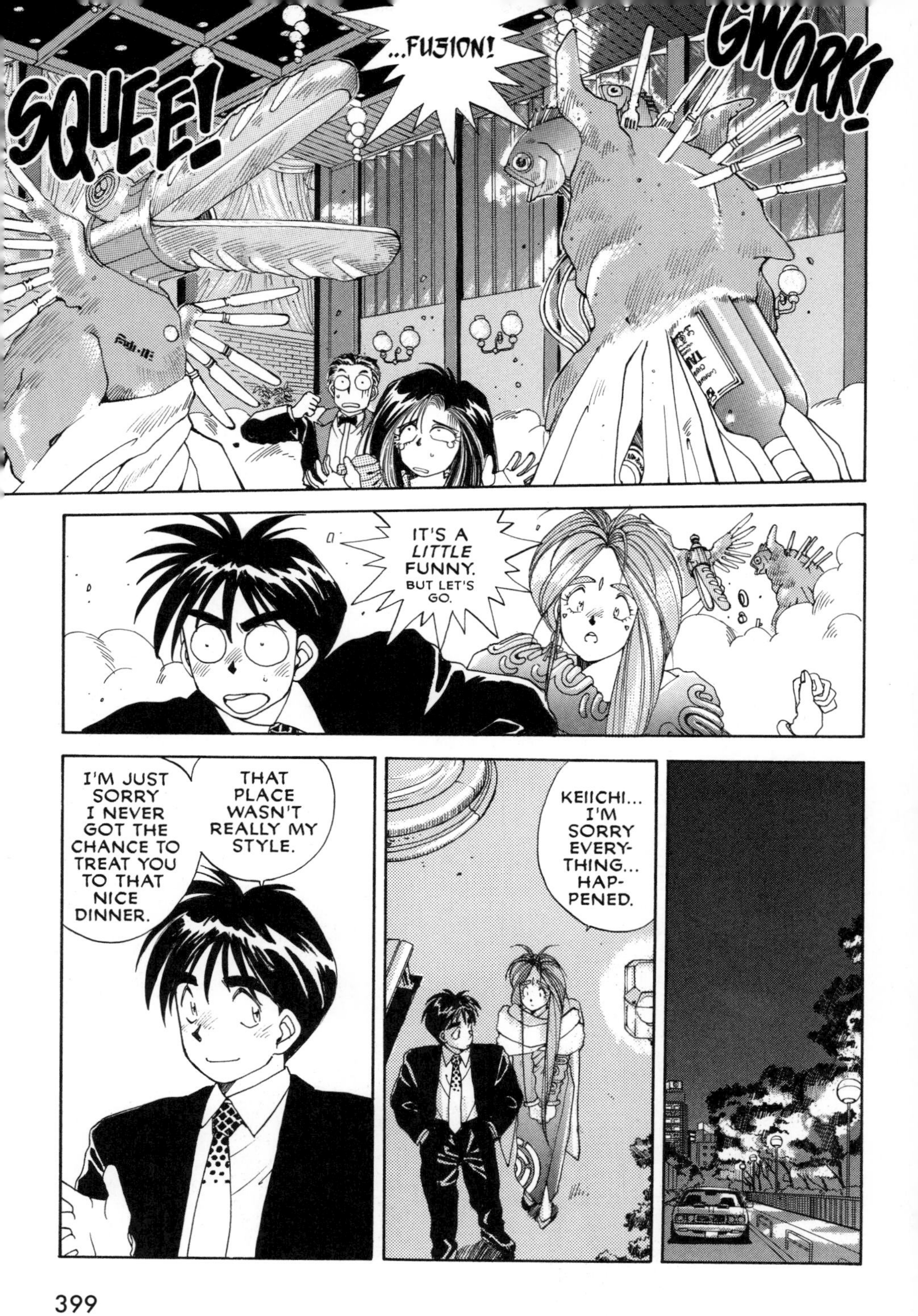
GWORK!
...FUSION!
SQUEEE!
IT'S A *LITTLE* FUNNY. BUT LET'S GO.
KEIICHI... I'M SORRY EVERY-THING... HAP-PENED.
THAT PLACE WASN'T REALLY MY STYLE.
I'M JUST SORRY I NEVER GOT THE CHANCE TO TREAT YOU TO THAT NICE DINNER.

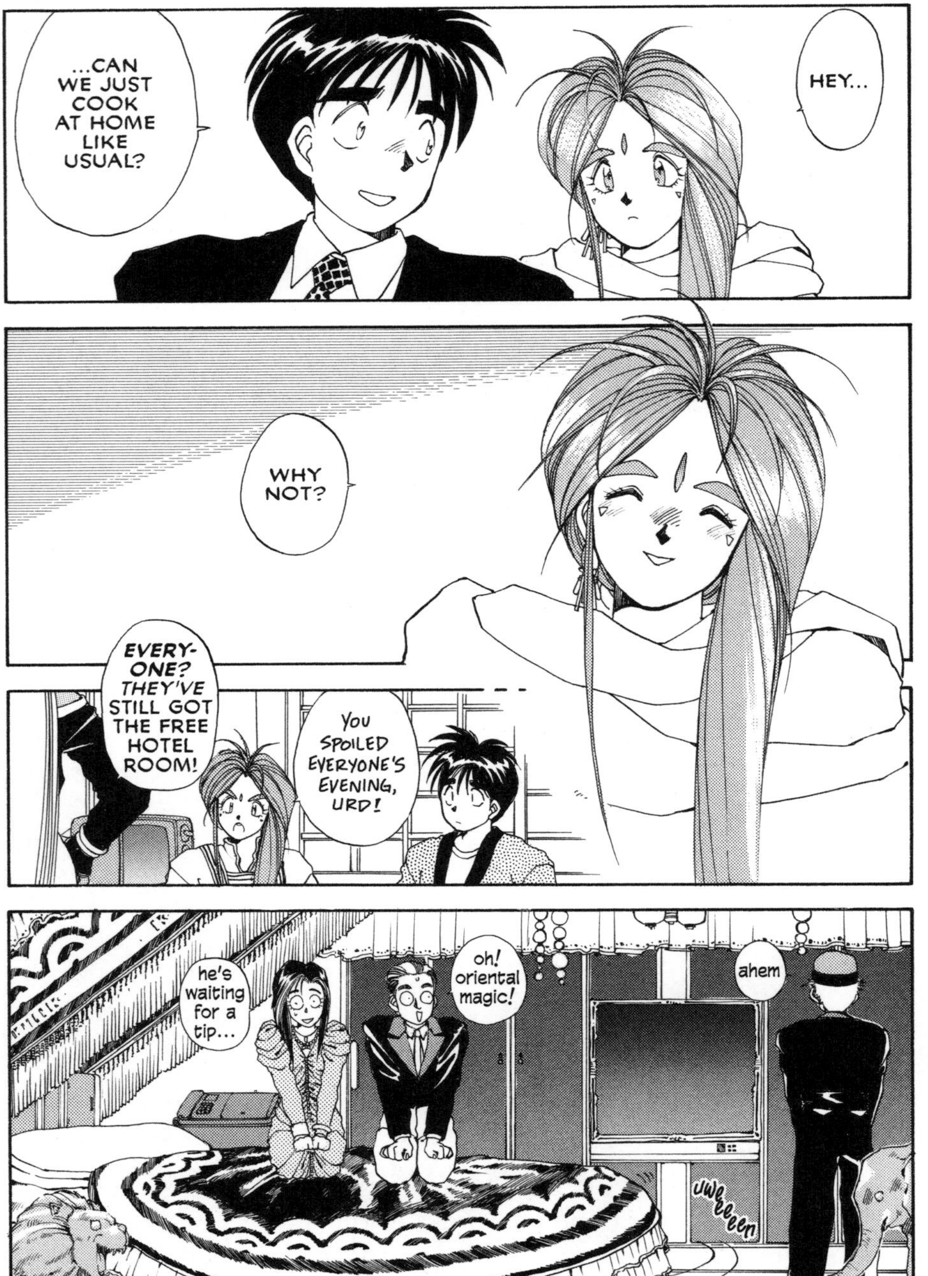
HEY...
...CAN WE JUST COOK AT HOME LIKE USUAL?
WHY NOT?
You SPOILED EVERYONE'S EVENING, URD!
EVERY-ONE? THEY'VE STILL GOT THE FREE HOTEL ROOM!
ahem
oh! oriental magic!
he's waiting for a tip...
uweeeeen

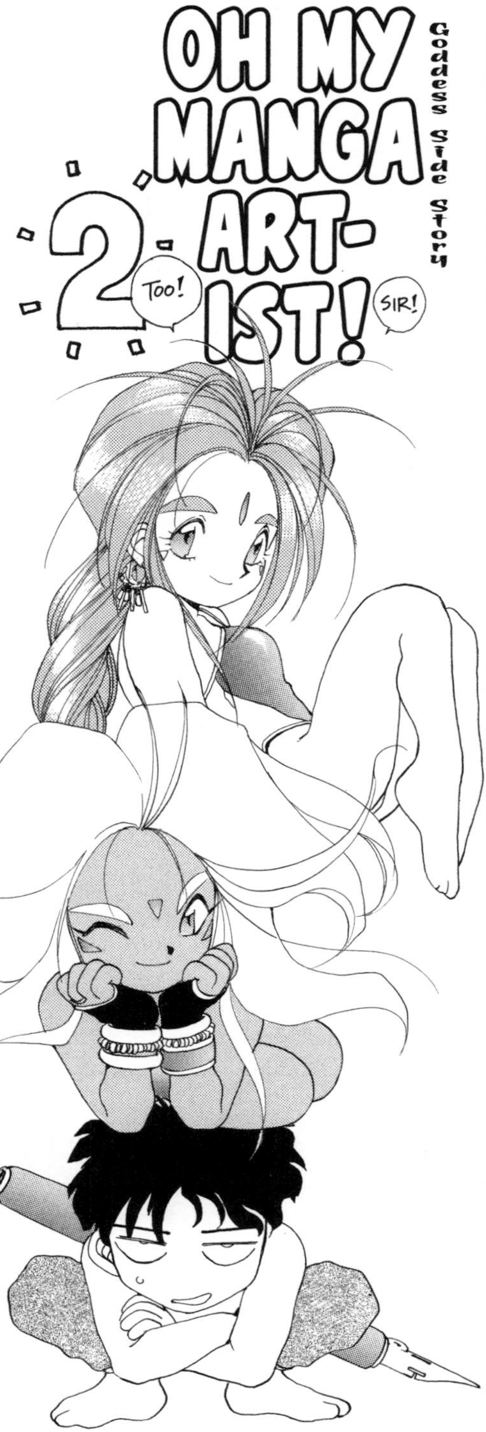
OH MY MANGA ART-IST!
Goddess Side Story
2
Too!
SIR!

THE BACK END

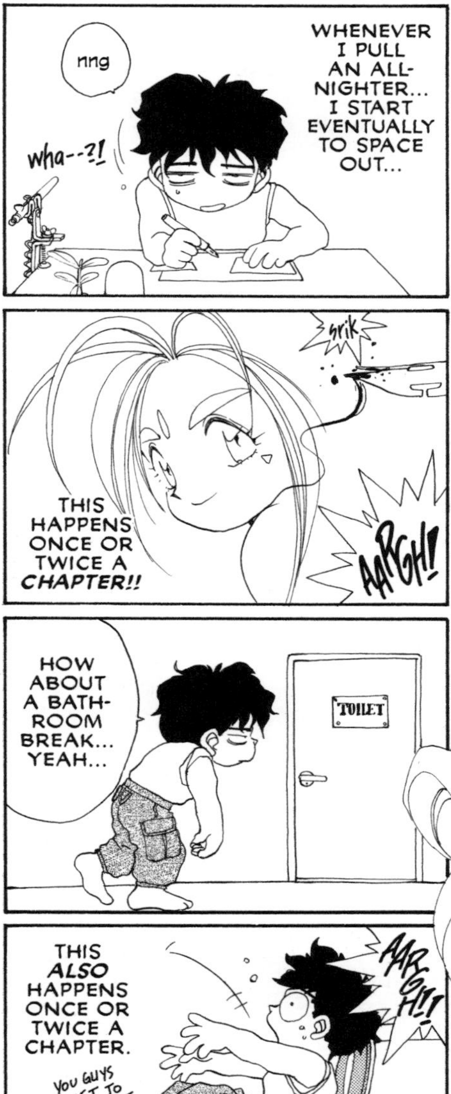
WHENEVER I PULL AN ALL-NIGHTER... I START EVENTUALLY TO SPACE OUT...
nng
wha--?!
srik
THIS HAPPENS ONCE OR TWICE A *CHAPTER!!*
AARGH!!
HOW ABOUT A BATH-ROOM BREAK... YEAH...
TOILET
AARGH!!
THIS *ALSO* HAPPENS ONCE OR TWICE A CHAPTER.
YOU GUYS FORGET TO PUT THE SEAT DOWN SOME-TIMES... RIGHT...?

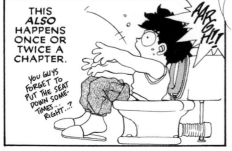

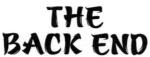

THE MYSTERY

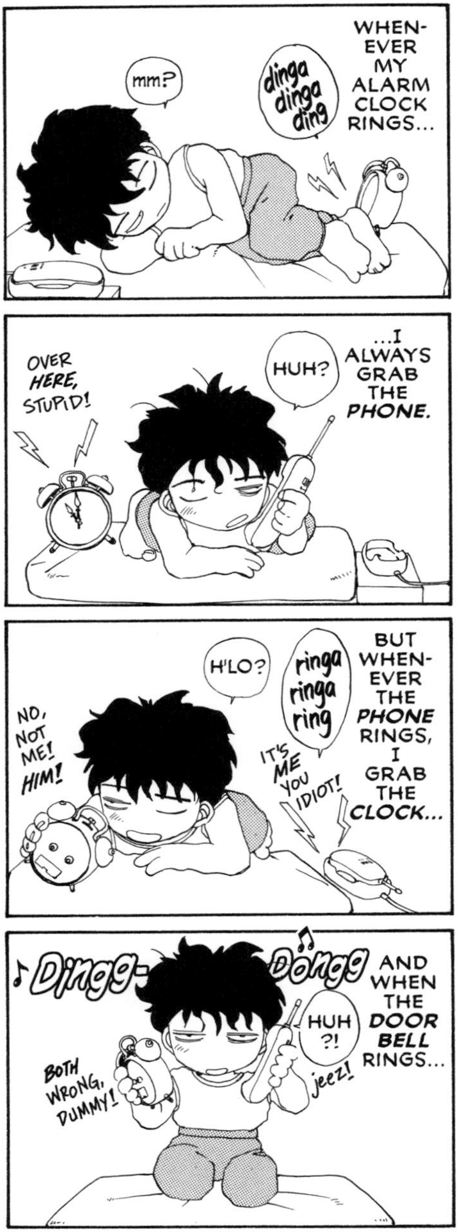
WHENEVER MY ALARM CLOCK RINGS...
dinga dinga ding
mm?
...I ALWAYS GRAB THE PHONE.
HUH?
OVER HERE, STUPID!
BUT WHENEVER THE PHONE RINGS, I GRAB THE CLOCK...
ringa ringa ring
H'LO?
IT'S ME YOU IDIOT!
NO, NOT ME! HIM!
AND WHEN THE DOOR BELL RINGS...
Dingg-Dongg
HUH ?!
jeez!
BOTH WRONG, DUMMY!

THE HOLE

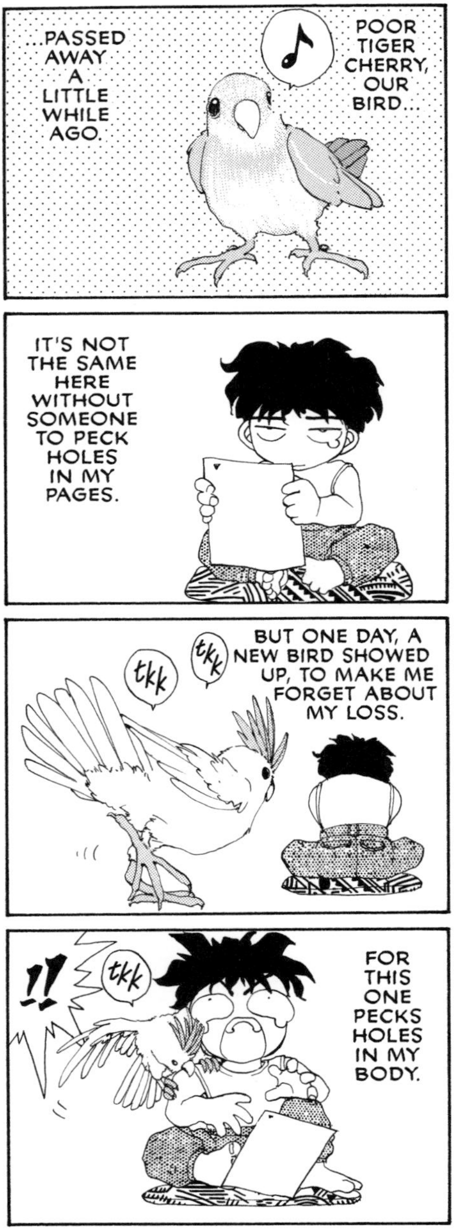
POOR TIGER CHERRY, OUR BIRD...
...PASSED AWAY A LITTLE WHILE AGO.
IT'S NOT THE SAME HERE WITHOUT SOMEONE TO PECK HOLES IN MY PAGES.
BUT ONE DAY, A NEW BIRD SHOWED UP, TO MAKE ME FORGET ABOUT MY LOSS.
tkk
tkk
FOR THIS ONE PECKS HOLES IN MY BODY.
tkk
!!

To Be Continued... eventually.

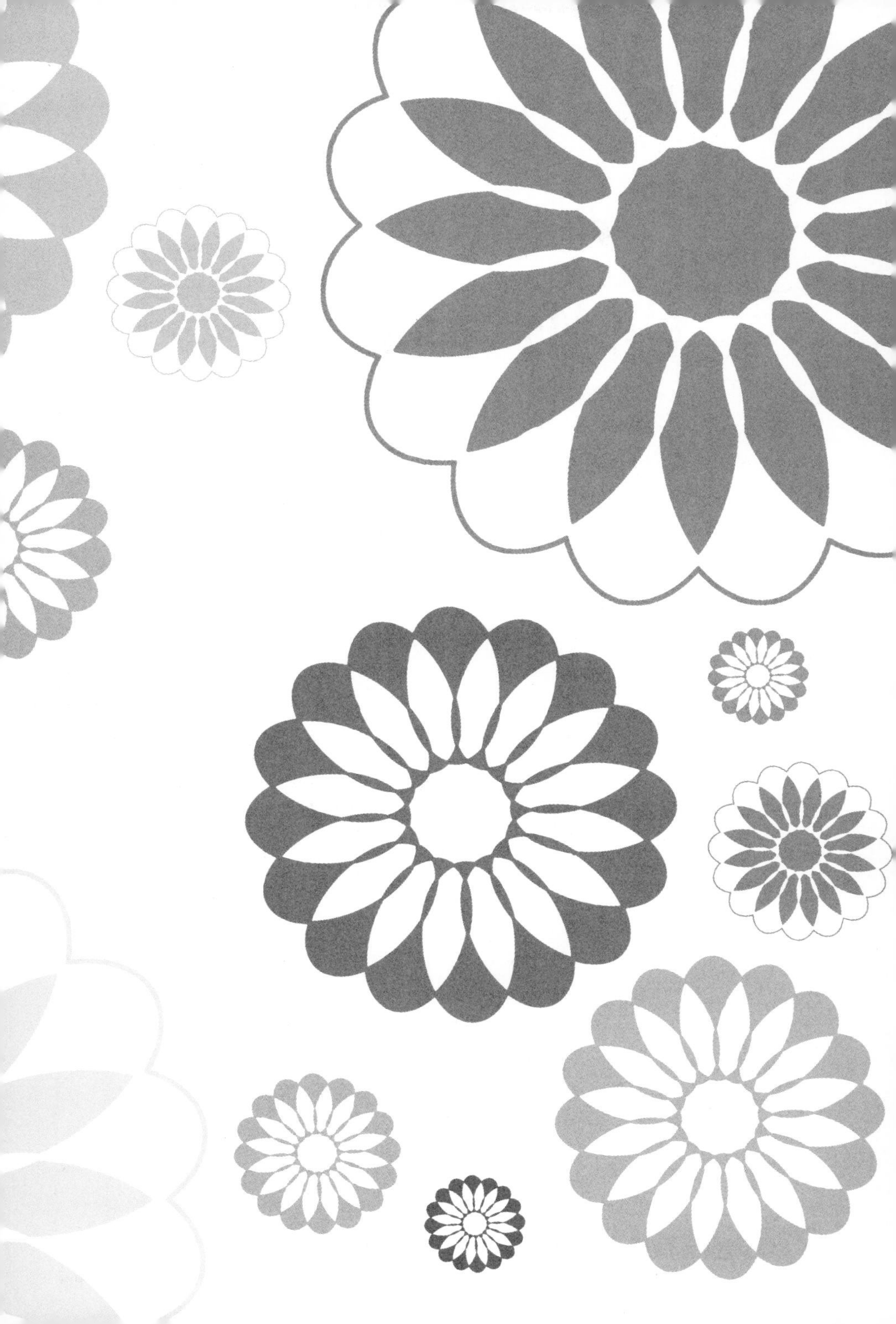

OH MY GODDESS!

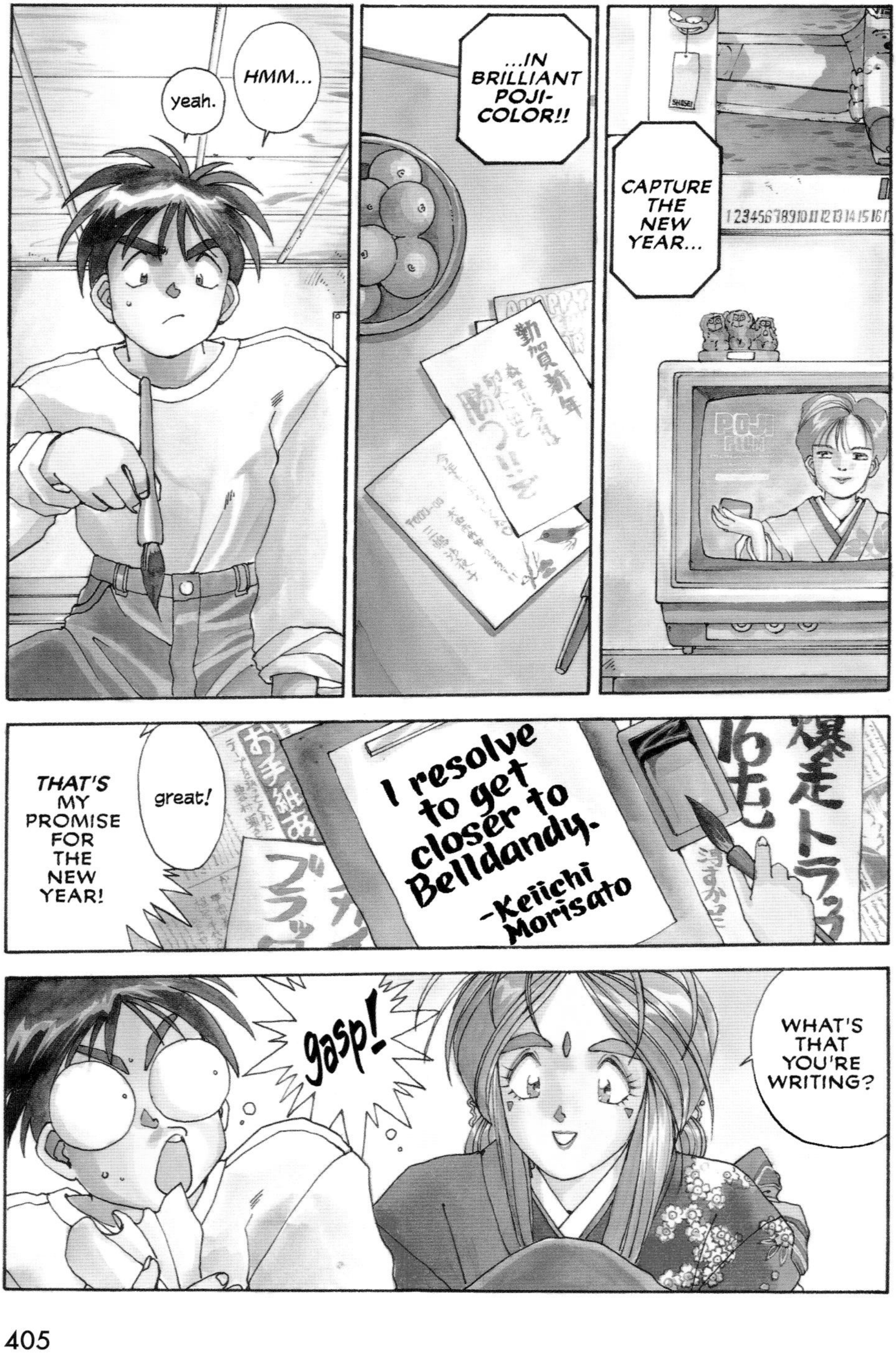
CAPTURE THE NEW YEAR...
...IN BRILLIANT POJI-COLOR!!
HMM...
yeah.
I resolve to get closer to Belldandy.
-Keiichi Morisato
great!
THAT'S MY PROMISE FOR THE NEW YEAR!
WHAT'S THAT YOU'RE WRITING?
gasp!

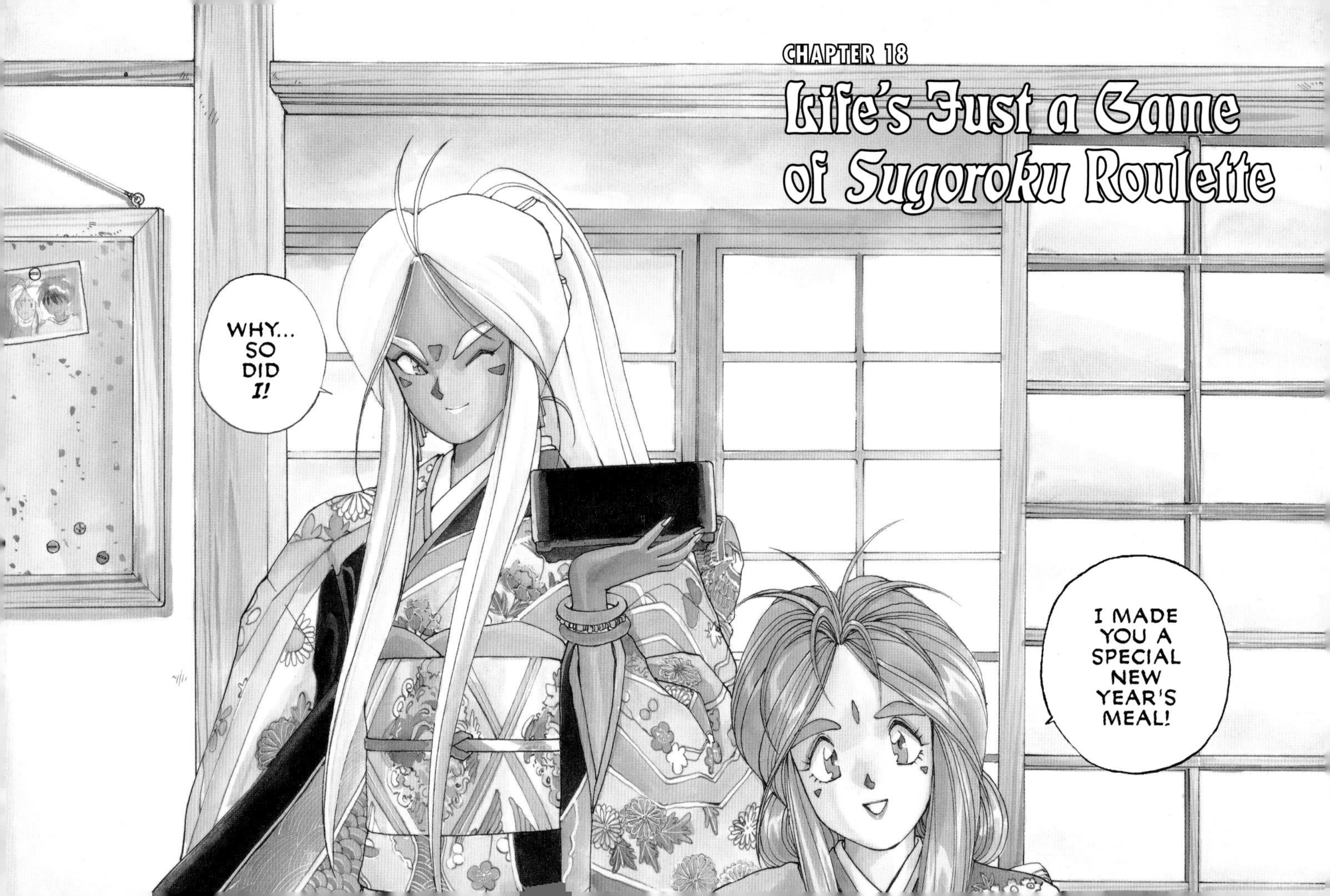
CHAPTER 18
Life's Just a Game of Sugoroku Roulette
I MADE YOU A SPECIAL NEW YEAR'S MEAL!
WHY... SO DID I!

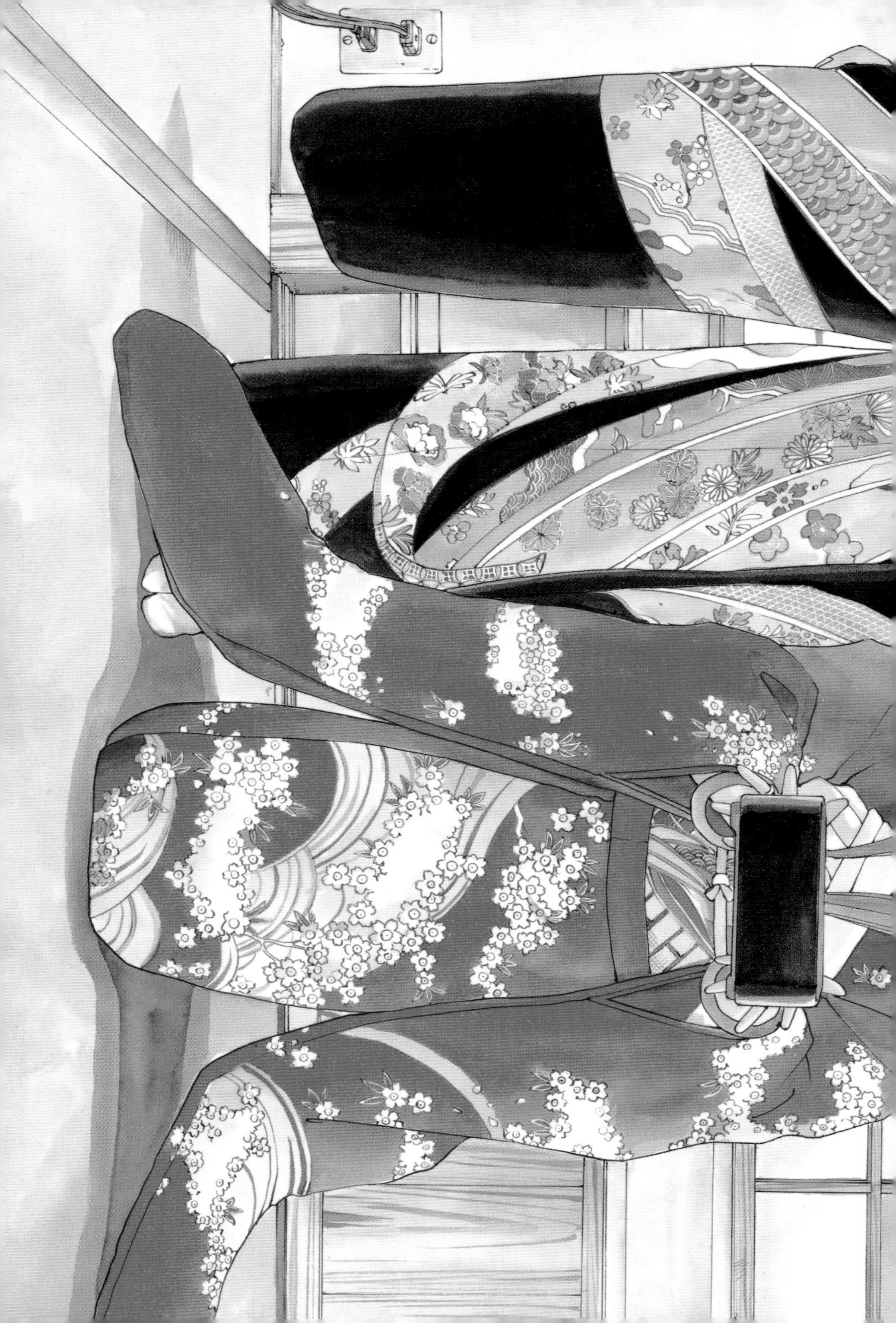

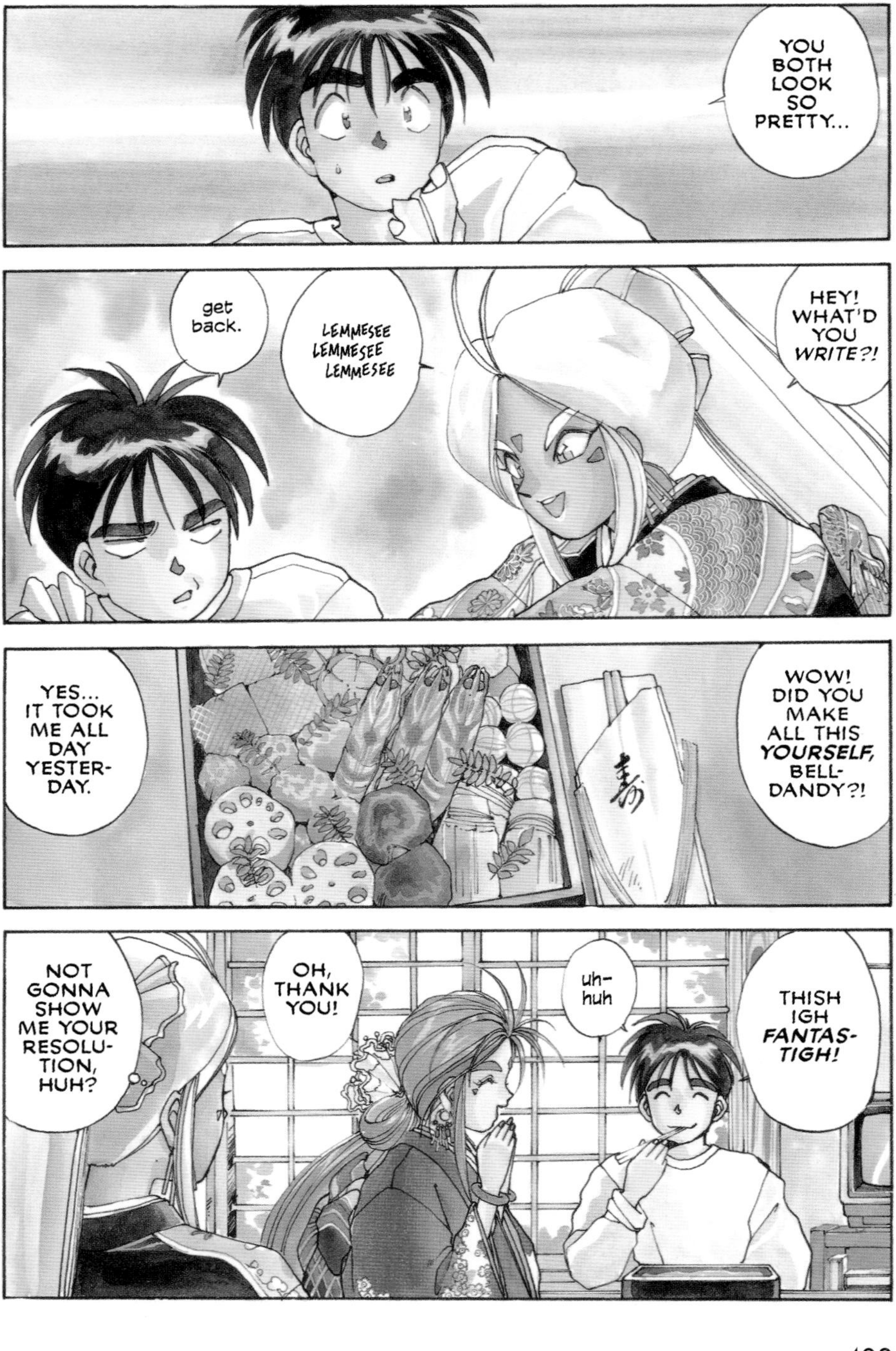
YOU BOTH LOOK SO PRETTY...
HEY! WHAT'D YOU WRITE?!
LEMMESEE LEMMESEE LEMMESEE
get back.
WOW! DID YOU MAKE ALL THIS YOURSELF, BELL-DANDY?!
YES... IT TOOK ME ALL DAY YESTER-DAY.
THISH IGH FANTAS-TIGH!
uh-huh
OH, THANK YOU!
NOT GONNA SHOW ME YOUR RESOLU-TION, HUH?

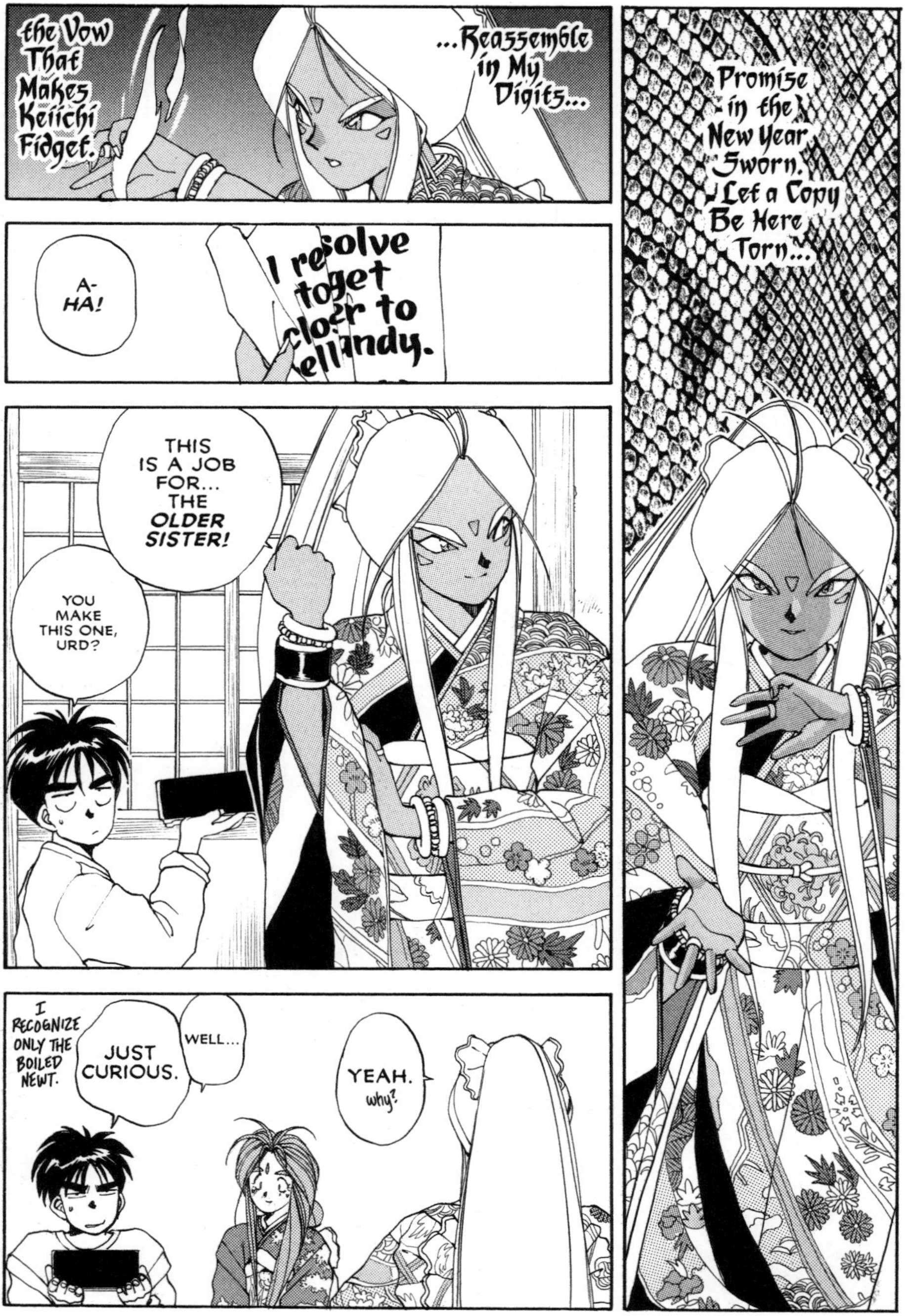
Promise in the New Year Sworn. Let a Copy Be Here Torn...
...Reassemble in My Digits...
the Vow That Makes Keiichi Fidget.
I resolve toget closer to ellandy.
A-HA!
THIS IS A JOB FOR... THE OLDER SISTER!
YOU MAKE THIS ONE, URD?
YEAH. why?
WELL...
JUST CURIOUS.
I RECOGNIZE ONLY THE BOILED NEWT.

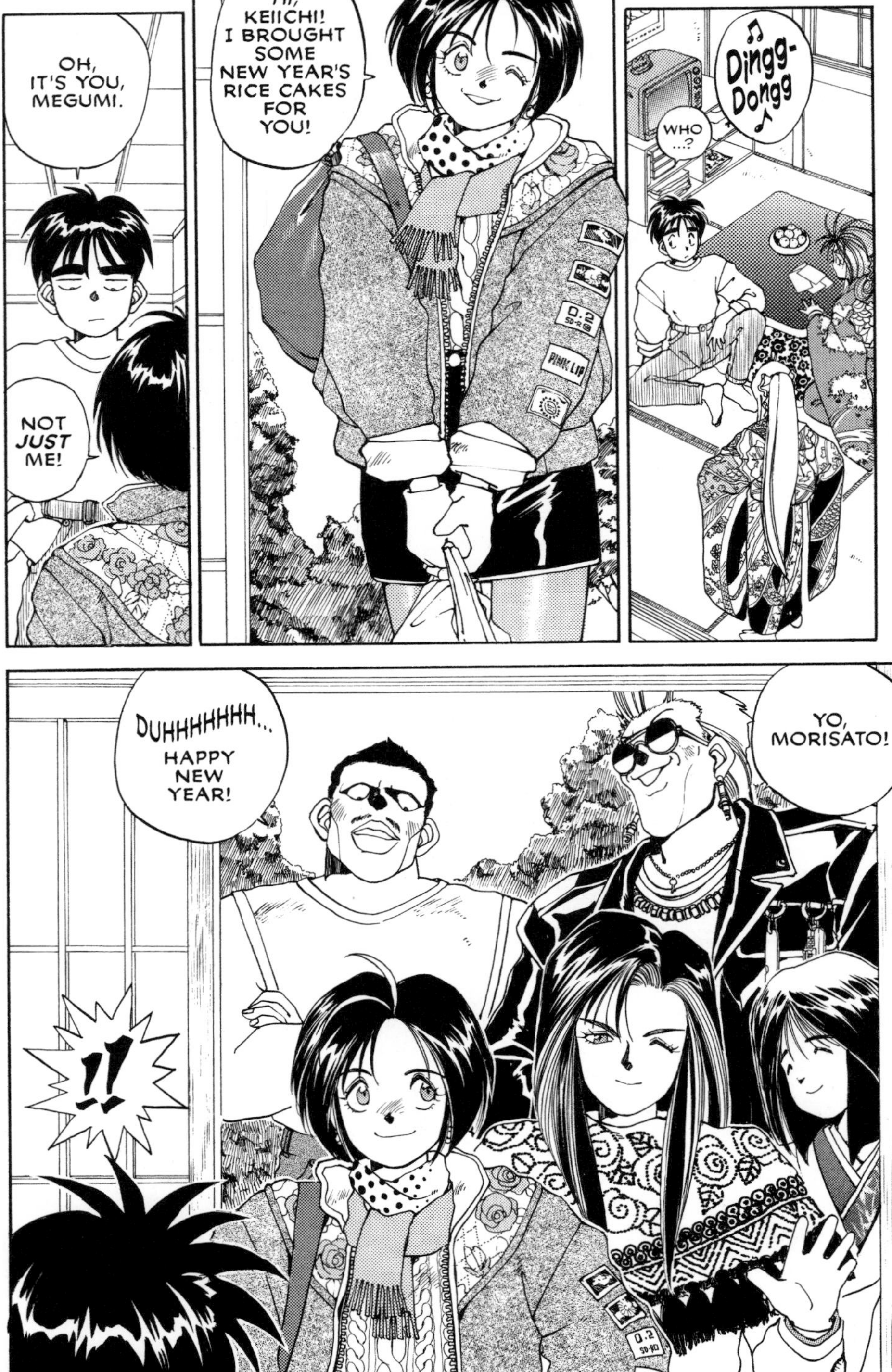
Dingg-Dongg
WHO ...?
HI, KEIICHI! I BROUGHT SOME NEW YEAR'S RICE CAKES FOR YOU!
OH, IT'S YOU, MEGUMI.
NOT JUST ME!
YO, MORISATO!
DUHHHHHHH... HAPPY NEW YEAR!
!!

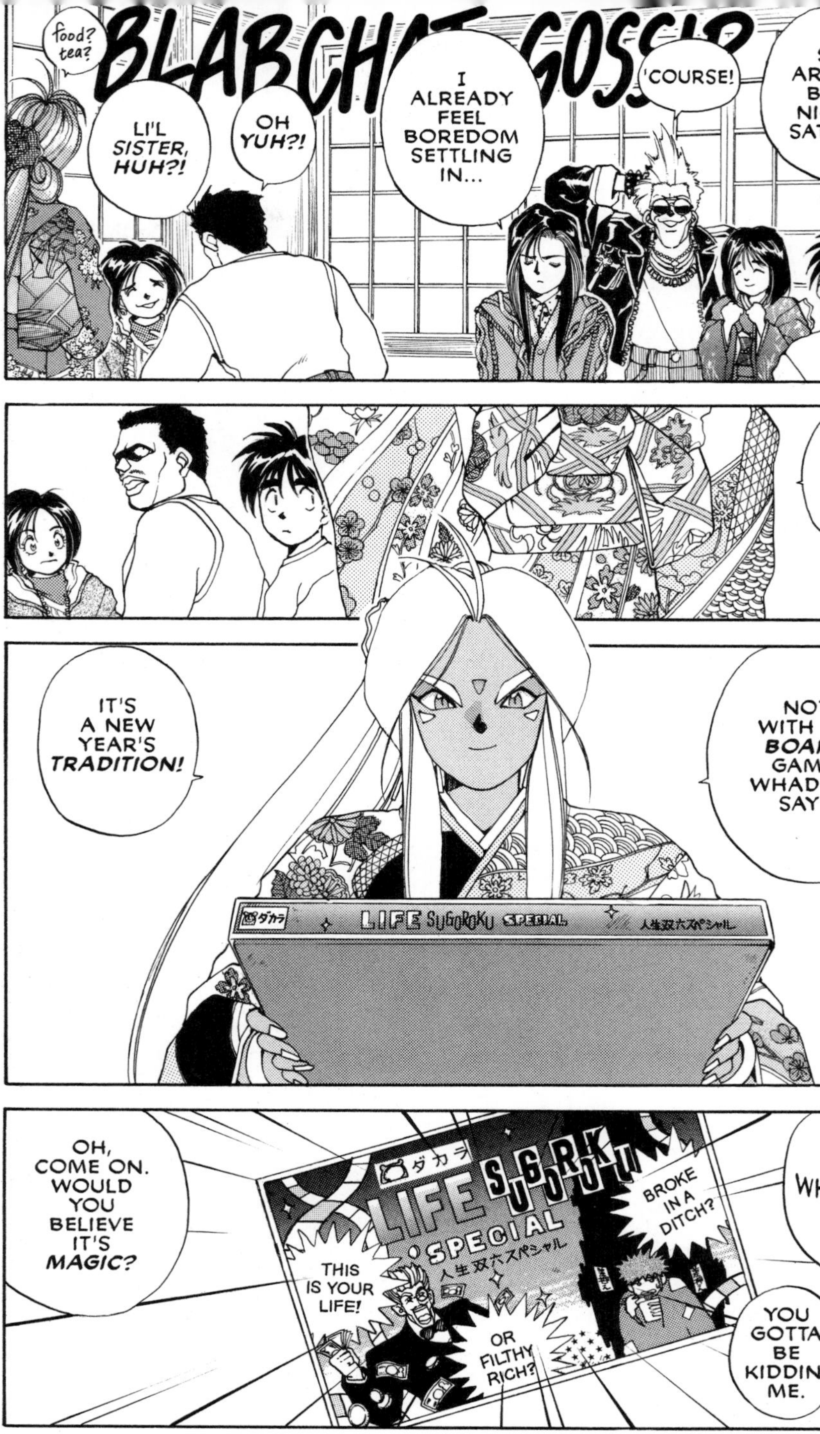
SO-- ARE YOU BEING NICE TO SATOKO?
'COURSE!
I ALREADY FEEL BOREDOM SETTLING IN...
BLABCHAT GOSSIP
OH *YUH?!*
LI'L *SISTER, HUH?!*
food? tea?
BORE-DOM?!
NOT WITH MY *BOARD* GAME! WHADDYA SAY?
IT'S A NEW YEAR'S *TRADITION!*
ダカラ LIFE SUGOROKU SPECIAL 人生双六スペシャル
WHAAAAT ...?
YOU GOTTA BE KIDDIN' ME.
ダカラ LIFE SUGOROKU SPECIAL 人生双六スペシャル
BROKE IN A DITCH?
THIS IS YOUR LIFE!
OR FILTHY RICH?
OH, COME ON. WOULD YOU BELIEVE IT'S *MAGIC?*

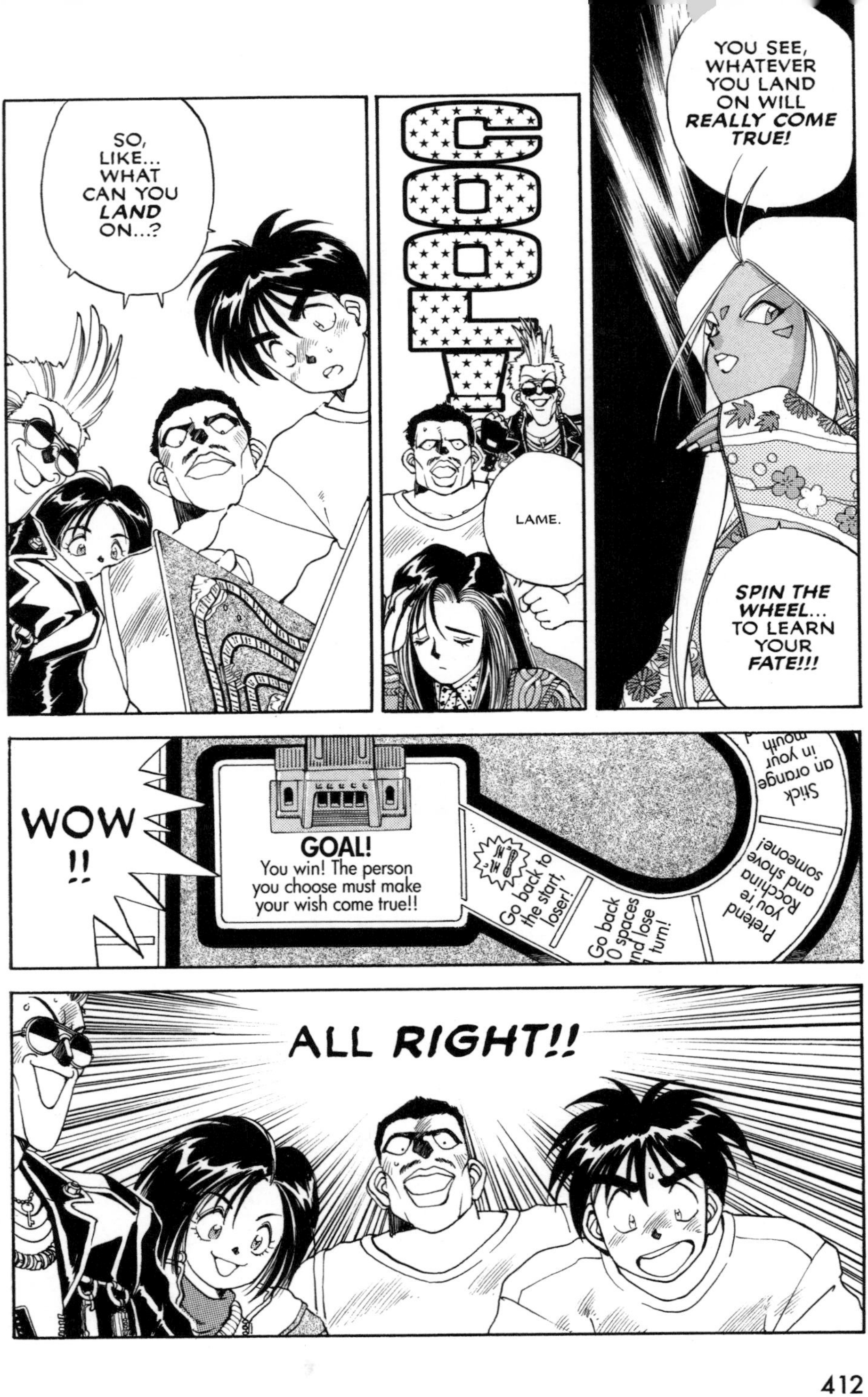

YOU SEE, WHATEVER YOU LAND ON WILL REALLY COME TRUE!
SPIN THE WHEEL... TO LEARN YOUR FATE!!!
COOL!
LAME.
SO, LIKE... WHAT CAN YOU LAND ON...?
Stick an orange in your mouth
Pretend you're Rocchina and shove someone!
Go back 0 spaces nd lose turn!
Go back to the start, loser!
GOAL!
You win! The person you choose must make your wish come true!!
WOW !!
ALL RIGHT!!

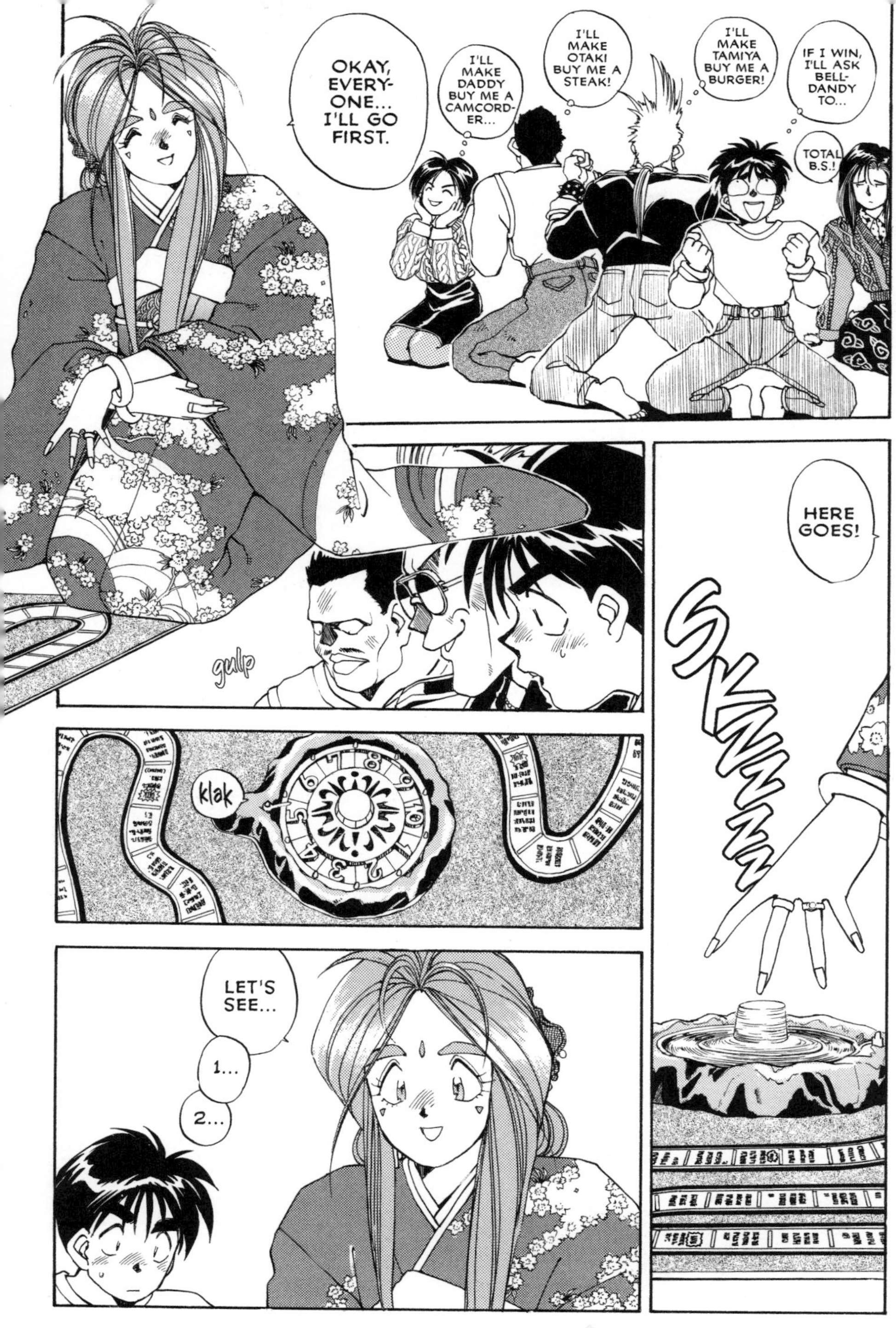
IF I WIN, I'LL ASK BELL-DANDY TO...
TOTAL B.S.!
I'LL MAKE TAMIYA BUY ME A BURGER!
I'LL MAKE OTAKI BUY ME A STEAK!
I'LL MAKE DADDY BUY ME A CAMCORDER...
OKAY, EVERYONE... I'LL GO FIRST.
HERE GOES!
gulp
klak
LET'S SEE...
1...
2...

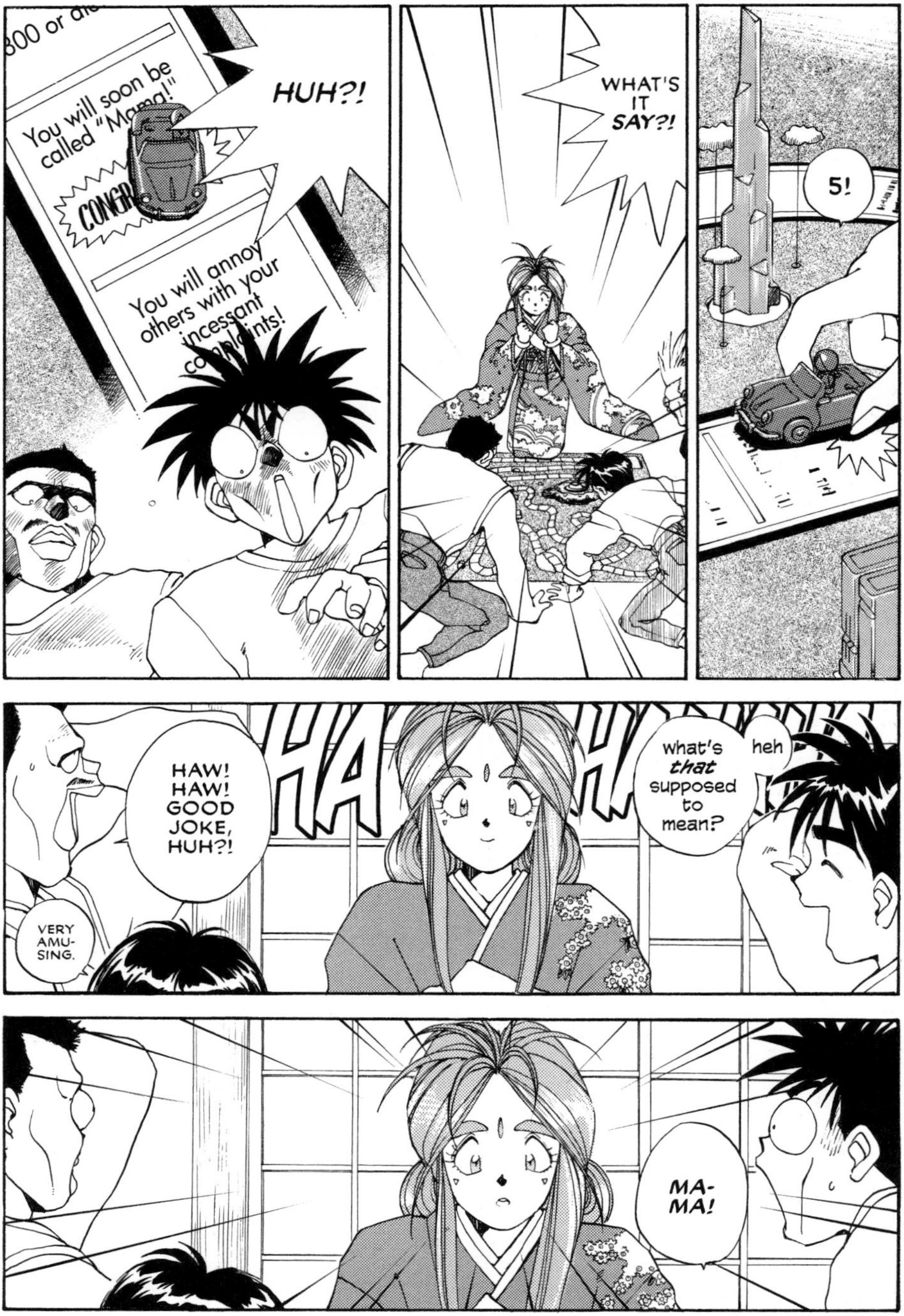
5!
WHAT'S IT SAY?!
You will soon be called
You will annoy others with your incessant
HUH?!
heh
what's that supposed to mean?
HAW! HAW! GOOD JOKE, HUH?!
VERY AMUSING.
MA-MA!

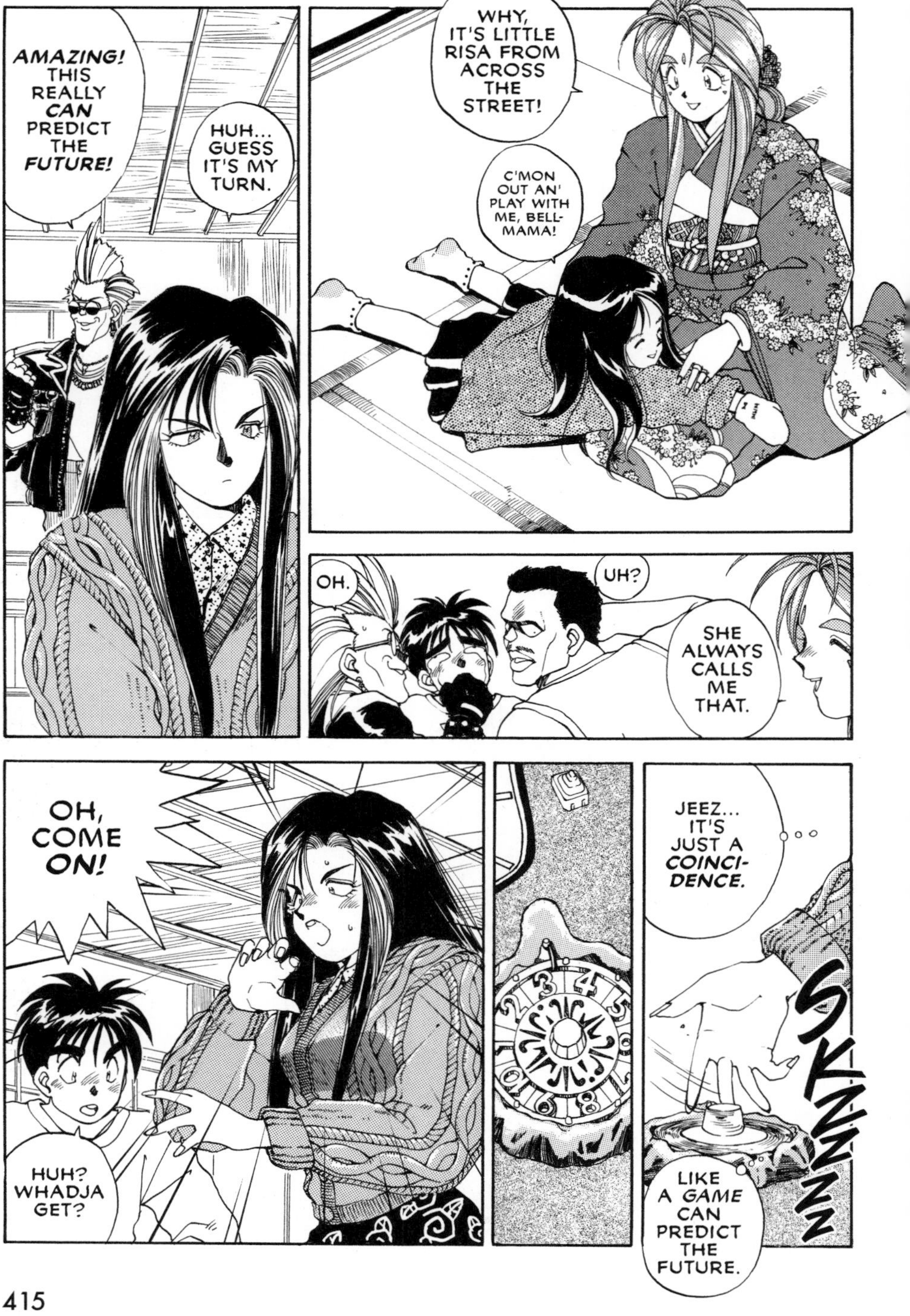
WHY, IT'S LITTLE RISA FROM ACROSS THE STREET!
C'MON OUT AN' PLAY WITH ME, BELL-MAMA!
UH?
OH.
SHE ALWAYS CALLS ME THAT.
AMAZING! THIS REALLY *CAN* PREDICT THE *FUTURE!*
HUH... GUESS IT'S MY TURN.
JEEZ... IT'S JUST A *COINCIDENCE.*
SKZZZZ
LIKE A *GAME* CAN PREDICT THE FUTURE.
OH, COME *ON!*
HUH? WHADJA GET?

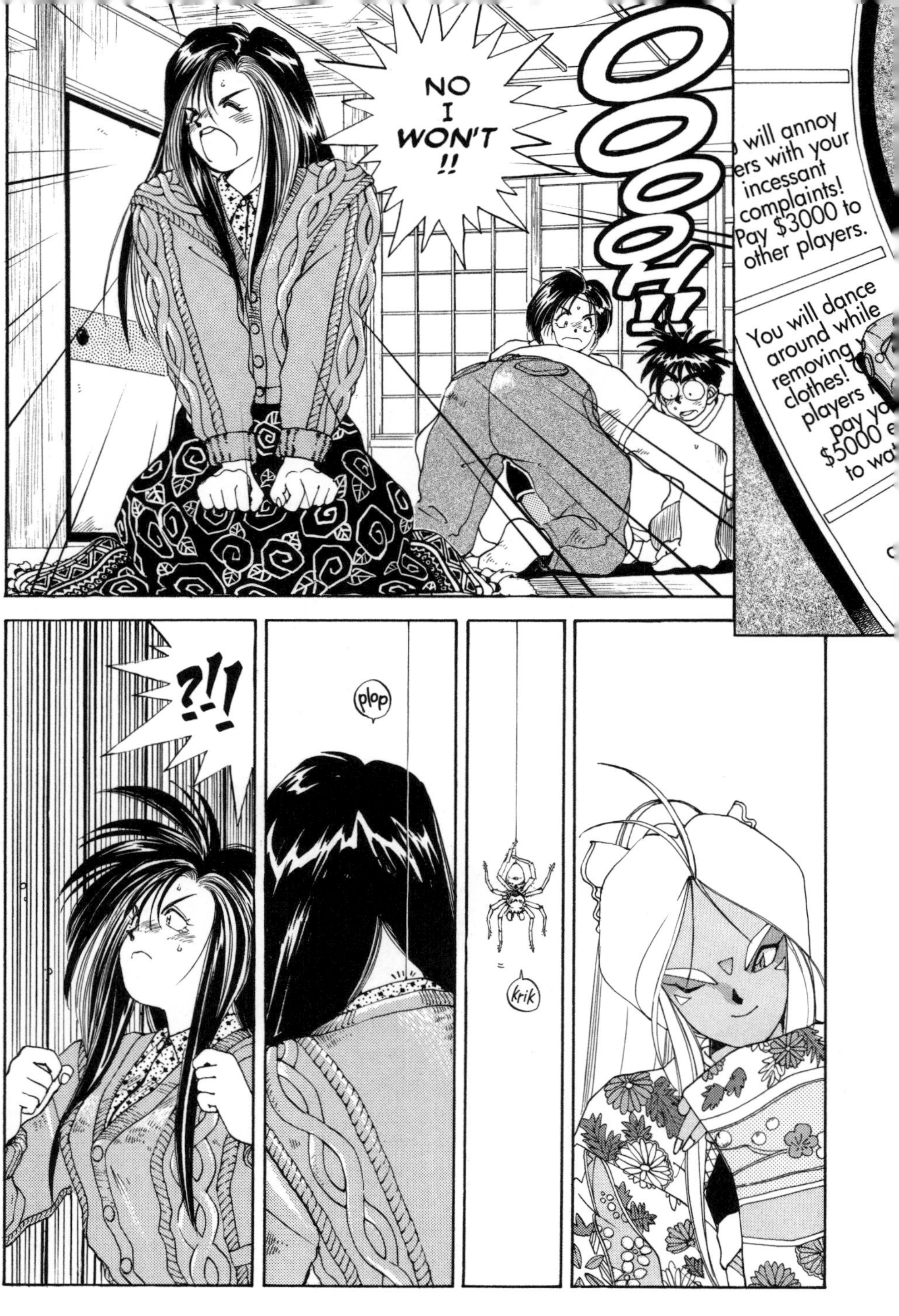
u will annoy
ers with your
incessant
complaints!
Pay $3000 to
other players.
You will dance
around while
removing
clothes!
players
pay yo
$5000 e
to wat
OOOOH!!
NO I WON'T !!
plop
krik
?!!

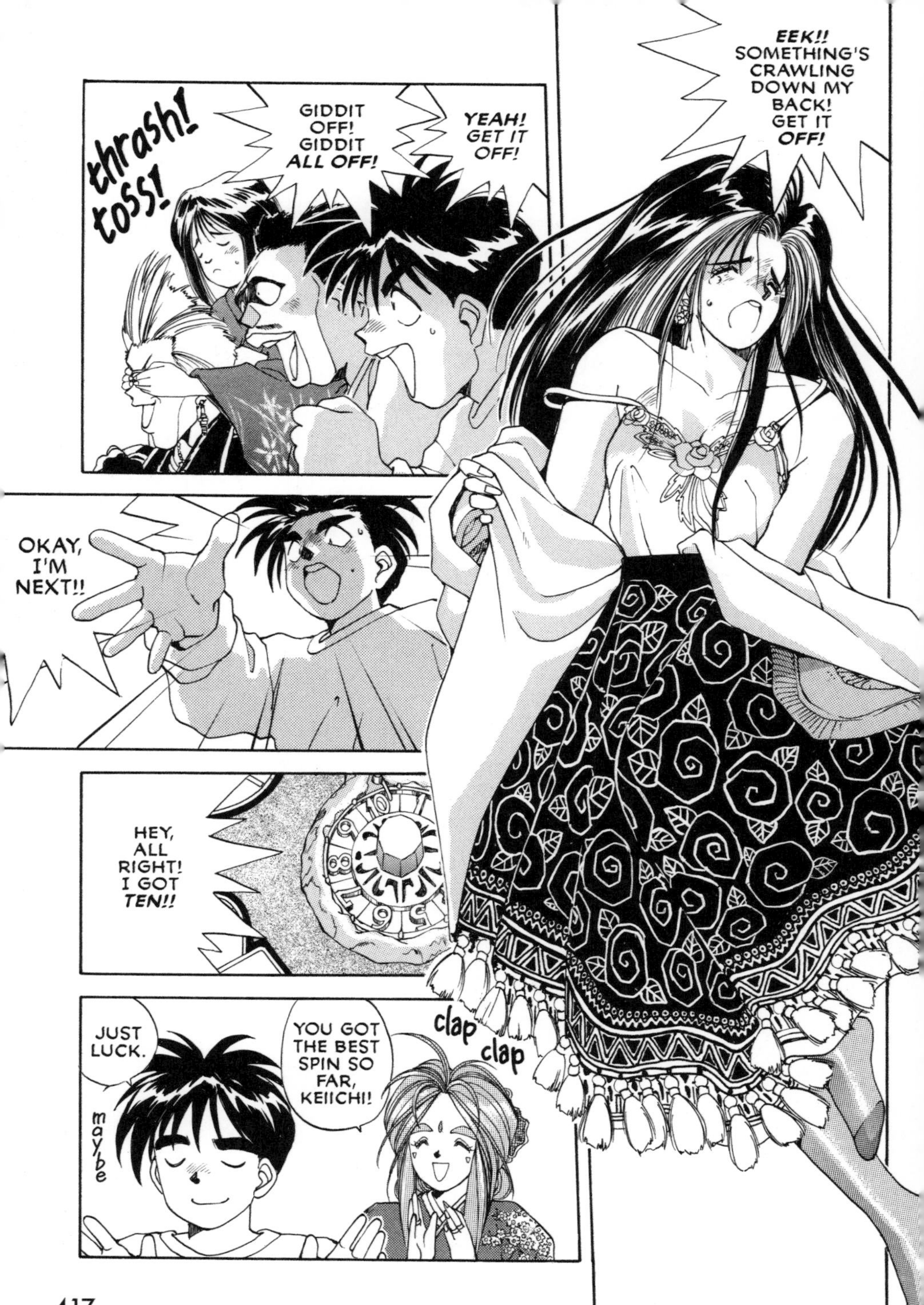
EEK!! SOMETHING'S CRAWLING DOWN MY BACK! GET IT OFF!
YEAH! GET IT OFF!
GIDDIT OFF! GIDDIT ALL OFF!
thrash! toss!
OKAY, I'M NEXT!!
HEY, ALL RIGHT! I GOT TEN!!
clap clap
YOU GOT THE BEST SPIN SO FAR, KEIICHI!
JUST LUCK.
maybe

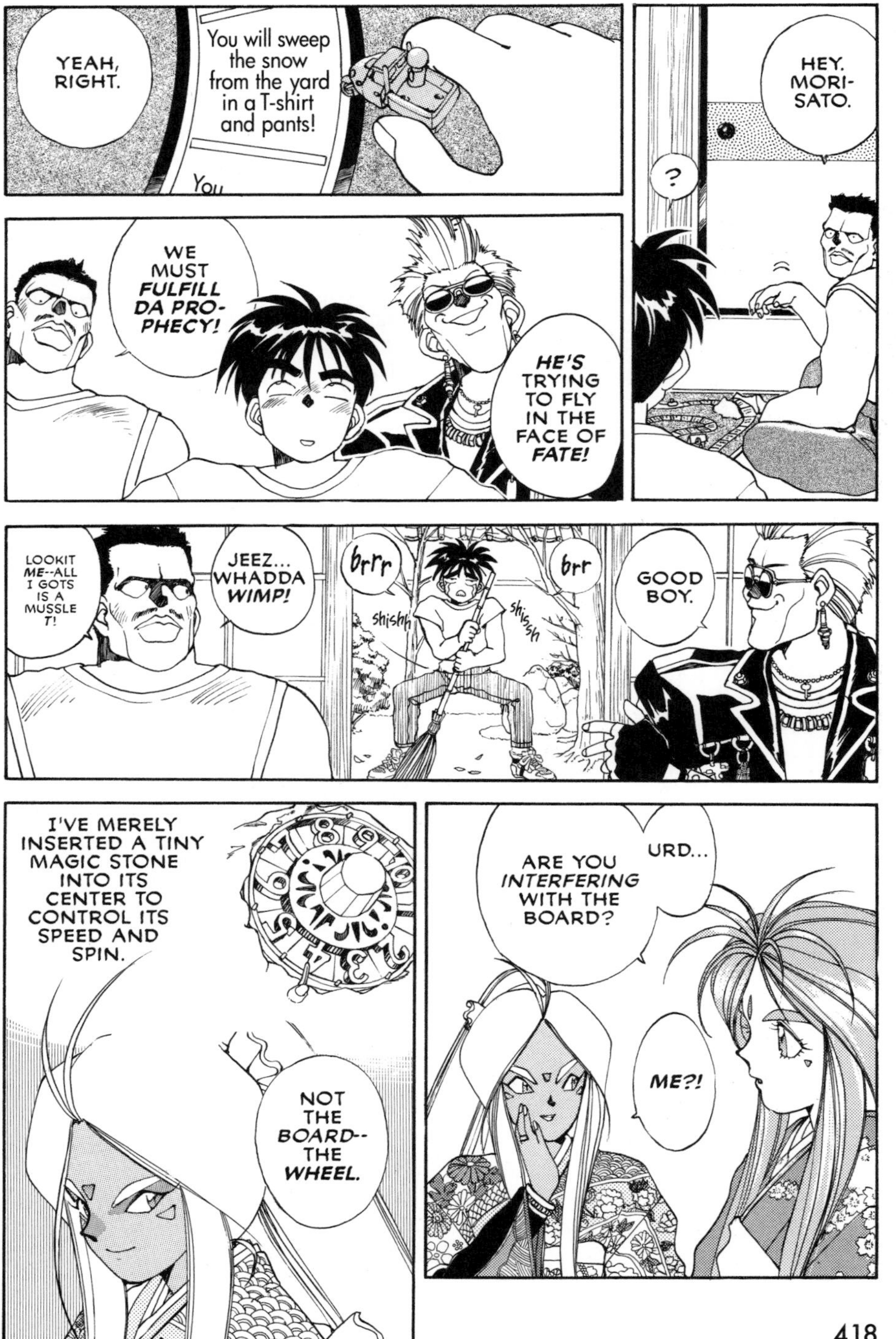
HEY. MORI-SATO.
?
You will sweep the snow from the yard in a T-shirt and pants!
You
YEAH, RIGHT.
HE'S TRYING TO FLY IN THE FACE OF FATE!
WE MUST FULFILL DA PRO-PHECY!
GOOD BOY.
brr
shissh
brrr
shishh
JEEZ... WHADDA WIMP!
LOOKIT ME--ALL I GOTS IS A MUSSLE T!
URD...
ARE YOU INTERFERING WITH THE BOARD?
ME?!
I'VE MERELY INSERTED A TINY MAGIC STONE INTO ITS CENTER TO CONTROL ITS SPEED AND SPIN.
NOT THE BOARD-- THE WHEEL.

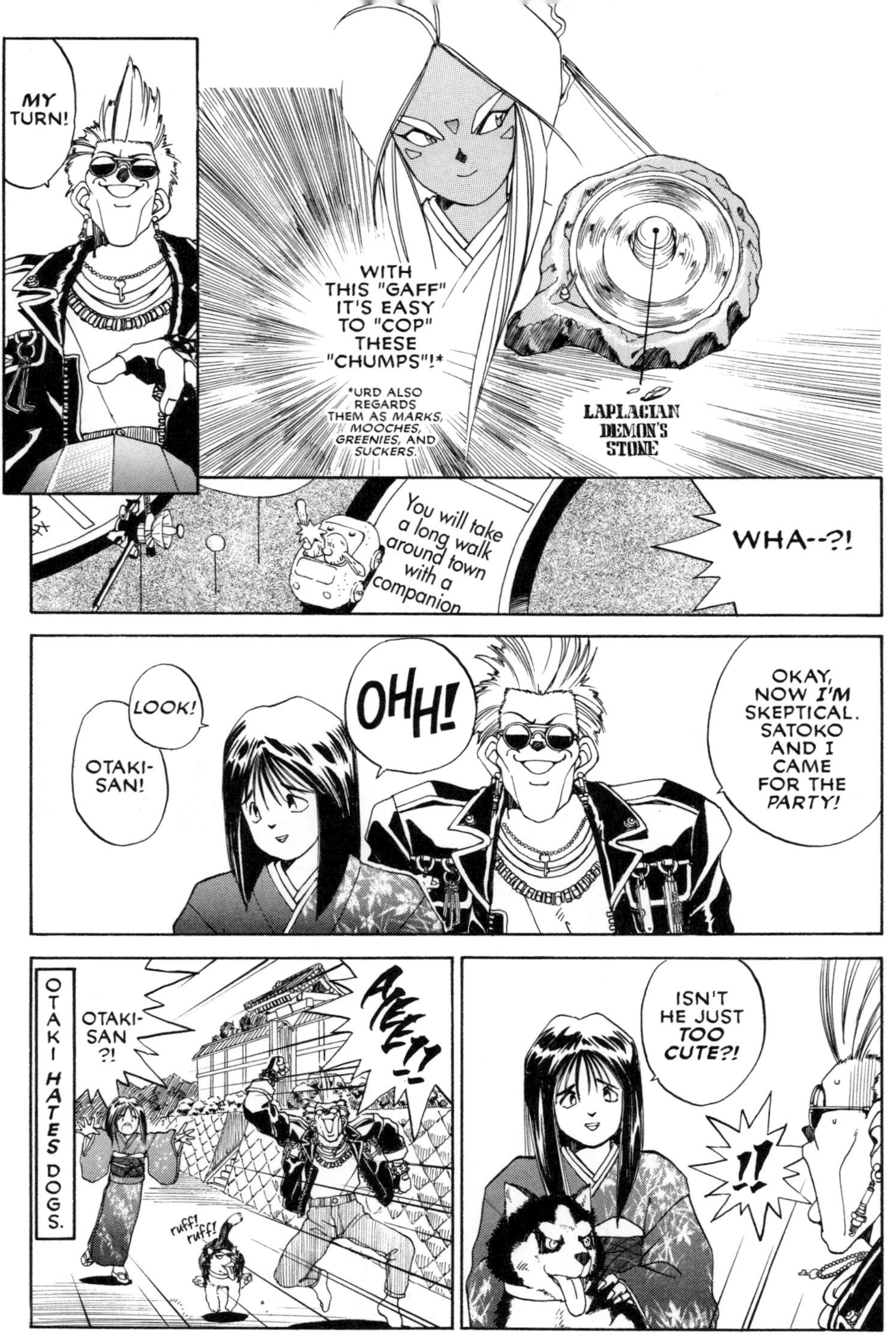
WITH THIS "GAFF" IT'S EASY TO "COP" THESE "CHUMPS"!*
*URD ALSO REGARDS THEM AS MARKS, MOOCHES, GREENIES, AND SUCKERS.
LAPLACIAN DEMON'S STONE
MY TURN!
WHA--?!
You will take a long walk around town with a companion
OKAY, NOW I'M SKEPTICAL. SATOKO AND I CAME FOR THE PARTY!
OHH!
LOOK!
OTAKI-SAN!
ISN'T HE JUST TOO CUTE?!
!!
AIEEE?!
OTAKI-SAN ?!
ruff! ruff!
OTAKI HATES DOGS.

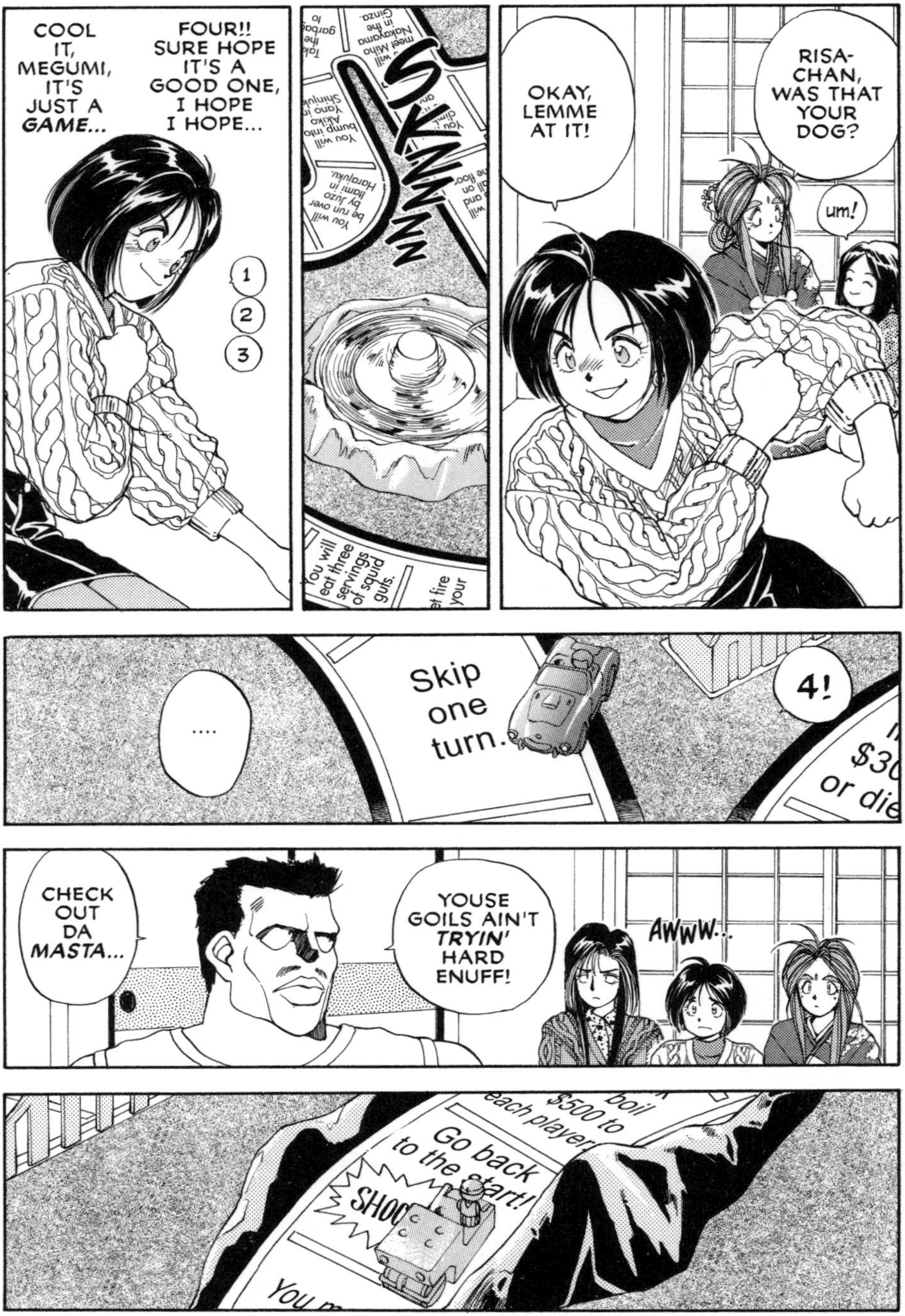
RISA-CHAN, WAS THAT YOUR DOG?
um!
OKAY, LEMME AT IT!
You will meet Miho Nakayama in the Ginza.
You will be run over by Juzo Itami in Harajuku.
You will bump into Aiko Yano in Shinjuku.
You will eat three servings of squid guts.
FOUR!! SURE HOPE IT'S A GOOD ONE, I HOPE I HOPE...
COOL IT, MEGUMI, IT'S JUST A GAME...
1
2
3
4!
Skip one turn.
....
AWWW...
YOUSE GOILS AIN'T TRYIN' HARD ENUFF!
CHECK OUT DA MASTA...
Go back to the start!

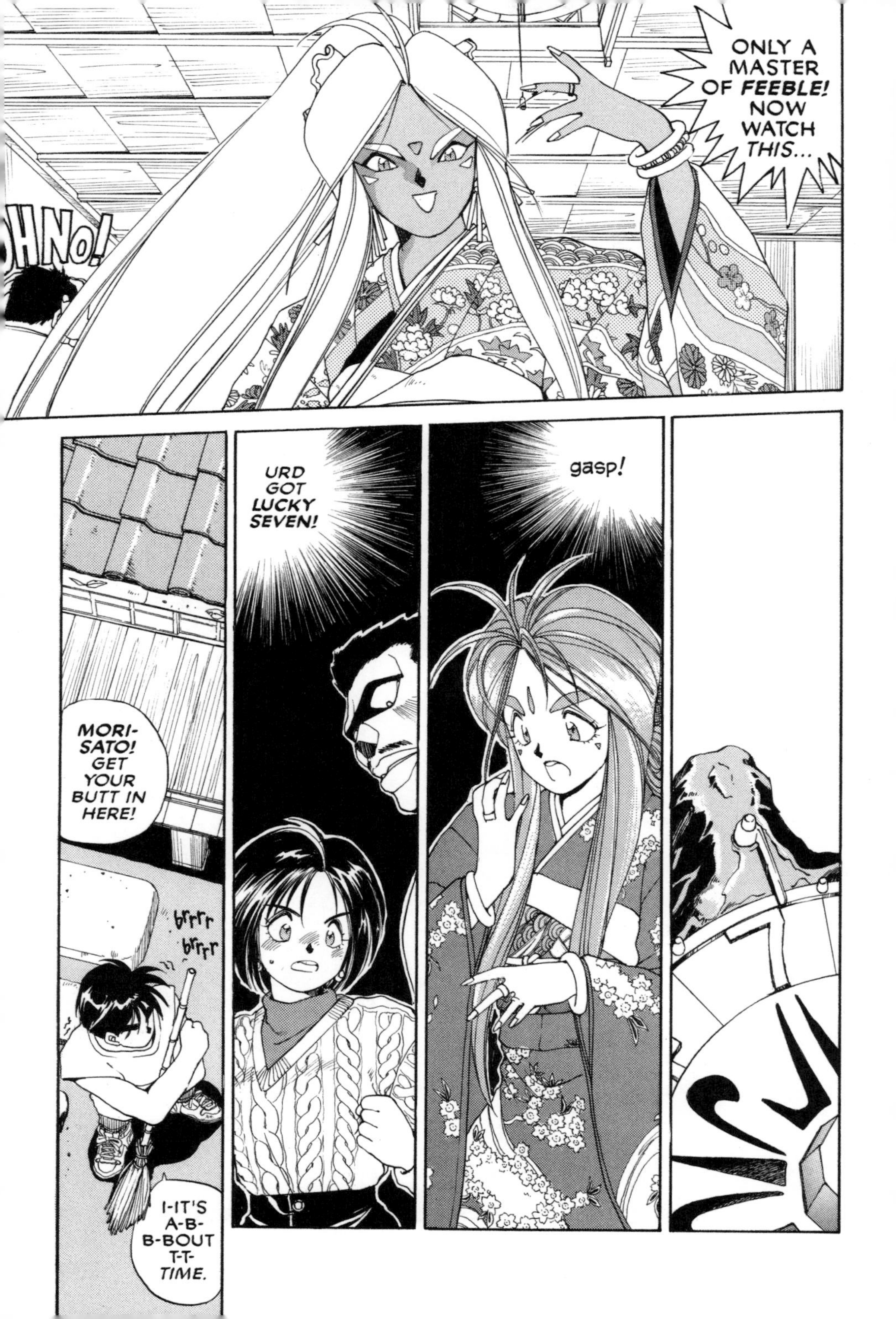
ONLY A MASTER OF FEEBLE! NOW WATCH THIS...
OH NO!
gasp!
URD GOT LUCKY SEVEN!
MORI-SATO! GET YOUR BUTT IN HERE!
brrrr brrrr
I-IT'S A-B-B-BOUT T-T-TIME.

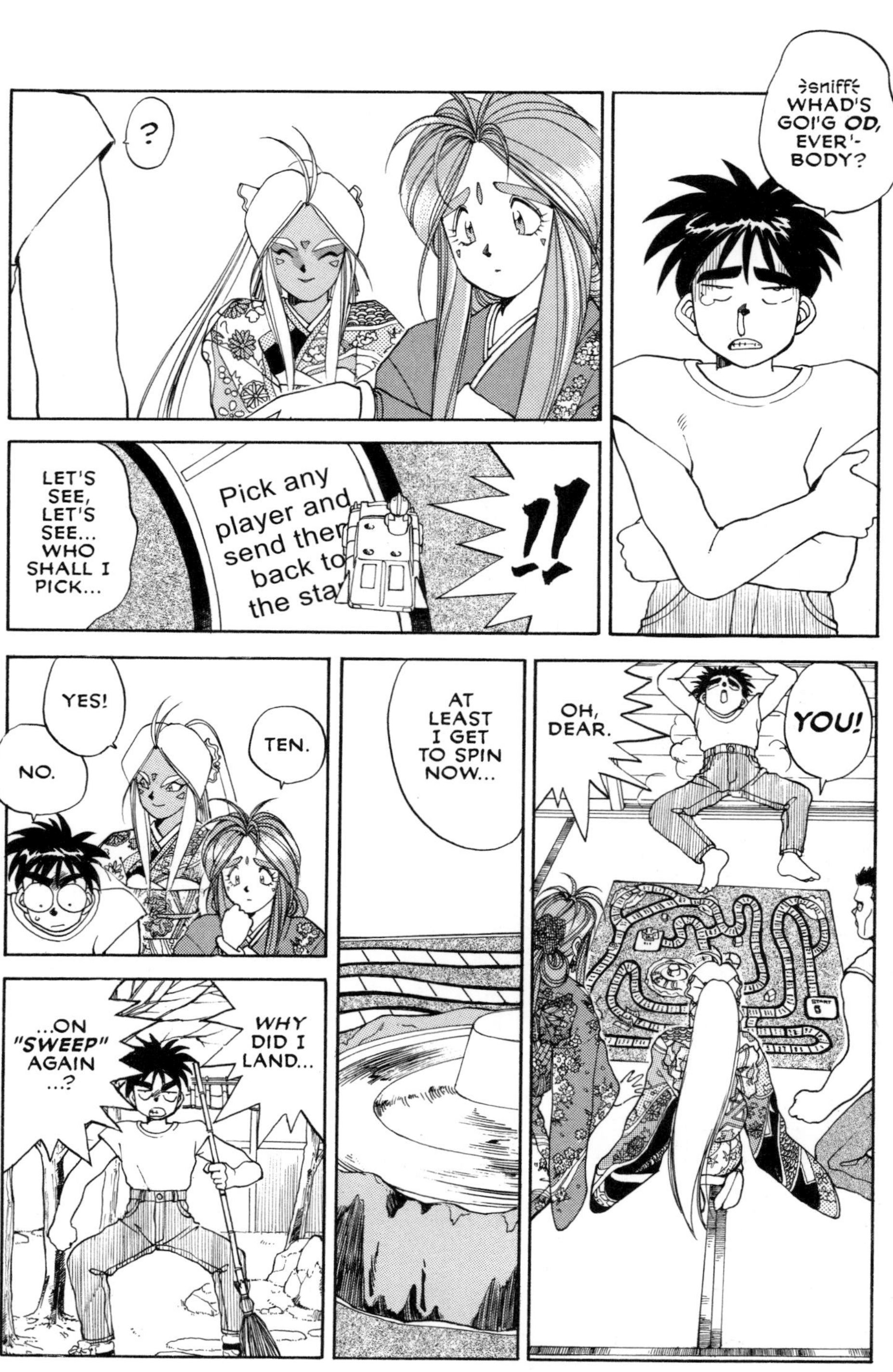

≶sniff≶ WHAD'S GOI'G *OD*, EVER'-BODY?
?
LET'S SEE, LET'S SEE... WHO SHALL I PICK...
Pick any player and send them back to the start
!!
YOU!
OH, DEAR.
AT LEAST I GET TO SPIN NOW...
YES!
TEN.
NO.
WHY DID I LAND...
...ON *"SWEEP"* AGAIN ...?

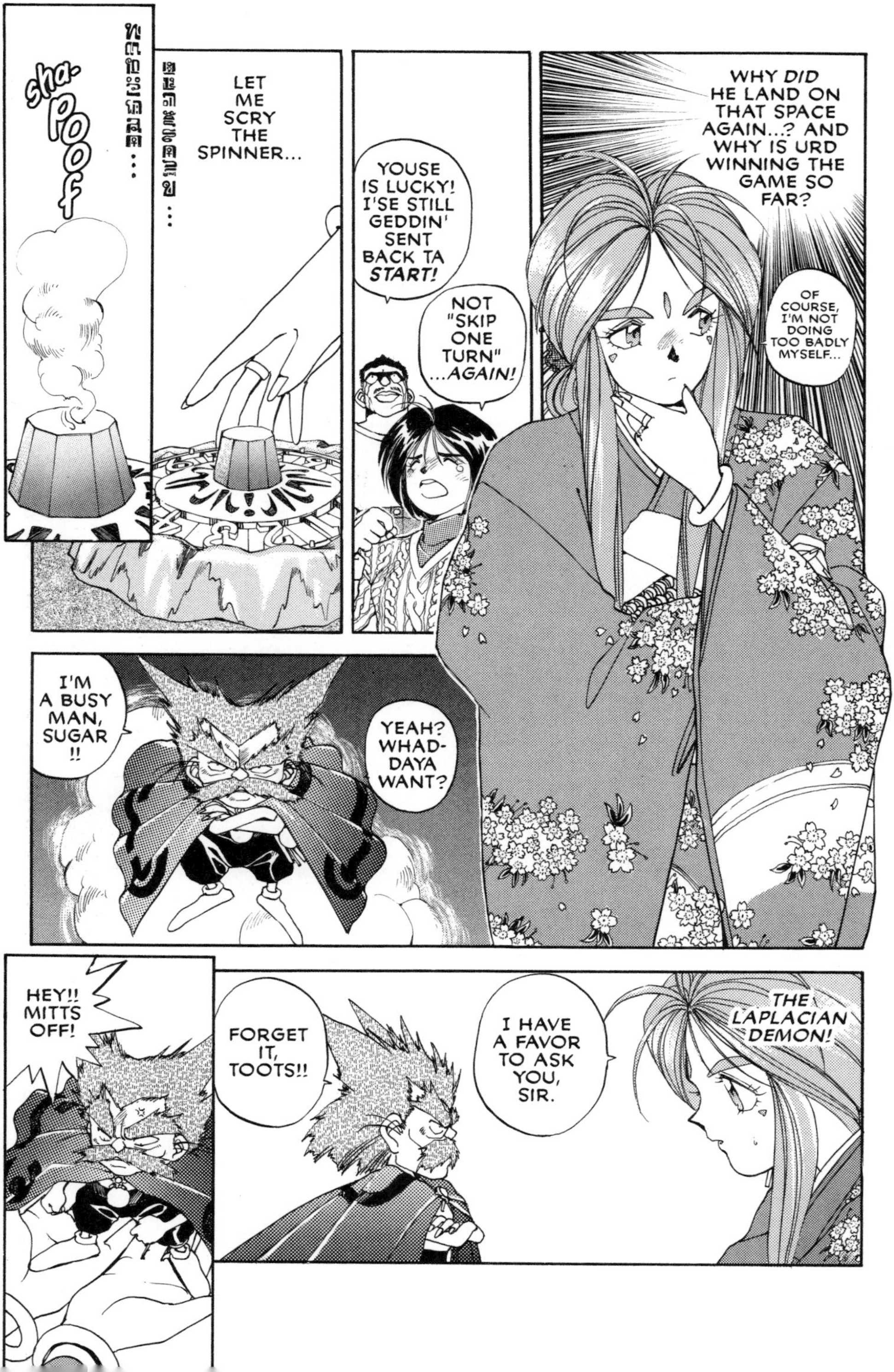
WHY DID HE LAND ON THAT SPACE AGAIN...? AND WHY IS URD WINNING THE GAME SO FAR?
OF COURSE, I'M NOT DOING TOO BADLY MYSELF...
YOUSE IS LUCKY! I'SE STILL GEDDIN' SENT BACK TA START!
NOT "SKIP ONE TURN" ...AGAIN!
LET ME SCRY THE SPINNER...
sha-poooof
YEAH? WHAD-DAYA WANT?
I'M A BUSY MAN, SUGAR!!
THE LAPLACIAN DEMON!
I HAVE A FAVOR TO ASK YOU, SIR.
FORGET IT, TOOTS!!
HEY!! MITTS OFF!

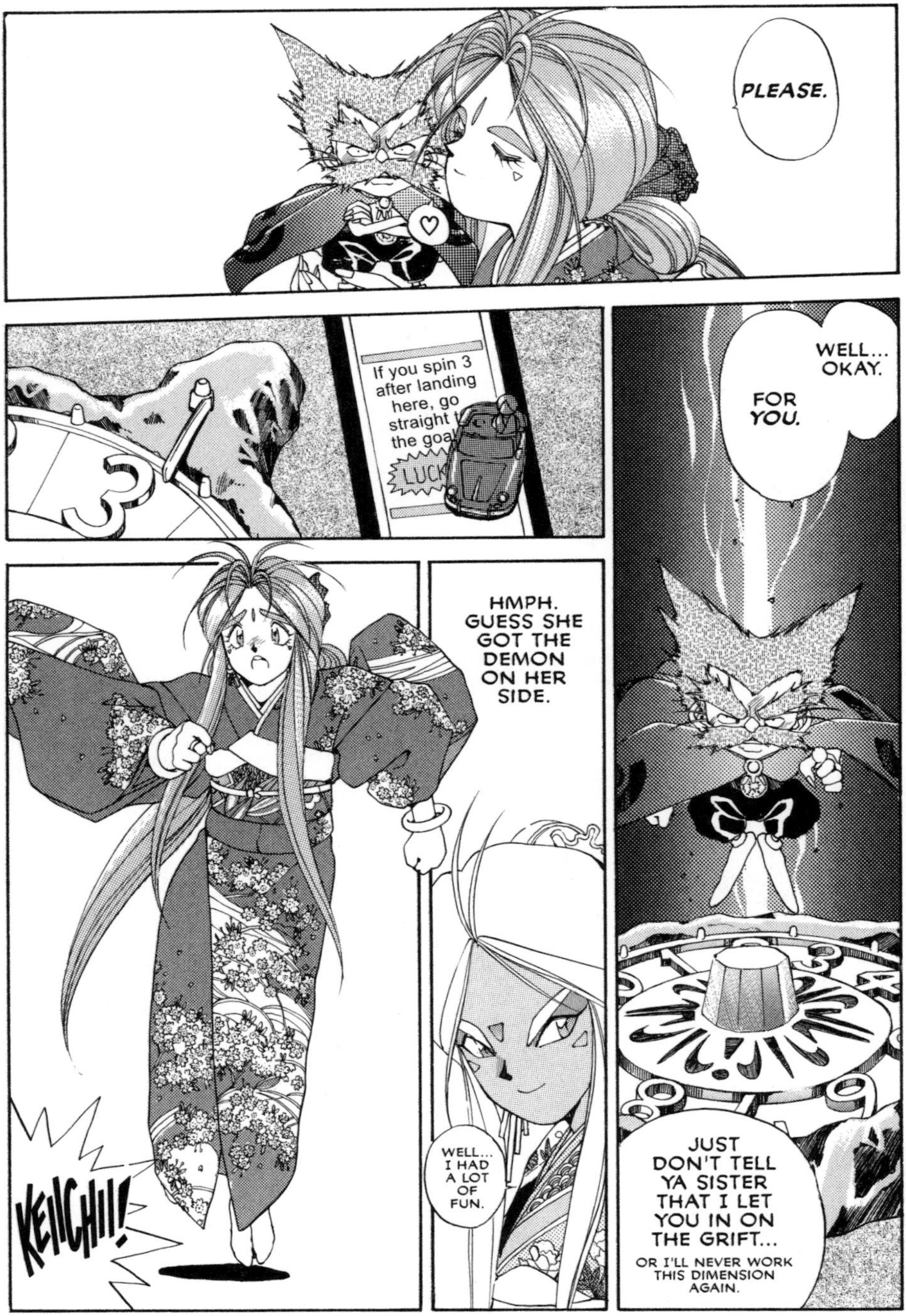
PLEASE.
WELL... OKAY.
FOR YOU.
JUST DON'T TELL YA SISTER THAT I LET YOU IN ON THE GRIFT...
OR I'LL NEVER WORK THIS DIMENSION AGAIN.
If you spin 3 after landing here, go straight to the goal
HMPH. GUESS SHE GOT THE DEMON ON HER SIDE.
WELL... I HAD A LOT OF FUN.
KEIICHI!

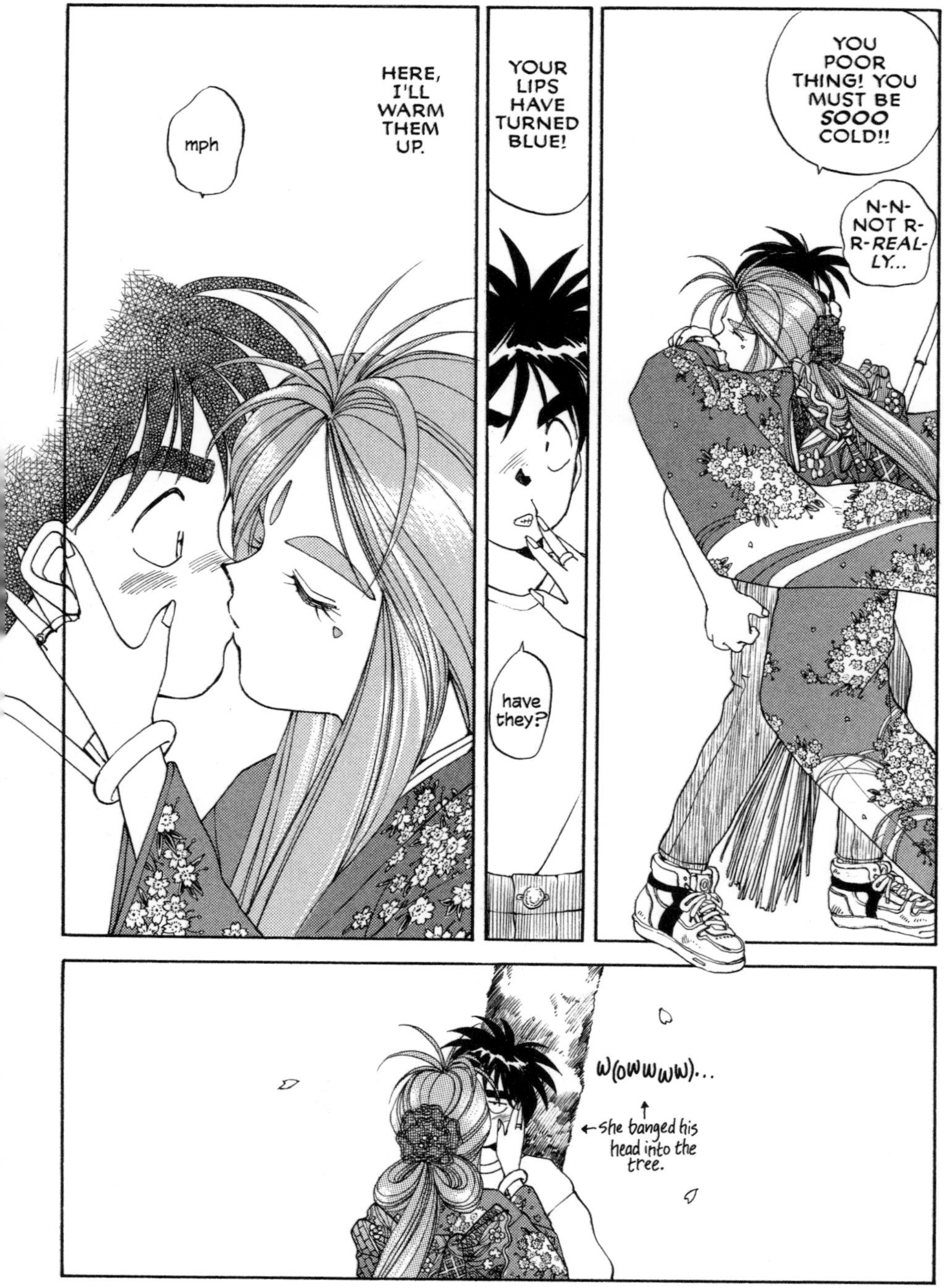
YOU POOR THING! YOU MUST BE *SOOO* COLD!!
N-N-NOT R-R-*REAL-LY*...
YOUR LIPS HAVE TURNED BLUE!
have they?
HERE, I'LL WARM THEM UP.
mph
W(OWWWW)...
she banged his head into the tree.

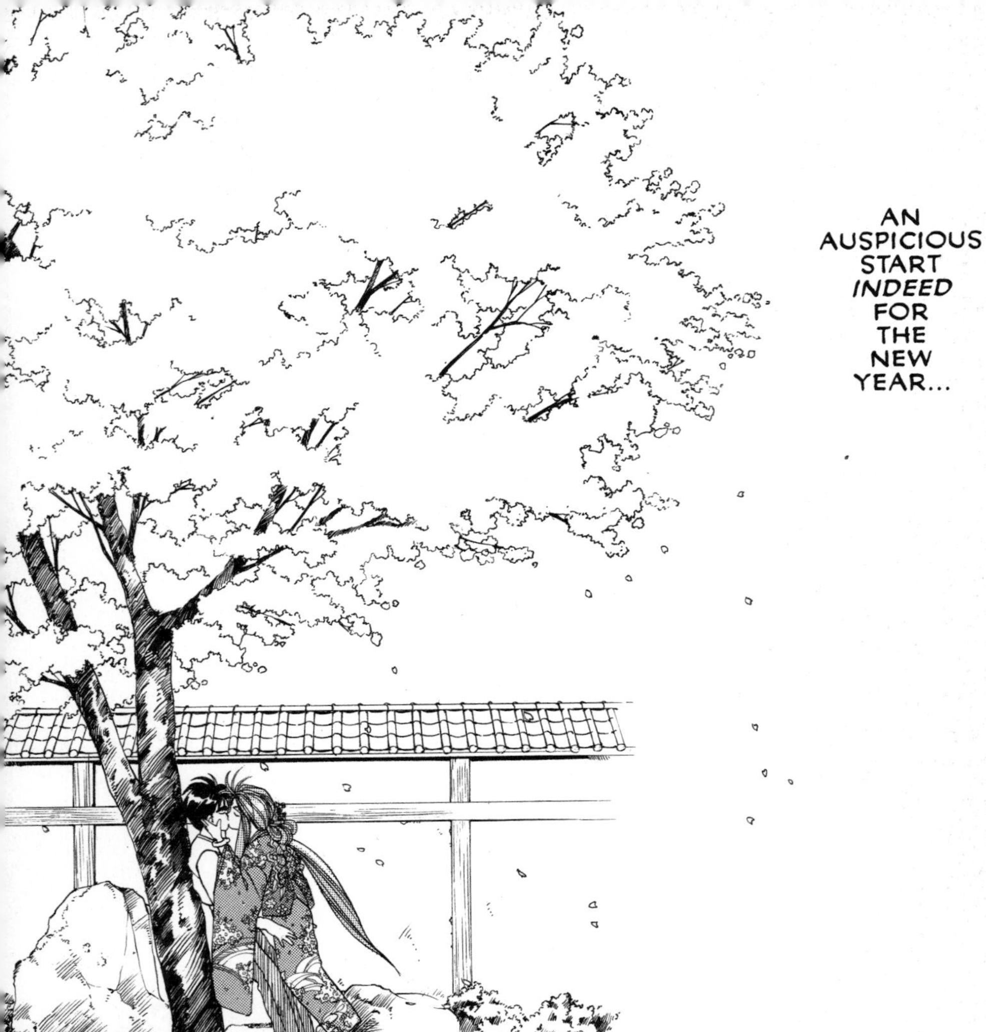
AN AUSPICIOUS START *INDEED* FOR THE NEW YEAR...

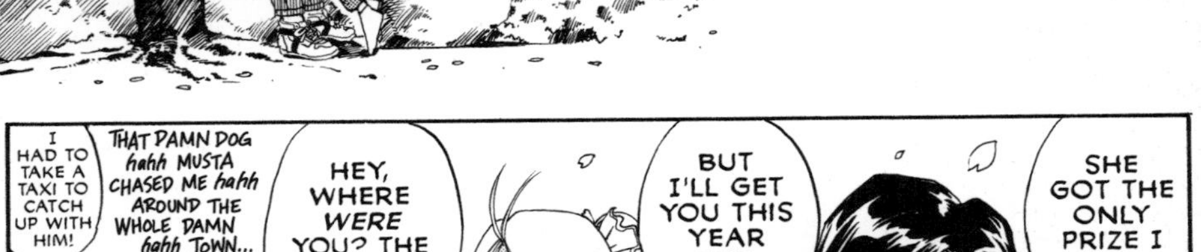
SHE GOT THE ONLY PRIZE I WANT-ED...
BUT I'LL GET YOU THIS YEAR FOR SURE.
HEY, WHERE *WERE* YOU? THE GAME'S OVER!
THAT DAMN DOG *hahh* MUSTA CHASED ME *hahh* AROUND THE WHOLE DAMN *hahh* TOWN...
I HAD TO TAKE A TAXI TO CATCH UP WITH HIM!

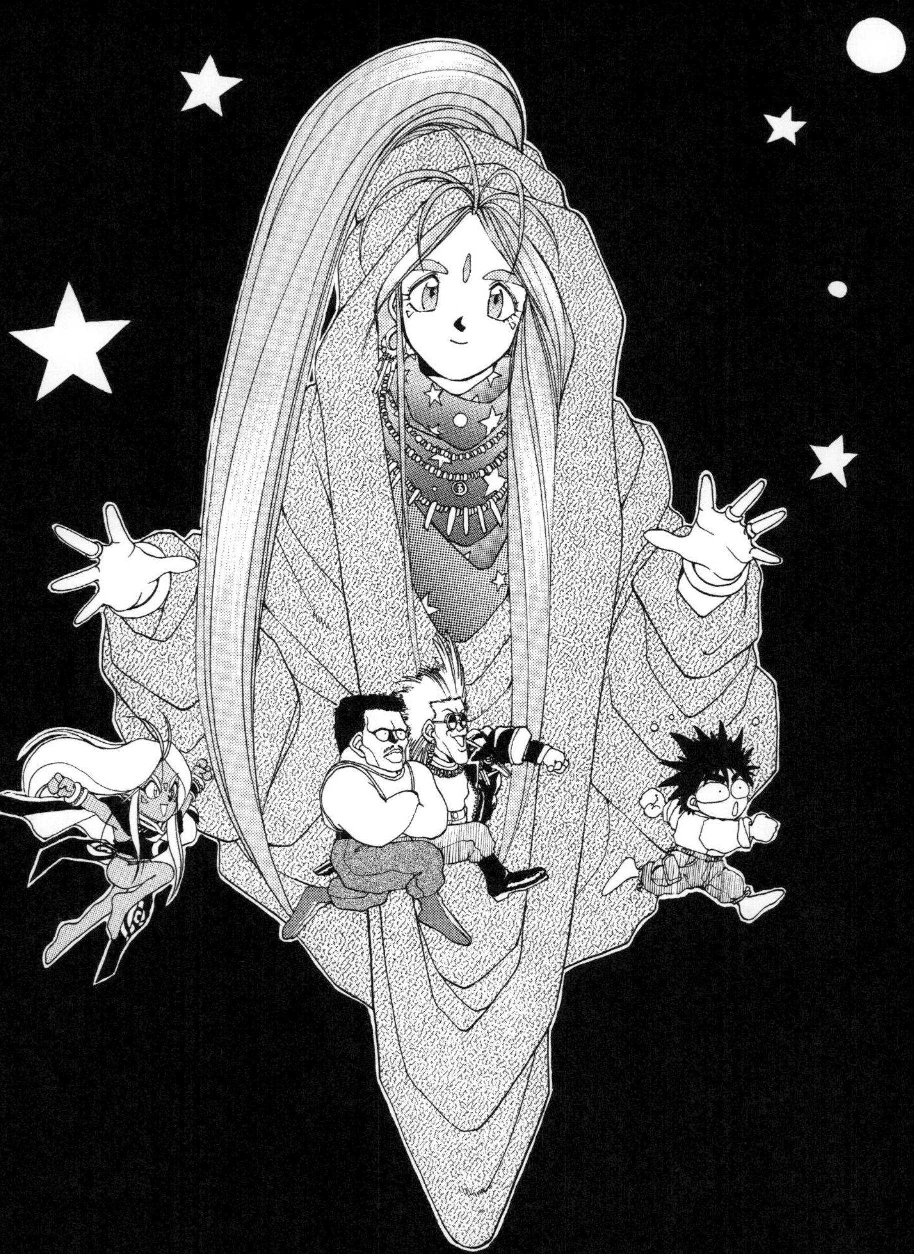

CHAPTER 19

Upon Close Examination

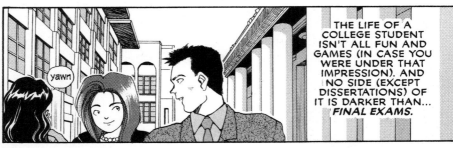

THE LIFE OF A COLLEGE STUDENT ISN'T ALL FUN AND GAMES (IN CASE YOU WERE UNDER THAT IMPRESSION). AND NO SIDE (EXCEPT DISSERTATIONS) OF IT IS DARKER THAN... *FINAL EXAMS.*
yawn
huh?
wha?
I'll never identify this substance in an hour!
It's just soy sauce, dummy.
CHEMISTRY
COMP SCI
DUE TO A SYSTEM CRASH THE COMPUTER LAB WILL BE CLOSED UNTIL FURTHER NOTICE.
NO NO *NOOO!!* IF I CAN'T USE IT TODAY I'LL *NEVER* GET MY PAPER DONE IN TIME!
KEIICHI
twitch
KEIICHI, DEAR?
I CAN'T HELP BUT NOTICE HOW TIRED YOU LOOK.
grunt

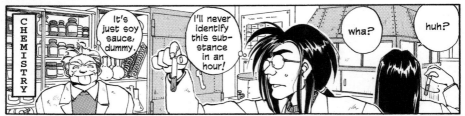

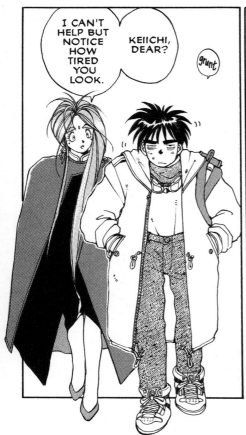

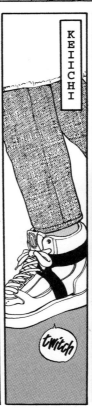

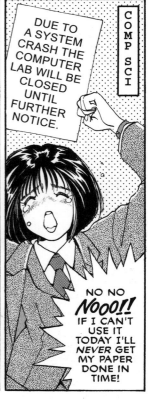

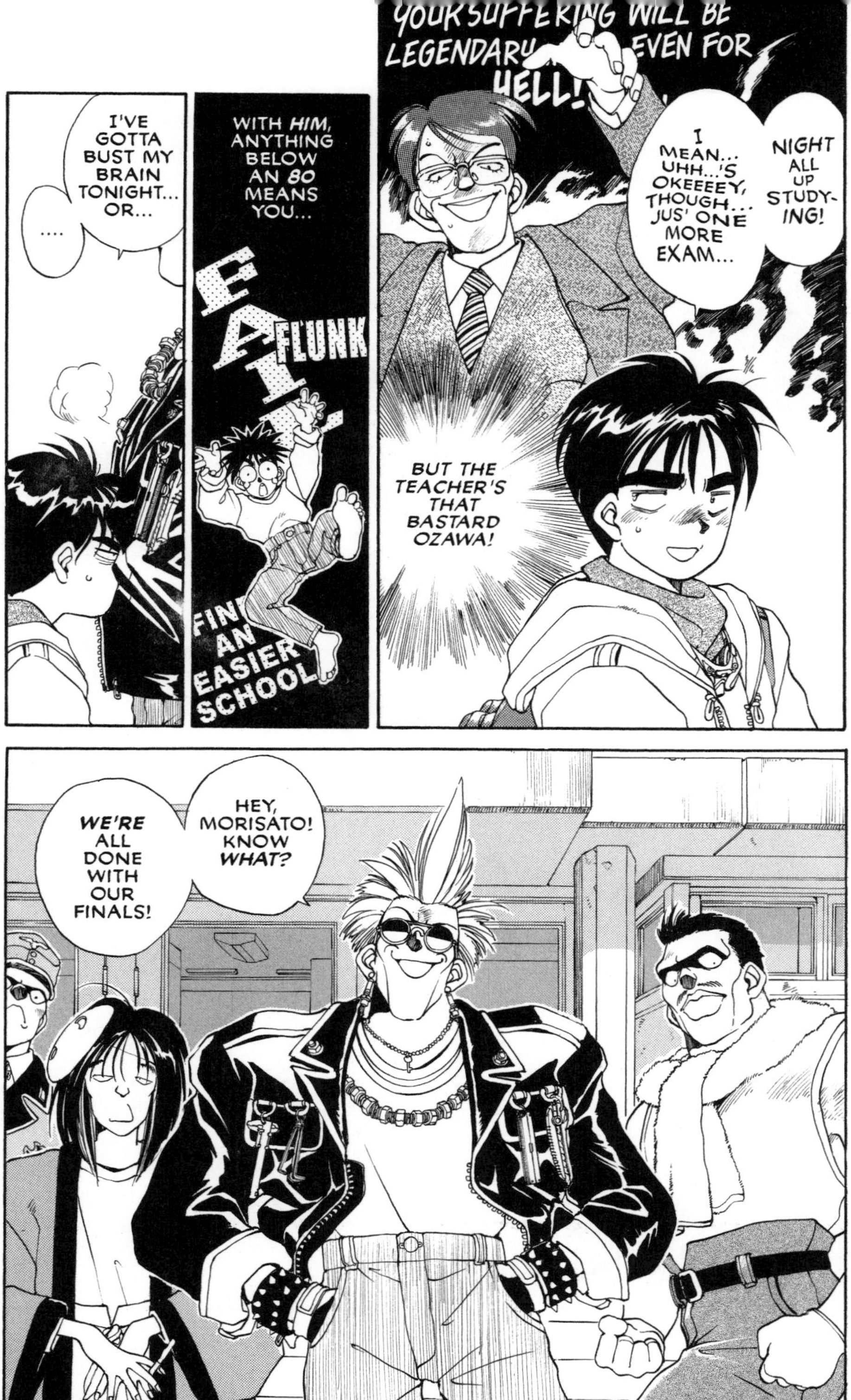
I MEAN... UHH...'S OKEEEEY, THOUGH... JUS' ONE MORE EXAM...
NIGHT ALL UP STUDY-ING!
BUT THE TEACHER'S THAT BASTARD OZAWA!
YOUR SUFFERING WILL BE LEGENDARY... EVEN FOR HELL!
WITH HIM, ANYTHING BELOW AN 80 MEANS YOU...
FAIL
FLUNK
FIN
AN EASIER SCHOOL
I'VE GOTTA BUST MY BRAIN TONIGHT... OR...
....
HEY, MORISATO! KNOW WHAT?
WE'RE ALL DONE WITH OUR FINALS!

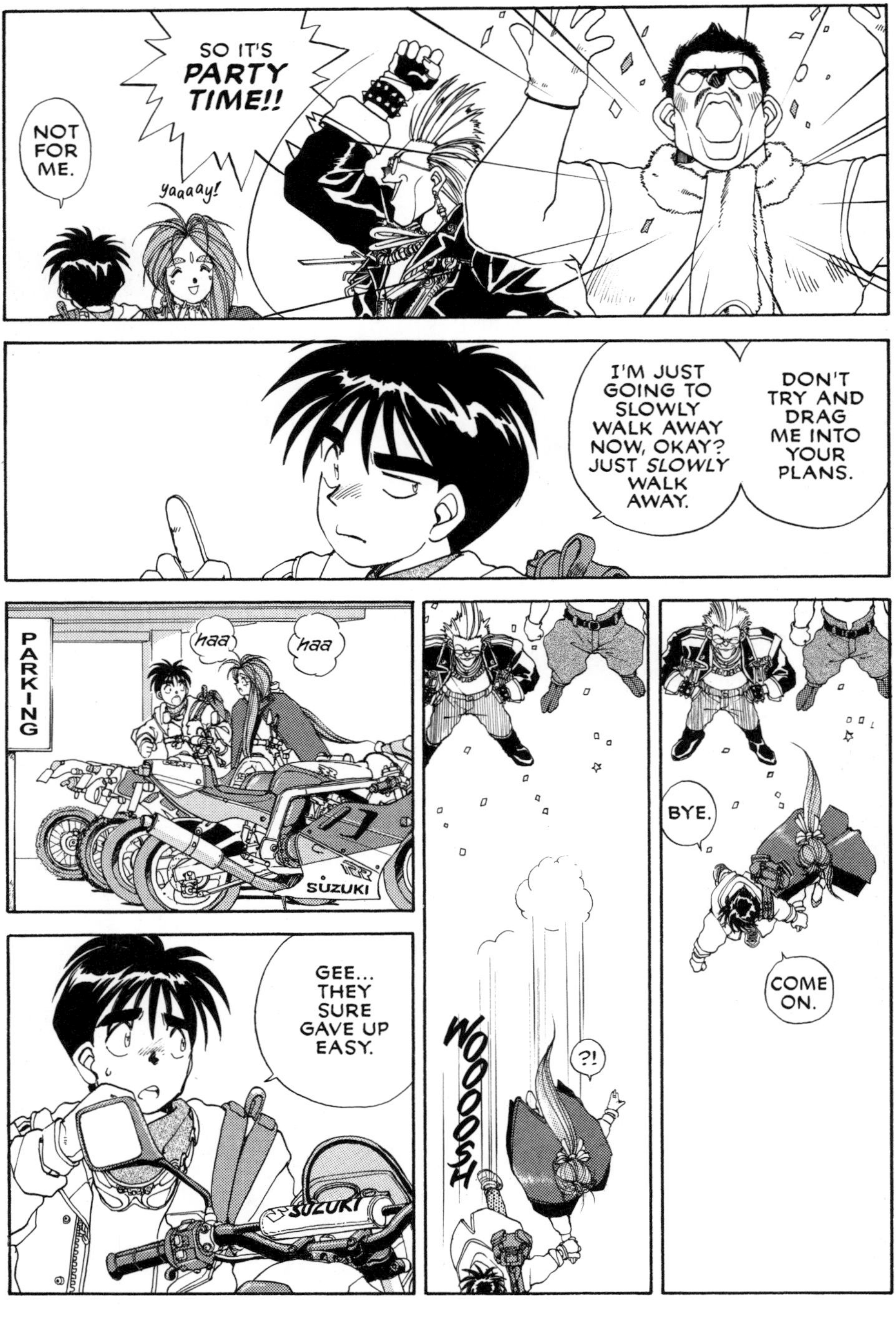
SO IT'S PARTY TIME!!
yaaaay!
NOT FOR ME.
DON'T TRY AND DRAG ME INTO YOUR PLANS.
I'M JUST GOING TO SLOWLY WALK AWAY NOW, OKAY? JUST SLOWLY WALK AWAY.
BYE.
COME ON.
?!
WOOOOOSH
haa
haa
PARKING
SUZUKI
GEE... THEY SURE GAVE UP EASY.
SUZUKI

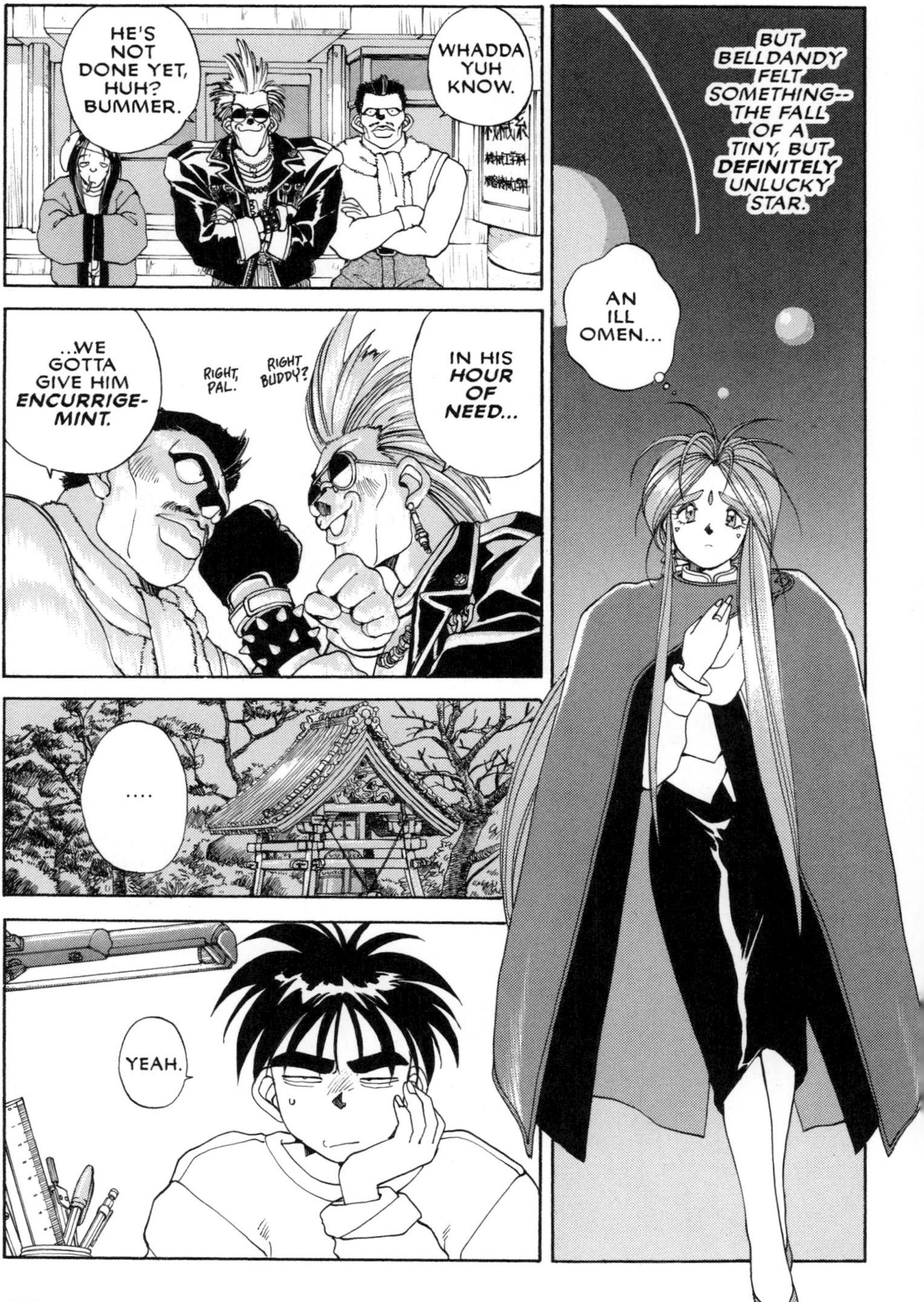
BUT BELLDANDY FELT SOMETHING-- THE FALL OF A TINY, BUT DEFINITELY UNLUCKY STAR.
AN ILL OMEN...
WHADDA YUH KNOW.
HE'S NOT DONE YET, HUH? BUMMER.
IN HIS HOUR OF NEED...
RIGHT BUDDY?
RIGHT, PAL.
...WE GOTTA GIVE HIM ENCURRIGE-MINT.
....
YEAH.

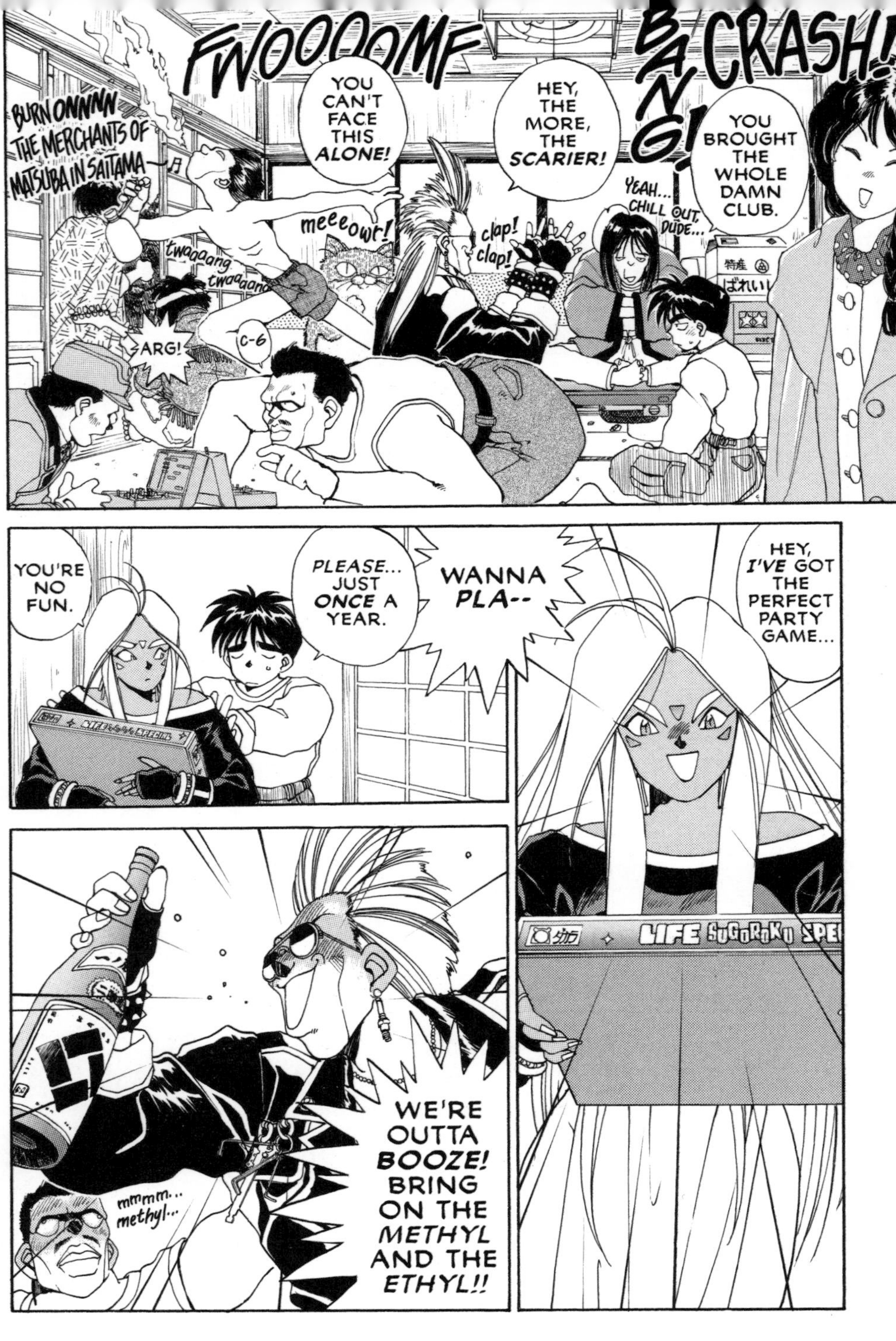
CRASH!
BANG!
YOU BROUGHT THE WHOLE DAMN CLUB.
YEAH... CHILL OUT, DUDE...
HEY, THE MORE, THE SCARIER!
clap! clap!
FWOOOOMF
YOU CAN'T FACE THIS ALONE!
meeeowr!
BURN ONNNN THE MERCHANTS OF MATSUBA IN SAITAMA~
twaaaang twaaaang
C-6
ARG!
HEY, I'VE GOT THE PERFECT PARTY GAME...
LIFE SUGOROKU
WANNA PLA--
PLEASE... JUST ONCE A YEAR.
YOU'RE NO FUN.
WE'RE OUTTA BOOZE! BRING ON THE METHYL AND THE ETHYL!!
mmmm... methyl...

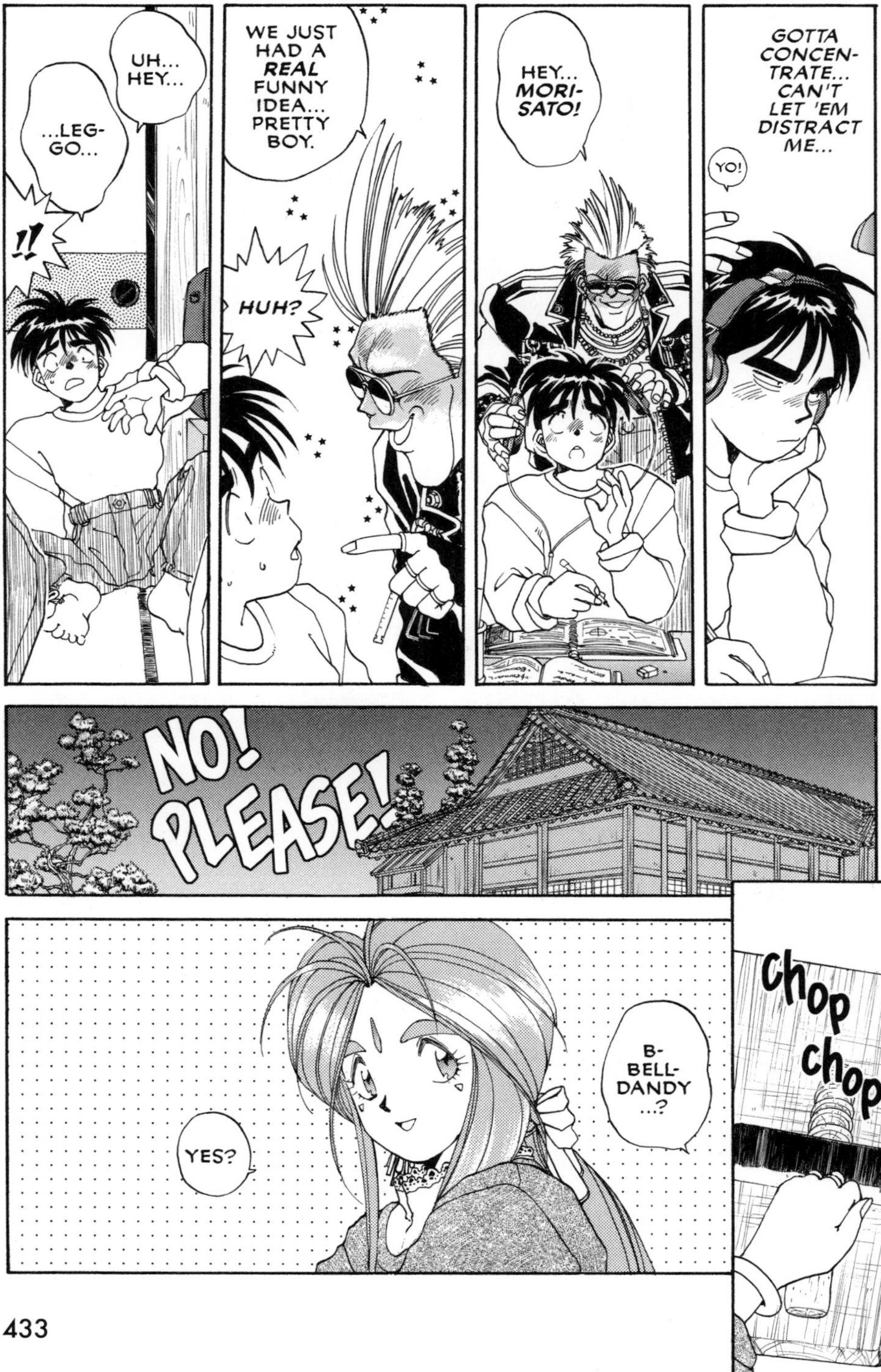
GOTTA CONCENTRATE... CAN'T LET 'EM DISTRACT ME...
YO!
HEY... MORISATO!
WE JUST HAD A REAL FUNNY IDEA... PRETTY BOY.
HUH?
UH... HEY...
...LEG-GO...
!!
NO! PLEASE!
chop chop
B-BELL-DANDY ...?
YES?

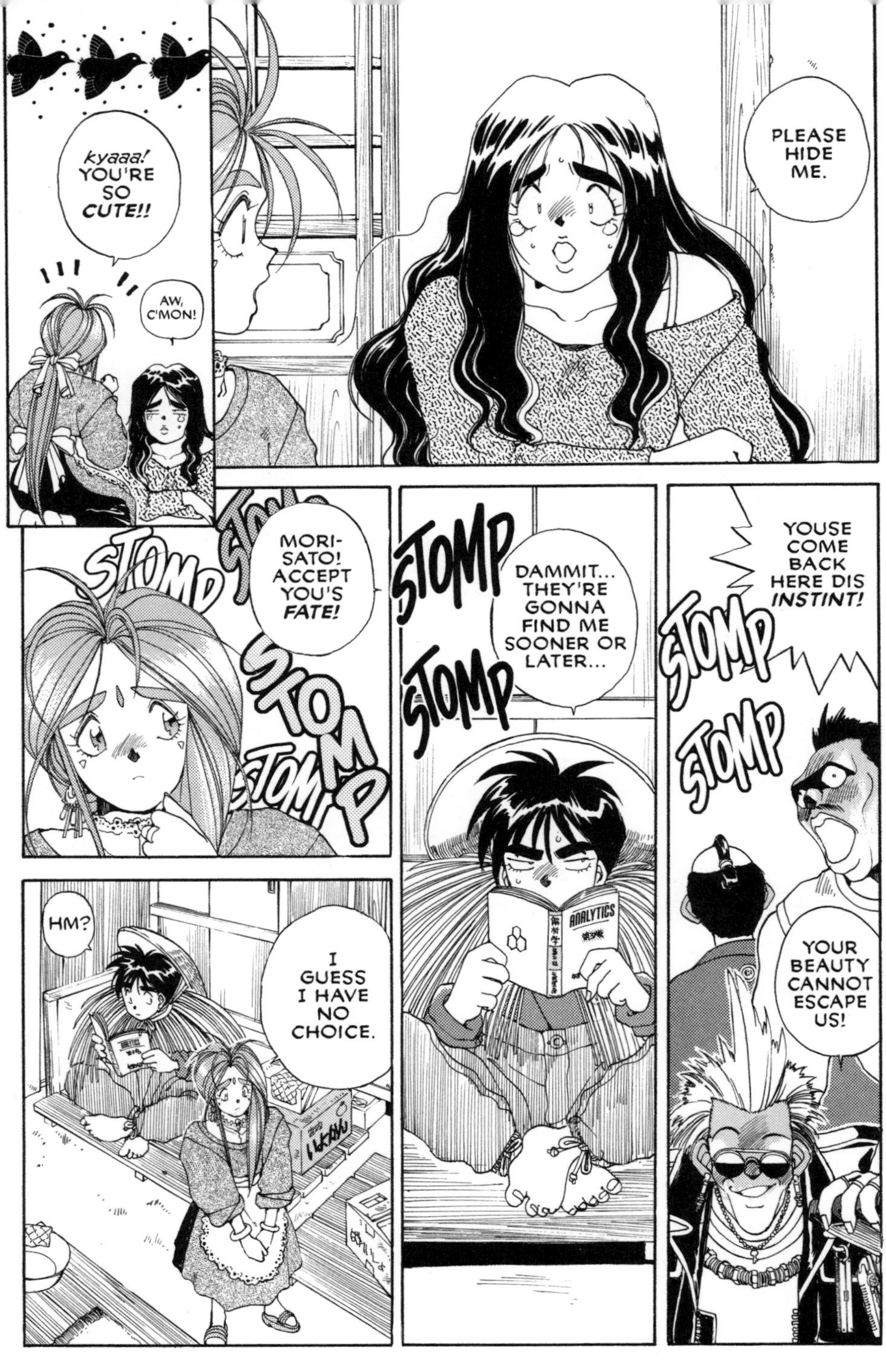
PLEASE HIDE ME.
kyaaa! YOU'RE SO CUTE!!
AW, C'MON!
YOUSE COME BACK HERE DIS INSTINT!
STOMP
STOMP
YOUR BEAUTY CANNOT ESCAPE US!
STOMP
DAMMIT... THEY'RE GONNA FIND ME SOONER OR LATER...
STOMP
ANALYTICS
STOMP
STOMP
MORI-SATO! ACCEPT YOU'S FATE!
STOMP
STOMP
STOMP
HM?
I GUESS I HAVE NO CHOICE.

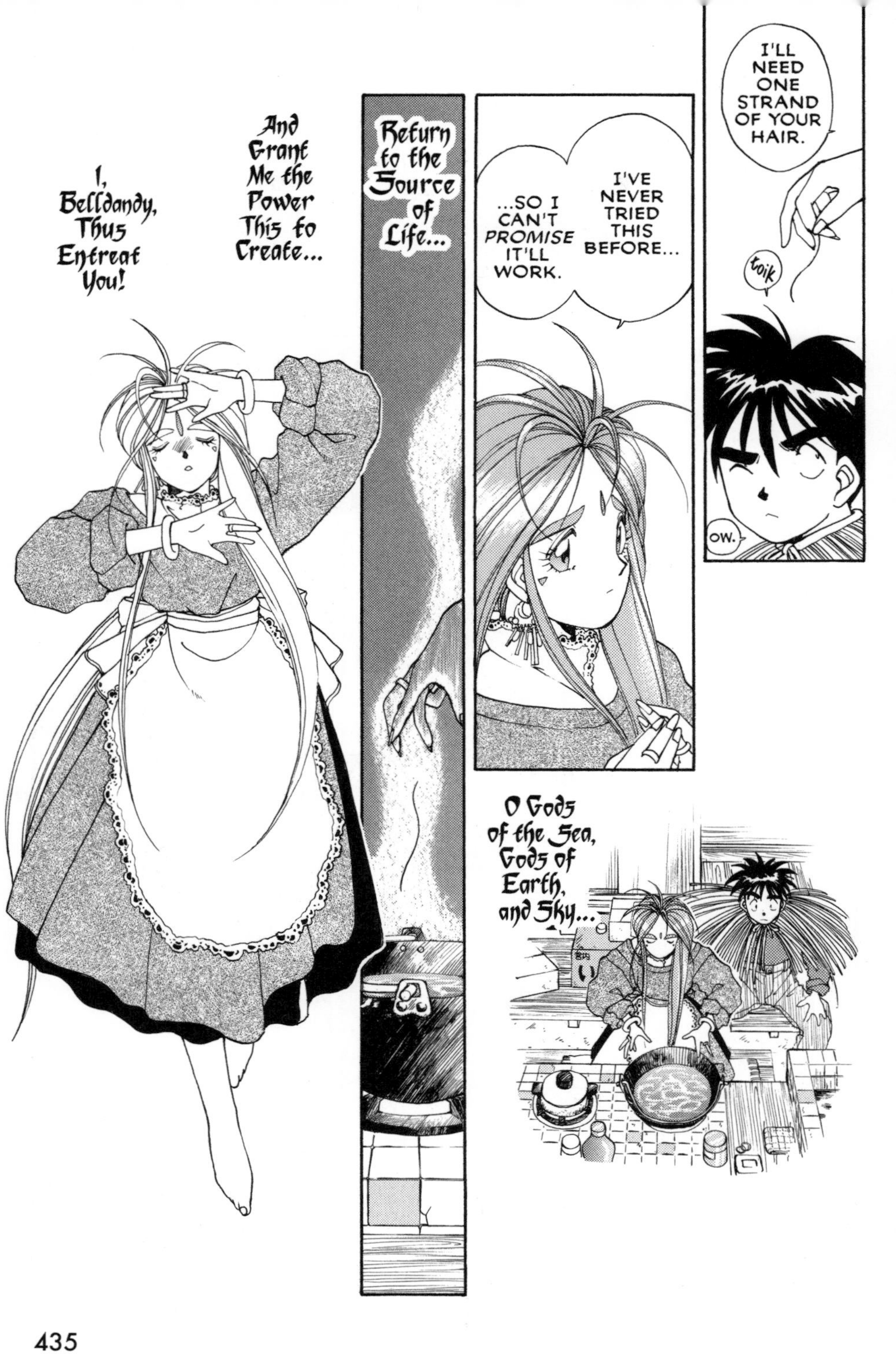
I'LL NEED ONE STRAND OF YOUR HAIR.
toik
OW.
I'VE NEVER TRIED THIS BEFORE...
...SO I CAN'T *PROMISE* IT'LL WORK.
O Gods of the Sea, Gods of Earth, and Sky...
Return to the Source of Life...
And Grant Me the Power This to Create...
I, Belldandy, Thus Entreat You!

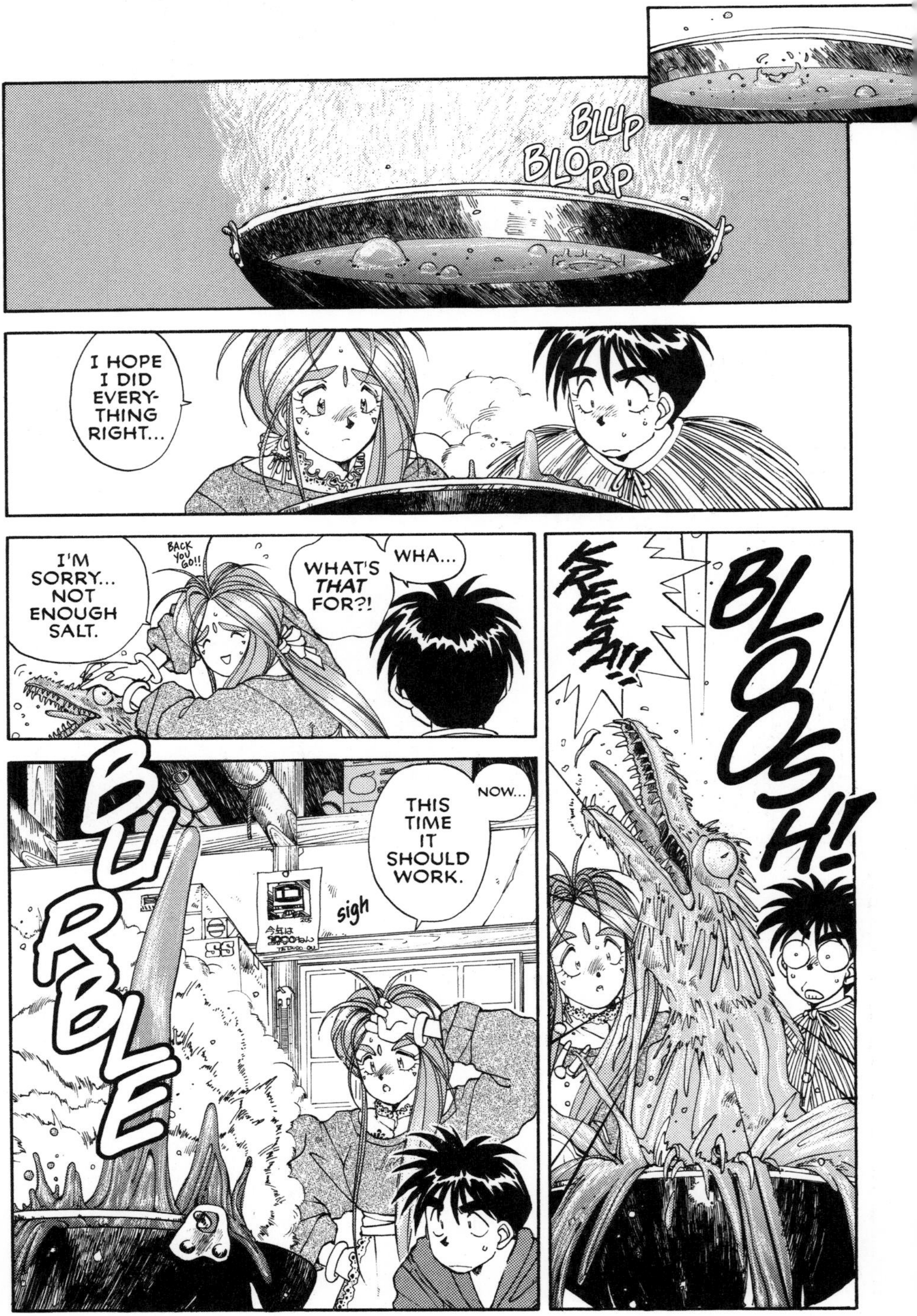
BLUP
BLORP
I HOPE I DID EVERYTHING RIGHT...
KREEEA!!!
BLOOSH!
WHA...
WHAT'S THAT FOR?!
BACK YOU GO!!
I'M SORRY... NOT ENOUGH SALT.
NOW...
THIS TIME IT SHOULD WORK.
sigh
BURBLE

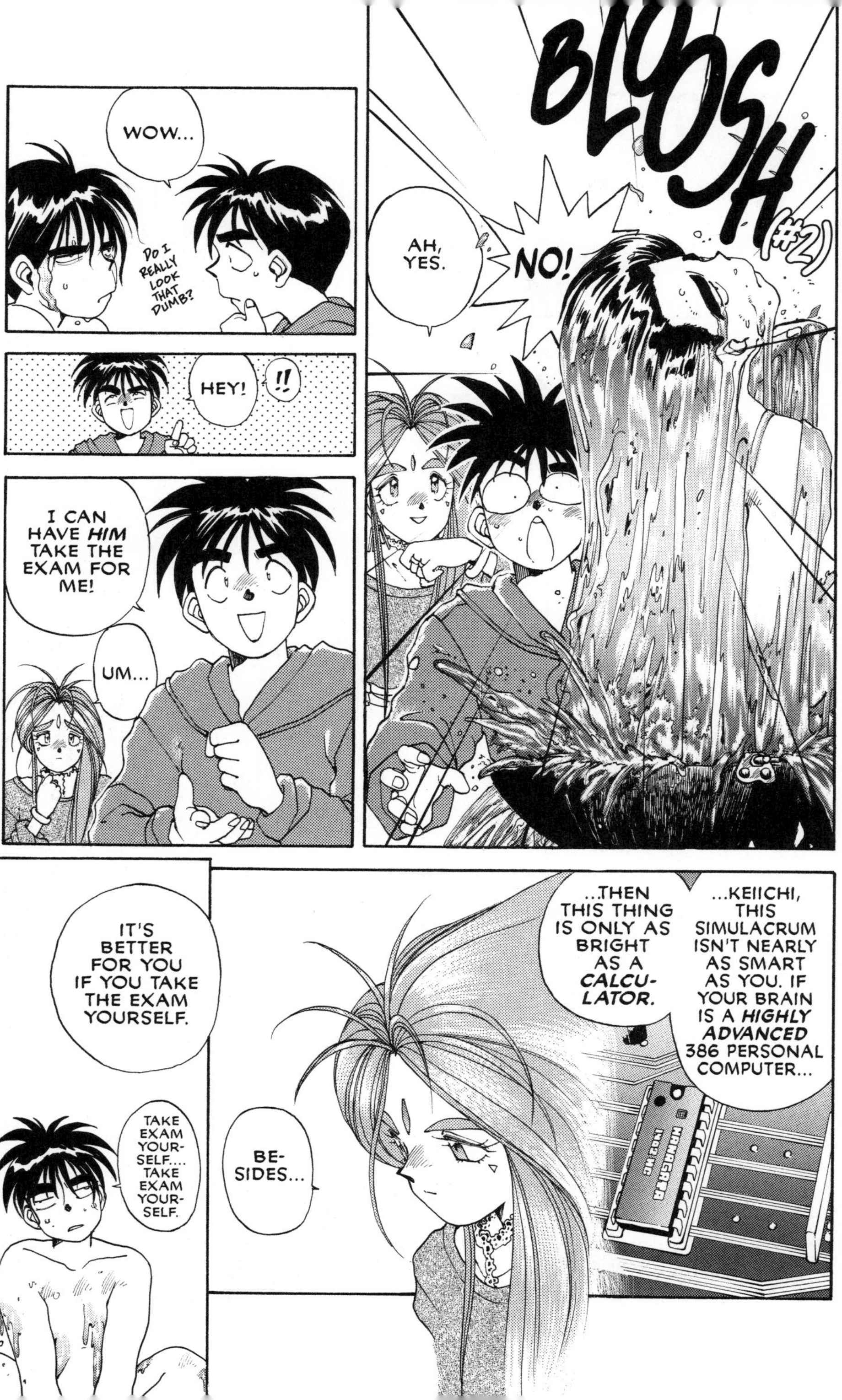
BLOOSH (#2)
NO!
AH, YES.
WOW...
DO I REALLY LOOK THAT DUMB?
!!
HEY!
I CAN HAVE *HIM* TAKE THE EXAM FOR ME!
UM...
...KEIICHI, THIS SIMULACRUM ISN'T NEARLY AS SMART AS YOU. IF YOUR BRAIN IS A *HIGHLY ADVANCED* 386 PERSONAL COMPUTER...
...THEN THIS THING IS ONLY AS BRIGHT AS A *CALCULATOR.*
BE-SIDES...
IT'S BETTER FOR YOU IF YOU TAKE THE EXAM YOURSELF.
TAKE EXAM YOUR-SELF.... TAKE EXAM YOUR-SELF.

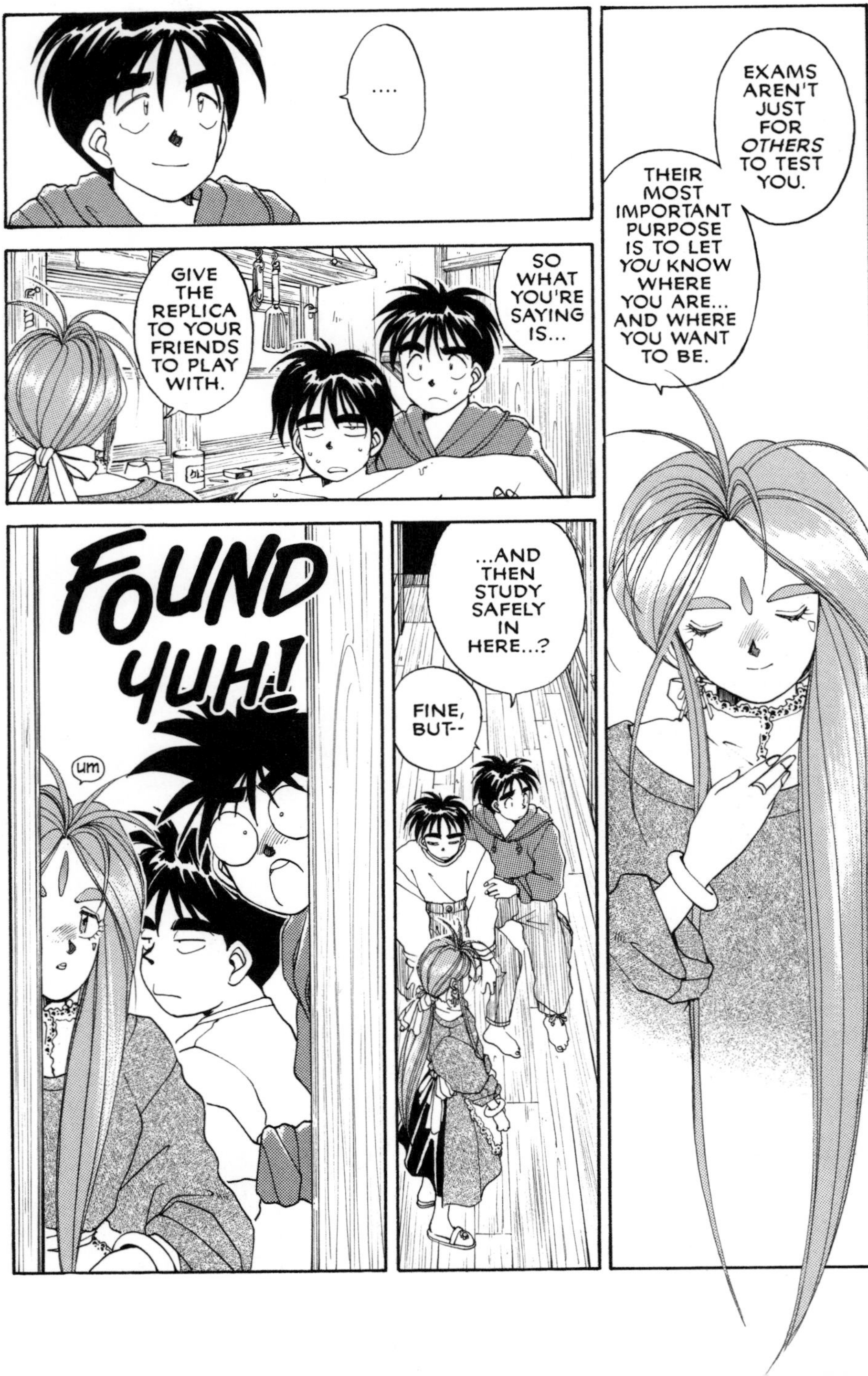
EXAMS AREN'T JUST FOR *OTHERS* TO TEST YOU.
THEIR MOST IMPORTANT PURPOSE IS TO LET *YOU* KNOW WHERE YOU ARE... AND WHERE YOU WANT TO BE.
....
SO WHAT YOU'RE SAYING IS...
GIVE THE REPLICA TO YOUR FRIENDS TO PLAY WITH.
...AND THEN STUDY SAFELY IN HERE...?
FINE, BUT--
FOUND YUH!
um

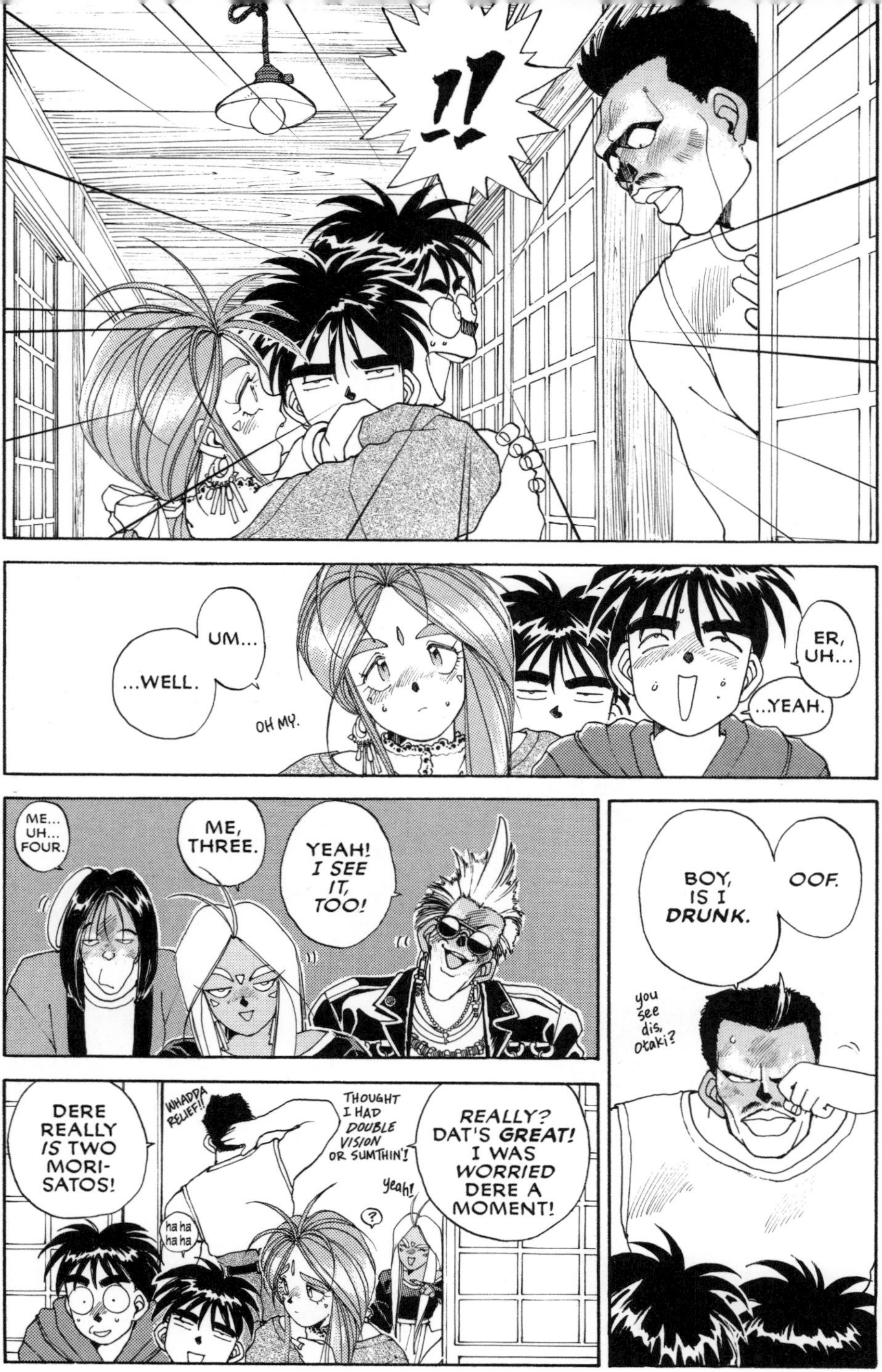
!!
ER, UH...
...YEAH.
UM...
...WELL.
OH MY.
OOF.
BOY, IS I DRUNK.
you see dis, Otaki?
YEAH! I SEE IT, TOO!
ME, THREE.
ME... UH... FOUR.
REALLY? DAT'S GREAT! I WAS WORRIED DERE A MOMENT!
THOUGHT I HAD DOUBLE VISION OR SUMTHIN'!
WHADDA RELIEF!!
yeah!
?
ha ha ha ha
DERE REALLY IS TWO MORI-SATOS!

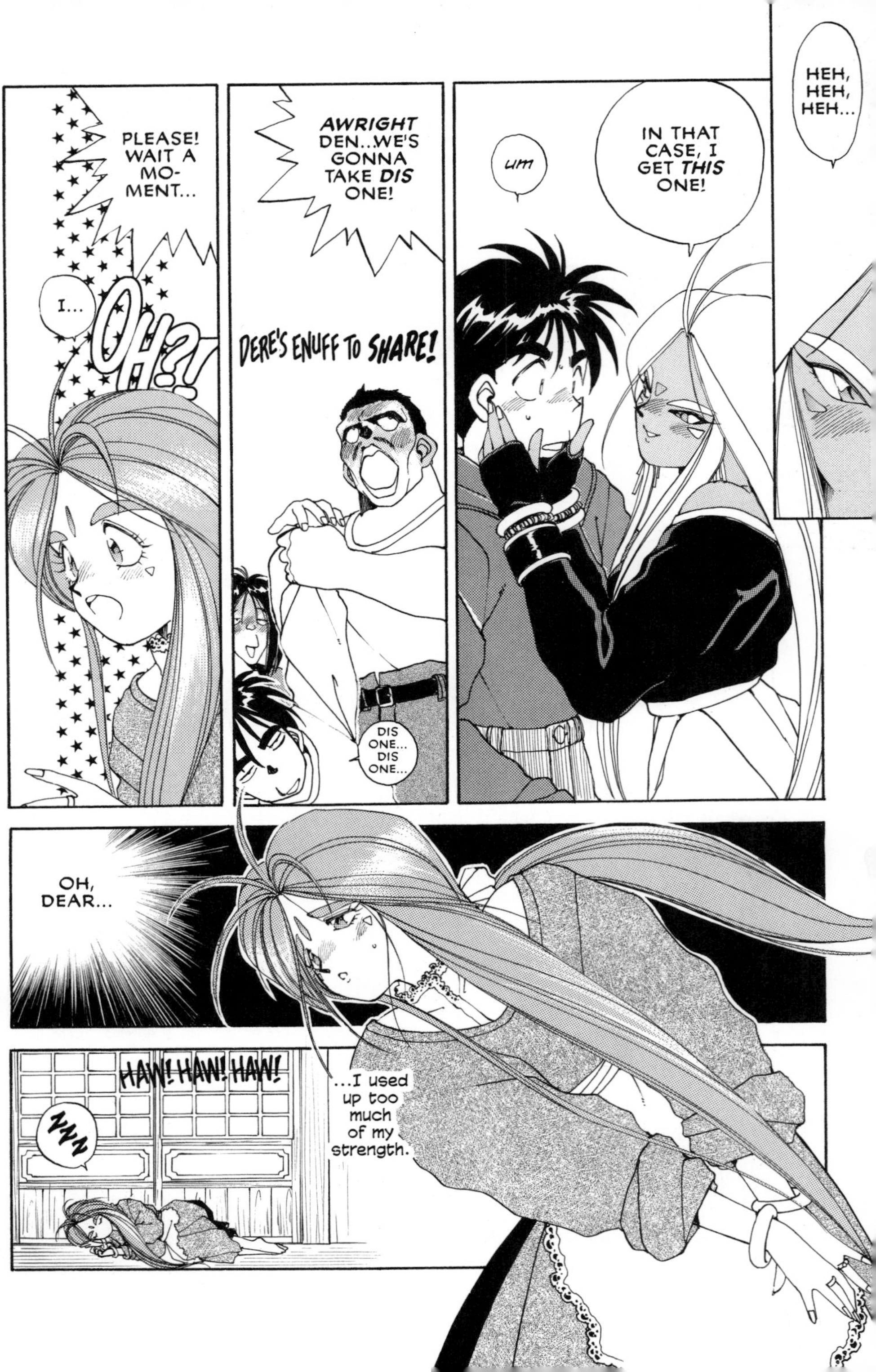
HEH, HEH, HEH...
IN THAT CASE, I GET THIS ONE!
um
AWRIGHT DEN...WE'S GONNA TAKE DIS ONE!
DERE'S ENUFF TO SHARE!
DIS ONE... DIS ONE...
PLEASE! WAIT A MO-MENT...
OH?!
I...
OH, DEAR...
...I used up too much of my strength.
HAW! HAW! HAW!
NNN

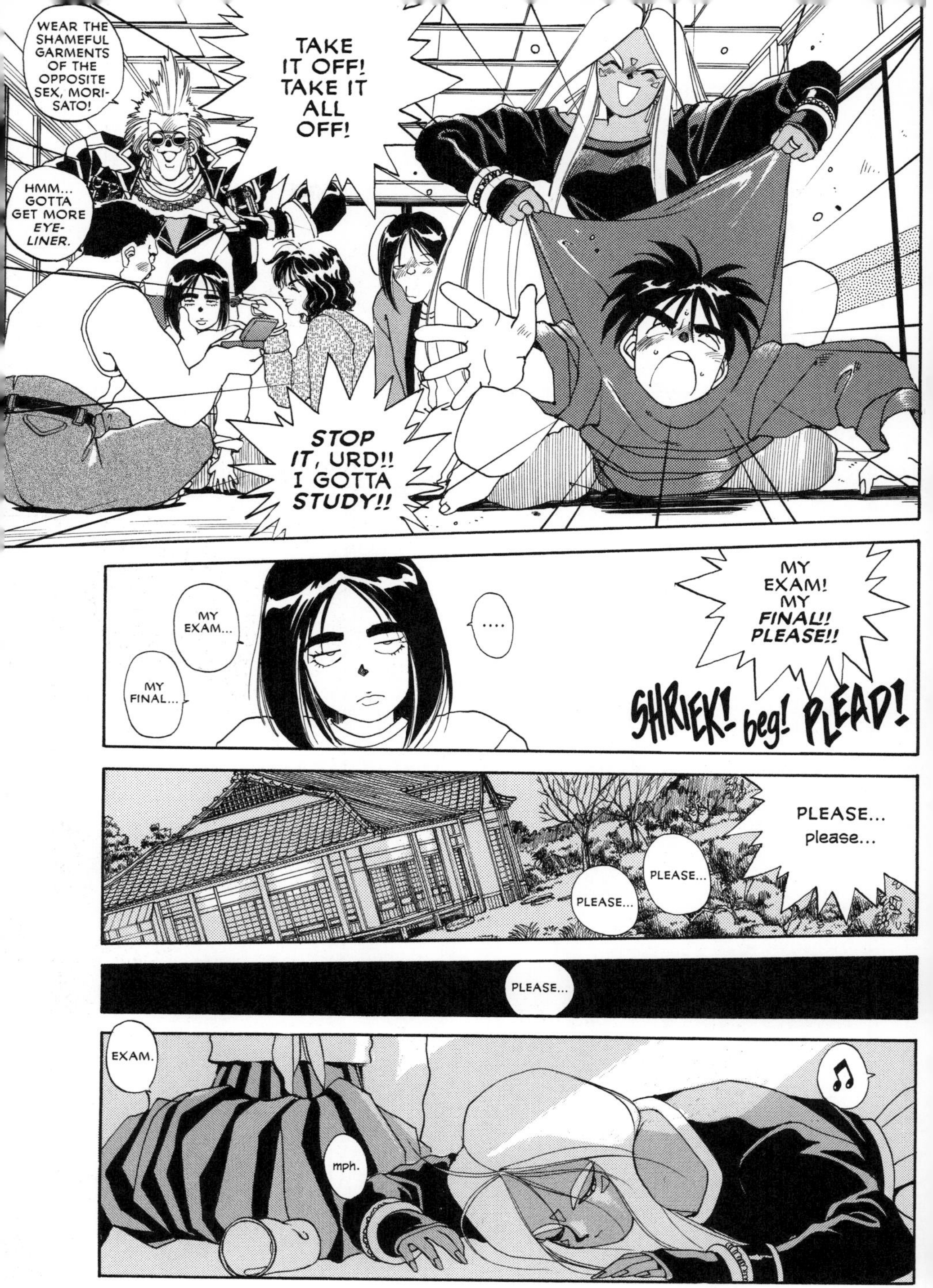
TAKE IT OFF! TAKE IT ALL OFF!
WEAR THE SHAMEFUL GARMENTS OF THE OPPOSITE SEX, MORI-SATO!
HMM... GOTTA GET MORE EYE-LINER.
STOP IT, URD!! I GOTTA STUDY!!
MY EXAM! MY FINAL!! PLEASE!!
SHRIEK! beg! PLEAD!
....
MY EXAM...
MY FINAL...
PLEASE... please...
PLEASE...
PLEASE...
PLEASE...
♪
mph.
EXAM.

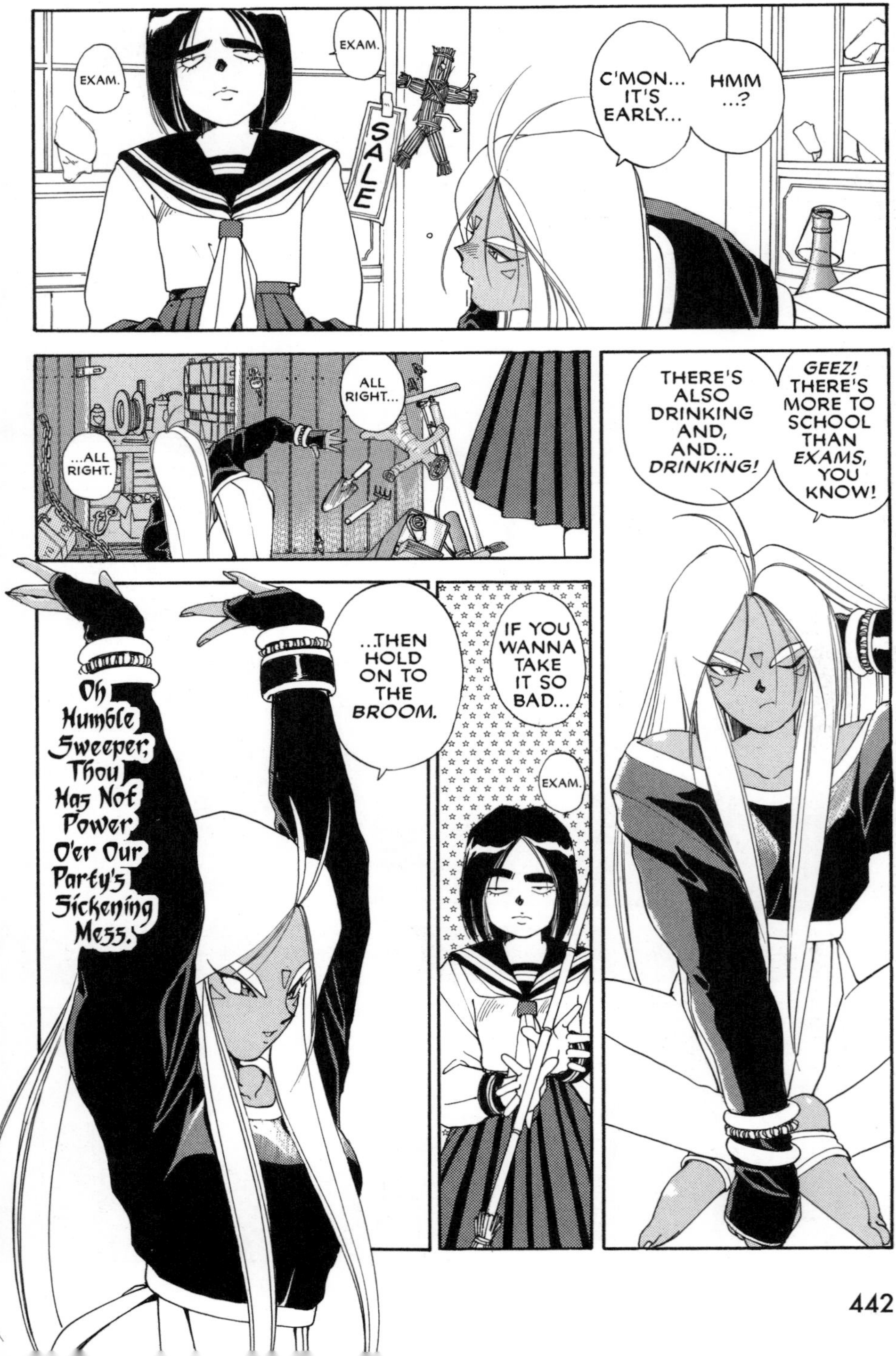
HMM ...?
C'MON... IT'S EARLY...
EXAM.
EXAM.
SALE
GEEZ! THERE'S MORE TO SCHOOL THAN *EXAMS,* YOU KNOW!
THERE'S ALSO DRINKING AND, AND... *DRINKING!*
ALL RIGHT...
...ALL RIGHT.
IF YOU WANNA TAKE IT SO BAD...
EXAM.
...THEN HOLD ON TO THE *BROOM.*
Oh Humble Sweeper; Thou Has Not Power O'er Our Party's Sickening Mess.

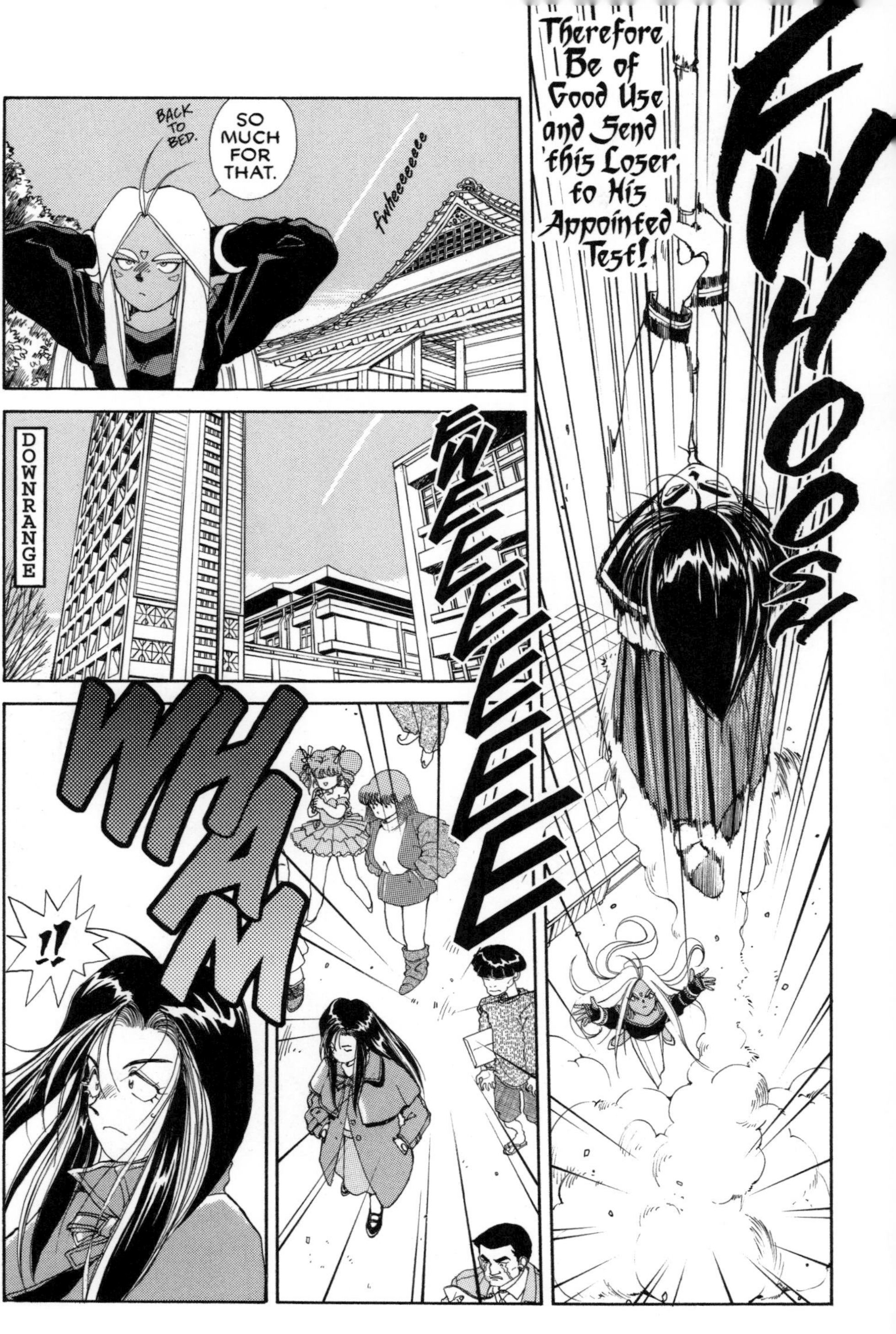
Therefore Be of Good Use and Send this Loser to His Appointed Test!
FWHOOSH
SO MUCH FOR THAT.
BACK TO BED.
fwheeeeeeee
DOWNRANGE
FWEEEEEEEE
WHAM
!!

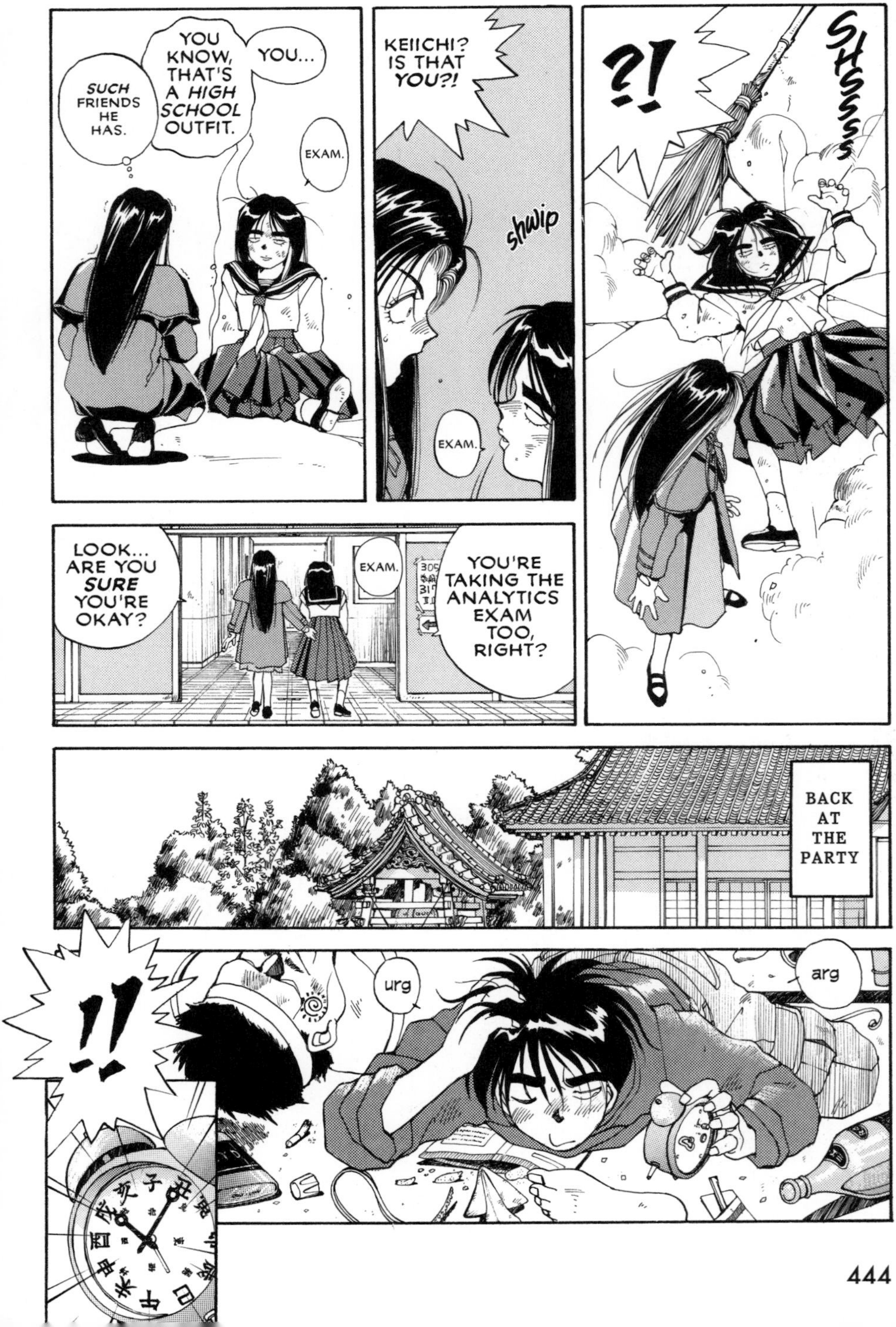
SHSSSSS
?!
KEIICHI? IS THAT YOU?!
shwip
EXAM.
YOU...
YOU KNOW, THAT'S A HIGH SCHOOL OUTFIT.
SUCH FRIENDS HE HAS.
EXAM.
YOU'RE TAKING THE ANALYTICS EXAM TOO, RIGHT?
EXAM.
LOOK... ARE YOU SURE YOU'RE OKAY?
BACK AT THE PARTY
arg
urg
!!

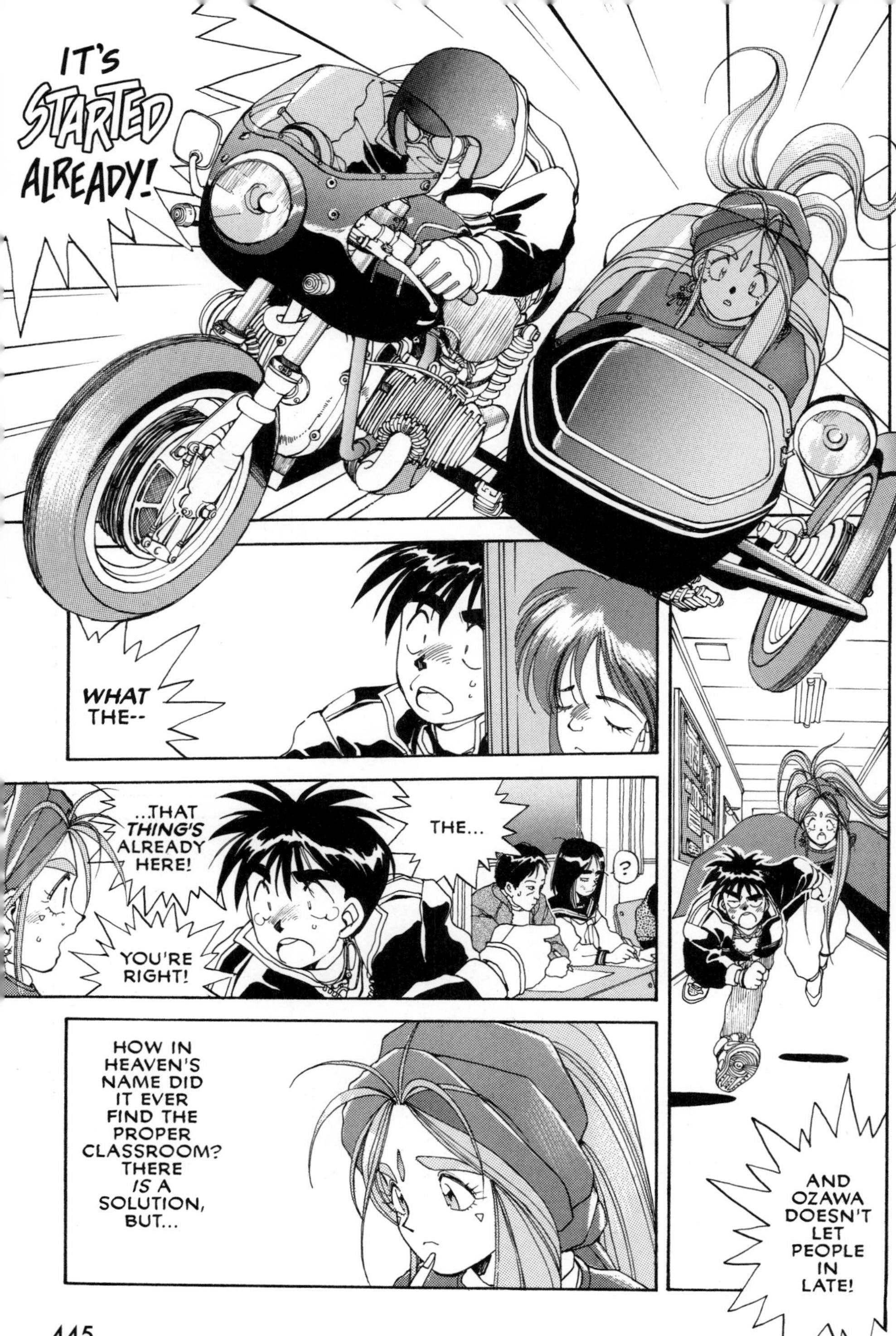
IT'S STARTED ALREADY!
AND OZAWA DOESN'T LET PEOPLE IN LATE!
WHAT THE--
THE...
?
...THAT THING'S ALREADY HERE!
YOU'RE RIGHT!
HOW IN HEAVEN'S NAME DID IT EVER FIND THE PROPER CLASSROOM? THERE IS A SOLUTION, BUT...

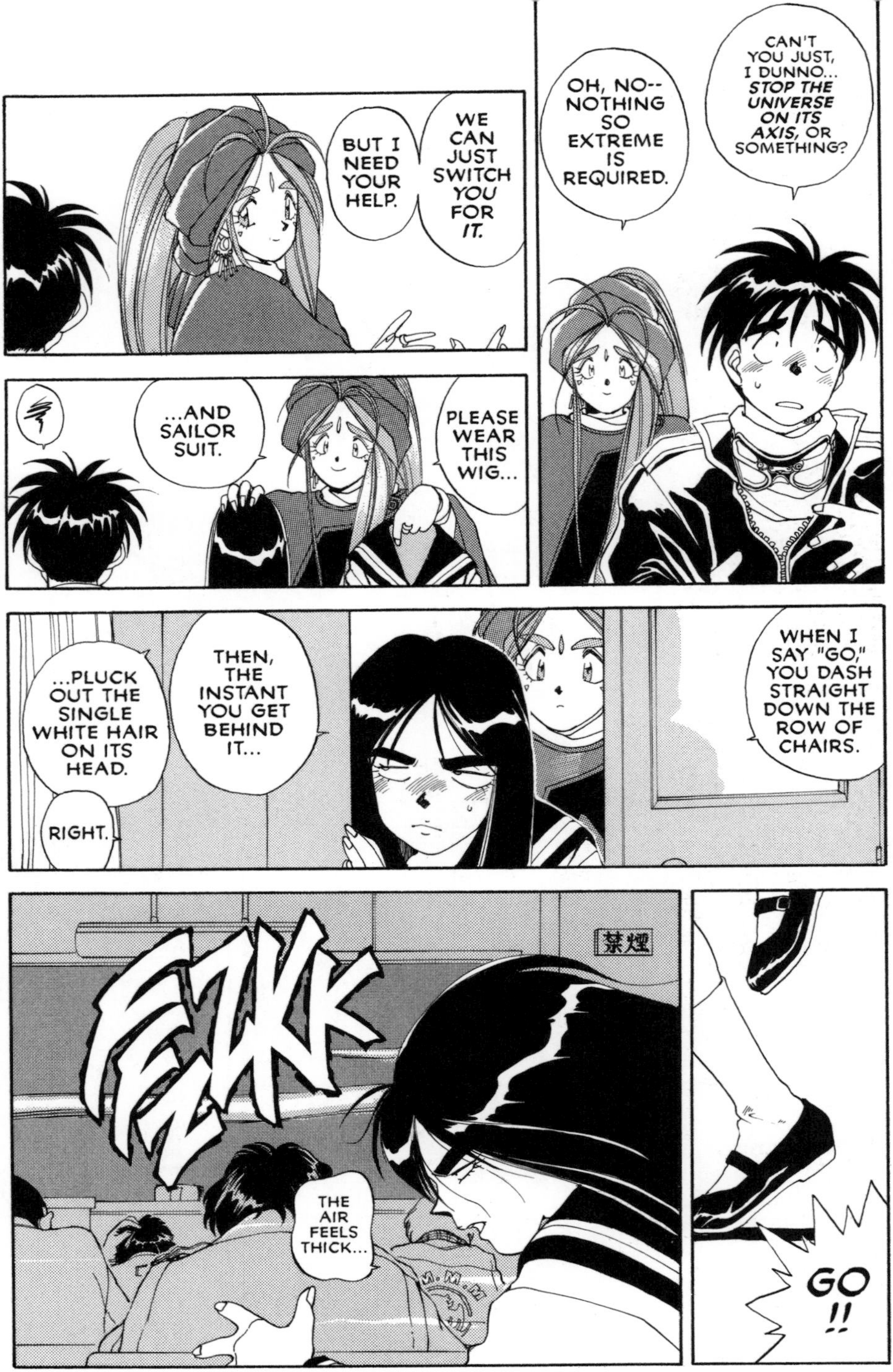
CAN'T YOU JUST, I DUNNO... *STOP THE UNIVERSE ON ITS AXIS,* OR SOMETHING?
OH, NO--NOTHING SO EXTREME IS REQUIRED.
WE CAN JUST SWITCH *YOU* FOR *IT.*
BUT I NEED YOUR HELP.
PLEASE WEAR THIS WIG...
...AND SAILOR SUIT.
WHEN I SAY "GO," YOU DASH STRAIGHT DOWN THE ROW OF CHAIRS.
THEN, THE INSTANT YOU GET BEHIND IT...
...PLUCK OUT THE SINGLE WHITE HAIR ON ITS HEAD.
RIGHT.
GO!!
禁煙
THE AIR FEELS THICK...

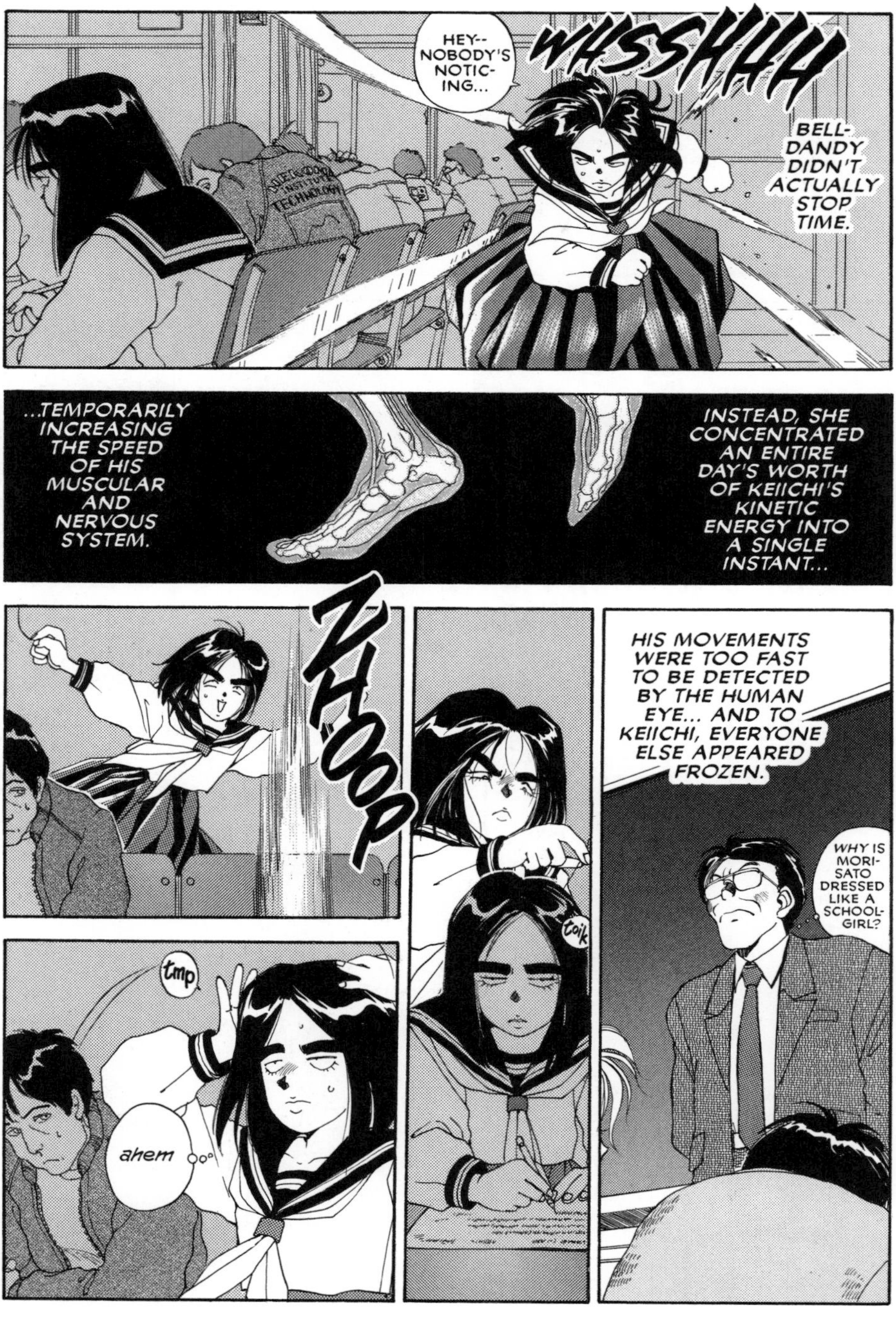
WHSSHHH
BELL-DANDY DIDN'T ACTUALLY STOP TIME.
HEY--NOBODY'S NOTICING...
INSTEAD, SHE CONCENTRATED AN ENTIRE DAY'S WORTH OF KEIICHI'S KINETIC ENERGY INTO A SINGLE INSTANT...
...TEMPORARILY INCREASING THE SPEED OF HIS MUSCULAR AND NERVOUS SYSTEM.
HIS MOVEMENTS WERE TOO FAST TO BE DETECTED BY THE HUMAN EYE... AND TO KEIICHI, EVERYONE ELSE APPEARED FROZEN.
WHY IS MORI-SATO DRESSED LIKE A SCHOOL-GIRL?
toik
ZHOOOP
tmp
ahem

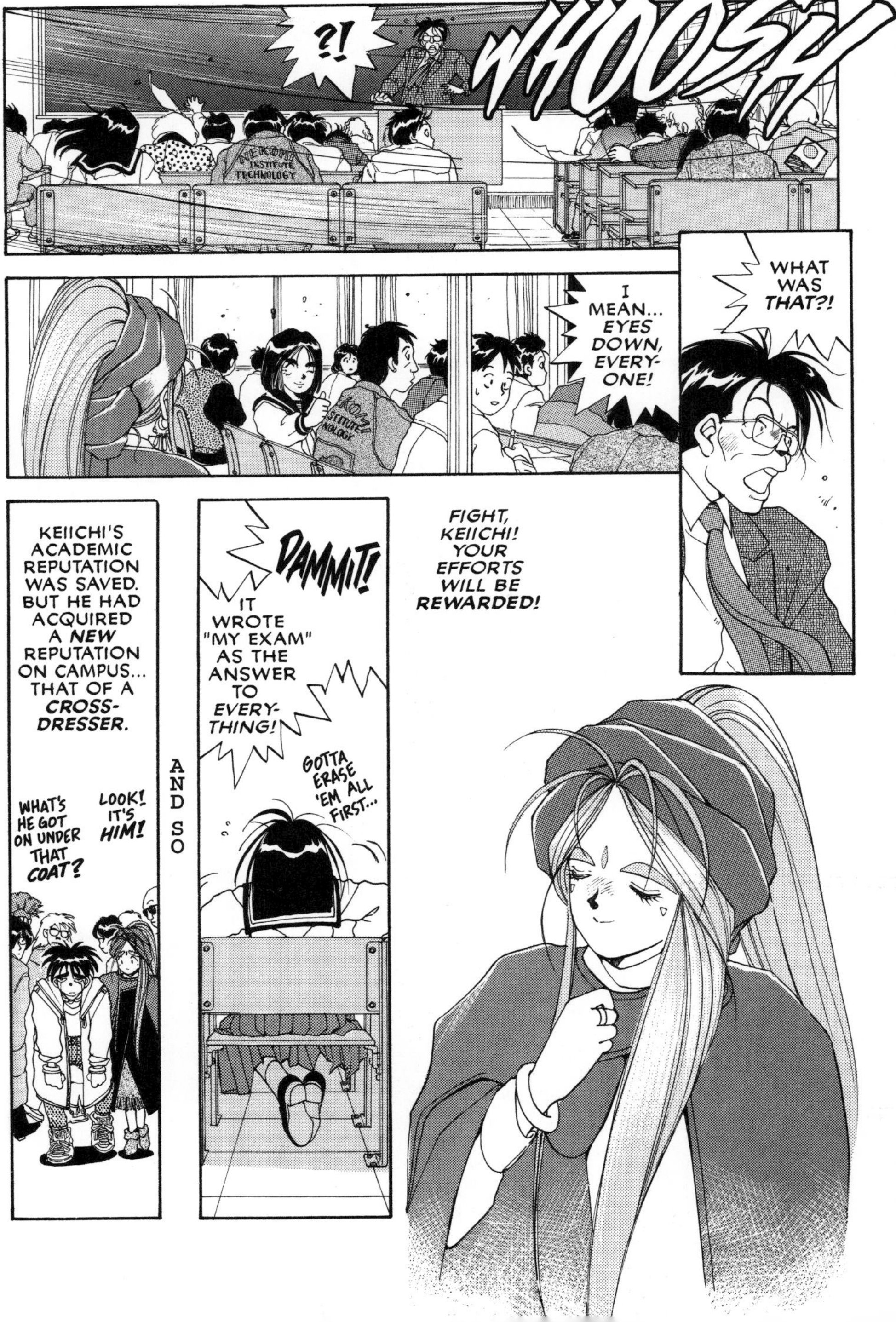
WHOOSH
?!
WHAT WAS THAT?!
I MEAN... EYES DOWN, EVERY-ONE!
FIGHT, KEIICHI! YOUR EFFORTS WILL BE REWARDED!
DAMMIT!
IT WROTE "MY EXAM" AS THE ANSWER TO EVERY-THING!
GOTTA ERASE 'EM ALL FIRST...
AND SO
KEIICHI'S ACADEMIC REPUTATION WAS SAVED. BUT HE HAD ACQUIRED A NEW REPUTATION ON CAMPUS... THAT OF A CROSS-DRESSER.
LOOK! IT'S HIM!
WHAT'S HE GOT ON UNDER THAT COAT?

CHAPTER 20

Belldandy in Danger

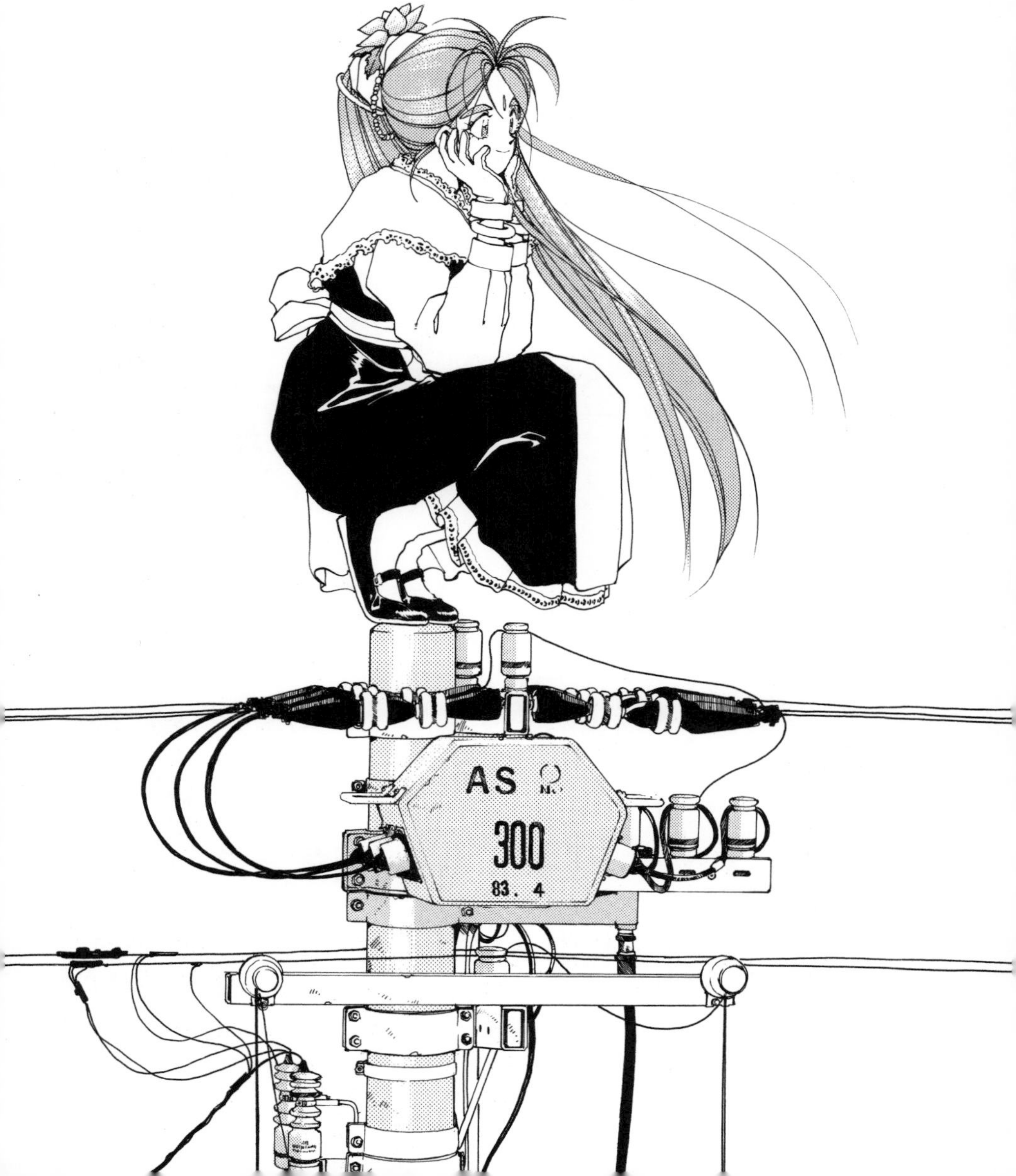
AS
300
83. 4

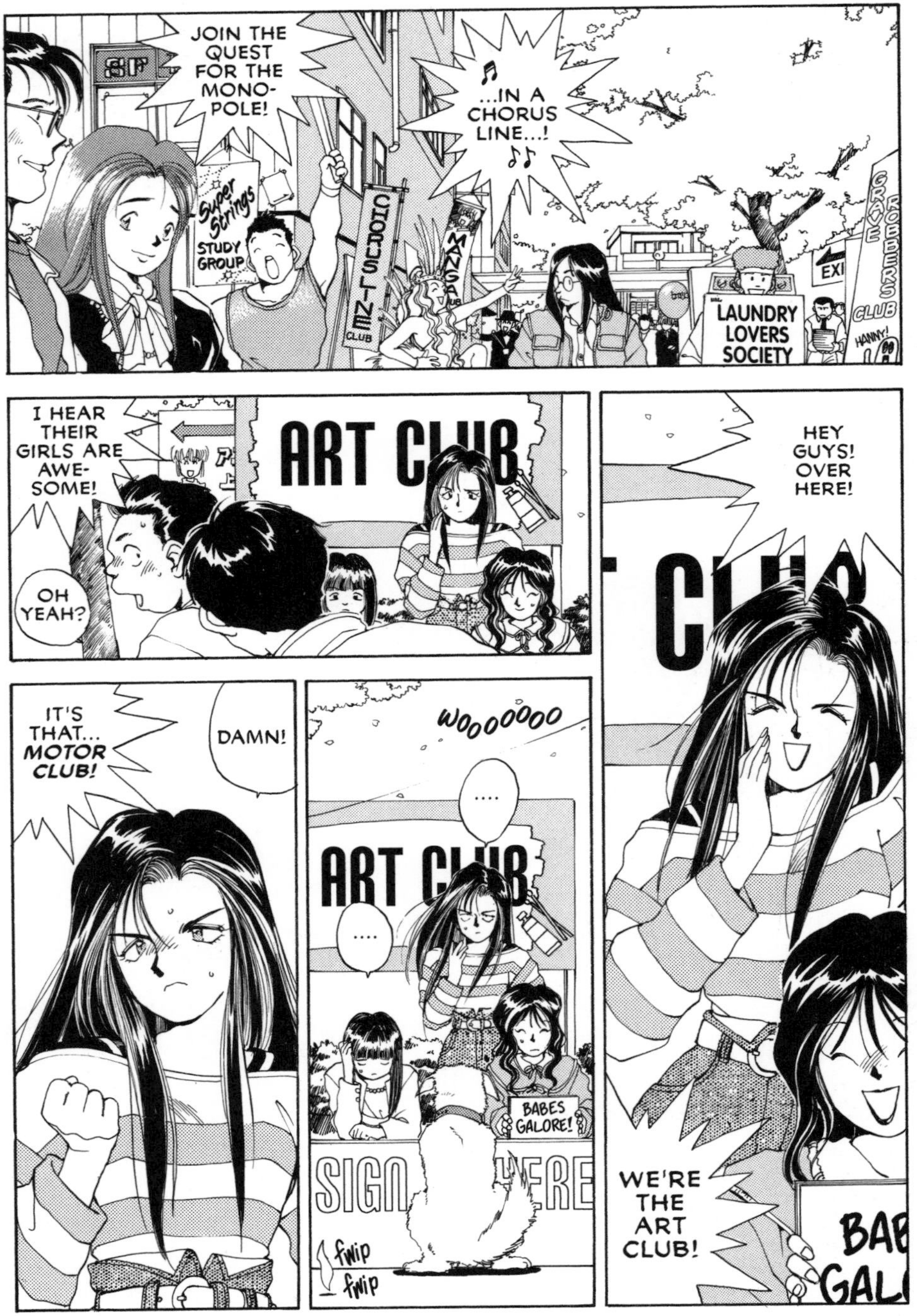
...IN A CHORUS LINE...!
JOIN THE QUEST FOR THE MONO-POLE!
GRAVE ROBBERS CLUB
LAUNDRY LOVERS SOCIETY
MANGA CLUB
CHORUS LINE CLUB
Super Strings STUDY GROUP
HEY GUYS! OVER HERE!
WE'RE THE ART CLUB!
I HEAR THEIR GIRLS ARE AWE-SOME!
ART CLUB
OH YEAH?
WOOOOOOO
....
ART CLUB
....
BABES GALORE!
fwip
fwip
DAMN!
IT'S THAT... *MOTOR CLUB!*

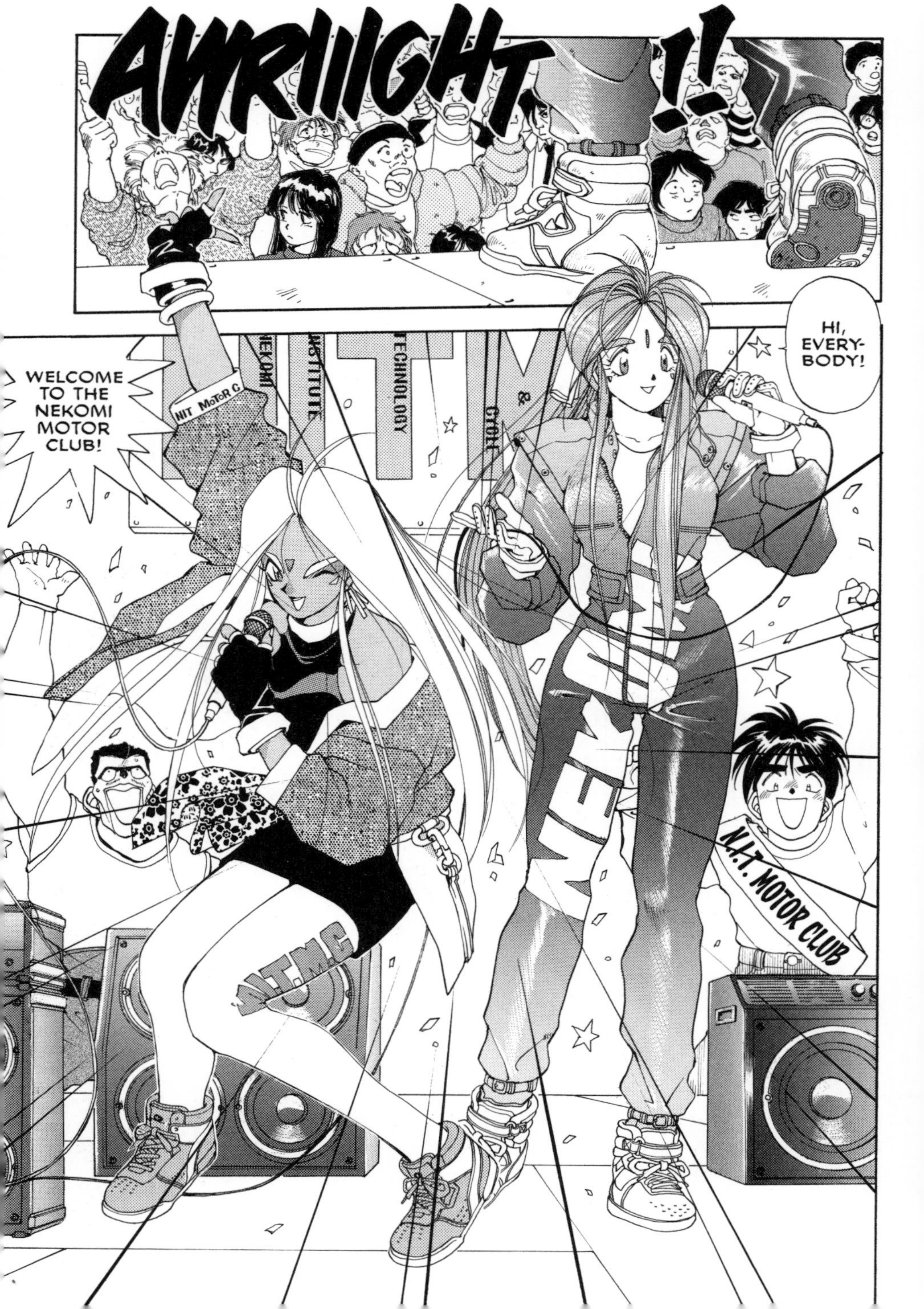
AWRIIIGHT!!
HI, EVERYBODY!
WELCOME TO THE NEKOMI MOTOR CLUB!
N.I.T. MOTOR CLUB
N.I.T.M.C

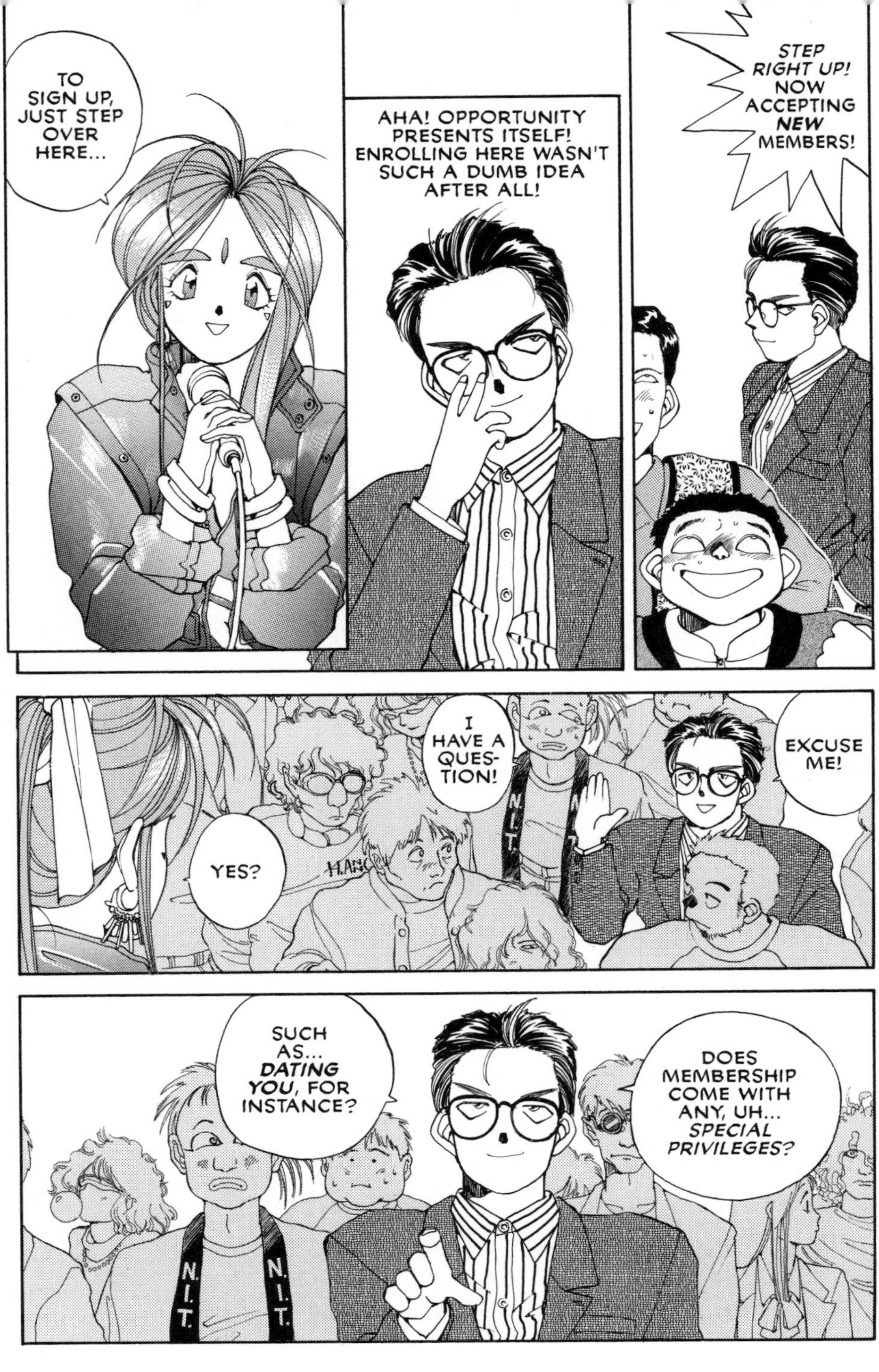
STEP RIGHT UP! NOW ACCEPTING NEW MEMBERS!
AHA! OPPORTUNITY PRESENTS ITSELF! ENROLLING HERE WASN'T SUCH A DUMB IDEA AFTER ALL!
TO SIGN UP, JUST STEP OVER HERE...
EXCUSE ME!
I HAVE A QUES-TION!
YES?
DOES MEMBERSHIP COME WITH ANY, UH... SPECIAL PRIVILEGES?
SUCH AS... DATING YOU, FOR INSTANCE?

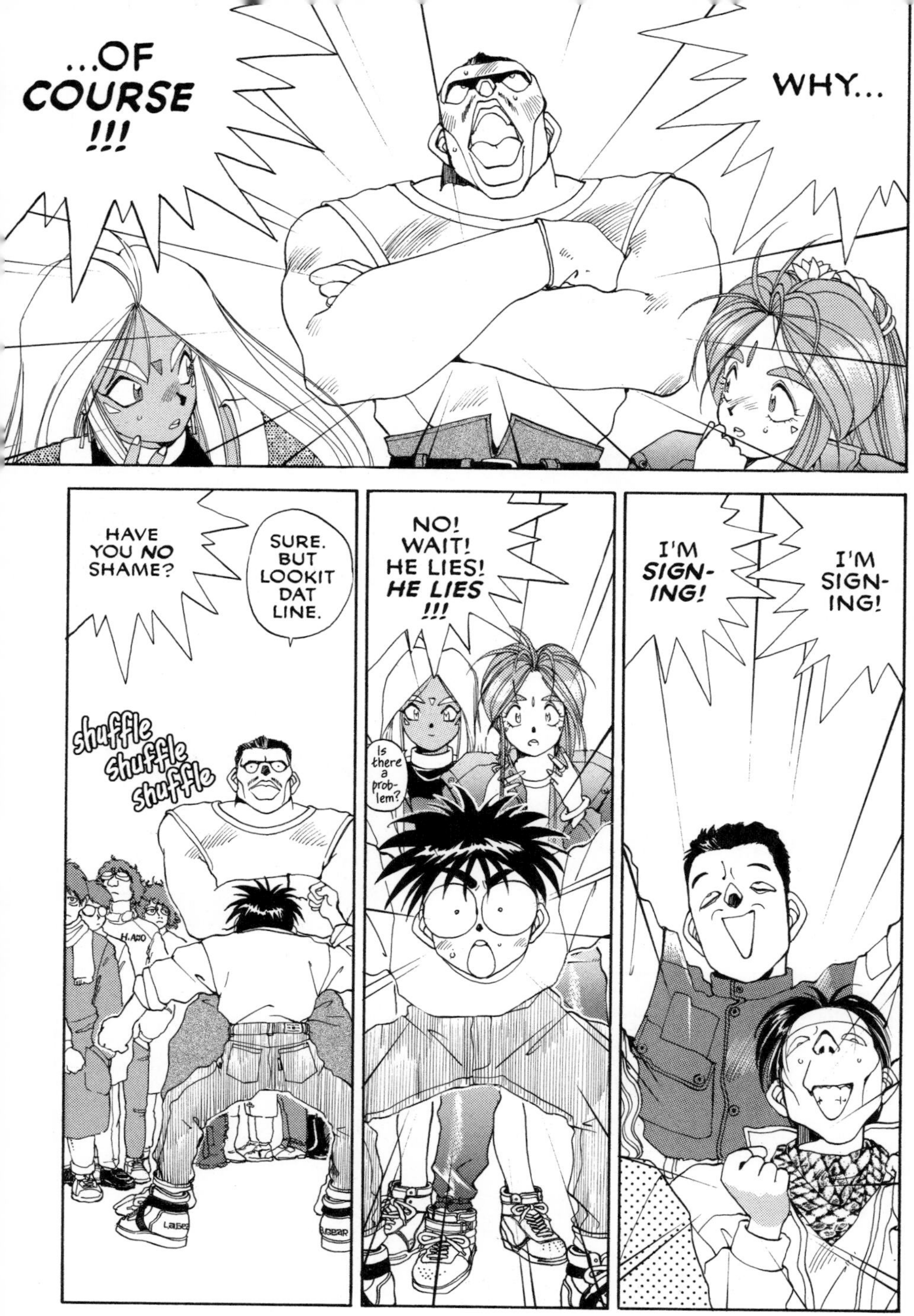
WHY...
...OF COURSE !!!
I'M SIGN-ING!
I'M *SIGN-ING!*
NO! WAIT! HE LIES! *HE LIES* !!!
Is there a prob-lem?
SURE. BUT LOOKIT DAT LINE.
HAVE YOU *NO* SHAME?
shuffle shuffle shuffle

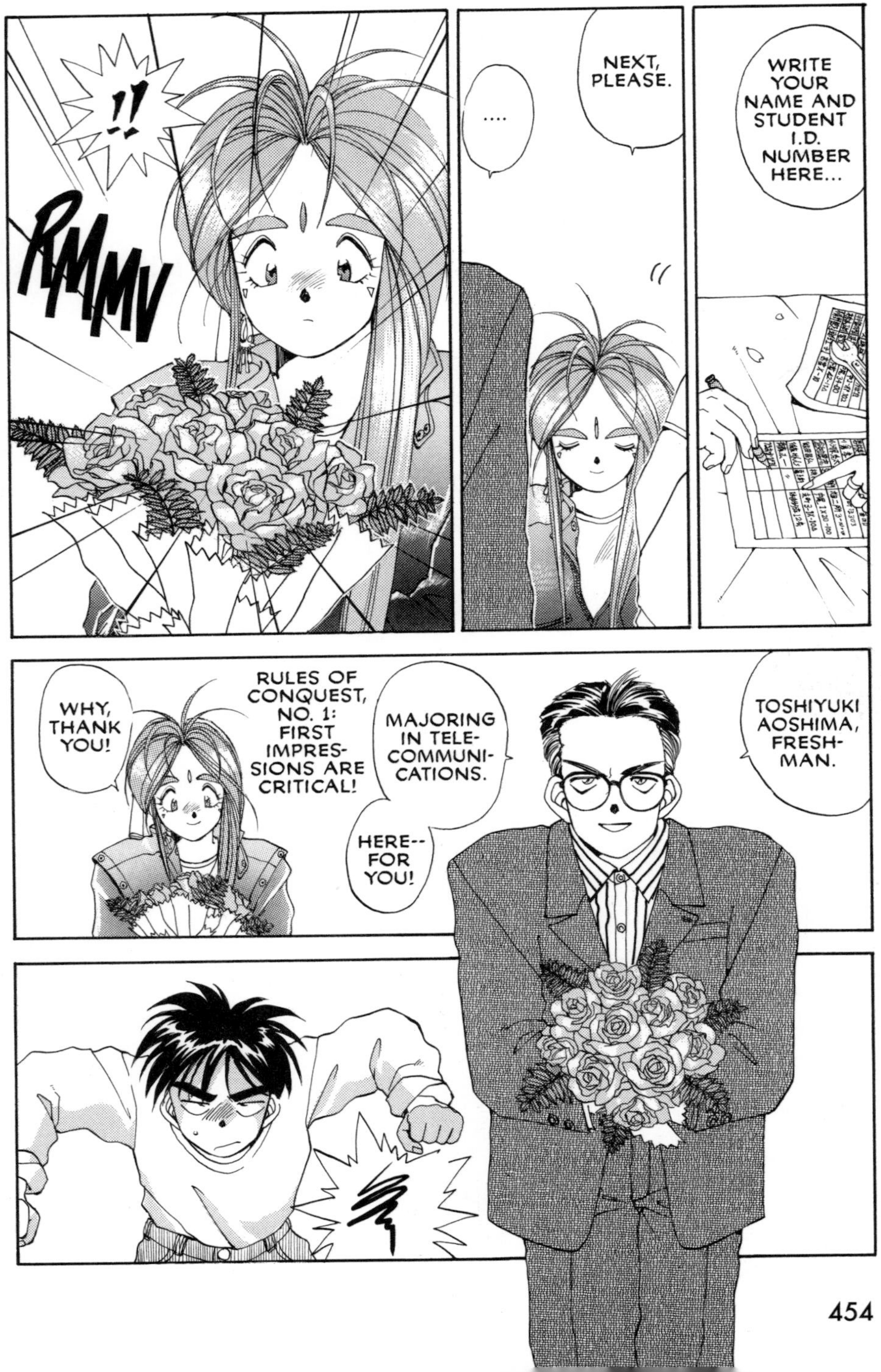
WRITE YOUR NAME AND STUDENT I.D. NUMBER HERE...
NEXT, PLEASE.
....
!!
RMMV
TOSHIYUKI AOSHIMA, FRESHMAN.
MAJORING IN TELE-COMMUNICATIONS.
HERE-- FOR YOU!
RULES OF CONQUEST, NO. 1: FIRST IMPRESSIONS ARE CRITICAL!
WHY, THANK YOU!

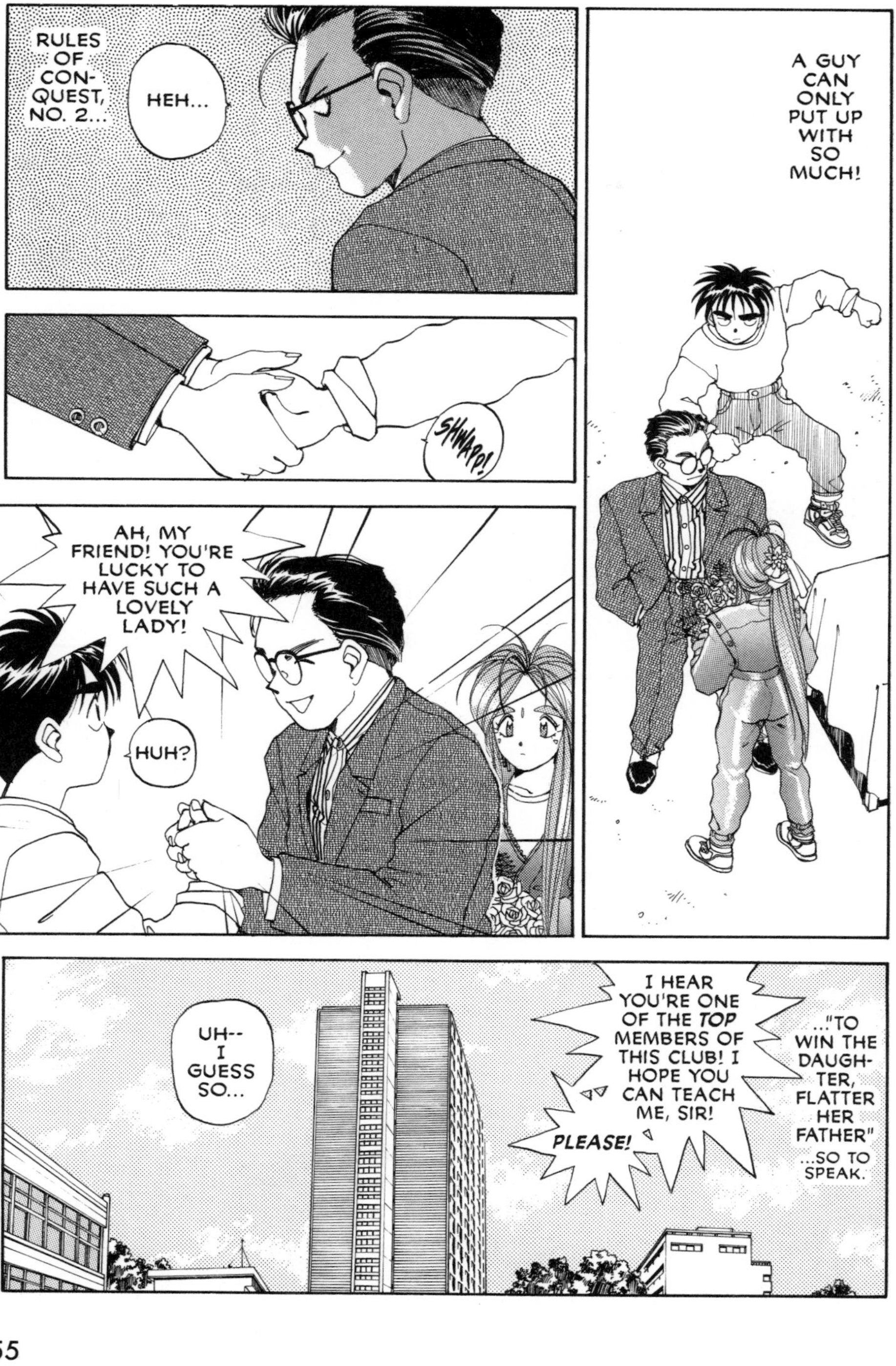
A GUY CAN ONLY PUT UP WITH SO MUCH!
HEH...
RULES OF CONQUEST, NO. 2...
SHWAPP!
AH, MY FRIEND! YOU'RE LUCKY TO HAVE SUCH A LOVELY LADY!
HUH?
UH--
..."TO WIN THE DAUGHTER, FLATTER HER FATHER" ...SO TO SPEAK.
I HEAR YOU'RE ONE OF THE *TOP* MEMBERS OF THIS CLUB! I HOPE YOU CAN TEACH ME, SIR!
PLEASE!
UH-- I GUESS SO...

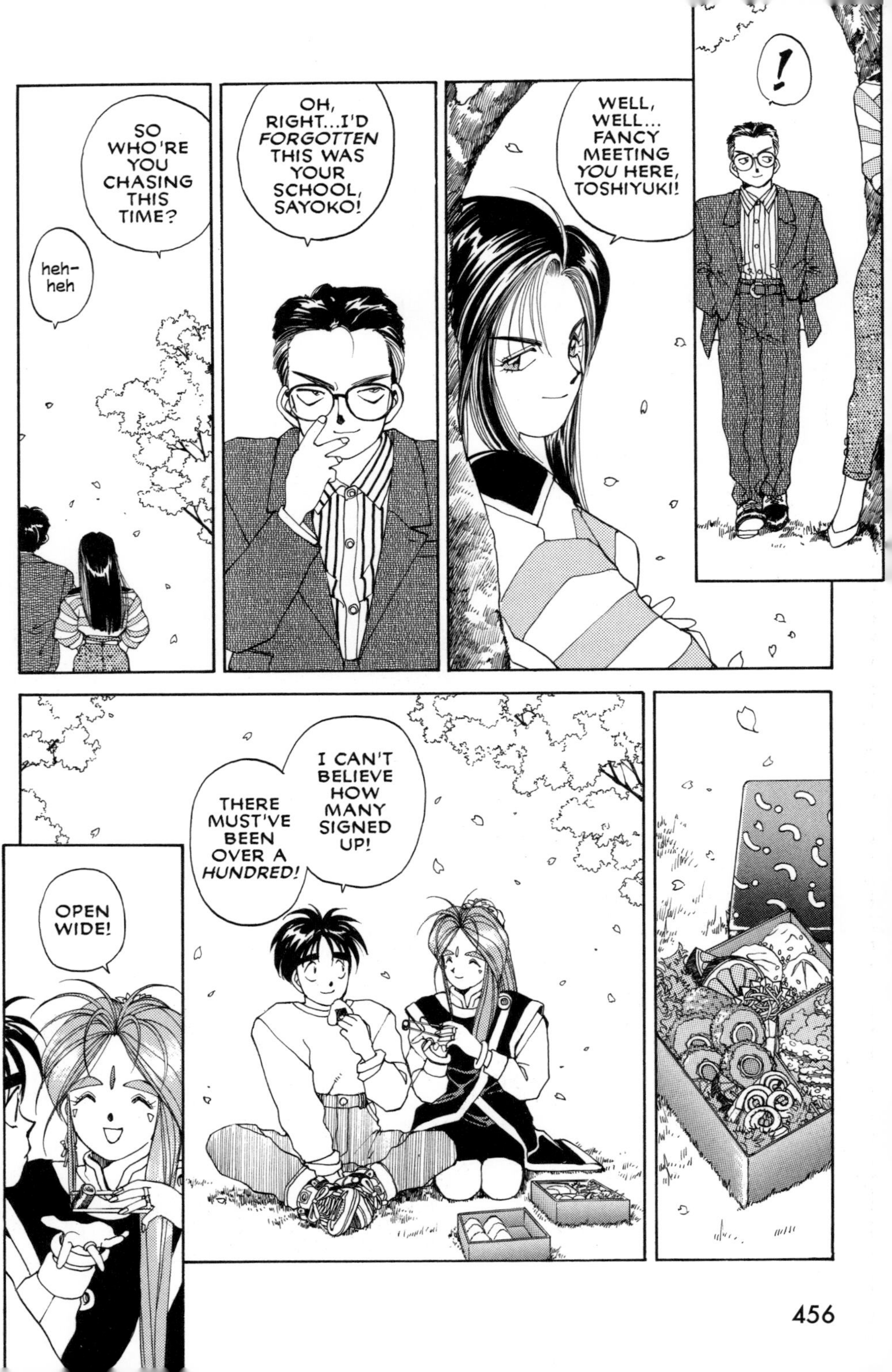
!
WELL, WELL... FANCY MEETING YOU HERE, TOSHIYUKI!
OH, RIGHT...I'D FORGOTTEN THIS WAS YOUR SCHOOL, SAYOKO!
SO WHO'RE YOU CHASING THIS TIME?
heh-heh
I CAN'T BELIEVE HOW MANY SIGNED UP!
THERE MUST'VE BEEN OVER A HUNDRED!
OPEN WIDE!

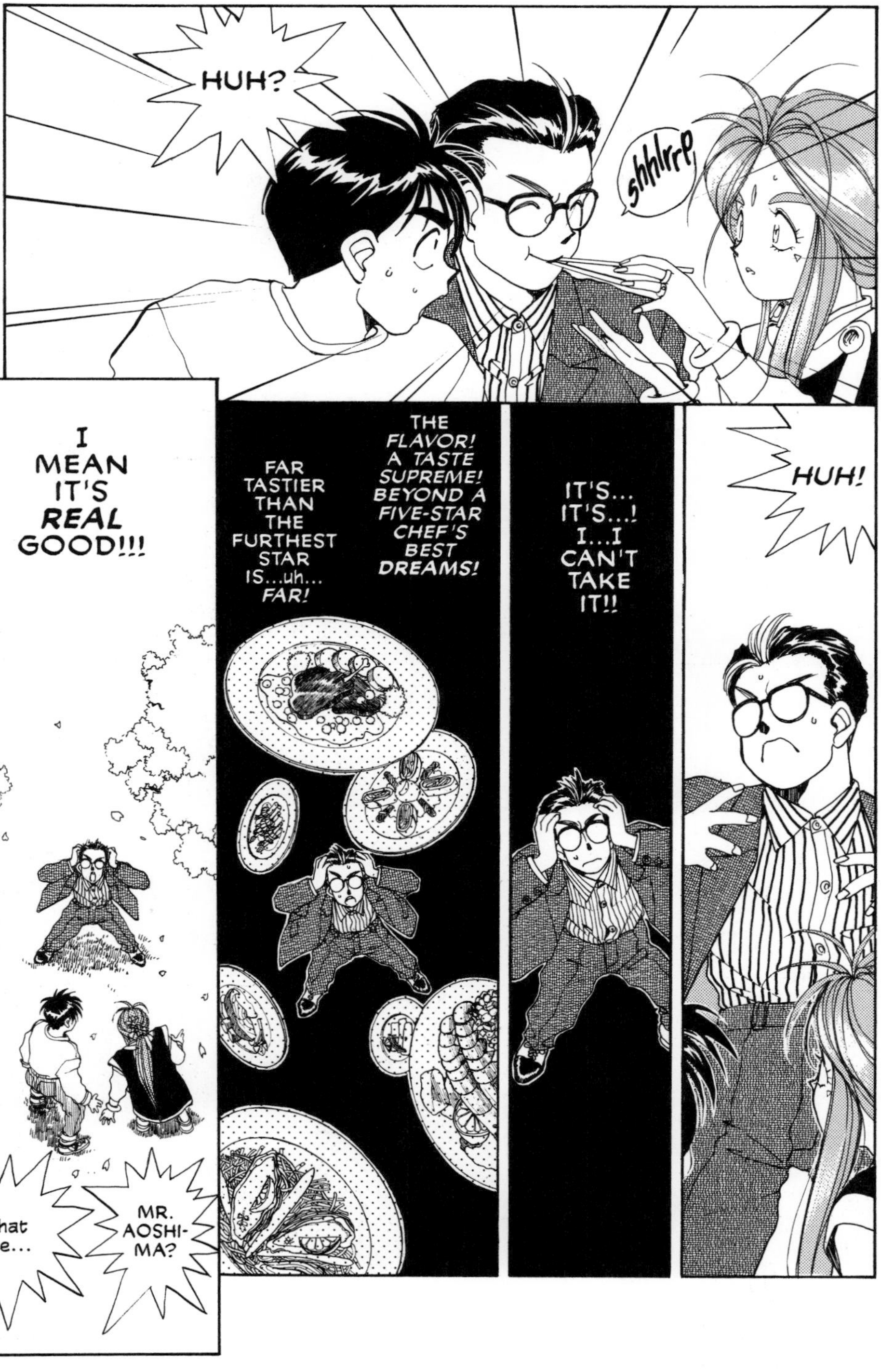
shhlrrp
HUH?
HUH!
IT'S... IT'S...! I...I CAN'T TAKE IT!!
THE FLAVOR! A TASTE SUPREME! BEYOND A FIVE-STAR CHEF'S BEST DREAMS!
FAR TASTIER THAN THE FURTHEST STAR IS...uh... FAR!
I MEAN IT'S REAL GOOD!!!
MR. AOSHIMA?
what the...

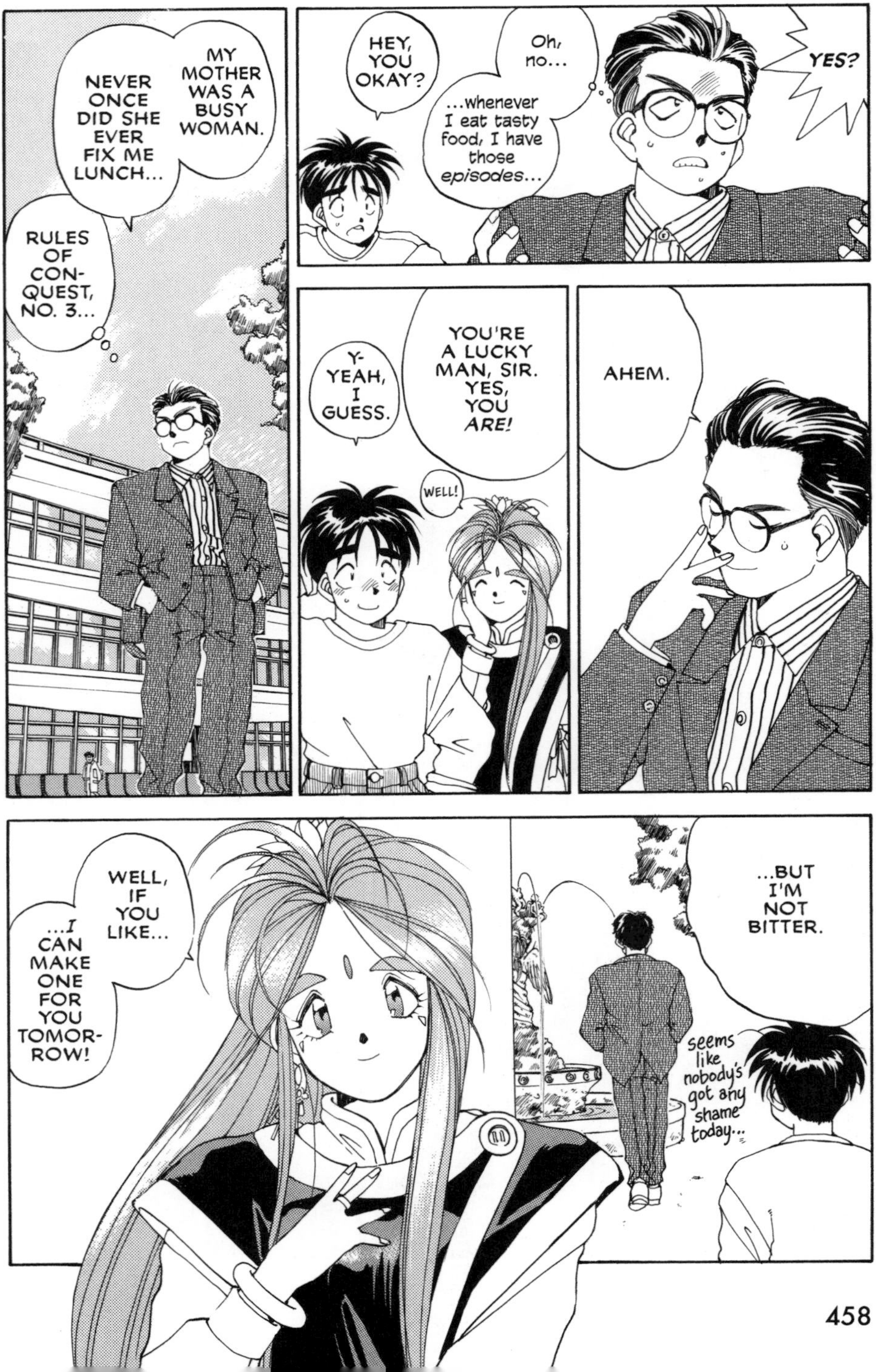
YES?
Oh, no...
...whenever I eat tasty food, I have those *episodes*...
HEY, YOU OKAY?
AHEM.
YOU'RE A LUCKY MAN, SIR. YES, YOU *ARE!*
WELL!
Y-YEAH, I GUESS.
MY MOTHER WAS A BUSY WOMAN.
NEVER ONCE DID SHE EVER FIX ME LUNCH...
RULES OF CONQUEST, NO. 3...
...BUT I'M NOT BITTER.
seems like nobody's got any shame today...
WELL, IF YOU LIKE...
...*I* CAN MAKE ONE FOR YOU TOMORROW!

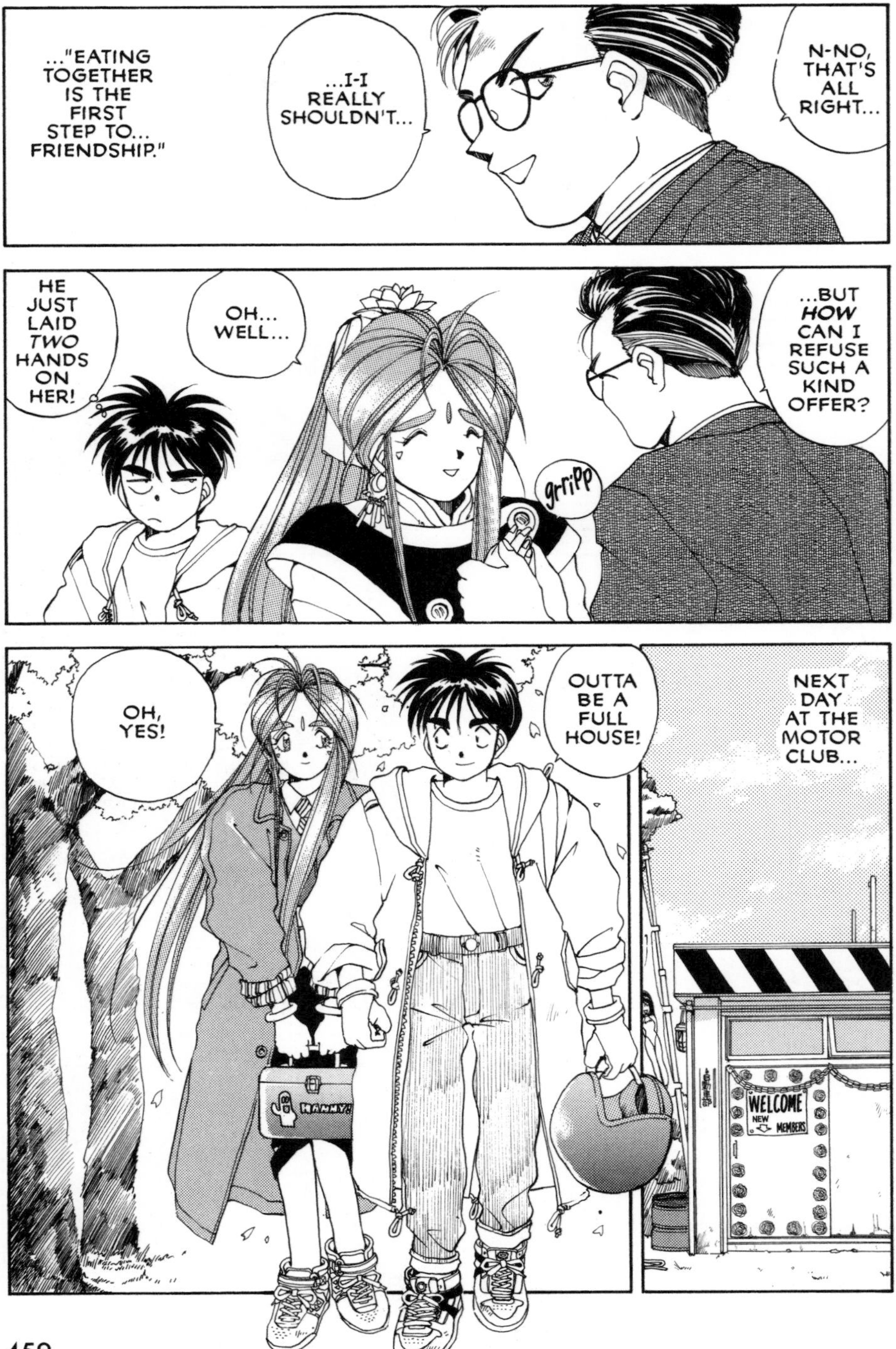
N-NO, THAT'S ALL RIGHT...
...I-I REALLY SHOULDN'T...
..."EATING TOGETHER IS THE FIRST STEP TO... FRIENDSHIP."
...BUT *HOW* CAN I REFUSE SUCH A KIND OFFER?
grripp
OH... WELL...
HE JUST LAID *TWO* HANDS ON HER!
NEXT DAY AT THE MOTOR CLUB...
WELCOME NEW MEMBERS
OUTTA BE A FULL HOUSE!
OH, YES!
HANNY!

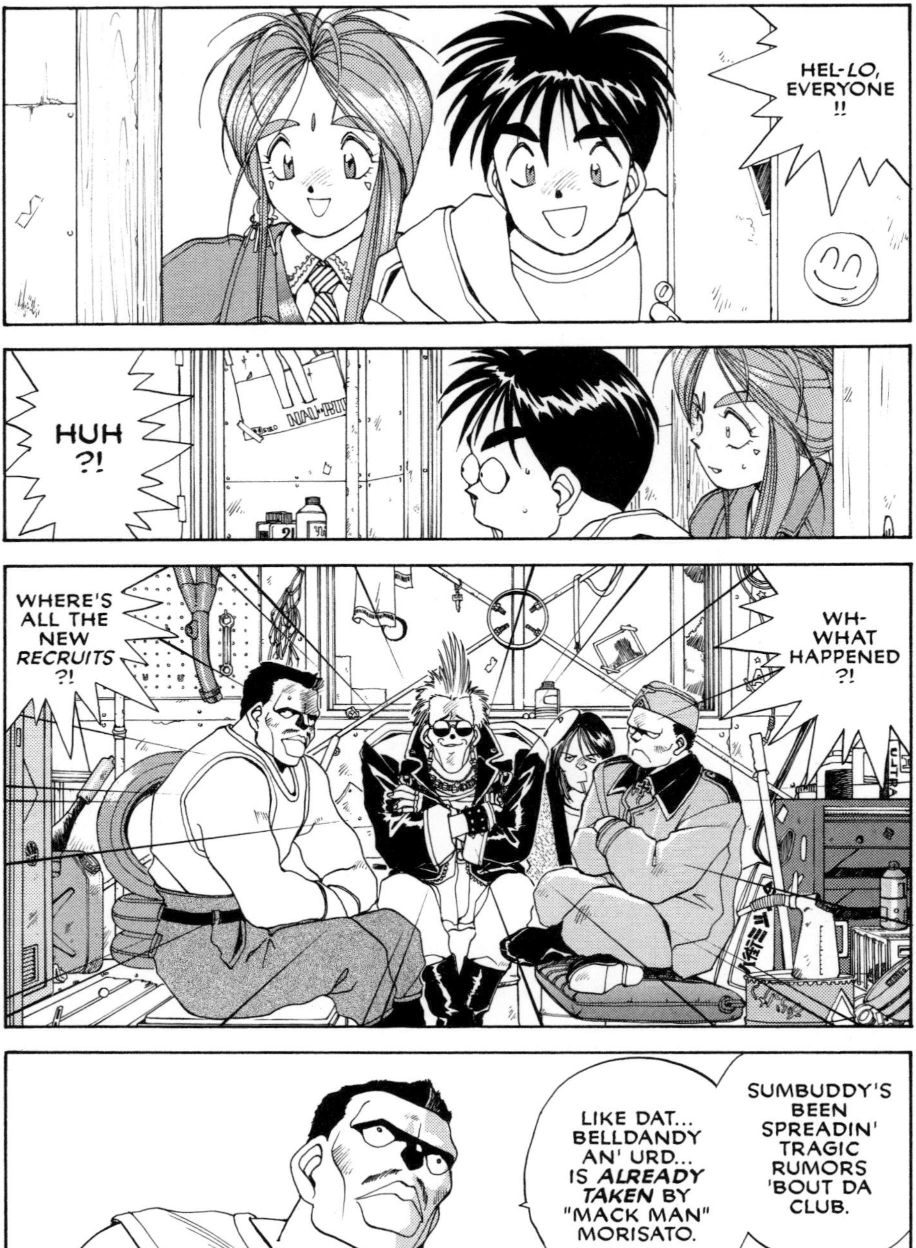
HEL-LO, EVERYONE !!
HUH ?!
WH- WHAT HAPPENED ?!
WHERE'S ALL THE NEW RECRUITS ?!
SUMBUDDY'S BEEN SPREADIN' TRAGIC RUMORS 'BOUT DA CLUB.
LIKE DAT... BELLDANDY AN' URD... IS ALREADY TAKEN BY "MACK MAN" MORISATO.

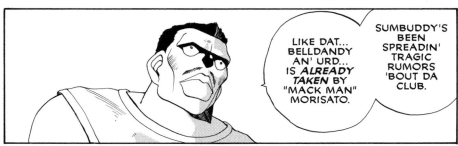

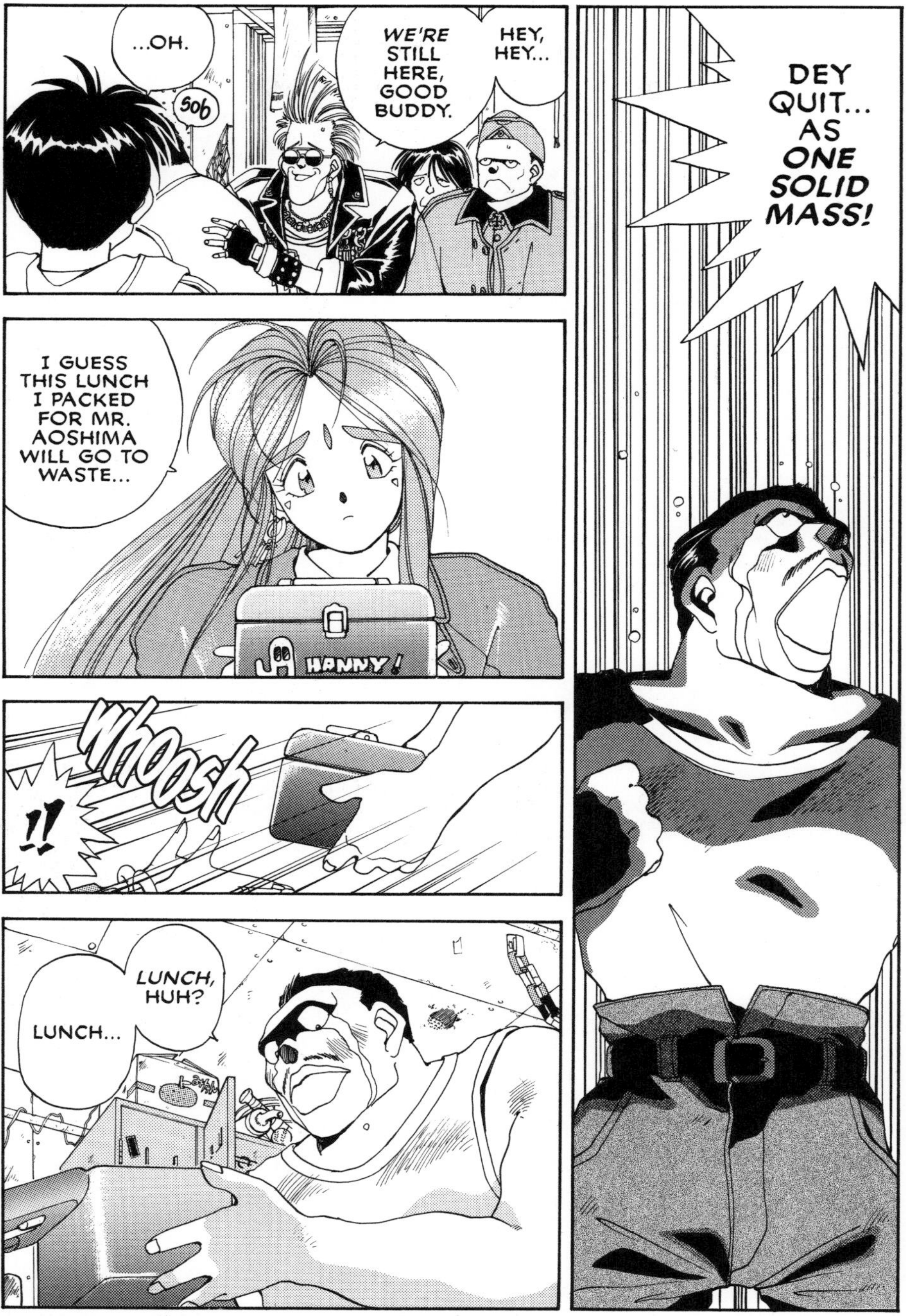

DEY QUIT... AS *ONE SOLID MASS!*
HEY, HEY...
WE'RE STILL HERE, GOOD BUDDY.
...OH.
sob
I GUESS THIS LUNCH I PACKED FOR MR. AOSHIMA WILL GO TO WASTE...
HANNY!
whoosh
!!
LUNCH, HUH?
LUNCH...

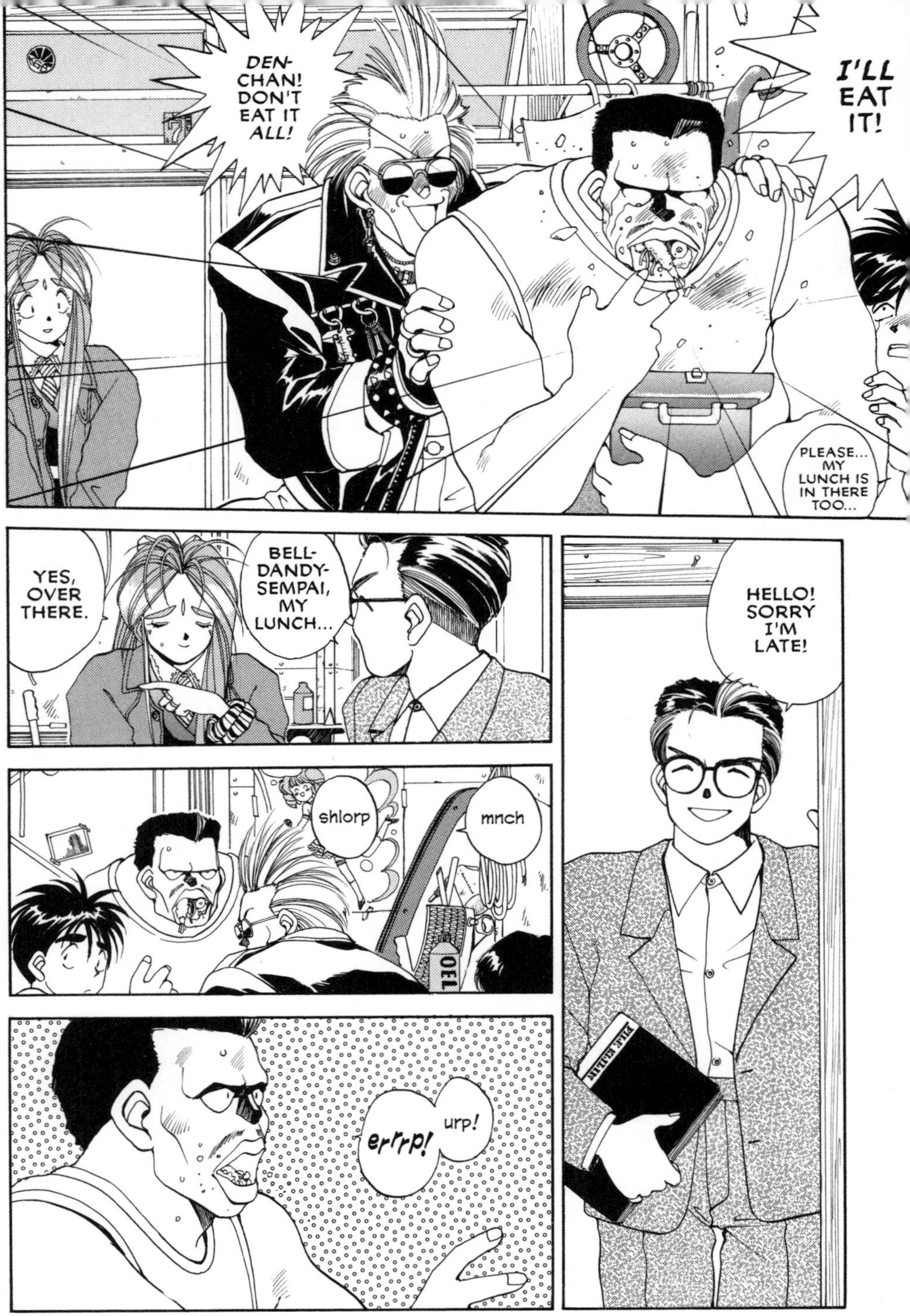
I'LL EAT IT!
DEN-CHAN! DON'T EAT IT ALL!
PLEASE... MY LUNCH IS IN THERE TOO...
HELLO! SORRY I'M LATE!
BELL-DANDY-SEMPAI, MY LUNCH...
YES, OVER THERE.
mnch
shlorp
urp!
errrp!

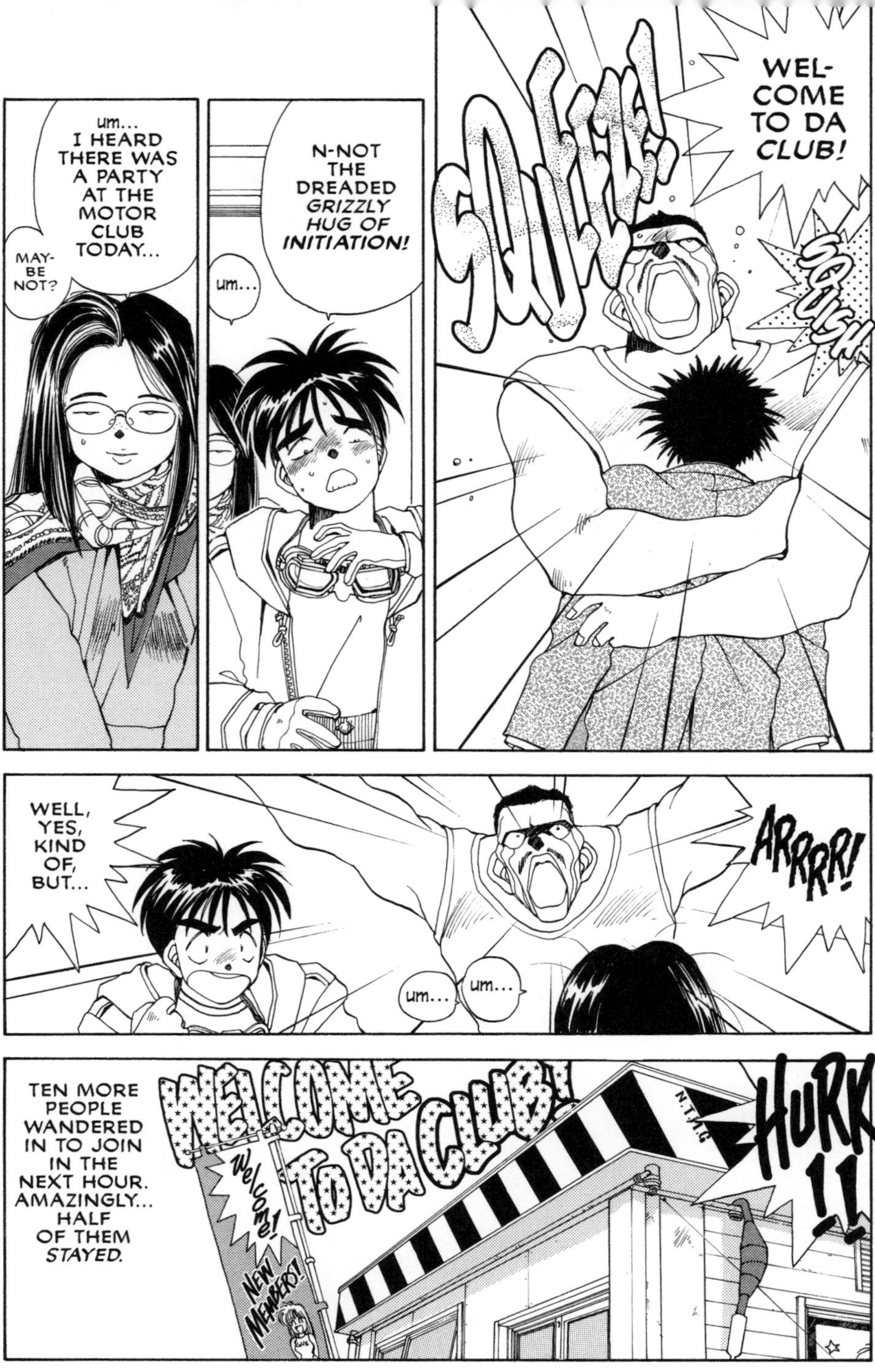
WEL-
COME
TO DA
CLUB!
SQUEEZE!
SQUISH
N-NOT THE DREADED GRIZZLY HUG OF INITIATION!
um...
um... I HEARD THERE WAS A PARTY AT THE MOTOR CLUB TODAY...
MAY-BE NOT?
ARRRR!
um...
um...
WELL, YES, KIND OF, BUT...
HURK!!
WELCOME TO DA CLUB!
Welcome!
NEW MEMBERS!
TEN MORE PEOPLE WANDERED IN TO JOIN IN THE NEXT HOUR. AMAZINGLY... HALF OF THEM STAYED.

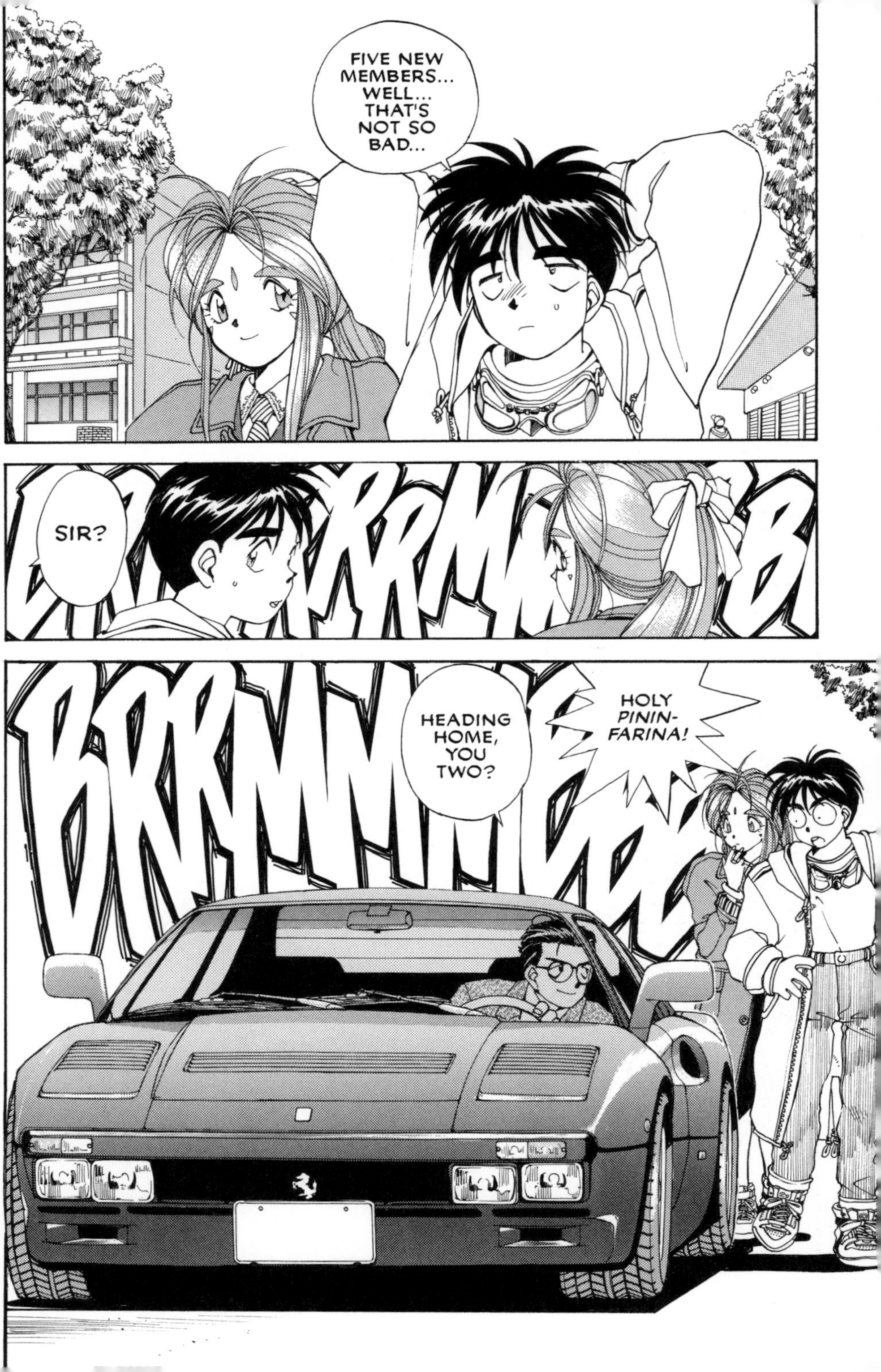
FIVE NEW MEMBERS... WELL... THAT'S NOT SO BAD...
SIR?
HOLY PININ-FARINA!
HEADING HOME, YOU TWO?

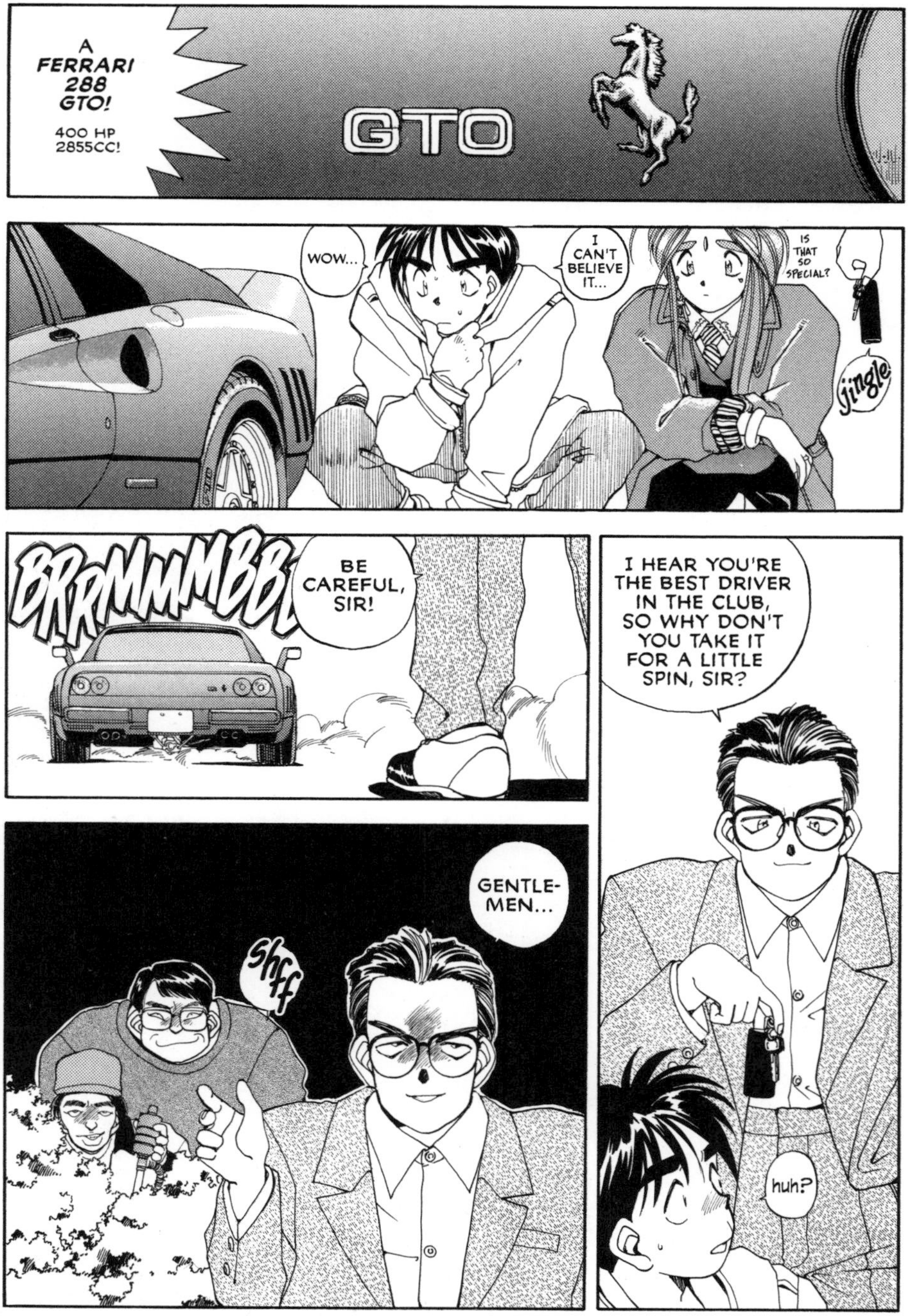
A FERRARI 288 GTO!
400 HP 2855CC!
GTO
IS THAT SO SPECIAL?
jingle
I CAN'T BELIEVE IT...
WOW...
I HEAR YOU'RE THE BEST DRIVER IN THE CLUB, SO WHY DON'T YOU TAKE IT FOR A LITTLE SPIN, SIR?
huh?
BE CAREFUL, SIR!
BRRMMMBB
GENTLE-MEN...
shff

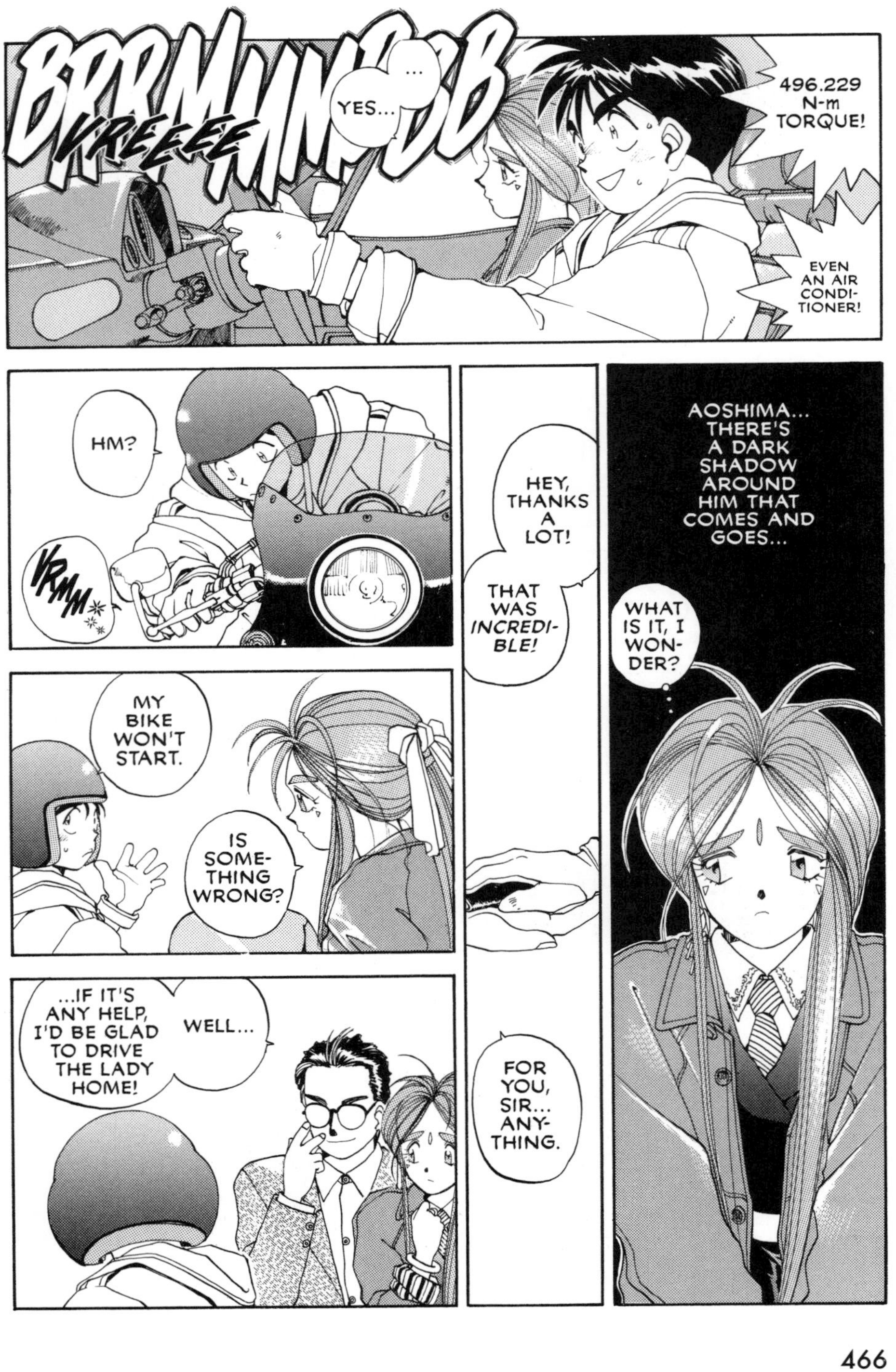

496.229 N-m TORQUE!
EVEN AN AIR CONDITIONER!
...
YES...
VREEEEE
AOSHIMA... THERE'S A DARK SHADOW AROUND HIM THAT COMES AND GOES...
WHAT IS IT, I WONDER?
HEY, THANKS A LOT!
THAT WAS *INCREDIBLE!*
FOR YOU, SIR... ANYTHING.
HM?
VRMM
MY BIKE WON'T START.
IS SOMETHING WRONG?
WELL...
...IF IT'S ANY HELP, I'D BE GLAD TO DRIVE THE LADY HOME!

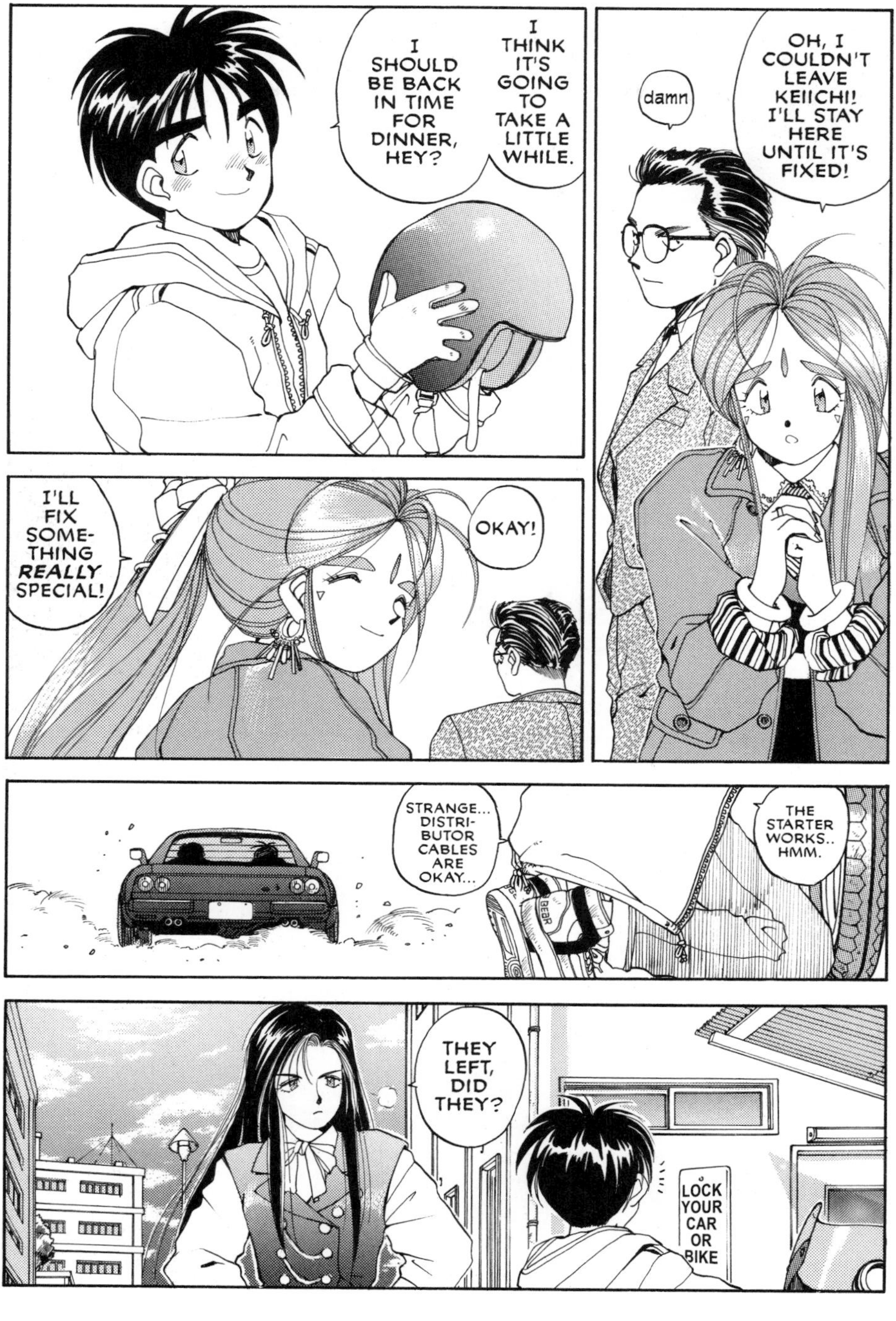
OH, I COULDN'T LEAVE KEIICHI! I'LL STAY HERE UNTIL IT'S FIXED!
damn
I THINK IT'S GOING TO TAKE A LITTLE WHILE.
I SHOULD BE BACK IN TIME FOR DINNER, HEY?
OKAY!
I'LL FIX SOME-THING REALLY SPECIAL!
THE STARTER WORKS.. HMM.
STRANGE... DISTRI-BUTOR CABLES ARE OKAY...
THEY LEFT, DID THEY?
LOCK YOUR CAR OR BIKE

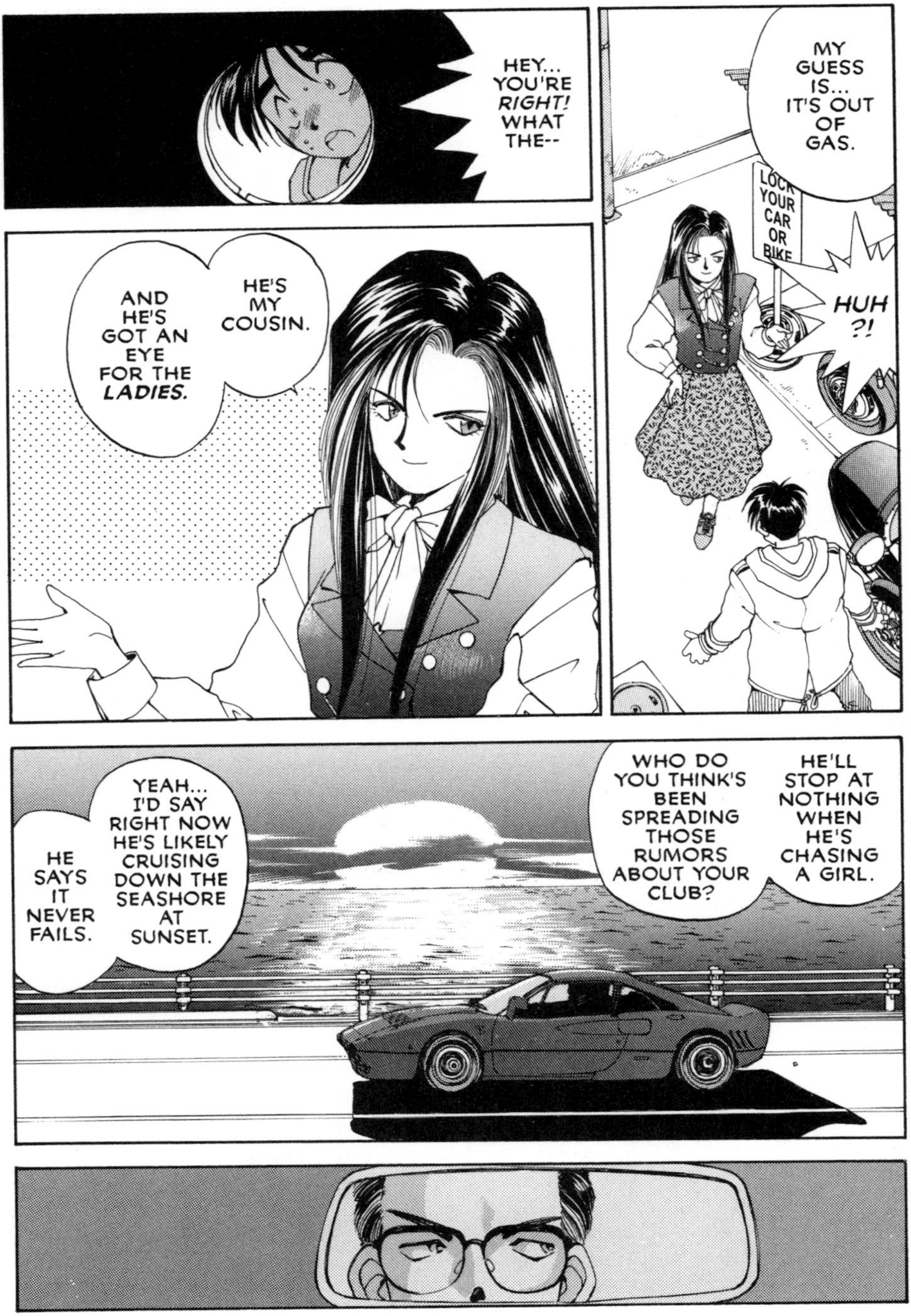
MY GUESS IS... IT'S OUT OF GAS.
LOCK YOUR CAR OR BIKE
HUH ?!
HEY... YOU'RE RIGHT! WHAT THE--
HE'S MY COUSIN.
AND HE'S GOT AN EYE FOR THE LADIES.
HE'LL STOP AT NOTHING WHEN HE'S CHASING A GIRL.
WHO DO YOU THINK'S BEEN SPREADING THOSE RUMORS ABOUT YOUR CLUB?
YEAH... I'D SAY RIGHT NOW HE'S LIKELY CRUISING DOWN THE SEASHORE AT SUNSET.
HE SAYS IT NEVER FAILS.

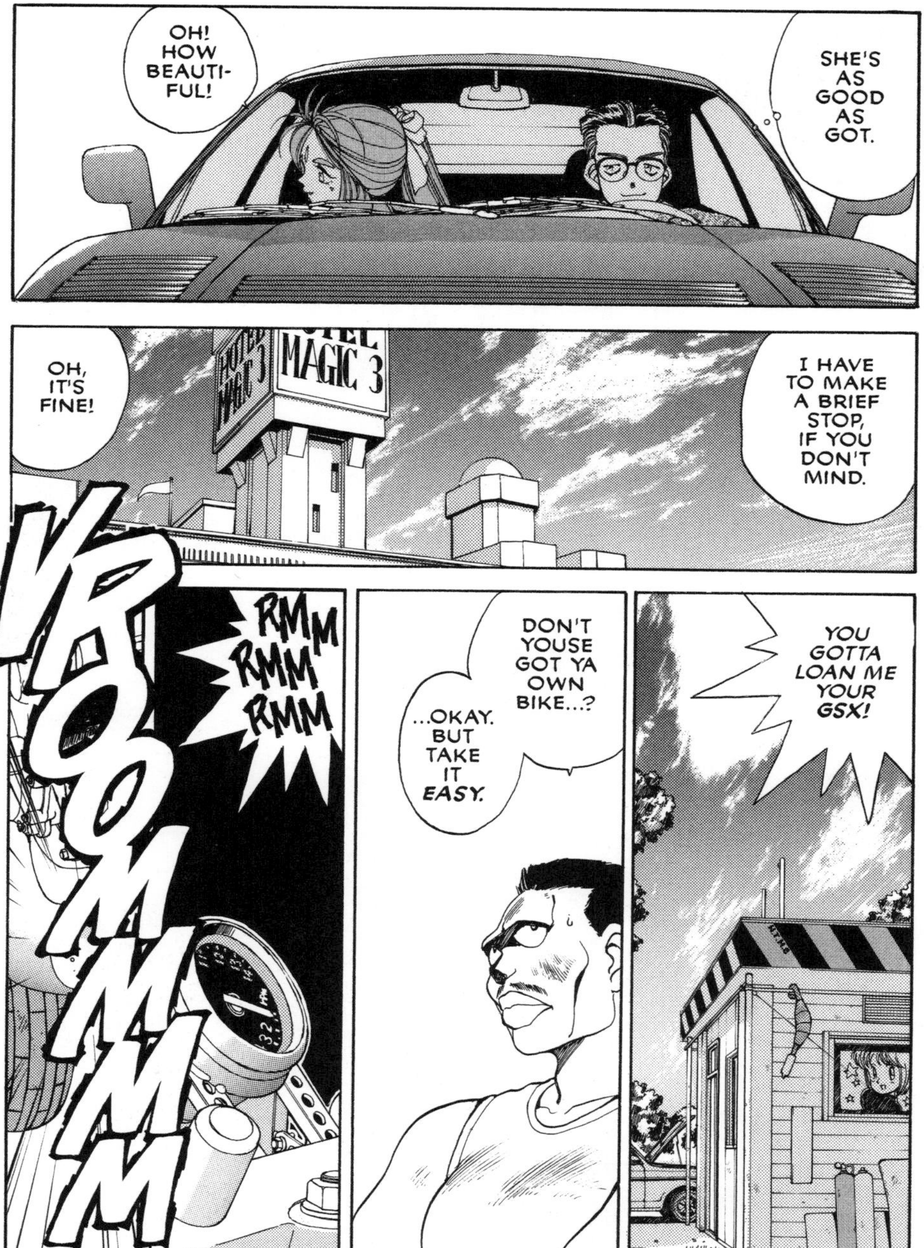
SHE'S AS GOOD AS GOT.
OH! HOW BEAUTI-FUL!
I HAVE TO MAKE A BRIEF STOP, IF YOU DON'T MIND.
MAGIC 3
OH, IT'S FINE!
YOU GOTTA LOAN ME YOUR *GSX!*
DON'T YOUSE GOT YA OWN BIKE...?
...OKAY. BUT TAKE IT *EASY.*
RMMM RMMM RMM
VROOMMMMM

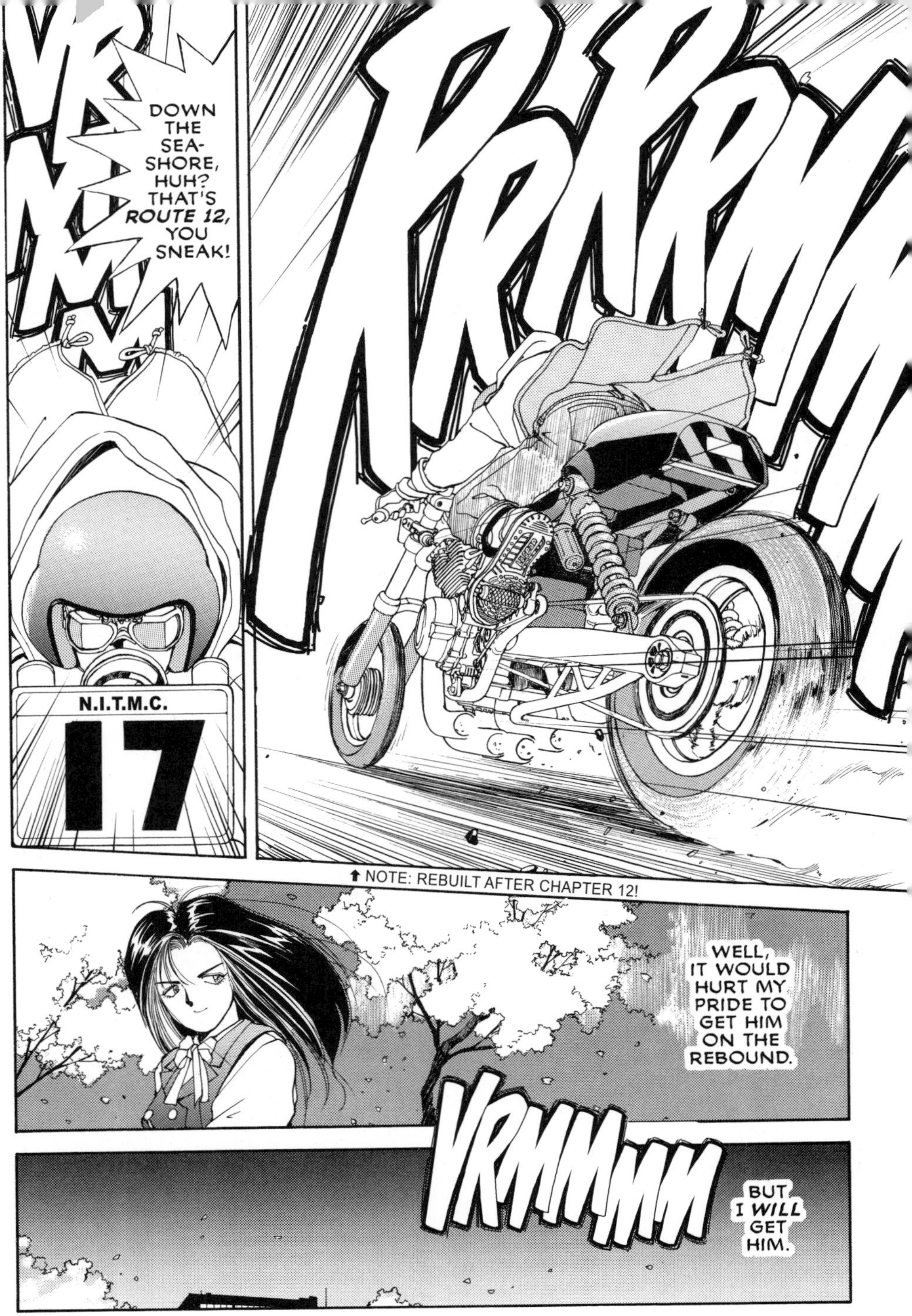
↑ NOTE: REBUILT AFTER CHAPTER 12!
DOWN THE SEA-SHORE, HUH? THAT'S ROUTE 12, YOU SNEAK!
N.I.T.M.C.
17
WELL, IT WOULD HURT MY PRIDE TO GET HIM ON THE REBOUND.
VRMMMMM
BUT I WILL GET HIM.

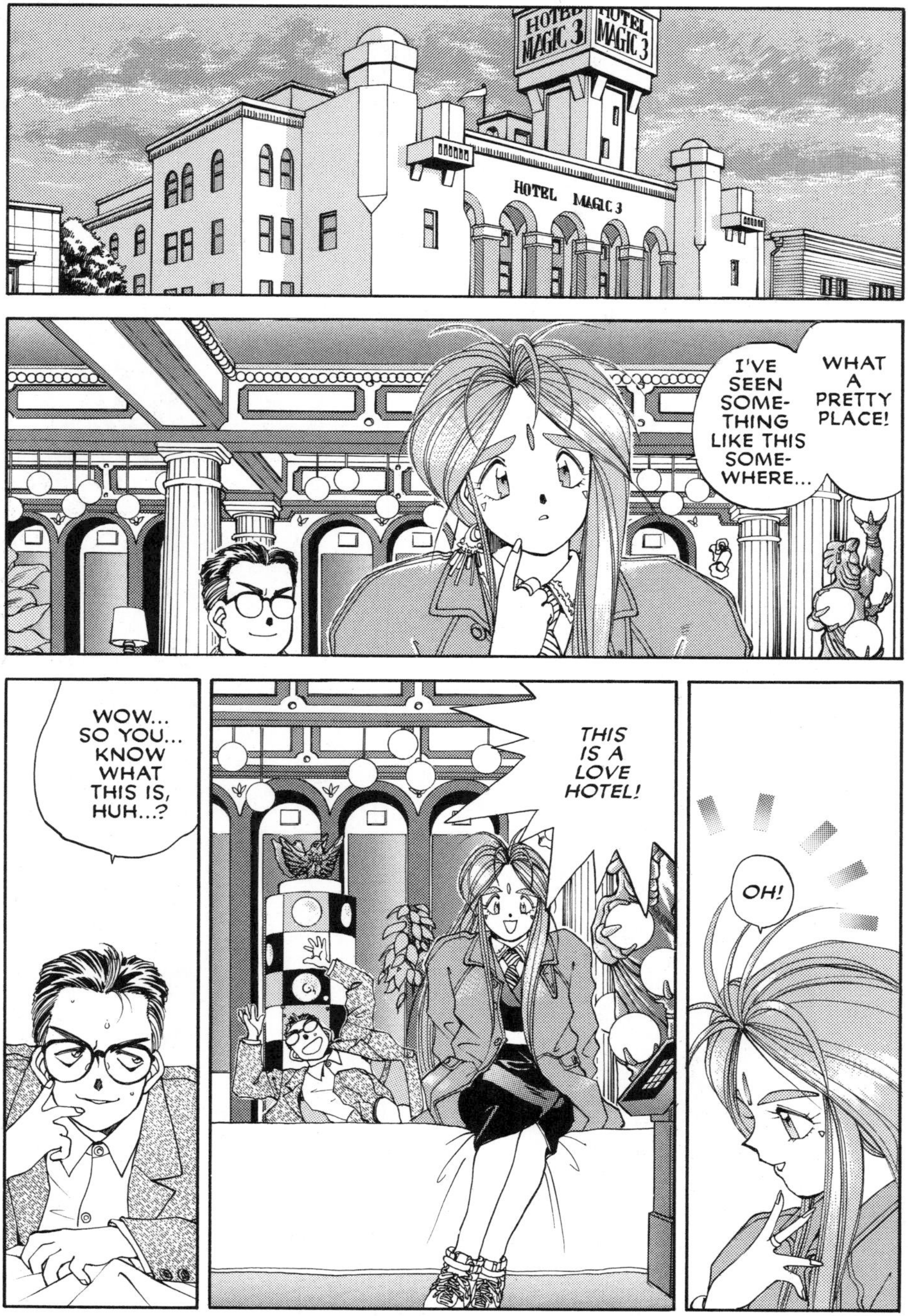
HOTEL MAGIC 3
HOTEL MAGIC 3
HOTEL MAGIC 3
WHAT A PRETTY PLACE!
I'VE SEEN SOME-THING LIKE THIS SOME-WHERE...
OH!
THIS IS A LOVE HOTEL!
WOW... SO YOU... KNOW WHAT THIS IS, HUH...?

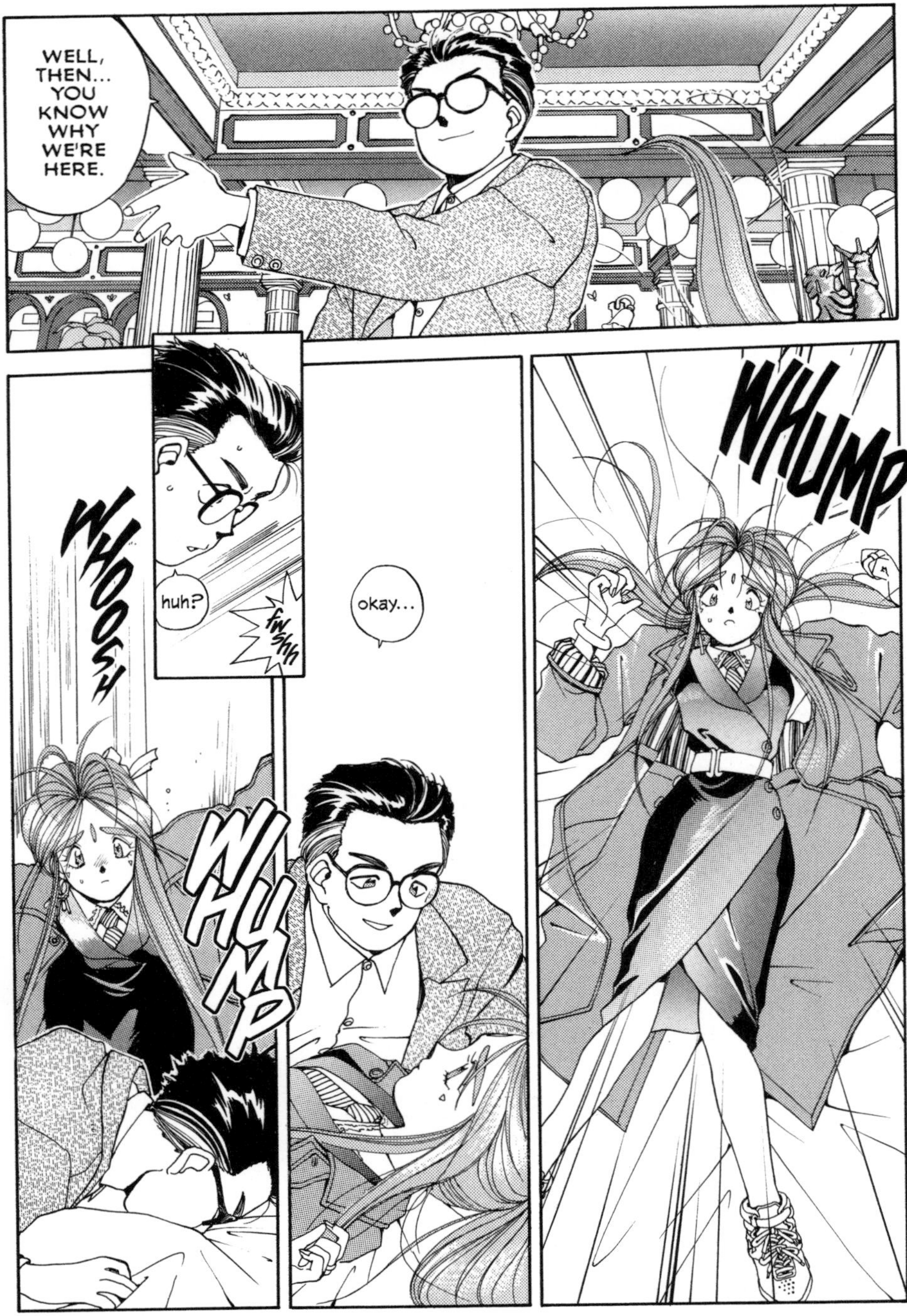
WELL, THEN... YOU KNOW WHY WE'RE HERE.
WHUMP
okay...
huh?
fwshh
WHOOOSH
WHUMP

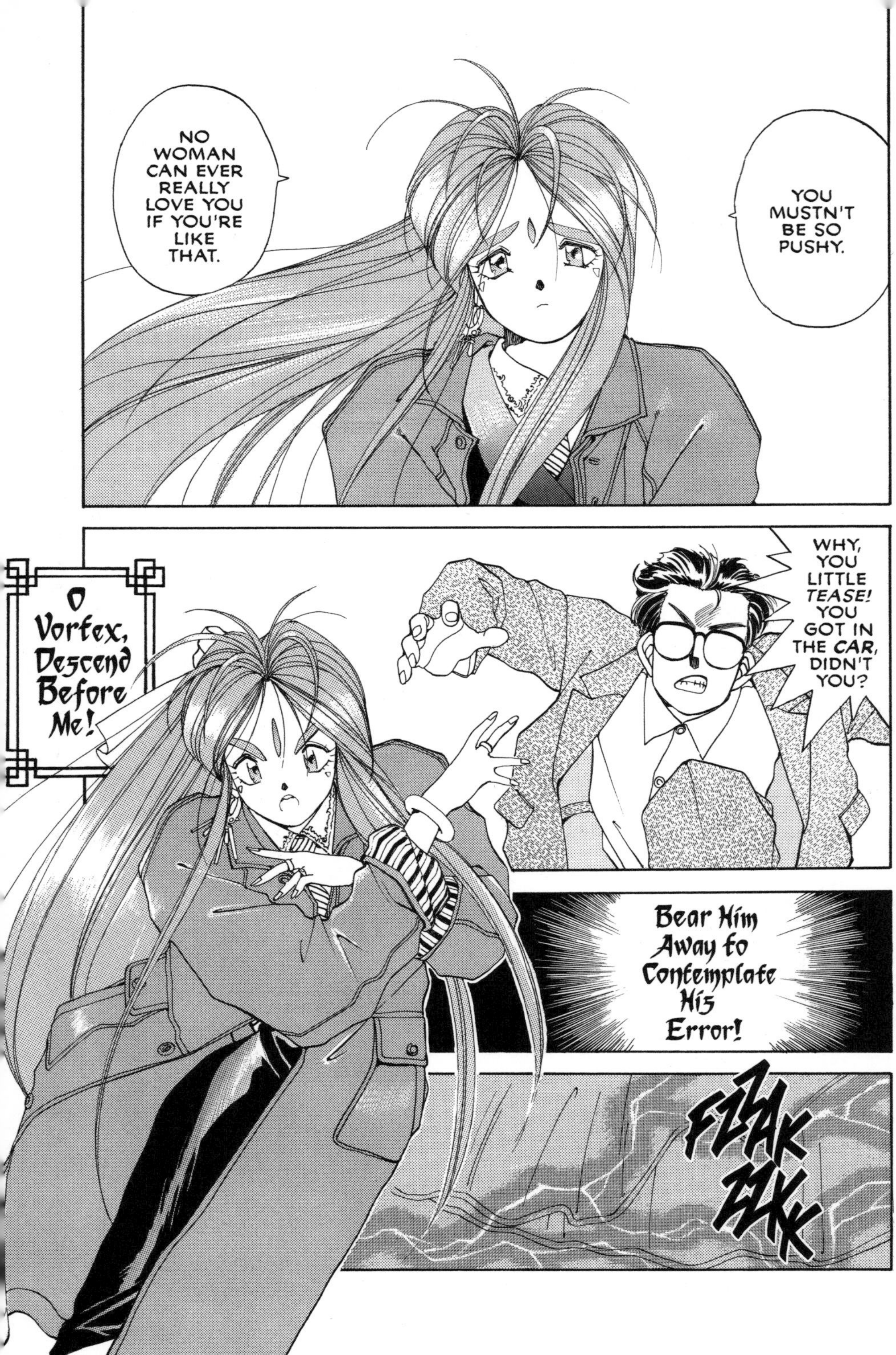
YOU MUSTN'T BE SO PUSHY.
NO WOMAN CAN EVER REALLY LOVE YOU IF YOU'RE LIKE THAT.
WHY, YOU LITTLE *TEASE!* YOU GOT IN THE *CAR*, DIDN'T YOU?
Bear Him Away to Contemplate His Error!
FZZAK
ZZKK
O Vortex, Descend Before Me!

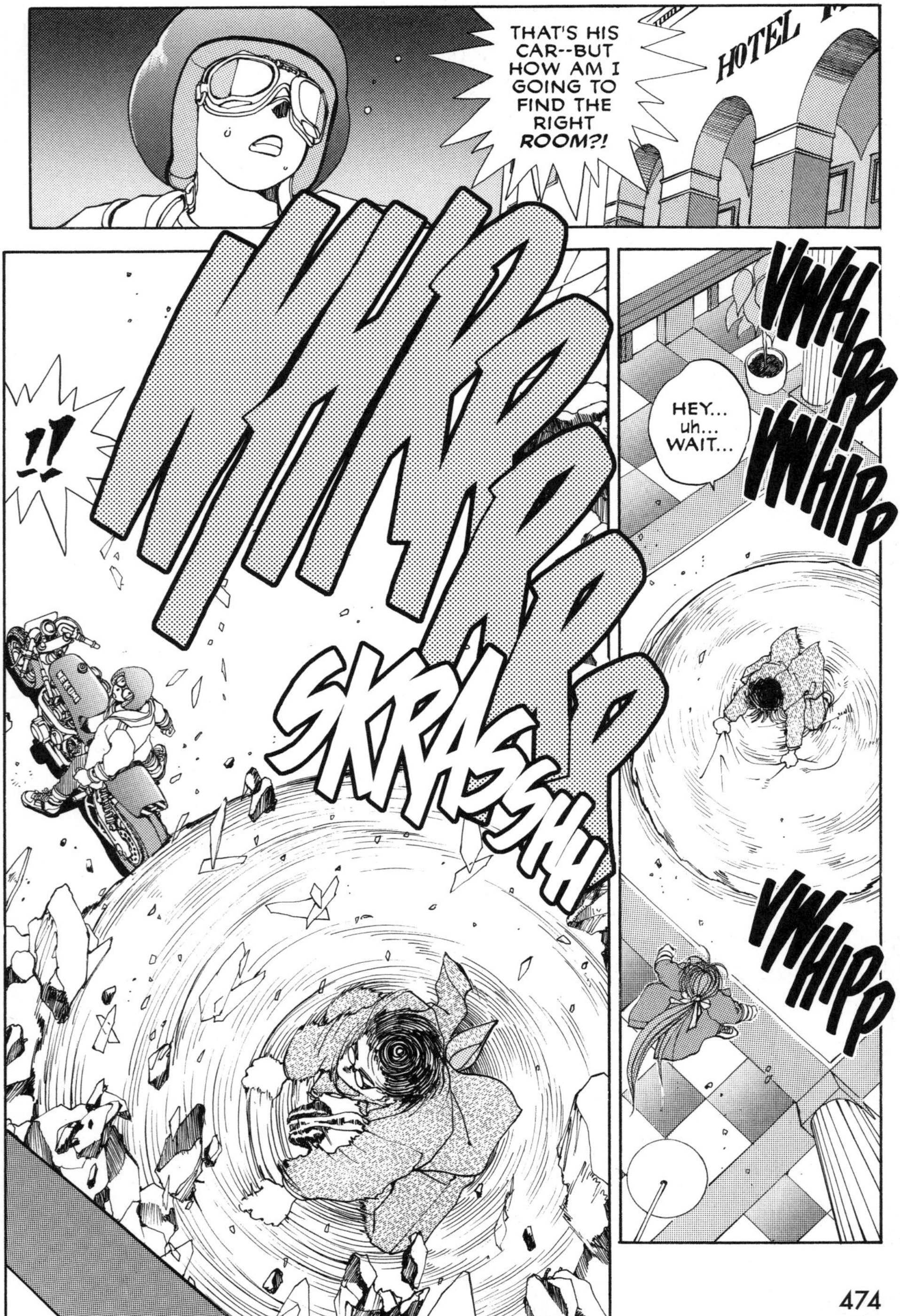
THAT'S HIS CAR--BUT HOW AM I GOING TO FIND THE RIGHT *ROOM?!*
HOTEL
HEY... uh... WAIT...
VWHIPP
VWHIPP
VWHIPP
!!
SKRASSHH

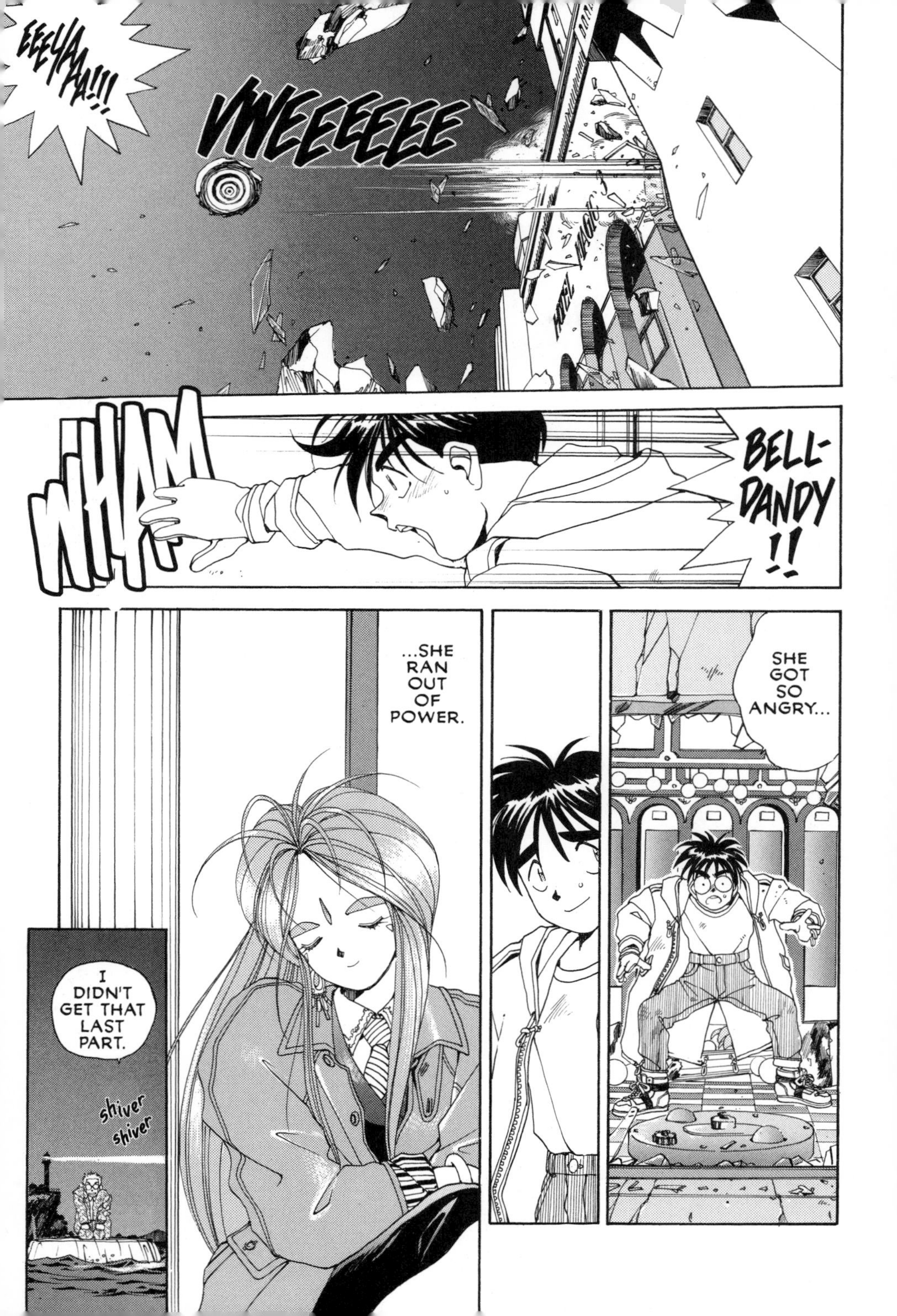
HOTEL MAGIC
VWEEEEEEE
EEEYAAA!!!
BELL-DANDY!!
WHAM
SHE GOT SO ANGRY...
...SHE RAN OUT OF POWER.
I DIDN'T GET THAT LAST PART.
shiver shiver

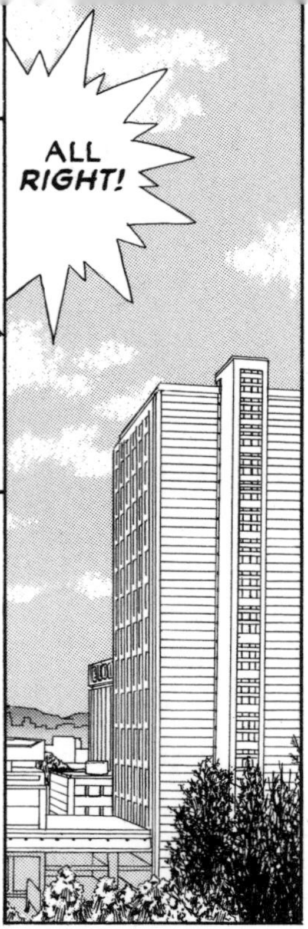
ALL RIGHT!
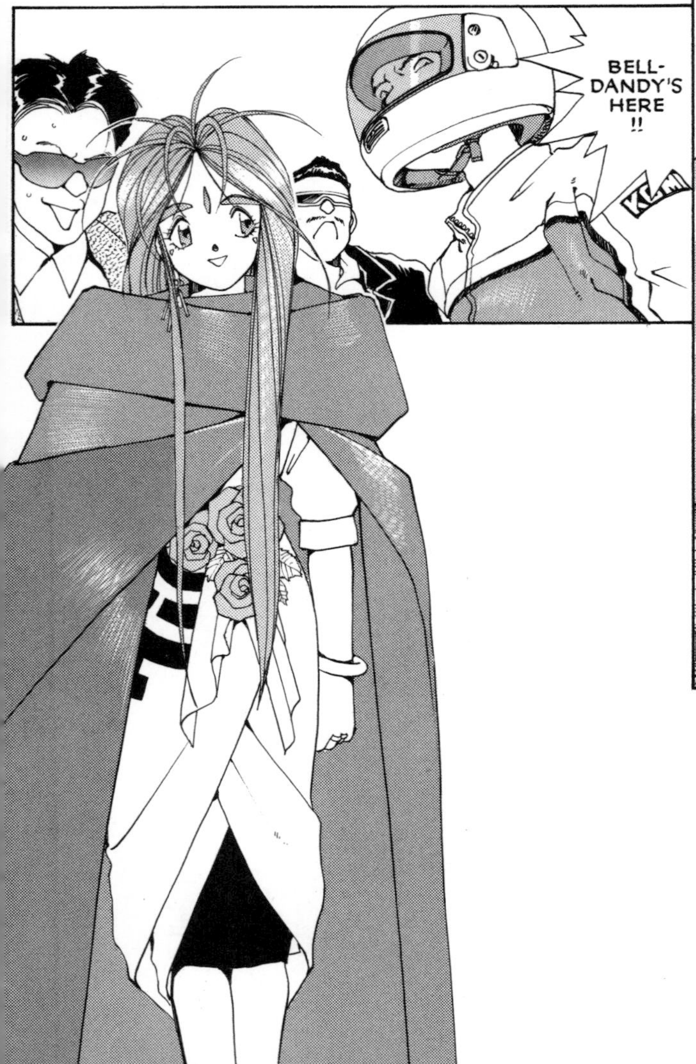
BELL-DANDY'S HERE !!

CHAPTER 21

Exposing a Secret

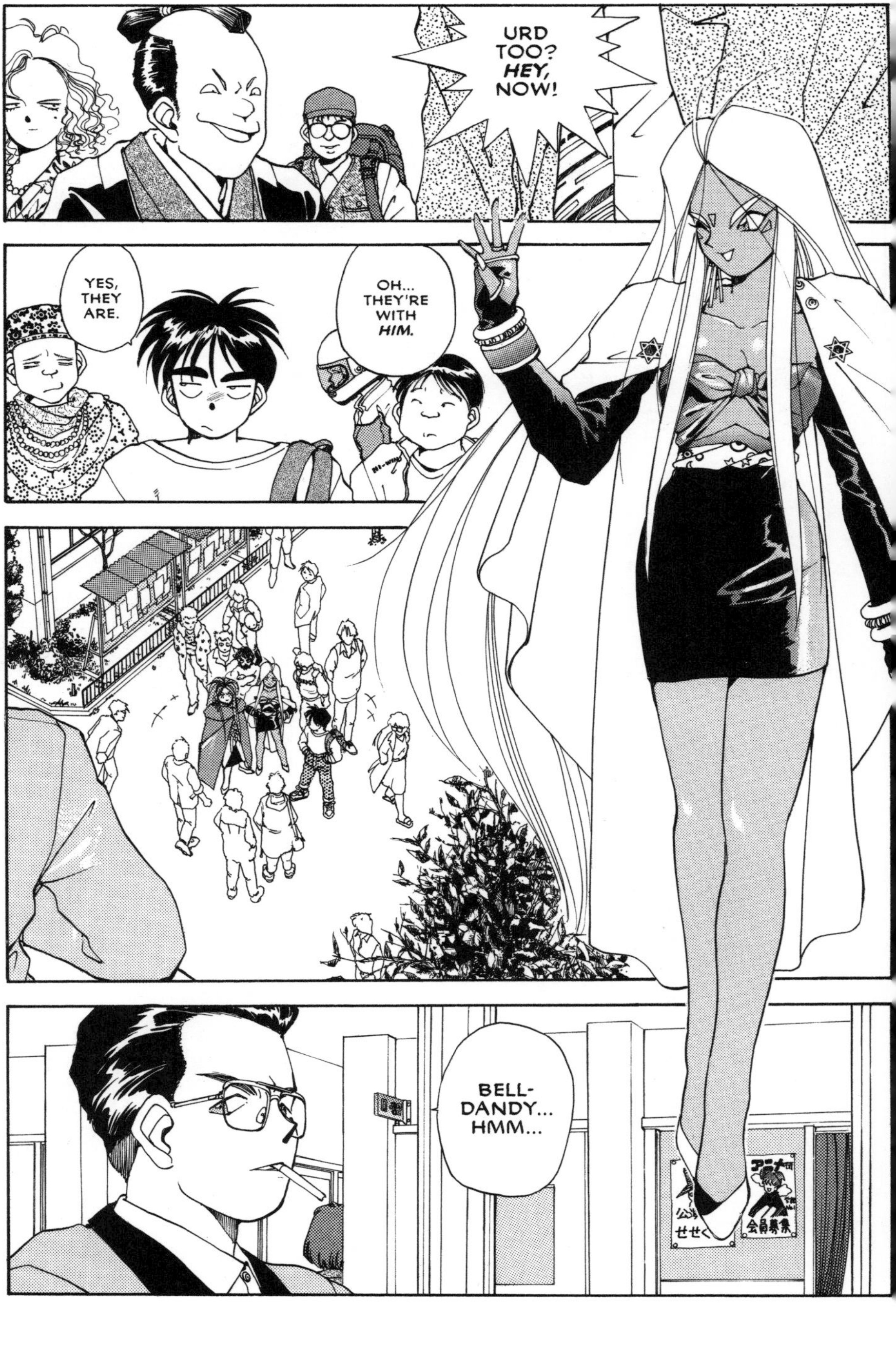
URD TOO? HEY, NOW!
OH... THEY'RE WITH HIM.
YES, THEY ARE.
BELL-DANDY... HMM...

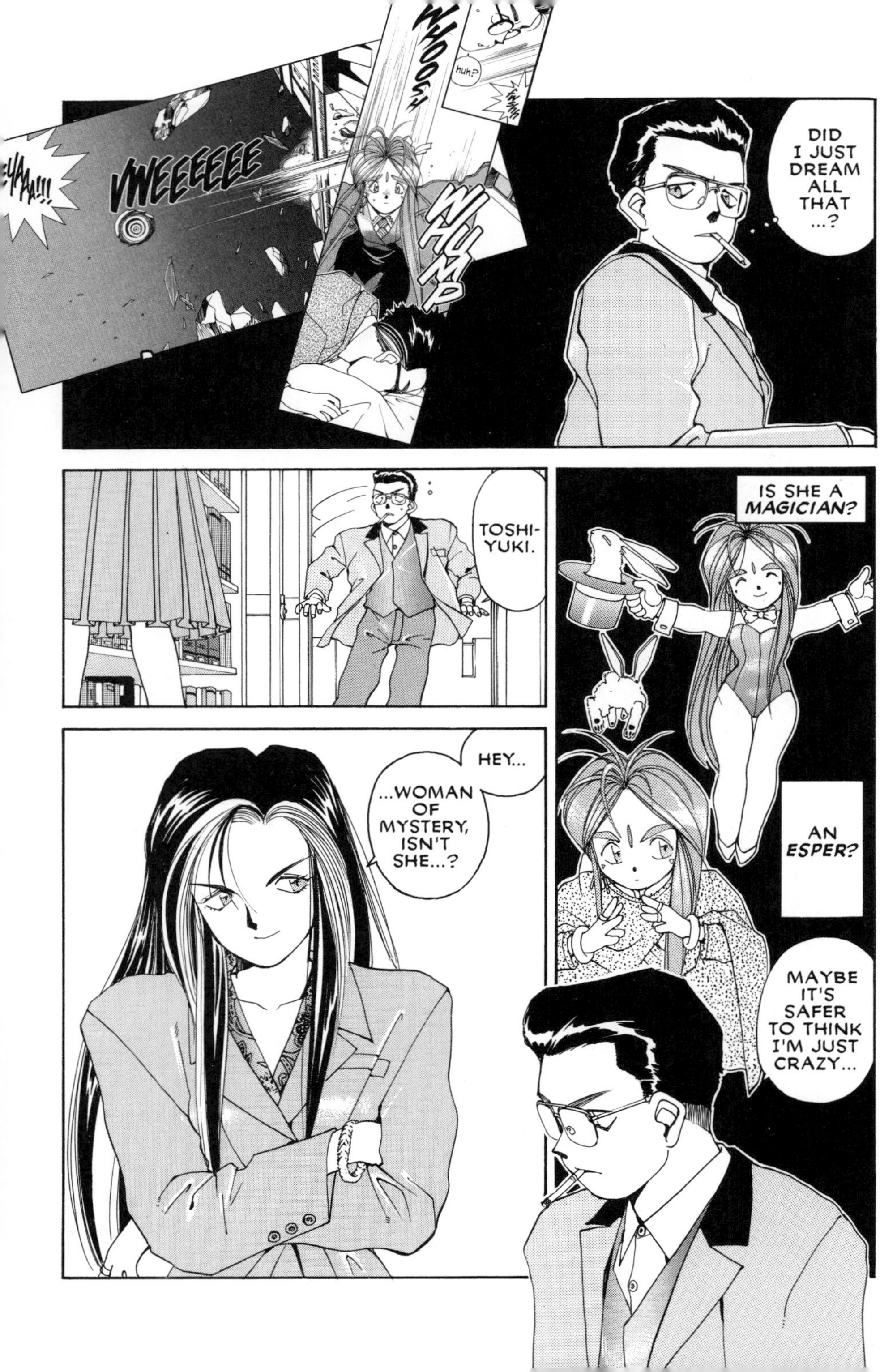
DID I JUST DREAM ALL THAT ...?
huh?
WHUMP
VWEEEEEE
IS SHE A MAGICIAN?
AN ESPER?
MAYBE IT'S SAFER TO THINK I'M JUST CRAZY...
TOSHI-YUKI.
HEY...
...WOMAN OF MYSTERY, ISN'T SHE...?

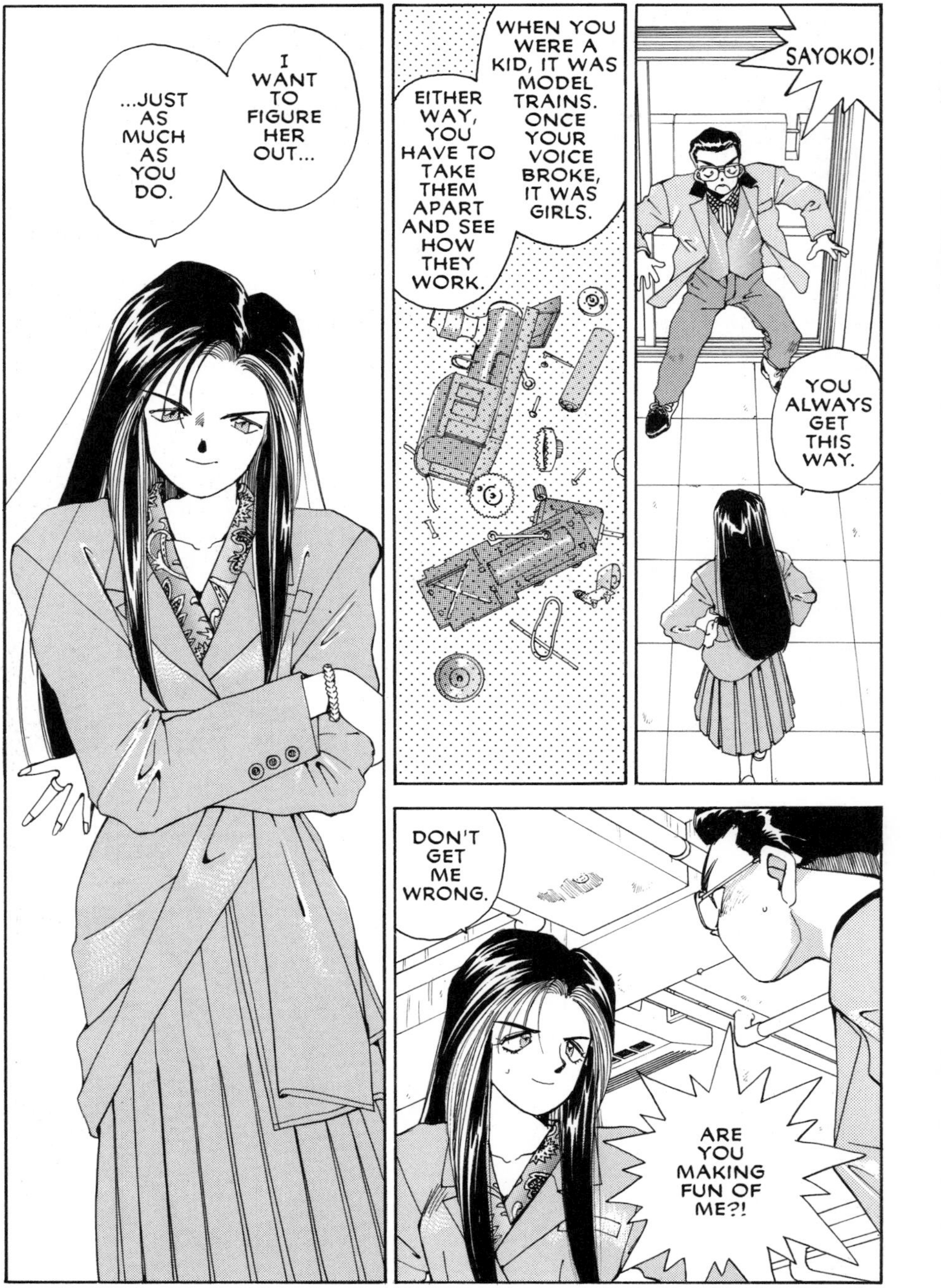
SAYOKO!
YOU ALWAYS GET THIS WAY.
WHEN YOU WERE A KID, IT WAS MODEL TRAINS. ONCE YOUR VOICE BROKE, IT WAS GIRLS.
EITHER WAY, YOU HAVE TO TAKE THEM APART AND SEE HOW THEY WORK.
ARE YOU MAKING FUN OF ME?!
DON'T GET ME WRONG.
I WANT TO FIGURE HER OUT...
...JUST AS MUCH AS YOU DO.

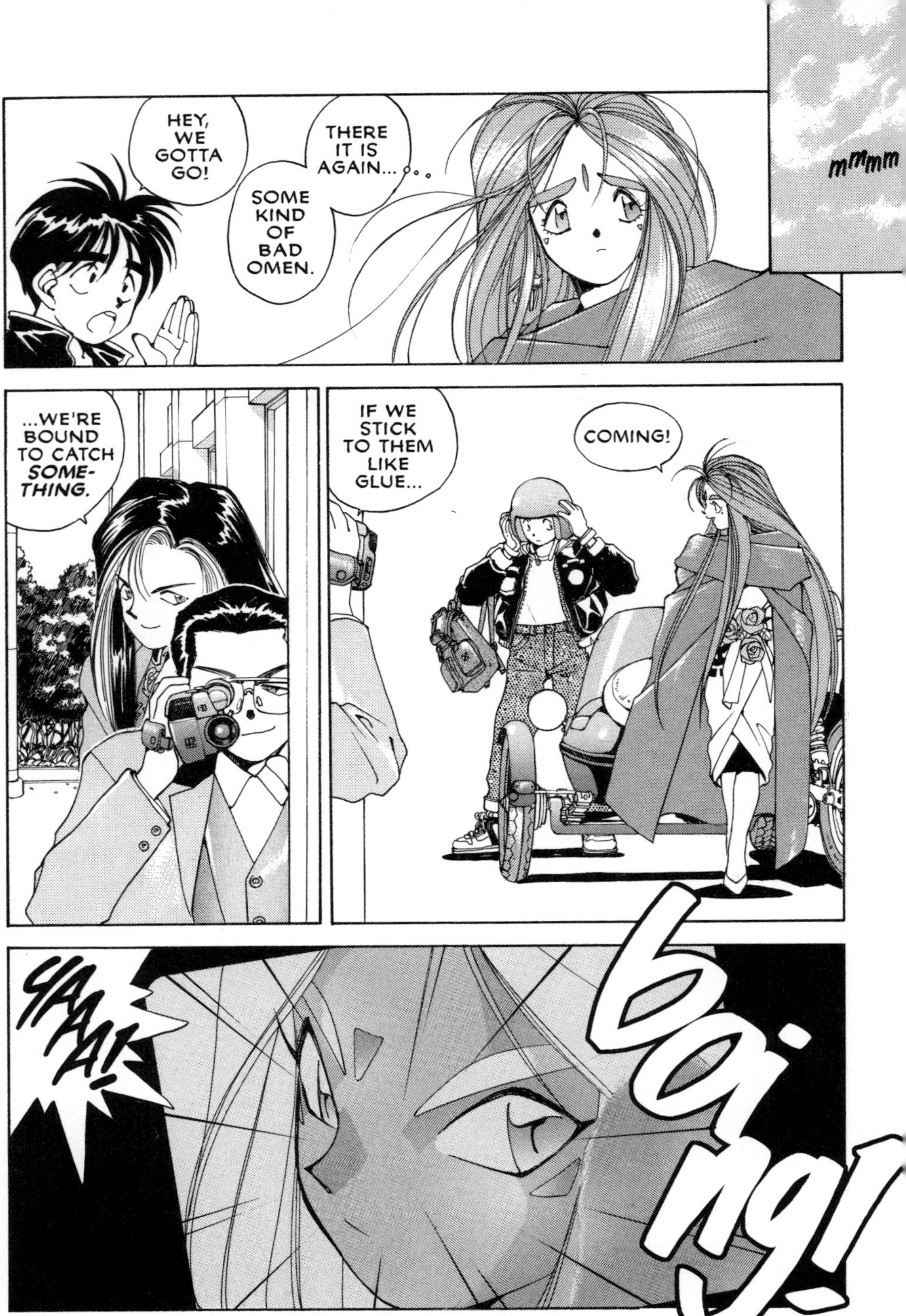
mmmm
THERE IT IS AGAIN...
SOME KIND OF BAD OMEN.
HEY, WE GOTTA GO!
COMING!
IF WE STICK TO THEM LIKE GLUE...
...WE'RE BOUND TO CATCH *SOME-THING.*
baing!
YAAAA!

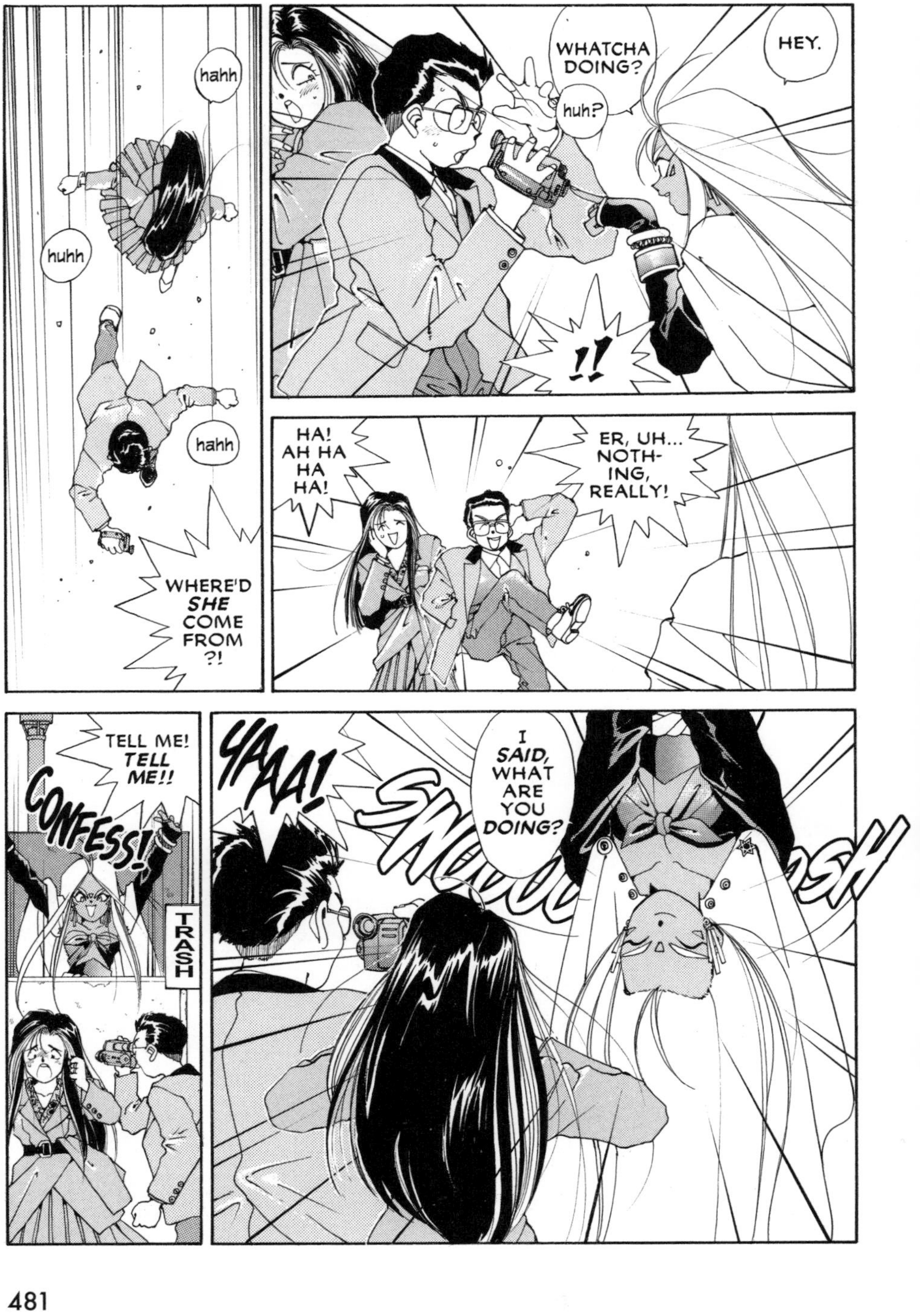

HEY.
WHATCHA DOING?
huh?
!!
ER, UH... NOTHING, REALLY!
HA! AH HA HA HA!
hahh
huhh
hahh
WHERE'D SHE COME FROM?!
I SAID, WHAT ARE YOU DOING?
YAAAA!
TELL ME! TELL ME!!
CONFESS!
TRASH

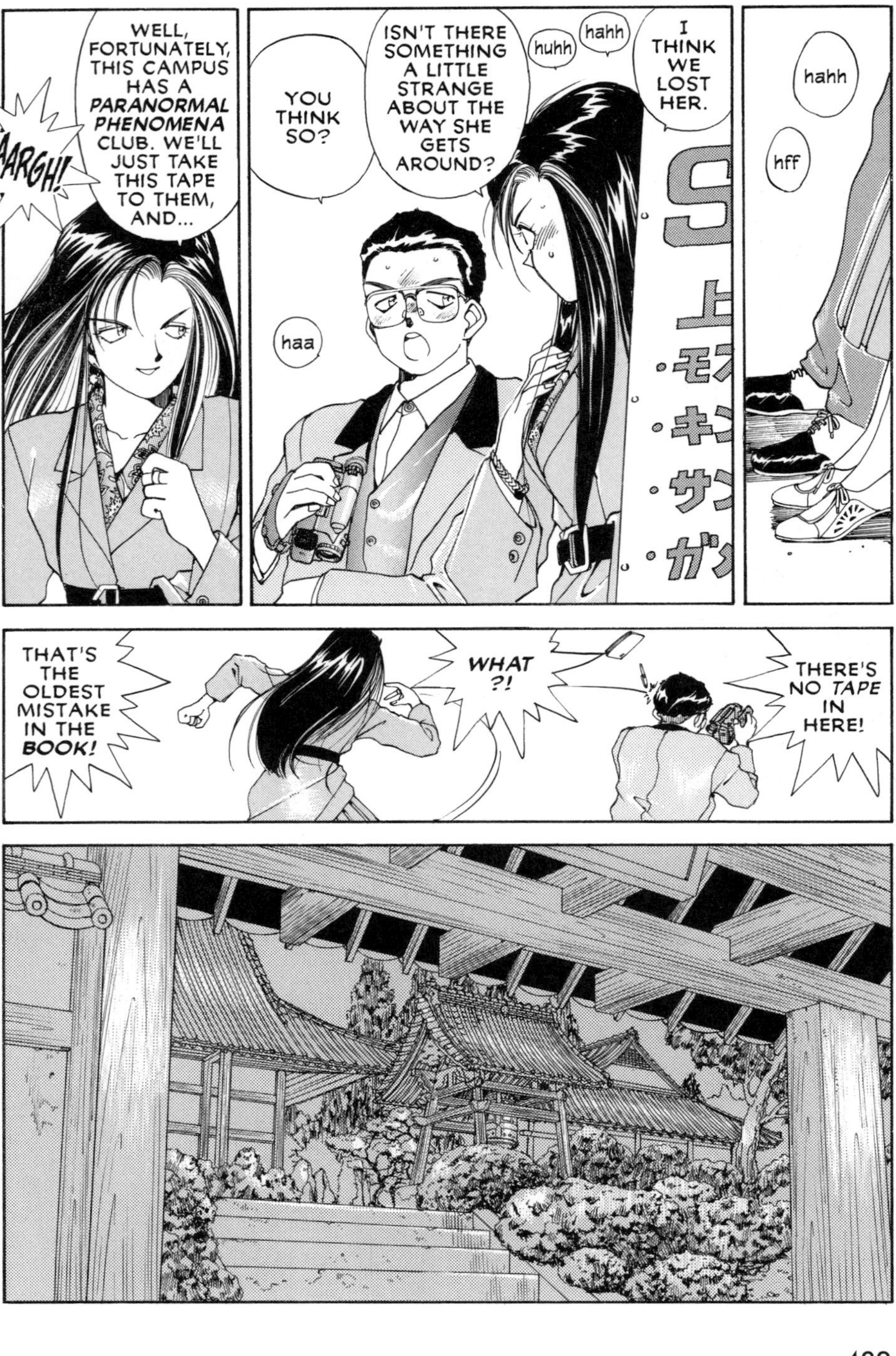

hahh
hff
I THINK WE LOST HER.
hahh
huhh
ISN'T THERE SOMETHING A LITTLE STRANGE ABOUT THE WAY SHE GETS AROUND?
YOU THINK SO?
haa
WELL, FORTUNATELY, THIS CAMPUS HAS A *PARANORMAL PHENOMENA* CLUB. WE'LL JUST TAKE THIS TAPE TO THEM, AND...
AARGH!
THERE'S NO *TAPE* IN HERE!
WHAT ?!
THAT'S THE OLDEST MISTAKE IN THE *BOOK!*

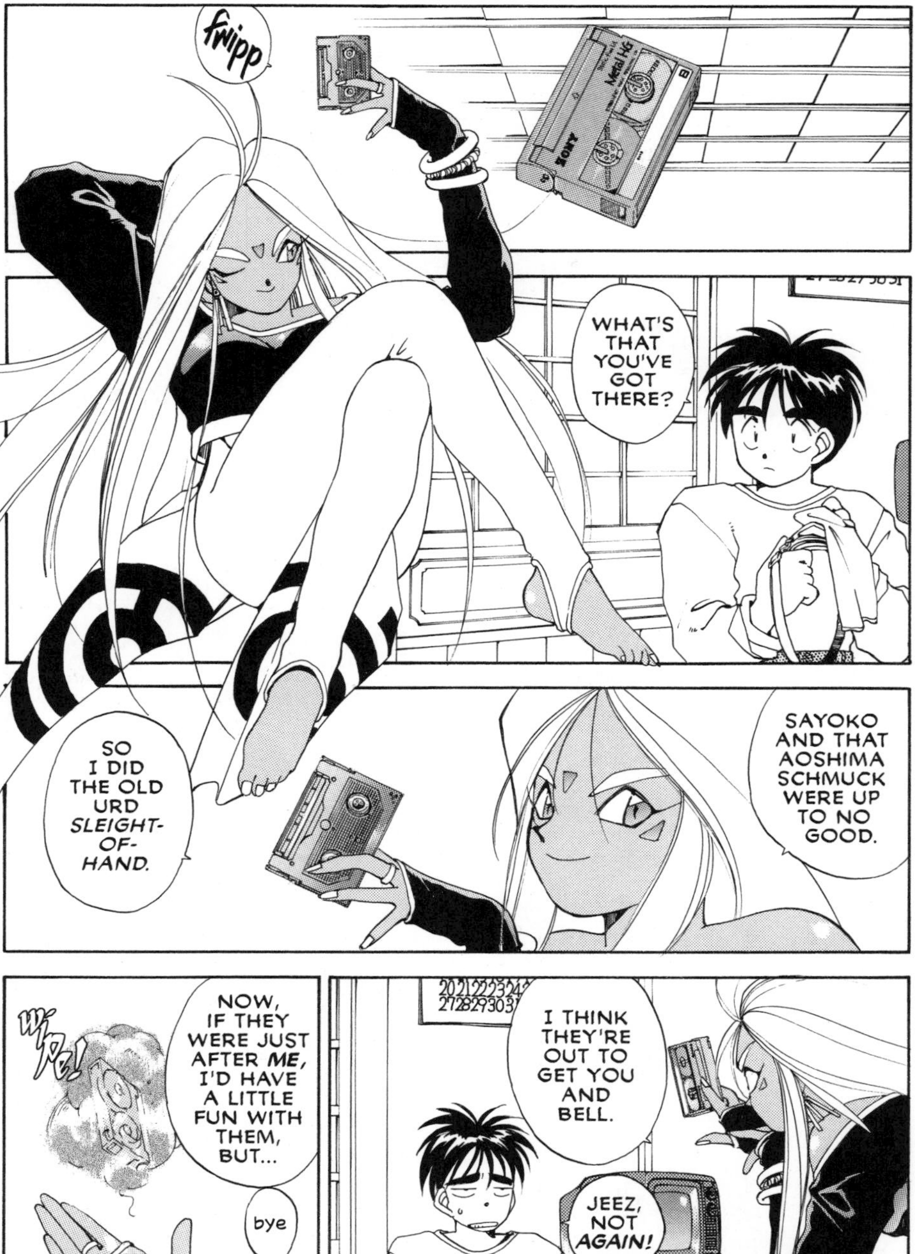
fripp
WHAT'S THAT YOU'VE GOT THERE?
SAYOKO AND THAT AOSHIMA SCHMUCK WERE UP TO NO GOOD.
SO I DID THE OLD URD *SLEIGHT-OF-HAND.*
I THINK THEY'RE OUT TO GET YOU AND BELL.
JEEZ, NOT *AGAIN!*
NOW, IF THEY WERE JUST AFTER *ME,* I'D HAVE A LITTLE FUN WITH THEM, BUT...
bye
wipe!

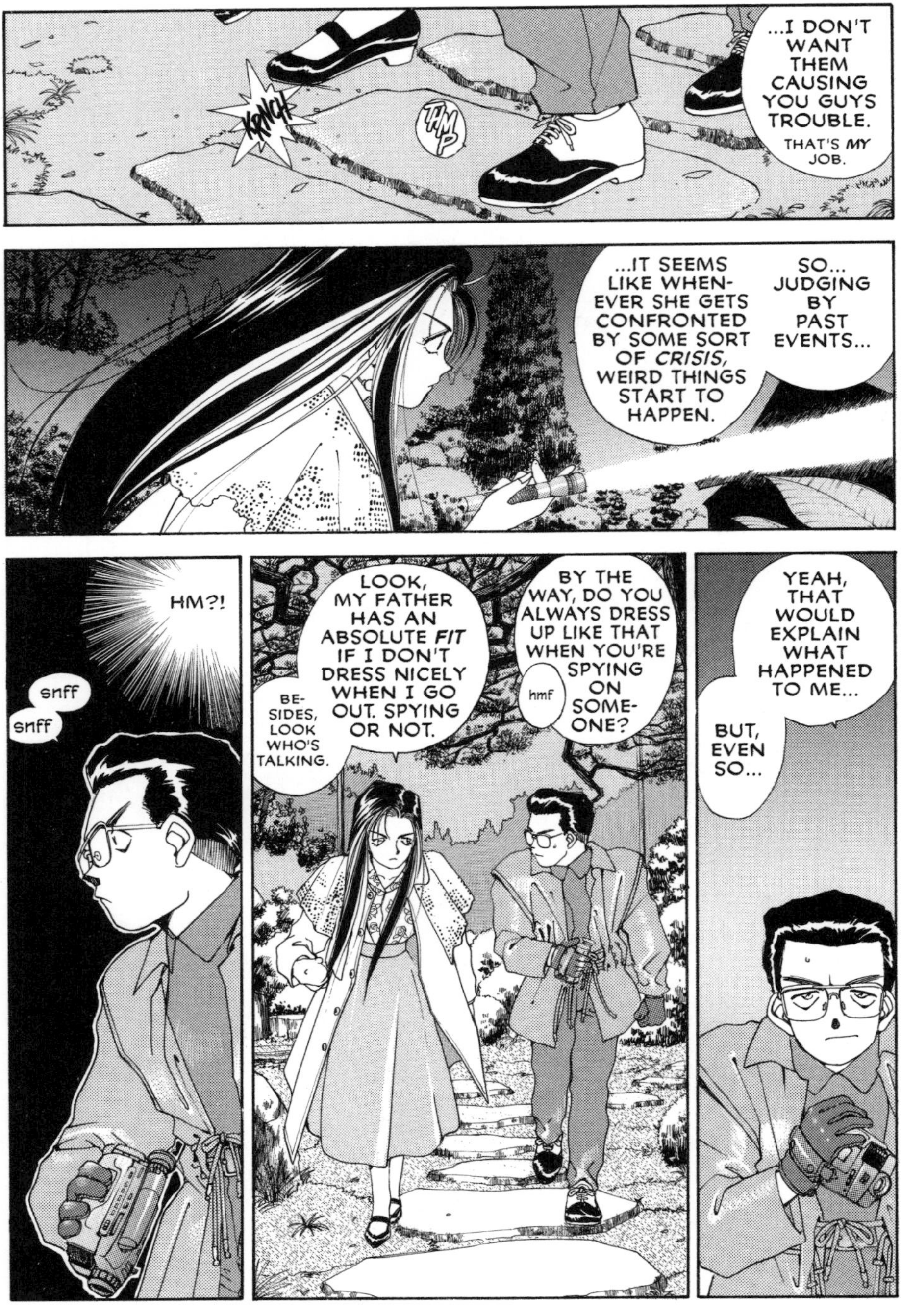
...I DON'T WANT THEM CAUSING YOU GUYS TROUBLE.
THAT'S *MY* JOB.
THMP
KRNCH
SO... JUDGING BY PAST EVENTS...
...IT SEEMS LIKE WHEN-EVER SHE GETS CONFRONTED BY SOME SORT OF *CRISIS,* WEIRD THINGS START TO HAPPEN.
YEAH, THAT WOULD EXPLAIN WHAT HAPPENED TO ME...
BUT, EVEN SO...
BY THE WAY, DO YOU ALWAYS DRESS UP LIKE THAT WHEN YOU'RE SPYING ON SOME-ONE?
hmf
LOOK, MY FATHER HAS AN ABSOLUTE *FIT* IF I DON'T DRESS NICELY WHEN I GO OUT. SPYING OR NOT.
BE-SIDES, LOOK WHO'S TALKING.
HM?!
snff
snff

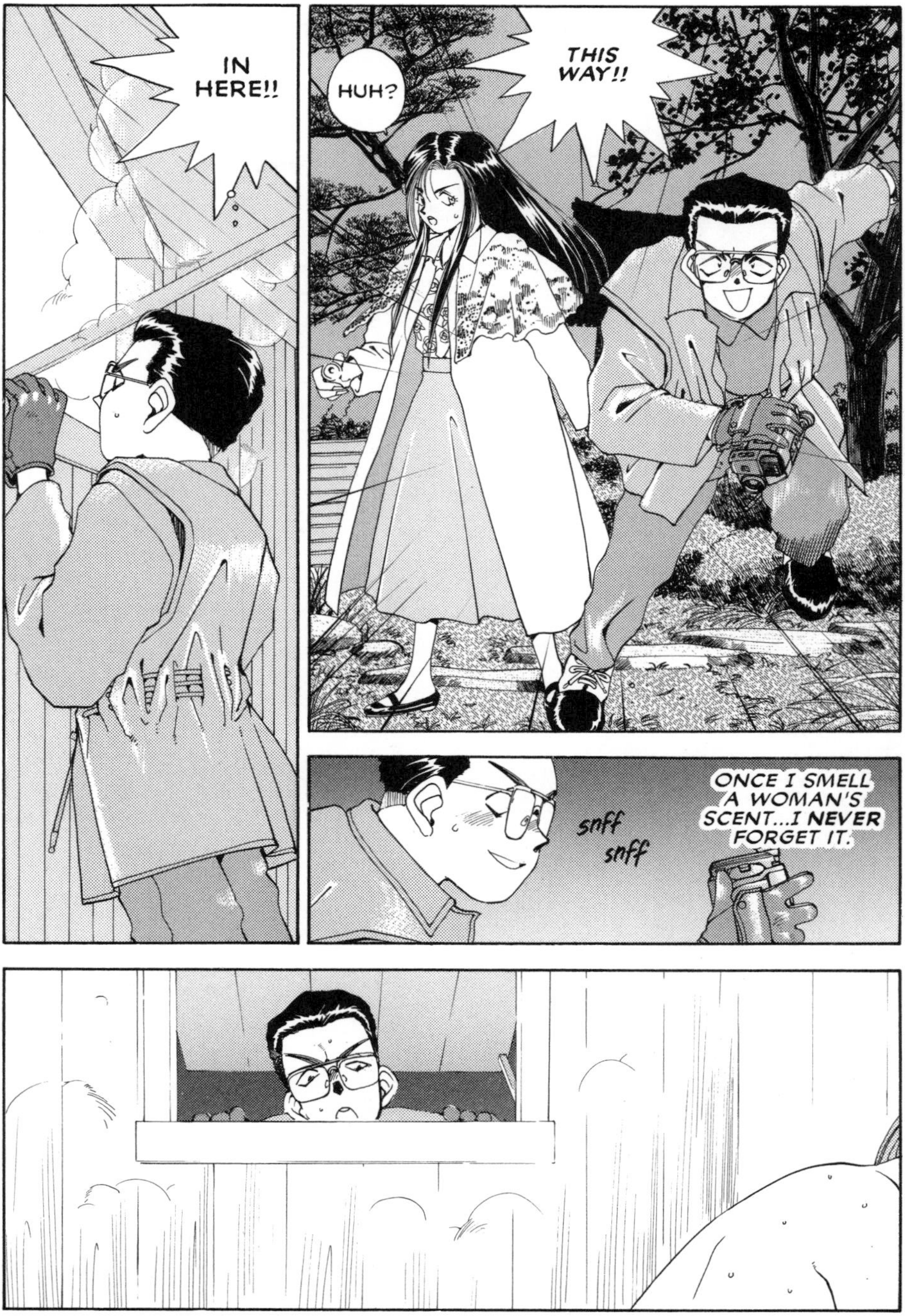
THIS WAY!!
HUH?
ONCE I SMELL A WOMAN'S SCENT...I NEVER FORGET IT.
snff snff
IN HERE!!

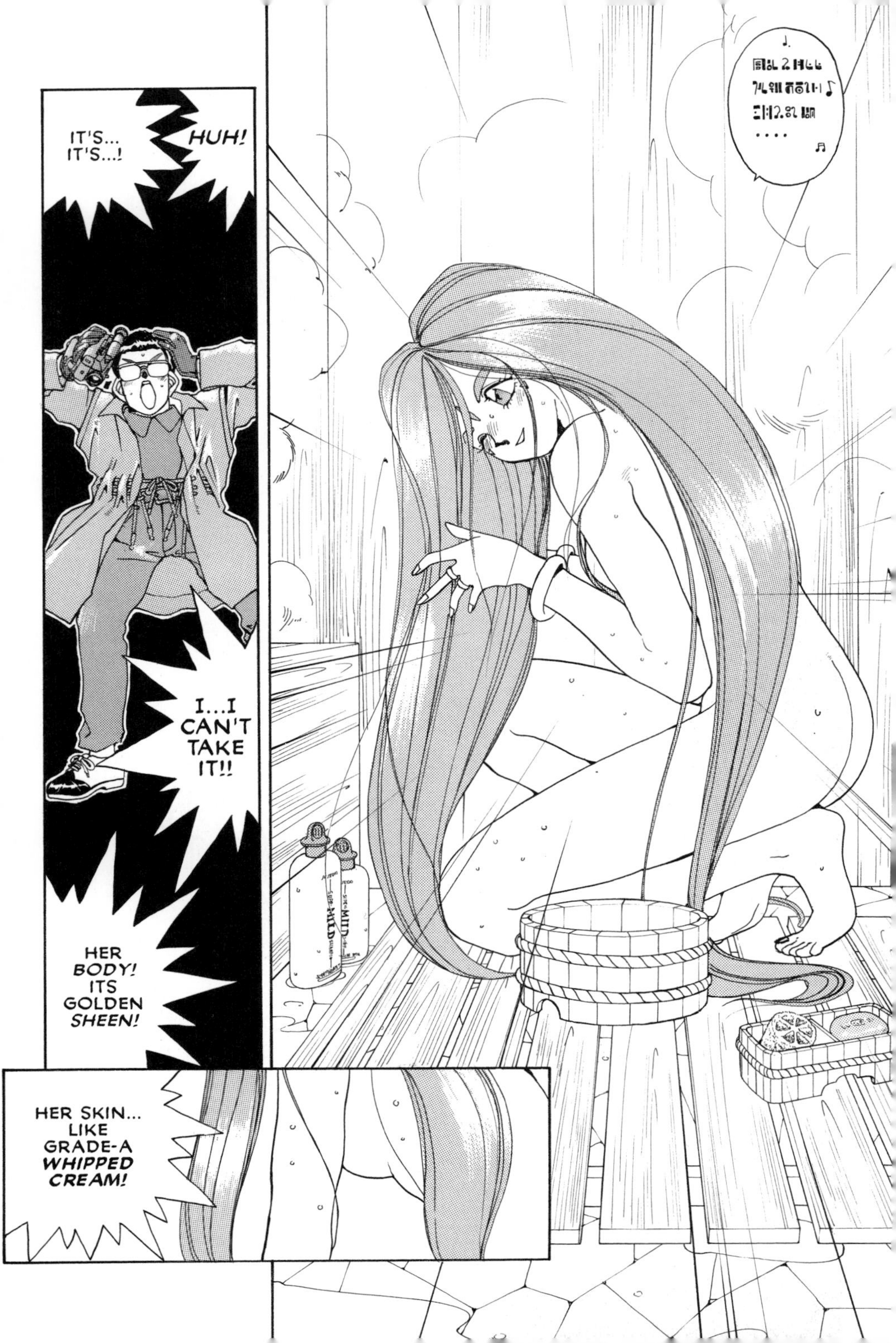
HUH!
IT'S... IT'S...!
I...I CAN'T TAKE IT!!
HER *BODY!* ITS GOLDEN *SHEEN!*
HER SKIN... LIKE GRADE-A *WHIPPED CREAM!*

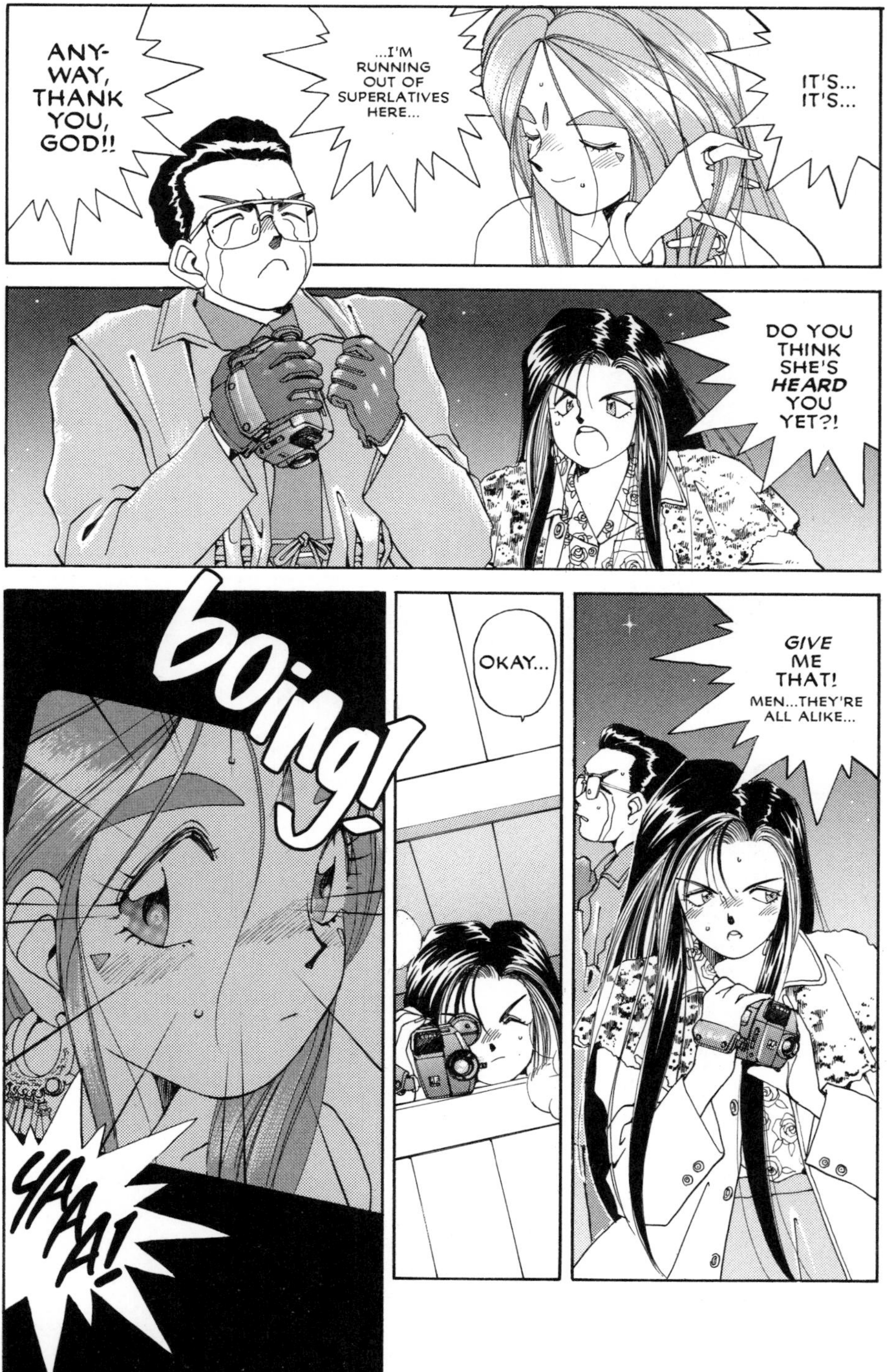
IT'S... IT'S...
...I'M RUNNING OUT OF SUPERLATIVES HERE...
ANY-WAY, THANK YOU, GOD!!
DO YOU THINK SHE'S *HEARD* YOU YET?!
GIVE ME THAT!
MEN...THEY'RE ALL ALIKE...
OKAY...
boing!
YAAAA!

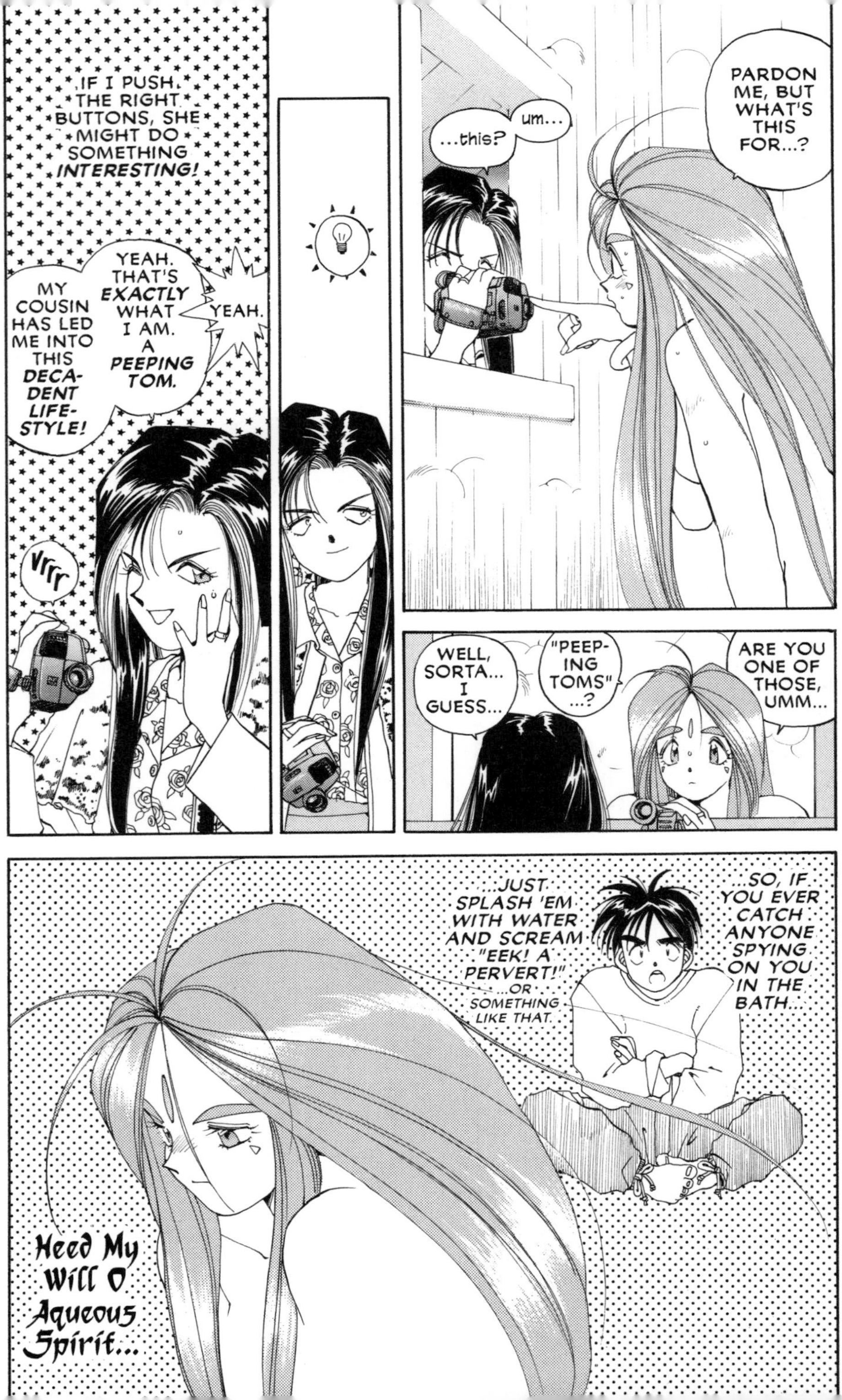
PARDON ME, BUT WHAT'S THIS FOR...?
um...
...this?
ARE YOU ONE OF THOSE, UMM...
"PEEPING TOMS" ...?
WELL, SORTA... I GUESS...
IF I PUSH THE RIGHT BUTTONS, SHE MIGHT DO SOMETHING INTERESTING!
YEAH.
YEAH. THAT'S EXACTLY WHAT I AM. A PEEPING TOM.
MY COUSIN HAS LED ME INTO THIS DECADENT LIFESTYLE!
Vrrr
...SO, IF YOU EVER CATCH ANYONE SPYING ON YOU IN THE BATH...
JUST SPLASH 'EM WITH WATER AND SCREAM "EEK! A PERVERT!" ...OR SOMETHING LIKE THAT.
Heed My Will O Aqueous Spirit...

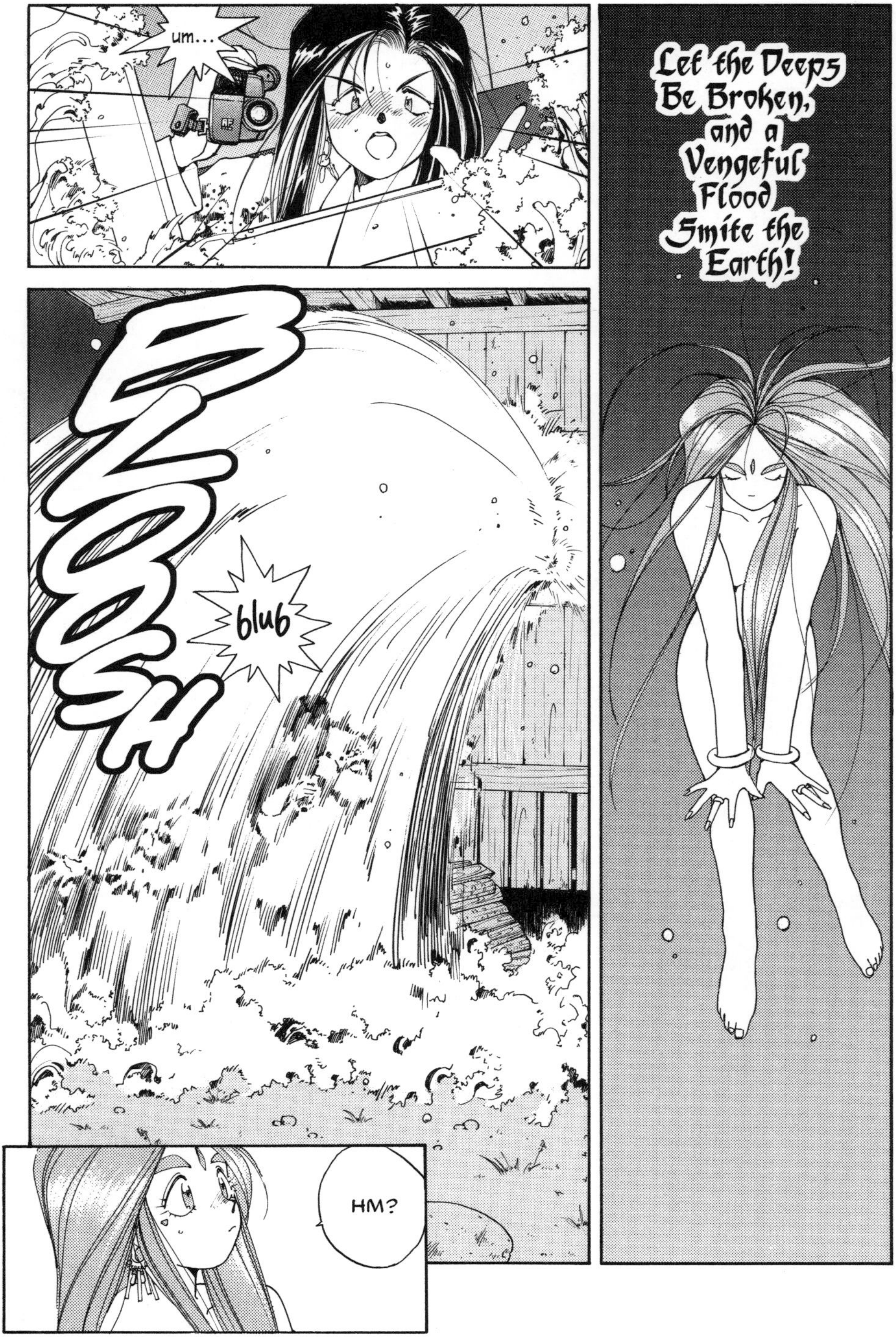
Let the Deeps Be Broken, and a Vengeful Flood Smite the Earth!
um...
BLOOSH
blub
HM?

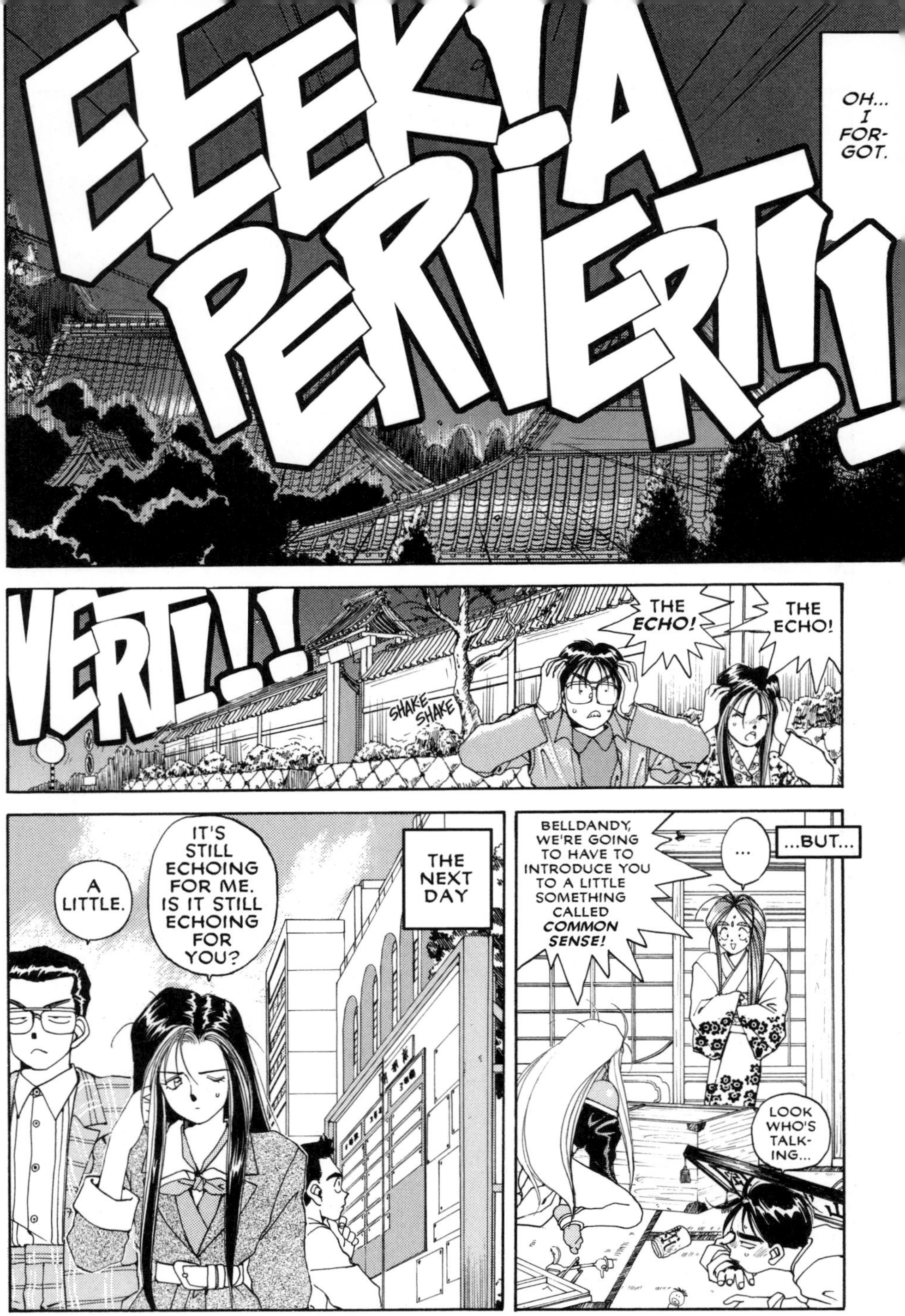
OH... I FOR-GOT.
EEK! A PERVERT!!!
THE ECHO!
THE ECHO!
SHAKE SHAKE
VERT!!!
...BUT...
...
BELLDANDY, WE'RE GOING TO HAVE TO INTRODUCE YOU TO A LITTLE SOMETHING CALLED COMMON SENSE!
LOOK WHO'S TALK-ING...
THE NEXT DAY
IT'S STILL ECHOING FOR ME. IS IT STILL ECHOING FOR YOU?
A LITTLE.

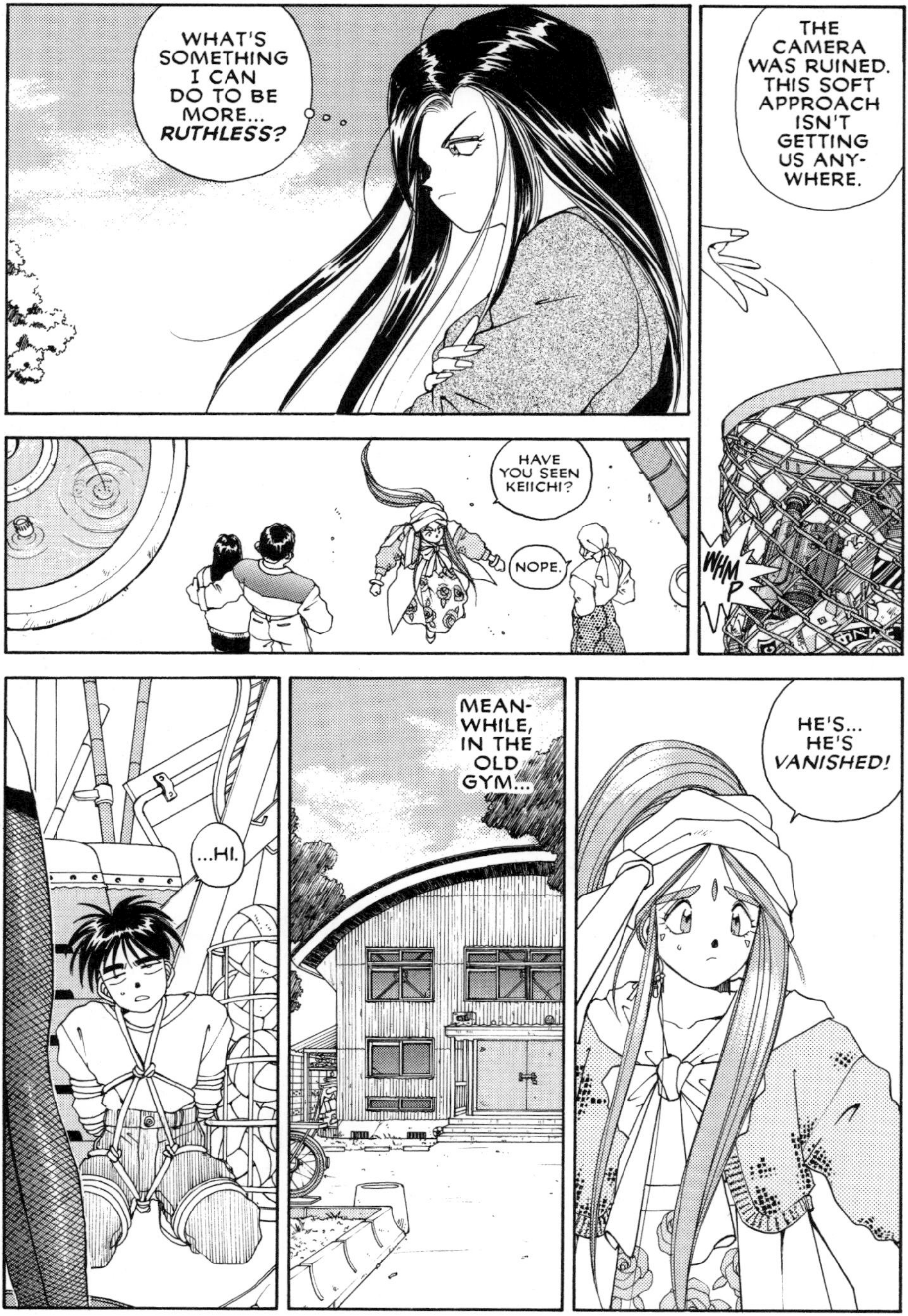
THE CAMERA WAS RUINED. THIS SOFT APPROACH ISN'T GETTING US ANY-WHERE.
WHMP
WHAT'S SOMETHING I CAN DO TO BE MORE... *RUTHLESS?*
HAVE YOU SEEN KEIICHI?
NOPE.
HE'S... HE'S *VANISHED!*
MEAN-WHILE, IN THE OLD GYM...
...HI.

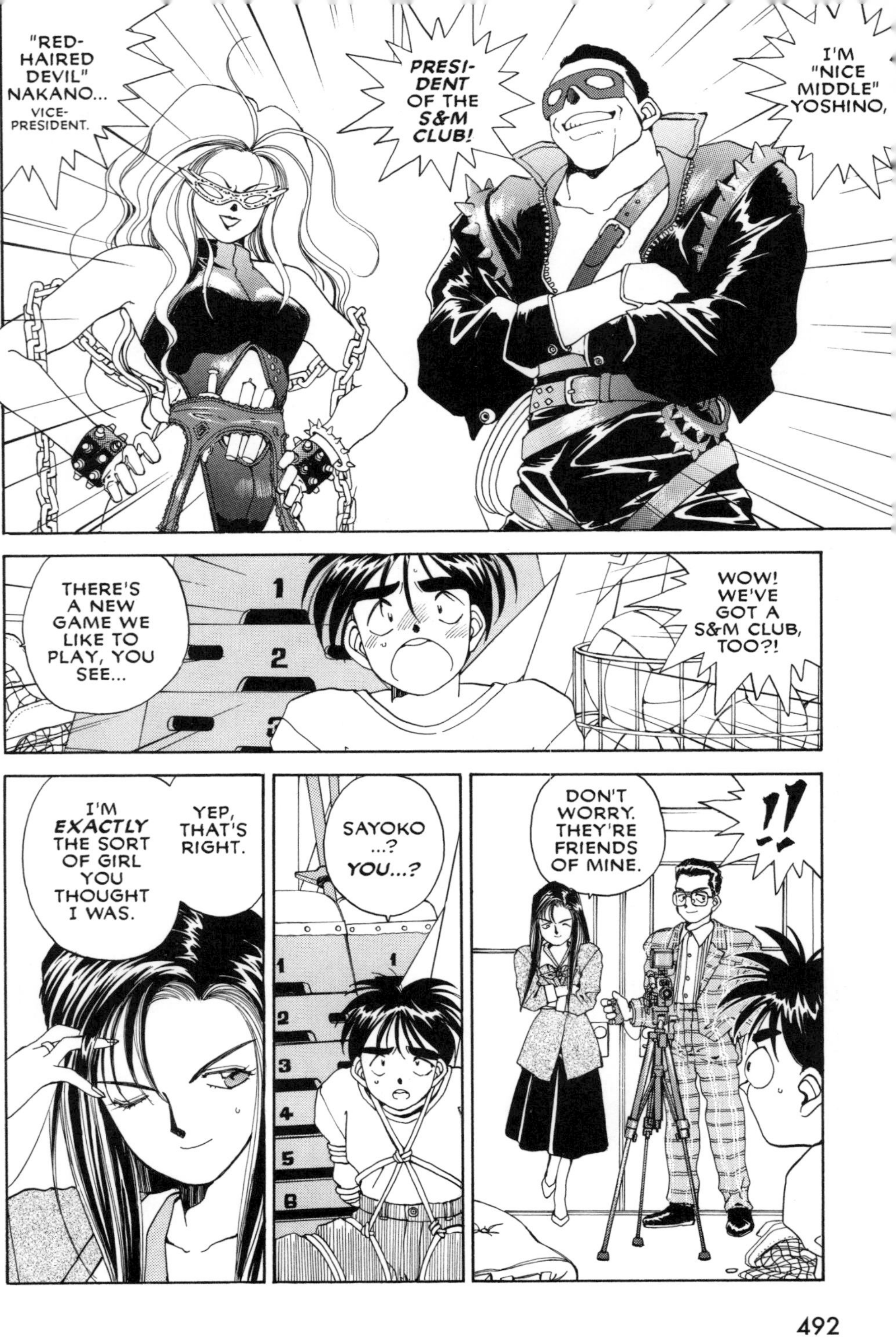
I'M "NICE MIDDLE" YOSHINO,
PRESIDENT OF THE S&M CLUB!
"RED-HAIRED DEVIL" NAKANO... VICE-PRESIDENT.
WOW! WE'VE GOT A S&M CLUB, TOO?!
THERE'S A NEW GAME WE LIKE TO PLAY, YOU SEE...
!!
DON'T WORRY. THEY'RE FRIENDS OF MINE.
SAYOKO ...? YOU...?
YEP, THAT'S RIGHT.
I'M EXACTLY THE SORT OF GIRL YOU THOUGHT I WAS.

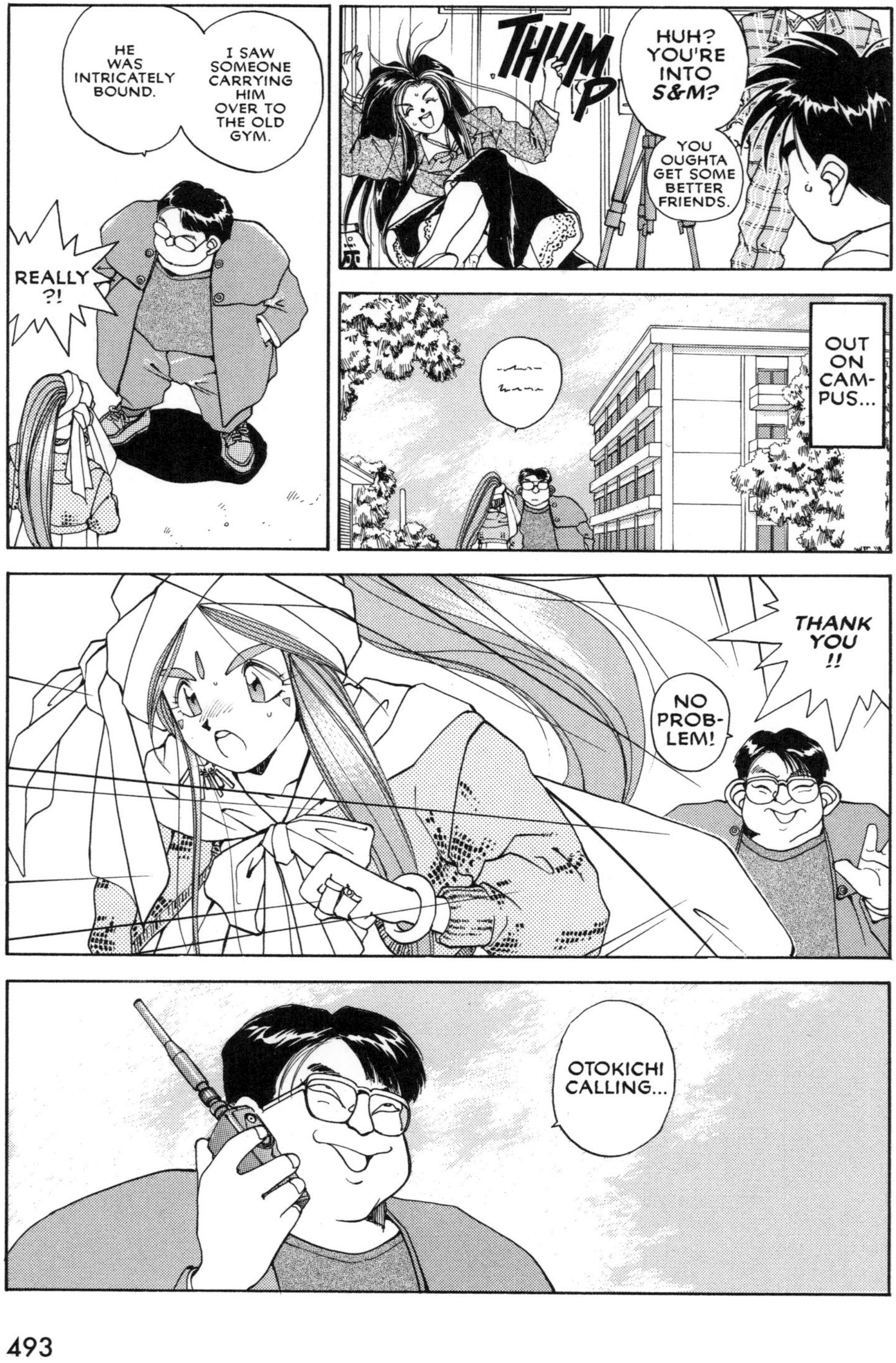
HUH? YOU'RE INTO S&M?
YOU OUGHTA GET SOME BETTER FRIENDS.
THUMP
OUT ON CAM-PUS...
I SAW SOMEONE CARRYING HIM OVER TO THE OLD GYM.
HE WAS INTRICATELY BOUND.
REALLY ?!
THANK YOU !!
NO PROB-LEM!
OTOKICHI CALLING...

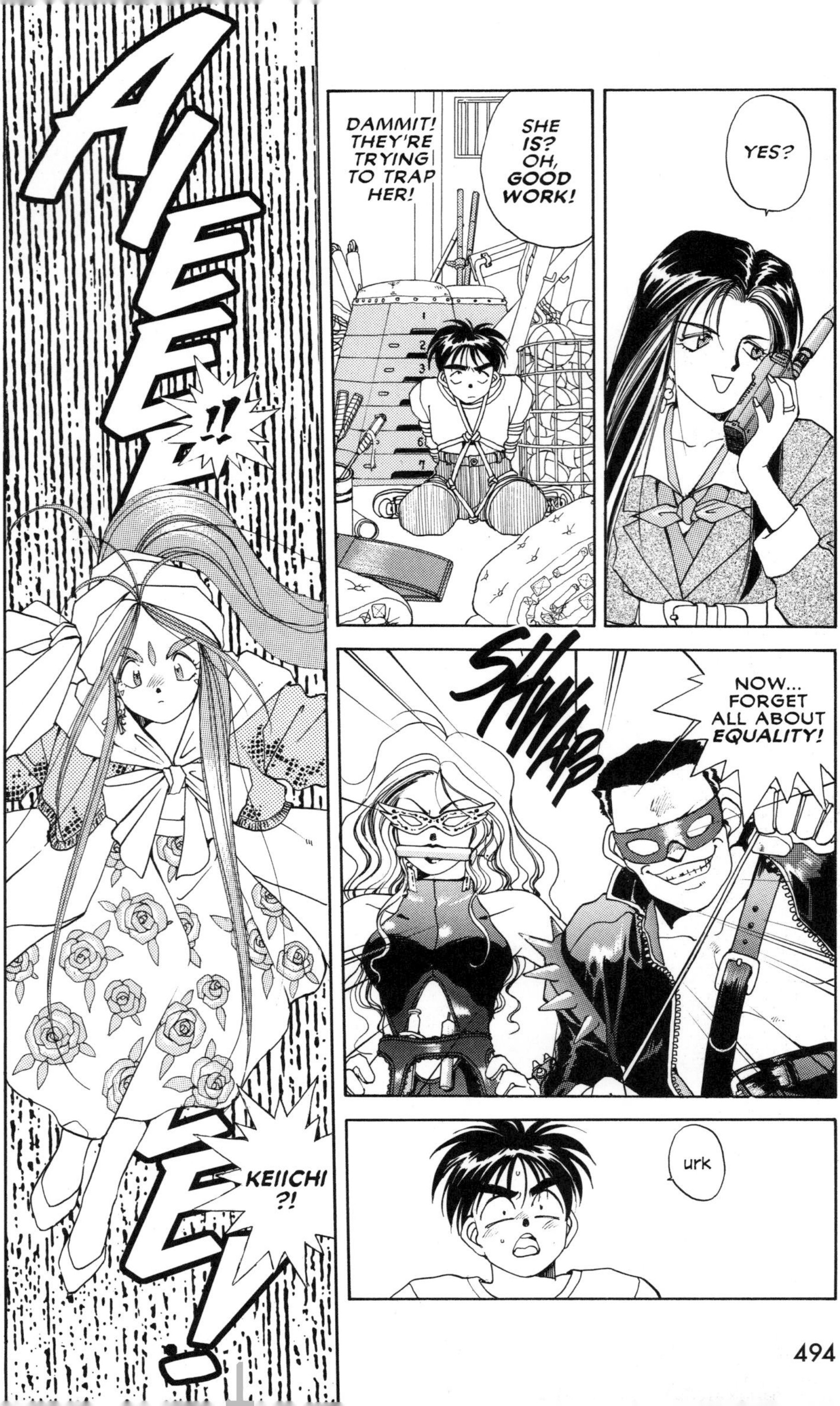
YES?
SHE IS? OH, GOOD WORK!
DAMMIT! THEY'RE TRYING TO TRAP HER!
SHWAP
NOW... FORGET ALL ABOUT EQUALITY!
urk
AIEEE
!!
KEIICHI ?!

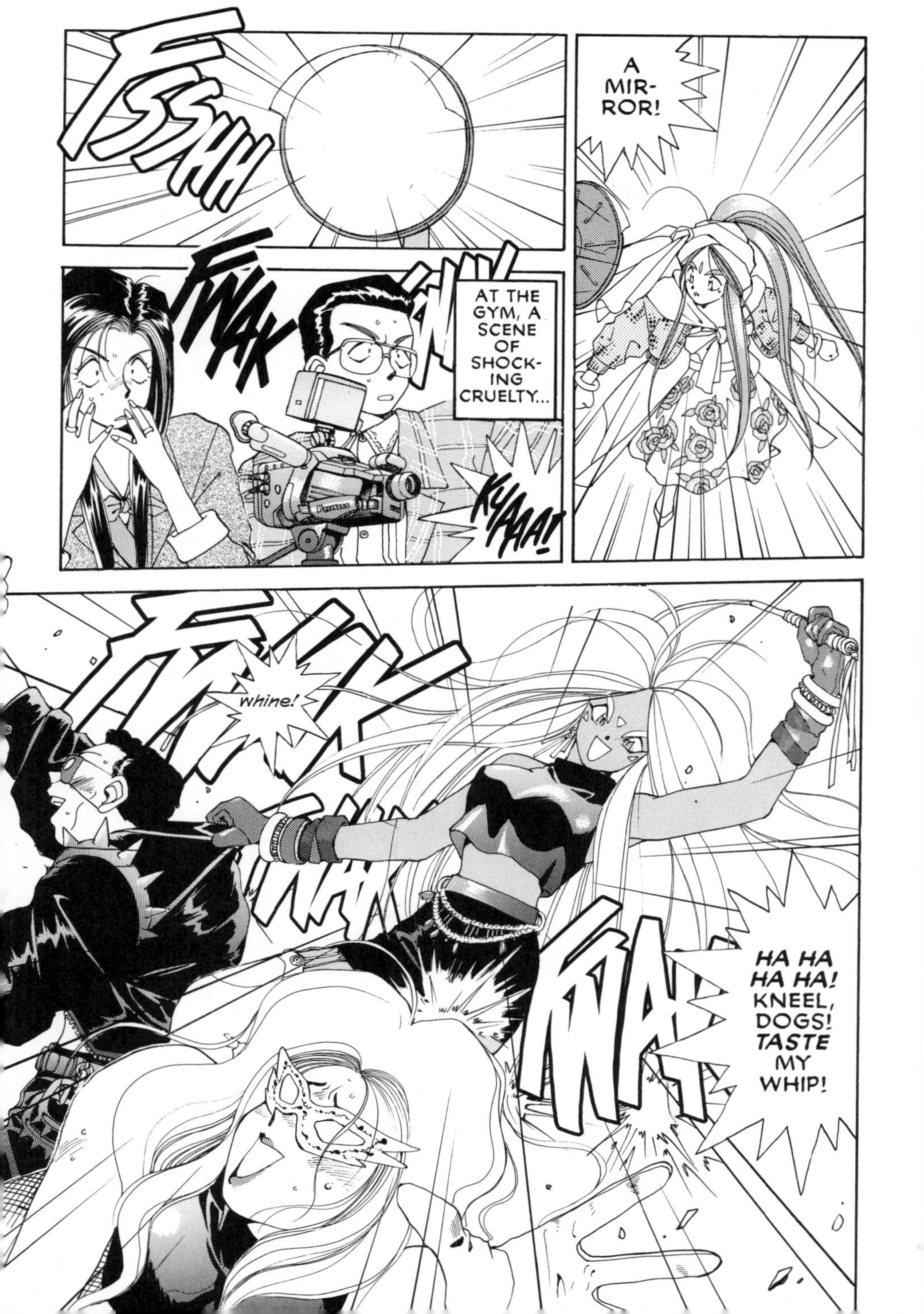
A MIR-ROR!
FSSHH
AT THE GYM, A SCENE OF SHOCKING CRUELTY...
FWAK
KYAAAA!
HA HA HA HA! KNEEL, DOGS! TASTE MY WHIP!
FWAK
whine!
FWAK

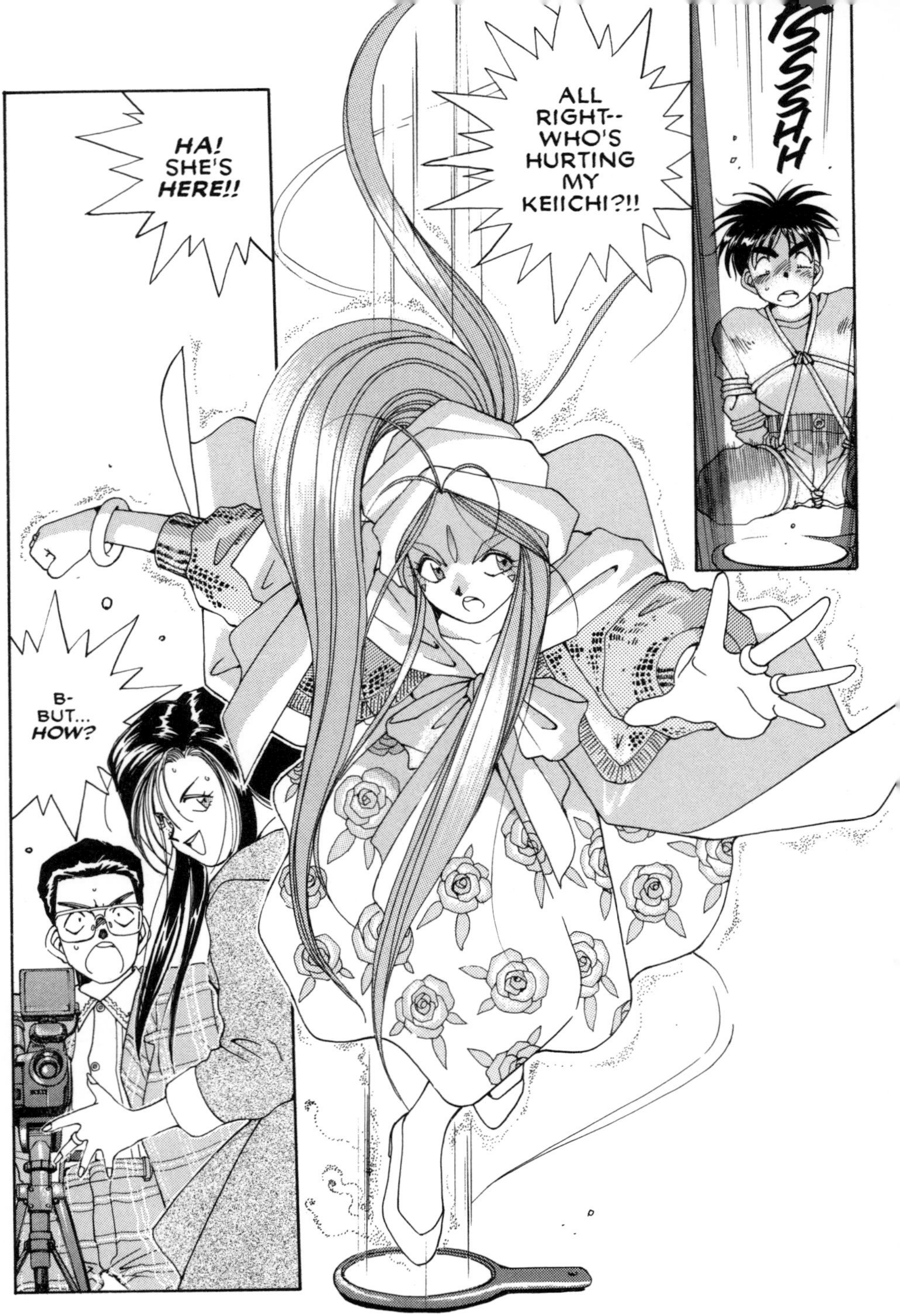
SSSSHH
ALL RIGHT-- WHO'S HURTING MY KEIICHI?!!
HA! SHE'S HERE!!
B-BUT... HOW?

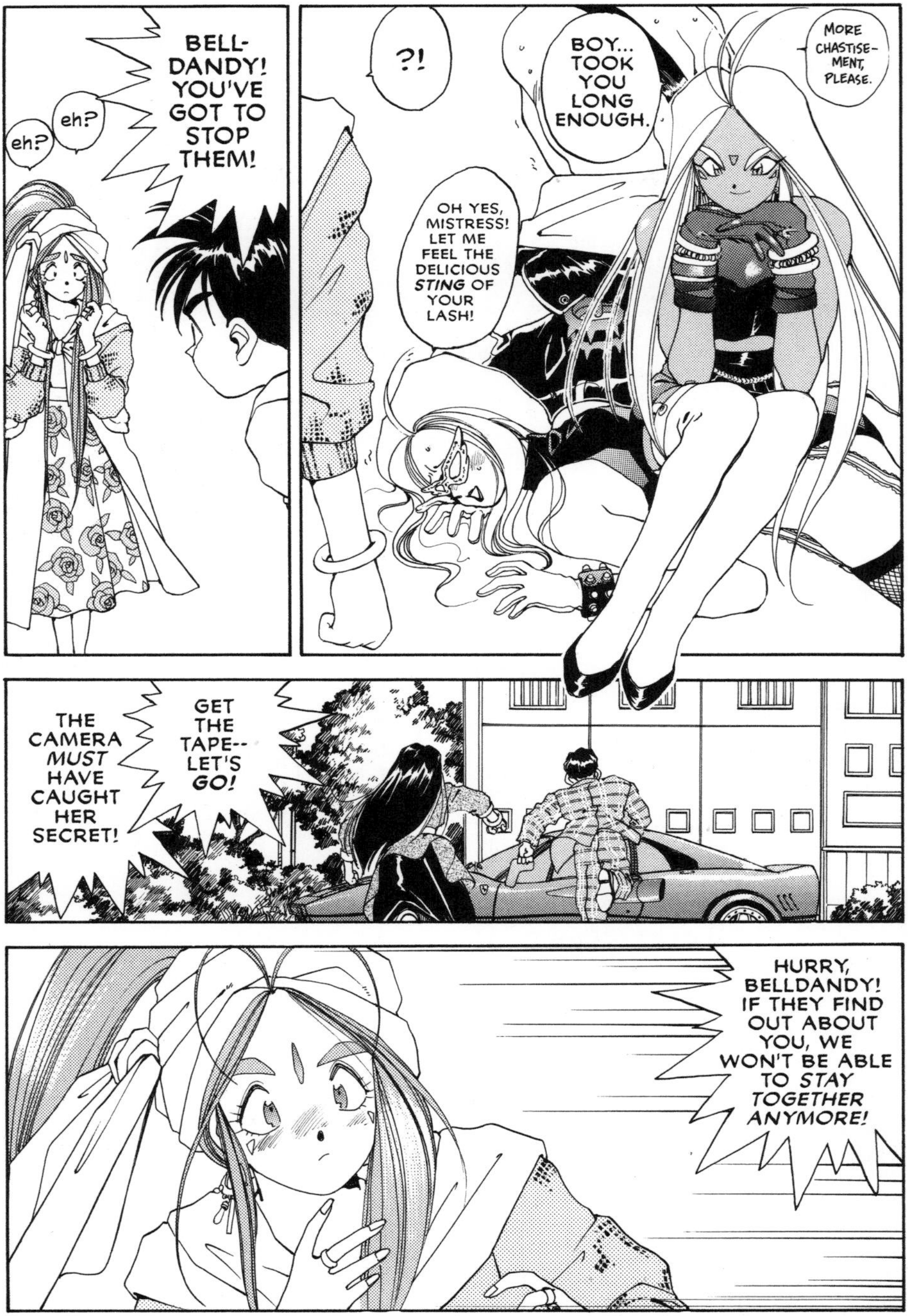
MORE CHASTISE-MENT, PLEASE.
BOY... TOOK YOU LONG ENOUGH.
?!
OH YES, MISTRESS! LET ME FEEL THE DELICIOUS *STING* OF YOUR LASH!
BELL-DANDY! YOU'VE GOT TO STOP THEM!
eh?
eh?
GET THE TAPE-- LET'S *GO!*
THE CAMERA *MUST* HAVE CAUGHT HER SECRET!
HURRY, BELLDANDY! IF THEY FIND OUT ABOUT YOU, WE WON'T BE ABLE TO *STAY TOGETHER ANYMORE!*

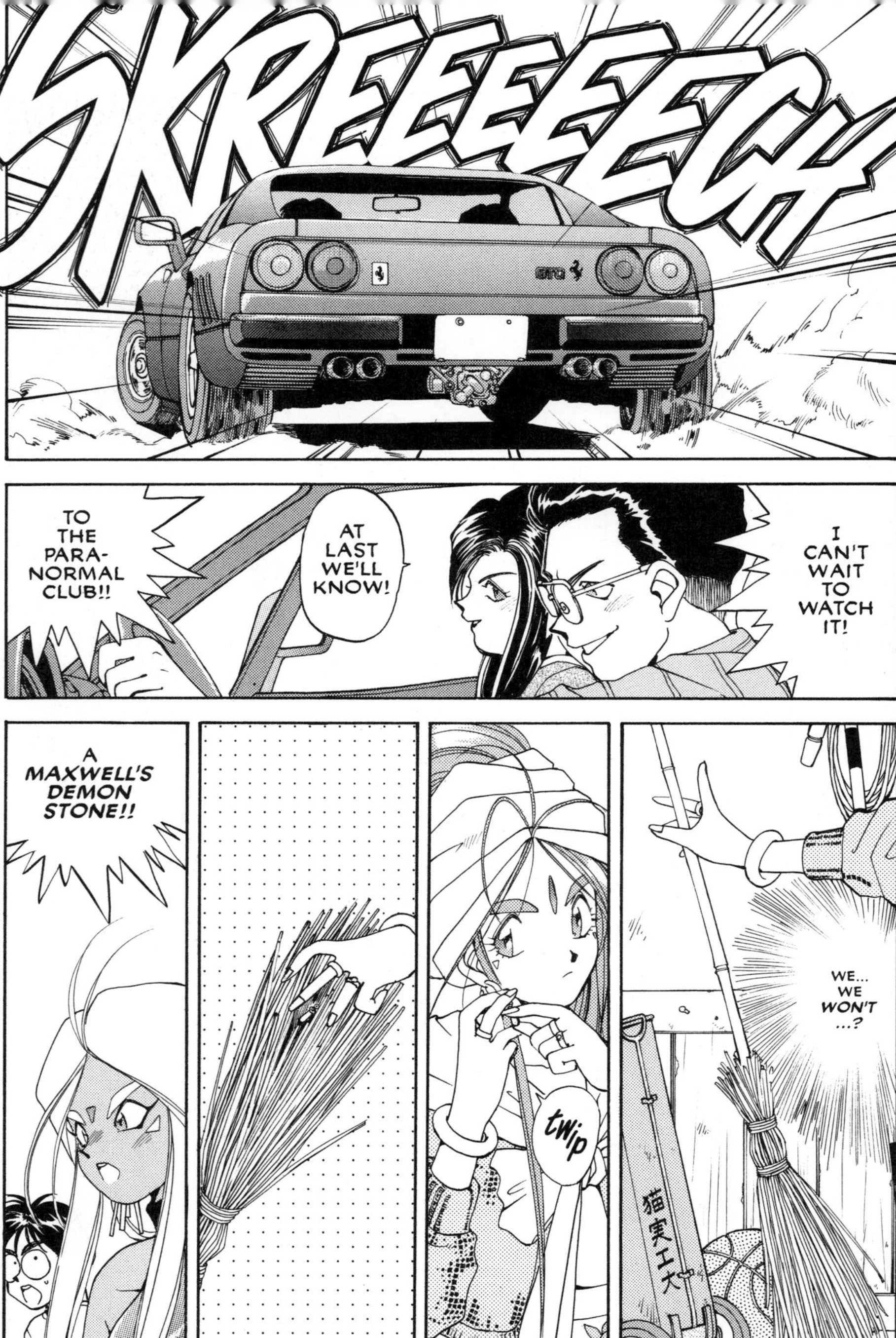
SKREEEEECH
I CAN'T WAIT TO WATCH IT!
AT LAST WE'LL KNOW!
TO THE PARA-NORMAL CLUB!!
WE... WE WON'T ...?
猫実工大
twip
A MAXWELL'S DEMON STONE!!

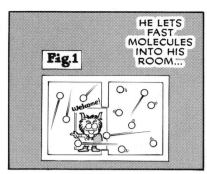

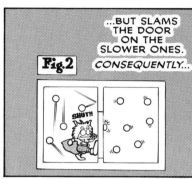

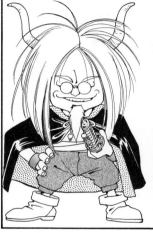

LIKE THE LAPLACIAN DEMON STONE, THIS IS A POWERFUL SPIRIT-STONE.
MAXWELL'S DEMON HAS THE ABILITY TO SEPARATE *FAST* MOLECULES FROM *SLOW* MOLECULES.
HE LETS FAST MOLECULES INTO HIS ROOM...
Fig.1
Welcome!
...BUT SLAMS THE DOOR ON THE SLOWER ONES.
CONSEQUENTLY...
Fig.2
SHUT!!
...AS THE ROOM FILLS WITH FAST MOLECULES, IT QUICKLY HEATS UP DUE TO THEIR ENERGY. THE DEMON PUSHES THE HOT GAS OUT, THEN FILLS THE ROOM UP AGAIN, OVER AND OVER.
YOU TAKE CARE OF THINGS HERE, URD!
THAT HOT AIR SERVES AS LIFT AND THRUST. AND NOW *YOU* KNOW THE SCIENCE BEHIND...

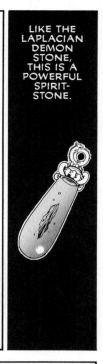

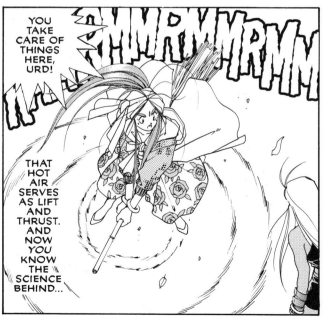

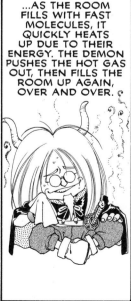

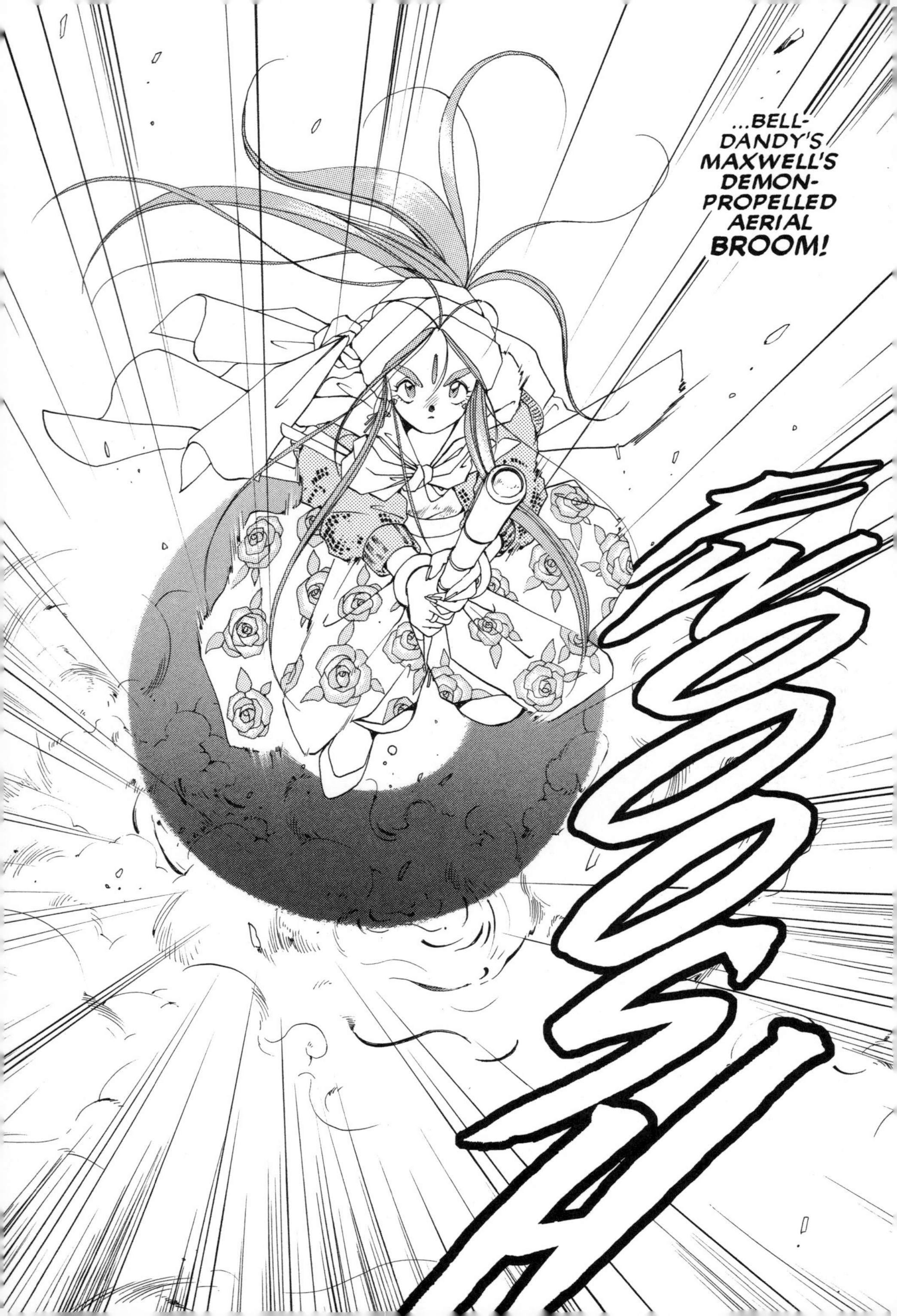
...BELL-DANDY'S MAXWELL'S DEMON-PROPELLED AERIAL BROOM!

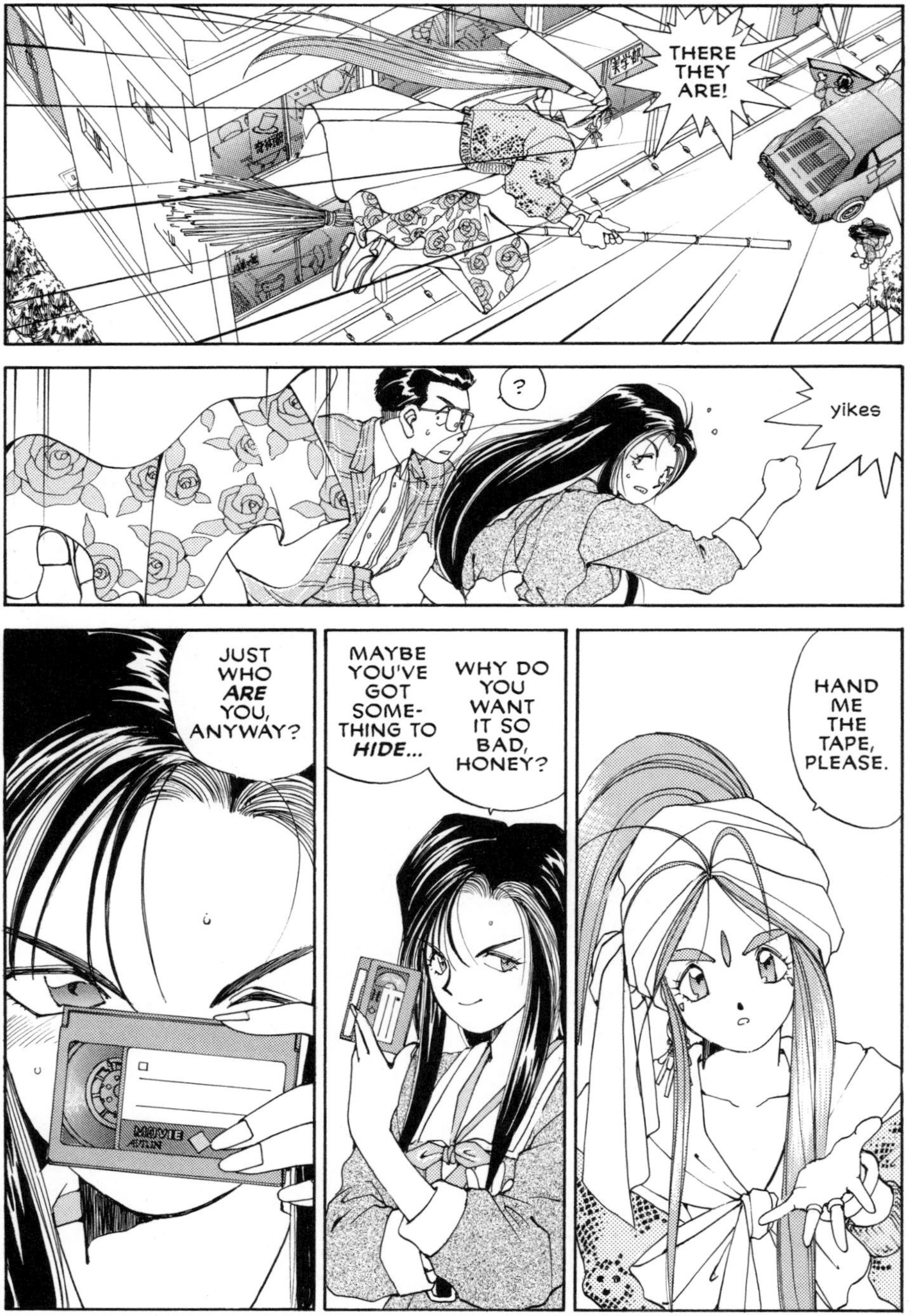
THERE THEY ARE!
yikes
?
HAND ME THE TAPE, PLEASE.
WHY DO YOU WANT IT SO BAD, HONEY?
MAYBE YOU'VE GOT SOME-THING TO ***HIDE...***
JUST WHO ***ARE*** YOU, ANYWAY?

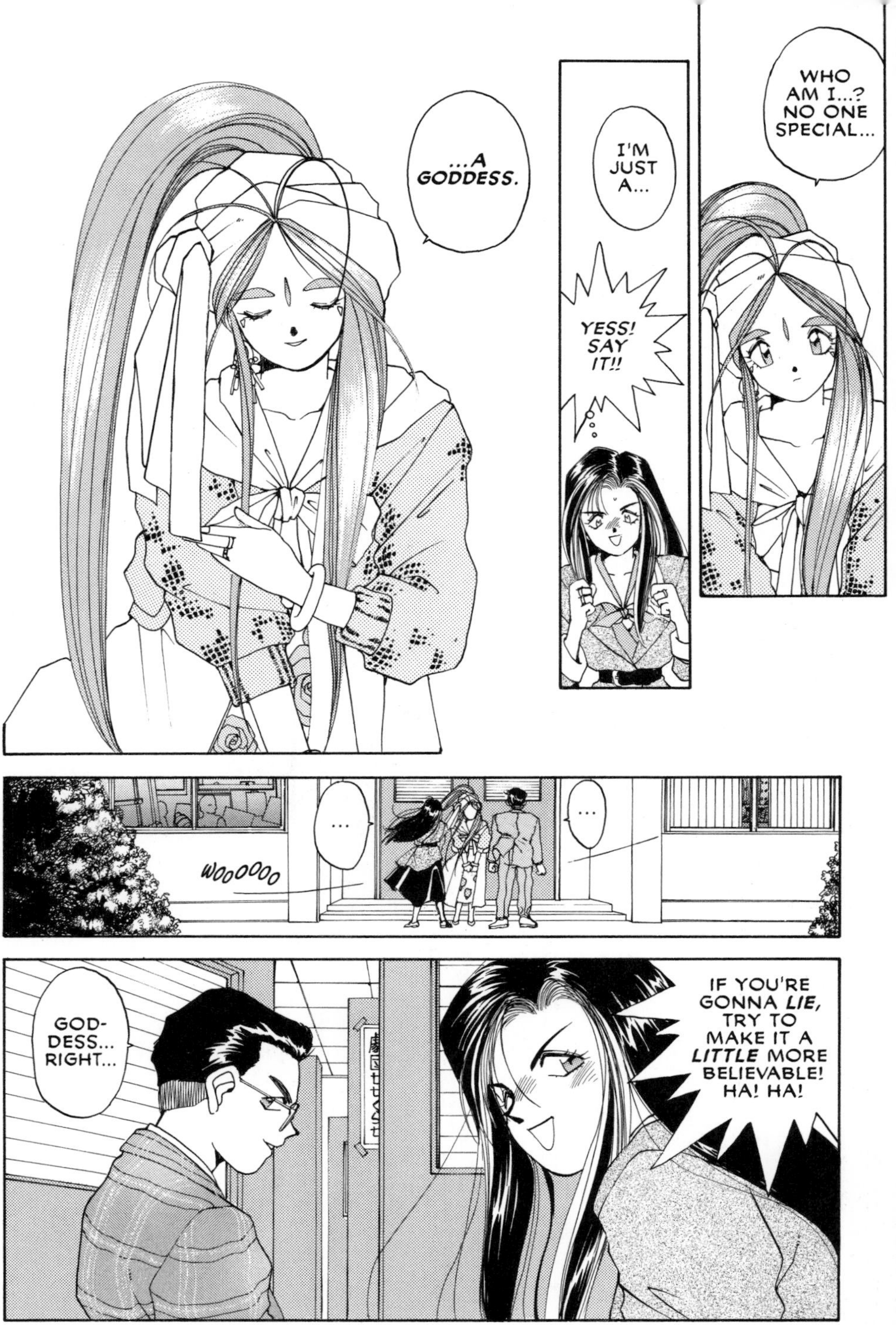
WHO AM I...? NO ONE SPECIAL...
I'M JUST A...
YESS! SAY IT!!
...A GODDESS.
...
...
WOOOOOO
IF YOU'RE GONNA LIE, TRY TO MAKE IT A LITTLE MORE BELIEVABLE! HA! HA!
GOD-DESS... RIGHT...

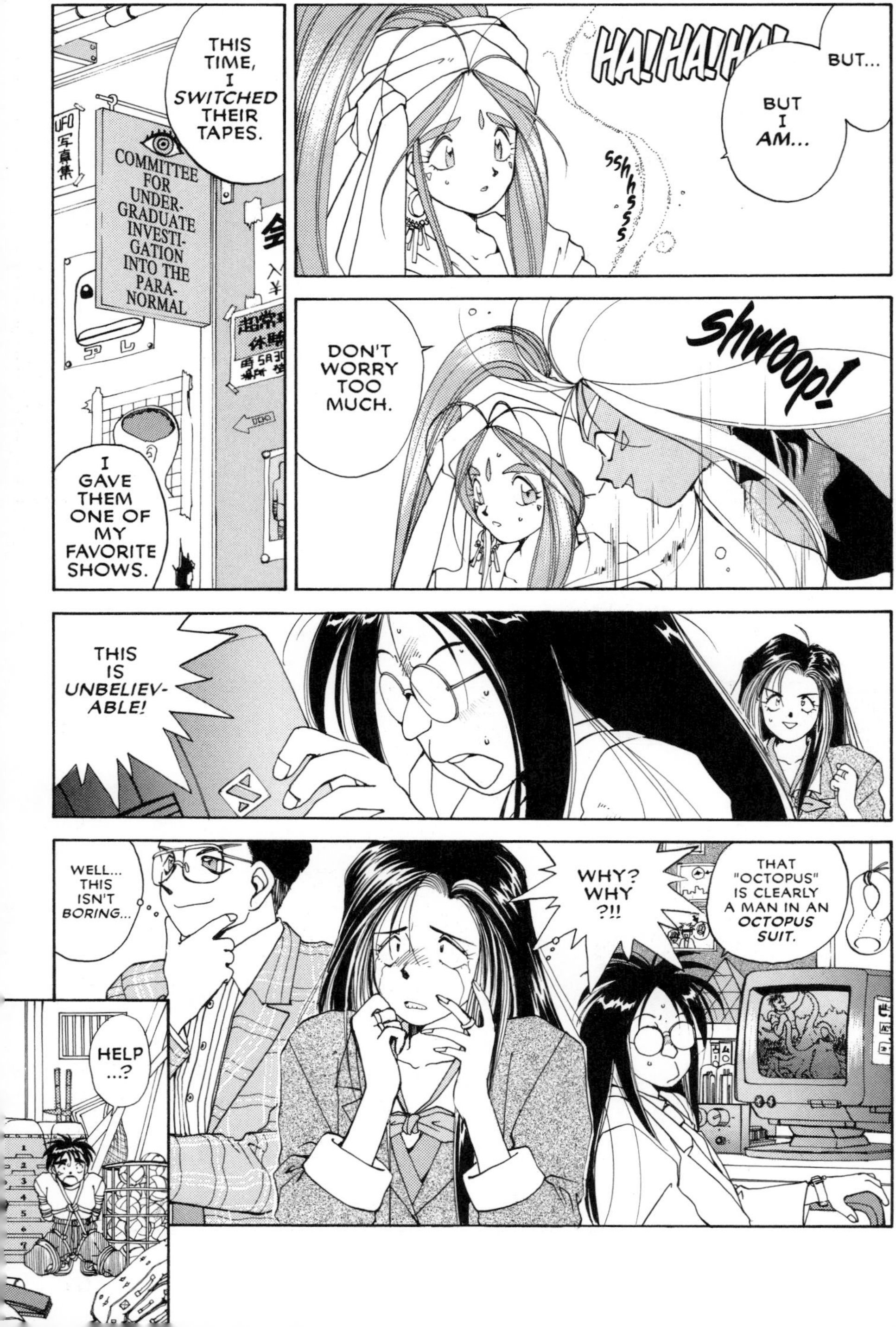
BUT...
BUT I AM...
HA!HA!HA!
sshhsss
shwoop!
DON'T WORRY TOO MUCH.
THIS TIME, I SWITCHED THEIR TAPES.
UFO 写真集
COMMITTEE FOR UNDER-GRADUATE INVESTI-GATION INTO THE PARA-NORMAL
I GAVE THEM ONE OF MY FAVORITE SHOWS.
THIS IS UNBELIEVABLE!
THAT "OCTOPUS" IS CLEARLY A MAN IN AN OCTOPUS SUIT.
WHY? WHY ?!!
WELL... THIS ISN'T BORING...
HELP ...?

SPECIAL BONUS! CONCEPT DRAWINGS FOR THE "MINI-BELLDANDY" AND "MINI-URD" DOLLS

RIGHT SIDE REAR FRONT

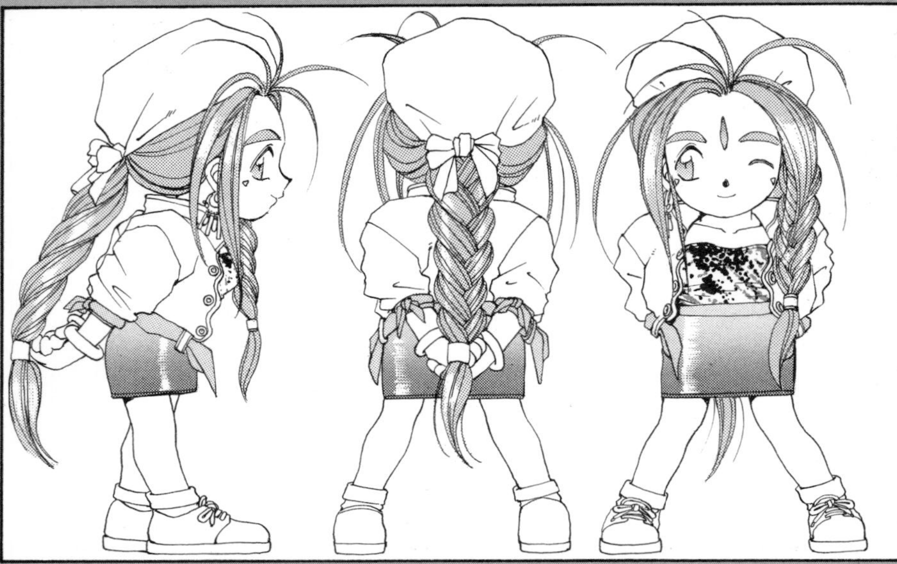

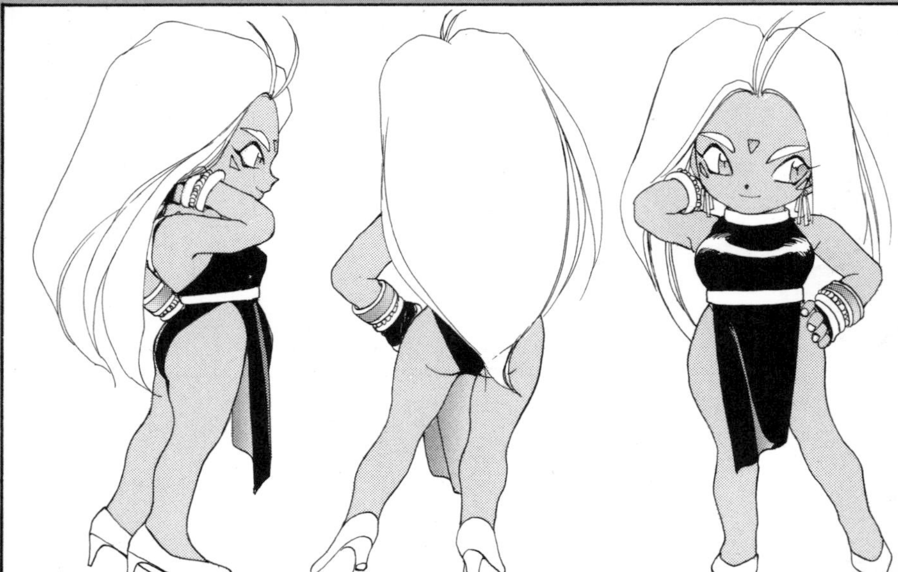

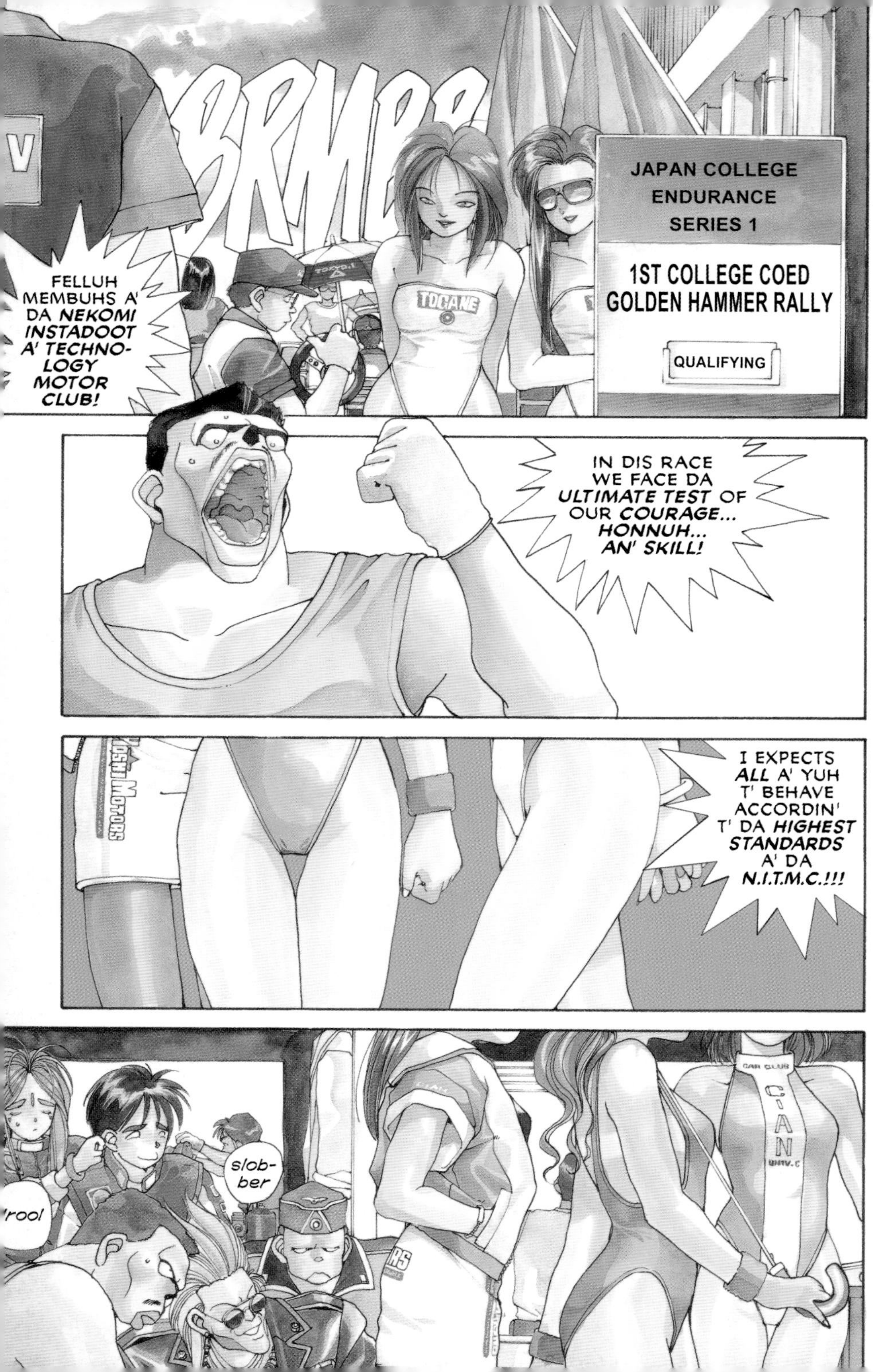
JAPAN COLLEGE ENDURANCE SERIES 1
1ST COLLEGE COED GOLDEN HAMMER RALLY
QUALIFYING
TOGANE
FELLUH MEMBUHS A' DA NEKOMI INSTADOOT A' TECHNOLOGY MOTOR CLUB!
IN DIS RACE WE FACE DA ULTIMATE TEST OF OUR COURAGE... HONNUH... AN' SKILL!
I EXPECTS ALL A' YUH T' BEHAVE ACCORDIN' T' DA HIGHEST STANDARDS A' DA N.I.T.M.C.!!!
CAR CLUB
C I A N
slob-ber
'rool

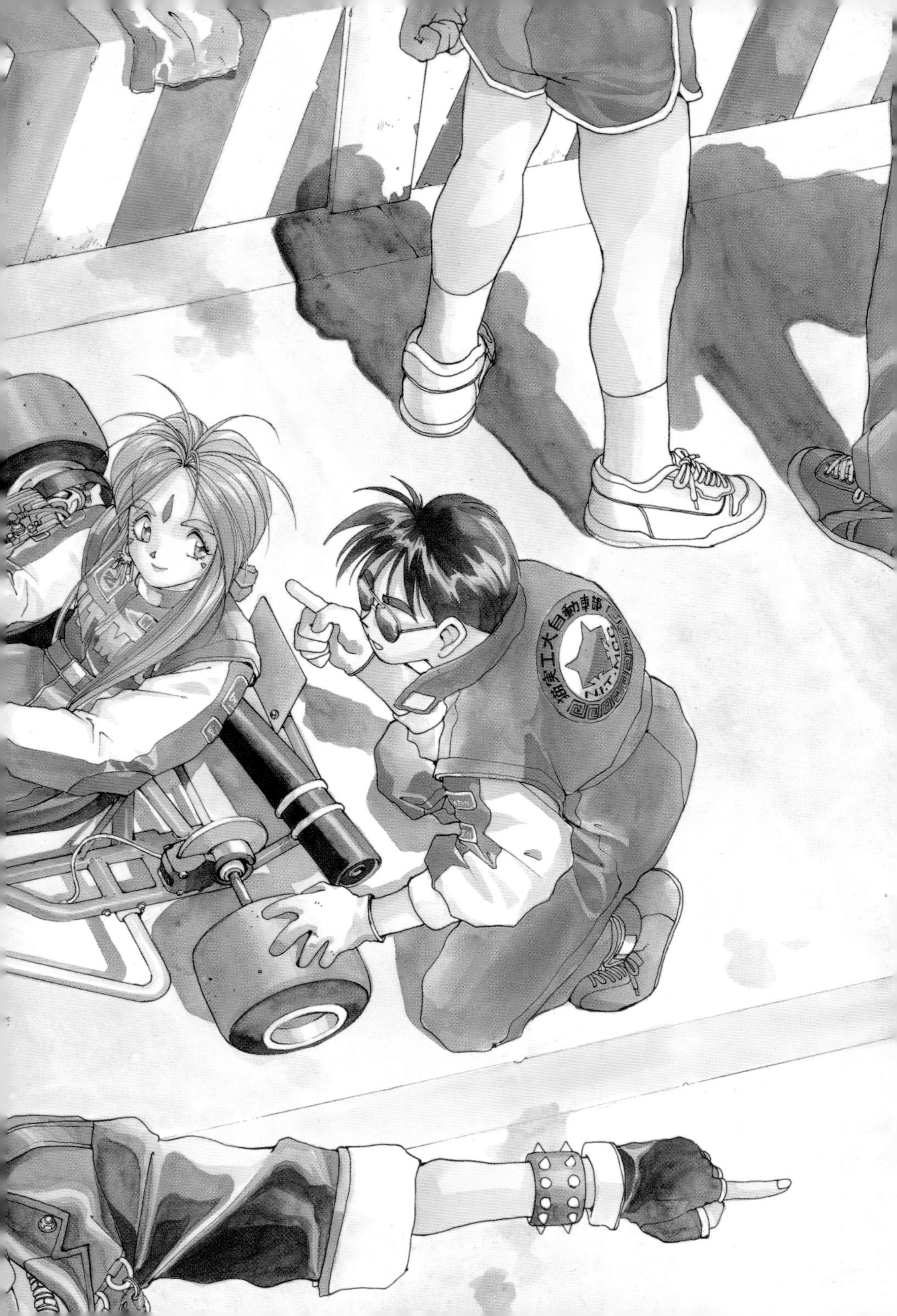
猫実工大自動車部
N.I.T. M.C.C.

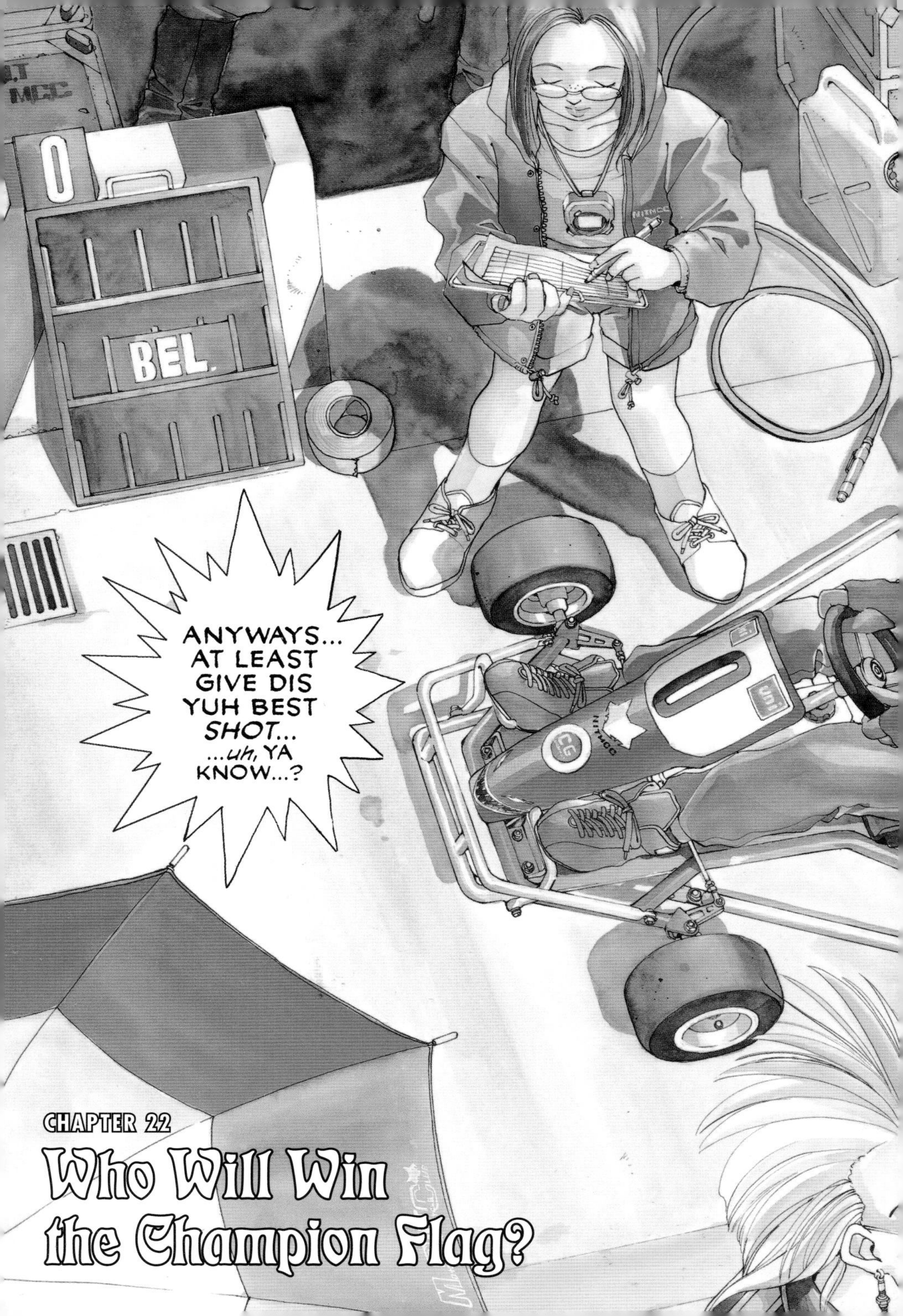
ANYWAYS... AT LEAST GIVE DIS YUH BEST *SHOT*... ...*uh,* YA KNOW...?

CHAPTER 22

Who Will Win the Champion Flag?

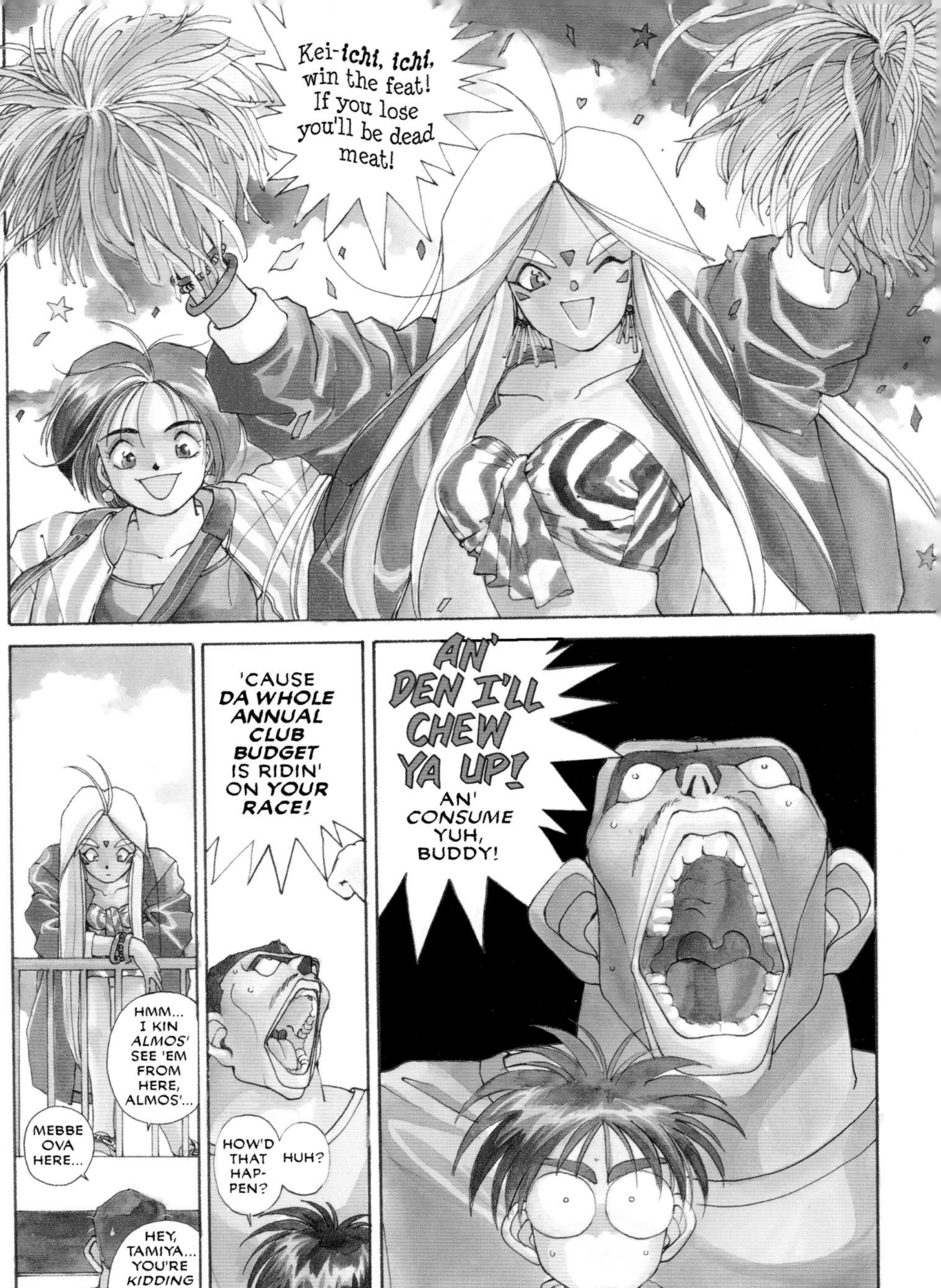
Kei-ichi, ichi, win the feat! If you lose you'll be dead meat!
AN' DEN I'LL CHEW YA UP!
AN' CONSUME YUH, BUDDY!
'CAUSE DA WHOLE ANNUAL CLUB BUDGET IS RIDIN' ON YOUR RACE!
HUH?
HOW'D THAT HAP-PEN?
HMM... I KIN ALMOS' SEE 'EM FROM HERE, ALMOS'...
MEBBE OVA HERE...
HEY, TAMIYA... YOU'RE KIDDING ABOUT OUR BUDGET, RIGHT?

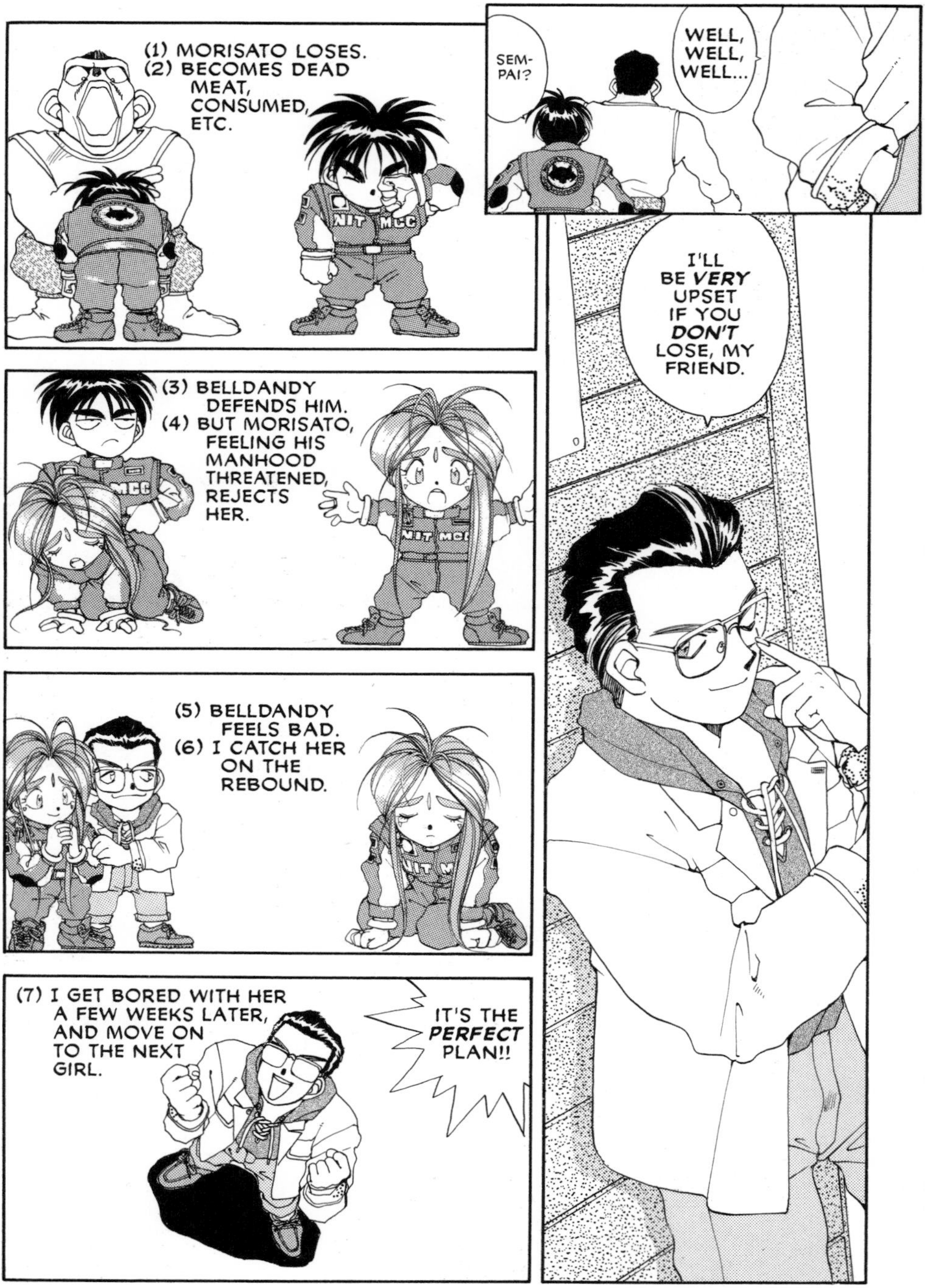
WELL, WELL, WELL...
SEM-PAI?
I'LL BE VERY UPSET IF YOU DON'T LOSE, MY FRIEND.
(1) MORISATO LOSES.
(2) BECOMES DEAD MEAT, CONSUMED, ETC.
NIT MCC
(3) BELLDANDY DEFENDS HIM.
(4) BUT MORISATO, FEELING HIS MANHOOD THREATENED, REJECTS HER.
(5) BELLDANDY FEELS BAD.
(6) I CATCH HER ON THE REBOUND.
(7) I GET BORED WITH HER A FEW WEEKS LATER, AND MOVE ON TO THE NEXT GIRL.
IT'S THE PERFECT PLAN!!

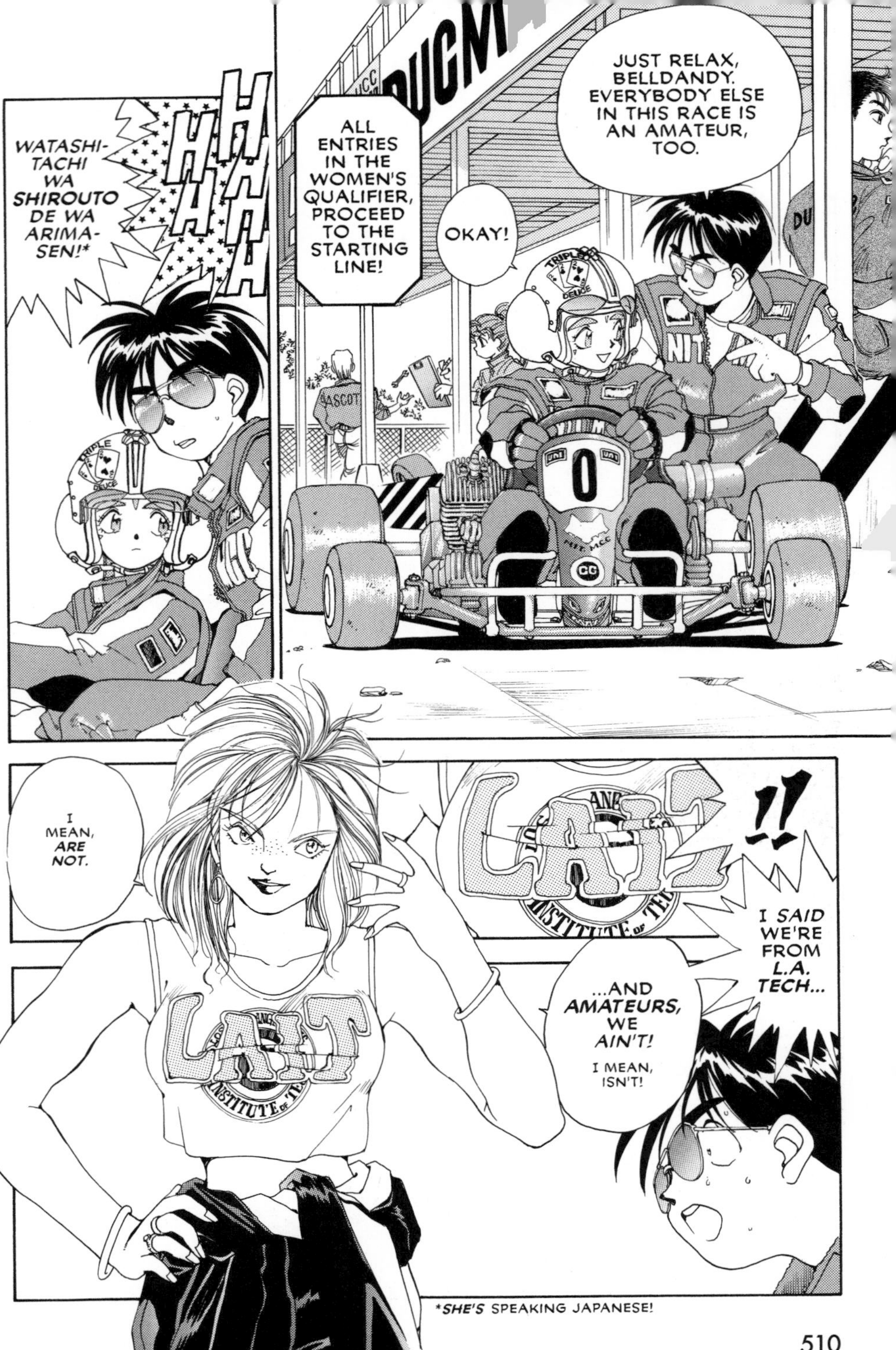
JUST RELAX, BELLDANDY. EVERYBODY ELSE IN THIS RACE IS AN AMATEUR, TOO.
ALL ENTRIES IN THE WOMEN'S QUALIFIER, PROCEED TO THE STARTING LINE!
OKAY!
HHHHHHH
WATASHI-TACHI WA SHIROUTO DE WA ARIMA-SEN!*
!!
I SAID WE'RE FROM L.A. TECH...
...AND AMATEURS, WE AIN'T!
I MEAN, ISN'T!
I MEAN, ARE NOT.

*SHE'S SPEAKING JAPANESE!

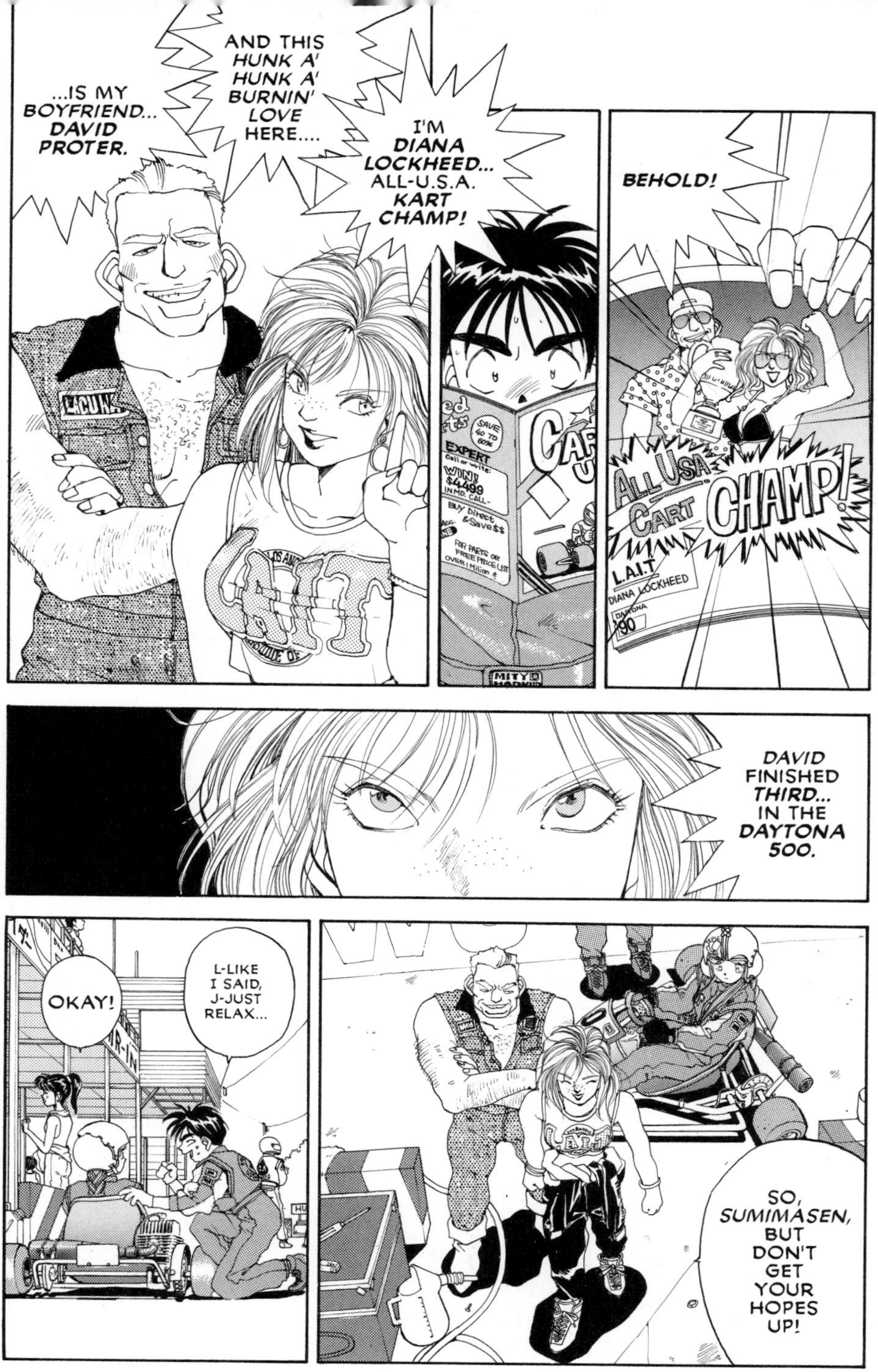
BEHOLD!
ALL USA CART CHAMP!
L.A.I.T
DIANA LOCKHEED
DAYTONA 90
SAVE 40 TO 60%
EXPERT
Call or write:
WIN! $4499
Buy Direct &Save$$
FREE PRICE LIST
I'M DIANA LOCKHEED... ALL-U.S.A. KART CHAMP!
AND THIS HUNK A' HUNK A' BURNIN' LOVE HERE....
...IS MY BOYFRIEND... DAVID PROTER.
DAVID FINISHED THIRD... IN THE DAYTONA 500.
SO, SUMIMASEN, BUT DON'T GET YOUR HOPES UP!
L-LIKE I SAID, J-JUST RELAX...
OKAY!

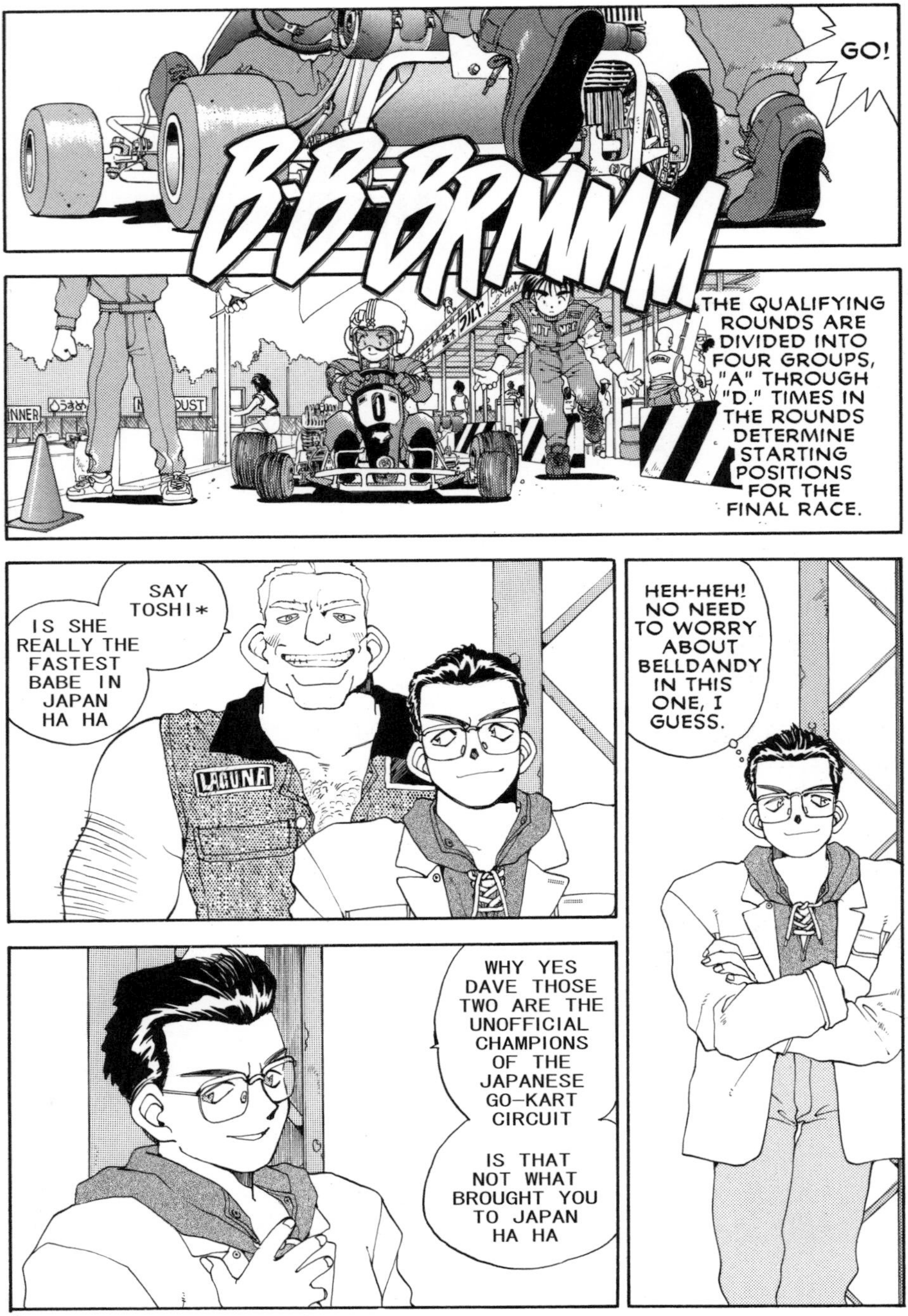
GO!
B-B-BRMMMM
THE QUALIFYING ROUNDS ARE DIVIDED INTO FOUR GROUPS, "A" THROUGH "D." TIMES IN THE ROUNDS DETERMINE STARTING POSITIONS FOR THE FINAL RACE.
HEH-HEH! NO NEED TO WORRY ABOUT BELLDANDY IN THIS ONE, I GUESS.
SAY TOSHI* IS SHE REALLY THE FASTEST BABE IN JAPAN HA HA
LAGUNA
WHY YES DAVE THOSE TWO ARE THE UNOFFICIAL CHAMPIONS OF THE JAPANESE GO-KART CIRCUIT
IS THAT NOT WHAT BROUGHT YOU TO JAPAN HA HA

*THEY'RE SPEAKING ENGLISH!

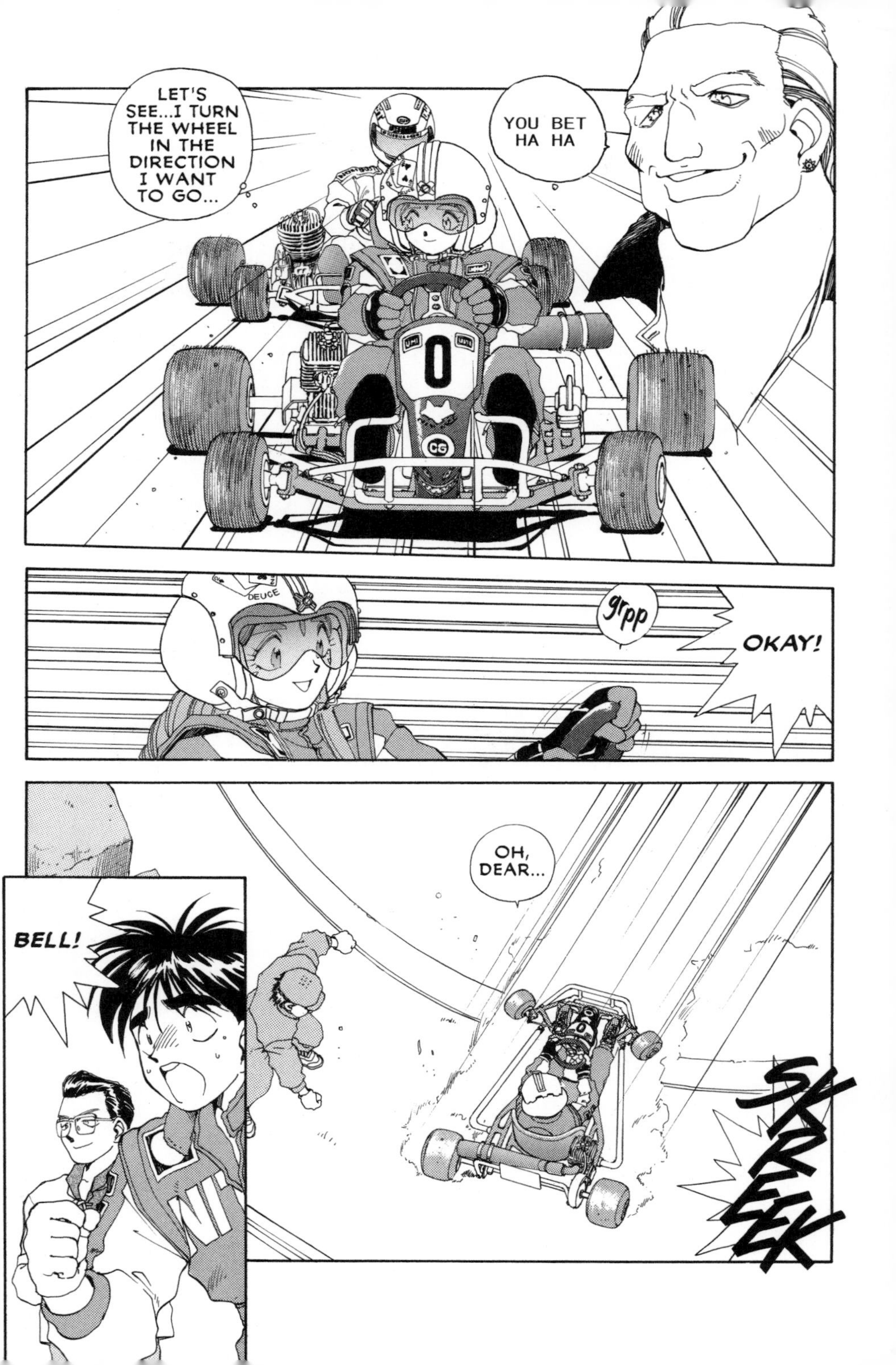
LET'S SEE...I TURN THE WHEEL IN THE DIRECTION I WANT TO GO...
YOU BET HA HA
OKAY!
grpp
OH, DEAR...
SKREEEK
BELL!

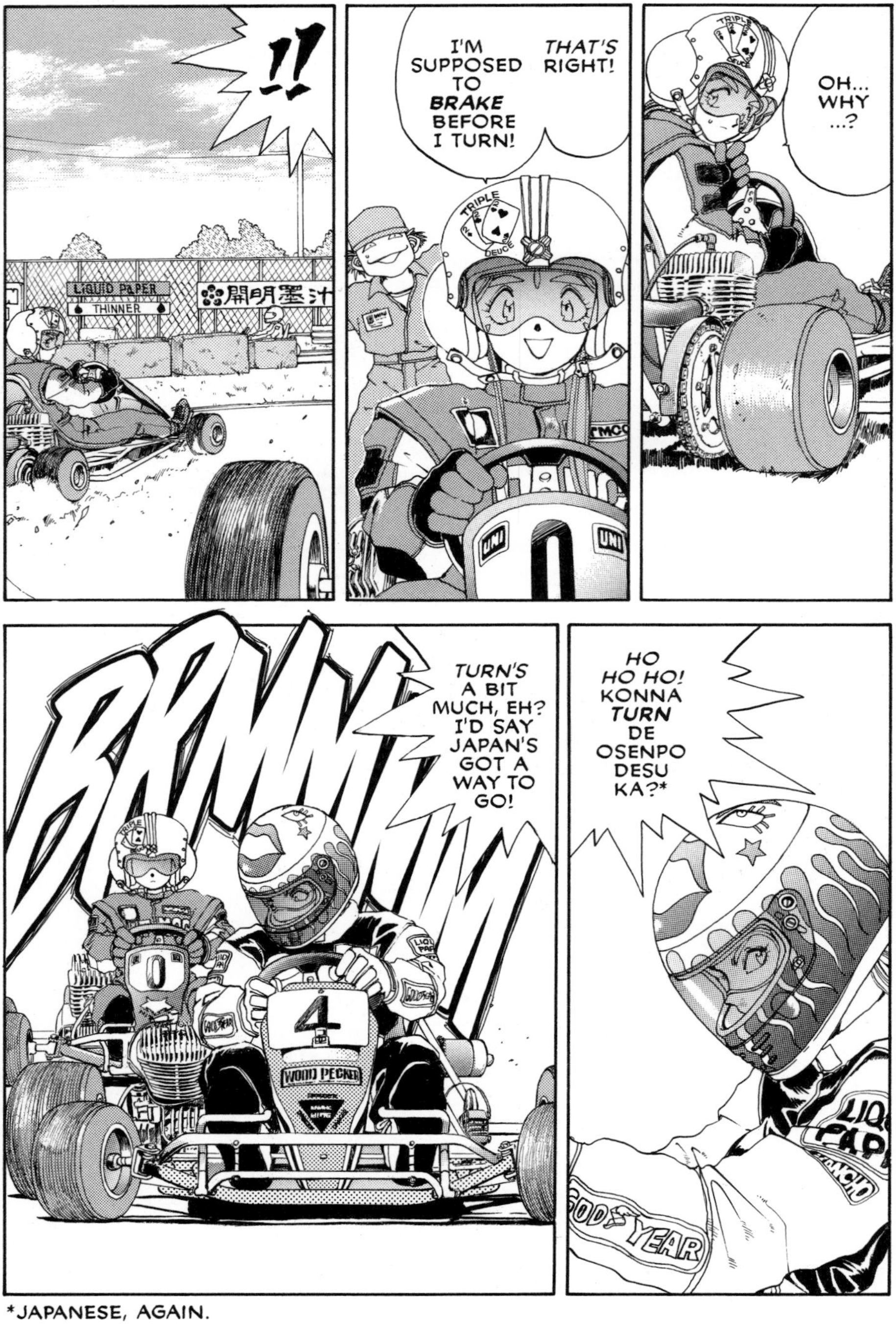
OH... WHY ...?
I'M SUPPOSED TO BRAKE BEFORE I TURN!
THAT'S RIGHT!
!!
LIQUID PAPER
THINNER
開明墨汁
HO HO HO! KONNA TURN DE OSENPO DESU KA?*
TURN'S A BIT MUCH, EH? I'D SAY JAPAN'S GOT A WAY TO GO!
BRMMMMM

*JAPANESE, AGAIN.

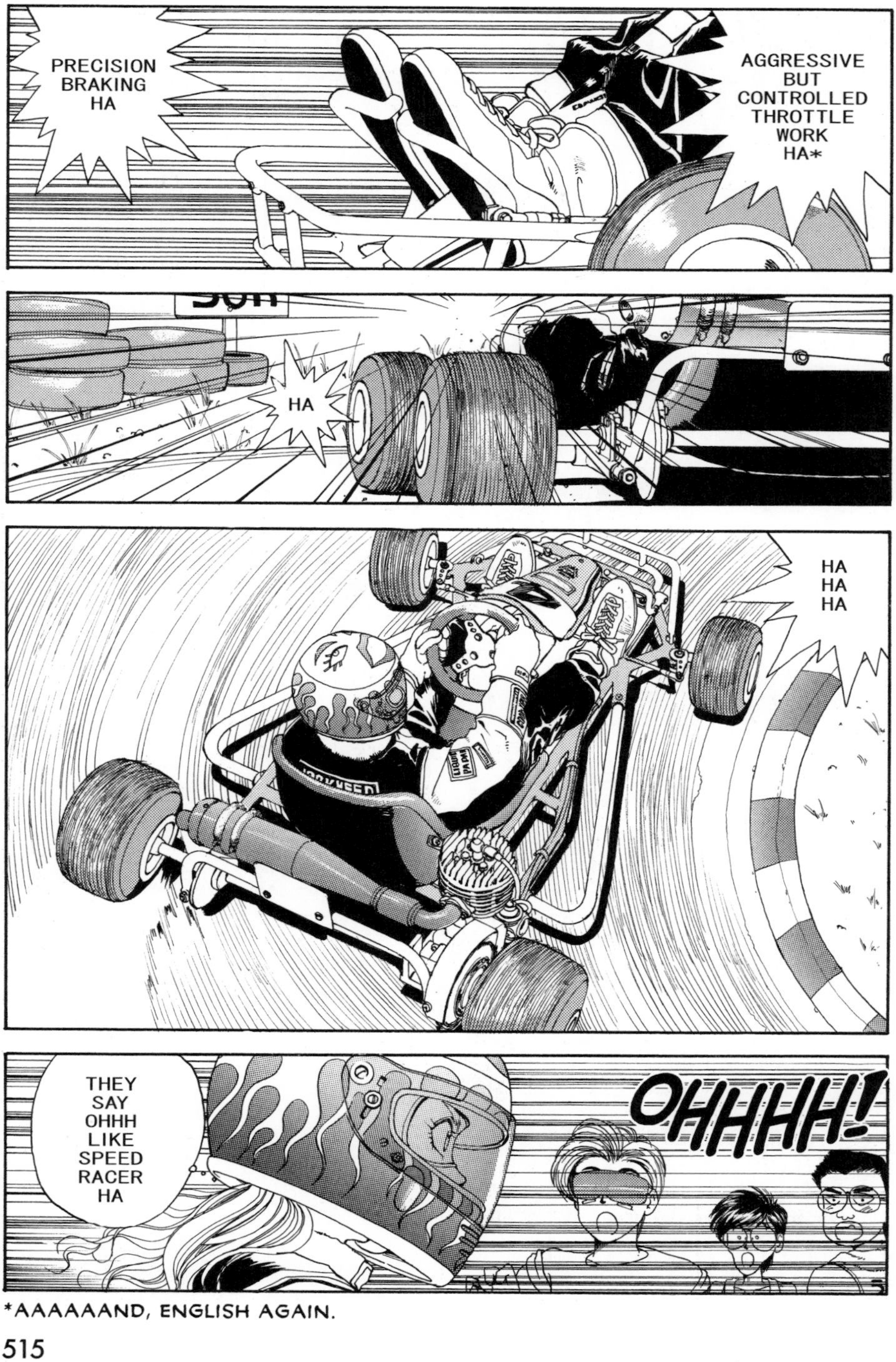
AGGRESSIVE BUT CONTROLLED THROTTLE WORK HA*
PRECISION BRAKING HA
HA
HA HA HA
OHHHH!
THEY SAY OHHH LIKE SPEED RACER HA

*AAAAAAND, ENGLISH AGAIN.

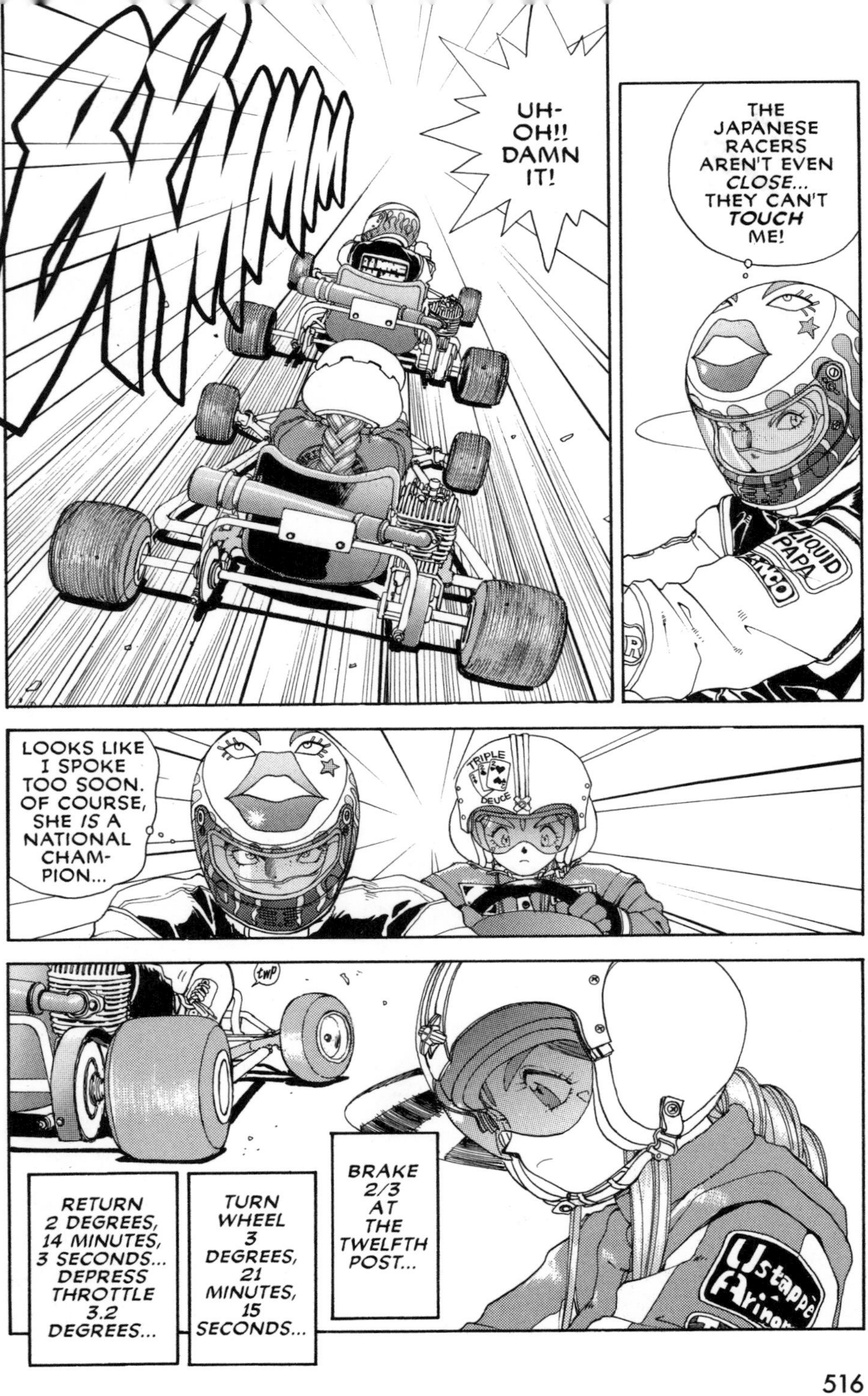

THE JAPANESE RACERS AREN'T EVEN *CLOSE*... THEY CAN'T *TOUCH* ME!
UH-OH!! DAMN IT!
LOOKS LIKE I SPOKE TOO SOON. OF COURSE, SHE *IS* A NATIONAL CHAMPION...
BRAKE 2/3 AT THE TWELFTH POST...
TURN WHEEL 3 DEGREES, 21 MINUTES, 15 SECONDS...
RETURN 2 DEGREES, 14 MINUTES, 3 SECONDS... DEPRESS THROTTLE 3.2 DEGREES...

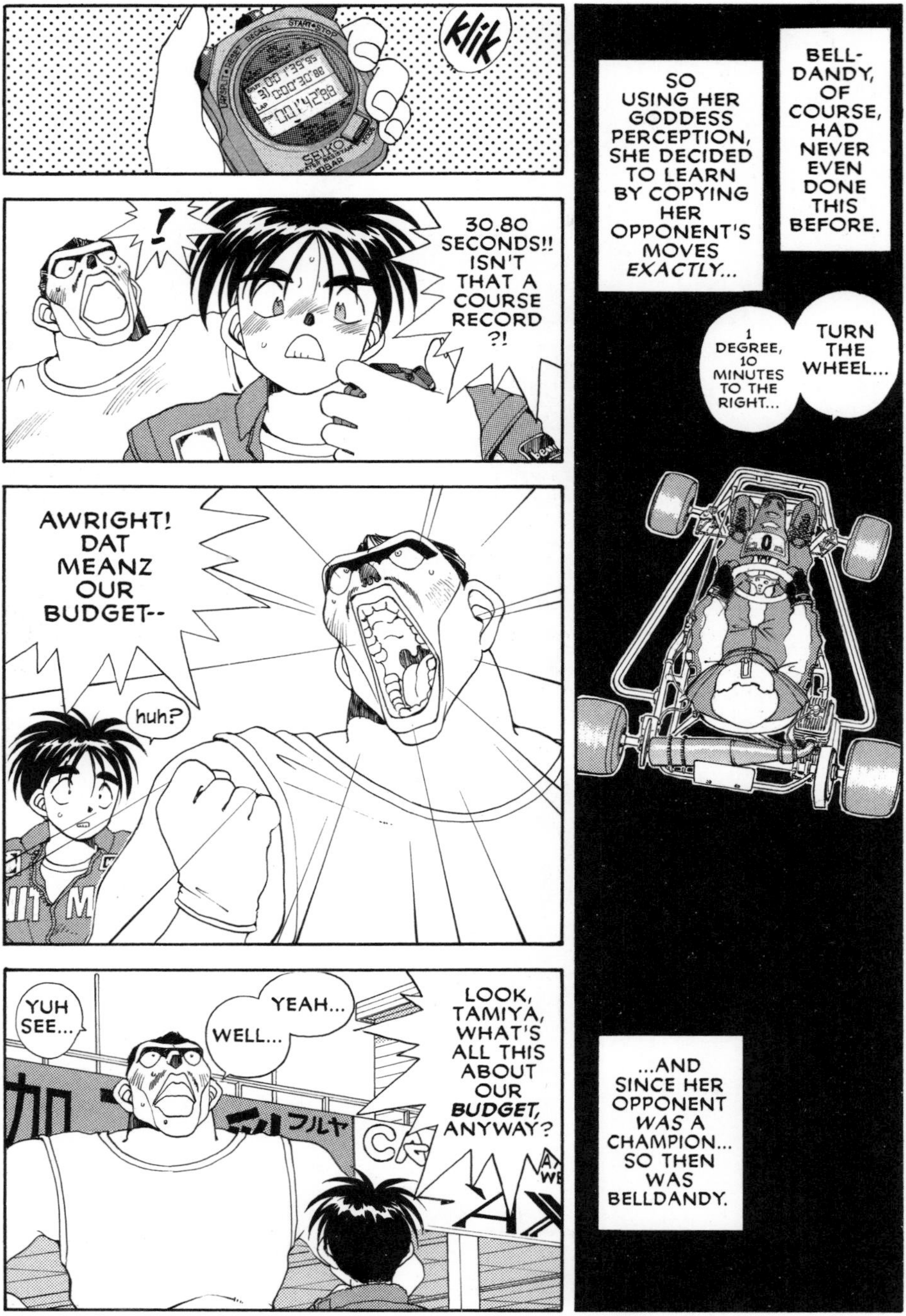
BELL-DANDY, OF COURSE, HAD NEVER EVEN DONE THIS BEFORE.
SO USING HER GODDESS PERCEPTION, SHE DECIDED TO LEARN BY COPYING HER OPPONENT'S MOVES *EXACTLY*...
TURN THE WHEEL...
1 DEGREE, 10 MINUTES TO THE RIGHT...
...AND SINCE HER OPPONENT *WAS* A CHAMPION... SO THEN WAS BELLDANDY.
klik
SEIKO
!
30.80 SECONDS!! ISN'T THAT A COURSE RECORD ?!
AWRIGHT! DAT MEANZ OUR BUDGET--
huh?
LOOK, TAMIYA, WHAT'S ALL THIS ABOUT OUR ***BUDGET***, ANYWAY?
YEAH...
WELL...
YUH SEE...

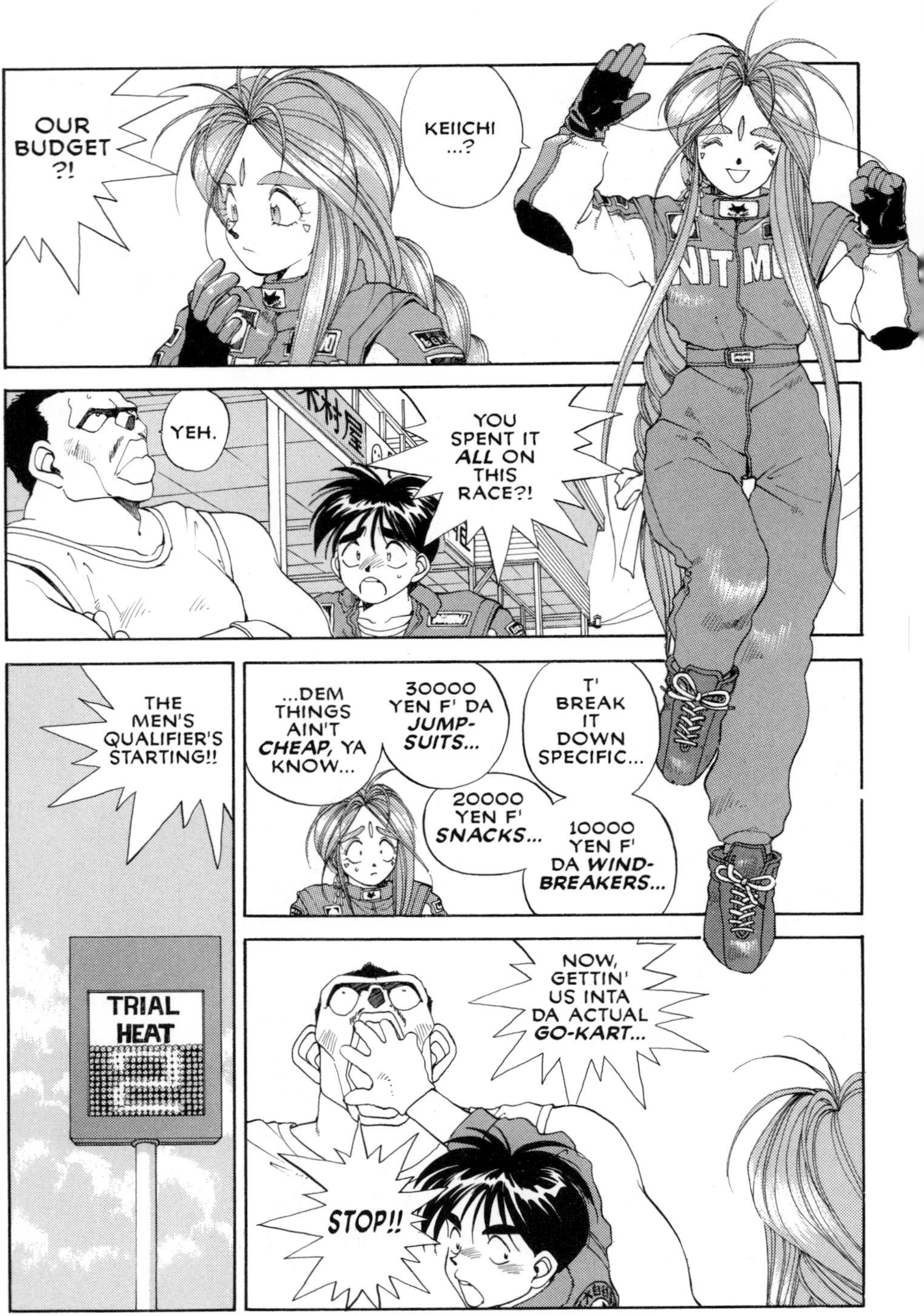
KEIICHI ...?
OUR BUDGET ?!
YOU SPENT IT ALL ON THIS RACE?!
YEH.
T' BREAK IT DOWN SPECIFIC...
30000 YEN F' DA JUMP-SUITS...
...DEM THINGS AIN'T CHEAP, YA KNOW...
20000 YEN F' SNACKS...
10000 YEN F' DA WIND-BREAKERS...
NOW, GETTIN' US INTA DA ACTUAL GO-KART...
STOP!!
THE MEN'S QUALIFIER'S STARTING!!
TRIAL HEAT

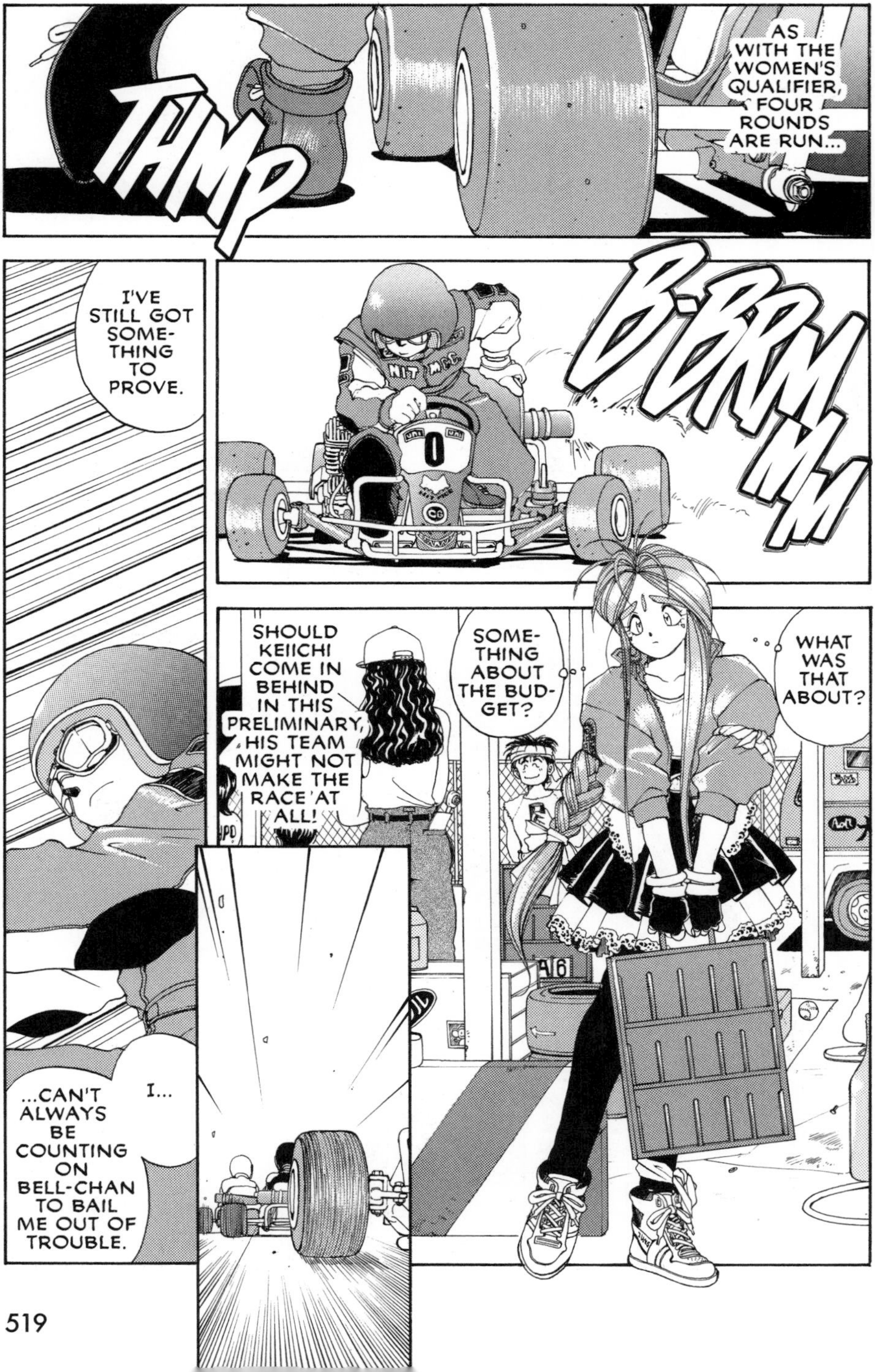

AS WITH THE WOMEN'S QUALIFIER, FOUR ROUNDS ARE RUN...
THAMP
B-BRMMMM
I'VE STILL GOT SOME-THING TO PROVE.
WHAT WAS THAT ABOUT?
SOME-THING ABOUT THE BUD-GET?
SHOULD KEIICHI COME IN BEHIND IN THIS PRELIMINARY, HIS TEAM MIGHT NOT MAKE THE RACE AT ALL!
I...
...CAN'T ALWAYS BE COUNTING ON BELL-CHAN TO BAIL ME OUT OF TROUBLE.

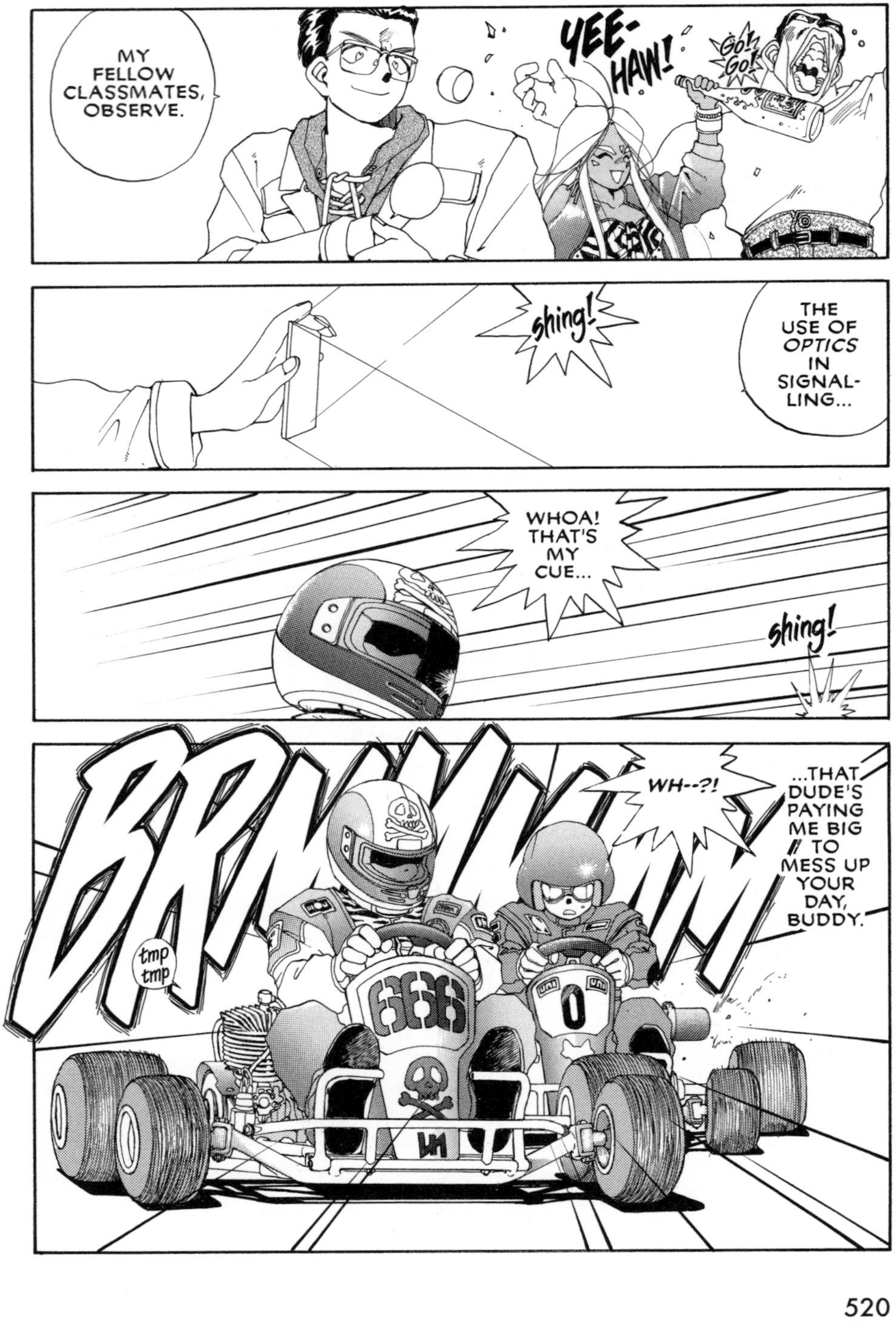
Go! Go!
YEE-HAW!
MY FELLOW CLASSMATES, OBSERVE.
THE USE OF *OPTICS* IN SIGNAL-LING...
shing!
WHOA! THAT'S MY CUE...
shing!
...THAT DUDE'S PAYING ME BIG TO MESS UP YOUR DAY, BUDDY.
WH--?!
tmp tmp

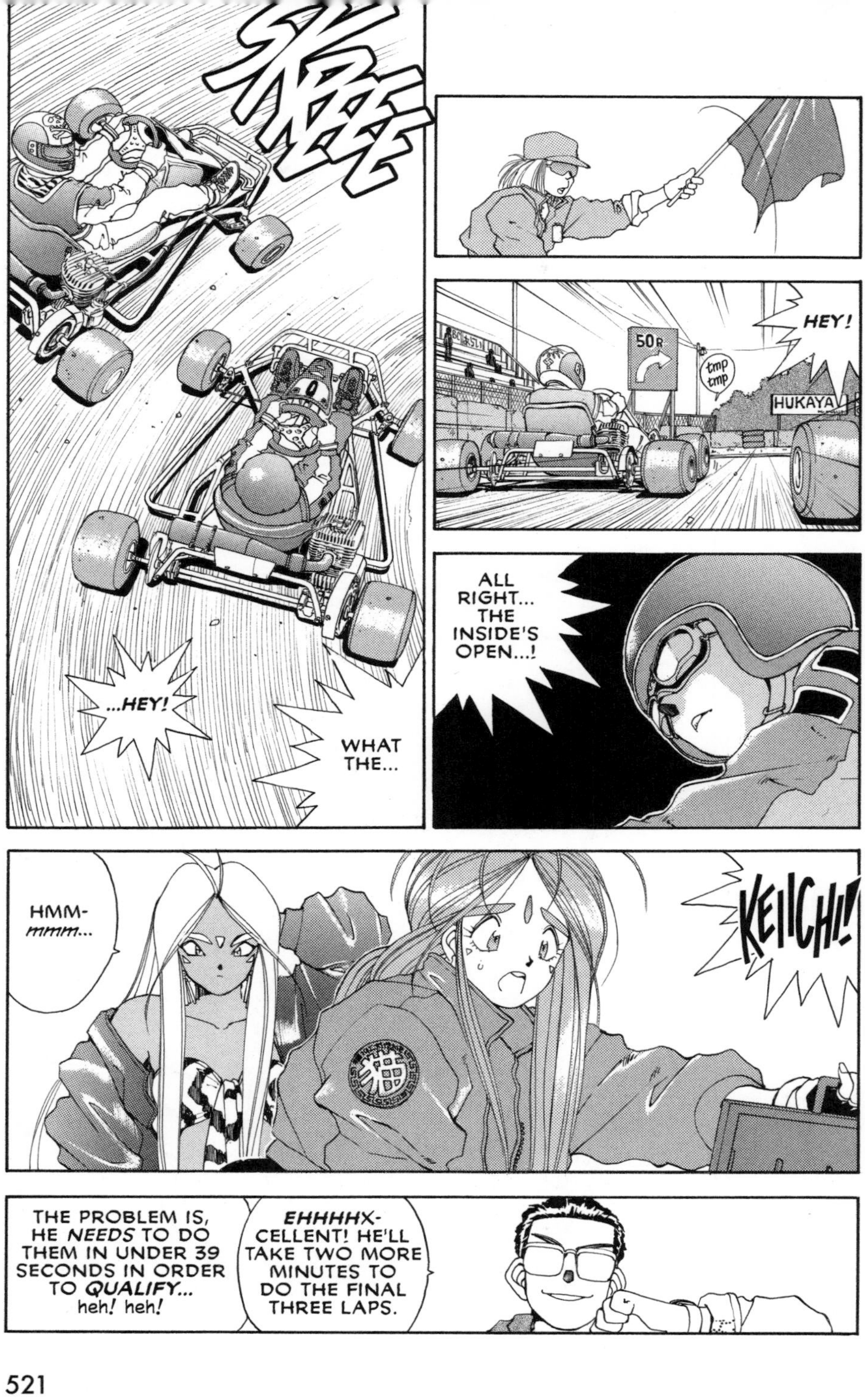

50R
tmp tmp
HEY!
HUKAYA
ALL RIGHT... THE INSIDE'S OPEN...!
SKREEE
...HEY!
WHAT THE...
KEIICHI!!
HMM-mmmm...
EHHHHX-CELLENT! HE'LL TAKE TWO MORE MINUTES TO DO THE FINAL THREE LAPS.
THE PROBLEM IS, HE NEEDS TO DO THEM IN UNDER 39 SECONDS IN ORDER TO QUALIFY... heh! heh!

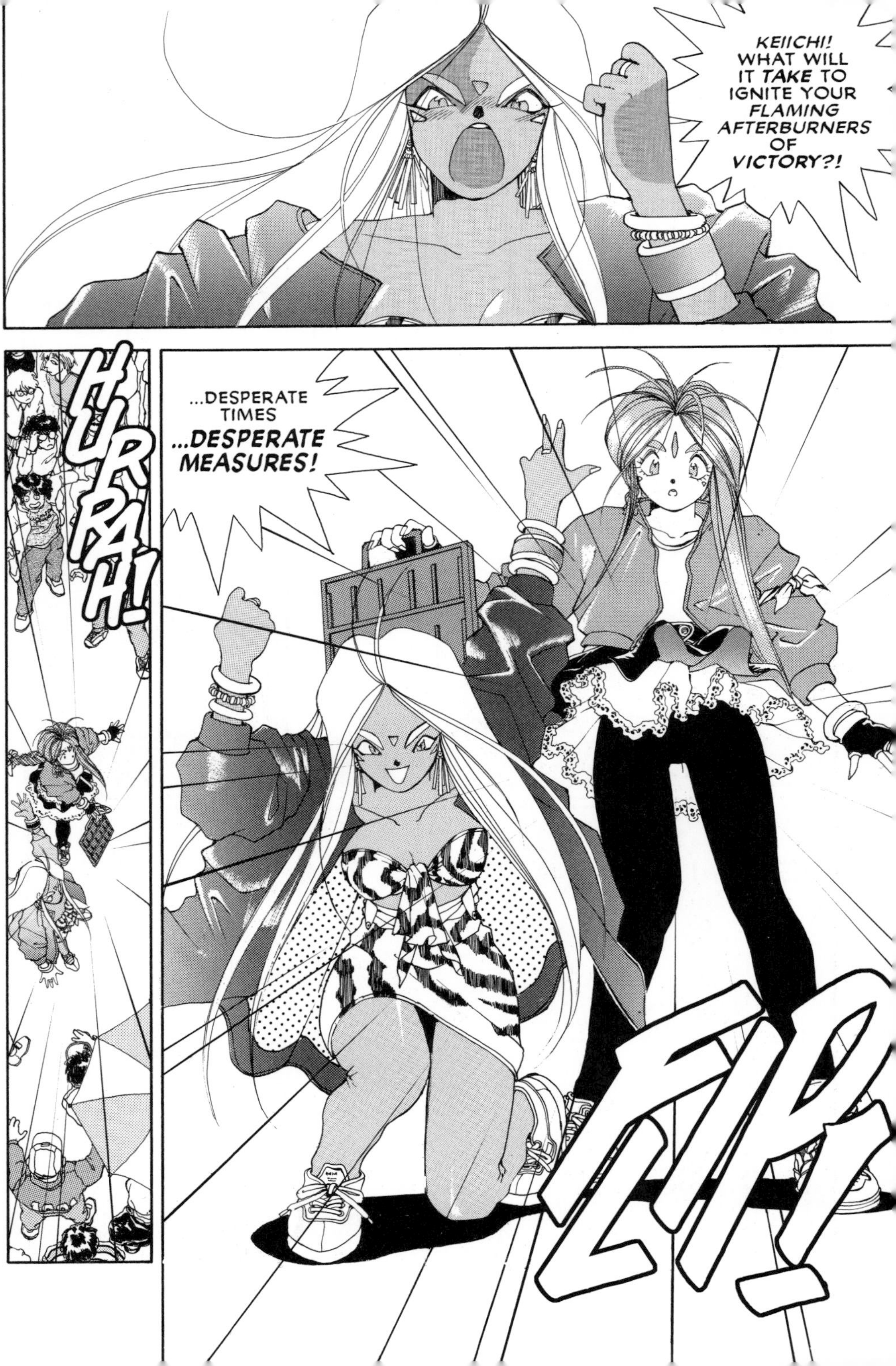
KEIICHI! WHAT WILL IT TAKE TO IGNITE YOUR FLAMING AFTERBURNERS OF VICTORY?!
...DESPERATE TIMES ...DESPERATE MEASURES!
HURRAH!

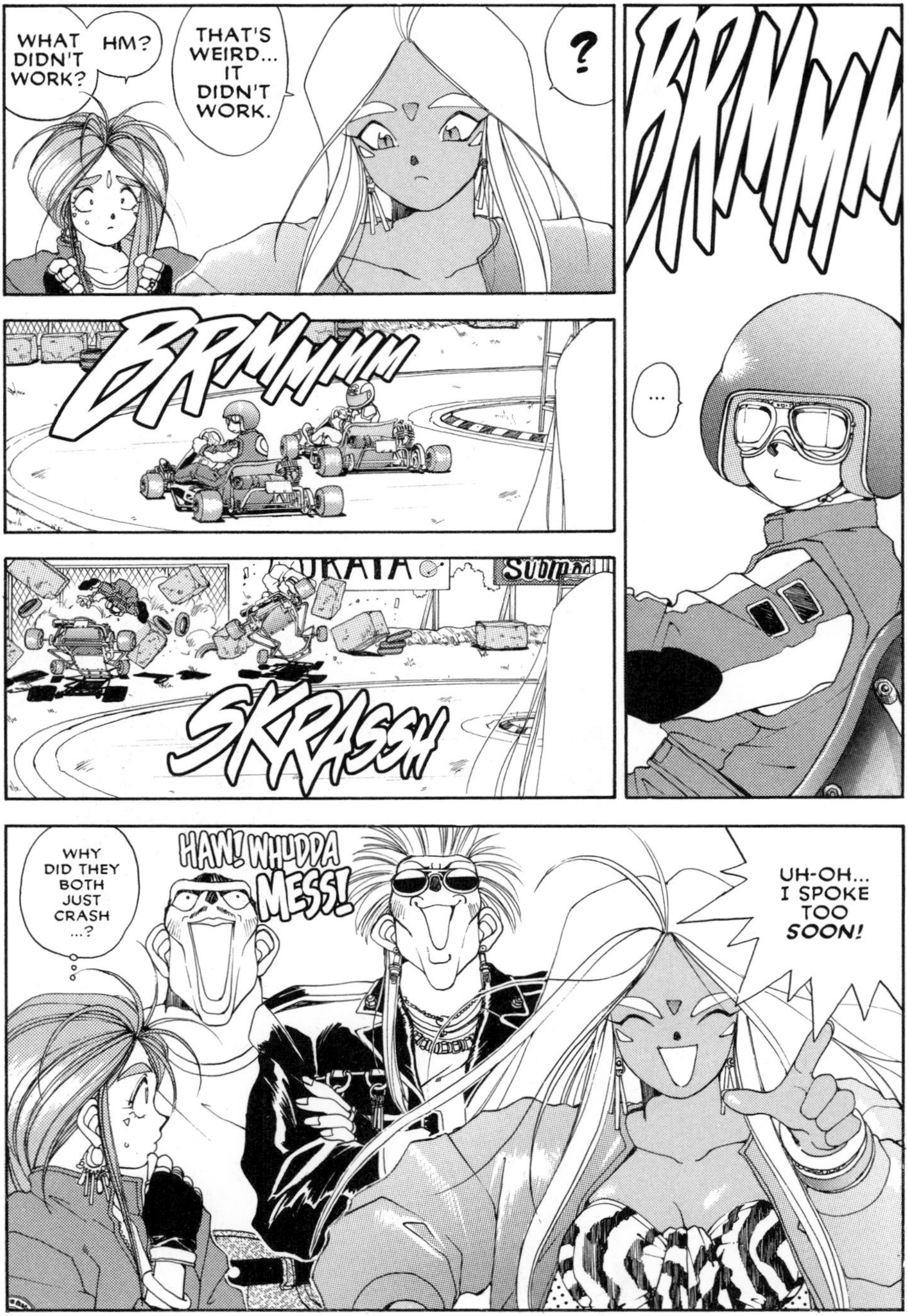
BRMMMM
...
?
THAT'S WEIRD... IT DIDN'T WORK.
HM?
WHAT DIDN'T WORK?
BRMMMMM
SKRASSH
UH-OH... I SPOKE TOO *SOON!*
HAW! WHUDDA MESS!
WHY DID THEY BOTH JUST CRASH ...?

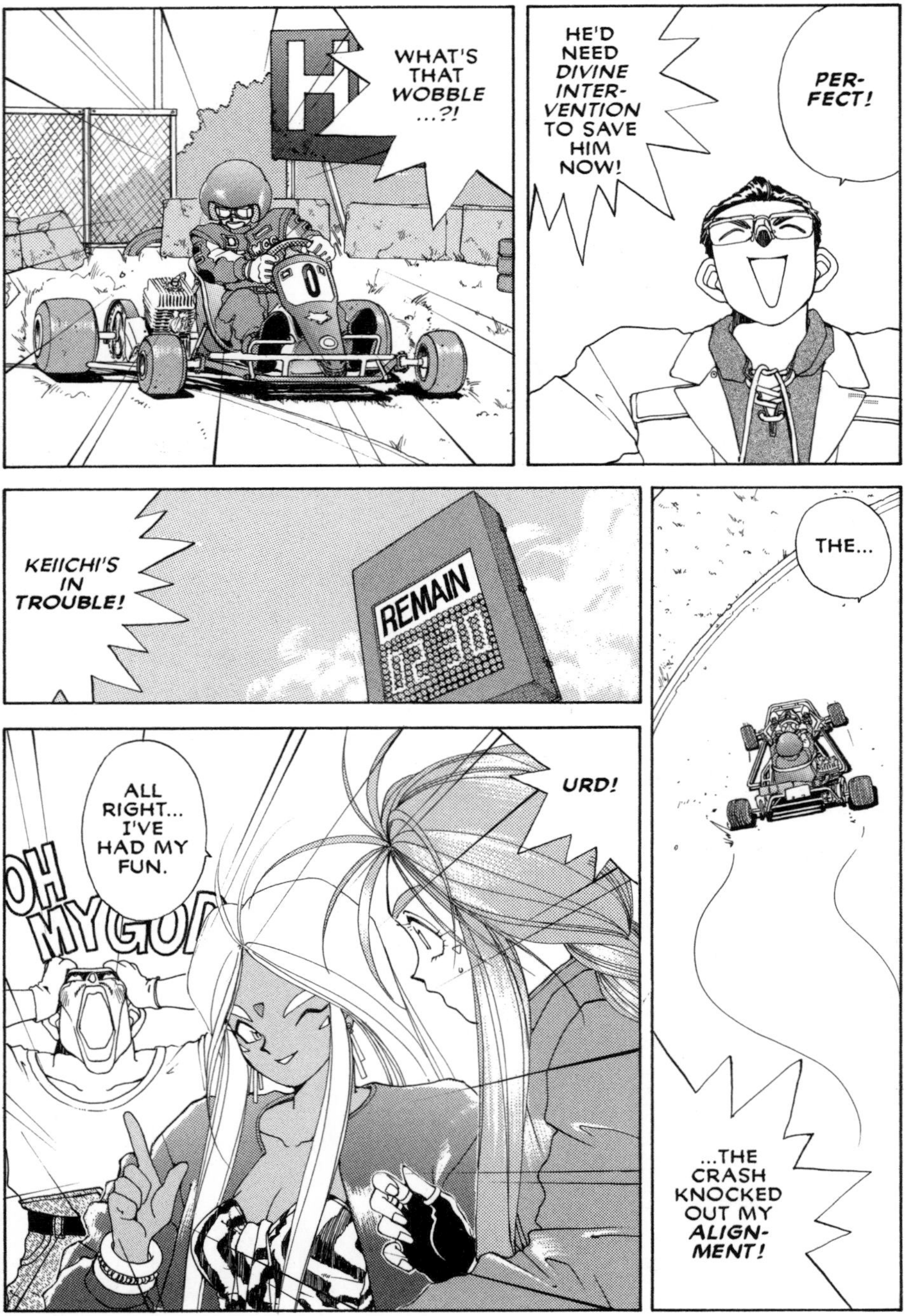
PER-FECT!
HE'D NEED DIVINE INTER-VENTION TO SAVE HIM NOW!
WHAT'S THAT WOBBLE ...?!
THE...
...THE CRASH KNOCKED OUT MY ALIGN-MENT!
KEIICHI'S IN TROUBLE!
REMAIN
URD!
ALL RIGHT... I'VE HAD MY FUN.
OH MYGOD

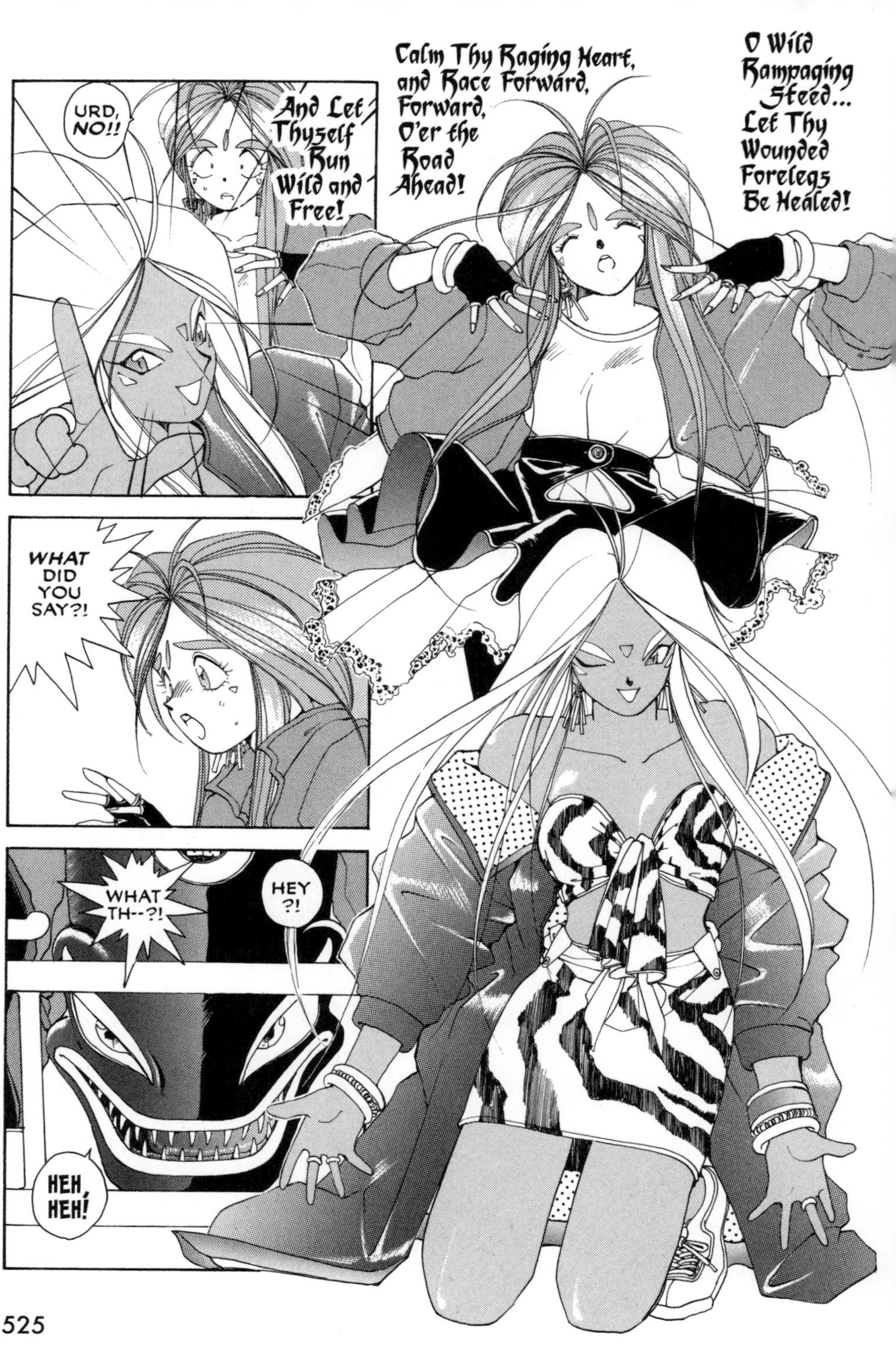
O Wild Rampaging Steed... Let Thy Wounded Forelegs Be Healed!
Calm Thy Raging Heart, and Race Forward, Forward, O'er the Road Ahead!
And Let Thyself Run Wild and Free!
URD, NO!!
WHAT DID YOU SAY?!
HEY?!
WHAT TH--?!
HEH, HEH!

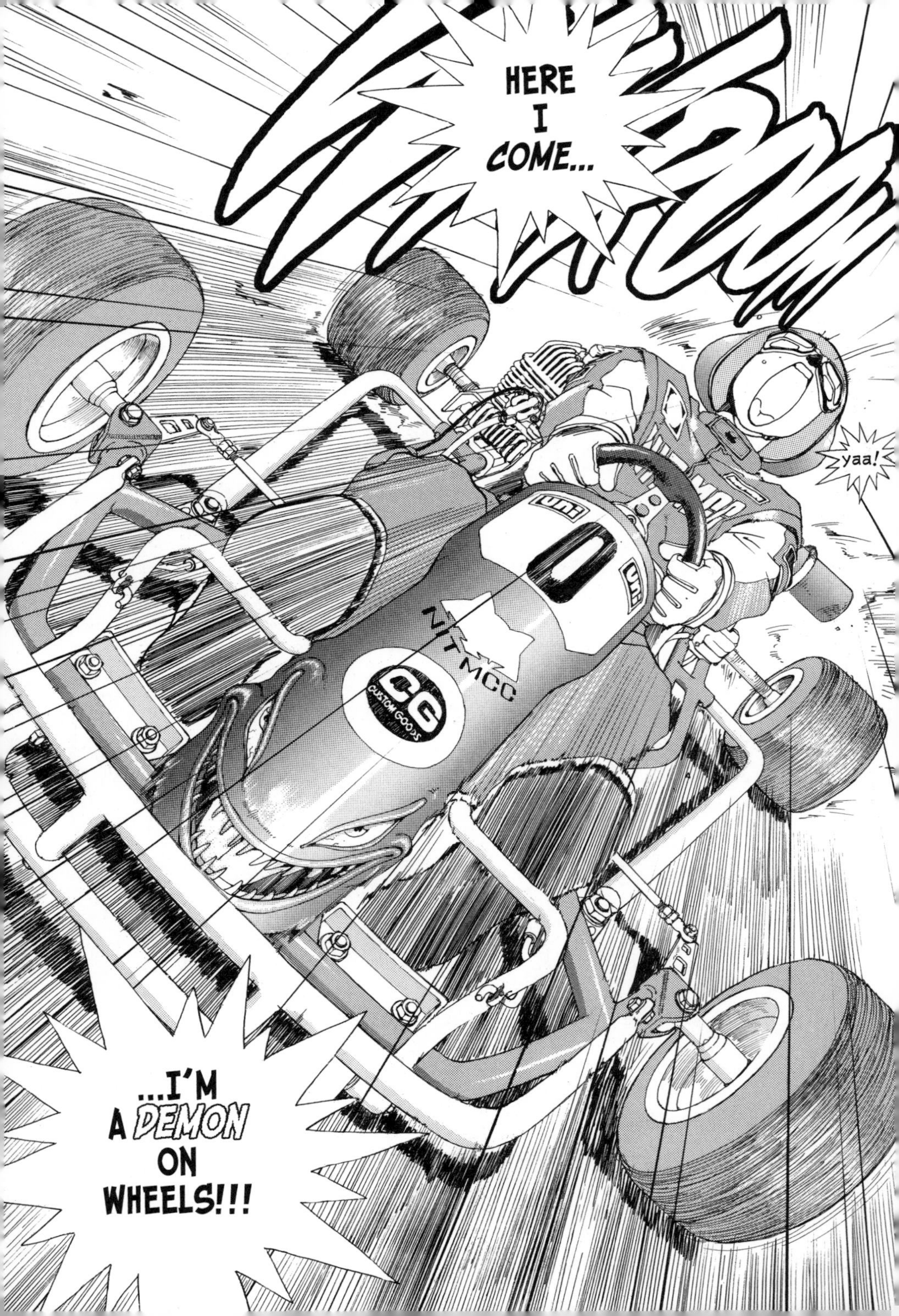
HERE I COME...
yaa!
...I'M A DEMON ON WHEELS!!!

W-WHAT THE HELL...?!
NO ONE CAN SURVIVE CORNERING AT SPEEDS LIKE THAT!
I'M GAININ' ON YA, SO YOU BETTER LOOK *ALIVE!*
aieee!
HAW! HAW!
GACK!
H-HE *PASSED* ME...
...LIKE IT WAS *NUTHIN'*...!!

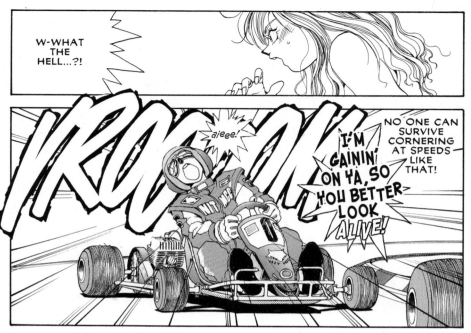

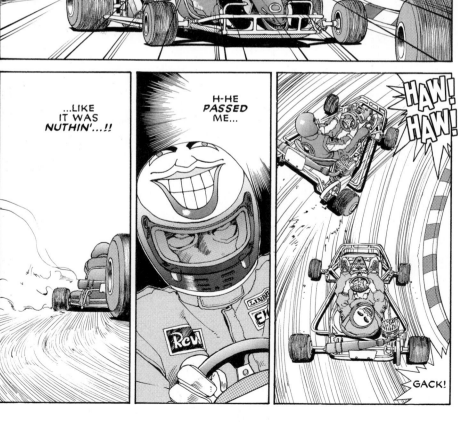

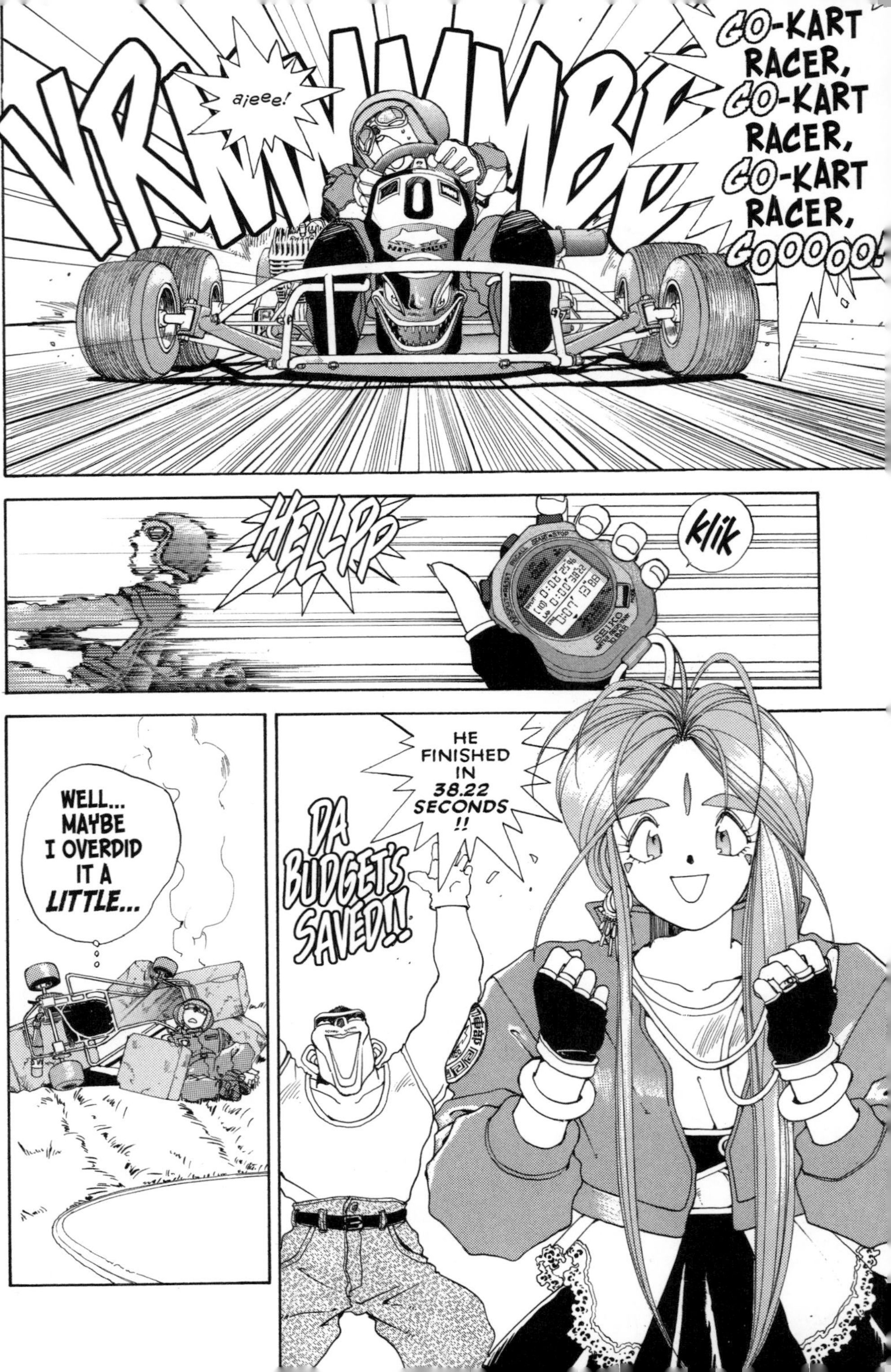
GO-KART RACER, GO-KART RACER, GO-KART RACER, GOOOOO!
aieee!
klik
HELLPP
HE FINISHED IN 38.22 SECONDS !!
DA BUDGET'S SAVED!!
WELL... MAYBE I OVERDID IT A LITTLE...

OH MY GODDESS!

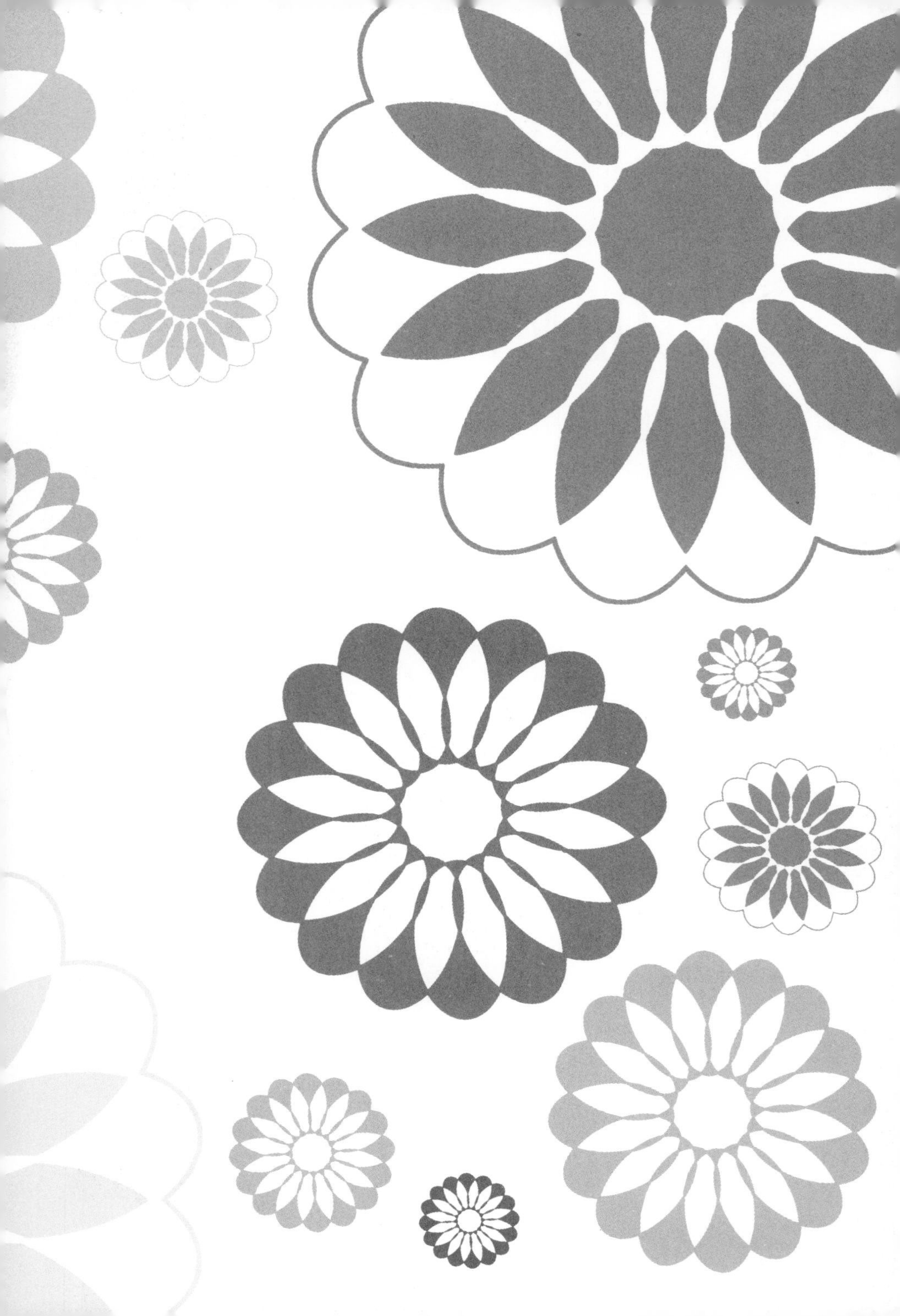

CHAPTER 23

What a Miracle

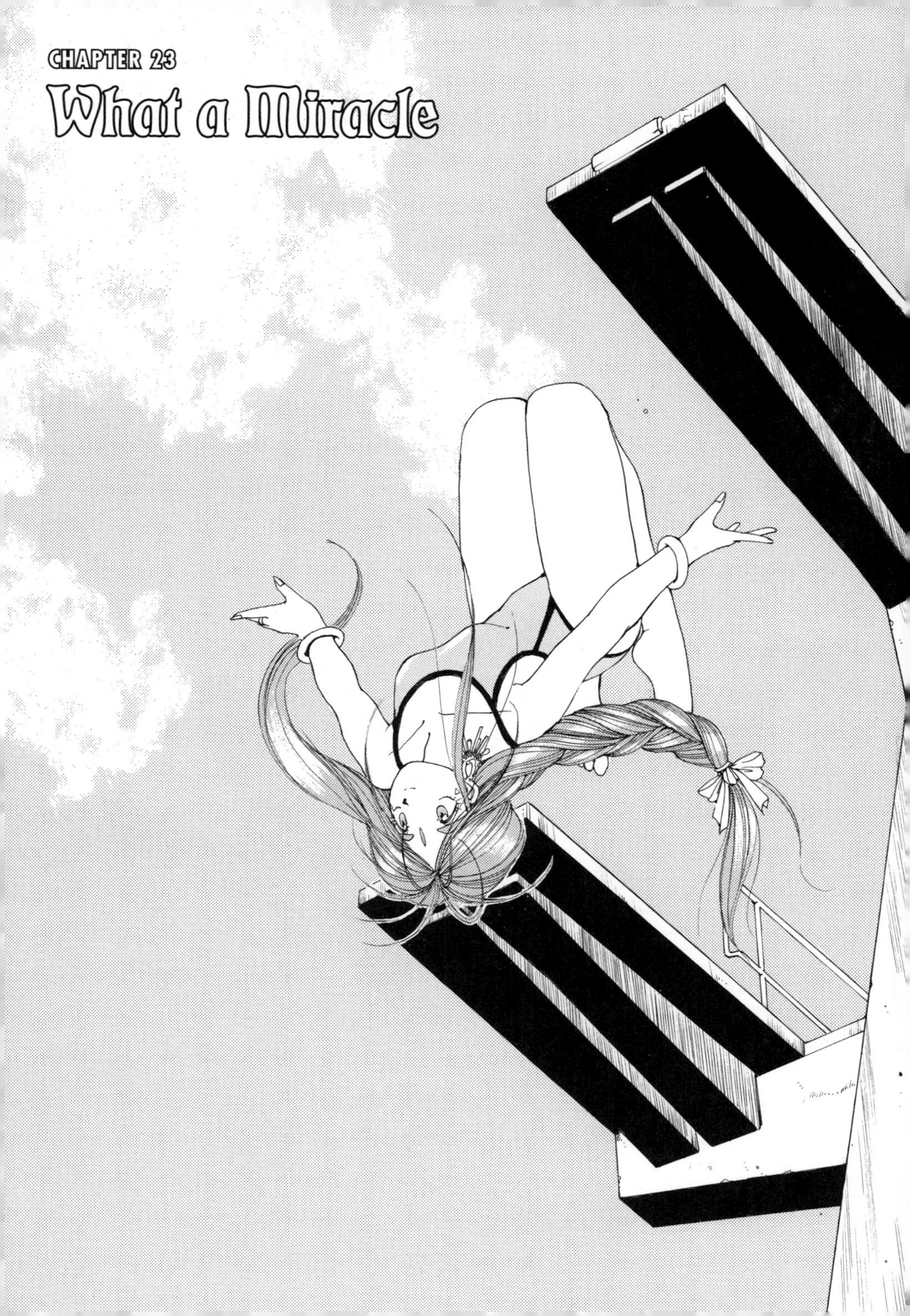

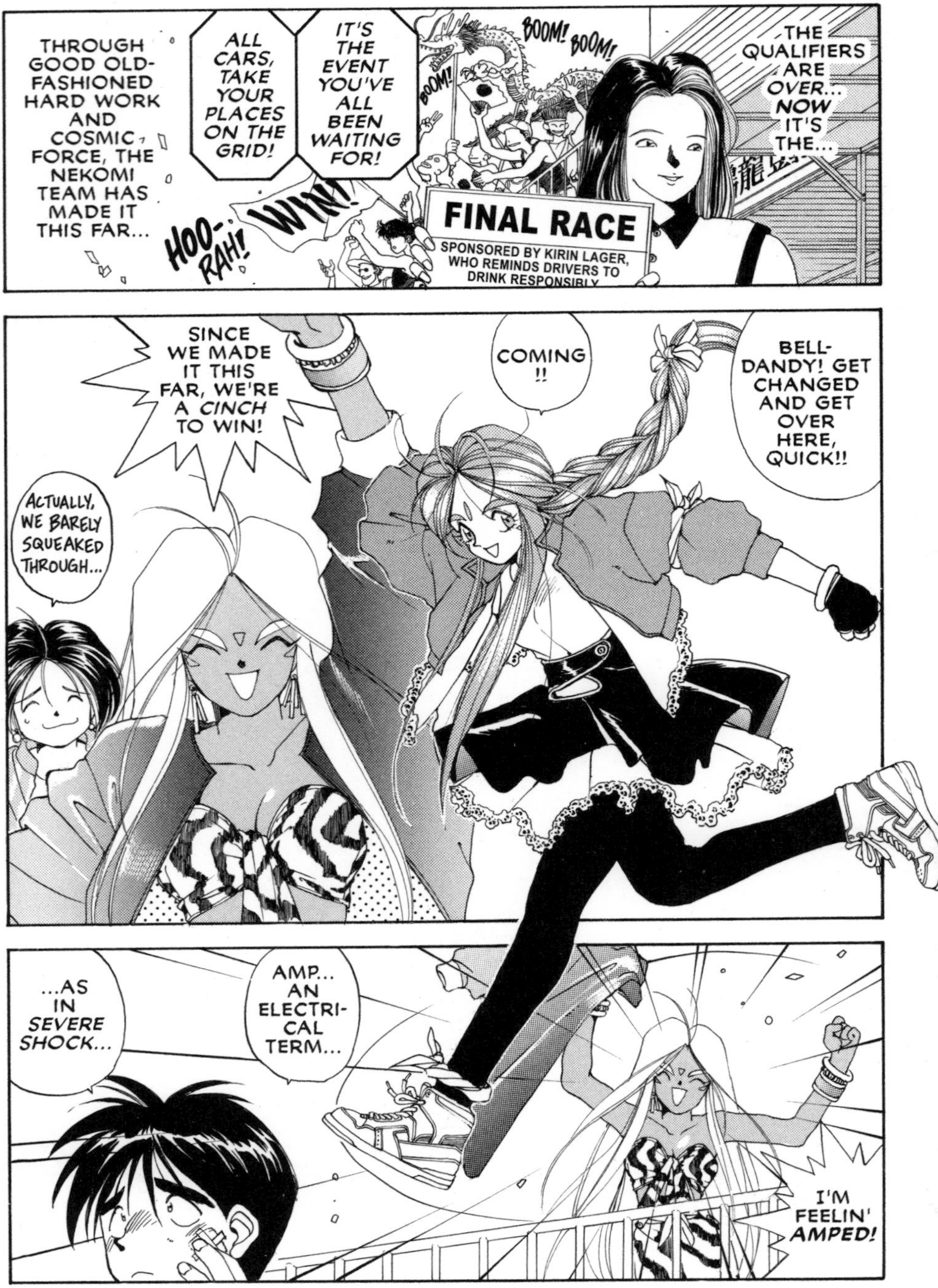
THE QUALIFIERS ARE OVER... NOW IT'S THE...
FINAL RACE
SPONSORED BY KIRIN LAGER, WHO REMINDS DRIVERS TO DRINK RESPONSIBLY
BOOM! BOOM!
BOOM!
IT'S THE EVENT YOU'VE ALL BEEN WAITING FOR!
ALL CARS, TAKE YOUR PLACES ON THE GRID!
WIN!
HOO-RAH!
THROUGH GOOD OLD-FASHIONED HARD WORK AND COSMIC FORCE, THE NEKOMI TEAM HAS MADE IT THIS FAR...
BELL-DANDY! GET CHANGED AND GET OVER HERE, QUICK!!
COMING!!
SINCE WE MADE IT THIS FAR, WE'RE A CINCH TO WIN!
ACTUALLY, WE BARELY SQUEAKED THROUGH...
I'M FEELIN' AMPED!
AMP... AN ELECTRICAL TERM...
...AS IN SEVERE SHOCK...

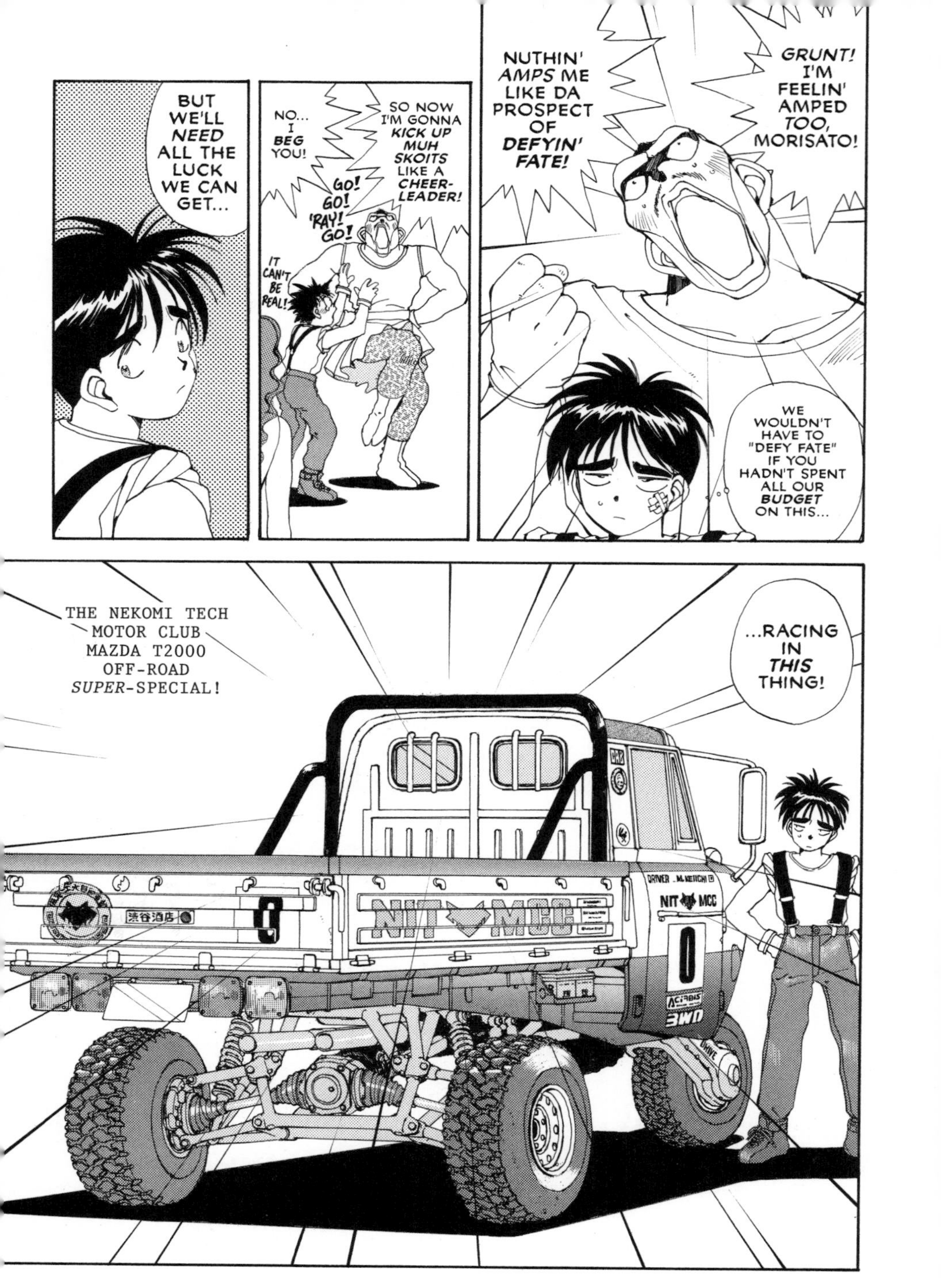
GRUNT! I'M FEELIN' AMPED TOO, MORISATO!
NUTHIN' AMPS ME LIKE DA PROSPECT OF DEFYIN' FATE!
WE WOULDN'T HAVE TO "DEFY FATE" IF YOU HADN'T SPENT ALL OUR BUDGET ON THIS...
SO NOW I'M GONNA KICK UP MUH SKOITS LIKE A CHEERLEADER!
NO... I BEG YOU!
GO! GO! 'RAY! GO!
IT CAN'T BE REAL!
BUT WE'LL NEED ALL THE LUCK WE CAN GET...
...RACING IN THIS THING!
THE NEKOMI TECH MOTOR CLUB MAZDA T2000 OFF-ROAD SUPER-SPECIAL!
NIT MCC
0
NIT MCC
0

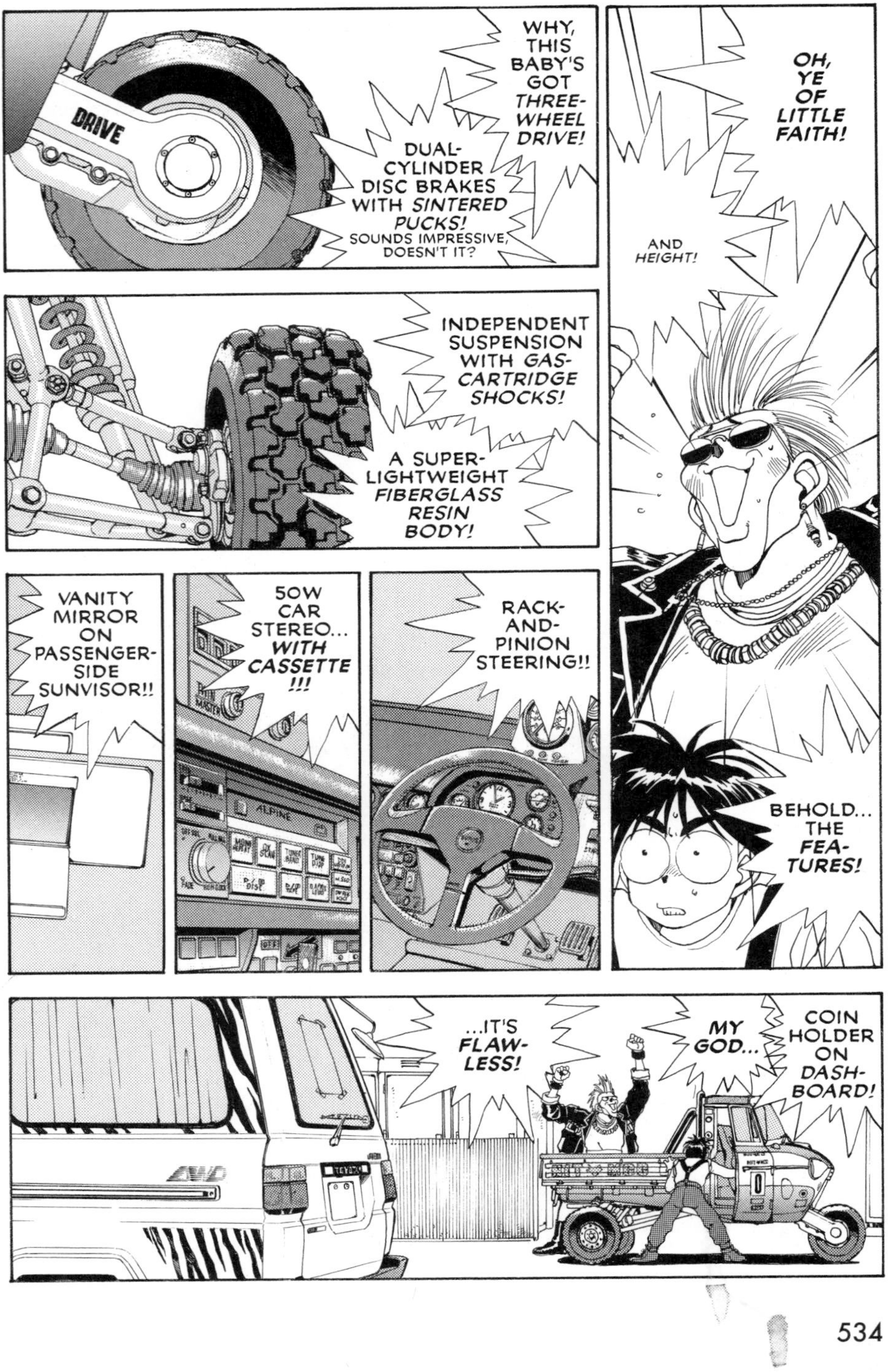
OH, YE OF LITTLE FAITH!
AND HEIGHT!
BEHOLD... THE FEATURES!
WHY, THIS BABY'S GOT THREE-WHEEL DRIVE!
DRIVE
DUAL-CYLINDER DISC BRAKES WITH SINTERED PUCKS! SOUNDS IMPRESSIVE, DOESN'T IT?
INDEPENDENT SUSPENSION WITH GAS-CARTRIDGE SHOCKS!
A SUPER-LIGHTWEIGHT FIBERGLASS RESIN BODY!
RACK-AND-PINION STEERING!!
50W CAR STEREO... WITH CASSETTE !!!
ALPINE
VANITY MIRROR ON PASSENGER-SIDE SUNVISOR!!
COIN HOLDER ON DASHBOARD!
MY GOD...
...IT'S FLAWLESS!

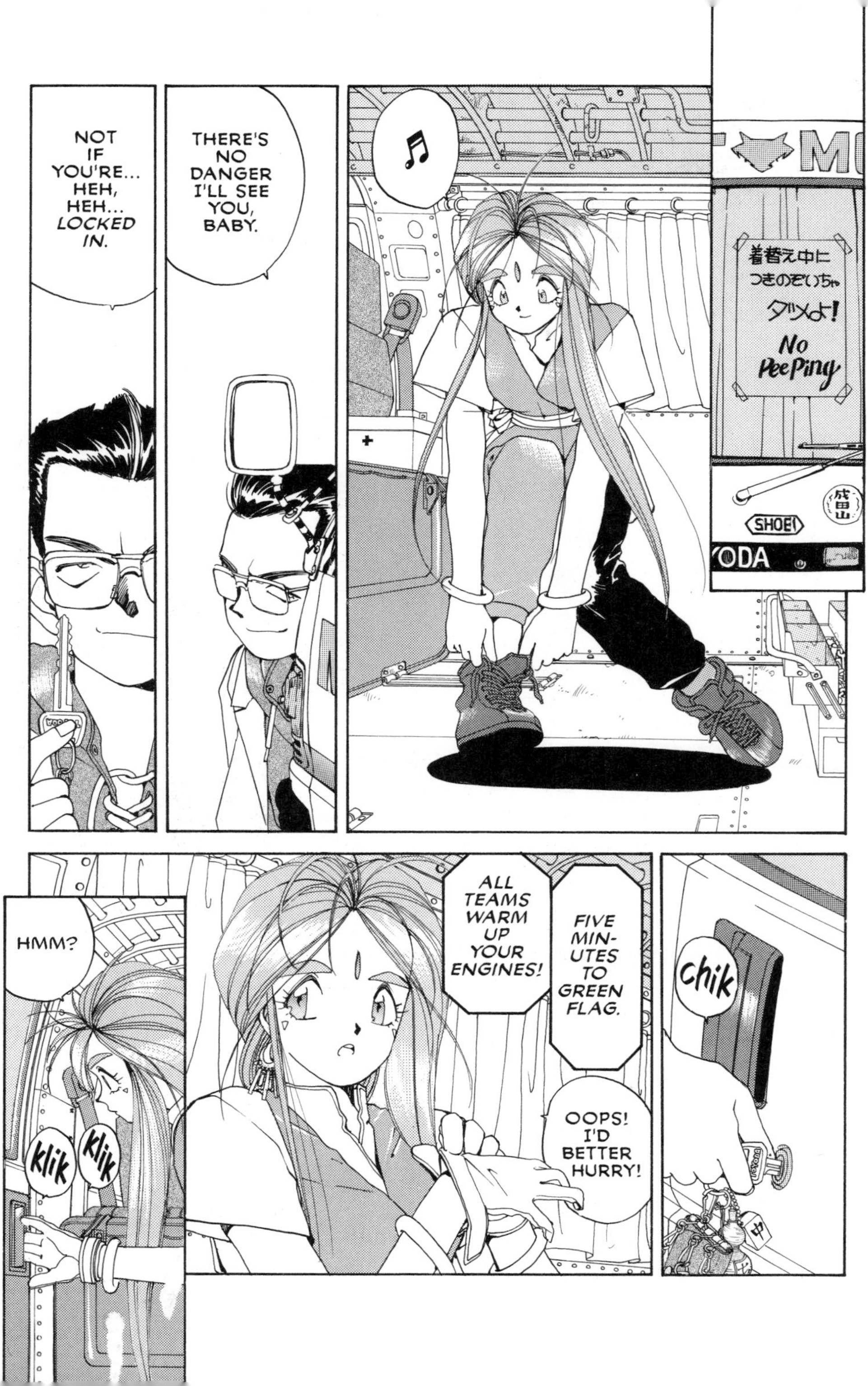

着替え中に
つきのぞいちゃ
ダメよ!
No PeePing
SHOEI
♪
THERE'S NO DANGER I'LL SEE YOU, BABY.
NOT IF YOU'RE... HEH, HEH... *LOCKED IN.*
chik
FIVE MIN-UTES TO GREEN FLAG.
ALL TEAMS WARM UP YOUR ENGINES!
OOPS! I'D BETTER HURRY!
HMM?
klik
klik

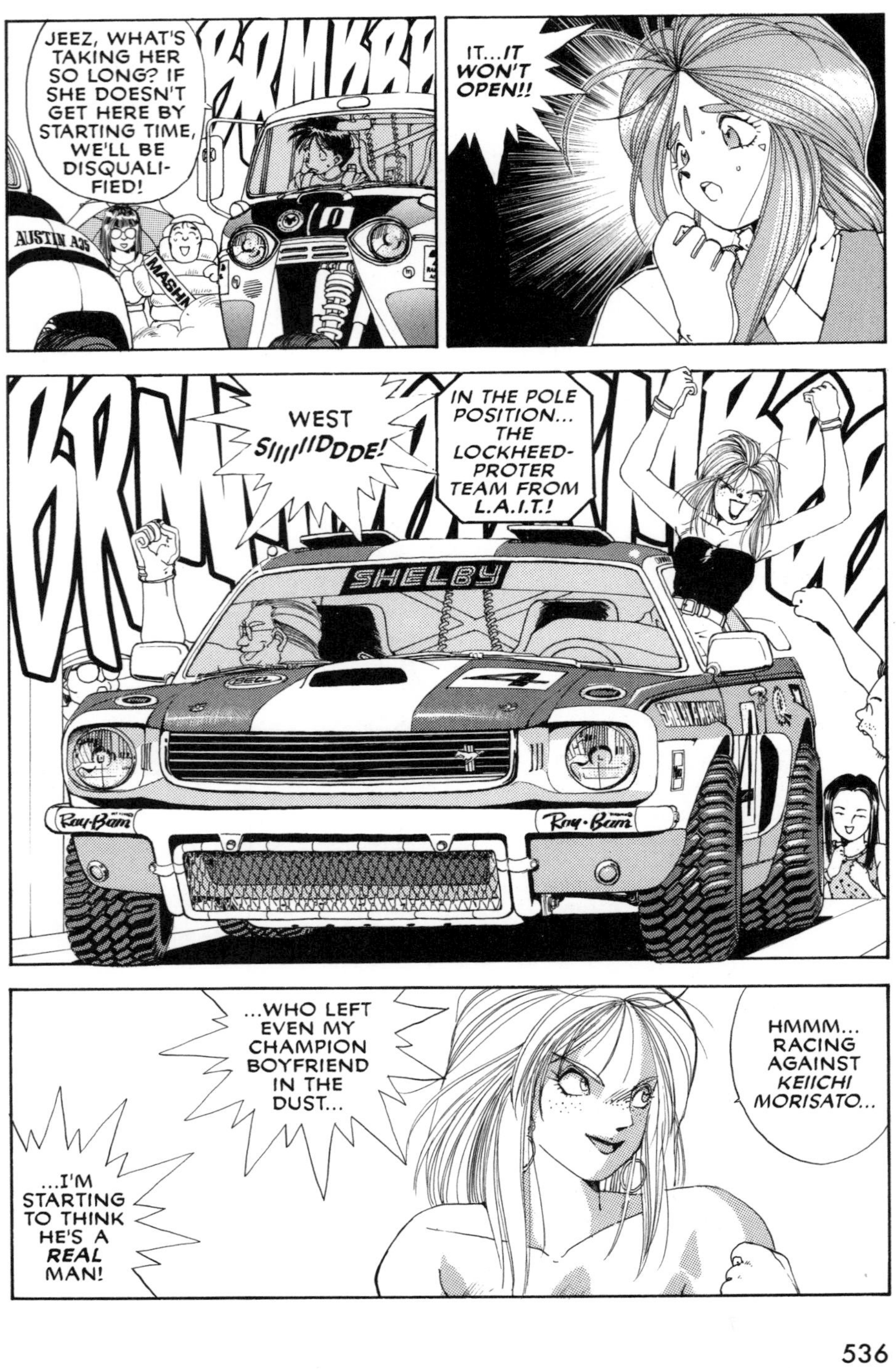

IT...IT WON'T OPEN!!
JEEZ, WHAT'S TAKING HER SO LONG? IF SHE DOESN'T GET HERE BY STARTING TIME, WE'LL BE DISQUALIFIED!
AUSTIN A35
IN THE POLE POSITION... THE LOCKHEED-PROTER TEAM FROM L.A.I.T.!
WEST SIIIIIDDDE!
SHELBY
HMMM... RACING AGAINST KEIICHI MORISATO...
...WHO LEFT EVEN MY CHAMPION BOYFRIEND IN THE DUST...
...I'M STARTING TO THINK HE'S A REAL MAN!

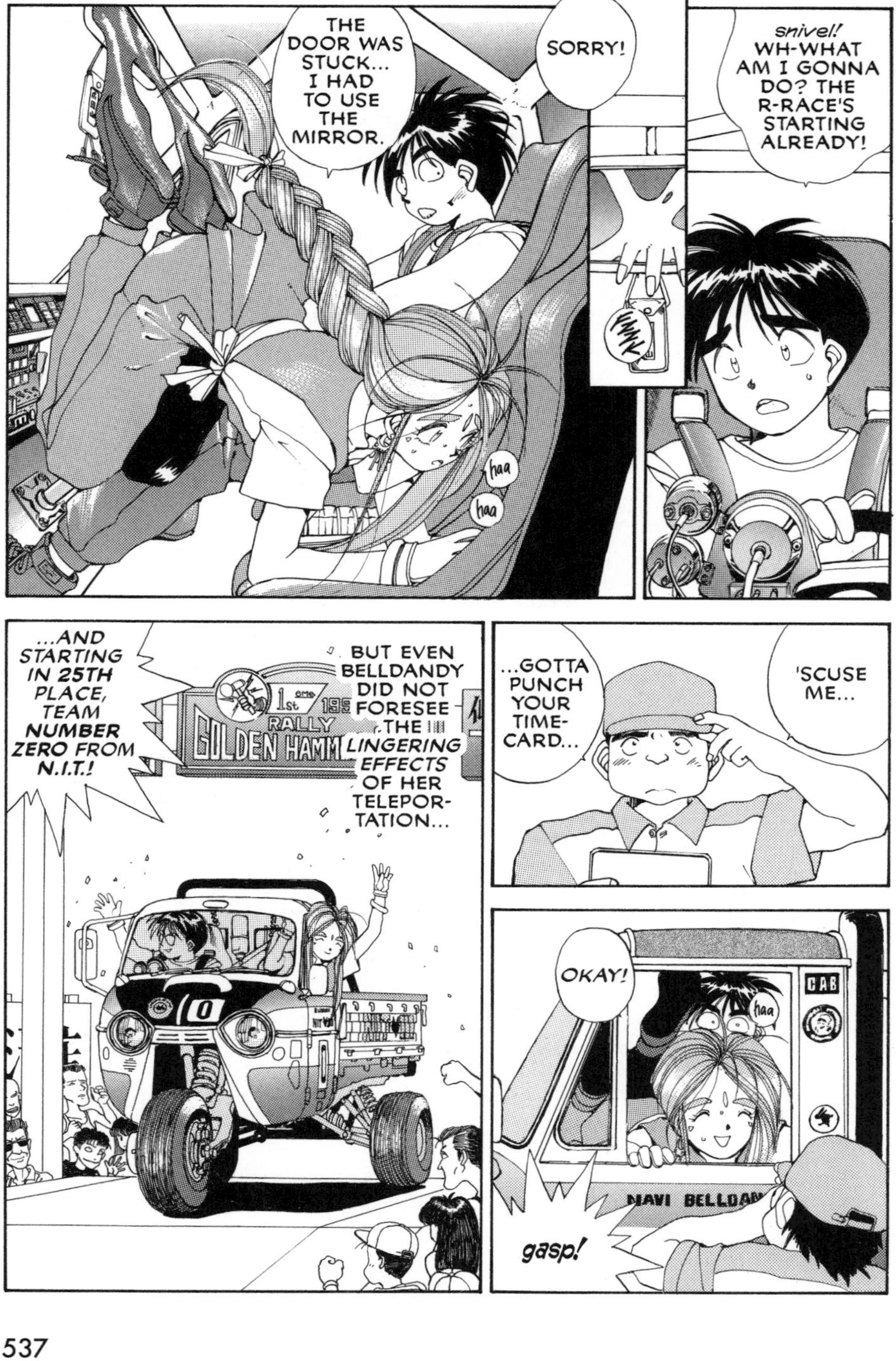
snivel! WH-WHAT AM I GONNA DO? THE R-RACE'S STARTING ALREADY!
SORRY!
THE DOOR WAS STUCK... I HAD TO USE THE MIRROR.
haa
haa
'SCUSE ME...
...GOTTA PUNCH YOUR TIME-CARD...
CAB
haa
OKAY!
gasp!
BUT EVEN BELLDANDY DID NOT FORESEE THE *LINGERING EFFECTS* OF HER TELEPORTATION...
...AND STARTING IN 25TH PLACE, TEAM **NUMBER ZERO FROM N.I.T.!**

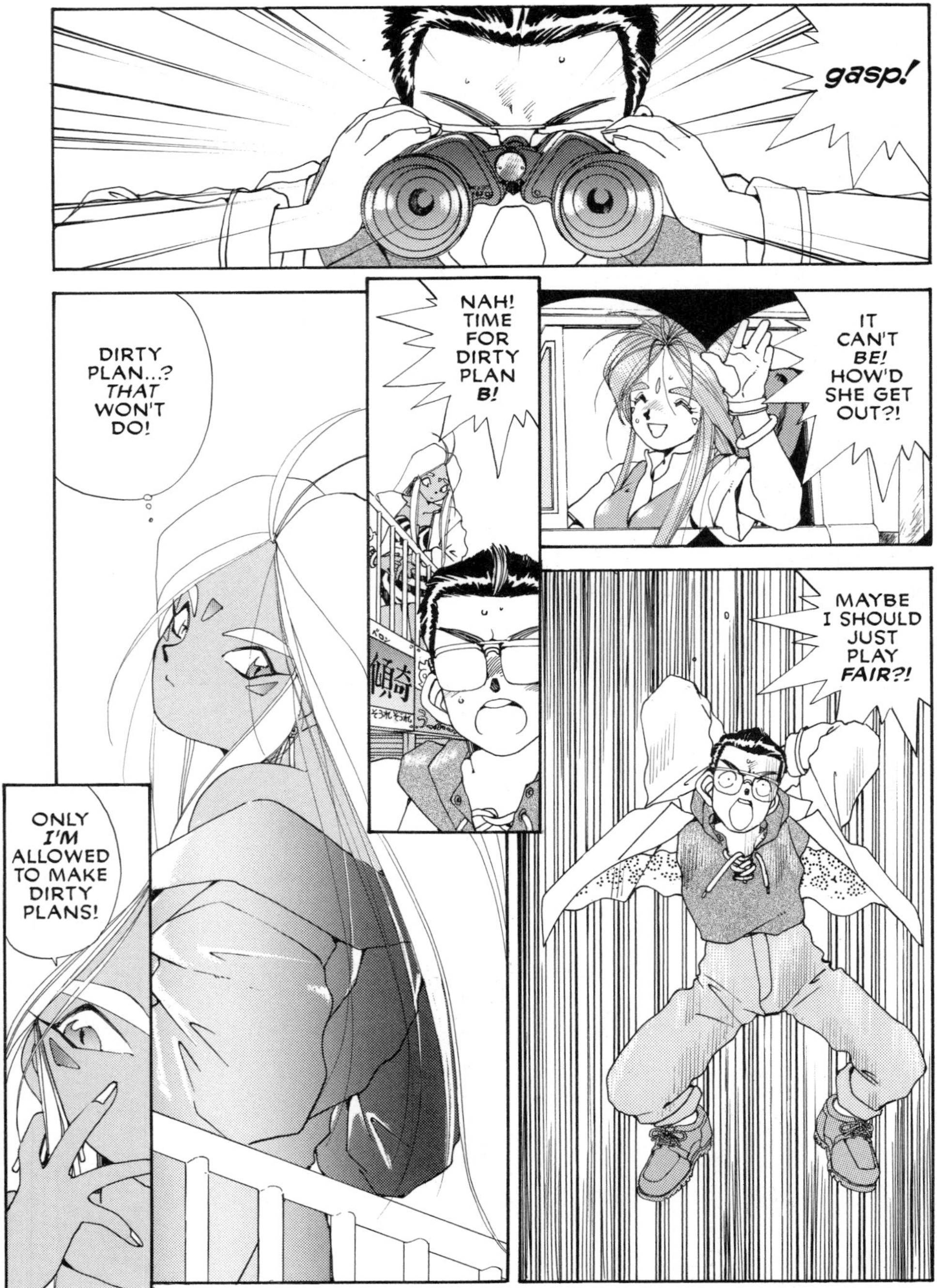
gasp!
IT CAN'T BE! HOW'D SHE GET OUT?!
NAH! TIME FOR DIRTY PLAN B!
MAYBE I SHOULD JUST PLAY FAIR?!
DIRTY PLAN...? THAT WON'T DO!
ONLY I'M ALLOWED TO MAKE DIRTY PLANS!

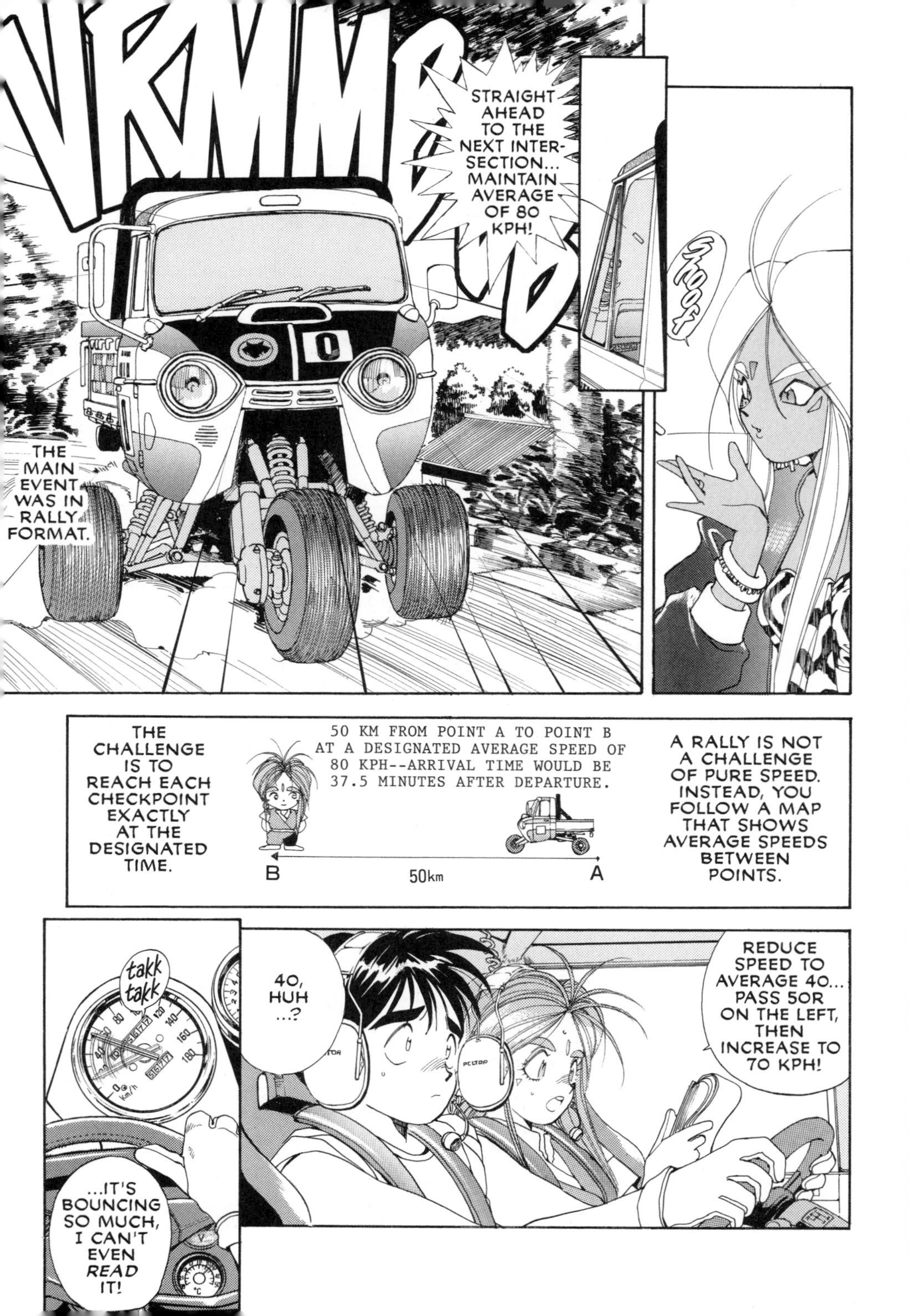
SHOOF
VRMMM
STRAIGHT AHEAD TO THE NEXT INTER-SECTION... MAINTAIN AVERAGE OF 80 KPH!
THE MAIN EVENT WAS IN RALLY FORMAT.
A RALLY IS NOT A CHALLENGE OF PURE SPEED. INSTEAD, YOU FOLLOW A MAP THAT SHOWS AVERAGE SPEEDS BETWEEN POINTS.
50 KM FROM POINT A TO POINT B AT A DESIGNATED AVERAGE SPEED OF 80 KPH--ARRIVAL TIME WOULD BE 37.5 MINUTES AFTER DEPARTURE.
B
50km
A
THE CHALLENGE IS TO REACH EACH CHECKPOINT EXACTLY AT THE DESIGNATED TIME.
REDUCE SPEED TO AVERAGE 40... PASS 50R ON THE LEFT, THEN INCREASE TO 70 KPH!
40, HUH ...?
takk takk
...IT'S BOUNCING SO MUCH, I CAN'T EVEN *READ* IT!

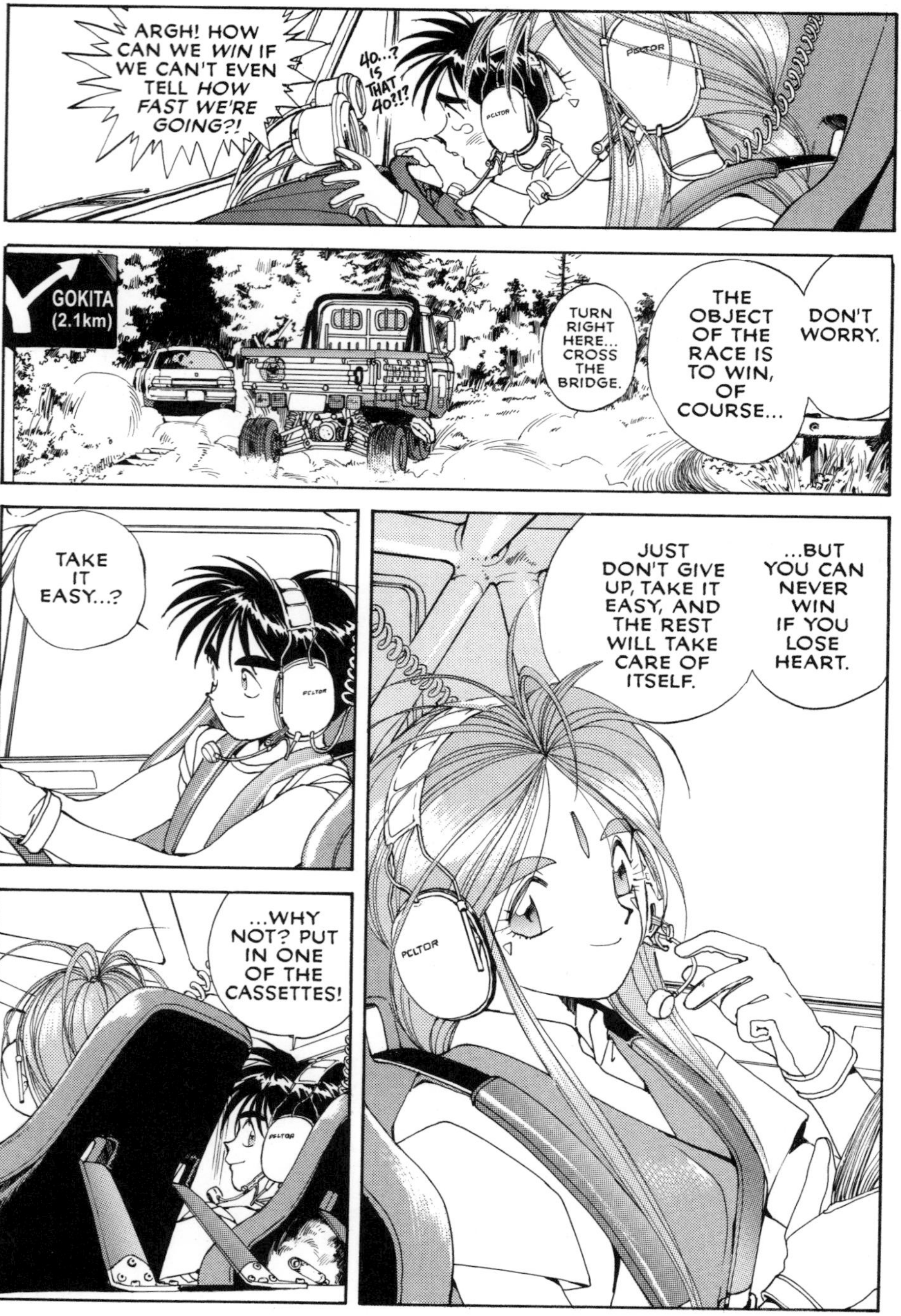
40...? IS THAT 40?!?
ARGH! HOW CAN WE WIN IF WE CAN'T EVEN TELL HOW FAST WE'RE GOING?!
DON'T WORRY.
THE OBJECT OF THE RACE IS TO WIN, OF COURSE...
TURN RIGHT HERE... CROSS THE BRIDGE.
GOKITA (2.1km)
...BUT YOU CAN NEVER WIN IF YOU LOSE HEART.
JUST DON'T GIVE UP, TAKE IT EASY, AND THE REST WILL TAKE CARE OF ITSELF.
TAKE IT EASY...?
...WHY NOT? PUT IN ONE OF THE CASSETTES!

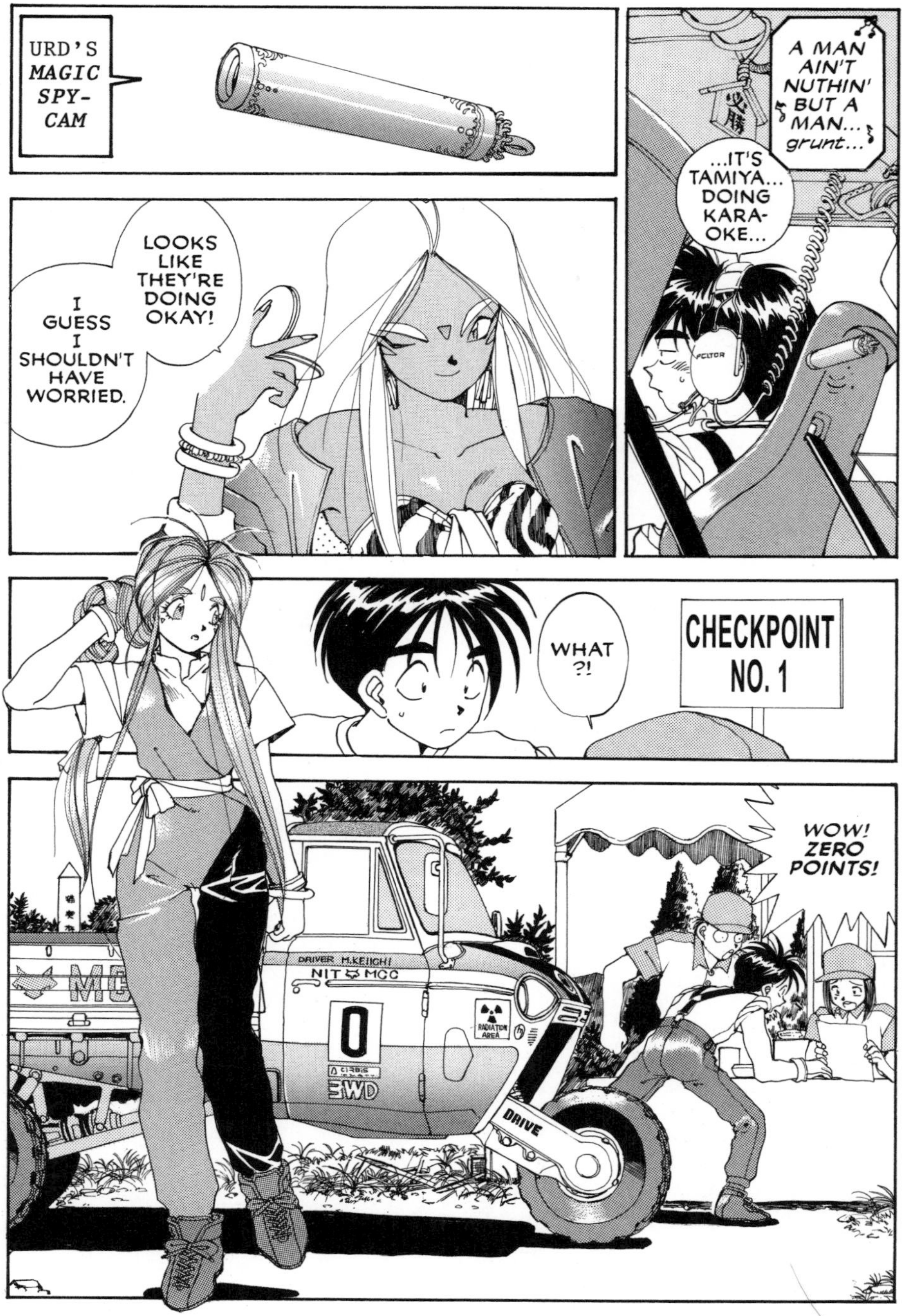
A MAN AIN'T NUTHIN' BUT A MAN... grunt...
...IT'S TAMIYA... DOING KARA-OKE...
URD'S MAGIC SPY-CAM
LOOKS LIKE THEY'RE DOING OKAY!
I GUESS I SHOULDN'T HAVE WORRIED.
CHECKPOINT NO. 1
WHAT ?!
WOW! ZERO POINTS!
DRIVER M.KEIICHI
NIT MCC
0
RADIATION AREA
DRIVE

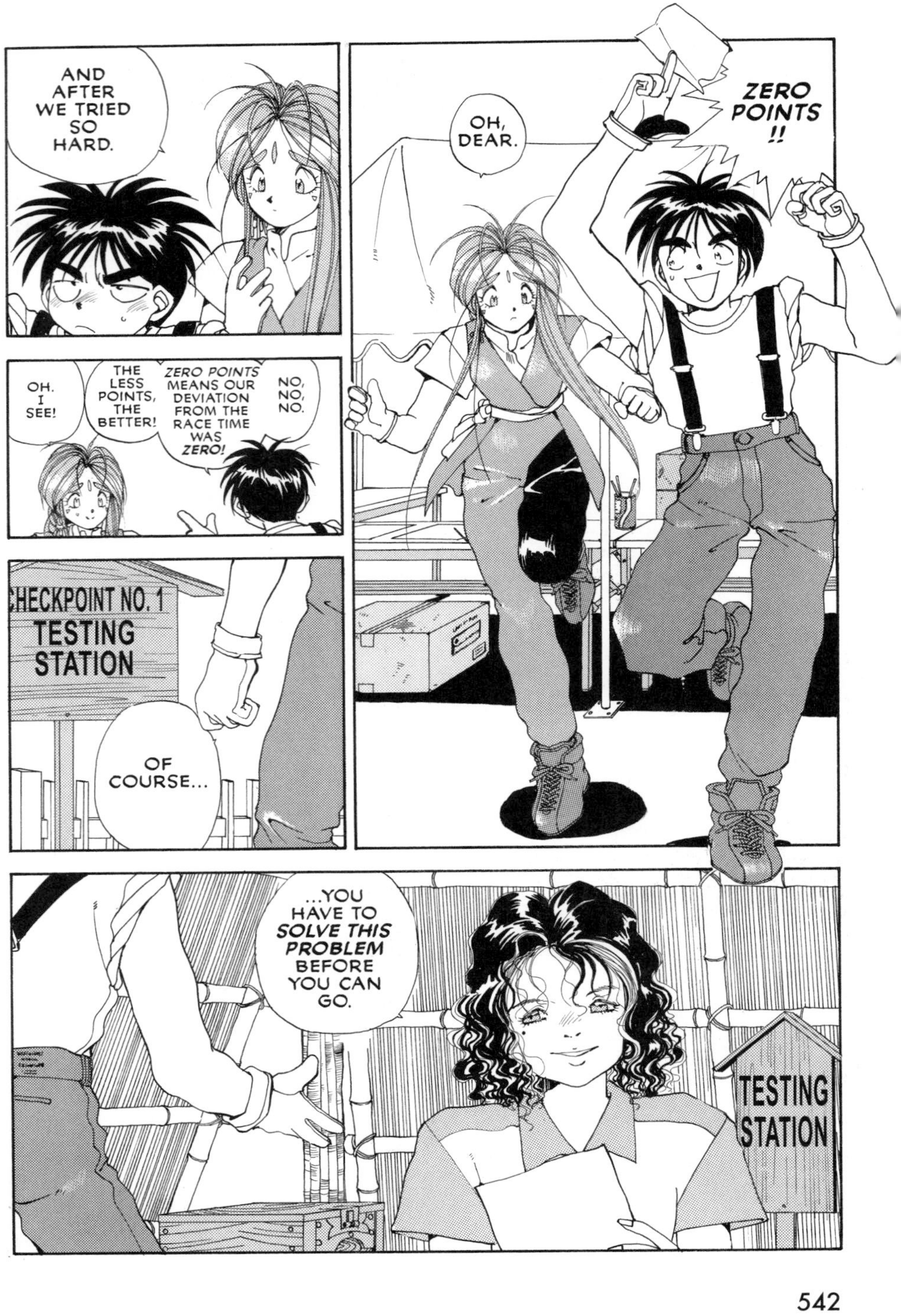
ZERO POINTS !!
OH, DEAR.
AND AFTER WE TRIED SO HARD.
NO, NO, NO.
ZERO POINTS MEANS OUR DEVIATION FROM THE RACE TIME WAS ZERO!
THE LESS POINTS, THE BETTER!
OH. I SEE!
CHECKPOINT NO. 1 TESTING STATION
OF COURSE...
TESTING STATION
...YOU HAVE TO SOLVE THIS PROBLEM BEFORE YOU CAN GO.

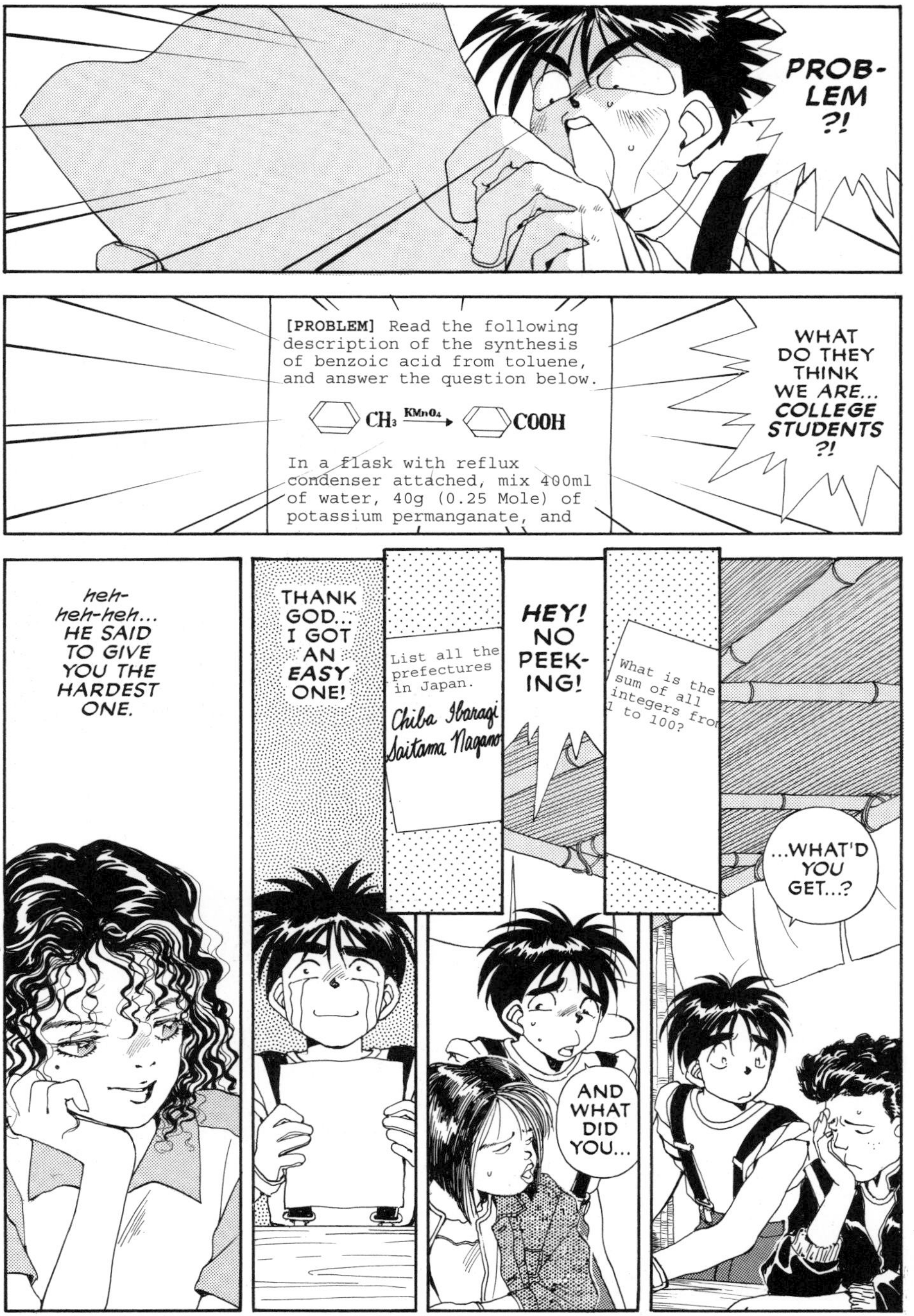
PROB-LEM ?!
WHAT DO THEY THINK WE ARE... COLLEGE STUDENTS ?!
[PROBLEM] Read the following description of the synthesis of benzoic acid from toluene, and answer the question below.
CH3 KMnO4 COOH
In a flask with reflux condenser attached, mix 400ml of water, 40g (0.25 Mole) of potassium permanganate, and
What is the sum of all integers fro
to 100?
...WHAT'D YOU GET...?
HEY! NO PEEK-ING!
AND WHAT DID YOU...
List all the prefectures in Japan.
Chiba Ibaragi Saitama Nagano
THANK GOD... I GOT AN EASY ONE!
heh-heh-heh... HE SAID TO GIVE YOU THE HARDEST ONE.

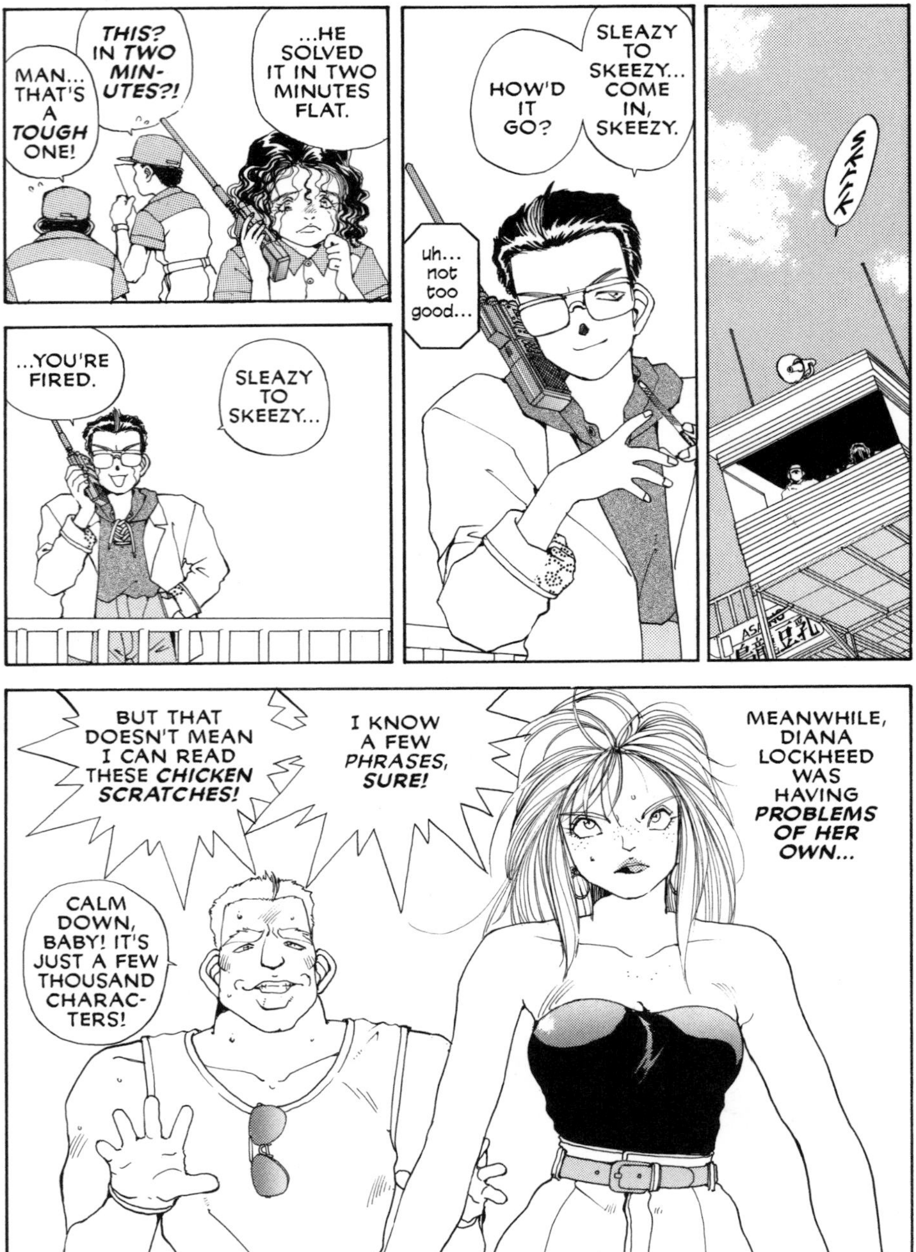
SKLIK
SLEAZY TO SKEEZY... COME IN, SKEEZY.
HOW'D IT GO?
uh... not too good...
...HE SOLVED IT IN TWO MINUTES FLAT.
THIS? IN TWO MIN-UTES?!
MAN... THAT'S A TOUGH ONE!
SLEAZY TO SKEEZY...
...YOU'RE FIRED.
MEANWHILE, DIANA LOCKHEED WAS HAVING PROBLEMS OF HER OWN...
I KNOW A FEW PHRASES, SURE!
BUT THAT DOESN'T MEAN I CAN READ THESE CHICKEN SCRATCHES!
CALM DOWN, BABY! IT'S JUST A FEW THOUSAND CHARAC-TERS!

YOU OKAY, BELL...?

...?!

ALL *RIGHT!* WHAT PERFECT TIMING!

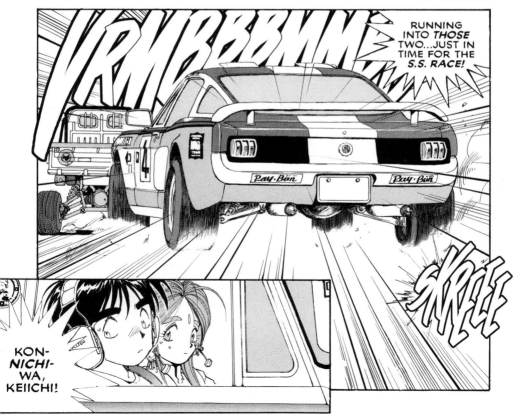

RUNNING INTO *THOSE* TWO...JUST IN TIME FOR THE *S.S. RACE!*

VRMBBBMM

SKREEE

KON-NICHI-WA, KEIICHI!

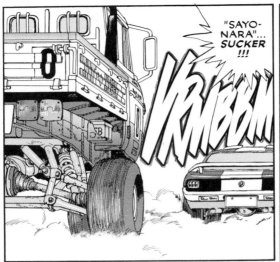

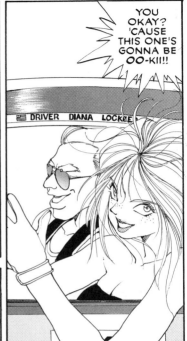

YOU OKAY? 'CAUSE THIS ONE'S GONNA BE OO-KII!!
DRIVER DIANA
"SAYO-NARA"... SUCKER !!!
WHY DID THEY PASS US?
WELL, YOU SEE...
S.S. STANDS FOR SPECIAL STAGE-- ONE WITH A DESIGNATED TIME OF ZERO-- IN OTHER WORDS, THE LESS TIME YOU TAKE, THE MORE POINTS YOU GET.
OKAY, AFTER 180 R...
...THERE'S A DIP...

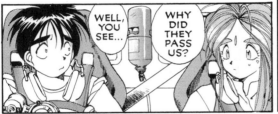

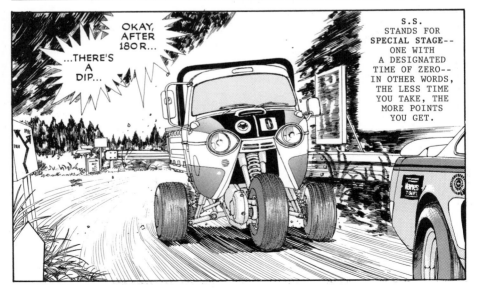

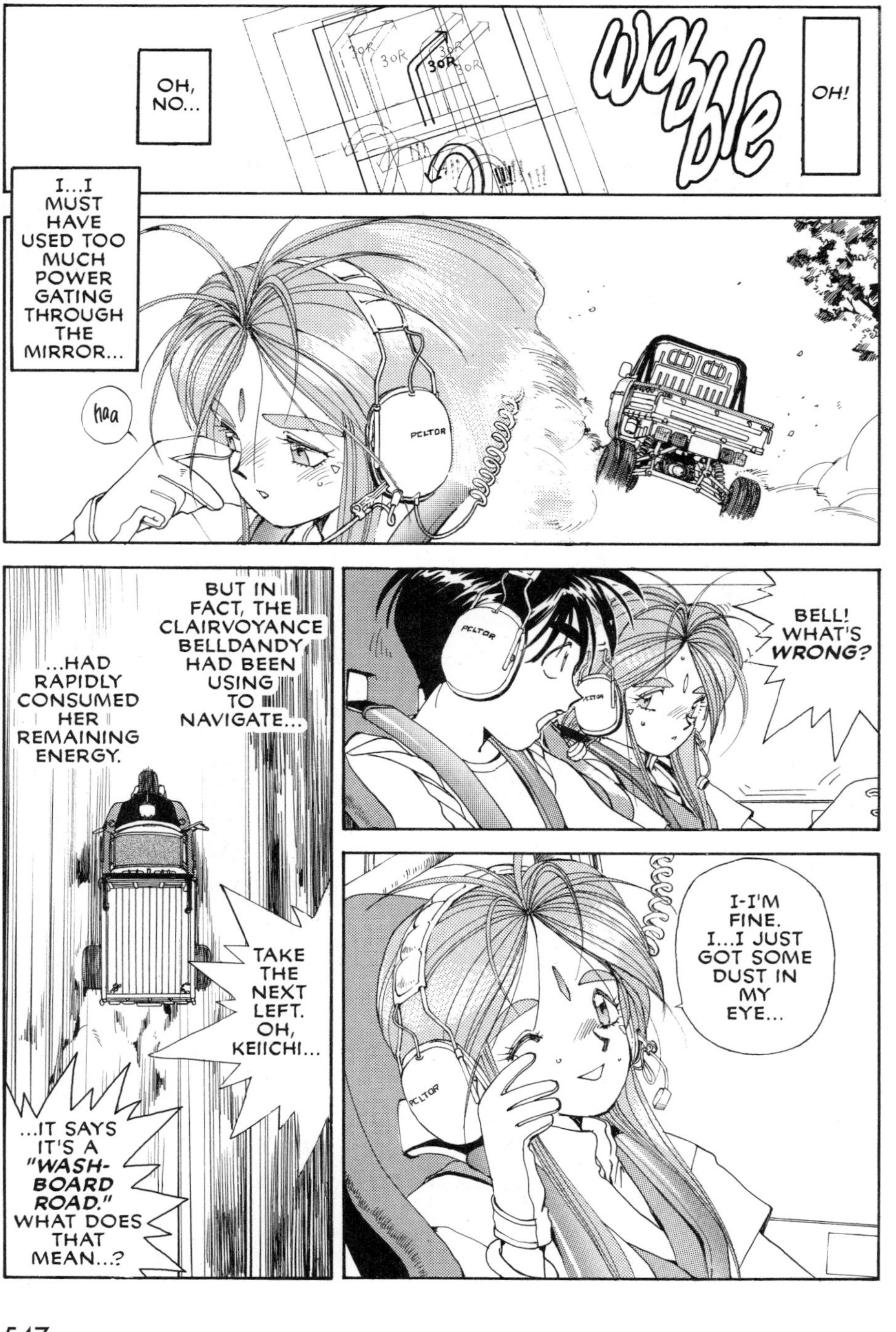
OH!
wobble
OH, NO...
I...I MUST HAVE USED TOO MUCH POWER GATING THROUGH THE MIRROR...
haa
BELL! WHAT'S *WRONG?*
I-I'M FINE. I...I JUST GOT SOME DUST IN MY EYE...
BUT IN FACT, THE CLAIRVOYANCE BELLDANDY HAD BEEN USING TO NAVIGATE...
...HAD RAPIDLY CONSUMED HER REMAINING ENERGY.
TAKE THE NEXT LEFT. OH, KEIICHI...
...IT SAYS IT'S A *"WASH-BOARD ROAD."* WHAT DOES THAT MEAN...?

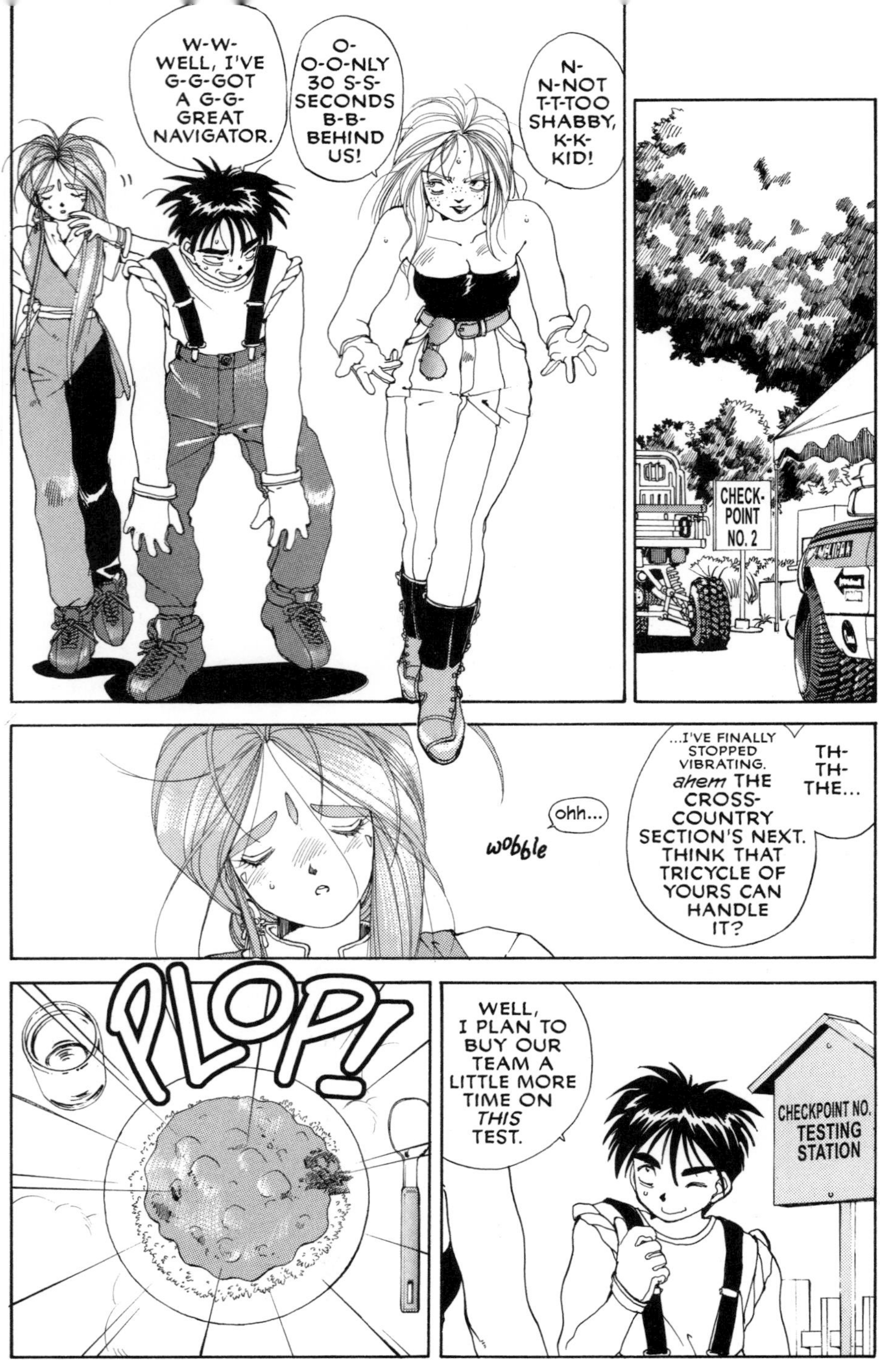
CHECK-POINT NO. 2
N-N-NOT T-T-TOO SHABBY, K-K-KID!
O-O-O-NLY 30 S-S-SECONDS B-B-BEHIND US!
W-W-WELL, I'VE G-G-GOT A G-G-GREAT NAVIGATOR.
TH-TH-THE...
...I'VE FINALLY STOPPED VIBRATING. *ahem* THE CROSS-COUNTRY SECTION'S NEXT. THINK THAT TRICYCLE OF YOURS CAN HANDLE IT?
ohh...
wobble
WELL, I PLAN TO BUY OUR TEAM A LITTLE MORE TIME ON *THIS* TEST.
CHECKPOINT NO.
TESTING STATION
PLOP!

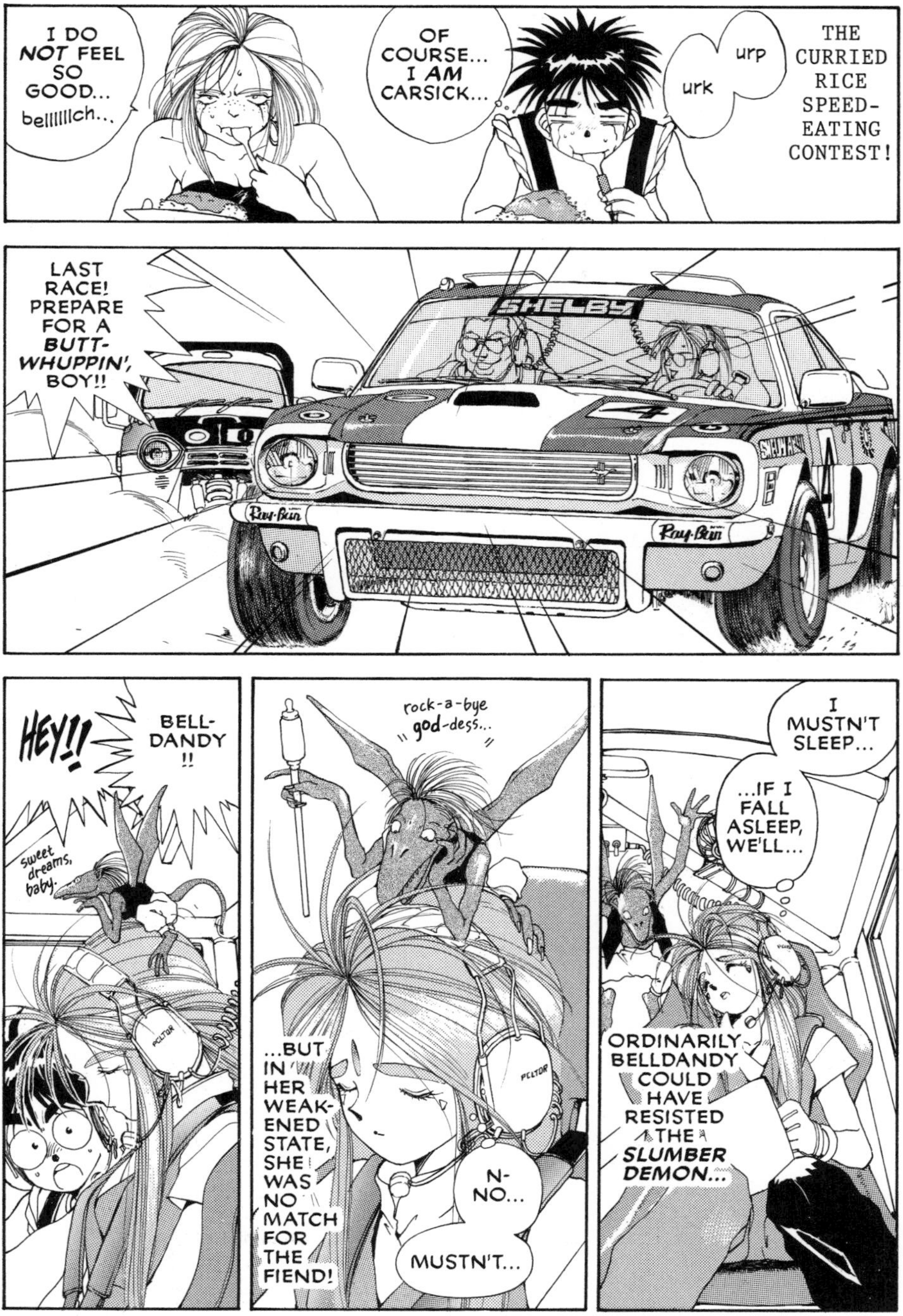
THE CURRIED RICE SPEED-EATING CONTEST!
urp
urk
OF COURSE... I AM CARSICK...
I DO NOT FEEL SO GOOD... belllllllch...
LAST RACE! PREPARE FOR A BUTT-WHUPPIN', BOY!!
I MUSTN'T SLEEP...
...IF I FALL ASLEEP, WE'LL...
ORDINARILY BELLDANDY COULD HAVE RESISTED THE SLUMBER DEMON...
rock-a-bye god-dess...
...BUT IN HER WEAKENED STATE, SHE WAS NO MATCH FOR THE FIEND!
N-NO...
MUSTN'T...
BELL-DANDY!!
HEY!!
sweet dreams, baby.

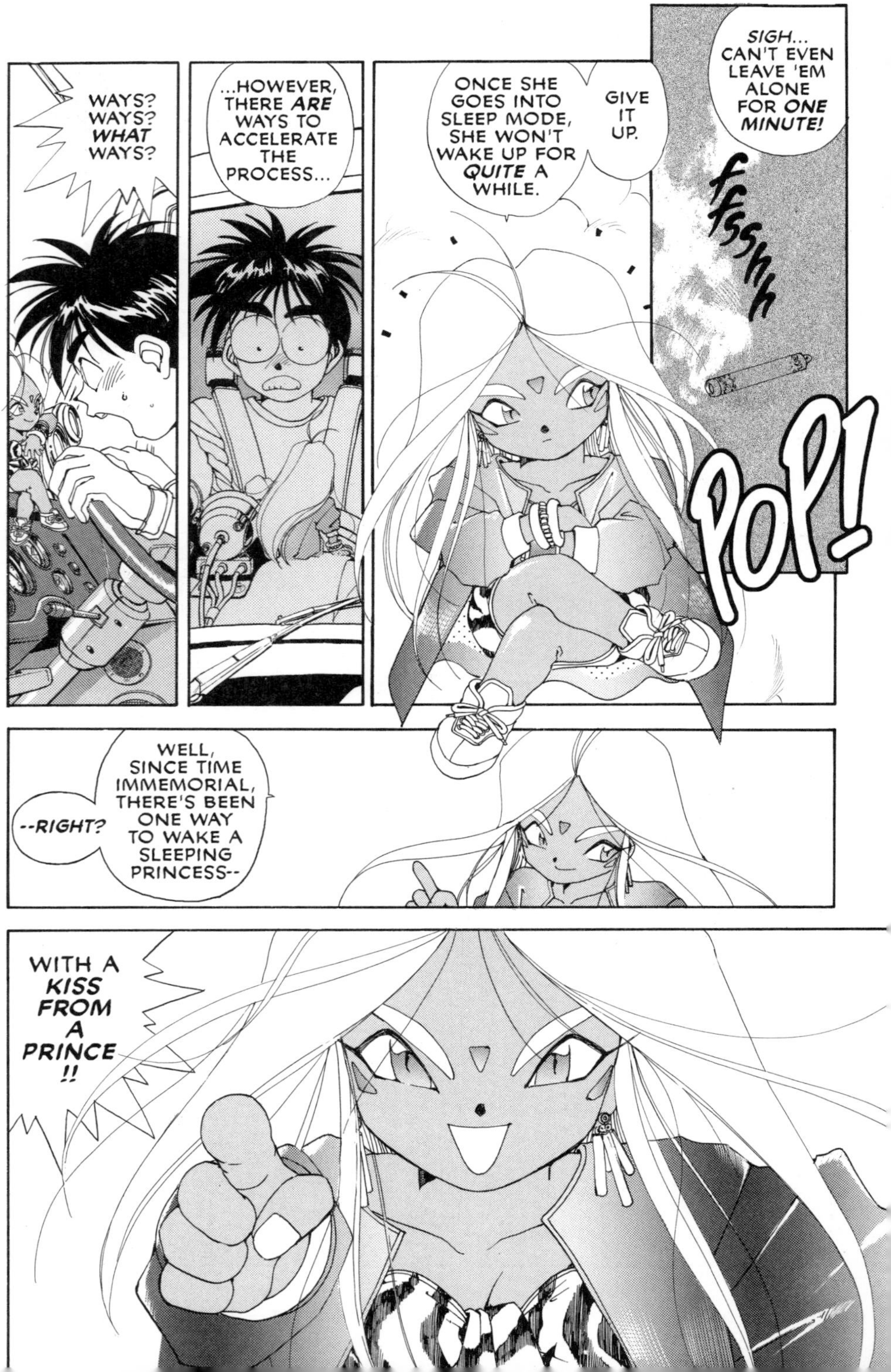
SIGH... CAN'T EVEN LEAVE 'EM ALONE FOR ONE MINUTE!
ffssnn
POP!
GIVE IT UP.
ONCE SHE GOES INTO SLEEP MODE, SHE WON'T WAKE UP FOR QUITE A WHILE.
...HOWEVER, THERE ARE WAYS TO ACCELERATE THE PROCESS...
WAYS? WAYS? WHAT WAYS?
WELL, SINCE TIME IMMEMORIAL, THERE'S BEEN ONE WAY TO WAKE A SLEEPING PRINCESS--
--RIGHT?
WITH A KISS FROM A PRINCE!!

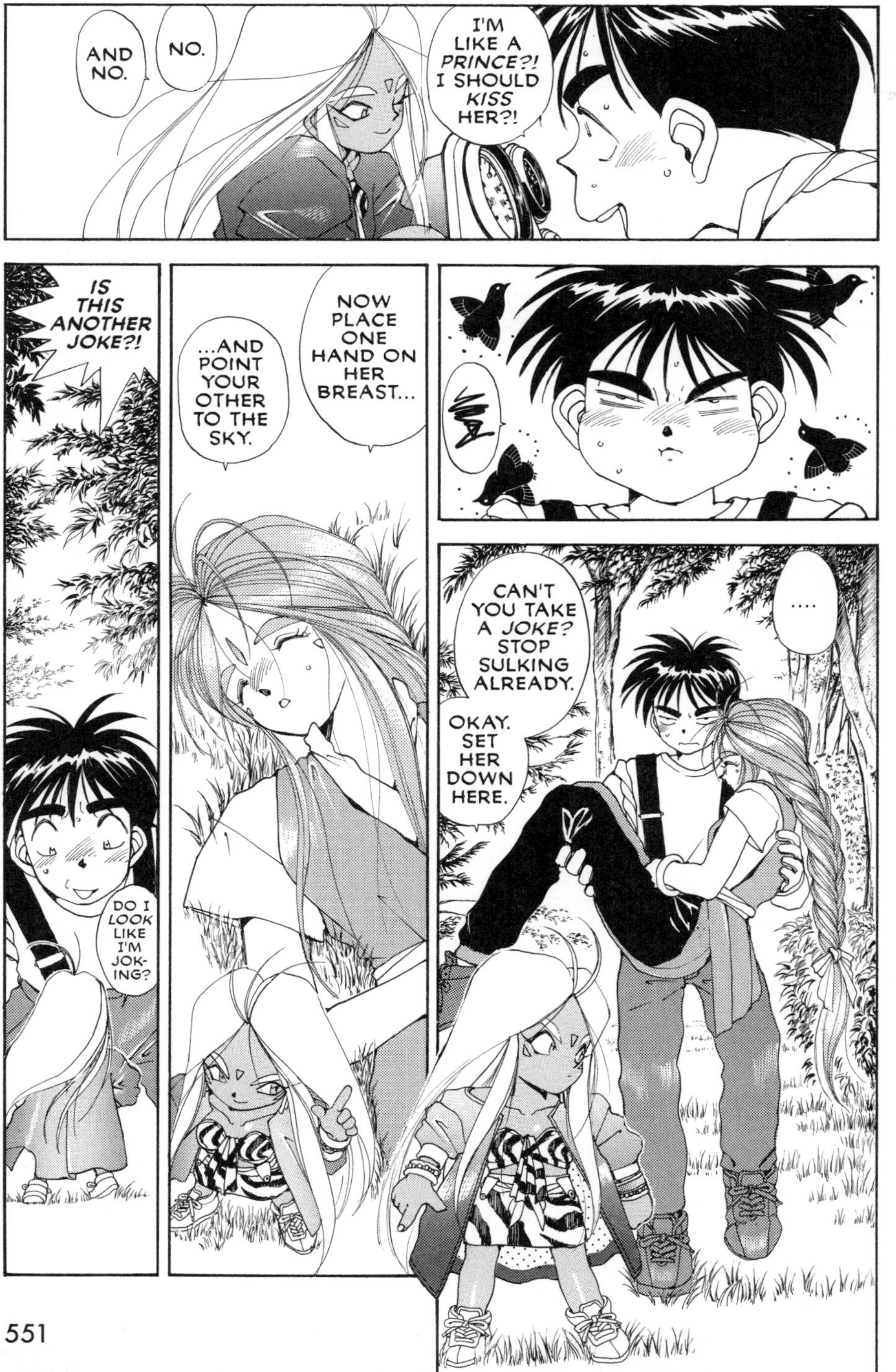
I'M LIKE A PRINCE?! I SHOULD KISS HER?!
NO.
AND NO.
....
CAN'T YOU TAKE A JOKE? STOP SULKING ALREADY.
OKAY. SET HER DOWN HERE.
NOW PLACE ONE HAND ON HER BREAST...
...AND POINT YOUR OTHER TO THE SKY.
IS THIS ANOTHER JOKE?!
DO I LOOK LIKE I'M JOKING?

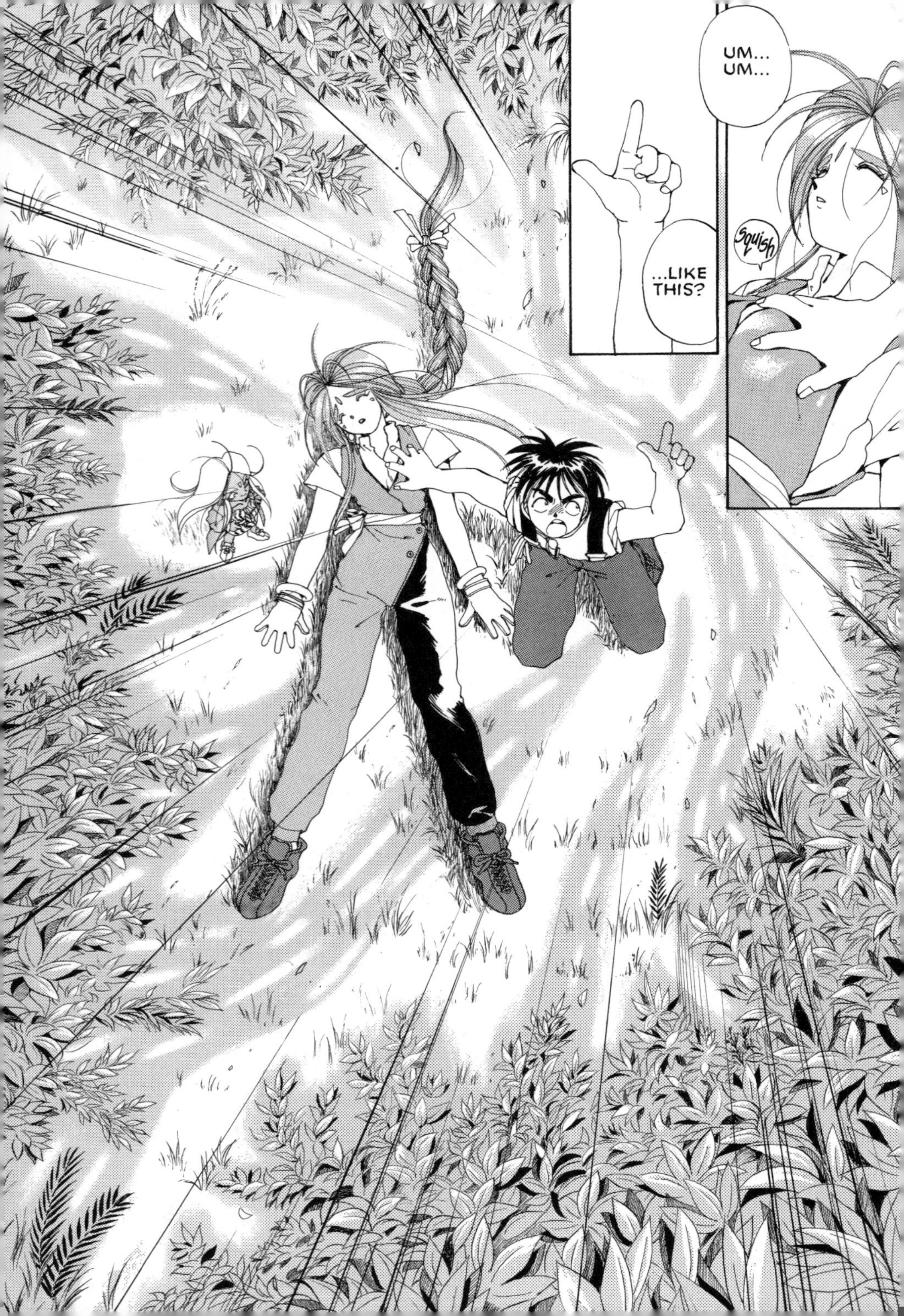
UM... UM...
Squish
...LIKE THIS?

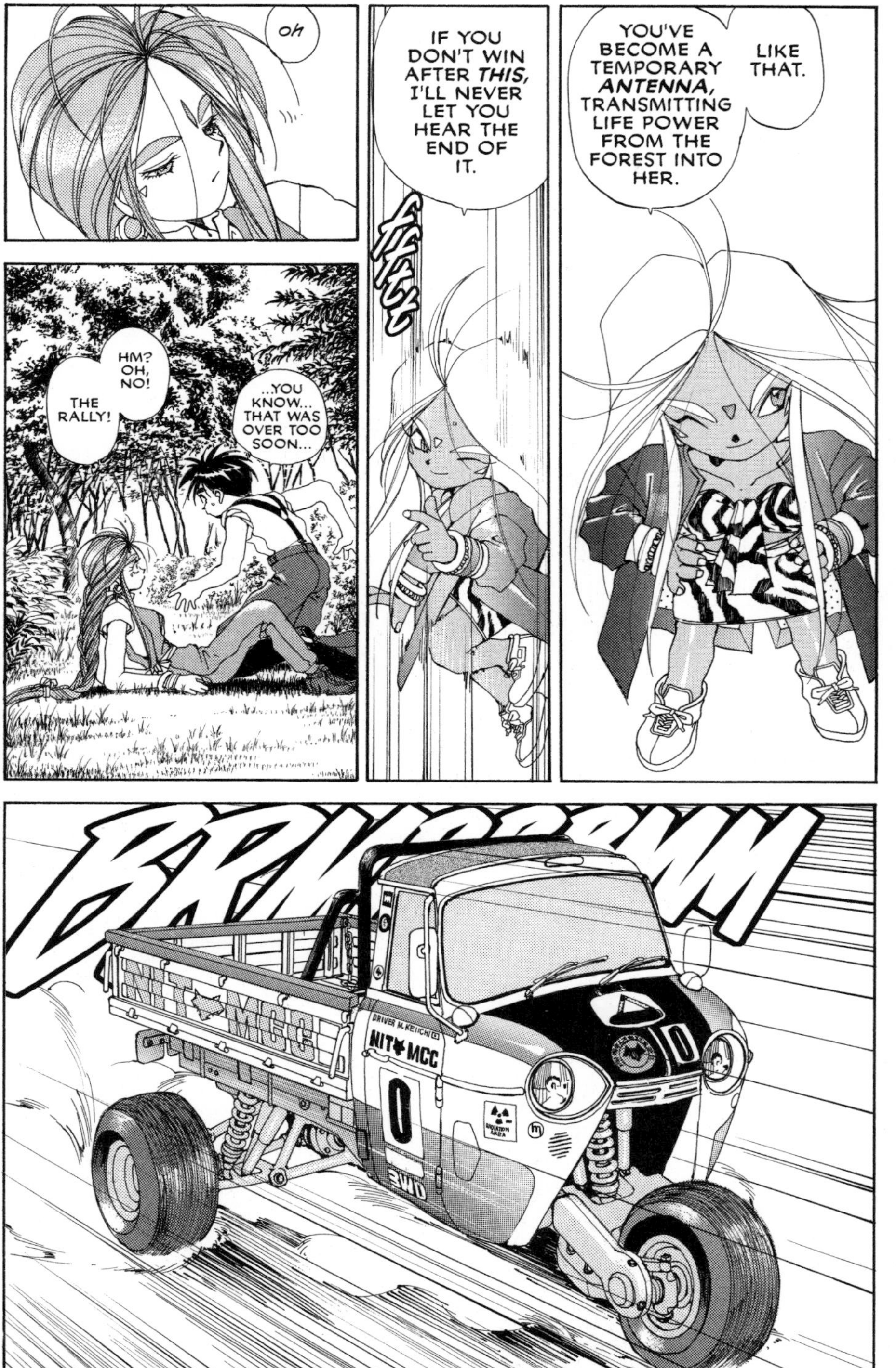
YOU'VE BECOME A TEMPORARY ANTENNA, TRANSMITTING LIFE POWER FROM THE FOREST INTO HER.
LIKE THAT.
IF YOU DON'T WIN AFTER THIS, I'LL NEVER LET YOU HEAR THE END OF IT.
oh
...YOU KNOW... THAT WAS OVER TOO SOON...
HM? OH, NO!
THE RALLY!
NIT MCC
DRIVER M. KEIICHI
NIT MCC
0
3WD

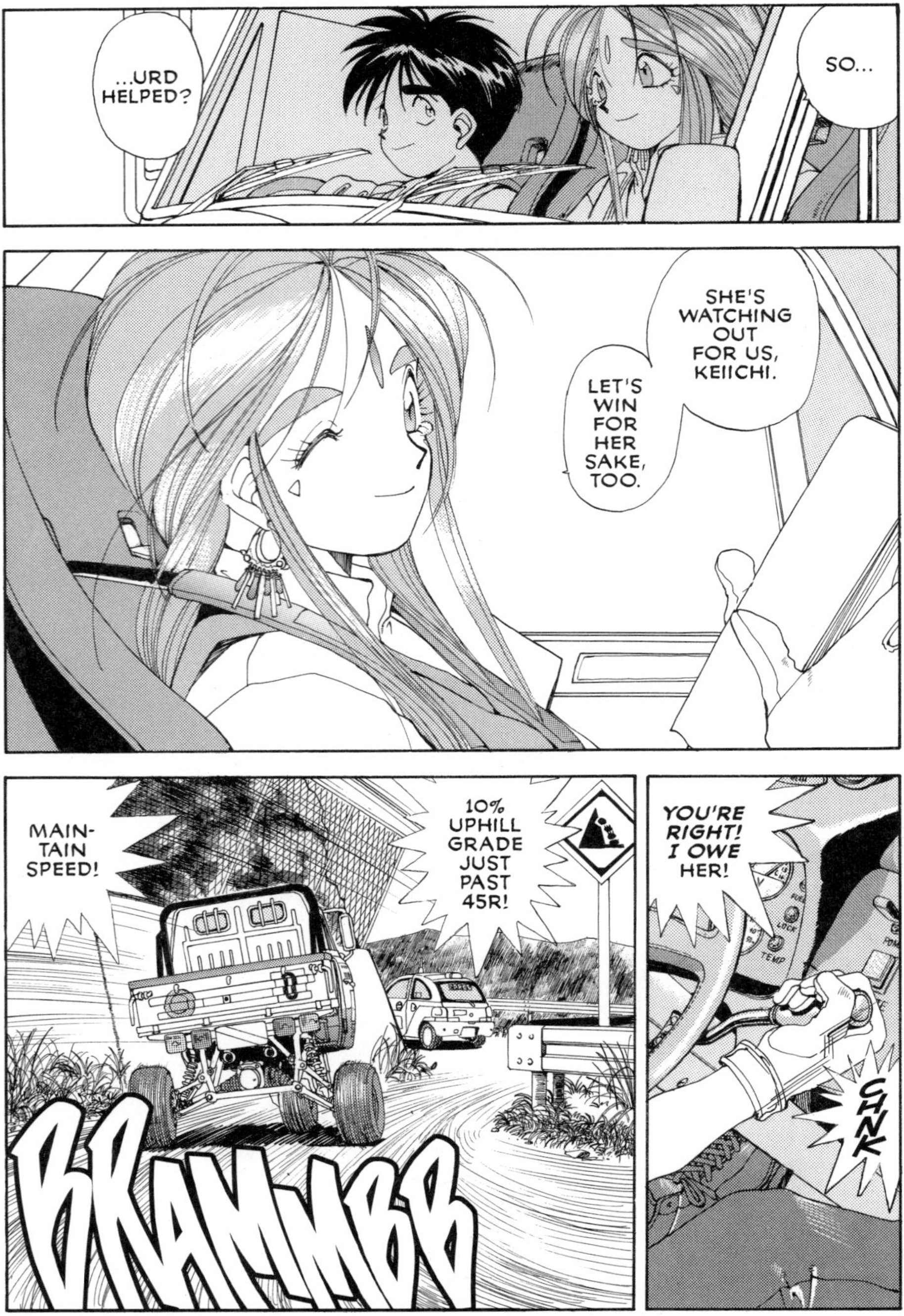
SO...
...URD HELPED?
SHE'S WATCHING OUT FOR US, KEIICHI.
LET'S WIN FOR HER SAKE, TOO.
YOU'RE RIGHT! I OWE HER!
CHNK
10% UPHILL GRADE JUST PAST 45R!
MAIN-TAIN SPEED!
BRAMMBB

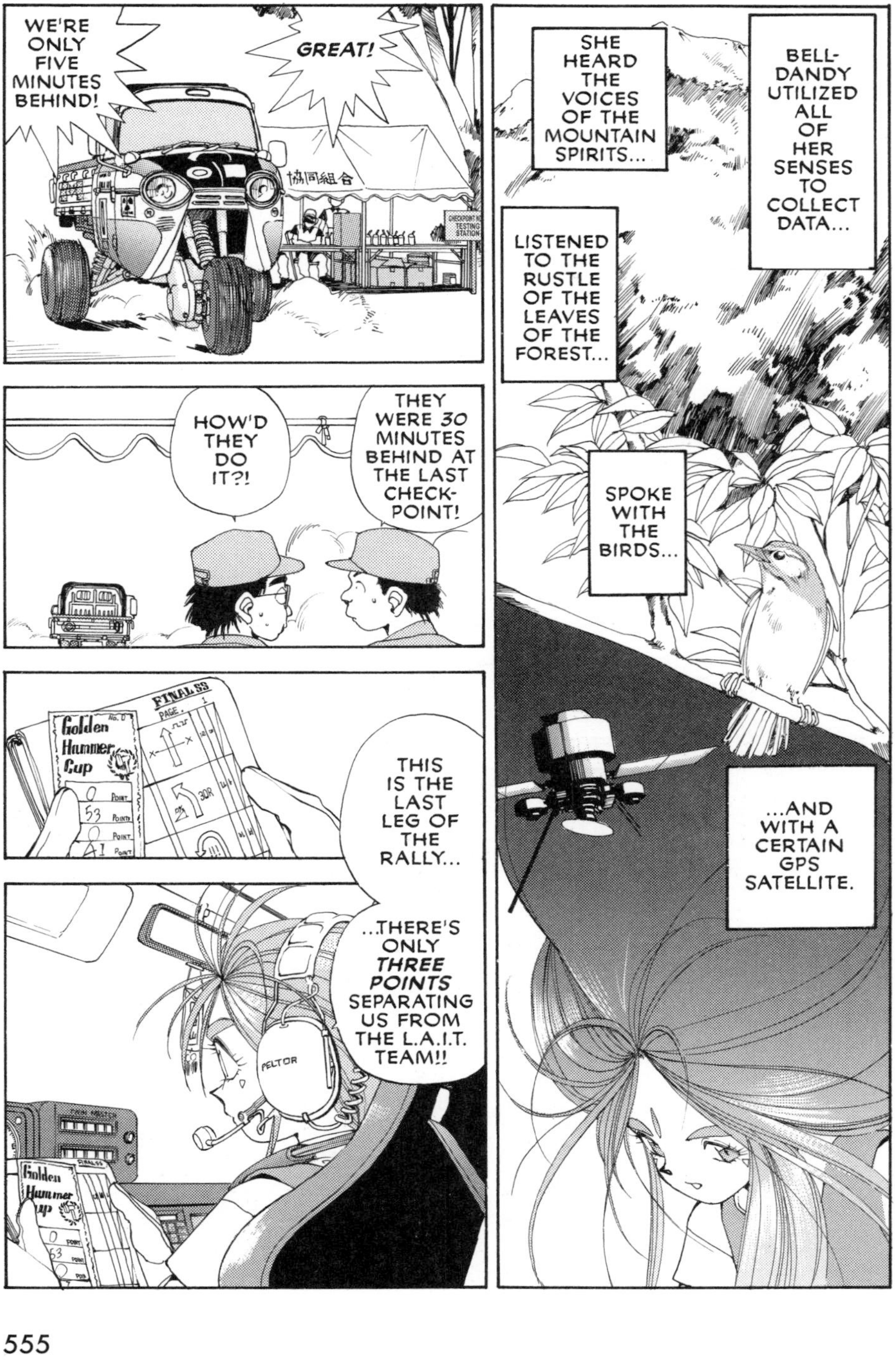
BELL-DANDY UTILIZED ALL OF HER SENSES TO COLLECT DATA...
SHE HEARD THE VOICES OF THE MOUNTAIN SPIRITS...
LISTENED TO THE RUSTLE OF THE LEAVES OF THE FOREST...
SPOKE WITH THE BIRDS...
...AND WITH A CERTAIN GPS SATELLITE.
GREAT!
WE'RE ONLY FIVE MINUTES BEHIND!
協同組合
TESTING STATION
THEY WERE *30* MINUTES BEHIND AT THE LAST CHECK-POINT!
HOW'D THEY DO IT?!
FINAL SS
Golden Hammer Cup
THIS IS THE LAST LEG OF THE RALLY...
...THERE'S ONLY **THREE POINTS** SEPARATING US FROM THE L.A.I.T. TEAM!!
PELTOR

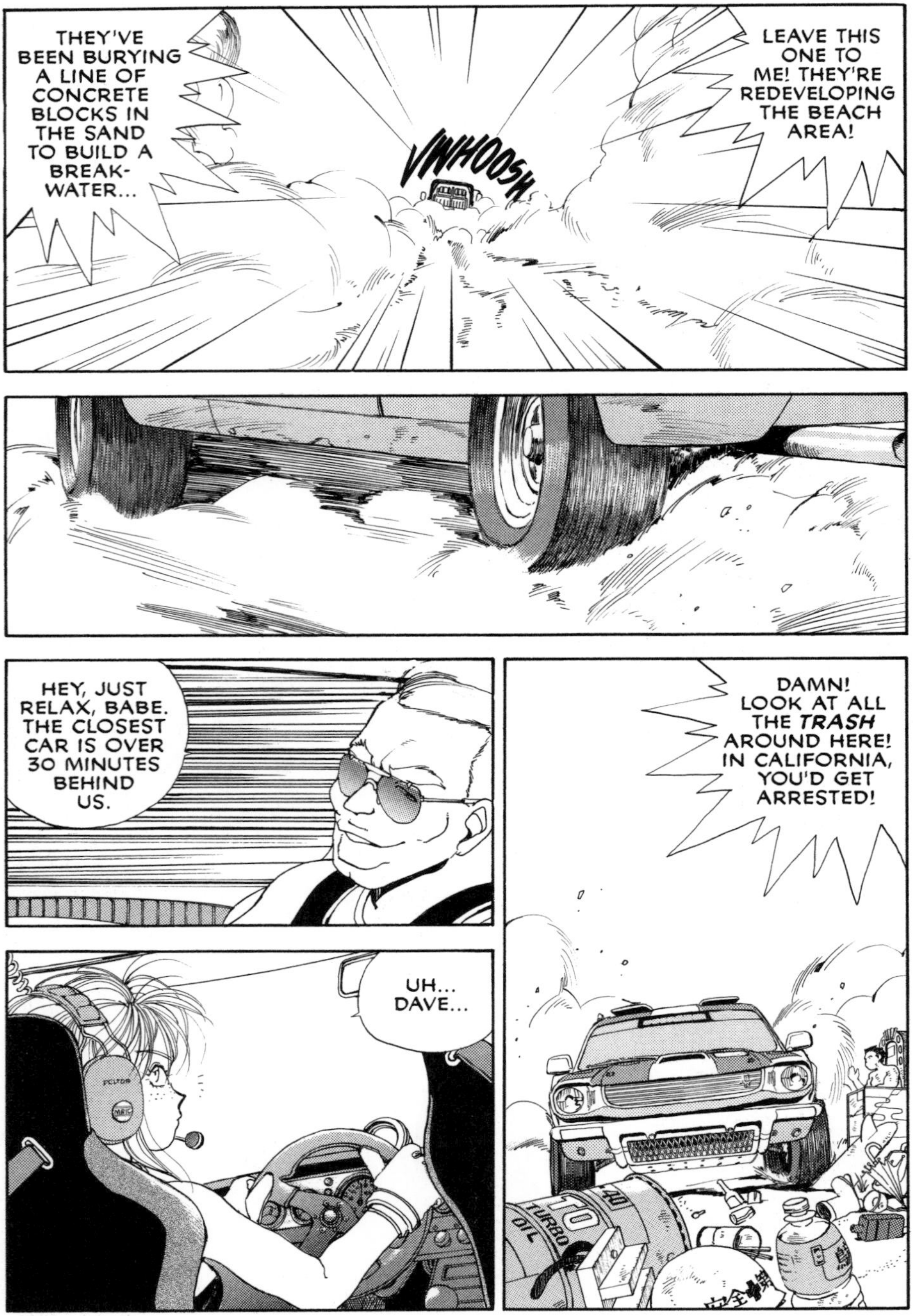
LEAVE THIS ONE TO ME! THEY'RE REDEVELOPING THE BEACH AREA!
THEY'VE BEEN BURYING A LINE OF CONCRETE BLOCKS IN THE SAND TO BUILD A BREAK-WATER...
VWHOOSH
DAMN! LOOK AT ALL THE *TRASH* AROUND HERE! IN CALIFORNIA, YOU'D GET ARRESTED!
HEY, JUST RELAX, BABE. THE CLOSEST CAR IS OVER 30 MINUTES BEHIND US.
UH... DAVE...

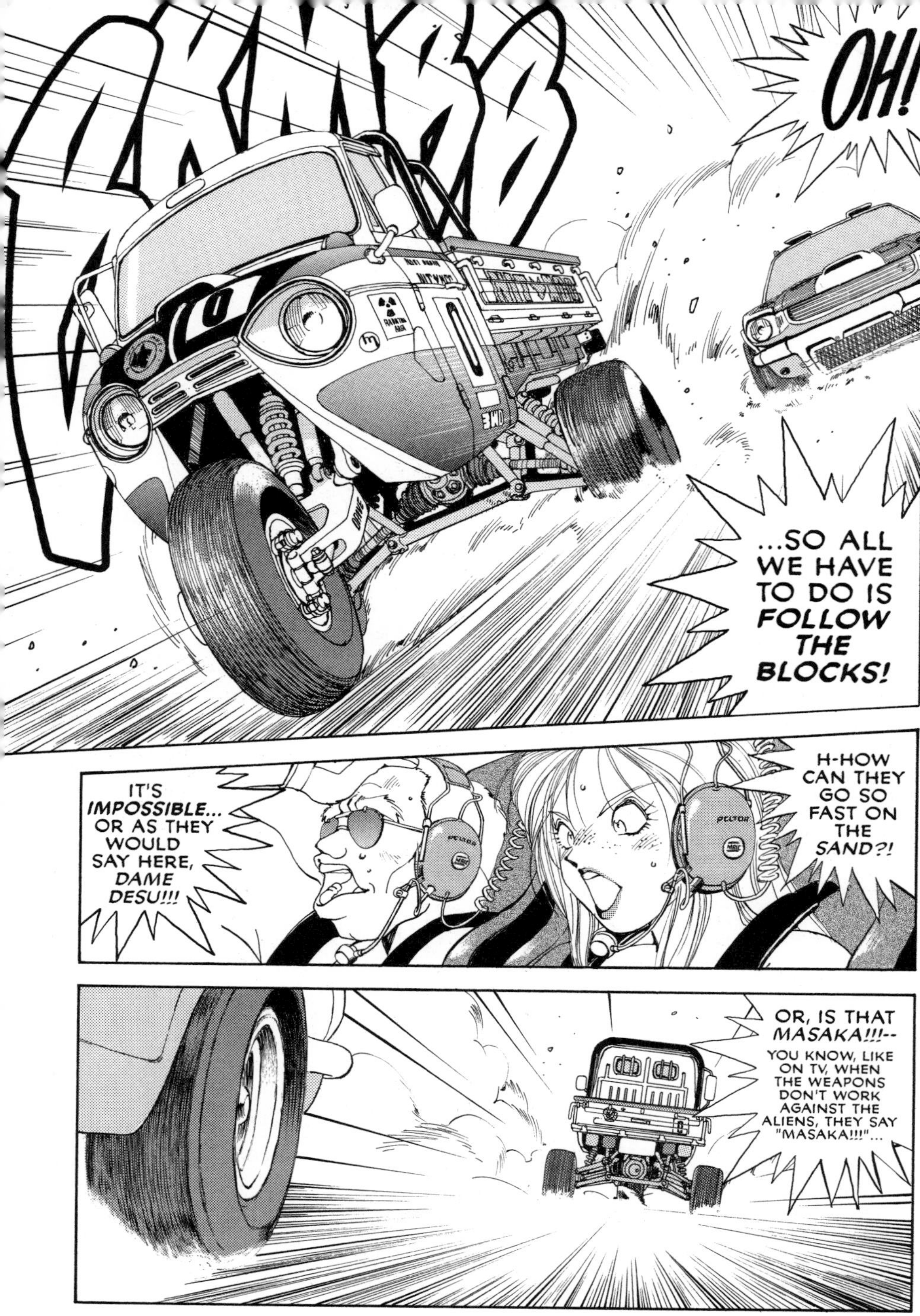
OH!
...SO ALL WE HAVE TO DO IS FOLLOW THE BLOCKS!
H-HOW CAN THEY GO SO FAST ON THE SAND?!
IT'S IMPOSSIBLE... OR AS THEY WOULD SAY HERE, DAME DESU!!!
OR, IS THAT MASAKA!!!--
YOU KNOW, LIKE ON TV, WHEN THE WEAPONS DON'T WORK AGAINST THE ALIENS, THEY SAY "MASAKA!!!"...

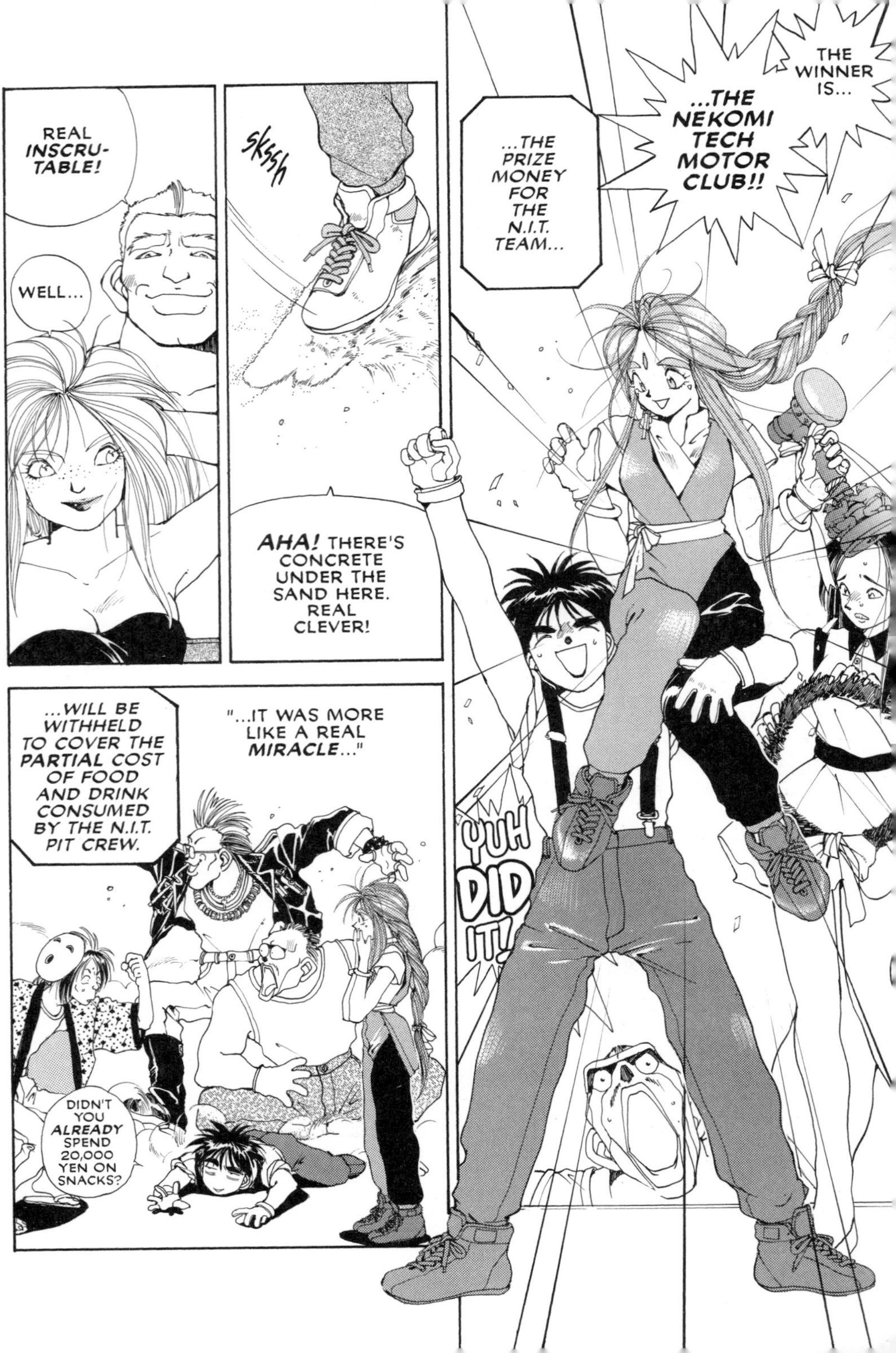
THE WINNER IS...
...THE NEKOMI TECH MOTOR CLUB!!
...THE PRIZE MONEY FOR THE N.I.T. TEAM...
YUH DID IT!
SKSSH
AHA! THERE'S CONCRETE UNDER THE SAND HERE. REAL CLEVER!
REAL INSCRU-TABLE!
WELL...
"...IT WAS MORE LIKE A REAL MIRACLE..."
...WILL BE WITHHELD TO COVER THE PARTIAL COST OF FOOD AND DRINK CONSUMED BY THE N.I.T. PIT CREW.
DIDN'T YOU ALREADY SPEND 20,000 YEN ON SNACKS?

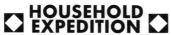

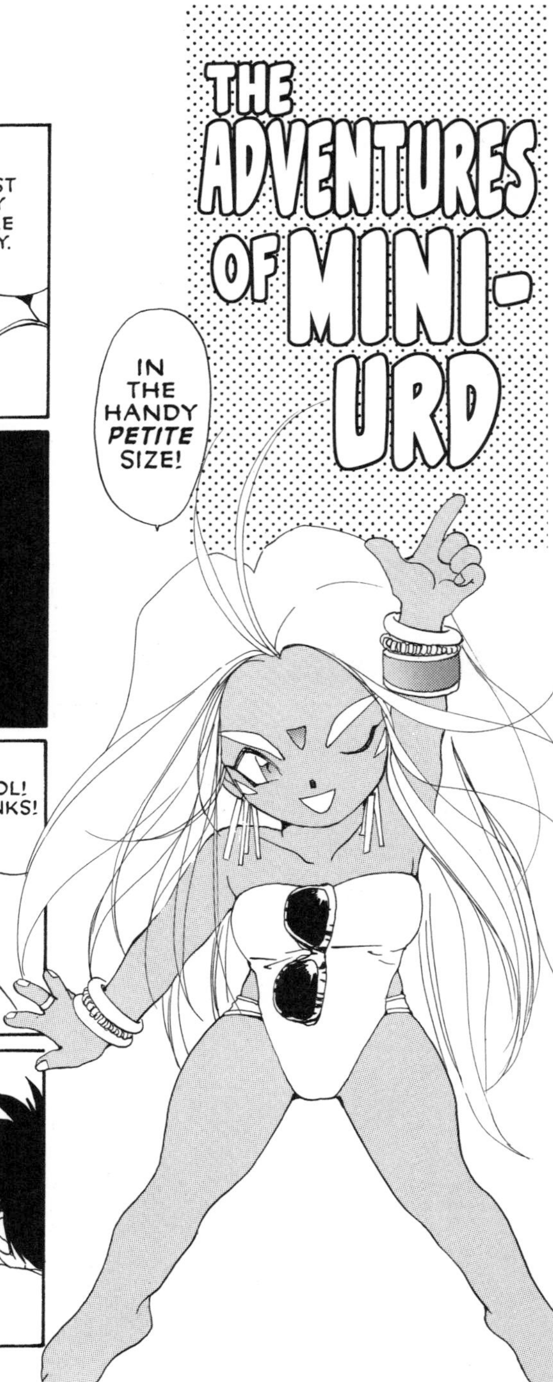
THE ADVENTURES OF MINI-URD
IN THE HANDY PETITE SIZE!

HOUSEHOLD EXPEDITION

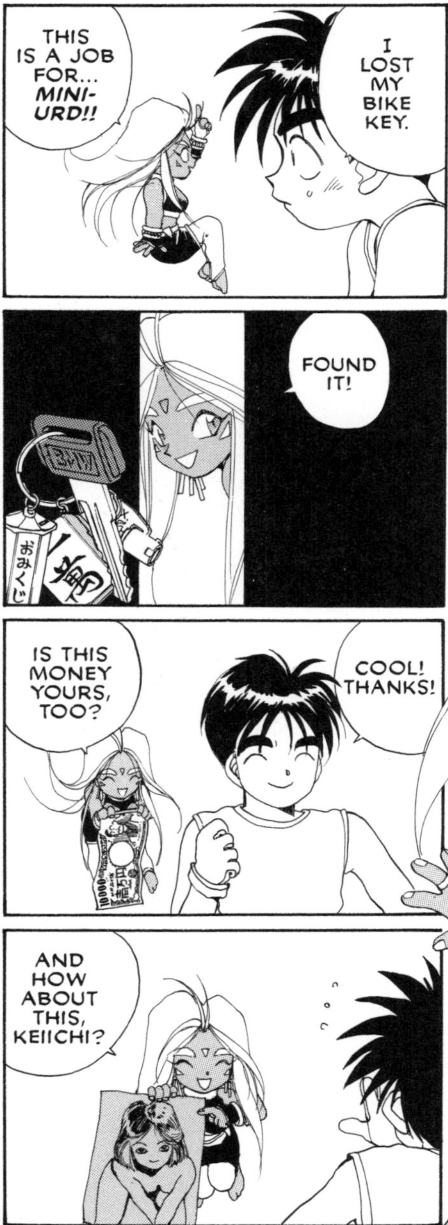
I LOST MY BIKE KEY.
THIS IS A JOB FOR... MINI-URD!!
FOUND IT!
おみくじ
COOL! THANKS!
IS THIS MONEY YOURS, TOO?
AND HOW ABOUT THIS, KEIICHI?

◆VACATION◆

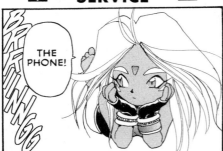

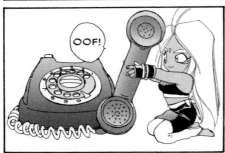

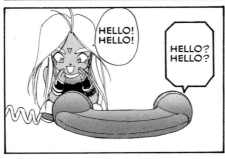

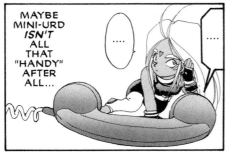

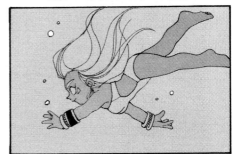

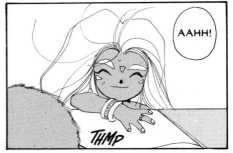

AAHH!
THMP
....
skitter skitter
THIS KITCHEN IS A LOUSY PLACE...
...FOR A VACATION...
gnaw gnaw

◆ ANSWERING SERVICE ◆

THE PHONE!
BRRIIINNGG
OOF!
HELLO? HELLO?
HELLO! HELLO!
....
....
MAYBE MINI-URD *ISN'T* ALL THAT "HANDY" AFTER ALL...

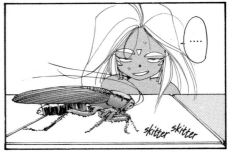

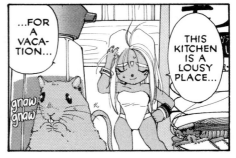

Oh My Goddess!

ああっ女神さまっ

2

OMNIBUS

藤島康介
KOSUKE FUJISHIMA

Oh My Goddess! Omnibus Book 2 introduces the third of the goddess sisters—the youngest, Skuld. It seems Keiichi's life wasn't complicated enough with Belldandy's magic and Urd's potions, so now Skuld is here with her personal form of weirdness—engineering! No sooner has she arrived at Nekomi Tech than Skuld appoints Keiichi's own little sister Megumi to be her archrival and challenges her to a robot battle . . . to the death?

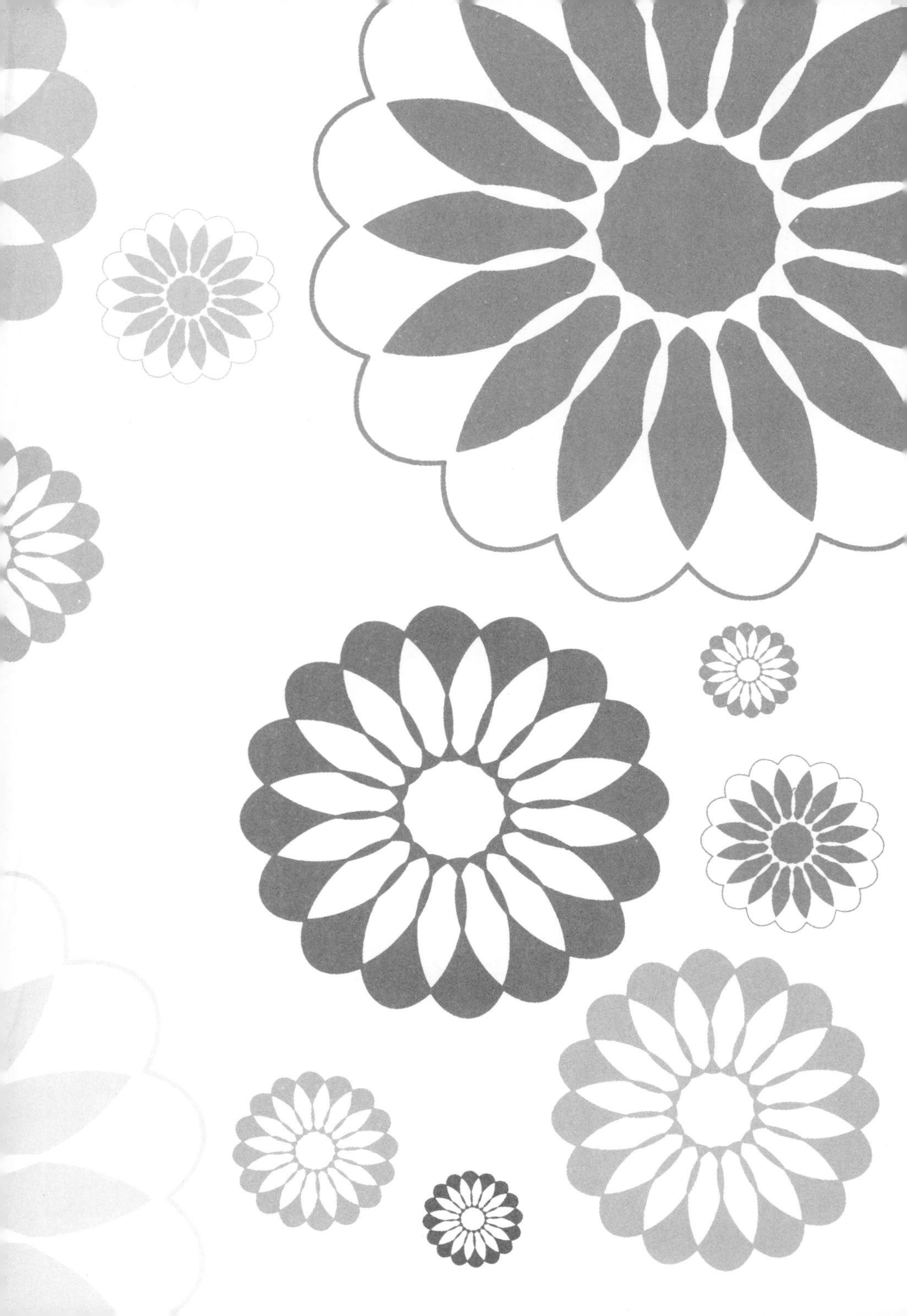

EDITOR
Carl Gustav Horn

DESIGNER
Kat Larson

PUBLISHER
Mike Richardson

English-language version
produced by Dark Horse Comics

Published by Dark Horse Manga
A division of Dark Horse Comics, Inc.
10956 SE Main Street
Milwaukie, OR 97222
DarkHorse.com

To find a comics shop in your area,
call the Comic Shop Locator Service
toll-free at 1-888-266-4226.

First edition: July 2015
ISBN 978-1-61655-740-9

1 3 5 7 9 10 8 6 4 2

Printed in China

Oh My Goddess!

ああっ女神さまっ

MANGA

VISIT THE
MANGA ZONE ON
DARKHORSE.COM
TO EXPLORE GREAT
FEATURES LIKE:

+ EXCLUSIVE CONTENT FROM
  EDITORS ON UPCOMING
  PROJECTS!

+ DOWNLOADABLE,
  EXCLUSIVE DESKTOPS!

+ ONLINE PREVIEWS, GAMES,
  AND OTHER FEATURES

+ MESSAGE BOARDS!

+ UP-TO-DATE INFORMATION
  ON THE LATEST RELEASES

+ LINKS TO OTHER COOL
  MANGA SITES!

Visit **DARKHORSE.COM**
for more details!

NEON GENESIS EVANGELION

Dark Horse Manga is proud to present these volumes that take a new look at the events
and characters from the groundbreaking *Neon Genesis Evangelion* universe!

NEON GENESIS EVANGELION: THE SHINJI IKARI RAISING PROJECT

Story and art by Osamu Takahashi

Volume 1
ISBN 978-1-59582-321-2
Volume 2
ISBN 978-1-59582-377-9
Volume 3
ISBN 978-1-59582-447-9
Volume 4
ISBN 978-1-59582-454-7
Volume 5
ISBN 978-1-59582-520-9
Volume 6
ISBN 978-1-59582-580-3
Volume 7
ISBN 978-1-59582-595-7
Volume 8

ISBN 978-1-59582-694-7
Volume 9
ISBN 978-1-59582-800-2
Volume 10
ISBN 978-1-59582-879-8
Volume 11
ISBN 978-1-59582-932-0
Volume 12
ISBN 978-1-61655-033-2
Volume 13
ISBN 978-1-61655-315-9
Volume 14
ISBN 978-1-61655-432-3
Volume 15
ISBN 978-1-61655-607-5

$9.99 each

NEON GENESIS EVANGELION: CAMPUS APOCALYPSE

Story and art by Mingming

Volume 1
ISBN 978-1-59582-530-8
Volume 2
ISBN 978-1-59582-661-9

Volume 3
ISBN 978-1-59582-680-0
Volume 4
ISBN 978-1-59582-689-3

$10.99 each

NEON GENESIS EVANGELION COMIC TRIBUTE

Story and art by various creators
ISBN 978-1-61655-114-8
$10.99

NEON GENESIS EVANGELION: THE SHINJI IKARI DETECTIVE DIARY

Story and art by Takumi Yoshimura

Volume 1
ISBN 978-1-61655-225-1

Volume 2
ISBN 978-1-61655-418-7

$9.99 each

TONY TAKEZAKI'S NEON GENESIS EVANGELION

Story and art by Tony Takezaki
ISBN 978-1-61655-736-2
$12.99

MANGA BY
CLAMP

Fourth grader Sakura Kinomoto has found a strange book in her father's library—a book made by the wizard Clow to store dangerous spirits sealed within a set of magical cards. But when Sakura opens it up, there is nothing left inside but Kero-chan, the book's cute little guardian beast…who informs Sakura that since the Clow cards seem to have escaped while he was asleep, it's now her job to capture them!

With remastered image files straight from CLAMP, Dark Horse is proud to present *Cardcaptor Sakura* in omnibus form! Each book collects three volumes of the original twelve-volume series, and features thirty bonus color pages!

OMNIBUS BOOK 1
ISBN 978-1-59582-522-3

OMNIBUS BOOK 2
ISBN 978-1-59582-591-9

OMNIBUS BOOK 3
ISBN 978-1-59582-808-8

OMNIBUS BOOK 4
ISBN 978-1-59582-889-7

$19.99 each!

東京 TOKYO BABYLON

CLAMP

CLAMP's early epic of dangerous work
—and dangerous attraction!

It's 1991, the last days of Japan's bubble economy,
and money and elegance run through the streets. So
do the currents of darkness beneath them, nourishing
the evil spirits that only the arts of the *onmyoji*—
Japan's legendary occultists—can combat. The two most
powerful *onmyoji* are in the unlikely guises of a handsome
young veterinarian, Seishiro, and the teenage heir to the
ancient Sumeragi clan, Subaru—just a couple
of guys whom Subaru's sister Hokuto has
decided are destined to be together!

*"Tokyo Babylon is CLAMP's
first really great work."*
—Manga: The Complete Guide

Each omnibus-sized
volume features over
a dozen full-color
bonus pages!

VOLUME ONE
ISBN 978-1-61655-116-2
$19.99

VOLUME TWO
ISBN 978-1-61655-189-6
$19.99

DARK HORSE MANGA
DarkHorse.com

AVAILABLE AT YOUR LOCAL COMICS SHOP OR BOOKSTORE!
To find a comics shop in your area, call 1-888-266-4226
For more information or to order direct: • On the web: DarkHorse.com
E-mail: mailorder@darkhorse.com • Phone: 1-800-862-0052 Mon.–Fri. 9 AM to 5 PM Pacific Time
Tokyo Babylon © CLAMP. Dark Horse Manga™ and the Dark Horse logo are trademarks of Dark Horse Comics, Inc. All
rights reserved. (BL 7032)

ANGELIC LAYER

Story and Art by
CLAMP

YOUNG TEEN MISAKI SUZUHARA
has just arrived in Tokyo to attend the
prestigious Eriol Academy. But what really
excites her is Angelic Layer, the game where
you control an Angel—a miniature robot
fighter whose moves depend on your mind!
Before she knows it, Misaki is an up-and-
coming contender in Angelic Layer . . . and in
way over her not-very-tall head! How far can
enthusiasm take her in an arena full of much
more experienced fighters . . . and a game
full of secrets?

Don't miss the thrilling prequel to the
acclaimed CLAMP manga *Chobits*! These
omnibus-sized volumes feature not only the
full story of *Angelic Layer* but also gorgeous,
exclusive bonus color illustrations!

VOLUME ONE
978-1-61655-021-9

VOLUME TWO
978-1-61655-128-5

$19.99 each

CLAMP オキモノ キモノ
Mokona's OKIMONO KIMONO

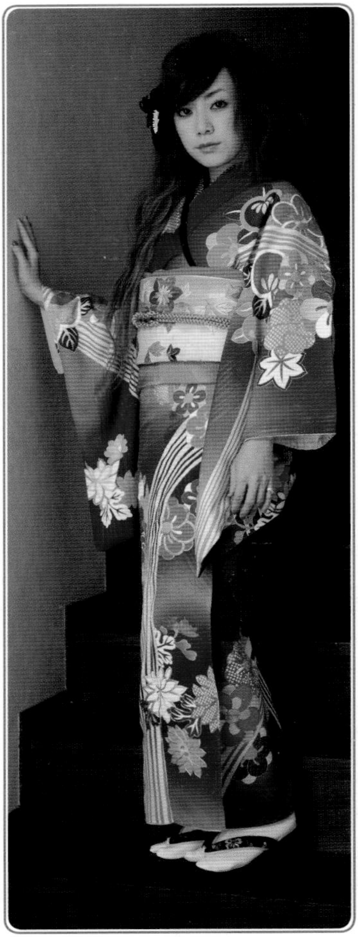

CLAMP artist Mokona loves the art of traditional Japanese kimono. In fact, she designs kimono and kimono accessories herself and shares her love in *Okimono Kimono*, a fun and lavishly illustrated book full of drawings and photographs, interviews (including an interview with Onuki Ami of the J-pop duo Puffy AmiYumi), and exclusive short manga stories from the CLAMP artists!

From the creators of such titles as *Clover, Chobits, Cardcaptor Sakura, Magic Knight Rayearth,* and *Tsubasa, Okimono Kimono* is now available in English for the first time ever!

ISBN 978-1-59582-456-1

$12.99

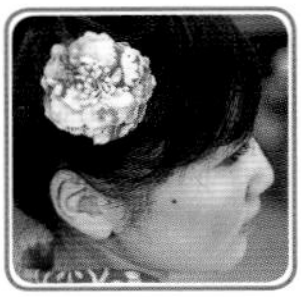

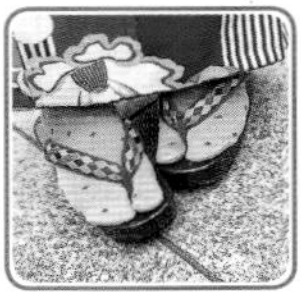

CLAMP

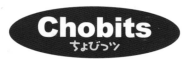

Chobits
ちょびっツ

IN NEAR-FUTURE JAPAN, the hottest style for your personal computer, or "persocom," is in the shape of an attractive android! Hideki, a poor student, finds a persocom seemingly discarded in an alley. He takes the cute, amnesiac robot home and names her "Chi."

But who is this strange new persocom in his life? Hideki finds himself having to teach Chi how to get along in the everyday world, even while he and his friends try to solve the mystery of her origins. Is she one of the urban-legendary *Chobits*—persocoms built to have the riskiest functions of all: real emotions and free will?

CLAMP's best-selling manga in America is finally available in omnibus form! Containing dozens of bonus color pages, *Chobits* is an engaging, touching, exciting story.

BOOK 1
ISBN 978-1-59582-451-6
$24.99

BOOK 2
ISBN 978-1-59582-514-8
$24.99

DARK HORSE MANGA
DarkHorse.com

AVAILABLE AT YOUR LOCAL COMICS SHOP OR BOOKSTORE

To find a comics shop in your area, call 1.888.266.4226. For more information or to order direct: •On the web: DarkHorse.com •E-mail: mailorder@darkhorse.com •Phone: 1.800.862.0052 Mon.–Fri. 9 AM to 5 PM Pacific Time.

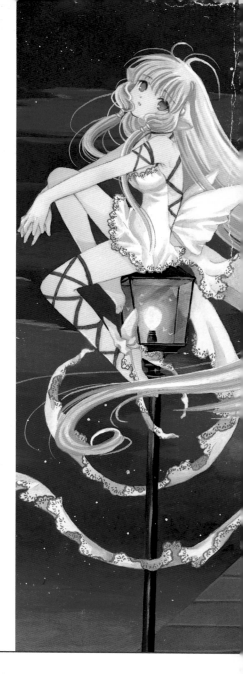

STOP! This is the back of the book!

This manga collection is translated into English, but arranged in right-to-left reading format to maintain the artwork's visual orientation as originally drawn and published in Japan. If you've never read comics this way before, take a look at the diagram below to give yourself an idea of how to go about it. Basically, you'll be starting in the upper right-hand corner, and will read each word balloon and panel moving right to left. It may take a little getting used to, but you should get the hang of it very quickly. Have fun! If this is the millionth manga you've read this way, never mind. ^_^

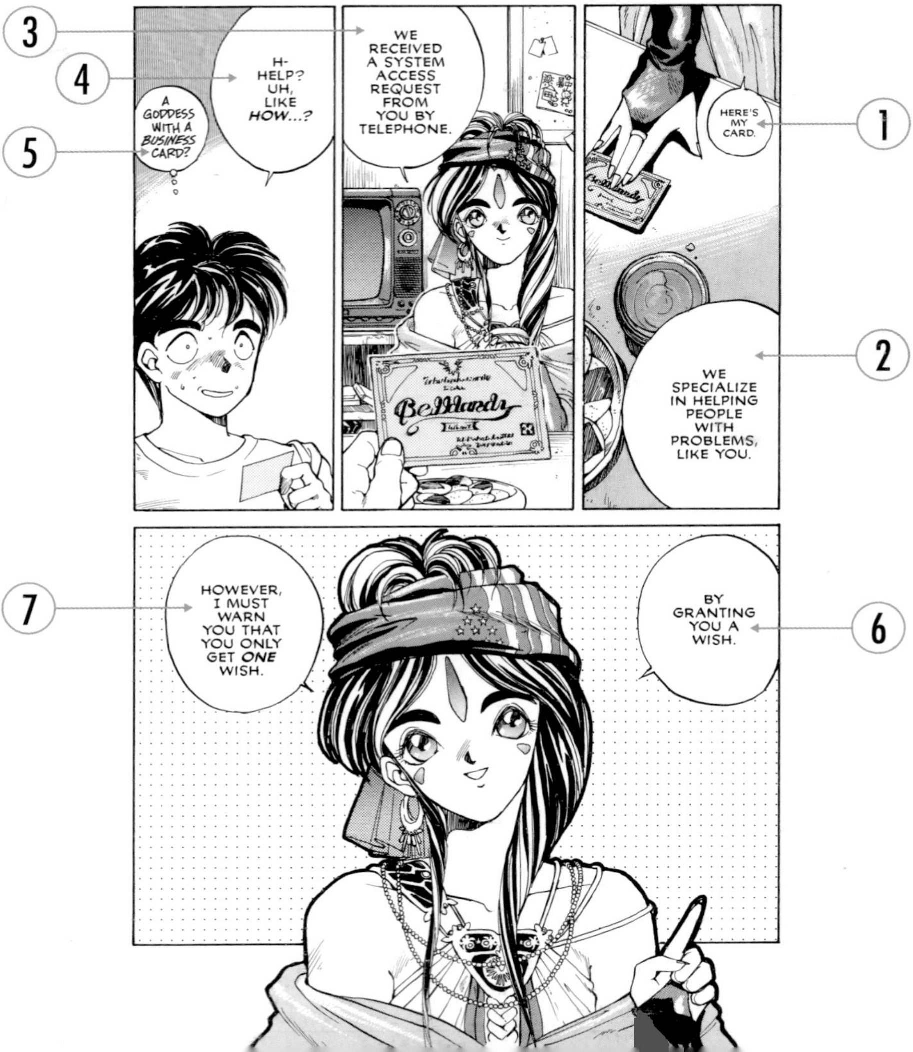
1
HERE'S MY CARD.
2
WE SPECIALIZE IN HELPING PEOPLE WITH PROBLEMS, LIKE YOU.
3
WE RECEIVED A SYSTEM ACCESS REQUEST FROM YOU BY TELEPHONE.
4
H-HELP? UH, LIKE *HOW*...?
5
A GODDESS WITH A *BUSINESS* CARD?
6
BY GRANTING YOU A WISH.
7
HOWEVER, I MUST WARN YOU THAT YOU ONLY GET *ONE* WISH.